A CASEBOOK ON TORT

AUSTRALIA AND NEW ZEALAND
The Law Book Company Ltd.
Sydney : Melbourne : Perth

CANADA AND U.S.A.
The Carswell Company Ltd.
Agincourt, Ontario

INDIA
N. M. Tripathi Private Ltd.
Bombay

and

Eastern Law House Private Ltd.
Calcutta
M.P.P. House
Bangalore

ISRAEL
Steimatzky's Agency Ltd.
Jerusalem : Tel Aviv : Haifa

A CASEBOOK ON TORT

SIXTH EDITION

by

TONY WEIR

Fellow of Trinity College, Cambridge

LONDON
SWEET & MAXWELL
1988

First Edition 1967
Second Edition 1970
Third Edition 1974
Fourth Edition 1979
Fifth Edition 1983
Sixth Edition 1988

Published in 1988 by
Sweet & Maxwell Limited of
11 New Fetter Lane, London
and printed in Great Britain by
Richard Clay (The Chaucer Press) Ltd.,
Bungay, Suffolk.

British Library Cataloguing in Publication Data

Weir, Tony
A casebook on tort.—6th ed.
1. Torts—Great Britain—Cases
I. Title
344.1063'0264   KD1948
ISBN 0-421-36390-8
ISBN 0-421-36400-9 Pbk

©
Sweet and Maxwell
1988

PREFACE TO SIXTH EDITION

THIS is the first edition since the second in which it has been possible to express pleasure at the intervening changes in the law of tort. The question last time was whether to give *Junior Books* pride of place over *Donoghue v. Stevenson*; this time the question was whether to include it at all. That is the measure of the change in just five years.

To call such a change a counterrevolution would be no exaggeration, but it might suggest that there had previously been a revolution where in reality there was only self-satisfied drift. Even when described as "logical development," drift is not at all easy to counteract, so our senior judges deserve great credit for their stalwart shredding and shedding of *Junior Books*, for their skill in containing both aspects of *Anns*, whose seeds were dragon's teeth, and most recently, for their neat stitch just in time to prevent *McGhee* from quite unravelling the law; *McGhee* had seemed to imply that you could make someone pay for harm without showing that he had caused it, perhaps, indeed, pay in proportion to the chance that he might have avoided it. These are valiant rescue operations, owing nothing to academic lawyers, ever liberal with other people's money, and of greater benefit to clients than to lawyers in practice, who had waxed fat enough in the previous confusion.

If liability for economic harm caused by negligence is now under better control, liability for *deliberately* causing economic loss still needs Herculean treatment, for that is another stable fouled by the why-nottery and "let-it-all-hang-out" school of the last twenty-odd years. *Torquay Hotel* needs to be flushed in the interests of freedom as well as sense, but as it may be some time before a suitable case for treatment emerges it is just possible that some assistance may come from academics.

The manuscript was submitted in January 1988, and little account is taken of subsequent events. It may be thought, indeed, that even of previous events too little account is taken, since there are no excerpts from such important decisions as *The Aliakmon*, *The Mineral Transporter* and *Muirhead*. The reason is that, Aladdin-like, these cases gave us old for new; and one may map a highway cleared of purprestures without recounting the details of their demolition.

Trinity College, Cambridge
April 1988

Tony Weir

v

PREFACE TO FIRST EDITION

A CASEBOOK has several uses. It may be taught with (American publishers sometimes give the teacher a little book of answers); it may be learnt from (which is a very different thing); or it may be used as a *bibliothèque de chevet*. Any casebook should answer all these purposes, but its structure will be affected by the purpose which the compiler had principally in mind. This one is designed primarily to be learnt from.

This is designed primarily to be learnt from. The best way to learn from cases is to study them and then read a Note on them in one of the learned periodicals—the references are easily found in the *Current Law Citator*. In practice students rarely do this—perhaps just because two books are worse than one. I should have liked to quote extensively from these Notes, but then either the book would be enormous or it would contain fewer cases. Accordingly, I have included, in tiny print, a fair amount of my own comment and criticism, occasionally extreme, in the hope of stimulating a response and of dispelling the aura of inevitability which the judgments themselves properly exhale.

The book is planned to be read straight through; on no account, however, must it be read in isolation. A casebook cannot contain everything, and this one in particular omits references to further reading; thus the conjunction of a standard textbook is essential—my own preference being for *Winfield*. I hope, too, that the book may be read with pleasure. There seems to be no good reason why law books designed for undergraduate eyes should be quite as solemn as those fashioned for judicial lips; explanation and exposition call for different styles.

Dr. Ellis Lewis, of Trinity Hall, Cambridge, very generously agreed to read the proofs and did so with the kindliest care. I am most grateful to him, and also to my colleagues in the College and the University whose contribution is none the less real for being less specific or even unconscious.

Trinity College, Cambridge
October 1966

Tony Weir

vi

CONTENTS

ACKNOWLEDGMENTS

THE Publishers and Compiler would like to record their grateful thanks to the following for permission to reprint parts of the publications indicated.

Butterworth & Co. (Publishers) Ltd.: *The All England Law Reports*.
The Incorporated Council of Law Reporting for England and Wales: *The Law Reports*; *The Weekly Law Reports*.
Charles Knight & Co. Ltd.: *Knight's Local Government Reports*.
Kenneth Mason Publications Ltd.: *Road Traffic Reports*.
Longman Group UK Ltd.: *Solicitors Journal*.
The Scottish Council of Law Reporting: *Session Cases*.
The Times Publishing Co. Ltd.: *The Times Law Reports*: *The Times* of March 13, 1953, and October 29, 1960.

TABLE OF CASES

*[Cases in capitals are excerpted at the page denoted in **bold** type. Only the first of successive page references is given.]*

TABLE OF STATUTES

[Excerpts are given at the page indicated in **bold** *type. Of successive page references, only the first is given.]*

OTHER INSTRUMENTS

SUBORDINATE LEGISLATION

PROSPECTIVE LEGISLATION

INTRODUCTION

In almost all the cases in this book the plaintiff is claiming money (damages); only occasionally does he ask the judge to stop the defendant doing something (injunction). In almost every case the plaintiff claims this money as compensation for harm he has suffered; only very rarely is the defendant required to pay more, as a punishment (*Rookes* v. *Barnard*, below, p. 292). The plaintiff's claim is grounded on the argument that the defendant (or someone for whom he is responsible) did wrong to cause this harm. Thus the law of torts determines when one person must pay another compensation for harm wrongfully caused. At any rate that is its primary function: it also helps to decide what conduct may be stopped by court order, and serves as a forum for the vindication of individual rights—quite an important function.

A tort suit, then, is very unlike an action of debt, which is a claim for a specific sum not measured by the amount of the plaintiff's loss (*e.g.*, a tax claim, or an action for the price of goods or the repayment of a loan). It is unlike an action on a property-insurance policy, where the claim *is* limited to the plaintiff's loss, because in such an action it is not claimed that the insurance company *caused* the loss. It is not like a claim for compensation after an expropriation; for there it is not claimed that the loss was *wrongfully* caused (*e.g. Burmah Oil Co.* v. *Lord Advocate* [1965] A.C. 75). But a tort suit is very like an action for damages for breach of contract, where also the amount claimed is claimed as compensation for harm which the defendant has caused wrongfully, namely, by breaking his word. Indeed many actions for damages may be based indifferently on contract or on tort.

A contractual claim can arise only where there is a transaction of some kind between the parties, such as sale, employment, carriage and so on: if there is no transaction, but only a collision between strangers, then any claim must be in tort. But a collision may well take place between the parties to a transaction, and it has long been the law that in such a case the victim may have both a tort and a contract claim. Now people involved in collisions usually suffer physical harm, that is, they actually get hurt, whereas the normal outcome when a transaction goes sour is that the affected party is just worse off, that is, suffers merely economic harm. The law of tort used to be interested mainly in physical harm but recently it has become increasingly ready to redress purely economic harm, and the result of this is that more and more breaches of contract simultaneously constitute torts as well. People who are not minding the kids or going to the pub are often doing a job they are paid to do or providing a service for reward, and if they do it wrong, that is usually a breach of their contractual duty to the person paying them. Under English law it is only that particular person who can complain of their conduct as being a breach of contract; a third party must found his claim in tort alone, but if the third party can do so, so can the contractor.

The law of tort is at bottom common law, the work of judges reacting, in the light of what has already been laid down, to the grievances of individuals. But a great deal of it has been replaced or overlaid by statute, the work of Parliament responding to social problems in the light of what is desirable and under pressure from various lobbyists, such as law reform bodies. Often Parliament has intervened to reverse individual rules laid down by the judges. Thus the common law denied any remedy to the widow and orphans of a person tortiously killed: such a remedy was provided by the Fatal Accidents Act 1846, now 1976, last amended in 1982. Until the Law Reform Act of 1934 a personal injury claim was lost if the tortfeasor died, and only after the Law Reform Act of 1945 could a person claim even reduced damages if he himself had been partly to blame for his injuries. The Crown Proceedings Act 1947 was needed to render the central government liable in tort at all, and the Consumer Protection Act 1987, which sprouted in Brussels, has abolished the rule that the person injured by a defective product must show that the manufacturer was at fault. Less frequently Parliament has sought to tidy up an area of the law of tort rather than to reverse a specific rule: examples would be the Occupiers' Liability Act 1957, the Animals Act 1971 and the Torts (Interference with Goods) Act 1977. There has, however, been no serious proposal to embark on a complete codification of the law of tort.

Whether it is wise to try to codify depends on the coherence of the area and the generality of the rules it is proposed to codify, and on whether the draftsmen possess the requisite technique. In both regards the present situation in England is unpropitious: while it is true that judicial synthesis of principle and legislative excision of anomalies have rendered the rules of tort much more general and abstract (and thereby reduced their number), tort as a whole is still far from homogeneous, thanks to the presence in it of eccentric native bodies such as defamation and conversion; and if the drafting technique displayed in the Animals Act 1971 (a product of the Law Commission itself) were adopted for codification, our code of tort alone would be nearly as long as (and less readable than) the American Restatement, whose 951 sections occupy four whole volumes.

Continental lawyers are more concise. The French law of delict is contained in five articles, of which the first reads: "Every act whatever of man which causes damage to another binds the person whose fault it was to repair it" (French Civil Code (1804), Art. 1382). The German Civil Code of 1900 deals with the law of unlawful acts in 31 paragraphs, whose principal one reads: "A person who on purpose or carelessly injures another contrary to law in his life, body, health, freedom, property or other right is liable to compensate that other for the resulting damage" (§ 823). Of course, these legislative provisions have received very many judicial glosses since their promulgation, but there has been no major legislative reformulation despite the vast changes in social structure and physical environment which have taken place since their enactment. Students might well test the results of the cases in this book against the words of these statutes.

If there is no demand for codification in England there are plenty of suggestions for further reform. Important proposals came from the Royal Commission on Civil Liability and Compensation for Personal Injury, set up in 1973 under the chairmanship of Lord Pearson (Cmnd. 7054, 1978). The Commission was not empowered to consider the whole of the law of tort, since *only* personal injury fell within its purview, nor yet could it investigate the compensation, by whatever means, of *all* personal injury, since apart from injuries to employees, consumers and persons on the highway, it could consider only injuries in respect of which tort liability now exists. But the Commission did review in great detail the roles and rules of tort law in relation to what might be called the total compensation situation.

The main concern of the Commission was that the law of tort be henceforth seen in relation to the other methods of alleviating harm which exist in the welfare state, especially social security. The moral value-judgment underlying the law of tort, namely that only wrongdoers need pay for the harm they cause, is at odds with the modern view, represented by social security, that all those who suffer harm should receive alleviation whether anyone is to blame or not: after all, the National Health Service does not ask *how* a patient came to need treatment.

The Commission proposed to mitigate this conflict by extending the role of social security, especially by providing all persons injured in motor accidents with benefits like those now paid to persons injured at work, and by diminishing the role of tort, not by depriving anyone of an existing right to sue, but by reducing the amount of damages payable, notably by refusing any compensation for pain and suffering during the first three months and by deducting all social security benefits.

The law of tort was thus subjected to a critical examination by the Commission, and it passed that examination, though not with flying colours: the Commission made 188 recommendations, of which the government has implemented about 15.

Those who think it wrong to discriminate in any way between persons suffering similar injuries will be displeased that a person who has only himself to blame for his injuries continues to be worse off than the person he injures, but others will be relieved that even in the Welfare State some role is to be allowed to private law, especially in so far as it reflects the view that everyone should conduct himself with due regard for the physical well-being of his follow-citizens, on pain of a monetary sanction proportioned to the harm he causes if he does not.

Two important institutions ensure that a person tortiously injured actually receives the money he is entitled to; the Motor Insurers' Bureau, still an informal body, meets the claim of a person injured on the highway by a motorist who is not only at fault but also uninsured or untraceable, and the Criminal Injuries Compensation Board, now finally on a statutory basis, disburses public funds to the victims of violent crime.

Neither of these bodies helps with damage to property; nor, of course, does social security; the owner must look to the law of tort unless he has private insurance cover. In cases where insured property has been tortiously damaged the courts have resolutely held that the owner's claim against the tortfeasor is unaffected by the fact that the owner has insurance. Of course the owner cannot keep both the insurance proceeds and the tort damages: he must refund the insurance proceeds out of the tort damages or, as most often happens, allow the insurance company to prosecute his claim against the tortfeasor. The unsatisfactoriness of the result is concealed from us by the fact that the insurance company, by "subrogation," sues in the name of the insured owner: we therefore fail to realise that money is being claimed by a company which was paid to take the risk of losing it. Insurance has another role, however, for liability in tort is one of the hazards one can (and should) insure against. The prevalence of such insurance induces the judges to impose liability on defendants whom they would be very reluctant to make pay out of their own pockets. As Lord Denning said in 1967 "We assume that the defendant in an action of tort is insured unless the contrary appears." (*Post Office* v. *Norwich Union Fire Ins.* [1967] 1 All E.R. 577, 580).

The law of tort covers a wide range of situations, from the tragic to the trivial. In this book one will come across an urchin who was blown out of a manhole (p. 196), a politician riled by criticism (p. 469), a credulous advertising agent (p. 44) and a television mogul miffed at being photographed (p. 317). Every situation, however, can be broken down into just a few structural elements which affect the outcome, and it would be right to say a preliminary word about each of them. They are (i) the victim's loss, (ii) the actor's behaviour, (iii) the relationship between the loss of behaviour, (iv) the relationship between the plaintiff and the actor or defendant and (v) the plaintiff's behaviour. As each case in this book is read, its facts should be classified under each of these heads; and then the conceptual devices which are used to justify the decision should be studied.

1. THE VICTIM'S LOSS

A judge once said "It is difficult to see why liability as such should depend on the nature of the damage." The difficulty is not apparent. Liability "as such" never exists; liability is always liability *for* something, and in tort it is liability to pay for the harm caused. To cause harm means to have an adverse effect on something good. There are several good things in life, such as liberty, bodily integrity, land, possessions, reputation, wealth, privacy, dignity, perhaps even life itself. Lawyers call these goods "interests." These interests are all good, but they are not all *equally* good. This is evident when they come into conflict (one may jettison cargo to save passengers, but not vice versa, and one may detain a thing, but not a person, as security for a debt). Because these interests are not equally good, the protection afforded to them by the law is not equal: the law protects the better interests better. Accordingly, the better the interest invaded, the more readily does the law give compensation for that harm. In other words, whether you get the money you claim depends on what you are claiming it for. It would be surprising if it were otherwise.

The kinds of damage most frequently complained of are personal injury, property damage and financial loss, *i.e.* damage to three of the best things of life, namely, health, property and wealth.

As between health and wealth, the priority would seem to be clear: it is better to be well than wealthy. But people who are poorly soon become poor, because they cannot earn their living and have to buy medicaments: personal injury has economic consequences. Is it *because* of those economic consequences that we protect people's bodies, seen as units of production and consumption rather than as sources of pleasure? If the question appears cynical, one should ponder the recommendation of the

Pearson Commission that victims of personal injury should receive a full indemnity in tort for their lost earnings and extra expenses, but nothing for their pain and suffering for the first three months.

That people are more important than things has been said often enough. But are things more important than money? The question is topical, because the law of tort has recently started to extend to money interests the protection it has long given to tangible property, and it is serious, for its answer may tell us something about the values of our society.

Things, unlike people, can be bought and sold, that is, they can be exchanged for money. Things are "money's worth." But there are valuables, *e.g.*, stocks and shares, which are not things. Things are defined as objects which can be touched: if it is invisible and intangible, it isn't a thing. Thus things appeal not only to economists but also to the human senses. The car which is merely an asset to the finance house which owns it is a positive pleasure to the hire-purchaser who drives it. The point is clearer with regard to immovables: a house has a human value to the family who live in it and make their home there, but to the building society which has lent the money to buy it, its value is purely economic. A legal system which was concerned with human values would be right to give greater protection to tangible property than to intangible wealth. This is what the law has done until recently: claims for property damage have been welcomed while claims for mere financial loss have been rejected; and the law has been much readier to grant a claim to the possessor of a chattel—the person who is enjoying it—than to the owner out of possession—the person who only profits from it. Of course there is one class of person, the artificial or legal person, to which this distinction between the thing and the mere asset can have no meaning whatever: that is because artificial persons have no senses. For companies it is immaterial whether there is one item less on the stock book or one item less on the credit side of the ledger. For people without senses, things are merely values, and a society without sensibility would so treat them. Our society is showing signs of doing so.

We have spoken thus far as if damage were requisite and as if the question whether there were damage or not was a pure question of fact. But suppose that I am locked up for five minutes. It would be difficult for me to show that this outrage had caused me any actual harm, unless I broke my leg trying to escape or missed an important engagement. Yet the person responsible should be made to pay. It is possible to hold him liable by saying that he has interfered with my right to liberty, and that my right to liberty is so important that to invade it is to cause me damage *ipso facto*. By using the concept of "right" we can gloss over the fact that no damage need be proved. It might, however, be better to admit that in addition to its more obvious function of redressing harms the law of tort also vindicates rights: it has a constitutional as well as a compensatory function.

2. THE ACTOR'S BEHAVIOUR

(a) *The act*

Positive acts trigger liability more easily than omissions to act: the duty not to cause harm precedes the duty not to let it happen, for it is worse to set fire to Rome than to fiddle while it burns. The thief and vandal are always liable; not so those who merely fail to forestall or deter them. The occupier of premises must certainly bestir himself for the safety of his visitors, and parents must try to protect children from themselves and from others (as well as others from them), but generally at common law if you want someone to do something for you, you must pay him, and then if he doesn't do it you can sue him for breach of contract. Duties to act are not readily imposed by the common law. The legislature, however, is constantly imposing such duties on people, usually on public bodies. Those bodies do not always live up to their obligations, and it is one of the urgent questions of tort law how far they may be made liable for failing to do so. We have come a long way from the view that "not doing is no trespass," but it remains true that one is more likely to be liable for creating a danger than for failing to remove one.

Thus we can oppose acts to omissions. We can also oppose acts to activities. A Lord Justice of Appeal once said: " . . . our law of torts is concerned not with activities but with acts" (*Read* v. *Lyons* [1945] 1 K.B. 216, 228 (Scott L.J.)), and he was apparently right. So if a person is run down in the street, he cannot say to the driver: "When you started driving, you enhanced the risk of people being hurt; I have been hurt, so you must compensate me." The victim must show that the defendant drove badly, that in the activity of driving just before the impact the defendant did some particular act he ought not to have done. But although this is generally true, there are areas of the law where liability is imposed because the defendant was running an activity, and although he himself has acted quite properly. Suppose the careless driver was employed by a firm and was on the firm's business at the time of the collision. The victim can sue the firm if he establishes the fault of the driver. The firm responds for careless conduct in its activity, though the firm itself is otherwise free from fault (p. 229).

After scrutinising our common and statutory law the Pearson Commission thought they could descry an embryo principle which "can be broadly stated as one of strict liability for personal injury caused by dangerous things or activities." One of their proposals was to implement and expand this principle by having a statute which would lay down a framework of liability and a series of statutory instruments which would specify the activities and things to which it would apply. The proposal is unlikely to be adopted.

The behaviour of things, as opposed to human acts, is of importance to the tort lawyer because most people who are hurt are hurt by things, especially by metal things. The French Civil Code says: "A person is responsible not only for the damage caused by his own act, but also for the damage caused by the act of those for whom he is responsible, or of the things which he has in his control" (Art. 1384). There is no such principle in the law of England, but there are instances in which a thing may involve liability. Thus if I am hurt by a thing under the control of the defendant, and the damage would not have occurred if the thing was properly controlled, then the behaviour of the thing, in the absence of explanation by the defendant, may bespeak carelessness on his part in looking after it. *Res ipsa loquitur* is the Latin form (p. 145). Again, if the defendant has brought an unusual thing on to his land, and it escapes and does damage to mine, he is liable as a matter of law (p. 391). If the defendant keeps a savage beast, and it gets out of control and bites me, then again, as a matter of law, the defendant is liable (p. 405). The rule is the same, in this regard, if the defendant's cattle escape and eat my tulips (p. 405).

Further, we can oppose acts to words. Lawyers have a tendency to confuse them (*Acts* of Parliament, *deeds* of individuals), and not only lawyers, since a Yuppie or a skinhead is said to "make a statement" when he drives his Porsche at breakneck speed or wears his skull bare, but we should try to keep acts and speech distinct, even if both can have harmful effects. First, speaking is an exercise of a specifically guaranteed freedom, in the way that driving a car, for example, is not; one must therefore be chary of unduly restraining verbal communication by too ready an imposition of liability if something goes wrong. Secondly, it is technically rather easy to impose liability for words, because one can *prove* the falsehood of what was said whereas one can only *argue* for the wrongfulness of what was done: it is not easy to remember that being wrong is not necessarily doing wrong. Finally, acts commonly impinge directly on the person hurt, whereas words operate by indirection, by inducing him to hurt himself or inducing others to hurt him. The concept of reliance is important here.

It should be stressed that the contrast between acts, on the one hand, and omissions, activities, words and things on the other, is drawn not to suggest that the former alone should or do attract liability, but to emphasise that one should be conscious of which is involved in a particular case, and that the law is probably right to have developed rather differently with regard to them.

(b) *Quality of the act*

In most cases it is not enough to show simply that the defendant acted, and thereby caused the damage. His act must be appraised and evaluated before liability follows. The pre-eminent test is whether the defendant acted *reasonably*. On the whole, a defendant who has acted reasonably is not going to have to pay damages. But there are exceptions, and it is very important to mark them when they occur. Sometimes the plaintiff's interest is so important that it is protected even against reasonable behaviour which infringes it. Thus a person's land is protected against persons who reasonably but erroneously believe themselves entitled to enter it (p. 312); a person's liberty may be protected against officials acting bona fide but in excess of their powers (p. 344); a person's stolen chattels are protected against persons who reasonably buy or sell them in the normal channels of commerce (p. 433); a person's reputation is protected even against imputations unintended by the writer (p. 460). These are also the cases where no damage need be proved.

Sometimes a person is not liable for acting unreasonably, even though he intended to bring about the damage in question. After all, businessmen are supposed to compete with vigour, that is, to beggar their neighbour, and labour is expected to wrestle with management: no one said they saw much wrong when the National Union of Mineworkers deliberately caused a loss of £6,000,000,000 by a strike in the year ending March 1985, though the associated sabotage and mayhem were, by reason of the kind of harm in issue, sternly discountenanced. Special protection is afforded to officials empowered by law to make decisions, often harmful in their results, as their freedom to decide would be inhibited if they were liable just because their decision could be described as unreasonable: they are liable in damages only if they have acted outside their powers, or at least very unreasonably indeed. Again, freedom of speech should not be unduly curtailed (though it is); Members of Parliament and those involved in litigation may say hurtful things with impunity, without liability for defamation, and even the private citizen may sometimes be free from liability unless he spoke with "malice," which means that good faith is protected (below p. 465). Again, since it is for the public good that suspected criminals be brought to book, the person who unreasonably brings a prosecution is not liable unless he was also in bad faith (below p. 536).

3. Relationship Between Behaviour and Damage

A person is not in general responsible for damage unless he has both caused it and been to blame for it. "Cause" and "blame" are not synonymous, yet as the component elements of responsibility they are not easily dissociated. On the one hand, even a person who is blameworthy does not have to pay for damage if it would have occurred anyhow; a person is not liable unless he "caused" the damage (below, p. 179). On the other hand, a blameworthy person is not necessarily liable for all the damage he can be said to have "caused."

What is "to cause"? Many words—often quite short, brutal Anglo-Saxon verbs like "kill," "burn," "break" or "stab"—contain causal notions, and designate an act, perhaps of a specific kind, which produces a result, possibly a special one, maybe in some particular manner. But where the effect of conduct is less typical or direct, especially outside the physical sphere, even the English language may have no single word to indicate the composite. Helena drew the distinction: "And though I kill him not, I am the cause His death was so effected" (*All's Well* III.ii). Causation at large is not a simple notion, and lawyers use it not simply in an explanatory manner but with the aim of fixing or denying responsibility.

In human affairs, present, past or fictional, effects result from a concatenation of causes, so one must not look for *the* cause, as if there were only one. One should rather ask "Did the conduct contribute to the harm?" Now it might be supposed that a person whose conduct had merely contributed to harm need only contribute to its compensation, that is, pay in proportion to his causal contribution. This is not the law. The causal contributor is liable to pay for the full effects to which his conduct conduced. It is not easy for the student to realise that a gallon of cause may go into the pint-pot of effect. But consider. If two people kill a third, neither has half-killed him: both have killed him. All each can say is that though he killed the deceased, another did so too. But that other may be penniless or hiding. So each contributor is held liable in full until the victim is fully paid.

Once a causal connection between the defendant's conduct and the plaintiff's harm is established in the sense that the harm would probably not have occurred without it, one must ask whether this connection is sufficient for it to be fair to impose liability on the defendant, for it is clear that one does not always have to pay for all the consequences of one's misconduct. A legal system might require that the harm be the *direct*, the *typical* or the *foreseeable* result of the conduct, or that it be a *proximate* consequence, not *too remote*, or that it be of the kind which the rule infringed was designed to guard against. All these formulae, and more, have been used. But their use should not conceal the fact that underneath the apparent factuality of causal vocabulary lurk value-judgments. This can be seen from the fact that the more reprehensible behaviour is, the more causally potent it tends to be, whether it is the behaviour of the defendant, the plaintiff or some third party.

4. RELATIONSHIP BETWEEN PLAINTIFF AND DEFENDANT

Whether you get the money you are claiming depends on whom you are claiming it from. In other words, the relationship between the plaintiff and the defendant is a material consideration in every tort suit. For example, suppose that the defendant is doing construction work under statutory powers in a main street, and that his crane is defective for want of repair. A load being lifted by it drops from a height on to a workman. Two people suffer shock at the sight of this tragedy, the craneman and a passer-by who has stopped to stare. It is probable that the craneman can sue and that the passer-by cannot (p. 77). Yet the behaviour of the defendant, the nature of the damage and the relationship between the damage and the behaviour are identical. The reason is that the defendant is in a protective relationship to the craneman, his employee, and is in no relationship with the pedestrian, save that constituted by physical proximity. Take another case. Antony is giving Balbus his second driving lesson, when, owing to lack of expertise, Balbus runs into a pedestrian, Cleopatra, and both Antony and Cleopatra are injured in the collision. The matter is controverted (since some people want just one rule for the road—see below p. 92), but the better view is that Cleopatra will recover and Antony will not.

In order to accommodate such difficulties the law has the device of "special relationship" which may either heighten or lower the duty which is owed when the relationship is merely spatial. But in many cases where the concept of "special relationship" is not mentioned, the results can only be rationalised on the basis that one exists. If one takes as standard the relationship, miscalled "neighbourhood," which is said to exist merely because the defendant should have been thinking of the plaintiff as a possible victim of his carelessness, then there are some relationships which are very different. Take actual neighbourhood, for example, the relationship between those who live next door to each other, or whose properties are adjacent. No legal system could treat such people as it treats those who collide on the highway. In England, the special regime for real neighbours is called "nuisance." Relationships differ widely, and the use of general terms should not conceal the fact. For instance, plaintiff and defendant may be parties to a contract, and a contract is a very special relationship indeed—there are whole books about it—because the parties have chosen to do business with each other.

In France the law of tort applies only in the absence of a contract; in other words, it applies only between strangers. The English law of tort applies between contractors, too, except in so far as it has been effectively excluded by the terms of the contract itself (effective exclusion now being difficult—see below p. 222). This concurrence of tort and contract leads to some difficulties. You bring the same action of trespass against the burglar

as against the landlord who evicts you. You bring the same action against a
thief as against the vendor who by mistake delivers to someone else the
thing he sold to you.

Two factors at least distinguish the voluntary from the involuntary relationship. On the one hand, where persons have come together, they must
know that they expose themselves to the risk of harm from the other. On
the other hand, the coming together of the parties may throw on one of
them a higher liability because he knows that the other party is relying on
him; the best example of this is master and servant.

5. THE PLAINTIFF'S BEHAVIOUR

A person who "has only himself to blame" for an accident cannot claim
from anyone else (except his insurer or social security). It would be monstrous if he could. Sometimes one feels that the plaintiff has only himself to
blame even though the defendant is at fault in some way. One feels this
mainly where the plaintiff's behaviour has been particularly unreasonable
in comparison with that of the defendant. In such cases, the plaintiff's
behaviour will be referable either to his relationship with the defendant, or
to the relationship between the defendant's behaviour and the damage—
one will say either. "The defendant doesn't have to pay *him*" or "The
defendant doesn't have to pay him for *that*." These points therefore can be
dealt with in terms of duty or causation. If the plaintiff's behaviour was not
very unreasonable, then the loss may be shared (below, p. 213).

While Western systems of law rather flatter themselves on paying no
heed to the personal merits or demerits of claimants, it is really undeniable
that good people get more and bad people less. Rescuers and other
altruists are favoured by the law of tort (below, p. 78), burglars and other
criminals disfavoured (below, p. 226).

6. THE DUTY CONCEPT

These are aspects of the facts of all cases which cannot fail to be relevant to
an acceptable decision; but the grounds of decision must be stated in terms
of legal concepts, which may or may not reflect the differences in the facts.
We have already seen how the concept of "right" may be used to conceal
the fact that the plaintiff has really suffered no damage; it may also be used
to make the defendant's act seem wrongful when it is really irreprehen-
sible. Here it must suffice to deal briefly with the very important concept of
"duty."

The word duty is used for two distinct purposes—to establish a relationship in law between the defendant and the plaintiff and to state the standard of behaviour which the law requires of the defendant in a question
with that plaintiff. But in certain cases liability is so clear that we bypass the
notion of duty. If A tells lies to B, we know that this is wrong, and do not
take the intermediate step of saying "A was under a duty to be honest."
People always are. So also we do not talk of a duty not to trespass, because
it is elementary that trespassers are liable. It is when liability is not clear
and when it is clear that there is no liability that we use the notion of
"duty," either by stating it (p. 44) or denying it (p. 29).

For example, where the plaintiff has suffered damage as a consequence of the defendant's behaviour, and the courts are unwilling for one reason or another to impose liability on the defendant but are yet unable to deny that what the plaintiff is complaining of is "damage" or that the defendant acted unreasonably or that that unreasonable behaviour caused the damage, then they say that the defendant did not owe the plaintiff any duty to take care. Thus, although the defendant has acted without care, his act is not a breach of duty to the plaintiff, because that duty is said not to exist. This was one of the grounds on which the Court of Appeal recently dismissed the claim of a congenitally deformed child who, but for the defendant's negligence, would never have been born at all (*McKay* v. *Essex Area Health Authority* [1982] Q.B. 1166). This was the reason given for absolving a barrister whose negligent advocacy has allegedly led to his client's conviction (*Rondel* v. *Worsley* [1969] 1 A.C. 191). No other reason can be given for preventing a wife suing for her undoubted personal loss resulting from the negligent emasculation of her husband (*Best* v. *Samuel Fox* [1952] A.C. 716). Similarly, where the plaintiff is complaining of financial loss only, and the court is unwilling to shift the burden of that loss to a merely negligent defendant, the court may use the duty device to deny recovery by holding that no duty was owed (p. 29). The courts cannot say "This kind of damage cannot be compensated," because in other circumstances it can; nor can they say "such behaviour in a defendant does not involve him in liability," because in other circumstances it does; nor can the courts deny causation, because frequently all the tests of causation are satisfied (*e.g.*, the defendant negligently damages a car insured by the plaintiff).

When does a duty exist? The question has been much discussed, though it is perhaps too generally phrased for the discussion to be useful. A duty should not be imposed unless it is "just and reasonable" to do so (*per* Lord Keith in *Peabody* [1984] 3 All E.R. 529, 534). In fact, a duty to take care to avoid causing foreseeable physical harm invariably exists, since one must not needlessly endanger people or their property; a duty to take positive steps to save others from such harm is found less commonly (below p. 53) and a duty to take care with regard to merely economic harm is rarely imposed in the absence of a special relationship.

Given that a duty exists, it must be a duty with a content. The duty fixes not only the relationship between the parties, but also the standard of behaviour to be required of the defendant. Here there is great flexibility. The flexibility can come either in the formulation of the duty or in its application to different sets of facts. Thus one can say that the person who hires out a ladder owes a duty to his contractor's employees to take reasonable care that it is not defective, whereas if they borrow a ladder from a neighbour, the neighbour's duty is only to disclose known defects. It is, however, just as satisfactory to say that both suppliers owe the same duty to take reasonable care, but that more extensive precautions are required to satisfy that duty in the one case than in the other. One expects both to take reasonable care, but one does not expect the housewife to test every rung; more is looked for in a business man than in a person doing a kindness. But this is satisfactory only so long as it is remembered that "reasonable care" means "reasonable care *in all the circumstances*." Otherwise one quickly goes wrong. (For a list of relevant circumstances, see Occupiers' Liability

Act 1957, s.2, below, p. 114). The present tendency of the common law is
to state the duty generally as being the duty to take reasonable care; "gross
negligence" is not required.

The "duty to take reasonable care" is a very satisfying one, because
"duty" calls up a picture of a standard of behaviour, measured by the possible; we do not in private life stigmatise someone for breach of a duty
unless it was within his power to fulfil it. But not all duties at common law
are of a level such that a person acting reasonably satisfies them, and duties
under statute usually are not. Cases will be found in this book where the
courts say "The defendant's contractor was negligent, so the defendant's
duty was not fulfilled." The defendant is accordingly in breach of his duty
although he himself has done nothing wrong. The content of the duty,
then, is not a pattern for behaviour, but a list of facts which must exist to
exonerate the defendant. For example, when the legislature requires that
dangerous parts of machinery be securely fenced (Factories Act 1961,
s.14), it is no excuse for a defendant, if a dangerous part is not securely
fenced, that the machine could not be operated if it were. Thus there are
duties which are broken only if the *defendant* was at fault (the duty owed
by one user of the highway to another). There are duties which are broken
only if *someone* was at fault—and the range of persons whose fault may
involve a breach of duty by the defendant is infinitely extensible (*e.g.*, liability for independent contractors), and there are duties which are broken
although *no one* was at fault (*e.g.*, some statutory duties, and the vendor's
liability to the purchaser of defective goods).

Dangers lurk, however, in the use of the word "duty." One such danger,
recently made manifest, is the danger of supposing that tort liability *must*
attach to behaviour which can be characterised as a breach of "duty." It is
tempting but misleading to say "You ought to have done that, *i.e.*, you
were under a duty to do it, so you must pay damages for not doing it." As
Lord Edmund-Davies has observed: "In most situations it is better to be
careful than careless, but it is quite another thing to elevate all carelessness
into a tort. Liability has to be based on a legal duty not to be careless, and I
can find none in this case." (*Moorgate Mercantile Co.* v. *Twitchings* [1977]
A.C. 890, 919).

Thus if A has promised B to do something, A clearly "ought" to do it,
and do it properly or carefully. His failure so to do it may injure C; but it
does not follow that C should be able to sue A, though we may be misled
into thinking that A is under some 'duty" to C just because there is a sense
in which A "ought" to have done what he promised. Likewise, it is elementary that public officials "ought" to perform their functions properly: that
is what they are there for and what they are paid for, and no one would
deny that they have "duties" to perform. However, it is not at all clear that
tort liability in damages is invariably the proper or sensible sanction for
their failure to perform them. Here again it is dangerously easy to infer
from the proposition that tort liability depends on breach of duty that every
breach of duty must lead to tort liability. It does so only if the relationship
between plaintiff and defendant is of a certain sort and if the damage is of a
certain sort and is caused in a certain way.

An Illustrative Case

THOMAS v. NATIONAL UNION OF MINEWORKERS (SOUTH WALES AREA)

Chancery [1986] Ch. 20; [1985] 2 W.L.R. 1081; [1985] 2 All E.R. 1; [1985] I.C.R. 886; [1985] I.R.L.R. 157

The plaintiff coal-miners decided to defy a strike but found it difficult and unpleasant to go to the pit because each morning several score of their striking colleagues gathered round the colliery gates and greeted them with vilification and abuse as they drove in under police escort. They sought an injunction against the union, and obtained it.

Scott J.: The right of the plaintiffs to relief in respect of the picketing at colliery gates raises three questions. First, there is the question whether the picketing sought to be restrained would represent the commission of a tort against a particular plaintiff or plaintiffs. As to this, I regard the phrase "unlawful picketing" as unhelpful and misleading. It is frequently used. Sometimes it is used to describe picketing in the course of which criminal offences are committed. Sometimes it is used to describe picketing which is tortious. And often it is used to describe picketing which is both tortious and criminal. This is a civil action in which the plaintiffs are asserting their private rights under the civil law. They can complain in a civil action of picketing which is tortious but not of picketing which is criminal. It is for the public prosecuting authorities or for the Attorney General to control the commission of criminal offences in the course of picketing. It is not for these plaintiffs to do so. The question for me, therefore, is whether the picketing is tortious. The question is not whether the picketing is criminal.

Counsel for the plaintiff helpfully put before me two papers . . . setting out in summary form his submissions as to the tortious nature of picketing. He relied on a number of torts. He began by referring to s.7 of the Conspiracy and Protection of Property Act 1875. His main argument was that the picketing constituted a criminal offence under that section and was therefore tortious.

[His Lordship discussed the authorities].

These authorities establish that conduct must, in order to be an offence under s.7, be tortious. The proposition that it can be shown to be tortious because it can be shown to be an offence under s.7 puts the cart before the horse, and in my judgment involves a misuse of s.7. I therefore reject counsel for the plaintiff's submission that the colliery gate picketing is tortious because it involves a breach of s.7. . . .

. . . After various repeals, amendments and re-enactments the relevant statutory immunity from tortious or criminal liability for acts done in the course of picketing is now to be found in s.16(1) of the Employment Act 1980. The statutory provision, which is expressed to be a substitution for s.15 of the Trade Union and Labour Relations Act 1974, is in these terms:

"**15.**—(1) It shall be lawful for a person in contemplation or furtherance of a trade dispute to attend—(*a*) at or near his own place of work, or (*b*) if he is an official of a trade union, at or near the place of work of a member of that union whom he is accompanying and whom he represents, for the purpose only of peacefully obtaining or communicating information, or peacefully persuading any person to work or abstain from working . . . "

I need not read the other subsections of the new s.15.

The position, therefore, is that the picketing in the present case of which complaint is made will not be actionable in tort if it can be brought within this substituted s.15. In my judgment, on any reasonable view of the defendants' own evidence, the immunity of this provision cannot be claimed for the persons who regularly assemble at the colliery gates. It may be that the six persons who are selected to stand close to the gates could bring themselves within the provision, but the many others who are present cannot do so. What is their purpose in attending? It is obviously not to obtain or communicate information. Is it peacefully to persuade the working miners to abstain from working? If that is the case what is the need for so many people, what is the need for the police, and what is the need for vehicles to bring the working miners safely into the collieries? It is fair to say that counsel for the first to seventh defendants, realistically, did not invite me to deal with this application on the footing that the colliery gate picketing could claim immunity under the substituted s.15. And, of course, picketing at people's houses or places of education cannot qualify for immunity under the section.

It does not, however, follow that, because picketing cannot be brought within the substituted s.15, the picketing is therefore tortious. In order to decide whether or to what extent picketing that falls outside the section is tortious, recourse must be had to the general law of tort.

I have already said that I am unable to accept counsel for the plaintiffs' basic approach, which was to start by asking whether the picketing represented an offence under s.7 of the 1875 Act. As a supplement to that approach he submitted that the picketing complained of was tortious under a number of heads. It represented, he said, the tort of assault in that the miners going to work were put in fear of violence. I cannot accept this. Assault is defined in *Clerk and Lindsell on Torts* (15th ed., 1982) para. 14/10 as "an overt act indicating an immediate intention to commit a battery, coupled with the capacity to carry that intention into effect." The tort of assault is not, in my view, committed, unless the capacity in question is present at the time the overt act is committed. Since the working miners are in vehicles and the pickets are held back from the vehicles, I do not understand how even the most violent of threats or gestures could be said to constitute an assault.

Alternatively, counsel for the plaintiffs submitted that the picketing involved obstruction of the highway for which the working miners could sue in tort. He referred me to *Broome* v. *D.P.P.* ([1974] A.C. 587), in which it was held that pickets had no right to insist that drivers or pedestrians stop and listen to what they have to say. Lord Reid said (at 597):

> "There was a suggestion that if a picket does not have a right to stop a driver or pedestrian the same result could be obtained lawfully by a large number of pickets gathering at the same place and doing nothing. The section does not limit the number of pickets and no limitation on numbers can be implied. So if a large number assemble it will not be physically possible in many cases for a driver or pedestrian to proceed. But if a picket has a purpose beyond those set out in the section, then his presence becomes unlawful and in many cases such as I have supposed it would not be difficult to infer as a matter of fact that pickets who assemble in unreasonably large numbers do have the purpose of preventing free passage. If that were the proper inference then their presence on the highway would become unlawful."

Counsel for the plaintiffs argued that in the present case the large numbers of pickets present at the colliery gates were almost bound to be obstructing some part of the highway, even if only the pavements. That may be so, but it does not follow that the obstruction would represent a tort actionable at the suit of the working miners. The present state of affairs, which I have no reason to suppose will not continue as long as the strike lasts, is that the working miners' entry into and egress from the colliery is not being physically prevented by the pickets. If the pickets are obstructing the highway, the obstruction is not causing any special damage to the working miners. On principle, therefore, the plaintiffs cannot, in my view, have a cause of action in tort for obstruction of the highway.

Counsel submitted that *Hubbard* v. *Pitt* ([1976] Q.B. 142) provided authority to the contrary effect.

[His Lordship discussed that case.]

Accordingly, this case cannot be regarded as any authority for the startling proposition that the plaintiffs can, without special damage, sue in tort for obstruction to the highway.

Counsel further submitted that the picketing was tortious at the suit of the plaintiffs in that it represented unlawful interference with the performance of the contracts of employment between them and the NCB.

The tort of interference with contract in the course of an industrial dispute has recently been considered by the House of Lords in *Merkur Island Shipping Corp.* v. *Laughton* ([1983] 2 A.C. 570). Lord Diplock, with whose speech the other members of the House agreed, described the interference necessary in order to constitute the tort as being the prevention of the performance of a primary obligation under the contract (see 608, 609). The picketing in the present case is not, as I understand it, having the effect of preventing the performance by the NCB of any primary obligation under the plaintiffs' employment contracts. The plaintiffs cannot, in my view, wield this tort as a weapon to attack the colliery gate picketing.

Counsel for the plaintiffs referred also to the tort of intimidation. By this he meant not the well-known tort of intimidation established by *Rookes* v. *Barnard* [below p. 517] a tort which has nothing at all to do with the present case, but the tort which he submitted was committed by a person who intimidated another. The working miners were, he submitted, being intimidated by the pickets at the colliery gates. This was another formulation of counsel's argument based on s.7 of the 1875 Act. He argued that the pickets were committing breaches of the section since, with a view to compelling the working miners to abstain from working, they were intimidating the working miners. But, on authority, the approach is wrong. First, the tortious conduct must be identified. Only then is it relevant to see whether there is a breach of s.7. None the less, although I cannot, for the reasons I have already given, accept counsel's approach, I am in full agreement with his general submissions regarding the state of affairs at the colliery gates, which, he said, represented intimidation.

The working miners are entitled to use the highway for the purpose of entering and leaving their respective places of work. In the exercise of that right they are at present having to suffer the presence and behaviour of the pickets and demonstrators. The law has long recognised that unreasonable interference with the rights of others is actionable in tort. The law of nuisance is a classic example and was classically described by Lindley M.R. in *J. Lyons & Sons Ltd.* v. *Wilkins* [1899] 1 Ch. 255, 267:

"The truth is that to watch or beset a man's house with a view to compel him to do or not to do what is lawful for him not to do or to do is wrongful and without lawful authority unless some reasonable justification for it is consistent with the evidence. Such conduct seriously interferes with the ordinary comfort of human existence and ordinary enjoyment of the house beset, and such conduct would support an action on the case for a nuisance at common law."

It is, however, not every act of interference with the enjoyment by an individual of his property rights that will be actionable in nuisance. The law must strike a balance between conflicting rights and interests. The point is made in *Clerk and Lindsell* para. 23/01:

"A variety of different things may amount to a nuisance *in fact* but whether

they are *actionable* as the *tort* of nuisance will depend upon a variety of considerations and a balance of conflicting interests."

Nuisance is strictly concerned with, and may be regarded as confined to, activity
which unduly interferes with the use or enjoyment of land or of easements. But
there is no reason why the law should not protect on a similar basis the enjoyment
of other rights. All citizens have the right to use the public highway. Suppose an
individual were persistently to follow another on a public highway, making rude
gestures or remarks in order to annoy or vex. If continuance of such conduct were
threatened no one can doubt but that a civil court would, at the suit of the victim,
restrain by an injunction the continuance of the conduct. The tort might be described as a species of private nuisance, namely unreasonable interference with the
victim's rights to use the highway. But the label for the tort does not, in my view,
matter.

In the present case, the working miners have the right to use the highway for the
purpose of going to work. They are, in my judgment, entitled under the general law
to exercise that right without unreasonable harassment by others. Unreasonable
harassment of them in their exercise of that right would, in my judgment, be tortious.

A decision whether in this, or in any other similar case, the presence or conduct
of pickets represents a tortious interference with the right of those who wish to go
to work to do so without harassment must depend on the particular circumstances
of the particular case. The balance to which I have earlier referred must be struck
between the rights of those going to work and the rights of the pickets.

It was made clear in *Ward Lock & Co. Ltd.* v. *Operative Printers' Assistants'
Society* ((1906) 22 T.L.R. 327) that picketing was not, *per se*, a common law nuisance. The Court of Appeal was in that case considering the question from the point
of view of the owner of the premises being picketed. The picketing was peaceful
and, *per* Vaughan Williams L.J. (at 329), "there was no evidence that the comfort
of the plaintiffs or the ordinary enjoyment of the Botolph Printing Works was
seriously interfered with by the watching and besetting." He held, in effect, that
there was no common law nuisance being committed.

Similarly, in the present case, the working miners cannot complain of picketing
per se or of demonstrations *per se*. They can only complain of picketing or demonstrations which unreasonably harass them in their entry into and egress from their
place of work.

From the comments I have already made earlier in this judgment it will be apparent that I think it plain from the evidence before me that the picketing at the colliery gates is of a nature and is carried out in a manner that represents an
unreasonable harassment of the working miners. A daily congregation on average
of 50 to 70 men hurling abuse and in circumstances that require a police presence
and require the working miners to be conveyed in vehicles do not in my view leave
any real room for argument. The working miners have the right to go to work.
Neither they nor any other working man should be required, in order to exercise
that right, to tolerate the situation I have described. Accordingly in my judgment
the colliery gates picketing is tortious at the suit of the plaintiff or plaintiffs who
work at the collieries in question.

I can deal more shortly with the picketing at Mr Lock's home and the picketing at
the entrance to the estate where Mr Fjaelberg lives. Regular picketing at the home
of a working miner would represent, in my opinion, regardless of the number of
people involved and regardless of the peaceful nature of their conduct, *per se* common law nuisance. The *Ward Lock* case was a case of picketing at business premises, which is a very different matter. Indeed, the bulk of the deponents on the
defendants' side very properly recognise the unreasonable character that picketing
at someone's home would have. They dissociate themselves from it.

The same would, in my judgment, also be true if Mr Sheehan were to return to work and if his college were then to be picketed. None of the defendants' deponents would seek to justify such a thing. . . .

Note:

This first-instance decision (noted at [1985] Camb.L.J. 374 (Ewing)) may not survive appellate scrutiny, but it illustrates

(a) the complex relationship between criminal law and the law of tort, as well as that between statute and common law;
(b) the typically English approach to tort cases, namely to run through all the possibly relevant "torts" in order to see whether the facts of the case fit the structure of any of them (fear of violence?, special damage?, contract interfered with?);
(c) the extension of liability to a new set of facts, by analogy with old decisions, it being hotly debated whether the extension in this instance was progressive or not;
(d) the fact that the law of tort is concerned not just with safety and wealth, but with freedom as well.

PART I

NEGLIGENCE

Chapter 1

DUTY

(M'ALISTER or) DONOGHUE v. STEVENSON

House of Lords [1932] A.C. 562; 101 L.J.P.C. 119; 147 L.T. 281; 48 T.L.R. 494; 76 S.J. 396; 37 Com.Cas. 350; [1932] All E.R.Rep. 1

Action by consumer against manufacturer in respect of personal injury

Mrs. Donoghue (*née* M'Alister) averred that a friend purchased a bottle of ginger-beer for her in Minchella's café in Paisley; that Minchella took the metal cap off the bottle, which was made of dark opaque glass, and poured some of the contents into a tumbler; that, having no reason to suspect that it was anything other than pure ginger-beer, she drank some of the contents; that when her friend refilled her glass from the bottle there floated out the decomposed remains of a snail; that she suffered from shock and severe gastro-enteritis as a result of the nauseating sight and of the impurities she had already consumed. She further averred that the ginger-beer was manufactured by the defender to be sold as a drink to the public (including herself), that it was bottled by him and labelled with a label bearing his name; and that the defender sealed the bottle with a metal cap. She also claimed that it was the duty of the defender to provide a system in his business which would prevent snails entering his ginger-beer bottles, and to provide an efficient system of inspection of bottles prior to their being filled with ginger-beer, and that his failure in both duties caused this accident.

The defender objected that the averments were irrelevant and insufficient (that is, that even if the pursuer established by proof all that she had averred, she would still not be entitled to judgment).

The Lord Ordinary overruled the defender's objection, and wanted to proceed with the evidence. The defender appealed to the Second Division of the Court of Session, who adhered to their judgment in *Mullen* v. *Barr & Co.*, 1929 S.C. 461, and allowed the appeal. The pursuer appealed to the House of Lords, who restored the interlocutor of the Lord Ordinary.

Lord Atkin: My Lords, the sole question for determination in this case is legal: Do the averments made by the pursuer in her pleading, if true, disclose a cause of action? I need not restate the particular facts. The question is whether the manufacturer of an article of drink sold by him to a distributor, in circumstances which prevent the distributor or the ultimate purchaser or consumer from discovering by inspection any defect, is under any legal duty to the ultimate purchaser or consumer to take reasonable care that the article is free from defect likely to cause injury to health. I do not think a more important problem has occupied your Lordships in your judicial capacity: important both because of its bearing on public health and because of the practical test which it applies to the system under which it arises . . . The law . . . appears to be that in order to support an action for damages for negligence the complainant has to show that he has been injured by the breach of a duty owed to him in the circumstances by the defendant to take reasonable care to avoid such injury. In the present case we are not concerned with the breach of the duty; if a duty exists, that would be a question of fact which is sufficiently averred and for present purposes must be assumed. We are solely concerned with the question

21

whether, as a matter of law in the circumstances alleged, the defender owed any duty to the pursuer to take care.

It is remarkable how difficult it is to find in the English authorities statements of general application defining the relations between parties that give rise to the duty. The Courts are concerned with the particular relations which come before them in actual litigation, and it is sufficient to say whether the duty exists in those circumstances. The result is that the Courts have been engaged upon an elaborate classification of duties as they exist in respect of property, whether real or personal, with further divisions as to ownership, occupation or control, and distinctions based on the particular relations of the one side or the other, whether manufacturer, salesman or landlord, customer, tenant, stranger, and so on. In this way it can be ascertained at any time whether the law recognizes a duty, but only where the case can be referred to some particular species which has been examined and classified. And yet the duty which is common to all the cases where liability is established must logically be based upon some element common to the cases where it is found to exist. To seek a complete logical definition of the general principle is probably to go beyond the function of the judge, for the more general the definition the more likely it is to omit essentials or to introduce non-essentials. The attempt was made by Brett M.R. in *Heaven* v. *Pender* ((1883) 11 Q.B.D. 503, 509), in a definition to which I will later refer. As framed, it was demonstrably too wide, though it appears to me, if properly limited, to be capable of affording a valuable practical guide.

At present I content myself with pointing out that in English law there must be, and is, some general conception of relations giving rise to a duty of care, of which the particular cases found in the books are but instances. The liability for negligence, whether you style it such or treat it as in other systems as a species of "culpa," is no doubt based upon a general public sentiment of moral wrongdoing for which the offender must pay. But acts or omissions which any moral code would censure cannot in a practical world be treated so as to give a right to every person injured by them to demand relief. In this way rules of law arise which limit the range of complainants and the extent of their remedy. The rule that you are to love your neighbour becomes in law, you must not injure your neighbour; and the lawyer's question, Who is my neighbour? receives a restricted reply. You must take reasonable care to avoid acts or omissions which you can reasonably foresee would be likely to injure your neighbour. **Who, then, in law is my neighbour? The answer seems to be—persons who are so closely and directly affected by my act that I ought reasonably to have them in contemplation as being so affected when I am directing my mind to the acts or omissions which are called in question.** This appears to me to be the doctrine of *Heaven* v. *Pender*, as laid down by Lord Esher (then Brett M.R.) when it is limited by the notion of proximity introduced by Lord Esher himself and A. L. Smith L.J. in *Le Lievre* v. *Gould* ([1893] 1 Q.B. 491, 497, 504). Lord Esher says: "That case established that, under certain circumstances, one man may owe a duty to another, even though there is no contract between them. If one man is near to another, or is near to the property of another, a duty lies upon him not to do that which may cause a personal injury to that other, or may injure his property." So A. L. Smith L.J.: "The decision of *Heaven* v. *Pender* was founded upon the principle, that a duty to take due care did arise when the person or property of one was in such proximity to the person or property of another that, if due care was not taken, damage might be done by the one to the other." **I think that this sufficiently states the truth if proximity be not confined to mere physical proximity, but be used, as I think it was intended, to extend to such close and direct relations that the act complained of directly affects a person whom the person alleged to be bound to take care would know would be directly affected by his careless act.** That this is the sense in which nearness or "proximity" was intended by Lord Esher is obvious from his own illustration in *Heaven* v. *Pender* of the application of his doctrine to the sale of goods. "This" (*i.e.*, the rule he has just formulated) "includes the case of goods, etc., supplied to be used immediately by a particular person or persons, or one of a class of persons, where it would be obvious to the person supplying, if he thought, that the goods would in all probability be used at once by such persons before a reasonable opportunity for discovering any defect which might exist, and where the thing supplied would be of such a nature that a neglect of ordinary care or skill as to its condition or the manner of supplying it would probably cause danger to the person or property of the person for whose use it was supplied, and who was about to use it. It would exclude a case in which the goods are supplied under circumstances in which it would be a chance by whom they would be used or whether they would be used or not, or whether they would be used before there would probably be means of observing any defect, or where the goods would be of such a nature that a want of care or skill as to their condition or the manner of supplying them would not probably produce danger of injury to person or property." I draw particular attention to the fact that Lord Esher emphasizes the necessity of goods having to be "used immediately" and "used at once before a reasonable opportunity of inspection." This is obviously to exclude the possibility of goods having their condition altered by lapse of time, and to call attention to the proximate relationship, which may be too remote where inspection even of the person using, certainly of an intermediate person, may reasonably be interposed. With this necessary qualification of proximate relationship as explained in *Le Lievre* v. *Gould*, I think the judgment of Lord Esher expresses the law of England; without the qualification, I think the majority of the Court in *Heaven* v. *Pender* were justified in thinking the principle was expressed in too general terms. **There will no doubt arise cases where it will be difficult to determine whether the contemplated relationship is so close that the duty arises.** But in the class of case now before the Court I cannot conceive any difficulty to arise. A manufacturer puts up an article of food in a container which he knows will be opened by the actual consumer. There can be no inspection by any purchaser and no reasonable preliminary inspection by the consumer. Negligently, in the course of preparation, he allows the contents to be mixed with poison. It is said that the law of England and Scotland is that the poisoned consumer has no remedy against the negligent manufacturer. If this were the result of the authorities I should consider the result a grave defect in the law, and so contrary to principle that I should hesitate long before following any decision to that effect which had not the authority of this House. I would point out that, in the assumed state of the authorities, not only would the consumer have no remedy against the manufacturer, he would have none against any one else, for in the circumstances alleged there would be no evidence of negligence against any one other than the manufacturer; and, except in the case of a consumer who was also a purchaser, no contract and no warranty of fitness, and in the case of the purchase of a specific article under its patent or trade name, which might well be the case in the purchase of some articles of food or drink, no warranty protecting even the purchaser-consumer. There are other instances than of articles of food and drink where goods are sold intended to be used immediately by the consumer, such as many forms of goods sold for cleaning purposes, where the same liability must exist. The doctrine supported by the decision below would not only deny a remedy to the consumer who was injured by consuming bottled beer or chocolates poisoned by the negligence of the manufacturer, but also to the user of what should be a harmless proprietary medicine, an ointment, a soap, a cleaning fluid or cleaning powder. I confine myself to articles of common household use, where every one, including the manufacturer, knows that the articles will be used by other persons than the actual ultimate purchaser— namely, by members of his family and his servants, and in some cases his guests. I do not think so ill of our jurisprudence as to suppose that its principles are so remote from the ordinary needs of civilized society and the ordinary claims it makes upon its members as to deny a legal remedy where there is so obviously a social wrong.

It will be found, I think, on examination that there is no case in which the circumstances have been such as I have just suggested where the liability has been negatived. There are numerous cases, where the relations were much more remote, where the duty has been held not to exist . . .

My Lords, if your Lordships accept the view that this pleading discloses a relevant cause of action you will be affirming the proposition that by Scots and English law alike a manufacturer of products, which he sells in such a form as to show that he intends them to reach the ultimate consumer in the form in which they left him with no reasonable possibility of intermediate examination, and with the knowledge that the absence of reasonable care in the preparation or putting up the products will result in an injury to the consumer's life or property, owes a duty to the consumer to take that reasonable care.

It is a proposition which I venture to say no one in Scotland or England who was not a lawyer would for one moment doubt. It will be an advantage to make it clear that the law in this matter, as in most others, is in accordance with sound common sense. I think that this appeal should be allowed.

Lord Macmillan: . . . The law takes no cognizance of carelessness in the abstract. It concerns itself with carelessness only where there is a duty to take care and where failure in that duty has caused damage. In such circumstances carelessness assumes the legal quality of negligence and entails the consequences in law of negligence. What, then, are the circumstances which give rise to this duty to take care? In the daily contacts of social and business life human beings are thrown into, or place themselves in, an infinite variety of relations with their fellows; and the law can refer only to the standards of the reasonable man in order to determine whether any particular relation gives rise to a duty to take care as between those who stand in that relation to each other. The grounds of action may be as various and manifold as human errancy; and the conception of legal responsibility may develop in adaptation to altering social conditions and standards. The criterion of judgment must adjust and adapt itself to the changing circumstances of life. The categories of negligence are never closed. The cardinal principle of liability is that the party complained of should owe to the party complaining a duty to take care, and that the party complaining should be able to prove that he has suffered damage in consequence of a breach of that duty. Where there is room for diversity of view, it is in determining what circumstances will establish such a relationship between the parties as to give rise, on the one side, to a duty to take care, and on the other side to a right to have care taken.

To descend from these generalities to the circumstances of the present case, I do not think that any reasonable man or any twelve reasonable men would hesitate to hold that, if the appellant establishes her allegations, the respondent has exhibited carelessness in the conduct of his business. For a manufacturer of aerated water to store his empty bottles in a place where snails can get access to them, and to fill his bottles without taking any adequate precautions by inspection or otherwise to ensure that they contain no deleterious foreign matter, may reasonably be characterized as carelessness without applying too exacting a standard. But, as I have pointed out, it is not enough to prove the respondent to be careless in his process of manufacture. The question is: Does he owe a duty to take care, and to whom does he owe that duty? Now I have no hesitation in affirming that a person who for gain engages in the business of manufacturing articles of food and drink intended for consumption by members of the public in the form in which he issues them is under a duty to take care in the manufacture of these articles. That duty, in my opinion, he owes to those whom he intends to consume his products. He manufactures his commodities for human consumption; he intends and contemplates that they shall be consumed. By reason of that very fact he places himself in a relationship with all the potential consumers of his commodities, and that relationship which he assumes and desires for his own ends imposes upon him a duty to take care to avoid injuring them. He owes them a duty not to convert by his own carelessness an article which he issues to them as wholesome and innocent into an article which is dangerous to life and health. It is sometimes said that liability can only arise where a reasonable man would have foreseen and could have avoided the consequences of his act or omission. In the present case the respondent, when he manufactured his ginger-beer, had directly in contemplation that it would be consumed by members of the public. Can it be said that he could not be expected as a reasonable man to foresee that if he conducted his process of manufacture carelessly he might injure those whom he expected and desired to consume his ginger-beer? The possibility of injury so arising seems to me in no sense so remote as to excuse him from foreseeing it. Suppose that a baker, through carelessness, allows a large quantity of arsenic to be mixed with a batch of his bread, with the result that those who subsequently eat it are poisoned, could he be heard to say that he owed no duty to the consumers of his bread to take care that it was free from poison, and that, as he did not know that any poison had got into it, his only liability was for breach of warranty under his contract of sale to those who actually bought the poisoned bread from him? Observe that I have said "through carelessness," and thus excluded the case of pure accident such as may happen where every care is taken. I cannot believe, and I do not believe, that neither in the law of England nor in the law of Scotland is there redress for such a case. The state of facts I have figured might well give rise to a criminal charge, and the civil consequence of such carelessness can scarcely be less wide than its criminal consequences. Yet the principle of the decision appealed from is that the manufacturer of food products intended by him for human consumption does not owe to the consumers whom he has in view any duty of care, not even the duty to take care that he does not poison them . . .

I am anxious to emphasise that the principle of judgment which commends itself to me does not give rise to the sort of objection stated by Parke B. in *Longmeid* v. *Holliday* ((1851) 6 Exch. 761, 768; 155 E.R. 752), where he said: "But it would be going much too far to say, that so much care is required in the ordinary intercourse of life between one individual and another, that if a machine not in its nature dangerous—a carriage, for instance—but which might become so by a latent defect entirely unknown, although discoverable by the exercise of ordinary care, should be lent or given by one person, even by the person who manufactured it, to another, the former should be answerable to the latter for a subsequent damage accruing by the use of it." I read this passage rather as a note of warning that the standard of care exacted in human dealings must not be pitched too high than as giving any countenance to the view that negligence may be exhibited with impunity. It must always be a question of circumstances whether the carelessness amounts to negligence, and whether the injury is not too remote from the carelessness. I can readily conceive that where a manufacturer has parted with his product and it has passed into other hands it may well be exposed to vicissitudes which may render it defective or noxious, for which the manufacturer could not in any view be held to be to blame. It may be a good general rule to regard responsibility as ceasing when control ceases. So, also, where between the manufacturer and the user there is interposed a party who has the means and opportunity of examining the manufacturer's product before he re-issues it to the actual user. But where, as in the present case, the article of consumption is so prepared as to be intended to reach the consumer in the condition in which it leaves the manufacturer, and the manufacturer takes steps to ensure this by sealing or otherwise closing the container so that the contents cannot be tampered with, I regard his control as remaining effective until the article reaches the consumer and the container is opened by him. The intervention of any exterior agency is intended to be excluded, and was in fact in the present case excluded . . .

The burden of proof must always be upon the injured party to establish that the defect which caused the injury was present in the article when it left the hands of the party whom he sues, that the defect was occasioned by the carelessness of that party, and that the circumstances are such as to cast upon the defender a duty to take care not to injure the pursuer. There is no presumption of negligence in such a case as the present, nor is there any justification for applying the maxim, res ipsa loquitur. Negligence must be both averred and proved . . .

Lord Thankerton: . . . A man cannot be charged with negligence if he has no obligation to exercise diligence . . . Unless the consumer can establish a special relationship with the manufacturer, it is clear, in my opinion, that neither the law of Scotland nor the law of England will hold that the manufacturer has any duty towards the consumer to exercise diligence . . . [But here there was a special relationship because the manufacturer] **in placing his manufactured article of drink upon the market, has intentionally so excluded interference with, or examination of, the article by any intermediate handler of the goods between himself and the consumer that he has, of his own accord, brought himself into direct relationship with the consumer, with the result that the consumer is entitled to rely upon the exercise of diligence by the manufacturer to secure that the article shall not be harmful to the consumer** . . .

Lord Buckmaster dissented on the ground that there were only two exceptions to the principle that "the breach of the defendant's contract with A. to use care and skill in and about the manufacture or repair of an article does not of itself give any cause of action to B. when he is injured by reason of the article proving to be defective" (*per* Lord Sumner in *Blacker* v. *Lake & Elliot Ltd*. (1912) 106 L.T. 533, 536), namely, where the article was dangerous in itself or had a defect known to the manufacturer. The majority decision was "simply to misapply to tort doctrine applicable to sale and purchase."

Lord Tomlin also dissented.

Quotation

> "There may be in the cup
> A spider steep'd, and one may drink, depart,
> And yet partake no venom, for his knowledge
> It is not infected; but if one present
> The abhorr'd ingredient to his eye, make known
> How he hath drunk, he cracks his gorge, his sides
> With violent hefts. I have drunk, and seen the spider."

Shakespeare, *The Winter's Tale*, II.i.37.

Explanation:
The passages printed in bold type above are especially endorsed by Lord Keith in *Yuen Kun Yeu*, below p. 31.

Questions
1. Suppose that Mrs. Donoghue bought a bottle of Stevenson's ginger beer for 10p. and took it home; and that when she opened it, she saw a decomposed snail at the top of the bottle, and suffered shock at the thought of what she might have drunk. Could she recover from the manufacturer (a) damages for shock; (b) 10p.?
2. Suppose that Stevenson got his bottles from Louis, and that Mrs. Donoghue had been injured because of a defect in the bottle which Stevenson couldn't have discovered. Would Louis or Stevenson be liable, or both?
3. Suppose that the victim is not a regular consumer like Mrs. Donoghue but a shop-lifter or a tester for *Which*? Would you make the manufacturer liable? If not, would this be because he owed no duty or for some other reason?

Note:
Donoghue v. *Stevenson* is hardly the Last Word on the tort of negligence, since it was decided over 50 years ago, but it still deserves to come first in the book. Its importance lies not

only in what it decided but also in how it was decided: it established, as its *ratio decidendi*, that a careless manufacturer of a dangerously defective product is liable to a consumer to whom it causes personal injury, but more importantly, it laid down in *obiter dicta* a general principle of liability for unintended harm, focussing on the duty of care.

The Manufacturer

Nowadays persons complaining of *personal injury* caused by defective products no longer need to rely on *Donoghue* v. *Stevenson* since under the Consumer Protection Act 1987 the manufacturer is liable without proof of fault. The EEC Directive underlying the Act is given below p. 28. *Donoghue* v. *Stevenson* continues to apply to most cases of *property damage*, however. Where mere *financial harm* is suffered by a distant consumer, the careless manufacturer is normally under no liability at all (*Muirhead* v. *Industrial Tank Specialities* [1985] 3 All E.R. 705 (C.A.)). The following paragraphs should be read in the light of this.

Lord Thankerton spoke of the special relationship between manufacturer and consumer, *i.e.* the person whose appetite the manufacturer seeks to stimulate ("Don't be Vague: Ask for Stevenson's Ginger Beer"). There is such a special relationship, but in fact the manufacturer also owes a duty to the innocent bystander with whom he has no such relationship: the pedestrian injured by the defective car can sue just as well as its owner (*Lambert* v. *Lewis* [1982] A.C. 225). So the special relationship is not necessary where the harm is physical and it is insufficient where the harm is merely financial.

Lord Macmillan suggested that it was for the plaintiff to prove that the manufacturer was careless, but of course the victim can hardly know what went on in the factory. In *Grant* v. *Australian Knitting Mills* [1936] A.C. 85, the plaintiff complained of dermatitis resulting from the use of underpants manufactured by the defendant which contained excess sulphites. The defendant led evidence that he had manufactured 4,737,600 pairs of underpants with never a complaint. Yet the plaintiff succeeded. No one can reasonably say that a manufacturer with a failure rate of only one in a million is not a reasonably careful manufacturer; it is, indeed, an astonishing performance which should earn a prize. And one cannot say that he was not reasonably careful with the pants in question, since there was no evidence as to them, save their defect. He was in fact made to pay because the pants were defective when they left his factory. Thus the principal case, though it expresses the duty in terms of taking reasonable care, virtually results in a guarantor's liability. (See, for example, *Hill* v. *James Crowe (Cases) Ltd.* [1978] 1 All E.R. 812.) Now that it is only in cases of commercial property damage that it matters whether the manufacturer was negligent or not, it is quite possible that the courts will be less ready to find him negligent.

Most things that are made are made to be sold. Indeed, there are many more sellers than makers. Even in this case the snail was sold not only by Stevenson (to Minchella) but also by Minchella (to Friend). Long before 1932 it was clear what the seller's duty was: his duty was to provide a good thing, not just to take care not to provide a bad one. The seller's liability was strict (*i.e.* not dependent on his carelessness) and it was triggered by the defect, even if the defect did not render the thing dangerous. (*i.e.* apt to cause physical harm). Now Friend bought the ginger-beer for Mrs. Donoghue ("Please can I have a ginger-beer for my lady-friend here?"), and Mrs. Donoghue was very close to Minchella, perhaps physically just as close as Friend himself. In many systems of law Mrs. Donoghue would have been able to sue Minchella on the contract of sale, as its beneficiary. English law, however, does not allow a beneficiary to sue (*Beswick* v. *Beswick* [1968] A.C. 68), either to enforce the contract or to claim damages for its breach.

The Principle

The decision did more than simply add manufacturer/consumer to the list of relationships which involved a duty to take care. It also laid down a principle much wider than the facts of the case required, *viz.* "You must take reasonable care to avoid causing foreseeable injury." It is because this principle acts as a unifying force that *Donoghue* v. *Stevenson* is said to denote the birth of negligence as a tort.

There are two areas in respect of which the principle is wider than the rule required by the facts of the case:

(1) In the actual case, the harm allegedly suffered was physical, indeed internal, injury. The principle did not seem to be so limited. Was the principle extensible to purely psychical harm and to purely financial harm? See *McLoughlin* v. *O'Brian* (below, p. 69) and *Junior Books* v. *Veitchi Co. Ltd.* [1983] A.C. 520 (H.L.).

(2) In the actual case Stevenson's conduct added a new danger to life. He positively caused the harm, he didn't just let it happen. Was the principle extensible to those who simply let the damage occur? See *Dorset Yacht* (below, p. 53) and *Anns* (below p. 60).

COUNCIL OF THE EUROPEAN COMMUNITIES
DIRECTIVE of JULY 25, 1985

Art. 1 The producer shall be liable for damage caused by a defect in his product.

Art. 2 For the purpose of this Directive "product" means all movables, with the exception of primary agricultural products and game, even though incorporated into another movable or into an immovable. "Primary agricultural products" means the products of the soil, of stock-farming and of fisheries, excluding products which have undergone initial processing. "Product" includes electricity.

Art. 3 (1) "Producer" means the manufacturer of a finished product, the producer of any raw material or the manufacturer of a component part and any person who, by putting his name, trade mark or other distinguishing feature on the product presents himself as its producer.
(2) Without prejudice to the liability of the producer, any person who imports into the Community a product for sale, hire, leasing or any form of distribution in the course of his business shall be deemed to be a producer within the meaning of this Directive and shall be responsible as a producer.
(3) Where the producer of the product cannot be identified, each supplier of the product shall be treated as its producer unless he informs the injured person, within a reasonable time, of the identity of the producer or of the person who supplied him with the product. The same shall apply, in the case of an imported product, if this product does not indicate the identity of the importer referred to in paragraph (2), even if the name of the producer is indicated.

Art. 4 The injured person shall be required to prove the damage, the defect and the causal relationship between defect and damage.

Art. 5 Where, as a result of the provisions of this Directive, two or more persons are liable for the same damage, they shall be liable jointly and severally, without prejudice to the provisions of national law concerning the rights of contribution or recourse.

Art. 6 (1) A product is defective when it does not provide the safety which a person is entitled to expect, taking all circumstances into account, including:

(a) the presentation of the product;
(b) the use to which it could reasonably be expected that the product would be put;
(c) the time when the product was put into circulation.

(2) A product shall not be considered defective for the sole reason that a better product is subsequently put into circulation.

Art. 7 The producer shall not be liable as a result of this Directive if he proves:

(a) that he did not put the product into circulation; or
(b) that, having regard to the circumstances, it is probable that the defect which caused the damage did not exist at the time when the product was put into circulation by him or that this defect came into being afterwards; or

(c) that the product was neither manufactured by him for sale or any form of distribution for economic purpose nor manufactured or distributed by him in the
course of his business; or

(d) that the defect is due to compliance of the product with mandatory regulations
issued by the public authorities; or

(e) that the state of scientific and technical knowledge at the time when he put the
product into circulation was not such as to enable the existence of the defect to
be discovered; or

(f) in the case of a manufacturer of a component, that the defect is attributable to
the design of the product in which the component has been fitted or to the
instructions given by the manufacturer of the product.

Art. 8 (1) Without prejudice to the provisions of national law concerning the right
of contribution or recourse, the liability of the producer shall not be reduced when
the damage is caused both by a defect in product and by the act or omission of a
third party.
(2) The liability of the producer may be reduced or disallowed when, having regard
to all the circumstances, the damage is caused both by a defect in the product and
by the fault of the injured person or any person for whom the injured person is
responsible.

Art. 9 For the purpose of Article 1, "damage" means:

(a) damage caused by death or by personal injuries;
(b) damage to, or destruction of, any item of property other than the defective
product itself, with a lower threshold of 500 ECU, provided that the item of
property:
 (i) is of a type ordinarily intended for private use or consumption, and
 (ii) was used by the injured person mainly for his own private use or consumption.

This Article shall be without prejudice to national provisions relating to non-
material damage.

Art. 10 This Directive shall not affect any rights which an injured person may have
according to the rules of the law of contractual or non-contractual liability or a
special liability system existing at the moment when this Directive is notified.

YUEN KUN YEU v. ATTORNEY-GENERAL of HONG KONG

Privy Council [1988] A.C. 175; [1987] 3 W.L.R. 776; [1987] 2 All E.R. 705

Action by depositors against Commissioner for Banking

The plaintiffs deposited large sums of money with a deposit-taking company which
the Commissioner had placed and maintained on the register of companies licensed
to accept deposits. The company went into liquidation less than a year later, and
the plaintiffs lost all their money.

Their statement of claim against the Commissioner, represented by th
Attorney-General, was struck out by the trial judge as disclosing no cause of actio

The Court of Appeal for Hong Kong dismissed the plaintiffs' appeal, and their further appeal to the Privy Council was likewise dismissed.

Lord Keith: The allegations of fault against the commissioner are, in substance, that he knew or ought to have known, had he taken reasonable care, that the affairs of the company were being conducted fraudulently, speculatively and to the detriment of its depositors; that he failed to exercise his powers under the ordinance so as to secure that the company complied with the obligations and restrictions thereby imposed on it (a considerable number of which are alleged to have been breached) and that he should either never have registered the company as a deposit-taking company or have revoked its registration before the appellants made their respective deposits with it, so as to save them from losing their money when the company eventually went into liquidation.

The issues in the appeal raise important issues of principle, having far-reaching implications as regards the potential liability in negligence of a wide variety of regulatory agencies carried on under the aegis of central or local government and also to some extent by non-governmental bodies. Such agencies are in modern times becoming an increasingly familiar feature of the financial, commercial, industrial and social scene.

The foremost question of principle is whether in the present case the commissioner owed to members of the public who might be minded to deposit their money with deposit-taking companies in Hong Kong a duty, in the discharge of his supervisory powers under the ordinance, to exercise reasonable care to see that such members of the public did not suffer loss through the affairs of such companies being carried on by their managers in a fraudulent or improvident fashion. That question is one of law, which is capable of being answered on the averments, assumed to be true, contained in the appellants' pleadings. If it is answered in the negative, the appellants have no reasonable cause of action, and their statement of claim was rightly struck out.

The argument for the appellants in favour of an affirmative answer to the question started from the familiar passage in the speech of Lord Wilberforce in *Anns* v. *Merton London Borough* [below p. 60]

"Through the trilogy of cases in this House, *Donoghue* v. *Stevenson* [above p. 21], *Hedley Byrne & Co.* v. *Heller & Partners* [below p. 44] and *Home Office* v. *Dorset Yacht Co.* [below p. 53] the position has now been reached that in order to establish that a duty of care arises in a particular situation, it is not necessary to bring the facts of that situation within those of previous situations in which a duty of care has been held to exist. Rather the question has to be approached in two stages. First one has to ask whether, as between the alleged wrongdoer and the person who has suffered damage there is a sufficient relationship of proximity or neighbourhood such that, in the reasonable contemplation of the former, carelessness on his part may be likely to cause damage to the latter, in which case a prima facie duty of care arises. Secondly, if the first question is answered affirmatively, it is necessary to consider whether there are any considerations which ought to negative, or to reduce or limit the scope of the duty or the class of person to whom it is owed or the damages to which a breach of it may give rise . . . "

This passage has been treated with some reservation in subsequent cases in the House of Lords, in particular by Lord Keith in *Governors of the Peabody Donation Fund* v. *Sir Lindsay Parkinson & Co.* ([1984] 3 All E.R. 529, 534, [1985] A.C. 210, 240) by Lord Brandon in *Leigh & Sillavan* v. *Aliakmon Shipping Co.* ([1986] 2 All E.R. 145, 153, [1986] A.C. 785, 815) and by Lord Bridge in *Curran* v. *Northern Ireland Co-ownership Housing Association* ([1987] 2 All E.R. 13, 17). The speeches containing these reservations were concurred in by all the other members of the

House who were party to the decisions. In *Sutherland Shire Council* v. *Heyman* ((1985) 60 A.L.R. 1) Brennan J. in the High Court of Australia indicated his disagreement with the nature of the approach indicated by Lord Wilberforce, saying (at 43–44):

> "Of course, if foreseeability of injury to another were the exhaustive criterion of a prima facie duty to act to prevent the occurrence of that injury, it would be essential to introduce some kind of restrictive qualification—perhaps a qualification of the kind stated in the second stage of the general proposition in *Anns*. I am unable to accept that approach. It is preferable, in my view, that the law should develop novel categories of negligence incrementally and by analogy with established categories, rather than by a massive extension of a prima facie duty of care restrained only by indefinable 'considerations which ought to negative, or to reduce or limit the scope of the duty or the class of person to whom it is owed.' The proper role of the 'second stage,' as I attempted to explain in *Jaensch* v. *Coffey* ((1984) 54 A.L.R. 417 at 437), embraces no more than 'those further elements [in addition to the neighbour principle] which are appropriate to the particular category of negligence and *which confine the duty of care within narrower limits* than those which would be defined by an unqualified application of the neighbour principle.' " (My emphasis.)

Their Lordships venture to think that the two-stage test formulated by Lord Wilberforce for determining the existence of a duty of care in negligence has been elevated to a degree of importance greater than it merits, and greater perhaps than its author intended. Further, the expression of the first stage of the test carries with it a risk of misinterpretation. As Gibbs C.J. pointed out in *Sutherland Shire Council* v. *Heyman* (at 13) there are two possible views of what Lord Wilberforce meant. The first view, favoured in a number of cases mentioned by Gibbs C.J., is that he meant to test the sufficiency of proximity simply by the reasonable contemplation of likely harm. The second view, favoured by Gibbs C.J. himself, is that Lord Wilberforce meant the expression "proximity or neighbourhood" to be a composite one, importing the whole concept of necessary relationship between plaintiff and defendant described by Lord Atkin in *Donoghue* v. *Stevenson*. In their Lordships' opinion the second view is the correct one. As Lord Wilberforce himself observed in *McLoughlin* v. *O'Brian* [below p. 69], it is clear that foreseeability does not of itself, and automatically, lead to a duty of care. There are many other statements to the same effect. The truth is that the trilogy of cases referred to by Lord Wilberforce each demonstrate particular sets of circumstances, differing in character, which were adjudged to have the effect of bringing into being a relationship apt to give rise to a duty of care. Foreseeability of harm is a necessary ingredient of such a relationship, but it is not the only one. Otherwise there would be liability in negligence on the part of one who sees another about to walk over a cliff with his head in the air, and forbears to shout a warning.

Donoghue v. *Stevenson* established that the manufacturer of a consumable product who carried on business in such a way that the product reached the consumer in the shape in which it left the manufacturer, without any prospect of intermediate examination, owed the consumer a duty to take reasonable care that the product was free from defect likely to cause injury to health. The speech of Lord Atkin stressed not only the requirement of foreseeability of harm but also that of a close and direct relationship of proximity. The relevant passages are:
[His Lordship cited the passages in bold type above, pp. 22–23]
Lord Atkin clearly had in contemplation that all the circumstances of the case, not only the foreseeability of harm, were appropriate to be taken into account in determining whether a duty of care arose. *Hedley Byrne & Co. Ltd.* v. *Heller & Partners Ltd.* [below p. 44] was concerned with the assumption of responsibility. On the facts of the case no liability was held to exist because responsibility for the

advice given had been disclaimed, but there was established the principle that a duty of care arises where a party is asked for and gives gratuitous advice on a matter within his particular skill or knowledge and knows or ought to have known that the person asking for the advice will rely on it and act accordingly. In such a case the directness and closeness of the relationship between the parties are very apparent. *Dorset Yacht Co. Ltd.* v. *Home Office* [below p. 53] was an example of the kind of situation where a special relationship between a defendant and a third party gives rise to a duty on the part of the defendant to take reasonable care to control the third party so as to prevent him causing damage to the plaintiff. Some borstal boys, under the supervision of prison officers, were encamped on an island off which yachts were moored. Some of the boys, in an attempt to escape from the island, boarded a yacht and manoeuvred it so as to damage another. This was the very thing that might reasonably be foreseen as likely to happen if the prison officers did not take reasonable care to control the activities of the boys. The relationship of the officers to the boys was analogous to that between parents and children, a relationship described by Dixon J. in *Smith* v. *Leurs* ((1945) to C.L.R. 256 at 261–262) as capable of giving rise to a duty of control, saying:

" . . . apart from vicarious responsibility, one man may be responsible to another for the harm done to the latter by a third person; he may be responsible on the ground that the act of the third person could not have taken place but for his own fault or breach of duty. There is more than one description of duty the breach of which may produce this consequence. For instance, it may be a duty of care in reference to things involving special danger. It may even be a duty of care with reference to the control of actions or conduct of the third person. It is, however, exceptional to find in the law a duty to control another's actions to prevent harm to strangers. The general rule is that one man is under no duty of controlling another man to prevent his doing damage to a third. There are, however, special relations which are the source of a duty of this nature. It appears now to be recognized that it is incumbent upon a parent who maintains control over a young child to take reasonable care so to exercise that control as to avoid conduct on his part exposing the person or property of others to unreasonable danger. Parental control, where it exists, must be exercised with due care to prevent the child inflicting intentional damage on others or causing damage by conduct involving unreasonable risk of injury to others."

It is true that in the *Dorset Yacht* case a question arose whether the decision of the Home Office to give borstal boys a measure of freedom in order to assist in their rehabilitation fell within the ambit of a discretionary power the exercise of which was not capable of being called in question. But that question did not reach into the conduct of the officers who were in charge of the boys in the circumstances prevailing on the island. Having regard to these circumstances, it was not difficult to arrive, as a matter of judgment, at the conclusion that a close and direct relationship of proximity existed between the officers and the owners of the yachts, sufficient to require the former, as a matter of law, to take reasonable care to prevent the boys from interfering with the yachts and damaging them.

The second stage of Lord Wilberforce's test is one which will rarely have to be applied. It can arise only in a limited category of cases where, notwithstanding that a case of negligence is made out on the proximity basis, public policy requires that there should be no liability. One of the rare cases where that has been held to be so is *Rondel* v. *Worsley* ([1969] 1 A.C. 191), dealing with the liability of a barrister for negligence in the conduct of proceedings in court. Such a policy consideration was invoked in *Hill* v. *Chief Constable of West Yorkshire* ([1987] 1 All E.R. 1173). In that case the mother of the last victim of a notorious murderer of young women, who was not apprehended until after he had perpetrated 13 murders and eight attempted murders, sued the chief constable of the area on the grounds of the negligence of his force in failing to apprehend the murderer before the death of her daughter. The Court of Appeal struck out the statement of claim as disclosing no reasonable cause of action, on the principal ground that no relationship of proximity had existed between the police and the deceased girl. Glidewell L.J., however, in a judgment concurred in by Sir Roualeyn Cumming-Bruce, said (at 1183):

"If the police were liable to be sued for negligence in the investigation of crime which has allowed the criminal to commit further crimes, it must be expected that actions in this field would not be uncommon. Investigative police work is a matter of judgment, often no doubt dictated by experience or instinct. The threat that a decision, which in the end proved to be wrong, might result in an action for damages would be likely to have an inhibiting effect on the exercise of that judgment. The trial of such actions would very often involve the retrial of matters which had already been tried at the Crown Court. While no doubt many such actions would fail, preparing for and taking part in the trial of such an action would inevitably involve considerable work and time for a police force, and thus either reduce the manpower available to detect crime or increase expenditure on police services. In short, the reasons for holding that the police are immune from an action of this kind are similar to those for holding that a barrister may not be sued for negligence in his conduct of proceedings in court: see *Rondel* v. *Worsley* ([1969] 1 A.C. 191)."

In view of the direction in which the law has since been developing, their Lordships consider that for the future it should be recognised that the two-stage test in *Anns* is not to be regarded as in all circumstances a suitable guide to the existence of a duty of care.

The primary and all-important matter for consideration, then, is whether in all the circumstances of this case there existed between the commissioner and would-be depositors with the company such close and direct relations as to place the commissioner, in the exercise of his functions under the ordinance, under a duty of care towards would-be depositors. Among the circumstances of the case to be taken into account is that one of the purposes of the ordinance (though not the only one) was to make provision for the protection of persons who deposit money. The restrictions and obligations placed on registered deposit-taking companies, fenced by criminal sanctions, in themselves went a long way to secure that object. But the discretion given to the commissioner to register or deregister such companies, so as effectively to confer or remove the right to do business, was also an important part of the protection afforded. No doubt it was reasonably foreseeable by the commissioner that, if an uncreditworthy company were placed on or allowed to remain on the register, persons who might in the future deposit money with it would be at risk of losing that money. But mere foreseeability of harm does not create a duty, and future would-be depositors cannot be regarded as the only persons whom the commissioner should properly have in contemplation. In considering the question of removal from the register, the immediate and probably disastrous effect on existing depositors would be a very relevant factor. It might be a very delicate choice whether the best course was to deregister a company forthwith or to allow it to continue in business with some hope that, after appropriate measures by the management, its financial position would improve. It must not be overlooked that the power to refuse registration, and to revoke or suspend it, is quasi-judicial in character, as is demonstrated by the right of appeal to the Governor in Council conferred on companies by s.34 of the ordinance, and the right to be heard by the commissioner conferred by s.47. The commissioner did not have any power to control the day-to-day management of any company, and such a task would require immense resources. His power was limited to putting it out of business or allowing it to continue. No doubt recognition by the company that the commissioner had power to put it out of business would be a powerful incentive impelling the company to carry on its affairs in a responsible manner, but if those in charge were determined on fraud it is doubtful if any supervision could be close enough to prevent it in time to forestall loss to depositors. In these circumstances their Lordships are unable to discern any intention on the part of the legislature that in considering whether to register or deregister a company the commissioner should owe any statutory duty to potential depositors. It would be strange that a common law duty of care should be superimposed on such a statutory framework.

On the appellants' case as pleaded the immediate cause of the loss suffered by the appellants in this case was the conduct of the managers of the company in carrying on its business fraudulently, improvidently and in breach of many of the provisions of the ordinance. Another cause was the action of the appellants in depositing their money with a company which in the event turned out to be uncreditworthy. Considerable information about the company was available from the documents required by the ordinance to be open to public inspection, and no doubt advice could have been readily obtained from investment advisers in Hong Kong. Before the appellants deposited their money with the company there was no relationship of any kind between them and the commissioner. They were simply a few among the many inhabitants of Hong Kong who might choose to deposit their money with that or any other deposit-taking company. The class to whom the commissioner's duty is alleged to have been owed must include all such inhabitants. It is true, however, that according to the appellants' averments there had been available to him information about the company's affairs which was not available to the public and which raised serious doubts, to say the least of it, about the company's stability. That raises the question whether there existed between the commissioner and the company and its managers a special relationship of the nature described by Dixon J. in *Smith* v. *Leurs* ((1945) 70 C.L.R. 256), and such as was held to exist between the prison officers and the borstal boys in the *Dorset Yacht* case, so as to give rise to a duty on the commissioner to take reasonable care to prevent the company and its managers from causing financial loss to persons who might subsequently deposit with it.

In contradistinction to the position in the *Dorset Yacht* case, the commissioner had no power to control the day-to-day activities of those who caused the loss and damage. As has been mentioned, the commissioner had power only to stop the company carrying on business, and the decision whether or not to do so was clearly well within the discretionary sphere of his functions. In their Lordships' opinion the circumstance that the commissioner had, on the appellants' averments, cogent reason to suspect that the company's business was being carried on fraudulently and improvidently did not create a special relationship between the commissioner and the company of the nature described in the authorities. They are also of opinion that no special relationship existed between the commissioner and those unascertained members of the public who might in future become exposed to the risk of financial loss through depositing money with the company. Accordingly, their Lordships do not consider that the commissioner owed to the appellants any duty of care on the principle which formed the ratio of the *Dorset Yacht* case. To hark back to Lord Atkin's words, there were not such close and direct relations between the commissioner and the appellants as to give rise to the duty of care desiderated.

The appellants, however, advanced an argument based on their averment of having relied on the registration of the company when they deposited their money with it. It was said that registration amounted to a seal of approval of the company, and that by registering the company and allowing the registration to stand the commissioner made a continuing representation that the company was creditworthy. In the light of the information in the commissioner's possession that representation was made negligently and led to the appellant's loss.

In *Hedley Byrne & Co. Ltd.* v. *Heller & Partners Ltd.* [below p. 44] the House of Lords held that a negligent misrepresentation about a customer's creditworthiness, given in answer to an inquiry, might give rise to a claim for damages at the instance of the party making the inquiry who had foreseeably relied on the representation and suffered financial loss thereby. Likewise in *Junior Books Ltd.* v. *Veitchi Co. Ltd.* ([1982] 3 All E.R. 201, [1983] 1 A.C. 520) it was held that a nominated specialist sub-contractor might be liable for economic loss caused to the building owner by negligent performance of the sub-contracted work, in circumstances where the building owner had, to the sub-contractor's knowledge, relied on his skill and experience. These decisions turned on the voluntary assumption of responsibility towards a particular party, giving rise to a special relationship. Lord Devlin in the *Hedley Byrne* case [below p. 48] proceeded on the proposition that wherever there is a relationship equivalent to a contract, there is a duty of care. In the present case there was clearly no voluntary assumption by the commissioner of any responsibility towards the appellants in relation to the affairs of the company. It was argued, however, that the effect of the ordinance was to place such a responsibility on him. Their Lordships consider that the ordinance placed a duty on the commissioner to supervise deposit-taking companies in the general public interest, but no special responsibility towards individual members of the public. His position is analogous to that of a police force, which in *Hill* v. *Chief Constable of West Yorkshire* ([1987] 1 All E.R. 1173) was held to owe no duty towards individual potential victims of crime. The ordinance was designed to give added protection to the public against unscrupulous or improvident managers of deposit-taking companies, but it cannot reasonably be regarded, nor should it have been by any investor, as having instituted such a far-reaching and stringent system of supervision as to warrant an assumption that all deposit-taking companies were sound and fully creditworthy. While the investing public might reasonably feel some confidence that the provisions of the ordinance as a whole went a long way to protect their interests, reliance on the fact of registration as a guarantee of the soundness of a particular company would be neither reasonable nor justifiable, nor should the commissioner reasonably be expected to know of such reliance, if it existed. Accordingly their Lordships are unable to accept the appellants' arguments about reliance as apt, in all the circumstances, to establish a special relationship between them and the commissioner such as to give rise to a duty of care.

The final matter for consideration is the argument for the Attorney-General that it would be contrary to public policy to admit the appellants' claim, on grounds similar to those indicated in relation to police forces by Glidewell L.J. in *Hill* v. *Chief Constable of West Yorkshire*. It was maintained that, if the commissioner were to be held to owe actual or potential depositors a duty of care in negligence, there would be reason to apprehend that the prospect of claims would have a seriously inhibiting effect on the work of his department. A sound judgment would be less likely to be exercised if the commissioner were to be constantly looking over his shoulder at the prospect of claims against him, and his activities would be likely to be conducted in a detrimentally defensive frame of mind. In the result, the effectiveness of his functions would be at risk of diminution. Consciousness of potential liability could lead to distortions of judgment. In addition, the principles leading to his liability would surely be equally applicable to a wide range of regulatory agencies, not only in the financial field, but also, for example, to the factory inspectorate and social workers, to name only a few. If such liability were to be desirable on any policy grounds, it would be much better that the liability were to be introduced by the legislature, which is better suited than the judiciary to weigh up competing policy considerations.

Their Lordships are of opinion that there is much force in these arguments, but as they are satisfied that the appellants' statement of claim does not disclose a cause of action against the commissioner in negligence they prefer to rest their decision on that rather than on the public policy argument.

For these reasons their Lordships will humbly advise Her Majesty that the appeal should be dismissed.

Note:
If this had happened in England, suit would have been brought against the Bank of England, on which the Banking Act 1979 conferred statutory powers and responsibilities akin to those of the Commissioner in Hong Kong. Those powers are now contained in the Banking Act 1987, whose s.1(4) reads:

"Neither the Bank nor any person who is a member of its Court of Directors or who is, or is acting as, an officer or servant of the Bank shall be liable in damages for anything done or omitted in the discharge or purported discharge of the functions of the Bank under this Act unless it is shown that the act or omission was in bad faith." The courts and the legislature are in rare agreement.

SPARTAN STEEL AND ALLOYS LTD. v. MARTIN & CO. (CONTRACTORS) LTD.

Court of Appeal [1973] 1 Q.B. 27; [1972] 3 W.L.R. 502; 116 S.J. 648; [1972] 3 All E.R. 557

Action by industrialist against highway contractor in respect of property damage and lost profits

Excavating with a mechanical shovel, the defendant carelessly damaged a cable and interrupted the supply of electricity to the plaintiffs' factory 400 yards away. In order to prevent damage to their furnace the plaintiffs had to damage its contents (on which they would have made a profit of £400) by £368, and they were prevented by the absence of electric current from processing four more "melts" which would have netted them £1,767.

Faulks J. held that the plaintiffs were entitled to all three sums; the Court of Appeal (Edmund Davies L.J. dissenting) held that they were entitled to the first two sums only.

Lord Denning M.R.: . . . At bottom I think the question of recovering economic loss is one of policy. Whenever the courts draw a line to mark out the bounds of *duty*, they do it as matter of policy so as to limit the responsibility of the defendant. Whenever the courts set bounds to the *damages* recoverable—saying that they are, or are not, too remote—they do it as matter of policy so as to limit the liability of the defendant.

In many of the cases where economic loss had been held not to be recoverable, it has been put on the ground that the defendant was under no *duty* to the plaintiff. Thus where a person is injured in a road accident by the negligence of another, the negligent driver owes a duty to the injured man himself, but he owes no duty to the servant of the injured man—see *Best* v. *Samuel Fox & Co. Ltd.* ([1952] A.C. 716, 731): nor to the master of the injured man—*Inland Revenue Commissioners* v. *Hambrook* ([1956] 2 Q.B. 641, 660): nor to anyone else who suffers loss because he had a contract with the injured man—see *Simpson & Co.* v. *Thomson* ((1887) 3 App.Cas. 279, 289): nor indeed to anyone who only suffers economic loss on account of the accident: see *Kirkham* v. *Boughey* ([1958] 2 Q.B. 338, 341). Likewise, when property is damaged by the negligence of another, the negligent tortfeasor owes a duty to the owner or possessor of the chattel, but not to one who suffers loss only because he had a contract entitling him to use the chattel or giving him a right to receive it at some later date: see *Elliot Steam Tug Co. Ltd.* v. *Shipping Controller* ([1922] 1 K.B. 127, 139) and *Margarine Union GmbH* v. *Cambay Prince Steamship Co. Ltd.* ([1969] 1 Q.B. 219, 251–252).

In other cases, however, the defendant seems clearly to have been under a duty to the plaintiff, but the economic loss has not been recovered because it is *too remote.* Take the illustration given by Blackburn J. in *Cattle* v. *Stockton Water-works Co.* ((1875) L.R. 10 Q.B. 453, 457), when water escapes from a reservoir and floods a coal mine where many men are working. Those who had their tools or clothes destroyed could recover: but those who only lost their wages could not. Similarly, when the defendants' ship negligently sank a ship which was being towed by a tug, the owner of the tug lost his remuneration, but he could not recover it from the negligent ship: though the same duty (of navigation with reasonable care) was owed to both tug and tow: see *Société Anonyme de Remorquage à Hélice* v. *Bennetts* ([1911] 1 K.B. 243, 248). In such cases if the plaintiff or his property had been physically injured, he would have recovered: but, as he only suffered economic loss, he is held not entitled to recover. This is, I should think, because the loss is regarded by the law as too remote: see *King* v. *Phillips* ([1953] 1 Q.B. 429, 439–440).

On the other hand, in the cases where economic loss by itself had been held to be recoverable, it is plain that there was a duty to the plaintiff and the loss was not too remote. Such as when one ship negligently runs down another ship, and damages it, with the result that the cargo has to be discharged and reloaded. The negligent ship was already under a duty to the cargo owners: and they can recover the cost of discharging and reloading it, as it is not too remote: see *Morrison Steamship Co. Ltd.* v. *Greystoke Castle (Cargo Owners)* ([1947] A.C. 265). Likewise, when a banker negligently gives a reference to one who acts on it, the duty is plain and the damage is not too remote: see *Hedley Byrne & Co. Ltd.* v. *Heller & Partners Ltd.* [below p. 44].

The more I think about these cases, the more difficult I find it to put each into its proper pigeon-hole. Sometimes I say "There was no duty." In others I say: "The damage was too remote." So much so that I think the time has come to discard those tests which have proved so elusive. It seems to me better to consider the particular relationship in hand, and see whether or not, as a matter of policy, economic loss should be recoverable, or not. Thus in *Weller & Co.* v. *Foot and Mouth Disease Research Institute* ([1966] 1 Q.B. 569) it was plain that the loss suffered by the auctioneers was not recoverable, no matter whether it is put on the ground that there was no duty or that the damage was too remote. Again in *Electrochrome Ltd.* v. *Welsh Plastics Ltd.* ([1968] 2 All E.R. 205), it is plain that the economic loss suffered by the plantiffs' factory (due to the damage to the fire hydrant) was not recoverable, whether because there was no duty or that it was too remote.

So I turn to the relationship in the present case. It is of common occurrence. The parties concerned are: the electricity board who are under a statutory duty to maintain supplies of electricity in their district; the inhabitants of the district, including this factory, who are entitled by statute to a continuous supply of electricity for their use; and the contractors who dig up the road. Similar relationships occur with other statutory bodies, such as gas and water undertakings. The cable may be damaged by the negligence of the statutory undertaker, or by the negligence of the contractor, or by accident without any negligence by anyone: and the power may have to be cut off whilst the cable is repaired. Or the power may be cut off owing to a short-circuit in the power house: and so forth. If the cutting off of the supply causes economic loss to the consumers, should it as matter of policy be recoverable? And against whom?

The first consideration is the position of the statutory undertakers. If the board do not keep up the voltage or pressure of electricity, gas or water—or, likewise, if they shut it off for repairs—and thereby cause economic loss to their consumers, they are not liable in damages, not even if the cause of it is due to their own negligence. The only remedy (which is hardly ever pursued) is to prosecute the board before the magistrates. Such is the result of many cases starting with a water board—*Atkinson* v. *Newcastle and Gateshead Waterworks Co.* ((1887) 2 Ex.D. 441); going on to a gas board—*Clegg, Parkinson & Co.* v. *Earby Gas Co* ([1896] 1 Q.B. 592); and then to an electricity company—*Stevens* v. *Aldershot Gas, Water &*

District Lighting Co. Ltd. (best reported in (1932) 31 L.G.R. 48; also in 102 L.J.K.B. 12). In those cases the courts, looking at the legislative enactments, held that Parliament did not intend to expose the board to liability for damages to the inhabitants en masse: see what Lord Cairns L.C. said in *Atkinson* v. *Newcastle and Gateshead Waterworks Co.* (2 Ex.D. 441, 445) and Wills J. in *Clegg, Parkinson & Co.* v. *Earby Gas Co.* ([1896] 1 Q.B. 592, 595). In those cases there was *indirect* damage to the plaintiffs, but it was not recoverable. There is another group of cases which go to show that, if the board, by their negligence in the conduct of their supply, cause direct physical damage or injury to person or property, they are liable: see *Milnes* v. *Huddersfield Corporation* ((1886) 11 App.Cas. 511, 530) by Lord Blackburn; *Midwood & Co. Ltd.* v. *Manchester Corporation* ([1905] 2 K.B. 597); *Heard* v. *Brymbo Steel Co. Ltd.* ([1947] 2 K.B. 692) and *Hartley* v. *Mayoh & Co.* ([1954] 1 Q.B. 383). But one thing is clear: the statutory undertakers have never been held liable for economic loss only. If such be the policy of the legislature in regard to electricity boards, it would seem right for the common law to adopt a similar policy in regard to contractors. If the electricity boards are not liable for economic loss due to negligence which results in the cutting off the supply, nor should a contractor be liable.

The second consideration is the nature of the hazard, namely, the cutting of the supply of electricity. This is a hazard which we all run. It may be due to a short circuit, to a flash of lightning, to a tree falling on the wires, to an accidental cutting of the cable, or even to the negligence of someone or other. And when it does happen, it affects a multitude of persons: not as a rule by way of physical damage to them or their property, but by putting them to inconvenience, and sometimes to economic loss. The supply is usually restored in a few hours, so the economic loss is not very large. Such a hazard is regarded by most people as a thing they must put up with—without seeking compensation from anyone. Some there are who install a stand-by system. Others seek refuge by taking out an insurance policy against breakdown in the supply. But most people are content to take the risk on themselves. When the supply is cut off, they do not go running round to their solicitor. They do not try to find out whether it was anyone's fault. They just put up with it. They try to make up the economic loss by doing more work next day. This is a healthy attitude which the law should encourage.

The third consideration is this: if claims for economic loss were permitted for this particular hazard, there would be no end of claims. Some might be genuine, but many might be inflated, or even false. A machine might not have been in use anyway, but it would be easy to put it down to the cut in supply. It would be well-nigh impossible to check the claims. If there was economic loss on one day, did the claimant do his best to mitigate it by working harder next day? And so forth. Rather than expose claimants to such temptation and defendants to such hard labour—on comparatively small claims—it is better to disallow economic loss altogether, at any rate when it stands alone, independent of any physical damage.

The fourth consideration is that, in such a hazard as this, the risk of economic loss should be suffered by the whole community who suffer the losses—usually many but comparatively small losses—rather than on the one pair of shoulders, that is, on the contractor on whom the total of them, all added together, might be very heavy.

The fifth consideration is that the law provides for deserving cases. If the defendant is guilty of negligence which cuts off the electricity supply and causes actual physical damage to person or property, that physical damage can be recovered: see *Baker* v. *Crow Carrying Co. Ltd.* ((unreported) February 1, 1960; Bar Library Transcript No. 45), referred to by Buckley L.J. in *S.C.M. (United Kingdom) Ltd.* v. *W.J. Whittall & Son Ltd.* ([1971] 1 Q.B. 337, 356); and also any economic loss truly consequential on the material damage: see *British Celanese Ltd.* v. *A.H. Hunt (Capacitors) Ltd.* ([1969] 1 W.L.R. 959) and *S.C.M. (United Kingdom) Ltd.* v. *W.J. Whittall & Son Ltd.* ([1971] 1 Q.B. 337). Such cases will be comparatively few.

They will be readily capable of proof and will be easily checked. They should be and are admitted.

These considerations lead me to the conclusion that the plaintiffs should recover for the physical damage to the one melt (£368), and the loss of profit on that melt consequent thereon (£400): but not for the loss of profit on the four melts (£1,767), because that was economic loss independent of the physical damage. I would, therefore, allow the appeal and reduce the damages to £768.

Edmund Davies L.J. (dissenting): . . . The facts giving rise to this appeal have already been set out . . . Their very simplicity serves to highlight a problem regarding which differing judicial and academic views have been expressed and which it is high time should be finally solved. The problem may be thus stated: Where a defendant who owes a duty of care to the plaintiff breaches that duty and, as both a direct and a reasonably foreseeable result of that injury, the plaintiff suffers only economic loss, is he entitled to recover damages for that loss?

In expressing in this way the question which now arises for determination, I have sought to strip away those accretions which would otherwise obscure the basic issue involved. Let me explain. We are not here concerned to inquire whether the defendants owed a duty of care to the plaintiffs or whether they breached it, for these matters are admitted. Nor need we delay to consider whether as a direct and reasonably foreseeable result of the defendants' negligence any harm was sustained by the plaintiffs, for a "melt" valued at £368 was admittedly ruined and the defendants concede their liability to make that loss good. But what *is* in issue is whether the defendants must make good (a) the £400 loss of profit resulting from that material being spoilt and (b) the £1,767 further loss of profit caused by the inability to put four more "melts" through the furnace before power was restored. As to (a), the defendants, while making no unqualified admission, virtually accept their liability, on the ground that the £400 loss was a *direct* consequence of the physical damage caused to the material in the furnace. But they reject liability in respect of (b), not because it was any the less a *direct* and reasonably foreseeable consequence of the defendants' negligence than was the £400, but on the ground that it was unrelated to any physical damage and that economic loss not anchored to and resulting from physical harm to person or property is not recoverable under our law as damages for negligence.

In my respectful judgment, however it may formerly have been regarded, the law is today otherwise. I am conscious of the boldness involved in expressing this view, particularly after studying such learned dissertations as that of Professor Atiyah on *Negligence and Economic Loss* ((1967) 83 L.Q.R. 243), where the relevant cases are cited. I recognise that proof of the necessary linkage between negligent acts and purely economic consequences may be hard to forge. I accept, too, that if economic loss of itself confers a right of action this may spell disaster for the negligent party. But this may equally be the outcome where physical damage alone is sustained, or where physical damage leads directly to economic loss. Nevertheless, when this occurs it was accepted in *S.C.M. (United Kingdom) Ltd.* v. *W.J. Whittall & Son Ltd.* ([1971] 1 Q.B. 337) that compensation is recoverable for both types of damage. It follows that this must be regardless of whether the injury (physical or economic, or a mixture of both) is immense or puny, diffused over a wide area or narrowly localised, provided only that the requirements as to foreseeability and directness are fulfilled. I therefore find myself unable to accept as factors determinant of legal principle those considerations of policy canvassed in the concluding passages of the judgment just delivered by Lord Denning M.R. . . .

For my part, I cannot see why the £400 loss of profit here sustained should be recoverable and not the £1,767. It is common ground that both types of loss were equally foreseeable and equally direct consequences of the defendants' admitted negligence and the only distinction drawn is that the former figure represents the profit lost as a result of the physical damage done to the material in the furnace at the time when power was cut off. But what has that purely fortuitous fact to do with legal principle? In my judgment, nothing . . .

Despite the frequency with which *Cattle* v. *Stockton Waterworks Co.* is cited as authority for the proposition that pecuniary loss, without more, can never sustain an action for negligence, I respectfully venture to think that Blackburn J. was there laying down no such rule. Had he intended to do so when, two years later as Lord Blackburn, he was a party to the decision in *Simpson & Co.* v. *Thomson* ((1877) 3 App.Cas. 279), this fact would surely have emerged when he concurred (at pp. 292 *et seq.*), in the dismissal of underwriters' claim for recoupment of the sum they had paid for a total loss. . . .

In *Hedley Byrne & Co. Ltd.* v. *Heller & Partners Ltd.* [below p. 44], one of those "exceptional cases" referred to by Lord Denning M.R. in *S.C.M. (United Kingdom) Ltd.* v. *W.J. Whittall & Son Ltd.* and a landmark in the branch of the law with which we are here concerned, Lord Devlin, referring to *Morrison Steamship Co. Ltd.* v. *Greystoke Castle (Cargo Owners)*, said (at p. 518): "Their Lordships did not in that case lay down any general principle about liability for financial loss in the absence of physical damage; but the case itself makes it impossible to argue that there is any general rule showing that such loss is of its nature irrecoverable." This is increasingly recognised as being the legal position, and ample illustrations of this are available. Thus in *Ministry of Housing* v. *Sharp* ([1970] 2 Q.B. 238), Salmon L.J. said (at p. 278): "So far, however, as the law of negligence relating to civil actions is concerned, the existence of a duty to take reasonable care no longer depends upon whether it is physical injury or financial loss which can reasonably be foreseen as a result of a failure to take such care." And in *Dutton* v. *Bognor Regis Urban District Council* ([1972] 1 Q.B. 372, 404) Sachs L.J. said that " . . . to pose the question: 'Is it physical damage or economic damage?' is to adopt a fallacious approach."

Having considered the intrinsic nature of the problem presented in this appeal, and having consulted the relevant authorities, my conclusion, as already indicated, is that an action lies in negligence for damages in respect of purely economic loss, provided that it was a reasonably foreseeable and direct consequence of failure in a duty of care. The application of such a rule can undoubtedly give rise to difficulties in certain sets of circumstances, but so can the suggested rule that economic loss may be recovered *provided* it is directly consequential upon physical damage. Many alarming situations were conjured up in the course of counsel's arguments before us. In their way, they were reminiscent of those formerly advanced against awarding damages for nervous shock; for example, the risk of fictitious claims and expensive litigation, the difficulty of disproving the alleged cause and effect, and the impossibility of expressing such a claim in financial terms. But I suspect that they (like the illustrations furnished by Lord Penzance in *Simpson & Co.* v. *Thomson* ((1877) 3 App.Cas. 279, 289 *et seq.*) would be for the most part be resolved either on the ground that no duty of care was owed to the injured party or that the damages sued for were irrecoverable *not* because they were simply financial but because they were too remote . . .

I should perhaps again stress that we are here dealing with economic loss which was both reasonably foreseeable and a direct consequence of the defendants' negligent act. What the position should or would be were the latter feature lacking (as in *Weller & Co.* v. *Foot and Mouth Disease Research Institute* ([1966] 1 Q.B. 569)) is not our present concern. By stressing this point one is not reviving the distinction between direct and indirect consequences which is generally thought to have been laid at rest by *The Wagon Mound* [below p. 185], for, in the words of Professor Atiyah, *Negligence and Economic Loss* (83 L.Q.R. 263), that case "was solely concerned with the question whether the directness of the damage is a *sufficient* test of liability, . . . In other words, *The Wagon Mound* merely decides that a plaintiff cannot recover for unforeseeable consequences even if they are direct; it does not decide that a plaintiff can always recover for foreseeable consequences even if they are indirect." Both directness and foreseeability being here established, it follows that I regard Faulks J. as having rightly awarded the sum of £2,535.

Lawton L.J.: This appeal raises neatly a question which has been asked from time to time since Blackburn J. delivered his well-known judgment in *Cattle* v. *Stockton Waterworks Co.* ((1875) L.R. 10 Q.B. 453) and more frequently since the decision in *Hedley Byrne & Co. Ltd.* v. *Heller & Partners Ltd.* [below p. 44], namely, whether a plaintiff can recover from a defendant, proved or admitted to have been negligent, foreseeable financial damage which is not consequential upon foreseeable physical injury or damage to property. Any doubts there may have been about the recovery of such consequential financial damage were settled by this court in *S.C.M. (United Kingdom) Ltd.* v. *W.J. Whittall & Son Ltd.* ([1971] 1 Q.B. 337). In my judgment the answer to this question is that such financial damage cannot be recovered save when it is the immediate consequence of a breach of duty to safeguard the plaintiff from that kind of loss.

This is not the first time a negligent workman has cut an electric supply cable nor the first claim for damages arising out of such an incident. When in practice at the Bar I myself advised in a number of such cases. Most practitioners acting for insurers under the so-called "public liability" types of policy will have had similar professional experiences; if not with electrical supply, with gas and water mains. Negligent interference with such services is one of the facts of life and can cause a lot of damage, both physical and financial. Water conduits have been with us for centuries; gas mains for nearly a century and a half; electricity supply cables for about three-quarters of a century; but there is not a single case in the English law reports which is an authority for the proposition that mere financial loss resulting from negligent interruption of such services is recoverable. Why?

Many lawyers would be likely to answer that ever since *Cattle* v. *Stockton Waterworks Co.* (L.R. 10 Q.B. 453), such damages have been irrecoverable. Edmund Davies L.J. has just stated that he doubts whether Blackburn J. laid down any such rule. Knowing that he had these doubts, I have re-read *Cattle* v. *Stockton Waterworks Co.* The claim was in negligence. The declaration was as follows: "that defendants, being a water company, so negligently laid down under a certain turnpike road their pipes for supplying water to a district, and so negligently kept and maintained the pipes in such insufficient repair, and in such imperfect and leaky condition, that, while plaintiff was lawfully constructing for reward to the plaintiff a tunnel across the turnpike road, and was lawfully using the road for such purpose, the pipes leaked, and large quantities of water flowed into the road, and upon the plaintiff's workings, and flooded them, and the plaintiff was hindered and delayed in the work, and suffered great loss." The declaration raised precisely the problem which has to be solved in this case; Blackburn J.'s answer was in these words, at p. 458: "In the present case there is no pretence for saying that the defendants were malicious or had any intention to injure anyone. They were, at most, guilty of a neglect of duty which occasioned injury to the property of Knight, but which did not injure any property of the plaintiff. The plaintiff's claim is to recover the damage which he has sustained by his contract with Knight becoming less profitable, or, it may be, a losing contract, in consequence of this injury to Knight's property. We think this does not give him any right of action."

Earlier in his judgment he had said (at p. 457): "No authority in favour of the plaintiff's right to sue was cited, and, as far as our knowledge goes, there was none that could have been cited." There is still no authority directly in point today. Blackburn J.'s judgment has been cited with approval and followed many times: the judgment of Hamilton J. in *Société Anonyme de Remorquage à Hélice* v. *Bennetts* ([1911] 1 K.B. 243, 248) and of Widgery J. in *Weller & Co.* v. *Foot and Mouth Disease Research Institute* ([1966] 1 Q.B. 569, 588) are instances. For nearly 100 years now contractors and insurers have negotiated policies and premiums have been calculated on the assumption that the judgment of Blackburn J. is a correct statement of the law; and those affected financially by the acts of negligent contractors have been advised time and time again that mere financial loss is irrecoverable.

It was argued that the law has developed since 1875, albeit the development was unnoticed by Hamilton J. and Widgery J. Has it? . . .

. . . If, in the *Greystoke Castle* case, the House of Lords overruled *Cattle* v. *Stockton Waterworks Co.* (L.R. 10 Q.B. 453), it did so by an unobserved flanking movement, not by a direct assault. The two leading counsel, Sir William McNair K.C. and Sir Robert Aske K.C. do not seem to have appreciated that a bastion of the common law was in danger of falling, as neither seems to have cited *Cattle* v. *Stockton Waterworks Co.* The only one of the Law Lords who did was Lord Simonds, who clearly did so with respect and approval: his speech, however, was a dissenting one. Lord Roche commented upon the judgment of Hamilton J. in *Société Anonyme de Remorquage à Hélice* v. *Bennetts* ([1911] 1 K.B. 243). He sought to explain it on the ground that the unsuccessful plaintiff had not proved a breach of duty. Had he intended to disapprove a long-standing judgment of such an eminent common lawyer as Blackburn J., I would have expected him to have done so in terms. The House did, however, by a majority, adjudge that the cargo owners had a direct claim against the owners of the colliding ship for a proportion of the general average contribution. The case was argued and speeches delivered on the basis that the House was considering a problem of maritime law. I would not have the temerity to express any opinion as to the extent to which maritime law and the common law differ as to the kinds of damage which are recoverable; but having regard to their differing historical developments it would not surprise me if there were divergencies. The policies governing their developments may well have been different. What I am satisfied about is that the House of Lords in the *Greystoke Castle case* ([1947] A.C. 265) cannot be said to have overruled *Cattle* v. *Stockton Waterworks Co.* (L.R. 10 Q.B. 453).

The differences which undoubtedly exist between what damage can be recovered in one type of case and what in another cannot be reconciled on any logical basis. I agree with Lord Denning M.R. that such differences have arisen because of the policy of the law. Maybe there should be one policy for all cases; the enunciation of such a policy is not, in my judgment, a task for this court . . . In my judgment the rule enunciated in 1875 by Blackburn J. is the correct one to apply in negligence cases.

When this principle is applied to the facts of this case it produces the result referred to by Lord Denning M.R. in his judgment. I too would allow the appeal and reduce the damages to £768.

Questions

1. If a company loses profits, its shareholders may lose dividends and its employees wages or jobs. If the company recovers damages, is it the shareholders or the employees who benefit? Could the shareholders or the employees themselves sue? If not, why not? Is it because they tend to be numerous? (See *Prudential Assur. Co.* v. *Newman Industries* [1982] 1 All E.R. 354, 366–7; and *Dynamco* v. *Holland & Hannen & Cubitts* 1971 S.C. 257).

2. An articulated lorry jack-knifes on the motorway. The following car collides with it, and the driver is injured. No one else suffers physical harm, but the motorway is closed for two hours, and many people miss valuable appointments. Do you think it would be reasonable to distinguish between the different types of harm caused by a single incident?

3. What class of litigants will bring an action for lost profits if such an action is allowed? What class of litigants can bring an action for personal injuries?

4. Does a proper sense of social responsibility require one to bear in mind the financial well-being of trading companies with limited liability?

5. Suppose that the defendant had been operating, with the plaintiff's permission, on the plaintiff's land. Would the result be the same?

6. The old idea that the law of tort should be determined by a moral view of the demands of social responsibility is being challenged by the theory that the law of tort should be determined by its function as a loss-distributing device. Might the results of the two views diverge in the present case?

Note:

A person's chances of obtaining the money he is claiming depend on what he is claiming it for and who he is claiming it from: in other words, both the type of injury he has suffered and the nature of his relationship with the defendant are material, perhaps vital, considerations.

Since *Donoghue* v. *Stevenson* people who act dangerously may have to pay even a complete stranger if the harm they cause is physical. So here Spartan Steel recovered for the physical harm they suffered (damage to the ore) but not for the purely financial harm (lost profits), though both results were equally foreseeable. Plaintiff and defendant were total strangers to each other. In *Muirhead* v. *Industrial Tank Specialities* [1985] 3 All E.R. 705 (C.A.) the careless manufacturer of a defective recycling pump had to pay the ultimate purchaser for the damage to his property (dead lobsters) but not the purely financial harm resulting from business interruption. But while in *Spartan Steel* the parties were complete strangers, in *Muirhead* they were not: they were in the relationship of consumer and manufacturer. As *Donoghue* v. *Stevenson* laid down, that is a special relationship, but when it comes to liability for purely economic loss, it is not special enough.

The economic loss in *Spartan Steel* occurred through the defendant's damaging an electricity cable which belonged to a third party. In cases where property has been damaged by carelessness the courts have long held that only those with a proprietary or possessory interest in the property may bring an action, not those who have merely a financial interest in the well-being of the property, whether that interest be positive, in the sense that they stand to gain if the property remains unimpaired, or negative, in the sense that they will have to pay out if it is damaged or destroyed. There are masses of cases: the courts have rejected claims by the insurer who had to pay out on the policy when the insured property was damaged (*Simpson* v. *Thomson* (1877) 3 App.Cas. 179), the salvor who lost his reward when the tow was sunk (*Société Anonyme de Remorquage à Hélice* v. *Bennetts* [1911] 1 K.B. 243), the buyer who was committed to paying for the goods (*The Aliakmon* [1986] 2 All E.R. 145, (noted [1986] Camb.L.J. 382 (Clarke), 384 (Markesinis)), the auctioneer who would have sold the property on commission (*Weller & Co.* v. *Foot and Mouth Disease Research Institute* [1966] 1 Q.B. 569), and the charterer who was paying for the use of the vessel (*The Mineral Transporter* [1985] 2 All E.R. 935, (noted [1986] Camb.L.J. 13 (Tettenborn), 102 L.Q.R. 13 (M. Jones)). The law could hardly have taken a clearer position, and it has now been reaffirmed so as to allay intervening doubts stemming from *Hedley Byrne* (below p. 44), *Anns* (below p. 60) and *Junior Books* v. *Veitchi Corp.* [1983] A.C. 520, [1982] 3 All E.R. 201).

The position adopted is also right and convenient. It is right to distinguish property damage from financial loss because things, being capable of gratifying the senses, are more significant than wealth, just as people are more significant than things. It would also be inconvenient not to distinguish property damage from financial loss because whereas property damage is always limited in extent (thanks to the physical laws of inertia), the incidence of financial loss knows no bounds, and the courts would have a fearful time trying to set them.

Take the interesting case of *Wimpey Constr. Co. (U.K.) Ltd.* v. *Martin Black & Co.*, 1982 S.L.T. 239. The pursuer was one of a consortium of firms engaged on a huge construction project in the Firth of Forth. The project depended on the availability of a certain crane-barge. This was obtained on hire by another member of the consortium, who procured wire slings from the defender. One day while a concrete pile belonging to the pursuer was being raised, the sling snapped. The pile sank and the crane-barge was so badly damaged that it was out of commission for eight weeks. The pursuer naturally recovered for the loss of its concrete pile, but it also sued for the vast expense involved in the delay to the construction work. The Inner House gave judgment on this point for the defenders. But then the House of Lords decided *Junior Books*. That decision so confused the law that the defenders settled for a huge sum (£1 m.) rather than face an appeal to the House of Lords constituted as it was. It is now happily clear that under the present law such an appeal would have been dismissed.

HEDLEY BYRNE & CO. v. HELLER & PARTNERS LTD.

House of Lords [1964] A.C. 465; [1963] 3 W.L.R. 101; 107 S.J. 454; [1963] 2 All E.R. 575; [1963] 1 Lloyd's Rep. 485

Action against gratuitous informant in respect of financial loss

The plaintiffs, advertising agents, had booked space and time on behalf of a customer, Easipower Ltd., under contracts making them personally liable. They then had doubts about Easipower's financial position, and asked their bankers to obtain from the defendants, merchant bankers with whom Easipower Ltd. had their account, a statement on Easipower's standing. This was done in the first instance by telephone, when the defendants said: "We believe that the company would not undertake any commitments they were unable to fulfil." Three months later the plaintiffs, through their bankers, asked whether Easipower were trustworthy to the extent of £100,000 per year. The defendants replied, in a letter headed "For your private use and without responsibility on the part of this bank or its officials," that Easipower Ltd. were a " . . . respectably constituted company, considered good for its ordinary business engagements" and that "Your figures are larger than we are accustomed to see." In reliance upon their view of what these statements meant the plaintiffs refrained from cancelling the advertising contracts, and when Easipower Ltd. went into liquidation lost sums calculated at £17,661 18s. 6d.

The plaintiffs abandoned an allegation of fraud, but maintained that the defendants' replies were given in breach of their duty of care. McNair J. held that the defendants were careless but that they owed no duty. The Court of Appeal affirmed judgment for the defendants on the same ground [1962] 1 Q.B. 396. The House of Lords affirmed the judgment on different grounds.

Lord Reid: My Lords, this case raises the important question whether and in what circumstances a person can recover damages for loss suffered by reason of his having relied on an innocent but negligent misrepresentation . . .

Before coming to the main question of law, it may be well to dispose of an argument that there was no sufficiently close relationship between these parties to give rise to any duty. It is said that the respondents did not know the precise purpose of the inquiries and did not even know whether the National Provincial Bank wanted the information for its own use or for the use of a customer: they knew nothing of the appellants. I would reject that argument. They knew that the inquiry was in connection with an advertising contract, and it was at least probable that the information was wanted by the advertising contractors. It seems to me quite immaterial that they did not know who these contractors were: there is no suggestion of any speciality which could have influenced them in deciding whether to give information or in what form to give it. I shall therefore treat this as if it were a case where a negligent misrepresentation is made directly to the person seeking information, opinion or advice, and I shall not attempt to decide what kind or degree of proximity is necessary before there can be a duty owed by the defendant to the plaintiff.

The appellants' first argument was based on *Donoghue* v. *Stevenson* [above p. 21]. That is a very important decision, but I do not think that it has any direct bearing on this case. That decision may encourage us to develop existing lines of authority, but it cannot entitle us to disregard them. Apart altogether from authority, I would think that the law must treat negligent words differently from negligent acts. The law ought so far as possible to reflect the standards of the reasonable man, and that is what *Donoghue* v. *Stevenson* sets out to do. The most obvious difference between negligent words and negligent acts is this. Quite careful people often express definite opinions on social or informal occasions even when they see that others are likely to be influenced by them; and they often do that without taking that care which they would take if asked for their opinion professionally or in a business connection. The appellant agrees that there can be no duty of care on such occasions, and we are referred to American and South African authorities where that is recognised, although their law appears to have gone much further than ours has yet done. But it is at least unusual casually to put into circulation negligently made articles which are dangerous. A man might give a friend a negligently prepared bottle of home-made wine and his friend's guests might drink it with dire results. But it is by no means clear that those guests would have no action against the negligent manufacturer.

Another obvious difference is that a negligently made article will only cause one accident, and so it is not very difficult to find the necessary degree of proximity or neighbourhood between the negligent manufacturer and the person injured. But words can be broadcast with or without the consent or the foresight of the speaker or writer. It would be one thing to say that the speaker owes a duty to a limited class, but it would be going very far to say that he owes a duty to every ultimate "consumer" who acts on those words to his detriment. It would be no use to say that a speaker or writer owes a duty but can disclaim responsibility if he wants to. He, like the manufacturer, could make it part of a contract that he is not to be liable for his negligence: but that contract would not protect him in a question with a third party, at least if the third party was unaware of it.

So it seems to me that there is good sense behind our present law that in general an innocent but negligent misrepresentation gives no cause of action. There must be something more than the mere misstatement. I therefore turn to the authorities to see what more is required. The most natural requirement would be that expressly or by implication from the circumstances the speaker or writer has undertaken some responsibility, and that appears to me not to conflict with any authority which is binding on this House. Where there is a contract there is no difficulty as regards the contracting parties: the question is whether there is a warranty. The refusal of English law to recognise any *jus quaesitum tertio* causes some difficulties, but they are not relevant here. Then there are cases where a person does not merely make a statement but performs a gratuitous service. I do not intend to examine the cases about that, but at least they show that in some cases that person owes a duty of care apart from any contract, and to that extent they pave the way to holding that there can be a duty of care in making a statement of fact or opinion which is independent of contract.

[Lord Reid considered *Derry* v. *Peek* (1889) 14 App.Cas. 337, which had erroneously been supposed to have decided that "To found an action for damages there must be a contract and breach, or fraud" (*per* Lord Bramwell at 347), quoted the view of Lord Haldane in *Nocton* v. *Lord Ashburton* [1914] A.C. 932, 947, and *Robinson* v. *National Bank of Scotland* 1916 S.C. (H.L.) 154, 157 and proceeded:]

This passage makes it clear that Lord Haldane did not think that a duty to take care must be limited to cases of fiduciary relationship in the narrow sense of relationships which had been recognised by the Court of Chancery as being of a fiduciary character. He speaks of other special relationships, and I can see no logical stopping place short of all those relationships where it is plain that the party seeking information or advice was trusting the other to exercise such a degree of care as the circumstances required, where it was reasonable for him to do that, and where the other gave the information or advice when he knew or ought to have known that the inquirer was relying on him. I say "ought to have known" because in questions of negligence we now apply the objective standard of what the reasonable man would have done.

A reasonable man, knowing that he was being trusted or that his skill and judgment were being relied on, would, I think, have three courses open to him. He could keep silent or decline to give the information or advice sought: or he could give an answer with a clear qualification that he accepted no responsibility for it or that it was given without that reflection or inquiry which a careful answer would require: or he could simply answer without any such qualification. If he chooses to adopt the last course he must, I think, be held to have accepted some responsibility for his answer being given carefully, or to have accepted a relationship with the inquirer which requires him to exercise such care as the circumstances require.

If that is right, then it must follow that *Candler* v. *Crane, Christmas & Co.* ([1951] 2 K.B. 164) was wrongly decided. There the plaintiff wanted to see the accounts of a company before deciding to invest in it. The defendants were the company's accountants, and they were told by the company to complete the company's accounts as soon as possible because they were to be shown to the plaintiff who was a potential investor in the company. At the company's request the defendants showed the completed accounts to the plaintiff, discussed them with him, and allowed him to take a copy. The accounts had been carelessly prepared and gave a wholly misleading picture. It was obvious to the defendants that the plaintiff was relying on their skill and judgment and on their having exercised that care which by contract they owed to the company, and I think that any reasonable man in the plaintiff's shoes would have relied on that. This seems to me to be a typical case of agreeing to assume a responsibility: they knew why the plaintiff wanted to see the accounts and why their employers, the company, wanted them to be shown to him, and agreed to show them to him without even a suggestion that he should not rely on them.

The majority of the Court of Appeal held that they were bound by *Le Lievre* v. *Gould* ([1893] 1 Q.B. 491) and that *Donoghue* v. *Stevenson* had no application . . . .

In *Le Lievre* v. *Gould* a surveyor, Gould, gave certificates to a builder who employed him. The plaintiffs were mortgagees of the builder's interest and Gould knew nothing about them or the terms of their mortgage; but the builder, without Gould's authority, chose to show them Gould's report. I have said that I do not intend to decide anything about the degree of proximity necessary to establish a relationship giving rise to a duty of care, but it would seem difficult to find such proximity in this case, and the actual decision in *Le Lievre* v. *Gould* may therefore be correct. But the decision was not put on that ground: if it had been, *Cann* v. *Willson* (1883) 39 Ch.D. 39) would not have been overruled.

Lord Esher M.R. held that there was no contract between the plaintiffs and the defendant and that this House in *Derry* v. *Peek* had "restated the old law that, in the absence of contract, an action for negligence cannot be maintained when there is no fraud" ([1893] 1 Q.B. 491, 498). Bowen L.J. gave a similar reason; he said (at 501): "Then *Derry* v. *Peek* decided this further point—*viz.*, that in cases like the present (of which *Derry* v. *Peek* was itself an instance) there is no duty enforceable in law to be careful"; and he added that the law of England "does not consider that what a man writes on paper is like a gun or other dangerous instrument, and, unless he intended to deceive, the law does not, in the absence of contract, hold him responsible for drawing his certificate carelessly." So both he and Lord Esher held that *Cann* v. *Willson* was wrong in deciding that there was a duty to take care. We now know on the authority of *Donoghue* v. *Stevenson* that Bowen L.J. was wrong in limiting duty of care to guns or other dangerous instruments, and I think that, for reasons which I have already given, he was also wrong in limiting the duty of care with regard to statements to cases where there is a contract. On both points Bowen L.J. was expressing what was then generally believed to be the law, but later statements in this House have gone far to remove those limitations. I would therefore hold that the ratio in *Le Lievre* v. *Gould* was wrong and that *Cann* v. *Willson* ought not to have been overruled.

Now I must try to apply these principles to the present case. What the appellants complain of is not negligence in the ordinary sense of carelessness, but rather misjudgment, in that Mr. Heller, while honestly seeking to give a fair assessment, in fact made a statement which gave a false and misleading impression of his customer's credit. It appears that bankers now commonly give references with regard to their customers as part of their business. I do not know how far their customers generally permit them to disclose their affairs, but, even with permission, it cannot always be easy for a banker to reconcile his duty to his customer with his desire to give a fairly balanced reply to an inquiry. And inquirers can hardly expect a full and objective statement of opinion or accurate factual information such as skilled men would be expected to give in reply to other kinds of inquiry. So it seems to me to be unusually difficult to determine just what duty beyond a duty to be honest a banker would be held to have undertaken if he gave a reply without an adequate disclaimer of responsibility or other warning . . .

But here the appellants' bank, who were their agents in making the inquiry, began by saying that "they wanted to know in confidence and without responsibility on our part," that is, on the part of the respondents. So I cannot see how the appellants can now be entitled to disregard that and maintain that the respondents did incur a responsibility to them.

The appellants founded on a number of cases in contract where very clear words were required to exclude the duty of care which would otherwise have flowed from the contract. To that argument there are, I think, two answers. In the case of a contract it is necessary to exclude liability for negligence, but in this case the question is whether an undertaking to assume a duty to take care can be inferred: and that is a very different matter. And, secondly, even in cases of contract general words may be sufficient if there was no other kind of liability to be excluded except liability for negligence: the general rule is that a party is not exempted from liability for negligence "unless adequate words are used"—*per* Scrutton L.J. in *Rutter* v. *Palmer* ([1952] 2 K.B. 87, 92). It being admitted that there was here a duty to give an honest reply, I do not see what further liability there could be to exclude except liability for negligence: there being no contract there was no question of warranty.

I am therefore of opinion that it is clear that the respondents never undertook any duty to exercise care in giving their replies. The appellants cannot succeed unless there was such a duty and therefore in my judgment this appeal must be dismissed.

Lord Morris of Borth-y-Gest: . . . My Lords, I consider that it follows and that it should now be regarded as settled that if someone possessed of a special skill undertakes, quite irrespective of contract, to apply that skill for the assistance of another person who relies upon such skill, a duty of care will arise. The fact that the service is to be given by means of or by the instrumentality of words can make no difference. Furthermore, if in a sphere in which a person is so placed that others could reasonably rely upon his judgment or his skill or upon his ability to make careful inquiry, a person takes it upon himself to give information or advice to, or allows his information or advice to be passed on to, another person who, as he knows or should know, will place reliance upon it, then a duty of care will arise . . .

Lord Devlin: . . . I think, therefore, that there is ample authority to justify your Lordships in saying now that the categories of special relationships which may give rise to a duty to take care in word as well as in deed are not limited to contractual relationships of fiduciary duty, but include also relationships which in the words of Lord Shaw in *Nocton* v. *Lord Ashburton* are "equivalent to contract," that is, where there is an assumption of responsibility in circumstances in which, but for the absence of consideration, there would be a contract. Where there is an express undertaking, an express warranty as distinct from mere representation, there can be little difficulty. The difficulty arises in discerning those cases in which the undertaking is to be implied. In this respect the absence of consideration is not irrelevant. Payment for information or advice is very good evidence that it is being relied upon and that the informer or adviser knows that it is. Where there is no consideration, it

will be necessary to exercise greater care in distinguishing between social and professional relationships and between those which are of a contractual character and
those which are not. It may often be material to consider whether the adviser is acting purely out of good nature or whether he is getting his reward in some indirect
form. The service that a bank performs in giving a reference is not done simply out
of a desire to assist commerce. It would discourage the customers of the bank if
their deals fell through because the bank had refused to testify to their credit when
it was good.

I have had the advantage of reading all the opinions prepared by your Lordships
and of studying the terms which your Lordships have framed by way of definition of
the sort of relationship which gives rise to a responsibility towards those who act
upon information or advice and so creates a duty of care towards them. I do not
understand any of your Lordships to hold that it is a responsibility imposed by law
upon certain types of persons or in certain sorts of situations. It is a responsibility
that is voluntarily accepted or undertaken, either generally where a general relationship, such as that of solicitor and client or banker and customer, is created, or
specifically in relation to a particular transaction. In the present case the appellants
were not, as in *Woods* v. *Martins Bank Ltd.* ([1959] 1 Q.B. 55), the customers or
potential customers of the bank. Responsibility can attach only to the single act,
that is, the giving of the reference, and only if the doing of that act implied a voluntary undertaking to assume responsibility. This is a point of great importance
because it is, as I understand it, the foundation for the ground on which in the end
the House dismisses the appeal. I do not think it is possible to formulate with exactitude all the conditions under which the law will in a specific case imply a voluntary
undertaking any more than it is possible to formulate those in which the law will
imply a contract. But in so far as your Lordships describe the circumstances in
which an implication will ordinarily be drawn, I am prepared to adopt any one of
your Lordships' statements as showing the general rule; and I pay the same respect
to the statement by Denning L.J. in his dissenting judgment in *Candler* v. *Crane,
Christmas & Co.* about the circumstances in which he says a duty to use care in
making a statement exists.

I do not go further than this for two reasons. The first is that I have found in the
speech of Lord Shaw in *Nocton* v. *Lord Ashburton* and in the idea of a relationship
that is equivalent to contract all that is necessary to cover the situation that arises in
this case. Mr. Gardiner does not claim to succeed unless he can establish that the
reference was intended by the respondents to be communicated by the National
Provincial Bank to some unnamed customer of theirs, whose identity was immaterial to the respondents, for that customer's use. All that was lacking was formal
consideration. The case is well within the authorities I have already cited and of
which *Wilkinson* v. *Coverdale* ((1793) 1 Esp. 75; 170 E.R. 284) is the most apposite
example.

I shall therefore content myself with the proposition that wherever there is a relationship equivalent to contract, there is a duty of care. Such a relationship may be
either general or particular. Examples of a general relationship are those of solicitor and client and of banker and customer. For the former *Nocton* v. *Lord Ashburton* has long stood as the authority and for the latter there is the decision of
Salmon J. in *Woods* v. *Martin Bank Ltd.* which I respectfully approve. There may
well be others yet to be established. Where there is a general relationship of this
sort, it is unnecessary to do more than prove its existence and the duty follows.
Where, as in the present case, what is relied on is a particular relationship created
ad hoc, it will be necessary to examine the particular facts to see whether there is an
express or implied undertaking of responsibility . . .

I regard this proposition as an application of the general conception of proximity.
Cases may arise in the future in which a new and wider proposition, quite independent of any notion of contract, will be needed. There may, for example, be cases in
which a statement is not supplied for the use of any particular person, any more

than in *Donoghue* v. *Stevenson* the ginger beer was supplied for consumption by any particular person; and it will then be necessary to return to the general conception of proximity and to see whether there can be evolved from it, as was done in *Donoghue* v. *Stevenson*, a specific proposition to fit the case. When that has to be done, the speeches of your Lordships today as well as the judgment of Denning L.J. to which I have referred—and also, I may add, the proposition in the *American Restatement of the Law of Torts*, Vol. III, p. 122, para. 552, and the cases which exemplify it—will afford good guidance as to what ought to be said. I prefer to see what shape such cases take before committing myself to any formulation, for I bear in mind Lord Atkin's warning, which I have quoted, against unnecessary restrictions on the adaptability of English law. I have, I hope, made it clear that I take quite literally the dictum of Lord Macmillan, so often quoted from the same case, that "the categories of negligence are never closed." English law is wide enough to embrace any new category or proposition that exemplifies the principle of proximity.

I have another reason for caution. Since the essence of the matter in the present case and in others of the same type is the acceptance of responsibility, I should like to guard against the imposition of restrictive terms notwithstanding that the essential condition is fulfilled. If a defendant says to a plaintiff: "Let me do this for you; do not waste your money in employing a professional, I will do it for nothing and you can rely on me," I do not think he could escape liability simply because he belonged to no profession or calling, had no qualifications or special skill and did not hold himself out as having any. The relevance of these factors is to show the unlikelihood of a defendant in such circumstances assuming a legal responsibility, and as such they may often be decisive. But they are not theoretically conclusive and so cannot be the subject of definition. It would be unfortunate if they were . . .

Questions

1. At whose risk does a business man lay out money on credit in the hope of profit?

2. If you had been so suspicious as to make repeated inquiries about Easipower's financial standing, how would you have understood the statement made by the defendant in this case? In what precise respects was the defendant negligent?

3. Suppose that the plaintiff had in his files, but had forgotten it, information suggesting that the defendant could not have meant what he appeared to be saying; would you allow the plaintiff to recover part of his loss on the ground that both were negligent? For the terms of the Law Reform (Contributory Negligence) Act 1945, see below, p. 213, and see Lord Reid at [1971] A.C. 793, 811. The Act has been held applicable where the defendant is in breach of a duty to take care in advice, but not, oddly enough, to a claim for breach of the precontractual duty of utmost good faith between insurer and insured: *Banque Keyser* [1987] 2 All E.R. 923, 958 (Steyn J.).

4. The disclaimer of responsibility apart, do you think the plaintiff should have recovered only what he had lost, or also his loss of profit on the transaction in question?

5. In these cases the debtor (here Easipower) will probably go into liquidation or bankruptcy, and it may be some time before it is clear what portion of their claims the creditors will receive. At what time may the plaintiff issue his writ against the defendant?

6. Are you amused that the leading case on misrepresentation should involve an advertising agent—as *plaintiff*?

7. Reflect for a moment on the conduct of Mr. Heller in writing the letter complained of. The trial judge unhesitatingly found it negligent, the House of Lords taking no view on the matter. Do *you* think that it was negligent to write such a letter? How would you have understood it? Suppose an employee wrote such a letter and thereby landed his employer with a liability for £17,000. Would it be fair for the employer to dismiss him? Is there a risk that conduct which causes financial harm is more likely to be held negligent than conduct which causes physical harm? Is such conduct more likely to occur? Have you ever copied out a paragraph of text with complete accuracy? Have you ever failed to spot a misprint, or struck out the wrong

50 DUTY

alternative in a form, or put a tick or cross in the wrong box? If liability is to be dependent on fault in such cases, should liability not be roughly proportional to fault?

Notes:

1. This is the first great case where a person merely negligent was, in principle, held liable for causing merely pecuniary loss to a non-contractor. There is a very interesting article on it by Robert Stevens in 27 M.L.R. 121 (1964).

The decision was thought by some to herald a general liability for causing foreseeable economic loss by negligent conduct, but *Spartan Steel* (above p. 36) shows that it has not had that effect.

Note that here there was no question of any *danger*. Dangerous misrepresentations ("Come on, it's perfectly safe" . . . *Crash!*) had led to liability before, but here the only possible harm was financial: the situation was commercial not collisional.

2. *Speech and Silence*

"Mere silence or inaction cannot amount to a misrepresentation unless there be a duty to disclose or act," *per* Lord Scarman said in *Tai Hing Cotton Mill* [1985] 2 All E.R. 947, 959. Even if Heller and Partners had known that Easipower were totally insolvent, they need not have said a word to Hedley Byrne. Thus one need not tell a complete stranger that he is about to fall over a cliff, and the witness of an accident is not liable for not divulging without *subpoena* the name and number of the fatal car (*Ricci* v. *Chow* [1987] 3 All E.R. 534; *Norwich Pharmacal* [1974] A.C. 133). By contrast, the occupier of premises is bound to warn his visitors about any dangers on them, and the doctor must tell the patient what has gone wrong: "the duty of candid disclosure . . . is but one aspect of the general duty of care, arising out of the patient/medical practitioner or hospital authority relationship and gives rise to rights both in contract and in tort" *per* Sir John Donaldson M.R. in *Naylor* v. *Preston AHA* [1987] 2 All E.R. 353, 360. The special relationship makes all the difference. So here. An insurer who knows that the insured's agent has been fraudulent in the past must tell the insured, but need not tell a mere applicant for insurance whose proposal is being rejected (*Banque Keyser* [1987] 2 All E.R. 923). Yet although it is only to a customer that a bank may be under a duty to explain the effect of a proposed guarantee, any explanation it gives to a stranger, if it chooses to give one, must be adequate (*Cornish* v. *Midland Bank* [1985] 3 All E.R. 513).

This duty of explanation must not be pitched too high: the duty to give correct information is not the same as the duty to give wise advice. Thus the Privy Council has held, by a bare majority, that a bank which supplied information requested by a customer was not liable for failing to add an explanation that it was an insufficient basis for a decision whether to invest or not: they had not undertaken to advise him (*Royal Bank Trust Co. (Trinidad)* v. *Pampallone* [1987] 1 Lloyd's Rep. 218).

3. *Duty to Whom?*

In the principal case the information was not only given to, but also requested by, the plaintiff. A request identifies the plaintiff: more people hear than ask to hear. Information which is volunteered attracts liability less easily, especially if it is widely published. Thus a municipality which published a development plan which had to be abandoned because it was infeasible was not liable to developers who had bought property on the strength of it: *San Sebastian Pty.* v. *Minister*, 68 A.L.R. 161 (H.Ct.Aus. 1986). Weather forecasting is a very clear example, even if the harm is physical in nature, as it tends to be.

Otherwise the duty is owed to the addressee, of whom there may be several, concurrent or consecutive. The range of persons to whom this duty is owed is not yet clear, but the courts may be expected to be hesitant, lest liability become rampant.

Persons may be affected by speech addressed to others. Can a duty be owed to them? In *Ministry of Housing and Local Government* v. *Sharp* [1970] 2 Q.B. 223 it was held that the Land Registry owed a duty to an incumbrancer not to tell a purchaser that there was no incumbrance, and *Ross* v. *Caunters* [1980] Ch. 297 implies that a solicitor who puts a £5,000 legacy in a will when the testator told him to put £50,000 will be liable to the disappointed legatee. In these cases the incumbrancer and legatee must have been in the very forefront of the defendant's mind, like the employee regarding whom an ex-employer was asked for a reference by a prospective employer (*Lawton* v. *BOC Transhield* [1987] 2 All E.R. 608). But the mere fact that the defendant was talking *about* the plaintiff rather than *to* him involves no assumption of duty: it is established law that in the absence of an antecedent relationship a person affected economically, rather than socially, by what the defendant said about him must show that the defendant either knew that what he was saying was false or had no business to be speaking on the subject at all (below p. 493): negligence is not enough, or, to put it another way, no duty of care is owed.

4. *Speech and Conduct*

Does the duty extend from communication to non-communicative conduct? Up to a point. In *Junior Books* [1983] A.C. 520 the defendants, selected by the plaintiffs to provide a floor, were held liable for economic loss due to its being defective, though there was no contract between them. The decision, ostensibly based on an extension of *Donoghue* v. *Stevenson*, has now been brought under the heading of *Hedley Byrne*, as a case where the defendant voluntarily undertook responsibility vis-à-vis the plaintiff. The accommodation is uneasy. The undertaking of responsibility is much clearer in *Al Kandari* v. *Brown* [1988] 1 All E.R. 833. The defendant solicitors undertook, in communication with the plaintiff's solicitors, to see that their client, her husband, did not get his hands on his passport. He did, and kidnapped the children after beating up the plaintiff. It was held that they owed a duty, and were liable for the consequences of its breach.

This involves that contractors owe each other a duty to take care of each other's economic interests. This very extensive overlap of contractual and tortious duties is unaesthetic, and can be noxious. Thus it is accepted that if the (novel) cause of action in tort accrues later than the cause of action in contract, the plaintiff may sue in tort though the (real) contract claim is barred. The courts have, however, stopped short of allowing the tort duty to increase the substantive obligations imposed on the parties. Thus it was established long before *Hedley Byrne* that a customer owes his bank a duty to draw each cheque in such a manner as to deter forgery, and to inform the bank of any forgeries which come to his notice. In *Tai Hing Cotton Mill* v. *Liu Chong Bank* [1985] 2 All E.R. 947 the bank argued that developments in tort law meant that the customer was now required to manage his business with care and to scrutinise his bank statements. Lord Scarman said: "Their Lordships do not believe that there is anything to the advantage of the law's development in searching for a liability in tort where the parties are in a contractual relationship."

5. Consider *Balsamo* v. *Medici* [1984] 2 All E.R. 304, noted 47 M.L.R. 86, 90–96 (1985) (Whitaker). Morris helped his friend Medici to sell a car, and when Medici had to return to Italy, agreed to collect the cheque and pay it to Zecchi at a given telephone number. Morris collected the cheque but lost the telephone number. Then Morris received a call from someone claiming to be Zecchi, and ultimately paid the money in cash to an emissary of the caller, bearing, apparently, one of Medici's business cards. The money was lost through this laxity of Morris's, but it was not really Medici's money, as Medici had been acting throughout on behalf of Balsamo, the plaintiff, who owned the car and wanted the money paid to Zecchi. Walton J. held that while Morris certainly owed a duty to Medici he owed none to Balsamo: *vis-a-vis* Balsamo, of whom he had never heard, Morris had assumed no responsibility.

6. Only one decision has really sought to limit *Hedley Byrne*. In *Mutual Life* v. *Evatt* [1971] A.C. 793, an investor had asked his insurance company about a subsidiary of theirs to which he was thinking of making unsecured loans at a high rate of interest. He got a positive answer and lost his money. He lost his lawsuit, too, because a majority of the Privy Council held that it was not the defendant's business to give such advice and that it was therefore not liable. Quite right, too. Lord Reid and Lord Hodson dissented strongly, on the ground that this was to pervert their own decision in *Hedley Byrne*, but their dissent has no special force: an author has no interpretational privilege. However, the High Court of Australia has rejected this limitation on the "principle" of *Hedley Byrne* (*Shaddock* v. *Parramatta* (1981) 36 A.L.R. 385, noted 2 Oxf.L.S. 440 (1982), and it is doubtful if it will be followed in England, though it would be useful to preserve us from pestilential questioners seeking free, or even inside information. Lord Denning has propounded a more flexible test, *viz.* was it clear that in all the circumstances the inquiry was directed towards obtaining considered advice rather than a quick answer? *Howard Marine* v. *Ogden & Sons* [1978] Q.B. 574, 591.

7. The disclaimer saved Heller & Partners from liability in this case. It might not do so today, in the light of the Unfair Contract Terms Act (below p. 222). Certainly surveyors

have been prevented from relying on such a disclaimer as against a house-purchaser (*Smith* v. *Eric Bush* [1987] 3 All E.R. 179; but see *Harris* v. *Wyre Forest D.C.* [1988] 1 All E.R. 691.

8. Professionals such as judges, arbitrators, valuers and architects, who decide how much people are to pay or be paid, are naturally very apt to cause financial loss by their decisions. Now that they may be sued by a party who did not employ them, the question of their liability has become very acute. That judges are immune from liability is well established (*Sirros* v. *Moore* [1975] Q.B. 118). That arbitrators are also immune was conceded by counsel in a recent case, though two of their Lordships doubted it (*Arenson* v. *Casson, Beckman Rutley & Co.* [1977] A.C. 405); the same case, following a decision about an architect's interim certificate of what was due to a builder (*Sutcliffe* v. *Thackrah* [1974] A.C. 727), held that mutual valuers have no immunity unless, perhaps, they are actually resolving a formulated dispute between the parties.

9. Here are some of the questions which have been raised since *Hedley Byrne.*

Does the bank on which a cheque is drawn owe a duty to the payee to take care in honouring their customer's cheque? No, *per* Kerr J. in *National Westminster Bank* v. *Barclay's Bank International* [1975] Q.B. 654.

Does a member of the organisation which receives, records and divulges information about the hire-purchase contracts affecting members' motor-cars owe a duty to fellow members to take care to supply relevant information? A bare majority of the House of Lords in *Moorgate Mercantile* v. *Twitchings* [1977] A.C. 890 thought not.

When a landlord had arranged insurance on tenanted premises did his successor owe a duty to the tenant to tell him that the insurance was not being continued? No, *per* Croom-Johnson J. in *Argy Trading* v. *Lapid Developments* [1977] 3 All E.R. 785 (*sed quaere.*)

Do the directors of a company owe a duty to the shareholders (as opposed to the company itself) to take care of the company's assets? No, *per* Templeman J. in *Daniels* v. *Daniels* [1978] Ch. 406 (though they may be liable if they profit from their negligence).

A house is surveyed at the instance of a building society. The surveyor negligently reports that the house is worth £25,000. The building society offers to lend £25,000 for the purchase of the house, which is worth much less. Can the purchaser sue the surveyor? Yes: *Yianni* v. *Edwin Evans & Sons* [1982] Q.B. 438.

X lends money to a company, taking a debenture. Y guarantees the company's debt. The company breaks, and X appoints Z as receiver to realise its assets. The less Z gets for those assets, the more Y will have to pay X. Does Z owe Y a duty to take care? Yes: *Standard Chartered Bank* v. *Walker* [1982] 3 All E.R. 938 (C.A.). But it may be reasonable for X to protect his own interests at the expense of Z, especially if he has a contractual right to do so (*Re Potters Oils (No. 2)* [1986] 1 All E.R. 890, 894).

Do the sequestrators of a company owe a duty to its creditors? Yes: *I.R.C.* v. *Hoogstraten* [1984] 3 All E.R. 25.

Does an adjudication officer whose decision is appealable owe a duty of care to an applicant for unemployment benefit? No, according to *Jones* v. *Department of Employment* ([1988] 1 All E.R. 725 (C.A.)).

Does a surveyor appointed to fix the rent under a lease with rent review owe a duty to both parties? Yes: *Palacath* v. *Flanagan* [1985] 2 All E.R. 161.

Does a litigant owe his opponent a duty to act reasonably? No, according to *Business Computers* v. *Registrar of Companies* [1987] 3 All E.R. 465.

Does a solicitor owe a duty to his client's opponent, if his client, being legally aided, is effectively unable to answer in costs? No, according to *Orchard* v. *South Eastern Elec. Bd.* [1987] 1 All E.R. 95, 99, unless the case is a very bad one (*Myers* v. *Elman* [1939] 4 All E.R. 484 (H.L.); *R.* v. *Oxfordshire C.C., ex p. Wallace* 137 New L.J. 542 (1987)).

Does a solicitor owe a duty to a prospective client to advise him about sources of support? Yes: *Crossan* v. *Ward Bracewell* ([1988] 1 All E.R. 364 (C.A.)).

Does a company solicitor owe a duty to directors who have guaranteed company debts and want a charge registered against its property? Yes: *Foster* v. *Crusts* 129 Sol.Jo. 333 (1985).

Does a solicitor advising his client on *inter vivos* transactions owe a duty to his client's residuary legatee? No: *Clarke* v. *Bruce Lance* ([1988] 1 All E.R. 364 (C.A.)).

Does the supplier of goods owe a duty to those whose intangible rights may foreseeably be infringed by the purchaser? No: *Amstrad Consumer Electronics* v. *British Phonographic Industries* 135 New L.J. 1186 (1985); *Paterson Zochonis & Co.* v. *Merfarken Packaging* [1986] 3 All E.R. 522.

HOME OFFICE v. DORSET YACHT CO.

House of Lords [1970] A.C. 1004; [1970] 2 W.L.R. 1140; [1970] 2 All E.R. 294; [1970] 1 Lloyd's Rep. 453; 114 S.J. 375

Action by owner against Home Office in respect of property damage done by runaway Borstal boys

Seven Borstal boys, five of whom had escaped before, were on a training exercise on Brownsea Island in Poole Harbour, and ran away one night when the three officers in charge of them were, contrary to instructions, all in bed. They boarded one of the many vessels in the harbour, started it and collided with the plaintiff's yacht, which they then boarded and damaged further.

To the preliminary question of law, whether on the facts as pleaded any duty of care capable of giving rise to a liability in damages was owed to the plaintiff by the defendant, their servants or agents, an affirmative answer was given by Thesiger J., by the Court of Appeal [1969] 2 Q.B. 412, and by the House of Lords (Viscount Dilhorne dissenting).

Lord Reid: . . . The case for the Home Office is that under no circumstances can Borstal officers owe any duty to any member of the public to take care to prevent trainees under their control or supervision from injuring him or his property. If that is the law, then inquiry into the facts of this case would be a waste of time and money because whatever the facts may be the respondents must lose. That case is based on three main arguments. First it is said that there is virtually no authority for imposing a duty of this kind. Secondly, it is said that no person can be liable for a wrong done by another who is of full age and capacity and who is not the servant or acting on behalf of that person. And thirdly it is said that public policy (or the policy of the relevant legislation) requires that these officers should be immune from any such liability.

The first would at one time have been a strong argument. About the beginning of this century most eminent lawyers thought that there were a number of separate torts involving negligence, each with its own rules, and they were most unwilling to add more. They were of course aware from a number of leading cases that in the past the courts had from time to time recognised new duties and new grounds of action. But the heroic age was over; it was time to cultivate certainty and security in the law; the categories of negligence were virtually closed. The Attorney-General invited us to return to those halcyon days, but, attractive though it may be, I cannot accede to his invitation.

In later years there has been a steady trend towards regarding the law of negligence as depending on principle so that, when a new point emerges, one should ask not whether it is covered by authority but whether recognised principles apply to it. *Donoghue* v. *Stevenson* ([1932] A.C. 562) may be regarded as a milestone, and the well-known passage in Lord Atkin's speech should I think be regarded as a statement of principle. It is not to be treated as if it were a statutory definition. It will require qualification in new circumstances. But I think that the time has come when we can and should say that it ought to apply unless there is some justification or valid explanation for its exclusion. For example, causing economic loss is a different matter; for one thing, it is often caused by deliberate action. Competition involves traders being entitled to damage their rivals' interests by promoting their own, and there is a long chapter of the law determining in what circumstances owners of land can and in what circumstances they may not use their proprietary rights so as to injure their neighbours. But where negligence is involved the tendency has been to apply principles analogous to those stated by Lord Atkin: *cf. Hedley Byrne & Co. Ltd.* v. *Heller & Partners Ltd.* ([1964] A.C. 465). And when a person has done nothing to put himself in any relationship with another person in

distress or with his property mere accidental propinquity does not require him to go
to that person's assistance. There may be a moral duty to do so, but it is not practicable to make it a legal duty. And then there are cases, *e.g.* with regard to landlord
and tenant, where the law was settled long ago and neither Parliament nor this
House sitting judicially has made any move to alter it. But I can see nothing to prevent our approaching the present case with Lord Atkin's principles in mind.

Even so, it is said that the respondents must fail because there is a general principle that no person can be responsible for the acts of another who is not his servant
or acting on his behalf. But here the ground of liability is not responsibility for the
acts of the escaping trainees; it is liability for damage caused by the carelessness of
these officers in the knowledge that their carelessness would probably result in the
trainees causing damage of this kind. So the question is really one of remoteness of
damage . . .

If the carelessness of the Borstal officers was the cause of the plaintiff's loss, what
justification is there for holding that they had no duty to take care? The first argument was that their right and power to control the trainees was purely statutory and
that any duty to exercise that right and power was only a statutory duty owed to the
Crown. I would agree, but there is a good authority for the proposition that if a person performs a statutory duty carelessly so that he causes damage to a member of
the public which would not have happened if he had performed his duty properly he
may be liable. In *Geddis* v. *Proprietors of Bann Reservoir* ((1873) 3 App.Cas 430)
Lord Blackburn said (at pp. 455–456): "For I take it, without citing cases, that it is
now thoroughly well established that no action will lie for doing that which the
legislature has authorised, if it be done without negligence, although it does
occasion damage to anyone; but an action does lie for doing that which the legislature has authorised, if it be done negligently." The reason for this is, I think, that
Parliament deems it to be in the public interest that things otherwise unjustifiable
should be done, and that those who do such things with due care should be immune
from liability to persons who may suffer thereby. But Parliament cannot reasonably
be supposed to have licensed those who do such things to act negligently in disregard of the interests of others so as to cause them needless damage.

Where Parliament confers a discretion the position is not the same. Then there
may, and almost certainly will, be errors of judgment in exercising such a discretion
and Parliament cannot have intended that members of the public should be entitled
to sue in respect of such errors. But there must come a stage when the discretion is
exercised so carelessly or unreasonably that there has been no real exercise of the
discretion which Parliament has conferred. The person purporting to exercise his
discretion has acted in abuse or excess of his power. Parliament cannot be supposed
to have granted immunity to persons who do that. The present case does not raise
this issue because no discretion was given to these Borstal officers. They were given
orders which they negligently failed to carry out. But the county court case of
Greenwell v. *Prison Commissioners* ((1951) 101 L.J. 486) was relied on and I must
deal with it.

Some 290 trainees were held in custody in an open Borstal institution. During the
previous year there had been no less than 172 escapes. Two trainees escaped and
took and damaged the plaintiff's motor truck; one of these trainees had escaped on
three previous occasions from this institution. For three months since his past
escape the question of his removal to a more secure institution had been under consideration but no decision has been reached. The learned judge held that the authorities there had been negligent. In my view, this decision could only be upheld if it
could be said that the failure of those authorities to deal with the situation was so
unreasonable as to show that they had been guilty of a breach of their statutory
duty and that that had caused the loss suffered by the plaintiff.

Governors of these institutions and other responsible authorities have a difficult
and delicate task. There was some argument as to whether the present system was
fully authorised by the relevant statutes, but I shall assume that it is. This system is

based on the belief that it assists the rehabilitation of trainees to give them as much freedom and responsibility as possible. So the responsible authorities must weigh on the one hand the public interest of protecting neighbours and their property from the depredations of escaping trainees and on the other hand the public interest of promoting rehabilitation. Obviously there is much room here for differences of opinion and errors of judgment. In my view there can be no liability if the discretion is exercised with due care. There could only be liability if the person entrusted with discretion either unreasonably failed to carry out his duty to consider the matter or reached a conclusion so unreasonable as again to show failure to do his duty.

It was suggested that these trainees might have been deliberately released at the time when they escaped and that then there could have been no liability. I do not agree. Presumably when trainees are released either temporarily or permanently some care is taken to see that there is no need for them to resort to crime to get food or transport. I could not imagine any more unreasonable exercise of discretion than to release trainees on an island in the middle of the night without making any provision for their future welfare.

We were also referred to *Holgate* v. *Lancashire Mental Hospitals Board* ([1937] 4 All E.R. 19), where the alleged fault was in releasing a mental patient. For similar reasons I think that this decision could only be supported if it could be said that the release was authorised so carelessly that there had been no real exercise of discretion.

If the appellants were right in saying that there can never be a right in a private individual to complain of negligent exercise of a duty to keep a prisoner under control, I do not see how *Ellis* v. *Home Office* ([1953] 2 All E.R. 149) can be correct. The plaintiff was in prison, and on one occasion, as he alleged, owing to inadequate control by warders another prisoner assaulted and injured him. It was assumed that he had a right of action, and the Attorney-General did not challenge this. But when the other prisoner assaulted Ellis he was not in fact under control or he would not have been permitted to carry out the assault. It would be very odd if the only persons entitled to complain of negligent performance of the statutory duty to control prisoners were other prisoners. If the main argument for the appellants were right I think that it would necessarily involve holding that *Ellis* was wrong.

It was suggested that a decision against the Home Office would have very far-reaching effects; it was, indeed, suggested in the Court of Appeal that it would make the Home Office liable for the loss occasioned by a burglary committed by a trainee on parole or a prisoner permitted to go out to attend a funeral. But there are two reasons why in the vast majority of cases that would not be so. In the first place it would have to be shown that the decision to allow any such release was so unreasonable that it could not be regarded as a real exercise of discretion by the responsible officer who authorised the release. And secondly it would have to be shown that the commission of the offence was the natural and probable, as distinct from merely a foreseeable, result of the release—that there was no novus actus interveniens. *Greenwell*'s case (101 L.J. 486) received a good deal of publicity at the time; it was commented on in the *Law Quarterly Review*, Vol. 68 (1952), p. 18. But it has not been followed by a series of claims. I think that the fears of the appellants are unfounded: I cannot believe that negligence or dereliction of duty is widespread among prison or Borstal officers.

Finally I must deal with public policy. It is argued that it would be contrary to public policy to hold the Home Office or its officers liable to a member of the public for this carelessness—or, indeed, any failure of duty on their part. The basic question is: who shall bear the loss caused by that carelessness—the innocent respondents or the Home Office, who are vicariously liable for the conduct of their careless officers? I do not think that the argument for the Home Office can be put better than it was put by the Court of Appeals of New York in *Williams* v. *State of New York* ((1955) 127 N.E. 2d 545, 550): " . . . public policy also requires that the

State be not held liable. To hold otherwise would impose a heavy responsibility upon the State, or dissuade the wardens and principal keepers of our prison systems from continued experimentation with 'minimum security' work details—which provide a means for encouraging better-risk prisoners to exercise their senses of responsibility and honour and so prepare themselves for their eventual return to society. Since 1917, the legislature has expressly provided for out-of-prison work, Correction Law, § 182, and its intention should be respected without fostering the reluctance of prison officials to assign eligible men to minimum security work, lest they thereby give rise to costly claims against the State, or indeed inducing the State itself to terminate this 'salutary procedure' looking toward rehabilitation." It may be that public servants of the State of New York are so apprehensive, easily dissuaded from doing their duty and intent on preserving public funds from costly claims that they could be influenced in this way. But my experience leads me to believe that Her Majesty's servants are made of sterner stuff. So I have no hesitation in rejecting this argument. I can see no good ground in public policy for giving this immunity to a government department. I would dismiss this appeal.

Viscount Dilhorne (dissenting): . . . If, applying Lord Atkin's test, it be held that a duty of care existed in this case, I do not think that such a duty can be limited to being owed only to those in the immediate proximity of the place from which the escape is made. In *Donoghue* v. *Stevenson* the duty was held to be owed to consumers wherever they might be. If there be such a duty, it must, in my view, be owed to all those who it can reasonably be foreseen are likely to suffer damage as a result of the escape. Surely it is reasonably foreseeable that those who escape may take a succession of vehicles, perhaps many miles from the place from which they escaped, to make their gateway. Surely it is reasonably foreseeable that those who escape from prisons, Borstals and other places of confinement will, while they are on the run, seek to steal food for their sustenance and money and are likely to break into premises for that purpose.

If the foreseeability test is applied to determine to whom the duty is owed, I am at a loss to perceive any logical ground for excluding liability to persons who suffer injury or loss, no matter how far they or their property may be from the place of escape, if the loss or injury was of a character reasonably foreseeable as the consequence of failure to take proper care to prevent the escape.

Lord Atkin's answer to the question "Who, then, in law is my neighbour?" while very relevant to determine to whom a duty of care is owed, cannot determine, in my opinion, the question whether a duty of care exists.

I find support for this view in the observations of du Parcq L.J. in *Deyong* v. *Shenburn* ([1946] K.B. 227). There the plaintiff has been employed in a theatre by the defendant. Some of his clothing had been stolen from his dressing room due, it was alleged, to the negligence of the defendant.

du Parcq L.J. said (at p. 233): "It is said that this is a case of tort, and we were reminded of observations which are very familiar to lawyers in *Heaven* v. *Pender* ((1883) 11 Q.B.D. 503) and *Donoghue* v. *Stevenson*. I do not think that I need cite them in terms. There are well known words of Lord Atkin in *Donoghue* v. *Stevenson* as to the duty towards one's neighbour and the method of ascertaining who is one's neighbour. It has been pointed out (and this only shows the difficulty of stating a general proposition which is not too wide) that unless one somewhat narrows the term of the proposition as it has been stated, one would be including in it something which the law does not support. It is not true to say that wherever a man finds himself in such a position that unless he does a certain act another person may suffer, or that if he does something another person will suffer, then it is his duty in the one case to be careful to do the act and in the other case to be careful not to do the act. Any such proposition is much too wide. There has to be a breach of a duty which the law recognises, and to ascertain what the law recognises regard must be had to the decisions of the courts. There has never been a decision that a master must, merely because of the relationship which exists between master and servant, take reasonable care for the safety of his servant's belongings in the sense that he must take steps to ensure, so far as he can, that no wicked person shall have an opportunity of stealing the servant's goods. That is the duty contended for here, and there is not a shred of authority to suggest that any such duty exists or ever has existed."

This was cited and followed by my learned and noble friends Lord Hodson and Lord Morris of Borth-y-Gest in *Edwards* v. *West Herts. Group Hospital Management Committee* ([1957] 1 W.L.R. 415, 420, 422).

In *Commissioner for Railways* v. *Quinlan* ([1964] A.C. 1054) the question was considered whether on the facts of that case and on the principle of *Donoghue* v. *Stevenson* (above, p. 21) a general duty of care and liability in negligence for its breach existed in relation to a trespasser. Viscount Radcliffe, delivering the judgment of the board, said (at p. 1070): " . . . such a duty, it was suggested, might be founded on a general principle derived from the House of Lords decision in *Donoghue* v. *Stevenson*. Their Lordships think this view mistaken. They cannot see that there is any general principle to be deduced from that decision which throws any particular light upon the legal rights and duties that arise when a trespasser is injured on a railway level crossing where he has no right to be . . . " Later he said (at p. 1084): " . . . passages occur in one or two of the other judgments that suggest that a trespasser can somehow become the occupier's 'neighbour,' within the meaning of the somewhat overworked shorthand of *Donoghue* v. *Stevenson* . . . " In the light of those passages I think that it is clear that the *Donoghue* v. *Stevenson* principle cannot be regarded as an infallible test of the existence of a duty of care, nor do I think that, if that test is satisfied, there arises any presumption of the existence of such a duty. . . .

Apart from [*Greenwell* v. *Prison Commissioners*] in which *Donoghue* v. *Stevenson* was applied, no shred of authority can be found to support the view that a duty of care, breach of which gives rise to liability in damages, is under the common law owed by the custodians of persons lawfully in custody to anyone who suffers damage or loss at the hands of persons who have escaped from custody.

Lord Denning M.R. in the course of his judgment in this case ([1969] 2 Q.B. 412, 424) said that he thought that the absence of authority was "because, until recently, no lawyer ever thought such an action would lie" on one of two grounds, first, that the damage was far too remote, the chain of causation being broken by the act of the person who had escaped; and, secondly, that the only duty owed was to the Crown.

Whatever be the reasons for the absence of authority, the significant fact is its absence and this leads me to the conclusion, despite the disclaimer of Mr. Fox-Andrews for the respondents of any such intention, that we are being asked to create in reliance on Lord Atkin's words an entirely new and novel duty and one which does not arise out of any novel situation.

I, of course, recognise that the common law develops by the application of well-established principles to new circumstances but I cannot accept that the application of Lord Atkin's words, which, though they applied in *Deyong* v. *Shenburn* ([1946] K.B. 227), and might have applied in *Commissioner for Railways* v. *Quinlan* ([1964] A.C. 1054), were not held to impose a new duty on a master to his servant or on an occupier to a trespasser, suffices to impose a new duty on the Home Office and on others in charge of persons in lawful custody of the kind suggested.

No doubt very powerful arguments can be advanced that there should be such a duty. It can be argued that it is wrong that those who suffer loss or damage at the hands of those who have escaped from custody as a result of negligence on the part of the custodians should have no redress save against the persons who inflicted the loss or damage who are unlikely to be able to pay; that they should not have to bear the loss themselves, whereas, if there is such a duty, liability might fall on the Home Office and the burden on the general body of taxpayers.

However this may be, we are concerned not with what the law should be but with what it is. The absence of authority shows that no such duty now exists. If there should be one, that is, in my view, a matter for the legislature and not for the courts . . .

Questions

1. What is the difference between the duty to take care that your ginger-beer doesn't hurt anyone and the duty to take care that other people don't?

2. Is it for the judges to decide whether a penal system has been (a) wisely instituted, (b) properly run? In what form of proceedings should such decisions be taken?

3. Why is it "not negligence to keep an open Borstal" (*per* Lord Denning M.R.) if it involves the risk that boys will sometimes escape and do damage?

4. Is it helpful to see this case as involving a conflict between property and liberty? Are warders likely to constrain detainees more carefully after this decision?

5. As between the state and the plaintiff's insurance company (who had been paid to take the risk of damage to the yacht) "on whom should the risk of negligence fall"?

6. Only those suffering personal injury, as opposed to property damage, can claim from the Criminal Injuries Compensation Board, which distributes public funds to the victims of crimes of violence. (See below p. 157). Why do you think this is?

7. Which of the following statements is accurate:

(a) The warders were responsible for the Borstal boys;

(b) the warders were responsible for the damage done by the Borstal boys;

(c) the warders were responsible for the damage they caused by letting the Borstal boys escape?

8. Jacqueline Hill was the last of the Yorkshire Ripper's 20 victims. Her estate sued the police for incompetently failing to catch him sooner. The claim was dismissed on the ground that "the cause of action contended for . . . does not fall within the principle of the *Dorset Yacht* case." (*Hill* v. *Chief Constable of West Yorkshire* [1987] 1 All E.R. 1173). Do you agree with (a) the decision, (b) that reason for it? (See also above pp. 32–35).

9. If warders carelessly permit a confidence trickster and a burglar to escape from prison, would a person duped by the former or raped by the latter have a claim against the Home Office?

10. After having 12 double whiskies in X's pub, A drove to Y's roadhouse; Y refused to serve him since he was obviously drunk but made no effort to stop him driving away. Just outside the roadhouse A collided with B, a pedestrian. Can B sue X or Y or both?

11. There are two major grounds of distinction between *Dorset Yacht* and *Ellis* v. *Home Office* (above p. 55). What are they?

12. From Harlow, *Compensation and Government Torts* (1982) pp. 154–155, we learn that the Home Office, regardless of whether it is at fault or not, regularly pays for property loss due to miscreants absconding from Borstal and open prisons, outside hospitals, working parties or escorted travel, provided that the property is in the "neighbourhood" and is not insured. A woman who was denied payment because she lived 17 miles away from the Borstal in question complained to the Ombudsman, who recommended a more generous interpretation of "neighbourhood." Do you think their Lordships knew of this scheme? Could counsel properly have informed them of it? Which side would have an interest in so informing the court?

13. Suppose that a convict escapes because the gaolers are on strike. Would you hold (a) them, (b) the Home Office, liable?

Note:

An employer has been held liable to an apprentice for letting another employee brutalise him (*Hudson* v. *Ridge Manufacturing Co.* [1957] 2 Q.B. 348) and an education authority has been held liable to a truck-driver who ran into a tree in order to avoid killing a child it had carelessly allowed to run on to the highway (*Carmarthenshire C.C.* v. *Lewis* [1955] A.C. 549). It is perhaps not surprising that the House of Lords should combine the two principles and hold an occupier liable for the property damage which adults who were carelessly allowed to escape were likely to cause. Only a very tiresome critic would seek to draw a distinction between, on the one hand, a young apprentice blown up with compressed air by a bully or a truck-driver sacrificing himself to save a toddler and, on the other hand, an insured yacht, doubly symbolic of capitalist excess, damaged by predictably incompetent outcasts.

The striking thing about *Dorset Yacht* is that the defendants were held liable to total strangers for not protecting them from the ravages of the boys: the yachts anchored in the harbour were just like cars parked on the road outside a borstal (except that walking is a bit easier than swimming). An occupier has been held liable to his neighbour (in the strict sense of the "person next door") for the escape of natural hazards which damaged his house (see *Leakey* v. *National Trust*, below p. 377), but the application of this principle to more distant chattels is doubtful. Of course, the Home Office didn't just fail to prevent the borstal boys escaping, it brought them to the island in the first place . . .

The judgment of Lord Diplock, too integrated for excerption and too long for inclusion, should be read with care. He emphasised that the duty in question, namely to control the Borstal boys, was very different from the duty to control one's property or one's own activities. He also emphasised that the power to detain the boys came from statute, and that the principal legal device for controlling the exercise of that power was the doctrine of *vires*; if, however, what the officers had done was *ultra vires*, as it would be if it were in breach of instructions or wholly unreasonable, the private law doctrine of negligence might enter, in favour of those immediately in the vicinity. His conclusion was that "any duty of a borstal officer to use reasonable care to prevent a borstal trainee from escaping from his custody was owed only to persons whom he could reasonably foresee had property situate in the vicinity of the place of detention of the detainee which the detainee was likely to steal or to appropriate and damage in the course of eluding immediate pursuit and recapture."

Viscount Dilhorne was certainly right to say that it will be very difficult to limit this duty to those in the immediate vicinity. In the shock cases, as we shall see, there was a well-established rule that only those *on the spot* could claim. That convenient limitation has now been discarded with scorn and derision because it was incompatible with the "foreseeability" formula, like the holding in this case (*McLoughlin* v. *O'Brian*, below p. 69).

We observed above (p. 27) that there were two respects in which Lord Atkin's principle was wider than the facts of the case. We have seen the extension from liability for causing physical harm to liability for causing economic harm. Now we see the extension from liability for causing harm to liability for letting others cause harm, in this case physical harm.

Now one can only be liable for letting someone cause harm if one has the power to prevent him. While it is true that some private people have certain powers of control (occupiers of premises, parents, employers), most of the powers to stop people doing things are vested in the government. It is amazing how many things the government can stop people doing, by refusing or withdrawing a licence, or permit them to do by granting one. *Yuen Kun-yeu*, above p. 29, is a good instance. That case, unlike *Dorset Yacht*, concerned mere financial loss, which is exactly the kind of harm most apt to ensue from governmental decisions or conduct in office. If, as in the next case, where the damage was of an ambiguous nature, really economic but apparently physical, liability is imposed on government, we are immediately caught up in a vast extension of governmental liability in the field of private law. The number of people entitled as of right (for tort claims can be brought as of right) to harass the government, especially local government, vastly increased as a result of *Anns*. The courts now realise what they have let loose and have decided that if one is questioning a decision of a governmental body in the area of public law, one must use the special procedure for such matters (R.S.C. Order 53) rather than an ordinary action. The special procedure permits an award of damages but allows the court much greater control and considerable discretion. (*Cocks* v. *Thanet D.C.* [1983] 2 A.C. 286, [1982] 3 All E.R. 1135 (H.L.)). It is a pity that the courts seem to be backtracking from this sensible attempt to put the winds of change back into the bag whence they fecklessly let them loose. In *Davy* v. *Spelthorne B.C.* [1983] 3 All E.R. 278 a plaintiff who could no longer challenge a planning decision of a local authority was allowed to sue it for negligence in advising him as to his rights in the matter (!).

In *Smith* v. *Scott* [1973] Ch. 314 the local authority installed a notoriously unruly and anti-social family in a house next the plaintiff's. The lease forbade the Scotts to cause a nuisance, but of course they did and the plaintiffs had to move out of their own house. The local authority was held to have committed no wrong to the plaintiffs: *Donoghue* v. *Stevenson* did not apply. The trial judge quoted the end of the third paragraph of Lord Reid's speech in *Dorset Yacht* as excerpted above p. 53.

ANNS v. MERTON LONDON BOROUGH COUNCIL

House of Lords [1978] A.C. 728; [1977] 2 W.L.R. 1024; 121 S.J. 377; [1977] 2 All E.R. 492

Action by householders against builder and local authority in respect of building defects

The plaintiffs were leaseholders of flats in a block built by Walcroft in 1962. In 1970 the wall began to crack and the floors started to tilt. According to the plaintiffs, this settlement was attributable to the inadequacy of the foundations. In 1972 they issued a writ against Walcroft, claiming damages for breach of contract and of the undertakings implied by section 6 of the Housing Act 1957; they also issued a writ against the local authority, claiming damages for negligent failure to inspect the foundations or to detect, on inspection, that they were shallower than was required by bye-laws or was indicated on the approved plans.

On the preliminary point whether the claim was time-barred the local authority appealed without success from an adverse decision of the Court of Appeal.

Lord Wilberforce: . . . before the appeal to this House came on, the council pre-sented a petition, asking for leave to argue the question whether the council was under any duty of care to the plaintiffs at all.

The question had not been considered by Judge Fay, or by the Court of Appeal, because it was thought, rightly in my opinion, that it was concluded by *Dutton's* case ([1972] 1 Q.B. 373) . . .

The factual relationship between the council and owners and occupiers of new dwellings constructed in their area must be considered in the relevant statutory set-ting, under which the council acts. That was the Public Health Act 1936. I must refer to the relevant provisions . . . [His Lordship did so] . . .

To summarise the statutory position. The Public Health Act 1936, in particular Part II, was enacted in order to provide for the health and safety of owners and occupiers of buildings, including dwelling houses, by, *inter alia*, setting standards to be complied with in construction, and by enabling local authorities, through build-ing byelaws, to supervise and control the operations of builders. One of the particu-lar matters within the area of local authority supervision is the foundations of buildings, clearly a matter of vital importance, particularly because this part of the building comes to be covered up as building proceeds. Thus any weakness or inade-quacy will create a hidden defect which whoever acquires the building has no means of discovering: in legal parlance there is no opportunity for intermediate inspec-tion. So, by the byelaws, a definite standard is set for foundation work (see byelaw 18(1)(*b*) [that the foundations of every building shall be taken down to such a depth, or be so designed and constructed as to safeguard the building against damage by swelling or shrinking of the subsoil]); the builder is under a statutory (*sc.* byelaw) duty to notify the local authority before covering up the foundations; the local authority has at this stage the right to inspect and to insist on any correc-tion necessary to bring the work into conformity with the byelaws. It must be in the reasonable contemplation not only of the builder but also of the local authority that failure to comply with the byelaws' requirement as to foundations may give rise to a hidden defect which in the future may cause damage to the building affecting the safety and health of owners and occupiers. And as the building is intended to last, the class of owners and occupiers likely to be affected cannot be limited to those who go in immediately after construction.

What then is the extent of the local authority's duty towards these persons? Although, as I have suggested, a situation of "proximity" existed between the council and owners and occupiers of the houses, I do not think that a description of the council's duty can be based on the "neighbourhood" principle alone or on merely any such factual relationship as "control" as suggested by the Court of Appeal. So to base it would be to neglect an essential factor which is that the local authority is a public body, discharging functions under statute: its powers and duties are definable in terms of public not private law. The problem which this type of action creates, is to define the circumstances in which the law should impose, over and above, or perhaps alongside, these public law powers and duties, a duty in private law towards individuals such that they may sue for damages in a civil court. It is in this context that the distinction sought to be drawn between duties and mere powers has to be examined.

Most, indeed probably all, statutes relating to public authorities or public bodies, contain in them a large area of policy. The courts call this "discretion," meaning that the decision is one for the authority or body to make, and not for the courts. Many statutes also prescribe or at least presuppose the practical execution of policy decisions: a convenient description of this is to say that in addition to the area of policy or discretion, there is an operational area. Although this distinction between the policy area and the operational area is convenient, and illuminating, it is probably a distinction of degree; many "operational" powers or duties have in them some element of "discretion." It can safely be said that the more "operational" a power or duty may be, the easier it is to superimpose on it a common law duty of care.

I do not think that it is right to limit this to a duty to avoid causing extra or additional damage beyond what must be expected to arise from the exercise of the power or duty. That may be correct when the act done under the statute *inherently* must adversely *affect* the interest of individuals. But many other acts can be done without causing any harm to anyone—indeed may be directed to preventing harm from occurring. In these cases the duty is the normal one of taking care to avoid harm to those likely to be affected.

Let us examine the Public Health Act 1936 in the light of this. Undoubtedly it lays out a wide area of policy. It is for the local authority, a public and elected body, to decide on the scale of resources which it can make available in order to carry out its functions under Part II of the Act—how many inspectors, with what expert qualifications, it should recruit, how often inspections are to be made, what tests are to be carried out, must be for its decision. It is no accident that the Act is drafted in terms of functions and powers rather than in terms of positive duty. As was well said, public authorities have to strike a balance between the claims of efficiency and thrift (du Parcq L.J. in *Kent and Porter* v. *East Suffolk Rivers Catchment Board* ([1940] 1 K.B. 319, 338)): whether they get the balance right can only be decided through the ballot box, not in the courts. It is said (there are reflections of this in the judgments in *Dutton's* case) that the local authority is under no duty to inspect, and this is used as the foundation for an argument, also found in some of the cases, that if it need not inspect at all, it cannot be liable for negligent inspection: if it were to be held so liable, so it is said, councils would simply decide against inspections. I think that this is too crude an argument. It overlooks the fact that local authorities are public bodies operating under statute with a clear responsibility for public health in their area. They must, and in fact do, make their discretionary decisions responsibly and for reasons which accord with the statutory purpose; cf. *Ayr Harbour Trustees* v. *Oswald, per* Lord Watson ((1883) 8 App.Cas. 623, 639):

> . . . the powers which [s.10] confers are discretionary . . . But it is the plain import of the clause that the harbour trustees . . . shall be vested with, and shall avail themselves of, these discretionary powers, whenever and as often as they may be of opinion that the public interest will be promoted by their exercise.

If they do not exercise their discretion in this way they can be challenged in the courts. Thus, to say that councils are under no duty to inspect, is not a sufficient statement of the position. They are under a duty to give proper consideration to the question whether they should inspect or not. Their immunity from attack, in the event of failure to inspect, in other words, though great is not absolute. And because it is not absolute, the necessary premise for the proposition "if no duty to inspect, then no duty to take care in inspection" vanishes.

Passing then to the duty as regards inspection, if made. On principle there must surely be a duty to exercise reasonable care. The standard of care must be related to the duty to be performed, namely to ensure compliance with the byelaws. It must be related to the fact that the person responsible for construction in accordance with the byelaws is the builder, and that the inspector's function is supervisory. It must be related to the fact that once the inspector has passed the foundations they will be covered up, with no subsequent opportunity for inspection. But this duty, heavily operational though it may be, is still a duty arising under the statute. There may be a discretionary element in its exercise, discretionary as to the time and manner of inspection, and the techniques to be used. A plaintiff complaining of negligence must prove, the burden being on him, that action taken was not within the limits of a discretion bona fide exercised, before he can begin to rely on a common law duty of care. But if he can do this, he should, in principle, be able to sue.

Is there, then, authority against the existence of any such duty or any reason to restrict it? It is said that there is an absolute distinction in the law between statutory duty and statutory power—the former giving rise to possible liability, the latter not; or at least not doing so unless the exercise of the power involves some positive act creating some fresh or additional damage.

My Lords, I do not believe that any such absolute rule exists: or perhaps, more accurately, that such rules as exist in relation to powers and duties existing under particular statutes, provide sufficient definition of the rights of individuals affected by their exercise, or indeed their non-exercise, unless they take account of the possibility that, parallel with public law duties there may coexist those duties which persons, private or public, are under at common law to avoid causing damage to others in sufficient proximity to them. This is, I think, the key to understanding of the main authority relied on by the council, *East Suffolk Rivers Catchment Board* v. *Kent* ([1941] A.C. 74) . . .

. . . the law, as stated in some of the speeches in the *East Suffolk* case, but not in those of Lord Atkin or Lord Thankerton, requires at the present time to be understood and applied with the recognition that, quite apart from such consequences as may flow from an examination of the duties laid down by the particular statute, there may be room, once one is outside the area of legitimate discretion or policy, for a duty of care at common law. It is irrelevant to the existence of this duty of care whether what is created by the statute is a duty or a power: the duty of care may exist in either case. The difference between the two lies in this, that, in the case of a power, liability cannot exist unless the act complained of lies outside the ambit of the power. In *Home Office* v. *Dorset Yacht Co. Ltd.* the officers may (on the assumed facts) have acted outside any discretion delegated to them and having disregarded their instructions as to the precautions which they should take to prevent the trainees from escaping (see *per* Lord Diplock ([1970] A.C. 1004, 1069)). So in the present case, the allegations made are consistent with the council or its inspector having acted outside any delegated discretion either as to the making of an inspection, or as to the manner in which an inspection was made. Whether they did so must be determined at the trial. In the event of a positive determination, and only so, can a duty of care arise. I respectfully think that Lord Denning M.R. in *Dutton's* case ([1972] 1 Q.B. 373, 392) put the duty too high.

To whom the duty is owed. There is, in my opinion, no difficulty about this. A reasonable man in the position of the inspector must realise that if the foundations are covered in without adequate depth or strength as required by the byelaws, injury to safety or health may be suffered by owners or occupiers of the house. The duty is owed to them, not of course to a negligent building owner, the source of his own loss. I would leave open the case of users, who might themselves have a remedy against the occupier under the Occupiers' Liability Act 1957. A right of action can only be conferred on an owner or occupier, who is such when the damage occurs (see below). This disposes of the possible objection that an endless, indeterminate class of potential plaintiffs may be called into existence.

The nature of the duty. This must be related closely to the purpose for which powers of inspection are granted, namely to secure compliance with the byelaws. The duty is to take reasonable care, no more, no less, to secure that the builder does not cover in foundations which do not comply with byelaw requirements. The allegations in the statements of claim, in so far as they are based on non-compliance with the plans, are misconceived.

The position of the builder. I agree with the majority in the Court of Appeal in thinking that it would be unreasonable to impose liability in respect of defective foundations on the council, if the builder, whose primary fault it was, should be immune from liability. So it is necessary to consider this point, although it does not directly arise in the present appeal. If there was at one time a supposed rule that the doctrine of *Donoghue* v. *Stevenson* did not apply to realty, there is no doubt under modern authority that a builder of defective premises may be liable in negligence to persons who thereby suffer injury: see *Gallagher* v. *N. McDowell Ltd.* ([1961] N.I. 26), *per* Lord MacDermott C.J., a case of personal injury. Similar decisions have been given in regard to architects (*Clayton* v. *Woodman & Son (Builders) Ltd.* ([1962] 2 Q.B. 533), *Clay* v. *A.J. Crump & Sons Ltd.* ([1964] 1 Q.B. 533). *Gallagher's* case expressly leaves open the question whether the immunity against action of builder-owners, established by older authorities (*e.g., Bottomley* v. *Bannister* ([1932] 1 K.B. 458)) still survives.

That immunity, as I understand it, rests partly on a distinction being made between chattels and real property, partly on the principle of "caveat emptor" or, in the case where the owner leases the property, on the proposition that (fraud apart) there is no law against letting a "tumbledown house" (*Robbins* v. *Jones* ((1863) 15 C.B.N.S. 221, 143 E.R. 768), *per* Erle C.J.). But leaving aside such cases as arise between contracting parties, when the terms of the contract have to be considered (see *Voli* v. *Inglewood Shire Council* ((1963) 110 C.L.R. 74, 85), *per* Windeyer J.), I am unable to understand why this principle or proposition should prevent recovery in a suitable case by a person, who has subsequently acquired the house, on the principle of *Donoghue* v. *Stevenson*: the same rules should apply to all careless acts of a builder: whether he happens also to own the land or not. I agree generally with the conclusions of Lord Denning M.R. on this point (*Dutton's* case). In the alternative, since it is the duty of the builder (owner or not) to comply with the byelaws, I would be of opinion that an action could be brought against him, in effect, for breach of statutory duty by any person for whose benefit or protection the byelaw was made. So I do not think that there is any basis here for arguing from a supposed immunity of the builder to immunity of the council.

Nature of the damages recoverable and arising out of the cause of action. There are many questions here which do not directly arise at this stage and which may never arise if the actions are tried. But some conclusions are necessary if we are to deal with the issue as to limitation. The damages recoverable include all those which foreseeably arise from the breach of the duty of care which, as regards the council, I have held to be a duty to take reasonable care to secure compliance with the byelaws. Subject always to adequate proof of causation, these damages may include damages for personal injury and damage to property. In my opinion they may also include damage to the dwelling-house itself; for the whole purpose of the byelaws in requiring foundations to be of a certain standard is to prevent damage arising from weakness of the foundations which is certain to endanger the health or safety of occupants.

To allow recovery for such damage to the house follows, in my opinion, from normal principle. If classification is required, the relevant damage is in my opinion material, physical damage, and what is recoverable is the amount of expenditure necessary to restore the dwelling to a condition in which it is no longer a danger to the health or safety of persons occupying and possibly (depending on the circumstances) expenses arising from necessary displacement . . .

Lord Diplock, Lord Simon of Glaisdale and Lord Russell of Killowen agreed with Lord Wilberforce. Lord Salmon delivered a concurring opinion.

Questions
1. There was "no subsequent opportunity for inspection" once the foundations had been filled in. Where have we met that phrase before? Why is that feature of the facts so important?
2. Is the following proposition true? "A *duty* says what you *must* do, while a *power* says what you *may* do, if you choose. In choosing what to do or how to do it, you are free, so far as liability in damages is concerned, to act unreasonably, within limits, but whatever you actually do must be done with reasonable care so as to avoid harm to others."
   In this context consider Building Act, 1984, s.91:

"(1) It is the duty of local authorities to carry this Act into execution . . . (2) It is the function of local authorities to enforce building regulations in their areas. . . . "

3. The local authority is the party held liable if the builder is bankrupt, as often happens, but who ultimately bears the cost? Is it the other purchasers of new houses (as under the National House Builders Council Scheme, (see below p. 000), all the ratepayers in the area of the local authority, or, if all local authorities insure against such liability, all ratepayers in the country? Suppose that the local authority's income ceases to be raised as rates assessed on occupiers of property in proportion to its value, and is raised on a *per capita*, or poll-tax, basis. Does this affect the fairness of the decision? Are such matters any concern of the courts?
4. Suppose that the builder bribes the building inspector to pass foundations as adequate when they are not? Is the local authority liable?

Note:
Like Lord Atkin in *Donoghue* v. *Stevenson*, Lord Wilberforce in *Anns* laid down both a general principle relating to duty and a more specific rule, relating to buildings. The principle is quoted and explained away in *Yuen*, above p. 29. The rule also has been contained. Courts had allowed it to be invoked by developers who had been badly advised by their architects, but it has now been held that the duty is owed only to those owners and the like whose health and safety are imperilled by the defect, *i.e.* human occupiers (*Investors in Industry* v. *South Beds. D.C.* [1986] 1 All E.R. 787). This was done by emphasising the purpose for which the local authority had been equipped with the powers it had allegedly been careless in exercising (*Peabody Donation Fund* v. *Sir Lindsay Parkinson* [1984] 3 All E.R. 529 (H.L.)). Even where the plaintiff is human, the more recent tendency has been to restrict the liability of local authorities: thus a local authority cannot be made liable on the basis that it paid an improvement grant in respect of work badly executed (*Curran* v. *Northern Ireland Co-ownership Housing Ass'n.* [1987] 2 All E.R. 13 (H.L.)).
Hedley Byrne*, however, remains available to the developer who asks the local authority whether a proposed building plan is suitable and receives a carelessly false answer, unless, indeed, one is to hold that he should really rely on his own people and not on the local authority.
Local authorities may now be relieved of their functions of inspection of buildings for compliance with Building Regulations (Building Act 1984, s.47–53); the functions would be performed by approved persons who are required to carry insurance.
The Builder. The distinction between realty and chattels permeates English law. The fact that Lord Wilberforce deplored it in this context shows how *general* the law of negligence aspires to become. A distinction seems to remain, however, for while, as this case holds, the careless builder is liable to an ultimate purchaser for the cost of repairing the structural defects, the careless manufacturer of a chattel does not seem to be liable for the cost of making his product safe or efficient. Note that damage to the product itself is expressly excluded from the Consumer Protection Act 1987 (see above p. 29).
The Damage. Did Stevenson damage Mrs. Donoghue's ginger beer? No, he didn't. The ginger beer he made was certainly disgusting, and it damaged her, but the kind of damage it

caused her was personal injury: she was well and was made ill. If she had thrown up over her clothes, that would have been property damage because her clothes would have been made worse than they had been, and the fact that the measure of damages would be the amount of the dry-cleaning bill, *i.e.*, what she spent to repair the damage, would not alter that fact.

Just as Stevenson did not damage Mrs. Donoghue's ginger beer (though he damaged her), so Walcroft the builder did not damage Mr. Anns's house (though he damaged him). Walcroft made a bad house and it damaged Mr. Anns. The kind of damage it caused him was pecuniary or purely economic: he was out of pocket because he paid too much for the house, too much by the amount it would cost him to put it right. He might have suffered personal injury if the house had fallen on him, and he might have suffered property damage if the house had fallen on his car or his pet or even on his carpet. None of these things happened. His loss was purely economic. No property of his was damaged. By making a bad thing you do not damage it: you damage a thing by making it worse than it was. It is idle for Lord Wilberforce to say that there was material, physical damage. You do not turn a horse into a cow by calling it a cow, as you will quickly discover when you try to milk it. This description of the damage in issue as material rather than financial has led to appalling chaos on the question of limitation.

Limitation. If one equivocates about the nature of the damage in issue it is naturally difficult to decide when it arises, and when, consequently, time starts to run on the right to sue for it. If we think of it as physical, we will say that damage to a building occurs when the cracks first appear (though the owner may not know of them); if we think of it as economic, we will say that the damage occurs when the owner buys the house, though he will not know of it until the cracks appear.

After sorry confusion in the courts (and handsome fees for lawyers) the legislature has intervened with the Latent Damage Act 1986, applicable to negligence claims causing damage other than personal injury. Even if more than six years have elapsed since the accrual of the cause of action, a suit will still lie if not more than three years have elapsed since suit could reasonably have been instituted, subject to this, that no suit may ever be brought more than 15 years after the last breach of duty by the defendant. Once time has started to run it runs against all successors, but it is no bar to a suit that the damage occurred to the property before the plaintiff acquired it, provided that no predecessor knew of the damage.

The date when the damage occurs is still important, for that is when the cause of action accrues. In suits against the local authority under *Anns*, the damage occurs when the property becomes dangerous or unhealthy to a human occupant, though this is not an easy moment to ascertain (*Jones* v. *Stroud Valley D.C.* [1986] 1 W.L.R. 1141 (C.A.)). As against builders sued for negligence, the damage occurs when it becomes manifest (*Pirelli Gen'l Cable Works* v. *Oscar Faber* [1983] 1 All E.R. 65 (H.L.)). In cases of clearly economic loss, as in *Forster* v. *Outred* [1982] 2 All E.R. 753, the damage may be held to occur when the plaintiff is exposed to loss rather than when it actually comes to light.

DEFECTIVE PREMISES ACT 1972

1.—(1) A person taking on work for or in connection with the provision of a dwelling (whether the dwelling is provided by the erection or by the conversion or enlargement of a building) owes a duty—

(*a*) if the dwelling is provided to the order of any person, to that person; and

(*b*) without prejudice to paragraph (*a*) above, to every person who acquires an interest (whether legal or equitable) in the dwelling;

to see that the work which he takes on is done in a workmanlike or, as the case may be, professional manner, with proper materials and so that as regards that work the dwelling will be fit for habitation when completed.

(2) A person who takes on any such work for another on terms that he is to do it in accordance with instructions given by or on behalf of that other shall, to the extent to which he does it properly in accordance with those instructions, be treated for the purposes of this section as discharging the duty imposed on him by subsection (1) above except where he owes a duty to that other to warn him of any defects in the instructions and fails to discharge that duty.

(3) A person shall not be treated for the purposes of subsection (2) above as having given instructions for the doing of work merely because he has agreed to the

work being done in a specified manner, with specified materials or to a specified design.

(4) A person who—

(a) in the course of a business which consists of or includes providing or arranging for the provision of dwellings or installations in dwellings; or

(b) in the exercise of a power of making such provision or arrangements conferred by or by virtue of any enactment;

arranges for another to take on work for or in connection with the provision of a dwelling shall be treated for the purposes of this section as included among the persons who have taken on the work.

(5) Any cause of action in respect of a breach of the duty imposed by this section shall be deemed, for the purposes of the Limitation Act 1939, the Law Reform (Limitation of Actions, etc.) Act 1954 and the Limitation Act 1963, to have accrued at the time when the dwelling was completed, but if after that time a person who has done work for or in connection with the provision of the dwelling does further work to rectify the work he has already done, any such cause of action in respect of that further work shall be deemed for those purposes to have accrued at the time when the further work was finished.

. . .

Questions

1. Does a local authority "arrange for the provision of dwellings" when it is exercising its powers to enforce Building Regulations?

2. Is a local authority responsible under this section for defects in council housing?

3. Does this section apply to office-blocks or shops?

4. What can be the purpose behind s.1(3)?

5. Suppose that the building materials are improper, but that this is not the builder's fault? Can he be held liable? (See *Young & Marten* v. *McManus Childs* [1969] 1 A.C. 454).

Note:

Here is the Parliamentary solution to the problem of defective housing which the court in *Anns* was tackling, though the court in that case wholly ignored the existence of the statute. The duty under s.1 differs from the common law duty:

(a) the common law duty is owed by the builder only to future occupants, not to owners or lessees not in occupation (*D & F Estates* v. *Church Commrs* (C.A., [1987] 1 F.T.L.R. 405)), whereas the statutory duty is owed to all those acquiring an interest in the building, provided it is a dwelling;

(b) the statutory duty is imposed equally on the developer, who thus becomes answerable for the builder's incompetence; at common law the developer was answerable only for his own faults, *e.g.* deciding to build in a bad place, drawing up bad plans etc. (*Batty* v. *Metropolitan Property Realizations* [1978] 2 All E.R. 445—a troublesome extempore opinion).

Satisfactory as the duty under s.1 may be, however, it will hardly ever be applied, because s.2 provides that "no action shall be brought . . . for breach of the duty imposed by s.1 . . . " if an approved scheme is in force. Nowadays purchasers of new houses invariably obtain a 10-year guarantee against defects from the National House Builders Council. As this is an approved scheme, s.1 does not apply. This is a striking and admirable instance of the ouster of tort law in cases where the plaintiff has adequate insurance cover against the risk in question; furthermore the costs are all borne by new house purchasers, and not, as under *Anns*, by other groups as well. It is, however, imaginable that the body paying under the policy might be subrogated to the owner's rights in tort against any party liable at common law.

CIVIL LIABILITY (CONTRIBUTION) ACT 1978

[*Preliminary Note*

Both in the Defective Premises Act 1972 and in the decision in *Anns* the law-makers were eager to give the house-purchaser someone to sue, over and above the actual builder. To have two people to sue is substantially advantageous to the plaintiff if one of the possible defendants is bankrupt, but even if they are both perfectly solvent he may sue them both, concurrently or consecutively, and obtain judgment against them both for the full amount of his compensable loss. Neither defendant is helped in the very least by the argument that the other is liable as well: a person who is liable for harm is liable for all of it, regardless of how many other people are liable too. Naturally the victim may only recover up to the amount of his loss: once he has been paid, all possible defendants are released from liability to him. Then arises the question whether the loss may be split between the defendants. Until 1935 the loss had to lie where the victim had cast it, since no tortfeasor who was at fault could claim contribution from anyone else. The 1978 Act, set out in part below, is an expanded version of the Law Reform (Married Women and Tortfeasors) Act 1935 which introduced the claim to contribution and, by making for fairness between tortfeasors, induced the judges to increase their number.

A good instance of multiple liability is provided by *Clay* v. *Crump* [1964] 1 Q.B. 533 (C.A.). When an old building was being demolished prior to the erection of a new one, the site-owner asked the architect if one of its walls could be left standing. The architect unwisely agreed, and the demolition contractor, who should have known better, proceeded to demolish the walls which supported it. The building contractor then sent his men onto the site without checking it for safety, and one of them was injured when the remaining wall fell on him. The victim sued the site-owner, the architect, the demolition contractor and his employer. The site-owner was let off because it was reasonable for him, as an amateur, to trust the professionals, but the demolition contractor was held liable because he should have known that he was making the wall unsafe, the building contractor was held liable for sending his men to a place he should have known to be dangerous, and the architect was held liable because he failed to show the professional skill the others were relying on him to display. The plaintiff obtained judgment in full against all the defendants who were held liable, and was entitled to collect from them as he pleased. As between themselves, the defendants were liable in the following proportions: architect 42 per cent.; demolition contractor 38 per cent.; building contractor/employer 20 per cent.]

1.—(1) Subject to the following provisions of this section, any person liable in respect of any damage suffered by another person may recover contribution from any other person liable in respect of the same damage (whether jointly with him or otherwise).

(2) A person shall be entitled to recover contribution by virtue of subsection (1) above notwithstanding that he has ceased to be liable in respect of the damage in question since the time when the damage occurred, provided that he was so liable immediately before he made or was ordered or agreed to make the payment in respect of which the contribution is sought.

(3) A person shall be liable to make contribution by virtue of subsection (1) above notwithstanding that he has ceased to be liable in respect of the damage in question since the time when the damage occurred, unless he ceased to be liable by virtue of the expiry of a period of limitation or prescription which extinguished the right on which the claim against him in respect of the damage was based.

(4) A person who has made or agreed to make any payment in bona fide settlement or compromise of any claim made against him in respect of any damage (including a payment into court which has been accepted) shall be entitled to recover contribution in accordance with this section without regard to whether or not he himself is or ever was liable in respect of the damage, provided, however, that he would have been liable assuming that the factual basis of the claim against him could be established.

(5) A judgment given in any action brought in any part of the United Kingdom by or on behalf of the person who suffered the damage in question against any per-

son from whom contribution is sought under this section shall be conclusive in the proceedings for contributions as to any issue determined by that judgment in favour of the person from whom the contribution is sought.

(6) . . .

2.—(1) Subject to subsection (3) below, in any proceedings for contribution under section 1 above the amount of the contribution recoverable from any person shall be such as may be found by the court to be just and equitable having regard to the extent of that person's responsibility for the damage in question.

(2) Subject to subsection (3) below, the court shall have power in any such proceedings to exempt any person from liability to make contribution, or to direct that the contribution to be recovered from any person shall amount to a complete indemnity.

(3) Where the amount of the damages which have or might have been awarded in respect of the damage in question in any action brought in England and Wales by or on behalf of the person who suffered it against the person from whom the contribution is sought was or would have been subject to—

(a) any limit imposed by or under any enactment or by any agreement made before the damage occurred;

(b) any reduction by virtue of section 1 of the Law Reform (Contributory Negligence) Act 1945 or section 5 of the Fatal Accidents Act 1976; or

(c) any corresponding limit or reduction under the law of a country outside England and Wales;

the person from whom the contribution is sought shall not by virtue of any contribution awarded under section 1 above be required to pay in respect of the damage a greater amount than the amount of those damages as so limited or reduced.

. . .

4. If more than one action is brought in respect of any damage by or on behalf of the person by whom it was suffered against persons liable in respect of the damage (whether jointly or otherwise) the plaintiff shall not be entitled to costs in any of those actions, other than that in which judgment is first given, unless the court is of the opinion that there was reasonable ground for bringing the action.

. . .

6.—(1) A person is liable in respect of any damage for the purposes of this Act if the person who suffered it (or anyone representing his estate or dependants) is entitled to recover compensation from him in respect of that damage (whatever the legal basis of his liability, whether tort, breach of contract, breach of trust or otherwise).

(2) References in this Act to an action brought by or on behalf of the person who suffered any damage include references to an action brought for the benefit of his estate or dependants.

. . .

Questions

1. A mother out shopping with her toddler carelessly loses sight of him. He scampers into the street and is run over by a motorist who is not paying quite enough attention. The child would naturally sue the (insured) motorist rather than his (uninsured) mother. Until 1935 when the predecessor to this Act was passed, the insurer would pay and that would be that. Now this Act permits the motorist's insurer to claim contribution from the mother, unless the court is ready to hold that a mother owes no duty to her child to take care that it is not injured.

Is this satisfactory?

2. P is injured by the combined faults of D1 and D2, and demands damages from both. D1 settles promptly for a sum which it genuinely believes to represent a fair proportion of the total damage. D2 refuses to settle, and it is some years before the case comes on for trial. In that trial D2's liability is naturally reduced by the amount that P has received from D1, but interest will run on the damages not yet paid. The Court of Appeal has held that under the Act D2 may claim contribution from D1 (*Logan* v. *Uttlesford D.C.* (1986) 136 New L.J. 541).

Is this consistent with the assumed aim of the legal system to encourage alleged tortfeasors to settle with the victim, so as to ensure that the victim is paid quickly and to relieve congestion in the court lists? Does the Act permit the court, in assessing contribution in such a case, to take account of the post-accident conduct of the parties?

3. We have seen that under the Latent Damage Act 1986 a party is not liable to the victim of property or economic damage once 15 years have elapsed from his last breach of duty (above p. 65). Does such a person nevertheless remain liable to contribute towards another tortfeasor who is still liable?

McLOUGHLIN v. O'BRIAN

House of Lords [1983] 1 A.C. 410; [1982] 2 W.L.R. 982; [1982] 2 All E.R. 298; [1982] R.T.R. 209

Action by mother against driver for shock at family's injuries

The plaintiff stayed at home one autumn afternoon while her husband was out in the car with three of the children, the eldest being at the wheel. About 5 p.m. a friend arrived with the grim news that an hour beforehand the car had been involved in a very bad accident about two miles away. The friend drove her to the hospital, where she found her husband and sons screaming, bloody and bemused, and learnt that her youngest child was dead.

These events, due to the defendant's negligence, were such as to cause her severe shock, organic depression and a change of personality, it being assumed that she was a person of normal fortitude.

Lord Wilberforce: . . . On these facts, or assumed facts, the trial judge, Boreham J., gave judgment for the respondents holding, in a most careful judgment reviewing the authorities, that the respondents owed no duty of care to the appellant because the possibility of her suffering injury by nervous shock, in the circumstances, was not reasonably foreseeable.

On appeal by the appellant, the judgment of Boreham J. was upheld, but not on the same ground ([1981] Q.B. 599). Stephenson L.J. took the view that the possibility of injury to the appellant by nervous shock *was* reasonably foreseeable and that the respondents owed the appellant a duty of care. However, he held that considerations of policy prevented the appellant from recovering. Griffiths L.J. held that injury by nervous shock to the appellant was "readily foreseeable" but that the respondents owed no duty of care to the appellant. The duty was limited to those on the road nearby. Cumming-Bruce L.J. agreed with both judgments. The appellant now appeals to this House. The critical question to be decided is whether a person in the position of the appellant, *i.e.* one who was not present at the scene of grievous injuries to her family but who comes on those injuries at an interval of time and space, can recover damages for nervous shock.

Although we continue to use the hallowed expression "nervous shock," English law, and common understanding, have moved some distance since recognition was given to this symptom as a basis for liability. Whatever is unknown about the mind-body relationship (and the area of ignorance seems to expand with that of knowledge), it is now accepted by medical science that recognisable and severe physical damage to the human body and system may be caused by the impact, through the senses, of external events on the mind. There may thus be produced what is as identifiable an illness as any that may be caused by direct physical impact. It is safe to say that this, in general terms, is understood by the ordinary man or woman who is hypothesised by the courts in situations where claims for negligence are made. Although in the only case which has reached this House (*Bourhill* v. *Young* [1943] A.C. 92) a claim for damages in respect of "nervous shock" was rejected on its facts, the House gave clear recognition to the legitimacy, in principle, of claims of that character. As the result of that and other cases, assuming that they are accepted as correct, the following position has been reached:

1. While damages cannot, at common law, be awarded for grief and sorrow, a claim for damages for "nervous shock" caused by negligence can be made without the necessity of showing direct impact or fear of immediate personal injuries for oneself. The reservation made by Kennedy J. in *Dulieu* v. *White & Sons* ([1901] 2 K.B. 669), though taken up by Sargant L.J. in *Hambrook* v. *Stokes Bros* ([1925] 1 K.B. 141), has not gained acceptance, and although the respondents, in the courts below, reserved their right to revive it, they did not do so in argument. I think that it is now too late to do so. The arguments on this issue were fully and admirably stated by the Supreme Court of California in *Dillon* v. *Legg* (1968) (A.L.R.) 3d 1316.

2. A plaintiff may recover damages for "nervous shock" brought on by injury caused not to him or herself but to a near relative, or by the fear of such injury. So far (subject to 5 below), the cases do not extend beyond the spouse or children of the plaintiff (*Hambrook* v. *Stokes Bros.*, *Boardman* v. *Sanderson* ([1964] 1 W.L.R. 1317), *Hinz* v. *Berry* [1970] 2 Q.B. 40 including foster children (where liability was assumed), and see *King* v. *Phillips* ([1953] 1 Q.B. 429).

3. Subject to the next paragraph, there is no English case in which a plaintiff has been able to recover nervous shock damages where the injury to the near relative occurred out of sight and earshot of the plaintiffs. In *Hambrook* v. *Stokes Bros* an express distinction was made between shock caused by what the mother saw with her own eyes and what she might have been told by bystanders, liability being excluded in the latter case.

4. An exception from, or I would prefer to call it an extension of, the latter case has been made where the plaintiff does not see or hear the incident but comes on its immediate aftermath. In *Boardman* v. *Sanderson* the father was within earshot of the accident to his child and likely to come on the scene; he did so and suffered damage from what he then saw. In *Marshall* v. *Lionel Enterprises* ((1971) D.L.R. (3d) 141) the wife came immediately on the badly injured body of her husband. And in *Benson* v. *Lee* ([1972] V.R. 879), a situation existed with some similarity to the present case. The mother was in her home 100 yards away, and, on communications by a third party, ran out to the scene of the accident and there suffered shock. Your Lordships have to decide whether or not to validate these extensions.

5. A remedy on account of nervous shock has been given to a man who came on a serious accident involving numerous people immediately thereafter and acted as a rescuer of those involved (*Chadwick* v. *British Transport Commission* ([1967] 1 W.L.R. 912)). "Shock" was caused neither by fear for himself nor by fear or horror on account of a near relative. The principle of "rescuer" cases was not challenged by the respondents and ought, in my opinion, to be accepted. But we have to consider whether, and how far, it can be applied to such cases as the present.

Throughout these developments, as can be seen, the courts have proceeded in the traditional manner of the common law from case to case, on a basis of logical necessity. If a mother, with or without accompanying children, could recover on account of fear for herself, how can she be denied recovery on account of fear for her accompanying children? If a father could recover had he seen his child run over by a backing car, how can he be denied recovery if he is in the immediate vicinity and runs to the child's assistance? If a wife and mother could recover if she had witnessed a serious accident to her husband and children, does she fail because she was a short distance away and immediately rushes to the scene? (*cf. Benson* v. *Lee*). I think that, unless the law is to draw an arbitrary line at the point of direct sight and sound, these arguments require acceptance of the extension mentioned above under principle 4 in the interests of justice.

If one continues to follow the process of logical progression, it is hard to see why the present plaintiff also should not succeed. She was not present at the accident, but she came very soon after on its aftermath. If, from a distance of some 100 yards (*cf. Benson* v. *Lee*), she had found her family by the roadside, she would have come within principle 4 above. Can it make any difference that she comes on them in an ambulance, or, as here, in a nearby hospital, when, as the evidence shows, they were in the same condition, covered with oil and mud, and distraught with pain? If Mr. Chadwick can recover when, acting in accordance with normal and irresistible human instinct, and indeed moral compulsion, he goes to the scene of an accident, may not a mother recover if, acting under the same motives, she goes to where her family can be found?

I could agree that a line can be drawn above her case with less hardship than would have been apparent in *Boardman's* and *Hinz's* cases, but so to draw it would not appeal to most people's sense of justice. To allow her claim may be, I think it is, on the margin of what the process of logical progression would allow. But where the facts are strong and exceptional, and, as I think, fairly analogous, her case ought, prima facie, to be assimilated to those which have passed the test.

To argue from one factual situation to another and to decide by analogy is a natural tendency of the human and legal mind. But the lawyer still has to inquire whether, in so doing, he has crossed some critical line behind which he ought to stop. That is said to be the present case. The reasoning by which the Lords Justices decided not to grant relief to the plaintiff is instructive. Both Stephenson and Griffiths L.JJ accepted that the "shock" to the plaintiff was foreseeable; but from this, at least in presentation, they diverge. Stephenson L.J. considered that the defendants owed a duty of care to the plaintiff, but that for reasons of policy the law should stop short of giving her damages: it should limit relief to those on or near the highway at or near the time of the accident caused by the defendants' negligence. He was influenced by the fact that the courts of this country, and of other common law jurisdictions, had stopped at this point: it was indicated by the barrier of commercial sense and practical convenience. Griffiths L.J. took the view that, although the injury to the plaintiff was foreseeable, there was no duty of care. The duty of care of drivers of motor vehicles was, according to decided cases, limited to persons and owners of property on the road or near to it who might be directly affected. The line should be drawn at this point. It was not even in the interest of those suffering from shock as a class to extend the scope of the defendants' liability: to do so would quite likely delay their recovery by immersing them in the anxiety of litigation.

I am deeply impressed by both of these arguments, which I have only briefly summarised. Though differing in expression, in the end, in my opinion, the two presentations rest on a common principle, namely that, at the margin, the boundaries of a man's responsibility for acts of negligence have to be fixed as a matter of policy. Whatever is the correct jurisprudential analysis, it does not make any essential difference whether one says, with Stephenson L.J., that there is a duty but, as a matter of policy, the consequences of breach of it ought to be limited at a certain point, or whether, with Griffiths L.J., one says that the fact that consequences may be foreseeable does not automatically impose a duty of care, does not do so in fact where policy indicates the contrary. This is an approach which one can see very clearly from the way in which Lord Atkin stated the neighbour principle in *Donoghue* v. *Stevenson* ([1932] A.C. 562, 580): " . . . persons who are so closely and directly affected by my act that I ought reasonably to have them in contemplation as being so affected . . . "

This is saying that foreseeability must be accompanied and limited by the law's judgment as to persons who ought, according to its standards of value or justice, to have been in contemplation. Foreseeability, which involves a hypothetical person, looking with hindsight at an event which has occurred, is a formula adopted by English law, not merely for defining, but also for limiting the persons to whom duty may be owed, and the consequences for which an actor may be held responsible. It is not merely an issue of fact to be left to be found as such. When it is said to result in a duty of care being owed to a person or a class, the statement that there is a "duty of care" denotes a conclusion into the forming of which considerations of policy have entered. That foreseeability does not of itself, and automatically, lead to a duty of care is, I think, clear. I gave some examples in *Anns* v. *Merton London Borough* ([1978] A.C. 728, 752), *Anns* itself being one. I may add what Lord Reid said in *McKew* v. *Holland & Hannen & Cubitts (Scotland) Ltd.* [below p. 208]: "A defender is not liable for a consequence of a kind which is not foreseeable. But it does not follow that he is liable for every consequence which a reasonable man could foresee."

We must then consider the policy arguments. In doing so we must bear in mind that cases of "nervous shock" and the possibility of claiming damages for it are not necessarily confined to those arising out of accidents in public roads. To state, therefore, a rule that recoverable damages must be confined to persons on or near the highway is to state not a principle in itself but only an example of a more general rule that recoverable damages must be confined to those within sight and sound of an event caused by negligence or, at least, to those in close, or very close, proximity to such a situation.

The policy arguments against a wider extension can be stated under four heads. First, it may be said that such extension may lead to a proliferation of claims, and possibly fraudulent claims, to the establishment of an industry of lawyers and psychiatrists who will formulate a claim for nervous shock damages, including what in America is called the customary miscarriage, for all, or many, road accidents and industrial accidents. Second, it may be claimed that an extension of liability would be unfair to defendants, as imposing damages out of proportion to the negligent conduct complained of. In so far as such defendants are insured, a large additional burden will be placed on insurers, and ultimately on the class of persons insured: road users or employers. Third, to extend liability beyond the most direct and plain cases would greatly increase evidentiary difficulties and tend to lengthen litigation. Fourth, it may be said (and the Court of Appeal agreed with this) that an extension of the scope of liability ought only to be made by the legislature, after careful research. This is the course which has been taken in New South Wales and the Australian Capital Territory.

The whole argument has been well summed up by Dean Prosser in *The Law of Torts* (4th edn, 1971) p. 256:

"The reluctance of courts to enter this zone even where the mental injury is clearly foreseeable, and the frequent mention of the difficulties of proof, the facility of fraud and the problem of finding a place to stop and draw the line, suggest that here it is the nature of the interest invaded and the type of damages which is the real obstacle."

Since he wrote, the type of damage has, in this country at least, become familiar and less deterrent to recovery. And some of the arguments are susceptible of answer. Fraudulent claims can be contained by the courts, which, also, can cope with evidentiary difficulties. The scarcity of cases which have occurred in the past, and the modest sums recovered, give some indication that fears of a flood of litigation may be exaggerated: experience in other fields suggests that such fears usually are. If some increase does occur, that may only reveal existence of a genuine social need; that legislation has been found necessary in Australia may indicate the same thing.

But, these discounts accepted, there remains, in my opinion, just because "shock" in its nature is capable of affecting so wide a range of people, a real need for the law to place some limitation on the extent of admissible claims. It is necessary to consider three elements inherent in any claim: the class of persons whose claims should be recognised; the proximity of such persons to the accident; and the means by which the shock is caused. As regards the class of persons, the possible range is between the closest of family ties, of parent and child, or husband and wife, and the ordinary bystander. Existing law recognises the claims of the first; it denies that of the second, either on the basis that such persons must be assumed to be possessed of fortitude sufficient to enable them to endure the calamities of modern life or that defendants cannot be expected to compensate the world at large. In my opinion, these positions are justifiable, and since the present case falls within the first class it is strictly unnecessary to say more. I think, however, that it should follow that other cases involving less close relationships must be very carefully scrutinised. I cannot say that they should never be admitted. The closer the tie (not merely in relationship, but in care) the greater the claim for consideration. The claim, in any case, has to be judged in the light of the other factors, such as proximity to the scene in time and place, and the nature of the accident.

As regards proximity to the accident, it is obvious that this must be close in both time and space. It is, after all, the fact and consequence of the defendant's negligence that must be proved to have caused the "nervous shock." Experience has shown that to insist on direct and immediate sight or hearing would be impractical and unjust and that under what may be called the "aftermath" doctrine, one who, from close proximity, comes very soon on the scene, should not be excluded. In my opinion, the result in *Benson* v. *Lee* ([1972] V.R. 879) was correct and indeed inescapable. It was based, soundly, on "direct perception of some of the events which go to make up the accident as an entire event, and this includes . . . the immediate aftermath." The High Court of Australia's majority decision in *Chester* v. *Waverley Municipal Council* ((1939) 62 C.L.R. 1), where a child's body was found floating in a trench after a prolonged search, may perhaps be placed on the other side of a recognisable line (Evatt J. in a powerful dissent placed it on the same side), but in addition, I find the conclusion of Lush J. in *Benson* v. *Lee* to reflect developments in the law.

Finally, and by way of reinforcement of "aftermath" cases, I would accept, by analogy with "rescue" situations, that a person of whom it could be said that one could expect nothing else than he or she would come immediately to the scene (normally a parent or a spouse) could be regarded as being within the scope of foresight and duty. Where there is not immediate presence, account must be taken of the possibility of alterations in the circumstances, for which the defendant should be responsible.

Subject only to these qualifications, I think that a strict test of proximity by sight or hearing should be applied by the courts.

Lastly, as regards communication, there is no case in which the law has compensated shock brought about by communication by a third party. In *Hambrook* v. *Stokes Bros* ([1925] 1 K.B. 141), indeed, it was said that liability would not arise in such a case, and this is surely right. It was so decided in *Abramzik* v. *Brenner* ((1967) 65 D.L.R. (2d) 651). The shock must come through sight or hearing of the event or of its immediate aftermath. Whether some equivalent of sight or hearing, *e.g.* through simultaneous television, would suffice may have to be considered.

My Lords, I believe that these indications, imperfectly sketched, and certainly to be applied with common sense to individual situations in their entirety, represent either the existing law, or the existing law with only such circumstantial extension as the common law process may legitimately make. They do not introduce a new principle. Nor do I see any reason why the law should retreat behind the lines already drawn. I find on this appeal that the appellant's case falls within the boundaries of the law so drawn. I would allow her appeal.

Lord Russell of Killowen. My Lords, I make two comments at the outset. First, we are not concerned with any problem that might have been posed had the accident been not wholly attributable to the negligence of the defendants, but partly attributable to negligent driving by the injured son of the plaintiff. Second, the plaintiff is to be regarded as of normal disposition or phlegm; we are therefore not concerned to investigate the applicability of the "thin skull" cases to this type of case. . . .

[His Lordship then stated that he could see no policy consideration which was sufficient to deprive "this plaintiff of just compensation for the reasonably foreseeable damage done to her."]

Lord Edmund-Davies, agreeing with Lord Wilberforce, objected to the application, in nervous shock cases, of physical limitations on what was reasonably foreseeable; he was prepared to treat the mother's visit to hospital as an act of rescue, he rejected the "floodgates" argument, and then very strongly objected to the view of Lord Bridge and Lord Scarman that "public policy" could not be invoked by a court in order to deprive of compensation a person who had suffered reasonably foreseeable harm. He agreed with Griffiths L.J. that "The test of foreseeability is not a universal touchstone to determine the extent of liability for the consequences of wrongdoing" ([1981] Q.B. 599, 618), but held that in this case there were no public policy considerations which would justify debarring the plaintiff.

Lord Bridge: . . . In approaching the question whether the law should, as a matter of policy, define the criterion of liability in negligence for causing psychiatric illness by reference to some test other than that of reasonable foreseeability it is well to remember that we are concerned only with the question of liability of a defendant who is, ex hypothesi, guilty of fault in causing the death, injury or danger which has in turn triggered the psychiatric illness. A policy which is to be relied on to narrow the scope of the negligent tortfeasor's duty must be justified by cogent and readily intelligible considerations, and must be capable of defining the appropriate limits of liability by reference to factors which are not purely arbitrary. A number of policy considerations which have been suggested as satisfying these requirements appear to me, with respect, to be wholly insufficient. I can see no ground whatever for suggesting that to make the defendant liable for reasonably foreseeable psychiatric illness caused by his negligence would be to impose a crushing burden on him out of proportion to his moral responsibility. However liberally the criterion of reasonable foreseeability is interpreted, both the number of successful claims in this field and the quantum of damages they will attract are likely to be moderate. I cannot accept as relevant the well-known phenomenon that litigation may delay recovery from a psychiatric illness. If this were a valid policy consideration, it would lead to the conclusion that psychiatric illness should be excluded altogether from the heads of damage which the law will recognise. It cannot justify limiting the cases in which damages will be awarded for psychiatric illness by reference to the circumstances of its causation. To attempt to draw a line at the furthest point which any of the decided cases happen to have reached, and to say that it is for the legislature, not the courts, to extend the limits of liability any further, would be, to my mind, an unwarranted abdication of the court's function of developing and adapting principles of the common law to changing conditions, in a particular corner of the common law which exemplifies, par excellence, the important and indeed necessary part which that function has to play. In the end I believe that the policy question depends on weighing against each other two conflicting considerations. On the one hand, if the criterion of liability is to be reasonable foreseeability simpliciter, this must, precisely because questions of causation in psychiatric medicine give rise to difficulty and uncertainty, introduce an element of uncertainty into the law and open the way to a number of arguable claims which a more precisely fixed criterion of liability would exclude. I accept that the element of uncertainty is an important factor. I believe that the "floodgates" argument, however, is, as it always has been, greatly exaggerated. On the other hand, it seems to me inescapable that any attempt to define the limit of liability by requiring, in addition to reasonable foreseeability, that the plaintiff claiming damages for psychiatric illness should have witnessed the relevant accident, should have been present at or near the place where it happened, should have come on its aftermath and thus have some direct perception of it, as opposed to merely learning of it after the event, should be related in some particular degree to the accident victim—to draw a line by reference to any of those criteria must impose a largely arbitrary limit of liability. I accept, of course, the importance of the factors indicated in the guidelines suggested by Tobriner J. in *Dillon* v. *Legg* ((1968) 68 Cal. 2d 728, 441, P. 2d 912) as bearing on the *degree* of foreseeability of the plaintiff's psychiatric illness. But let me give two examples to illustrate what injustice would be wrought by any such hard and fast lines of policy as have been suggested. First, consider the plaintiff who learned after the event of the relevant accident. Take the case of a mother who knows that her husband and children are staying in a certain hotel. She reads in her morning newspaper that it has been the scene of a disastrous fire. She sees in the paper a photograph of unidentifiable victims trapped on the top floor waving for help from the windows. She learns shortly afterwards that all her family have perished. She suffers an acute psychiatric illness. That her illness in these circumstances was a reasonably foreseeable consequence of the events resulting from the fire is undeniable. Yet, is the law to deny her damages as against a defendant whose negligence was responsible for the fire simply on the ground that an important link in the chain of causation of her psychiatric illness was supplied by her imagination of the agonies of mind and body in which her family died, rather than by direct perception of the event? Second, consider the plaintiff who is unrelated to the victims of the relevant accident. If rigidly applied, an exclusion of liability to him would have defeated the plaintiff's claim in *Chadwick* v. *British Transport Commission*. The Court of Appeal treated that case as in a special category because Mr Chadwick was a rescuer. Now, the special duty owed to a rescuer who voluntarily places himself in physical danger to save others is well understood, and is illustrated by *Haynes* v. *Harwood* ([1935] K.B. 146), the case of the constable injured in stopping a runaway horse in a crowded street. But, in relation to the psychiatric consequences of witnessing such terrible carnage as must have resulted from the Lewisham train disaster, I would find it difficult to distinguish in principle the position of a rescuer, like Mr Chadwick, from a mere spectator, as, for example, an uninjured or only slightly injured passenger in the train, who took no part in the rescue operations but was present at the scene after the accident for some time, perforce observing the rescue operations while he waited for transport to take him home.

My Lords, I have no doubt that this is an area of the law of negligence where we should resist the temptation to try yet once more to freeze the law in a rigid posture which would deny justice to some who, in the application of the classic principles of negligence derived from *Donoghue* v. *Stevenson* ought to succeed, in the interests of certainty, where the very subject matter is uncertain and continuously developing, or in the interests of saving defendants and their insurers from the burden of having sometimes to resist doubtful claims. I find myself in complete agreement with Tobriner J. that the defendant's duty must depend on reasonable foreseeability and—

> "must necessarily be adjudicated only upon a case-by-case basis. We cannot now predetermine defendant's obligation in every situation by a fixed category; no immutable rule can establish the extent of that obligation for every circumstance of the future."

To put the matter in another way, if asked where the thing is to stop, I should answer, in an adaptation of the language of Lord Wright and Stephenson L.J., "Where in the particular case the good sense of the judge, enlightened by progressive awareness of mental illness, decides."

My Lords, I would accordingly allow the appeal.

Lord Scarman [agreed with Lord Bridge. He went on to say that the judges must decide according to "principle" and that if the results were "socially unacceptable" it was for Parliament to legislate. Here] common law principle requires the judges to follow the logic of the "reasonably foreseeable test" so as, in circumstances where it is appropriate, to apply it untrammelled by spatial, physical or temporal limits. Space, time, distance, the nature of the injuries sustained and the relationship of the plaintiff to the immediate victim of the accident are factors to be weighed, but not legal limitations, when the test or reasonable foreseeability is to be applied.

But I am by no means sure that the result is socially desirable. The "floodgates" argument may be exaggerated. Time alone will tell; but I foresee social and financial problems if damages for "nervous shock" should be made available to persons other than parents and children who without seeing or hearing the accident, or being present in the immediate aftermath, suffer nervous shock in consequence of it. There is, I think, a powerful case for legislation such as has been enacted in New South Wales and the Australian Capital Territory.

Why then should not the courts draw the line, as the Court of Appeal manfully tried to do in this case? Simply, because the policy issue where to draw the line is not justiciable. The problem is one of social, economic, and financial policy. The considerations relevant to a decision are not such as to be capable of being handled within the limits of the forensic process.

Questions

1. What is the majority holding in this case?

2. Is it (a) easier, (b) much easier, to tell whether the plaintiff was (i) at the scene of the accident, (ii) a reasonably foreseeable victim of shock? Does the ease of application of a rule affect the number of claims and settlements respectively?

3. What is wrong with rules of thumb? Are judicial-foot-rules any better?

4. Is it true, as Lord Bridge asseverates, that any uncertainty there may be in the application of the foreseeability test in cases of psychical damage is due to the obscurity of its causation? Is the application of the foreseeability test easy when causation is clear, as in *The Wagon Mound (Nos. 1 and 2)*, below p. 185?

5. Would a policeman, fireman or doctor who suffered shock at a nasty accident occasioned by the defendant's negligence be likely to recover damages for his shock?

6. Under the Criminal Injuries Compensation Scheme shock suffered by a person is compensated only if it "is attributable to his having been put in fear of immediate physical injury to himself or another." See below p. 158.

7. Lord Wilberforce speaks of the "logical progression" of the common law, even of "logical necessity." Do you think he is a Hegelian? And how do you reconcile those observations with his view that "the boundaries of a man's responsibility for acts of negligence have to be fixed as a matter of policy"?

8. Would either Lord Wilberforce or Lord Bridge grant recovery in the following cases?

(i) Agatha has a fit when she sees her cat run over by a drunk driver who could easily, had he been sober, have avoided it;

(ii) Fred's car is involved in a collision solely because of a manufacturing defect. Fred's passenger is killed, and Fred, who is himself unhurt, is horrified at the thought that he has killed his friend;

(iii) Martha, holidaying in Majorca, receives a telegram "Father involved in bad accident. Come soonest." She is unable to effect telephonic communication and has great difficulty obtaining a flight. When she gets home, she is in a terrible condition and her father is dead. (Note: a child cannot sue for emotional harm occasioned by the death of a parent: see Fatal Accidents Act 1976 s.1A below p. 79).

9. Suppose that a mother is riding in a car being driven for his own purposes by her son, and that she suffers actual physical injury in a collision with an oncoming car carelessly driven. It is clear law that her claim against the oncoming driver is not affected by the fact (a) that her son was also to blame for the collision (below p. 214) and (b) that she was especially susceptible to injury. In the light of this, what do you make of Lord Russell's preliminary observations?

10. Distinctions are sometimes drawn between fear, shock and grief. If the distinction is between the emotional reactions to what may happen, what is happening and what has happened, which was involved in the present case?

11. Consider the application to the facts of this case of s.1A Fatal Accidents Act 1976 (introduced in 1982). Should the defendant now have to pay Mrs. McLoughlin extra for not killing the rest of her family?

12. Lord Bridge says that judgment for Mrs. McLoughlin was required by the "classic prin-

ciples of negligence as derived from *Donoghue* v. *Stevenson.*" Is this still true after *Yuen* (above p. 29)?

13. Suppose a very near miss between two jumbo jets, X and Y, over Gatwick, owing to the fault of the pilot of plane X. Shock is suffered by A, a passenger in plane X; B, the pilot of plane Y; C, the air traffic controller; D, a friend of A waiting at the airport and taking the air on the terrace; and by E, a farmer working in the field below. Rate the victims in order of probable success in the law courts.

14. Was Lord Wilberforce right to speak of the "modest sums recovered" in such cases? In *Brice* v. *Brown* [1984] 1 All E.R. 997 the plaintiff was riding in a taxi with her daughter when the taxi collided with an oncoming bus. The plaintiff's physical injuries were trivial, but her daughter was cut on the forehead, had to be in hospital for two or three nights, and was left with a four-inch scar. The mother suffered a total collapse after the incident, owing to a hysterical personality disorder. The judge awarded her £22,500 as general damages, quite apart from sums for all medical expenses and lost earnings, a very grand total of £56,045. Not bad for a taxi-ride.

Notes

1. *Shock.* There is no doubt that it is *harm* to be rendered unfit to cope with the daily exigencies of life, to have one's merriment turned to misery, to feel one's peace of mind shattered by a shocking occurrence. So, too, it is harm to lose a limb and have to hobble about. But there is equally no doubt that the public—crass and ignorant as it may be—draws a distinction between the neurotic and the cripple, between the man who loses his concentration and the man who loses his leg. It is widely felt that being frightened is less than being struck, that trauma to the mind is less than lesion to the body. Many people would consequently say that the duty to avoid injuring strangers is greater than the duty not to upset them. The law has reflected this distinction as one would expect, not only by refusing damages for grief altogether, but by granting recovery for other psychical harm only late and grudgingly, and then only in very clear cases. In tort, clear means close—close to the victim, close to the accident, close to the defendant.

The principal case involved a plaintiff who was close to the victims (mother/family), not very close to the accident in time or place, and a complete stranger to the defendant truck-drivers. In other cases the plaintiff is close to the defendant, and, as one would expect, that can make a big difference. Thus in *Dooley* v. *Cammell Laird* [1951] 1 Lloyd's Rep. 271 a crane-driver sued his employer for his shock when a defect in the crane caused the load which he was lifting to fall into the hold where his mates were working. Of course the plaintiff recovered damages: an employer owes a duty to his workmen regarding their peace of mind as well as their physical integrity. So do fellow-workmen; recovery was granted to a train-driver who was shocked by the death of a traveller struck by a door carelessly left open by the guard (*Wigg* v. *British Railways Board,* (1986) 136 New L.J. 446). Similarly one can expect that occupiers will fairly readily be held liable to shocked visitors (airline/passengers), and doctors, even psychiatrists, to their patients for brutal treatment. But what about husbands to wives, given the frequency of mental cruelty in days of yore?

Closeness was a feature in *Attia* v. *British Gas* [1987] 3 All E.R. 455 (C.A.). The defendant's men had been installing central heating in the plaintiff's house. When she came home that afternoon she found smoke coming out of the loft, and by the time the fire brigade arrived the house was full alight and burned for four hours. The Court of Appeal, unlike the trial judge, was not prepared to say that the plaintiff's shock was necessarily an unforeseeable consequence of the defendant's breach of duty: this was not a case where duty had to be established, it was simply a question of remoteness. It is because of the closeness of the parties that "In a proper case damages for mental distress can be recovered in contract, just as damages for shock can be recovered in tort," *per* Lord Denning M.R. in *Jarvis* v. *Swans Tours* [1973] Q.B. 233, 237–238. Jarvis got damages for pique when his Alpine holiday was less fun than promised by the tour operator. Mrs. Heywood got £150 from solicitors who negligently failed to stop a man harassing her (*Heywood* v. *Wellers* [1976] 1 All E.R. 300), and a man called Cox who suffered "vexation, frustration and distress" on being demoted got £500 from his employers (*Cox* v. *Philips Industries* [1976] 3 All E.R. 161). However *Cox* has been overruled by the Court of Appeal: "Where damages fall to be assessed for breach of contract rather than in tort it is not permissible to award general damages for frustration, mental distress, injured feelings or annoyance occasioned by the breach . . . " except " . . . where the contract which has been broken is itself a contract to provide peace of mind or freedom from distress." *Bliss* v. *S.E. Thames Regional Health Auth'y* [1985] I.R.L.R. 308, 316. This would meet with the approval of Kerr L.J. who in other cases would award damages for physical inconvenience, if actually suffered, but not for aggravation "because such aggravation is experienced by almost all litigants." (*Perry* v. *Sidney Phillips* [1982] 3 All E.R. 705, 712). The reason he gives, however, is false, because most litigants in contract cases are not human at all, and are incapable of suffering aggravation. The sums awarded are quite small, but they have a considerable nuisance value.

2. *Rescue.* In *Chadwick* the plaintiff, who lived nearby, nobly assisted the victims of the terrible train disaster at Lewisham in 1957, and the horror of it marked him for life. British Rail had to pay him, on the principle that a person who negligently causes an accident may be liable to those who come to help the victims and get injured themselves. The injury is usually physical. The three defences which the negligent party may seek to raise in such a case are unlikely to succeed: (i) "You weren't endangered; you came on the scene voluntarily, so I didn't owe you any duty"; (ii) "You weren't taking proper care of your own safety"; (iii) "Your intervention, not my negligence, was the cause of your injuries." Just as bad people pay more, so good people get more. (See *Baker* v. *Hopkins (T.E.) & Sons* [1959] 1 W.L.R. 966, [1959] 3 All E.R. 225 (C.A.)).

If the rescuer can sue A who negligently endangers B (regardless of whether B himself was negligent), can the rescuer equally sue B who negligently puts himself in apparent need of rescue? In *Harrison* v. *British Railways Board* [1981] 3 All E.R. 679 a railway employee, leaving work early, tried to leap on to a train already in motion. He was held liable to the guard on the train who tried to help him aboard and was himself pulled off.

In early 1983 the following sea-side tragedy occurred. A young man who was a strong swimmer was walking along the Blackpool promenade one very stormy day with his Jack Russell terrier and threw a ball for the dog to retrieve. The ball went over the sea-wall and the dog went after it. The young man followed his dog and got into difficulties in the high seas. Four police officers tried to save him and three of them were drowned. Analyse the situation in legal terms.

FATAL ACCIDENTS ACT 1976

1.—(1) If death is caused by any wrongful act, neglect or default which is such as would (if death had not ensued) have entitled the person injured to maintain an action and recover damages in respect thereof, the person who would have been liable if death had not ensued shall be liable to an action for damages, notwithstanding the death of the person injured.

(2) Subject to section 1A(2) below, every such action shall be for the benefit of the dependants of the person ("the deceased") whose death has been so caused.

(3) In this Act "dependant" means—

(a) the wife or husband or former wife or husband of the deceased;
(b) any person who—
    (i) was living with the deceased in the same household immediately before the date of the death; and
    (ii) had been living with the deceased in the same household for at least two years before that date; and
    (iii) was living during the whole of that period as the husband or wife of the deceased;
(c) any parent or other ascendant of the deceased;
(d) any person who was treated by the deceased as his parent;
(e) any child or other descendant of the deceased;
(f) any person (not being a child of the deceased) who, in the case of any marriage to which the deceased was at any time a party, was treated by the deceased as a child of the family in relation to that marriage;
(g) any person who is, or is the issue of, a brother, sister, uncle or aunt of the deceased.

(5) In deducing any relationship for the purposes of subsection (3) above—

(a) any relationship by affinity shall be treated as a relationship by consanguinity, any relationship of the half blood as a relationship of the whole blood, and the stepchild of any person as his child, and

(b) an illegitimate person shall be treated as the legitimate child of his mother and reputed father.

1A.—(1) An action under this Act may consist of or include a claim for damages for bereavement.

(2) A claim for damages for bereavement shall only be for the benefit—

(a) of the wife or husband of the deceased; and

(b) where the deceased was a minor who was never married—

(i) of his parents, if he was legitimate; and

(ii) of his mother, if he was illegitimate.

(3) Subject to subsection (5) below, the sum to be awarded as damages under this section shall be £3,500.

(4) Where there is a claim for damages under this section for the benefit of both the parents of the deceased, the sum awarded shall be divided equally between them.

(5) The Lord Chancellor may by order made by statutory instrument, subject to annulment in pursuance of a resolution of either House of Parliament, amend this section by varying the sum for the time being specified in subsection (3) above.

2.—(1) The action shall be brought by and in the name of the executor or administrator of the deceased. . . .

3.—(1) In the action such damages, other than damages for bereavement, may be awarded as are proportioned to the injury resulting from the death to the dependants respectively.

(2) After deducting the costs not recovered from the defendant any amount recovered otherwise than as damages for bereavement shall be divided among the dependants in such shares as may be directed.

(3) In an action under this Act where there fall to be assessed damages payable to a widow in respect of the death of her husband there shall not be taken into account the re-marriage of the widow or her prospects of re-marriage.

(4) In an action under this Act where there fall to be assessed damages payable to a person who is a dependant by virtue of section 1(3)(b) above in respect of the death of the person with whom the dependant was living as husband or wife there shall be taken into account (together with any other matter that appears to the court to be relevant to the action) the fact that the dependant had no enforceable right to financial support by the deceased as a result of their living together.

(5) If the dependants have incurred funeral expenses in respect of the deceased, damages may be awarded in respect of those expenses.

(6) Money paid into court in satisfaction of a cause of action under this Act may be in one sum without specifying any person's share.

4. In assessing damages in respect of a person's death in an action under this Act, benefits which have accrued or will or may accrue to any person from his estate or otherwise as a result of his death shall be disregarded.

5. Where any person dies as the result partly of his own fault and partly of the fault of any other person or persons, and accordingly if an action were brought for the benefit of the estate under the Law Reform (Miscellaneous Provisions) Act 1934 the damages recoverable would be reduced under section 1(1) of the Law Reform (Contributory Negligence) Act 1945, any damages recoverable in an action under this Act shall be reduced to a proportionate extent.

Note:

We have already seen how reluctant the common law was to compensate A for financial harm consequent on damage to the property of B (above p. 43). It was reluctant, too, to compensate A for harm consequent on personal injury to B, fatal or not.

Those affected by a person's *death* had, and have, no claim at common law at all. Any claim they may now have must stem from statute. The original Fatal Accidents Act was passed in 1846 when the other Stephenson's invention came of age. As amended in 1959, consolidated in 1976 and re-amended in 1982, it provides the leading example of liability in tort for negligently causing financial harm. It does not lay down that the tortfeasor owes a duty towards his victim's dependants: it simply enables them to sue the tortfeasor if the deceased could have done so when he died. Thus if the primary victim has settled with the tortfeasor or sued him to judgment or let his claim become time-barred, the dependants have no claim.

Only the persons specified in the statute, including now the ex-wife and the live-in lover, may sue. Many other people may suffer loss, such as the employer, the partner, the insurance company or the donee who becomes liable to tax. None of these may sue; indeed, a person cannot sue for the loss of his business partner even if he was married to her (*Burgess* v. *Florence Nightingale Hospital* [1955] 1 Q.B. 349 (*sed quaere*)).

The claim for bereavement is new. Until 1982 only financial loss was recoverable under the Act: no damages at all could be awarded for grief. This was particularly hard in the case where a small child was killed, for then there was no financial loss—indeed, rather a saving—and the appalling human loss went quite unalleviated. But the provision is odd in some respects. Why should a child not be able to sue when bereft of its mother? (Actually, it can sue, but for lost services rather than bereavement). And why did the legislator lay down a fixed sum rather than a ceiling? Under this rule Niobe could collect £49,000 from Apollo and Artemis.

Some of the problems in determining the amount of the award are discussed below at p. 559.

But the family may be affected by *non-fatal* injuries to one of its members. Here the very strong tendency is to allow only the primary victim to claim, and to dress up the loss to others as being the primary victim's loss. Thus if the husband is emasculated, the wife will clearly suffer; she cannot sue, however, for he will be paid for the pleasure he can neither receive nor give (*Best* v. *Samuel Fox* [1952] A.C. 716). Again, the wage-earner who will shortly die because of the injury can hardly be said to have lost the wages he will not be on earth to earn; he is, however, treated as having a present interest in providing for his survivors (*Pickett* v. *British Rail Engineering* [1980] A.C. 136). If the mother is incapacitated the family loses her services; she can sue for their value, though she doesn't seem to have lost anything except trouble, and her husband, who has, cannot (*Daly* v. *General Steam Navigation Co.* [1980] 3 All E.R. 696; Administration of Justice Act 1982, s.2). If the mother is rendered permanently unconscious, it is only the family that suffers (pointless visits to hospital, the near corpse in the upstairs room); they cannot sue, and the immense sum payable to the mother, which she can never use, seems to reflect the fact. (*West* v. *Shephard* (below p. 550)). If a child is injured, the mother may give up her job to nurse him; the child can sue for the value of the free services received, often equal to the wages given up (*Donnelly* v. *Joyce* [1974] Q.B. 454; *Housecroft* v. *Burnett* [1986] 1 All E.R. 332, 342–3).

Note that although the financial or human harm suffered by the ricochet victims is perfectly foreseeable, they themselves cannot sue. This should be borne in mind when one is making general statements about the law of negligence to the effect that one is responsible for the foreseeable consequences of one's unreasonable conduct. The law is that you do not owe a person any duty not to maim or kill his nearest and dearest unless you do it in his presence, or, after *McLoughlin*, vicinity. It is true that in 1976 Lord Kilbrandon said "The law now treats the employer as knowing that nearly all the men and many of the women he employs have dependants who are maintained out of the wages he pays and that those dependants will suffer grief as well as patrimonial loss if he, by neglect of his duty of care, occasions his employees physical harm. Those dependants are therefore persons to whom he owes that duty." (*Dick* v. *Burgh of Falkirk* 1976 S.L.T. 21, 25 (H.L.)). But this "revolutionary" observation was sternly denounced and disavowed by all the members of the House of Lords in *Robertson* v. *Turnbull* 1982 S.L.T. 96.

CONGENITAL DISABILITIES (CIVIL LIABILITY) ACT 1976

1.—(1) If a child is born disabled as the result of such an occurrence before its birth as is mentioned in subsection (2) below, and a person (other than the child's own mother) is under this section answerable to the child in respect of the occurrence, the child's disabilities are to be regarded as damage resulting from the wrongful act of that person and actionable accordingly at the suit of the child.

(2) An occurrence to which this section applies is one which—

(a) affected either parent of the child in his or her ability to have a normal, healthy child; or

(b) affected the mother during her pregnancy, or affected her or the child in the course of its birth, so that the child is born with disabilities which would not otherwise have been present.

(3) Subject to the following subsections, a person (here referred to as "the defendant") is answerable to the child if he was liable in tort to the parent or would, if sued in due time, have been so; and it is no answer that there could not have been such liability because the parent suffered no actionable injury, if there was a breach of legal duty which, accompanied by injury, would have given rise to the liability.

(4) In the case of an occurrence preceding the time of conception, the defendant is not answerable to the child if at the time either or both of the parents knew the risk of their child being born disabled (that is to say, the particular risk created by the occurrence); but should it be the child's father who is the defendant, this subsection does not apply if he knew of the risk and the mother did not.

(5) The defendant is not answerable to the child, for anything he did or omitted to do when responsible in a professional capacity for treating or advising the parent, if he took reasonable care having due regard to then received professional opinion applicable to the particular class of case; but this does not mean that he is answerable only because he departed from received opinion.

(6) Liability to the child under this section may be treated as having been excluded or limited by contract made with the parent affected, to the same extent and subject to the same restrictions as liability in the parent's own case; and a contract term which could have been set up by the defendant in an action by the parent, so as to exclude or limit his liability to him or her, operates in the defendant's favour to the same, but no greater, extent in an action under this section by the child.

(7) If in the child's action under this section it is shown that the parent affected shared the responsibility for the child being born disabled, the damages are to be reduced to such extent as the court thinks just and equitable having regard to the extent of the parent's responsibility.

2. A woman driving a motor vehicle when she knows (or ought reasonably to know) herself to be pregnant is to be regarded as being under the same duty to take care for the safety of her unborn child as the law imposes on her with respect to the safety of other people; and if in consequence of her breach of that duty her child is born with disabilities which would not otherwise have been present, those disabilities are to be regarded as damage resulting from her wrongful act and actionable accordingly at the suit of the child. . . .

4.—(1) . . .

(2) In this Act—

(a) "born" means born alive (the moment of a child's birth being when it first has a life separate from its mother), and "birth" has a corresponding meaning . . .

(5) This Act applies in respect of births after (but not before) its passing, and in respect of any such birth it replaces any law in force before its passing, whereby a person could be liable to a child in respect of disabilities with which it might be born; . . .

Note:

This Act was passed because it was uncertain whether any duty could be owed to a person not yet born, not yet viable or not yet conceived. This uncertainty weakened the case of the Thalidomide victims against the distributors of that drug: see *Att.-Gen.* v. *Times Newspapers* [1973] 3 All E.R. 54.

In *McKay* v. *Essex Area Health Authority* [1982] Q.B. 1166 the allegations were that the defendant doctor had negligently failed (a) to diagnose rubella in the pregnant mother, (b) to recommend an abortion, and (c) to take steps which might have reduced the disabilities with which the infant plaintiff was born. The Court of Appeal held that while the mother could sue for the pain and expense of having a disabled child, and while the infant could sue on the ground that its disabilities were greater than they would have been if the doctor had treated the mother properly, the infant could not claim damages on the ground that the doctor had negligently prevented her being aborted. Stephenson L.J. said " . . . neither defendant was under any duty to the child to give the child's mother an opportunity to terminate the child's life. That duty may be owed to the mother, but it cannot be owed to the child." (at 1180). *McKay* was decided under the common law which was abrogated by the above statute. What would the position be under the statute today?

In *McKay* the mother wanted the child, if well, but in many cases she doesn't, and sues the doctor who performed the sterilisation operation negligently. The courts now allow her to claim for the expense of bringing up the child, even if it is perfectly healthy, as well as the pain and associated expenses of pregnancy and childbirth, with no real set-off, except possibly against the trouble of upbringing, for the joys of reluctant maternity. The House of Lords should perhaps consider whether such involuntary children should be "on the parish" in this way and so learn that they were not wanted. Where the operation is properly performed but nevertheless ineffectual, the doctor is liable only for culpable failure to warn of the risk of further impregnation or conception (*Eyre* v. *Measday* [1986] 1 All E.R. 488): a clear warning that the operation is normally irreversible is no longer taken to be a guarantee of its success (*Thake* v. *Maurice* [1984] 2 All E.R. 513, rev'd on this point, Kerr L.J. dissenting, [1986] 1 All E.R. 497; *Gold* v. *Haringey Health Auth'y* [1987] 2 All E.R. 888). See Rogers, Legal Implications of Ineffective Sterilization, (1985) 5 L.S. 296.

Questions:
1. Under s.1(1) why should the mother not be liable if the father is?
2. Under s.1(7) why should the parents' contributory negligence be imputed to the unborn child when it is not imputed to the child once born? (*Oliver* v. *Birmingham & Midland Omnibus Co.* [1933] 1 K.B. 35).
3. Under s.2 why should the mother be liable if the foetus is injured by her bad driving but not by her falling downstairs pickled with gin?
4. Can a mother claim bereavement damages under the Fatal Accidents Act for the death of a viable foetus killed by the defendant's fault?

WHEAT v. E. LACON & CO.

House of Lords [1966] A.C. 552; [1966] 2 W.L.R. 581; 110 S.J. 149; [1966] 1 All E.R. 582

Action against occupier in respect of visitor's death

On the facts stated below, Winn J. held that Lacons, as occupier, owed the deceased a duty to take care, but that their breach did not cause his death. In the Court of Appeal a majority held that Lacons owed the deceased no duty as occupier ([1966] 1 Q.B. 335). The plaintiff's appeal to the House of Lords was dismissed on the grounds that, although Lacons owed an occupier's duty to the deceased, the duty was not broken.

Lord Denning: My Lords, The "Golfers Arms" at Great Yarmouth is owned by the brewery company, E. Lacon & Co. Ltd. The ground floor was run as a public-house by Mr. Richardson as manager for the brewery company. The first floor was used by Mr. and Mrs. Richardson as their private dwelling. In the summer Mrs. Richardson took in guests for her private profit. Mr. and Mrs. Wheat and their family were summer guests of Mrs. Richardson. About 9 p.m. one evening, when it was getting dark, Mr. Wheat fell down the back staircase in the private portion and was killed.

Winn J. held that there were two causes: (i) the handrail was too short because it did not stretch to the foot of the stairs; (ii) someone had taken the bulb out of the light at the top of the stairs.

The case raises this point of law: did the brewery company owe any duty to Mr. Wheat to see that the handrail was safe to use or to see that the stairs were properly lighted? That depends on whether the brewery company was "an occupier" of the private portion of the "Golfers Arms," and Mr. Wheat its "visitor" within the Occupiers' Liability Act 1957: for, if so, the brewery company owed him the "common duty of care." . . .

In the Occupiers' Liability Act 1957, the word "occupier" is used in the same sense as it was used in the common law cases on occupiers' liability for dangerous premises. It was simply a convenient word to denote a person who had a sufficient degree of control over premises to put him under a duty of care towards those who came lawfully on to the premises . . . This duty is simply a particular instance of the general duty of care which each man owes to his "neighbour." When Lord Esher first essayed a definition of this general duty, he used the occupiers' liability as an instance of it: see *Heaven* v. *Pender* ((1883) 11 Q.B.D. 503, 508–509); and when Lord Atkin eventually formulated the general duty in acceptable terms, he, too, used occupier's liability as an illustration: see *Donoghue* v. *Stevenson* (above p. 22), and particularly his reference to *Grote* v. *Chester Railway Company* ((1848) 2 Ex. 251, 154 E.R. 485). Translating this general principle into its particular application to dangerous premises, it becomes simply this: wherever a person has a sufficient degree of control over premises that he ought to realise that any failure on his part to use care may result in injury to a person coming lawfully there, then he is an "occupier" and the person coming lawfully there is his "visitor": and the "occupier" is under a duty to his "visitor" to use reasonable care. In order to be an "occupier" it is not necessary for a person to have entire control over the premises. He need not have exclusive occupation. Suffice it that he has some degree of control. He may share the control with others. Two or more may be "occupiers." And whenever this happens, each is under a duty to use care towards persons coming lawfully on to the premises, dependent on his degree of control. If each fails in his duty, each is liable to a visitor who is injured in consequence of his failure, but each may have a claim to contribution from the other.

In *Salmond on Torts*, 14th ed. (1965), p. 372, it is said that an "occupier" is "he who has the immediate supervision and control and the power of permitting or prohibiting the entry of other persons." . . . There is no doubt that a person who fulfils that test is an "occupier." He is the person who says "come in." But I think that test is too narrow by far. There are other people who are "occupiers," even though they do not say "come in." If a person has any degree of control over the state of the premises it is enough. The position is best shown by examining the cases in four groups.

First, where a landlord let premises by demise to a tenant, he was regarded as parting with all control over them. He did not retain any degree of control, even though he had undertaken to repair the structure. Accordingly, he was held to be under no duty to any person coming lawfully on to the premises, save only to the tenant under the agreement to repair. In *Cavalier* v. *Pope* ([1906] A.C. 428) it was argued that the premises were under the control of the landlord because of his agreement to repair: but the House of Lords rejected that argument. That case has now been overruled by section 4 of the Act of 1957 to the extent therein mentioned.

Secondly, where an owner let floors or flats in a building to tenants, but did not demise the common staircase or the roof or some other parts, he was regarded as having retained control of all parts not demised by him. Accordingly, he was held to be under a duty in respect of those retained parts to all persons coming lawfully on to the premises. So he was held liable for a defective staircase in *Miller* v. *Hancock* ([1893] 2 Q.B. 177); for the gutters in the roof of *Hargroves, Aronson & Co.* v. *Hartopp* ([1905] 1 K.B. 472); and for the private balcony in *Sutcliffe* v. *Clients*

Investment Co. Ltd. ([1924] 2 K.B. 746). . . . The extent of the duty is now simply the common duty of care. But the old cases still apply so as to show that the landlord is responsible for all parts not demised by him, on the ground that he is regarded as being sufficiently in control of them to impose on him a duty of care to all persons coming lawfully on to the premises.

Thirdly, where an owner did not let premises to a tenant but only licensed a person to occupy them on terms which did not amount to a demise, the owner still having the right to do repairs, he was regarded as being sufficiently in control of the structure to impose on him a duty towards all persons coming lawfully on to the premises. So he was held liable for a visitor who fell on the defective step to the front door in *Hawkins* v. *Coulsdon and Purley U.D.C.* ([1954] 1 Q.B. 319); and to the occupier's wife for the defective ceiling which fell on her in *Greene* v. *Chelsea Borough Council* ([1954] 2 Q.B. 127) . . .

Fourthly, where an owner employed an independent contractor to do work on premises or a structure, the owner was usually still regarded as sufficiently in control of the place as to be under a duty towards all those who might lawfully come here. In some cases he might fulfil that duty by entrusting the work to the independent contractor: see *Haseldine* v. *C.A. Daw & Son* ([1941] 2 K.B. 343) and section 2(4) of the Act of 1957. In other cases he might only be able to fulfil it by exercising proper supervision himself over the contractor's work, using due diligence himself to prevent damage from unusual danger: see *Thomson* v. *Cremin* ([1956] 1 W.L.R. 103n.), as explained by Lord Reid in *Davie* v. *New Merton Board Mills Ltd.* ([1959] A.C. 604). But in addition to the owner, the courts regarded the independent contractor as himself being sufficiently in control of the place where he worked as to owe a duty of care towards all persons coming lawfully there. He was then said to be an "occupier" also: see *Hartwell's* case ([1947] K.B. 901); but this is only a particular instance of his general duty of care: see *Billings (A.C.) & Sons Ltd.* v. *Riden* ([1958] A.C. 240), *per* Lord Reid.

In the light of these cases, I ask myself whether the brewery company had a sufficient degree of control over the premises to put them under a duty to a visitor. Obviously they had complete control over the ground floor and were "occupiers" of it. But I think that they had also sufficient control over the private portion. They had not let it out to Mr. Richardson by a demise. They had only granted him a licence to occupy it, having a right themselves to do repairs. That left them with a residuary degree of control which was equivalent to that retained by the Chelsea Corporation in *Greene's* case. They were in my opinion "an occupier" within the Act of 1957. Mr. Richardson, who had a licence to occupy, had also a considerable degree of control. So had Mrs. Richardson, who catered for summer guests. All three of them were, in my opinion, "occupiers" of the private portion of the "Golfers Arms." There is no difficulty in having more than one occupier at one and the same time, each of whom is under a duty of care to visitors. The Court of Appeal so held in the recent case of *Crockfords Club* ([1965] 1 W.L.R. 1093).

What did the common duty of care demand of each of these occupiers towards their visitors? Each was under a duty to take such care as "in all the circumstances of the case" was reasonable to see that the visitor would be reasonably safe. So far as the respondents were concerned, the circumstances demanded that on the ground floor they should, by their servants, take care not only of the structure of the building, but also the furniture, the state of the floors and lighting, and so forth, at all hours of day or night when the premises were open. In regard to the private portion, however, the circumstances did not demand so much of the respondents. They ought to have seen that the structure was reasonably safe, including the handrail, and that the system of lighting was efficient; but I doubt whether they were bound to see that the lights were properly switched on or the rugs laid safely on the floor. The respondents were entitled to leave those day-to-day matters to Mr. and Mrs. Richardson. They, too, were occupiers. The circumstances of the case demanded that Mr. and Mrs. Richardson should take care of those matters in the private portion of the house. And of other matters, too. If they had realised that the handrail was dangerous, they should have reported it to the respondents.

We are not concerned here with Mr. and Mrs. Richardson. The judge has absolved them from any negligence and there is no appeal. We are only concerned with the respondents. They were, in my opinion, occupiers and under a duty of care . . . but . . . I can see no evidence of any breach of duty by the respondents. So far as the handrail was concerned, the evidence was overwhelming that no-one had any reason before this accident to suppose that it was in the least dangerous. So far as the light was concerned, the proper inference was that it was removed by some stranger shortly before Mr. Wheat went down the staircase. Neither the respondents nor Mr. and Mrs. Richardson could be blamed for the act of a stranger.

I would, therefore, dismiss this appeal.

Lord Pearce: . . . I agree . . . that the respondents were under a duty of care to the deceased under the Occupiers' Liability Act 1957. But that Act may impose a duty of care on more than one person. And in my opinion the Richardsons were also under a duty of care. The safety of premises may depend on the acts or omissions of more than one person, each of whom may have a different right to cause or continue the state of affairs which creates the danger and on each a duty of care may lie. But where separate persons are each under a duty of care the acts or omissions which would constitute a breach of that duty may vary very greatly. That which would be negligent in one may well be free from blame in the other. If the Richardsons had a dangerous hole in the carpet which they chose to put down in their sitting-room that would be negligent in them towards a visitor who was injured by it. But the respondents could fairly say that they took no interest in the Richardson's private furnishings and that no reasonable person in their position would have noticed or known of or taken any steps with regard to the dangerous defect. If the construction of the staircase was unsafe that would be negligence on the respondents' part. Whether the Richardsons would also be negligent in not warning their visitors or taking steps to reveal the danger would depend on whether a reasonable person in their position would have done so. Once the duty of care is imposed, the question whether a defendant failed in that duty becomes a question of fact in all the circumstances. In the present case the respondents are not shown to have failed in their duty of care . . .

I would dismiss the appeal.

Note:

The manufacturer is responsible for the condition of the ginger-beer; the occupier is responsible for the state of the premises; both are under a duty to take reasonable care. This equation is delusive, however, since the duties differ in their basis and in their extent. The manufacturer is responsible because he *does* make the thing dangerous, whereas the occupier is responsible because he *can* make the thing safe; the manufacturer's duty arises from his action, the occupier's from his capacity to act (he must because he can). And the extent of the duties differs. Unlike the manufacturer, the occupier is not just under a duty not to cause harm to people; he must prevent harm to them; he must mend the premises and tend the visitor. For example, he must protect the visitor against other visitors. Those other visitors of course owe a duty to everyone present or probably present, but that duty is only the standard one of not hurting them; they are not responsible save in so far as they make the place dangerous; the occupier must make it reasonably safe.

The occupier's duty extends also to goods on his premises with his permission; he must protect them from damage, but he need not, unless he is a hotelier, protect them from theft. The distinction is sensible; thieves are not dangerous. The duty to protect goods from theft comes not from *being* in charge of the place where they are but *taking* charge of the goods themselves, *assuming* control of them; the bailee's duty arises not from his capacity to protect the goods but from his undertaking to do so. Indeed, there may be an assumption of responsibility sufficient to give rise to a duty to take positive steps to protect the goods even if there is no proper bailment or contract (*Fairline Shipping Co.* v. *Adamson* [1975] Q.B. 180). Liability for failure to take such positive steps is somewhat easier to exclude than liability for damage caused by positive negligence (*Johnson Matthey* v. *Constantine Terminals* [1976] 2 Lloyd's Rep. 215).

Thus we have three different sources of duties in tort; the manufacturer's stems from his act, the occupier's from his power to act and the bailee's from his undertaking to act. They are all (need it be said?) under a duty to take reasonable care; but that simplistic formula masks the difference between the obligation not to act unreasonably and the obligation to act reasonably.

DEFECTIVE PREMISES ACT 1972

4. Landlord's duty of care in virtue of obligation or right to repair premises demised

(1) Where premises are let under a tenancy which puts on the landlord an obligation to the tenant for the maintenance or repair of the premises, the landlord owes to all persons who might reasonably be expected to be affected by defects in the state of the premises a duty to take such care as is reasonable in all the circumstances to see that they are reasonably safe from personal injury or from damage to their property caused by a relevant defect.

(2) The said duty is owed if the landlord knows (whether as the result of being notified by the tenant or otherwise) or if he ought in all the circumstances to have known of the relevant defect.

(3) In this section "relevant defect" means a defect in the state of the premises existing at or after the material time and arising from, or continuing because of, an act or omission by the landlord which constitutes or would if he had had notice of the defect, have constituted a failure by him to carry out his obligation to the tenant for the maintenance or repair of the premises; and for the purposes of the foregoing provision "the material time" means—

   (a) where the tenancy commenced before this Act, the commencement of this Act; and
   (b) in all other cases, the earliest of the following times, that is to say—
      (i) the time when the tenancy commences;
      (ii) the time when the tenancy agreement is entered into;
      (iii) the time when possession is taken of the premises in contemplation of the letting.

(4) Where premises are let under a tenancy which expressly or impliedly gives the landlord the right to enter the premises to carry out any description of maintenance or repair of the premises, then, as from the time when he first is, or by notice or otherwise can put himself, in a position to exercise the right and so long as he is or can put himself in that position, he shall be treated for the purposes of subsections (1) to (3) above (but for no other purpose) as if he were under an obligation to the tenant for that description of maintenance or repair of the premises; but the landlord shall not owe the tenant any duty by virtue of this subsection in respect of any defect in the state of the premises arising from, or continuing because of, a failure to carry out an obligation expressly imposed on the tenant by the tenancy.

(5) For the purposes of this section obligations imposed or rights given by any enactment in virtue of a tenancy shall be treated as imposed or given by the tenancy.

(6) This section applies to a right of occupation given by contract or any enactment and not amounting to a tenancy as if the right were a tenancy, and "tenancy" and cognate expressions shall be construed accordingly.

Note:
Since the very reason one pays rent is in order to occupy the rented premises, it is, as Lord Denning explained in *Wheat* v. *Lacon*, the tenant rather than the landlord who is under the

occupier's duty to take steps to see that visitors are reasonably safe. But tenants who pay very low rents probably cannot afford to do repairs, and short-term tenants cannot be expected to do substantial work, so section 6 of the Housing Act 1957 requires the landlord of low-rent housing to keep it fit for human habitation and section 11 of the Landlord and Tenant Act 1985 (below) specifies the matters which the landlord must attend to in leases of up to seven years. These provisions only affect the contract between the landlord and the tenant. It is section 4 of the Defective Premises Act 1972 which imposes on the landlord a duty to save third parties from physical harm by taking reasonable steps to discover and remedy defects in the premises which are his responsibility rather than that of the tenant-occupier.

LANDLORD AND TENANT ACT 1985

11.—(1) In a lease to which this section applies (as to which see sections 13 and 14) there is implied a covenant by the lessor—

(a) to keep in repair the structure and exterior of the dwelling-house (including drains, gutters and external pipes),
(b) to keep in repair and proper working order the installations in the dwelling-house for the supply of water, gas and electricity and for sanitation (including basins, sinks, baths and sanitary conveniences, but not other fixtures, fittings and appliances for making use of the supply of water, gas or electricity), and
(c) to keep in repair and proper working order the installations in the dwelling-house for space heating and heating water.

(2) The covenant implied by subsection (1) ("the lessor's repairing covenant") shall not be construed as requiring the lessor—

(a) to carry out works or repairs for which the lessee is liable by virtue of his duty to use the premises in a tenant-like manner, or would be so liable but for an express covenant on his part,
(b) to rebuild or reinstate the premises in the case of destruction or damage by fire, or by tempest, flood or other inevitable accident, or
(c) to keep in repair or maintain anything which the lessee is entitled to remove from the dwelling-house.

(3) In determining the standard of repair required by the lessor's repairing covenant, regard shall be had to the age, character, and prospective life of the dwelling-house and the locality in which it is situated. . . .

13.—(1) Section 11 (repairing obligations) applies to a lease of a dwelling-house granted on or after 24th October 1961 for a term of less than seven years. . . .

OCCUPIERS' LIABILITY ACT 1984

1.—(1) The rules enacted by this section shall have effect, in place of the rules of the common law, to determine—

(a) whether any duty is owed by a person as occupier of premises to persons other than his visitors in respect of any risk of their suffering injury on the premises by reason of any danger due to the state of the premises or to things done or omitted to be done on them; and
(b) if so, what that duty is.

(2) For the purposes of this section, the persons who are to be treated respectively as an occupier of any premises (which, for those purposes, include any fixed or movable structure) and as his visitors are—

(a) any person who owes in relation to the premises the duty referred to in section 2 of the Occupiers' Liability Act 1957 (the common duty of care), and
(b) those who are his visitors for the purposes of that duty.

(3) An occupier of premises owes a duty to another (not being his visitor) in respect of any such risk as is referred to in subsection (1) above if—

(a) he is aware of the danger or has reasonable grounds to believe that it exists;
(b) he knows or has reasonable grounds to believe that the other is in the vicinity of the danger concerned or that he may come into the vicinity of the danger (in either case, whether the other has lawful authority for being in that vicinity or not); and
(c) the risk is one against which, in all the circumstances of the case, he may reasonably be expected to offer the other some protection.

(4) Where, by virtue of this section, an occupier of premises owes a duty to another in respect of such a risk, the duty is to take such care as is reasonable in all the circumstances of the case to see that he does not suffer injury on the premises by reason of the danger concerned.

(5) Any duty owed by virtue of this section in respect of a risk may, in an appropriate case, be discharged by taking such steps as are reasonable in all the circumstances of the case to give warning of the danger concerned or to discourage persons from incurring the risk.

(6) No duty is owed by virtue of this section to any person in respect of risks willingly accepted as his by that person (the question whether a risk was so accepted to be decided on the same principles as in other cases in which one person owes a duty of care to another).

(7) No duty is owed by virtue of this section to persons using the highway, and this section does not affect any duty owed to such persons.

(8) Where a person owes a duty by virtue of this section, he does not, by reason of any breach of the duty, incur any liability in respect of any loss of or damage to property.

(9) In this section—

"highway" means any part of a highway other than a ferry or waterway;
"injury" means anything resulting in death or personal injury, including any disease and any impairment of physical or mental condition; and
"movable structure" includes any vessel, vehicle or aircraft.

Note:

As regards the safety of his premises, the old common law used to impose on the occupier a very high duty towards his contractors, a highish duty towards his invitees (such as the employees of his contractors) and a rather lower duty towards his licensees, such as social guests. Since the Occupiers' Liability Act 1957 he owes them all the same duty, the "common duty of care" (see below p. 114). These people are compendiously called "visitors."

Of those who were not "visitors," because they had no right or permission to be there, the main class were *trespassers*. The duty owed to them was meagre indeed, perhaps just the duty to "treat them with common humanity." The common law rule on the matter, last enunciated in *Herrington* [1972] A.C. 877, is now supplanted by the statute above, though, as Spencer has pointed out, it is arguable that the common law remains applicable to property damage, because (i) it is only with regard to "injury" (defined in s.1(9) as personal injury) that the common law is displaced by this section, and (ii) it is only liability for property damage "under this section" which is barred by s.1(8).

s.1(3)(c). Burglars cannot reasonably expect much to be done for their safety, but children can. However

s.1(4) seems to suggest that if any protection can be expected, the precautions must be the same in the two cases.

s.1(7). This sub-section was doubtless thought desirable because those using a highway or private right of way are not "visitors," but it may have been unnecessary since it is not certain that the highway authority is actually the "occupier." See *Holden* v. *White* [1982] 2 All E.R. 328 (C.A.). Highway authorities *do* owe a duty towards highway users (see below p. 115) and presumably the same duty whether the users are trespassers or not.

s.1(8). Note this clear preference for persons over property. Damage intentionally done to a trespasser's property (cars, dogs etc.) will fall under the law of trespass (below p. 275). The occupier's privilege is merely to disembarrass his premises of the intruding chattels, and the manner of its exercise must be reasonable although the decision to exercise it need not be.

WOOLDRIDGE v. SUMNER

Court of Appeal [1963] 2 Q.B. 43; [1962] 3 W.L.R. 616; 106 S.J. 489; [1962] 2 All E.R. 978

Action by spectator against participant in respect of personal injury

During a competition for heavyweight hunters at the National Horse Show the plaintiff was taking photographs from between some potted shrubs on the edge of the arena. One of the horses competing was "Work of Art," owned by the first defendant and ridden by Ronald Holladay. It came down the far side of the course, rounded the bend at great speed, and then galloped furiously and apparently out of control down the line of shrubs to where the plaintiff was standing. In fright, the plaintiff tried to pull another spectator out of the way, but fell back into the horse's path and was seriously hurt. The horse returned and won.

Barry J. held that the rider had been negligent in allowing the horse to go so fast, and in attempting to bring it back on course when there were people in the way. He gave judgment for the plaintiff for £6,500. The defendant's appeal was allowed.

Diplock L.J.: . . . It is a remarkable thing that in a nation where during the present century so many have spent so much of their leisure in watching other people take part in sports and pastimes there is an almost complete dearth of judicial authority as to the duty of care owed by the actual participants to the spectators. In *Cleghorn* v. *Oldham* ((1927) 43 T.L.R. 465) the act relied on as constituting negligence by a golfer was not done in the actual course of play and the case, which was tried by a jury and only very briefly reported, throws little light upon the extent of the duty of care. So, too, in the Canadian case of *Payne & Payne* v. *Maple Leaf Gardens Ltd.* ([1949] 1 D.L.R. 369) the negligent act was not committed in the course of play but in the course of a private fight between two players over the possession of an ice hockey stick at the opposite side of the arena to that in which the game was going on at the relevant time. There have been other cases—*Hall* v. *Brooklands Auto Racing Club* ([1933] 1 K.B. 205) itself is one of them—in which the actual participants in the game or competition have been sued as well as the occupiers of the premises on which it took place, but juries have acquitted the participants of negligence and the cases are reported only upon the duty owed by an occupier of premises to invitees. Such duty is not based upon negligence simpliciter but flows from a consensual relationship between the occupier and the invitee; there is thus no conceptual difficulty in implying a term in that consensual relationship (which in the reported cases has in fact been a contractual relationship) that the occupier need take no precautions to protect the invitee from all or from particular kinds of risks incidental to the game or competition which the spectator has come upon the premises to watch.

In the case of a participant, however, any duty of care which he owed to the spectator is not based upon any consensual relationship between them but upon mere "proximity," if I may use that word as a compendious expression of what makes one person a "neighbour" of another in the sense of Lord Atkin's definition in *Donoghue* v. *Stevenson* as expanded in *Hay (or Bourhill)* v. *Young*. Nevertheless, some assistance is to be gathered from the invitee cases, for the term as to the duty of the occupier to take precautions to prevent damage being sustained upon the premises by his invitee, which was implied at common law, was closely analogous to the duty a breach of which constitutes negligence simpliciter, namely, "to use reasonable care to ensure safety" (*Hall* v. *Brooklands Auto Racing Club, per* Scrutton L.J.), "that reasonable skill and care have been used to make [the premises] safe" (*per* Greer L.J.).

To treat Lord Atkin's statement: "You must take reasonable care to avoid acts or omissions which you can reasonably foresee would be likely to injure your neighbour," as a complete exposition of the law of negligence is to mistake aphorism for exegesis. It does not purport to define what is reasonable care and was directed to identifying the persons to whom the duty to take reasonable care is owed. What is reasonable care in a particular circumstance is a jury question and where, as in a case like this, there is no direct guidance or hindrance from authority it may be answered by inquiring whether the ordinary reasonable man would say that in all the circumstances the defendant's conduct was blameworthy.

The matter has to be looked at from the point of view of the reasonable spectator as well as the reasonable participant; not because of the maxim volenti non fit injuria, but because what a reasonable spectator would expect a participant to do without regarding it as blameworthy is as relevant to what is reasonable care as what a reasonable participant would think was blameworthy conduct in himself. The same idea was expressed by Scrutton L.J. in *Hall* v. *Brooklands:* "What is reasonable care would depend upon the perils which might be reasonably expected to occur, *and the extent to which the ordinary spectator might be expected to appreciate and take the risk of such perils.*"

A reasonable spectator attending voluntarily to witness any game or competition knows and presumably desires that a reasonable participant will concentrate his attention upon winning, and if the game or competition is a fast-moving one, will have to exercise his judgment and attempt to exert his skill in what, in the analogous context of contributory negligence, is sometimes called "the agony of the moment." If the participant does so concentrate his attention and consequently does exercise his judgment and attempt to exert his skill in circumstances of this kind which are inherent in the game or competition in which he is taking part, the question whether any mistake he makes amounts to a breach of duty to take reasonable care must take account of those circumstances.

The law of negligence has always recognised that the standard of care which a reasonable man will exercise depends upon the conditions under which the decision to avoid the act or omission relied upon as negligence has to be taken. The case of the workmen engaged on repetitive work in the noise and bustle of the factory is a familiar example. More apposite for present purposes are the collision cases, where a decision has to be made upon the spur of the moment. "A's negligence makes collision so threatening that though by the appropriate measure B could avoid it, B has not really time to think and by mistake takes the wrong measure. B is not to be held guilty of any negligence and A wholly fails" (*Admiralty Commissioners* v. *S.S. Volute* [1922] 1 A.C. 129, 136). A fails not because of his own negligence; there never has been any contributory negligence rule in Admiralty. He fails because B has exercised such care as is reasonable in circumstances in which he has not really time to think. No doubt if he has got into those circumstances as a result of a breach of duty of care which he owes to A, A can succeed upon this antecedent negligence; but a participant in a game or competition gets upon the circumstances in which he has no time or very little time to think by his decision to take part in the game or competition at all. It cannot be suggested that the participant, at any rate if he has some modicum of skill is, by the mere act of participating, in breach of his duty of care to a spectator who is present for the very purpose of watching him do so. If, therefore, in the course of the game or competition, at a moment when he really has not time to think, a participant by mistake takes a wrong measure, he is not, in my view, to be held guilty of any negligence.

Furthermore, the duty which he owes is a duty of care, not a duty of skill. Save where a consensual relationship exists between a plaintiff and a defendant by which the defendant impliedly warrants his skill, a man owes no duty to his neighbour to exercise any special skill beyond that which an ordinary reasonable man would acquire before indulging in the activity in which he is engaged at the relevant time. It may well be that a participant in a game or competition would be guilty of negligence to a spectator if he took part in it when he knew or ought to have known that his lack of skill was such that even if he exerted it to the utmost he was likely to cause injury to a spectator watching him. No question of this arises in the present case. It was common ground that Mr. Holladay was an exceptionally skilful and experienced horseman.

The practical result of this analysis of the application of the common law of negligence to participant and spectator would, I think, be expressed by the common man in some such terms as these: "A person attending a game or competition takes the risk of any damage caused to him by any act of a participant done in the course of and for the purposes of the game or competition notwithstanding that such act may involve an error of judgment or a lapse of skill, unless the participant's conduct is such as to evince a reckless disregard of the spectator's safety." . . .

Beyond saying that the question is one of degree, the judge has not expressly stated in his judgment anything which would indicate the considerations which he had in mind in determining that Mr. Holladay was in breach of the duty of care owed by a participant in a competition of this character to a spectator who had chosen to watch the event in the arena in which it was taking place. There is, however, no reference in his judgment to the fact, which is, in my view, of the utmost relevance, that Mr. Holladay's decisions as to what he should do once the signal for the gallop has been given had to be made in circumstances in which he had no time to exercise an unhurried judgment. It is, I think, clear that if the trial judge gave any weight to this factor he did not make proper allowance for it.

As regards the speed at which Mr. Holladay went round the bandstand end of the arena, I doubt whether his error of judgment would have amounted to negligence even if one were to ignore completely the fact that his judgment had to be exercised rapidly in the excitement of the contest although not at a moment of intense crisis. For it does not seem to me that any miscalculation of the speed at which "Work of Art" could take the corner could be reasonably foreseen to be likely to injure any spectator sitting on or standing by the benches 20 to 30 yards from the point at which a horse taking the corner at too great a speed would cross the line demarcated by the shrubs . . . The horse was deflected from its course before it reached the benches and no spectator would have been injured had not the plaintiff, in a moment of panic, stepped or stumbled back out of his proper and safe place among the other spectators in the line of benches into the path of the horse. Such panic in the case of a person ignorant of equine behaviour and, as the judge found, paying little or no attention to what was going on, is understandable and excusable, but, in my view, a reasonable competitor would be entitled to assume that spectators actually in the arena would be paying attention to what was happening, would be knowledgeable about horses, and would take such steps for their own safety as any reasonably attentive and knowledgeable spectator might be expected to take.

When due allowance is made for the circumstances in which Mr. Holladay had in fact to exercise his judgment as to the speed at which to take the corner, his conduct in taking the corner too fast could not, in my view, amount to negligence.

As regards the second respect in which the judge found Mr. Holladay to be negligent, namely, in his attempt to bring back the horse into the arena after it had come into contact with the first shrub, I have already stated the reasons why I am unable to accept the judge's inference of fact that the course taken by the horse along the line of shrubs was due to Mr. Holladay's attempt to bring it back into the arena instead of letting it run out on to the cinder track. But even if the judge's inference of fact be accepted, here was a classic case where Mr. Holladay's decision what to do had to be taken in the "agony of the moment," when he had no time to think, and if he took the wrong decision that could not in law amount to negligence.

The most that can be said against Mr. Holladay is that in the course of and for the purposes of the competition he was guilty of an error or errors of judgment or a lapse of skill. That is not enough to constitute a breach of the duty of reasonable care which a participant owes to a spectator. In such circumstances something in the nature of a reckless disregard of the spectator's safety must be proved, and of this there is no suggestion in the evidence. I, too, would allow this appeal.

Note:

The formula adopted by Diplock L.J. was doubted in a later case where a spectator was suing a participant in a motor-cycle scramble (*Wilks* v. *Cheltenham Car Club* [1971] 2 All E.R. 369 (neither occupier nor participant shown to be at fault)). It was ignored entirely in the first reported case between participants. In *Condon* v. *Basi* [1985] 2 All E.R. 453 (C.A.) (noted 102 L.Q.R. 11 (Hudson)), the defendant was held liable for breaking the plaintiff's leg in a soccer match in the Leamington Local League by a tackle which "was made in a reckless and dangerous manner not with malicious intent but in an 'excitable manner without thought of the consequences'." It seems that the plaintiff had got rid of the ball at the time.

Players are ready to get hurt and to cause hurt, within limits and if need be, in order to win, and spectators go there to see them so conduct themselves. The limits cannot be determined by the rules of the game, since not all rules are safety-orientated, and it is certain that play is not rendered tortious just because the commentators think it bad play: they must be shocked before liability arises. The judgment of Diplock L.J. seems right.

It was cited in a very different kind of case. The defendant policeman was chasing, in an unmarked car, a car in which the plaintiff was travelling, knowing it to have been stolen. The plaintiff's car stopped and the policeman intended to drive his car alongside it, but collided with it and injured the plaintiff, who had descended with alacrity (*Marshall* v. *Osmond* [1982] 2 All E.R. 610). Milmo J. said, at first instance: "It would be a sorry state of affairs if the police in this country involved in the pursuit of criminals were to be held to owe the same duty of care to the criminals whom they are endeavouring to arrest as they owe to ordinary law-abiding users of the highway." On appeal the Master of the Rolls said "I think that the duty owed by a police driver to the suspect is . . . the same duty as that owed to anyone else, namely to exercise such care and skill as is reasonable in all the circumstances," but held that as the circumstances were "stressful," the police driver's error of judgment was not a breach of duty ([1983] 2 All E.R. 225, 227).

Question:

Package tourists in Mallorca go on an outing to the Santa Ponsa go-kart track one after-noon. The plaintiff is very timid and crawls along on the very outside of the track. The defend-ant who, like most of the others, was going as fast as possible, makes an error of judgment and collides with the plaintiff, who suffers a hand injury. The defendant was held liable for £5,500 and costs. Both parties were legally aided. (*Denyer* v. *Heaney*, C.A., February 19, 1985). Do you agree with the result?

NETTLESHIP v. WESTON

Court of Appeal [1971] 2 Q.B. 691; [1971] 3 W.L.R. 370; 115 S.J. 624; [1971] 3 All E.R. 581

Action in respect of personal injuries by driving instructor against learner driver

The defendant asked the plaintiff, who was a friend and not a professional driving instructor, to teach her to drive her husband's car. On being assured that there was fully comprehensive insurance cover, he agreed to do so. During the third lesson the defendant stopped at a junction prior to turning left. The plaintiff engaged first gear for her, and she started to turn slowly to the left. Her grip on the steering wheel tightened implacably, and despite the plaintiff's advice and efforts, the car followed a perfect curve, mounted the nearside pavement and struck a lamp post with sufficient impact to fracture the plaintiff's knee.

The trial judge dismissed the plaintiff's claim on the ground that the defendant's only duty to him was to do her best, and this she had done, poor though it was. The

Court of Appeal allowed the plaintiff's appeal, subject (Megaw L.J. dissenting) to a reduction of the damages by 50 per cent. in respect of his contributory negligence.

Megaw L.J.: . . . The important question of principle which arises is whether, because of Mr. Nettleship's knowledge that Mrs. Weston was not an experienced driver, the standard of care which was owed to him by her was lower than would otherwise have been the case.

In *The Insurance Commissioner* v. *Joyce* ((1948) 77 C.L.R. 39, 56–60), Dixon J. stated persuasively the view that there is, or may be, a "particular relation" between the driver of a vehicle and his passenger resulting in a variation of the standard of duty owed by the driver. He said (at p. 56): "The case of a passenger in a car differs from that of a pedestrian not in the kind or degree of danger which may come from any want of care or skill in driving but in the fact that the former has come into a more particular relation with the driver of the car. It is because that relation may vary that the standard of duty or of care is not necessarily the same in every case . . . the gratuitous passenger may expect prima facie the same care and skill on the part of the driver as is ordinarily demanded in the management of a car. Unusual conditions may exist which are apparent to him or of which he may be informed and they may affect the application of the standard of care that is due. If a man accepts a lift from a car driver whom he knows to have lost a limb or an eye or to be deaf, he cannot complain if he does not exhibit the skill and competence of a driver who suffers from no defect." He summarised the same principle in these words (at p. 59): "It appears to me that the circumstances in which the defendant accepts the plaintiff as a passenger and in which the plaintiff accepts the accommodation in the conveyance should determine the measure of duty . . . " Theoretically, the principle as thus expounded is attractive. But, with very great respect, I venture to think that the theoretical attraction should yield to practical considerations.

As I see it, if this doctrine of varying standards were to be accepted as part of the law on these facts, it could not logically be confined to the duty of care owed by learner drivers. There is no reason in logic why it should not operate in a much wider sphere. The disadvantages of the resulting unpredictability, uncertainty and, indeed, impossibility of arriving at fair and consistent decisions outweigh the advantages. The certainty of a general standard is preferable to the vagaries of a fluctuating standard.

As a first example of what is involved, consider the converse case: the standard of care (including skill) owed, not by the driver to the passenger, but by the passenger instructor to the learner driver. Surely the same principle of varying standards, if it is a good principle, must be available also to the instructor, if he is sued by the driver for alleged breach of the duty of care in supervising the learner driver. On this doctrine, the standard of care, or skill, owed by the instructor, *vis-à-vis* the driver, may vary according to the knowledge which the learner driver had, at some moment of time, as to the skill and experience of the particular instructor. Indeed, if logic is to prevail, it would not necessarily be the knowledge of the driver which would be the criterion. It would be the expectation which the driver reasonably entertained of the instructor's skill and experience, if that reasonable expectation were greater than the actuality. Thus, if the learner driver knew that the instructor had never tried his hand previously even at amateur instructing, or if, as may be the present case, the driver knew that the instructor's experience was confined to two cases of amateur instructing some years previously, there would, under this doctrine, surely be a lower standard than if the driver knew or reasonably supposed that the instructor was a professional or that he had had substantial experience in the recent past. But what that standard would be, and how it would or should be assessed, I know not. For one has thus cut oneself adrift from the standard of the competent and experienced instructor, which up to now the law has required without regard to the particular personal skill, experience, physical characteristics or temperament of the individual instructor, and without regard to a third party's knowledge or assessment of those qualities or characteristics.

Again, when one considers the requisite standard of care of the learner driver, if this doctrine were to apply, would not logic irresistibly demand that there should be something more than a mere single, conventional, standard applicable to anyone who falls into the category of learner driver: that is, of anyone who has not yet qualified for (or perhaps obtained) a full licence? That standard itself would necessarily vary over a wide range, not merely with the actual progress of the learner, but also with the passenger's knowledge of that progress: or, rather, if the passenger has in fact over-estimated the driver's progress, it would vary with the passenger's reasonable assessment of that progress at the relevant time. The relevant time would not necessarily be the moment of the accident.

The question, what is the relevant time, would itself have to be resolved by reference to some principle. The instructor's reasonable assessment of the skill and competence of the driver (and also the driver's assessment of the instructor's skill and competence) might alter drastically between the start of the first lesson and the start of a later lesson, or even in the course of one particular spell of driving. I suppose the principle would have to be that the relevant time is the last moment when the plaintiff (whether instructor or driver) could reasonably have refused to continue as passenger or driver in the light of his then knowledge. That factor in itself would introduce yet another element of difficulty, uncertainty and, I believe, serious anomaly.

I, for my part, with all respect, do not think that our legal process could successfully or satisfactorily cope with the task of fairly assessing or applying to the facts of a particular case such varying standards, depending on such complex and elusive factors, including the assessment by the court, not merely of a particular person's actual skill or experience, but also of another person's knowledge or assessment of that skill or experience at a particular moment of time.

Again, if the principle of varying standards is to be accepted, why should it operate, in the field of driving motor vehicles, only up to the stage of the driver qualifying for a full licence? And why should it be limited to the quality of inexperience? If the passenger knows that his driver suffers from some relevant defect, physical or temperamental, which could reasonably be expected to affect the quality of his driving, why should not the same doctrine of varying standards apply? Dixon J. thought it should apply. Logically there can be no distinction. If the passenger knows that his driver, though holding a full driving licence, is blind in one eye or has the habit of taking corners too fast, and if an accident happens which is attributable wholly or partly to that physical or that temperamental defect, why should not some lower standard apply, *vis-à-vis* the fully informed passenger, if standards are to vary?

Why should the doctrine, if it be part of the law, be limited to cases involving the driving of motor cars? Suppose that to the knowledge of the patient a young surgeon, whom the patient has chosen to operate on him, has only just qualified. If the operation goes wrong because of the surgeon's inexperience, is there a defence on the basis that the standard of skill and care is lower than the standard of a competent and experienced surgeon? Does the young newly qualified solicitor owe a lower standard of skill and care when the client chooses to instruct him with the knowledge of his experience?

True, these last two examples may fall within the sphere of contract; and a contract may have express terms which deal with the question, or it may have implied terms. But in relationships such as are involved in this case, I see no good reason why a different term should be implied where there is a contract from the term which the law should attach where there is, or may be, no contract. Of course, there may be a difference—not because of any technical distinction between cases which fall within the law of tort and those which fall within the law of contract—but because the very factor or factors which create the contractual relationship may be relevant to the question of the implication of terms. Thus, if it is a contract because of consideration consisting of the promise of payment, that very fact may be relevant. I do not say that it is relevant. I do say that it may be relevant. Or the amount or the circumstances of the payment may be relevant. That is not a question which arises here, and I think that it would be unwise to consider it hypothetically.

In my judgment, in cases such as the present it is preferable that there should be a reasonably certain and reasonably ascertainable standard of care, even if on occasion that may appear to work hardly against an inexperienced driver or his insurers. The standard of care required by the law is the standard of the competent and experienced driver: and this is so, as defining the driver's duty towards a passenger who knows of his inexperience, as much as towards a member of the public outside the car; and as much in civil as in criminal proceedings.

It is not a valid argument against such a principle that it attributes tortious liability to one who may not be morally blameworthy. For tortious liability has in many cases ceased to be based on moral blameworthiness. For example, there is no doubt whatever that if Mrs. Weston has knocked down a pedestrian on the pavement when the accident occurred, she would have been liable to the pedestrian. Yet so far as any moral blame is concerned, no different considerations would apply in respect of the pedestrian from those which apply in respect of Mr. Nettleship.

In criminal law also, the inexperience of the driver is wholly irrelevant. In the phrase commonly used in directions to juries in charges of causing death by dangerous driving, the driver may be guilty even though the jury think that he was "doing his incompetent best": see *Reg.* v. *Evans* ([1963] 1 Q.B. 412, 418) and *Reg.* v. *Scammell* ((1967) 51 Cr.App.R. 398). There can be no doubt that in criminal law, further, it is no answer to a charge of driving without due care and attention that the driver was inexperienced or lacking in skill: see *McCrone* v. *Riding* ([1938] 1 All E.R. 157). In the present case, indeed, there was a conviction for that offence.

If the criminal law demands of an inexperienced driver the standard of care and competence of an experienced driver, why should it be wrong or unjust or impolitic for the civil law to require that standard, even *vis-à-vis* an injured passenger who knew of the driver's inexperience?

Different considerations may, indeed, exist when a passenger has accepted a lift from a driver whom the passenger knows to be likely, through drink or drugs, to drive unsafely. There may in such cases sometimes be an element of aiding and abetting a criminal offence; or, if the facts fall short of aiding and abetting, the passenger's mere assent to benefit from the commission of a criminal offence may involve questions of *turpis causa*. For myself, with great respect, I doubt the correctness on its facts of the decision in *Dann* v. *Hamilton* ([1939] 1 K.B. 509). But the present case involves no such problem . . .

Lord Denning M.R.: . . . The driver owes a duty of care to every passenger in the car, just as he does to every pedestrian on the road; and he must attain the same standard of care in respect of each . . .

. . . Seeing that the law lays down, for all drivers of motor-cars, a standard of care to which all must conform, I think that even a learner-driver, so long as he is the sole driver, must attain the same standard towards all passengers in the car, including an instructor. But the instructor may be debarred . . . because he has voluntarily agreed to waive any claim for any injury that may befall him. Otherwise he is not debarred. He may, of course, be guilty of contributory negligence and have his damages reduced on that account. . . . But apart from contributory negligence, he is not excluded unless it be that he had voluntarily agreed to incur the risk. . . .

Salmon L.J.: I need not recite the facts which have been so lucidly stated by Lord Denning M.R. I entirely agree with all he says about the responsibility of a learner driver in criminal law. I also agree that a learner driver is responsible and owes a duty in civil law towards persons on or near the highway to drive with the same degree of skill and care as that of the reasonably competent and experienced driver. The duty in civil law springs from the relationship which the driver, by driving on the highway, has created between himself and persons likely to suffer damage by his bad driving. This is not a special relationship. Nor, in my respectful view, is it affected by whether or not the driver is insured. On grounds of public policy, neither this criminal nor civil responsibility is affected by the fact that the driver in question may be a learner, infirm or drunk. The onus, of course, lies on anyone claiming damages to establish a breach of duty and that it has caused the damages which he claims.

Any driver normally owes exactly the same duty to a passenger in his car as he does to the general public, namely, to drive with reasonable care and skill in all the relevant circumstances. As a rule, the driver's personal idiosyncrasy is not a relevant circumstance. In the absence of a special relationship what is reasonable care and skill is measured by the standard of competence usually achieved by the ordinary driver. In my judgment, however, there may be special facts creating a special relationship which displaces this standard or even negatives any duty, although the onus would certainly be upon the driver to establish such facts. With minor reservations I respectfully agree with and adopt the reasoning and conclusions of Sir Owen Dixon in his judgment in *The Insurance Commissioner* v. *Joyce* ((1948) 77 C.L.R. 39). I do not agree that the mere fact that the driver has, to the knowledge of his passenger, lost a limb or an eye or is deaf can affect the duty which he owes the passenger to drive safely. It is well known that many drivers suffering from such disabilities drive with no less skill and competence than the ordinary man. The position, however, is totally different when, to the knowledge of the passenger, the driver is so drunk as to be incapable of driving safely. Quite apart from being negligent, a passenger who accepts a lift in such circumstances clearly cannot expect the driver to drive other than dangerously.

The duty of care springs from relationship. The special relationship which the passenger has created by accepting a lift in the circumstances postulated surely cannot entitle him to expect the driver to discharge a duty of care or skill which *ex hypothesi* the passenger knows the driver is incapable of discharging. Accordingly, in such circumstances, no duty is owed by the driver to the passenger to drive safely, and therefore no question of *volenti non fit injuria* can arise.

The alternative view is that if there is a duty owed to the passenger to drive safely, the passenger by accepting a lift has clearly assumed the risk of the driver failing to discharge that duty. What the passenger has done goes far beyond establishing mere "scienter." If it does not establish "volens," it is perhaps difficult to imagine what can.

Such a case seems to me to be quite different from *Smith* v. *Baker & Sons* ([1891] A.C. 325) and *Slater* v. *Clay Cross Co. Ltd.* ([1956] 2 Q.B. 264). Like Sir Owen Dixon, I prefer to rest on the special relationship between the parties displacing the prima facie duty on the driver to drive safely rather than on the ground of *volenti non fit injuria*. Whichever view is preferable, it follows that, in spite of the very great respect I have for any judgment of Lord Asquith, I do not accept that *Dann* v. *Hamilton* ([1939] 1 K.B. 509) was correctly decided. Although Sir Owen Dixon's judgment was delivered in 1948, I cannot think of anything which has happened since which makes it any less convincing now than it was then.

I should like to make it plain that I am not suggesting that whenever a passenger accepts a lift knowing that the driver has had a few drinks, this displaces the prima facie duty ordinarily resting on a driver, let alone that it establishes *volenti non fit injuria*. Indeed, Sir Owen Dixon dissented in *Joyce's* case, because he did not agree that the evidence was capable of establishing that the plaintiff passenger knew that the driver was so drunk as to be incapable of exercising ordinary care and skill. In practice it would be rare indeed that such a defence could be established.

There are no authorities which bear directly on the duty owed by a learner driver to his instructor. I have dwelt upon the authorities concerning the relationship between a drunken driver and his passenger because to some extent there is an analogy between those two classes of case. But the analogy is by no means exact. The drunken driver is in sole charge of the car. His condition may be such that the passenger knows that it is impossible for him to drive with any care or skill. On the other hand, the learner driver and his instructor are jointly in charge of the car. The instructor is entitled to expect the learner to pay attention to what he is told, perhaps to take exceptional care, and certainly to do his best. The instructor, in most cases such as the present, knows, however, that the learner has practically no driving experience or skill and that, for the lack of this experience and skill the learner will almost certainly make mistakes which may well injure the instructor unless he takes adequate steps to correct them. To my mind, therefore, the relationship is usually such that the beginner does not owe the instructor a duty to drive with the skill and competence to be expected of an experienced driver. The instructor knows that the learner does not possess such skill and competence. The alternative way of putting the case is that the instructor voluntarily agrees to run the risk of injury resulting from the learner's lack of skill and experience.

The point may be tested in this way: suppose that the instructor is paid for the lessons he gives and there is a contract governing the relationship between the parties, but the contract is silent about the duty owed by the learner to the instructor. It is well settled that the law will not imply any term into such a contract unless it is necessary to do so for the purpose of giving to the contract ordinary business efficacy. Could it really be said that in order to give this contract ordinary business efficacy; it is necessary to imply a term that the learner owed the instructor a duty to drive with the degree of skill and competence which both parties know that he does not possess? If the law were to imply such a term, far from it giving the contract efficacy, it would, in my view, only make itself and the contract look absurd.

Nor can I think that even when there is no payment and no contract, the special relationship between the parties can as a rule impose any such duty upon the learner. Indeed such a duty is excluded by that relationship.

If, however, the learner, for example, refuses to obey instructions or suddenly accelerates to a high speed or pays no attention to what he is doing and as a result the instructor is injured, then, in my view, the learner is in breach of duty and liable to the instructor in damages. The duty is still the duty to use reasonable care and skill in all the relevant circumstances. What is reasonable depends, however, on the special relationship existing between the learner and his instructor. This relationship, in my view, makes the learner's known lack of skill and experience a highly relevant circumstance.

I do not think that the learner is usually liable to his instructor if an accident occurs as a result of some mistake which any prudent beginner doing his best can be expected to make. I recognise that on this view, cases in which a driving instructor is injured while his pupil is driving may raise difficult questions of fact and degree. Equally difficult questions of fact and degree are, however, being assessed and decided in our courts every day. The law lays down principles but not a rule of thumb for deciding issues arising out of any special relationship between the parties. A rule of thumb, if it existed, might no doubt remove difficulties, but could hardly produce justice either in practice or in theory.

It does not appear to me to be incongruous that a learner is responsible for acts or omissions in criminal law and indeed to the public at large in civil law and yet not necessarily responsible for such acts or omissions to his instructor. The learner has no special relationship with the public. The learner is certainly not liable to his instructor if his responsibility is excluded by contract. I can see no reason why, in the absence of contract, the same result should not follow from the special relationship between the parties.

For the reasons I have stated, I would, but for one factor, agree with the judge's decision in favour of the defendant. I have, however, come to the conclusion, not without doubt, that this appeal should be allowed. Mr. Nettleship when he gave evidence was asked: "Q. Was there any mention made of what the position would be if you were involved in an accident? A. I had checked with Mr. and Mrs. Weston regarding insurance, and I was assured that they had fully comprehensive insurance which covered me as a passenger in the event of an accident." Mrs. Weston agreed, when she gave evidence, that this assurance had been given before Mr. Nettleship undertook to teach her. In my view this evidence completely disposes of any possible defence of *volenti non fit injuria*. Moreover, this assurance seems to me to be an integral part of the relationship between the parties. In *Hedley Byrne & Co. Ltd. v. Heller & Partners Ltd.* ([1964] A.C. 465), the House of Lords decided that the relationship which there existed between the parties would have imposed a duty of care upon the defendants in giving the plaintiffs information but for the fact that the defendants gave the information "without responsibility." This disclaimer of responsibility was held to colour the whole relationship between the parties by negativing any duty of care on the part of the defendants.

Much the same result followed when a passenger accepted a lift in a car which exhibited a notice stating: "Warning. Passengers travelling in this vehicle do so *at their own risk*": *Bennett* v. *Tugwell* ([1971] 2 Q.B. 267). The present case is perhaps the converse of the cases of *Hedley Byrne* and *Bennett* v. *Tugwell*.

On the whole, I consider, although with some doubt, that the assurance given to Mr. Nettleship altered the nature of the relationship which would have existed between the parties but for the assurance. The assurance resulted in a relationship under which Mrs. Weston accepted responsibility for any injury which Mr. Nettleship might suffer as a result of any failure on her part to exercise the ordinary driver's standards of reasonable care and skill . . .

Questions

1. Suppose that the lessons had been given in the plaintiff's car and he sued in respect of damage suffered by it. Same result?

2. Would the result have been the same if the means of harm had been a motorised lawn-mower in the use of which the plaintiff was giving the defendant instruction on the defendant's premises? Suppose Albert was teaching Bella how to play Frisbee in a public park and, owing to her lack of deftness, he is struck in the eye by it.

3. Why must learner drivers carry visible "L" plates on the car?

4. Personal factors, irrelevant to criminal guilt, may be taken into account in sentencing. If personal factors are made irrelevant to civil liability, can or should they be taken into account in assessing damages? Were they taken into account in this case?

5. What is the duty of a driving examiner? And what is the duty of the candidate towards him? The answers are in a case involving a collision between two candidates: *British School of Motoring* v. *Simms* [1971] 1 All E.R. 317.

6. Are you surprised to learn that a teacher may sue his pupil for being inept?

Note:

Lord Denning said that the professional—as opposed to the amateur—instructor might be unable to sue by reason of an implied term to that effect in the contract. Such a term, if express, would be void by s.142 Road Traffic Act 1972 (if the accident took place on the highway). Thus the only way to prevent recovery by the professional instructor is to hold that the pupil is not guilty of negligence at all simply by reason of his lack of *savoir faire*. The High Court of Australia so held in *Cook* v. *Cook* 68 A.L.R. 353 (1986), and expressly disapproved of the reasoning of Lord Denning and of Megaw L.J. The defendant who had hardly ever driven a car before and had no licence of any kind was nevertheless urged by the plaintiff to take the wheel. She mismanaged a corner and thought she was going to strike a stationary car: to avoid doing so she accelerated and struck a stobie pole which she had failed to observe. The Court held that a collision with the stationary car would not have been actionable, since it would be attributable to mere inexperience, but that to accelerate into the unseen stobie pole was actionable imprudence rather than excusable inexperience.

Brennan J. said (at p. 365): " . . . the driver was under a duty of care to the passenger because it was reasonably foreseeable that a failure to exercise reasonable care in driving was likely to result in injury to the plaintiff; the circumstances out of which the duty arose included the plaintiff's knowledge, when she accepted carriage in the vehicle, that the driver was inexperienced; the standard of care required to discharge the driver's duty in the circumstances is the standard of an inexperienced driver of ordinary prudence."

The splendid judgment of Mason, Wilson, Deane & Dawson JJ. contains the following passage: "In relation to other users of the highway, the duty of care of both instructor and pupil will ordinarily fall to be measured by the same objective standard since the relevant relationship will be the ordinary one between a driver and another user of the highway. As between themselves, however, it would be to state a half-truth to say that the relationship was, if the pupil was driving, that of driver and passenger. The special circumstances of such a case remove the relationship into a distinct category or class which, while possessing the requisite degree of proximity, could not rationally be seen as giving rise to a duty to drive with the skill reasonably to be expected of a competent and experienced driver. Indeed, it is the very absence of that skill which lies at the heart of the special relationship between the driving instructor and his pupil. In such a case, the standard of care which arises from the relationship of pupil and instructor is that which is reasonably to be expected of an unqualified and inexperienced driver in the circumstances in which the pupil is placed. The standard of care remains an objective one. It is, however, adjusted to fit the special relationship under which it arises."

But driving is not the only activity which can only be learnt by doing it: doctoring is another. The difference is that while no social obloquy attaches to the incompetent driver, a doctor who is held negligent suffers a very serious professional set-back. Thus in *Wilsher* v. *Essex AHA* [1986] 3 All E.R. 801 at 833, the Vice-Chancellor said: "The houseman had to take up his post in order to gain full professional qualification; anyone who . . . wishes to obtain specialist skills has to learn those skills by taking a post in a specialist unit. In my judgment, such doctors cannot in fairness be said to be at fault if, at the start of their time, they lack the skills which they are seeking to acquire." This was countered by Glidewell L.J. at 831: "In my view, the law requires the trainee or learner to be judged by the same standard as his more experienced colleagues. If it did not, inexperience would frequently be urged as a defence to an action for professional negligence." Mustill L.J. took an intermediate line: "In a case such as the present, the standard is not just that of the average competent and well-informed junior houseman (or whatever the position of the doctor) but of such a person who fills a post in a unit offering a highly specialised service. But, even so, it must be recognised that different posts make different demands. If it is borne in mind that the lower rank will be occupied by those of whom it would be wrong to expect too much, the risk of abuse by litigious patients can be mitigated . . . " (*id.* at 813).

Further Note:
One's only purpose in asking whether a duty is to do one's best or to do as well as others do (subjective/objective?) is to find out whether what the defendant actually did constituted a breach of his duty, whichever it was. That is the subject-matter of the next chapter.

Take *Roberts* v. *Ramsbottom*, for example ([1980] 1 All E.R. 7). One morning a 73-year old accountant was about to drive his wife to the office some $2\frac{1}{2}$ miles away when he suffered a quite unheralded stroke which impaired his consciousness considerably. He forgot all about his wife and drove off. He managed to negotiate a few corners but then struck a parked van. He told the van-driver he felt all right and continued his progress. Next he knocked a boy off his bike and finally rammed the plaintiff's stationary car and injured the family by it. He was held liable despite his curious condition since it fell short of automatism and complete loss of consciousness, and because after striking the van he should have realised (though he could not) that he was unfit to continue driving. "An impairment of judgment does not provide a defence." In *Waugh* v. *James K. Allen* (1964) S.L.T. 269 (H.L.) by contrast, the man at the wheel could not be said to be driving at all, as he had suffered a total black-out, and he was not liable for remaining at the wheel since there was no premonition of the heart-attack.

Many people think that one should get damages if one is run into by a driver who has had a heart attack; but is this very different from suffering a heart attack oneself?

Chapter 2

BREACH

Section 1.—Specific or General?

QUALCAST (WOLVERHAMPTON) LTD. v. HAYNES

House of Lords [1959] A.C. 743; [1959] 2 W.L.R. 510; 103 S.J. 310; [1959] 2 All E.R. 38

Action by employee against employer in respect of personal injury

The plaintiff was an experienced metal moulder, employed by the defendants; he burnt his left foot when the ladle of molten metal he was holding slipped from his grasp. He was wearing ordinary leather boots at the time. His employers had a stock of protective spats for the asking and of reinforced boots at a price, but they had never urged the plaintiff to wear them. The county court judge felt bound by authority to hold that the employers were under a duty to urge the plaintiff to wear protective clothing, and gave judgment for the plaintiff, subject to 75 per cent. contributory negligence. He also said: "I think he knew of all the risks involved and quite voluntarily decided to wear the boots which he was wearing, and I believe that since the accident and since his return to work as a moulder he has not worn any protective clothing."

The Court of Appeal affirmed the judgment for the plaintiff [1958] 1 W.L.R. 225. The defendants appealed to the House of Lords, and their appeal was allowed.

Lord Somervell of Harrow: My Lords, I also would allow the appeal. In the present case the county court judge, after having found the facts, had to decide whether there was, in relation to this plaintiff, a failure by the defendants to take reasonable care for his safety. It is, I think, clear from the passage cited by my noble and learned friend that he would have found for the defendants but for some principle laid down, as he thought, by the authorities, to which he referred.

I hope it may be worth while to make one or two general observations on the effect on the precedent system of the virtual abolition of juries in negligence actions. Whether a duty of reasonable care is owed by A to B is a question of law. In a special relationship such as that of employer to employee the law may go further and define the heads and scope of the duty. There are cases in your Lordships' House which have covered this ground, I would have thought by now, exhaustively (*Wilson's and Clyde Coal Co. Ltd.* v. *English* ([1938] A.C. 57); *Latimer* v. *A.E.C. Ltd.* ([1953] A.C. 643); *General Cleaning Contractors Ltd.* v. *Christmas* [below p. 104]; and there are, of course, others). There would seem to be little, if anything, that can be added to the law. Its application in borderline cases may, of course, still come before appellate tribunals. When negligence cases were tried with juries the judge would direct them as to the law as above. The question whether on the facts in that particular case there was or was not a failure to take reasonable care was a question for the jury. There was not, and could not be, complete uniformity of standard. One jury would attribute to the reasonable man a greater degree of prescience than would another. The jury's decision did not become part of our law citable as a precedent. In those days it would only be in very exceptional circumstances that a judge's direction would be reported or be citable.

100

So far as the law is concerned they would all be the same. Now that negligence cases are mostly tried without juries, the distinction between the functions of judge and jury is blurred. A judge naturally gives reasons for the conclusion formerly arrived at by a jury without reasons. It may sometimes be difficult to draw the line, but if the reasons given by a judge for arriving at the conclusion previously reached by a jury are to be treated as "law" and citable, the precedent system will die from a surfeit of authorities. In *Woods* v. *Durable Suites Ltd.* ([1953] 1 W.L.R. 857) counsel for the plaintiff was seeking to rely on a previous decision in a negligence action. Singleton L.J. said this: "That was a case of the same nature as that which is now under appeal. It is of the greatest importance that it should be borne in mind that though the nature of the illness and the nature of the work are the same, the facts were quite different. Mr. Doughty claims that the decision of this court in *Clifford* v. *Charles H. Challen & Son Ltd.* ([1951] 1 K.B. 495) lays down a standard to be adopted in a case of this nature. In other words, he seeks to treat that decision as deciding a question of law rather than as being a decision on the facts of that particular case."

In the present case, and I am not criticising him, the learned county court judge felt himself bound by certain observations in different cases which were not, I think, probably intended by the learned judges to enunciate any new principles or gloss on the familiar standard of reasonable care. It must be a question on the evidence in each case whether, assuming a duty to provide some safety equipment, there is a duty to advise everyone, whether experienced or inexperienced, as to its use. . . .

I have come to the conclusion that the learned judge's first impulse was the right conclusion on the facts as he found them, and for the reasons which he gives. I will not elaborate these reasons or someone might cite my observations as part of the law of negligence.

Lord Denning: My Lords, in 1944 du Parcq L.J. gave a warning which is worth repeating today: "There is danger, particularly in these days when few cases are tried with juries, of exalting to the status of propositions of law what really are particular applications to special facts of propositions of ordinary good sense"; see *Easson* v. *London & North Eastern Railway Co.* ([1944] K.B. 421, 426).

In the present case the only proposition of law that was relevant was the well-known proposition—with its threefold sub-division—that it is the duty of a master to take reasonable care for the safety of his workmen. No question arose on that proposition. The question that did arise was this: What did reasonable care demand of the employers in this particular case? That is not a question of law at all but a question of fact. To solve it the tribunal of fact—be it judge or jury—can take into account any proposition of good sense that is relevant in the circumstances, but it must beware not to treat it as a proposition of law. I may perhaps draw an analogy from the Highway Code. It contains many propositions of good sense which may be taken into account in considering whether reasonable care has been taken, but it would be a mistake to elevate them into propositions of law.

Applying this to the present case: You start with the fact that, when a moulder in an iron foundry carries a ladle full of hot molten metal and pours it into the moulding box, there is a danger that the hot metal may splash over onto his feet. In order to safeguard him from injury, the employers ought, I should have thought, to provide protective footwear for him. But in saying so, I speak as a juryman, for it is not a proposition of law at all, but only a proposition of good sense. If the employers fail to provide protective footwear, the tribunal of fact can take it into account in deciding whether the employers took reasonable care for the safety of their men.

But the question here is not whether the employers ought to provide protective footwear for the men—for they clearly did so. The question is whether, having provided spats and boots, they ought to go further and *urge* the men to wear them. Here too I should have thought that the employers ought to advise and encourage the men to wear protective footwear. But again I speak as a juryman and not as a judge: because it is not a proposition of law at all, but a proposition of good sense. And that is the very point where the county court judge fell into error. He treated it as matter of strict law. He thought that, as this man "was never told that they must be worn," he was *bound by authority* to find that the employers were negligent. He treated it almost as on a par with a statutory regulation: whereas it was nothing of the kind. The distinction was taken by Lord Wright 25 years ago: "Whereas at the ordinary law the standard of duty must be fixed by the verdict of a jury, the statutory duty is conclusively fixed by the statute"; see *Lochgelly Iron & Coal Co. Ltd.* v. *M'Mullan* ([1934] A.C. 1). So here, this being a case governed by the common law and not by any statute or regulation, the standard of care must be fixed by the judge as if he were a jury, without being rigidly bound by authorities. What is "a proper system of work" is a matter for evidence, not for law books. It changes as the conditions of work change. The standard goes up as men become wiser. It does not stand still as the law sometimes does.

I can well see how it came about that the county court judge made this mistake. He was presented with a number of cases in which judges of the High Court had given reasons for coming to their conclusions of fact. And those reasons seemed to him to be so expressed as to be rulings in point of law: whereas they were in truth nothing more than propositions of good sense. This is not the first time this sort of thing has happened. Take accidents on the road. I remember well that in several cases Scrutton L.J. said that "if a person rides in the dark he must ride at such a pace that he can pull up within the limits of his vision" (*Baker* v. *E. Longhurst & Sons Ltd.* ([1933] 2 K.B. 461, 468)). That was treated as a proposition of law until the Court of Appeal firmly ruled that it was not (*Tidy* v. *Battman* ([1934] 1 K.B. 319); *Morris* v. *Luton Corporation* ([1946] K.B. 114)). So also with accidents in factories. I myself once said that an employer must, by his foreman, "do his best to keep [the men] up to the mark" (*Clifford* v. *Charles H. Challen & Son Ltd.* ([1951] 1 K.B. 495)). Someone shortly afterwards sought to treat me as having laid down a new proposition of law, but the Court of Appeal, I am glad to say, corrected the error (*Woods* v. *Durable Suites Ltd.* ([1953] 1 W.L.R. 857)). Such cases all serve to bear out the warning which has been given in this House before. " . . . we ought to beware of allowing tests or guides which have been suggested by the court in one set of circumstances, or in one class of cases, to be applied to other surroundings," and thus by degrees to turn that which is at bottom a question of fact into a proposition of law. That is what happened in the cases under the Workmen's Compensation Act and it led to a "wagon-load of cases"; see *Harris* v. *Associated Portland Cement Manufacturers Ltd.* ([1939] A.C. 71, 78) by Lord Atkin. Let not the same thing happen to the common law, lest we be crushed under the weight of our own reports.

Seeing, then, that the county court judge fell into error, what should the Court of Appeal have done? The answer seems to me this: the Court of Appeal should have done as the judge would have done if he had not felt bound by authority. He would have found that the employers had not been guilty of negligence. . . . In this case I would not myself be prepared to differ from the judge's view that there was no negligence on the part of the employers in regard to this particular workman. He knew all there was to know, without being told; and he voluntarily decided to wear his own boots, which he had bought for the purpose.

Only one word more. It is on causation. Even if it had been the duty of the employers to urge this workman to wear spats, I do not think their omission should be taken to be one of the causes of the accident. It is often said that a person who omits to do his duty "cannot be heard to say" that it would have made no difference even if he had done it: see *Roberts* v. *Dorman Long & Co. Ltd.* ([1953] 1 W.L.R. 942, 946). But this is an overstatement. The judge *may* infer the omission to be a cause, but he is not bound to do so. If, at the end of the day, he thinks that, whether the duty was omitted or fulfilled, the result would have been the same, he is at liberty to say so. So here, this workman, after he recovered from the injury, went back to work and did the same as before. He never wore spats. If the warning given by the accident made no difference, we may safely infer that no advice beforehand would have had any effect.

I would allow the appeal.

Question

If this case says, as it seems to, that all fact situations are as a matter of law distinguishable, what becomes of the principle of *stare decisis*, if that principle is based on the view that like cases should be treated alike?

Note:

This decision should deter counsel from citing decisions on breach as authority for the case in hand, and dissuade the student faced with a problem from hunting down cases "on all fours," like a housewife seeking a matching thread in a haberdashery. But the student may have to read a good many cases in order to gain vicariously the experience which lies at the root of sound judgment. Despite the best efforts of the higher courts, however, counsel (who are paid by the day) continue to cite enormous numbers of cases (see *Lambert* v. *Lewis* [1982] A.C. 225) and county court judges (who are paid to use their judgment) continue to apply decisions on breach as if they laid down fixed rules ("inching forward into traffic isn't negligence," *Worsfold* v. *Howe* [1980] 1 All E.R. 1028).

Another effect of the principal decision is to emphasise that the proper form of question, when one is dealing with breach of duty, is "Did the defendant take reasonable care?" One must not pick on some feature of the defendant's acts and say: "Was he under a duty not to do that?" (see also *A.C. Billings & Sons* v. *Riden* [1958] A.C. 240, 264, *per* Lord Somervell of Harrow). Of course, the plaintiff must normally identify what it was in the defendant's behaviour that he finds objectionable—*e.g.*, that he omitted to give a signal before turning right on the highway. But the question remains "Did the defendant drive with reasonable care, considering that he gave no signal?" and does not become "Was the defendant under a duty to give a signal?" Matters of detail are to be treated as part of the question of breach, not as raising sub-duties with a specific content.

A different approach is, however, to be found in *Smith* v. *Littlewoods Organisation* [1987] 1 All E.R. 710 (H.L.), where youths entered the defendant's unoccupied and unguarded cinema and started a fire which spread to, and burnt, the plaintiffs' buildings next door. It was agreed, Lord Goff dissenting, that the defendant owed his neighbours a "general duty" to exercise reasonable care to prevent his building becoming a source of danger to theirs. So far, so good. But then, as Lord Brandon put it, "The second question is whether that general duty encompassed a specific duty to exercise reasonable care to prevent young persons obtaining unlawful access to the cinema and, having done so, unlawfully setting it on fire," and Lord Mackay speaks of "the duty to take a particular precaution."

This approach is unsatisfactory for practical as well as aesthetic reasons. For even if it is now accepted that the *foreseeability* of resultant harm is not of itself a sufficient reason for imposing a duty to take care to avoid it, but that in all the circumstances it must be *reasonable* to impose such a duty, nevertheless it is more clearly established that the test of *breach of duty* is not whether the harm was foreseeable or not but whether the defendant's behaviour was reasonable or not (in the light of what might have been foreseen, and how likely it was and how harmful it was likely to be and how much it would have cost to avoid it etc. etc.).

Lord Goff very appropriately observes that "it would be quite wrong if householders were to be held liable in negligence for acting in a socially acceptable manner," but the reason they are not to be held liable is not that they owe their neighbours no duty to behave in a normally prudent householderly manner but that they have, in fact, so behaved and have not breached the duty incumbent upon them.

In *Smith* v. *Littlewoods Organisation* the real question was whether the defendant should be blamed for not having mounted a 24-hour guard on their premises, which were not especially attractive or inflammable or situated in an area rife with vandalism, seeing that they did not know, and were not at fault in not knowing, that vandals had already tried their hand at arson there. It is the same question as the question in *Bolton* v. *Stone* (below p. 107), namely whether the cricket club, who clearly owed a duty to passersby outside, were to be blamed for continuing to play cricket; or in *Glasgow Corp.* v. *Muir* (below p. 116) whether the manageress of the tea-room was to be blamed for not clearing the premises when a tea-urn was being carried through.

The approach of Lord Griffiths in *Smith* is to be preferred: "I agree that mere foreseeability of damage is certainly not a sufficient basis to found liability. But with this warning I doubt that more can be done than to leave it to the good sense of the judges to apply realistic standards in conformity with generally accepted patterns of behaviour to determine whether in the particular circumstances of a given case there has been a breach of duty sounding in negligence."

So, too, with regard to doctors. The general duty of the doctors treating the plaintiff, is, in the words of Lord Diplock, "not subject to dissection into a number of component parts to which different criteria of what satisfy the duty of care apply" (see [1985] A.C. 871, 893) cited by Stephen Brown J. in *Gold* v. *Haringey Health Auth'y* [1987] 2 All E.R. 888, 896.

GENERAL CLEANING CONTRACTORS LTD. v. CHRISTMAS

House of Lords [1953] A.C. 180; [1953] 2 W.L.R. 6; 97 S.J. 7; [1952] 2 All E.R. 1110; 51
L.G.R. 109

Action by employee against employer in respect of personal injury

The plaintiff was cleaning the library windows of the Caledonian Club on the instructions of his employers for whom he had worked for 20 years. After cleaning the inside, he went outside on to the sill, which was 6¼ inches wide and 27 feet above the ground. He cleaned the outside top sash and pushed it up, leaving the bottom sash slightly open so as to afford himself a grip on the underside of the top sash. Then the bottom sash suddenly fell as such sashes were known to do; it dislodged the plaintiff's fingers and caused him to fall.

He sued both the occupiers and his employers, and succeeded against both at first instance [1951] W.N. 294. The Court of Appeal reversed the decision against the Club (and there was no appeal against that reversal), but affirmed the judgment against the employers [1952] 1 K.B. 141. The employers appealed to the House of Lords, and their appeal was dismissed.

Lord Reid: My Lords, it appears that it has for long been the general practice of window cleaners to clean the outsides of ordinary two-sash windows while standing on the window sill outside the window. When the sill is narrow, as it often is, the window cleaner must have something to hold on to, and it is unusual for there to be anything for the cleaner to grasp except part of the window itself. If the window is completely closed there is nothing to grasp, but if either the top or bottom sash is even slightly open there is room for the cleaner to insert his fingers between the wooden bar which forms the bottom of the top sash and the panes of glass in the lower sash. It might seem that, even with this hold, the cleaner's position is precarious and unsafe, but the evidence in this case is not to that effect. A window cleaner with this hold does not appear to be in greater danger than men who work in many other trades in exposed places high above the ground with apparently little to assist them to keep their balance. But a peculiar danger in window cleaning arises from the fact that sometimes a sash moves down unexpectedly so as to deprive the man of his hold, and the evidence shows that it is not very uncommon for this to happen and to cause a serious accident. The respondent in this case was severely injured by an accident of this kind.

The main case made for the respondent in his pleadings and at the trial was that this method of cleaning windows is in itself so unsafe that a master who requires his servants to adopt it is in breach of his duty to provide a safe system of working. Two other methods of doing this kind of work were advocated. In the first place it was said that it could be done by men standing on ladders. It was proved that it would have been practicable and reasonably safe to use this method to clean the outside of the window where this accident happened: this window was on the first floor. But there was no evidence about the general applicability of this method, and it seems fairly obvious that it would not be practicable in a large number of cases. The main objection to using it where it is practicable is that it takes longer and is more expensive to clean windows in this way than by standing on the sill. The other method advocated is to support the man on the sill by a safety belt. Such a belt must be attached to two hooks—one on either side of the window—and these hooks must be firmly attached to the building so as to support his whole weight if he slips. It was not disputed that, to get sufficient strength, the shaft of the hook must be driven right through the wall of the building from the outside and then anchored in some way on the inside of the wall. No evidence was led about the cost or difficulty of doing this, but it is plainly an operation which could not be carried out by a window cleaner, and, if this is to be the only alternative to using ladders, I think that I must assume that vast numbers of these hooks would be needed: the evidence shows that such hooks have only been provided in a very small proportion of existing buildings. The evidence is that even where hooks are available the men generally do not use them.

A plaintiff who seeks to have condemned as unsafe a system of work which has been generally used for a long time in an important trade undertakes a heavy onus: if he is right it means that all, or partically all, the numerous employers in the trade have been habitually neglecting their duty to their men. The evidence in this case appears to me to be quite inadequate to establish either that the window sill method is so inherently dangerous that it cannot be made reasonably safe by taking proper precautions, or that the ladder method or the safety belt method are as a general rule reasonably practicable alternatives.

That brings me to what I have found to be the most difficult part of the case. The evidence does prove that the window sill method is often dangerous if no precautions are taken, and in this case no precautions were taken; and if the respondent is to succeed it must, I think, be on the ground that it was the duty of the appellants to devise for the window sill method a proper system of precautions and instruct their servants to follow that system, and that, if they had done so and their orders had been obeyed, this accident would, or at least would probably, have been prevented. No such case is made in the pleadings and no attempt was made to prove it at the trial. The best that can be said is that the pleadings can perhaps be read so as not to exclude it, and there are a number of bits of evidence which, if eked out with common knowledge, lend support to it. I would not think it proper or fair to the appellants to consider this case were it not for the fact that the appellants' counsel in effect asked us to treat the case as a test case and enlighten employers in the trade as to their duty. In the circumstances I think that I can properly consider this case on such evidence as there is to support it.

The need to provide against the danger of a sash moving unexpectedly appears to me to be so obvious that, even if it were proved that it is the general practice to neglect this danger, I would hold that it ought not to be neglected and that precautions should be taken. It is at this point that lack of evidence causes difficulty, for there is no evidence as to what would be reasonably practicable or effective precautions. But I cannot believe that there would be any great difficulty in devising a simple method of preventing the lower sash from closing. I do not know what the best method would be. Generally the plaintiff ought to put forward some method which can be tested by evidence. But in this case I am assisted by the fact that the appellants in their defence allege negligence against the respondent " . . . (b) if he knew of the said defect, [the tendency of this window to move easily] in taking no or no adequate steps to wedge or secure the said window; (c) if he did not know of the said defect, in taking no or no adequate steps to ascertain whether it was safe to rely on the sashes of the said window for handhold." This is in line with the impression which I get from the evidence, that a simple test would show whether a sash is loose or not and that if it moved at all easily it could be wedged or something could be placed across the window sill which would prevent the sash from closing fully. It does appear from the evidence that very simple tests after the accident showed that this sash was loose and ran down very easily. I think that this ought to have been discovered before the accident, and I think that I am entitled to assume that if it had been discovered some simple and effective precaution could have been taken. But I must confess that even in this case I make this assumption with some reluctance in the absence of evidence and I would not be prepared to do so in a less clear case.

The question then is whether it is the duty of the appellants to instruct their servants what precautions they ought to take and to take reasonable steps to see that those instructions are carried out. On that matter the appellants say that their men are skilled men who are well aware of the dangers involved and as well able as the appellants to devise and take any necessary precautions. That may be so but, in my opinion, it is not a sufficient answer. Where the problem varies from job to job it may be reasonable to leave a great deal to the man in charge, but the danger in this case is one which is constantly found, and it calls for a system to meet it. Where a practice of ignoring an obvious danger has grown up I do not think that it is reasonable to expect an individual workman to take the initiative in devising and using precautions. It is the duty of the employer to consider the situation, to devise a suitable system, to instruct his men what they must do and to supply any implements that may be required such as, in this case, wedges or objects to be put on the window sill to prevent the window from closing. No doubt he cannot be certain that his men will do as they are told when they are working alone. But if he does all that is reasonable to ensure that his safety system is operated he will have done what he is bound to do. In this case the appellants do not appear to have done anything as they thought they were entitled to leave the taking of precautions to the discretion of each of their men. In this I think that they were in fault, and I think that this accident need not have happened if the appellants had done as I hold they ought to have done. I therefore agree that the appeal should be dismissed.

Question

If the plaintiff had been employed cleaning windows for 20 years, did he or his employer know more about the risks of cleaning windows?

Note:

Here we have the backside of the point made in *Qualcast* v. *Haynes* (above, p. 100). The employers wanted to be told authoritatively exactly what they must do to comply with the requirement of the common law that they take reasonable care of their employees. They didn't learn much from their appeal to the House of Lords; they were told that they must do what was reasonable; and they knew that before.

This illustrates something about the common law of negligence. It says after the event whether something was done badly or not; it does not give instructions about how to act well. That is for the legislature to do; and we shall see shortly (below, p. 168) how the judges react when the legislature has done so.

In the Court of Appeal [1952] 1 K.B. 141, 149, Denning L.J. said: "If employers employ men on this dangerous work for their own profit, they must take proper steps to protect them, even if they are expensive. If they cannot afford to provide adequate safeguards, then they should not ask them to do it at all. It is not worth the risk." Is it worth the risk that, in a country without full employment, the employee's family should have a weekly pay packet rather than unemployment benefit only? An employee has even brought an action against an employer on the ground that it was careless of the employer to give the employee a job she had asked for. The action failed only on appeal (*Withers* v. *Perry Chain Co.* [1961] 1 W.L.R. 1314). In Scotland a man with no sight in one eye and defective vision in the other has success-fully alleged that his employer was negligent in letting him do outside work (*Porteous* v. *National Coal Board*, 1967 S.L.T. 117).

A recent decision is more sensible. A person who had been employed as a labourer for three months was offered and accepted a job as a grinder. Grinders are inevitably apt to be affected by Raynaud's Phenomenon, or VIF (vibration-induced white finger) which is at least disagreeable and may be worse. The plaintiff was thus affected and had to revert to a less well-paid job. He lost his suit. Lawton L.J. said: " . . . if a job has risks to health and safety which are not common knowledge but of which an employer knows or ought to know and against which he cannot guard by taking precautions, then he should tell anyone to whom he is offer-ing the job what those risks are if, on the information then available to him, knowledge of those risks would be likely to affect the decision of a sensible level-headed prospective employee about accepting the offer." (*White* v. *Holbrook Precision Castings* [1985] I.R.L.R. 215 (C.A.)).

All employees at work—some 21 million of them—are covered by the industrial injuries compensation scheme, under which a claim does not depend on proof that anyone was to blame or that the claimant was not. The scheme provides a reduced earnings allowance and, regardless of reduced earnings, a disability pension if the disability exceeds 14 per cent. (Social Security Act 1986, s.39). The practice of paying a lump sum for disability of less than 20 per cent. was terminated in 1986: we may therefore expect an increase in the number of minor tort claims. As it is, plaintiffs in 48 per cent. of personal injury cases in the Royal Courts of Justice, and 29 per cent. overall, have trade union support for their litigation.

Note that the occupier of the premises which had the defective window-sash was held not liable. This result is now endorsed by Occupiers' Liability Act 1957, s.2(3)(*b*), (below, p. 114).

Section 2.—What is Reasonable?

BOLTON v. STONE

House of Lords [1951] A.C. 850; [1951] 1 T.L.R. 977; [1951] 1 All E.R. 1078; 50 L.G.R. 32; 95 S.J. 333

Action by pedestrian against occupier of land adjoining the highway in respect of personal injury

On August 9, 1947, Miss Stone was standing on the highway outside her home and was struck by a cricket ball hit by a visiting batsman from the grounds of the Cheetham Cricket Club which adjoined the highway. She sued the committee and members of the Club, not including the batsman in question.

The ground had been used for cricket since 1864, long before the surrounding houses were built. Balls were only rarely hit over the fence during a match, and committee members could not recall an accident. A nearer neighbour said that balls had been hit into his yard. This particular ball had travelled 78 yards before passing over the fence (the top of which was seven feet above the highway and 17 feet above the pitch) and about 25 yards further before striking Miss Stone.

The plaintiff claimed damages on the ground of negligence and nuisance. The particulars of negligence alleged were that the defendants "(a) pitched the cricket pitch too near to the said road; (b) failed to erect a . . . fence . . . of sufficient height to prevent balls being struck into the said road; (c) failed to ensure that cricket balls would not be hit into the said road."

Oliver J. gave judgment for the defendants [1949] 1 All E.R. 237. The Court of Appeal, by a majority, allowed the plaintiff's appeal, on the grounds that the defendants were guilty of negligence [1950] 1 K.B. 201. The defendants' appeal to the House of Lords was allowed.

Lord Radcliffe: My Lords, I agree that this appeal must be allowed. I agree with regret, because I have much sympathy with the decision that commended itself to the majority of the members of the Court of Appeal. I can see nothing unfair in the appellants being required to compensate the respondent for the serious injury that she has received as a result of the sport that they have organised on their cricket ground at Cheetham Hill. But the law of negligence is concerned less with what is fair than with what is culpable, and I cannot persuade myself that the appellants have been guilty of any culpable act or omission in this case.

I think that the case is in some respects a peculiar one, not easily related to the general rules that govern liability for negligence. If the test whether there has been a breach of duty were to depend merely on the answer to the question whether this accident was a reasonably foreseeable risk, I think that there would have been a breach of duty, for that such an accident might take place some time or other might very reasonably have been present to the minds of the appellants. It was quite foreseeable, and there would have been nothing unreasonable in allowing the imagination to dwell on the possibility of its occurring. But there was only a remote, perhaps I ought to say only a very remote, chance of the accident taking place at any particular time, for, if it was to happen, not only had a ball to carry the fence round the ground but it had also to coincide in its arrival with the presence of some person on what does not look like a crowded thoroughfare and actually to strike that person in some way that would cause sensible injury.

Those being the facts, a breach of duty has taken place if they show the appellants guilty of a failure to take reasonable care to prevent the accident. One may phrase it as "reasonable care" or "ordinary care" or "proper care"—all these phrases are to be found in decisions of authority—but the fact remains that, unless there has been something which a reasonable man would blame as falling beneath the standard of conduct that he would set for himself and require of his neighbour, there has been no breach of legal duty. And here, I think, the respondent's case breaks down. It seems to me that a reasonable man, taking account of the chances against an accident happening, would not have felt himself called upon either to abandon the use of the ground for cricket or to increase the height of his surrounding fences. He would have done what the appellants did: in other words, he would have done nothing. Whether, if the unlikely event of an accident did occur and his play turn to another's hurt, he would have thought it equally proper to offer no more consolation to his victim than the reflection that a social being is not immune from social risks, I do not say, for I do not think that that is a consideration which is relevant to legal liability.

I agree with the others of your Lordships that if the respondent cannot succeed in negligence she cannot succeed on any other head of claim.

Questions

1. Would the defendants be liable if a similar accident occurred today?

2. Would the result have been the same if Miss Stone had been sitting in her garden at the time the ball struck her?

3. Suppose that the ball had been struck during practice at the nets rather than during a match. Same result?

4. Suppose that Miss Stone had been (a) a spectator or (b) the tea-lady in the pavilion. In

what terms would one decide her suit against (a) the cricket club and (b) the batsman? (See *Wooldridge* v. *Sumner*, above, p. 89).

Note:

The reason for selecting this speech (rather than Lord Reid's, for example) is that Viscount Radcliffe makes it quite clear that the ultimate and vital question is "Was the conduct unreasonable?" and not "Was the harm foreseeable?" Of course if behaviour is apparently innocuous, *i.e.*, such that no one would foresee any harm resulting from it, yet unpredictably causes some freak damage, we would not make the defendant pay. If behaviour is dangerous, on the other hand, *i.e.* such that one could foresee harm resulting from it, we are tempted to castigate it. But it is not *all* dangerous conduct which renders a person liable, it is only *unreasonably* dangerous conduct, conduct which, in the light (*inter alia*) of the recognisable danger, is *unreasonable*.

Sixteen years later Lord Reid was still in some perplexity over this case. In *The Wagon Mound (No. 2)* [1967] 1 A.C. 617, he said this:

"*Bolton* v. *Stone* posed a new problem. There a member of a visiting team drove a cricket ball out of the ground on to an unfrequented adjacent public road and it struck and severely injured a lady who happened to be standing in the road. That it might happen that a ball would be driven on to this road could not have been said to be a fantastic or far-fetched possibility: according to the evidence it had happened about six times in 28 years. Moreover it could not have been said to be a far-fetched or fantastic possibility that such a ball would strike someone in the road: people did pass along the road from time to time. So it could not have been said that, on any ordinary meaning of the words, the fact that a ball might strike a person in the road was not foreseeable or reasonably foreseeable. It was plainly foreseeable; but the chance of its happening in the foreseeable future was infinitesimal. A mathematician given the data could have worked out that it was only likely to happen once in so many thousand years. The House of Lords held that the risk was so small that in the circumstances a reasonable man would have been justified in disregarding it and taking no steps to eliminate it.

It does not follow that, no matter what the circumstances may be, it is justifiable to neglect a risk of such a small magnitude. A reasonable man would only neglect such a risk if he had some valid reason for doing so: *e.g.*, that it would involve considerable expense to eliminate the risk. He would weigh the risk against the difficulty of eliminating it. If the activity which caused the injury to Miss Stone had been an unlawful activity there can be little doubt but that *Bolton* v. *Stone* would have been decided differently. In their lordships' judgment *Bolton* v. *Stone* did not alter the general principle that a person must be regarded as negligent if he does not take steps to eliminate a risk which he knows or ought to know is a real risk and not a mere possibility which would never influence the mind of a reasonable man. What that decision did was to recognise and give effect to the qualification that it is justifiable not to take steps to eliminate a real risk if it is small and if the circumstances are such that a reasonable man, careful of the safety of his neighbour, would think it right to neglect it.

In the present case there was no justification whatever for discharging the oil into Sydney Harbour. Not only was it an offence to do so, but also it involved considerable loss financially. If the ship's engineer had thought about the matter there could have been no question of balancing the advantages and disadvantages. From every point of view it was both his duty and his interest to stop the discharge immediately."

Cricket has given trouble more recently. In *Miller* v. *Jackson* [1977] Q.B. 966 a couple who had bought a new house on the edge of a small village cricket ground sought to have the cricket stopped and claimed damages. Contrast the views of Lord Denning M.R. and Geoffrey Lane L.J.:

Lord Denning M.R.: "The club were entitled to use this ground for cricket in the accustomed way. It was not a nuisance, nor was it negligence of them so to run it. Nor was the batsman negligent when he hit the ball for six. All were doing simply what they were entitled to do. So if the club had put it to the test, I would have dismissed the claim for damages also."

Geoffrey Lane L.J.: "The evidence . . . makes it clear that the risk of injury to property at least was both foreseeable and foreseen. It is obvious that such injury is going to take place so long as cricket is being played on this field. It is the duty of the cricketers so to conduct their operations as not to harm people they can or ought reasonably to foresee may be affected . . . The risk of injury to persons and property is so great that on each occasion when a ball comes over the fence and causes damage to the plaintiffs, the defendants are guilty of negligence."

Cumming-Bruce L.J. agreed with Geoffrey Lane L.J. in holding the cricket club liable in damages for negligence, but agreed with Lord Denning that the cricket should be allowed to continue: "So on the facts of this case a court of equity must seek to strike a fair balance between the right of the plaintiffs to have quiet enjoyment of their house and garden without exposure to cricket balls occasionally falling like thunderbolts from the heavens, and the opportunity of the inhabitants of the village in which they live to continue to enjoy the manly sport which constitutes a summer recreation for adults and young persons . . ."

But can the common law of negligence itself not "seek to strike a fair balance"? Surely the test of what is reasonable in all the circumstances (unlike the question whether harm was foreseeable) is an apt one for the purpose. Safety first equal?

So important is it to see that the question here is "was the conduct unreasonable?" rather than "was the harm foreseeable?" that at the risk of labouring the point we cite a glaring example of judicial confusion. *Smith* v. *Blackburn* [1974] R.T.R. 533 involved a head-on collision. Since the plaintiff was driving impeccably and the defendant was driving like a madman, the only question was whether the plaintiff's damages should be reduced on the ground that his failure to wear a seat-belt constituted contributory negligence. The judge said this:

> "The accident happened in an unusual place, the Bushey Road Flyover. Here was a one-way road going up to a rise to a crest and along that road Mr. Smith was driving his car absolutely normally. He was doing nothing wrong at all, and yet it was really suggested that he should have foreseen that a madman would drive up the flyover in the wrong direction, travelling along a one-way street in the opposite direction to that which he should have been, and at high speed, so that when he did meet somebody minding his own business, they collided head on.
>
> To start with in my judgment the law does not require a person in the position of Mr. Smith in the place where he was to foresee that that kind of accident will occur. He may foresee that he may come upon a broken-down vehicle or all sorts of things, but I see no ground for assuming that the law required Mr. Smith to foresee that.
>
> If the law does not require him to foresee it, why should the law be said to require him to take precautions against the possible event?"

Even if the accident was unforeseeable by Mr. Smith it was unreasonable of him not be wearing a seat-belt: seat-belts are no trouble to put on and they do in fact reduce the incidence of serious injury, so reasonable people wear them. Whether Mr. Smith's injuries would actually have been reduced by a seat-belt is a quite different question, but pointing to the improbability of the collision which took place does not help us to answer it.

Take another case. A man was employed to stamp the initials "CA" on steel tyres. The way everyone does this is to hold the stamp and hit it firmly with a heavy hammer. One day, after many many days of doing this more than 100 times a day, the plaintiff mishit the stamp and broke his thumb. The judge held that the accident was foreseeable (which no one who has used a hammer could deny) and that *therefore* the employer was negligent. The Court of Appeal reversed, because the judge "did not ask the proper and right question." *Pindall* v. *British Steel Corp.* (March 7, 1980). The proper question was whether the employer had acted reasonably, *i.e.* whether the system adopted or endorsed by him exposed the employee to unreasonable risk of harm, and the answer would depend on whether a rubber hammer or a thumb–guard should have been provided, whether there were any avoidable distractions in the workplace, whether the employee was kept at the task too long at a time, and so on, virtually *ad infinitum*.

WATT v. HERTFORDSHIRE COUNTY COUNCIL

Court of Appeal [1954] 1 W.L.R. 835; 118 J.P. 377; 98 S.J. 372; [1954] 2 All E.R. 368; 52 L.G.R. 383

Action by employee against employer in respect of personal injury

The plaintiff had for 12 years been a fireman at the Watford Fire Station. He was on duty on July 27, 1951, when an emergency call was received; a woman was trapped under a heavy vehicle only 200 or 300 yards away. The sub-officer in charge left the station immediately after giving instructions that the plaintiff's team should follow in a Fordson lorry and bring a large jack for lifting heavy weights. The jack, which stood on four small wheels and weighed two or three hundredweights, was put on the back of the lorry, where the plaintiff with two others steadied it. There was no mechanical means of securing the jack, since the lorry had a smooth floor and there was nothing to which the jack could be lashed. The driver had to brake suddenly. The three men in the back were thrown off balance, and the jack slewed forward, catching the plaintiff's ankle and causing him serious injuries. The fire station normally had a vehicle suitable for carrying the jack safely, but it was not in the station at the time. When that vehicle was not available and the jack was needed, it was the practice to notify another fire station; to follow that practice in this case would have involved a delay of at least 10 minutes.

The plaintiff failed before Barry J. [1954] 1 W.L.R. 208. The Court of Appeal, in unreserved judgments, dismissed his appeal.

Singleton L.J.: I am in complete agreement with the judgment of Barry J. but it is right that I should state my reasons for having formed that opinion.

The fire service is a service which must always involve risk for those who are employed in it, and, as Mr. Baker on behalf of the plaintiff pointed out, they are entitled to expect that their equipment shall be as good as reasonable care can secure. An emergency arose, as often happens. The sub-officer who had given the order, was asked in re-examination: "From your point of view you thought it was a piece of luck, with this unfortunate woman under the bus, that the Fordson was available and you could use it? (A.) Yes. It is recognised in the service that we use our initiative at all times, and in doing so any reasonable step you take is considered satisfactory if it is a question of saving life. You have to make a sudden decision."

It is not alleged that there was negligence on the part of any particular individual, nor that the driver was negligent in driving too fast, nor that the sub-officer was negligent in giving the order which he did. The case put forward in this court is that as the defendants had a jack, it was their duty to have a vehicle fitted in all respects to carry that jack, from which it follows, I suppose, that it is said that there must be a vehicle kept at the station at all times, or that if there is not one the lifting jack must not be taken out; indeed, Mr. Baker claimed that in the case of a happening such as this, if there was not a vehicle fitted to carry the jack the sub-officer ought to have telephoned to the fire station at St. Albans and arranged that they should attend to the emergency. St. Albans is some seven miles away, and it was said that an extra 10 minutes or so would have elapsed if that had been done. I cannot think that that is the right way to approach the matter. There was a real emergency; the woman was under a heavy vehicle; these men in the fire service thought that they ought to go promptly and to take a lifting jack, and they did so. Most unfortunately this accident happened.

What is the duty owed by employers? It has been stated often, and never more clearly than it was by Lord Herschell in *Smith* v. *Baker & Sons* ([1891] A.C. 325, 362), in these words: "It is quite clear that the contract between employer and employed involves on the part of the former the duty of taking reasonable care to provide proper appliances, and to maintain them in a proper condition, and so to carry on his operations as not to subject those employed by him to unnecessary risk."

The employee in this case was a member of the fire service, who always undertake some risk—but, said Mr. Baker, not this risk. Is it to be said that if an emergency call reaches a fire station the one in charge has to ponder on the matter in this way: "Must I send out my men with the lifting jack in these circumstances, or must I telephone to St. Albans, seven miles away, to ask them to undertake the task?" I suppose he must think about his duty; but what would a reasonable man do, faced as he was? Would the reasonably careful head of the station have done anything other than that which the sub-officer did? I think not. Can it be said, then, that there is a duty on the employers here to have a vehicle built and fitted to carry this jack at all times, or if they have not, not to use the jack for a short journey of 200 or 300 yards? I do not think that that will do.

Asquith L.J., in *Daborn* v. *Bath Tramways Motor Co. Ltd.* said ([1946] 2 All E.R. 333, 336): "In determining whether a party is negligent, the standard of reasonable care is that which is reasonably to be demanded in the circumstances. A relevant circumstance to take into account may be the importance of the end to be served by behaving in this way or in that. As has often been pointed out, if all the trains in this country were restricted to a speed of five miles an hour, there would be fewer accidents, but our national life would be intolerably slowed down. The purpose to be served, if sufficiently important, justifies the assumption of abnormal risk."

The purpose to be served in this case was the saving of life. The men were prepared to take that risk. They were not, in my view, called on to take any risk other than that which normally might be encountered in this service. I agree with Barry J. that on the whole of the evidence it would not be right to find that the employers were guilty of any failure of the duty which they owed to their workmen. In my opinion the appeal should be dismissed.

Denning L.J.: It is well settled that in measuring due care you must balance the risk against the measures necessary to eliminate the risk. To that proposition there ought to be added this: you must balance the risk against the end to be achieved. If this accident had occurred in a commercial enterprise without any emergency there could be no doubt that the servant would succeed. But the commercial end to make profit is very different from the human end to save life or limb. The saving of life or limb justifies taking considerable risk, and I am glad to say that there have never been wanting in this country men of courage ready to take those risks, notably in the fire service.

In this case the risk involved in sending out the lorry was not so great as to prohibit the attempt to save life. I quite agree that fire engines, ambulances and doctors' cars should not shoot past the traffic lights when they show a red light. That is because the risk is too great to warrant the incurring of the danger. It is always a question of balancing the risk against the end. I agree that this appeal should be dismissed.

Questions
1. Suppose the plaintiff had been a pedestrian run over by the driver in his haste to reach the scene of the emergency. Would his case have been stronger or weaker than that of the present plaintiff?
2. Could Watt recover from the person who carelessly provoked the emergency?
3. Would the answer have been any different if the cause of the injury had been a defective wheel on the jack?
4. Do you think that the pension schemes of local fire services take account of the risks of the calling?

WARD v. HERTFORDSHIRE COUNTY COUNCIL

Court of Appeal [1970] 1 W.L.R. 356; 114 S.J. 87; 68 L.G.R. 151; [1970] 1 All E.R. 535

Action for personal injuries by pupil against school

Lord Denning M.R. On 29th April 1966, Mrs. Ward took her two small children to the junior primary school at Sarratt in Hertfordshire. Timothy (the infant plaintiff) was about eight years of age, and Sarah five. She left them at the school at about 8.50 a.m. The school started at about 8.55 a.m. After she left them there, the infant plaintiff played with the other boys in the playground until school was ready. They decided to have a race up and down the playground. As the infant plaintiff was running, he tumbled. He tripped and fell against a wall at one side of the playground.

The wall was of a common type. It was built about 100 years ago. It had brick pillars and in between flints set in mortar. Just an ordinary flint wall. It was quite a low wall, 3 feet to 3 feet 6 inches high. The flints only came up to about 2 feet 3 inches above the ground, and there was a brick coping above. The infant plaintiff fell headlong, almost as it were diving into the wall. His head hit one of the flints. It must have had rather a sharp edge. He was seriously injured. Fortunately, he has made a remarkably good recovery. He had to have a plate put into his head, but he is now nearly normal. He can do most of the things a boy likes to do, except that he must not dive in the swimming bath, and he must not head the ball, and so forth. Naturally, the infant plaintiff's parents were very upset at this accident. They felt that the wall was dangerous; and, further, that there had not been proper supervision. So they brought this action against the local education authority for negligence and breach of duty.

The judge found ([1969] 1 W.L.R. 790, 794) that the playground "with its flint walls and sharp and jagged flints protruding, was inherently dangerous"; and that the local education authority was wrong in allowing it to be in that condition. He said that it ought to have rendered the wall or put up some railings or netting, or something of that kind, to prevent a child falling against it. Furthermore, he held that one of the teachers ought to have been in the playground supervising from the time when the children came in. The local education authority appeals to this court.

I must say, reviewing all the evidence, that I do not think that this wall was dangerous. One has only to look at the pictures to see that it is a wall of the commonest type. It is an ordinary flint wall. It was built in the days when flints were picked off the ground and used to make walls. One-third of this Hertfordshire village has flint walls like this; 16 of the schools in Hertfordshire have; and goodness knows how many in the country at large. At that time all the church schools were made in this way. These flint walls have, of course, their angles and sharp edges. But that does not mean that they are dangerous. We have lived with them long enough to know.

The infant plaintiff's parents sought to rely on previous accidents; but, when examined, they come to nothing. They happened to boys who were at the school some years ago, but have now grown up to be men. Each hurt himself against the wall. Mr. Bidderstaff was there over 30 years ago. He had been playing a game of football, and hit his head on the top of the wall, not on the flints. He had a bruise about the size of an egg. Mr. Parker was there 14 years ago. He was rushing across to see his father. He ran into the wall and hurt his knee, and the teacher bandaged it up. Mr. Styles was there 14 or 15 years ago. He tripped and fell into the wall and lost his front teeth. He said he hit against the flints, but he did not say that it was against the sharp edge. Those three incidents are just the ordinary sort of thing which happens in any playground. They do not show that the wall was dangerous.

I may add that the infant plaintiff's mother herself said that it never occurred to her to think that the wall was dangerous before the accident, and she was quite happy about it. I cannot see any evidence that the wall was dangerous.

The judge also held that there should have been supervision over the children in the playground. But I do not think that that was established. The headmaster said that the teachers took charge of the children from the moment they were due to be in school at 8.55 a.m. until the time when they were let out. Before the school began the staff were indoors preparing for the day's work. They cannot be expected to be in the playground, too. He said that even if he had been in the playground, he would not have stopped the children playing. It often happens that children run from one side of the playground to the other. It is impossible so to supervise them that they never fall down and hurt themselves. I cannot think that this accident shows any lack of supervision by the local education authority.

Great as is the respect which I have for the judge, I am afraid on this occasion I cannot go with him. It is a case where a small boy playing at school hurt himself badly, but the local education authority is not liable for it. . . .

Salmon L.J. delivered a concurring opinion.

Cross L.J. This wall is undoubtedly somewhat less suitable as a boundary wall to a school playground than the ordinary brick wall would be, because in unusual circumstances, such as most unfortunately arose in this case, a child falling against it may suffer much more serious injury than he would suffer from falling against an ordinary brick wall; but although I naturally hesitate to differ from a judge whose experience in this field is so much greater than my own, I cannot bring myself to think that this wall, which has stood in the school playground since 1862, has been such a source of danger that those in charge of the school were guilty of negligence in not having it rendered with a smooth surface or masked by a wooden fence or wire netting. I agree with Salmon L.J. that increased supervision would have been useless because it would be unreasonable for any supervisor to prevent or attempt to prevent children from running races between the walls. In the course of his judgment the judge said that—"a prudent parent of a large family would have realised that this playground, with its flint walls and sharp and jagged flints protruding, was inherently dangerous." But, as my Lords have pointed out, the parents of the children in this village seem not to have so regarded it, for they have never represented to the local education authority that this wall was a source of danger. With reluctance I agree that this appeal should be allowed.

Note:
  Things have come to a pretty pass when it can solemnly be argued that a local authority should put a fence round a wall, but the trial judge had "no hesitation at all in finding . . . that the defendant was guilty of a breach of its common law duty."

OCCUPIERS' LIABILITY ACT 1957

2.—(1) An occupier of premises owes the same duty, the "common duty of care," to all his visitors, except in so far as he is free to and does extend, restrict, modify or exclude his duty to any visitor or visitors by agreement or otherwise.

(2) The common duty of care is a duty to take such care as in all the circumstances of the case is reasonable to see that the visitor will be reasonably safe in using the premises for the purposes for which he is invited or permitted by the occupier to be there.

(3) The circumstances relevant for the present purpose include the degree of care, and of want of care, which would ordinarily be looked for in such a visitor, so that (for example) in proper cases—

  (*a*) an occupier must be prepared for children to be less careful than adults; and
  (*b*) an occupier may expect that a person, in the exercise of his calling, will appreciate and guard against any special risks ordinarily incident to it, so far as the occupier leaves him free to do so.

(4) In determining whether the occupier of premises has discharged the common duty of care to a visitor, regard is to be had to all the circumstances, so that (for example)—

  (*a*) where damage is caused to a visitor by a danger of which he had been warned by the occupier, the warning is not to be treated without more as absolving the occupier from liability, unless in all the circumstances it was enough to enable the visitor to be reasonably safe; and

(b) where damage is caused to a visitor by a danger due to the faulty execution of any work of construction, maintenance or repair by an independent contractor employed by the occupier, the occupier is not to be treated without more as answerable for the danger if in all the circumstances he had acted reasonably in entrusting the work to an independent contractor and had taken such steps (if any) as he reasonably ought in order to satisfy himself that the contractor was competent and that the work had been properly done.

(5) The common duty of care does not impose on an occupier any obligation to a visitor in respect of risks willingly accepted as his by the visitor (the question whether a risk was so accepted to be decided on the same principles as in other cases in which one person owes a duty of care to another).

(6) For the purposes of this section, persons who enter premises for any purpose in the exercise of a right conferred by law are to be treated as permitted by the occupier to be there for that purpose, whether they in fact have his permission or not.

Note:
According to s.1(1) these rules displace the common law. This is not always appreciated. See, *e.g.*, *Kealey* v. *Heard* [1983] 1 All E.R. 973, incorrectly following *Wheeler* v. *Copas* [1981] 3 All E.R. 405, where another ground of liability (bailee/bailor) existed. *Ogwo* v. *Taylor* [1987] 3 All E.R. 961 (H.L.) is also doubtful on this point.

HIGHWAYS ACT 1980

58.—(1) In an action against a highway authority in respect of damage resulting from their failure to maintain a highway maintainable at the public expense it is a defence (without prejudice to any other defence or the application of the law relating to contributory negligence) to prove that the authority had taken such care as in all the circumstances was reasonably required to secure that the part of the highway to which the action relates was not dangerous for traffic.

(2) For the purposes of a defence under subsection (1) above, the court shall in particular have regard to the following matters:

(a) the character of the highway, and the traffic which was reasonably to be expected to use it;

(b) the standard of maintenance appropriate for a highway of that character and used by such traffic;

(c) the state of repair in which a reasonable person would have expected to find the highway;

(d) whether the highway authority knew, or could reasonably have been expected to know, that the condition of the part of the highway to which the action relates was likely to cause danger to users of the highway;

(e) where the highway authority could not reasonably have been expected to repair that part of the highway before the cause of action arose, what warning notices of its condition had been displayed;

but for the purposes of such a defence it is not relevant to prove that the highway authority had arranged for a competent person to carry out or supervise the maintenance of the part of the highway to which the action relates unless it is also proved that the authority had given him proper instructions with regard to the maintenance of the highway and that he had carried out the instructions.

Note:
The House of Lords must soon resolve a disagreement in the Court of Appeal regarding the intensity and scope of the duty to maintain the highway (s.41, Highways Act 1980) to which

this section provides a defence. In *Haydon* v. *Kent C.C.* [1978] Q.B. 343 Lord Denning held that once it was shown that the highway was dangerous (though the mere fact of an accident did not establish that (*Meggs* v. *Liverpool Corp.* [1968] 1 All E.R. 1137)), the duty was absolute but covered only failure to repair structural defects and did not extend to the removal of adventitious hazards such as water, snow or ice. Goff and Shaw L.JJ. seemed to hold that the duty might extend beyond repair, but that the plaintiff must show a "culpable breach of [the] duty to maintain." In *Bartlett* v. *Department of Transport* (1984) 83 L.G.R. 579 a very careless driver was killed on the A34 in Oxfordshire which was dreadfully icy because the National Union of Public Employees forbade its members to salt or grit it. Boreham J. would have preferred to follow Lord Denning, but was able in any case to hold that the local authority could not be blamed for the continued icy condition of the highway.

GLASGOW CORPORATION v. MUIR

House of Lords [1943] A.C. 448; 112 L.J.P.C. 1; 169 L.T. 53; 107 J.P. 140; 59 T.L.R. 266; 87 S.J. 182; 41 L.G.R. 173; [1943] 2 All E.R. 44

Action by visitor against occupier in respect of personal injury

One Saturday afternoon in June 1940 a party of 30 to 40 members of the Milton Road Free Church were to have a picnic in the King's Park, Glasgow. It came on to rain, so their leader, McDonald, went to the defender's tearooms and asked the manageress, Mrs. Alexander, if they might eat their food there. Mrs. Alexander agreed, and charged them 12s. 6d. She then went back to serving a group of children at the sweet counter in the hall. McDonald and a boy of his party accordingly brought the urn of tea down to the building. As they entered the hall, the children at the sweet counter were about five feet away from them, and Mrs. Alexander had her back to the scene as she was scooping ice-cream from the freezer. McDonald suddenly lost his grip on the back handle of the urn and six children, including the pursuer, were scalded by its contents. No one knew why McDonald lost his grip on the urn, since the pursuer did not call him as a witness. The urn itself was a perfectly ordinary metal one with a lid, about 16 inches high, 15 inches in diameter, and weighing, when full, not more than 100 pounds.

After the evidence, the Lord Ordinary dismissed the action; the First Division of the Court of Session (the Lord President dissenting) allowed the pursuer's appeal, 1942 S.C. 126. The Corporation appealed to the House of Lords, who allowed the appeal.

Lord Macmillan: My Lords, the degree of care for the safety of others which the law requires human beings to observe in the conduct of their affairs varies according to the circumstances. There is no absolute standard, but it may be said generally that the degree of care required varies directly with the risk involved. Those who engage in operations inherently dangerous must take precautions which are not required of persons engaged in the ordinary routine of daily life. It is, no doubt, true that in every act which an individual performs there is present a potentiality of injury to others. All things are possible, and, indeed, it has become proverbial that the unexpected always happens, but, while the precept *alterum non laedere* requires us to abstain from intentionally injuring others, it does not impose liability for every injury which our conduct may occasion. In Scotland, at any rate, it has never been a maxim of the law that a man acts at his peril. Legal liability is limited to those consequences of our acts which a reasonable man of ordinary intelligence and experience so acting would have in contemplation. "The duty to take care," as I essayed to formulate it in *Bourhill* v. *Young* ([1943] A.C. 92, 104), "is the duty to avoid doing or omitting to do anything the doing or omitting to do which may have as its reasonable and probable consequence injury to others, and the duty is owed to those to whom injury may reasonably and probably be anticipated if the duty is not observed." This, in my opinion, expresses the law of Scotland and I apprehend that it is also the law of England. The standard of foresight of the reasonable man is, in one sense, an impersonal test. It eliminates the personal equation and is independent of the idiosyncrasies of the particular person whose conduct is in question. Some persons are by nature unduly timorous and imagine every path beset with lions. Others, of more robust temperament, fail to foresee or nonchalantly disregard even the most obvious dangers. The reasonable man is presumed to be free both from over-apprehension and from over-confidence, but there is a sense in which the standard of care of the reasonable man involves in its application a subjective element. It is still left to the judge to decide what, in the circumstances of the particular case, the reasonable man would have had in contemplation, and what, accordingly, the party sought to be made liable ought to have foreseen. Here there is room for diversity of view, as, indeed, is well illustrated in the present case. What to one judge may seem far-fetched may seem to another both natural and probable.

With these considerations in mind I turn to the facts of the occurrence on which your Lordships have to adjudicate. Up to a point the facts have been sufficiently ascertained . . . The question, as I see it, is whether Mrs. Alexander, when she was asked to allow a tea urn to be brought into the premises under her charge, ought to have had in mind that it would require to be carried through a narrow passage in which there were a number of children and that there would be a risk of the contents of the urn being spilt and scalding some of the children. If, as a reasonable person, she ought to have had these considerations in mind, was it her duty to require that she should be informed of the arrival of the urn, and, before allowing it to be carried through the narrow passage, to clear all the children out of it in case they might be splashed with scalding water? The urn was an ordinary medium-sized cylindrical vessel of about 15 inches diameter and about 16 inches in height made of light sheet metal with a fitting lid, which was closed. It had a handle at each side. Its capacity was about nine gallons, but it was only a third or a half full. It was not in itself an inherently dangerous thing and could be carried quite safely and easily by two persons exercising ordinary care. A caterer called as a witness on behalf of the pursuers, who had large experience of the use of such urns, said that he had never had a mishap with an urn while it was being carried. The urn was in charge of two responsible persons, McDonald, the church officer, and the lad, Taylor, who carried it between them. When they entered the passage way they called out to the children there congregated to keep out of the way and the children drew back to let them pass. Taylor, who held the front handle, had safely passed the children, when, for some unexplained reason, McDonald loosened hold of the other handle, the urn tilted over, and some of its contents were spilt, scalding several of the children who were standing by. The urn was not upset, but came to the ground on its base.

In my opinion, Mrs. Alexander had no reason to anticipate that such an event would happen as a consequence of granting permission for a tea urn to be carried through the passage way where the children were congregated, and, consequently, there was no duty incumbent on her to take precautions against the occurrence of such an event. I think that she was entitled to assume that the urn would be in charge of responsible persons (as it was) who would have regard for the safety of the children in the passage (as they did have regard), and that the urn would be carried with ordinary care, in which case its transit would occasion no danger to bystanders. The pursuers have left quite unexplained the actual cause of the accident. The immediate cause was not the carrying of the urn through the passage, but McDonald's losing grip of his handle. How he came to do so is entirely a matter of speculation. He may have stumbled or he may have suffered a temporary muscular failure. We do not know, and the pursuers have not chosen to enlighten us by calling McDonald as a witness. Yet it is argued that Mrs. Alexander ought to have foreseen the possibility, nay, the reasonable probability of an occurrence the nature of which is unascertained. Suppose that McDonald let go his handle through carelessness. Was Mrs. Alexander bound to foresee this as reasonably probable and to take precautions against the possible consequences? I do not think so. The only ground on which the view of the majority of the learned judges of the First Division can be justified is that Mrs. Alexander ought to have foreseen that some accidental injury might happen to the children in the passage if she allowed an urn containing hot tea to be carried through the passage, and ought, therefore, to have cleared out the children entirely during its transit, which Lord Moncrieff describes as "the only effective step." With all respect, I think that this would impose on Mrs. Alexander a degree of care higher than the law exacts. . . .

Lord Wright: My Lords, it is impossible not to feel a desire that the children, by or on behalf of whom these proceedings have been taken, should be compensated for the injuries sustained by them. It is true that the accident could not have occurred but for the action of Mrs. Alexander, the appellants' manageress, in giving permission that the tea urn should be carried through the short but narrow passage in which the children, about a dozen in number, were waiting as customers at the appellants' sweet counter to buy ices or sweets, but, to establish liability, the court has to be satisfied that the appellants owed a duty to the children, that that duty was broken, and that the children were injured in consequence of the breach.

That the appellants owed a duty to the children is not open to question. Your Lordships are not, therefore, on this occasion exercised by the problem which was presented recently in *Bourhill* v. *Young* ([1943] A.C. 92), which was whether the person injured came within the limits of foreseeable harm from the dangerous acts complained of. Here the children were on the appellants' premises in full view of Mrs. Alexander, the appellants' responsible servant, and were plainly liable to be injured if the place in which they were was rendered dangerous to them by Mrs. Alexander's act in consenting to the urn being carried through the place. The question thus is whether Mrs. Alexander knew or ought to have known that what she was permitting involved danger to the children. The same criterion applies in this connection as applied in the kindred problem in *Bourhill's* case, that is to say, the criterion of reasonable foreseeability of danger to the children. It is not a question of what Mrs. Alexander actually foresaw, but what the hypothetical reasonable person in Mrs. Alexander's situation would have foreseen. The test is what she ought to have foreseen. I may quote again as in *Bourhill's* case Lord Atkin's words in *Donoghue* v. *Stevenson*: "You must take reasonable care to avoid acts or omissions which you can reasonably foresee would be likely to injure your neighbour." On this occasion the children were "the neighbours." The act or omission to be avoided was creating a new danger in the premises by allowing the church party to transport the urn. If that issue is decided against the appellants, they must be held responsible in the action.

The issue can be stated on the general principles of the law of negligence without any reference to the special rules relating to the position of those who come as invitees upon premises. The children were clearly invitees within the rules laid down in *Indermaur* v. *Dames* ((1866) L.R. 1 C.P. 274), because they were customers at the appellants' shop, but that authority does no more than lay down a special sub-head of the general doctrine of negligence. . . .

Before dealing with the facts, I may observe that in cases of "invitation" the duty has most commonly reference to the structural condition of the premises, but it may clearly apply to the use which the occupier (or whoever has control so far as material) of the premises permits a third party to make of the premises. Thus, the occupier of a theatre may permit an independent company to give performances, or the person holding a fair may grant concessions to others to conduct side shows or subsidiary entertainments, which may, in fact, involve damage to persons attending the theatre or fair, and in such and similar cases the same test of reasonable foreseeability of danger may operate to impose liability on the person authorising what is done. The immediate cause of damage in such cases is generally the action of third parties who are neither servants nor agents of the defendant, but are mere licensees or concessionaires for whose acts as such the defendants are not directly liable. If the occupiers are held liable for what is done, it is because they are in law responsible in proper cases at an earlier stage because of the permission which they gave for the use of their premises. This is the cause of action against them. Thus, in the present case the appellants are not primarily concerned with the manner in which the members of the church party carried the urn as they would have been if these members had been their servants or agents. The two men were mere licensees in the matter. The appellants were not directly responsible for their acts. If they are to be held responsible, it must be because, by the permission which Mrs. Alexander, their manageress, gave to the members of the church party, they created an unusual danger affecting the invitees, in particular, the children. The breach of duty (if any) may thus be stated to have been that in granting the permission they did not use reasonable foresight to guard the children from unusual danger arising from the condition or use of the premises. If the tea urn had been upset by the negligence of the appellants' servants, the appellants would have been liable in negligence. Whether or not they would have been liable as invitors in the alternative would depend on other considerations. The cause of action in invitation is different, because it depends primarily, not on what actually happened (except in the sense that what actually happened would be essential to complete the cause of action by showing damage), but on whether the invitor (it is convenient to use the word) knew or ought to have known that the invitee was being exposed to unusual danger. Where the unusual danger was due to structural defects the question can be stated to be whether the invitor knew or ought to have known of the defects. In a case like the present the question is whether it can be said of Mrs. Alexander that she either knew or ought to have known that the children would be exposed to unusual danger by reason of the uses to which the premises were put by her permission for the tea urn to be carried into and down the passage. It is not, of course, a question of what she actually thought at the moment but what the hypothetical reasonable person would have foreseen. That is the standard to determine the scope of her duty. This involves the question: Was the operation of carrying the tea urn something which a reasonable person in Mrs. Alexander's position should have realised would render the place in which it was performed dangerous to the children in the circumstances? This is the crucial issue of fact and the acid test of liability. On this crucial issue I agree with the Lord President. He said (1942 S.C. 126, 145): "I find myself unable to assent to the proposition that anything was authorised by the defenders or their servant in this case which obviously involved a danger which could not be avoided by the care of the men who carried the urn. The respondents [*i.e.*, the defenders] were not bound to take precautions against dangers which were not apparent to persons of ordinary intelligence and prudence."

A distinction has been drawn in some cases between things intrinsically dangerous or dangerous *per se* and other things which are not dangerous in the absence of negligence. The correctness or value of that distinction has been doubted by eminent judges. I think, however, that there is a real and practical distinction between the two categories. Some things are obviously and necessarily dangerous unless the danger is removed by appropriate precautions. These are things dangerous *per se*. Other things are only dangerous if there is negligence. It is only in that contingency that they can cause danger. Thus, to introduce, not a tea urn, but a savage animal, such as a lion or a tiger, into the passage way would have been of the former class. Another illustration of the same class may be afforded by the performance in a circus on the flying trapeze. The ocupier who permits such a performance owes a duty to the members of the audience to protect them by sufficient netting or otherwise against the obvious risk of the performer missing his hold. The present case, however, in my opinion, falls under the other category. It was not, in my opinion, *per se* dangerous. I do not think that the safe carriage of the tea urn presented any reasonably foreseeable difficulty. The urn was about 16 inches high and about 15 inches in diameter. It was a cylinder of metal about one-eighth of an inch thick with a lid which was in position. It weighed at most about 100 pounds with the quantity of tea it contained. The handles for carrying it were about 18 inches apart. Two men should have had no difficulty in carrying it safely even if one had to go in front and one behind because of the narrow space, as the men actually did. There is no explanation of how the accident happened.

There seem to be only two possible alternatives, either a mere accident or negligence. In my opinion, neither hypothesis could impose liability on the appellants. As to negligence, the two men were not their servants. They were not responsible for their acts. That the men should be negligent in so simple an operation was not likely to happen. It was a mere possibility, not a reasonable probability. The men, if negligent, were, no doubt, responsible for their own negligence, but from the standpoint of the appellants the risk of negligence was a mere unlikely accident which no reasonable person in Mrs. Alexander's position could naturally be expected to foresee. The same is true of an accidental slip or loss of grip. To hold the appellants liable on either basis would be to make them insurers, which under the authorities they are not. In my opinion, no breach of duty or negligence by the appellants to the respondents has been established. . . .

In the present case, as I have stated, as the permitted operation was intrinsically innocuous, I do not think any obligation rested on Mrs. Alexander to attempt to supervise it. As a reasonable person, not having any ground for anticipating harm, she was entitled to go on with her proper work and leave the church party to do what was proper. There might, of course, be circumstances in which, because there was an obvious risk, a duty might rest on the occupier to supervise the actual conducting of the operation if the permission was given. I do not see what Mrs. Alexander could have done in that respect unless she had seen that all the children were removed from the passage when the urn was being carried through. That might be her obligation if the operation she permitted had been intrinsically dangerous, but it was not so in the circumstances as I apprehend them. No doubt, some difficult questions of fact may arise in these cases. In the present case, however, as I think that there was no reasonably foreseeable danger to the children from the use of the premises which the appellants permitted to be made, I think the respondents' claim cannot be supported. In my judgment the appeal should be allowed.

Questions

1. Would the defenders have been liable if the urn had been carried in and dropped by a catering firm under contract with them?

2. Could the defenders have been held liable here without also making liable the inn-keeper whose guest drives his car into the car of another guest in the car-park?

Note:

McDonald would have been liable, because he could foresee that *if* he was careless the children might well be hurt, and he *was* careless. Mrs. Alexander could equally well foresee that *if* McDonald were careless the children might be hurt, but *she* was not careless, since she could not foresee that McDonald would in fact be clumsy, and only such a premonition would require her to put the children out in the rain.

Sometimes, however, one must foresee the carelessness of others. It is not careful to act on the assumption that other people will be careful when it is known that they are not. Drivers do in fact emerge without warning from side-roads. In *London Passenger Transport Board* v. *Upson* [1949] A.C. 155, 173, Lord Uthwatt said: "A driver is not, of course, bound to anticipate folly in all its forms, but he is not, in my opinion, entitled to put out of consideration the teachings of experience as to the form those follies commonly take."

Where wickedness rather than folly can be foreseen, it is more difficult to forestall its effects and consequently less unreasonable to proceed regardless (see below p. 000). But in all cases the irreducible question is whether the defendant behaved *reasonably*.

WYNGROVE'S CURATOR BONIS v. SCOTTISH OMNIBUSES LTD.

House of Lords, 1966 S.C.(H.L.) 47; 1966 S.L.T. 273

Action by passenger against carrier in respect of personal injuries

Lord Reid: On July 25, 1961, the late Mr. Wyngrove was a passenger in a bus operated by the appellants. The bus was travelling from Edinburgh to Glasgow and he intended to alight at a stop in Broxburn. Some distance before the bus reached the stop he fell from the rear platform and sustained very serious injuries. . . . He died recently and [the respondent] is now his executrix. The Lord Ordinary held that the appellants were in fault but that the deceased had been guilty of contributory negligence. He assessed damages at £12,500 but awarded one-quarter of that sum. The Second Division (Lord Wheatley and Lord Walker, Lord Strachan dissenting) also held that the appellants were in fault but they increased the sum awarded to three-quarters of £12,500. The appellants appeal on the ground that no fault has been proved against them. Alternatively they seek to have the Lord Ordinary's award of damages restored.

The bus was double-decked, the body being of Bristol Lodeka type. The entrance and exit are through a doorway on the near side at the rear. The doorway is 3 feet 6 inches wide and the door can be folded back when it is open, and made secure against the partition between the rear platform and the lower saloon by means of a catch. When the door is open, the aperture through which passengers alight is reduced to a width of 3 feet 2 inches.

The practice in operating buses of this type is to keep the door open in built-up areas where stops are frequent, but to shut it at least in bad weather when there is a long interval between stops. There is no central vertical pillar or rail in this doorway similar to the pillars which are generally provided in buses with open rear platforms. The case for the respondent is that, if such a door was to be kept open between stops, a central pillar in the doorway ought to have been provided as a handhold for passengers on the rear platform, or alternatively that the door ought to have been kept shut between stops: if either of these courses had been followed, this accident would have been prevented.

. . . The deceased was seated in the lower saloon. Some considerable distance before the bus reached the stop, he rose from his seat and stepped on to the rear platform. The bus was being driven smoothly and properly. There were two adequate handholds on the right-hand side, a vertical rail by the side of the saloon door, and a horizontal handrail on the folded door between the door of the saloon and the near side of the bus. But before he had grasped either of them, for some reason he lost his balance and fell outwards. He seems to have tried to grasp the horizontal rail but failed to do so. His left arm swung outwards and the respondent says that, if there had been a vertical pillar or rail in the middle of the doorway, he could have saved himself by grasping it, or at least it would have arrested his fall. The Lord Ordinary reached the opinion that a central pillar probably would have prevented the accident. This finding was attacked by the appellants and no doubt it is a matter of speculation what would have happened had there been a central pillar. But I see no ground for disagreeing with this finding. So the main question is whether such a pillar ought to have been provided. The Lord Ordinary and the majority of the Second Division have held that it ought to have been provided.

It is admitted that the appellants were aware that it was a general practice for passengers to leave their seats and move on to the rear platform before the bus reached the stop at which they intended to alight. And it is not denied that they were therefore under a duty to take all reasonable precautions for the safety of passengers while they were on the rear platform. Their defence is that there were already ample handholds on the rear platform—nine in all—and that a central pillar in the doorway was unnecessary and would have been inconvenient in obstructing passengers boarding or alighting from the bus.

It is convenient at this point to deal with the respondent's alternative case that the door should have been kept shut between stops. It appears from the evidence for the appellants that the door is not intended as a safety precaution: its sole purpose is to keep out bad weather. It is left to the discretion of the conductor to close the door when practicable in bad weather. In my view it is clearly proved that it is impracticable to close the door in parts of the route where stops are close together. If it is closed, the conductor must be beside it in time to open it at the next stop, and his ordinary duty of collecting fares would, if the bus were at all crowded, prevent him from being at the door in time for every stop.

So the substantial question is whether there ought to have been a central pillar bisecting the doorway vertically. There was no engineering difficulty in fitting such a pillar and its cost would have been small. The appellants' defence was that experience had proved that it was unnecessary and that it would have been an obstruction to passengers boarding or alighting from the bus. Buses of this type had been on the road for six years or more before the accident. The evidence is that in a year a bus carries some 200,000 passengers. Evidence was given by the appellants' manager and the managers of two other large bus companies. Between them they operate over 600 of this type of bus. None of these buses is fitted with a central pillar in the doorway. They are all operated on the same system of leaving it to the conductor to shut the door when that is practicable and desirable for the comfort of the passengers. The managers said that they all received reports of all accidents but that they were unaware of any case where an accident had been attributable to the absence of a central pillar or of any complaint that such pillars should be provided. We do not know how many of the many hundreds of millions of passengers carried by these buses had stood on the rear platforms when the doors were open while the bus was in motion but the number must have been very large. Accordingly the chance that a passenger, who for any reason lost his balance while standing on the rear platform, would be unable to save himself by grasping one of the nine handholds provided but would be saved by the presence of a central pillar, must on the evidence be held to be extremely small.

The evidence with regard to the inconvenience of having a central pillar in the doorway was not very specific. If there were a central pillar, neither half of the bisected doorway would have been more than 1 foot 7 inches wide and the minimum width for a doorway required by paragraph 27 of the Public Service Vehicles (Conditions of Fitness) Regulations 1958 (S.I. 1958/473) is 1 foot 9 inches. The third proviso in that paragraph is not easy to understand and I do not find it necessary to decide whether putting a central pillar in a doorway 3 feet 2 inches wide would infringe the Regulations. But I am satisfied that it would be an inconvenient obstruction if there were many passengers trying to alight from or board the bus at the same stop.

The Lord Ordinary held "that the pursuer has established the need for a central pillar, if the bus was to be operated with the door open, and that the defenders have not shown any sufficient reason why a central pillar should not have been provided." His main reasons for the first of these findings were that a passenger at the forward end of the platform might need a rail that could be grasped with his left hand as well as a rail he could grasp with his right hand, and that a central pillar would have reduced the risk of a passenger falling or being thrown off the platform. I think that he underestimated the importance of the evidence as to the use of hundreds of these buses for years without any accident of this kind being known. And there was no sufficient evidence that it is customary in any type of bus for there always to be available for any passenger moving in the bus while it is in motion two things to grasp—one for each hand. Indeed common knowledge strongly suggests the contrary. As regards his second finding he had held that a central pillar could not be placed in a doorway of this width, but he said that this could be overcome by making the entrance slightly wider. Clearly that could not be done without redesigning the rear part of the body of the bus. So he has in effect found that this type of bus is unsuitable for use on routes where it is often impracticable to keep the door shut between stops. In face of the evidence of the use of hundreds of these buses for years I am quite unable to agree that their design is unsafe.

Lord Wheatley held that "the reasonable provision of safety required a hand-rail or support available to either hand," and that even if it was inconvenient to have a central pillar in this doorway, safety must come before convenience. He was of opinion that the defenders could have kept the door closed at all times when the bus was in motion, even if this might require in practice a conductor on each deck. Lord Walker held that "reasonable care required a system of closing the door when passengers might be expected to be on the platform on approaching stopping places."

These findings also appear to me necessarily to lead to the conclusion that the design of these buses makes them unsafe for use in the way in which they are habitually used. It needs no evidence to show that it would be impracticable to have two conductors: the cost would be prohibitive without an increase in fares. And if it is impracticable always to keep the door shut between stops with only one conductor, and the provision of a central pillar in the doorway would at least cause frequent inconvenience, I see no escape from the conclusion that the buses are badly designed—a conclusion which on the evidence I am not prepared to accept.

I think that it is necessary to recall the well-established principles of law regarding the duty of a person towards passengers or other persons who are in his vehicle or on his premises. He must take all precautions for their safety which a reasonable and careful person in his position would take, and he must anticipate such a degree of inadvertence on their part as experience shows to be not uncommon. But he is entitled to have regard to his own experience and to that of others in a similar situation with regard to what precautions have been found to be adequate hitherto. It may be that these precautions ought to have been seen by him to be in fact inadequate, but the more extensive the past experience of safe working has been, the more difficult it will be to prove that he ought to have seen that enough was not being done. It is clearly foreseeable that a person leaving his seat in a moving vehicle may for some reason lose his balance, and if he is near the door, he may fall out. So adequate means must be provided to enable him to save himself, and the recognised means are handholds. Nine handholds are provided on the rear platform of this type of bus. There is evidence that in operating hundreds of this type of bus for a period of years in the way in which this bus was operated, no accident has been reported as attributable to the absence of a central pillar. So it appears to me to be clear that a reasonable person operating such a bus would not have thought that there was more than a very remote chance of a passenger who failed to grasp one of these nine handholds gaining any benefit from the presence of a central pillar. And if the risk of injury is so small, the reasonable man will consider the disadvantages of providing something additional which might in some very exceptional circumstances serve to prevent an accident. Here the disadvantage was the general inconvenience to many passengers in the regular use of the bus. In my opinion the evidence shows that it would have been unreasonable to fit central pillars in the doorway of these buses.

That is sufficient to decide the case in favour of the appellants. . . .

Note:

Scottish Omnibuses Ltd. is not, of course, an organ of government, but the decision impugned by the plaintiff here, namely to purchase buses of the construction in question, was a fairly high-level decision, and if the courts had held that decision to be a ground of liability, the financial consequences would have been enormous. In making decisions of such an order, safety is naturally an important consideration, but it is by no means the only one; in a tort case brought by a particular injured plaintiff, the tendency is to give too much importance to safety, simply because other factors may seem less important. In *Levine* v. *Morris* [1970] 1 W.L.R. 71 there was an accident on a highway built to less than the optimum specifications and the plaintiff was injured in a collision with the stanchion of a road-sign. The highway authority was held liable for siting the road-sign where it did, but not liable for building a less than splendid road. The latter holding is clearly right; but the former holding is justifiable only on the ground that the authority did not show that it had considered the question of safety at all when it was decided to site the sign where it did. In another case a person was killed at a delusive intersection; a "Give-Way" sign would clearly have reduced the chances of a collision. The point was not argued, but soon it will be, whether an authority may not be liable for failing to erect such a sign (*Macintyre* v. *Coles* [1966] 1 W.L.R. 831) or having traffic lights which change quickly (*Radburn* v. *Kemp* [1971] 1 W.L.R. 1502) or not keeping up a side road while a main road is being constructed (*Rider* v. *Rider* [1973] 1 Q.B. 505). It does not seem that courts are better qualified to weigh the conflicting interests of safety and traffic flow, or safety and visibility, or safety and expense, than experts in the field. A decision disturbing for analogous reasons is *Barnes* v. *Hampshire County Council* [1971] 1 W.L.R. 892. There the local authority had to pay a school-child aged five the sum of £10,000. She had been let out of school four minutes early on the day before the Whitsun break, had not waited for her mother (who was slightly late) and had been run over in the main street some yards away. Considering that many children were not met at all, the decision seems a doubtful one; but at least the House of Lords did not accede to the suggestion of the plaintiff's counsel that it was negligence in the school authority not to have a system of "pairing-off" whereby the kids would be kept by the teachers until someone appeared to take them individually away. Such a decision would not be an appropriate one for a court of justice to make.

The common law of trespass has been extremely useful in limiting the abuses of power by members of the executive; the common law of negligence seems a much less satisfactory form in which to challenge, at the instance of particular interests, decisions of a high order and political nature. Reference should be made again to the opinion of Lord Diplock in the *Dorset Yacht Co.* case [1970] A.C. 1004, 1057 and to the opinion of Lord Wilberforce in *Anns* (above, p. 60) with its distinction between the discretionary and the operational areas of government, invoked in *Haydon* (above p. 116) where the local authority responsible for miles and miles of roads had failed to salt and grit a particular icy footpath. One must also remember that it may be an abuse of process to try to question a public law decision in an ordinary action at law rather than by application for judicial review (*O'Reilly* v. *Mackman* [1982] 3 All E.R. 1124).

Question

Not long ago in the United States cars of a certain make tended to explode if rear-ended. This was because the petrol tank was situated in a relatively exposed position. When suit was brought on the part of incinerated passengers, it was discovered that the manufacturer had compared the cost of siting the tank in a safer place (as reflected in reduced income from sales by reason of the higher price) with the probable cost of paying damages to the victims injured by its being in the less safe place. People were outraged. Were they right to be so? Was the manufacturer's conduct reasonable (a) socially, (b) economically, (c) legally?

The outrage is manifest, for example, in *Ford* v. *Dunhill* 714 S.W.2d 329 (Tex.App. 1986) where a jury awarded $106,500,000, later reduced to a mere $12,311,000 (death by burning of young unmarried woman).

Section 3.—Special Plaintiffs

HALEY v. LONDON ELECTRICITY BOARD

House of Lords [1965] A.C. 778; [1964] 3 W.L.R. 479; 129 J.P. 14; 108 S.J. 637; [1964] 3 All E.R. 185

Action by pedestrian against person working on highway in respect of personal injury

The plaintiff, a blind man, was walking carefully with a stick along the pavement in a London suburb when he fell into a trench dug there by the defendants pursuant to statutory powers. He suffered personal injury subsequently evaluated at £7,000. In front of the trench the defendants had put a long-handled hammer, its head resting on the pavement and the handle on some railings two feet high. This was an adequate protection for pedestrians with sight, but it was insufficient for blind people.

Marshall J. gave judgment for the defendants, and the Court of Appeal affirmed this decision [1964] 2 Q.B. 121. The plaintiff's appeal to the House of Lords was allowed.

Lord Reid: . . . The trial judge held that what the respondents' men did gave adequate warning to ordinary people with good sight, and I am not disposed to disagree with that. The excavation was shallow and was to be filled in before nightfall, and the punner (or the pick and shovel) together with the notice boards and the heap of spoil on the pavement beside the trench were, I think, sufficient warning to ordinary people that they should not try to pass along the pavement past the trench. I agree with Somervell L.J. in saying that a person walking along a pavement does not have "to keep his eyes on the ground to see whether or not there is any obstacle in his path" (*Almeroth* v. *W.E. Chivers & Sons Ltd.* [1948] 1 All E.R. 53, 54). But even allowing for that degree of inadvertence of which most people are often guilty when walking along a pavement, I think that what the respondents' men did was just sufficient to attract the attention of ordinary people with good sight exercising ordinary care.

On the other hand, if it was the duty of the respondents to have in mind the needs of blind or infirm pedestrians I think that what they did was quite insufficient. Indeed, the evidence shows that an obstacle attached to a heavy weight and only nine inches above the ground may well escape detection by a blind man's stick and is for him a trap rather than a warning.

So the question for your Lordships' decision is the nature and extent of the duty owed to pedestrians by persons who carry out operations on a city pavement. The respondents argue that they were only bound to have in mind or to safeguard ordinary able-bodied people and were under no obligation to give particular consideration to the blind or infirm. If that is right, it means that a blind or infirm person who goes out alone goes at his peril. He may meet obstacles which are a danger to him but not to those with good sight because no one is under any obligation to remove or protect them. And if such an obstacle causes him injury he must suffer the damage in silence.

I could understand the respondents' contention if it was based on an argument that it was not reasonably foreseeable that a blind person might pass along that pavement on that day; or that, although foreseeable, the chance of a blind man coming there was so small and the difficulty of affording protection to him so great that it would have been in the circumstances unreasonable to afford that protection. Those are well recognised grounds of defence. But in my judgment neither is open to the respondents in this case.

In deciding what is reasonably foreseeable one must have regard to common knowledge. We are all accustomed to meeting blind people walking alone with their white sticks on city pavements. No doubt there are many places open to the public where for one reason or another one would be surprised to see a blind person walking alone, but a city pavement is not one of them. And a residential street cannot be different from any other. The blind people we meet must live somewhere and most of them probably left their homes unaccompanied. It may seem surprising that blind people can avoid ordinary obstacles so well as they do, but we must take account of the facts. There is evidence in this case about the number of blind people in London and it appears from Government publications that the proportion in the whole country is near one in 500. By no means all are sufficiently skilled or confident to venture out alone, but the number who habitually do so must be very large. I find it quite impossible to say that it is not reasonably foreseeable that a blind person may pass along a particular pavement on a particular day.

No question can arise in this case of any great difficulty in affording adequate protection for the blind. In considering what is adequate protection again one must have regard to common knowledge. One is entitled to expect of a blind person a high degree of skill and care because none but the most foolhardy would venture to go out alone without having that skill and exercising that care. We know that in fact blind people do safely avoid all ordinary obstacles on pavements; there can be no question of padding lamp posts as was suggested in one case. But a moment's reflection shows that a low obstacle in an unusual place is a grave danger: on the other hand, it is clear from the evidence in this case and also, I think, from common knowledge that quite a light fence some two feet high is an adequate warning. There would have been no difficulty in providing such a fence here. The evidence is that the Post Office always provide one, and that the respondents have similar fences which are often used. Indeed the evidence suggests that the only reason there was no fence here was that the accident occurred before the necessary fences had arrived. So if the respondents are to succeed it can only be on the ground that there was no duty to do more than safeguard ordinary able-bodied people. . . .

I can see no justification for laying down any hard-and-fast rule limiting the classes of persons for whom those interfering with a pavement must make provision. It is said that it is impossible to tell what precautions will be adequate to protect all kinds of infirm pedestrians or that taking such precautions would be unreasonably difficult or expensive. I think that such fears are exaggerated, and it is worth recollecting that when the courts sought to lay down specific rules as to the duties of occupiers the law became so unsatisfactory that Parliament had to step in and pass the Occupiers' Liability Act 1957. It appears to me that the ordinary principles of the common law must apply in streets as well as elsewhere, and that fundamentally they depend on what a reasonable man, careful of his neighbour's safety, would do having the knowledge which a reasonable man in the position of the defendant must be deemed to have. I agree with the statement of law at the end of the speech of Lord Sumner in *Glasgow Corporation* v. *Taylor* ([1922] 1 A.C. 44, 67): "a measure of care appropriate to the inability or disability of those who are immature or feeble in mind or body is due from others, who know of or ought to anticipate the presence of such persons within the scope and hazard of their own operations." I would therefore allow this appeal.

Question
If a sighted person had fallen into the trench, guarded as it was, would that person have recovered (a) nothing, or (b) a sum reduced by reason of his contributory negligence, (i) before this case, and (ii) after it?

Note:
Many of the people to whom accidents happen are people to whom accidents are particularly likely to happen. Wyngrove (last case) had no fingers on his right hand. The susceptible

plaintiff causes difficulties. The susceptibility may be physical—the sensitive housewife who contracts dermatitis from a "safe" detergent (*Board* v. *Thos. Hedley* [1951] 2 All E.R. 431; *Ingham* v. *Emes* [1955] 2 Q.B. 366); or mental—the child who takes a bomb for a toy (*Yachuk* v. *Oliver Blais* [1949] A.C. 386); or emotional—(*Bourhill* v. *Young* [1943] A.C. 92). It is usually impossible to use the concept of contributory negligence to limit liability to the sensitive—though if an epileptic takes to working at heights, his recovery may be restricted (*Cork* v. *Kirby Maclean* [1952] W.N. 399). The "thin-skull" rule (below, p. 191) makes it difficult to limit the amount of recovery once liability is admitted. One can feel some disquiet at the reaction of the law when a neurotic is totally unhinged by a shock which would cause transitory discomfort to a normal person, and it is really unacceptable that £56,045 be paid out to an emotionally labile mother who has a hysterical reaction to the slight injuries suffered by her nine-year old daughter in a minor accident due to the negligence of the driver of the taxi in which they were travelling (*Brice* v. *Brown* [1984] 1 All E.R. 997). But if one's claim for pain and suffering will not be reduced just because others would not have suffered so acutely, one's claim for loss of earnings will be reduced if a pre-existing ailment would in any case have shortened one's earning life. It is sometimes possible to say that no special duty was owed to the abnormally accident-prone (see *Phipps* v. *Rochester Corpn.*, next case); but not when the susceptibility is known (*Paris* v. *Stepney Borough Council* [1951] A.C. 367), or foreseeable (the principal case). The question of liability then turns on breach, and becomes a question of fact.

PHIPPS v. ROCHESTER CORPORATION

Queen's Bench [1955] 1 Q.B. 450; [1955] 2 W.L.R. 23; 119 J.P. 92; 99 S.J. 45; [1955] 1 All E.R. 129; 53 L.G.R. 80

Action by infant visitor against occupier of land in respect of personal injury

The plaintiff, a boy of five, and his sister, aged seven, crossed the defendant's land in order to go blackberrying. The defendant knew that people crossed its land, and apparently did not mind. The land was being developed as a housing estate, and, preparatory to the insertion of a sewer, the defendant had dug a trench about two and a half feet wide, eight or nine feet deep, and about a hundred yards long. The girl negotiated this hazard safely, but the plaintiff fell in and broke his leg. His claim was dismissed.

Devlin J.: . . . The trench was neither an allurement to a child nor a danger concealed from an adult or even from a big child. It was, however, a danger imperceptible by a little child of the plaintiff's age simply because he was not old enough to see the necessity of avoiding it or of taking special care; whether or not it was obvious to his eye, it was concealed from his understanding. The question of law is whether he is entitled to protection against that sort of danger.

Mr. Van Oss submits that, irrespective of any question of allurement, the duty towards little children should not be judged by adult standards. But he admits that the duty cannot be so high as to require the licensor to make the premises absolutely safe for them. The difficulty is to see upon what principle one stops short of that, once one gets away from the test of obviousness as perceived by the adult. A commonplace feature of a building or of land may be a danger to a little child; he may see much but apprehend little; he is usually impervious to warning. Is, then, the licensor, in the words of Hamilton L.J. in *Latham* v. *R. Johnson & Nephew Ltd.* ([1913] 1 K.B. 398, 414), "practically bound to see that the wandering child is as safe as in a nursery?" If the duty of a licensor towards such a child is converted into an obligation to make the premises safe, it means that the normal relationship of licensor and licensee has entirely ceased to apply. . . .

I have not been able to find in the cases which have been cited to me any clearly authoritative formulation of the licensor's duty towards little children. I think that the cases do show that judges have not allowed themselves to be driven to the conclusion that licensors must make their premises safe for little children; but they have chosen different ways of escape from that conclusion. . . .

I think that the general principle which governs the relationship between licensors and licensees can be made to work in the case of little children without the employment of any special device. The general principle is that a licensor must give warning of any danger which would not be perceived by a licensee using reasonable care for his own safety. In many cases the application of the rule raises the question whether the licensee has been guilty of contributory negligence. But that does not mean that, because a little child cannot be guilty of contributory negligence, the rule breaks down. The licensor's duty is not unbounded unless he can prove contributory negligence. There are limits to his duty which exist quite independently of the behaviour of the licensee in any particular case. His duty is to consider with reasonable care whether there are on his premises, so far as he knows their condition, any dangers that would not be obvious to the persons whom he has permitted to use them; and if there are, to give warning of them or to remove them. If he rightly determines a danger to be obvious, he will not be liable because some individual licensee, albeit without negligence in the special circumstances of his case, fails to perceive it. He must be taken to know generally the "habits, capacities and propensities" of those whom he himself has licensed, but not their individual peculiarities. In the light of that general knowledge and on the assumption that they will behave reasonably, he must determine what steps he will take. If he makes that determination carefully, he cannot be made liable, whatever may subsequently happen.

I think that it would be an unjustifiable restriction of the principle if one were to say that although the licensor may in determining the extent of his duty have regard to the fact that it is the habit, and also the duty, of prudent people to look after themselves, he may not in that determination have a similar regard to the fact that it is the habit, and also the duty, of prudent people to look after their little children. If he is entitled, in the absence of evidence to the contrary, to assume that parents will not normally allow their little children to go out unaccompanied, he can decide what he should do and consider what warnings are necessary on that basis. He cannot then be made liable for the exceptional child that strays, nor will he be required to prove that any particular parent has been negligent. It is, I think, preferable that this result should be achieved by allowing the general principle to expand in a natural way rather than by restricting its influence and then having to give it artificial aids in order to make it work at all in the case of little children.

The principle I am seeking to express is that contained in the passage from the speech of Lord Shaw in *Glasgow Corporation* v. *Taylor* ([1922] 1 A.C. 44, 61) where he says that the municipality is entitled to take into account that reasonable parents will not permit their children to be sent into danger without protection; that the guardians of the child and of the park must each act reasonably; and that each is entitled to assume of the other that he will. That passage was not spoken in reference to the English law of licence, but nevertheless it seems to me to express perfectly the way in which the English law can reasonably be applied. A licensor who tacitly permits the public to use his land without discriminating between its members must assume that the public may include little children. But as a general rule he will have discharged his duty towards them if the dangers which they may encounter are only those which are obvious to a guardian or of which he has given a warning comprehensible by a guardian. To every general rule there are, of course, exceptions. A licensor cannot divest himself of the obligation of finding out something about the sort of people who are availing themselves of his permission and the sort of use they are making of it. He may have to take into account the social habits of the neighbourhood. No doubt there are places where little children go to play unaccompanied. If the licensor knows or ought to anticipate that, he may have to take steps accordingly. But the responsibility for the safety of little children must rest primarily upon the parents; it is their duty to see that such children are not allowed to wander about by themselves, or at the least to satisfy themselves that the places to which they do allow their children to go unaccompanied are safe for them to go to. It would not be socially desirable if parents were, as a matter of course, able to shift the burden of looking after their children from their own shoulders to those of persons who happen to have accessible bits of land. Different consider-ations may well apply to public parks or to recognised playing grounds where parents allow their children to go unaccompanied in the reasonable belief that they are safe. . . .

If this be the true principle to apply, then I have to consider whether the corpor-ation ought in the present case to have anticipated the presence of the infant plain-tiff unaccompanied. I say "unaccompanied" because the sister, while doubtless able to take care of herself as is shown by her own avoidance of the trench, was not old enough to take care of her little brother as well. There is no evidence in this case to show that little children frequently went unaccompanied on the open space in a way which ought to have brought home to the corporation that that was the use which was being made of its licence. Apart from evidence of that sort, I do not think that the corporation ought to have anticipated that it was a place in which children of five would be sent out to play by themselves. It is not an overcrowded neighbourhood; it is not as if it were the only green place in the centre of a city. The houses had gardens in which small children could play; if it be material, I believe that at the relevant time the plaintiff's garden was in fact fenced. The parents of children who might be expected to play there all live near and could have made themselves familiar with the space. They must have known that building operations were going on nearby and ought to have realised that that might involve the digging of trenches and holes. Even if it be prudent, which I do not think it is, for a parent to allow two small children out in this way on an October evening, the parents might at least have satisfied themselves that the place to which they allowed these little children to go held no dangers for them. Any parent who looked could have seen the trench and taken steps to prevent his child going there while it was still open. In my judgment, the corporation is entitled to assume that parents would behave in this naturally prudent way, and is not obliged to take it upon itself, in effect, to discharge parental duties. I conclude, therefore, that the infant plaintiff was on the land as a licensee, but that there was no breach of the corporation's duty towards him.

Questions

1. The applicable law is now the Occupiers' Liability Act 1957 (above p. 114). Is the approach of Devlin J. still valid?

2. How much would you bet that the child was trying to jump across the trench when he fell in? How could you prove it? Would it make any difference if you could?

3. Why not simply ask whether the defendants had behaved reasonably? Should they have (a) not dug the trench in the first place, (b) put a warning notice on top of the spoil, (c) filled the trench in for the weekend or (d) fenced off the whole area?

Note:

Wilde's Selfish Giant, who kept out of his garden the children who wanted to play in it, had read his law-books. He knew that if he didn't chase them out, he would be held to have per-mitted them to be there. Once there, they would fall off his apple-trees and eat the berries on his precious but poisonous shrubs. There would be endless litigation to determine the concep-tual grounds of his liability or non-liability. So he kept them out. And they no doubt played in the street.

ROLES v. NATHAN

Court of Appeal [1963] 1 W.L.R. 1117; 107 S.J. 680; [1963] 2 All E.R. 908

Action by widow of visitor against occupier

The Manchester Assembly Rooms, owned and occupied by the defendant, were heated by an old coke-burning boiler which smoked badly. Two chimney sweeps were called to clean it, but it was no better after they had done so. An expert, Collingwood, was called, saw that the boiler-room was dangerous through fumes and succeeded, though only by force, in removing the sweeps from it. He said that the sweep-hole and inspection chamber should be sealed before the boiler was lit, and the sweeps undertook to do that. On Friday evening the defendant's son-in-law, Mr. Corney, went to the boiler-room and found the sweeps working there with the fire on. They had not finished sealing off the apertures, and were to return the next day with more cement. On Saturday morning they were found there dead, the fire still burning brightly.

Elwes J. gave judgment for the widows of the sweeps, but the Court of Appeal allowed the defendant's appeal, Pearson L.J. dissenting.

Lord Denning: . . . The judge found Mr. Corney guilty of negligence because "he failed to take such care as should have ensured that there was no fire lit until the sweep-hole had been sealed up." He said: "Unfortunately Mr. Corney did not tell the caretaker to draw the fire, or at any rate not to stoke it up." On this account he held that Mr. Corney was at fault, and the occupier liable. But he found the two sweeps guilty of contributory negligence, and halved the damages. The judge said: "That negligence"—that is to say, of the chimney sweeps—"consisted in the knowledge that there was gas about, or probably would be, the way they ignored explicit warnings and showed complete indifference to the danger which was pointed out to them in plain language, and this strange indifference to the fact that the fire was alight, when Mr. Collingwood had said it ought not to be, until the sweep-hole had been sealed."

The occupier now appeals and says that it is not a case of negligence and contributory negligence, but that, on the true application of the Occupiers' Liability Act 1957, the occupier was not liable at all. This is the first time we have had to consider that Act. It has been very beneficial. . . .

"The common duty of care," the Act says, "is a duty to take such care as in all the circumstances of the case is reasonable to see that the visitor"—note the visitor, not the premises—"will be reasonably safe in using the premises for the purposes for which he is invited or permitted by the occupier to be there." That is comprehensive. All the circumstances have to be considered. But the Act goes on to give examples of the circumstances that are relevant. The particular one in question here is in subsection (3) of section 2: "The circumstances relevant for the present purpose include the degree of care, and of want of care, which would ordinarily be looked for in such a visitor, so that (for example) in proper cases . . . (*b*) an occupier may expect that a person, in the exercise of his calling, will appreciate and guard against any special risks ordinarily incident to it, so far as the occupier leaves him free to do so."

That subsection shows that *General Cleaning Contractors* v. *Christmas* [above p. 104] is still good law under this new Act. There a window cleaner (who was employed by independent contractors) was sent to clean the windows of a club. One of the windows was defective; it had not been inspected and repaired as it should have been. In consequence, when the window cleaner was cleaning it, it ran down quickly and trapped his hand, thus causing him to fall. It was held that he had no cause of action against the club. If it had been a guest who had his fingers trapped by the defective window, the guest could have recovered damages from the club. But the window cleaner could not do so. The reason is this: the householder is concerned to see that the windows are safe for his guests to open and close, but he is not concerned to see that they are safe for a window cleaner to hold on to. The risk of a defective window is a special risk, but it is ordinarily incident to the calling of a window cleaner, and so he must take care for himself, and not expect the householder to do so. Likewise in the case of a chimney sweep who comes to sweep the chimneys or to seal up a sweep-hole. The householder can reasonably expect the sweep to take care of himself so far as any dangers from the flues are concerned. These chimney sweeps ought to have known that there might be dangerous fumes about and ought to have taken steps to guard against them. They ought to have known that they should not attempt to seal up a sweep-hole whilst the fire was still alight. They ought to have had the fire withdrawn before they attempted to seal it up, or at any rate they ought not to have stayed in the alcove too long when there might be dangerous fumes about. All this was known to these two sweeps; they were repeatedly warned about it, and it was for them to guard against the danger. It was not for the occupier to do it, even though he was present and heard the warnings. When a householder calls in a specialist to deal with a defective installation on his premises, he can reasonably expect the specialist to appreciate and guard against the dangers arising from the defect. The householder is not bound to watch over him to see that he comes to no harm. I would hold, therefore, that the occupier here was under no duty of care to these sweeps, at any rate in regard to the dangers which caused their deaths. If it had been a different danger, as for instance if the stairs leading to the cellar gave way, the occupier might no doubt be responsible, but not for these dangers which were special risks ordinarily incidental to their calling.

Even if I am wrong about this point, and the occupier was under a duty of care to these chimney sweeps, the question arises whether the duty was discharged by the warning that was given to them. This brings us to subsection (4) which states: "In determining whether the occupier of premises has discharged the common duty of care to a visitor, regard is to be had to all the circumstances, so that (for example)— (a) where damage is caused to a visitor by a danger of which he had been warned by the occupier, the warning is not to be treated without more as absolving the occupier from liability, unless in all the circumstances it was enough to enable the visitor to be reasonably safe."

We all know the reason for this subsection. It was inserted so as to clear up the unsatisfactory state of the law as it had been left by the decision of the House of Lords in *London Graving Dock Co.* v. *Horton* ([1951] A.C. 737). That case was commonly supposed to have decided that, when a person comes onto premises as an invitee, and is injured by the defective or dangerous condition of the premises (due to the default of the occupier), it is nevertheless a complete defence for the occupier to prove that the invitee knew of the danger, or had been warned of it. Suppose, for instance, that there was only one way of getting into and out of premises, and it was by a footbridge over a stream which was rotten and dangerous. According to *Horton's* case, the occupier could escape all liability to any visitor by putting up a notice: "This bridge is dangerous," even though there was no other way by which the visitor could get in or out, and he had no option but to go over the bridge. In such a case, section 2(4) makes it clear that the occupier would nowadays be liable. But if there were two footbridges, one of which was rotten, and the other safe a hundred yards away, the occupier could still escape liability, even today, by putting up a notice: "Do not use this footbridge. It is dangerous. There is a safe one further upstream." Such a warning is sufficient because it does enable the visitor to be reasonably safe.

I think that the law would probably have developed on these lines in any case; see *Greene* v. *Chelsea Borough Council* ([1954] 2 Q.B. 127), where I ventured to say "knowledge or notice of the danger is only a defence when the plaintiff is free to act upon that knowledge or notice so as to avoid the danger." But the subsection has now made it clear. A warning does not absolve the occupier, unless it is enough to enable the visitor to be reasonably safe.

Apply subsection (4) to this case. I am quite clear that the warnings which were given to the sweeps were enough to enable them to be reasonably safe. The sweeps would have been quite safe if they had heeded these warnings. They should not have come back that evening and attempted to seal up the sweep-hole while the fire was still alight. They ought to have waited till next morning, and then they should have seen that the fire was out before they attempted to seal up the sweep-hole. In any case they should not have stayed too long in the sweep-hole. In short, it was entirely their own fault. The judge held that it was contributory negligence. I would go further and say that under the Act the occupier has, by the warnings, discharged his duty.

I would therefore be in favour of allowing this appeal and entering judgment for the defendants.

Note:

1. Platform 4 at Neasden Station can be left in three ways—by subway at the North end, by footbridge at the South end, or across the (electrified) tracks. One morning the subway was flooded, and a notice was posted at the entrance to it saying "Subway flooded—do not cross tracks. Please go round by footbridge." The plaintiff followed others across the tracks and was run over by a train. The defendants were held liable, subject to 75 per cent. contributory negligence, for not warning the train drivers that people were crossing the tracks despite the warning. *Umeh* v. *London Transp. Exec.* (1984) 134 New L.J. 522 (McNeill J.).

2. Visiting firemen brought quite a lot of lawsuits in the past decade, and ended with a signal victory. It is now clear from *Ogwo* v. *Taylor* [1987] 3 All E.R. 961 (H.L.) that a householder who negligently starts a fire (in that case with a blow-lamp on a fascia board) is liable to an injured fireman even if there is nothing whatever peculiar about the fire or the premises. It is not that the fireman does not know his business or that you should help him with it: it is that he is only there about his dangerous business because you have been negligent. Nevertheless, the householder's liability to the fireman is not as extensive as his liability for burning down his neighbour's house: see below p. 394. Observations that the occupier's liability to the fireman is not based on the Occupiers' Liability Act seem groundless.

Section 4.—Skilful Defendants

WELLS v. COOPER

Court of Appeal [1958] 2 Q.B. 265; [1958] 3 W.L.R. 128; 102 S.J. 508; [1958] 2 All E.R. 527

Action by visitor against occupier in respect of personal injury

The plaintiff went to the defendant's house to deliver fish and was asked to stay for a cup of tea. After drinking it, he left by the back door. As he pulled it shut, with the force required by a strong wind and the draught-excluder, the door-handle came away in his hand, and he fell four feet to the ground from the top of the back steps. The door-handle, which was of the lever type, had been screwed on with three-quarter inch screws by the defendant himself, a "do-it-yourself" man who frequently did such jobs around the house; he replaced the previous door-handle since he thought it was unsafe.

Stable J. dismissed the action on the ground that the accident was not one which was reasonably foreseeable; the plaintiff appealed to the Court of Appeal without success.

Jenkins L.J.: . . . the duty owed by the defendant to the plaintiff was a duty to take reasonable care for his safety, and the question is whether on the facts of this case the defendant did take reasonable care to that end. . . .

As above related, the defendant did the work himself. We do not think the mere fact that he did it himself instead of employing a professional carpenter to do it constituted a breach of his duty of care. No doubt some kinds of work involve such highly specialised skill and knowledge, and create such serious dangers if not properly done, that an ordinary occupier owing a duty of care to others in regard to the safety of premises would fail in that duty if he undertook such work himself instead of employing experts to do it for him. See *Haseldine* v. *C.A. Daw & Son Ltd.*, *per* Scott L.J. ([1941] 2 K.B. 343, 356). But the work here in question was not of that order. It was a trifling domestic replacement well within the competence of a householder accustomed to doing small carpentering jobs about his home, and of a kind which must be done every day by hundreds of householders up and down the country.

Accordingly, we think that the defendant did nothing unreasonable in undertaking the work himself. But it behoved him, if he was to discharge his duty of care to persons such as the plaintiff, to do the work with reasonable care and skill, and we think the degree of care and skill required of him must be measured not by reference to the degree of competence in such matters which he personally happened to possess, but by reference to the degree of care and skill which a reasonably competent carpenter might be expected to apply to the work in question. Otherwise, the extent of the protection that an invitee could claim in relation to work done by the invitor himself would vary according to the capacity of the invitor, who could free himself from liability merely by showing that he had done the best of which he was capable, however good, bad or indifferent that best might be.

Accordingly, we think the standard of care and skill to be demanded of the defendant in order to discharge his duty of care to the plaintiff in the fixing of the new handle in the present case must be the degree of care and skill to be expected of a reasonably competent carpenter doing the work in question. This does not mean that the degree of care and skill required is to be measured by reference to the contractual obligations as to the quality of his work assumed by a professional carpenter working for reward, which would, in our view, set the standard too high. The question is simply what steps would a reasonably competent carpenter wishing to fix a handle such as this securely to a door such as this have taken with a view to achieving that object.

In fact the only complaint made by the plaintiff in regard to the way in which the defendant fixed the new handle is that three-quarter inch screws were inadequate and that one inch screws should have been used. The question may, therefore, be stated more narrowly as being whether a reasonably competent carpenter fixing this handle would have appreciated that three-quarter inch screws such as those used by the defendant would not be adequate to fix it securely and would accordingly have used one inch screws instead. . . .

In relation to a trifling and perfectly simple operation such as the fixing of the new handle we think that the defendant's experience of domestic carpentry is sufficient to justify his inclusion in the category of reasonably competent carpenters. The matter then stands thus. The defendant, a reasonably competent carpenter, used three-quarter inch screws, believing them to be adequate for the purpose of fixing the handle. There is no doubt that he was doing his best to make the handle secure and believed that he had done so. Accordingly, he must be taken to have discharged his duty of reasonable care, unless the belief that three-quarter inch screws would be adequate was one which no reasonably competent carpenter could reasonably entertain, or, in other words, an obvious blunder which should at once have been apparent to him as a reasonably competent carpenter. The evidence adduced on the plaintiff's side failed, in the judge's view, to make that out. He saw and heard the witnesses, and had demonstrated to him the strength of attachment provided by three-quarter inch screws. We see no sufficient reason for differing from his conclusion. Indeed, the fact that the handle remained secure during the period of four or five months between the time it was fixed and the date of the accident, although no doubt in constant use throughout that period, makes it very difficult to accept the view that the inadequacy of the three-quarter inch screws should have been obvious to the defendant at the time when he decided to use them. . . .

Each case of this kind depends on its own particular facts, to which the broad principle of reasonable care must be applied with common sense. The task of finding the facts and applying the principle to them is eminently a matter for the court of first instance. On the facts of this case, we find it impossible to hold that the judge came to a wrong conclusion, having regard in particular to the view which he took, and was entitled to take, of the expert evidence on the strength of which it was sought, after the event, to show that the defendant knew or ought to have known at the time when he fixed the handle that the three-quarter inch screws were inadequate, notwithstanding that they in fact sufficed to hold the handle securely for the four or five months of constant use which preceded the accident.

Accordingly, we would dismiss this appeal.

Questions
1. Which of the following statements are correct?

   (i) The question is not whether the defendant did his best.
  (ii) The question is not whether he did as well as a professional carpenter would have done, acting under contract.
 (iii) The question is whether he did as well as a professional carpenter working for himself on a Sunday afternoon.
 (iv) If the defendant was a carpenter of some experience, the question is whether he did his best, except in the case where he should have known that what he was doing would strike a professional carpenter as an obvious blunder.

2. If the defendant here had hired a carpenter to do the job, and that carpenter had done it as the defendant did here, and the defendant had fallen downstairs as a result, would the carpenter have been liable to the defendant? To the plaintiff? Would the defendant have been liable to the plaintiff?

Note:
Most of the cases so far have been concerned with care rather than with skill, but the distinction is not very clear. Some tasks call for expertise if they are to be properly executed. Those who embark on them without having that expertise are careless in embarking; those who have the expertise but do not use it are liable for the faulty execution. It is where, as in this case, it is not clear that only an expert would undertake the job that one has the problem of whether to apply the standard of the expert or not.

Cases involving professional skill are less amenable to a jury. The jury knows what should be done by a person in the shoes of Mrs. Alexander (*Glasgow Corpn.* v. *Muir,* above, p. 116), but cannot say, except at second hand and after conflicting expert evidence, what a man in a surgeon's mask should have done. Nevertheless, the same standard is applied, and a ruling which required gross negligence in a doctor was overruled in *Hunter* v. *Hanley,* 1955 S.L.T. 213. A deviation from proper practice generates liability. But this involves considerations of time and place. A doctor will not be liable for not having the latest equipment, or for not having read the latest number of an American learned periodical. One cannot demand from a garage in the West Highlands of Scotland the same standard of expedition and professional competence which can be hoped for in the metropolis. These factors can easily be taken into account in the professional negligence cases, since the plaintiff and defendant are almost always in a "special relationship," whether payment passes or not. If you *choose* to go to a jeweller in Hatton Garden to have your ears pierced, you cannot expect a Harley Street puncture (*Philips* v. *Whiteley* [1938] 1 All E.R. 566). But see the views of Megaw L.J. above, p. 94.

BOLAM v. FRIERN HOSPITAL MANAGEMENT COMMITTEE

Queen's Bench [1957] 1 W.L.R. 582; 101 S.J. 357; [1957] 2 All E.R. 118

Action by patient against hospital in respect of personal injury

The plaintiff broke his pelvis during electro-convulsive therapy treatment at the defendants' hospital. He alleged that the doctor was negligent in not warning him of the risks of the treatment, in not giving relaxant drugs before the treatment, and in not holding him down during the treatment. The trial took place before McNair J. and a jury. After the evidence the learned judge summed up as follows.

McNair J.: Members of the jury, it is now my task to try to help you to reach a true verdict, bearing in mind that you take the law from me and that the facts are entirely a matter for your consideration. You will only give damages if you are satisfied that the defendants have been proved to be guilty of negligence. Counsel for the plaintiff quite squarely faces up to that and accepts that he has to satisfy you that there was some act of negligence, in the sense which I will describe in a moment, on behalf of the defendants—and that primarily means Dr. Allfrey—and that that proved negligence did cause the injuries which the plaintiff suffered, or at least that the defendants negligently failed to take some precaution which would have minimised the risk of those injuries.

Before dealing with the law, it is right that I should say this, that you must look at this case in its proper perspective. You have been told by Dr. Page that he had only seen one acetabular fracture in 50,000 cases, involving a quarter of a million treatments, and it is clear, is it not, that the particular injury which produced these disastrous results in the plaintiff is one of extreme rarity. Another fact which I think it is right that you should bear in mind is this, that whereas some years ago when a patient went into a mental institution afflicted with mental illness, suffering from one of the most terrible ills from which a man can suffer, he had very little hope of recovery—in most cases he could only expect to be carefully and kindly treated until in due course merciful death released him from his sufferings—today, according to the evidence, the position is entirely changed. The evidence shows that today a man who enters one of these institutions suffering from particular types of mental disorder has a real chance of recovery. Dr. Marshall told you that in his view that change was due almost entirely to the introduction of physical methods of treatment of mental illness, and of those physical methods the electric convulsive therapy which you have been considering during the last few days is the most important. When you approach this case and consider whether it has been proved against this hospital that negligence was committed, you have to consider that against that background, and bearing in mind the enormous benefits which are conferred upon unfortunate men and women by this form of treatment.

Another general comment which I would make is this: on the evidence it is clear, is it not, that the use of E.C.T. is a progressive science. You have had it traced for you historically over the quite few years in which it has been used in this country, and you may think on the evidence that even today there is no standard settled technique upon all points, to which all competent doctors will agree. The doctors called before you have mentioned in turn different variants of the technique they use. Some use restraining sheets, some use relaxants, some use manual control; but the final question you have got to make up your minds about is this, whether Dr. Allfrey, following upon the practice he had learnt at Friern and following upon the technique which he had shown to him by Dr. Bastarrechea, was negligent in failing to use relaxant drugs or, if he decided not to use relaxant drugs, that he was negligent in failing to exercise any manual control over the patient beyond merely arranging for his shoulders to be held, the chin supported, a gag used, and a pillow put under his back. No one suggests that there was any negligence in the diagnosis or in the decision to use E.C.T. Furthermore, no one suggests that Dr. Allfrey or anyone at the hospital was in any way indifferent to the care of their patients. The only question is really a question of professional skill.

Before I turn to that I must tell you what in law we mean by "negligence." In the ordinary case which does not involve any special skill, negligence in law means a failure to do some act which a reasonable man in the circumstances would do, or the doing of some act which a reasonable man in the circumstances would not do; and if that failure or the doing of that act results in injury, then there is a cause of action. How do you test whether this act or failure is negligent? In an ordinary case it is generally said you judge it by the action of the man in the street. He is the ordinary man. In one case it has been said you judge it by the conduct of the man on the top of a Clapham omnibus. He is the ordinary man. But where you get a situation which involves the use of some special skill or competence, then the test as to whether there has been negligence or not is not the test of the man on the top of a Clapham omnibus, because he has not got this special skill. The test is the standard of the ordinary skilled man exercising and professing to have that special skill. A man need not possess the highest expert skill; it is well established law that it is sufficient if he exercises the ordinary skill of an ordinary competent man exercising that particular art. I do not think that I quarrel much with any of the submissions in law which have been put before you by counsel. Mr. Fox-Andrews put it in this way, that in the case of a medical man, negligence means failure to act in accordance with the standards of reasonably competent medical men at the time. That is a perfectly accurate statement, as long as it is remembered that there may be one or more perfectly proper standards; and if he conforms with one of those proper standards, then he is not negligent. Mr. Fox-Andrews also was quite right, in my judgment, in saying that a mere personal belief that a particular technique is best is no defence unless that belief is based on reasonable grounds. That again is unexceptionable. But the emphasis which is laid by the defence is on this aspect of negligence, that the real question you have to make up your minds about on each of the three major topics is whether the defendants, in acting in the way they did, were acting in accordance with a practice of competent respected professional opinion. Mr. Stirling submitted that if you are satisfied that they were acting in accordance with a practice of a competent body of professional opinion, then it would be wrong for you to hold that negligence was established. In a recent Scottish case, *Hunter* v. *Hanley* (1955 S.L.T. 213, 217), Lord President Clyde said: "In the realm of diagnosis and treatment there is ample scope for genuine difference of opinion and one man clearly is not negligent merely because his conclusion differs from that of other professional men, nor because he has displayed less skill or knowledge than others would have shown. The true test for establishing negligence in diagnosis or treatment on the part of a doctor is whether he has been proved to be guilty of such failure as no doctor of ordinary skill would be guilty of, if acting with ordinary care." If that statement of the true test is qualified by the words "in all the circumstances," Mr. Fox-Andrews would not seek to say that that expression of opinion does not accord with the English law. It is just a question of expression. I myself would prefer to put it this way, that he is not guilty of negligence if he has acted in accordance with a practice accepted as proper by a responsible body of medical men skilled in that particular art. I do not think there is much difference in sense. It is just a different way of expressing the same thought. Putting it the other way round, a man is not negligent, if he is acting in accordance with such a practice, merely because there is a body of opinion who would take a contrary view. At the same time, that does not mean that a medical man can obstinately and pig-headedly carry on with some old technique if it has been proved to be contrary to what is really substantially the whole of informed medical opinion. Otherwise you might get men today saying: "I do not believe in anaesthetics. I do not believe in antiseptics. I am going to continue to do my surgery in the way it was done in the eighteenth century." That clearly would be wrong.

Before I get to the details of the case, it is right to say this, that it is not essential for you to decide which of two practices is the better practice, as long as you accept that what the defendants did was in accordance with a practice accepted by responsible persons; if the result of the evidence is that you are satisfied that his practice is better than the practice spoken of on the other side, then it is really a stronger case. Finally, bear this in mind, that you are now considering whether it was negligent for certain action to be taken in August 1954, not in February 1957; and in one of the well-known cases on this topic it has been said you must not look with 1957 spectacles at what happened in 1954.

The plaintiff's case, as it has developed in the evidence, primarily depends upon three points. Firstly, that the defendants were negligent in failing to give to the plaintiff a warning of the risks involved in the treatment, so that he might have a chance to decide whether he was going to take those risks or not. Secondly, that they were negligent in failing to use any relaxant drugs which admittedly, if used, would have to all intents and purposes excluded the risk of fracture altogether. Thirdly—and this was, I think, the point upon which Mr. Fox-Andrews laid the most emphasis—that if relaxants are not used, then at least some form of manual control beyond shoulder control, support of the chin, and pillow under the back, must be used. . . .

Having considered the evidence on this point, you have to make up your minds whether it has been proved to your satisfaction that when the defendants adopted the practice they did (namely, the practice of saying very little and waiting for questions from the patient), they were falling below a proper standard of competent professional opinion on this question of whether or not it is right to warn. Members of the jury, though it is a matter entirely for you, you may well think that when dealing with a mentally sick man and having a strong belief that his only hope of cure is E.C.T. treatment, a doctor cannot be criticised if he does not stress the dangers which he believes to be minimal involved in that treatment.

If you do come to the conclusion that proper practice requires some warning to be given, the second question which you have to decide is: If a warning had been given, would it have made any difference? The only man who really can tell you the answer to that question is the plaintiff, and he was never asked the question. . . .

I have not said anything about Dr. Allfrey in detail, though he is primarily the man under attack, for it was during his operation that the disaster occurred. You have got to form your judgment of Dr. Allfrey, and make up your minds whether you think that he was a careful practitioner interested in his art, giving thought to the different problems, or whether he was a man who was quite content just to follow the swim. You may recall that on quite a number of occasions in the course of his evidence he gave instances where he had really applied his inquiring mind to the problem and come to a conclusion. On the use of restraint, he told you that during his training he knew that there was a school of thought that favoured restraint, but that he got the impression that the general view was against it. He recalls how he was taught by the man responsible for his training that there was a greater danger of fracture if two ends of a rigid member like a stick were held firm than if one was left swinging or both were left swinging, and that rather persuaded him that there was something in the view that restraint should not be used. He, at his hospital, Knole, adopted under tuition (and, as he got older, on his own responsibility) the practice of leaving the limbs free to move, merely holding down the shoulders. When he got to Friern he found the same practice was being carried out by his chief there, Dr. Bastarrechea. Having had his technique shown to him, he followed it. The question you have got to make up your minds about is whether he is, in following that practice, doing something which no competent medical practitioner using due care would do, or whether, on the other hand, he is acting in accordance with a perfectly well-recognised school of thought. Dr. Marshall at Netherne adopts the same practice. Dr. Baker at Banstead adopts the same practice. It is true, and in fact interesting as showing the diversity of practice, that Dr. Page at the Three Counties mental institution adopts a modification of that, inasmuch as he prefers to carry out the treatment in bed, with the patient controlled to some extent by the blanket, sheets and counterpane. That may be of interest to you as showing the diversity of practice; but it would not be right, would it, to take that as a condemnation of the practice adopted by the defendants? . . .

After a retirement of 40 minutes the jury returned a verdict for the defendants.

Note:

The words of McNair J. were enthusiastically endorsed as "true doctrine" by Lord Edmund-Davies in *Whitehouse* v. *Jordan* [1981] 1 All E.R. 267. That case involved a charge of negligence against a senior registrar in charge of a childbirth in which the child suffered brain damage. The defendant realised that normal birth by contraction was impossible and attempted a trial by forceps in order to see whether delivery by forceps, a better method than Caesarean section, might be possible. The question was whether he pulled too long and too hard. The trial judge found that he had; the Court of Appeal, by a majority, differed; and the House of Lords unanimously upheld the Court of Appeal. Lord Russell said this: "Some passages in the Court of Appeal might suggest that if a doctor makes an error of judgment he cannot be found guilty of negligence. This must be wrong. An error of judgment is not *per se* incompatible with negligence . . . I would accept the phrase 'a mere error of judgment' if the impact of the word 'mere' is to indicate that not all errors of judgment show a lapse from the standard of skill and care required to be exercised to avoid a charge of negligence."

Compare with that of McNair J. the instruction given to the jury by Tindal C.J. in *Lanphier* v. *Phipos* (1838) 8 C. & P. 475; 173 E.R. 581. Frightened by a cow, Mrs. Lanphier had fallen and broken her wrist. The defendant applied splints, which he left on for seven weeks, and nursed the inflammation with vinegar; Mrs. Lanphier's condition did not improve.

"What you will have to say is this, whether you are satisfied that the injury sustained is attributable to the want of a reasonable and proper degree of care and skill in the defendant's treatment. Every person who enters into a learned profession undertakes to bring to the exercise of it a reasonable degree of care and skill. He does not undertake, if he is an attorney, that at all events you shall gain your case, nor does a surgeon undertake that he will perform a cure; nor does he undertake to use the highest possible degree of skill. There may be persons who have higher education and greater advantages than he has, but he undertakes to bring a fair, reasonable and competent degree of skill, and you will say whether, in this case, the injury was occasioned by the want of such skill in the defendant. . . . " The jury found a verdict for the plaintiff, £100 damages.

Until fairly recently British people displayed a decent distaste for suing their doctors. While one can sympathise with the parental grief which turns to grievance and fuels a hopeless vendetta through the courts (*Kay* v. *Ayrshire & Arran H.B.* [1987] 2 All E.R. 417 (H.L.)), one can ponder the virtue of claiming damages for a child's blindness from the very doctors whose remarkable devotion and skill kept it alive at all (*Wilsher* v. *Essex A.H.A.* [1987] 1 All E.R. 871 (H.L.)). Claims against doctors and hospitals are on the increase (up by 400 per cent. in the four years to 1986) and the premiums which doctors must pay for the liability insurance they are required to carry are increasing correspondingly (up from £575 to £1,080 in 1988). The medical protection societies play a valuable social role both in paying out (£23.7m. in 1986) on claims which are meritorious and in resisting those which are not. Indeed it is because settlement is prompt in so many cases and the defence so vigorous in the others that most medical negligence claims which reach the courts are lost. Despite the probable fact that in the three million operations which take place annually in the U.K. nearly a thousand patients die unnecessarily (*The Independent* December 9, 1987, p. 5), it is true (and right) that judges are more sympathetic to doctors than to drivers, especially in the higher courts where they are not distracted by seeing the actual victim. This judicial forbearance does not apply to non-disclosure of medical records and reports.

There are, of course, some gross and disastrous errors, for which compensation should be paid, but one should bear in mind the foolish and unmeritorious claimants also: the parents of a girl who claimed damages for shock when the doctor diagnosed as gonorrhoea what was *herpes simplex,* the relatives of an attempted suicide whose doctor wrongly identified the poison, and the patient who sued the psychiatrist for letting her fall in love with him. That legal aid committees and judges should be slow to extend litigation and liability is suggested by the advice of the protection society to its members that they should communicate with it before embarking on experimental procedures.

ROE v. MINISTER OF HEALTH

Court of Appeal [1954] 2 Q.B. 66; [1954] 2 W.L.R. 915; 98 S.J. 319; [1954] 2 All E.R. 131

Action by patients against hospital and anaesthetist in respect of personal injury

The two plaintiffs in these consolidated actions entered hospital for minor surgery and emerged permanently paralysed from the waist down. The reason was that the ampoules of the anaesthetic, nupercaine, which was injected spinally, had tiny cracks in them, and some phenol, the disinfectant in which they were kept, had percolated through those cracks and had contaminated the anaesthetic.

The action was brought against the Minister of Health, as successor in title to the trustees of the Chesterfield and North Derbyshire Royal Hospital, and the anaesthetist, Dr. Graham, who had a private practice but was under an obligation to provide a regular service at the hospital.

The trial judge dismissed the plaintiffs' actions ([1954] 1 W.L.R. 128), and the Court of Appeal dismissed their appeal.

Denning L.J.: No one can be unmoved by the disaster which has befallen these two unfortunate men. They were both working men before they went into the Chesterfield Hospital in October 1947. Both were insured contributors to the hospital, paying a small sum each week, in return for which they were entitled to be admitted for treatment when they were ill. Each of them was operated on in the hospital for a minor trouble, one for something wrong with a cartilage in his knee, the other for a hydrocele. The operations were both on the same day, October 13, 1947. Each of them was given a spinal anaesthetic by a visiting anaesthetist, Dr. Graham. Each of them has in consequence been paralysed from the waist down.

The judge has said that those facts do not speak for themselves, but I think that they do. They certainly call for an explanation. Each of these men is entitled to say to the hospital: "While I was in your hands something has been done to me which has wrecked my life. Please explain how it has come to pass." The reason why the judge took a different view was because he thought that the hospital authorities could disclaim responsibility for the anaesthetist, Dr. Graham: and, as it might be his fault and not theirs, the hospital authorities were not called upon to give an explanation. I think that that reasoning is wrong. In the first place, I think that the hospital authorities are responsible for the whole of their staff, not only for the nurses and doctors, but also for the anaesthetists and the surgeons. It does not matter whether they are permanent or temporary, resident or visiting, whole-time or part-time. The hospital authorities are responsible for all of them. The reason is because, even if they are not servants, they are the agents of the hospital to give the treatment. The only exception is the case of consultants or anaesthetists selected and employed by the patient himself. I went into the matter with some care in *Cassidy* v. *Ministry of Health* ([1951] 2 K.B. 343) and I adhere to all I there said. In the second place, I do not think that the hospital authorities and Dr. Graham can both avoid giving an explanation by the simple expedient of each throwing responsibility on to the other. If an injured person shows that one or other or both of two persons injured him, but cannot say which of them it was, then he is not defeated altogether. He can call on each of them for an explanation: see *Baker* v. *Market Harborough Industrial Co-operative Society* ([1953] 1 W.L.R. 1472).

I approach this case, therefore, on the footing that the hospital authorities and Dr. Graham were called on to give an explanation of what has happened. But I think that they have done so. They have spared no trouble or expense to seek out the cause of the disaster. The greatest specialists in the land were called to give evidence. In the result, the judge has found that what happened was this: In October 1947, a spinal anaesthetic was in use at the hospital called nupercaine. It was a liquid supplied by the makers in closed glass ampoules. These were test tubes sealed with glass. When the time came to use it, a nurse filed off the glass top, the anaesthetist inserted his needle and drew off the nupercaine, which he then injected into the spine of the patient. It so happened that in this process there was some risk of the needle becoming infected. The reason was because the outside of the ampoule might become contaminated with a germ of some kind: and the needle might touch it as the anaesthetist was filling it. That this risk was a real one is shown by the fact that quite a number of cases became complicated by some infection or other.

In order to avoid this risk, the senior anaesthetist at the hospital, Dr. Pooler, decided to keep the ampoules in a jar of disinfectant called phenol, which was a form of carbolic acid. This disinfectant was made in two strengths. The stronger was tinted light blue and the weaker was tinted pale red. This was so as to distinguish it from water. Following Dr. Pooler, the junior anaesthetist, Dr. Graham, thought that it was a good thing to disinfect the ampoules in this way and he adopted the same system. By a great misfortune this new system of disinfecting had in it a danger of which Dr. Pooler and Dr. Graham were quite unaware. The danger was this: the ampoules in the jar might become cracked; the cracks might be so fine or so placed that they could not be detected by ordinary inspection, and the carbolic disinfectant would then seep through the cracks into the nupercaine, and no one would realise that it had taken place. Thus the anaesthetist, who thought he was inserting pure nupercaine into the spine of the patient, was in fact inserting nupercaine mixed with carbolic acid. That is the very thing which happened in the case of these two men. Carbolic acid was inserted into their spines and corroded all the nerves which controlled the lower half of their bodies.

That is the explanation of the disaster, and the question is: were any of the staff negligent? I pause to say that once the accident is explained, no question of *res ipsa loquitur* arises. The only question is whether on the facts as now ascertained anyone was negligent. Mr. Elwes said that the staff were negligent in two respects: (1) in not colouring the phenol with a deep dye; (2) in cracking the ampoules. I will take them in order: (1) The deep tinting. If the anaesthetists had foreseen that the ampoules might get cracked with cracks that could not be detected on inspection they would no doubt have dyed the phenol a deep blue; and this would have exposed the contamination. But I do not think that their failure to foresee this was negligence. It is so easy to be wise after the event and to condemn as negligence that which was only a misadventure. We ought always to be on our guard against it, especially in cases against hospitals and doctors. Medical science has conferred great benefits on mankind, but these benefits are attended by considerable risks. Every surgical operation is attended by risks. We cannot take the benefits without taking the risks. Every advance in technique is also attended by risks. Doctors, like the rest of us, have to learn by experience; and experience often teaches in a hard way. Something goes wrong and shows up a weakness, and then it is put right. That is just what happened here. Dr. Graham sought to escape the danger of infection by disinfecting the ampoule. In escaping that known danger he unfortunately ran into another danger. He did not know that there could be undetectable cracks, but it was not negligent for him not to know it at that time. We must not look at the 1947 accident with 1954 spectacles. The judge acquitted Dr. Graham of negligence and we should uphold his decision.

(2) The cracks. In cracking the ampoules, there must, I fear, have been some carelessness by someone in the hospital. The ampoules were quite strong and the sisters said that they should not get cracked if proper care was used in handling them. They must have been jolted in some way by someone. This raises an interesting point of law. This carelessness was, in a sense, one of the causes of the disaster; but the person who jolted the ampoule cannot possibly have foreseen what dire conse-

quences would follow. There were so many intervening opportunities of inspection that she might reasonably think that if the jolting caused a crack, it would be discovered long before any harm came of it. As Somervell L.J. has pointed out, she herself would probably examine the ampoule for a crack, and seeing none, would return it to the jar. The anaesthetist himself did in fact examine it for cracks, and finding none, used it. The trouble was that nobody realised that there might be a crack which could not be detected on ordinary examination. What, then, is the legal position?

It may be said that, by reason of the decision of this court in *Re Polemis* ([1921] 3 K.B. 560) the hospital authorities are liable for all the consequences of the initial carelessness of the nurse, even though the consequences could not reasonably have been foreseen. But the decision in *Re Polemis* is of very limited application. The reason is because there are two preliminary questions to be answered before it can come into play. The first question in every case is whether there was a duty of care owed to the plaintiff; and the test of duty depends, without doubt, on what you should foresee. There is no duty of care owed to a person when you could not reasonably foresee that he might be injured by your conduct: see *Hay or Bourhill* v. *Young* ([1943] A.C. 92), *Woods* v. *Duncan* ([1946] A.C. 401, 437), *per* Lord Russell and *per* Lord Porter.

The second question is whether the neglect of duty was a "cause" of the injury in the proper sense of that term; and causation, as well as duty, often depends on what you should foresee. The chain of causation is broken when there is an intervening action which you could not reasonably be expected to foresee: see *Woods* v. *Duncan* (421, 431, 432), *per* Lord Simon, Lord Macmillan, and Lord Simonds. It is even broken when there is an intervening omission which you could not reasonably expect. For instance, in cases based on *Donoghue* v. *Stevenson* a manufacturer is not liable if he might reasonably contemplate that an intermediate examination would probably be made. It is only when those two preliminary questions—duty and causation—are answered in favour of the plaintiff that the third question, remoteness of damage, comes into play.

Even then your ability to foresee the consequences may be vital. It is decisive where there is intervening conduct by other persons: see *Stansbie* v. *Troman* ([1948] 2 K.B. 48), *Lewis* v. *Carmarthenshire County Council* ([1953] 1 W.L.R. 1439). It is only disregarded when the negligence is the immediate or precipitating cause of the damage, as in *Re Polemis* and *Thurogood* v. *Van den Berghs & Jurgens Ltd.* ([1951] 2 K.B. 537). In all these cases you will find that the three questions, duty, causation, and remoteness, run continually into one another. It seems to me that they are simply three different ways of looking at one and the same problem. Starting with the proposition that a negligent person should be liable, within reason, for the consequences of his conduct, the extent of his liability is to be found by asking the one question: Is the consequence fairly to be regarded as within the risk created by the negligence? If so, the negligent person is liable for it: but otherwise not.

Even when the three questions are taken singly, they can only be determined by applying common sense to the facts of each particular case: see as to duty, *King* v. *Phillips* ([1953] 1 Q.B. 429, 437), as to causation, *Stapley* v. *Gypsum Mines Ltd.* ([1953] A.C. 663, 681), *per* Lord Reid; and as to remoteness, *Liesbosch, Dredger* v. *Edison S.S. (Owners)* ([1933] A.C. 449), *per* Lord Wright. Instead of asking three questions, I should have thought that in many cases it would be simpler and better to ask the one question: is the consequence within the risk? And to answer it by applying ordinary plain common sense. That is the way in which Singleton L.J. and Hodson L.J. approached a difficult problem in *Jones* v. *Livox Quarries Ltd.* ([1952] 2 Q.B. 608), and I should like to approach this problem in the same way.

Asking myself, therefore, what was the risk involved in careless handling of the ampoules, I answer by saying that there was such a probability of intervening examination as to limit the risk. The only consequence which could reasonably be anticipated was the loss of a quantity of nupercaine, but not the paralysis of a patient. The hospital authorities are therefore not liable for it.

When you stop to think of what happened in the present case, you will realise that it was a most extraordinary chapter of accidents. In some way the ampoules must have received a jolt, perhaps while a nurse was putting them into the jar or while a trolley was being moved along. The jolt cannot have been very severe. It was not severe enough to break any of the ampoules or even to crack them so far as anyone could see. But it was just enough to produce an invisible crack. The crack was of a kind which no one in any experiment has been able to reproduce again. It was too fine to be seen, but it was enough to let in sufficient phenol to corrode the nerves, whilst still leaving enough nupercaine to anaesthetise the patient. And this very exceptional crack occurred not in one ampoule only, but in two ampoules used on the self-same day in two successive operations; and none of the other ampoules was damaged at all. This has taught the doctors to be on their guard against invisible cracks. Never again, it is to be hoped, will such a thing happen. After this accident a leading textbook was published in 1951 which contains the significant warning: "Never place ampoules of local anaesthetic solution in alcohol or spirit. This common practice is probably responsible for some of the cases of permanent paralysis reported after spinal analgesia." If the hospitals were to continue the practice after this warning, they could not complain if they were found guilty of negligence. But the warning had not been given at the time of this accident. Indeed, it was the extraordinary accident to these two men which first disclosed the danger. Nowadays it would be negligence not to realise the danger, but it was not then.

One final word. These two men have suffered such terrible consequences that there is a natural feeling that they should be compensated. But we should be doing a disservice to the community at large if we were to impose liability on hospitals and doctors for everything that happens to go wrong. Doctors would be led to think more of their own safety than of the good of their patients. Initiative would be stifled and confidence shaken. A proper sense of proportion requires us to have regard to the conditions in which hospitals and doctors have to work. We must insist on due care for the patient at every point, but we must not condemn as negligence that which is only a misadventure. I agree with my Lord that these appeals should be dismissed.

Questions

1. Does the question formulated by Denning L.J. in terms of "risk" invite any other answer than "Yes" or "No"? And would it be better if judges answered it in one word? (See *Qualcast*, above, p. 100).

2. Contrast the attitudes of Lord Denning to fire brigades (*Watt*, above, p. 110), employers (*Christmas*, above, p. 104), village cricketers (*Miller*, above, p. 109) and hospitals (the principal case). Would the reasons he gives for denying liability in this case apply with equal force to industrial development during the last century? Or now? What about pharmaceutical companies?

Note:

The requirement of fault clearly entails that a defendant must be judged by the standard prevalent at the time of the conduct being impugned: a person cannot be blamed for not knowing what no one yet knows. But what if fault is not required? What if a product is as safe as it could be made at the time of its manufacture but could be made safer at the time of the injury or the law-suit? The Brussels Directive (above p. 28) left it to the various member states to decide whether to impose liability or not. Britain decided not to impose liability (Consumer Protection Act 1987, s.4(1)(*e*), a defence "that the state of scientific and technical knowledge at the relevant time was not such that a producer of products of the same description as the product in question might be expected to have discovered the defect if it had existed in his products while they were under his control . . . "). Does this formula match Art.. 7(3) of the Directive?

STOKES v. GUEST, KEEN & NETTLEFOLD (BOLTS AND NUTS) LTD.

Assizes [1968] 1 W.L.R. 1776; 112 S.J. 821

Action by widow against husband's employer

The plaintiff's husband was frequently required, in the course of his employment as a toolsetter by the defendants, to lean over oily machines; he died of scrotal cancer. The plaintiff alleged that the defendants ought to have known of the risks of this disease and were negligent in not warning her husband and in not giving him periodic medical examinations. Judgment was given for the plaintiff.

Swanwick J.: . . . This brings me to the third and most difficult question, were there any steps or precautions that as employers the defendants or their servants ought to have taken and did not take either to protect Mr. Stokes from the risk of contracting the disease or towards detecting it at an earlier stage?

There were cited to me and I have perused some of the standard line of authorities dealing with the duties of employers towards their workmen, especially where errors of omission are alleged.These included *Paris* v. *Stepney Borough Council* ([1951] A.C. 367), including the well-known passage from Lord Normand's speech quoting Lord Dunedin's famous dictum and putting what has been called his own "gloss" upon it, *Morris* v. *West Hartlepool Steam Navigation Co. Ltd.* ([1956] A.C. 552), *Cavanagh* v. *Ulster Weaving Co. Ltd.* ([1960] A.C. 145), and the dicta, *obiter* but still persuasive, of Devlin J. in *Graham* v. *Co-operative Wholesale Society Ltd.* ([1957] 1 W.L.R. 511); also the convenient summary of these and other cases in the sixth edition of Mr. Munkman's useful book on *Employers' Liability at Common Law*, 6th ed. (1966), pp. 34 to 47.

From these authorities I deduce the principles, that the overall test is still the conduct of the reasonable and prudent employer, taking positive thought for the safety of his workers in the light of what he knows or ought to know; where there is a recognised and general practice which has been followed for a substantial period in similar circumstances without mishap, he is entitled to follow it, unless in the light of common sense or newer knowledge it is clearly bad; but, where there is developing knowledge, he must keep reasonably abreast of it and not be too slow to apply it; and where he has in fact greater than average knowledge of the risks, he may be thereby obliged to take more than the average or standard precautions. He must weigh up the risk in terms of the likelihood of injury occurring and the potential consequences if it does; and he must balance against this the probable effectiveness of the precautions that can be taken to meet it and the expense and inconvenience they involve. If he is found to have fallen below the standard to be properly expected of a reasonable and prudent employer in these respects, he is negligent.

There is, however, an additional complication in this case, not directly covered by authority so far as I am aware. For in this case the negligence alleged against the defendants lies largely in the sphere of vicarious responsibility for the actions or inaction of Dr. Lloyd, who was in their full-time employment as factory doctor and was thus their servant. It is of course plain that, if an employer delegates to a servant the performance of any part of his duty towards his workmen, he is responsible for the servant's negligence, however skilled the task; and I myself would take the view that, where the task requires a special skill or art, the servant must be judged by the standards pertaining to that skill or art, in so far as he is possessed of and exercising it. In the case of a doctor those standards are well set out by McNair J. when charging the jury in *Bolam* v. *Friern Hospital Management Committee* [above, p. 135], to which along with *Mahon* v. *Osborne* ([1939] 2 K.B. 14) I was referred.

A factory doctor, however, as emerged from the evidence, when advising his employers on questions of safety precautions is subject to pressures and has to give weight to considerations which do not apply as between a doctor and his patient and is expected to give and in this case regularly gave to his employers advice based partly on medical and partly on economic and administrative considerations. For instance he may consider some precaution medically desirable but hesitate to recommend expanding his department to cope with it, having been refused such an expansion before; or there may be questions of frightening workers off the job or of interfering with production. An example of this last type of consideration is the final sentence of Dr. Lloyd's memorandum of January 8, 1962, to the defendants' labour manager, Mr. Powis, on the subject of a man Aldridge, who had been advised by Dr. Senter and his own general practitioner to cease working in oil for fear of contracting scrotal cancer. After disagreeing with this high-powered medical opinion and urging the man to stay at work and keep his earnings up, Dr. Lloyd finished his memorandum, "If we took the medical advice given in this case, we might as well close the works and much of British industry."

Where, therefore, the advice to management and its acceptance are based on mixed considerations of this sort, it is to the medical aspect only that I would apply the perhaps rather special tests indicated by McNair J. in the passage I have indicated; and the economic and administrative aspect would be covered by the more general principles that I have endeavoured to summarise. In any event McNair J. emphasises and I agree that, while adherence to the views of a recognised body of medical opinion even if a minority is not negligence in a doctor, where the doctor is acting on his own personal opinion only he must be judged by the standard of what is reasonable. . . .

Note:

Part of this judgment was cited with approval by Mustill J. in his splendid decision regarding the liability of employers in the ship-building business for deafness suffered by their employees. The problem of noxious noise had been recognised but generally ignored for many years—by employers, unions and government alike—despite the increasing availability of alleviating devices. To decide the point of time at which it became negligent to fail to take any steps he asked: "From what date would a reasonable employer, with proper but not extraordinary solicitude for the welfare of his workers, have identified the problem of excessive noise in his yard, recognised that it was capable of solution, found a possible solution, weighed up the potential advantages and disadvantages of that solution, decided to adopt it, acquired a supply of the protectors, set in train the programme of education necessary to persuade the men and their representatives that the system was useful and not potentially deleterious, experimented with the system and finally put it into full effect?" *Thompson* v. *Smiths Shiprepairers* [1984] 1 All E.R. 881.

Section 5.—Proof of Breach

In his statement of claim a plaintiff must disclose a cause of action, that is, he must aver facts which, if proved, would entitle him to succceed. If he does not, he may fail right at the outset (*Price* v. *Gregory* [1959] 1 W.L.R. 177; *Fowler* v. *Lanning,* below, p. 285). On the whole however, English judges prefer to let the case go to trial; facts involving liability may emerge, and the plaintiff may be allowed to amend his pleadings so as to bring them into line with those facts. On the other hand, if what was proved diverges very widely from what he alleged, he may still fail (*Esso Petroleum Co.* v. *Southport Corporation* [1956] A.C. 218, 241; *Waghorn* v. *George Wimpey & Co.* [1970] 1 All E.R. 474).

At the trial itself, the plaintiff must lead some evidence. He will always know what the damage is, and he will be able to show the circumstances in which he was placed when it was suffered. He may not be able to show exactly what caused the damage he complains of, and he may very well not be able to show the other thing that must ultimately be established, namely, that one of its causes was some fault in the behaviour of the defendant. If all the facts come out at the trial, as in *Roe,* then the only question is whether those facts show a breach of duty in the defendant. The question is not whether it was more probable or not that he was negligent, but simply whether he was negligent. As to that, of course, there may be two views; appellate courts are quite ready to substitute their view for that of the judge, unless he is a county court judge and not much money is involved.

But all the facts may not emerge—indeed, they rarely do. The defendant may not want to tell all he knows, though the process of discovery limits his power of secrecy. The question then is whether the plaintiff has proved enough. If you do not know what the defendant did (a matter of proof), you cannot decide (a matter of judgment) whether what he did was careless or not. It may, however, be possible to say that it is more probable than not that the defendant was careless; this is an elliptical and confusing way of saying that from the facts proved it is possible to *infer* other facts which, if proved, would entitle one to conclude that the defendant had fallen short of the required standard. For example, from the fact that a well-made machine worked badly one may infer that it was not very well maintained; whether that lack of maintenance, if one infers it, amounts to a shortfall in the defendant depends on how expert and frequent the maintenance incumbent on him, as a matter of law, is. But one may not infer bad maintenance at all. The machine may have been badly handled. If the person responsible for maintenance is also responsible for the faults of the operator of the machine, it does not matter which is inferred, and it is enough that it is more likely than not that it must have been one or the other.

When one can infer from the facts proved that the defendant was careless in some respect not specifically shown, then it is said that *res ipsa loquitur.* People have tried to say under what circumstances such an inference is possible or permissible or unavoidable, but it appears from the nature of the matter that there can be no real rules about it. If there are few rules to tell us when a defendant *was* careless, there must be even fewer to tell us when he *must have been* careless.

If *res ipsa loquitur,* a matter which need not be specifically pleaded (*Bennett* v. *Chemical Construction (G.B.) Ltd.* [1971] 1 W.L.R. 1571), the defendant will lead evidence. His aim is to show that he behaved properly. He may try to prove the physical cause of the accident and that it is not attributable to his fault; but it is enough, even if he cannot do that, to clear himself of fault by showing that he behaved properly throughout. If the facts he proves make it appear less likely than not that there are unproved facts suggesting that he was at fault, then the plaintiff loses.

Take an example. A shopper falls on some spilt yoghourt on the floor of a supermarket. She naturally has no idea how long it has lain there. The supermarket is not responsible just because the yoghourt was dropped (unless by an employee), but only if it has lain there an unreasonable time.

So the supermarket is probably not at fault unless the yoghourt is more likely than not to have been there an unreasonable time—and there is no evidence either way on that point. Certainly if the supermarket proves that the floor was swept 10 minutes or so before the accident, the plaintiff will fail, but in a case where the supermarket did not prove when it last swept the floor but only that it normally swept the floor five or six times a day, a divided Court of Appeal upheld the judge's holding for the plaintiff. The same court would not necessarily have reversed a judge's finding for the defendant. (*Ward* v. *Tesco Stores* [1976] 1 All E.R. 219).

Take another example. Suppose that the defendant shows that the physical cause of the accident was a defect in his machine. Proof of that fact excludes the inference that the machine was badly operated. It leaves quite open the inference that the machine was badly maintained (*Colvilles* v. *Devine* [1969] 1 W.L.R. 475 (H.L.)). Suppose that the defendant then proves that his system of maintenance was in accordance with general practice, and that the system was being properly implemented. Then the defendant has very nearly rebutted the inference that there was some respect in which he behaved carelessly. But if he is a specialist, the court may require him to show in addition that he had a system of informing himself of those events which called for more than normal maintenance, and that that system operated properly (*Henderson* v. *Jenkins* [1970] A.C. 282). Or it may not.

A pedestrian who offers to prove only that she was run down in the street by the defendant motorist probably does not offer to prove enough—such accidents are commonly caused by plaintiffs who emerge suddenly from behind buses (*Kinnaird* v. *O'Donnell*, 1964 S.L.T.(Sh.Ct.) 51). A pedestrian who proves that she was on a controlled pedestrian crossing at the time probably does establish a prima facie case. So, too, if the pedestrian was on the sidewalk at the time she was struck by the defendant's vehicle. But in the last case, if the defendant proves that the driver was dead at the wheel by reason of a cardiac attack, then the inference of facts indicating negligence (the driver can't have been keeping a proper look-out, etc.) vanishes, and the defendant does not then have to go further and show that it was not negligent of the driver to set out when he was about to collapse (*Waugh* v. *James K. Allen Ltd.*, 1964 S.L.T. 269; [1964] 2 Lloyd's Rep. 1 (H.L.)).

Where the defendant's duty is high (as in the pedestrian crossing instance), it is easier to infer that facts occurred which constituted a breach of it, because there are more sets of such facts. Thus in the tort of public nuisance the burden of proof is said to be reversed. This reversal of the burden of proof may make it practically easier to recover, even if the defendant's duty is stated in terms of reasonable care. There is a positive rule of law that the bailee of a chattel who fails to return it to the bailor must either pay its value or show that he was not at fault in not having it to give back; the plaintiff need prove only the delivery and the unsuccessful demand (*Houghland* v. *Low*, below, p. 438). Yet the duty of the compensated bailee is always said to be the duty to take reasonable care only. In law he bears the risk of carelessness only; in fact he bears the risk of not being able to prove that he was careful.

Chapter 3

CRIME AND TORT

Introduction

ONE might think that if *unreasonable* behaviour can give rise to liability for resulting harm, *unlawful* behaviour must certainly do so. Behaviour is constantly being rendered unlawful by statutes and regulations emanating from Parliament or Ministers, telling people to do this or not do that. When someone has done or not done what such a rule forbids or requires, it is an important question whether he may be sued by a person injured in consequence. It is not, however, an easy question, since statutes and regulations cover a vast range of situations and are drafted in very various terms.

Sometimes the primary purpose of a statute is to change the rules of tort law (*e.g.*, Occupiers' Liability Act 1957, Defective Premises Act 1972, Consumer Protection Act 1987). More often an enactment seeks to change human behaviour. It may do this either by empowering people to do what otherwise they could not lawfully do, or by requiring them to do or abstain from doing what they were previously free to do or not to do. It is important to note the distinction. The statutes in *Anns* and *Dorset Yacht* did not require, but merely empowered, the defendants to stop the building or confine the boys: it was the common law which required the defendants to take care how they exercised their statutory powers. The claims in this chapter, by contrast, are founded on the unlawfulness, not the unreasonableness, of the defendant's behaviour.

An enactment may simply provide that in certain circumstances liability is to exist (Civil Aviation Act 1982, s.76; Control of Pollution Act 1974, s.88; Data Protection Act 1984, ss.22, 23). It may impose a duty to act in a certain way and then provide that liability is to ensue if the duty is broken (Health and Safety at Work Act 1974, s.47(2) (safety regulations); Building Act 1984, s.38 (building regulations); Telecommunications Act 1984, s.18; Race Relations Act 1976, s.57; Consumer Credit Act 1974, s.92(3)). Sometimes an enactment imposes a duty but provides that there is to be no civil liability for breach (Post Office Act 1969, s.9; Health and Safety at Work Act 1974, s.47(1)(*a*)). Sometimes conduct is made into an offence and civil liability is excluded (Fire Precautions Act 1971, s.27A; Fair Trading Act 1973, s.26; Safety of Sports Grounds Act 1975, s.13). Quite often, however, an enactment imposes a duty or creates an offence and remains wholly silent about civil liability (Crossbows Act 1987 (!)). In such a case it falls to the judges to determine whether civil liability is to exist or not.

In the French view it is obvious that a person who can be punished by the State can be sued by his victim: indeed, they let the victim claim his damages in the criminal prosecution itself. Criminal courts in England can now make limited compensation orders in favour of victims (see below p. 156) but the civil courts, which do not even impose liability on all com-

mon law criminals (*Hargreaves* v. *Bretherton* [1959] 1 Q.B. 45 (perjury),
Chapman v. *Honig* [1963] 2 Q.B. 502 (contempt of court)), are most reluctant to impose liability on statutory offenders. This is not so unreasonable.
It is one thing to make a person pay a small fine and quite another to make
him pay for all the consequences of his conduct, especially if the fine is so
small that it is exacted even if he is not really to blame at all. Furthermore,
since the common law of tort already holds people liable if their unreasonable behaviour causes physical harm, the only result of imposing liability
on statutory offenders would be to make people pay when they have
behaved quite reasonably or have caused only financial harm to strangers.

How is one to determine whether breach of a particular statutory provision leads to civil liability? In Germany the judges ask if the law in question was designed to protect people like the plaintiff from harm of that
type. In England that is certainly a factor to be taken into account, but the
principal question is, was it the intention of Parliament that there should be
civil liability? This is rather an odd question to ask when there is no evidence of the intention it seeks to ascertain, rather like the question in contract cases whether a statute which prohibits an act impliedly prohibits a
contract which involves the act (*e.g., St. John Shipping Corpn.* v. *Rank*
[1957] 1 Q.B. 267, 285). In both situations it is really the courts which make
the decision, and in making the decision they are naturally affected by the
same considerations which weigh with them in other cases. They are much
more ready to impose liability in tort if the damage is physical, if the relationship is close and if the defendant was at fault—though if liability
already exists at common law the judges may always say that statutory liability is unnecessary (*McCall* v. *Abelesz* [1976] Q.B. 585). In other cases if
Parliament wants civil liability to exist, it had better say so in clear terms
(Resale Prices Act 1976, s.25(3); Restrictive Trade Practices Act 1976,
s.35(2)).

Damage

A water authority is under a duty to maintain a certain pressure in its
pipes; it fails to do so and a ratepayer's house is burned down in consequence; the water authority is subject to a fine, but not to liability in
damages (*Atkinson* v. *Newcastle Waterworks Co.* (1877) 2 Ex.D. 441). The
same Act requires the water to be wholesome; it is not, and a ratepayer
suffers personal injury from drinking it; the water authority is liable in
damages as well as to a fine (*Read* v. *Croydon Corpn.* [1938] 4 All E.R.
631). Take another pair of cases. An education authority is under a duty to
provide school accommodation; it fails to do so and a parent is put to the
expense of fees at a private school; he cannot recover them (*Watt* v. *Keste-
ven C.C.* [1955] 1 Q.B. 408). The same Act requires that safety in schools
be reasonably assured; a child cuts her hand on a thin pane of glass; she can
recover (*Reffell* v. *Surrey C.C.*, below, p. 162).

Relationship

The occupier of a factory buys and instals machinery whose dangerous
parts are insufficiently fenced; a workman injures himself on it. The victim
can recover from the occupier, but not from the vendor, though both are
liable to a fine (*Biddle* v. *Truvox Engineering Co.* [1952] 1 K.B. 101: the
relationship of vendor and consumer (unlike vendor/purchaser and manu-

facturer/consumer) is rather weak, whereas the relationship of occupier and visitor or employer and employee is extremely strong. Indeed, most of the successful suits for breach of statutory duty are brought by workmen against their employer or the occupier of their place of work. The relevant statutes (Mines and Quarries Act 1954, Factories Act 1961, and Offices Shops and Railway Premises Act 1963) will eventually be replaced by regulations under the Health and Safety at Work Act 1974.

The relationship of common users of the highway, on the other hand, is much less protective and strong. The pedestrian, certainly, can recover from the driver who mows him down on a pedestrian crossing (*London Passenger Transport Board* v. *Upson* [1949] A.C. 155), but those duties breach of which may injure both pedestrians and other motorists, and property as well as person, are not generally so construed as to give a right of action to the person hurt thereby (*Phillips* v. *Britannia Hygienic Laundry Co.*, below, p. 165). And where the duty is imposed, not on a motorist using the highway, but on a manufacturer, vendor or repairer, the grounds for denying liability seem even stronger.

Where the common law relationship is extremely weak, as it is between rival traders, statutes regulating the subject-matter will hardly ever be held impliedly to give a right of action, even although the breach in such cases may be quite deliberate (*London Armoury Co.* v. *Ever Ready Co.* [1941] 1 K.B. 742).

Fault

German law has an admirable provision: "Liability also attaches to a person who contravenes a statute designed for the protection of another. If the statute may, according to its terms, be contravened even in the absence of fault, liability in damages attaches only where fault is present" (§ 823, German Civil Code). In England, however, Parliament declined to implement the recommendation of the Monckton Committee on Alternative Remedies that a workman should not be able to recover damages for breach of statutory duty when that breach could not reasonably have been avoided by the defendant or his servants working in the course of their employment (Cmd. 6860, para. 82).

If the statutory duty is one which gives rise to liability on breach, there will be liability no matter how the breach arose. Because of this rule, the courts, which dislike imposing liability without fault, are tempted either to deny that a particular statutory duty which can be broken without fault gives rise to liability at all or to construe it in such a manner that unless there is some fault there is no breach.

Subject to all this, the plaintiff who sues for breach of statutory duty has the one great advantage that, depending on its terms, he may not have to persuade the court that the defendant behaved unreasonably: proof that the situation was dangerous may suffice without the further proof that it was the defendant's fault. But there are special hurdles, too. The plaintiff must bring both himself and his harm within the ambit of the legislative intention. Thus only the ratepayer, and not his family, may found on the water company's duty to provide wholesome water (*Read* v. *Croydon Corp.* [1938] 4 All E.R. 631), and no compensation is payable to the owner of sheep which were drowned owing to breach of a duty intended to save them from contagion (*Gorris* v. *Scott,* below, p. 194).

"In every case where a plaintiff has alleged a breach of statutory duty, he is entitled to allege negligence at common law and to ask the court to answer the question whether he has proved negligence, irrespective of his having proved a breach of statutory duty" (*Bux* v. *Slough Metals* [1974] 1 All E.R. 262, 273, *per* Stephenson L.J.). The fact that the defendant has satisfied his statutory obligations does not entail, though it may go some way to suggest, that he has taken reasonable steps to safeguard the plaintiff: for example, an employer who is bound by statute to see that a safety appliance is available for use may be bound at common law to take steps to see that it is actually used.

The Pearson Commission paid particular attention to the compensation of injuries at work. While it made proposals for the extension of the industrial injuries scheme of social security benefits, it was content with the operation of the present law of tort, including the action for breach of statutory duty.

Common law crimes

So far as the common law is concerned, there appear to be only two cases where the qualification of the defendant's behaviour as criminal is relevant to render him liable to pay damages to a person hurt in consequence of that behaviour. One is conspiracy (see later, p. 529); the other, much more important, is public nuisance. Public nuisance is a crime committed, in the main, by unreasonably impeding proper use of the Queen's highway, whether by obstruction or danger. If the defendant has been guilty of public nuisance (by creation or failure to abate), a plaintiff who suffers special damage may sue. Public nuisance, indeed, is the matrix out of which the modern law of negligence between co-users of the highway has sprung; the two torts co-exist uneasily.

Now the public interest in interferences with the highway is primarily in their removal; the Attorney-General seeks an injunction. There is good reason to grant an injunction to abate a proved nuisance even if the defendant was not at fault in causing it; he will be at fault if he doesn't remove it after being put on notice by the action. It is, of course, another question whether he should be amenable to a fine or liable to pay damages if he was not at fault in creating the nuisance. Nevertheless, liability in public nuisance came to be independent of the qualification of the defendant's conduct as reasonable or not; if the obstruction or the danger was unreasonable, it is immaterial how the defendant acted in causing it. On this, however, one must put the gloss that obstructions or dangers which are produced without negligence in the course of a reasonable user of the highway do not constitute nuisances; thus a car does not become a nuisance the minute it has unforeseeably broken down, though the person responsible for its being there must show that it was not his fault it was there at all or so long (*Moore* v. *Maxwell's of Emsworth* [1968] 1 W.L.R. 1077).

There are three possible points of divergence between public nuisance and negligence—the fault, the damage, and the factor which links them.

Fault is necessary in negligence, as we have seen. Public nuisance, on the other hand, is based more on causing an unreasonable danger than on causing a danger unreasonably. Accordingly, bearing in mind the gloss mentioned above, we must say that fault in the defendant or his servant is not a necessary element of liability in public nuisance. The faultless instigator of faulty work on the highway and the landlord of dilapidated premises adjoining it are liable. (The first case may be subsumed under the general law of negligence by styling it an instance of liability for the fault of an independent contractor, but the second cannot.) Where, however, an unreasonable danger exists without the fault of anyone at all, the present tendency appears to be to deny liability in public nuisance (*British Road Services* v. *Slater* [1964] 1 W.L.R. 498).

Until recently the tort of negligence remedied primarily physical damage. In other words, negligence was about *dangers*. Public nuisance admittedly includes dangers on the highway, but it also extends to *obstructions*. Obstructions typically cause delay; and time is not blood, but money. "Obstruction damage," therefore, tended to found liability not in negligence but only, if at all, in public nuisance—delay to a traveller (*Anglo-Algerian S.S. Co.* v. *Houlder Line* [1908] 1 K.B. 659), the cutting-off of a valuable view (*Campbell* v. *Paddington Borough Council* [1911] 1 K.B. 869), loss of profit through inability to get goods out (*Iveson* v. *Moore* (1699) 1 Ld.Raym. 486; 91 E.R. 1224), or customers or vehicles in (*Wilkes* v. *Hungerford Market Co.* (1835) 2 Bing.N.C. 281; 132 E.R. 110; *Tate & Lyle Indus.* v. *G.L.C.* [1983] 1 All E.R. 1159 (H.L.)).

What of the link between the conduct and the damage? Negligence remedies primarily foreseeable damage. Suppose that a nuisance by obstruction unpredictably turns out to be a danger and directly causes unforeseeable physical damage. Is this damage compensable? A cogent judgment from New South Wales held that it was, but the Judicial Committee disagreed and said: "It is not sufficient that the injury suffered . . . was the direct result of the nuisance if that injury was in the relevant sense unforeseeable." *The Wagon Mound (No. 2)* [1967] 1 A.C. 617, 640, on appeal from [1963] 1 Lloyd's Rep. 402. In this respect, then, public nuisance has been analogised to negligence, at any rate where physical damage has been caused. Must obstruction damage also be foreseeable? The Judicial Committee said: "the choice is between [foreseeability] being a necessary element in all cases of nuisance or in none," but there will be difficulty in applying this to nuisance by obstruction, at any rate if "necessary" is taken to mean "sufficient"—for how many people foreseeably lose money when a bridge collapses or a level-crossing gate gets stuck or someone floods a road?

CHAPMAN v. HONIG

Court of Appeal [1963] 2 Q.B. 502; [1963] 3 W.L.R. 19; 107 S.J. 374; [1963] 2 All E.R. 513

This was an action of trespass brought by a tenant against his landlord. The plaintiff had given evidence against the defendant in a previous action by another tenant, and the defendant out of pique served a notice to quit on the plaintiff, under such circumstances that the defendant could have been punished for contempt of court. The plaintiff stayed on in the flat after the expiry of the notice to quit, and the defendant entered and padlocked the doors.

The county court judge awarded £50 damages. The defendant appealed, and his appeal was allowed by the Court of Appeal (Lord Denning M.R. dissenting).

Davies L.J.: . . . One cannot help but sympathise with the proposition that in general a person injured by a wrongful act should have a remedy in damages against the wrongdoer. But it has to be considered whether, in the first place, that proposition is universally true, and, secondly, whether in the circumstances of this case the defendant's action in serving a notice to quit was, as against the plaintiff, wrongful at all.

It is, no doubt, true that in most cases a person injured by a criminal offence has a right of action against the criminal. That is because most crimes are torts. Acts of criminal violence to person or property would be trespasses; larceny would be conversion; most frauds would give rise to an action of deceit; and so on. But not all crimes give rise to a cause of action. For example, it is well established that perjury does not give rise to a cause of action at the suit of a person injured by the perjury; see the decision of Lord Goddard C.J. in *Hargreaves* v. *Bretherton* ([1959] 1 Q.B. 45), and the authorities there cited. It is true that there may be special features relating to the offence of perjury which might make it difficult to permit of an action based upon it. But this line of authority shows that there is no general rule that all crimes give rise to a cause of action.

Equally relevant to this inquiry is the great body of case-law dealing with the question whether the commission of an act forbidden or made punishable by statute gives a cause of action to a person injured by the act. On this question it is notoriously difficult to enunciate any guiding principle. The authorities are discussed in the dissenting *obiter* judgment of Somervell L.J. in *Solomons* v. *R. Gertzenstein Ltd.* [1954] 2 Q.B. 243. As examples may be cited the well-known case of *Groves* v. *Lord Wimborne* ([1898] 2 Q.B. 402), the *alma genetrix* of so much litigation under the provisions of the Factories Acts, on the one side of the line, and, on the other, *Phillips* v. *Britannia Hygienic Laundry Co. Ltd.* [below, p. 165]. Perhaps the nearest that one gets to a statement of principle is in the words of Atkin L.J. in the last-cited case, in a passage adopted by Somervell L.J. in *Solomons'* case: "Therefore the question is," said Atkin L.J., "whether these regulations, viewed in the circumstances in which they were made and to which they relate, were intended to impose a duty which is a public duty only or whether they were intended, in addition to the public duty, to impose a duty enforceable by an individual aggrieved." It is, of course, implicit in this principle that not in every case is an individual who has been injured by a wrongful act entitled to sue, even though the wrongful act is prohibited or made punishable by statute. And the principle can, in my judgment, be applied in the present case by inquiring whether the concept of, and proceedings for, contempt of court are concerned with the preservation of the inviolability of the administration and course of justice and its proper conduct or whether, in addition, they are intended in all cases to give a remedy in damages to an individual injured by the contempt. . . .

Pearson L.J.: . . . I have considered a number of cases in which the court had to decide, in relation to some particular enactment, whether an individual, adversely affected by breach of a statutory duty, had a right of action for damages against the person who had committed the breach. . . . The answer depends on the construction of the particular enactment, *i.e.*, on the intention which it manifests. Here there is no enactment which is directly relevant and I can only consider, perhaps in a rather metaphorical way, what intention is to be inferred from the nature and exercise of the jurisdiction. So far as I know, no individual ever has been awarded, or has even claimed, damages or other compensation for contempt of court until the present case. The jurisdiction exists and is exercised *alio intuitu,* for the protection of the administration of justice and not for the protection of individuals. So to speak, the hypothetical enactment should be notionally construed as not conferring on an individual affected by a contempt of court any right of action for damages for the contempt of court as such although of course he may have a right of action for damages on other grounds. . . .

LONRHO LTD. v. SHELL PETROLEUM CO. LTD.

House of Lords [1982] A.C. 173; [1981] 3 W.L.R. 33; [1981] 2 All E.R. 456

The claimants owned a pipeline, leading from the Mozambique coast to Southern Rhodesia, which the respondent oil companies paid to use. After the government of that country had declared itself independent, Orders in Council in the United Kingdom rendered it an offence to supply crude oil to Southern Rhodesia, and oil ceased to flow along the claimants' pipeline to their loss. In arbitration proceedings the claimants claimed over £100m. on the basis that the illegal regime would have collapsed and the profitable use of their pipeline recommenced much sooner had the respondents not supplied the regime with oil in breach of the Orders. It was held by the House of Lords that none of the claimants' allegations stated a cause of action, and the extract printed below gives the opinion of Lord Diplock in answer to question 5, namely " . . . if there were breaches by the Respondents of the 1965 and 1968 Orders [sc. the sanctions orders] (a) Whether breaches of those Orders would give rise to a right of action in the Claimants for damage alleged to have been caused by those breaches . . . "

Lord Diplock: . . . My Lords, it is well settled by authority of this House in *Cutler* v. *Wandsworth Stadium Ltd.* ([1949] A.C. 398) that the question whether legislation which makes the doing or omitting to do a particular act a criminal offence renders the person guilty of such offence liable also in a civil action for damages at the suit of any person who thereby suffers loss or damage is a question of construction of the legislation. . . .

[His Lordship considered the provisions of the Southern Rhodesia Act 1965 and the 1965 sanctions order] . . .

The sanctions order thus creates a statutory prohibition on the doing of certain classes of acts and provides the means of enforcing the prohibition by prosecution for a criminal offence which is subject to heavy penalties including imprisonment. So one starts with the presumption laid down originally by Lord Tenterden C.J. in *Doe d. Bishop of Rochester* v. *Bridges* ((1831) 1 B. & Ad. 847, 859) where he spoke of the "general rule" that "where an Act creates an obligation, and enforces the performance in a specified manner . . . that performance cannot be enforced in any other manner," a statement that has frequently been cited with approval ever since, including on several occasions in speeches in this House. Where the only manner of enforcing performance for which the Act provides is prosecution for the criminal offence of failure to perform the statutory obligation or for contravening the statutory prohibition which the Act creates, there are two classes of exception to this general rule.

The first is where on the true construction of the Act it is apparent that the obligation or prohibition was imposed for the benefit or protection of a particular class of individuals, as in the case of the Factories Acts and similar legislation. As Lord Kinnear put it in *Black* v. *Fife Coal Co. Ltd.* ([1912] A.C. 149, 165), in the case of such a statute:

"There is no reasonable ground for maintaining that a proceeding by way of penalty is the only remedy allowed by the statute . . . We are to consider the scope and purpose of the statute and in particular for whose benefit it is intended. Now the object of the present statute is plain. It was intended to compel mine owners to make due provision for the safety of the men working in their mines, and the persons for whose benefit all these rules are to be enforced are the persons exposed to danger. But when a duty of this kind is imposed for the benefit of particular persons there arises at common law a correlative right in those persons who may be injured by its contravention."

The second exception is where the statute creates a public right (*i.e.* a right to be enjoyed by all those of Her Majesty's subjects who wish to avail themselves of it) and a particular member of the public suffers what Brett J. in *Benjamin* v. *Storr* ((1874) L.R. 9 C.P. 400, 407) described as "particular, direct and substantial" damage "other and different from that which was common to all the rest of the public." Most of the authorities about this second exception deal not with public rights created by statute but with public rights existing at common law, particularly in respect of use of highways. *Boyce* v. *Paddington Borough Council* ([1903] 1 Ch. 109) is one of the comparatively few cases about a right conferred on the general public by statute. It is in relation to that class of statute only that Buckley J.'s oft-cited statement (at 114) as to the two cases in which a plaintiff, without joining the Attorney-General, could himself sue in private law for interference with that public right must be understood. The two cases he said were:

"first, where the interference with the public right is such as that some private right of his is at the same time interfered with . . . and, secondly, where no private right is interfered with, but the plaintiff, in respect of his public right, suffers special damage peculiar to himself from the interference with the public right."

The first case would not appear to depend on the existence of a public right in addition to the private one; while to come within the second case at all it has first to be shown that the statute, having regard to its scope and language, does fall within that class of statutes which create a legal right to be enjoyed by all of Her Majesty's subjects who wish to avail themselves of it. A mere prohibition on members of the public generally from doing what it would otherwise be lawful for them to do is not enough.

My Lords, it has been the unanimous opinion of the arbitrators with the concurrence of the umpire, of Parker J. and of each of the three members of the Court of Appeal that the sanctions orders made pursuant to the Southern Rhodesia Act 1965 fell within neither of these two exceptions. Clearly they were not within the first category of exception. They were not imposed for the *benefit* or *protection* of a particular class of individuals who were engaged in supplying or delivering crude oil or petroleum products to Southern Rhodesia. They were intended to put an end to such transactions. Equally plainly they did not create any public right to be enjoyed by all those of Her Majesty's subjects who wished to avail themselves of it. On the contrary, what they did was to withdraw a previously existing right of citizens of, and companies incorporated in, the United Kingdom to trade with Southern Rhodesia in crude oil and petroleum products. Their purpose was, perhaps, most aptly stated by Fox L.J. He said:

"I cannot think that they were concerned with conferring rights either on individuals or the public at large. Their purpose was the destruction, by economic pressure, of the UDI regime in Southern Rhodesia; they were instruments of state policy in an international matter."

Until the United Nations called on its members to impose sanctions on the illegal regime in Southern Rhodesia it may not be strictly accurate to speak of it as an international matter, but from the outset it was certainly state policy in affairs external to the United Kingdom.

In agreement with all those present and former members of the judiciary who have considered the matter I can see no ground on which contraventions by Shell and BP of the sanctions orders, though not amounting to any breach of their contract with Lonrho, nevertheless constituted a tort for which Lonrho could recover in a civil suit any loss caused to them by such contraventions.

Briefly parting from this part of the case, however, I should mention briefly two cases, one in the Court of Appeal of England, *Ex parte Island Records Ltd.* ([1978] Ch. 122), and one in the High Court of Australia, *Beaudesert Shire Council* v. *Smith* ((1966) 120 C.L.R. 145), which counsel for Lonrho, as a last resort, relied on as showing that some broader principle has of recent years replaced those long-established principles that I have just stated for determining whether a contravention of a particular statutory prohibition by one private individual makes him liable in tort to another private individual who can prove that he has suffered damage as a result of the contravention.

Ex parte Island Records Ltd. was an unopposed application for an Anton Piller order against a defendant who, without the consent of the performers, had made records of musical performances for the purposes of trade. This was an offence, punishable by a relatively small penalty under the Dramatic and Musical Performers' Protection Act 1958. The application for the Anton Piller order was made by performers whose performances had been "bootlegged" by the defendant without their consent and also by record companies with whom the performers had entered into exclusive contracts. So far as the application by performers was concerned, it could have been granted for entirely orthodox reasons. The Act was passed for the protection of a particular class of individuals, dramatic and musical performers; even the short title said so. Whether the record companies would have been entitled to obtain the order in a civil action to which the performers whose performances had been bootlegged were not parties is a matter which for present purposes it is not necessary to decide. Lord Denning M.R., however, with whom Waller L.J. agreed (Shaw L.J. dissenting) appears to enunciate a wider general rule, which does not depend on the scope and language of the statute by which a criminal offence is committed, that whenever a lawful business carried on by one individual in fact suffers damage as the consequence of a contravention by another individual of any statutory prohibition the former has a civil right of action against the latter for such damage.

My Lords, with respect, I am unable to accept that this is the law; and I observe that in his judgment rejecting a similar argument by the appellants in the instant appeal Lord Denning M.R. accepts that the question whether a breach of sanctions orders gives rise to a civil action depends on the object and intent of those orders, and refers to *Ex parte Island Records Ltd.* as an example of a statute passed for the protection of private rights and interests, *viz.* those of the performers.

Beaudesert Shire Council v. *Smith* is a decision of the High Court of Australia. It appeared to recognise the existence of a novel innominate tort of the nature of an "action for damages upon the case" available to "a person who suffers harm or loss as the inevitable consequence of the unlawful, intentional and positive acts of another." The decision, although now 15 years old, has never been followed in any Australian or other common law jurisdiction. In subsequent Australian cases it has invariably been distinguished, most recently by the Privy Council in *Dunlop* v. *Woollahra Municipal Council* ([1982] A.C. 158), on appeal from the Supreme Court of New South Wales. It is clear now from a later decision of the Australian High Court in *Kitano* v. *Commonwealth of Australia* ((1974) 129 C.L.R. 151) that the adjective "unlawful" in the definition of acts which give rise to this new action for damages on the case does not include *every* breach of statutory duty which in fact causes damage to the plaintiff. It remains uncertain whether it was intended to include acts done in contravention of a wider range of statutory obligations or prohibitions than those which under the principles that I have discussed above would give rise to a civil action at common law in England if they are contravened. If the tort described in *Beaudesert* was really intended to extend that range, I would invite your Lordships to declare that it forms no part of the law of England. . . .

Lord Edmund-Davies, Lord Keith, Lord Scarman and Lord Bridge all agreed with Lord Diplock.

Note:
The terms in which this opinion are rendered seem to have been affected by the decision in *Gouriet,* which was concerned with another point of contact between private law and criminal law, with the question when an individual can seek an injunction to restrain a threatened

breach of statutory law. It is true that in that case the plaintiff did not allege that he would suffer any damage as a result of the crime, were it committed, and it is true that even if he had, he could not have sued the trade union for encouraging it (trade unions being then immune to liability in tort) nor yet the Post Office or any of its employees (Post Office Act 1969 s.9). In that case, however, Viscount Dilhorne said that although " . . . only the Attorney-General can sue on behalf of the public for the purpose of preventing public wrongs . . . a private individual . . . may be able to do so if he will sustain injury as a result of a public wrong" ([1978] A.C. 435, 494). Lord Diplock here says that a private individual cannot sue for proven damage resulting from a public wrong; indeed his dismissive analysis of the observations of Buckley J. which he cites robs them of content entirely. Do you think that Lonrho would have been allowed to seek an injunction to prevent the respondents' conduct if (unimaginably) the Attorney-General had refused his consent to a relator action?

POWERS OF CRIMINAL COURTS ACT 1973

35.—(1) Subject to the provisions of this Part of this Act, a court by or before which a person is convicted of an offence, in addition to dealing with him in any other way, may, on application or otherwise, make an order (in this Act referred to as "a compensation order") requiring him to pay compensation for any personal injury, loss or damage resulting from that offence or any other offence which is taken into consideration by the court in determining sentence, or to make payments for funeral expenses or bereavement in respect of a death resulting from any such offence, other than a death due to an accident arising out of the presence of a motor vehicle on a road; and a court shall give reasons, on passing sentence, if it does not make such an order in a case where this section empowers it to do so.

(2) In the case of an offence under the Theft Act 1968, where the property in question is recovered, any damage to the property occurring while it was out of the owner's possession shall be treated for the purposes of subsection (1) above as having resulted from the offence, however and by whomsoever the damage was caused.

(3) A compensation order may only be made in respect of injury, loss or damage (other than loss suffered by a person's dependants in consequence of his death) which was due to an accident arising out of the presence of a motor vehicle on a road, if—

(a) it is in respect of damage which is treated by subsection (2) above as resulting from an offence under the Theft Act 1968; or
(b) it is in respect of injury, loss or damage as respects which
  (i) the offender is uninsured in relation to the use of the vehicle; and
  (ii) compensation is not payable under any arrangements to which the Secretary of State is a party;

and, where a compensation order is made in respect of injury, loss or damage due to such an accident, the amount to be paid may include an amount representing the whole or part of any loss of or reduction in preferential rates of insurance attributable to the accident.

(3B) A compensation order in respect of funeral expenses may be made for the benefit of anyone who incurred the expenses.

(3C) A compensation order in respect of bereavement may only be made for the benefit of a person for whose benefit a claim for damages for bereavement could be made under section 1A of the Fatal Accidents Act 1976.

(3D) The amount of compensation in respect of bereavement shall not exceed the amount for the time being specified in section 1A(3) of the Fatal Accidents Act 1976.

(4) In determining whether to make a compensation order against any person, and in determining the amount to be paid by any person under such an order, the court shall have regard to his means so far as they appear or are known to the court.

(5) The compensation to be paid under a compensation order made by a magistrates' court in respect of any offence of which the court has convicted the offender shall not exceed £2,000; and the compensation or total compensation to be paid under a compensation order or compensation orders made by a magistrates' court in respect of any offence or offences taken into consideration in determining sentence shall not exceed the difference (if any) between the amount or total amount which under the preceding provisions of this subsection is the maximum for the offence or offences of which the offender has been convicted and the amount or total amounts (if any) which are in fact ordered to be paid in respect of that offence or those offences.

. . .

38.—(1) This section shall have effect where a compensation order has been made in favour of any person in respect of any injury, loss or damage and a claim by him in civil proceedings for damages in respect of the injury, loss or damage subsequently falls to be determined.

(2) The damages in the civil proceedings shall be assessed without regard to the order; but the plaintiff may only recover an amount equal to the aggregate of the following—

(a) any amount by which they exceed the compensation; and
(b) a sum equal to any portion of the compensation which he fails to recover,

and may not enforce the judgment, so far as it relates to a sum such as is mentioned in paragraph (b) above, without the leave of the court.

Note:
It was in 1972 that criminal courts in England were first given the power to order a convict to pay compensation to the victim. In 1986 they issued over 100,000 compensation orders, including 94,000 in magistrates' courts and 6,500 in the Crown Court; about 40 per cent. of the former were of £25 or less and 25 per cent of £100 or more, as were over half of the latter. Despite a certain ambivalence in the Court of Appeal towards this new institution, it has been resoundingly confirmed by the Criminal Justice Bill 1988 which adds, *inter alia*, the final words to s.35(1) above. A compensation order may be granted even if no civil liability exists (*R.* v. *Chappell* (1984) 80 Cr.App.R. 31 (C.A.), noted Wasik, 48 M.L.R. 707 (1985)). Thus criminal courts need not face the tricky question whether breach of a particular statutory duty attracts civil liability as well as a criminal sanction.

CRIMINAL JUSTICE BILL 1988

Note:
The numbers and texts of the sections in the eventual Act may well differ from those given below).

106.—(1) The Criminal Injuries Compensation Board ("the Board") shall by that name be a body corporate.

(2) The Board shall administer the scheme for the payment of compensation for criminal injuries established by the following provisions of this Part of this Act (in this Act referred to as "the scheme") and shall be responsible for determining claims for compensation under the scheme and for paying compensation due under it.

107.—(1) In this Part of this Act "criminal injury" means any personal injury caused by—

(a) conduct constituting—
(i) an offence which is specified in subsection (3) below; or
(ii) an offence which is not so specified but which requires proof of intent to cause death or personal injury or recklessness as to whether death or personal injury is caused; or
(b) any of the following activities—

    (i) the apprehension or attempted apprehension of an offender or sus-
pected offender;

    (ii) the prevention or attempted prevention of the commission of an
offence; or

    (iii) assisting a constable engaged in any of the activities mentioned in sub-
paragraph (i) or (ii) above;

and "personal injury" includes any disease, any harm to a person's physical or mental condition and pregnancy.

    (2) Harm to a person's mental condition is only a criminal injury if it is attributable—

    (a) to his having been put in fear of immediate physical injury to himself or
another; or

    (b) to his being present when another sustained a criminal injury other than
harm to his mental condition.

    (3) [lists offences including rape, arson, kidnapping and false imprisonment,
assault, trespass on a railway and certain offences under the Explosive Substances
Act 1883, the Firearms Act 1968 and the Public Order Act 1986.]

108.—(1) Compensation for a criminal injury shall only be payable under this
Part of this Act if the injury is a qualifying injury.

109.—(1) An award of compensation may be made—

    (a) to any person who satisfies the Board that he has sustained a qualifying injury;

    (b) to any person who satisfies the Board that he is a dependant of a person who died
after sustaining a qualifying injury (whether or not he died as a result of it);

and in this subsection "satisfies" means satisfies on a balance of probabilities.

    (3) If a person dies as a result of a qualifying injury, the compensation that may
be awarded in respect of that injury includes—

    (a) compensation for reasonable funeral expenses paid in respect of him; and

    (b) compensation for bereavement not exceeding the amount specified at the
time of his death in section 1A(3) of the Fatal Accidents Act 1976.

    (5) The only persons to whom an award under subsection (3)(b) above may be
made are persons for whose benefit damages for bereavement may be awarded
under the Fatal Accidents Act 1976.

    (7) In this Part of this Act "dependant" . . . has the same meaning as in the Fatal
Accidents Act 1976.

110.—(1) It is for the claimant to satisfy the Board, on a balance of probabilities—

    (a) that he took all reasonable steps within a reasonable time to inform the police,
or such other authority as the Board consider appropriate, of the circumstances
of the injury to which his claim relates and that he has co-operated fully with the
police, or with such other authority as the Board consider appropriate, in bringing to justice any person responsible for causing the injury;

    (b) that he has given the Board, or such other authority as the Board consider
appropriate, all the assistance in connection with his claim which it is reasonable for him to give; and

    (c) that there is no possibility that a person responsible for causing the injury
will benefit from an award,

and if a claimant fails so to satisfy the Board, they may, if they think fit, refuse an
award or award less than they would otherwise have awarded.

    (2) The Board may also, if they think fit, refuse an award or award less than they
would otherwise have awarded because of any of the following—

    (a) criminal convictions or unlawful conduct of the claimant;

    (b) conduct on his part connected with the injury.

(3) The references to convictions and conduct in subsection (2) above are references to convictions and conduct at any time, including a time after the injury.

111.—(1) An appeal on any ground which involves a question of law alone shall lie—

(a) to the High Court from a decision of the Board under the law of England and Wales; . . .

112.—(1) The Secretary of State may by order provide that the Board shall not make any award of compensation, other than an award in respect of funeral expenses, which is less than the minimum amount specified in the order.

113.—(1) Where—

(a) a person has been convicted . . . of an offence; and
(b) the Board have made an award of compensation in respect of an injury which is a criminal injury by virtue of the offence,

proceedings may be brought by the Board, for the reimbursement by the offender to the Board of the whole or any specified part of the award.

(SCHEDULE 7)

9.—(1) In the case of an award under section 109(1)(a) above, compensation shall be payable—

(a) for the personal injury to the claimant; and
(b) for any loss of or damage to property of his which occurred in the course of his sustaining the injury to which the claim relates,

but compensation shall only be payable under paragraph (b) above if he relied on the property as a physical aid and for damage only if the damage impaired the utility of the property as a physical aid.

(2) The amount of compensation payable under this paragraph shall, subject to the provisions of this Part of this Act, be assessed in accordance with the principles for the time being applicable under the appropriate law to the assessment of damages on a civil claim . . .

(3) Compensation payable under this paragraph shall not include any element—

(a) in respect of interest; or
(b) corresponding to exemplary or aggravated damages.

(4) In assessing compensation payable under this paragraph no account shall be taken of any expenses incurred in respect of private medical treatment unless the Board are satisfied that such treatment is or was essential; and where the Board are so satisfied in relation to any such treatment, compensation for the expenses incurred in respect of that treatment shall not exceed a reasonable amount.

9.—(1) Where—

(a) the injury to which the claim relates was sustained in the course of rape; and
(b) the claimant has given birth to a child conceived as a result of the rape; and
(c) she intends to keep the child,

a sum of £5,000 shall be payable as compensation in addition to any compensation payable under paragraph 5 above.

(2) Compensation payable under that paragraph in respect of loss suffered in consequence of such an injury shall not include any sum in respect of the maintenance of such a child.

12.—(1) The Board may award compensation to a dependant of a person who died otherwise than as a result of a qualifying injury in respect—

(a) of any loss of earnings (not being prospective earnings) by the deceased; and

(b) of expenses and liabilities incurred by the deceased, as a result of the injury but the award shall be limited to the amount of the dependant's loss.

13.—(1) For the purposes of assessing compensation payable under this Part of this Act, the earning capacity of the person who sustained the injury to which the claim in question relates shall be taken not to be or to have been in excess of one-and-a-half times the gross average industrial wage.

14.—(1) Compensation, other than compensation for rape under paragraph 9 above or compensation in respect of funeral expenses, shall be assessed on the basis that the loss to be compensated is reduced by the value of any entitlement to benefits which the claimant has in consequence of the injury to which the claim relates or, as the case may be, the death of the person who sustained that injury.

(2) In this paragraph—

"benefit" means—

(a) any social security benefits payable under the laws of any part of the United Kingdom and any similar benefits payable under the laws of any other country or territory;

(b) any award under the scheme established by the Criminal Injuries (Compensation) (Northern Ireland) Order 1977, or any order replacing that Order, or under any similar scheme established in any other country or territory;

(c) benefits (including any return of premiums) under any insurance arrangements, other than private insurance arrangements. . . .

15.—(1) Compensation payable, other than compensation for rape under paragraph 9 above or compensation in respect of funeral expenses, shall be assessed on the basis that the loss to be compensated is reduced by the value of any pension rights, other than private pension rights, which—

(a) where the claimant is the person who sustained the injury to which the claim relates, are enjoyed by him in consequence of that injury and by virtue of any office or employment of his; or

(b) where the claimant is a dependant of the person who sustained the injury to which the claim relates, are enjoyed by him in consequence of that person's death and by virtue of any office or employment of that person.

(4) For the purposes of this paragraph, "pension rights" includes sums paid under insurance arrangements, other than private insurance arrangements, and gratuities.

16. Where the Board are satisfied that, by virtue of—

(a) a judgment or decree in, or the settlement of, any action for damages; or

(b) any order under . . . the Powers of Criminal Courts Act 1973,

a claimant has received any payment which compensates him for any loss in respect of which compensation is payable to him under this Part of this Act, the compensation so payable to him shall be assessed on the basis that that loss is reduced by the amount of that payment.

17. If—

(a) a deceased person has become entitled to compensation under this Part of this Act; and

(b) a claim for such compensation for the same injury is made by one of his dependants,

the dependant's compensation shall be reduced by the amount of the deceased's compensation; and proportionate reductions shall be made if claims are made by two or more dependants.

Comments:

s.107(2). Train drivers will be pleased by the inclusion of the offence of endangering persons on railways, for the Court of Appeal had held that no award could be made to a driver shocked by running over a trespasser on the line. Anna Karenina's example is followed by about 250 people per year, and 250 claims by engine drivers were pending before the Board at the time of *R.* v. *Criminal Injuries Compensation Board, ex p. Warner* [1986] 2 All E.R. 478.

s.108. The following are *not* qualifying injuries:

(a) injury sustained by a minor residing with the offender, unless the offender has been prosecuted and the minor has ceased to reside with him, or there is a good reason why not;
(b) accidental injury falling within s.107(1)(*b*) unless the risk taken by the claimant was exceptional and justified;
(c) injuries caused by motor vehicles where cover is provided by a compulsory policy or by the Motor Insurers Bureau.

s.109(7). Under the previous non-statutory scheme no claim could be brought by the survivor of an unmarried couple.

s.110. The Board's power to reduce compensation is very much wider than that of the courts under the Contributory Negligence Act or, in the case of battery, common law (see below p. 213).

s.112. The minimum amount under the previous Scheme was £550. For smaller claims, one should seek a compensation order from the criminal courts, since the County Court will be too expensive.

Schedule

Para. 8(3). Aggravated damages would be a common feature of claims at law against a violent criminal.

Para. 8(4). This is in sensible derogation from the rule in Law Reform (Personal Injuries) Act 1948, s.2(4).

Para. 12. At law a claim for the decedent's pain and suffering may be brought by his estate—a silly rule, well excluded here.

Para. 13. Very democratic. The gross average industrial wage is announced from time to time (probably late) by the Secretary of State.

Para. 14. "Private insurance arrangements" do not include arrangements made by an employer, so sums payable thereunder are deductible. The same is true of "private pension arrangements" under para. 15.

Para. 17. At law, dependants may not claim if the decedent has settled his claim or obtained judgment.

Note:

The Criminal Injuries Compensation Scheme was started in 1964 and proceeded on a non-statutory basis until this enactment. Review by the courts was originally embarrassed (*R.* v. *Criminal Injuries Compensation Board, ex p. Lain* [1967] 2 All E.R. 770), but became increasingly frequent. In the year ending March 31, 1986 the Board received 39,697 new applications and made 22,534 awards—5 per cent. of more than £5,000, 57 per cent. of less than £1,000 and the rest in between—a total of £41,600,000. In the following year the total payout exceeded £48m., and the number of applications increased by 2,620.

CIVIL EVIDENCE ACT 1968

11.—(1) In any civil proceedings the fact that a person has been convicted of an offence by or before any court in the United Kingdom or by a court-martial there or elsewhere shall (subject to subsection (3) below) be admissible in evidence for the purpose of proving, where to do so is relevant to any issue in those proceedings, that he committed that offence, whether he was so convicted upon a plea of guilty or otherwise and whether or not he is a party to the civil proceedings; but no conviction other than a subsisting one shall be admissible in evidence by virtue of this section.

. . .

Section 1.—Statutory Duties and Civil Liability

BARNA v. HUDES MERCHANDISING CORPORATION

Court of Appeal (1962) 106 S.J. 194; Crim.L.R. 321

Action by motorist against motorist in respect of property damage

The plaintiff was driving his Citroen along West Heath Avenue to where it ended by forming a T-junction with North End Road, where he planned to turn right. At the junction he stopped. To his left, on the crown of the main road, was a line of cars waiting to turn right into the street from which he was emerging. To his right was a line of parked cars which impeded his vision. He edged slowly forward, and then saw, about 40 yards away, the defendant's car approaching from his right at a speed which the defendant admitted was in excess of the legal limit. The plaintiff stopped, but as there was not enough room between his car and those waiting to turn right, the defendant collided with him, and both vehicles were damaged. The plaintiff claimed the cost of repairs, and the defendant counterclaimed. The county court judge dismissed the claim and allowed the counterclaim. The plaintiff appealed without success to the Court of Appeal.

Ormerod L.J. said that, since the amount of the claim was under £200, there was no appeal on a question of fact and the Court of Appeal could only interfere if the judge's inference could not be reasonably drawn from the evidence. There was no doubt that the . . . defendant had exceeded the speed limit and had committed an offence, but that did not make his speed excessive for the purposes of civil liability and did not of itself constitute negligence. The . . . defendant, driving on a fast busy main road, had no reason to anticipate that it would be blocked as it was. In those circumstances the judge's inference, that the speed of the . . . defendant was not excessive and that the plaintiff alone was negligent, was one that could be reasonably drawn from the evidence.

REFFELL v. SURREY COUNTY COUNCIL

Queen's Bench [1964] 1 W.L.R. 358; 128 J.P. 261; 108 S.J. 119; 62 L.G.R. 186; [1964] 1 All E.R. 743

Action by pupil against education authority in respect of personal injury

The plaintiff, a girl of 12 and a pupil at the defendant's school, hurried down a corridor to the cloakroom. One of its two glazed doors was swinging towards her, so she put out her right hand to stop it. Her hand went through one of the panes of glass which was only one-eighth of an inch thick. It had been installed by a competent architect when the school was built in 1919, and there had never been an accident with that door before. Broken panes were always replaced by toughened glass. The local authority was responsible for over 700 educational establishments, and had about 11 accidents per year involving broken glass.

Veale J.: . . . It is in those circumstances that the plaintiff puts her case in two ways. She alleges that the local education authority have been guilty of a breach of their statutory duty. Secondly, she alleges that they are guilty of negligence at common law.

I will deal first with the question of statutory duty. The Education Act 1944, provides by section 10(1): "The Minister shall make regulations prescribing the standards to which the premises of schools maintained by local education authorities are to conform, and such regulations may prescribe different standards for such descriptions of schools as may be specified in the regulations." Section 10(2) provides: "Subject as hereinafter provided, it shall be the duty of a local education authority to secure that the premises of every school maintained by them conform to the standards prescribed for schools of the description to which the school belongs." Be it noted that the duty is a duty to secure conformity with the prescribed standards.

In accordance with the duty laid upon him, the Minister has made regulations. The relevant ones for my consideration are the Standards for School Premises Regulations 1959. Regulation 51, under the heading "Precautions for Health and Safety," reads as follows [His Lordship read regulation 51 and continued:] Omitting irrelevant words, that regulation therefore reads: "In all parts of the buildings of every school . . . the design, the construction . . . and the properties of the materials shall be such that the health and safety of the occupants . . . shall be reasonably assured."

Three points really arise. First, do the statute and regulation 51 give a right of action to a pupil at the school? Secondly, if so, what is the nature and extent of the duty? Thirdly, was there any breach of duty which caused this accident?

. . . The question whether or not a private person has a right of action for the breach of a statutory duty is always a very difficult one. Reliance is placed by the plaintiff on cases such as *Groves* v. *Wimborne* ([1898] 2 Q.B. 402) and on the observations of their Lordships in *Cutler* v. *Wandsworth Stadium* ([1949] A.C. 398). It is said that there is a strong presumption that a private right of action can be enforced by a private individual in cases where the statute provides no penalty for the breach. That is the case here, because the Education Act 1944, by section 99, gives powers to the minister to issue directions to an education authority and, if necessary, an application can be made for mandamus.

I think that the best approach to this kind of question is that set out in *Charlesworth on Negligence* (4th ed., 1962), paragraph 963, at p. 454: "It has been said: 'No universal rule can be formulated which will answer the question whether in any given case an individual can sue in respect of a breach of statutory duty.' In addition to the general rule set out in the preceding section, however, the most important matters to be taken into consideration appear to be: (a) Is the action brought in respect of the kind of harm which the statute was intended to prevent? (b) Is the person bringing the action one of the class which the statute desired to protect? (c) Is the special remedy provided by the statute adequate for the protection of the person injured? If the first two questions are answered in the affirmative and the third in the negative then, in most cases, the individual can sue."

I do not think that there has been any express decision on section 10 of the Education Act 1944, and regulation 51 of the Standards for School Premises Regulations 1959, and I confess that I have had some doubt about the matter; but I have come to the conclusion that the answers in this case to the three questions set out in the paragraph I have just read are "yes" to the first two and "no" to the third. Bearing in mind that no penalty is laid down by the statute for a breach, I think that an action does lie by a pupil or master at a school who can prove a breach of the regulation.

What then is the nature of the duty? Counsel for the plaintiff says that, if in fact there is a breach in the sense that premises are not reasonably safe or that safety is not reasonably assured, this statutory duty is wider than any duty at common law, because—so the argument runs—the test is objective; that is to say, it matters not what this authority or other authorities knew or did not know, did or did not do, or what the past experience was. If safety was not reasonably assured, that, says counsel, is an end of the matter, though he concedes that, at common law, such matters as past experience, would indeed be relevant. The local education authority, on the other hand, say that the regulation adds nothing to the common law duty. On the facts as I find them to be in this case I think this argument is largely academic; but it is an important point and I think it right to express my view upon it.

In my judgment, the argument of the plaintiff on this point is right. I think the duty to secure (that is the word in the section) that safety shall be reasonably assured (which are the words of the regulation) is an absolute duty and the test of breach or no is objective. Putting it another way, if safety is not reasonably assured in the premises in fact, then there is a breach.

That leads to the third question. Were the premises on July 15, 1960, with this $\frac{1}{8}$ inch glass in the cloakroom door, at a height of four feet, reasonably safe? I have no hesitation in saying that they were not. This $\frac{1}{8}$ inch glass in a cloakroom door was, in my view, asking for trouble. True, there had been no previous accident at this door, but there had been accidents of some sort at such doors elsewhere, and there had been an accident at the boys' cloakroom door in 1937, and the boys' cloakroom door was altered because of the danger of unruly boys. Boys are more unruly than girls, or so a witness told me. Boys will be boys; but, equally, I should have thought, girls will be girls. Even if they do not fight like small boys and generally behave with more decorum, they nevertheless have been known to chase each other and to run in corridors. It is easy to visualise one girl following another, the one in front swinging the cloakroom door to and the following girl putting out a hand to arrest it, without any element of horse play at all. I cannot help thinking that the defendants have been lucky that there has been no previous accident at this door.

The distinction between boys and girls has not been drawn by the local education authority since the war. All doors in new schools have toughened glass in doors and all breakages of glass in doors have involved toughened glass as a replacement. One sympathises, of course, with the position of a local education authority with a number of old schools to manage. I have no doubt at all that this local education authority appreciated the risk. But no evidence has been called before me by the local education authority to show that they considered this question; or if they did, to what conclusion they came and why; or that the replacements involved enormous expense which was out of proportion to the risk; or that some form of grille or wooden slat was impracticable. For all I know (and, indeed, the position seems to be this) the local education authority merely waited for either a major adaptation of the buildings, or a breakage to occur, before they did anything at all.

The Middlesex County Council are said now to be gradually changing $\frac{1}{8}$ inch glass in school doors. The Essex County Council are said to have issued, only last month, a directive to the same effect to a Mr. Jefferson, who takes his orders from the Essex County architect and follows their advice. But I have the evidence of a practical man and a convincing witness whose evidence I accept. This $\frac{1}{8}$ inch glass, he said, should have been changed years ago. I am not, I hope, being wise after the event, and I exclude, I hope, the wisdom of hindsight; but, if instead of considering whether there was a breach of regulation 51 on an objective basis I were to approach the matter on a common law basis, I should still say, and indeed I find, that the defendants were negligent. This is not the case of an isolated hit for six out of a cricket ground as in *Bolton* v. *Stone.*

It is said for the local education authority that their common law duty *qua* their premises is the common duty of care under the Occupiers' Liability Act 1957 and is a somewhat lower duty than the duty of a school master as a good and prudent father of a family. That is, I think, correct. But it makes very little, if any, difference, on the facts of this case. I am content to take their duty as the common duty of care, which is defined by section 2(2) of the Occupiers' Liability Act 1957 as a duty "to take such care as in all the circumstances of the case is reasonable to see that the visitor will be reasonably safe in using the premises for the purposes for which he is invited or permitted by the occupier to be there." The circumstances here include the circumstance that this was a school and that the door was in constant use by children. I do not accept that the risk was minimal, as was urged upon me by counsel for the local education authority. If it is too much to ask an education authority, confronted with this problem of glass in doors, to change every door with ⅛ inch in it, it is not too much to ask them to do something more than merely wait for major adaptations or breakages. Whatever may be the vulnerability of other doors, I should have said that a cloakroom door at the end of a straight corridor was more vulnerable than most. Not only, in my judgment, was the risk of accident a real risk, but it was both a foreseeable risk and was in fact foreseen. If it had not been foreseen there would not have been the policy of replacing broken ⅛ inch glass with toughened glass.

In the result, I find the local education authority liable to the plaintiff both under the statute and regulation and at common law.

Questions

1. Are there any situations in which the plaintiff would have recovered in an action for breach of statutory duty and would have failed to recover at common law?

2. Suppose you want to *make* someone perform his statutory duty, rather than wait for harm and then claim compensation from him. For what remedy should you apply if the duty is (a) public, (b) private? Would the appropriate remedy ever be granted or refused when damages for any harm suffered would not?

3. Suppose that the education authority had decided, after meeting a pay claim by intransigent teachers, that it simply could not afford to replace thin glass by thick glass. Would the plaintiff still succeed, or could the defendant deploy the operational/policy distinction of *Dorset Yacht* (above p. 53) and *Anns* (above p. 60)?

4. Suppose that the person injured by the glass was (a) a master, (b) the school janitor, (c) a parent fetching a child, or (d) a burglar. Would recovery be allowed?

Read:

Buckley, "Liability in Tort for Breach of Statutory Duty," 100 L.Q.R. 204 (1984).

Note:

The plaintiff here, who had suffered no financial loss, recovered (tax free) a sum about equal to half her teacher's annual salary, or the cost of a thousand panes of toughened glass.

No injunction will issue to prevent an education authority's setting up a new school in premises which fall short of the standards laid down by Regulations: the only remedy of the parent is to apply to the Secretary of State: *Bradbury* v. *Enfield Borough* [1967] 3 All E.R. 434 (C.A.).

Many statutory duties imposed on public bodies involve the provision of benefits to specified classes of people. Can a disappointed claimant sue for breach of statutory duty? A two-man Court of Appeal so held in *Thornton* v. *Kirklees Metropolitan B.C.* [1979] Q.B. 626, a decision entirely out of line with previous holdings, but of course quite consonant with *Anns* (above p. 60) which imposed liability for financial harm caused by the unreasonable exercise of statutory powers, though only in the operational area. The consequent harassment of local authorities has led the courts to undo some of this wretched work by insisting that what are really matters of public law must be resolved in proper proceedings, namely by judicial review, in which damages may be awarded, rather than by ordinary action of tort.

PHILLIPS v. BRITANNIA HYGIENIC LAUNDRY CO.

Court of Appeal [1923] 2 K.B. 832; 93 L.J.K.B. 5; 129 L.T. 777; 39 T.L.R. 530; 68 S.J. 102; 21 L.G.R. 709; [1923] All E.R.Rep. 127

Action by highway user against highway user in respect of property damage

Bankes L.J.: This is an appeal from the Divisional Court reversing the county court judge in an action brought by the plaintiff for damage done to his motor van. The axle of the defendants' motor lorry broke and caused the damage. The action in the county court was founded on an alleged breach of a statutory provision contained in the Motor Cars (Use and Construction) Order 1904 and alternatively on the alleged negligence of the defendant. The county court judge absolved the defendant from negligence in relation either to the management of the motor lorry or to the state of its axle, but he found negligence on the part of the repairers to whom the motor lorry had been sent, in not having executed the repairs efficiently, and gave judgment for the plaintiff on the ground that the lorry was not in the condition required by cl. 6 of art. II of the Order. On an appeal by the defendants the Divisional Court reversed this judgment. The plaintiff appeals to this court.

I agree with the conclusion of the Divisional Court. If the judgment of the county court judge were to stand it would have very far-reaching consequences. It is unnecessary to consider what they would be, as in this case there is only one point to be considered, and that has long been governed by well-established rules; and when those rules are applied to the facts of this case, it is clear that the Divisional Court came to the right conclusion.

The only point of substance argued for the appellant was that the Motor Cars (Use and Construction) Order 1904 conferred on him a statutory right of action for breach of its conditions. Two well-known rules relate to this question; the first is stated by Kennedy L.J. in *Dawson & Co.* v. *Bingley Urban Council* ([1911] 2 K.B. 149, 159) in these words: "Now, the general law as to the remedy of a person who has been injured by the infringement of a statutory right or the breach of a statutory obligation for his benefit is clear. Where the statute has not in express terms given a remedy, the remedy which by law is properly applicable to the right or the obligation follows as an incident. The law is, I think, correctly stated in *Addison on Torts*, 8th ed., p. 104, referring to *Comyn's Digest*: 'In every case where a statute enacts or prohibits a thing for the benefit of a person, he shall have a remedy upon the same statute for the thing enacted for his advantage, or for the recompense of a wrong done to him contrary to the said law': Com.Dig. Action upon Statute (F). Accordingly, where the statute is silent as to the remedy, the Legislature is to be taken as intending the ordinary result; and the proper remedy for breach of the statute is an action for damages and, in a proper case, for an injunction." In these cases it may be material to consider whether the right conferred or the act prohibited is for the benefit of a particular class of persons or of the public generally. The second rule is thus stated by Lord Halsbury in *Pasmore* v. *Oswaldtwistle Urban Council* ([1898] A.C. 387, 394): "The principle that where a specific remedy is given by a statute, it thereby deprives the person who insists upon a remedy of any other form of remedy than that given by the statute, is one which is very familiar and which runs through the law. I think Lord Tenterden accurately states that principle in the case of *Doe* v. *Bridges* ((1831) 1 B. & Ad. 847, 859; 109 E.R. 1001, 1006). He says: 'Where an Act creates an obligation, and enforces the performance in a specified manner, we take it to be a general rule that performance cannot be enforced in any other manner.'" In the same case of *Pasmore* v. *Oswaldtwistle Urban Council* Lord Macnaghten said: "Whether the general rule is to prevail, or an exception to the general rule is to be admitted, must depend on the scope and language of the Act which creates the obligation and on considerations of policy and convenience." In the case we are considering the statute creates an obligation and provides a remedy for its non-observance, and the question is whether the scope and language of the statute indicate that the general rule is to prevail so that the remedy provided is the only remedy, or whether an exception to that general rule is to be admitted. The order of the Local Government Board was made under section 6 of the Locomotives on Highways Act 1896, which empowered the Local Government Board to make regulations with respect to the use of light locomotives on highways, their construction, and the conditions under which they may be used. Section 7 of the Act provides that a breach of any regulation made under the Act may be punished by a fine not exceeding £10. The language of the Act includes the expressions the "use of light locomotives" their "construction" and "conditions under which they may be used"; and its scope is the public user of highways, which has been for years subject to rules regulating and controlling it. Thus the Act deals with rights which have always been sufficiently protected by the common law. Under this Act the Local Government order was made. It is divided into sections or articles, five in number. The provision relied on is art. II: "No person shall cause or permit a motor car to be used on any highway, or shall drive or have charge of a motor car when so used, unless the conditions hereinafter set forth are satisfied." Then follow the conditions on which a motor car may be used on any highway. They are contained in seven clauses. It is clear that some of them are introduced not to protect persons using the highway but to preserve the highway itself; those for instance relating to the width of wheels and the weight of motor cars. If the appellant's contention is to prevail everyone injured by a motor car which does not comply with the regulations has a right of action. There is no reason for differentiating between those who are injured as a legal consequence of a breach from those who are injured in fact irrespective of the breach of the regulations. Take cl. 7 for example. That clause provides that a car must have lamps exhibiting a white light in front and a red light in the rear. According to the appellant's contention a foot passenger crossing in front of a motor car would have a right of action if injured without any negligence of the driver, merely because the car had no red light in the rear. That cannot have been the intention of the Legislature. The absence of a red light in the rear may concern the safety of the car itself, or it may be a wise police regulation for other vehicles overtaking it, but it cannot affect the safety of a foot passenger passing in front of the car. This seems to indicate that it is not the intention of the Act to confer a right of action on every person injured by a car which does not conform to the regulations and to confer this right even though the breach of the regulations has no effect on the injury of which he complains. The matter might have been more doubtful if cl. 6 had stood alone. It provides that the car and all its fittings "shall be in such a condition as not to cause, or to be likely to cause, danger to any person on the motor car or on any highway." We have not to consider the case of a person injured on the highway. The injury here was done to the appellant's van; and the appellant, a member of the public, claims a right of action as one of a class for whose benefit cl. 6 was introduced. He contends that the public using the highway is the class so favoured. I do not agree. In my view the public using the highway is not a class; it is itself the public and not a class of the public. The clause therefore was not passed for the benefit of a class or section of the public. It applies to the public generally, and it is one among many regulations for breach of which it cannot have been intended that a person aggrieved should have a civil remedy by way of action in addition to the more appropriate remedy provided, namely a fine. In my opinion therefore this case is not an exception to the general rule; that rule applies, and the appeal must be dismissed.

Note:

In *Monk* v. *Warbey*, the plaintiff, a bus-driver, was injured by X, who was carelessly driving a car he had borrowed from the defendant. X was not insured against liability to the plaintiff—he had no policy of his own, and he was not an additional insured under the defendant's policy. The defendant had therefore unwittingly committed an offence under the Road Traffic Act 1930, s.35 (now Road Traffic Act 1972, s.143). X had no money with which to pay the plaintiff, so the plaintiff was allowed to recover from the defendant (who had at least the car).

The decision is striking, both because the plaintiff was complaining of financial harm (the defendant's breach of duty did not cause the injuries, but only the plaintiff's failure to get compensation for them), and because offences under the section in question are so easily committed. Nevertheless, the decision fits very well into the policy of the law that victims of *negligence* on the highway should not only be entitled to compensation, but should actually receive it. The scheme is now completed by the institution of the Motor Insurers' Bureau, which compensates those victims of motor-vehicles who should, by statute, have been able to recover from an insurance company). (See Hepple and Matthews, *Tort: Cases and Materials* (3rd ed. 1985) 781–783).

But if the policy of the law were to indemnify the victims of traffic *accidents*, then *Phillips* would appear as the anomalous decision. If the offence of putting an *uninsured* vehicle on the roads leads to liability, then why not also the offence of putting a *dangerous* car on the road? The distinction is particularly curious when one considers that, had *Phillips* gone the other way, most of the people caught under it would have the statutory insurance cover against liability to pay those damages, whereas defendants caught under *Monk* v. *Warbey* will normally have to pay out of their own pocket.

FACTORIES ACT 1961

14.—(1) Every dangerous part of any machinery . . . shall be securely fenced. . . .

Note:
It might be supposed that this section gave a claim for damages to every workman injured in a factory by a machine. Not so.

Dangerous part: The mere fact that a piece of machinery hurt someone does not show that it was dangerous. A part is dangerous only if a person looking at it could reasonably imagine it hurting a person acting the way people do.

Machinery: All factory equipment, installed or not, but not the factory product, is capable of being machinery; but not all parts of a machine are parts of its machinery (just as "poems very seldom consist of poetry and nothing else" (Housman)).

Securely fenced: A fence is secure if it keeps the workman from bringing his person (and perhaps his clothing, but perhaps not his tools) into contact with the dangerous part, notwithstanding that it does not prevent his being bombarded by pieces of the material being worked on or of the machinery itself. Since secure fencing can be got round by workmen determined to do so, mere proof that the workman came in contact with the dangerous part does not conclusively show that the fence was not secure.

Shall be: The imperative is absolute in the sense that it is unqualified by reasonableness; but, as has been seen, it is conditioned on foreseeability.

F. E. CALLOW (ENGINEERS) v. JOHNSON

House of Lords [1971] A.C. 335; [1970] 3 W.L.R. 982; 114 S.J. 846; [1970] 3 All E.R. 639

Action for personal injuries by employee against occupier of factory

A stainless-steel workpiece rotated every two seconds while a boring-bar to which a cutting tool was attached moved very slowly forward inside it. Between the workpiece and the bar was a space varying from half an inch on the operative's side to four inches on the far side. While the plaintiff was manually injecting the necessary coolant—a practice disapproved of by his employers who provided an automatic system—his hand, inserted into the larger space, was caught in the narrower space and his fingers were crushed.

The trial judge found no breach of Factories Act 1961, s.14, and dismissed the action. The Court of Appeal allowed the plaintiff's appeal ([1970] 1 All E.R. 129). The defendant appealed and his appeal was dismissed by the House of Lords (Viscount Dilhorne dissenting).

Lord Hailsham of St. Marylebone L.C.: My Lords, this appeal is another example of litigation arising from section 14 of the Factories Act 1961.

Section 14 forms part of a group of five sections (sections 12 to 16) which deal with the liability of an employer in a factory to fence part of the machinery for the protection of his employees. These sections are clearly intended to form, as it were, a single code and should be read together. Section 12 deals with prime movers. Section 13 deals with transmission machinery. Section 14 deals with dangerous parts of machinery, other than prime movers and transmission machinery.

The obligation cast on the employer is not unqualified, and section 15 deals with the operation of machinery which, under the exceptions to the preceding sections, is unfenced. Section 16 deals with the construction and maintenance of fences in cases where the duty to fence applies under the preceding sections. It provides (in language which may be material to this appeal) that the fences are to be kept in position while the parts required to be fenced are "in motion or in use," thereby implying that there may be cases in which the parts are in motion but not in use and equally cases in which the parts required to be fenced are in use but not in motion.

At first sight the code provided by this group of five sections is deceptively simple. In point of fact, however, its provisions, especially those of section 14 which are now under discussion, have given rise to a considerable degree of difference of opinion. In some ways the duty cast on employers has seemed at times unduly harsh. In others the protection afforded to the worker has seemed illusory and unreal.

The sanction behind the sections imposed by the Act is primarily penal and this is the only sanction contained expressly in the Act. But for many years a breach of the provisions of the code has been held to give rise to a civil action for damages for personal injury at the suit of the injured workman. As a matter of social policy the necessity for this connection between the judicially recognised remedy and the statutory offence is not logically plain. For, while it might appear to be reasonable and even self-evident that if an employer is guilty of an offence against the code any workman injured thereby should be entitled to damages for the breach, the converse is by no means so obvious; it is not so plain that in the absence of negligence the only correct basis for the compensation by an employer of his workman injured or killed by dangerous machinery is his commission of a criminal offence. It is clearly the law now. But it is not self-evident that it should be so.

But, while the policy of the Act is well established, some of the protection to the workman which at first sight might be thought to be available turns out on closer scrutiny to be illusory. Thus: (1) since it is only *parts* of the machinery which have to be fenced there is no obligation to fence a machine under section 14 if it is dangerous *as a whole* but without having dangerous parts (*cf. Liptrot* v. *British Railways Board* [1969] 1 A.C. 136, *per* Lord Reid at p. 159); (2) it is now established that under section 14 what is referred to as a part of the machinery does not include a workpiece moving under power and held in the machinery by a chuck; nor does it include other material in the machine as distinct from parts of the machinery (see, for instance, *Eaves* v. *Morris Motors Ltd.* [1961] 2 Q.B. 385; *Bullock* v. *G. John Power (Agencies) Ltd.* [1956] 1 W.L.R. 171); (3) the dangers against which the fencing is required do not include dangers to be apprehended from the ejection of flying material from the machine whether this is part of the material used in the machine (see *Nicholls* v. *F. Austin (Leyton) Ltd.* [1946] A.C. 493) or part of the machine itself (see *Close* v. *Steel Co. of Wales Ltd.* [1962] A.C. 367); (4) the workman is not ordinarily protected if what comes into contact with the dangerous part of a machine is a hand tool operated by the workman as distinct from the workman's body or his clothes (see *Sparrow* v. *Fairey Aviation Co. Ltd.* [1964] A.C. 1019), nor if the danger created arises because of the proximity of moving machinery to some stationary object extraneous to the machine (*Pearce* v. *Stanley-Bridges Ltd.* [1965] 1 W.L.R. 931).

In these circumstances it is not surprising that arguments about the protection afforded by section 14 of the Factories Act were described by Holroyd Pearce L.J. as "technical" and "artificial" and the protection itself as "in some respects illusory" (see *Eaves* v. *Morris Motors Ltd.* [1961] 2 Q.B. 385, 396). It is equally not surprising that the decisions in *Nicholls* v. *F. Austin (Leyton) Ltd.* ([1946] A.C. 493) and *Close* v. *Steel Co. of Wales Ltd.* ([1962] A.C. 367) were strongly criticised by Lord MacDermott and by Lord Reid in *Sparrow* v. *Fairey Aviation Co. Ltd.* ([1964] A.C. 1019, 1046–1048, 1033–1034), in spite of the fact that Lord Reid regarded himself as bound by the decisions which he criticised. It has been pointed out more than once that the position would be ameliorated by the use by the Minister of his regulatory powers under section 14(6) of the Act of 1961 (for this purpose equivalent to section 14(3) of its predecessor of 1937). But no use has so far been made of this power, not, I apprehend, through inadvertence, but as a matter of departmental policy. No one contemplating the situation set up by this series of decisions can wholly avoid the conclusion reached by Holroyd Pearce L.J. in the passage cited above that the gap in the protection afforded by the statute is one "which neither logic nor common sense appears to justify." It is however too late for the courts to close the gap. The gap can only be closed by legislation or to some extent by the use of the regulatory powers of the Minister. It has however to be said that I for one would be slow to enlarge the gap or to extend the ambit of the criticised decisions beyond the limits required by the facts of the cases concerned and the reasoning of the judgments in them. . . .

Lord Hailsham, having intimated that in his view the defendants were guilty of common law negligence in permitting an unsafe system of work, held that the boring bar, though nearly stationary, could be a dangerous part of machinery by reason of its juxtaposition to the moving workpiece (which there was no obligation to fence), an accident of this type being in the light of the defendant's knowledge foreseeable. Lord Hodson and Lord Gardiner concurred. Lord Donovan held that it was possible to regard the boring bar as a dangerous part of the machine only because the employers knew of the system of injecting coolant by hand. Viscount Dilhorne, dissenting, held that the boring bar was not made into a dangerous part of the machinery of the lathe by the mere fact that coolant was being injected by hand, and that consequently there was no duty to fence it.

NIMMO v. ALEXANDER COWAN & SONS

House of Lords [1968] A.C. 107; [1967] 3 W.L.R. 1169; 111 S.J. 668; [1967] 3 All E.R. 187; 3 K.I.R. 277; 1967 S.L.T. 277

Action by employee against employer in respect of personal injuries

The pursuer was injured while working, and alleged that the working-place was not safe, and claimed that the employer was in breach of Factories Act 1961, s.29(1), which requires that "every such place shall, so far as is reasonably practicable, be made and kept safe for any person working there." He did not plead that it was reasonably practicable for the employer to make the place safe, and the Lord Ordinary accordingly dismissed his claim. The pursuer's appeal to the Inner House of the Court of Session was dismissed (1966 S.L.T. 266). His further appeal to the House of Lords was allowed, and the case returned for trial.

Lord Guest, Lord Upjohn and Lord Pearson allowed the appeal on the ground that it must have been the intention of Parliament that the onus be on the employer of showing that it was not reasonably practicable to make the working-place safe, since this would give better protection to the workman, and the employer was in a better position to know, and was under a duty to know, whether safety was reasonably practicable or not.

Lord Reid (dissenting): My Lords, a considerable number of statutes prescribe, or enable regulations to prescribe, what steps an employer or occupier must take to promote the safety of persons working in factories, mines and other premises where work is carried on. Sometimes the duty imposed is absolute: certain things must be done and it is no defence that it was impossible to prevent an accident because it was caused by a latent defect which could not have been discovered—still less is it a defence to prove that it was impracticable to carry out the statutory requirement.

But in many cases the statutory duty is qualified in one way or another so that no offence is committed if it is impracticable or not reasonably practicable to comply with the duty. Unfortunately there is great variety in the drafting of such provisions. Sometimes the duty is expressed in absolute terms in one section and in another section it is provided that it shall be a defence to prove that it was impracticable or not reasonably practicable to comply with the duty. Sometimes the form adopted is that the occupier shall, so far as reasonably practicable, do certain things. Sometimes it is that the occupier shall take all practicable steps to achieve or prevent a certain result. And there are other provisions which do not exactly fit into any of these classes. Often it is difficult to find any reason for these differences.

There has been much doubt where the onus rests in these cases. About the first class it may well be it is sufficient for the prosecutor or pursuer to aver and prove a breach of the duty set out in the one section, leaving it to the accused or defender to avail himself of the statutory defence if he can. But in the other cases there is much room for doubt. In the present case the pleadings have been deliberately drawn in such a way as to require a decision at least with regard to the section on which the pursuer relies.

The pursuer, the present appellant, avers that on May 18, 1964, he had, within a factory, to unload railway wagons filled with bales of pulp. In doing this he had to stand on some of the bales, and while he was standing on one of the bales it tipped up and caused him to fall and fracture his skull and three ribs. He founds on section 29(1) of the Factories Act 1961, which is in these terms: "There shall, so far as is reasonably practicable, be provided and maintained safe means of access to every place at which any person has at any time to work, and every such place shall, so far as is reasonably practicable, be made and kept safe for any person working there."

He avers that the bales were insecurely placed in the wagons so that the place at which he had to work was not made and kept safe for his working there. He deliberately avoids averring that it was reasonably practicable for the respondents, his employers, to make that place safe. He says that he has averred a relevant case because under this section it is for the defender to aver and prove, if he can, that it was not reasonably practicable to make the place safe. The respondents, of course, had no control over the loading of the bales in the wagon: that no doubt was done by the seller who sold the pulp to them. They make averments to show that it was not reasonably practicable for them to make the place safe, and they also plead that, the pursuer's averments being irrelevant, the action should be dismissed. This plea to the relevancy was sustained by the Lord Ordinary and the First Division adhered to his interlocutor.

This matter is not a mere technicality. It has important practical consequences. If the respondents are right the pursuer must not only aver in general terms that it was reasonably practicable to make the place safe—such an averment without more would be lacking in specification—he must also make sufficient positive averments to give notice to the defender of the method of making the place safe which he proposes to support by evidence. But if the appellant is right he can simply wait for the evidence which the respondent would have to lead to discharge the onus on him to show that it was not reasonably practicable to make the place safe, and then cross-examine the respondent's witness in any relevant way he chooses. He would only have to make positive averments if he intended to lead evidence that some particular method of making the place safe could have been adopted by the defender.

In my opinion, this question should be approached by considering first what a prosecutor would have to allege and prove in order to obtain a conviction. For civil liability only arises if there has been a breach of the statutory duty, and I cannot see how a pursuer could succeed in a civil action without averring and proving all the facts essential to establish the commission of an offence. It is true that the standard of proof is lower in a civil case so that the pursuer only has to show that it is probable that an offence was committed. But that cannot mean that the onus of proof is different with regard to any of the essential elements of the offence.

The appellant's argument is that, although the statute says that every working place "shall, so far as is reasonably practicable, be made and kept safe," a prosecutor need only allege and prove that the place was not made and kept safe, leaving it to the accused to show that this was not reasonably practicable. . . .

Lord President Clyde, having analysed the section with which we are concerned, said (1966 S.L.T. 266, 271): "The words 'so far as is reasonably practicable' consequently become, in my view, an integral part of the duty imposed and define the ambit of what is made obligatory." Lord Guthrie said (*ibid.* at 272): "No breach of the section is committed, and no failure on the part of the defenders can take place, unless it is reasonably practicable to take steps to make and keep the working place safe." And Lord Migdale said (*ibid.* at 273) that the section "is not a command to make the place safe but to make it safe so far as is reasonably practicable." I agree with these views.

It would be very convenient if one could avoid examination of the method of drafting and have a general rule either that in all these cases the onus is on the pursuer or that it is on the defender. But I do not think that is possible. On the one hand, where the provision is that it "shall be a defence to prove" something, it would not be reasonable to require the pursuer to disprove that defence. But, on the other hand, take, for example, section 31 of this Act which requires that "all practicable steps shall be taken" to prevent an explosion, to restrict its spread, and to remove fumes, etc. I cannot see how a prosecutor or pursuer could frame a relevant complaint or condescendence by merely alleging that an explosion occurred, or that it spread, or that fumes were not removed, leaving it to the accused or the defender to show that no practicable steps could have been taken to avoid that. The offence here must be failure to take practicable steps and the prosecutor or pursuer must allege and prove such failure.

I get no assistance in this case from any general presumption that a person is not required to prove a negative or that a person is required to prove facts peculiarly within his own knowledge. I do not lay any stress on the fact that, if the appellant is right, the defender would have to prove a negative—that it was not reasonably practicable to make the place safe. And I do not think that the question whether this was reasonably practicable is a matter peculiarly within the knowledge of the defender—an expert witness for the pursuer should be just as well able to deal with this as the defender.

I would dismiss this appeal.

Lord Wilberforce also dissented.

Note:
It is perfectly true, as Lord Reid said in *Jenkins* v. *Allied Ironfounders* ([1970] 1 W.L.R. 304, 307), that " . . . after the evidence has been led it is only in very rare cases that onus of proof is material," but it is very material indeed when one is deciding whether to sue or not.

THE INTERPRETATION OF STATUTES

Law Commission Paper No. 21 (1969)

APPENDIX A

DRAFT CLAUSES

. . .

4. Where any Act passed after this Act imposes or authorises the imposition of a duty, whether positive or negative and whether with or without a special remedy for its enforcement, it shall be presumed, unless express provision to the contrary is made, that a breach of the duty is intended to be actionable (subject to the defences and other incidents applying to actions for breach of statutory duty) at the suit of any person who sustains damage in consequence of the breach.

Questions

1. Is the rule that compensation is given only for harm of the type Parliament intended to prevent (below, p. 194) an "incident applying to actions for breach of statutory duty"? If so, will the present proposal, if implemented, greatly curtail the inquiry by the courts into the intentions of Parliament?

2. Does a statute which enacts that it will be an offence to do an act impose a duty not to do that act? (No, *per* Harman J. in *Shelley* v. *Cunane* [1983] F.S.R. 390, 397, strongly dissented from by Hobhouse J. in *Rickless* v. *United Artists* [1986] F.S.R. 202).

3. Could Parliament consistently attempt to prevent harm happening and not attempt to remedy it if it does happen?

4. Would Lonrho (above p. 153) be wise to lobby for the enactment of this proposal?

Note:

One form of the question running through this chapter has been "Can the victim of unlawful conduct claim damages?" A new twist has been given to this question by our accession to the Common Market and its legal regime. Some of the articles of the Treaty of Rome impose obligations and confer rights on states and private persons. To the rights resulting from articles which have "direct effect" the member states are required to give protection, and English courts are required to do so under s.2 of the European Communities Act 1972. It is left to the member states to decide the precise legal protection to be afforded to such rights, but it must be effective and it must be comparable with the protection afforded to similar rights arising under the national law. Hence the problem. Our cases on when a victim can claim damages for breach of statutory duty never talk in terms of rights at all, and it would be excessively difficult to try to define the class of rights inferable from the imposition of statutory duties, invasion of which attracts the sanction of damages. Now art. 30 of the Treaty of Rome prohibits member states from imposing quantitative restrictions on imports except on the grounds specified in art. 36. Our Minister banned imports of French turkey meat, and was held by the European Court to be in breach of art. 30. French turkey importers claimed damages from the Minister for trade lost through the unlawful ban. It was held by a majority of the Court of Appeal that no action for damages lay on the mere ground that the plaintiff's right had been infringed: he could claim judicial review of the Minister's order, and that was effective protection. (*Bourgoin S.A.* v. *Ministry of Agriculture* [1985] 3 All E.R. 585). Oliver L.J., dissenting on this point, held that the plaintiff's right was to import goods free of any restriction, unless valid, that the right had been invaded by the invalid restriction, and that the right was not adequately protected by a petition for review of the validity of the ban. It seems that the crux lies in the words of Nourse L.J.: "It is axiomatic that if the duty had been imposed by an Act of the United Kingdom Parliament the action would not lie" (at 632). If so, to deny an action to the French turkey importers was not to deny comparable protection, and we can avoid the jurisprudential twaddle. It appears that one must ask whether, on the hypothesis that Parliament had enacted the various articles of the Treaty of Rome, it would be held to have been its intention in each case that a claim for damages should lie. Breach of art. 86 by a private person (abuse of dominant position) does, however, give rise to a claim for damages, though a British statute in like terms would not be held to confer one. That is because the protection of the right must be effective, and (a) no other remedy is provided by the article, and (b) it is said to be unknown in English law for an injunction to be available against the continuation of unlawful harm without damages also being available for harm already done (*Garden Cottage Foods* v. *Milk Marketing Board* [1984] A.C. 130; [1983] 2 All E.R. 770).

Section 2.—Public Nuisance and Civil Liability

BENJAMIN v. STORR

Common Pleas (1874) L.R. 9 C.P. 400; 43 L.J.C.P. 162; 30 L.T. 362; 22 W.R. 631

Action by frontager against highway-user in respect of financial loss

The plaintiff ran a coffee-house in Rose Street, near Covent Garden, adjoining the exit from the defendant's auction rooms. The defendant had many horse-drawn vans to collect and deliver goods. The constant presence of the vans and the intermittent urination of the horses made the plaintiff's premises incommodious by obstructing the light and fouling the air.

The jury gave a verdict for the plaintiff, damages £75. The defendant, pursuant to leave, obtained a rule *nisi* for a non-suit or a new trial, but the rule was discharged.

Brett J.: This action is founded upon alleged wrongful acts by the defendants, *viz.*, the unreasonable use of a highway—unreasonable to such an extent as to amount to a nuisance. That alone would not give the plaintiff a right of action; but the plaintiff goes on to allege in his declaration that the nuisance complained of is of such a kind as to cause him a particular injury other than and beyond that suffered by the rest of the public, and therefore he claims damages against the defendants. The first point discussed was whether it was necessary that the plaintiff should show something more than an injury to his business, an actual injury to his property; and cases decided under the Lands Clauses Consolidation Act (8 & 9 Vict. c. 18) were cited. In this case I think the action is maintainable without showing injury to property. In the class of cases referred to, the action is brought to recover compensation for lands taken or injuriously affected; and there, of course, injury to property must be shown, and not merely injury to the trade of the occupier. Those cases, therefore, do not at all affect the present. Before the passing of the Lands Clauses Consolidation Act, by the common law of England, a person guilty of a public nuisance might be indicted; but, if injury resulted to a private individual, other and greater than that which was common to all the Queen's subjects, the person injured had his remedy by action. The cases referred to upon this subject show that there are three things which the plaintiff must substantiate, beyond the existence of the mere public nuisance, before he can be entitled to recover. In the first place, he must show a particular injury to himself beyond that which is suffered by the rest of the public. It is not enough for him to show that he suffers the same inconvenience in the use of the highway as other people do, if the alleged nuisance be the obstruction of a highway. The case of *Hubert* v. *Groves* ((1794) 1 Esp. 148; 170 E.R. 308) seems to me to prove that proposition. There, the plaintiff's business was injured by the obstruction of a highway, but no greater injury resulted to him therefrom than to anyone else, and therefore it was held that the action would not lie. . . . Other cases show that the injury to the individual must be direct, and not a mere consequential injury; as, where one way is obstructed, but another (though possibly a less convenient one) is left open; in such a case the private and particular injury has been held not to be sufficiently direct to give a cause of action. Further, the injury must be shown to be of a substantial character, not fleeting or evanescent. If these propositions be correct, in order to entitle a person to maintain an action for damage caused by that which is a public nuisance, the damage must be particular, direct, and substantial. The question then is, whether the plaintiff here has brought himself within the rule so laid down.

The evidence on the part of the plaintiff showed that from the too long standing of horses and wagons of the defendants in the highway opposite his house, the free passage of light and air to his premises was obstructed, and the plaintiff was in consequence obliged to burn gas nearly all day, and so to incur expense. I think that brings the case within all the requirements I have pointed out; it was a particular, a direct, and a substantial damage. As to the bad smell, that also was a particular injury to the plaintiff, and a direct and substantial one. So, if by reason of the access to his premises being obstructed for an unreasonable time and in an unreasonable manner, the plaintiff's customers were prevented from coming to his coffee-shop, and he suffered a material diminution of trade, that might be a particular, a direct, and a substantial damage. As to that part of the rule which seeks to enter a nonsuit, assuming the evidence objected to to have been properly received, I think it cannot be sustained. . . .

Note:
Public nuisance is a crime because it is likely to cause at least widespread inconvenience; stopping it is a matter for the state enforcement authorities. It would be intolerable if all those who were inconvenienced could bring a private action, even if the defendant is acting wrongfully; the courts therefore insist that the plaintiff show a particular damage suffered by himself. The requirement of particular damage was strictly insisted on in the mid-nineteenth century, lest the construction of railways, which was necessarily disruptive, become too expensive (*Ricket* v. *Metropolitan Ry.* (1867) L.R. 2 H.L. 175); today it is certain that proved business loss is recoverable.

Read:
Kodilinye, "Public Nuisance and Particular Damage in the Modern Law," (1986) 6 L.S. 182.

Question
Every evening people waiting at the bus-stop outside your house throw into your front garden the remnants of the fish-and-chips they have bought from a fish restaurant close by. Have you any remedy against the bus company or the fish restaurant?

MINT v. GOOD

Court of Appeal [1951] 1 K.B. 517; 94 S.J. 822; [1950] 2 All E.R. 1159; 49 L.G.R. 495

Action by highway-user against owner of adjoining property in respect of personal injury

A boy of 10 years of age was walking along a public footpath when a wall collapsed on him and injured him. The wall, some four feet in length and two feet six inches high, separated the footpath from the forecourt of two houses owned by the defendant and let by him to persons (not sued) on weekly tenancies. The defendant had not specifically reserved the right to enter the premises for examination or repairs.

Stable J. found that the wall was in imminent danger of collapse, and that a competent person would have realised this after a reasonable inspection; accordingly the wall was technically a nuisance. But he dismissed the action on the ground that the defendant was not liable for it, since he had not reserved the right to enter the premises, and therefore had no control of the wall.

The plaintiff's appeal to the Court of Appeal was allowed in unreserved judgments.

Denning L.J.: The law of England has always taken particular care to protect those who use a highway. It puts on the occupier of adjoining premises a special responsibility for the structures which he keeps beside the highway. So long as those structures are safe, all well and good; but if they fall into disrepair, so as to be a potential danger to passers-by, then they are a nuisance, and, what is more, a public nuisance; and the occupier is liable to anyone using the highway who is injured by reason of the disrepair. It is no answer for him to say that he and his servants took reasonable care; for, even if he has employed a competent independent contractor to repair the structure, and has every reason for supposing it to be safe, the occupier is still liable if the independent contractor did the work badly: see *Tarry* v. *Ashton* ((1876) 1 Q.B.D. 314).

The occupier's duty to passers-by is to see that the structure is as safe as reasonable care can make it; a duty which is as high as the duty which an occupier owes to people who pay to come on to his premises. He is not liable for latent defects, which could not be discovered by reasonable care on the part of anyone, nor for acts of trespassers of which he neither knew, nor ought to have known: see *Barker* v. *Herbert* ([1911] 2 K.B. 633, 645); but he is liable when structures fall into dangerous disrepair, because there must be some fault on the part of someone or other for that to happen; and he is responsible for it to persons using the highway, even though he was not actually at fault himself. That principle was laid down in this court in *Wringe* v. *Cohen* ([1940] 1 K.B. 233), where it is to be noted that the principle is confined to "premises on a highway," and is, I think, clearly correct in regard to the responsibility of an occupier to passers-by.

The question in this case is whether the owner, as well as the occupier, is under a like duty to passers-by. I think that in many cases he is. The law has shown a remarkable development on this point during the last 16 years. The three cases of *Wilchick* v. *Marks and Silverstone* ([1934] 2 K.B. 56), *Wringe* v. *Cohen* ([1940] 1 K.B. 229), and *Heap* v. *Ind, Coope & Allsopp Ltd.* ([1940] 2 K.B. 476), show that the courts are now taking a realistic view of these matters. They recognise that the occupying tenant of a small dwelling-house does not in practice do the structural repairs, but the owner does; and that if a passer-by is injured by the structure being in dangerous disrepair, the occupier has not the means to pay damages, but the owner has, or, at any rate, he can insure against it. If a passer-by is injured by its falling on him, he should be entitled to damages from someone, and the person who ought to pay is the owner, because he is in practice responsible for the repairs. This practical responsibility means that he has *de facto* control of the structure for the purpose of repairs and is therefore answerable in law for its condition. Parliament has long made owners responsible under the Public Health Acts for nuisances arising from defects of a structural character: see section 94 of the Public Health Act 1875 and section 93(*b*) of the Public Health Act 1936; and the common law now also in many cases makes them responsible for public nuisances due to the disrepair of the structure.

This seems to me to be a logical consequence of the cases to which we have been referred. In *Wilchick* v. *Marks and Silverstone* the landlord had covenanted to repair; in *Heap* v. *Ind, Coope & Allsopp Ltd.* he had not covenanted to repair, but had reserved a right to enter. In the present case he has not reserved a right to enter, but he has in practice always done the structural repairs. I cannot think that the liability of the owner to passers-by depends on the precise terms of the tenancy agreement between the owner and the tenant, that is to say, on whether he has expressly reserved a right to enter or not. It depends on the degree of control exercised by the owner, in law or in fact, for the purpose of repairs. If a landlord is liable when he reserves an express right to enter, he is also liable when he has an implied right; and even if he has no strict right, but has been given permission to enter whenever he asked, it should make no difference. The landlord has in practice taken the structural repairs on himself and should be responsible for any disrepair.

That is sufficient for the decision of this case, but I venture to doubt whether in these days a landlord can in all cases exempt himself from liability to passers-by by taking a covenant from a tenant to repair the structure adjoining the highway. I know that in *Pretty* v. *Bickmore* ((1873) L.R. 8 C.P. 401) a landlord managed to escape liability for a coal-plate which was, at the beginning of the lease, in dangerous disrepair, because he took from the tenant a covenant to repair. I doubt whether he would escape liability today. Again, suppose that a landlord of small houses took from weekly tenants a covenant to repair the structure, and then did not trouble to enforce the covenant or to repair himself? Could he escape liability by so doing? I doubt it. It may be that in such cases the landlord owes a duty to the public which he cannot get rid of by delegating it to another. These questions do not however arise here because there was no such covenant. In this case the judge found that the condition of the wall was a nuisance, and that a reasonable examination of the wall by a competent person would have detected the condition in which it was. That means that the duty of the landlord was not fulfilled. His duty was to see that the structure was as safe as reasonable care could make it. It was not so safe.

I agree, therefore, that the appeal should be allowed, and judgment entered accordingly.

Note:

This vigorous unreserved judgment makes the law appear perhaps simpler than it is.

One starts with the proposition that if a person is hurt by something on the highway, he must first find out whether the act which hurt him was incidental to a reasonable user of the highway. If it was, then, subject to *res ipsa loquitur*, he must prove carelessness in the actor. If the act was something the actor had no right to do on the highway at all, the victim need not prove carelessness but will recover only for foreseeable damage.

People may also be hurt by things falling on to the highway from adjoining land. Some legal systems make the occupier of the premises from which they fall strictly liable to the person injured by them; but in England there is no law of *res dejectae vel effusae* (see Buckland, *Textbook of Roman Law*, 598). If a chattel (*e.g.*, Miss Stone's cricket ball) falls into the highway, the person struck by it must prove negligence; but the chattel may help him to establish it by speaking for itself (*Byrne* v. *Boadle* (1863) 2 H. & C. 722, 159 E.R. 299; but see *Walsh* v. *Holst & Co.* [1958] 1 W.L.R. 800).

The biggest things that frequently fall into the highway are trees and bits of houses; the law of England appears to distinguish between them. A house involves liability if, had a competent person looked at it just before it collapsed, he would have seen that it needed repair. A tree makes the occupier liable only if he should have procured a competent person to look at it, and that person would have seen that action was called for (*Caminer* v. *Northern & London Investment Trust* [1951] A.C. 88; *British Road Services* v. *Slater* [1964] 1 W.L.R. 498; *Quinn* v. *Scott* [1965] 2 All E.R. 588). This is the difference between liability in nuisance and liability in negligence.

Now what are the grounds for distinction between a tree and a bit of a house? Is it that a house is used and a tree is not? (*Sedleigh-Denfield* v. *O'Callaghan*, [1940] A.C. 880). Is it because a house is always built and a tree is not always planted? (It would be absurd to distinguish between planted and self-sown trees, *Davey* v. *Harrow Corporation* [1958] 1 Q.B.

60). Is it because a tree is uncommonly lovely and a house is commonly unlovely? Or is it because people are supposed to know about houses and not about trees, trees being subject, as houses are usually not, to *secret unobservable processes of nature*?

The italicised phrase occurs in *Wringe* v. *Cohen* [1940] 1 K.B. 229, an action in respect of property damage between neighbours adjoining the highway. That case established that an occupier was liable if his house, or part of it, collapsed owing to want of repair, independently of the question whether he was negligent or not. It would be a defence to show that the collapse was caused by the act of a trespasser (and enemy bombers were treated as trespassers in *Cushing* v. *Peter Walker & Son* [1942] 2 All E.R. 693) or a secret unobservable process of nature. The decision has been very adversely commented on, but, as Somervell L.J. said in the present case, "It is a plain decision, laying down plain principles." The French Civil Code, Art. 1386, provides: "The owner of a building is liable for the damage caused by its collapse, if it collapses by reason of want of repair or fault in construction."

In English law we think of the occupier and not the owner as being the person responsible, but the principal case shows one of the great advantages of public nuisance as a ground of action. Once the plaintiff has been injured by a thing which can be characterised as a nuisance, he is in a better position than the plaintiff in negligence who has to look around for a person who *acted* badly. The plaintiff in nuisance only has to study the thing and he can catch anyone connected with that thing—here the landlord as well as the occupier. So if I fall into an unguarded trench dug illegally on the highway, I can sue not only the careless person who dug it, but also the perfectly careful person who procured the digging.

But the rules of public nuisance protect only those on the highway, that is, those outside buildings. People injured inside buildings must generally use the Occupiers' Liability Act 1957. For this purpose the landlord as well as the tenant may be the occupier (see *Wheat* v. *Lacon*, above, p. 82); even if he is not the occupier, the landlord may still be held liable to an injured visitor under the Defective Premises Act 1972, s.4 (above, p. 86), provided that he is in breach of obligations owed, or deemed by s.4(4) to be owed, to the tenant. Note, however, that the landlord's liability under the Defective Premises Act 1972 extends also to persons outside the premises, while not, presumably, diminishing their rights, if wider, under the common law of which the principal case is an example.

Chapter 4

CAUSATION

Section 1.—No Cause

McWILLIAMS v. SIR WILLIAM ARROL & CO.

House of Lords [1962] 1 W.L.R. 295; 106 S.J. 218; 1962 S.C.(H.L.) 70; 1962 S.L.T. 121;
[1962] 1 All E.R. 623

Action by widow against employer of husband

The pursuer appealed to the House of Lords from an order of the First Division of
the Court of Session (1961 S.L.T. 265) affirming judgment given by the Lord
Ordinary in favour of the defender. Her appeal was dismissed.

Lord Reid: My Lords, the appellant is the widow of William McWilliams, a steel
erector who was killed on May 27, 1956, when he fell from a steel tower which was
being erected in a shipyard occupied by the second respondents. The first respondents were his employers. McWilliams was setting up a working platform for
riveters on the outside of the tower about seventy feet from the ground. This had to
be placed on "needles" which are battens projecting some four feet from the tower.
They were secured to the tower by lashings. A lashing of one of the needles was not
properly fixed so that when the deceased put his weight on this needle it tilted and
he fell to the ground. It is not clear whether he was responsible for not fixing it
properly or not inspecting it, and in this action no fault is alleged against the
respondents with regard to the needle.

The case made by the appellant is that both respondents were at fault in not providing safety belts. These belts have about fifteen feet of rope attached to them so
that the end of the rope can be tied to some convenient part of the structure near
where the man is working: then if he falls the rope prevents him from falling more
than its length. It is not denied that if McWilliams had been wearing a safety belt
when he fell he would not have been killed. The employers do not deny that it was
general practice to provide such belts but they do not admit any duty to provide
them. The courts below have held that they had this duty and also that, by reason of
the shipyard being a factory within the meaning of the Factories Act 1937, section
26(2) of that Act required the second respondents to provide these belts. I need not
consider whether this was right, because the main defence of both respondents is
that if such belts had been available on the day of the accident McWilliams would
not have worn one and, therefore, any failure to provide a belt was not the cause of
his death. I shall assume in the case of both respondents that they were in breach of
duty in not providing belts.

There can be no certainty as to whether the deceased would or would not have
worn a belt on this day, but the defenders maintain that it is highly probable that he
would not. Work on this tower had been proceeding for many weeks and at least
for a good part of that time he had been doing work similar to that which he was
doing when he fell. Throughout this period safety belts had to his knowledge been
available in a hut near-by and it is clear that it was not his practice to wear a belt.
Steel erectors were neither required nor exhorted to wear belts, and several wit-

179

nesses with long experience say that they had never seen any steel erector wear a belt, and in particular that they had never seen McWilliams wear one. And there is evidence that the condition of the belts showed that they had seldom if ever been used. But one witness says that he saw McWilliams wearing a belt on two occasions when working in an exposed position. The Lord Ordinary thought this extremely doubtful, but I am prepared to assume in the appellant's favour that this evidence can be accepted. It was left to the discretion of each man to decide whether to wear a belt, and it appears that the reason why belts were not generally worn was not mere prejudice against them. They are cumbersome and some witnesses say they might be dangerous in certain circumstances.

For some reason, the belts were taken away to another site two or three days before the accident. So after that the defenders were in breach of their duty to provide belts. We do not know whether the deceased knew that they had been removed, and there is nothing to suggest that during those two or three days he may have considered changing his normal practice not to wear a belt. So it appears to me to be a natural, and indeed almost inevitable, inference that he would not have worn a belt on this occasion even if it had been available. And that inference is strengthened by the general practice of other men not to wear belts.

It was argued that the law does not permit such an inference to be drawn because what a man did on previous occasions is no evidence of what he would have done on a later similar occasion. This argument was based on the rule that you cannot infer that a man committed a particular crime or delict from the fact that he has previously committed other crimes or delicts. But even that is not an unqualified rule (see, for example, *Moorov* v. *Lord Advocate,* 1930 J.C. 68), and there are reasons for that rule which would not apply to a case like the present. It would not be right to draw such an inference too readily because people do sometimes change their minds unexpectedly. But the facts of this case appear to me to be overwhelming.

I would have had much more difficulty if the only evidence had been that there was a general practice not to wear belts. One would assume, in the absence of evidence to the contrary, that the deceased was a reasonable and careful man, and it may be that if the evidence proved that a reasonable and careful man would not have worn a belt on such an occasion that would be sufficient. But I would reserve my opinion about a case which merely depended on evidence of general practice. I regard the evidence about general practice in this case as corroborating the inference to be drawn from McWilliams' own past conduct.

The appellant founded on the case of *Roberts* v. *Dorman Long & Co. Ltd.* ([1953] 1 W.L.R. 942). There a steel erector who was not wearing a safety belt was killed during the erection of a steel building to which building regulations of 1948 applied. They required that belts should be available which would "so far as practicable enable such persons who elect to use them to carry out the work without risk of serious injury." The employers did have belts but they were kept so far away from the site that they were held not to be available. One question in the case was whether the employers' breach of statutory duty could be founded on in face of evidence of a general practice to elect not to use such belts. The evidence is not fully reported and it is not clear whether the deceased himself had ever had an opportunity to use such belts, or whether the evidence merely related to the practice of other men not to use them at other sites where they were available. Lord Goddard C.J. said: "It may very well be that the judge could form the opinion on the evidence that it was unlikely that if safety belts had been available the deceased would have used one." But he went on to say: "I think that if a person is under a duty to provide safety belts or other appliances and fails to do so, he cannot be heard to say: 'Even if I had done so they would not have been worn.' "

In my view, this is not correct. "He cannot be heard to say" suggests to me personal bar or estoppel: indeed, I know of no other ground on which a defender can be prevented from proving a fact vital for his defence. If I prove that my breach of duty in no way caused or contributed to the accident I cannot be liable in damages.

And if the accident would have happened in just the same way whether or not I fulfilled my duty, it is obvious that my failure to fulfil my duty cannot have caused or contributed to it. No reason has ever been suggested why a defender should be barred from proving that his fault, whether common law negligence or breach of statutory duty, had nothing to do with the accident.

Hodson L.J. (as he then was) put the matter rather differently. His view was that there was no possibility of finding out whether the man would have exercised his election one way or another. If my noble and learned friend meant that if a man is dead you can never prove what he would have done I would not agree with him. Proof in civil cases depends on probability, and I think that the ordinary man would be surprised if told that you can never say that it is probable that in certain circumstances a deceased man would have done one thing and not another. But if his observation was directed to the facts of that particular case I am not prepared to say that it was wrong without fuller knowledge of the evidence which had been led. I have already said that I wish to reserve my opinion about a case where the only evidence relates to the practice of other men engaged on other work: much may depend on the precise nature of that evidence. . . .

It has been suggested that the decision of this House in *Bonnington Castings Ltd.* v. *Wardlaw* ([1956] A.C. 613) lays down new law and increases the burden on pursuers. I do not think so. It states what has always been the law—a pursuer must prove his case. He must prove that the fault of the defender caused, or contributed to, the danger which he has suffered. But proof need not be by direct evidence. If general practice or a regulation requires that some safety appliance shall be provided, one would assume that it is of some use, and that a reasonable man would use it. And one would assume that the injured man was a reasonable man. So the initial onus on the pursuer to connect the failure to provide the appliance with the accident would normally be discharged merely by proving the circumstances which led to the accident, and it is only where the evidence throws doubt on either of these assumptions that any difficulty would arise. Normally it would be left to the defender to adduce evidence, if he could, to displace these assumptions. So in practice it would be realistic, even if not theoretically accurate, to say that the onus is generally on the defender to show that the man would not have used the appliance even if it had been available. But in the end, when all the evidence has been brought out, it rarely matters where the onus originally lay, the question is which way the balance of probability has come to rest. . . .

Lord Devlin: . . . Mr. Stott, for the appellant, based his case upon the proposition tht the failure to provide the safety belt was the cause of the [workman's] death. In my opinion, this proposition is incomplete. There is a missing link. The immediate cause of the deceased's death was the fact that at the time of the fall he was not wearing a safety belt. The cause or reason he was not wearing a safety belt may have been the fact that one was not provided, but the failure to provide operates only through the failure to wear. The correct way of stating the appellant's case is, I think, as follows: The immediate cause of the deceased's death was that at the time of the fall he was not wearing a safety belt: but for the fault of his employers, he would have been wearing a safety belt: therefore the fault of his employers was an effective cause of his death. So stated, it is plain that the reason why the deceased was not wearing a safety belt must be a proper subject for inquiry. . . .

This question of the burden of proof is frequently important when what is in issue is what a dead workman in fact did. Without his evidence it may be difficult to prove that negligence by the employers was an effective cause of the death: once negligence is proved, the fact that the workman cannot be called to account for his actions often defeats the proof of contributory negligence. But in the present case the question is not what the deceased actually did but what he would have done in circumstances that never arose. Whether the workman is alive or dead, this cannot be proved positively as a matter of fact but can only be inferred as a matter of likelihood or probability. Even when the workman himself is perforce silent, there may be plenty of material, as there is in this case, from which an inference can be drawn one way or the other; and then the question of burden of proof is unimportant. . . .

Question

Was "death by falling" within the risk envisaged by the legislature when it required safety-belts to be provided? Did the defendant's failure to provide safety-belts enhance the risk of death by falling? Did it enhance the risk that McWilliams might fall to his death?

Note:

The judges here were confident the McWilliams would not have worn the safety-belt on the day in question, because the evidence was that he never wore one. But suppose he sometimes did and sometimes didn't, that he wore a safety-belt on average once every four days. The judges would then be trying to decide what would have happened on a hypothetical state of facts, namely that safety-belts were provided (as they were not). Would there be any basis for awarding one-fourth of the damages due to his death?

In *Hotson* v. *East Berks. A.H.A.* [1987] 2 All E.R. 909 the trial judge, upheld by the Court of Appeal, had awarded the plaintiff 25 per cent. of the value of his harm on the basis that the defendant's negligent diagnosis had robbed him of a one-in-four chance of recovery. The House of Lords reversed on the ground that at the time of the negligent diagnosis the plaintiff's physical condition either was or was not such as to permit recovery with proper treatment: it was a case of doubts, not chances, and the evidence was that he was (very probably) doomed. Unfortunately chances as to the future can easily be converted into doubts about the past just by using the future participle in conjunction with the past tense—"Was he 'going to recover'?" The House of Lords' decision is in line with the traditional all-or-nothing approach of the common law, with its reluctance to split the difference or announce a draw. This results in some people getting too much and some too little, as determined by the scales of justice and mercy respectively, but it probably reduces the number of persons who bring claims in the hope of getting a consolation prize from the bran-tub.

The people who get too much do so under decisions such as *Bonnington Castings* v. *Wardlaw* [1956] A.C. 613 and *McGhee* v. *National Coal Board* [1972] 3 All E.R. 1008 (H.L.). In the former case the plaintiff's lung disease was due to his prolonged inhalation of polluted air, for only part of which the defendant employer was responsible, but because the defendant's fault had made a not insubstantial contribution to the plaintiff's condition the plaintiff was allowed to recover in full. Resistance to this doctrine can be inferred from cases such as *Thompson* v. *Smiths Shiprepairers*, the deafness case (above p. 144), where the plaintiffs recovered only in proportion to the noxious noise for which the defendant was responsible ([1984] 1 All E.R. 881, 905–910), and *Brooks* v. *J. & P. Coates* [1984] 1 All E.R. 702 (Boreham J.) where a byssinosis victim had his damages reduced by half, without reference to the Contributory Negligence Act, because smoking had also contributed to his disability.

In *McGhee* the House of Lords had seemed to hold that proof that the defendant's conduct rendered the harm more probable was tantamount to proof that the conduct probably caused the harm; and the astonishing principle was inferred "that the defendant was liable to a plaintiff where his conduct enhanced an existing risk that injury would ensue, nothwithstanding either that the conduct in question was merely one of several possible risk factors, any one of which might have caused the injury, or that the existence and extent of the contribution made by the defendant's breach of duty to the plaintiff's injury could not be ascertained." (*Bryce* v. *Swan Hunter Group* (Phillips J., *The Times*, February 19, 1987)). Mercifully the House of Lords has now held that *McGhee* "laid down no new principle of law whatever. On the contrary, it affirmed the principle that the onus of proving causation lies on the plaintiff." (*Wilsher* v. *East Sussex A.H.A.* [1988] 1 All E.R. 871, 881).

Puzzles

1. The defendant carelessly injures the plaintiff, causing him to lose 30 per cent. of the use of his left leg. Three years later gangsters shoot the plaintiff in the same leg and it has to be amputated. Does the defendant have to pay for 30 per cent. of the leg for life or only 30 per cent. of the leg for three years? *Baker* v. *Willoughby* ([1970] A.C. 467) said for life.

2. A person who might have been expected to work until 1985 had an accident in 1973 owing to his employer's fault. This reduced his earning capacity by 50 per cent. In 1976 a dis-

ease quite unconnected with the accident incapacitated him totally. Does he get 50 per cent. of his lost earnings for three years or for twelve? *Jobling* v. *Associated Dairies* ([1982] A.C. 794) said for three.

In that case Lord Wilberforce drew "the conclusion that no general, logical, or universally fair rules can be stated which will cover, in a manner consistent with justice, cases of supervening events, whether due to tortious, partially tortious, non-culpable or wholly accidental events."

3. A school is under a duty not to let children out till 3.30 p.m., since that is when their mothers fetch them. One day the school lets a child out at 3.25 p.m., and at 3.29 p.m. the child is run over in the street. It is proved that on that day the mother would have been 15 minutes late. Is the school liable for causing the death of the child?

4. George is injured when Henry runs him over in the street. Henry wasn't looking where he was going and didn't apply the brakes at all. If he had been paying attention he could have braked and if the brakes had worked he would not have hit George. The brakes would not have worked, however, because Ian, a mechanic, had failed to fix them properly. Has either Henry or Ian contributed to George's injuries? Have both?

Section 2.—Directness and Foreseeability

RE AN ARBITRATION between POLEMIS and FURNESS, WITHY & Co.

Court of Appeal [1921] 3 K.B. 560; 90 L.J.K.B. 1353; 126 L.T. 154; 37 T.L.R. 940; 27 Com.Cas. 25; 15 Asp.M.L.C. 398; [1921] All E.R.Rep. 40

Claim by owners against charterers in respect of destruction of ship

This was a dispute between the charterers and owners of a ship which was destroyed while under charter. At Casablanca, the charterers had employed Arab stevedores to unload the cargo. One of them dropped a heavy plank into the hold, which was full of petrol vapour. On impact, the plank caused a spark, the spark ignited the vapour, and the ship was destroyed. The arbitrator found that it was careless to drop the plank, that some damage to the ship was foreseeable, but that the causing of the spark and the ensuing fire were not. He awarded the owners damages of £196,165-odd (the equivalent of 20 months' hire). Sankey J. confirmed the award, and so did the Court of Appeal.

Bankes L.J.: . . . In the present case the arbitrators have found as a fact that the falling of the plank was due to the negligence of the defendants' servants. The fire appears to me to have been directly caused by the falling of the plank. Under these circumstances I consider that it is immaterial that the causing of the spark by the falling of the plank could not have been reasonably anticipated. The appellants' junior counsel sought to draw a distinction between the anticipation of the extent of damage resulting from a negligent act, and the anticipation of the type of damage resulting from such an act. He admitted that it could not lie in the mouth of a person whose negligent act had caused damage to say that he could not reasonably have foreseen the extent of the damage, but he contended that the negligent person was entitled to rely upon the fact that he could not reasonably have anticipated the type of damage which resulted from his negligent act. I do not think that the distinction can be admitted. Given the breach of duty which constitutes the negligence, and given the damage as a direct result of that negligence, the anticipations of the person whose negligent act has produced the damage appear to me to be irrelevant. I consider that the damages claimed are not too remote. . . .

Warrington L.J.: . . . The result may be summarised as follows: The presence or absence of reasonable anticipation of damage determines the legal quality of the act as negligent or innocent. If it be thus determined to be negligent, then the question whether particular damages are recoverable depends only on the answer to the question whether they are the direct consequence of the act. Sufficient authority for the proposition is afforded by *Smith* v. *London and South Western Ry.* ((1870) L.R. 6 C.P. 14), in the Exchequer Chamber, and particularly by the judgments of Channell B. and Blackburn J. . . .

Scrutton L.J.: . . . The second defence is that the damage is too remote from the negligence as it could not be reasonably foreseen as a consequence. On this head we were referred to a number of well-known cases in which vague language, which I cannot think to be really helpful, has been used in an attempt to define the point at which damage becomes too remote from, or not sufficiently directly caused by, the breach of duty, which is the original cause of action, to be recoverable. For instance, I cannot think it useful to say the damage must be the natural and probable result. This suggests that there are results which are natural but not probable, and other results which are probable but not natural. I am not sure what either adjective means in this connection; if they mean the same thing, two need not be used; if they mean different things, the difference between them should be defined. And as to many cases of fact in which the distinction has been drawn, it is difficult to see why one case should be decided one way and one another. Perhaps the House of Lords will some day explain why, if a cheque is negligently filled up, it is a direct effect of the negligence that someone finding the cheque should commit forgery: *London Joint Stock Bank* v. *Macmillan* ([1918] A.C. 777); while if someone negligently leaves a libellous letter about, it is not a direct effect of the negligence that the finder should show the letter to the person libelled: *Weld-Blundell* v. *Stephens* ([1920] A.C. 956). In this case, however, the problem is simpler. To determine whether an act is negligent, it is relevant to determine whether any reasonable person would foresee that the act would cause damage; if he would not, the act is not negligent. But if the act would or might probably cause damage, the fact that the damage it in fact causes is not the exact kind of damage one would expect is immaterial, so long as the damage is in fact directly traceable to the negligent act, and not due to the operation of independent causes having no connection with the negligent act, except that they could not avoid its results. Once the act is negligent, the fact that its exact operation was not foreseen is immaterial. This is the distinction laid down by the majority of the Exchequer Chamber in *Smith* v. *London and South Western Ry.*, and by the majority of the Court in Banc in *Rigby* v. *Hewitt* and *Greenland* v. *Chaplin* ((1850) 5 Ex. 240, 243; 155 E.R. 103, 104), and approved recently by Lord Sumner in *Weld-Blundell* v. *Stephens* and Sir Samuel Evans in *H.M.S. London* ([1914] P. 76). In the present case it was negligent in discharging cargo to knock down the planks of the temporary staging, for they might easily cause some damage either to workmen, or cargo, or the ship. The fact that they did directly produce an unexpected result, a spark in an atmosphere of petrol vapour which caused a fire, does not relieve the person who was negligent from the damage which his negligent act directly caused. . . .

Questions

1. A borrows a car from B. When the day comes for returning it, A says, "Oh, I'm very sorry, I haven't got it. My chauffeur was getting into the car with a heavy picture I had just bought, and he rather carelessly struck the cigar-lighter on the dash-board. This must have set up some kind of electrical trouble, for the next thing we knew was that the car was on fire, and we were lucky to escape before the whole thing blew up. As to the car, it was just an unfortunate accident, I'm afraid." Is this a satisfactory answer to B's claim for the car?

2. If, under *Hadley* v. *Baxendale* ((1854) 9 Exch. 341; 156 E.R. 145), there is implied in a contract of carriage a term that the carrier will not be liable for more than the value of the thing to be carried, what is the limit of liability in a contract whereby one person contracts for the use of another person's chattel (*e.g.* a ship)?

3. The charterparty in question in this case exempted the charterers from liability for "act of God, the King's enemies, loss or damage from fire on board, etc.," and all the judges agreed that this did not cover fire caused by the charterer's negligence. Does the presence of this clause suggest which party agreed to bear the risk of loss not covered by the exemption clause?

4. Suppose the cause of the fire were wholly unknown. Would the charterers pay (a) in the absence of the exemption clause, (b) when it is present?

OVERSEAS TANKSHIP (U.K.) LTD. v. MORTS DOCK & ENGINEERING CO. THE WAGON MOUND

Privy Council [1961] A.C. 388; [1961] 2 W.L.R. 126; 105 S.J. 85; [1961] 1 All E.R. 404; [1961] 1 Lloyd's Rep. 1

Action by frontager against highway user in respect of property damage

A large quantity of oil was carelessly allowed to spill from *The Wagon Mound*, a ship under the defendant's control, during bunkering operations in Sydney Harbour on October 30, 1951. This oil spread to the plaintiff's wharf about 200 yards away, where a ship, *The Corrimal*, was being repaired. The plaintiff asked whether it was safe to continue welding, and was assured (in accordance with the best scientific opinion) that the oil could not be ignited when spread on water. On November 1, a drop of molten metal fell on a piece of floating waste; this ignited the oil, and the plaintiff's wharf was consumed by fire.

Kinsella J. found that the destruction of the wharf by fire was a direct but unforeseeable consequence of the carelessness of the defendant in spilling the oil, but that some damage by fouling might have been anticipated. He gave judgment for the plaintiff [1958] 1 Lloyd's Rep. 575. The Full Court of the Supreme Court of New South Wales affirmed his decision [1959] 2 Lloyd's Rep. 697. The defendant appealed to the Judicial Committee of the Privy Council, and the appeal was allowed.

Viscount Simonds: . . . the authority of *Polemis* has been severely shaken though lip-service has from time to time been paid to it. In their Lordships' opinion it should no longer be regarded as good law. It is not probable that many cases will for that reason have a different result, though it is hoped that the law will be thereby simplified, and that in some cases, at least, palpable injustice will be avoided. For it does not seem consonant with current ideas of justice or morality that for an act of negligence, however slight or venial, which results in some trivial foreseeable damage the actor should be liable for all consequences however unforeseeable and however grave, so long as they can be said to be "direct." It is a principle of civil liability, subject only to qualifications which have no present relevance, that a man must be considered to be responsible for the probable consequences of his act. To demand more of him is too harsh a rule, to demand less is to ignore that civilised order requires the observance of a minimum standard of behaviour.

This concept applied to the slowly developing law of negligence has led to a great variety of expressions which can, as it appears to their Lordships, be harmonised with little difficulty with the single exception of the so-called rule in *Polemis*. For, if it is asked why a man should be responsible for the natural or necessary or probable consequences of his act (or any other similar description of them) the answer is that it is not because they are natural or necessary or probable, but because, since they have this quality, it is judged by the standard of the reasonable man that he ought to have foreseen them. Thus it is that over and over again it has happened that in different judgments in the same case, and sometimes in a single judgment, liability for a consequence has been imposed on the ground that it was reasonably foresee-able or, alternatively, on the ground that it was natural or necessary or probable. The two grounds have been treated as coterminous, and so they largely are. But, where they are not, the question arises to which the wrong answer was given in *Polemis*. For, if some limitation must be imposed upon the consequences for which the negligent actor is to be held responsible—and all are agreed that some limi-tation there must be—why should that test (reasonable foreseeability) be rejected which, since he is judged by what the reasonable man ought to foresee, corresponds with the common conscience of mankind, and a test (the "direct" consequence) be substituted which leads to nowhere but the never-ending and insoluble problems of causation. "The lawyer," said Sir Frederick Pollock, "cannot afford to adventure himself with philosophers in the logical and metaphysical controversies that beset the idea of cause." Yet this is just what he has most unfortunately done and must continue to do if the rule in *Polemis* is to prevail. A conspicuous example occurs when the actor seeks to escape liability on the ground that the "chain of causation" is broken by a "nova causa" or "novus actus interveniens."

The validity of a rule or principle can sometimes be tested by observing it in oper-ation. Let the rule in *Polemis* be tested in this way. In the case of the *Liesbosch* ([1933] A.C. 449) the appellants, whose vessel had been fouled by the respondents, claimed damages under various heads. The respondents were admittedly at fault; therefore, said the appellants, invoking the rule in *Polemis*, they were responsible for all damage whether reasonably foreseeable or not. Here was the opportunity to deny the rule or to place it secure upon its pedestal. But the House of Lords took neither course; on the contrary, it distinguished *Polemis* on the ground that in that case the injuries suffered were the "immediate physical consequences" of the negli-gent act. It is not easy to understand why a distinction should be drawn between "immediate physical" and other consequences, nor where the line is to be drawn. It was perhaps this difficulty which led Denning L.J. in *Roe* v. *Minister of Health* ([1954] 2 Q.B. 66, 85; above, p. 139) to say that foreseeability is only disregarded when the negligence is the immediate or *precipitating* cause of the damage. This new word may well have been thought as good a word as another for revealing or disguising the fact that he sought loyally to enforce an unworkable rule.

In the same connection may be mentioned the conclusion to which the Full Court finally came in the present case. Applying the rule in *Polemis* and holding therefore that the unforeseeability of the damage by fire afforded no defence, they went on to consider the remaining question. Was it a "direct" consequence? Upon this Man-ning J. said: "Notwithstanding that, if regard is had separately to each individual occurrence in the chain of events that led to this fire, each occurrence was improb-able and, in one sense, improbability was heaped upon improbability, I cannot escape from the conclusion that if the ordinary man in the street had been asked, as a matter of common sense, without any detailed analysis of the circumstances, to state the cause of the fire at Mort's Dock, he would unhesitatingly have assigned such cause to spillage of oil by the appellant's employees." Perhaps he would, and probably he would have added: "I never should have thought it possible." But with great respect to the Full Court this is surely irrelevant, or, if it is relevant, only serves to show that the *Polemis* rule works in a very strange way. After the event even a fool is wise. But it is not the hindsight of a fool; it is the foresight of the reasonable man which alone can determine responsibility. The *Polemis* rule by sub-stituting "direct" for "reasonably foreseeable" consequence leads to a conclusion equally illogical and unjust.

At an early stage in this judgment their Lordships intimated that they would deal with the proposition which can best be stated by reference to the well-known dic-tum of Lord Sumner: "This however goes to culpability not to compensation." It is with the greatest respect to that very learned judge, and to those who have echoed his words, that their Lordships find themselves bound to state their view that this proposition is fundamentally false.

It is, no doubt, proper when considering tortious liability for negligence to analyse its elements and to say that the plaintiff must prove a duty owed to him by the defendant, a breach of that duty by the defendant, and consequent damage. But there can be no liability until the damage has been done. It is not the act but the consequences on which tortious liability is founded. Just as (as it has been said) there is no such thing as negligence in the air, so there is no such thing as liability in the air. Suppose an action brought by A for damage caused by the carelessness (a neutral word) of B, for example, a fire caused by the careless spillage of oil. It may, of course, become relevant to know what duty B owed to A, but the only liability that is in question is the liability for damage by fire. It is vain to isolate the liability from its context and to say that B is or is not liable, and then to ask for what damage he is liable. For his liability is in respect of that damage and no other. If, as admittedly it is, B's liability (culpability) depends on the reasonable foreseeability of the consequent damage, how is that to be determined except by the foreseeability of the damage which in fact happened—the damage in suit? And, if that damage is unforeseeable so as to displace liability at large, how can the liability be restored so as to make compensation payable?

But, it is said, a different position arises if B's careless act has been shown to be negligent and has caused some foreseeable damage to A. Their Lordships have already observed that to hold B liable for consequences however unforeseeable of a careless act, if, but only if, he is at the same time liable for some other damage however trivial, appears to be neither logical nor just. This becomes more clear if it is supposed that similar unforeseeable damage is suffered by A and C but other foreseeable damage, for which B is liable, by A only. A system of law which would hold B liable to A but not to C for the similar damage suffered by each of them could not easily be defended. Fortunately, the attempt is not necessary. For the same fallacy is at the root of the proposition. It is irrelevant to the question whether B is liable for unforeseeable damage that he is liable for foreseeable damage, as irrelevant as would the fact that he had trespassed on Whiteacre be to the question whether he has trespassed on Blackacre. Again, suppose a claim by A for damage by fire by the careless act of B. Of what relevance is it to that claim that he has another claim arising out of the same careless act? It would surely not prejudice his claim if that other claim failed: it cannot assist it if it succeeds. Each of them rests on its own bottom, and will fail if it can be established that the damage could not reasonably be foreseen. We have come back to the plain common sense stated by Lord Russell of Killowen in *Bourhill* v. *Young* ([1943] A.C. 92, 101). As Denning L.J. said in *King* v. *Phillips* ([1953] 1 Q.B. 429, 441): "there can be no doubt since *Bourhill* v. *Young* that the test of *liability for shock* is foreseeability of *injury by shock.*" Their Lordships substitute the word "fire" for "shock" and endorse this statement of the law.

Their Lordships conclude this part of the case with some general observations. They have been concerned primarily to displace the proposition that unforeseeability is irrelevant if damage is "direct." In doing so they have inevitably insisted that the essential factor in determining liability is whether the damage is of such a kind as the reasonable man should have foreseen. This accords with the general view thus stated by Lord Atkin in *Donoghue* v. *Stevenson*: "The liability for negligence, whether you style it such or treat it as in other systems as a species of 'culpa,' is no doubt based upon a general public sentiment of moral wrongdoing for which the offender must pay." It is a departure from this sovereign principle if liability is made to depend solely on the damage being the "direct" or "natural" consequence of the precedent act. Who knows or can be assumed to know all the processes of nature? But if it would be wrong that a man should be held liable for damage unpredictable by a reasonable man because it was "direct" or "natural," equally it would be wrong that he should escape liability, however "indirect" the damage, if he foresaw or could reasonably foresee the intervening events which led to its being done: *cf. Woods* v. *Duncan* ([1946] A.C. 401, 442). Thus foreseeability becomes the effective test. In reasserting this principle their Lordships conceive that they do not depart from, but follow and develop, the law of negligence as laid down by Baron Alderson in *Blyth* v. *Birmingham Waterworks Co.* ((1856) 11 Exch. 781, 784; 156 E.R. 1047).

It is proper to add that their Lordships have not found it necessary to consider the so-called rule of "strict liability" exemplified in *Rylands* v. *Fletcher* ((1868) L.R. 3 H.L. 330; below, p. 391) and the cases that have followed or distinguished it. Nothing that they have said is intended to reflect on that rule. . . .

Their Lordships will humbly advise Her Majesty that this appeal should be allowed, and the respondents' action so far as it related to damage caused by the negligence of the appellants be dismissed with costs, but that the action so far as it related to damage caused by nuisance should be remitted to the Full Court to be dealt with as that court may think fit. The respondents must pay the costs of the appellants of this appeal and in the courts below.

Questions

1. Did their Lordships deny that the spillage of oil caused the fire?

2. Could *you* defend a legal system which held "B liable to A but not to C for the similar damage suffered by each of them" if there was a contract or other special relationship between B and A but not between B and C, or vice versa?

3. Do you have any difficulty in distinguishing the immediate physical consequences of an act from its immediate non-physical consequences (*e.g. The Edison*, below, p. 563) or from its mediate physical consequences (*e.g. Best* v. *Samuel Fox*, [1952] A.C. 716)?

4. Suppose that their Lordships had wanted to maintain the result of *Re Polemis* and to decide the present case in favour of the defendants. On which of the following grounds of distinction could they most properly have done so?

(a) the difference between three days and one second;
(b) the difference between 200 yards horizontally and about 20 feet vertically;
(c) the difference between a case where there was an intervening act (*viz.*, the dropping of the molten metal) and a case where there was not;
(d) the difference between strangers and contractors?

5. Does what the plaintiff complains of have to be merely foreseeable, or does it have to be a foreseeable *consequence* of the defendant's behaviour? If the latter, how do we escape from the "never-ending and insoluble problems of causation"?

6. Do you have any difficulty with the following case (*The Trecarrell* [1973] 1 Lloyd's Rep. 402 (Brandon J.))? A ship lying alongside X's quay was having its tank painted by Y. Z, one of Y's men, tripped as he was carrying a drum of paint across the quay to the ship and the paint drum fell on an electrical cable lying on the ground and cut it. Sparks came from the cut cable, ignited the spilt paint and caused a fire which burnt the ship. Y was held liable because Z should have taken more care with the paint which he knew to be very inflammable though he didn't know that there was a source of ignition close by. X was held not liable since it was not normal practice to give extra insulation to such cables.

Small Notes:

1. "But it is not the hindsight of a fool. . . . " One of the characters in Congreve's *Love for Love* is named Foresight. He is described as "An illiterate old Fellow, peevish and positive, superstitious and pretending to understand Astrology, Palmistry, Phisiognomy, Omens, Dreams &c."

2. All the incendiary bombs and high explosives of the Royal Air Force were incapable of setting fire to the oil which spread on to the English Channel from the wreck of the *Torrey Canyon* after it collided with Lands End in 1967. Presumably experts thought otherwise.

Long Note:

In *The Wagon Mound (No. 2)* the same defendant was sued by the owners of the ship which was being repaired at Morts Dock. The trial judge held that there could be no recovery in negligence, since the fire was unforeseeable, but that unforeseeability of consequences was irrelevant in nuisance. The Judicial Committee held that there was no difference in this respect between nuisance and negligence, but found that the fire was foreseeable after all and gave judgment for the plaintiff in negligence ([1967] 1 A.C. 617, on appeal from [1963] 1 Lloyd's Rep. 402). (Appeals from Australia have now been abolished.)

So the defendants paid the owner of the burnt ship. Could they then claim contribution (above, p. 66) from Morts Dock? That depends on whether Morts Dock would have been liable to the owners of the ship they were repairing. Now that the fire has been held to have been foreseeable, could one properly say that it was negligent of the *Wagon Mound's* engineer to let the oil spill, but not negligent of the wharf-owners to carry on welding? Probably one could, since liability depends on the unreasonableness of behaviour as well as the foreseeability of the results. Remember the words of Lord Reid: "If a real risk is one which would occur to the mind of a reasonable man . . . and which he would not brush aside as far-fetched, and if the criterion is to be what that reasonable man would have done in the circumstances, then surely he would not neglect such a risk if action to eliminate it presented no difficulty, involved no disadvantage and required no expense." ([1967] 1 A.C. 617, 643–644).

The Wagon Mound (No. 2) discusses how foreseeable the damage must be in order to satisfy the test laid down by *The Wagon Mound (No. 1)*. As Lord Upjohn put it in *The Heron II* [1969] 1 A.C. 350, 422, "the tortfeasor is liable for any damage which he can reasonably foresee may happen as a result of the breach however unlikely it may be, unless it can be brushed aside as far-fetched." According to *The Heron II* the rules of remoteness are different in contract and tort: a contractor is not, like the tortfeasor, liable for consequences which are just foreseeable, but only for those which are so foreseeable that one would actually have predicted them. Now although the rules of remoteness certainly operate differently depending on the features of the case in hand, it is far from clear that the distinction between contract and tort is the correct one to draw or that it is useful to spend time on such verbal formulae. If we accept that the outcome of a damages suit is a function of (a) the type of harm complained of, (b) the relationship between the parties and (c) the blameworthiness of the defendant, then we can be sure that liability for consequences will be more extensive if (a) the harm is physical, especially personal injury, (b) there is a special relationship, and (c) the defendant was greatly to blame. Whereas features (a) and (c) are often missing in contract cases, feature (b) is invariably present; in tort cases, on the other hand, (a) and (c) are usually present but (b) often is not (as in *The Wagon Mound* itself). In *Parsons* v. *Uttley Ingham* [1978] Q.B. 791 the defendants sold the plaintiff a hopper for pig-food. Because its ventilator was stuck, the nuts inside went mouldy. The plaintiff's pigs got a rare disease from the mouldy nuts and 254 of them died. Here was physical harm (as Lord Denning emphasised) caused by a careless breach of contract. The defendants were held liable.

SMITH v. LEECH BRAIN & CO.

Queen's Bench [1962] 2 Q.B. 405; [1962] 2 W.L.R. 148; 106 S.J. 77; [1961] 3 All E.R. 1159

Action by widow against employer of husband

Smith was employed by the defendant as labourer and galvaniser; his job was to remove galvanised articles from a tank of molten metal. One day in 1950 he was burnt on the lip by a drop of molten metal when a large object was immersed in the tank. The defendants were negligent in not providing adequate protection. Smith died of cancer in 1953. He had previously worked in a gasworks for nine years and was consequently at the time of the accident in a condition such that a burn or scratch might induce the malignancy from which he died.

Lord Parker C.J.: . . . Accordingly, I find that the burn was the promoting agency of cancer in tissues which already had a pre-malignant condition. In those circumstances, it is clear that the plaintiff's husband, but for the burn, would not necessarily ever have developed cancer. On the other hand, having regard to the number of matters which can be promoting agencies, there was a strong likelihood that at some stage in his life he would develop cancer. But that the burn did contribute to, or cause in part, at any rate, the cancer and the death, I have no doubt.

The third question is damages. Here I am confronted with the recent decision of the Privy Council in *Overseas Tankship (U.K.) Ltd.* v. *Morts Dock and Engineering Co. Ltd. (The Wagon Mound).* But for that case, it seems to me perfectly clear that, assuming negligence proved, and assuming that the burn caused in whole or in part the cancer and the death, the plaintiff would be entitled to recover. It is said on the one side by Mr. May that although I am not strictly bound by the *Wagon Mound* since it is a decision of the Privy Council, I should treat myself as free, using the arguments to be derived from that case, to say that other cases in these courts— other cases in the Court of Appeal—have been wrongly decided, and particularly that *Re Polemis and Furness Withy & Co.* was wrongly decided, and that a further ground for taking that course is to be found in the various criticisms that have from time to time in the past been made by members of the House of Lords in regard to the *Polemis* case.

It is said, on the other hand, by Mr. Martin Jukes, that I should hold that the *Polemis* case was rightly decided and, secondly, that even if that is not so I must treat myself as completely bound by it. Thirdly, he said that in any event, whatever the true view is in regard to the *Polemis* case, the *Wagon Mound* has no relevance at all to this case.

For my part, I am quite satisfied that the Judicial Committee in the *Wagon Mound* case did not have what I may call, loosely, the thin skull cases in mind. It has always been the law of this country that a tortfeasor takes his victim as he finds him. It is unnecessary to do more than refer to the short passage in the decision of Kennedy J. in *Dulieu* v. *White & Sons,* where he said ([1901] 2 K.B. 669, 679): "If a man is negligently run over or otherwise negligently injured in his body, it is no answer to the sufferer's claim for damages that he would have suffered less injury, or no injury at all, if he had not had an unusually thin skull or an unusually weak heart."

To the same effect is a passage in the judgment of Scrutton L.J. in *The Arpad* ([1934] P. 189, 202). But quite apart from those two references, as is well known, the work of the courts for years and years has gone on on that basis. There is not a day that goes by where some trial judge does not adopt that principle, that the tort-feasor takes his victim as he finds him. If the Judicial Committee had any intention of making an inroad into that doctrine, I am quite satisfied that they would have said so.

It is true that if the wording in the advice given by Lord Simonds in the *Wagon Mound* case is applied strictly to such a case as this, it could be said that they were dealing with this point. But, as I have said, it is to my mind quite impossible to con-ceive that they were and, indeed, it has been pointed out that they disclose the dis-tinction between such a case as this and the one they were considering when they comment on *Smith* v. *London & South Western Ry.* ((1870) L.R. 6 C.P. 14). Lord Simonds, in dealing with that case, said: "Three things may be noted about this case: the first, that for the sweeping proposition laid down no authority was cited; the second, that the point to which the court directed its mind was not unforesee-able damage of a different kind from that which was foreseen, but more extensive damage of the same kind." In other words, Lord Simonds is clearly there drawing a distinction between the question whether a man could reasonably anticipate a type of injury, and the question whether a man could reasonably anticipate the extent of injury of the type which could be foreseen.

The Judicial Committee were, I think, disagreeing with the decision in the *Pole-mis* case that a man is no longer liable for the type of damage which he could not reasonably anticipate. The Judicial Committee were not, I think, saying that a man is only liable for the extent of damage which he could anticipate, always assuming the type of injury could have been anticipated. I think that view is really supported by the way in which cases of this sort have been dealt with in Scotland. Scotland has never, so far as I know, adopted the principle laid down in *Polemis,* and yet I am quite satisfied that they have throughout proceeded on the basis that the tortfeasor takes the victim as he finds him.

In those circumstances, it seems to me that this is plainly a case which comes within the old principle. The test is not whether these employers could reasonably have foreseen that a burn would cause cancer and that he would die. The question is whether these employers could reasonably foresee the type of injury he suffered, namely, the burn. What, in the particular case, is the amount of damage which he suffers as a result of that burn depends upon the characteristics and constitution of the victim.

Accordingly, I find that the damages which the widow claims are damages for which the defendants are liable. Before leaving that part of the case, I should say, in case the matter goes further, that I would follow, sitting as a trial judge, the decision in the *Wagon Mound* case; or rather, more accurately, I would treat myself, in the light of the arguments in that case, able to follow other decisions of the Court of Appeal prior to the *Polemis* case, rather than the *Polemis* case itself. As I have said, that case has been criticised by individual members of the House of Lords, although followed by the Court of Appeal in *Thurogood* v. *Van Den Berghs & Jurgens Ltd.* ([1951] 2 K.B. 537). I should treat myself as at liberty to do that, and for my part I would do so the more readily because I think it is important that the common law, and the development of the common law, should be homogeneous in the various sections of the Commonwealth. I think it would be lamentable if a court sitting here had to say that while the common law in the Commonwealth and Scotland has been developed in a particular way, yet we in this country, and sitting in these courts, are going to proceed in a different way. However, as I have said, that does not strictly arise in this case.

[His Lordship considered the question of damages, observed that he must make a substantial reduction from the figure taken for the dependency because of the fact that the plaintiff's husband might have developed cancer even if he had not suffered the burn, and awarded the plaintiff £3,064 17s. 0d.]

Questions

1. Was this a claim in respect of "immediate physical consequences" which were unforeseeable?

2. Was the claim in respect of damage of the same *type* as could have been foreseen?

3. Complete the following: "The test of liability for fire is foreseeability of injury by fire. The test of liability for cancer is foreseeability of injury by—."

4. Does the "thin-skull" rule apply every time some injury to the plaintiff is foreseeable and a different injury occurs?

5. If it be true, as Lord Denning suggests below p. 205, that policy is an element in questions of remoteness of damage, would it be right to make a distinction between claims for personal injury (this case) and property damage (*The Wagon Mound*)? If the claim is for purely financial loss, is the rule of remoteness likely to be applied in a manner favourable to the plaintiff?

Note:

"You must take your victim as you find him" is a perplexing saying in some ways. The principal case seems to hold that a claim for unforeseeable consequences of careless conduct is not defeated if their unforeseeability results from an unsuspected pre-existing susceptibility of the victim, given that some injury was foreseeably caused. The susceptibility is an old cause, not a new one. Here, then, is a difference between culpability and compensation, since if one knows or should know of the susceptibility one may have to take extra steps to avoid that damage (*Paris* v. *Stepney B.C.* [1951] A.C. 367; *Haley* v. *London Electricity Board* (above p. 125)).

But there may be a new cause which triggers the old susceptibility. In one case the plaintiff proved tragically allergic to an anti-tetanus serum which was foreseeably injected after he suffered an abrasion on a ladder which was oily owing to the defendant employer's negligence. In upholding judgment for the plaintiff, the Court of Appeal said: " . . . the principle that a defendant must take the plaintiff as he finds him involves that if a wrongdoer ought reasonably to foresee that as a result of his wrongful act the victim may require medical treatment he is, subject to the principle of novus actus interveniens, liable for the consequences of the treatment applied although he could not reasonably foresee those consequences or that they could be serious." (*Robinson* v. *Post Office* [1974] 2 All E.R. 737, 750). Can this be reconciled with the decision for the defendant in a South African case where the victim of a traffic accident who was taking Parstellin as prescribed died as a result of eating a cheese sandwich, it not being known at that time that the drug and cheese made a fatal mixture? (*Alston* v. *Marine & Trade Ins. Co.* 1964 (4) S.A. 112).

The saying also sometimes works to the benefit of the defendant. If the young man whom the motorist injures has a secret ailment which would in any case have curtailed his working life, the motorist pays less by way of damages. Again, if you carelessly dent a car you expect to have to pay for a respray; but if it already needed a respray by reason of a prior dent, you don't have to pay (*sed quaere*) (*Performance Cars* v. *Abraham* [1962] 1 Q.B. 33).

Where personal injury is suffered and there is no intervening event, the injury has to be really freaky to excuse a negligent person who caused it. One can contrast two master and servant cases. In *Bradford* v. *Robinson Rentals Ltd.* ([1967] 1 W.L.R. 337) in the depths of the worst winter for years the plaintiff radio engineer was required to drive in unheated vans from Honiton to Bedford and back, a trip of 24 hours in two days; he suffered frostbite, a rare complaint in England, and recovered damages. In *Tremain* v. *Pike* ([1969] 1 W.L.R. 1556) a farm worker contracted Weil's disease owing to contact with the urine of rats which his employer allowed to proliferate; the employer was held not liable.

Note that Lord Russell in *McLoughlin* (above p. 69) emphasised that the shock victim in that case was not abnormally susceptible. Can his implication be reconciled with true doctrine? In *Malcolm* v. *Broadhurst* [1970] 3 All E.R. 508, Geoffrey Lane J. had observed that there was no difference in principle between an egg-shell skull and an egg-shell personality. In that case the defendant was liable for causing physical injury to husband and wife. The wife recovered from the physical injuries by June 1967, but their psychical consequences lasted until February 1968 because she had a nervous condition before the accident. For six months thereafter she was still unfit for work because with her vulnerable personality she was unable to cope with her husband's changed behaviour due to the accident. She recovered damages for all three periods of unfitness for work. And in *Brice* v. *Brown* [1984] 1 All E.R. 997 a neurotic mother who had a hysterical reaction to the minor injury suffered by her nine-year-old daughter travelling with her in a taxi was awarded damages of £56,045.

McGOVERN v. BRITISH STEEL CORP.

Court of Appeal [1986] I.C.R. 608

Action for personal injuries against employer

A walkway on scaffolding 20 metres above the ground was bordered by toe-boards, planks eight inches broad and nine feet long, lying on their edge, one-and-a-half inches thick. Some time in the late morning one of these boards fell inwards and lay in the walkway, and the plaintiff, using the walkway for the fourth time that day, tripped over it. He was quite unharmed, and decided to replace the board (of which he later said that he could carry half-a-dozen without difficulty). In this apparently innocuous manoeuvre he ricked his back badly for reasons which remained entirely unexplained.

The trial judge found that the accident was unforeseeable in the *Wagon Mound* sense, and that there was therefore no liability at common law, but he gave judgment for the plaintiff on the ground of breach of Reg. 30(2) of the Construction (Working Places) Regulations 1966: "Every . . . gangway . . . shall be kept free from any unnecessary obstruction and material." The defendant's appeal was dismissed, Ralph Gibson L.J. dissenting.

Sir John Donaldson M.R.: I agree that the only live issues in this appeal are (a) causation—whether the injury suffered by the plaintiff was caused by the defendants' breach of regulation 30 of the Construction (Working Places) Regulations

1966, and (b) mischief—whether the injury suffered by the plaintiff was of a kind against which the regulation was intended to guard.

I start with the mischief issue. As Lord Reid said in *Grant* v. *National Coal Board* ([1956] A.C. 649, 661):

"In every case the problem is to ascertain the intention of Parliament from the terms of the statute . . . If the statute is only aimed at preventing a certain kind of injury, then it seems reasonable to hold (as in *Gorris* v. *Scott*) that civil liability only results if that kind of injury is caused by a breach. But in this case there is no question of limitation to a particular kind of injury: . . . "

The same can, in my judgment, be said of the present case. The regulation is designed to avoid the mischief of obstruction in gangways. If injury is caused by the obstruction, it must fall within the regulation. The mischief issue is thus indistinguishable from that of causation.

I turn therefore to causation. The "but for" test was much canvassed in argument. However, it is of limited value. As the learned editors of *Clerk & Lindsell on Torts*, 15th ed. (1982) put it, at para. 11–37:

"In the main the courts appear to isolate, first, the possible factors but for which the damage would not have been sustained, and then to pick out what appears to be the most responsible cause. The so-called 'but for' test serves an exclusionary purpose, namely, to reject from further consideration any factor which did not affect the event."

It so happened that in *Millard* v. *Serck Tubes Ltd.* ([1969] 1 W.L.R. 211), the "but for" test was conclusive, because there was no other competing cause, but it is fallacious to reply upon it to establish positive causation where there is.

There is no doubt that the toe-board caused the plaintiff to trip and "but for" his having tripped he would never have noticed the toe-board, tried to move it or suffered his injury. However, it was quite clear that the trip did not cause him any injury. The chain of causation was broken. The starting point is thus, at the earliest, the time at which, having noticed the obstruction, he sought to remove it. The judge, who had the advantage of seeing and hearing the witness and getting a "feel" for the situation which is denied to us, concluded that it was very probable that if anyone saw the board they would take steps to move it out of the way. I therefore see no reason to disagree with the judge when he held that the presence of the board obstructing the gangway in breach of the regulation was a cause of the plaintiff trying to remove it. However, this is not sufficient unless the removal of the board was a cause of the plaintiff's injury.

I confess that it is this aspect which has given me the greatest difficulty. The toe-board was of no great weight and it is difficult to see why the accident happened at all. All would have been explained if it had emerged that the plaintiff had tried to move the toe-board in a negligent manner, such as trying to break it in two for more convenient handling. Then his negligence and not the obstruction would have been the cause of his injury. But in the absence of any evidence of an intervening cause, I am driven to the conclusion that the removal of the board was the cause of the plaintiff's injury. How this came about is another matter. If, of course, the process of removal could not possibly by itself have caused the injury, the plaintiff would fail, but I do not think that that was the position. It looks as if the toe-board was jammed in some peculiar way such that, once it was moved, compressive forces were released and transmitted to the plaintiff causing the injury to his back. This is sufficient to establish the plaintiff's claim.

I would dismiss the appeal.

Note:

In *Millard* v. *Serck Tubes Ltd.* [1969] 1 W.L.R. 211, a case turning on the Factories Act 1961, s.14 (duty to fence dangerous machinery), Salmon L.J. said "the fact that the accident occurred in an entirely unforeseeable way is wholly irrelevant in this case." Whether any accident was foreseeable is, of course, material to determine whether the machinery was dangerous and therefore bound to be fenced. We therefore here have an example of the application of Lord Sumner's dictum that foreseeability "goes to culpability not to compensation," though that observation was said to be fundamentally false in *The Wagon Mound* (above, p. 186).

Section 3.—The Risk Envisaged

GORRIS v. SCOTT

Court of Exchequer (1874) L.R. 9 Exch. 125; 43 L.J.Ex. 92; 30 L.T. 431; 22 W.R. 575

Action by owner against carrier in respect of loss of property

Kelly C.B.: This is an action to recover damages for the loss of a number of sheep which the defendant, a shipowner, had contracted to carry, and which were washed overboard and lost by reason (as we must take it to be truly alleged) of the neglect to comply with a certain order made by the Privy Council, in pursuance of the Contagious Diseases (Animals) Act 1869. The Act was passed merely for sanitary purposes, in order to prevent animals in a state of infectious disease from communicating it to other animals with which they might come in contact. Under the authority of that Act, certain orders were made; amongst others, an order by which any ship bringing sheep or cattle from any foreign ports to ports in Great Britain is to have the place occupied by such animals divided into pens of certain dimensions, and the floor of such pens furnished with battens or foot-holds. The object of this order is to prevent animals from being overcrowded, and so brought into a condition in which the disease guarded against would be likely to be developed. This regulation has been neglected, and the question is, whether the loss, which we must assume to have been caused by that neglect, entitles the plaintiffs to maintain an action.

The argument of the defendant is, that the Act has imposed penalties to secure the observance of its provisions, and that, according to the general rule, the remedy prescribed by the statute must be pursued; that although, when penalties are imposed for the violation of a statutory duty, a person aggrieved by its violation may sometimes maintain an action for the damage so caused, that must be in cases where the object of the statute is to confer a benefit on individuals and to protect them against the evil consequences which the statute was designed to prevent, and which have in fact ensued; but that if the object is not to protect individuals against the consequences which have in fact ensued, it is otherwise; that if, therefore, by reason of the precautions in question not having been taken, the plaintiffs had sustained that damage against which it was intended to secure them, an action would lie, but that when the damage is of such a nature as was not contemplated at all by the statute, and as to which it was not intended to confer any benefit on the plaintiffs, they cannot maintain an action founded on the neglect. The principle may be well illustrated by the case put in argument of a breach by a railway company of its duty to erect a gate on a level crossing, and to keep the gate closed except when the crossing is being actually and properly used. The object of the precaution is to prevent injury from being sustained through animals or vehicles being upon the line at unseasonable times; and if by reason of such a breach of duty, either in not erecting the gate, or in not keeping it closed, a person attempts to cross with a carriage at an improper time, and injury ensues to a passenger, no doubt an action would lie against the railway company, because the intention of the legislature was that, by the erection of the gates and by their being kept closed individuals should be protected against accidents of this description. And if we could see that it was the object, or among the objects of this Act, that the owners of sheep and cattle coming from a foreign port should be protected by the means described against the danger of their property being washed overboard, or lost by the perils of the sea, the present action would be within the principle.

But, looking at the Act, it is perfectly clear that its provisions were all enacted with a totally different view; there was no purpose, direct or indirect, to protect against such damage; but, as is recited in the preamble, the Act is directed against the possibility of sheep or cattle being exposed to disease on their way to this country. The preamble recites that "it is expedient to confer on Her Majesty's most honourable Privy Council power to take such measures as may appear from time to time necessary to prevent the introduction into Great Britain of contagious or infectious diseses among cattle, sheep, or other animals, by prohibiting or regulating the importation of foreign animals," and also to provide against the "spreading" of such diseases in Great Britain. Then follow numerous sections directed entirely to this object. Then comes section 75, which enacts that "the Privy Council may from time to time make such orders as they think expedient for all or any of the following purposes." What, then, are these purposes? They are "for securing for animals brought by sea to ports in Great Britain a proper supply of food and water during the passage and on landing," "for protecting such animals from unnecessary suffering during the passage and on landing," and so forth; all the purposes enumerated being calculated and directed to the prevention of disease, and none of them having any relation whatever to the danger of loss by the perils of the sea. That being so, if by reason of the default in question the plaintiffs' sheep had been overcrowded, or had been caused unnecessary suffering, and so had arrived in this country in a state of disease, I do not say that they might not have maintained this action. But the damage complained of here is something totally apart from the object of the Act of Parliament, and it is in accordance with all the authorities to say that the action is not maintainable.

Pigott B.: . . . The object, then, of the regulations which have been broken was, not to prevent cattle from being washed overboard, but to protect them against contagious disease. . . . If, indeed, by reason of the neglect complained of, the cattle had contracted a contagious disease, the case would have been different. But as the case stands on this declaration, the answer to the action is this: Admit there has been a breach of duty; admit there has been a consequent injury; still the legislature was not legislating to protect against such an injury, but for an altogether different purpose; its object was not to regulate the duty of the carrier for all purposes, but only for one particular purpose.

Pollock B.: . . . Here no other negligence is alleged than the omission of that precaution; we must assume that the sheep were washed overboard merely in consequence of that omission and the question is whether that washing away gives a cause of action to the plaintiffs. Now, the Act of Parliament was passed *alio intuitu;* the recital in the preamble and the words of section 75 point out that what the Privy Council have power to do is to make such orders as may be expedient for the purpose of preventing the introduction and the spread of contagious and infectious diseases amongst animals. Suppose, then, that the precautions directed are useful and advantageous for preventing animals from being washed overboard, yet they were never intended for that purpose, and a loss of that kind caused by their neglect cannot give a cause of action.

Quote
"It is one thing to say that if the damage suffered is of a kind totally different from that which it is the object of the regulation to prevent, there is no civil liability. But it is quite a

different thing to say that civil liability is excluded because the damage, though precisely of the kind which the regulation was designed to prevent, happened in a way not contemplated by the maker of the regulation. The difference is comparable with that which caused the decision in *Overseas Tankship (U.K.) Ltd.* v. *Morts Dock & Engineering Co. Ltd. (The Wagon Mound)* ([1961] A.C. 388; above, p. 185) to go one way and the decision in *Hughes* v. *Lord Advocate* ([1963] A.C. 837, next below) to go the other way." *Donaghey* v. *Boulton & Paul Ltd.* ([1968] A.C. 1, 26, *per* Lord Reid).

Note:

    This may be an old decision but recent use has been made of the doctrine that liability may be restricted by reference to the purpose of the rule infringed. Readers will recall that in *Anns* (above p. 60) it was held that a local authority might be under a common law duty to take care in the (operational) exercise of its statutory powers. Among the first to get their snouts in this new trough were building developers who had made less than the expected profit because the local authority had failed to correct their plans. This scandal was eventually stopped when the House of Lords held that there could be liability only in respect of the harm against which the powers negligently exercised were directed. (*Peabody Donation Fund* v. *Sir Lindsay Parkinson* [1984] 3 All E.R. 529). As it was put in a later case: "The purpose for which the legislature has conferred the supervisory powers over building operations on local authorities is to protect the occupiers of buildings built in the local authority's area and also members of the public generally against dangers to health or personal safety. It is not to safeguard the building developer himself against economic loss incurred in the course of a building project, or indeed anyone else against purely economic loss." (*Investors in Industry* v. *South Beds. D.C.* [1986] 1 All E.R. 787, 805, *per* Slade L.J.).

HUGHES v. LORD ADVOCATE

House of Lords [1963] A.C. 837; [1963] 2 W.L.R. 779; 107 S.J. 232; [1963] 1 All E.R. 705; 1963 S.C.(H.L.) 31; 1963 S.L.T. 150

Action by pedestrian against person working on highway in respect of personal injury

The defenders, acting under statutory powers, opened a manhole in an Edinburgh street in order to do underground telephone repairs. Above the manhole their workmen placed a tent, and round the tent they placed warning paraffin lamps. At five o'clock one winter evening all the workmen left for tea. The pursuer, a boy of eight, and his uncle, a boy of ten, came along, took a lamp and entered the manhole. As they emerged, the lamp was knocked into the hole and a violent explosion took place, with flames shooting 30 feet into the air. The pursuer was knocked back into the hole where he sustained serious burns.

    The Lord Ordinary, after hearing evidence, gave judgment for the defenders, and this decision was upheld by the First Division of the Court of Session (Lord Carmont dissenting), 1961 S.C. 310. The pursuer's appeal to the House of Lords was allowed.

Lord Guest: . . . It might very well be that paraffin lamps by themselves, if left in the open, are not potentially dangerous even to children. But different considerations apply when they are found in connection with a shelter tent and a manhole, all of which are allurements to the inquisitive child. It is the combination of these factors which renders the situation one of potential danger.

    In dismissing the appellant's claim the Lord Ordinary and the majority of the judges of the First Division reached the conclusion that the accident which happened was not reasonably foreseeable. In order to establish a coherent chain of causation it is not necessary that the precise details leading up to the accident should have been reasonably foreseeable: it is sufficient if the accident which occurred is of a type which should have been foreseeable by a reasonably careful person (*Miller* v. *South of Scotland Electricity Board* (1958 S.C.(H.L.) 20, 34), Lord Keith of Avonholm; *Harvey* v. *Singer Manufacturing Co. Ltd.* (1960 S.C. 155, 168), Lord Patrick) or as Lord Mackintosh expressed it in the *Harvey* case, the precise concatenation of circumstances need not be envisaged. Concentration has been placed in the courts below on the explosion which, it was said, could not have been foreseen because it was caused in a unique fashion by the paraffin forming into vapour and being ignited by the naked flame of the wick. But this, in my opinion, is to concentrate on what is really a non-essential element in the dangerous situation created by the allurement. The test might better be put thus: Was the igniting of paraffin outside the lamp by the flame a foreseeable consequence of the breach of duty? In the circumstances, there was a combination of potentially dangerous circumstances against which the Post Office had to protect the appellant. If these formed an allurement to children it might have been foreseen that they would play with the lamp, that it might tip over, that it might be broken, and that when broken the paraffin might spill and be ignited by the flame. All these steps in the chain of causation seem to have been accepted by all the judges in the courts below as foreseeable. But because the explosion was the agent which caused the burning and was unforeseeable, therefore the accident, according to them, was not reasonably foreseeable. In my opinion, this reasoning is fallacious. An explosion is only one way in which burning can be caused. Burning can also be caused by the contact between liquid paraffin and a naked flame. In the one case paraffin vapour and in the other case liquid paraffin is ignited by fire. I cannot see that these are two different types of accident. They are both burning accidents and in both cases the injuries would be burning injuries. Upon this view the explosion was an immaterial event in the chain of causation. It was simply one way in which burning might be caused by the potentially dangerous paraffin lamp. I adopt, with respect, Lord Carmont's observation in the present case: "The defender cannot, I think, escape liability by contending that he did not foresee all the possibilities of the manner in which allurements—the manhole and the lantern—would act upon the childish mind."

The respondent relied upon the case of *Muir* v. *Glasgow Corporation* [above, p. 116] and particularly on certain observations by Lords Thankerton and Macmillan. There are, in my view, essential differences between the two cases. The tea urn was, in that case, not, like the paraffin lamp in the present circumstance, a potentially dangerous object. Moreover, the precise way in which the tea came to be spilled was never established, and, as Lord Romer said (at 467): "It being thus unknown what was the particular risk that materialised, it is impossible to decide whether it was or was not one that should have been within the reasonable contemplation of Mrs. Alexander or of some other agent or employee of the appellants, and it is, accordingly, also impossible to fix the appellants with liability for the damage that the respondents sustained."

I have therefore reached the conclusion that the accident which occurred and which caused burning injuries to the appellant was one which ought reasonably to have been foreseen by the Post Office employees and that they were at fault in failing to provide a protection against the appellant entering the shelter and going down the manhole.

I would allow the appeal.

Lord Pearce: My Lords, I agree with the opinion of my noble and learned friend, Lord Guest.

The dangerous allurement was left unguarded in a public highway in the heart of Edinburgh. It was for the defenders to show by evidence that, although this was a public street, the presence of children there was so little to be expected that a reasonable man might leave the allurement unguarded. But, in my opinion, their evidence fell short of that, and the Lord Ordinary rightly so decided.

The defenders are therefore liable for all the foreseeable consequences of their neglect. When an accident is of a different type and kind from anything that a defender could have foreseen he is not liable for it (see *The Wagon Mound*). But to demand too great precision in the test of foreseeability would be unfair to the pursuer since the facets of misadventure are innumerable. . . . In the case of an allurement to children it is particularly hard to foresee with precision the exact shape of the disaster that will arise. The allurement in this case was the combination of a red paraffin lamp, a ladder, a partially closed tent, and a cavernous hole within it, a setting well fitted to inspire some juvenile adventure that might end in calamity. The obvious risks were burning and conflagration and a fall. All these in fact occurred, but unexpectedly the mishandled lamp instead of causing an ordinary conflagration produced a violent explosion. Did the explosion create an accident and damage of a different type from the misadventure and damage that could be foreseen? In my judgment it did not. The accident was but a variant of the foreseeable. It was, to quote the words of Denning L.J. in *Roe* v. *Minister of Health* (above, p. 139), "within the risk created by the negligence." No unforeseeable, extraneous, initial occurrence fired the train. The children's entry into the tent with the ladder, the descent into the hole, the mishandling of the lamp, were all foreseeable. The greater part of the path to injury had thus been trodden, and the mishandled lamp was quite likely at that stage to spill and cause a conflagration. Instead, by some curious chance of combustion, it exploded and no conflagration occurred, it would seem, until after the explosion. There was thus an unexpected manifestation of the apprehended physical dangers. But it would be, I think, too narrow a view to hold that those who created the risk of fire are excused from the liability for the damage by fire because it came by way of explosive combustion. The resulting damage, though severe, was not greater than or different in kind from that which might have been produced had the lamp spilled and produced a more normal conflagration in the hole.

I would therefore allow the appeal.

Lord Reid: . . . So we have (first) a duty owed by the workmen, (secondly) the fact that if they had done as they ought to have done there would have been no accident, and (thirdly) the fact that the injuries suffered by the appellant, though perhaps different in degree, did not differ in kind from injuries which might have resulted from an accident of a foreseeable nature. The ground on which this case has been decided against the appellant is that the accident was of an unforeseeable type. Of course, the pursuer has to prove that the defender's fault caused the accident, and there could be a case where the intrusion of a new and unexpected factor could be regarded as the cause of the accident rather than the fault of the defender. But that is not this case. The cause of this accident was a known source of danger, the lamp, but it behaved in an unpredictable way. . . .

Note:
This decision has been taken as an authority in favour of the risk principle in so far as it "typifies" the means whereby the injury accrues. Lord Jenkins said: "To my mind, the distinction drawn between burning and explosion is too fine to warrant acceptance." Yet the distinction between fire and explosion as separate risks is a commonplace of insurance law. For example, the 1943 Standard Fire Policy of New York specifically excludes the liability of the insurer for damage caused by explosion. And the following is an extract from a Consequential Loss policy in everyday use in Great Britain: "The Company agrees . . . that if . . . any building . . . be destroyed or damaged by 1. Fire (whether resulting from explosion or otherwise); 2. Lightning; 3. Explosion . . . the Company will pay to the Insured . . . the amount of loss. . . . As will be seen from that extract, however, a fire caused by explosion falls within the *fire* risk. What the Court of Session did was to distinguish between risks created by a wrongdoer more subtly than do those whose business it is to distinguish the risks they choose to accept. It is satisfactory that the House of Lords has corrected them. But it remains a question whether a person who has admittedly and wrongfully created a danger should have his

liability for the consequent damage determined as if he were a person who had been paid to accept that risk and that risk alone.

Question:

Would the defender have been held liable if the pursuers had drunk the paraffin in the lamps?

Section 4.—Intervening Act

THE OROPESA

Court of Appeal [1943] P. 32; 112 L.J.P. 91; 168 L.T. 364; 74 Lloyd's Rep. 86; 59 T.L.R. 103; [1943] 1 All E.R. 211

Action by dependants of seaman against owners of colliding vessel

The *Manchester Regiment* and the *Oropesa* collided off Nova Scotia in December 1939. Both vessels were to blame, and both were badly damaged. The captain of the *Manchester Regiment* put 50 of his crew of 74 in a lifeboat and they reached the *Oropesa* in safety. Then, more than an hour after the collision, he decided to go and discuss the salvage of his ship with the captain of the *Oropesa*, already over a mile away. He embarked in a lifeboat with the rest of his crew. The lifeboat capsized in the heavy seas after half-an-hour and nine persons, including the plaintiffs' son, were drowned. The others reached the *Oropesa* and Nova Scotia in safety. The *Manchester Regiment* sank.

Langton J. gave judgment for the plaintiffs [1942] P. 140, and the Court of Appeal dismissed the defendants' appeal.

Lord Wright: . . . On the main question, the plaintiffs sue on the basis that the owners of the *Oropesa* owed a duty, not only to the owners of the *Manchester Regiment*, but also to her officers and crew, to navigate with care and skill so as not to injure them. Negligent navigation would obviously be a breach of that duty, and, therefore, it is said there was here a breach of duty towards the deceased. The defendants deny liability on the ground that there was no legal connection between the breach of duty and the death of the deceased. Certain well-known formulae are invoked, such as that the chain of causation was broken and that there was a *novus actus interveniens*. These phrases, sanctified as they are by standing authority, only mean that there was not such a direct relationship between the act of negligence and the injury that the one can be treated as flowing directly from the other. Cases have been cited which show great difference of opinion on the true answer in the various circumstances to the question whether the damage was direct or too remote. I find it very difficult to formulate any precise and all-embracing rule. I do not think that the authorities which have been cited succeed in settling that difficulty. It may be said that in dealing with the law of negligence it is possible to state general propositions, but when you come to apply those principles to determine whether there has been actionable negligence in any particular case, you must deal with the case on its facts.

What were the facts here? The master of the *Manchester Regiment* was faced with a very difficult proposition. His ship was helpless, without any means of propulsion or of working any of her important auxiliary apparatus, a dead lump in the water, and he had only the saving thought that she might go on floating so long as her bulk-heads did not give way. He had great faith in his ship, but he realised that there was a heavy sea, with a heavy gale blowing and that he was in a very perilous plight. As Sir Robert Aske pointed out in his argument, the captain of a ship is guilty of a misdemeanour under section 220 of the Merchant Shipping Act 1894 if he "refuses or omits to do any lawful act proper and requisite to be done by him for preserving his ship from immediate loss, destruction or serious danger, or for preserving any person belonging to or on board ship from immediate danger to life or limb." In those circumstances the master decided to go to the *Oropesa* where, no doubt, he thought he would find valuable help and advice. Nobody suggests that he was acting unreasonably or improperly in doing so, or, indeed, that he was doing anything but his duty. Nor can anyone say that the deceased acted unreasonably in getting into the boat. If he had not obeyed the lawful orders of his captain, he would have committed a criminal offence under section 225(1)(*b*) of the Merchant Shipping Act 1894. If, therefore, the test is whether what was done was reasonable, there can be no question that the actions of both the master and the deceased were reasonable. Whether the master took exactly the right course is another matter. He may have been guilty of an error of judgment, but, as I read the authorities, that would not affect the question whether the action he took and its consequences flowed directly from the negligence of the *Oropesa*. I am not sure that Mr. Sellers does not agree with that view, anyhow to some extent, but he also argued that the deceased was merely a spectator of the collision. He received no personal injury nor shock, and there was no need for special steps to be taken on his behalf in the emergency. That being so, in obeying the master's orders and getting into the boat, he was merely doing a voluntary act which was in no legal sense associated or connected with the negligence of the *Oropesa*. As for the master, Mr. Sellers argued that what he did had no legal connection with the casualty. In my view, that is not a correct reading of the position. Having regard to the situation of the *Manchester Regiment* and those on board her, I think that the hand of the casualty lay heavily on her and that the conduct both of the master and of the deceased was directly caused by and flowed from it. There was an unbroken sequence of cause and effect between the negligence which caused the *Oropesa* to collide with the *Manchester Regiment*, and their action, which was dictated by the exigencies of the position. It cannot be severed from the circumstances affecting both ships. To that must be joined the duty which they were under in their positions as captain and sixth engineer.

There are some propositions which are beyond question in connection with this class of case. One is that human action does not *per se* sever the connected sequence of acts. The mere fact that human action intervenes does not prevent the sufferer from saying that injury which is due to that human action as one of the elements in the sequence is recoverable from the original wrongdoer. *The City of Lincoln* ((1889) 15 P.D. 15) is a useful case. It is short and the judges of the Court of Appeal were all agreed so we do not get the complications which are present in some of the cases in the House of Lords on this point. In *The City of Lincoln* the question was whether the injury was directly caused by the casualty. On the point of what was meant by "the ordinary course of things," Lindley L.J. said: "Sir Walter Phillimore has asked us to exclude from it all human conduct. I can do nothing of the kind. I take it that reasonable human conduct"—I stress that expression—"is part of the ordinary course of things. So far as I can see my way to any definite proposition I should say that the ordinary course of things does not exclude all human conduct, but includes at least the reasonable conduct of those who have sustained the damage, and who are seeking to save further loss." Mr. Sellers said that those words must not be pressed too hard, but you must look at the facts. The facts were that there had been a collision between a steamer and a barque, and the steamer was held alone to blame. "The steering compass, charts, log and log glass of the barque were lost through the collision," the headnote states. "The captain of the barque made for a port of safety, navigating his ship by a compass which he found on board. The barque, while on her way, without any negligence on the part of the captain or crew, and owing to the loss of the requisites for navigation above mentioned, grounded, and was necessarily abandoned." It was held by the Court of Appeal that "the grounding of the barque was a natural and reasonable consequence of the collision, and that the owners of the steamer were liable for the damages caused thereby." In principle, that case is not different from the present. The captain, being placed in a difficulty, went on navigating the ship. He thought that that was the reasonable course to adopt, and it was held to be reasonable in the emergency. The plaintiffs thus recovered, although there was a long interval, both in time and distance, between the collision and the physical grounding of the vessel. If the vessel had remained where she was, she might have been picked up or many other things might have happened. She might still have become a total wreck, but not a total wreck in the way in which the event happened in fact, but there it was held, notwithstanding the human action, that the grounding was a natural and reasonable consequence of the collision. In *Summers* v. *Salford Corporation* ([1942] W.N. 224), a woman cleaning a window was injured because the sash cord broke. That is far removed from the facts with which we have to deal here, but it involves the same principle. Assuming, as was held in that case, that there was a breach of duty to her, the mere fact that no harm would have happened to her if she had not been cleaning the window was immaterial because she was doing something which was reasonable and in the ordinary course of events. If the master and the deceased in the present case had done something which was outside the exigencies of the emergency, whether from miscalculation or from error, the plaintiffs would be debarred from saying that a new cause had not intervened. The question is not whether there was new negligence, but whether there was a new cause. I think that is what Lord Sumner emphasised in *The Paludina* ([1927] A.C. 16). To break the chain of causation it must be shown that there is something which I will call ultroneous, something unwarrantable, a new cause which disturbs the sequence of events, something which can be described as either unreasonable or extraneous or extrinsic. I doubt whether the law can be stated more precisely than that. Lord Haldane gave a fuller description in *Canadian Pacific Ry.* v. *Kelvin Shipping Co. Ltd.* ((1927) 138 L.T. 369, 370), where the whole of the ultimate damage was due to a handling of the vessel after the collision. Lord Haldane said: "I therefore turn at once to the crucial question in the case, was there fault in those responsible for the ship in reference to the use of her engines when she was on the north bank? Now this is a question of evidence, and in weighing the evidence in order to draw the proper inferences, there are certain principles which have to be kept steadily in view. When a collision takes place by the fault of the defending ship in an action for damages, the damage is recoverable if it is the natural and reasonable result of the negligent act, and it will assume this character if it can be shown to be such a consequence as in the ordinary course of things would flow from the situation which the offending ship had created. Further, what those in charge of the injured ship do to save it may be mistaken, but if they do whatever they do reasonably, although unsuccessfully, their mistaken judgment may be a natural consequence for which the offending ship is responsible, just as much as is any physical occurrence. Reasonable human conduct is part of the ordinary course of things which extends to the reasonable conduct of those who have sustained the damage and who are seeking to save further loss." He takes that final proposition from *The City of Lincoln.* I think that is an important statement of principle—"if they do whatever they do reasonably, although unsuccessfully, their mistaken judgment may be a natural consequence for which the offending ship is responsible." Here it may be said that, even if the master of the *Manchester Regiment* was not doing quite the right thing, his mistake might be regarded as the natural consequence of the emergency in which he was placed by the negligence of the *Oropesa.* There was a difference of opinion in *Canadian Pacific Ry.* v. *Kelvin Shipping Co. Ltd.* on the final issue of fact. There was again a difference of opinion in *The Paludina,* but I should like to quote a few words of Lord Sumner: "Cause and consequence in such a matter do not depend on the question whether the first action, which intervenes,

is excusable or not, but on the question whether it is new and independent or not."
There the master of the *Singleton Abbey* had not stopped his engines at a particular
moment, and that resulted in trouble with the *Paludina* and the *Sara*. It was held
that there had been a miscalculation which broke the chain of causation. That,
again, was a decision on the facts. It does not take the matter any further, except,
possibly, by way of comparison. The statement of the principles applicable by the
majority of their Lordships does not in any way contradict what I have said. A mere
voluntary act would clearly cause a breaking in the sequence of cause and effect as,
for instance, in *The Amerika* ([1917] A.C. 38), one of the claims made by the
Admiralty by way of damages for loss due to the collision was that they had paid
bounties to relatives of members of the ship's crew who had lost their lives. It was
held that those payments were purely voluntary. That is an extreme, but obvious,
illustration of a loss resulting from a collision which did not impose any legal liability. It was a loss incurred by purely ultroneous conduct.

The real difficulty in the present case is the application of the principle, which is a
question of fact. I agree entirely with Langton J. in the way in which he has dealt
with the question. I am not prepared to say in all the circumstances that the fact
that the deceased's death was due to his leaving the ship in the lifeboat and to the
unexpected capsizing of that boat prevented his death being a direct consequence
of the casualty. It was a risk, no doubt, but a boat would not generally capsize in
those circumstances. In my opinion, the appeal should be dismissed.

Scott L.J.: I agree. We have been advised, as Langton J. was advised, that the position throughout in these happenings was one of critical danger to all those on
board the *Manchester Regiment*. I am satisfied that the action taken by the master
to save the lives of those for whom he was responsible was reasonable, and, therefore, that there was no break in the chain of causation. I agree entirely with the
judgment which has just been delivered.

Questions
1. Suppose that the captain of the *Manchester Regiment* had been the only person drowned.
Would his dependants have recovered?
2. Suppose that, owing to the unreasonable behaviour of the captain, the life-boats of the
Manchester Regiment were incapable of being used, would the defendants have been liable to
the dependants of persons drowned in consequence?
3. Suppose that, though the life-boats could be used, the captain of the *Manchester Regiment* unreasonably declined to allow the crew to leave the sinking ship; would the dependants
of the crew recover from the defendants?

Note:
When the question is asked whether the captain behaved "reasonably" or not, one is not
asking whether he behaved without negligence, but whether his decision to act as he did, that
decision having turned out to be wrong, was voluntary or not. If the decision was made in the
stress of danger, it will not be really voluntary ("the hand of casualty lay heavily on her"), and
it may be called a reasonable response to the emergency, notwithstanding that it turned out to
be wrong. Behaviour which is unreasonable only in the sense of being careless is much less
potent casually than a voluntary act even if that act can be called "reasonable." Though
"sciens" is not "volens," voluntariness is affected by knowledge, perhaps dependent on it.
Thus a failure to remedy a known defect or danger is a better insulator than a failure to discover it. For example, in *Taylor* v. *Rover Co.* [1966] 1 W.L.R. 1491, an employee was injured
by a chisel which had carelessly been overhardened by the supplier's sub-contractor. The
employer, however, had prior knowledge that the chisel was dangerous and had failed to
remove it from circulation. Baker J. held that this insulated the supplier from possible liability. In *Lambert* v. *Lewis* [1982] A.C. 225, on the other hand, where the plaintiffs were
injured on the highway when the first defendant's trailer came loose from his Land-Rover
owing to a defect in the coupling badly designed by the manufacturer, the fourth defendant,
the manufacturer was held liable to the victims although the first defendant knew that the coupling was defective and dangerous.

Question
Is there an explanation in terms of causation of s.1(4) of the Congenital Disabilities (Civil
Liability) Act 1976 (above p. 80)?

LAMB v. CAMDEN LONDON BOROUGH COUNCIL

Court of Appeal [1981] Q.B. 625; [1981] 2 W.L.R. 1038; [1981] 2 All E.R. 408

*Action by houseowner against careless local authority for damage done by
vandals*

In 1973 the defendant's contractors broke a water-main outside the plaintiff's house
near Hampstead Heath. The water washed away the foundations and the plaintiff's
tenant moved out. In the summer of 1974 the plaintiff returned from the United
States, moved her furniture out and arranged for some building works to be
started. In October squatters moved in. The plaintiff had them evicted when she
returned again at Christmas, and had some boarding put up. In the summer of 1975
more squatters moved in and were not expelled until May 1977, by which time they
had done damage amounting to £30,000. This was the item in issue.

The plaintiff's claim for it was rejected by the official referee, and her appeal to
the Court of Appeal was dismissed.

Watkins L.J.: . . . This appeal involves but a single issue. Was the damage done to
Mrs. Lamb's house by squatters too remote to be a consequence of the council's
initial negligent and damaging act which partly destroyed support for the house and
for which they have to compensate her?

Counsel for the plaintiffs contends that, since the official referee intimated in his
judgment that if thereby he was applying the only relevant and correct test he
would be disposed to hold that an invasion of the undermined house by squatters
was a risk reasonably foreseeable by the defendants, the case should go back to him
so that he can positively make that finding and give judgment for Mrs. Lamb for the
sum claimed in respect of the squatters' damage. For, he says, reasonable foreseeability simpliciter of the fresh kind of damage done is, since *The Wagon Mound
(No. 2)* [1967] 1 A.C. 617, the sole test which determines whether fresh damage
caused by an act which is independent of and committed later than the initial tortious act is too remote: whether, in other words, it is truly a novus actus interveniens for the damage caused by which a defendant is not liable.

He submits that Lord Reid was out of step with the *Wagon Mound* test which
should always be followed nowadays when in *Home Office* v. *Dorset Yacht Co. Ltd.*
([1970] A.C. 1004, 1030) he said:

" . . . where human action forms one of the links between the original wrongdoing of the defendant and the loss suffered by the plaintiff, that action must at
least have been something very likely to happen if it is not to be regarded as
novus actus interveniens breaking the chain of causation. I do not think that a
mere foreseeable possibility is or should be sufficient, for then the intervening
human action can more properly be regarded as a new cause than as a consequence of the original wrongdoing. But if the intervening action was likely to
happen I do not think that it can matter whether that action was innocent or tortious or criminal. Unfortunately, tortious or criminal action by a third party is
often the "very kind of thing" which is likely to happen as a result of the wrongful
or careless act of the defendant."

So by adopting, as he did, the opinion of Lord Reid the official referee was also
out of step with *The Wagon Mound (No. 2)* and applied the wrong test to the issue

of remoteness. If he had allowed himself to be governed by *The Wagon Mound (No. 2)* he would inevitably have found for Mrs. Lamb for the considerable damage deliberately and criminally caused by the squatters.

I feel bound to say with respect that what Lord Reid said in the *Dorset Yacht* case does nothing to simplify the task of deciding for or against remoteness, especially where the fresh damage complained of has been caused by the intervening act of a third party. It may be that in respect of such an act he is to be understood as saying, without using his remarkable and usual clarity of expression, that damage is inevitably too remote unless it can reasonably be foreseen as likely to occur. If that be so, it could be said that he was not intending to depart from the *Wagon Mound* test save in cases involving intervening human action to which he would apply a rather stricter than usual test by placing acts which are *not likely to occur* within the realm of remoteness. . . .

It seems to me that if the sole and exclusive test of remoteness is whether the fresh damage has arisen from an event or act which is reasonably foreseeable, or reasonably foreseeable as a possibility, or likely or quite likely to occur, absurd, even bizarre, results might ensue in actions for damages for negligence. Why, if this test were to be rigidly applied to the facts in the *Dorset Yacht* case, one can envisage the Home Office being found liable for the damage caused by an escaped borstal boy committing a burglary in John O'Groats. This would plainly be a ludicrous conclusion.

I do not think that words such as, among others, "possibility," "likely" or "quite likely" assist in the application of the test of reasonable foreseeability. If the crisply stated test which emanates from *The Wagon Mound (No. 2)* is to be festooned with additional words supposedly there for the purpose of amplification or qualification, an understandable application of it will become impossible.

In my view the *Wagon Mound* test should always be applied without any of the gloss which is from time to time being applied to it.

But when so applied it cannot in all circumstances in which it arises conclude consideration of the question of remoteness, although in the vast majority of cases it will be adequate for this purpose. In other cases, the present one being an example of these in my opinion, further consideration is necessary, always providing, of course, a plaintiff survives the test of reasonable foreseeability.

This is because the very features of an event or act for which damages are claimed themselves suggest that the event or act is not on any practical view of it remotely in any way connected with the original act of negligence. These features will include such matters as the nature of the event or act, the time it occurred, the place where it occurred, the identity of the perpetrator and his intentions, and responsibility, if any, for taking measures to avoid the occurrence and matters of public policy.

A robust and sensible approach to this very important area of the study of remoteness will more often than not produce, I think, an instinctive feeling that the event or act being weighed in the balance is too remote to sound in damages for the plaintiff. I do not pretend that in all cases the answer will come easily to the inquirer. But that the question must be asked and answered in all these cases I have no doubt.

To return to the present case, I have the instinctive feeling that the squatters' damage is too remote. I could not possibly come to any other conclusion, although on the primary facts I, too, would regard that damage or something like it as reasonably foreseeable in these times.

We are here dealing with unreasonable conduct of an outrageous kind. It is notorious that squatters will take the opportunity of entering and occupying any house, whether it be damaged or not, which is found to be unoccupied for more than a very temporary duration. In my opinion this kind of antisocial and criminal behaviour provides a glaring example of an act which inevitably, or almost so, is too remote to cause a defendant to pay damages for the consequences of it.

Accordingly, I would hold that the damage caused by the squatters in the present case is too remote to be recovered from these defendants.

Lord Denning M.R. [rejected the "very likely to happen" test of Lord Reid, on the ground that it led to too wide a range of liability in some cases and that it was inconsistent with *Stansbie* v. *Troman* ([1948] 2 K.B. 48), and also rejected the "reasonably foreseeable" test for the same reason. The test should be one of policy]. . . .

Looking at the question as one of policy, I ask myself: whose job was it to do something to keep out the squatters? And, if they got in, to evict them? To my mind the answer is clear. It was the job of the owner of the house, Mrs. Lamb, through her agents. That is how everyone in the case regarded it. It has never been suggested in the pleadings or elsewhere that it was the job of the council. No one ever wrote to the council asking them to do it. The council were not in occupation of the house. They had no right to enter it. All they had done was to break the water main outside and cause the subsidence. After they had left the site, it was Mrs. Lamb *herself* who paved the way for the squatters by moving out all her furniture and leaving the house unoccupied and unfurnished. There was then, if not before, on the judge's findings, a reasonably foreseeable risk that squatters might enter. She ought to have taken steps to guard against it. She says that she locked the doors and pulled the shutters. That turned out to be insufficient, but it was her responsibility to do more. At any rate, when the squatters did get in on the first occasion in 1974, it was then her agents who acted on her behalf. They got the squatters out. Then, at any rate, Mrs. Lamb or her agents ought to have done something effective. But they only put up a few boards at a cost of £10. Then there was the second invasion in 1975. Then her agents did recognise her responsibility. They did what they could to get the squatters out. They eventually succeeded. But no one ever suggested throughout that it was the responsibility of the council. . . .

On broader grounds of policy, I would add this: the criminal acts here, malicious damage and theft, are usually covered by insurance. By this means the risk of loss is spread throughout the community. It does not fall too heavily on one pair of shoulders alone. The insurers take the premium to cover just this sort of risk and should not be allowed, by subrogation, to pass it on to others. Just as in *Stansbie* v. *Troman* [1948] 2 K.B. 48, the householder was no doubt insured against theft of the diamond bracelet. She should have recovered its value from the insurers and not from the decorator whose only fault was that he forgot to put the latch down. It might be decided differently today. It is commonplace nowadays for the courts, when considering policy, to take insurance into account. It played a prominent part in *Photo Production Ltd.* v. *Securicor Transport Ltd.* ([1980] A.C. 827). The House of Lords clearly thought that the risk of fire should be borne by the fire insurers, who had received the full premium for fire risk, and not by Securicor's insurers, who had only received a tiny premium. That, too, was a policy decision. It was a direct consequence of the Unfair Contract Terms Act 1977. Before that Act, the doctrine of fundamental breach was an essential part of our legal system: so as to protect the small consumer from unjust exemption clauses.

So here, it seems to me, that, if Mrs. Lamb was insured against damage to the house and theft, the insurers should pay the loss. If she was not insured, that is her misfortune.

Taking all these policy matters into account, I think the council are not liable for the acts of these squatters.

I would dismiss this appeal.

Oliver L.J.: [considered the observation of Lord Reid cited by Watkins L.J. above, and continued]. As it seems to me, all that Lord Reid was saying was this, that, where as a matter of fact the consequence which the court is considering is one which results from, or would not have occurred but for, the intervention of some independent human agency over which the tortfeasor has no control it has to approach the problem of what could be reasonably foreseen by the tortfeasor, and thus of the damage for which he is responsible, with particular care. The immediate cause is known: it is the independent human agency; and one has therefore to ask: on what basis can the act of that person be attributed back to the tortfeasor? It may be because the tortfeasor is responsible for his actions or because the third party act which has precipitated the damage is the very thing that the tortfeasor is employed to prevent. But what is the position in the absence of some such consideration? Few things are less certainly predictable than human behaviour, and if one is asked whether in any given situation a human being may behave idiotically, irrationally or even criminally the answer must always be that that is a possibility, for every society has its proportion of idiots and criminals. It cannot be said that you cannot foresee the possibility that people will do stupid or criminal acts, because people are constantly doing stupid or criminal acts. But the question is not what is foreseeable merely as a possibility but what would the reasonable man actually foresee if he thought about it, and all that Lord Reid seems to me to be saying is that the hypothetical reasonable man in the position of the tortfeasor cannot be said to foresee the behaviour of another person unless that behaviour is such as would, viewed objectively, be very likely to occur. Thus, for instance, if by my negligent driving I damage another motorist's car, I suppose that theoretically I *could* foresee that, whilst he leaves it by the roadside to go and telephone his garage, some ill-intentioned passer-by may jack it up and remove the wheels. But I cannot think that it could be said that, merely because I have created the circumstances in which such a theft might become possible, I ought reasonably to foresee that it would happen. . . .

The critical finding here is, to my mind, that the incursion of squatters was in fact unlikely.

Given this finding, it seems to me that, accepting Lord Reid's test as correct (which counsel for the plaintiff challenges), it must be fatal to the plaintiff's contentions on this appeal, because it constitutes in effect a finding that the damage claimed is not such as could be reasonably foreseen. And that, indeed, seems to me to accord with the common sense of the matter. . . .

. . . whether or not it is right to regard questions of remoteness according to some flexible test of the policy of the law from time to time (on which I prefer at the moment to express no view) I concur with Lord Denning M.R. in regarding the straight test of foreseeability, at least in cases where the acts of independent third parties are concerned, as one which can, unless subjected to some further limitation, produce results which extend the ambit of liability beyond all reason. Speaking for myself, I would respectfully regard Lord Reid's test as a workable and sensible one, subject only to this, that I think that he may perhaps have understated the *degree* of likelihood required before the law can or should attribute the free act of a responsible third person to the tortfeasor. Such attribution cannot, as I think, rationally be made simply on the basis of some geographical or temporal proximity, and even "likelihood" is a somewhat uncertain touchstone. It may be that some more stringent standard is required. There may, for instance, be circumstances in which the court would require a degree of likelihood amounting almost to inevitability before it fixes a defendant with responsibility for the act of a third party over whom he has and can have no control. On the official referee's finding, however, that does not arise here, and the problem can be left for a case in which it directly arises.

Notes:

1. These opinions are pretty desperate. Watkins L.J. relies on intuition like a lay-judge in medieval Germany; Lord Denning, as usual, where law and sense deviate, opts for sense; Oliver L.J. is reduced to semantics. The difficulties inherent in remoteness have certainly been enhanced as liability in tort has been imposed ever more widely, but the despair comes, it is fair to say, from the delusive simplicity of *The Wagon Mound*. "Foreseeability rules,

O.K.?" is simply inadequate to cope with the complexities of life and litigation. Given the trouble caused by the foreseeability formula in this area, we may be glad that it has been abandoned as the sole determinant of the existence of a duty to take care. The substitution of "proximity" in that context reminds us that in the United States it is only if a tortfeasor's conduct is a "proximate cause" of harm that he is responsible for it.

Many recent lawsuits have sought, mainly without success, to make the defendant liable for facilitating or not preventing theft or damage by third parties: *Dorset Yacht* (above p. 53), *Perl* v. *Camden L.B.C.* [1983] 3 All E.R. 161, *King* v. *Liverpool C.C.* [1986] 3 All E.R. 544, and *Smith* v. *Littlewoods* (above p. 103) were decided in terms of duty, while *Ward* v. *Cannock Chase* [1985] 3 All E.R. 537, like the principal case, but with a different result, was decided in terms of remoteness.

2. Another recent case in which the opinion seems rather incoherent, though the result is not wrong, is *Knightley* v. *Johns* [1982] 1 All E.R. 851 (C.A.). The first defendant had negotiated the blind bend in a one-way tunnel in Birmingham and nearly reached the exit when he negligently crashed his car and blocked the tunnel. The police were called, but the inspector failed to obey standing orders and close off the entrance to the tunnel. When it began to fill with traffic, the inspector told the plaintiff constable to get on his bike and ride back up the tunnel to the entrance. As the plaintiff was doing this he was struck and badly injured by a car which had just entered the tunnel and was being driven quite carefully. The trial judge held that the original motorist was liable to the plaintiff policeman and that the police inspector was not, but the Court of Appeal reversed both holdings.

Stephenson L.J. said: "The ordinary course of things took an extraordinary course. The length and irregularities of the line leading from the first accident to the second have no parallel in the reported rescue cases, in all of which the plaintiff succeeded in establishing the original wrongdoer's liability. It was natural, it was probable, it was foreseeable, it was indeed certain, that the police would come to the overturned car and control the tunnel traffic. It was also natural and probable and foreseeable that some steps would be taken in controlling the traffic and clearing the tunnel and some things be done that might be more courageous than sensible. The reasonable hypothetical observer would anticipate some human errors, some forms of what might be called folly, perhaps even from trained police officers, and some unusual and unexpected accidents in the course of their rescue duties. But would he anticipate such a result as this from so many errors as these, so many departures from the common sense procedure prescribed by the standing orders for just such an emergency as this?"

3. In motorway pile-ups, which are normally caused by successive acts of carelessness, the person responsible for the original danger tends to be liable for all the damage. In *Rouse* v. *Squires* ([1973] Q.B. 889) the driver of an articulated lorry, A, carelessly let it skid: it jack-knifed and blocked the slow and centre lanes. B, in a car, collided with it. C, in a lorry, drove past, parked and returned to help. D pulled his lorry up 15 feet short and illuminated the scene with his headlights. Five or ten minutes after the original accident E, driving too fast, braked too late and skidded into D's lorry which was pushed forward on to C, who was killed. E, held liable to C's widow, was able to claim 25 per cent. contribution from A.

4. In the cases excerpted so far in this section the harm complained of would not have occurred at all but for the act of the third party. In other cases harm for which the defendant is clearly responsible is prolonged or aggravated by an incompetent doctor, an indolent garage, a neurotic mother or a dilatory solicitor. Are there any grounds for distinguishing cases of the two types?

5. In *Salsbury* v. *Woodland* (below, p. 268) the Court of Appeal expressed relief that the judge's finding on causation was not questioned. Do you think that the facts of that case raised any difficult question of causation?

McKEW v. HOLLAND & HANNEN & CUBITTS (SCOTLAND) LTD.

House of Lords [1969] 3 All E.R. 1621; 8 K.I.R. 921; 1970 S.C.(H.L.) 20

Action by employee against employer for personal injuries

The pursuer, who had suffered trivial injuries at work by reason of the defender's fault, which had made him stiff and weakened his left leg, went some days later to inspect a tenement flat, in the company of some members of his family. The stair was steep, with walls on either side, but no hand-rail. As the pursuer left the apartment with his daughter, he raised his right foot to go down the stairs. His left leg "went" and he was about to fall. Rather than fall, he jumped, and landed heavily on his right foot, breaking the right ankle and a bone in his left leg.

The Court of Session disallowed the claim for the consequences of the second accident, and the House of Lords dismissed the pursuer's appeal.

Lord Reid: My Lords, the appellant sustained in the course of his employment trivial injuries which were admittedly caused by the fault of the respondents. His back and hips were badly strained, he could not bend, and on several occasions his left leg suddenly "went away from" him. I take this to mean that for a short time he lost control of his leg and it became numb. He would have recovered from his injuries in a week or two but for a second accident in which he suffered a severe fracture of his ankle. The question in this case is whether the respondents are liable for the damage caused by this second accident. If they are so liable then damages have been agreed at £4,915; if they are not so liable then damages are agreed at £200, the sum awarded in the Court of Session. . . .

The appellant's case is that this second accident was caused by the weakness of his left leg which in turn had been caused by the first accident. The main argument for the respondents is that the second accident was not the direct or natural and probable or foreseeable result of their fault in causing the first accident.

In my view the law is clear. If a man is injured in such a way that his leg may give way at any moment he must act reasonably and carefully. It is quite possible that in spite of all reasonable care his leg may give way in circumstances such that as a result he sustains further injury. Then that second injury was caused by his disability which in turn was caused by the defender's fault. But if the injured man acts unreasonably he cannot hold the defender liable for injury caused by his own unreasonable conduct. His unreasonable conduct is novus actus interveniens. The chain of causation has been broken and what follows must be regarded as caused by his own conduct and not by the defender's fault or the disability caused by it. Or one may say that unreasonable conduct of the pursuer and what follows from it is not the natural and probable result of the original fault of the defender or of the ensuing disability. I do not think that foreseeability comes into this. A defender is not liable for a consequence of a kind which is not foreseeable. But it does not follow that he is liable for every consequence which a reasonable man could foresee. What can be foreseen depends almost entirely on the facts of the case, and it is often easy to foresee unreasonable conduct or some other novus actus interveniens as being quite likely. But that does not mean that the defender must pay for damage caused by the novus actus. It only leads to trouble that if one tries to graft on to the concept of foreseeability some rule of law to the effect that a wrongdoer is not bound to foresee something which in fact we could readily foresee as quite likely to happen. For it is not at all unlikely or unforeseeable that an active man who has suffered such a disability will take some quite unreasonable risk. But if he does he cannot hold the defender liable for the consequences.

So in my view the question here is whether the second accident was caused by the appellant doing something unreasonable. It was argued that the wrongdoer must take his victim as he finds him and that that applies not only to a thin skull but also to his intelligence. But I shall not deal with that argument because there is nothing in the evidence to suggest that the appellant is abnormally stupid. This case can be dealt with equally well by asking whether the appellant did something which a moment's reflection would have shown him was an unreasonable thing to do.

He knew that his left leg was liable to give way suddenly and without warning. He knew that this stair was steep and that there was no hand-rail. He must have realised, if he had given the matter a moment's thought, that he could only safely descend the stair if he either went extremely slowly and carefully so that he could sit down if his leg gave way, or waited for the assistance of his wife and brother-in-law. But he chose to descend in such a way that when his leg gave way he could not stop himself. . . .

But I think it right to say a word about the argument that the fact that the appellant made to jump when he felt himself falling is conclusive against him. When his leg gave way the appellant was in a very difficult situation. He had to decide what to do in a fraction of a second. He may have come to a wrong decision; he probably did. But if the chain of causation had not been broken before this by his putting himself in a position where he might be confronted with an emergency, I do not think that he would put himself out of court by acting wrongly in the emergency unless his action was so utterly unreasonable that even on the spur of the moment no ordinary man would have been so foolish as to do what he did. In an emergency it is natural to try to do something to save oneself and I do not think that his trying to jump in this emergency was so wrong that it could be said to be no more than an error of judgment. But for the reasons already given I would dismiss this appeal.

Note:

Some commentators think that judgment should have been given for the pursuer subject to a deduction for contributory negligence. Yet there must come a time when "the buck passes" (as perhaps it did to the police in *Knightley* v. *Johns* (above p. 207), to the manufacturer in *Taylor* v. *Rover Co.* (above p. 200), and certainly to Mrs. Lamb in Hampstead. If the buck passes to a person, it may well pass from the previous holder.

McKew may have had a sore leg, but his mind was unimpaired. Not so in the notorious case of *Meah* v. *McCreamer* [1985] 1 All E.R. 367, followed by [1986] 1 All E.R. 935 and [1986] 1 All E.R. 943. Meah, a 26–year-old borstal graduate and ex-skinhead, was badly injured in a Jaguar driven by the very drunk McCreamer, since vanished. He suffered brain damage analogous to that resulting from leukotomy. Before the accident Meah had been self-indulgent and promiscuous in sexual matters but not generally violent or inconsiderate, but some three years after the accident he viciously attacked two women, and six months later, while on bail for those offences, raped and savaged a third. He was sentenced to life imprisonment and as a category A prisoner would probably not be released for very many years.

In the first suit Meah claimed damages from the driver for the imprisonment as well as the injury. The defendant insurer expressly disclaimed any argument arising from remoteness of damage or public policy, so the only question was whether there was a causal link between the injury and the crimes. The judge held that there was: the plaintiff would probably have committed, and perhaps have been jailed for, other minor crimes, but would not have committed such crimes as these but for the injury, though the injury would not have caused him to commit them had he not been a latent aggressive psychopath particularly susceptible to being so affected by such an injury. General damages of £60,000 were awarded, reduced by 25 per cent. because it was careless of the plaintiff to travel with an obviously drunken driver.

Then two of the victims claimed damages from Meah, now richer by £45,000. There was no problem about liability, of course, and damages of £6,750 and £10,250 were awarded (as compared with £3,600 from the Criminal Injuries Compensation Board in the latter case; a Master awarded £12,500 to the third victim). There was the predictable howl of outraged ignorance in the Press: "Rapist Gets More Than Victims!"

Meah then claimed an indemnity from the defendant for the sums he had just been held liable to pay to his victims. At this stage the defendant did raise arguments of remoteness of damage and of public policy. On both grounds the judge dismissed Meah's claim.

It is important to note that the judge never held that Meah's imprisonment was not too remote a consequence of the injury, but it is clear that he would sooner have given damages for the imprisonment than for the loss resulting from Meah's having to pay his victims, and he was certain that the victims had no claim of their own against the driver.

GINTY v. BELMONT BUILDING SUPPLIES LTD.

Queen's Bench [1959] 1 All E.R. 414

Action by employee against employer in respect of personal injury

The plaintiff was employed by the first defendant. He was told to replace the asbestos roofing at the factory of the second defendant and told that the existing roofing was unsafe. Crawling boards were provided by the second defendant but the plaintiff did not use them and consequently fell through the roof and was seriously injured. The plaintiff's failure to use the boards constituted a breach of statutory regulations on the part both of himself and of his employers.

Pearson J. gave judgment for the defendants.

Pearson J.: . . . This accident was caused manifestly by the plaintiff working on an asbestos roof, which was a fragile roof, without using boards. The special feature of this case is that that wrongful act of his constitutes a breach by him of his instructions and of the regulations as they apply to him; but it also constitutes, technically at any rate, a breach by his employer under his obligation under reg. 31(3)(*a*) [Building (Safety, Health and Welfare) Regulations 1948] to use the boards. The actual wrongful act was the plaintiff's wrongful act, but in one aspect it constitutes a breach by himself and in another aspect it constitutes a breach by his employer. So what is the position?

There has been a number of cases, to which I shall refer in a moment, in which it has been considered whether or not the employer delegated to the employee the performance of the statutory duty. In my view, the law which is applicable here is clear and comprehensible if one does not confuse it by seeking to investigate this very difficult and complicated question whether or not there was a delegation. In my view, the important and fundamental question in a case like this is not whether there was a delegation, but simply the usual question: Whose fault was it? I shall refer to some of the decided cases to demonstrate what I have said. If the answer to that question is that in substance and reality the accident was solely due to the fault of the plaintiff, so that he was the sole author of his own wrong, he is disentitled to recover. But that has to be applied to the particular case and it is not necessarily conclusive for the employer to show that it was a wrongful act of the employee plaintiff which caused the accident. It might also appear from the evidence that something was done or omitted by the employer which caused or contributed to the accident; there may have been a lack of proper supervision or lack of proper instructions; the employer may have employed for this purpose some insufficiently experienced men, or he may in the past have acquiesced in some wrong behaviour on the part of the men. Therefore, if one finds that the immediate and direct cause of the accident was some wrongful act of the man, that is not decisive. One has to inquire whether the fault of the employer under the statutory regulations consists of, and is co-extensive with, the wrongful act of the employee. If there is some fault on the part of the employer which goes beyond or is independent of the wrongful act of the employee, and was a cause of the accident, the employer has some liability. I have stated what, in my view, the proper rule is. For this rule several explanations can be given and several bases can be provided, and I will mention three. First, there is the common law principle that a person cannot derive any advantage from his own wrong. As applied to this case, that means that a person cannot by his own wrongful act impose on his employers the liability to pay damages to him. On that, I will refer to a recent case, *Goulandris Bros. Ltd.* v. *B. Goldman & Sons Ltd.* ([1957] 3 All E.R. 100), in which that principle of the common law was considered in relation to a different subject-matter.

Secondly (and this is, at any rate, closely allied to the first explanation or principle which I have mentioned), let us consider the effect of the plaintiff's own negligence at common law, that is, before the passing of the Law Reform (Contributory Negligence) Act 1945. If the accident was caused wholly or in part by the plaintiff's own negligence, he was barred from recovering anything, and his action failed. The Law Reform (Contributory Negligence) Act 1945, s.1(1), modified that position and provides: "Where any person suffers damage as the result partly of his own fault and partly of the fault of any other person or persons, a claim in respect of that damage shall not be defeated by reason of the fault of the person suffering the damage, but the damages recoverable in respect thereof shall be reduced to such extent as the court thinks just and equitable having regard to the claimant's share in the responsibility for the damage. . . . "

That applies only in a case where the accident is caused partly by the fault of the plaintiff and partly by the fault of somebody else; but the peculiarity of a situation such as we have here is that the accident is caused wholly by one wrongful act, and that act constitutes in one aspect a breach of obligation by the plaintiff and in another aspect a breach of obligation by his employer. Therefore, although one could say that the accident was wholly caused by the fault of the plaintiff, one could also say that the accident was wholly caused by the fault of the first defendant. In my view, that takes a case of this kind outside the scope of the Law Reform (Contributory Negligence) Act 1945 and one has to revert to common law principles to see what the position is. If one does that, the common law principle is still valid to this extent, that, if the accident is wholly caused by the plaintiff's own fault, he is disentitled to recover.

Then there is a third explanation, or basis, which can be provided; that is, the need for avoiding circuity of action. Circuity of action would arise in this way. Suppose that the plaintiff said that his employer committed a breach of statutory obligation whereby damage was caused to him, and he was entitled to recover damages from his employer. The employer would reply that by the contract of employment the employee owed a duty to his employer, who, therefore, was entitled to recover damages against the employee, and that the amount of damages which the employer was entitled to recover was equal to the amount of the damages which the employee was supposedly entitled to recover against the employer. If that were the position, the litigation would go round in a circle, and for that reason there is, in my view, a valid plea of circuity of action. The plea of circuity of action is not usually found in these days because that situation is usually sufficiently provided for by the modern provisions for set-off and counterclaim; but it is a valid plea, and again I would cite *Goulandris Bros. Ltd.* v. *B. Goldman & Sons Ltd.* and certain previously decided cases which are mentioned in that case.

Those are three explanations of the rule, which, in my view, is a valid one, and there may be other explanations too. I ought to say that I think the theory of delegation of the performance of the employer's statutory duty is not a sound explanation. It may be that another explanation suggested, namely, the principle "*ex turpi causa non oritur actio,*" is also unsound. . . .

That being the position, we have here the case in which the fault of the employer—and it is a fault under the definition of "fault" contained in the definition section, section 4, of the Law Reform (Contributory Negligence) Act 1945— was a breach of statutory obligation by the employer because, through the employee, the employer did not use the boards; but that fault of the employer consisted of, and was co-extensive with, that of the plaintiff, and in substance this unfortunate accident was due to the fault of the plaintiff in breach of, and in defiance of, his instructions and of regulations which were well known to him. He decided to do the work on this roof without the use of boards. It would not be right, however, to take too severe a view; he was not in any direct sense going to gain anything for himself; he was taking the risk for himself with a view to getting the work done. Yet it is quite impossible to impose a liability on his employer, because the plaintiff himself decided to take the risk and not to use the boards, and in those circumstances the plaintiff must fail.

Question
How can you solve a problem of causation by asking: "Whose fault was it?"?

Note:
The defendant's liability for breach of statutory duty is not neutralised by the fact that it was the plaintiff's breach of duty which constituted it. If the defendant does not show that there was adequate supervision of the job, instruction about dangers and explanation of the regulations he remains liable, even if a failure in those regards would not amount to common law negligence. *Boyle* v. *Kodak Ltd.* [1969] 1 W.L.R. 661 (H.L.).

Circuity of action proved to be a good defence in *Post Office* v. *Hants. C.C.* [1979] 2 All E.R. 818 (C.A.). The defendant's employees had dug up and damaged a cable belonging to the plaintiff which the plaintiff's engineer had told them was not there. Anyone who damaged such a cable was by statute absolutely and automatically liable for the damage, but the plaintiff's claim was nevertheless dismissed: since the defendant could have counterclaimed, on the basis of *Hedley Byrne*, for an amount equal to any damages for which it might have been held liable, circuity of action provided a good defence.

Chapter 5

DEFENCES

Section 1.—Contributory Negligence

LAW REFORM (CONTRIBUTORY NEGLIGENCE) ACT 1945

1.—(1) Where any person suffers damage as the result partly of his own fault and partly of the fault of any other person or persons, a claim in respect of that damage shall not be defeated by reason of the fault of the person suffering the damage, but the damages recoverable in respect thereof shall be reduced to such extent as the court thinks just and equitable having regard to the claimant's share in the responsibility for the damage: . . .

(2) Where damages are recoverable by any person by virtue of the foregoing subsection subject to such reduction as is therein mentioned, the court shall find and record the total damages which would have been recoverable if the claimant had not been at fault. . . .

4. The following expressions have the meanings hereby respectively assigned to them, that is to say—

"damage" includes loss of life and personal injury;
"fault" means negligence, breach of statutory duty or other act or omission which gives rise to a liability in tort or would, apart from this Act, give rise to the defence of contributory negligence.

Notes:
   Until this very important Act, a plaintiff was unlikely to recover any damages at all if his own fault had contributed to the injury of which he complained. Many questions are raised by the Act, not all of which have yet been answered.
   1. In determining the proportion by which the plaintiff's damages are to be reduced, attention must be paid to the respective blameworthiness of the parties as well as to the causative potency of their acts or omissions: if attention were not paid to causative potency, a careless plaintiff would recover nothing from a defendant who was free from fault but strictly liable, and if blameworthiness were not taken into account the results would be unfair. But the reduction is to be by an amount which is "just and equitable" having regard to the plaintiff's responsibility for the harm, and it has been suggested that it may not be just and equitable to reduce at all the damages payable by an employer to a mildly careless employee (*Hawkins* v. *Ian Ross (Castings) Ltd.* [1970] 1 All E.R. 180). It had, indeed, already been held, before the Act was passed, that an employee who made a careless mistake in the heat and stress of factory conditions was not, as against an occupier in breach of safety regulations, to be treated as careless, but this new approach is more extensive. Contrariwise, " . . . there is no principle of law which requires that, even where there is a breach of statutory duty in circumstances . . . where the intention of the statute is to provide protection, *inter alia*, against folly on the part of a workman, there cannot be 100 per cent. contributory negligence on the part of the workman." (*Jayes* v. *I.M.I. (Kynoch)* [1985] I.C.R. 155, 159, *per* Robert Goff L.J.). In fact reductions are very commonly made, and the Court of Appeal quite frequently varies them, though it says it doesn't.
   2. It is well established that contributory negligence, unlike defendant's negligence, need not be a breach of a duty to take care. The terms of *Tremayne* v. *Hill* [1987] R.T.R. 131 (C.A.) are therefore puzzling. The defendant carelessly drove through a red light and ran

213

over the plaintiff who was crossing the road where there was no pedestrian-crossing. In repelling the (impertinent) defence of contributory negligence, Sir Roger Ormrod said: "The only question . . . is whether the plaintiff owed any duty of care, either to himself or to other drivers on the road, to act in any way other than that which he did," and Ralph Gibson L.J. said "The plaintiff was not shown to have been in breach of a self-regarding duty."

3. Unlike the use of a Walkman or a car telephone, failure to wear a seat-belt does not cause accidents, though it may aggravate injuries. Failure to wear a seat-belt is normally unreasonable and damages will be reduced if the defendant can show that it made a difference. Lord Denning suggested standard reductions of 15 per cent. if the injuries would have been less serious, 25 per cent. if they would have been avoided (*Froom* v. *Butcher* [1976] Q.B. 286). The unlawfulness of failure to wear a seat-belt is of course irrelevant. If a driver is injured because the seat-belt is defective, the manufacturer may invoke his faulty driving (*Kaye* v. *Alfa Romeo* (1984) 134 New L.J. 126).

4. Contributory negligence must be pleaded by the defendant: *Fookes* v. *Slaytor* [1979] 1 All E.R. 137 (C.A.). For a case where the particulars of contributory negligence offered by the defendant resulted in his own liability for failure to take those very precautions, see *General Cleaning Contractors* v. *Christmas*, above p. 104.

5. Apart from the doctrine of mitigation of damage (see for example *Darbishire* v. *Warran* below, p. 565) this Act provides the only admitted means of giving the plaintiff something by way of damages, but less than the full amount. (Other systems are more flexible—in Switzerland damages may be reduced if the defendant was not greatly at fault, and in France judges have a *de facto* discretion because no final appeal lies on questions of quantum.) It is therefore a pity that the courts of England have not applied the Act against trespassers (*Westwood* v. *Post Office* [1974] A.C. 1), and that they are so unwilling to find that a child has been contributorily negligent (*Gough* v. *Thorne* [1966] 1 W.L.R. 1387). The Pearson Commission recommended that the defence of contributory negligence should not be available in cases of motor vehicle injury where the victim was under the age of 12 at the time.

6. Damages claimed for loss of support by dependants of a person killed by the defendant are reduced by the amount of carelessness of the deceased. A child's damages are not reduced by reason of the concurrent carelessness of a parent or guardian, but the parent or guardian may, at a pinch, be brought in as a third party by the tortfeasor and held liable to pay contribution (above, p. 66). Neither a passenger in a vehicle nor its owner is affected by the contributory negligence of the driver unless he is driving as their servant or agent. Note, however, the position under s.1(7) of the Congenital Disabilities (Civil Liability) Act 1976, and consider the position if there is a collision between a car negligently driven by a pregnant mother and one negligently driven by a stranger and the child is born deformed as a result.

7. Rescuers are frequently and nobly indifferent to their own safety but their recovery is not often barred or limited on that account. In a case where the rescuer's negligence contributed to the emergency which called for the rescue, Boreham J. overcame his "distaste about finding a rescuer guilty of contributory negligence" (*Harrison* v. *British Railways Board* [1981] 3 All E.R. 679).

8. This Act is designed to split the loss between plaintiff and defendant; where there is more than one defendant the loss may be apportioned between them under the 1978 Act (above, p. 66). Where the plaintiff as well as two others have been at fault, both Acts apply, and one must establish the extent to which each contributed to the harm complained of by the plaintiff (*The Miraflores and The Abadesa* [1967] 1 A.C. 826). Now there is a rule, except in maritime collision cases (where all parties could be supposed solvent, at least until the appearance of one-ship companies), that a person liable for a loss is liable for the whole of that loss even though some third party or parties were just as much or more at fault than he. This rule produces complexities where the plaintiff also is at fault. Suppose, as happened in the case last cited, that the plaintiff is found 40 per cent. to blame, and the two defendants (D1 and D2) are found 40 per cent. and 20 per cent. to blame respectively. If effect is given to the rule just mentioned, and to the terms of the Contributory Negligence Act, D2 would be bound to pay 60 per cent. of the plaintiff's loss although he was only half as much to blame as the plaintiff; D2 could then try to recover two-thirds of that sum from D1.

In Germany the matter is resolved in a much more sophisticated manner. Suppose that the plaintiff's loss is £12,000. The plaintiff, being 40 per cent. to blame, can collect in all 60 per cent. of his loss, or £7,200. Since D1 is equally to blame with the plaintiff, the plaintiff can collect up to 50 per cent. of his loss from D1, or £6,000; D2, only half as much to blame as the plaintiff, need pay only one-third of his loss, or £4,000. If, as one would expect, the plaintiff collects £6,000 from D1 and the balance of £1,200 from D2, how much contribution can D1 collect from D2? Since the first £3,200 paid by D1 did not reduce the amount of D2's liability at all (for at that stage the plaintiff was still entitled to collect £4,000, the total amount of D2's liability) only £2,800 of the money paid by D1 had the effect of reducing the liability of D2. To this sum D2 must contribute, but since D1 was twice as negligent as D2, D2 pays only one-third of it, or £933. In the result, then, D1 pays £5,067 and D2 pays £2,133. Since in England D1 would pay £4,800 and D2 would pay £2,400, the difference may not seem material. But if D1 were insolvent, D2 in Germany would pay £4,000 and in England would pay £7,200, and this difference is not immaterial.

Such sophistication is too much for our Court of Appeal, but they went half-way towards it in their erroneous judgment in *Fitzgerald* v. *Lane* [1987] 2 All E.R. 455. The plaintiff pedestrian walked briskly on to a pelican crossing whose lights were against him and was struck first by D1, a motorist carelessly proceeding South and then by D2, a motorist carelessly proceeding North. The trial judge held all three parties equally to blame. He proceeded to say that each defendant should pay one-third of the plaintiff's damages but plaintiff's counsel reminded him of the rule of liability *in solidum*, so he corrected himself and ordered that the plaintiff should have judgment against both defendants for two-thirds of his claim, the defendants to contribute equally as between themselves. This order was correct, but the Court of Appeal reversed it, and ordered that the plaintiff have judgment for only 50 per cent. of his claim against both defendants. This is quite wrong because s.1(1) of the 1945 Act does *not* say "the damages recoverable . . . shall be reduced to such extent as the court thinks just and equitable having regard to the claimant's share *as against each of those persons separately* in the responsibility for the damage." See Fleming, 104 L.Q.R. 6 (1988).

9. The Act applies only where the defendant's conduct is tortious. Thus if the defendant has broken his contract without committing any tort, a plaintiff whose fault has conduced to the harm will recover all or nothing (*Quinn* v. *Burch Bros.* [1966] 2 Q.B. 370, affirming [1965] 3 All E.R. 801; *Lambert* v. *Lewis*—all in the Court of Appeal, nothing in the House of Lords [1982] A.C. 225). Increasingly often, however, the defendant's breach of contract will also constitute a tort, in which case the Act will apply (*Sole* v. *W. J. Hallt* [1973] Q.B. 574), unless the parties have expressly excluded apportionment (*Forsikrings Vesta* v. *Butcher* [1986] 2 All E.R. 488, 507–510).

Very dubious is the holding in *Banque Keyser* v. *Skandia Ins. Co.* [1987] 2 All E.R. 923, 958, that while the 1945 Act does apply to a claim for breach of the duty of care owed by one negotiator to another, it does not apply to a damages claim by one party to an insurance contract against the other for breach of the precontractual duty to disclose material circumstances, the so-called duty of the utmost good faith. After all, it can hardly not be "fault" to fall short of the level of conduct required by law, and if a damages claim is not contractual, what else can it be but tortious?

10. Since the legislature has seen fit to enact that "Contributory negligence is no defence in proceedings founded on conversion, or on intentional trespass to goods" (Torts (Interference with Goods) Act 1977, s.11), it is still important to distinguish the form of action being used. In cases of nuisance, where the plaintiff is complaining that the defendant's conduct is rendering life on his real property intolerable, the obvious defence in some cases is that the plaintiff was aware of the situation when he bought the property. Traditionally however, it is no defence that "the plaintiff came to the nuisance." See *Miller* v. *Jackson*, below p. 386.

11. The existence of this Act has induced the judges to reduce the scope of the defence of *volenti non fit injuria*, by which a plaintiff who has accepted the risk of the injury which has occurred is barred from recovery in respect of it. The reaction is perfectly understandable, but it is not wholly justifiable, since respect for the self-determination of the individual requires the legal system to make him suffer the consequences of *voluntarily* exposing himself to physical risk, even if it was not in the circumstances an *unreasonably* dangerous thing to do.

12. A person who has taken out insurance against liability can naturally recover from his insurer in full although he was at fault in incurring the liability: that is the whole point of the policy (though he may have problems if his fault was very grave, like rape). So also a person who insures against his property being damaged or lost may recover under the policy though it was his fault the damage or loss occurred: a term in the policy that he must take care is construed as a term that he must not act recklessly (*W. J. Lane* v. *Spratt* [1970] 2 Q.B. 480). But people other than insurers do not often promise to pay people for the consequences of their own carelessness, so indemnity clauses are rigorously construed (*Thompson* v. *T. Lohan Ltd.* [1987] 2 All E.R. 631 (C.A.)) and will be invalid against a consumer unless reasonable (Unfair Contract Terms Act 1977, s.4).

13. In France motorists have been strictly liable for traffic accidents for over 50 years, but until recently had to pay only reduced damages if the victim had been careless. The widespread feeling that such a reduction was unfair led to a striking decision by the Court of Cassa-

tion that any reduction was unlawful. Subsequent legislation provides that the damages are not to be reduced unless the victim was himself at the wheel. In Britain where the victim can recover only if the motorist is at fault, we do not feel it unfair that damages should be reduced if the victim was also at fault, but it would be possible to argue that if one can recover from one's own insurer though one is at fault, one should equally be able to recover from someone else's insurer.

BILL v. SHORT BROS. & HARLAND LTD.

House of Lords [1963] N.I. 1

Action by employee against employer in respect of personal injury

The plaintiff was an experienced workman with 14 years' service with the defend-ants. One day after his lunch-break, he fell over a 1½-inch rubber pipe laid across the floor of the building for the purpose of carrying compressor air. His view of the floor was slightly obstructed by the presence in front of him of a fellow-workman, but he knew that the pipe might be there.

At the trial before Sheil J. and a jury, the plaintiff gave evidence of those facts, said that he knew of two previous accidents caused in a similar way, and that in other factories the air-pipes were laid along a wall or suspended from the roof. Sheil J. withdrew the case from the jury, and dismissed the plaintiff's claim. The Court of Appeal of Northern Ireland dismissed the plaintiff's appeal (Lord Mac-Dermott C.J. dissenting). Curran L.J. said: "This was the case of a man who decided to cross the working floor of a factory and who stumbled on an obstacle which he knew was there." The House of Lords allowed the plaintiff's appeal and ordered a new trial.

Lord Denning: My Lords, it appears to me that the claim at common law depends on three simple propositions. First, it is the duty of the employer to take reasonable care so to carry on his operations as not to subject those employed by him to unnecessary risk. Secondly, if the employer has failed in that duty, then the fact that the employee was fully aware of the risk may go to show that he was guilty of contributory negligence, but it does not by itself disentitle him from recovering. Thirdly, it is for the judge to say where there is any evidence from which the jury *could* infer that there was negligence on the part of the employer or contributory negligence on the part of the employee, but if there is such evidence then it must be left to the jury to say whether it *ought* to be inferred.

There was, in my opinion, evidence on which the jury *could* find that the employers were negligent. I base this particularly on the previous accidents which were drawn to their attention and on the means taken in other workshops to elimi-nate the risk. There was evidence on which the jury *could* find that the workman was guilty of contributory negligence. I base this particularly on his knowledge of the facts and of the risk. The jury *might* even find that his negligence was so pre-dominant a factor that he was solely responsible for the accident—in short that he was one hundred per cent. to blame—but they were not bound so to find. They *could* find him less to blame. And if so, it was for the jury to apportion the responsi-bility.

I think, therefore, that the common law claim should have been left to the jury. . . .

Section 2.—Volenti Non Fit Injuria

IMPERIAL CHEMICAL INDUSTRIES v. SHATWELL

House of Lords [1965] A.C. 656; [1964] 3 W.L.R. 329; 108 S.J. 578; [1964] 2 All E.R. 999

Action by employee against employer in respect of personal injury

On the facts, sufficiently stated in the judgment of Lord Reid, Elwes J. gave judgment for the plaintiff, subject to a reduction of damages by 50 per cent. for contributory negligence. The Court of Appeal affirmed this judgment. The defendant's appeal was allowed by the House of Lords.

Lord Reid: My Lords, this case arises out of the accidental explosion of a charge at a quarry belonging to the appellants which caused injuries to the respondent George Shatwell and his brother James, who were both qualified shot firers. On June 28, 1960, these two men and another shot firer, Beswick, had bored and filled fifty shot holes and had inserted electric detonators and connected them up in series. Before firing it was necessary to test the circuit for continuity. This should have been done by connecting long wires so that the men could go to a shelter some eighty yards away and test from there. They had not sufficient wire with them and Beswick went off to get more. The testing ought not to have been done until signals had been given so that other men could take shelter and these signals were not due to be given for at least another hour.

Soon after Beswick had left George said to his brother: "Must we test them?" meaning shall we test them, and James said "Yes." The testing is done by passing a weak current through the circuit in which a small galvanometer is included and if the needle of the instrument moves when a connection is made the circuit is in order. So George got a galvanometer and James handed two short wires to him. Then George applied the wires to the galvanometer and the needle did not move. This showed that the circuit was defective so the two men went round inspecting the connections. They saw nothing wrong and George said that that meant there was a dud detonator somewhere, and decided to apply the galvanometer to each individual detonator. James handed two other wires to him and George used them to apply the galvanometer to the first detonator. The result was an explosion which injured both men.

This method had been regularly used without mishap until the previous year. Then some research done by the appellants showed that it might be unsafe and in October 1959, the appellants gave orders that testing must in future be done from a shelter and a lecture was given to all the shot firers, including the Shatwells, explaining the position. Then in December 1959, new statutory regulations were made (1959, No. 2259) probably because the Ministry had been informed of the results of the appellants' research. These regulations came into operation in February 1960, and the Shatwells were aware of them. But some of the shot firers appear to have gone on in the old way. An instance of this came to the notice of the management in May 1960, and the management took immediate action and revoked the shot firing certificate of the disobedient man, and told the other shot firers about this. George admitted in evidence that he knew all this. He admitted that they would only have had to wait ten minutes until Beswick returned with the long wires. When asked why he did not wait, his only excuse was that he could not be bothered to wait.

George now sues the appellants on the ground that he and his brother were equally to blame for this accident, and that the appellants are vicariously liable for his brother's conduct. He has been awarded £1,500, being half the agreed amount of his loss. There is no question of the appellants having been in breach of the regulations because the duty under the regulation is laid on the shot firer personally. So counsel for George frankly and rightly admitted that if George had sued James personally instead of suing his employer the issue would have been the same. If this decision is right it means that if two men collaborate in doing what they know is dangerous and is forbidden and as a result both are injured, each has a cause of action against the other.

The appellants have two grounds of defence, first that James' conduct had no causal connection with the accident, the sole cause being George's own fault, and secondly, *volenti non fit injuria*. I am of opinion that they are entitled to succeed on the latter ground but I must deal shortly with the former ground because it involves the decision of this House in *Stapley* v. *Gypsum Mines Ltd.* ([1953] A.C. 663), and I think that there has been some misunderstanding of that case. Stapley and a man named Dale were working together in the mine. They found that a part of the roof was dangerous. They tried to bring it down but failed. Then, contrary to the foreman's orders and to statutory regulations, they decided to go on with their ordinary work and Stapley went to work below that part of the roof. It fell on him and he was killed. The only issue before the House was whether the conduct of Dale had contributed to cause the accident, and the House decided by a majority that it had. There was little, if any, difference of opinion as to the principles to be applied; the difference was in their application to the facts of the case. The case gives authoritative guidance on the question of causation but beyond that it decides nothing. It clearly appears from the argument of counsel that the defence *volenti non fit injuria* was never taken and nothing about it was said by any of their Lordships.

Applying the principles approved in Stapley's case, I think that James' conduct did have a causal connection with this accident. It is far from clear that George would have gone on with the test if James had not agreed with him. But perhaps more important James did collaborate with him in making the test in a forbidden and unlawful way. His collaboration may not have amounted to much but it was not negligible. If I had to consider the allocation of fault I would have difficulty in finding both men equally to blame. If James had been suing in respect of his damage it would, I think, be clear that both had contributed to cause the accident but that the greater part of the fault must be attributed to George. So I do not think that the appellants could succeed entirely on this defence and I turn to consider their second submission.

The defence *volenti non fit injuria* has had a chequered history. At one time it was very strictly applied. Today one can hardly read the robust judgment of Cockburn C.J. in *Woodley* v. *Metropolitan District Railway* (1877) 2 Ex.D. 384) without some astonishment. But one must remember that his views were in line with those of the judges who a generation or two before had invented the doctrine of common employment. Then the tide began to turn. The modern view can be seen emerging in the judgments of the majority in *Yarmouth* v. *France* ((1887) 19 Q.B.D. 647). No one denied that a man who freely and voluntarily incurs a risk of which he has full knowledge cannot complain of injury if that risk materialises and causes him damage. The controversy was whether acceptance of the risk can (or must) be inferred from the mere fact that the man goes on working in full knowledge of the risk involved. The point was finally settled by this House in *Smith* v. *Baker & Sons* ([1891] A.C. 325). The opposing views were tersely stated by Hawkins J. in *Thrussell* v. *Handyside* ((1888) 20 Q.B.D. 359, 364)—"his poverty, not his will, consented to incur the danger"—and by Lord Bramwell in *Membery* v. *Great Western Railway* ((1889) 14 App.Cas. 179, 188): "The master says here is the work, do it or let it alone. . . . The master says this, the servant does the work and earns his wages, and is paid, but is hurt. On what principle of reason or justice should the master be liable to him in respect of that hurt?"

The ratio in *Smith* v. *Baker and Sons* was, I think, most clearly stated by Lord Herschell: "The maxim is founded on good sense and justice. One who has invited or assented to an act being done towards him cannot, when he suffers from it, complain of it as a wrong. The maxim has no special application to the case of employer and employed, though its application may well be invoked in such a case." Then he pointed out that a person undertaking to do work which is intrinsically dangerous, notwithstanding that care has been taken to make it as little dangerous as possible, cannot if he suffers complain that a wrong has been done him. And then he continued: "But the argument for the respondents went far beyond this. The learned counsel contended that, even though there had been negligence on the part of the defendants, yet the risk created by it was known to the plaintiff; and inasmuch as he continued in the defendants' employment, doing their work under conditions, the risk of which he appreciated, the maxim, '*Volenti non fit injuria*,' applied, and he could not recover." And later he said: "If, then, the employer thus fails in his duty towards the employed, I do not think that because he does not straightaway refuse to continue his service, it is true to say that he is willing that his employer should thus act towards him. I believe it would be contrary to fact to assert that he either invited or assented to the act or default which he complains of as a wrong."

More recently it appears to have been thought in some quarters that, at least as between master and servant, *volenti non fit injuria* is a dead or dying defence. That I think is because in most cases where the defence would now be available it has become usual to base the decision on contributory negligence. Where the plaintiff's own disobedient act is the sole cause of the injury it does not matter in the result whether one says 100 per cent. contributory negligence or *volenti non fit injuria*. But it does matter in a case like the present. If we adopt the inaccurate habit of using the word "negligence" to denote a deliberate act done with full knowledge of the risk it is not surprising that we sometimes get into difficulties. I think that most people would say, without stopping to think of the reason, that there is a world of difference between two fellow-servants collaborating carelessly so that the acts of both contribute to cause injury to one of them, and two fellow-servants combining to disobey an order deliberately though they know the risk involved. It seems reasonable that the injured man should recover some compensation in the former case but not in the latter. If the law treats both as merely cases of negligence it cannot draw a distinction. But in my view the law does and should draw a distinction. In the first case only the partial defence of contributory negligence is available. In the second *volenti non fit injuria* is a complete defence if the employer is not himself at fault and is only liable vicariously for the acts of the fellow-servant. If the plaintiff invited or freely aided and abetted his fellow-servant's disobedience, then he was *volens* in the fullest sense. He cannot complain of the resulting injury either against the fellow-servant or against the master on the ground of his vicarious responsibility for his fellow-servant's conduct. I need not here consider the common case where the servant's disobedience puts the master in breach of a statutory obligation and it would be wrong to decide in advance whether that would make any difference. There remain two other arguments for the respondent which I must deal with.

It was argued that in this case it has not been shown that George had a full appreciation of the risk. In my view it must be held that he had. He knew that those better qualified than he was took the risk seriously. He knew that his employers had forbidden this practice and that it had then been prohibited by statutory regulation. And he knew that his employers were taking strong measures to see that the order was obeyed. If he did not choose to believe what he was told I do not think that he could for that reason say that he did not fully appreciate the risk. He knew that the risk was that a charge would explode during testing, and no shot firer could be in any doubt about the possible consequences of that.

Finally the respondent argues that there is a general rule that the defence of *volenti non fit injuria* is not available where there has been a breach of a statutory obligation. It would be odd if that were so. In the present case the prohibition of testing except from a shelter had been imposed by the appellants before the statutory prohibition was made. So it would mean that if the respondent had deliberately done what he did in full knowledge of the risk the day before the statutory prohibition was made this defence would have been open to the appellants, but if he had done the same thing the day after the regulation came into operation it would not. . . .

I entirely agree that an employer who is himself at fault in persistently refusing to comply with a statutory rule could not possibly be allowed to escape liability because the injured workman had agreed to waive the breach. If it is still permissible for a workman to make an express agreement with his employer to work under an unsafe system, perhaps in consideration of a higher wage—a matter on which I need express no opinion—then there would be a difference between breach of statutory obligation by the employer and breach of his common law obligation to exercise due care: it would be possible to contract out of the latter but not out of the former type of obligation. But all that is very far removed from the present case. . . .

I can find no reason at all why the facts that these two brothers agreed to commit an offence by contravening a statutory prohibition imposed on them as well as agreeing to defy their employer's orders should affect the application of the principle *volenti non fit injuria* either to an action by one of them against the other or to an action by one against their employer based on his vicarious responsibility for the conduct of the other. I would therefore allow this appeal.

Viscount Radcliffe: . . . On one view George simply blew himself up. . . . After all, if a man decides to test an unexploded mine by tapping it with a hammer and he asks someone standing by to find the hammer and hand it to him, the complier would not naturally be thought of as being in any degree the author of any injury that is inflicted on the tester if the mine explodes. . . .

I do not see how either can succeed against the other, since, where both were joined in carrying through the whole operation and each in what he did was the agent of the other to achieve it, there was nothing that one did against the other that the other did not equally do against himself. This, in my view, is the true result of a joint unlawful enterprise, in which what is wrong is the whole enterprise and neither of the joint actors has contributed a separate wrongful act to the result. Each emerges as the author of his own injury. . . .

Note:
    This case shows the practical advantages of keeping all possible concepts available, however offensive their overlap may be to the intellectual aesthete. *Stapley's* case was on its facts indistinguishable. If the concept of *volenti* has been destroyed—and many have wished for its destruction (*e.g.*, James, "Assumption of Risk," 61 Yale L.J. 141, 169 (1952))—the difficulty of reaching the proper result would have been enhanced.

Questions
    1. Is there a big difference between doing something bad and doing something badly?
    2. If *Shatwell* applies only where the defendant's liability is purely vicarious and *Ginty* (above, p. 210) applies only where the plaintiff has been fully apprised of the regulations, is *Shatwell* very like *Ginty* or not?
    3. Should all those who agree to play Russian Roulette be liable to the loser's widow?

WOOLDRIDGE v. SUMNER

Court of Appeal [1963] 2 Q.B. 43; [1962] 3 W.L.R. 616; 106 S.J. 489; [1962] 2 All E.R. 978

The facts are given above, p. 89.

Diplock L.J.: . . . The practical result of this analysis of the application of the common law of negligence to participant and spectator would, I think, be expressed by the common man in some such terms as these: "A person attending a game or competition takes the risk of any damage caused to him by any act of a participant done in the course of and for the purposes of the game or competition notwithstanding that such act may involve an error of judgment or a lapse of skill, unless the participant's conduct is such as to evince a reckless disregard of the spectator's safety."

The spectator takes the risk because such an act involves no breach of the duty of care owed by the participant to him. He does not take the risk by virtue of the doctrine expressed or obscured by the maxim *volenti non fit injuria*. That maxim states a principle of estoppel applicable originally to a Roman citizen who consented to being sold as a slave. Although pleaded and argued below it was only faintly relied upon by Mr. Everett in this court. In my view, the maxim in the absence of expressed contract has no application to negligence *simpliciter* where the duty of care is based solely upon proximity or "neighbourship" in the Atkinian sense. The maxim in English law presupposes a tortious act by the defendant. The consent that is relevant is not consent to the risk of injury but consent to the lack of reasonable care that may produce that risk (see *Kelly* v. *Farrans Ltd.* ([1954] N.I. 41, 45) *per* Lord MacDermott) and requires on the part of the plaintiff at the time at which he gives consent full knowledge of the nature and extent of the risk he ran (*Osborne* v. *London and North Western Railway* ((1888) 21 Q.B.D. 220, 224), *per* Wills J., approved in *Letang* v. *Ottawa Electric Railway* ([1926] A.C. 725)). In *Dann* v. *Hamilton* ([1939] 1 K.B. 509) Asquith J. expressed doubts as to whether the maxim ever could apply to license in advance a subsequent act of negligence, for if the consent precedes the act of negligence the plaintiff cannot at that time have full knowledge of the extent as well as the nature of the risk which he will run. Asquith J., however, suggested that the maxim might nevertheless be applicable to cases where a dangerous physical condition had been brought about by the negligence of the defendant, and the plaintiff with full knowledge of the existing danger elected to run the risk thereof. With the development of the law of negligence in the last twenty years a more consistent explanation of this type of case is that the test of liability on the part of the person creating the dangerous physical condition is whether it was reasonably foreseeable by him that the plaintiff would so act in relation to it as to endanger himself. This is the principle which has been applied in the rescue cases (see *Cutler* v. *United Dairies (London) Ltd.* ([1933] 2 K.B. 297), and contrast *Haynes* v. *Harwood* ([1935] 1 K.B. 146)) and that part of Asquith J.'s judgment in *Dann* v. *Hamilton* dealing with the possible application of the maxim to the law of negligence which was not approved by the Court of Appeal in *Baker* v. *T.E. Hopkins & Son* ([1959] 1 W.L.R. 966). In the type of case envisaged by Asquith J., if I may adapt the words of Morris L.J. in *Baker* v. *T.E. Hopkins & Son*, the plaintiff could not have agreed to run the risk that the defendant might be negligent for the plaintiff would only play his part after the defendant had been negligent.

Since the maxim has in my view no application to this or any other case of negligence *simpliciter*, the fact that the plaintiff owing to his ignorance of horses did not fully appreciate the nature and extent of the risk he ran did not impose upon Mr. Holladay any higher duty of care towards him than that which he owed to any ordinary reasonable spectator with such knowledge of horses and vigilance for his own safety as might be reasonably expected to be possessed by a person who chooses to watch a heavyweight hunter class in the actual arena where the class is being judged. He cannot rely upon his personal ignorance of the risk any more than the plaintiff in *Murray* v. *Harringay Arena* ([1951] 2 K.B. 529) could rely upon his ignorance of the risk involved in ice-hockey, excusable though such ignorance may have been in a six-year-old child. . . .

Note:
It is clear that the voluntary act of a person in exposing himself to a danger of which he knows, already created by the carelessness of another, may well deprive him of a claim on the grounds of causation (*McKew* v. *Holland & Hannen & Cubitts (Scotland)* (above, p. 207)). It

is clear also from *Shatwell* that a person may be deprived of a claim if he participated deliberately in a dangerous enterprise. Furthermore, it is clear that a person may deprive himself in advance of a claim in respect of subsequent negligence, by means of an agreement by which the defendant exempts himself from liability or the plaintiff undertakes not to sue, so far as the Unfair Contract Terms Act 1977 permits. The question is whether there is a doctrine related neither to causation nor to participation nor to contract which may operate to deprive a person of a claim on the ground that he accepted the risk of injury caused by the defendant's carelessness. Diplock L.J. denies it in the previous case, but it does seem strange that a person who has voluntarily exposed himself to the risk of subsequent carelessness can invariably sue, subject only to a reduction of damages under the 1945 Act if it was unreasonably dangerous of him so to act.

Legislators admit the existence of the defence. The Occupiers' Liability Act 1957, s.2(5) reads: "The common duty of care does not impose on an occupier any obligation to a visitor in respect of risks willingly accepted as his by the visitor (the question whether a risk was so accepted to be decided on the same principles as in other cases in which one person owes a duty of care to another)." Acceptance of risk is also a specific defence to a claim under the Control of Pollution Act 1974, s.88. Note, however, that the Road Traffic Act 1972, s.148(3), provides that "the fact that a person so carried [*i.e.* carried in a vehicle whose use is such that a policy of insurance is required] has willingly accepted as his the risk of negligence on the part of the user shall not be treated as negativing any such liability of the user." This section reverses the effect of such decisions as *Birch* v. *Thomas* [1972] 1 W.L.R. 294 (C.A.), which will, however, remain useful to repel claims by pillion passengers on toboggans and by water-skiers against the motorman.

In his *Last Journal*, Captain Scott wrote: "I do not regret this journey; we took risks, we knew we took them, things have come out against us, therefore we have no cause for complaint."

Question

A's dog and B's dog are fighting on the highway. C intervenes to separate them and is bitten by A's dog. *Volenti non fit injuria*? Is it different if they are fighting in C's garden? Is it different if B intervenes and is bitten by A's dog?

Read:
Jaffey, "Volenti Non Fit Injuria," [1985] Camb.L.J. 87.

Section 3.—Agreement and Notice

UNFAIR CONTRACT TERMS ACT 1977

1.—(1) For the purposes of this Part of this Act, "negligence" means the breach—

 (*a*) of any obligation, arising from the express or implied terms of a contract, to take reasonable care or exercise reasonable skill in the performance of the contract;
 (*b*) of any common law duty to take reasonable care or exercise reasonable skill (but not any stricter duty);
 (*c*) of the common duty of care imposed by the Occupiers' Liability Act 1957 or the Occupiers' Liability Act (Northern Ireland) 1957.

. . .

(3) In the case of both contract and tort, sections 2 to 7 apply (except where the contrary is stated in section 6(4)) only to business liability, that is liability for breach of obligations or duties arising—

 (*a*) from things done or to be done by a person in the course of a business (whether his own business or another's); or (*b*) from the occupation of premises used for business purposes of the occupier;

and references to liability are to be read accordingly, but liability of an occupier of premises for breach of an obligation or duty towards a person obtaining access to the premises for recreational or educational purposes, being liability for loss or damage suffered by reason of the dangerous state of the premises, is not a business liability of the occupier unless granting that person such access for the purposes concerned falls within the business purposes of the occupier.

(4) In relation to any breach of duty or obligation, it is immaterial for any purpose of this Part of this Act whether the breach was inadvertent or intentional, or whether liability for it arises directly or vicariously.

2.—(1) A person cannot by reference to any contract term or to a notice given to persons generally or to particular persons exclude or restrict his liability for death or personal injury resulting from negligence.

(2) In the case of other loss or damage, a person cannot so exclude or restrict his liability for negligence except insofar as the term or notice satisfies the requirement of reasonableness.

(3) Where a contract term or notice purports to exclude or restrict liability for negligence a person's agreement to or awareness of it is not of itself to be taken as indicating his voluntary acceptance of any risk.

11. . . .

(3) In relation to a notice (not being a notice having contractual effect), the requirement of reasonableness under this Act is that it should be fair and reasonable to allow reliance on it, having regard to all the circumstances obtaining when the liability arose or (but for the notice) would have arisen.

(4) Where by reference to a contract term or notice a person seeks to restrict liability to a specified sum of money, and the question arises (under this or any other Act) whether the term or notice satisfies the requirement of reasonableness, regard shall be had in particular (but without prejudice to subsection (2) above in the case of contract terms) to—

(*a*) the resources which he could expect to be available to him for the purpose of meeting the liability should it arise; and

(*b*) how far it was open to him to cover himself by insurance.

(5) It is for those claiming that a contract term or notice satisfies the requirement of reasonableness to show that it does.

13.—(1) To the extent that this Part of this Act prevents the exclusion or restriction of any liability it also prevents—

(*a*) making the liability or its enforcement subject to restrictive or onerous conditions;

(*b*) excluding or restricting any right or remedy in respect of the liability, or subjecting a person to any prejudice in consequence of his pursuing any such right or remedy;

(*c*) excluding or restricting rules of evidence or procedure;

and (to that extent) sections 2 and 5 to 7 also prevent excluding or restricting liability by reference to terms and notices which exclude or restrict the relevant obligation or duty.

14. In this Part of this Act—

"business" includes a profession and the activities of any government department or local or public authority;

. . .

"negligence" has the meaning given by section 1(1);

"notice" includes an announcement, whether or not in writing, and any other communication or pretended communication;

. . .

Note:

The value-judgments of the draftsmen of the Act are clear enough: (i) personal injury is more serious than property damage (even a reasonable exclusion of liability for causing personal injury by negligence is void); (ii) conduct is particularly objectionable if it is careless (strict liability for even personal injury may be excluded, though not vicarious liability for negligence causing it); (iii) businesses are subject to greater liability than persons in private life.

The classic instance of the defence which this Act so severely restricts arises where a person is allowed to take a short-cut across the land of another on the published terms that he is to have no claim against the occupier even if he is negligently injured. The Court of Appeal upheld this defence in *Ashdown* v. *Williams* [1957] 1 Q.B. 409, and the legislator endorsed the decision in the Occupiers' Liability Act 1957, s.2(1). But this extremely paternalistic Unfair Contract Terms Act used to invalidate any notice whereby the business occupier of premises (such as the farmer) purported to exempt himself from liability for personal injury suffered by a visitor. Thereafter—believe it or not, such is the wickedness of landowners, about time capitalism was abolished and everyone could go where they wanted *and* be able to sue if hurt, let the state provide the money—farmers who had theretofore let ramblers cross their land, reluctantly enough but as long as it cost them nothing, started to stop everyone crossing their land because, no matter what any notice might say and be perfectly understood as saying, they might be held liable in massive damages to a rambler who caught his foot in a moorland beck, if only some bench-bound judge in London would say, as he doubtless might, that there should have been a notice saying "Danger, Concealed Rivulet!," if, indeed, it shouldn't have been covered over against such errant feet. So in 1984 the legislator had to add the final lemma to s.1(3) above, though he cannot have needed to add it so cumbrously, and he should have forestalled the need to add it at all. Let it not be supposed that it was added out of any sense of fairness to landowners: it was added to deter them from being wicked and selfish.

Section 4.—Illegality

MURPHY v. CULHANE

Court of Appeal [1977] Q.B. 94; [1976] 3 W.L.R. 458; 120 S.J. 506; [1976] 3 All E.R. 533

Action by widow of assailant against criminal killer

Lord Denning M.R.: In this case we do not know the true facts. We only know the allegations in the pleadings. According to them Timothy Murphy was a man of 29. He was a self-employed builder, that is, on the "lump" earning between £60 and £70 a week. On 19th September 1974 he, with some other men, made a wicked plot together. They decided to beat up another man called John Joseph Culhane, the defendant. They went to an address at 20 Grove Place in Greater London. We do not know anything of what took place except that there was a "criminal affray." During it John Culhane is said to have struck Timothy Murphy on the head with a plank and killed him. John Culhane was charged with murder. He was tried at the Central Criminal Court on 25th April 1975. At first, he pleaded not guilty, but after the case had been opened and some evidence heard, he changed his plea to guilty of manslaughter. He was sentenced to eight years which was reduced to five years by the Court of Appeal.

Timothy Murphy's widow now brings an action against John Culhane for damages under the Fatal Accidents Acts, claiming damages on behalf of herself and her baby daughter. I do not suppose he has any money to pay any damages as he is still in prison. But legal aid has, I believe, been granted to both sides. The question is whether or not Mrs. Murphy is entitled to judgment on the pleadings without any trial. The statement of claim says:

"On or about the nineteenth day of September, 1974, near Grove Place, in the area of Greater London, the Defendant assaulted and beat the Deceased by striking him on the head with a plank. The said assault was unlawful. The Plaintiff intends to adduce evidence pursuant to Section 11 of the Civil Evidence Act, 1968, that the Defendant was on the 25th day of April, 1975, convicted on his own plea of guilty before the Central Criminal Court of manslaughter of the Deceased."

The defence admits those allegations and further admits that, by reason of the assault, Mr. Murphy was killed. It then says:

"The said assault occurred during and as part of a criminal affray which was initiated by the Deceased and others who had together come to 20 Grove Place on the occasion in question with the joint criminal intent of assaulting and beating the Defendant."

That is followed by legal contentions of *ex turpi causa non oritur actio, volenti non fit injuria*, and that the deceased's said death was caused in part by his own aforesaid fault.

On those pleadings Mrs. Murphy applied for judgment under RSC Ord. 27, r. 3, which gives the court power to give judgment on admissions. The master and the judge both felt that, on the state of the authorities, they were bound to give judgment for Mrs. Murphy and shut out these defences of Mr. Culhane. Judgment was given for damages to be assessed. I gather that the judge felt most unwilling to do this, but thought he was bound by the cases. So I must deal with them. There are two cases which seem to show that, in a civil action for damages for assault, damages are not to be reduced because the plaintiff was himself guilty of provocation. Provocation, it was said, can be used to wipe out the element of exemplary damages but not to reduce the actual figure of pecuniary damages. It was so said by the High Court of Australia in 1962 in *Fontin* v. *Katapodis* ((1962) 108 C.L.R. 177) and followed by this court in 1967 in *Lane* v. *Holloway* ([1968] 1 Q.B. 379). But those were cases where the conduct of the injured man was trivial—and the conduct of the defendant was savage—entirely out of proportion to the occasion. So much so that the defendant could fairly be regarded as solely responsible for the damage done. I do not think they can or should be applied where the injured man, by his own conduct, can fairly be regarded as partly responsible for the damage he suffered. So far as general principle is concerned, I would like to repeat what I said in the later case of *Gray* v. *Barr* ([1971] 2 Q.B. 554, 569):

"In an action for assault, in awarding damages, the judge or jury can take into account, not only circumstances which go to aggravate damages, but also those which go to mitigate them."

That is the principle I prefer rather than the earlier cases. Apart altogether from damages, however, I think there may well be a defence on liability. If Murphy was one of a gang which set out to beat up Culhane, it may well be that he could not sue for damages if he got more than he bargained for. A man who takes part in a criminal affray may well be said to have been guilty of such a wicked act as to deprive himself of a cause of action or, alternatively, to have taken on himself the risk. I put the case in the course of argument: suppose that a burglar breaks into a house and the householder, finding him there, picks up a gun and shoots him, using more force maybe than is reasonably necessary. The householder may be guilty of manslaughter and liable to be brought before the criminal courts. But I doubt very much whether the burglar's widow could have an action for damages. The householder might well have a defence either on ground of *ex turpi causa non oritur actio* or *volenti non fit injuria*. So in the present case it is open to Mr. Culhane to raise both those defences. Such defences would go to the whole claim.

There is another point, too, even if Mrs. Murphy were entitled to damages under the Fatal Accidents Acts, they fall to be reduced under the Law Reform (Contributory Negligence) Act 1945 because the death of her husband might be the result partly of his own fault and partly of the default of the defendant: see s.1(1) and (4) of the 1945 Act. On this point I must explain a sentence in *Gray* v. *Barr* where the widow of the dead man was held to be entitled to full compensation without any reduction. Her husband had not been guilty of any "fault" within s.4 of the 1945 Act because his conduct had not been such as to make him liable in an action of tort or, alternatively, was not such that he should be regarded as responsible in any degree for the damage. So also in *Lane* v. *Holloway*, as Winn L.J. pointed out. But in the present case the conduct of Mr. Murphy may well have been such as to make him liable in tort.

It seems to me that this is clearly a case where the facts should be investigated before any judgment is given. It should be open to Mr. Culhane to be able to put forward his defences so as to see whether or not and to what extent he is liable in damages.

I would therefore allow the appeal. The judgment should be set aside and the case go for trial accordingly.

Orr L.J. and Waller J. agreed.

Note:
Earlier in the book we saw that unlawful as well as unreasonable behaviour might render a *defendant* liable, though often it does not. Unreasonable conduct on the part of the *plaintiff* may reduce or extinguish his claim, as we have just seen. What if his conduct is unlawful?

Judges are naturally unwilling to award damages to plaintiffs they think should be in the dock. Bad people get less. This is reflected in the Latin tag *ex turpi causa non oritur actio*. Although it is of general application throughout the law, it has different effects in the different branches of the law of obligations. In contract, for example, if we agree that I shall kill your mother-in-law for £500 and I do kill her, I cannot claim the £500—the judges will not reward a person for doing wrong: and if I change my mind, you cannot sue me for non-performance— the judges will not make a person pay for not doing wrong. These principles are so strong in contract law that they apply even if the illegality is quite technical and the parties morally innocent. In restitution the principle operates less fiercely. It is true that if I decide not to murder your mother-in-law, I can keep any down-payment you made me, not because I have earned it (since I have not), but because you will be disentitled from reclaiming it; here the normal right to reclaim is lost only if the claimant is tainted with turpitude. Again, when one tortfeasor is claiming contribution from another, he is founding on his own wrong. This was enough to bar his claim at common law, unless he was wholly innocent: negligent tortfeasors may now claim under the statute (above, p. 66) but a wicked claimant might well find himself in difficulties.

In tort cases the wickedness of the plaintiff plays a slighter role, because the interests traditionally in issue are basic—liberty, life and limb, property. Of course the liberty of criminals is not as well protected as that of honest citizens, for criminals are subject to arrest and imprisonment, but they are no longer hanged or beaten, and their property is not forfeit, though they may be bankrupted (Powers of Criminal Courts Act 1973, ss.39–41). So if I run someone over in the street, it can hardly be relevant that he was on his way to or from a robbery (unless in the former case he was claiming for lost swag or in the latter for damage to his booty).

Yet in recent years there has been a revival of the defence, actually upheld in *Ashton* v. *Turner* [1981] Q.B. 137 (burglar hurt by bad driving of fellow-burglar in get-away car). On one view, that is due to the growing moralism which accompanies the levelling process in society. Technically, perhaps, it is due to the restriction in the scope of the other defences— no duty, contributory negligence, *volenti non fit injuria*. Suppose a person is injured by a defective product he has stolen from the retailer. Can we say that the manufacturer owed the shoplifter no duty? Suppose that a burglar is injured by a danger on the burgled premises: contributory negligence does not apply if he was looking out for his own safety (*Westwood* v. *Post Office* [1974] A.C. 1). Suppose that a hitch-hiker pulls a gun on the person who gives him a lift and forces him to drive to a specified destination: the Road Traffic Act 1972, s.148(3) makes it impossible for us to say that the gunman takes the risk of bad driving, and *Nettleship*

v. *Weston* (above, p. 92) makes it difficult for us to qualify the competence required of the driver.

It is therefore not surprising that in recent years it has been suggested in *obiter dicta* that the defence of illegality might bar a claim by a burglar bitten by a guard-dog (*Cummings* v. *Grainger* [1977] Q.B. 397), a patron of a pub who had been drinking after hours and was injured on the way out (*Stone* v. *Taffe* [1974] 3 All E.R. 1016) and a passenger in a car whose driver was known to be the worse for drink or drugs (*Nettleship* v. *Weston*, above, p. 95).

In *Burns* v. *Edman* [1970] 2 Q.B. 541 a criminal had been killed in a motor accident for which the defendant was principally responsible. Not only was the claim for loss of life reduced because the criminal's lot, like the policeman's, is not a happy one, but his widow and children were not allowed to claim for the loss of their share of the proceeds of his prevented crimes. Again, it has been held that a person running an illicit business cannot claim damages from a tortfeasor who interferes with it (*Columbia Pictures Indus.* v. *Robinson* [1985] 3 All E.R. 338, 379) and that if the proceeds of a cheque represent the fruits of a fraud in which he was implicated the payee whose endorsement has been forged cannot sue the bank which negligently cashes it and credits a third party (*Thackwell* v. *Barclays Bank* [1986] 1 All E.R. 676).

Significant, too, is the decision in *Ashmore, Benson, Pease & Co.* v. *A. V. Dawson* [1973] 2 All E.R. 856, where the Court of Appeal dismissed a claim in respect of damage negligently caused to the plaintiffs' property while it was being carried by the defendants on a vehicle which, as the plaintiffs knew, was illegally and dangerously inadequate for the load. Lord Denning said: " . . . the question is whether the illegality prevents Ashmores from suing for that negligence. This depends on whether the contract itself was unlawful, or its performance was unlawful." But suppose a doctor agrees to perform an illegal abortion and carelessly injures the patient. Surely the patient would not be debarred from suing just because she knew the operation was unlawful?

There is another straw in the wind. Having recommended that social security benefits be payable to victims of motor accidents regardless of any question of negligence or contributory negligence, the Pearson Commission suggested that the Secretary of State be given discretionary power to withhold such payments from convicts injured during the commission of the offence or on the way there or back. Note also that under the previous Scheme the Criminal Injuries Compensation Board could reduce or refuse an award "having regard to the conduct of the applicant before, during or after the events giving rise to the claim or to his character and way of life" (*R.* v. *Criminal Injuries Compensation Board, ex p. Thompstone* [1984] 3 All E.R. 572); and that while s.1(3)(*b*) of the Fatal Accidents Act permits an award to the survivor of an unmarried couple, the Scheme did not. There has been a slight improvement now the Scheme is on a statutory basis: the latter restriction has gone and the former discretion has been slightly diminished (see Criminal Justice Bill 1988, s.110, above p. 157). Still, to fare well in the welfare state you must be good!

A recent case in the Court of Appeal appears to have backtracked on *Murphy* v. *Culhane*. The defendant had undoubtedly struck the plaintiffs' mother a fatal blow with a machete, and sought to defend on the ground that before he reacted so violently he and his family had been subjected to an unbearably prolonged course of abuse, harassment, vilification and minor injury by the plaintiff and her family who lived next door, ending in an actual attack on his own children in his presence. He was not allowed to adduce any such proof. May L.J. held, notwithstanding Lord Denning's overdue abandonment in *Murphy* of the Australian decision in *Fontin* v. *Katapodis*, that it is still the law of England that a person who unforgivably provokes a response may claim full compensatory damages if the response is disproportionately effective. (*Barnes* v. *Nayer, The Times*, December 19, 1986)).

PART II

LIABILITY THROUGH OTHERS

INTRODUCTION

MANY of the plaintiffs we have encountered have been real people of flesh and blood—after all, only they can suffer personal injury—but very few of the defendants have been the individuals whose misbehaviour caused the injury: the defendants have mostly been constructive non-entities such as the London Borough of Merton or the Britannia Hygienic Laundry Co. Such legal persons, with their rights and powers and duties and liabilities, may be immensely significant in the metaworld of law, but they cannot actually *do* anything in the world of perceptible fact. We may say,if we choose to, that the London Borough of Merton did something wrong, but we should realise that we are speaking shorthand or metaphor or nonsense, since the London Borough of Merton cannot do anything whatever, right or wrong: in law it has the power to render further building unlawful, but it does not in fact have eyes with which to peek into the foundations nor a mind with which to judge of their adequacy. Likewise, however many vans the Britannia Hygienic Laundry Co. may *own*, it cannot *drive* any of them or knock over a single pedestrian. Physical harm can be caused only by physical acts, of which notional creatures are incapable. But incapable though they may be of acting, they are perfectly capable of paying: so we can make them pay for those they pay to act for them.

Of those human beings who are lucky enough to have a job at all, a few are self-employed; the great majority, however, are employed by someone else, almost always by a legal non-entity rather than by another human being. But while the odd employer may still be human, there has never been an employee who was anything else but human. A company can no more be an employee than it can be a husband: dependent status is reserved for mankind. Of course you can get a company to do something for you or, more accurately, to get things done for you, through its employees or others, but you will be paying the company a fee rather than wages (the hallmark of employment), you will be a customer rather than an employer, and the company will be an independent contractor rather than your humble servant. The company's customers may well include other companies, but they are often human beings, eagerly consuming the goods and services promised by companies and provided by their employees.

Those being the facts, suppose that one were challenged to produce formal rules with the substantial effect that companies must pay for people but not *vice versa*. One could hardly do better than lay down that liability should attach to employers but not to customers, that one should be liable for one's permanent staff but not for any other persons whom one might pay to do things or get things done—in brief, that there should be liability for employees but not for independent contractors. That is more or less the position in English law (and, indeed, in most other Western systems of law as well).

But although in general an employer (even human) is liable for servants and a customer (even corporate) is not liable for contractors, one is not

231

liable for everything one's servants do wrong, and one may in certain situations be liable for the misdoings of one's independent contractor.

An employer is liable for what his servant does only if the servant was acting in the course and scope of his employment at the time. Since the victim's claim is really that the defendant's business hurt him, he must establish a relationship between the servant's act and the master's business. The question will be whether the servant was just doing his job badly or not doing the job at all, doing his own thing instead. Considerations of time, place, equipment and purpose will all be relevant to this purely factual determination.

This vicarious liability of employer for employee is said to be a general principle. This is true in the sense that the victim need not set up any special relationship between himself and the employer. But it is not true that an employer is invariably liable for the torts of his employees in the course and scope of their employment. A special relationship between plaintiff and defendant may reduce the defendant's liability. Suppose, for example, that the plaintiff is trespassing on the defendant's premises and is injured there by the carelessness of one of the defendant's servants: to hold the occupier liable for the faults of his employees towards the intruder would be inconsistent with the low duty owed by the occupier to the trespasser (above p. 114). The same is true where there is a valid exclusion or disclaimer clause: to say that the careless representation by Heller and Partners was made by their employee in the course and scope of his clerkly employment would not have helped Hedley Byrne to obtain damages from the bank.

The cases in English law where a person may be liable although his own organisation has operated flawlessly are exceptional and heterogeneous. First, a person may be subject to a statutory duty such as to make him liable if the required result is not brought about. Thus section 14 of the Factories Act 1961 renders the occupier of a factory liable to a workman injured by an inadequately fenced piece of dangerous machinery even if the occupier had consulted the best engineer in the world and had retained him to fence it. To take another instance, the property developer is liable under section 1 of the Defective Premises Act 1972 (above p. 65) if the house is badly built: it will not help him in the least to say that it was built by an independent company working under contract. So, too, the financier who has arranged for the supply of goods on credit may be liable to the consumer for the supplier's misrepresentation or breach of contract (Consumer Credit Act 1974, s.75). In each case it will be a question of construction whether the statute imposes a liability stern enough to catch the defendant when the fault lies with an independent third party.

Secondly, a contractor who has promised actual results may be liable despite his best efforts. For example, a defect in a building may be entirely attributable to the carelessness of the brick company, but the builder may still have to pay the bill (*Young & Marten* v. *McManus Childs* [1969] 1 A.C. 454). Again it is a question of construction how strict a liability is assumed under the contract or imposed by it.

The judges are thus quite accustomed to making defendants pay damages where the blame attached not to them or to their staff but to an independent third party. Are there any such cases at common law, leaving aside statute and contract?

It seems that it is only for injuries on the highway that one may be liable to a complete stranger for the harm done to him by one's careless contractor. People who are simply using the highway are not caught by this extended liability (the driver does not answer for the mechanic), but those responsible for works on the highway or buildings alongside it may be liable if their contractors are incompetent in the work or the repairs (see the 1961 Act, above p. 115). These can be classified as instances of public nuisance (above p. 178). In private nuisance also one may have to answer for one's contractor's doings, but there is a special relationship between neighbours in the strict sense, and a special relationship can give rise to higher as well as to lower liabilities or, which is the same thing, liabilities for wider or narrower ranges of assistants.

We must now slightly extend the cast of characters and concepts. Just as a person may loosely be called a "trustee" if he is trusted with property "for" another, so a person who does some act "for" another can be called an "agent." This term is too general to be of direct use: after all, servants and independent contractors both do things "for" the person who pays them and we have seen that we must distinguish between them. We need to draw two further distinctions, one relating to the nature of the service performed, the other to the terms on which the service is performed. First, we distinguish those who are retained to do something in the world of fact from those who are retained to do something in the world of law: on the one hand, the airline which actually flies me across the Atlantic and, on the other, the travel agency which gets me the ticket. An agent in this sense is retained to transact rather than just to act. Such an agent (who may be either a servant or an independent contractor, often a firm) will render the principal liable for faults in the transaction: such faults characteristically take the form of misrepresentation and result in financial rather than physical harm. This liability is an outcrop of the main function of the agent-negotiator, which is to effect contractual relations between his principal and the other party, and it is here that we come across the notion of "authority" which is the source of the agent's power to do so.

But if one of the functions of an agent in this sense is to *create* obligations on behalf of the principal, another may be to *perform* obligations on his behalf or to execute his powers. In this sense the agent might be styled a "delegate," a person through whom the principal seeks to perform his obligations. In such a case, if the agent misperforms, the innocent principal may well be held liable for the agent's negligent breach of his duties or negligent exercise of his powers. Such a strong duty does not normally exist at common law in the absence of a special relationship, but it may well arise, like special powers, under statute.

Secondly we must distinguish the business world from the social scene. Servants and independent contractors act because they are paid to. People who do things for others without any thought of payment (actually, even the "bob-a-job" boy scout) may well be independent, but they are not contractors. If such a service is unsolicited, the recipient will not be liable, but a person who asks another to do him a favour may well be responsible if his "agent" hurts a third party in the process, especially if he equips the "agent" with the means, as well as the occasion, of causing harm.

Some final points remain to be made. The first is that the liability of the superior is additional to the liability of the actual tortfeasor, not alternative to it. The workman is liable even if his master is liable as well. Indeed, the workman is primarily liable, and may have to pay his employer if his employer has to pay the victim (*Lister* v. *Romford Ice & Cold Storage Co.* [1957] A.C. 555).

The second point is that a superior employee, such as the managing director of a company or a ranking civil servant, is not liable for employees lower down the hierarchy: only the master, the paymaster, is vicariously liable. Of course a managing director might be liable for unreasonably making or letting an inferior do something dangerous, but that would be a personal rather than an imputed liability.

That takes us to the third point. In each case one must consider all the possible bases of liability—the personal liability of the defendant as well as his vicarious liability both as employer and as principal. In one case, for example, an apprentice was bullied by a fellow-employee. The master was not liable in his capacity as the employer of the bully, since the bully was not acting in the scope of his employment, but he was personally liable as the employer of the plaintiff apprentice, for failing to take reasonable steps to protect him from the bully (*Hudson* v. *Ridge Manufacturing Co.* [1957] 2 Q.B. 348). Likewise, if the tortfeasor is an independent contractor, it is worth asking whether it was not careless of the defendant to select him for the task. Again, if an employee carelessly injures his mate while driving him to work, the employer will not be liable as employer, since driving to work is not driving at work; but if the driving was being done at the employer's request, the driver may well be the employer's "agent" and the employer will be liable as principal (*Vandyke* v. *Fender* [1970] 2 Q.B. 292.).

Chapter 6

WHERE THE OTHER IS A SERVANT

Section 1.—Who is a Servant?

STEVENSON JORDAN & HARRISON LTD. v. MACDONALD & EVANS

Court of Appeal [1952] 1 T.L.R. 101

Denning L.J.: I fully agree with all that my Lord has said on all the issues in this case. It raises the troublesome question of the distinction between a contract of service and a contract for services. The test usually applied is whether the employer has the right to control the manner of doing the work. Thus in *Collins* v. *Herts County Council* ([1947] K.B. 598, 615) Hilbery J. said: "The distinction between a contract for services and a contract of service can be summarised in this way: In the one case the master can order or require what is to be done, while in the other case he can not only order or require what is to be done but how it shall be done." But in *Cassidy* v. *Ministry of Health* ([1951] 2 K.B. 343, 352), Somervell L.J. pointed out that that test is not universally correct. There are many contracts of service where the master cannot control the manner in which the work is to be done, as in the case of a captain of a ship. Somervell L.J. went on to say: "One perhaps cannot get much beyond this 'Was the contract a contract of service within the meaning which an ordinary person would give under the words?' " I respectfully agree. As my Lord has said, it is almost impossible to give a precise definition of the distinction. It is often easy to recognise a contract of service when you see it, but difficult to say wherein the difference lies. A ship's master, a chauffeur, and a reporter on the staff of a newspaper are all employed under a contract of service; but a ship's pilot, a taxi-man, and a newspaper contributor are employed under a contract for services. One feature which seems to run through the instances is that, under a contract of service, a man is employed as part of the business, and his work is done as an integral part of the business; whereas, under a contract for services, his work, although done for the business, is not integrated into it but is only accessory to it.

It must be remembered, however, that a man who is employed under a contract of service may sometimes perform services outside the contract. A good illustration is *Byrne* v. *Statist Co.* ([1914] 1 K.B. 622), where a man on the regular staff of a newspaper made a translation for the newspaper in his spare time. It was held that the translation was not made under a contract of service but under a contract for services. Other instances occur, as when a doctor on the staff of a hospital or a master on the staff of a school is employed under a contract of service to give lectures or lessons orally to students. If, for his own convenience, he puts the lectures into writing, then his written work is not done under the contract of service. It is most useful as an accessory to his contracted work, but it is not really part of it. The copyright is in him and not in his employers. . . .

235

ROE v. MINISTER OF HEALTH

Above, p. 139.

Note:
   The question whether the relationship of two people is that of employer and employee may arise in many contexts other than vicarious liability. For example, employees are owed special duties by their employers (*Ferguson* v. *John Dawson & Partners (Contractors)* [1976] 3 All E.R. 817; *Quinn* v. *Burch Brothers (Builders)* [1966] 2 Q.B. 370), have special statutory protection against unfair dismissal (*Massey* v. *Crown Life Ins. Co.* [1978] 2 All E.R. 576) and have a special place in the tax and social security systems (*Ready Mixed Concrete (South East) Ltd.* v. *Minister of Pensions and National Insurance* [1968] 2 Q.B. 497). Parties may seek to avoid being classified as employer and employee, but while people are in general entitled to decide what their relationship is to be, they are not entitled to fix the rules which are to apply to the relationship they have actually entered.

POLICE ACT 1964

48.—(1) The chief officer of police for any police area shall be liable in respect of torts committed by constables under his direction and control in the performance or purported performance of their functions in like manner as a master is liable in respect of torts committed by his servants in the course of their employment, and accordingly shall in respect of any such tort be treated for all purposes as a joint tortfeasor.

   (2) There shall be paid out of the police fund—

   (*a*) any damages or costs awarded against the chief officer of police in any proceedings brought against him by virtue of this section and any costs incurred by him in any such proceedings so far as not recovered by him in the proceedings; and

   (*b*) any sum required in connection with the settlement of any claim made against the chief officer of police by virtue of this section, if the settlement is approved by the police authority.

Note:
   In 1985 a total of £193,588 was paid out to claimants by the Commissioner for the Metropolitan Police, of which £13,949 was by court order. In the same year 175 civil suits were initiated against the Metropolitan Police. On the size of awards, see below p. 342.

CHILDREN AND YOUNG PERSONS ACT 1933

55.—(1) Where—

   (*a*) a child or young person is convicted or found guilty of any offence for the commission of which a fine or costs may be imposed or a compensation order may be made under section 35 of the Powers of Criminal Courts Act 1973; and

   (*b*) the court is of opinion that the case would best be met by the imposition of a fine or costs or the making of such an order, whether with or without any other punishment,

it shall be the duty of the court to order that the fine, compensation or costs awarded be paid by the parent or guardian of the child or young person instead of by the child or young person himself, unless the court is satisfied—

   (i) that the parent or guardian cannot be found; or

   (ii) that it would be unreasonable to make an order for payment, having regard to the circumstances of the case.

Note:
   In care proceedings comparable power exists under the Children and Young Persons Act 1969, s.3(6) (Criminal Justice Act 1982, s.27).

In 1986 parents had compensation orders made against them in 3,200 cases.

A local authority which has a child or young person under its care is not liable under the principal section. It may, however, be liable under *Dorset Yacht* (above p. 53) if its operational fault has contributed to the harm done (*obiter* in *Leeds C.C.* v. *West Yorkshire Police* [1983] 1 A.C. 29). Such a case will not be easy to establish.

Section 2.—Whose is the Servant?

MERSEY DOCKS & HARBOUR BOARD v. COGGINS & GRIFFITH (LIVERPOOL) LTD.

House of Lords [1947] A.C. 1; 115 L.J.K.B. 465; 175 L.T. 270; 62 T.L.R. 533; [1946] 2 All E.R. 345

McFarlane was injured at Liverpool Docks when a crane-driver, Newall, carelessly drove into him. Newall was employed by the appellants who let crane and driver to the respondent stevedores under a contract providing that "the drivers so provided shall be the servants of the [respondent]." Newall himself gave evidence, and said: "I take no orders from anybody."

Croom-Johnson J. gave judgment against the crane-owners on the ground that Newall was in their employment at the time of the accident, and judgment in favour of the stevedores on the ground that he was not. The Court of Appeal dismissed the crane-owners' appeal [1945] K.B. 301, and their further appeal to the House of Lords was also dismissed.

Lord Porter: My Lords, I need not repeat the facts giving rise to the question to be determined in this appeal. That question is whose servant was the crane driver, Francis Newall, at the time of the accident. As to this matter I find myself in agreement with those members of your Lordships' House who sat to hear the appeal and only desire to add a few observations as to the principles concerned. In determining this question it has to be borne in mind that the employee's position is an important consideration. A contract of service is made between master and man and an arrangement for the transfer of his services from one master to another can only be effected with the employee's consent, express or implied. His position is determined by his contract. No doubt by finding out what his work is and how he does it and how he fulfils the task when put to carry out the requirements of an employer other than his own, one may go some way towards determining the capacity in which he acts, but a change of employer must always be proved in some way, not presumed. The need for a careful consideration of the circumstances said to bring about the change of employment has latterly been accentuated by the statutory provisions now in force for compulsory health and accident insurance and, in the case of many firms, by the existence of funds accumulated under a trust for the benefit of employees who will not lightly incur the risk of losing such benefits by a transfer of their services from one master to another. Nor is it legitimate to infer that a change of masters has been effected because a contract has been made between the two employers declaring whose servant the man employed shall be at a particular moment in the course of his general employment by one of the two. A contract of this kind may of course determine the liability of the employers *inter se,* but it has only an indirect bearing upon the question which of them is to be regarded as master of the workman on a particular occasion.

The indicia from which the inference of a change is to be derived have been stated in many different ways. . . .

. . . For myself, I do not find much assistance in the circumstances of the present case from such expressions, especially as they were used with reference to men who had left their ordinary employment and taken on work for another employer, as distinguished from those who continued to do their ordinary work, though no doubt from time to time subjected to the directions of a third party as to the work they were to do.

Many factors have a bearing on the result. Who is paymaster, who can dismiss, how long the alternative service lasts, what machinery is employed, have all to be kept in mind. The expressions used in any individual case must always be considered in regard to the subject-matter under discussion but amongst the many tests suggested I think that the most satisfactory, by which to ascertain who is the employer at any particular time, is to ask who is entitled to tell the employee the way in which he is to do the work upon which he is engaged. If someone other than his general employer is authorised to do this he will, as a rule, be the person liable for the employee's negligence. But it is not enough that the task to be performed should be under his control, he must also control the method of performing it. It is true that in most cases no orders as to how a job should be done are given or required: the man is left to do his own work in his own way. But the ultimate question is not what specific orders, or whether any specific orders, were given but who is entitled to give the orders as to how the work should be done. Where a man driving a mechanical device, such as a crane, is sent to perform a task, it is easier to infer that the general employer continues to control the method of performance, since it is his crane and the driver remains responsible to him for its safe keeping. In the present case if the appellants' contention were to prevail, the crane driver would change his employer each time he embarked on the discharge of a fresh ship. Indeed, he might change it from day to day, without any say as to who his master should be and with all the concomitant disadvantages of uncertainty as to who should be responsible for his insurance in respect of health, unemployment and accident. I cannot think that such a conclusion is to be drawn from the facts established. I would dismiss the appeal.

Question
If one is not liable for one's independent contractor, would it not be odd if one were liable for one's independent contractor's servants?

Note:
It is one thing to supply a manned machine, especially if it is the machine which does the harm; it is another thing to supply just men, especially if they are to man the machines of others. Nevertheless "Just as with employers who let out a man with a machine, so also with an employer who sends out a skilled man to do work for another, the general rule is that he remains the servant of the general employer throughout." *Savory* v. *Holland & Hannen & Cubitts (Southern) Ltd.* [1964] 1 W.L.R. 1158, 1163, *per* Lord Denning M.R.

Section 3.—To whom is there Liability?

STAVELEY IRON & CHEMICAL CO. v. JONES

House of Lords [1956] A.C. 627; [1956] 2 W.L.R. 479; 100 S.J. 130; [1956] 1 All E.R. 403; [1956] 1 Lloyd's Rep. 65

Action by employee against employer in respect of personal injury

The plaintiff was an experienced coremaker employed in the defendant's ironworks at Hollingwood, Derbyshire; he was injured when a pan of cores being lifted by crane swung towards him and caught his arm against a railway truck. The crane-driver, Bertha Howett, had lowered the crab of the crane, from which hung four chains, over a pan of cores, but from her position she could not see clearly whether the crab was central, and this was necessary to prevent the pan slewing sideways when lifted. The plaintiff fixed two of the chains to his corners of the pan while an assistant (whom the plaintiff could not see for the height of the cores) fixed the other two chains to the remaining corners. Then the crane-driver, without any signal and without testing the balance of the pan, suddenly lifted it, and the accident occurred.

The plaintiff alleged that the defendant failed to provide a safe system of work or safe plant and equipment, but this claim was rejected. He further alleged that the crane-driver was negligent in not keeping a look-out to see that the crab was central over the pan, in raising the load when it was not safe to do so, and in failing to control the crane. The defendant pleaded that the plaintiff was contributorily negligent in not paying sufficient regard to the centralisation of the crab, in not instructing the crane-driver that the crab was not central, in not signalling to the crane driver to lower the crab, and in not standing clear of the pan.

Sellers J. gave judgment for the defendant. The Court of Appeal allowed the plaintiff's appeal, and entered judgment for him [1955] 1 Q.B. 474. The defendant's appeal to the House of Lords was dismissed.

Lord Reid: . . . My Lords, it is proved that the proper practice is not to raise the load at once but only to take the weight on the chains and then to pause to see whether everything is in order. For some reason which she could not explain the crane-driver did not do this, and, if she had done, the lack of centring ought to have been noticed and the accident would almost certainly have been avoided. The question is whether her failure to pause in lifting the load was negligence for which the appellants, her employers, are responsible.

Sellers J. held that both Jones and the crane-driver were guilty of errors of judgment but not of negligence, but, at least as regards the crane-driver, I do not think that he applied the right test of negligence. As regards Jones, I do not find it necessary to decide whether he applied the right test of contributory negligence because, as I have already said, the evidence is too indefinite to warrant a finding of contributory negligence on any test. His reasons appear from the following passages in his judgment:

"It is a type of action which seems to be increasingly entertained in the courts at the present time. To my mind it does give rise to a serious question as to whether these acts of carelessness, or inadvertence, which arise in factories in the course of work where people are collaborating together and working in a team should be described, except in exceptional circumstances where the conduct is so excessively bad as to require the description, as acts of negligence or errors of judgment. The question is not without considerable importance because, as I have said, these accidents are very common. . . .

I think there was some fault on the crane-driver's part, but I think there was at least as great, and probably greater, fault on the part of the plaintiff himself and, as I say, it raises quite acutely the question whether the court here ought to characterize this failure to do that which ought to have been done in the circumstances as acts of negligence—which would mean that the plaintiff would recover some damages, but only a proportion which is ultimately assessed to be his due having regard to his own conduct—or whether in circumstances such as this where there is both team work, routine work, work which necessitates a close co-operation with both and where there is a mistake which results, but only just results, in an accident as here, whether it is not more appropriate to regard them in such a case as this as errors of judgment on the part of both.

"I recognize that errors of judgment which might have been so described at any rate a hundred years ago perhaps have tended to be described in more recent years as acts of negligence, but when the question arose as to the conduct of operatives in a factory some years ago as to whether their inadvertent careless acts ought to be characterized as contributory negligence, the court took the view, and the House of Lords, the higher court, took the view, that it was not every act of inadvertence and carelessness which might arise in the course of a day's work where operatives were subject to noise, fatigue and diversions of one sort and another which ought to be contributory negligence. I should not describe the acts of either the plaintiff himself or the crane-driver in the circumstances of this case as acts of negligence but of errors of judgment. . . .

"I think it was one of those accidents which occur and are bound to occur in the rough and tumble of industry and can quite properly be described as an error of judgment."

This seems to me to be based on the view that conduct which would amount to negligence if a stranger were injured may not amount to negligence if the person injured is a fellow servant. If that was the view of the learned judge I cannot agree with it. One can imagine a case where the conduct of a servant has caused injury both to a fellow servant and to a passer-by in the street. If that conduct is negligence *vis-à-vis* the stranger I cannot see how it could be other than negligence *vis-à-vis* the fellow servant; if the servant is liable to the one he is equally liable to the other (apart from any question of contributory negligence); and if the servant is liable so is the master. Moreover, the abolition of the doctrine of common employment appears to me to make it necessary to hold that the test of negligence is the same whether the person injured is a fellow servant or a stranger: to hold otherwise would mean that if a servant causes damage then by reason of their common employment a fellow servant would not have as full a remedy against his master as a stranger would have.

It was argued that this view of the law would lead to grave anomalies and, indeed, is not consistent with *Caswell* v. *Powell Duffryn Associated Collieries Ltd.* ([1940] A.C. 152). That case decided, at least with regard to cases of breach of statutory duty—I express no opinion whether it goes farther—that what I may call excusable lapses do not amount to contributory negligence. It was suggested that two fellow servants might be injured by such lapses on the part of both of them: then, unless Sellers J. is right, each could sue the employer founding on the negligence of the other but neither could be held guilty of contributory negligence, and it was argued that this could not be right. It may be that some such result is inevitable—again I express no opinion until the case arises—but that would not be a reason, in my view, for trying to make *Caswell's* case apply to negligence as well as to contributory negligence. In that case this House was only dealing with contributory negligence and most of the reasoning is quite inapplicable to anything else. It may be that a servant can say to his employer, "You cannot complain of my lapse because you put me in a situation where a careful and prudent man might well have a lapse like mine" but neither he nor his employer can say that to a fellow servant. All either of them could say would be: "You cannot complain because when you took on the work you must have known that lapses of this kind were bound to happen"; in other words, *scienti non fit injuria*. But that would just be reviving the doctrine of common employment which Parliament has abolished.

The Court of Appeal reversed the decision of Sellers J., but different views were expressed on the law. Denning L.J., as I read his judgment, did not find it necessary to hold that the crane-driver was herself negligent. He said: "The employer is made liable, not so much for the crane-driver's fault, but rather for his own fault committed through her. . . . He acts by his servant; and his servant's acts are, for this purpose, to be considered as his acts. *Qui facit per alium facit per se.* He cannot escape by the plea that his servant was thoughtless or inadvertent or made an error of judgment. If he takes the benefit of a machine like this, he must accept the burden of seeing that it is properly handled. It is for this reason that the employer's responsibility for injury may be ranked greater than that of the servant who actually made the mistake."

My Lords, if this means that the appellants could be held liable even if it were held that the crane-driver was not herself guilty of negligence, then I cannot accept that view. Of course, an employer may be himself in fault by engaging an incompetent servant or not having a proper system of work or in some other way. But there is nothing of that kind in this case. Denning L.J. appears to base his reasoning on a literal application of the maxim *qui facit per alium facit per se*, but, in my view, it is rarely profitable and often misleading to use Latin maxims in that way. It is a rule of law that an employer, though guilty of no fault himself, is liable for damage done by the fault or negligence of his servant acting in the course of his employment. The maxims *respondeat superior* and *qui facit per alium facit per se* are often used, but I do not think that they add anything or that they lead to any different results. The former merely states the rule baldly in two words, and the latter merely gives a fictional explanation of it. "It has long been the established law of this country that a master is liable to third persons for any injury or damage done through the negligence or unskilfulness of a servant acting in his master's employ. The reason of this is, that every act which is done by a servant in the course of his duty is regarded as done by his master's orders, and consequently is the same as if it were the master's own act, according to the maxim, *qui facit per alium facit per se*" (*per* Lord Chelmsford L.C. in *Bartonshill Coal Co.* v. *McGuire* ((1858) 3 Macq. 300, 306)). On the same occasion Lord Cranworth used the two maxims apparently without thinking that there was any difference between them (*Bartonshill Coal Co.* v. *Reid* ((1858) 3 Macq. 266, 283)) and later authorities do not appear to me to establish any material difference. I do not think that the foregoing passage from Lord Chelmsford's speech will support an employer being held liable for something which was not negligent or wrongful on the part of his servant. . . .

Hodson and Romer L.JJ. do not follow Denning L.J. on this point and they appear to me to base their judgments on the crane-driver having been negligent. I think she was negligent. The system was that there were two safety checks. Jones was supposed to see to the first, centring, and the crane-driver was responsible for the second, pausing after taking the weight of the load. The first was not done but, as I have said, there is insufficient evidence to find that Jones was guilty of contributory negligence. But the fact that the first check was omitted is no excuse for failure to carry out the second, and the crane-driver gave no reason to explain her failure. I am therefore of opinion that this appeal should be dismissed.

Lord Morton of Henryton: . . . My Lords, what the court has to decide in the present case is: Was the crane-driver negligent? If the answer is "Yes," the employer is liable vicariously for the negligence of his servant. If the answer is "No," the employer is surely under no liability at all. Cases such as this, where an employer's liability is vicarious, are wholly distinct from cases where an employer is under a personal liability to carry out a duty imposed upon him as an employer by common law or statute. In the latter type of case the employer cannot discharge himself by saying: "I delegated the carrying out of this duty to a servant, and he failed to carry it out by a mistake or error of judgment not amounting to negligence." To such a case one may well apply the words of Denning L.J.: "[The employer] remains responsible even though the servant may, for some reason, be immune." These words, however, are, in my view, incorrect as applied to a case where the liability of the employer is not personal but vicarious. In such a case if the servant is "immune," so is the employer. . . .

Lord Tucker: . . . My Lords, I think I have already sufficiently indicated that I do not consider that recent legislation has in any way altered the standard of care which is required from workmen or employers or that the standard can differ according to whether the workman is being sued personally or his employer is being sued in respect of his acts or omissions in the course of his employment. It is true that, in accordance with what was said in this House in *Caswell's* case, there may be cases, such as those involving breach of statutory duty, where an employer who is in breach of his duty cannot be heard as against his own servant who has been injured thereby to say that some risky act due to familiarity with the work or some inattention resulting from noise or strain amounts to contributory negligence. In this respect it is possible the same act may have different consequences when the injured man is the plaintiff suing his employers and where the employer is being sued by a third party (including another employee) in respect of the same act or omission. This is not so illogical as may appear at first sight when it is remembered that contributory negligence is not founded on breach of duty (cf. Nance v. British Columbia Electric Ry. Co. Ltd. ([1951] A.C. 601) and Lewis v. Denye ([1939] 1 K.B. 540, 544) and the cases there referred to), although it generally involves a breach of duty, and that in Factory Act cases the purpose of imposing the absolute obligation is to protect the workmen against those very acts of inattention which are sometimes relied upon as constituting contributory negligence so that too strict a standard would defeat the object of the statute.

This doctrine cannot be used so as to require any modification in the standard of care required from a workman in relation to his fellow servants or other third parties or the resulting liability of his employers. . . .

Note:

In *Lister* v. *Romford Ice & Cold Storage Co.* [1957] A.C. 555 the House of Lords decided that an employer who had been held vicariously liable to servant A for the fault of servant B could recover from B the damages paid to A, even if the employer had insurance cover against such liability. It is true that the insurance companies have now agreed not to enforce their rights and that employers are not likely to, but in law Bertha Howett is liable to pay Jones, through their employer, the full amount of his damage, although the trial judge found that they were equally at fault. "Fair's fair," isn't it?

ROSE v. PLENTY

Court of Appeal [1976] 1 W.L.R. 141; 119 S.J. 592; [1976] 1 All E.R. 97

Action by illicit passenger against driver's employer

Lord Denning M.R.: Mr. Plenty was a milk roundsman employed at Bristol by the Co-operative Retail Services Ltd. He started working for them at Easter 1970. There were notices up at the depot making it quite clear that the roundsmen were not allowed to take children on the vehicles. One notice said: "Children and young persons *must not in any circumstances be employed by you* in the performance of your duties." Both employers and trade union did their utmost to stop it. No doubt Mr. Plenty knew it was not allowed. But in spite of all these warnings, the practice still persisted. Boys used to hang about the depot waiting to be taken on and some of the roundsmen used to take them.

Soon after Mr. Plenty started work as a milk roundsman a boy, Leslie Rose, who was just over 13, went up to Mr. Plenty and asked if he could help him. Mr. Plenty agreed to let him do it. The boy described his part in these words: "I would jump out of the milk float, grab the milk, whatever had to go into the house, collect the money if there was any there and bring the bottles back." That is what he did. The milk roundsman paid the boy 6 shillings for the weekends and 4 shillings for the week days. While the boy was going round some houses the roundsman would go to others. On June 21, 1970, unfortunately, there was an accident. After going to one house, the boy jumped on to the milk float. He sat there with one foot dangling down so as to be able to jump off quickly. But at that time the milk roundsman, I am afraid, drove carelessly and negligently. He went too close to the kerb. As the milk float went round the corner, the wheel caught the boy's leg. He tried to get his leg away, but he was dragged out of the milk float. His foot was broken with a compound fracture, but it was mended. So it was not very serious.

Afterwards he, by his father as his next friend, brought an action for damages against the roundsman and against his employers. The judge found that the milk roundsman was negligent, but he felt that the boy was old enough to bear some part of the blame himself. He assessed the responsibility for the accident at 75 per cent. to the milk roundsman and 25 per cent. to the boy. He assessed the total damages at £800. He gave judgment against the milk roundsman for three-quarters of it: £600. But he exempted the employers from any liability. He held that the roundsman was acting outside the scope of his employment and that the boy was a trespasser on the float. The boy, through his father, now appeals to this court. He says the employers are liable for the acts of their milk roundsman.

This raises a nice point on the liability of a master for his servant. I will first take the notices to the roundsmen saying they must not take the boys on. Those do not necessarily exempt the employers from liability. The leading case is *Limpus* v. *London General Omnibus Co.* (1862) 1 H. & C. 526, 158 E.R. 993. The drivers of omnibuses were furnished with a card saying they "must not on any account race with or obstruct another omnibus." Nevertheless the driver of one of the defendants' omnibuses did obstruct a rival omnibus and caused an accident in which the plaintiff's horses were injured. Martin B. directed the jury that, if the defendants' driver did it for the purposes of his employer, the defendants were liable, but if it was an act of his own, and in order to effect a purpose of his own, the defendants were not responsible. The jury found for the plaintiff. The Court of Exchequer Chamber held that the direction was correct. It was a very strong court which included Willes J. and Blackburn J. Despite the prohibition, the employers were held liable because the injury resulted from an act done by the driver in the course of his service and for his masters' purposes. The decisive point was that it was *not* done by the servant for his own purposes, but for his masters' purposes.

I will next take the point about a trespasser. The boy was a trespasser on the milk float so far as the employers were concerned. They had not given him any permission to be on the float and had expressly prohibited the milk roundsman from taking him on. There are two early cases where it was suggested that the employer of a driver is not liable to a person who is a trespasser on the vehicle. They are *Twine* v. *Bean's Express Ltd.* (1946) 62 T.L.R. 458 and *Conway* v. *George Wimpey & Co. Ltd. (No. 2)* [1951] 2 K.B. 266. But these cases are to be explained on other grounds and the statements about a trespasser are no longer correct. . . . So far as vehicles are concerned, I venture to go back to my own judgment in *Young* v. *Edward Box & Co. Ltd.* [1951] 1 T.L.R. 789, 793, when I said: "In every case where it is sought to make a master liable for the conduct of his servant the first question is to see whether the servant was liable. If the answer is Yes, the second question is to see whether the employer must shoulder the servant's liability." That way of putting it is, I think, to be preferred to the way I put it later in *Jones* v. *Staveley Iron and Chemical Co. Ltd.* [1955] 1 Q.B. 474, 480.

Applying the first question in *Young* v. *Edward Box & Co. Ltd.*, it is quite clear that the driver, the milk roundsman, was liable to the boy for his negligent driving of the milk float. He actually invited the boy to ride on it. So the second question arises, whether his employers are liable for the driver's negligence. That does not depend on whether the boy was a trespasser. It depends, as I said in *Young* v. *Edward Box & Co. Ltd.*, on whether the driver, in taking the boy on the milk float, was acting in the course of his employment.

In considering whether a prohibited act was within the course of the employment, it depends very much on the purpose for which it is done. If it is done for his employers' business, it is usually done in the course of his employment, even though it is a prohibited act. That is clear from *Limpus* v. *London General Omnibus Co.*, *Young* v. *Edward Box & Co. Ltd.* and *Ilkiw* v. *Samuels* [1963] 1 W.L.R.

991. But if it is done for some purpose other than his masters' business, as, for instance, giving a lift to a hitchhiker, such an act, if prohibited, may not be within the course of his employment. Both *Twine* v. *Bean's Express Ltd.* and *Conway* v. *George Wimpey & Co. Ltd. (No. 2)* are to be explained on their own facts as cases where a driver had given a lift to someone else, contrary to a prohibition and not for the purposes of the employers. *Iqbal* v. *London Transport Executive* (1973) 16 K.I.R. 329 seems to be out of line and should be regarded as decided on its own special circumstances. In the present case it seems to me that the course of the milk roundsman's employment was to distribute the milk, collect the money and to bring back the bottles to the van. He got or allowed this young boy to do part of that business which was the employers' business. It seems to me that although prohibited, it was conduct which was within the course of the employment; and on this ground I think the judge was in error. I agree it is a nice point in these cases on which side of the line the case falls; but, as I understand the authorities, this case falls within those in which the prohibition affects only the conduct within the sphere of the employment and did not take the conduct outside the sphere altogether. I would hold that the conduct of the roundsman was within the course of his employment and the masters are liable accordingly, and I would allow the appeal.

In parting with the case, it may be interesting to notice that this type of case is unlikely to arise so much in the future, since a vehicle is not to be used on a road unless there is in force an insurance policy covering, inter alia, injury to passengers.

Lawton L.J. (dissenting): Ever since 1946 employers of drivers have been entitled to arrange their affairs on the assumption that if they gave clear and express instructions to their drivers that they were not to carry passengers on the employers' vehicles, the employers would not be liable in law for any injury sustained by such passengers. They were entitled to make that assumption because of the decision of this court in *Twine* v. *Bean's Express Ltd.*, 62 T.L.R. 458. No doubt since 1946 employers when negotiating with their insurers have sought to get reductions in premiums and have done so because of the assumption which, so it seems to me, they were entitled to make about freedom from liability to unauthorised passengers. . . . If between 1946 and 1951 any employers had the kind of doubts about *Twine's* case which in more recent years have been expressed by academic writers, their minds would have been put at rest by another decision of this court in 1951, namely, *Conway* v. *George Wimpey & Co. Ltd. (No. 2)* [1951] 2 K.B. 266. That was a case in which a lorry driver employed by a firm of contractors on a site where many other contractors were working, contrary to his express instructions, gave an employee of another firm of contractors a lift in his lorry. This man was injured while a passenger. The problem for the court was whether the injured man could claim against the employers of the lorry driver who had given him a lift. This court, in a unanimous decision, adjudged that the injured man could not claim. The leading judgment was given by Asquith L.J. and he gave his reason for saying that what the lorry driver had done had not been done in the course of his employment. He said, at p. 276: "I should hold that taking men not employed by the defendants on to the vehicle was not merely a wrongful mode of performing the act of the class this driver was employed to perform, but was the performance of an act of a class which he was not employed to perform at all." These two cases have not been over-ruled by the House of Lords. Insurers have proceeded ever since on the assumption that these cases are properly decided. It would I think be most unfortunate if this court departed from clear decisions save on good and clear grounds. What has been submitted is that those two judgments should not be followed because when the driver of the milk float employed the boy to carry bottles for him, he was employing him to do acts which furthered the employers' business interests. In my judgment he was doing nothing of the sort. The driver had been employed to drive the milk float and deliver the milk. He had not been authorised to sub-contract his work. What he was doing was setting the boy to do the job for which he had been employed and for which he was getting paid. In my judgment in so doing he was acting outside the scope of his employment—just as in the same way as was the driver in *Conway* v. *George Wimpey & Co. Ltd. (No. 2)*.

If a general principle should be relied upon to justify my opinion in this case, I would adopt the same approach as Lord Greene M.R. in *Twine's* case. What duty did the employers owe to the boy? The plaintiff's counsel says: "Oh well, they put the driver with the milk float on the road: they put him into a position to take passengers if he were minded to disobey his instructions and therefore it is socially just that they should be responsible." I do not agree. When they put the driver with his float on the road they put him into a position where he had to take care not to injure those with whom he was reasonably likely to have dealings or to meet, that is all other road users and his customers. They expressly excluded anyone travelling as a passenger on his milk float. He was instructed specifically that he was not to carry passengers. Had he obeyed his instructions, he would not have had a passenger to whom he owes a duty of care. It was his disobedience which brought the injured boy into the class of persons to whom the employers vicariously owed a duty of care. He had not been employed to do anything of the kind. In my judgment, the injured boy has failed to establish that the employers owed him any duty of care.

I appreciate that in *Ilkiw* v. *Samuels* [1963] 1 W.L.R. 991 . . . Diplock L.J. did say that a broad approach must be made to this problem. But the broad approach must not be so broad that it obscures the principles of law which are applicable. Therein lies the danger of too broad an approach. That can be illustrated by examining Diplock L.J.'s suggested general question, namely, what was the job on which he, the employee, was engaged for his employer? If that general question is asked without reference to the particular circumstances, the answer in *Twine's* case would have been to make Bean's Express liable for his injuries. The van driver in that case had been employed to drive carefully. He had not been employed to drive negligently. When Twine was injured the driver was doing the job he had been employed to do, namely, to drive. Unless this court is prepared to say that *Twine* v. *Bean's Express Ltd.* was wrongly decided, for my part I cannot see how that case can be distinguished from this. In the course of the argument an illustrative example was put to Mr. Rawlins, the plaintiff's counsel. He was asked whether if in *Twine's* case the driver had asked the passenger to do some map reading for him in order that he could get more quickly to the place where in the course of his employment he wanted to go, whether that fact would have made the employers liable. Mr. Rawlins said it would. In my judgment fine distinctions of that kind should have no place in our law, particularly in a branch of it which affects so many employers and their insurers. Having regard to what has been decided in the past, in my judgment it would be wrong now, without the authority either of the House of Lords or of Parliament not to follow the 1946 and 1951 cases. I would dismiss the appeal.

Scarman L.J. agreed with Lord Denning in allowing the appeal, not because the master's work was being advanced, but on the ground that the prohibitions did not limit the sphere of the roundsman's employment and that his disregard of them did not take him outside it. Scarman L.J. consequently approved of *Iqbal* v. *London Transport Executive* (1973) 16 K.I.R. 329, which Lord Denning regarded as "out of line": in that case the employer was held not liable for a bus conductor who, to be helpful, tried to drive a bus.

Questions
1. Did Master Rose become one of the dairy's employees when Mr. Plenty agreed to pay him for helping with his work?
2. Is it relevant whether or not Master Rose knew of the prohibitions?
3. Do you agree with the general principle formulated as a question by Lawton L.J.?

4. If the relationship between the plaintiff and the employer is irrelevant, why does one ask whether it was within the scope of the roundsman's employment to enlist the boy's help rather than whether the bad driving occurred in the scope of the employment?

5. Alf parks his car without permission in an awkward place on Bert's premises. Charlie, one of Bert's servants, has to extricate a lorry in order to make a delivery for Bert. In his manoeuvres Charlie carelessly collides with Alf's car. Is Bert liable to Alf? Is Charlie?

6. Were the Shatwell brothers (above p. 217) acting in the course and scope of their employment?

7. Does it follow from this case that an employer is now liable to a hitchhiker to whom the employee has, in breach of instructions prominently displayed on the dash-board, given a lift and whom the employee has injured through negligent driving?

Note:

The House of Lords has recently considered the question when C, invited by B to enter A's premises, is a trespasser *vis-à-vis* A. If B had no actual authority to issue the invitation, it depends on whether A had made him look as if he had such authority (ostensible authority). C will be a trespasser if he knew or should have realised that B had no such authority. In *Ferguson* v. *Welsh* [1987] 3 All E.R. 777 it was held that a demolition contractor who had been forbidden to subcontract nevertheless had, as a result of being invited on to the premises, ostensible authority to invite subcontractors on to the premises. It is clear, however, that unless B had actual authority, A may turn C off the premises on due notice.

Section 4.—For what Acts of the Servant?

CENTURY INSURANCE CO. v. NORTHERN IRELAND ROAD TRANSPORT BOARD

House of Lords [1942] A.C. 509; 111 L.J.P.C. 138; 167 L.T. 404; [1942] 1 All E.R. 491

The respondents provided Holmes, Mullin & Dunn Ltd. with tankers and drivers for the delivery of petrol to their customers. On August 2, 1937, a driver, Davison, collected 300 gallons of petrol from that firm and drove the tanker to Catherwood's garage in Belfast. He backed the tanker into the garage, inserted the nozzle of the delivery pipe into the manhole of Catherwood's storage tank, and turned on the stop-cock on the side of the tanker. He then lit a cigarette and threw away the match. The match ignited some material on the ground, and the fire spread to the manhole. Catherwood attacked the manhole with a fire-extinguisher; Davison, without turning off the stopcock, drove the tanker into the street. The fire followed the trail of petrol from the delivery pipe, and when it reached the tanker, the tanker exploded and did damage to Catherwood's car and the neighbouring houses.

The respondents paid the claims of those suffering property damage, and sought an indemnity from the appellants, who had insured them against liability to third parties arising out of the use of the tanker in question. The appellants denied liability on the grounds that Davison was acting as the servant of Holmes, Mullin & Dunn Ltd. and not of the respondents, and that in any case he was not acting in the course of his employment at the time he caused the fire. On the first point, the appellants failed before every tribunal but one; on the second point they failed before every tribunal without exception.

Viscount Simon L.C.: . . . On the second question, every judge who has had to consider the matter in Northern Ireland agrees with the learned arbitrator in holding that Davison's careless act which caused the conflagration and explosion was an act done in the course of his employment. Admittedly, he was serving his master when he put the nozzle into the tank and turned on the tap. Admittedly, he would be serving his master when he turned off the tap and withdrew the nozzle from the tank. In the interval, spirit was flowing from the tanker to the tank, and this was the very delivery which the respondents were required under their contract to effect. Davison's duty was to watch over the delivery of the spirit into the tank, to see that it did not overflow, and to turn off the tap when the proper quantity had passed from the tanker. In circumstances like these, "they also serve who only stand and wait." He was presumably close to the apparatus, and his negligence in starting smoking and in throwing away a lighted match at that moment is plainly negligence in the discharge of the duties on which he was employed by the respondents. This conclusion is reached on principle and on the evidence, and does not depend on finding a decided case which closely resembles the present facts, but the decision of the English Court of Appeal twenty years ago in *Jefferson* v. *Derbyshire Farmers Ltd.* ([1921] 2 K.B. 281) provides a very close parallel. As for the majority decision, nearly sixty years before that, of the Exchequer Chamber in *Williams* v. *Jones* ((1865) 3 H. & C. 602; 159 E.R. 668) it may be possible to draw distinctions, as the court in *Jefferson's* case sought to do, but this House is free to review the earlier decision, and for my part I prefer the view expressed in that case by the minority, which consisted of Blackburn and Mellor JJ. The second question must also be answered adversely to the appellants. I move that the appeal be dismissed with costs. . . .

Notes:

1. In April 1954, eight coal-miners at the Whiterigg Colliery in West Lothian were injured in an explosion caused when one of them left the working-face during a lull in work, entered the "waste" and lit a cigarette. The use of naked lights and the possession of matches or cigarettes was forbidden by statute. All five judges held that the employers were not liable for the smoker's negligence. *Kirby* v. *N.C.B.*, 1958 S.C. 514. Lord President Clyde said: "In the first place, if the master actually authorised the particular act, he is clearly liable for it. Secondly, where the workman does some work which he is appointed to do, but does it in a way which his master has not authorised and would not have authorised had he known of it, the master is nevertheless still responsible, for the servant's act is still within the scope of his employment. On the other hand, in the third place, if the servant is employed only to do a particular work or a particular class of work, and he does something outside the scope of that work, the master is not responsible for any mischief the servant may do to a third party. Lastly, if the servant uses his master's time or his master's place or his master's tools for his own purposes, the master is not responsible." *Ibid.* at 532–533.

2. Apprentices on day-release from their various employers were members of a joinery class at a technical college. Gregory and Llewendon had finished their assignment and went to tease and harass Powell, who was still working at the same bench as the plaintiff. Llewendon jabbed at Powell's handiwork and Gregory picked up a chisel, apparently in order to do likewise. Powell told him to put it down, and when Gregory failed to do so, grabbed for it. In the ensuing struggle the chisel flew into the air and hit the plaintiff in the eye. Gregory and Powell were held equally to blame but Powell's employer was held liable and Gregory's was not. *Duffy* v. *Thanet D.C.* (1984) 134 New L.J. 680 (McCowan J.).

3. A person on the way to work has not yet arrived; the transit is *hors d'oeuvre*, for the course of employment has not yet started. Thus a master is not in general liable to those run over by his men on their way to work, or from it. However, the work may involve driving, as does that of a commercial traveller, so it may be held that the work started or stopped at home (*Elleanor* v. *Cavendish Woodhouse* (1973) 30 M.L.R. 310 (C.A.)). Furthermore, the driver may be bringing others to work at the employer's request; the driver may then make his master liable, not because he is doing his work, but because he is doing a job for the master—the master will be liable for him as agent, not as servant. See, in this connection, *Vandyke* v. *Fender* [1970] 2 Q.B. 292. Those who leave work early may also take themselves outside the course of their employment: *Harrison* v. *British Railways Board* [1981] 3 All E.R. 679 ("Mr. Howard was no longer at work. He should have been, but he was not.") And this is so although he was allowed to use his employer's transport to go home in. By a bare majority, the Pearson Commission recommends that industrial injuries benefits should be extended to workers injured on the way to or from work.

4. To hold that a person is not vicariously liable does not mean that he is not liable at all, even where it is his servant who did the damaging act. If the management of Whiterigg colliery had known that miners were smoking and did nothing to stop it, they would be liable for breach of their own duty to take reasonable steps to prevent their employees being exposed to unnecessary danger. See *Hudson* v. *Ridge Manufacturing Co.* [1957] 2 Q.B. 348.

Introductory Note:
"Dishonest conduct is of a different character from blundering attempts to promote the employer's business interests, involving negligent ways of carrying out the employee's work or excessive zeal and errors of judgment in the performance of it. Dishonest conduct perpetrated with no intention of benefiting the employer but solely with that of procuring a personal gain or advantage to the employee is governed, in the field of vicarious liability, by a set of principles and a line of authority of peculiar application." (*per* Lord Keith in *Armagas* v. *Mundogas, The Ocean Frost*, [1986] 2 All E.R. 385, 392).

MORRIS v. C.W. MARTIN & SONS LTD.

Court of Appeal [1966] 1 Q.B. 716; [1965] 3 W.L.R. 276; 109 S.J. 451; [1965] 2 Lloyd's Rep. 63; [1965] 2 All E.R. 725

Action by owner of goods against person in lawful possession of them in respect of their loss by theft

The plaintiff wanted her mink stole cleaned, and delivered it to one Beder. Beder could not clean it himself, so he delivered it to the defendants for that purpose. The contract between Beder and the defendants contained a clause limiting the defendants' liability in certain circumstances. The trial judge found that Beder contracted as principal and not as agent for the plaintiff, but that he had the plaintiff's authority to sub-contract the job of cleaning the stole. One of the defendants' servants, Morrissey, who had been told by the defendants to deal with the fur, stole it instead of cleaning it, and it was never recovered.

The trial judge felt bound by *Cheshire* v. *Bailey* [1905] 1 K.B. 237 to give judgment for the defendants. The Court of Appeal allowed the plaintiff's appeal.

Lord Denning M.R.: . . . The case raises the important question of how far a master is liable for theft or dishonesty by one of his servants. If the master has himself been at fault in not employing a trustworthy man, of course he is liable. But what is the position when the master is not himself at fault at all?

The law on this subject has developed greatly over the years. During the nineteenth century it was accepted law that a master was liable for the dishonesty or fraud of his servant if it was done in the course of his employment *and* for his master's benefit. Dishonesty or fraud by the servant for his *own* benefit took the case out of the course of his employment. The judges took this simple view: No servant who turns thief and steals is acting in the course of his employment. He is acting outside it altogether. But in 1912 the law was revolutionised by *Lloyd* v. *Grace, Smith & Co.* ([1912] A.C. 716), where it was held that a master was liable for the dishonesty or fraud of his servant if it was done within the course of his employment, no matter whether it was done for the benefit of the master or for the benefit of the servant. Nevertheless there still remains the question: What is meant by the phrase "in the course of his employment"? When can it be said that the dishonesty or fraud of a servant, done for his *own* benefit, is in the course of his employment?

On this question the cases are baffling. In particular those cases, much discussed before us, where a bailee's servant dishonestly drives a vehicle for his own benefit. These stretch from *Coupé Co.* v. *Maddick* ([1891] 2 Q.B. 413) to the present day.

Let me take an illustration well fitted for a moot. Suppose the owner of a car takes it to a garage to be repaired. It is repaired by a garage hand who is then told to drive it back to the owner. But instead, he takes it out on a "frolic of his own" (to use the nineteenth-century phrase) or on a "joyride" (to come into the twentieth century). He takes it out, let us say, on a drunken escapade or on a thieving expedition. Nay more, for it is all the same, let us suppose the garage hand steals the car himself and drives off at speed. He runs into a motor-cyclist. Both the car and the motor-cycle are damaged. Both owners sue the garage proprietor for the negligence of his servant. The motor-cyclist clearly cannot recover against the garage proprietor for the simple reason that at the time of the accident the servant was not acting in the course of his employment: see *Storey* v. *Ashton* ((1869) L.R. 4 Q.B. 476). You might think also that the owner of the car could not recover, and for the self-same reason, namely, that the servant was *not* acting in the course of his employment. And before 1912 the courts would undoubtedly have so held: see *Sanderson* v. *Collins* ([1904] 1 K.B. 628) and *Cheshire* v. *Bailey* ([1905] 1 K.B. 237), as explained by Lord Shaw in *Lloyd* v. *Grace, Smith & Co.* itself. But since 1912 it seems fairly clear that the owner of the damaged car could recover from the garage proprietor, see *Central Motors (Glasgow) Ltd.* v. *Cessnock Garage & Motor Co.* (1925 S.C. 796), on the ground that, although the garage hand was using the car for his own private purposes, "he should be regarded as still acting in the course of his employment," see *Aitchison* v. *Page Motors* ((1935) 52 T.L.R. 137, 138), and even if he stole the car on the journey, it was a conversion "in the course of the employment": see *United Africa Co. Ltd.* v. *Saka Owoade* ([1955] A.C. 130, 144). I ask myself, How can this be? How can the servant, on one and the same journey, be acting both within and without the course of his employment? Within *qua* the car owner. Without *qua* the motor-cyclist. It is time we got rid of this confusion. And the only way to do it, so far as I can see, is by reference to the duty laid by the law on the master. The duty of the garage proprietor to the owner of the car is very different from his duty to the motor-cyclist. He owes to the owner of the car the duty of a bailee for reward, whereas he owes no such duty to the motor-cyclist on the road. He does not even owe him a duty to use care not to injure him.

If you go through the cases on this difficult subject, you will find that, in the ultimate analysis, they depend on the nature of the duty owed by the master towards the person whose goods have been lost or damaged. If the master is under a duty to use due care to keep goods safely and protect them from theft and depredation, he cannot get rid of his responsibility by delegating his duty to another. If he entrusts that duty to his servant, he is answerable for the way in which the servant conducts himself therein. No matter whether the servant be negligent, fraudulent, or dishonest, the master is liable. But not when he is under no such duty. The cases show this:

(i) *Gratuitous bailment.* Suppose I visit a friend's house and leave my coat with his servant in the hall, so that my friend becomes a gratuitous bailee of it: see *Ultzen* v. *Nicols* ([1894] 1 Q.B. 92). On my departure, I find my coat has gone. The servant who was entrusted with it has stolen it without my friend's fault. He has converted it, it may be said, in the course of his employment. But nevertheless my friend is not liable for the loss, because he was not under any duty to prevent it being stolen, but only to keep it as his own. "The law is not so unreasonable," said Holt C.J., "as to charge a man for doing such a friendly act for a friend": see *Coggs* v. *Bernard* ((1703) 2 Ld.Raym. 909, 914; 92 E.R. 107, 110) and *Giblin* v. *McMullen* ((1869) L.R. 2 P.C. 317), where it was assumed, rightly or wrongly, that the bank was a gratuitous bailee.

(ii) *Occupier's liability for visitor's belongings.* Suppose an actor leaves his belongings in his dressing-room. The porter negligently leaves the stage door unattended. A thief slips in and steals the actor's belongings. The porter was negligent in the course of his employment. But nevertheless the occupiers of the theatre are not liable for the loss, for the simple reason that they were under no duty to protect the actor's belongings from theft: see *Deyong* v. *Shenburn* ([1946] K.B. 227) and *Edwards* v. *West Herts. Group Hospital Management Committee* ([1957] 1 W.L.R. 415).

(iii) *Bailment for reward.* Once a man has taken charge of goods as a bailee for reward, it is his duty to take reasonable care to keep them safe; and he cannot escape that duty by delegating it to his servant. If the goods are lost or damaged, whilst they are in his possession, he is liable unless he can show—and the burden is on him to show—that the loss or damage occurred without any neglect or default or misconduct of himself or of any of the servants to whom he delegated his duty. This is clearly established by *Reeve* v. *Palmer* ((1858) 5 C.B.(N.S.) 84; 141 E.R. 33), *Coldman* v. *Hill* ([1919] 1 K.B. 443) and *Building and Civil Engineering Holidays Scheme Management Ltd.* v. *Post Office* ([1966] 1 Q.B. 247). There is an old case at nisi prius apparently to the contrary. It is *Finucane* v. *Small* ((1795) 1 Esp. 315; 170 E.R. 369). Lord Kenyon is there reported to have said that the bailor must prove that the loss was caused by the negligence of the bailee. That was clearly wrong. The bailee, to excuse himself, must show that the loss was without any fault on his part or on the part of his servants. If he shows that he took due care to employ trustworthy servants, and that he and his servants exercised all diligence, and yet the goods were stolen, he will be excused: but not otherwise. Take a case where a cleaner hands a fur to one of his servants for cleaning, and it is stolen. If the master can prove that thieves came in from outside and stole it without the fault of any of his servants, the master is not liable. But if it appears that the servant to whom he entrusted it was negligent in leaving the door unlocked—or collaborated with the thieves—or stole the fur himself, then the master is liable: see *Southcote's* case ((1601) 4 Co.Rep. 836; 76 E.R. 1061), *United Africa Co. Ltd.* v. *Saka Owoade* ([1955] A.C. 130) and *Reg.* v. *Levy Bros. Co. Ltd.* ([1961] S.C.R. 189).

(iv) *Contract to take care to protect the goods.* Although there may be no bailment, nevertheless circumstances often arise in which a person is under a contractual duty to take care to protect goods from theft or depredation: see, for instance, *Stansbie* v. *Troman* ([1948] 2 K.B. 48). The most familiar case is the keeper of a boarding house or a private hotel. He is under an implied contract to take reasonable care for the safety of property brought into the house by a guest. If his own servants are negligent and leave the place open so that thieves get in and steal he is liable: see *Dansey* v. *Richardson* ((1854) 3 E. & B. 144; 118 E.R. 1095) and *Scarborough* v. *Cosgrove* ([1905] 2 K.B. 805). So also if they are fraudulent and collaborate with the thieves. Again, when a job-master lets out a brougham and coachman, he undertakes impliedly that the coachman will take care to protect the goods in the brougham. If they are stolen owing to the coachman's negligence, the job-master is liable. So also if the coachman steals them himself.

(v) *Apparent authority of servant.* In *Lloyd* v. *Grace, Smith & Co.* a solicitor's clerk, acting within the *apparent* scope of his authority from his principals, accepted Mrs. Lloyd's deeds so as to sell her cottages on her behalf and to call in a mortgage. When he accepted her instructions, he intended to misappropriate the deeds for his own benefit, and he did so. His principals were held liable. The essence of that case as stressed in all the speeches (and especially in the judgment of Scrutton J.) was that the clerk was acting within his *apparent* authority in receiving the deeds and thus his principals had them in their charge. (And this was afterwards stressed by Sir Wilfrid Greene M.R. in *Uxbridge Permanent Benefit Building Society* v. *Pickard* ([1939] 2 K.B. 248, 252).) In consequence of this *apparent* authority, the firm of solicitors were clearly under a *duty* to deal honestly and faithfully with Mrs. Lloyd's property: and they could not escape that duty by delegating it to their agent. They were responsible for the way he conducted himself therein, even though he did it dishonestly for his own benefit.

(vi) *Where there is only opportunity to defraud.* There are many cases in the books where a servant takes the opportunity afforded by his service to steal or defraud another for his own benefit. It has always been held that the master is not on that account liable to the person who has been defrauded: see *Ruben* v. *Great Fingall Consolidated* ([1906] A.C. 439). If a window cleaner steals a valuable article from my flat whilst he is working there, I cannot claim against his employer unless he was negligent in employing him: see *De Parrell* v. *Walker* ((1932) 49 T.L.R. 37). In order for the master to be liable there must be some circumstances imposing a duty on the master: see *Coleman* v. *Riches, per* Williams J. ((1855) 16 C.B. 104, 121; 139 E.R. 695).

From all these instances we may deduce the general proposition that when a principal has in his charge the goods or belongings of another in such circumstances that he is under a duty to take all reasonable precautions to protect them from theft or depredation, then if he entrusts that duty to a servant or agent, he is answerable for the manner in which that servant or agent carries out his duty. If the servant or agent is careless so that they are stolen by a stranger, the master is liable. So also if the servant or agent himself steals them or makes away with them. It follows that I do not think that *Cheshire* v. *Bailey* ([1905] 1 K.B. 237) can be supported. The jobmaster was clearly under a duty to take all reasonable precautions to protect the goods from being stolen, either as a bailee for reward or under the contract. He entrusted that duty to the coachman and must be answerable for the way in which the coachman carried out that duty; and it is all the same whether he did it negligently or fraudulently and whether he did it for his master's benefit or his own benefit. The decision cannot survive *Lloyd* v. *Grace, Smith & Co.* and should be overruled.

So far I have been dealing with the cases where the owner himself has entrusted the goods to the defendant. But here it was not the owner, the plaintiff, who entrusted the fur to the cleaners. She handed it to Beder, who was a bailee for reward. He in turn, with her authority, handed it to the cleaners who were sub-bailees for reward. Mr. Beder could clearly himself sue the cleaners for loss of the fur and recover the whole value, see *The Winkfield* case ([1902] P. 42; below, p. 427), unless the cleaners were protected by some exempting conditions. But can the plaintiff sue the cleaners direct for the misappropriation by their servant? And if she does, can she ignore the exempting conditions?

These are questions of the first importance. At one time the owner of goods who bailed them to another could not sue a third person who had wrongfully lost or damaged or detained the goods. He could only sue the bailee; and the bailee could sue the third person. See the history of the matter fully discussed in Holmes, *The Common Law* (1881), pp. 164–180. But now an action does lie by the owner direct against the wrongdoer if he has the right to immediate possession: see *Kahler* v. *Midland Bank Ltd.* ([1950] A.C. 24, 33, 56). Even if he has no right to immediate possession, he can sue for any permanent injury to, or loss of, the goods by a wrongful act of the defendant: see *Mears* v. *London & South Western Ry.* ((1862) 11 C.B.(N.S.) 850; 142 E.R. 1029). But what is a wrongful act as between the owner and the sub-bailee? What is the duty of the sub-bailee to the owner? Is the sub-bailee liable for misappropriation by his servant? There is very little authority on this point. *Pollock and Wright on Possession* (1888), p. 169, say: "If the bailee of a thing sub-bails it by authority . . . and there is no direct privity of contract between the third person and the owner . . . *it would seem that both the owner and the first bailee have concurrently the rights of a bailor against the third person according to the nature of the sub-bailment.*" By which I take it that if the sub-bailment is for reward, the sub-bailee owes to the owner all the duties of a bailee for reward: and the owner can sue the sub-bailee direct for loss of or damage to the goods; and the sub-bailee (unless he is protected by any exempting conditions) is liable unless he can prove that the loss or damage occurred without his fault or that of his servants. So the plaintiff can sue the defendants direct for the loss of the goods by the misappropriation by their servant, and the cleaners are liable unless they are protected by the exempting conditions.

Now comes the question: Can the defendants rely, as against the plaintiff, on the exempting conditions although there was no contract directly between them and her? There is much to be said on each side. On the one hand, it is hard on the plaintiff if her just claim is defeated by exempting conditions of which she knew nothing and to which she was not a party. On the other hand, it is hard on the defendants if they are held liable to a greater responsibility than they agreed to undertake. As long ago as 1601 Lord Coke advised a bailee to stipulate specially that he would not be responsible for theft, see *Southcote's* case, a case of theft by a servant. It would be strange if his stipulation was of no avail to him. The answer to the problem lies, I think, in this: the owner is bound by the conditions if he has expressly or impliedly consented to the bailee making a sub-bailment containing those conditions, but not otherwise. . . .

Diplock L.J.: . . . The defendants cannot in my view escape liability for the conversion of the plaintiff's fur by their servant Morrissey. They accepted the fur as bailees for reward in order to clean it. They put Morrissey as their agent in their place to clean the fur and to take charge of it while doing so. The manner in which he conducted himself in doing that work was to convert it. What he was doing, albeit dishonestly, he was doing in the scope or course of his employment in the technical sense of that infelicitous but time-honoured phrase. The defendants as his masters are responsible for his tortious act.

I should add that we are not concerned here with gratuitous bailment. That is a relationship in which the bailee's duties of care in his custody of the goods are different from those of a bailee for reward. It may be that his duties being passive rather than active, the concept of vicarious performance of them is less apposite. However this may be, I express no views as to the circumstances in which he would be liable for conversion of the goods by his servant. Nor are we concerned with what would have been the liability of the defendants if the fur had been stolen by another servant of theirs who was not employed by them to clean the fur or to have the care or custody of it. The mere fact that his employment by the defendants gave him the opportunity to steal it would not suffice. The crucial distinction between *Lloyd* v. *Grace, Smith & Co.* ([1912] A.C. 716) and *Ruben* v. *Great Fingall Consolidated* ([1906] A.C. 439) is that in the latter case the dishonest servant was neither actually nor ostensibly employed to warrant the genuineness of certificates for shares in the company which employed him. His fraudulent conduct was facilitated by the access which he had to the company's seal and documents in the course of his employment for another purpose: but the fraud itself which was the only tort giving rise to a civil liability to the plaintiffs was not committed in the course of doing that class of acts which the company had put the servant in its place to do.

I base my decision in this case on the ground that the fur was stolen by the very servant whom the defendants as bailees for reward had employed to take care of it and clean it.

I agree that the appeal should be allowed.

Salmon L.J.: . . . I accordingly agree with my Lords that the appeal should be allowed. I am anxious, however, to make it plain that the conclusion which I have reached depends upon Morrissey being the servant through whom the defendants chose to discharge their duty to take reasonable care of the plaintiff's fur. The words of Willes J. in *Barwick's* case ((1867) L.R. 2 Exch. 259) are entirely applicable to these facts. The defendants "put the agent (Morrissey) in (the defendants') place to do that class of acts and . . . must be answerable for the manner in which that agent has conducted himself in doing the business which it was the act of his master to put him in." A bailee for reward is not answerable for a theft by any of his servants but only for a theft by such of them as are deputed by him to discharge some part of his duty of taking reasonable care. A theft by any servant who is not employed to do anything in relation to the goods bailed is entirely outside the scope of his employment and cannot make the master liable. So in this case, if someone employed by the defendants in another depot had broken in and stolen the fur, the defendants would not have been liable. Similarly in my view if a clerk employed in the same depot had seized the opportunity of entering the room where the fur was kept and had stolen it, the defendants would not have been liable. The mere fact that the master, by employing a rogue, gives him the opportunity to steal or defraud does not make the master liable for his depredations: *Ruben* v. *Great Fingall Consolidated* ([1906] A.C. 439). It might be otherwise if the master knew or ought to have known that his servant was dishonest, because then the master could be liable in negligence for employing him. . . .

Questions

1. You take your car to a garage for repair. When you go to pick it up, the garage owner says: "I'm very sorry. One of my men sneaked back last night after we were closed, got in with a duplicate key he had had made somewhere, took your car—it was the nicest one in the garage—and wrecked it." Is this, or should it be, a satisfactory answer? See *Leesh River Tea Co.* v. *British India Steam Navigation Co.* [1967] 2 Q.B. 250, 278, *per* Salmon L.J.

2. Do you agree with the following decisions?

(a) Long-distance telephone calls costing nearly £1,500 were made from the plaintiff's office by a cleaner employed by the defendant cleaning firm. Although the cleaning contracted for included the cleaning and sterilisation of the plaintiff's telephones, the defendants were held not liable. *Heasmans* v. *Clarity Cleaning* (1987) 137 New L.J. 101 (C.A.).

(b) In *Swiss Bank* v. *Brink's-MAT* [1986] 2 Lloyd's Rep. 79 a security firm was held not liable for a valuable cargo stolen by robbers tipped off by an employee who learnt of its arrival while on the job.

3. Does this case mean that a patient assaulted by a nurse may sue the hospital but that a patient assaulted by a floor-cleaner cannot?

4. Is there any connection between the two following statements?

(a) The very bad act of a third party tends to insulate a previous tortfeasor from liability.

(b) The worse a servant's act is, the less likely is the master to be held vicariously responsible.

5. Was it essential to the defendant's liability that Morrissey was their servant, or was it sufficient that he was a person to whom they had entrusted the plaintiff's coat in order to fulfil their promise to clean it?

6. If it is the relationship between the plaintiff and the defendant which determines whether the defendant is liable for his employee's theft (this case), why is the relationship irrelevant when the question is whether the defendant is liable for his employee's negligence (*Rose* v. *Plenty*, above, p. 242)?

Note:

Wilful acts

In *Keppel Bus Co.* v. *Sa'ad bin Ahmad* [1974] 2 All E.R. 700 a passenger took verbal exception to the bus conductor's behaviour and the conductor struck him in the eye with the ticket-punch. The courts of Singapore had held the bus company liable, but the Privy Council reversed them, on the rather odd ground that "there was no evidence which would justify the ascription of the act of the conductor to any authority, express or implied, vested in him by his employers." Considering that the plaintiff had paid the defendant to carry him with care and that one of the conductor's functions must be to try to protect the passengers from harm, the decision is rather surprising.

Contrast *Photo Production Ltd.* v. *Securicor Transport Ltd.* [1980] A.C. 827. The defendants had contracted to guard the plaintiff's factory but the man they sent to guard it deliberately set fire to it. It was accepted that the defendants would be liable unless their exemption clause protected them, as the House of Lords held it did. Yet the bus conductor's assault apparently did not constitute even an unfundamental breach of the contract of carriage!

Theft

Judges are rather reluctant to hold one person liable for theft committed by another. This reluctance is justifiable on the ground that theft is a risk against which sensible owners insure themselves (so that plaintiffs are either stupid owners or insurers in disguise), though it is also true that employers can take out fidelity insurance against the risk of an employee's dishonesty. (See Vann, "Insuring Against Fraud and Dishonesty," ((1987) 137 New L.J. 624). Conceptually the judicial reluctance may be expressed in two ways, or even three, for in addition to denying the duty or the causation, it may be held that in the circumstances it was not unreasonable to guard against the theft which occurred.

If one person is to be liable for theft by another, then his duty must be the duty to take positive steps to protect the goods against theft. This is higher than the normal duty in tort, namely, to take care not to damage the goods. Such a higher duty can arise either by contract or by reason of an "undertaking" by the defendant followed by a "reliance" by the plaintiff. (Was there any "reliance" by the plaintiff on the defendant in the principal case, or only on Beder? And was the defendant's "undertaking" not qualified by the exemption clause?) The undertaking-reliance duty will exist in every bailment situation *inter partes*, and will subsist though the contract be tainted by fraud or illegality. In the absence of such an undertaking, the higher duty will not rest on an employer (*Edwards* v. *West Herts. Group Hospital Management Committee* [1957] 1 W.L.R. 415) or on a neighbour (*Perl* v. *Camden L.B.C.* [1983] 3 All E.R. 161) or on an occupier (*Tinsley* v. *Dudley* [1951] 2 K.B. 18). Goods which are lawfully on another's premises may be there by mere licence—a bicycle in a college bicycle shed—or because the occupier has possession of them—a bicycle being repaired at the bicycle shop. (For a case distinguishing parking ("May I leave it here?") and garaging ("Will you look after it?"), see *Ashby* v. *Tolhurst* [1937] 2 K.B. 242.) In the second case the occupier is also bailee; the mental element necessary for possession being the same as that required to constitute an "undertaking" in tort.

Alternatively, one can say that, even if the defendant was careless, the voluntary and unlawful act of the thief breaks the chain of causation between the carelessness and the loss. This may be said when either there was no duty to guard or the duty was fulfilled (*Brook's Wharf & Bull Wharf* v. *Goodman Bros.* [1937] 1 K.B. 534), but it is difficult to say it when there has been a failure to guard, there being a contract or undertaking to do so (*Stansbie* v. *Troman* [1948] 2 K.B. 48), since the theft which has intervened is the very thing that should have been guarded against; for the difficulties, see *Mercantile Credit Co.* v. *Hamblin* ([1965] 2 Q.B. 242, 275, and now *Lamb* v. *London Borough of Camden* (above p. 203)).

None of this, however, need mean that a person who is under a duty to guard and has fulfilled it either personally or through the servant to whom he has entrusted the job (*e.g.*, a nightwatchman) should not still be liable for theft by one of his other servants. But the law is that he is not.

Wholly different considerations apply where the defendant has done an unpermitted act which results in the loss of the thing or where the defendant has come into possession of the thing subsequent to the theft (below, p. 433).

Chapter 7

WHERE THE OTHER IS NOT A SERVANT

Section 1.—The Employer

DAVIE v. NEW MERTON BOARD MILLS LTD.

House of Lords [1959] A.C. 604; [1959] 2 W.L.R. 331; 103 S.J. 177; [1959] 1 All E.R. 346;
[1959] 2 Lloyd's Rep. 587

Action by employee against employer in respect of personal injury

During his employment by the first defendants, the plaintiff wanted to separate two pieces of a machine; for this purpose he needed a drift, a pointed metal bar about a foot long. He went to a cupboard and chose one which was apparently sound, but at the second stroke of his hammer a piece of the drift broke off and entered his left eye. The drift was too hard to be safe, because the manufacturers, the second defendants, had given it the wrong heat treatment; once this was done, however, the defect in the drift was undiscoverable, short of a test which it would have been unreasonable to expect the employers to carry out. The employers had not bought the drift directly from the manufacturers but from a reputable middleman.

Ashworth J. gave judgment for the plaintiff against both defendants, the employers to be indemnified by the manufacturers [1957] 2 Q.B. 368. The employers' appeal to the Court of Appeal was allowed (Jenkins L.J. dissenting) [1958] 1 Q.B. 210. The workman's appeal to the House of Lords was dismissed.

Viscount Simonds: . . . Before I turn to the examination of the cases by which it may be supposed that guiding authority is given, I would remind your Lordships that this action was founded in tort. The accident, it was said, was caused by the negligence of the respondents, their servants or agents, and their negligence consisted in this, that they failed to provide a suitable drift which could be hammered safely without the risk of pieces flying off. I have deliberately used the language of the statement of claim which has been repeatedly used in these proceedings. It may be relevant to observe that it is not strictly accurate. The accident occurred not through a failure to supply a suitable drift—a failure that could result in nothing— but through the supply of an unsuitable drift. Therein lay their alleged negligence, and I pause to analyse that allegation. It may mean one of two things. First, it may mean that it was the duty of the respondents to supply suitable drifts: they supplied an unsuitable one: they did not do their duty: therefore they were negligent. This is a bare statement of absolute obligation. But, secondly, it may mean that the supply of an unsuitable drift was due to a want of reasonable care on their part. It must, then, be shown wherein lay the want of reasonable care, and at once the question arises, for whose negligence, acts, I suppose, of omission and commission, the employer is liable in the long chain which ends with the supply by him of a tool to his workman but may begin with the delving of the raw material of manufacture in a distant continent. In the case before us the chain is long enough. The respondents were not guilty of any negligence nor was any servant or agent of theirs nor was the reputable firm who supplied the drifts, but at the end of the chain were the manufacturers. The respondents stood in no contractual relation to them: so little con-

255

nection was there between them that it was long in dispute whether the fatal drift had been manufactured by them and delivered by them to the suppliers. But it is for their negligence in manufacture that the appellant would make the respondents liable. Remembering, my Lords, that the essence of the tort of negligence lies in the failure to take reasonable care, I am constrained to wonder how this thing can be. But it is made clear by the powerful dissenting judgment of Jenkins L.J. that, if such a result cannot commend itself to reason, it yet may find support in authority. I say that it cannot commend itself to reason; for, if indeed it is the law, every man employing another and supplying him with tools for his job acts at his peril: if someone at some time has been careless, then, for any flaw in the tools, it is he who is responsible, be he himself ever so careful. I observe that such a view of the law is usually accompanied by a disclaimer of any idea that an employer warrants the fitness of the tool he supplies and do not find the reconciliation easy.

My Lords, in the consideration of the very numerous cases which may be thought to have some bearing on this matter, two things should be borne in mind. In the first place, in England for the 100 years between the decision in *Priestley* v. *Fowler* ((1837) 3 M. & W. 1; 150 E.R. 1030) and the abolition of the doctrine of common employment, and for a somewhat shorter period in Scotland, the determination to avert, or at least reduce, the consequences of that decision led to a great deal of artificiality and refinement which would have been otherwise unnecessary. The shadow of it is still upon us. But we can at least return to the simple question which is at the bottom of it all; "Has the employer taken reasonable care for the safety of the workman?," a question which can only be answered in each case by a consideration of all its circumstances. In the second place, it is well to remember that we are dealing with a case of tort. The same act or omission by an employer may support an action in tort or for breach of an implied term of the contract of employment but it can only lead to confusion if, when the action is in tort, the court embarks on the controversial subject of implied contractual terms. I would venture a third general observation. Just as the law imposes a certain standard of care upon an employer in relation to his workman, so it imposes on the occupier of land a certain standard of care in relation to those who enter on it, and in this regard there were refinements which may now be forgotten. It may well be that the standard of reasonable care in both relations is in certain circumstances the same. It may, too, be useful to argue by way of analogy from one to another. But I would deprecate any direct appeal to cases between invitor and invitee for the purpose of determining the measure of responsibility of an employer to his workman. Particularly I think it is inept where the question is as to the liability of the employer for acts of a third party, independent contractor or another, of which he had not, and could not reasonably have had, knowledge. To that I now return, for it is in this case the very heart of the matter.

My Lords, let me remind your Lordships that the respondents are liable (if they are liable) for the accident to the appellant because the manufacturers were careless, and for that carelessness they must assume vicarious responsibility. That is a conclusion, said Jenkins L.J., which the Court of Appeal was constrained on the authorities to adopt. He observed ([1958] 1 Q.B. 210, 236) that that did not "entail the substitution of an absolute duty to ensure safety for the duty of reasonable care enunciated in *Smith* v. *Charles Baker & Sons* ([1891] A.C. 325, 362) and accepted passim by the House of Lords in *Wilsons & Clyde Coal Co. Ltd.* v. *English* ([1938] A.C. 57)." "The duty," he said, "remains a duty of reasonable care, but the obligation to take that degree of care *per se* or *per alios* is an absolute obligation." With great respect to the Lord Justice, I find this a difficult proposition to interpret and apply. If indeed it means that the employer is responsible for lack of care shown by anyone in the long chain to which I referred earlier in this opinion, then it is for practical purposes indistinguishable from the standard of absolute obligation which is disclaimed. If it means anything else, if it is necessary to determine who are the *alii* for whose default the employer is responsible, then the question is once more open. At what stage is the act or omission of a third party something for which the employer is responsible or no longer responsible?

My Lords, I would begin, as did Parker L.J., with a reference to the familiar words of Lord Herschell in *Smith* v. *Charles Baker & Sons* in which he describes the duty of a master at common law as "the duty of taking reasonable care to provide proper appliances, and to maintain them in a proper condition, and so to carry on his operations as not to subject those employed by him to unnecessary risk," words that are important both in prescribing the positive obligation and in negativing by implication anything higher. The content of the duty at common law, thus described by Lord Herschell, must vary according to the circumstances of each case. Its measure remains the same: it is to take reasonable care, and the subject-matter may be such that the taking of reasonable care may fall little short of absolute obligation. I find nothing in the earlier cases, in either the English or Scottish courts, to which our attention was called, that requires any qualification of this statement, though there are dicta which, taken out of their context, might appear to do so.

But, my Lords, as I have said, the difficulty arises, not on the primary statement of liability, but upon the question for whom is the employer responsible. Clearly he is responsible for his own acts, and clearly, too, for those of his servants. To them at least the maxims *respondeat superior* and *qui facit per alium facit per se* will apply. It is the next step that is difficult. The employer is said to be liable for the acts of his "agents" and, with greater hesitation, for the acts of "independent contractors." My Lords, fortunately we are not troubled here with the word "agent." No one could say that a manufacturer who makes a tool and supplies it to a merchant who in turn sells it to an employer is in any sense an agent of the latter for providing his workman with a tool. Is he then an independent contractor? It is perhaps a striking commentary on the artificiality of this concept that it should for a moment be thought possible to regard as an independent contractor with an employer a manufacturer with whom he never contracted, of whom he may never have heard and from whom he may be divided in time and space by decades and continents. It may lead your Lordships to the conclusion that the liability of the employer in such a case can only be sustained if his obligation is absolute. But that *ex hypothesi* it is not. . . .

As I have tried to show, the contention, as stated in its first form, that the employer is liable for the acts of himself, his servants and agents and, subject to whatever limitations might be thought fit, independent contractors, could not lead to success in this action: for the manufacturer could not by any legitimate use of language be considered the servant or agent of, or an independent contractor with, the employer who buys his manufactures in the market. It was then sought to reach the same result by a different road. The employer, it was said, was under a duty to take reasonable care to supply his workmen with proper plant and machinery. It was assumed that this included tools such as drifts, and I, too, will, without deciding it, assume it. It was then said that the employer could not escape responsibility by employing a third party, however expert, to do his duty for him. So far, so good. That is what Lord Maugham said, and I agree. But then comes the next step—but I would rather call it a jump, and a jump that would unhorse any rider. Therefore, it was said, the employer is responsible for the defect in goods that he buys in the market, if it can be shown that that defect was due to the want of skill or care on the part of anyone who was concerned in its manufacture. But, my Lords, by what use or misuse of language can the manufacturer be said to be a person to whom the employer delegated a duty which it was for him to perform? How can it be said that it was as the delegate or agent of the employer that the manufacturer failed to exhibit due skill and care? It is, to my mind, clear that he cannot and equally clear that Lord Maugham was not contemplating such a case nor using language which was apt to cover it. . . .

. . . It was said that an employer might, instead of purchasing tools of a standard design, either from the manufacturer direct or in the market, order them to be made to his own design. If he did so and if they were defective and an accident resulted, it was clear (so the argument ran) that he would be responsible. I agree that he would, if the fault lay in the design and was due to lack of reasonable care or skill on his part. There is no reason why he should not. A more difficult question would arise if the defect was not due to any fault in design (for which the employer was responsible) but to carelessness in workmanship. But that is a far cry from the present case, and recognising, as I do, that in this area of the law there is a border-line of difficult cases, I do not propose to say more than I need. I must, however, refer, since I mentioned it some time since, to a case tried by Finnemore J. at Chester Assizes. No authority having been cited to him, he said ([1955] 1 W.L.R. 549, 551): "Employers have to act as reasonable people, they have to take reasonable care; but if they buy their tools from well-known makers, such as the second defendants are, they are entitled to assume that the tools will be proper for the pur-poses for which both sides intended them to be used, and not require daily, weekly or monthly inspection to see if in fact all is well." My Lords, a prolonged examin-ation of the authorities could not have led him to a sounder conclusion.

As I have already said, a large number of authorities were cited to us, many of them relating to the liability of an employer or more often of an occupier of land, for the default of an independent contractor. It may one day fall to the House to explain and, perhaps, to reconcile these cases. It is not the occasion for that task when the fault lies at the door of one who was not an "independent contractor," however wide a meaning may be given to those words.

One more thing I must say. It was at one time suggested—I do not use a more emphatic word, for learned counsel was rightly discreet in his approach—that the House should take into consideration the fact that possibly or even probably the employer would, but the workman would not, be covered by insurance, and for that reason should be the more ready to fasten upon the employer liability for an accident due neither to his nor to the workman's carelessness. I will only say that this is not a consideration to which your Lordships should give any weight at all in your determination of the rights and obligations of the parties. The legislature has thought fit in some circumstances to impose an absolute obligation upon employers. The Factories Acts and the elaborate regulations made under them testify to the care with which the common law has been altered, adjusted and refined in order to give protection and compensation to the workman. It is not the function of a court of law to fasten upon the fortuitous circumstance of insurance to impose a greater burden on the employer than would otherwise lie upon him.

For these reasons, therefore, which I will sum up by saying that the claim was against reason, contrary to principle, and barely supported by authority, I would dismiss the appeal with costs.

Lord Reid: . . . even if it were open on the authorities to reach a conclusion in favour of the appellant, I would think such a conclusion to be wrong in principle. A master's duty to his servant with regard to the safety of plant supplied should, I think, be regarded as a part of the law of tort. Vicarious liability is well recognised and I see no difficulty in principle in extending vicarious liability beyond liability for those who are, strictly speaking, servants, but it would, I think, be going far beyond anything reasonable to extend it to cover a case where there was no relationship whatever between the master and the negligent person or his employer at the time when the negligence occurred. Then I take the other possible way of regarding the master's duty. It was common at one time to regard it as depending on the contract of employment, and, indeed, it was this view which was largely responsible for the invention of the rule of common employment. No doubt this view leaves the court much scope, but I think that it has always been recognised that an implied term must at least be reasonable. I could understand that it might be thought reasonable to make the master absolutely liable in certain cases. This has been done exten-sively by statute. But it seems to me wholly unreasonable to make the master's liability depend on the conduct of the servants of some person who may be a complete stranger. . . .

Where, then, is the line to be drawn? On the one hand it appears that an employer is liable for the negligence of an independent contractor whom he has engaged to carry out one of what have been described as his personal duties on his own premises and whose work might normally be done by the employer's own servant—at least if the negligent workmanship is discoverable by reasonable inspection. On the other hand, for the reasons which I have given, I am of opinion that he is not liable for the negligence of the manufacturer of an article which he has bought, provided that he has been careful to deal with a seller of repute and has made any inspection which a reasonable employer would make. That leaves a wide sphere regarding which it is unnecessary, and it would, I think, be undesirable, to express any opinion here. Various criteria have been suggested, and it must be left for the further development of the law to determine which is correct. In my judgment this appeal should be dismissed.

Lord Tucker: . . . My Lords, I do not think that the introduction of the independent contractor into this discussion presents any difficulty. It may well be that in some cases the employer may delegate the performance of his obligations in this sphere to someone who is more properly described as a contractor than a servant, but this will not affect the liability of the employer, he will be just as much liable for his negligence as for that of his servant. Such a contractor is entrusted by the employer with the performance of the employer's personal duty. But this does not mean that every person with whom the employer may have entered into some contractual relationship connected with the manufacture or supply of some machinery, appliance or tool which is ultimately used in his business automatically becomes a person entrusted by the employer with the performance of his common law duty. Still less can the negligence of some person with whom the employer has never been in contact contractually or otherwise, or of whom perhaps he has never even heard, be imputed to him. . . .

Note:

The law on the precise point decided in this case was changed 10 years later by the Employers' Liability (Defective Equipment) Act 1969, which rendered the employer liable for personal injury suffered by an employee in consequence of a defect in equipment provided by the employer which was due to the fault of a "third party," "third party" including an unidentifiable manufacturer (*Cullum* v. *Anill Hire* (Raymond Kidwell Q.C., June 9, 1986), and "equipment" including a ship on which the employee serves (*The Derbyshire* [1987] 3 All E.R. 1068 (H.L.)). The statutory requirement that the third party be at fault before the employer can be held liable remains unmodified by the Consumer Protection Act 1987, although that enactment renders the manufacturer liable without fault. Can you think of any good reason for this? However, the employee can require the employer's supplier, on pain of being held strictly liable himself, to reveal the name of the manufacturer or, if he is outside the E.E.C., the importer. (Consumer Protection Act 1987, s.2(4).)

The same year saw the enactment of the Employers' Liability (Compulsory Insurance) Act 1969 which required employers to take out the insurance against liability to his employees which Viscount Simonds insisted on ignoring.

Davie remains an illuminating case, however. The outcome was far from being as obvious as the opinions assert. The person who lets out tools on hire used to warrant that they were as fit as care and skill could make them, that is, that they were not defective by reason of any want of care or skill (*White* v. *John Warwick* [1953] 1 W.L.R. 1285); the warranty of the lessor is now statutory and absolute, like that of the seller of goods (Supply of Goods and Services Act 1982, s.4(2) and 4(5)). It would have been perfectly easy to imply into the relationship of employer and employee an undertaking by the employer that equipment provided by him would be safe and suitable. The opinions gain plausibility by insisting that the case was one of tort, not because there are not contractual duties merely to take care (rather than guarantee a result) or because there are no strict liabilities in tort, but because whereas the higher duty appears more natural in contract, the duty in tort tends to be only the duty to take care, through oneself and one's servants, unless there is some very good reason why it should be higher.

McDERMID v. NASH DREDGING AND RECLAMATION CO.

House of Lords [1987] A.C. 906; [1987] 3 W.L.R. 212; [1987] I.C.R. 917; [1987] 2 All E.R. 878; [1987] 2 Lloyd's Rep. 201

Action for personal injury by employee against employer

The plaintiff was employed by the defendant as a deckhand on a tug, whose captain was employed by a third party (the defendant's parent company). The plaintiff's job was to untie the hawsers attaching the tug to a dredger and then to knock twice on the wheelhouse door to tell the captain that it was safe to start the tug. One day the captain started the tug before the knocks were given, and the plaintiff, pulled into the sea by the snaking ropes, suffered a serious leg injury.

The trial judge held that the captain was to be treated as the defendant's servant, even if he were not. The Court of Appeal held the defendant liable, even though the captain was not their servant. The House of Lords unanimously dismissed the defendant's appeal.

Lord Brandon: My Lords, the Court of Appeal regarded the case as raising difficult questions of law on which clear authority was not easy to find. With great respect to the elaborate judgment of that court, I think that it has treated the case as more difficult than it really is. A statement of the relevant principle of law can be divided into three parts. First, an employer owes to his employee a duty to exercise reasonable care to ensure that the system of work provided for him is a safe one. Second, the provision of a safe system of work has two aspects: (a) the devising of such a system and (b) the operation of it. Third, the duty concerned has been described alternatively as either personal or non-delegable. The meaning of these expressions is not self-evident and needs explaining. The essential characteristic of the duty is that, if it is not performed, it is no defence for the employer to show that he delegated its performance to a person, whether his servant or not his servant, whom he reasonably believed to be competent to perform it. Despite such delegation the employer is liable for the non-performance of the duty.

In the present case the relevant system of work in relation to the plaintiff was the system for unmooring the tug *Ina*. In the events which occurred the defendants delegated both the devising and the operating of such system to Captain Sas, who was not their servant. An essential feature of such system, if it was to be a safe one, was that Captain Sas would not work the tug's engines ahead or astern until he knew that the plaintiff had completed his work of unmooring the tug. The system which Captain Sas devised was one under which the plaintiff would let him know that he had completed that work by giving two knocks on the outside of the wheelhouse. I have already said that I agree with the Court of Appeal that there was scope, on the evidence, for a finding that that system was not a safe one. I shall assume, however, in the absence of any contrary finding by Staughton J., that that system, as devised by Captain Sas, was safe. The crucial point, however, is that, on the occasion of the plaintiff's accident, Captain Sas did not operate that system. He negligently failed to operate it in that he put the tug's engines astern at a time when the plaintiff had not given, and he, Captain Sas, could not therefore have heard, the prescribed signal of two knocks by the plaintiff on the outside of the wheelhouse. For this failure by Captain Sas to operate the system which he had devised, the defendants, as the plaintiff's employers, are personally, not vicariously, liable to him.

It was contended for the defendants that the negligence of Captain Sas was not negligence in failing to operate the safe system which he had devised. It was rather casual negligence in the course of operating such system, for which the defendants, since Captain Sas was not their servant, were not liable. I cannot accept that contention. The negligence of Captain Sas was not casual but central. It involved abandoning the safe system of work which he had devised and operating in its place a manifestly unsafe system. In the result there was a failure by the defendants, not in devising a safe system of work for the plaintiff, but in operating one.

On these grounds, which while not differing in substance from those relied on by the Court of Appeal are perhaps more simply and directly expressed, I agree with that court that the defendants are liable to the plaintiff.

Questions

1. Would Lord Brandon have held the defendant liable if the reason the tug started had been (a) that Captain Sas had had a sudden heart attack and fallen against the wheel, (b) that another deckhand, whether or not employed by the defendant, had deliberately given the signal to start?

2. Is the operation of a system of work delegated to every person working under the system?

3. Is there any reason why an entrepreneur should not arrange to have each workman employed by a different company? See *Porr* v. *Shaw, The Marabu Porr* [1979] 2 Lloyd's Rep. 331 (C.A.).

Note:

The High Court of Australia has held an employer liable to an employee injured by an unsafe system of work adopted by a crane-driver, an independent contractor. *Kondis* v. *State Transp. Auth'y* (1984) 154 C.L.R. 672.

Section 2.—The Carrier

RIVERSTONE MEAT CO. PTY. LTD. v. LANCASHIRE SHIPPING CO. LTD.

House of Lords [1961] A.C. 807; [1961] 2 W.L.R. 269; 105 S.J. 148; [1961] 1 All E.R. 495; [1961] 1 Lloyd's Rep. 57

Action by cargo owner against carrier for damage to goods

The trial judge dismissed the action [1959] 1 Q.B. 74; the Court of Appeal affirmed [1960] 1 Q.B. 536; the House of Lords allowed the plaintiff's appeal.

Lord Radcliffe: My Lords, I have no doubt that this case is important in its implications and that it has merited the full consideration that it has received at all its hearings. Nevertheless, it appears to me that the answer to be returned to the problem it raises depends upon a very short question, what kind of obligation is imported by the words "shall be bound . . . to exercise due diligence to make the ship seaworthy" that appears in article III (1) of the Rules scheduled to the Australian Sea Carriage of Goods Act 1924. As we know, these are in fact the Hague Rules. Read them in one way, the answer must necessarily be for the appellants, the cargo owners: read them in another, it must be for the respondents, the carriers.

The relevant facts are of the simplest. Cargo has been damaged in the course of a voyage and it was damaged because the ship on which it was carried was unseaworthy. The unseaworthiness was caused by the carelessness of a fitter employed by skilled repairers working for the carriers. The work that they were doing was in connection with the ship's No. 2 special survey and annual load-line survey, in other words, work which was reasonably required in order to keep the ship in a seaworthy condition.

Now, I am quite satisfied that, treating the carriers as a legal person, a limited company whose mind, will and actions are determined by its officers and servants, they did nothing but what they should have done as responsible and careful persons in the carrying business. They were not themselves in the repairing business and there is no reason why they should have been, but they were mindful of their duty to have their ship in good order for its voyage or voyages and they not only entrusted her to a ship-repairing company of repute for reception in dry-dock but also employed an experienced and competent marine superintendent to act on their behalf. He, in his turn, acted with more than usual caution in requiring all the ship's storm-valves to be opened up for inspection and, although it was the carelessness of one of the repairers' fitters that left one of these valves ineffectively closed, it was ordinary prudent practice to entrust the work of closing up to a fitter and not to subject such work to an independent inspection.

I see no ground, therefore, for saying that the carriers themselves were negligent in anything that they did. If the content of their obligation is that they should, as a legal person, observe the standard of reasonable care that would be required at common law in a matter of this sort, which involves skilled and technical work, and if there is nothing more in their obligation than that, then I should not regard them as in default or, consequently, as liable to the cargo owners. Full and instructive as are the several judgments of the members of the Court of Appeal, I do not think that in the end they amount to more than an acceptance of this standard of obligation and a drawing of the necessary conclusion from the facts.

But there is, on the other hand, a way of looking at the intrinsic nature of the obligation that is materially different from this. It is to ask the question, when there has been damage to cargo and that damage is traceable to unseaworthiness of the vessel, whether that unseaworthiness is due to any lack of diligence in those who have been implicated by the carriers in the work of keeping or making the vessel seaworthy. Such persons are then agents whose diligence or lack of it is attributable to the carriers. An inquiry on these lines is not concerned with the distinctions between carelessness on the part of officers or servants of the carriers or their supervising agents, on the one hand, and carelessness on the part of their contractors or those contractors' contractors, on the other. The carriers must answer for anything that has been done amiss in the work. It is the work itself that delimits the area of the obligation, just as it is the period "before or at the beginning of the voyage" that delimits the time at which any obligation imputed to the carriers can be thought to begin. If these last points are borne in mind, I think that the difficulties about "an almost unlimited retrogression" (see *W. Angliss & Co. (Australia) Proprietary Ltd.* v. *P. & O. Steam Navigation Co.* ([1927] 2 K.B. 456, 461)) tend to disappear: for there is a point in each case at which defective work is not the work of any agent of the carrier and the duty to be diligent is no more than a duty to be skilled and careful in inspection. But the inspection that is relevant in such a case is not merely the carrier's inspection of his contractor's work: it is inspection on the part of anyone working for the carrier who is concerned to make sure that he does not accept defective materials or use defective tools.

If one had to choose between these two alternatives without any background in the way of previous authority or opinion with regard to the interpretation of this section of the Hague Rules, I think it would be very difficult to know which way one ought to turn. The natural meaning of the words does not seem to me to accord well with either reading. Whatever the responsibility is, it is imposed on the carrier and no one else—that is clear—but it is equally clear that no one would regard the carrier as being in the wrong merely because he gets whatever requires to be done, inspection, survey or work, done for him by someone else. If the respondents' reading is adopted, the one that has commended itself to McNair J. and the Court of Appeal, one must treat the words "due diligence to make the ship seaworthy" as if they were equivalent to "due diligence to see that the ship is made seaworthy," and that is not the same thing. On the other hand, the reading for which the appellants contend is not in truth consistent with the grammatical meaning of the words they have to rely upon, for the exercise of due diligence to which the carrier would be held would include the performance or omission of acts that were not in law the acts of the carrier at all.

Such general considerations as occur to me appear to favour the cargo owner's claim. He is not in any sense behind the scenes with regard to what is done to the vessel or how or when it is done. His concern with it begins and ends with the loading and discharge of his goods. The carrier, on the other hand, must have some form of ownership of the vessel and some measure of responsibility for seeing that it is fit and in proper condition for the carriage undertaken. He may qualify that responsibility by stipulation, if the law allows him to; or the law may write out the terms of his responsibility for him; but within those limits the responsibility is there. I should regard it as unsatisfactory, where a cargo owner has found his goods damaged through a defect in the seaworthiness of the vessel, that his rights of recovering from the carrier should depend on particular circumstances in the carrier's situation and arrangements with which the cargo owner has nothing to do; as, for instance, that liability should depend upon the measure of control that the carrier had exercised over persons engaged on surveying or repairing the ship or upon such questions as whether the carrier had, or could have done, whatever was needed by the hands of his own servants or had been sensible or prudent in getting it done by other hands. Carriers would find themselves liable or not liable, according to circumstances quite extraneous to the sea carriage itself. . . .

Lord Keith of Avonholm: . . . The obligation is a statutory obligation imposed in defined contracts between the carrier and the shipper. There is nothing novel in a statutory obligation being held to be incapable of delegation so as to free the person bound of liability for breach of the obligation, and the reasons for this become, I think, more compelling where the obligation is made part of a contract between parties. We are not faced with a question in the realm of tort, or negligence. The obligation is a statutory contractual obligation. The novelty, if there is one, is that the statutory obligation is expressed in terms of an obligation to exercise due diligence, etc. There is nothing, in my opinion, extravagant in saying that this is an inescapable personal obligation. The carrier cannot claim to have shed his obligation to exercise due diligence to make his ship seaworthy by selecting a firm of competent ship repairers to make his ship seaworthy. Their failure to use due diligence to do so is his failure. The question, as I see it, is not one of vicarious responsibility at all. It is a question of statutory obligation. Perform it as you please. The performance is the carrier's performance. As was said in a corresponding case under the Harter Act: "The Act requires due diligence in the work itself"—*The Colima* (82 F. 665 (D.C.N.Y. 1897)). Ample other authority in the same direction has already been cited by my noble and learned friends. I am only concerned here to say that it seems to me to proceed on sound principle. I should only add that when I refer to repairers I include sub-contractors brought on to the ship by the repairers to enable them to perform the work which they contracted to do. Their failure, in my opinion, must also be the failure of the carrier on whom the statutory duty rests, unless in some very exceptional circumstances their employment can be said to be without any authority, express or implied, of the carrier, a case which can be considered if ever it arises. . . .

Note:

The Hague Rules have been updated, but the duty "to exercise due diligence" remains unchanged: Carriage of Goods by Sea Act 1971, Sched., Art. III(1).

The carrier of goods, like the warehouseman, the dry-cleaner and the repairman, is a bailee. The common-law duty of the bailee, though it may be expressed in terms of reasonable care or due diligence, always tends to be rather higher than it sounds. Thus the burden of disproof of breach of duty lies on the defendant (below, p. 438), and the duty is a duty to take positive, though reasonable, steps to guard the goods from harm, and not just the usual duty to take reasonable care not to damage them.

The Court of Appeal has said that a warehouseman is liable to the bailor if the goods are stolen in consequence of the carelessness of nightwatchmen supplied by an independent security firm. *B.R.S.* v. *Arthur V. Crutchley* [1968] 1 All E.R. 811. Does it follow that the warehouseman would be equally liable if the goods were damaged by rainwater entering in consequence of the carelessness of the building firm which constructed or repaired the warehouse?

Questions:

1. Why do textbooks on Contract not have a chapter on vicarious liability?

2. Did you suppose that the careless Arab stevedore in *Re Polemis* (above p. 183) was one of the charterer's employees? (A charterer is not a bailee of the vessel or coach or plane, but simply has a contractual right to use it and, within limits, to direct its staff, who remain the owner's servants. The person who hires a car, on the other hand, does become a bailee of it).

3. As regards liability for stevedores, where better to see how it differs in contract and tort than the judgment of Robert Goff L.J. in *The Aliakmon* [1985] 2 All E.R. 44, 78?

ROGERS v. NIGHT RIDERS

Court of Appeal [1983] R.T.R. 324; (1984) 134 New L.J. 61; [1983] C.A.T. 22

Action by customer against minicab firm for personal injuries

The plaintiff was injured while travelling in a minicab owned and driven by L. when, owing to a defective door-catch, the door flew open, struck a parked car and slammed shut again. The minicab had been sent by the defendant firm in response to a telephone call by the plaintiff's mother. The defendant owned no cabs and employed no drivers, but had a list of independent driver-owners such as L. who agreed to pay the defendant a weekly sum for the hire of a car-radio and to collect customers as instructed by the defendant. The driver kept the whole fare paid by the customer.

Eveleigh L.J.: . . . In my opinion, this is not a case where we are concerned to consider vicarious liability or whether there is liability for the act of an independent contractor. We are concerned to consider a case of primary duty on the part of the defendants. It was never suggested, and it was not put to the plaintiff, that she knew that the defendants were simply a kind of post box to put her in touch with someone else with whom she would be able to make an independent contract. On the fact of this case, in my opinion, the defendants undertook to provide a car and driver to take the plaintiff to her destination. They did not undertake, and neither did she request them, to put her in touch with someone else who would undertake this obligation. Now in those circumstances of undertaking to provide a car and its driver to take her to her destination the defendants could foresee that she might be injured if the vehicle were defective, and so they owed a duty arising out of this relationship to take care to see that the vehicle was safe. They relied upon the driver to do this. Whether he was a servant or an independent contractor matters not, he was a third person upon whom they relied to perform their duty arising from their relationship with the plaintiff, and it is well-established law that such a duty cannot be delegated.

Dunn L.J.: agreed.

The firm Night Riders or A1 Cars hold themselves out to the general public as a car hire firm and they undertook to provide a hire-car to take the plaintiff to Euston Station. In those circumstances, they owed the plaintiff a duty to take reasonable steps to ensure that the car was reasonably fit for that purpose. It matters not whether the duty is put in contract or in tort, either way it is a duty they could not delegate to a third person so as to evade responsibility if the car was not fit for that purpose. There was no suggestion in the evidence in the court below, and it was never put to the plaintiff, that she was told of the true position of the firm, that is to say, the car did not belong to them and that the firm was no more than a booking agent for owner-driven cars over which they had no control. If there had been such evidence and if the true nature of the defendants' business had been known to the plaintiff, then the situation would have been different. But so far as the plaintiff was concerned, she was dealing with a car-hire firm not a mere booking agency and, accordingly, the defendants were under a primary duty to her.

For those reasons, and the reasons given by Eveleigh L.J., I too would allow the appeal.

Note:

Readers should be warned that no authority supports this unprincipled and unreserved decision whose practical effect is doubtless to render minicabs as expensive as the taxicabs which the Yellow Pages inform the world minicabs are not.

The contract here was not one of *hire* of the vehicle. Had it been a contract of hire, it would certainly have contained a warranty that the vehicle was not defective for want of care (now a strict warranty under Supply of Goods and Services Act 1982, s.2). But it was not a contract of hire, and the plaintiff's erroneous supposition that it was would not make it one. The contract was not a contract of *carriage*, either, whatever the plaintiff supposed. Had it been a contract of carriage, the words of Lord Radcliffe in *Barkway* v. *South Wales Transp.* would apply: " . . . a carrier's obligation to his passenger, whether it be expressed in contract or in tort, is to provide a carriage that is as free from defects as the exercise of all reasonable care can make it" ([1950] 1 All E.R. 392, 403). But the carrier is liable in tort because he actually carries, and in contract because he promises to carry. Here the defendant did not carry and did not promise to carry. In one case, admittedly, a freight forwarder was held to be a carrier (*Claridge & Holt* v. *King & Ramsay* (1920) 3 L.L.R. 197 (Bailhache J.)), but it had announced, contrary to the fact, that it owned and operated a fleet of liners whereas there was nothing in our case to estop the defendant from asserting that it had not undertaken to carry the plaintiff or even to provide a vehicle which it owned or manned. It is the defendant's assumpsit, not the plaintiff's assumption, which imposes responsibility. In any case the plaintiff here had not relied on any such supposed undertaking: she simply wanted a ride to the station. The contract—or contact—here was so marginal that it is not easy to discern the consideration. Certainly the plaintiff was not to pay the defendant, but doubtless the agreement was "If you agree to pay the driver, I shall send one to pick you up." The defendant here was a sort of telephone commissionnaire, the modern equivalent of the man in the street you ask to call you a taxi. The idea that business efficiency requires the implication into such a contract of such a heavy duty as the court here found is ludicrous. Doubtless the contract would now fall under s.12 of the Supply of Goods and Services Act 1982, with the result that, under s.13, "there is an implied term that the supplier will carry out the service with reasonable care and skill." The service here, however, was to get the driver to call, and that service was punctiliously performed.

But even if one took a different view of the *contract* involved, one could not conclude that the defendant owed any such duty in *tort* as was here held. After all, the defendant was not even the occupier of the defective vehicle—and a person is not turned into an occupier by the visitor's erroneous supposition that he is one.

Question:

Would the result have been the same if the plaintiff's injury had arisen solely by reason of L.'s negligent driving? If not, why not?

Section 3.—The Occupier

GREEN v. FIBREGLASS LTD.

Assizes [1958] 2 Q.B. 245; [1958] 3 W.L.R. 71; 102 S.J. 472; [1958] 2 All E.R. 521

Action by visitor against occupier in respect of personal injury

The plaintiff was caretaker of a building in Newcastle in which the defendants rented some offices; she contracted with the defendants to have their offices regularly cleaned, and this she did with the aid of charwomen employed by herself.

On July 31, 1956, the plaintiff was dusting an electric fire in the defendants' offices when she received severe electrical burns, as a consequence of which the fingers of her right hand had to be amputated. There was nothing wrong with the fire itself, and it was switched off at the wall; but although it was cold, the element was charged with electricity. This was because the wall-switch cut out the neutral wire instead of the live wire; and this had been made possible because the reputable electrical contractors who had rewired the offices five years previously at the instance of the defendants had done the job badly, by using only red wires instead of the distinctive red, black and green wires commonly used.

The plaintiff's action against the occupier was dismissed.

Salmon J.: The question arises whether the defendants are responsible for the negligent wiring which caused this accident. I have held that the plaintiff was not a servant of the defendants; at the time of the accident she was the defendants' invitee. It is clearly settled that the defendants, as invitors, owe a duty to exercise due care for the safety of their invitee, the plaintiff. An invitor must use reasonable care to prevent damage from an unusual danger of which he knows or ought to know: *Indermaur* v. *Dames* ((1866) L.R. 1 C.P. 274). What is reasonable care must depend upon the circumstances of each particular case. When the defendants took over these offices in 1951 they knew nothing about the wiring; the wiring, for all they knew, might then have been dangerously defective. They took the precaution, however, of having the offices completely rewired by Cairns (Newcastle) Ltd. I find that this company was, and the defendants reasonably believed them to be, a long-established firm with a high reputation as electrical contractors. It is true that the information before me on this point is not very detailed, but it appears from the documents that have been put in evidence that that company has been in business in Newcastle since 1905, and that its directors are well-qualified electrical engineers. No evidence was called by the plaintiff, nor were any questions put in cross-examination, to suggest that Cairns (Newcastle) Ltd. are other than competent experts, or that the defendants had any reason to doubt that fact. It is obvious that unless the electrical wiring of any premises is put into a safe condition, anyone using the premises may be exposed to danger of an unusual kind. Electrical wiring, however, is a matter for expert electrical contractors and is not ordinarily carried out by the occupier himself. How were the defendants to fulfil their duty to use reasonable care? I cannot think it was incumbent on them to send one of their directors or servants to a Polytechnic to take a course in electrical engineering and then attempt the rewiring themselves. In my view, they would discharge their duty of care by employing reputable and competent experts; and this they did. Nor had the defendants at any time thereafter any reason to suppose that the experts had been negligent, or that the electrical installation was unsafe.

This case seems to me to be indistinguishable from *Haseldine* v. *Daw & Son Ltd.* ([1941] 2 K.B. 343), in which it was held that the owners of lifts discharge their duty of care to invitees by employing competent experts to attend to the lift for them. In that case, the lift in question became dangerous by reason of the negligence of one of the expert's servants and the plaintiff thereby suffered damage. It was held by the Court of Appeal that the defendants were not liable for the negligence of the servants of their independent contractor experts. Scott L.J. held that the plaintiff was an invitee; Goddard and Clauson L.JJ. did not decide whether he was a licensee or an invitee, but said that even if he were an invitee, his claim must still fail against the occupier. Mr. Stanley Price, on behalf of the plaintiff, has sought to distinguish that decision on the ground that in the present case the defendants did not employ experts to make regular inspections of the electrical installation. I am not impressed by that point. An ordinarily prudent man, it is true, would have his lift regularly examined and serviced by an expert. I cannot believe, however, that an ordinarily prudent man who had had his premises wholly rewired by experts would think of having the wiring examined within five years of its installation unless there was any special reason, such as an apparent fault, for him to do so. Here, there was no such reason. *Haseldine* v. *Daw & Son Ltd.* was distinguished, but no doubt was cast upon it, by du Parcq L.J. in *Woodward* v. *Mayor of Hastings* ([1945] K.B. 174, 182), and by Parker J. in *Bloomstein* v. *Railway Executive* ([1952] 2 All E.R. 418). Those were cases where the safety of the invitee depended upon the careful performance of some act which called for no technical knowledge or experience but upon acts which the courts held that the invitor could and should have done himself and which he neglected to do. In such cases, the invitor is liable for his neglect to do the act. It is no excuse for his failure to do that act that, for purposes of his own, he chooses to employ an independent contractor who has neglected to perform the act or to perform it carefully. du Parcq L.J. and Parker J. reaffirmed that in the *Haseldine* v. *Daw* class of case—to which the present case, in my judgment, clearly belongs—the invitor, because of his inherent lack of technical knowledge or experience, discharges his duty of care to the invitee, not by attempting to do the act himself but by employing a properly qualified independent contractor to do it for him. In another context, *Phillips* v. *Britannia Hygienic Laundry Co. Ltd.* ([1923] 2 K.B. 832) and *Stennett* v. *Hancock* ([1939] 2 All E.R. 578) are illustrations of the same principle.

It is well settled that generally in an action for negligence a man is not vicariously liable for the carelessness of an independent contractor. There are, of course, cases where, by virtue of a contract or by the operation of law, an obligation may be imposed on a man to do an act, or to ensure that it is done and done carefully. In such cases, the defendant cannot shelter behind any independent contractor whom he may have employed. If he breaches the obligation he is liable, not in negligence but in contract, as in *Maclenan* v. *Segar* ([1917] 2 K.B. 325), or by reason of some breach of duty other than a duty to take care, as in *Dalton* v. *Angus* ((1881) 6 App. Cas. 740). The master, too, owes special duties to his servant which he cannot delegate. Those duties, however, spring from the nature of the contract of service. I can find no authority for holding that an invitor owes the same duty to his invitee as a master does to his servant. "Ever since *Quarman* v. *Burnett* ((1840) 6 M. & W. 499; 151 E.R. 509) it has been considered settled law that one employing another is not liable for his collateral negligence unless the relation of master and servant existed between them. So that a person employing a contractor to do work is not liable for the negligence of that contractor or his servants. On the other hand, a person causing something to be done, the doing of which casts on him a duty, cannot escape from the responsibility attaching on him of seeing that duty performed by delegating it to a contractor": *Dalton* v. *Angus, per* Lord Blackburn (at 829). It is important to observe that the duty cast upon the defendant in that case was not a duty to take care but a duty not to let down the plaintiff's adjoining buildings whilst excavating on his own land, the plaintiff having acquired a right of support by twenty years' enjoyment of such support.

Hughes v. *Percival* ((1883) 8 App.Cas. 443), *Honeywill & Stein Ltd.* v. *Larkin Bros. Ltd.* ([1934] 1 K.B. 191) and *Black* v. *Christchurch Finance Co. Ltd.* ([1894]

A.C. 48) are exceptional cases because there the defendants were employing contractors to do extra-hazardous acts, that is, acts which in their very nature involve in the eyes of the law special danger to others. It may be that such cases, like the master and servant cases, are an exception to the general rule that persons employing a contractor are not vicariously liable for his negligence or for the negligence of his servants. . . .

. . . With great diffidence, I doubt whether it is helpful to import into this branch of the law the conception of warranty. That seems to me to belong exclusively to the law of contract. The obligation of an invitor to an invitee has nothing to do with the law of contract or quasi-contract, but is part of the law of tort. The invitee's cause of action lies in negligence and nothing else. The only obligation of the invitor in essence is an obligation imposed by law to take reasonable care and nothing more. In each case the question must be posed: How ought that obligation to be performed? The answer to that question must depend on the particular facts of each case. If, as in the present case and in *Haseldine* v. *Daw & Son Ltd.*, some act is to be performed which calls for special knowledge and experience which the invitor cannot be expected to possess, then, in my judgment, he fulfils his duty of care as a prudent man by employing a qualified and reputable expert to do the act.

In my judgment, it follows that the claim fails against the present defendants. I would add that on the facts as I have found them it would appear that there could have been no answer to the claim had it been brought against Cairns (Newcastle) Ltd.

Note:
See now Occupiers' Liability Act 1957, s.2(4)(*b*), above, p. 114.

Questions
1. If, in *Glasgow Corporation* v. *Muir* (above, p. 116), the question was whether it was foreseeable that the person carrying the urn might drop it, why in this case was the question not asked whether it was foreseeable that the electrical contractor might do his job badly?

2. Would the result have been any different if the plaintiff had been a secretary employed by the defendant? Does *Davie's* case help us to answer this? See *Cook* v. *Broderip* (1968) 112 S.J. 193. Not being an employee, Mrs. Green would fall outside the terms of the Employers' Liability (Defective Equipment) Act 1969. If she had been an employee, would the statute have allowed her to recover?

3. Suppose I call a tree-felling firm to come and trim the trees on my estate. I see one of their workmen astride a limb which he is busily sawing through at a point between himself and the trunk of the tree. I must clearly warn visitors, such as the postman, on whom he and the limb are likely to fall, but am I liable to the workman himself if I fail to warn him? *Ferguson* v. *Welsh* [1987] 3 All E.R. 777 (H.L.) suggests not.

Section 4.—The Organiser of Dangerous Works

SALSBURY v. WOODLAND

Court of Appeal [1970] 1 Q.B. 324; [1969] 3 W.L.R. 29; 113 S.J. 327; [1969] 3 All E.R. 863

Action in respect of personal injuries by highway user against adjacent occupier

Telephone wires led from a pole on the far side of the highway to the eaves of a house 40 feet away. The first defendant, who had just bought the house, wanted a large hawthorn tree, some 25 feet high, eradicated by an expert. The second defendant, apparently competent, undertook the task at the instance of the first defendant's wife, but mismanaged it so badly that a branch of the falling tree broke the wires near the house and they fell across the highway. The plaintiff who had been watching from next door went on to the highway to try to remove the wires which were a danger to traffic, but before he could do anything the third defendant rounded the corner at speed. To avoid being struck by the wires with which the third defendant collided, the plaintiff flung himself down on the grass verge, an action which, thanks to a pre-existing back condition, caused him fairly severe injuries.

The trial judge gave judgment for the plaintiff against all three defendants. The appeal of the third defendant, the motorist, was dismissed, and the appeal of the first defendant, the occupier, was allowed.

Widgery L.J.: . . . It is trite law that an employer who employs an independent contractor is not vicariously responsible for the negligence of that contractor. He is not able to control the way in which the independent contractor does the work, and the vicarious obligation of a master for the negligence of his servant does not arise under the relationship of employer and independent contractor. I think that it is entirely accepted that those cases—and there are some—in which an employer has been held liable for injury done by the negligence of an independent contractor are in truth cases where the employer owes a direct duty to the person injured, a duty which he cannot delegate to the contractor on his behalf. The whole question here is whether the occupier is to be judged by the general rule, which would result in no liability, or whether he comes within one of the somewhat special exceptions— cases in which a direct duty to see that care is taken rests upon the employer throughout the operation.

This is clear from authority; and for convenience I take from *Salmond on Torts* this statement of principle: "One thing can, however, be said with confidence: the mere fact that the work entrusted to the contractor is of a character which may cause damage to others unless precautions are taken is not sufficient to impose liability on the employer. There are few operations entrusted to an agent which are not capable, if due precautions are not observed, of being sources of danger and mischief to others; and if the principal was responsible for this reason alone, the distinction between servants and independent contractors would be practically eliminated from the law." I am satisfied that that statement is supported by authority, and I adopt it for the purposes of this judgment.

One can compare at once that statement with the statement of principle upon which the judge relied. Having referred to some of the considerations to which I have myself already referred, he said: "The principal, unlike the employer, is not liable for incidental acts of negligence during the work; for instance, dropping a hammer on someone's head; but he is liable if the very act he orders to be done contains in it a risk of injury to others, and someone is injured as a result of the contractor's negligence as a consequence of that risk. In this case"—he meant the instant case—"there can be no doubt that there was an inherent risk of injury to others when the tree was felled unless proper care was taken to get rid of the risk." I make two observations upon those words of the judge. First, the evidence makes it perfectly clear that the tree could have been felled by a competent contractor, using proper care, without any risk of injury to anyone. The undisputed evidence of an expert was that the proper way to fell it, in its confined situation, was to lop the branches respectively until there was left a stump of only eight to ten feet in height. All that could be done without any danger to anyone, if, at any rate, all appropriate precautions were taken, and the resultant stump eight to ten feet high could then have been winched out of the ground, again without risk to anyone. So when the judge referred to it as being an operation in which "there was an inherent risk," he was, in my view, putting the matter too high. If he meant that there was a risk which even due care could not avoid, he was, in my judgment, quite wrong upon the undisputed evidence that was before him.

Secondly, I would venture to criticise the statement of principle which he applied as being too wide. Taken literally, it would mean that the fare who hired a taxicab to drive him down the Strand would be responsible for negligence of the driver en route because the negligence would be negligence in the very thing which the contractor had been employed to do. No one is disposed to suggest that the liability of the employer is that high; and although the judge reinforced himself by certain observations of Romer L.J. in *Penny* v. *Wimbledon Urban District Council* ([1899] 2 Q.B. 72, 78), in my opinion, the test which he applied was far too stringent.

In truth, according to the authorities there are a number of well-determined classes of case in which this direct and primary duty upon an employer to see that care is taken exists. Two such classes are directly relevant for consideration in the present case. The first class concerns what have sometimes been described as "extra-hazardous acts"—acts commissioned by an employer which are so hazardous in their character that the law has thought it proper to impose this direct obligation on the employer to see that care is taken. An example of such a case is *Honeywill & Stein Ltd.* v. *Larkin Bros.* ([1934] 1 K.B. 191). Other cases which one finds in the books are cases where the activity commissioned by the employer is the keeping of dangerous things within the rule in *Rylands* v. *Fletcher* [below p. 391] and where liability is not dependent on negligence at all.

I do not propose to add to the wealth of authority on this topic by attempting further to define the meaning of "extra-hazardous acts"; but I am confident that the act commissioned in the present case cannot come within that category. The act commissioned in the present case, if done with ordinary elementary caution by skilled men, presented no hazard to anyone at all.

The second class of case, which is relevant for consideration, concerns dangers created in a highway. There are a number of cases on this branch of the law, a good example of which is *Holliday* v. *National Telephone Co.* ([1899] 2 Q.B. 392). These, on analysis, will all be found to be cases where work was being done in a highway and was work of a character which would have been a nuisance unless authorised by statute. It will be found in all these cases that the statutory powers under which the employer commissioned the work were statutory powers which left upon the employer a duty to see that due care was taken in the carrying out of the work, for the protection of those who passed on the highway. In accordance with principle, an employer subject to such a direct and personal duty cannot excuse himself, if things go wrong, merely because the direct cause of the injury was the act of the independent contractor.

This again is not a case in that class. It is not a case in that class because in the instant case no question of doing work in the highway, which might amount to a nuisance if due care was not taken, arises. In my judgment, the present case is clearly outside the well defined limit of the second class to which I have referred. Mr. Bax, accordingly, invited us to say that there is a third class into which the instant case precisely falls, and he suggested that the third class comprised those cases where an employer commissions work to be done *near* a highway in circumstances in which, if due care is not taken, injury to passers-by on the highway may be caused. If that be a third class of case to which the principle of liability of the employer applies, no doubt the present case would come within that description. The question is, is there such a third class?

Reliance was placed primarily on three authorities. The first was *Holliday* v. *National Telephone Co.* ([1899] 2 Q.B. 392). That was a case of work being done in a highway by undertakers laying telephone wires. The injury was caused by the negligent act of a servant of the independent contractor who was soldering joints in the telephone wires. The cause of the injury was the immersion of a defective blowlamp in a pot of solder, and the pot of solder was physically upon the highway—according to the report, on the footpath. The Earl of Halsbury L.C., holding the employers responsible for that negligence, in my view, on a simple application of the cases applicable to highway nuisance to which I have already referred, said (at p. 399): "Therefore works were being executed in proximity to a highway, in which in the ordinary course of things an explosion might take place." Mr. Bax drew our attention to the phrase "in proximity to a highway" and submitted that that supported his contention on this point. I am not impressed by that argument, because the source of danger in *Holliday's* case was itself on the highway and also because I do not think it follows (although one need not decide the point today), that in the true highway cases to which I have referred the actual source of injury must arise on the highway itself. Mr. Bax said that in *Holliday* it would have been ridiculous if there had been liability because the pot of solder was on the highway, but no liability if it was two feet off the highway. That is an observation with which I entirely sympathise; but I can find nothing in Lord Halsbury's use of the word "proximity" to justify the view that there is , therefore, a special class of case on the lines he submitted.

The second case relied upon was *Tarry* v. *Ashton* ((1876) 1 Q.B.D. 314). That was a case where a building adjoining the highway had attached to it a heavy lamp, which was suspended over the footway and which was liable to be a source of injury to passers-by if allowed to fall into disrepair. It fell into disrepair, and injury was caused. The defendant sought to excuse himself by saying that he had employed a competent independent contractor to put the lamp into good repair and that the cause of the injury was the fault of the independent contractor. Mr. Bax argued that that case illustrated the special sympathy with which the law regards passers-by on the highway. He said that it demonstrated that the law has always been inclined to give special protection to persons in that category and so supported his argument that any action adjacent to the highway might be subject to special rights. But, in my judgment, that is not so. *Tarry* v. *Ashton* seems to me to be a perfectly ordinary and straightforward example of a case where the employer was under a positive and continuing duty to see that the lamp was kept in repair. That duty was imposed upon him before the contractor came and after the contractor had gone; and on the principle that such a duty cannot be delegated the responsibility of the employer in that case seems to me to be fully demonstrated. I cannot find that it produces on a side-wind, as it were, anything in support of Mr. Bax's contention.

The last case relied upon was *Walsh* v. *Holst & Co. Ltd.* ([1958] 1 W.L.R. 800), a decision of this court. In that case the occupier of premises adjoining the highway was carrying out works of reconstruction, which involved knocking out large areas of the front wall. He employed for that purpose a contractor, who employed a sub-contractor. It was obvious to all that such an operation was liable to cause injury to passers-by by falling bricks unless special precautions against that eventuality were taken. Indeed, very considerable precautions were so taken. However, on a day when the only workman employed was an employee of the sub-contractor, one brick escaped the protective net, fell in the street and injured a passer-by. The passer-by sued the occupier, the contractor, and the sub-contractor, relying on the doctrine of *res ipsa loquitur*. In my judgment, the only thing decided by that case was that on those facts the precautions which had been taken against such an injury rebutted the presumption of negligence which might otherwise have arisen under the doctrine of *res ipsa loquitur*. . . .

Accordingly, in my judgment, there is no third class of cases of the kind put forward by Mr. Bax; and it was for those reasons that I concurred in the court's decision that the occupier's appeal should be allowed and the judgment against him set aside. . . .

Note:
    One justification for the very different treatment of employee and independent contractor is that the latter, being in business for himself, is much more likely to be substantial and insured than the person in employment. Furthermore, the independent contractor will very

often *be* a business whereas an employee is invariably a mere human being. In the principal case the tree-feller seems to have been in business in the smallest possible way, and he would surely have been bankrupted if the motorist's liability insurer had chosen to exercise its right to claim contribution under the Act.

Question
Would you describe an accident of the sort that happened as falling within the road traffic risk or the householder's risk, as understood by insurers?

Further Note:
Widgery L.J. referred to *Honeywill & Stein* v. *Larkin Brothers* [1934] 1 K.B. 191. It is a strange case. The plaintiffs did some work in a cinema, obtained the permission of the cinema company to have the work photographed and then contracted with the defendants to go to the cinema and do the photography. In doing so, the defendants' employee carelessly set light to the curtains and caused a fire. The plaintiffs paid the cinema company's bill for the damage but on suing to recover this sum from the defendants they met the trumpery defence that they need not have paid the cinema company at all. The Court of Appeal held that the plaintiffs had indeed been liable to the cinema company for the negligence of the defendants, independent contractors though they were, since the task (which in those days involved igniting magnesium powder on a tin tray) was extra hazardous. It is hardly surprising that a decision on such facts has not proved very fertile.

Section 5.—The Owner of a Vehicle

ORMROD v. CROSVILLE MOTOR SERVICES LTD. (MURPHIE, THIRD PARTY)

Court of Appeal [1953] 1 W.L.R. 1120; 97 S.J. 570; [1953] 2 All E.R. 753

Actions for personal injury and property damage arising out of a highway accident

There was a collision in fog between an Austin Healey car, belonging to Murphie, the third party, and a bus belonging to the corporate defendant and driven by the personal defendant. Both vehicles were damaged, and both the male plaintiff, who was driving the Austin Healey, and the female plaintiff, his wife and passenger, suffered personal injuries. The plaintiffs sued the defendants in respect of their personal injuries, and the corporate defendant claimed the cost of repairing its bus from Murphie.

Devlin J. held that the accident was caused solely by the fault of the male plaintiff and dismissed the actions. He gave judgment for the bus company against Murphie, as being responsible for the male plaintiff's negligence [1953] 1 W.L.R. 409.

The plaintiffs were taking Murphie's car to Monte Carlo for him, where he was driving another car in the Rally; thereafter they were all to go on holiday together. On the way to Monte Carlo the plaintiffs were going to visit friends in Bayeux; the accident took place on the way to the Channel port.

Murphie appealed, as did the plaintiffs. The Court of Appeal dismissed Murphie's appeal on point of liability, but subsequently, on hearing further evidence, allowed the plaintiffs' appeals, holding that the two drivers were equally to blame.

Singleton L.J.: . . . It has been said more than once that a driver of a motor-car must be doing something for the owner of the car in order to become an agent of the owner. The mere fact of consent by the owner to the use of a chattel is not proof of agency; but the purpose for which the car was being taken down the road on the morning of the accident was, either that the car should be used by the owner or that it should be used for the joint purposes of the owner and the plaintiffs when it reached Monte Carlo.

In those circumstances, it appears to me that the judgment of Devlin J. that at the time of the accident the male plaintiff was the agent of the third party was right, and the third party's appeal on that head should be dismissed.

Denning L.J.: It has often been supposed that the owner of a vehicle is only liable for the negligence of the driver if that driver is his servant acting in the course of his employment. But that is not correct. The owner is also liable if the driver is his agent, that is to say, if the driver is, with the owner's consent, driving the car on the owner's business or for the owner's purposes. In the present case the driver was, by mutual arrangement, driving the car partly for his own purposes and partly for the owner's purposes. The owner wanted the car taken to Monte Carlo, and the driver himself wanted to go with his wife to Monte Carlo, and he intended to visit friends in Normandy on the way. On this account he started two or three days earlier than he would have done if he had been going solely for the owner's purposes. Mr. Scholefield Allen says that this should exempt the owner from liability for the driver's negligence, because the accident might never have happened if he had started later. He says that the owner would not have been liable for any negligence of the driver on the trip from Calais to Normandy and should not be liable for negligence on the early start. I do not think that this argument is correct. The law puts an especial responsibility on the owner of a vehicle who allows it out on to the road in charge of someone else, no matter whether it is his servant, his friend, or anyone else. If it is being used wholly or partly on the owner's business or for the owner's purposes, then the owner is liable for any negligence on the part of the driver. The owner only escapes liability when he lends it out or hires it out to a third person to be used for purposes in which the owner has no interest or concern: see *Hewitt* v. *Bonvin* ([1940] 1 K.B. 188). That is not this case. The trip to Monte Carlo must be considered as a whole, including the proposed excursion to Normandy, and, as such, it was undertaken with the owner's consent for the purposes of both of them, and the owner is liable for any negligence of the driver in the course of it. I agree that the appeal should be dismissed.

(At first instance)

Devlin J.: . . . It is clear that there must be something more than the granting of mere permission in order to create liability in the owner of a motor-car for the negligence of the driver to whom it has been lent. But I do not think that it is necessary to show a legal contract of agency. It is in an area between the two that this case is to be found, and it may be described as a case where, in the words of du Parcq L.J., there is a "social or moral" obligation to drive the owner's car ([1940] 1 K.B. 196). Mr. Ormrod was under such a duty as this; for if he had not driven the car as arranged, then the third party would have had a legitimate grievance. I think that the arrangement amounted to a request to Mr. Ormrod to drive the car. He who complies with such a request is the agent of the other, since he who makes the request has an interest in its being done. In this case the car was wanted for the purpose of a joint holiday; that was enough to give the third party an interest in the arrival of the car, so that the driving became an act done for his benefit. In the case of mere permission the person permitting has no interest in whether the act is done or not.

Questions
  1. Could Mrs. Ormrod have claimed damages for her personal injuries from Murphie?
  2. Was Ormrod an "independent contractor" of Murphie's?

3. Could Murphie claim (a) damages, (b) statutory contribution, (c) a quasi-contractual indemnity from Ormrod in respect of the damages paid by Murphie to the bus company? Would Warbey face any extra difficulties if he brought an action of relief against the person to whom he lent his car (*Monk* v. *Warbey*, above, p. 167)?

4. Would Murphie's claim against the defendants for damage to his Austin Healey be reduced by reason of Ormrod's negligence?

5. Suppose, in *Salsbury* v. *Woodland* (above p. 268), that instead of paying a tree-feller the occupier had asked his adolescent son or house-guest to cut down the hawthorn tree. Would the occupier be liable?

6. If a hitch-hiker sues the employer of the person who gives him a lift, could one impute the driver's negligence to the hitch-hiker on the basis that the driver was his agent?

Note:

The seeds planted by Lord Denning at the end of his judgment came to harvest in *Launchbury* v. *Morgans* [1971] 2 Q.B. 245. A husband frequently used his wife's car to go to work and to go drinking with his friends thereafter. His wife had asked him to get a friend to drive him home when he was the worse for drink, and one such evening he did so. The friend drove off at 90 m.p.h. in the wrong direction and collided with a bus; husband and friend were killed, the plaintiff passengers injured. The question was whether the wife was liable. The trial judge and a majority of the Court of Appeal held that she was. According to Lord Denning the wife would have been liable even if she had not asked her husband to procure a substitute driver, because she had an "interest or concern" in the return of her car (and of her husband), and the return of her husband and her car was what the friend was engaged on or for.

The House of Lords, in distinctly acid judgments, unanimously reversed ([1973] A.C. 127). It was emphasised that there were no special common law rules for cars and that in order to make the owner liable the driver, if not his servant, must be shown to be his agent. Not everyone who does something in the interests of another is his agent: an agent is a person who does something at another's request. It must be a request rather than a permission, and in order to discover which it is it may be useful to ask whether the alleged principal had any interest in the matter: after all, you *ask* people to do things for you, you *let* them do things for themselves, and letting someone do something, even with your property, does not make you liable for his negligence.

Of course A may be liable for B's driving of C's car—as in *Launchbury* v. *Morgans* the friend was certainly the agent of the husband—on this see *Nottingham* v. *Aldridge* ([1971] 2 Q.B. 739).

It may be useful to place this doctrine of agency in the context of the other rules relating to liability for traffic accidents.

Where A, a pedestrian, suffers personal injury because of the bad driving by B of C's car, A can sue C if

(1) C was careless in allowing B to drive (because C should have known that either B or the car was dangerous);

(2) C is B's employer, and B was driving in the course of his employment;

(3) C has *asked* B (servant or not) to drive the car (*Carberry* v. *Davies* [1968] 1 W.L.R. 1103, [1968] 2 All E.R. 817).

(4) C has *permitted* B (whoever he is) to drive the car (on any business whatever), and neither B nor C has a policy covering the liability of either to A.

In *Monk* v. *Warbey* (above, p. 167) although the defendant had lent the car to the driver for the driver's own purposes, the defendant still had to compensate the plaintiff, because there was no policy in force as statute required. Now either there is a policy in force or there is not. If there is, the plaintiff can sue the person covered by it; if there is not, he can sue the owner of the car (or the Motor Insurers' Bureau). Does the decision in *Ormrod*, then, add anything? It does, because under *Monk* v. *Warbey* the plaintiff can recover only in respect of personal injuries, insurance not being compulsory against liability for property damage in England, though it is elsewhere in Europe. Accordingly, the rule in the *Ormrod* case benefits only a person who is complaining of property damage. Now if the owner of the car is not required to be insured against this risk, the chances are high that he will not in fact be insured against it. It is accordingly a nice question whether the doctrine of the principal case should exist at all, if its only effect is to make an innocent person liable in respect of risks which are probably uninsured. It certainly ought not to be extended, as it was (in favour of a pedestrian) in *Scarsbrook*

v. *Mason* [1961] 3 All E.R. 767 (doubted by Oliver L.J. in *S* v. *Walsall M.D.C.* [1985] 3 All E.R. 294, 296, a case on whether a local authority which has received a child into care is answerable to the child for injury due to the negligence of the foster-parents).

But although *Ormrod* extends civil liability in a doubtful manner, it correspondingly restricts criminal liability. No offence is committed under the Road Traffic Act 1972, s.143, if any of the persons liable in respect of a victim's personal injuries is insured against liability to compensate him; if there is someone who is both liable and insured, it is immaterial that the driver personally is not insured (*Lees* v. *Motor Insurers' Bureau* [1952] 2 All E.R. 513). Thus, after the decision in *Ormrod*, where C has a policy which covers his liability while the car is being driven by B, personally uninsured, C will not be guilty of an offence when B is driving at C's request. Had the decision gone the other way, an offence would be committed in those circumstances, because B would not be insured, and C, though insured, would not be liable.

A further point requires mention. An insurance policy may consist of a promise by the company to indemnify only the insured (C), either while the car is being driven by C or a named driver, or while the car is being driven by anyone having C's permission. In such a case, it is C whom one must sue in order to be in a position to claim from his insurer, if the driver was a permitted one; if he is not, C will be liable for breach of statutory duty to insure. On the other hand, many policies contain in addition a promise by the company to indemnify anyone driving the car with C's permission. In such a case, the victim should sue B, and will be able, despite the fact that B is not a party to the policy, to recover from C's insurer. This will be of particular benefit to the victim in the common case where B is a servant driving the master's vehicle with his permission, but on his own business, and therefore outside the scope of his employment by C. In such a case, C will not be liable at all, either at common law (B being neither in the scope of his employment nor driving at C's request) nor for breach of statutory duty (because there is in fact a policy in force). Recovery in these circumstances can be had *only* by suing B personally.

With regard to the compensation of victims of motor accidents, the Pearson Commission decided not to extend the role of tort law but to propose the introduction of a system of social security payments. Such payments would be made automatically, without proof of fault or reduction for contributory negligence, to all those injured and to the dependants of all those killed by a motor vehicle in a public place. The sums so payable would not be as handsome as those now received by a successful plaintiff, but tort claims would continue to be available as now, subject to two qualifications as to amount: damages would include nothing for any pain and suffering during the first three months, and would be reduced by the full amount of any social security payments received or receivable.

PART III

TRESPASS

INTRODUCTION

IT was barely 50 years ago that the tort of negligence was born, or synthesised, but it has thrived so mightily and grown so lusty that one could be forgiven for wondering whether there was room left for any other tort at all. Negligence is always trying to edge out the other torts in the hope of elevating into a completely general and comprehensive principle its own proposition that it is actionable *unreasonably* to cause *foreseeable* harm to another. Although we shall later have to record the sad death of detinue (p. 436), a few torts have managed to survive the competition. Trespass has survived in part. Trespass existed long before negligence—long enough, indeed, to figure in the Lord's Prayer. Trespass had its principle, too. Its principle was that any *direct invasion* of a *protected interest* was actionable, subject to justification. This needs a word of explanation.

The first wrongdoers a system has to catch are the worst—the footpad, the highwayman, the kidnapper, the burglar and the thief. They should be brought before the King's Bench forthwith. If there is no police force to prosecute them, the victim must be encouraged to bring suit. This was done by the writ of trespass. In sanctioning these miscreants, the law was protecting the citizen's interests in bodily safety, security from attack, liberty of movement and possession of property. These are very important interests (which are missing?). So important are they that perhaps they should be protected against *all* invasions, not just criminal invasions, and not just those invasions which result in provable harm. It would be too much, however, if everyone whose conduct somehow resulted in such an invasion were held liable, so a doubly restrictive device was adopted: the invasion had to result *directly* from a *positive act*. If the invasion was *indirect*, however foreseeable, there was no liability in trespass, and there was no liability in trespass for *omissions*, however clear the duty to act. Those who had encompassed the plaintiff's ruin by indirection or indolence might well be liable in some other form of action, but trespassers they were not.

This trespass system was not a bad one in a society where parties could not be witnesses and where the jury consequently knew nothing but the *res gestae*. Most invasions in fact cause actual damage, and the jury could always award very small sums if no damage was caused. Again, most acts which directly cause an invasion are acts likely to cause such an invasion, even if they are not actually designed to produce it. However, some invasions do not involve any damage (shaking your fist at a bouncer, tiptoeing through a stubble-field), and sometimes an act directly results in an invasion which is neither designed nor foreseeable (a gamekeeper aiming at a pheasant hits a concealed picnicker). Thus trespass not only failed to catch some scoundrels (the ones who sat idly by or who caused indirect harm), but also caught some people who were quite innocent.

There was bound to be a categorical conflict between negligence, with its insistence on unreasonableness of conduct and foreseeability of harm, and trespass, with its emphasis on positive action and directness of invasion. The conflict was joined in *Fowler* v. *Lanning* in 1959 (below, p. 285). The plaintiff asserted simply that the defendant shot him. There could hardly be a terser statement of a claim in trespass. "He shot" establishes the positive act: "shot me" establishes the direct invasion. It entails, however, no assertion that there was anything unreasonable about the defendant's conduct, or that the plaintiff's being shot was a foreseeable result of the defendant's shooting. Diplock J. held that this statement of claim disclosed no cause of action: Fowler must allege that it was either intentionally or negligently that Lanning shot him.

This means that a person is not responsible for an unintended invasion (a) if his conduct was reasonable, or (b) even supposing his conduct was unreasonable, if the invasion was an unforeseeable consequence of it (*The Wagon Mound,* above, p. 185). It is thus no longer sufficient that the act be positive—it must be unreasonable; or that the invasion be direct—it must be foreseeable. To this extent the rules of negligence have completely trumped those of trespass, at least so far as actual damage is concerned.

That leaves intended invasions. Here the rules of trespass remain unimpaired, especially the vital rule that it is not for the plaintiff to show that the defendant's conduct was unreasonable but rather for the defendant to justify it. When the plaintiff has established an intentional invasion against his will, he will recover damages unless the defendant can establish a justification. This is the most important, as well as the oldest, rule in the book. The Cheetham Cricket Club (above, p. 107) was not liable for hitting Miss Stone because they did not intend to touch her at all, and what they did was reasonable; but no one in Britain, *no one,* can justify deliberately touching even a hair on Miss Stone's head, or entering her garden—much less depriving her of her liberty—merely on the ground that it was reasonable to do so, or on the more insidious ground that he reasonably thought he was entitled to do so. Trespass trips up the zealous bureaucrat, the eager policeman and the officious citizen; indeed, punitive damages can be awarded against the first two. It is not enough to *think* you are entitled; you must actually *be* entitled. Sometimes you will be entitled because of what you reasonably think (*e.g.*, a policeman's power to arrest criminals extends to arresting those he reasonably but erroneously believes guilty); sometimes not (a bailiff may enter A's house to find B; but only if B is actually there: *Southam* v. *Smout* [1964] 1 Q.B. 308).

This point has to be insisted on, since it is in danger of being overlooked. The law of tort does not have one function only; few things do. It is true that most tort claimants want compensation for harm caused to them by someone else and that in this sense (and in this sense only) the main function of the law of tort is to ordain such compensation. It has another function, however, which, though traditional, has rarely been more important than now, namely to vindicate constitutional rights. Not every infraction of a right causes damage. That is precisely why the law of trespass does not insist on damage. But if jurists believe that damage is of the essence of a tort claim, they will regard trespass as anomalous, deride it as antiquated, ignore the values it enshrines and proceed to diminish the protection it affords to the rights of the citizen. When constitutional rights are in issue what matters is whether they have been infringed, not whether the defendant can really be blamed for infringing them. But if jurists think of negligence as the paradigm tort (and they do so for no better reason than that a great many people are mangled on the highway) they will regard it as the overriding principle of the law of tort that you do not have to pay unless you were at fault (and, equally, that you always have to pay if you were at fault); the old cases where liability was imposed despite the absence of fault (or not imposed despite its presence) are then to be restricted or over-ruled as vestigial exceptions. If a defendant can say that he acted reasonably, a negligence lawyer will let him off, without bothering to distinguish the reasonable but erroneous belief that the projected behaviour was *authorised* from the reasonable but erroneous belief that it was *safe*.

It is especially important in Britain to make this distinction, because we can sue officials and the government, local or central, as if they were private persons. Officials are no less liable by reason of their office. That is all very well and good. But they are no more liable either; and that may not be so good, for it means that if you diminish the circumstances under which the citizen can sue another citizen you likewise diminish the circumstances under which the citizen can sue the state or its officials. Fortunately one can still claim punitive damages from an official who behaves outrageously; but one should also be able to claim damages from an official who, though behaving reasonably after the manner of officials, has nevertheless invaded those basic rights which are protected by the law of trespass. For it must be remembered (or learnt) that those who invade our rights generally do so on reasonable grounds, *viz.*, for our own good or for someone else's good or for the public good (which may, perhaps, be no one's).

The person who has committed a trespass must justify it. In creating the grounds of justification, the law is using the same process as it used in *Watt* v. *Hertfordshire C.C.* (above, p. 110); it balances the interests of the plaintiff against the interests sought to be furthered by the defendant. But here the rules are a little more precise, partly because they were formed under a system of strict pleading, and partly because there must be stricter limitations on those who intentionally invade the interests of others than on those who merely imperil them.

There is no reason to suppose that the categories of justification are closed, but they should be extended with the greatest caution, since every extension of a defence constitutes an erosion of a right. The present justifications exist for the purposes of promoting the most important interests—maintenance of public order, enforcement of the law, and preservation of life and property—and they frequently overlap. In addition, an act cannot be unlawful if it is authorised by the legislature, a judge or a proper custom.

Order is the precondition of justice: without public order social life is impossible. Thus anyone may stop a person committing, or from committing, a breach of the peace (*Albert* v. *Lavin* [1982] A.C. 546). But even when order is not threatened the law must be enforced: criminals must be caught however orderly they are. When they are caught in the act, there are not too many problems, but once they have got away, it is less clear that a crime has been committed and whether the suspects are guilty. A policeman may safely arrest a person whom he reasonably suspects of having committed certain crimes, but a private person had better let a policeman do any arresting that needs to be done, since if he does it himself he must show that the offence in question was actually committed. In other words, the private citizen must not only be reasonable about the suspect; he must be right about the crime. These powers are now largely statutory (below, p. 332). Arrest by warrant is safer, provided it is the person named in it who is arrested; here there is a second ground of justification—the order of a magistrate. There may, of course, also be a statutory power. May one trespass to land in order to catch a thief? It would be idle to say that a person who is subject to arrest can be taken only at home or on the highway. Thus policemen may enter premises if they have reasonable grounds for supposing the suspect to be there. There is, of course, no common law power to go on premises to look for evidence, but some striking statutory powers exist and have given cause for concern (*Inland Revenue Commissioners* v. *Rossminster Ltd.* [1980] A.C. 952).

If you can thus justify a trespass against a man who threatens the public, you can also justify one against a man who threatens you. Self-defence against aggressor, defence of property against burglar and thief are of course permitted. But now we happen upon a peculiarity. Under the old system of pleading, only trespassers could be thrown off land and only assailants could be struck in self-defence: in other words, if B used force against A in defence of person or property, B's liability depended on whether A was a trespasser or not. "Trespassers" must therefore include not only those who ought to be held liable in damages but also those whom one may evict or strike in self-defence. Now we see why a person who has no right to stay on land must be called a trespasser even if he came there without any negligence at all and even if he is doing no harm whatever. Likewise a person must be called an assailant if he appeared to be about to strike, whatever his real intentions may have been.

Take a famous case about whether someone was guilty of assault. S. and T. had exchanged disobliging words in the street; T. put his hand on the hilt of his sword, rather like the man in the Western going for his gun, but said as he did so "If 'twere not assize-time I should not take such language from you." The main question was whether T.'s behaviour constituted an assault, but of course T. was not being sued for assault—even in the seventeenth century you didn't sue someone for not hitting you; T. was suing S. for battery, because S. had then actually drawn his sword and poked T. in the eye with it. But whether S. was guilty of battery for blinding T. depended on whether T. was guilty of assault. In the event T. won, despite his act of putting his hand to his sword, since it was clear from what he said that he was not going to draw it (*Tuberville* v. *Savage* (1669) 1 Mod. 3, 86 E.R. 684).

In these cases one justifies self-defence by calling the other party a wrongdoer. But suppose my neighbour's prize cat is about to eat my canary; if the cat got the bird, my neighbour might well not be responsible, but I would surely be justified in hurling a brickbat at the cat in order to deter it, and I would not be liable to its owner if I hit it and caused it injury. Suppose that an accidental fire breaks out on my neighbour's land; if it appears likely to spread to my land, I can surely go on to his land to dig a fire-trench (though doubtless it would be better to call the Fire Brigade).

Now suppose that the danger in no way comes from the plaintiff, as the cat and fire did. A fire breaks out in my own house; may I seize my neighbour's fire-extinguisher and use it? This does not seem a wrongful thing to do, but it does seem that I should pay for the use of his thing. French law would unhesitatingly impose liability on the principle that one must not enrich himself (by cutting down fire damage) at the expense of another. English law has only two alternatives—to say (contrary to our belief) that the act was wrongful, or to say that it was not, and leave the plaintiff with the loss (contrary to our wish). The courts of England dislike the defence of necessity ("the tyrant's plea"), and vigorously rejected it in a case where squatters in council property said that they had nowhere else to live and that this was due to the council's breach of duty: *Southwark* v. *Williams* ([1971] Ch. 734 (C.A.)).

What of protection of property from loss? Must a storekeeper permit a child to leave his store with a thing its mother has stolen? Surely not. The Theft Act 1978, to be sure, empowers anyone to arrest a person who is dishonestly making off with goods without paying for them as required or expected, but there must also be some power at common law to retake chattels from someone in wrongful possession of them, and to enter land to retake stolen chattels or things which have been put there by the occupier.

But at this point self-defence or protection of property tends to become self-help; it is not preventing loss but remedying it; that is what the courts are for, and when the courts have a role, they like it to be an exclusive one. The legislature agrees with them, for it has enacted that a court order is required by an owner who wants to take back his goods from a hire-purchaser in default who has paid a third of the price (Consumer Credit Act 1974, s.90(1)), and also by a landlord who wants to evict a tenant on the expiry of the tenancy (Protection from Eviction Act 1977, s.3(1)).

One very important overriding qualification attaches to all these common law powers. They must be exercised reasonably. A person who would be lawfully arrested if he were told the reason is unlawfully arrested if he is not (PACE s.28, below p. 336). A trespasser who would go when asked may sue if pushed. A court will not order a stranger to return your thing if you have not demanded it (*Clayton* v. *Le Roy* [1911] 2 K.B. 1031); you may not take it back yourself in the absence of that courtesy.

There is no similar principle that statutory or contractual powers must be exercised reasonably. Granted that such a power exists, it may be exercised "for a good reason or a bad reason or no reason at all," *Chapman* v. *Honig* [1963] 2 Q.B. 502, 520, *per* Pearson L.J. But the law is not as helpless as it sounds. For although the judges will not admit that there is an overriding duty to exercise such powers reasonably, they are in a position to say exactly what those powers are, by construing the statute or contract in question. Except in an unusual case, the document will be held to grant the power conditionally on its reasonable use. Thus in one case the defendants had a power under statute to pull down the plaintiff's house. They did so. The plaintiff claimed damages for trespass. He recovered. The court held that there was in the statute an implied qualification of the power, namely, that notice of its intended exercise must be given. It would certainly have been reasonable for the defendant to have given notice, but the statute said nothing about it (*Cooper* v. *Wandsworth Board of Works* (1863) 14 C.B.(N.S.) 180; 143 E.R. 414).

Finally, judges and magistrates, who spend so much of their time causing people to be laid by the heels or locked up, have very considerable community from strict liability in trespass (see below p. 342).

These are the legal justifications which a defendant may adduce if he has deliberately invaded one of the plaintiff's protected interests and is therefore guilty of false imprisonment, assault, battery, or trespass to land or goods. But no justification is required if the plaintiff consented to the invasion: *volenti non fit injuria*. One boxer cannot sue another for a fair blow. There may be disputes of fact about the existence of the consent: did the suspect agree to go to the police station when asked to help, or was he taken willy nilly? Or about the extent of the licence—you may come here but not go there. Or about its duration—can the theatre manager eject a patron before the show is over? Or about the mode of exercise—does the patient consent to the surgeon's use of a dirty scalpel? Or about its validity—perhaps the consent was induced by fraud, or the invasion agreed to was illegal (can the masochist sue the sadist?). There may also be questions of law—can consent be given by a servant against his master's will (was Master Rose a trespasser?, above, p. 242), and what if there was apparently consent but really none?

Chapter 8

THE CAUSE OF ACTION

Section 1.—The Context of Trespass

(i) *Trespass and Negligence*

FOWLER v. LANNING

Queen's Bench [1959] 1 Q.B. 426; [1959] 2 W.L.R. 241; 103 S.J. 157; [1959] 1 All E.R. 290

Diplock J.: . . . The writ in this case claims damages for trespass to the person committed by the defendant at Corfe Castle, in the county of Dorset, on November 19, 1957. The statement of claim alleges laconically that at that place and on that date "the defendant shot the plaintiff," and that by reason thereof the plaintiff sustained personal injuries and has suffered loss and damage. By his defence the defendant, in addition to traversing the allegations of fact, raises the objection "that the statement of claim is bad in law and discloses no cause of action against him on the ground that the plaintiff does not allege that the said shooting was either intentional or negligent. . . . "

The point of law is not, however, a mere academic one even at the present stage of the action. The alleged injuries were, I am told, sustained at a shooting party; it is not suggested that the shooting was intentional. The practical issue is whether, if the plaintiff was in fact injured by a shot from a gun fired by the defendant, the onus lies upon the plaintiff to prove that the defendant was negligent, in which case, under the modern system of pleading, he must so plead and give particulars of negligence (see R.S.C., Ord. 19, r. 4), or whether it lies upon the defendant to prove that the plaintiff's injuries were not caused by the defendant's negligence, in which case the plaintiff's statement of claim is sufficient and discloses a cause of action (see R.S.C., Ord. 19, r. 25). The issue is thus a neat one of onus of proof. . . .

. . . It is fashionable today to regard trespass to the person as representing the historic principle that every man acts at his peril and is liable for all the consequences of his acts; negligence as representing the more modern view that a man's freedom of action is subject only to the obligation not to infringe any duty of care which he owes to others: see *per* Lord Macmillan in *Read* v. *J. Lyons & Co. Ltd.* ([1947] A.C. 156, 170). But however true this may have been of trespass in medieval times—and I respectfully doubt whether it ever was—the strict principle that every man acts at his peril was not applied in the case of trespass to the person even as long ago as 1617. It is true that in that year, in the much-cited case of *Weaver* v. *Ward* ((1617) Hob. 134; 80 E.R. 284) which arose out of a shooting accident during an exercise of trained bands, the Court of King's Bench held that a plea that "the defendant *casualiter et per infortuniam et contra voluntatem suam,* in discharging of his piece did hurt and wound the plaintiff" was demurrable. But it would seem that this was because the plea, which was a special plea, was insufficient because, although it denied intention, it did not negative negligence on the part of the defendant. It is clear from the report that the court was of opinion that the action of trespass to the person would fail if it should appear that the accident was "inevitable and that the defendant had committed no negligence to give occasion to the hurt."

This phrase is repeated in many of the later cases. . . . In any event, I can find no trace in the cases from the seventeenth century onwards that a defendant, in order to escape liability for unintentional trespass to the person, must comply with any higher standard of care than was needed to escape liability if the action were framed in trespass on the case. . . .

Apart from the question of onus of proof, which I must now examine, there does not appear by 1852 to have been any difference between the substantive law applicable whether the action were framed in trespass on the case or trespass to the person. Differences as regards pleading were, of course, in those days vital, but are not relevant for the purposes of the present case in 1959, except in so far as they throw any light upon where the onus of proof lay.

In trespass on the case the onus of proof of the defendant's negligence undoubtedly lay upon the plaintiff. Where it lay in trespass is much more difficult to determine. . . .

The majority of pre-Common Law Procedure Act cases in which the question of unintentional trespass to the person or to goods was discussed were, it is true, cases of collision on the highway either on land or on water. There is, however, no suggestion that I can find in any of the judgments that this was a relevant consideration, or that the law as to trespass *vi et armis* to the person or to goods was different according to whether the injury took place on a highway or not. Prima facie, therefore, one would suppose that the onus of proof lay upon the same party to the action in either case. If, then, it is conceded—as all agree that it must be at any rate today—that in the case of an involuntary trespass to the person on a highway the onus of proving negligence lies on the plaintiff, why should it be otherwise when the involuntary trespass to the person is not committed on a highway? There is, nevertheless, a formidable body of academic opinion—but not, I think, any binding judicial authority—that highway cases have in the last 100 years become an exception to a previously existing general rule that the onus of proof of absence of negligence on the part of a defendant in a case founded on trespass to the person lies upon the defendant himself. . . .

This brings me to *Stanley* v. *Powell* ([1891] 1 Q.B. 86), a case of a shooting accident, not on a highway, in which Denman J. held that trespass to the person would not lie in the absence of negligence by the defendant. . . .

Little assistance is to be obtained from any later cases. Since *Stanley* v. *Powell*, and perhaps as a result of that decision, there appears to be no case in the reports where unintentional trespass to the person has been relied upon as distinct from negligence, despite the encouragement of the learned authors of the article on "Trespass and Negligence" in *The Law Quarterly Review* in 1933 (45 L.Q.R. 359), and the continued appearance in successive editions of *Bullen & Leake* of a precedent of a pleading in trespass to the person in which neither intention nor negligence is alleged. No doubt in many cases it is the master who is sued for the act of his servant, and here trespass as opposed to case would never lie; but in the sixty-eight years which have passed since *Stanley* v. *Powell* there must have been many cases where the injury to the plaintiff was the direct consequence of the act of the defendant himself. But no practitioner seems to have thought, and certainly no court has decided, that to do so would affect the onus of proof.

I think that what appears to have been the practice of the profession during the present century is sound in law. I can summarise the law as I understand it from my examination of the cases as follows:

(1) Trespass to the person does not lie if the injury to the plaintiff, although the direct consequence of the act of the defendant, was caused unintentionally and without negligence on the defendant's part.

✗ (2) Trespass to the person on the highway does not differ in this respect from trespass to the person committed in any other place.

(3) If it were right to say with Blackburn J. in 1866 that negligence is a necessary ingredient of unintentional trespass only where the circumstances are such as to show that the plaintiff had taken upon himself the risk of inevitable injury (*i.e.*, injury which is the result of neither intention nor carelessness on the part of the defendant), the plaintiff must today in this crowded world be considered as taking upon himself the risk of inevitable injury from any acts of his neighbour which, in the absence of damage to the plaintiff, would not in themselves be unlawful—of which discharging a gun at a shooting party in 1957 or a trained band exercise in 1617 are obvious examples. For Blackburn J., in *Fletcher* v. *Rylands* [below p. 392] was in truth doing no more than stating the converse of the principle referred to by Lord Macmillan in *Read* v. *J. Lyons & Co. Ltd.* [below, p. 404], that a man's freedom of action is subject only to the obligation not to infringe any duty of care which he owes to others.

(4) The onus of proving negligence, where the trespass is not intentional, lies upon the plaintiff, whether the action be framed in trespass or in negligence. This has been unquestioned law in highway cases ever since *Holmes* v. *Mather* ((1875) L.R. 10 Ex. 261, 268), and there is no reason in principle, nor any suggestion in the decided authorities, why it should be any different in other cases. It is, indeed, but an illustration of the rule that he who affirms must prove, which lies at the root of our law of evidence. . . .

If, as I have held, the onus of proof of intention or negligence on the part of the defendant lies upon the plaintiff, then, under the modern rules of pleading, he must allege either intention on the part of the defendant, or, if he relies upon negligence, he must state the facts which he alleges constitute negligence. Without either of such allegations the bald statement that the defendant shot the plaintiff in unspecified circumstances with an unspecified weapon in my view discloses no cause of action. . . .

I do not see how the plaintiff will be harmed by alleging now the facts upon which he ultimately intends to rely. On the contrary, for him to do so will serve to secure justice between the parties. It offends the underlying purpose of the modern system of pleading that a plaintiff, by calling his grievance "trespass to the person" instead of "negligence," should force a defendant to come to trial blindfold; and I am glad to find nothing in the authorities which compels justice in this case to refrain from stripping the bandage at least from the defendant's eyes.

I hold that the statement of claim in its present form discloses no cause of action.

Questions

1. What more must the plaintiff say in his statement of claim in order to disclose a good cause of action in negligence?

2. Miss Stone might have sued the batsman in trespass to the person, but she did not sue him at all (*Bolton* v. *Stone*, above, p. 107). If she had, what do you think the House of Lords would have said? Could you distinguish Miss Stone's hypothetical claim against the batsman from the claim in *Brewer* v. *Delo* [1967] 1 Lloyd's Rep. 488 where the plaintiff, waiting to play on the sixth fairway, was struck on the head by a golf-ball badly hooked by the defendant on the eleventh?

Note:

At a subsequent trial the plaintiff could not even establish that the projectile which struck him came from the defendant's gun. Dworkin, "The Case of the Misguided Missile" (1959) 22 M.L.R. 538, 544. That is, he would have failed even if Diplock J. had decided the preliminary point of law the other way.

The High Court of Australia has declined to follow this decision (*McHale* v. *Watson* (1964) 111 C.L.R. 384).

LETANG v. COOPER

Court of Appeal [1965] 1 Q.B. 232; [1964] 3 W.L.R. 573; 108 S.J. 519; [1964] 2 Lloyd's Rep.
339; [1964] 2 All E.R. 929

The defendant appealed from a judgment for the plaintiff by Elwes J., who held
that the plaintiff's claim was not time-barred [1964] 2 Q.B. 53. The appeal was
allowed.

Lord Denning M.R.: On July 10, 1957, the plaintiff was on holiday in Cornwall. She
was staying at an hotel and thought she would sunbathe on a piece of grass where
cars were parked. While she was lying there the defendant came into the car park
driving his Jaguar motor-car. He did not see her. The car went over her legs and she
was injured.

On February 2, 1961, more than three years after the accident, the plaintiff
brought this action against the defendant for damages for loss and injury caused by
(1) the negligence of the defendant in driving a motor-car and (2) the commission
by the defendant of a trespass to the person.

The sole question is whether the action is statute-barred. The plaintiff admits
that the action for negligence is barred after three years, but she claims that the
action for trespass to the person is not barred until six years have elapsed. The
judge has so held and awarded her £575 damages for trespass to the person.

Under the Limitation Act 1939 the period of limitation was six years in all actions
founded "on tort"; but, in 1954, Parliament reduced it to three years in actions for
damages for personal injuries, provided that the actions come within these words of
section 2(1) of the Law Reform (Limitation of Actions, etc.) Act 1954, "actions for
damages for negligence, nuisance or breach of duty (whether the duty exists by virtue of a contract or of a provision made by or under a statute or independently of
any contract or any such provision) where the damages claimed by the plaintiff for
the negligence, nuisance or breach of duty consist of or include damages in respect
of personal injuries to any person."

The plaintiff says that these words do not cover an action for trespass to the person and that therefore the time bar is not the new period of three years, but the old
period of six years.

The argument, as it was developed before us, became a direct invitation to this
court to go back to the old forms of action and to decide this case by reference to
them. . . .

I must decline, therefore, to go back to the old forms of action in order to construe this statute. I know that in the last century Maitland said "the forms of action
we have buried, but they still rule us from their graves" (see Maitland, *Forms of
Action* (1909), p. 296), but we have in this century shaken off their trammels.
These forms of action have served their day. They did at one time form a guide to
substantive rights; but they do so no longer. Lord Atkin, in *United Australia Ltd.* v.
Barclays Bank Ltd. ([1941] A.C. 1, 29), told us what to do about them: "When
these ghosts of the past stand in the path of justice clanking their mediaeval chains
the proper course for the judge is to pass through them undeterred."

The truth is that the distinction between trespass and case is obsolete. We have a
different sub-division altogether. Instead of dividing actions for personal injuries
into trespass (direct damage) or case (consequential damage), we divide the causes
of action now according as the defendant did the injury intentionally or unintentionally. If one man intentionally applies force directly to another, the plaintiff has
a cause of action in assault and battery, or, if you so please to describe it, in trespass
to the person. "The least touching of another in anger is a battery," *per* Holt C.J. in

Cole v. *Turner* ((1704) 6 Mod. 149; 87 E.R. 907). If he does not inflict injury intentionally, but only unintentionally, the plaintiff has no cause of action today in trespass. His only cause of action is in negligence, and then only on proof of want of
reasonable care. If the plaintiff cannot prove want of reasonable care, he may have
no cause of action at all. Thus, it is not enough nowadays for the plaintiff to plead
that "the defendant shot the plaintiff." He must also allege that he did it intentionally or negligently. If intentional, it is the tort of assault and battery. If negligent
and causing damage, it is the tort of negligence.

The modern law on this subject was well expounded by Diplock J. in *Fowler* v.
Lanning [above, p. 285], with which I fully agree. But I would go this one step
further: when the injury is not inflicted intentionally, but negligently, I would say
that the only cause of action is negligence and not trespass. If it were trespass, it
would be actionable without proof of damage; and that is not the law today.

In my judgment, therefore, the only cause of action in the present case, where
the injury was unintentional, is negligence and is barred by reason of the express
provision of the statute. . . .

So we come back to construe the words of the statute with reference to the law of
this century and not of past centuries. So construed, they are perfectly intelligible.
The tort of negligence is firmly established. So is the tort of nuisance. These are
given by the legislature as sign-posts. Then these are followed by words of the most
comprehensive description: "Actions for . . . breach of duty (whether the duty
exists by virtue of a contract or of a provision made by or under a statute or independently of any contract or any such provision)." Those words seem to me to
cover not only a breach of a contractual duty, or a statutory duty, but also a breach
of any duty under the law of tort. Our whole law of tort today proceeds on the footing that there is a duty owed by every man not to injure his neighbour in a way forbidden by law. Negligence is a breach of such a duty. So is nuisance. So is trespass
to the person. So is false imprisonment, malicious prosecution or defamation of
character. Professor Winfield indeed defined "tortious liability" by saying that it
"arises from the breach of a duty primarily fixed by the law: this duty is towards
persons generally and its breach is redressible by an action for unliquidated
damages": See *Winfield on Tort*, 7th ed. (1963), p. 5.

In my judgment, therefore, the words "breach of duty" are wide enough to comprehend the cause of action for trespass to the person as well as negligence.

I come, therefore, to the clear conclusion that the plaintiff's cause of action here
is barred by the Statute of Limitations. Her only cause of action here, in my judgment, where the damage was unintentional, was negligence and not trespass to the
person. It is therefore barred by the word "negligence" in the statute. But even if it
was trespass to the person, it was an action for "breach of duty" and is barred on
that ground also. Accordingly, I would allow the appeal.

Note:
The statutory words being construed now appear, only immaterially altered, in Limitation
Act 1980, s.11(1).

Questions
1. Suppose the defendant had *intentionally* run over the plaintiff's foot. Would her claim
have been time-barred? See *Long* v. *Hepworth* [1968] 1 W.L.R. 1299, [1968] 3 All E.R. 248
(yes).

2. Why is there a shorter period of limitation for *any* actions in respect of personal injury?
Does the wording of the statute suggest that it was intended to cover *all* such claims? For
example, a claim against the vendor by the purchaser of goods in respect of personal injury
caused by a defect constituting a breach of the condition of quality implied by Sale of Goods
Act 1979, s.14?

(ii) *Trespass and Wilful Wrongs*

WILKINSON v. DOWNTON

Queen's Bench [1897] 2 Q.B. 57; 66 L.J.Q.B. 493; 76 L.T. 493; 45 W.R. 525; 13 T.L.R. 388; 41 S.J. 493

Wright J.: In this case the defendant, in the execution of what he seems to have regarded as a practical joke, represented to the plaintiff that he was charged by her husband with a message to her to the effect that her husband was smashed up in an accident, and was lying at The Elms at Leytonstone with both legs broken, and that she was to go at once in a cab with two pillows to fetch him home. All this was false. The effect of the statement on the plaintiff was a violent shock to her nervous system, producing vomiting and other more serious and permanent physical consequences at one time threatening her reason, and entailing weeks of suffering and incapacity to her as well as expense to her husband for medical attendance. These consequences were not in any way the result of previous ill-health or weakness of constitution; nor was there any evidence of predisposition to nervous shock or any other idiosyncrasy.

In addition to these matters of substance there is a small claim for 1s. 10½d. for the cost of railway fares of persons sent by the plaintiff to Leytonstone in obedience to the pretended message. As to this 1s. 10½d. expended in railway fares on the faith of the defendant's statement, I think the case is clearly within the decision in *Pasley* v. *Freeman* ((1789) 3 T.R. 51; 100 E.R. 450). The statement was a misrepresentation intended to be acted on to the damage of the plaintiff.

The real question is as to the £100, the greatest part of which is given as compensation for the female plaintiff's illness and suffering. It was argued for her that she is entitled to recover this as being damage caused by fraud, and therefore within the doctrine established by *Pasley* v. *Freeman* and *Langridge* v. *Levy* ((1837) 2 M. & W. 519; 150 E.R. 863). I am not sure that this would not be an extension of that doctrine, the real ground of which appears to be that a person who makes a false statement intended to be acted on must make good the damage naturally resulting from its being acted on. Here there is no *injuria* of that kind. I think, however, that the verdict may be supported upon another ground. The defendant has, as I assume for the moment, wilfully done an act calculated to cause physical harm to the plaintiff—that is to say, to infringe her legal right to personal safety, and has in fact thereby caused physical harm to her. That proposition without more appears to me to state a good cause of action, there being no justification alleged for the act. This wilful *injuria* is in law malicious, although no malicious purpose to cause the harm which was caused nor any motive of spite is imputed to the defendant.

It remains to consider whether the assumptions involved in the proposition are made out. One question is whether the defendant's act was so plainly calculated to produce some effect of the kind which was produced that an intention to produce it ought to be imputed to the defendant, regard being had to the fact that the effect was produced on a person proved to be in an ordinary state of health and mind. I think that it was. It is difficult to imagine that such a statement, made suddenly and with apparent seriousness, could fail to produce grave effects under the circumstances upon any but an exceptionally indifferent person, and therefore an intention to produce such an effect must be imputed, and it is no answer in law to say that more harm was done than was anticipated, for that is commonly the case with all wrongs. The other question is whether the effect was, to use the ordinary phrase, too remote to be in law regarded as a consequence for which the defendant is answerable. Apart from authority, I should give the same answer and on the same ground as the last question, and say that it was not too remote. . . .

. . . Suppose that a person is in a precarious and dangerous condition, and another person tells him that his physician has said that he has but a day to live. In such a case, if death ensued from the shock caused by the false statement, I cannot doubt that at this day the case might be one of criminal homicide, or that if a serious aggravation of illness ensued damages might be recovered. I think, however, that it must be admitted that the present case is without precedent. . . .

There must be judgment for the plaintiff for £100 1s. 10½d.

Questions

1. Suppose that what the defendant said was true. Which element of the tort would be lacking? Who has to prove its presence or absence?

2. Suppose that, though the statement was false, the defendant honestly believed it to be true (a) because there were reasonable grounds for that belief, and (b) because he was stupid and credulous. Would he be liable?

3. Would Mrs. Wilkinson have suffered shock if she had disbelieved the defendant? If not, why is there any difficulty in saying that she relied on the truth of what was said?

4. Suppose Mrs. Wilkinson had disbelieved the defendant. Would she have been justified in striking him?

5. Does this case become one of negligence if we say that there is a duty not to tell a known lie?

Notes:

1. In this very illustrative case, a deliberate lie destroyed the plaintiff's peace of mind and caused her physical harm. These facts did not, however, quite fit the form of any established tort. Although the appropriate interest (peace of mind) was affected, it was not quite *assault*, since the defendant did nothing but speak, and trespass requires an act. It was not quite *deceit*, since the plaintiff took no detrimental action, except for paying her friends to take the train. Nor was *negligence* appropriate, since shock damage resulting from unreasonable behaviour was not compensable in 1897. However, the defendant's behaviour was not just unreasonable, it was wilful; the harm was not just foreseeable, it was the calculated result; and there was a special relationship between the parties. So it was entirely correct of Wright J. to infer and state a new principle of liability. Of course negligence has grown a lot since then . . .

2. In one case the National Society for the Prevention of Cruelty to Children received information that the plaintiff was maltreating her child and sent an officer to investigate. The information was false and the plaintiff was severely shocked by the experience. The issue in the litigation was whether the Society was bound to disclose the name of the informant, but the demand for disclosure rested on a claim for damages against the Society of which Lord Denning, *obiter*, said this: "I can understand that where a false statement is made knowingly and intentionally without just cause or excuse and when it causes emotional distress, it may give rise to a cause of action. But it is a big step forward—or backward—to extend it to a statement which is made honestly in good faith. Many a person has occasion to investigate a complaint. It may be an employer or a police officer. Someone may report to him that goods have been stolen and that he believes that a man named AB is the thief. The employer or police officer sees the man AB and tells him that he is suspected. He is so shocked that he has a nervous breakdown. Has he a cause of action against the employer or police officer on the ground that he conducted the inquiry negligently? The question has only to be posed to see what an extension this would be." (*D.* v. *N.S.P.C.C.* [1976] 2 All E.R. 993, 998; [1978] A.C. 171, 189).

3. During the proceedings of the American Law Institute to consider the Tentative Draft for the new Restatement of the Law of Torts, Dean Prosser referred to the following story as an example of a case where the defendant would clearly *not* be liable. Mrs. Murphy was at home asleep one night while her husband worked on the night shift at a neighbouring coal-mine. She was woken by a noise outside, and threw up the window. The defendant, one of a group of colliers, shouted up "Are you the widow Murphy?" "My name is Murphy, but I'm no widow." "The hell you ain't." Her husband had been killed down the mine, and this was his colleagues' method of informing her. (1957 Proceedings of the American Law Institute 292.)

4. Telling lies, as in the principal case, is one thing; hurling abuse is another. Both may do harm. In the United States, the liability of carriers for the shock damage done to passengers by their abusive bus and train conductors is quite well established. Why should carriers in particular be liable? . . . except, of course, the Keppel Bus Co. (above, p. 253). Uttering threats

is a third thing, and there should be liability for damage caused by threatening to do a thing which, if done, would involve liability, provided that the damaging reaction to the threat was normal enough. See the cases reviewed in Handford, "Tort Liability for Threatening or Insulting Behaviour," (1976) 54 Can.Bar Rev. 563.

5. One fertile source of litigation in the United States has been the harassment of debtors by creditors or, more commonly, by debt collection agencies to which the debts have been assigned. The bulk assignment of debts is becoming more common in England and though the methods of collection adopted hitherto have been less outrageous, the Payne Committee reported that in their view harassment should be made an offence, but not a ground of civil liability (Cmnd. 3909 (1969), paras. 1240–1243). Accordingly the Administration of Justice Act 1970, s.40, made it an offence to indulge in behaviour calculated to subject the debtor or members of his family or household to alarm, distress or humiliation, but made no mention of a civil claim for damages. Similarly, it is an offence for a landlord to harass a tenant (now Protection from Eviction Act 1977, s.1), but the Court of Appeal has held that it gives rise to no statutory cause of action (*McCall* v. *Abelesz* [1976] Q.B. 585). In part this was because damages for distress may now be awarded for breach of contract (above, p. 77).

(iii) *Wilful Wrongs and Damages*

ROOKES v. BARNARD

House of Lords [1964] A.C. 1129; [1964] 2 W.L.R. 269; 108 S.J. 93; [1964] 1 All E.R. 367, [1964] 1 Lloyd's Rep. 28

The facts, which are not relevant to the purpose for which the following extract is given, are stated below, p. 517.

Lord Devlin: . . . Exemplary damages are essentially different from ordinary damages. The object of damages in the usual sense of the term is to compensate. The object of exemplary damages is to punish and deter. It may well be thought that this confuses the civil and criminal functions of the law; and indeed, so far as I know, the idea of exemplary damages is peculiar to English law. There is not any decision of this House approving an award of exemplary damages and your Lordships therefore have to consider whether it is open to the House to remove an anomaly from the law of England.

It must be remembered that in many cases of tort damages are at large, that is to say, the award is not limited to the pecuniary loss that can be specifically proved. In the present case, for example, and leaving aside any question of exemplary or aggravated damages, the appellant's damages would not necessarily be confined to those which he would obtain in an action for wrongful dismissal. He can invite the jury to look at all the circumstances, the inconveniences caused to him by the change of job and the unhappiness maybe by a change of livelihood. In such a case as this, it is quite proper without any departure from the compensatory principle to award a round sum based on the pecuniary loss proved.

Moreover, it is very well established that in cases where the damages are at large the jury (or the judge if the award is left to him) can take into account the motives and conduct of the defendant where they aggravate the injury done to the plaintiff. There may be malevolence or spite or the manner of committing the wrong may be such as to injure the plaintiff's proper feelings of dignity and pride. These are matters which the jury can take into account in assessing the appropriate compensation. Indeed, when one examines the cases in which large damages have been awarded for conduct of this sort, it is not at all easy to say whether the idea of compensation or the idea of punishment has prevailed.

But there are also cases in the books where the awards given cannot be explained as compensatory, and I propose therefore to begin by examining the authorities in order to see how far and in what sort of cases the exemplary principle has been recognised. The history of exemplary damages is briefly and clearly stated by Professor Street in *Principles of the Law of Damages* (1962) at p. 28. They originated just 200 years ago in the *cause célèbre* of John Wilkes and the *North Briton* in which the legality of a general warrant was successfully challenged. Mr. Wilkes' house had been searched under a general warrant and the action of trespass which he brought as a result of it is reported in *Wilkes* v. *Wood* ((1763) Lofft. 1; 98 E.R. 489). Serjeant Glynn on his behalf asked for "large and exemplary damages," since trifling damages, he submitted, would put no stop at all to such proceedings. Pratt C.J., in his direction to the jury, said: "Damages are designed not only as a satisfaction to the injured person, but likewise as a punishment to the guilty, to deter from any such proceeding for the future, and as a proof of the detestation of the jury to the action itself." The jury awarded £1,000. It is worth noting that the Lord Chief Justice referred to "office precedents" which, he said, were not justification of a practice in itself illegal, though they might fairly be pleaded in mitigation of damages. This particular direction exemplifies very clearly his general direction, for a consideration of that sort could have no place in the assessment of compensation. . . .

In *Benson* v. *Frederick* ((1766) 3 Burr. 1845; 97 E.R. 1130) the plaintiff, a common soldier, obtained damages of £150 against his colonel who had ordered him to be flogged so as to vex a fellow officer. Lord Mansfield C.J. said that the damages "were very great, and beyond the proportion of what the man had suffered." But the sum awarded was upheld as damages in respect of an arbitrary and unjustifiable action and not more than the defendant was able to pay.

These authorities clearly justify the use of the exemplary principle; and for my part I should not wish, even if I felt at liberty to do so, to diminish its use in this type of case where it serves a valuable purpose in restraining the arbitrary and outrageous use of executive power.

. . . There are three cases in the Court of Appeal in which the principle has been stated and applied.

In *Owen and Smith (trading as Nuagin Car Service)* v. *Reo Motors (Britain) Ltd.* ((1934) 151 L.T. 274) the plaintiff, a motor dealer, had on his premises for display a chassis belonging to the defendants which they were at liberty to remove at any time, except that it was specially provided that if the plaintiff had constructed a body on the vehicle he should be at liberty to dismantle it before removal. The defendants, without notice to the plaintiff, entered his garage, took the chassis and dismantled the body in the street, the process being observed by some members of the public including one of the plaintiff's creditors. It does not appear that any injury was done to the plaintiff's property, but the Court of Appeal said it was a case for exemplary damages and awarded £100.

Loudon v. *Ryder* ([1953] 2 Q.B. 202) was a case of trespass and assault. The plaintiff was a young girl, and the defendant broke into her flat and tried to turn her out. Her injuries were comparatively trivial, but his behaviour was outrageous. The jury awarded her £1,500 damages for trespass, and £1,000 for assault; and £3,000 as exemplary damages, making £5,500 in all. This award was upheld in the Court of Appeal.

In *Williams* v. *Settle* ([1960] 1 W.L.R. 1072) the defendant was a professional photographer who had taken photographs of the plaintiff's wedding, the copyright being vested in the plaintiff. Two years later, when an event had occurred which caused the plaintiff to be exposed to publicity, the defendant sold the photographs to two national newspapers, and the publication caused the plaintiff great distress. The county court judge awarded the plaintiff £1,000 damages for breach of copyright. This award was upheld in the Court of Appeal and in both courts it was described as one of exemplary damages. . . .

These authorities convince me of two things. First, that your Lordships could not, without a complete disregard of precedent, and indeed of statute, now arrive at a determination that refused altogether to recognise the exemplary principle. Secondly, that there are certain categories of cases in which an award of exemplary damages can serve a useful purpose in vindicating the strength of the law and thus affording a practical justification for admitting into the civil law a principle which ought logically to belong to the criminal. I propose to state what these two categories are; and I propose also to state three general considerations which, in my opinion, should always be borne in mind when awards of exemplary damages are being made. I am well aware that what I am about to say will, if accepted, impose limits not hitherto expressed on such awards and that there is powerful, though not compelling, authority for allowing them a wider range. I shall not, therefore, conclude what I have to say on the general principles of law without returning to the authorities and making it clear to what extent I have rejected the guidance they may be said to afford.

The first category is oppressive, arbitrary or unconstitutional action by the servants of the government. I should not extend this category—I say this with particular reference to the facts of this case—to oppressive action by private corporations or individuals. Where one man is more powerful than another, it is inevitable that he will try to use his power to gain his ends; and if his power is much greater than the other's, he might, perhaps, be said to be using it oppressively. If he uses his power illegally, he must of course pay for his illegality in the ordinary way; but he is not to be punished simply because he is the more powerful. In the case of the government it is different, for the servants of the government are also the servants of the people and the use of their power must always be subordinate to their duty of service. It is true that there is something repugnant about a big man bullying a small man and, very likely, the bullying will be a source of humiliation that makes the case one for aggravated damages, but it is not, in my opinion, punishable by damages.

Cases in the second category are those in which the defendant's conduct has been calculated by him to make a profit for himself which may well exceed the compensation payable to the plaintiff. . . . It is a factor also that is taken into account in damages for libel; one man should not be allowed to sell another man's reputation for profit. Where a defendant with a cynical disregard for a plaintiff's rights has calculated that the money to be made out of his wrongdoing will probably exceed the damages at risk, it is necessary for the law to show that it cannot be broken with impunity. This category is not confined to money-making in the strict sense. It extends to cases in which the defendant is seeking to gain at the expense of the plaintiff some object—perhaps some property which he covets—which either he could not obtain at all or not obtain except at a price greater than he wants to put down. Exemplary damages can properly be awarded whenever it is necessary to teach a wrongdoer that tort does not pay.

To these two categories which are established as part of the common law there must of course be added any category in which exemplary damages are expressly authorised by statute.

I wish now to express three considerations which I think should always be borne in mind when awards of exemplary damages are being considered. First, the plaintiff cannot recover exemplary damages unless he is the victim of the punishable behaviour. The anomaly inherent in exemplary damages would become an absurdity if a plaintiff totally unaffected by some oppressive conduct which the jury wished to punish obtained a windfall in consequence.

Secondly, the power to award exemplary damages constitutes a weapon that, while it can be used in defence of liberty, as in the *Wilkes* case, can also be used against liberty. Some of the awards that juries have made in the past seem to me to amount to a greater punishment than would be likely to be incurred if the conduct were criminal; and, moreover, a punishment imposed without the safeguard which the criminal law gives to an offender. I should not allow the respect which is traditionally paid to an assessment of damages by a jury to prevent me from seeing that the weapon is used with restraint. It may even be that the House may find it necessary to follow the precedent it set for itself in *Benham* v. *Gambling* ([1941] A.C. 157), and place some arbitrary limit on awards of damages that are made by way of punishment. Exhortations to be moderate may not be enough.

Thirdly, the means of the parties, irrelevant in the assessment of compensation, are material in the assessment of exemplary damages. Everything which aggravates or mitigates the defendant's conduct is relevant. . . .

But when this has been said, there remains one class of case for which the authority is much more precise. It is the class of case in which the injury to the plaintiff has been aggravated by malice or by the manner of doing the injury, that is, the insolence or arrogance by which it is accompanied. . . .

. . . The direct authority for exemplary damages in this category of case lies in the three modern decisions of the Court of Appeal. I think that your Lordships, if you agree with my conclusion, are bound to express your dissent from most of the reasoning in all of them. . . .

This conclusion will, I hope, remove from the law a source of confusion between aggravated and exemplary damages which has troubled the learned commentators on the subject. Otherwise, it will not, I think, make much difference to the substance of the law or rob the law of the strength which it ought to have. Aggravated damages in this type of case can do most, if not all, of the work that could be done by exemplary damages. In so far as they do not, assaults and malicious injuries to property can generally be punished as crimes, whereas the objectionable conduct in the categories in which I have accepted the need for exemplary damages are not, generally speaking, within the criminal law and could not, even if the criminal law was to be amplified, conveniently be defined as crimes. I do not care for the idea that in matters criminal an aggrieved party should be given an option to inflict for his own benefit punishment by a method which denies to the offender the protection of the criminal law. . . .

Questions

1. It is not difficult to distinguish the damage suffered by the plaintiff, which is the object of compensation, from the behaviour of the defendant, which is the object of punishment. If aggravated damages may be awarded when the defendant has behaved outrageously, but only then, does it not follow that either unaggravated damages are not compensation or aggravated damages are punitive?

2. Consider the case where the plaintiff is a corporation rather than an individual. Could it be awarded (a) aggravated, (b) punitive damages? See *Columbia Picture Indus.* v. *Robinson* [1986] 3 All E.R. 338, 379–380.

3. Should the Chief Constable (effectively the public purse) be liable to pay the punitive damages imposed on a policeman who wilfully abuses his powers? See the statute above p. 236.

4. Suppose that the defendant has been convicted in criminal proceedings and sentenced for the fraud in respect of which he is now sued. Is there any objection to making him pay (a) aggravated, (b) punitive damages? (See *Archer* v. *Brown* [1984] 2 All E.R. 267; *Ashgar* v. *Armed* (cited in Gray, *Elements of Land Law* 959)).

5. "Aggravated damages are a response to conduct that shocks the plaintiff whereas exemplary damages are a response to conduct which shocks the court." (Migdal in 129 New L.J. 84 (1979), varying Davies L.J. in *Broadway Approvals* [1965] 2 All E.R. 523, 538). Do you agree with this?

6. Should it be lawful to insure oneself against liability to pay punitive damages? See the question raised in *du Pont de Nemours* v. *Agnew*, (1987) 137 New L.J. 884 (C.A.).

Note:

Rookes must be unique among House of Lords decisions in that it was almost immediately reversed by statute on point of liability, and by the Court of Appeal on point of damages. In both cases the reversal was temporary.

"Lord Devlin's whole approach was based on a fundamental fallacy" (Salmon L.J.); "the

decision was clearly wrong and must be treated as delivered *per incuriam*" (Phillimore L.J.);
"The new doctrine is hopelessly illogical and inconsistent" (Lord Denning) . . . (*Broome* v.
Cassell & Co. [1971] 2 Q.B. 354). The Privy Council had not demurred when the High Court
of Australia refused to follow Lord Devlin's advice (*Australian Consolidated Press* v. *Uren*
[1969] 1 A.C. 590), but such overt disobedience from the Court of Appeal was something
else. When *Broome* v. *Cassell & Co.* went to the House of Lords ([1972] A.C. 1027) five out
of the seven Lords of Appeal refuted these criticisms and adhered to the new rules restricting
punitive damages, with a slight extension of the two permitted categories at common law: the
servants of government whose arbitrary conduct may make them liable to exemplary damages
include local government officials and the police, and exemplary damages may be awarded
against those who deliberately and recklessly break the law with a view to gain even if the gain
cannot be proved to have eventuated.

Lord Devlin's categories are not very satisfactory. How is it worse for an official to cow
someone by abuse of legal authority than for a bully to terrify him by brute force? Why should
a sadist pay less because he inflicts pain for fun rather than for profit? Nor are the general
grounds for restricting the award of punitive damages at all strong. Safeguards are required in
criminal cases because the State is pursuing the citizen in order to obtain money for itself; the
same considerations do not apply where an outraged citizen asks the State to make the black-
guard pay a fine to him.

It is not clear how much has actually changed as a result of all this flurry. When a landlord
unlawfully evicted a tenant and his girl friend, kept them out of the apartment for ten weeks
and refused to comply with an injunction requiring him to remove the people he had installed
there, the county court judge awarded £1,000, the largest sum then in his power. The Court of
Appeal upheld the award with enthusiasm (*Drane* v. *Evangelou* [1978] 2 All E.R. 437). Lord
Devlin would not have approved, in view of his observation that although *Loudon* v. *Ryder*
[1953] 2 Q.B. 202 involved assault and battery as well as trespass to a dwelling "The case was
not one in which exemplary damages ought to have been given as such." Note that although
the defendant in *Drane* v. *Evangelou* was clearly guilty of an offence, no prosecution was
brought and he would have remained unpunished had exemplary damages not been awarded
against him.

Where there are several plaintiffs, and the total of compensatory damages is insufficient to
punish the defendant, the extra punitive element should be divided equally between the plaintiffs, though the aggravated damages awarded to them may vary. *Riches* v. *News Group
Newspapers* [1985] 2 All E.R. 845 (C.A.).

Section 2.—False Imprisonment

(i) *The Act*

BIRD v. JONES

Queen's Bench (1845) 7 Q.B. 742; 15 L.J.Q.B. 82; 5 L.T.(o.s.) 406; 10 J.P. 4; 9 Jur. 870; 115
E.R. 668

The plaintiff obtained a verdict in a trial before Lord Denman C.J. The defendant
obtained a rule nisi for a new trial on the ground of misdirection. The rule for a new
trial was made absolute, Lord Denman C.J. dissenting.

Patteson J.: This was an action of trespass for an assault and false imprisonment.
The pleas were: as to the assault, *son assault demesne;* as to the imprisonment, that
the plaintiff, before the imprisonment, assaulted the defendant, wherefore the
defendant gave him into custody. The replication was *de injuria* to each plea. This
puts in issue, as to the first plea, who committed the first assault; and, as to the
second, whether the imprisonment was before or after the assault, if any, committed by the plaintiff. . . .

Now the facts of this case appear to be as follows. A part of Hammersmith Bridge which is ordinarily used as a public footway was appropriated for seats to view a regatta on the river, and separated for that purpose from the carriage way by a temporary fence. The plaintiff insisted on passing along the part so appropriated, and attempted to climb over the fence. The defendant, being clerk of the Bridge Company, seized his coat, and tried to pull him back: the plaintiff, however, succeeded in climbing over the fence. The defendant then stationed two policemen to prevent, and they did prevent, the plaintiff from proceeding forwards along the footway; but he was told that he might go back into the carriage way, and proceed to the other side of the bridge, if he pleased. The plaintiff would not do so, but remained where he was above half an hour: and then, on the defendant still refusing to suffer him to go forwards along the footway, he endeavoured to force his way, and, in so doing, assaulted the defendant: whereupon he was taken into custody.

It is plain from these facts that the first assault was committed by the defendant when he tried to pull the plaintiff back as he was climbing over the fence: and, as the jury have found the whole transaction to have been continuous, the plaintiff would be entitled to retain the verdict which he has obtained on the issue as to the first plea. Again, if what passed before the plaintiff assaulted the defendant was in law an imprisonment of the plaintiff, that imprisonment was undoubtedly continuous, and the assault by the plaintiff would not have been before the imprisonment as alleged in the second plea, but during it, and in attempting to escape from it: and the plaintiff would, in that case, be entitled to retain the verdict which he has obtained on the issue as to the second plea. But, if what so passed was not in law an imprisonment, then the plaintiff ought to have replied the right of footway and the obstruction by the defendant, and that he necessarily assaulted him in the exercise of the right, and, not having so replied, is not entitled to the verdict. So that the case is reduced to the question, whether what passed before the assault by the plaintiff was or was not an imprisonment of the plaintiff in point of law.

I have no doubt that, in general, if one man compels another to stay in any given place against his will, he imprisons that other just as much as if he locked him up in a room: and I agree that it is not necessary, in order to constitute an imprisonment, that a man's person should be touched. I agree, also, that the compelling a man to go in a given direction against his will may amount to imprisonment. But I cannot bring my mind to the conclusion that, if one man merely obstructs the passage of another in a particular direction, whether by threat of personal violence or otherwise, leaving him at liberty to stay where he is or to go in any other direction if he pleases, he can be said thereby to imprison him. He does him wrong, undoubtedly, if there was a right to pass in that direction, and would be liable to an action on the case for obstructing the passage, or of assault, if, on the party persisting in going in that direction, he touched his person, or so threatened him as to amount to an assault. But imprisonment is, as I apprehend, a total restraint of the liberty of the person, for however short a time, and not a partial obstruction of his will, whatever inconvenience it may bring on him. The quality of the act cannot, however, depend on the right of the opposite party. If it be an imprisonment to prevent a man passing along the public highway, it must be equally so to prevent him passing further along a field into which he has broken by a clear act of trespass.

. . . Upon the whole, I am of opinion that the only imprisonment proved in this case was that which occurred when the plaintiff was taken into custody after he had assaulted the defendant, and that the second plea was made out; I therefore think that the rule for a new trial ought to be made absolute.

Coleridge J.: . . . I lay out of consideration the question of right or wrong between these parties. The acts will amount to imprisonment neither more nor less from their being wrongful or capable of justification.

And I am of opinion that there was no imprisonment. To call it so appears to me

to confound partial obstruction and disturbance with total obstruction and detention. A prison may have its boundary large or narrow, visible and tangible, or,
though real, still in the conception only; it may itself be movable or fixed: but a
boundary it must have; and that boundary the party imprisoned must be prevented
from passing; he must be prevented from leaving that place, within the ambit of
which the party imprisoning would confine him, except by prison-breach. Some
confusion seems to me to arise from confounding imprisonment of the body with
mere loss of freedom: it is one part of the definition of freedom to be able to go
whithersoever one pleases; but imprisonment is something more than the mere loss
of this power; it includes the notion of restraint within some limits defined by a will
or power exterior to our own. . . .

Lord Denman C.J. (dissenting): I have not drawn up a formal judgment in this case,
because I hoped to the last that the arguments which my learned brothers would
produce in support of their opinion might alter mine. We have freely discussed the
matter both orally and in written communications; but, after hearing what they
have advanced, I am compelled to say that my first impression remains. If, as I must
believe, it is a wrong one, it may be in some measure accounted for by the circumstances attending the case. A company unlawfully obstructed a public way for their
own profit, extorting money from passengers, and hiring policemen to effect this
purpose. The plaintiff, wishing to exercise his right of way, is stopped by force, and
ordered to move in a direction which he wished not to take. He is told at the same
time that a force is at hand ready to compel his submission. That proceeding
appears to me equivalent to being pulled by the collar out of the one line and into
the other.

There is some difficulty perhaps in defining imprisonment in the abstract without
reference to its illegality; nor it is necessary for me to do so, because I consider
these acts as amounting to imprisonment. That word I understand to mean any
restraint of the person by force. In Buller's *Nisi Prius* (p. 22) it is said: "Every
restraint of a man's liberty under the custody of another, either in a gaol, house,
stocks or in the street, is in law an imprisonment; and whenever it is done without a
proper authority, is false imprisonment, for which the law gives an action; and this
is commonly joined to assault and battery; for every imprisonment includes a battery, and every battery an assault." It appears, therefore, that the technical
language has received a very large construction, and that there need not be any
touching of the person: a locking up would constitute an imprisonment, without
touching. From the language of Thorpe C.J., which Mr. Selwyn (Vol. ii, p. 915,
11th ed., tit. Imprisonment) cites from the *Book of Assizes* (22 Ass. fol. 104, B, pl.
85), it appears that, even in very early times, restraint of liberty by force was understood to be the reasonable definition of imprisonment.

I had no idea that any person in these times supposed any particular boundary to
be necessary to constitute imprisonment, or that the restraint of a man's person
from doing what he desires ceases to be an imprisonment because he may find some
means of escape.

It is said that the party here was at liberty to go in another direction. I am not
sure that in fact he was, because the same unlawful power which prevented him
from taking one course might, in case of acquiescence, have refused him any other.
But this liberty to do something else does not appear to me to affect the question of
imprisonment. As long as I am prevented from doing what I have a right to do, of
what importance is it that I am permitted to do something else? How does the
imposition of an unlawful condition show that I am not restrained? If I am locked in
a room, am I not imprisoned because I might effect my escape through a window,
or because I might find an exit dangerous or inconvenient to myself, as by wading
through water or by taking a route so circuitous that my necessary affairs would
suffer by delay?

It appears to me that this is a total deprivation of liberty with reference to the purpose for which he lawfully wished to employ his liberty: and, being effected by force, it is not the mere obstruction of a way, but a restraint of the person. The case cited as occurring before Lord Chief Justice Tindal, as I understand it, is much in point. He held it an imprisonment where the defendant stopped the plaintiff on his road till he had read a libel to him. Yet he did not prevent his escaping in another direction.

It is said that, if any damage arises from such obstruction, a special action on the case may be brought. Must I then sue out a new writ stating that the defendant employed direct force to prevent my going where my business called me, whereby I sustained loss? And, if I do, is it certain that I shall not be told that I have misconceived my remedy, for all flows from the false imprisonment, and that should have been the subject of an action of trespass and assault? For the jury properly found that the whole of the defendant's conduct was continuous: it commenced in illegality; and the plaintiff did right to resist it as an outrageous violation of the liberty of the subject from the very first.

Note:

This is the first decision we have had under the old system of pleading, and it is very illustrative.

First, the plaintiff was not, as might be thought on a cursory reading, complaining of being held up on Hammersmith Bridge for half an hour. He was complaining of having had to spend a night in jail after being arrested by the defendant for breach of the peace.

Secondly, the decision turned entirely on the pleadings. The question was not whether the plaintiff was entitled to recover on the facts—he was, indeed—but whether the replication framed for him by his counsel was appropriate in view of the facts.

As to the substance, students will recall the tort of public nuisance, and the rule that a person cannot sue unless he has suffered some particular damage as a result of the illegal obstruction (above, p. 174). The plaintiff here had not. If this obstruction had been held to constitute an imprisonment, that rule would have been wholly subverted, because in an action of false imprisonment no damage has to be proved.

Now a person is entitled to abate a thing which is a nuisance. That is why the plaintiff did no wrong in climbing over the fence. That is why he might have retained his verdict in assault against the defendant. But the defendant had stopped assaulting him by the time the plaintiff tried to force his way past; at that stage the defendant had stopped being an assailant and was merely a nuisance. People often are a nuisance, but you cannot hit them even so, though you may hit your gaoler. To put it differently, you may use force against people in order to get *out* but not in order to get *past*.

HERRING v. BOYLE

Court of Exchequer (1834) 1 Cr.M. & R. 377; 6 C. & P. 496; 4 Tyr. 801; 3 L.J.Ex. 344; 149 E.R. 1126

The plaintiff, having been nonsuited at the trial, obtained a rule nisi for a new trial. The rule was discharged.

Bolland B.: This was an action of trespass for assault and false imprisonment, brought by an infant by his next friend. The facts of the case were these: the plaintiff had been placed by his mother at the school kept by the defendant, and it appeared that she had applied to take him away. The schoolmaster very improperly refused to give him up to his mother, unless she paid an amount which he claimed to be due. The question is, whether it appears upon the judge's notes that there was any evidence of a trespass to go to the jury? I am of opinion that there was not, and, consequently, that this rule must be discharged. It has been argued on the part of the plaintiff that the misconduct of the defendant amounted to a false imprisonment. I cannot find any thing upon the notes of the learned judge which shows that the plaintiff was at all cognisant of any restraint. There are many cases which show that it is not necessary to constitute an imprisonment, that the hand should be laid upon the person; but in no case has any conduct been held to amount to an imprisonment in the absence of the party supposed to be imprisoned. An officer may make an arrest without laying his hand on the party arrested; but in the present case, as far as we know, the boy may have been willing to stay; he does not appear to have been cognisant of any restraint, and there was no evidence of any act whatsoever done by the defendant in his presence. I think that we cannot construe the refusal to the mother in the boy's absence, and without his being cognisant of any restraint, to be an imprisonment of him against his will; and therefore I am of opinion that the rule must be discharged.

Alderson B.: There was a total absence of any proof of consciousness of restraint on the part of the plaintiff. No act of restraint was committed in his presence; and I am of opinion that the refusal in his absence to deliver him up to his mother was not a false imprisonment. My brother Parke, who heard the rule moved, but who was not present at the argument, concurs in the opinion of the court.

Gurney B.: This plaintiff complains of an assault and false imprisonment. There was no evidence of any restraint upon him. There was no evidence that he had any knowledge of his mother having desired that he should be permitted to go home, nor that any thing passed between the plaintiff and defendant which showed that there was any compulsion upon the boy; and there was nothing to show that he was conscious that he was in any respect restrained.

Rule discharged.

Questions

1. Does this case say that the person imprisoned must know that he is imprisoned, or that the fact that a boy does not return from school does not show that he was not glad to stay there, or that the defendant must be shown to be guilty of an act, as opposed to uttering a threat, before he will be liable in trespass?

2. Suppose that in the written contract for schooling had been the term "Under no condition will boys be allowed to return home until outstanding fees are paid." Would this make any difference in a case where an imprisonment could be shown?

3. In *Meering* v. *Graham-White Aviation Co.* (1919) 122 L.T. 44, Atkin L.J. held that knowledge of the imprisonment was not an essential element in the plaintiff's cause of action. Does the principal case (which was not cited to him) conflict with that? If it does, which do you prefer? And what would you do with the case where a senile millionaire is kidnapped by the defendants, but is so kindly treated that he does not understand himself to be under constraint?

ROBINSON v. BALMAIN NEW FERRY CO. LTD.

Privy Council [1910] A.C. 295; 79 L.J.P.C. 84; 26 T.L.R. 143

The plaintiff, a lawyer, had a verdict for £100 from a jury before Darley C.J. The defendant obtained a rule nisi to set aside the verdict and for a new trial or nonsuit or verdict for the defendant. The Supreme Court of New South Wales discharged the rule. The High Court of Australia reversed that decision. The plaintiff appealed without success to the Judicial Committee of the Privy Council.

Lord Loreburn L.C.: . . . The plaintiff paid a penny on entering the wharf to stay there till the boat should start and then be taken by the boat to the other side. The defendants were admittedly always ready and willing to carry out their part of this contract. Then the plaintiff changed his mind and wished to go back. The rules as to the exit from the wharf by the turnstile required a penny for any person who went through. This the plaintiff refused to pay, and he was by force prevented from going through the turnstile. He then claimed damages for assault and false imprisonment.

There was no complaint, at all events there was no question left to the jury by the plaintiff's request, of any excessive violence, and in the circumstances admitted it is clear to their Lordships that there was no false imprisonment at all. The plaintiff was merely called upon to leave the wharf in the way in which he contracted to leave it. There is no law requiring the defendants to make the exit from their premises gratuitous to people who come there upon a definite contract which involves their leaving the wharf by another way; and the defendants were entitled to resist a forcible passage through their turnstile.

The question whether the notice which was affixed to these premises was brought home to the knowledge of the plaintiff is immaterial, because the notice itself is immaterial.

When the plaintiff entered the defendants' premises there was nothing agreed as to the terms on which he might go back, because neither party contemplated his going back. When he desired to do so the defendants were entitled to impose a reasonable condition before allowing him to pass through their turnstile from a place to which he had gone of his own free will. The payment of a penny was a quite fair condition, and if he did not choose to comply with it the defendants were not bound to let him through. He could proceed on the journey he had contracted for.

Under these circumstances their Lordships consider that, when the defendants at the end of the case submitted that there ought to be a nonsuit, the learned judge ought to have nonsuited the plaintiff. Their Lordships are glad that they can thus arrive, in accordance with law, at this decision, because they regard the plaintiff's conduct as thoroughly unreasonable in this case.

Questions

1. Was the plaintiff's complaint (a) "He shut me in," or (b) "He wouldn't let me out"?

2. Suppose that the plaintiff had no penny at all. Would he have to stay there for ever without being able to bring an action for false imprisonment? Would it matter whether he knew a penny to be exigible on exit?

3. Suppose that the plaintiff had a sixpence, and the defendants declined to change it for him, though they could?

4. The owner of a mansion looks out of his window and sees his two Dobermann Pinscher dogs growling at the bottom of an apple tree, which contains an infant trespasser. He does not call off the dogs, and the child remains there all night. Is there any liability for false imprisonment? Is there any liability at all?

Note:

Read Glanville Williams, "Two Cases on False Imprisonment," in *Law, Justice and Equity* (Essays in tribute to G. W. Keeton) (1967), 47–55.

False imprisonment is also a crime, given the necessary *mens rea*: see *R. v. D* [1984] 2 All E.R. 449 (H.L.) and *Mohammed Mogbular Rahman* (1985) 81 Cr.App.R. 349 (restraining one's own child).

Parties to a suit for false imprisonment are entitled to demand trial by jury, as in claims for defamation and malicious prosecution (Supreme Court Act 1981, s.69(1)). Even in a minor case of false imprisonment the question of exemplary damages must apparently be left to the jury: *Holden* v. *Chief Constable of Lancs.* [1986] 3 All E.R. 836 (C.A.). Why do you think that special provision is made for false imprisonment in this way? Would it be better to provide that all claims by individuals against the police be triable by jury?

(ii) *Directness*

FLEWSTER v. ROLE

Nisi Prius (1808) 1 Camp. 187; 170 E.R. 924

In October 1807 the defendant went to the naval recruitment centre, gave the plaintiff's name and address and said that he was liable to be conscripted as a sailor. The press-gang accordingly seized the plaintiff, and detained him on board until it emerged that the only time he had ever been on a ship before was a previous occasion when he had been wrongly impressed.

Lord Ellenborough (to the jury): This is not like a malicious prosecution, where the party gets a valid warrant or writ, and gives it to an officer to be executed. There was clearly a trespass here in seizing the plaintiff, and the defendant therefore was a trespasser in procuring it to be done.—Nor is any proof of malice necessary. If a person causes another to be impressed, he does it at his own peril, and is liable in damages if that person proves not to have been subject to the impress service. If the defendant in this case had said, that she believed the plaintiff was liable to be impressed, leaving it to the officer of the press-gang to make the necessary inquiries, and to act as he should think most advisable—for such a line of conduct, which a regard for the public service would have induced her to adopt, she would not have been amenable in this action. But she took upon herself positively to aver that he was compellable to serve in a King's ship, and she must therefore answer for the consequences.

The jury returned a verdict for the plaintiff (who was represented by the Attorney-General).

Note:
There must have been a great demand for sailors in England in October 1807, since the English fleet had just taken possession of the neutral Danish fleet, after a bombardment of Copenhagen which cost 2,000 civilian lives.

GOSDEN v. ELPHICK

Exchequer (1849) 4 Ex. 445; 19 L.J.Ex. 9; 14 L.T.(o.s.) 157; 14 J.P.38; 13 Jur. 989; 154 E.R. 1287

The plaintiff and a couple of friends were showing horses at a fair when one of the horses broke loose and injured a boy. The defendant Bennett, a constable, arrived on the scene and was about to arrest one of the plaintiff's mates when the defendant Elphick, a bystander, said: "That's not the man" and pointed to the plaintiff and said "That's the man." Bennett then arrested the plaintiff.

Alderson B. told the jury that Elphick would be liable if he had directed the constable to take the plaintiff into custody, but that he would not be liable if his object was merely to offer himself as a witness, and to tell the constable that the wrong man was in custody. The jury brought in a verdict for the defendant. The plaintiff moved for a new trial on the grounds of misdirection.

Rolfe B. (*arguendo*), after referring to *Flewster* v. *Role*: I must dissent from that ruling. The case may mean that the facts were evidence from which the jury might infer a wrongful imprisonment. . . .

Alderson B. (*arguendo*): . . . it would come to this, that if a constable in search of a delinquent says, "Which is the man?" the persons present must not point him out. Or, if I see a man who is perfectly innocent taken into custody, and the guilty man running away, I must not say so, or I shall be liable in trespass. The evidence in *Flewster* v. *Role* very likely showed that the defendant bore some spite to the plaintiff. . . .

The motion for a new trial was refused.

GRINHAM v. WILLEY

Exchequer (1859) 4 H. & N. 496; 28 L.J.Ex. 242; 33 L.T.(o.s.) 110; 23 J.P. 280; 5 Jur.(n.s.) 444; 7 W.R. 463; 157 E.R. 934

The defendant had his watch stolen in *The Crown* and offered a reward for its return. Shortly thereafter the plaintiff barmaid handed him a package, saying that a stranger had asked her to give it to him. Inside the package was the watch. The defendant then called a policeman and told him how the plaintiff had returned his watch after he had offered a reward for it. After putting some questions to the plaintiff, the policeman took her down to the police station where the defendant signed the charge-sheet.

The jury found that the defendant did not give the plaintiff into custody, but consented to her being taken into custody. Bramwell B. directed a verdict for the defendant, with leave to the plaintiff to move for a verdict in her favour. This she now did.

Pollock C.B.: There will be no rule. The circumstances of this case are, that the defendant appealed to the authorities who are charged with the preservation of the peace. The arrest and detention were the acts of the police officer, and the defendant did nothing more than he was bound to do, *viz.*, sign the charge-sheet. He may have been liable if he acted mala fide, but not otherwise. I agree with the observations of Lord Cranworth and Alderson B. as to the case of *Flewster* v. *Role*. We ought to take care that people are not put in peril for making complaint when a crime has been committed. If a charge be made mala fide, there are ample means of redress. But in the absence of mala fides we ought not to be too critical in our examination of the facts, to see if something is not done without which the charge against the suspected person could not have been proceeded with. A person ought not to be held responsible in trespass, unless he directly and immediately causes the imprisonment.

Bramwell B.: . . . An offence was committed; the defendant sent for a policeman, who made inquiry, and on his own authority arrested the plaintiff. The defendant signed the charge-sheet; but in doing so he did nothing but obey the direction of the police. It may have been hard upon the plaintiff that she was imprisoned, but it was the act of the constable.

I think the difficulty of the jury arose from their not being able to understand the distinction I pointed out between the defendant being the cause of the arrest in the sense that he had given the information which induced the officer to make it, and causing it in the sense that he directed the officer to make it. . . .

The rule for a verdict for the plaintiff was refused.

Question
Are the last three cases reconcilable?

RAFAEL v. VERELST

Common Pleas (1776) 2 Black.W. 1055; 96 E.R. 621

The plaintiff was an Armenian trader in Oudh, where Suja Dowla was the Nabob. The Nabob wrote to the defendant, who was Governor of Bengal, complaining of the behaviour of the traders; in his reply the defendant withdrew his support for the traders and invited the Nabob to arrest the plaintiff and send him to Calcutta. The Nabob then ordered the English sepoys stationed in Oudh to arrest the plaintiff, which they did.

The question was whether the defendant could be held responsible for the imprisonment by a Sovereign. The jury found that Suja Dowla acted "under the awe and influence of the defendant, and acted contrary to his own inclination, being fearful of offending him," and gave a verdict for the plaintiff with damages of £4,000. The verdict was upheld.

Blackstone J.: . . . The Nabob is a mere machine—an instrument and engine of the defendant. . . .

Note:
   Being an imperialist is a thankless task. Clive, the governor of Bengal before Verelst, committed suicide; Warren Hastings, governor after him, was impeached. Verelst himself, "a man of strict integrity and great industry," was "ruined by litigation raised by corrupt Bengal influences" and died in poverty at Boulogne (*Dictionary of National Biography*). The main corrupt influence was a Dutch adventurer called Willem Bolts, who quit his job with the East India Co. and made £90,000 by illegal trade and trafficking through agents such as Rafael before Verelst had him shipped back to England (see *Bolts* v. *Att.-Gen.* (1773) 1 Brown 421, 1 E.R. 661 and *Bolts* v. *Purvis* (1775) 2 W.Bl. 1023, 96 E.R. 601). Bolts too was ruined by litigation and the expense of a publishing campaign against Verelst; he became a colonel under Maria Theresa and returned to India where he set up six establishments for the Austrian East India Company.

HARNETT v. BOND

House of Lords [1925] A.C. 669; 94 L.J.K.B. 569; 133 L.T. 482; 89 J.P. 182; 41 T.L.R. 509; [1925] All E.R. Rep. 110

The plaintiff was an inmate of Malling Place, a licensed house for lunatics run by Dr. Adam, the second defendant. He was granted a month's leave, but Dr. Adam had the power to reconfine him during that period. On the second day the plaintiff went to the offices of the Commissioners of Lunacy and saw one of the Commissioners, Bond, the second defendant. Bond came to the conclusion that the plaintiff was not fit to be at large, so he telephoned Dr. Adam to send a car and detained the plaintiff until it arrived three hours later. Back at Malling Place Dr. Adam examined the plaintiff and decided that he was insane. The plaintiff was confined in various institutions for the next nine years, but then he escaped and was found to be quite sane.

The jury found that the plaintiff had not been of unsound mind at the time the first defendant had detained him in the Commissioners' offices with a view to his further detention at Malling Place. The judge instructed them that in fixing the damages to be paid by the first defendant they might take account of the subsequent period of confinement. The jury gave a verdict for the plaintiff for £5,000 against Bond alone and for £20,000 against both defendants.

The Court of Appeal directed judgment for the second defendant on the ground that there was no evidence that he had failed to exercise reasonable care and that he would not be liable unless he had so failed; they also ordered a new trial against Bond, the Commissioner.

The plaintiff's appeal to the House of Lords was dismissed.

Viscount Cave L.C.: . . . It is not disputed that, on the assumption that the findings of the jury as to the appellant's mental condition on December 14, 1912, were correct, Dr. Bond had no right to cause the appellant to be detained at the office pending the arrival of Dr. Adam's car, and is liable in damages for that illegal detention. But those damages must, on the authorities, be confined to such as were the direct consequence of the wrong committed; and to hold that the detention of the appellant at the offices for a few hours was the direct cause, not only of his being retaken and conveyed to Malling Place, but also of his being confined in that and other houses until October 1921 appears to me to be impossible. . . . The retaking and confinement were the independent acts of Dr. Adam, and each of them was a *novus actus interveniens* sufficient to break the chain of causation.

Lord Dunedin observed that although Bond wanted the plaintiff to be detained at Malling Place, he had no power to ensure that he should be detained there, and therefore could not be liable for his detention.

Section 3.—Assault

READ v. COKER

Common Pleas (1853) 13 C.B. 850; 22 L.J.C.P. 201; 21 L.T.(o.s.) 156; 17 Jur. 990; 1 W.R. 413; 138 E.R. 1437

The plaintiff was a paper-stainer in financial difficulties and in arrears with his rent. The defendant purchased his equipment and paid the rent under an agreement which secured to the plaintiff a weekly allowance. One day the defendant told the plaintiff to leave the premises, and when the plaintiff refused, the defendant collected together some of his workmen who mustered round the plaintiff, tucking up their sleeves and aprons, and threatened to break the plaintiff's neck if he did not leave. The plaintiff did leave, and now brought an action of trespass for assault.

At the trial Talfourd J. left it to the jury to say whether there was an intention on the part of the defendant to assault, and whether the plaintiff was apprehensive of personal violence if he did not retire. The jury found for the plaintiff, damages one farthing. The defendant asked for a new trial on the grounds of misdirection by the judge.

Byles Serjt. (*arguendo*): That which was proved as to the first count, clearly did not amount to an assault. [JERVIS C.J.: It was as much an assault as a sheriff's officer being in a room with a man against whom he has a writ, and saying to him "You are my prisoner," is an arrest.] To constitute an assault, there must be something more than a threat of violence. An assault is thus defined in Buller's *Nisi Prius,* p. 15: "An assault is an attempt or offer, by force or violence, to do a corporal hurt to another, as, by pointing a pitchfork at him, when standing within reach; presenting a gun at him [within shooting distance]; drawing a sword, and waving it in a menacing manner, &c., *The Queen* v. *Ingram* (1712) 1 Salk. 384; 91 E.R. 335. But no words can amount to an assault, though perhaps they may in some cases serve to explain a doubtful action,—1 Hawk.P.C. 133; as, if a man were to lay his hand upon his sword, and say, 'If it were not assize time, he would not take such language:' the words would prevent the action from being construed to be an assault, because they show he had no intent to do him any corporal hurt at that time: *Tuberville* v. *Savage* (1669) 1 Mod. 3; 86 E.R. 684." So, in Selwyn's *Nisi Prius*, 11th ed., 26, it is said: "An assault is an attempt, with force or violence, to do a corporal injury to another, as, by holding up a fist in a menacing manner; striking at another with a cane or stick, though the party striking may miss his aim; drawing a sword or bayonet; throwing a bottle or glass with intent to wound or strike; presenting a gun at a person who is within the distance to which the gun will carry; pointing a pitchfork at a person who is within reach,—*Genner* v. *Sparks* (1705) 6 Mod. 173; 1 Salk. 79; 87 E.R. 928—or by any other similar act, accompanied with such circumstances as denote at the time an intention coupled with a present ability,—see *Stephens* v. *Myers* (1830) 4 C. & P. 349; 172 E.R. 735—of using actual violence, against the person of another." So, in 3 Bl.Comm. 120, an assault is said to be "an attempt or offer to beat another, without touching him; as, if one lifts up his cane or his fist, in a threatening manner, at another; or strikes at him but misses him; this is an assault, *insultus,* which Finch (L. 202) describes to be 'an unlawful setting upon one's person.' " [JERVIS C.J.: If a man comes into a room, and lays his cane on the table, and says to another, "If you don't go out, I will knock you on the head," would not that be an assault?] Clearly not: it is a mere threat, unaccompanied by any gesture or action towards carrying it into effect. The direction of the learned judge as to this point was erroneous. He should have told the jury that, to constitute an assault, there must be an attempt, coupled with a present ability to do personal violence to the party; instead of leaving it to them, as he did, to say what the plaintiff thought, and not what they (the jury) thought was the defendant's intention. There must be some act done denoting a present ability and an intention to assault.

Jervis C.J.: . . . If anything short of actual striking will in law constitute an assault, the facts here clearly showed that the defendant was guilty of an assault. There was a threat of violence exhibiting an intention to assault, and a present ability to carry the threat into execution. . . .
Rule discharged on first count.

BALL v. AXTEN

Nisi Prius (1866) 4 F. & F. 1019; 176 E.R. 890

There was an altercation between a farmer and the defendant who was hunting without permission on his land. The defendant struck a blow at the farmer's dog, and hit his wife who was trying to protect it.

Lord Cockburn C.J.: . . . even though the defendant had not aimed the blow at the woman, there was no doubt an assault. . . .

Question
Even after *Fowler* v. *Lanning* (above, p. 285)?

Section 4.—Battery

GIBBONS v. PEPPER

King's Bench (1695) 1 Ld. Raym. 38; 4 Mod. 404; 2 Salk. 637; 91 E.R. 922

Per curiam: . . . for if I ride upon a horse, and J.S. whips the horse, so that he runs away with me and runs over any other person, he who whipped the horse is guilty of the battery, and not me. But if I by spurring was the cause of such accident, then I am guilty. In the same manner, if A. takes the hand of B. and with it strikes C., A. is the trespasser and not B.

FAGAN v. METROPOLITAN POLICE COMMISSIONER

Queen's Bench Division [1969] 1 Q.B. 439; [1968] 3 W.L.R. 1120; [1968] 3 All E.R. 443; 52 Cr.App.R. 700 (noted 85 L.Q.R. 162)

As Fagan was parking his car at the direction of a police constable, the car came to rest on the constable's foot. Urged by the constable to back off, Fagan became abusive and switched off the engine before eventually complying.

Fagan was convicted by the Willesden Magistrates of assaulting a police constable in the execution of his duty, and his appeal to Middlesex Quarter Sessions was dismissed, as was his present appeal to the Divisional Court, Bridge J. dissenting.

James J. (with whom **Lord Parker C.J.** agreed): . . . The justices . . . were left in doubt whether the mounting of the wheel on to the officer's foot was deliberate or accidental. They were satisfied, however, beyond all reasonable doubt that the appellant "knowingly, provocatively and unnecessarily" allowed the wheel to remain on the foot after the officer said "Get off, you are on my foot." They found that, on these facts, an assault was proved. . . .

In our judgment, the question arising, which has been argued on general principles, falls to be decided on the facts of the particular case. An assault is any act which intentionally—or possibly recklessly—causes another person to apprehend immediate and unlawful personal violence. Although "assault" is an independent crime and is to be treated as such, for practical purposes today "assault" is generally synonymous with the term "battery," and is a term used to mean the actual intended use of unlawful force to another person without his consent. On the facts of the present case, the "assault" alleged involved a "battery." Where an assault involved a battery, it matters not, in our judgment, whether the battery is inflicted directly by the body of the offender or through the medium of some weapon or instrument controlled by the action of the offender. An assault may be committed by the laying of a hand on another, and the action does not cease to be an assault if it is a stick held in the hand and not the hand itself which is laid on the person of the victim. So, for our part, we see no difference in principle between the action of stepping on to a person's toe and maintaining that position and the action of driving a car on to a person's foot and sitting in the car while its position on the foot is maintained.

To constitute this offence, some intentional act must have been performed; a *mere* omission to act cannot amount to an assault. Without going into the question whether words alone can constitute an assault, it is clear that the words spoken by the appellant could not alone amount to an assault; they can only shed a light on the appellant's action. For our part, we think that the crucial question is whether, in this case, the act of the appellant can be said to be complete and spent at the moment of time when the car wheel came to rest on the foot, or whether his act is to be regarded as a continuing act operating until the wheel was removed. In our judgment, a distinction is to be drawn between acts which are complete—though results may continue to flow—and those acts which are continuing. Once the act is complete, it cannot thereafter be said to be a threat to inflict unlawful force on the victim. If the act, as distinct from the results thereof, is a continuing act, there is a continuing threat to inflict unlawful force. If the assault involves a battery and that battery continues, there is a continuing act of assault. For an assault to be committed, both the elements of *actus reus* and *mens rea* must be present at the same time. The "*actus reus*" is the action causing the effect on the victim's mind. . . . The "*mens rea*" is the intention to cause that effect. It is not necessary that *mens rea* should be present at the inception of the *actus reus*; it can be superimposed on an existing act. On the other hand, the subsequent inception of *mens rea* cannot convert an act which has been completed without *mens rea* into an assault.

In our judgment, the justices at Willesden and quarter sessions were right in law. On the facts found, the action of the appellant may have been initially unintentional, but the time came when, knowing that the wheel was on the officer's foot, the appellant (i) remained seated in the car so that his body through the medium of the car was in contact with the officer, (ii) switched off the ignition of the car, (iii) maintained the wheel of the car on the foot, and (iv) used words indicating the intention of keeping the wheel in that position. For our part, we cannot regard such conduct as mere omission or inactivity. There was an act constituting a battery which at its inception was not criminal because there was no element of intention, but which became criminal from the moment the intention was formed to produce the apprehension which was flowing from the continuing act. The fallacy of the appellant's argument is that it seeks to equate the facts of this case with such a case as where a motorist has accidentally run over a person and, that action having been completed, fails to assist the victim with the intent that the victim should suffer.

We would dismiss this appeal.

Bridge J.: I fully agree with my lords as to the relevant principles to be applied. No mere omission to act can amount to an assault. Both the elements of *actus reus* and *mens rea* must be present at the same time, but the one may be superimposed on the other. It is in the application of these principles to the highly unusual facts of this case that I have, with regret, reached a different conclusion from the majority of the court. I have no sympathy at all for the appellant, who behaved disgracefully; but I have been unable to find any way of regarding the facts which satisfied me that they amounted to the crime of assault. This has not been for want of trying; but at every attempt I have encountered the inescapable question: after the wheel of the appellant's car had accidentally come to rest on the constable's foot, what was it that the appellant *did* which constituted the act of assault? However the question is approached, the answer which I feel obliged to give is: precisely nothing. The car rested on the foot by its own weight and remained stationary by its own inertia. The appellant's fault was that he omitted to manipulate the controls to set it in motion again.

Neither the fact that the appellant remained in the driver's seat nor that he switched off the ignition seem to me to be of any relevance. The constable's plight would have been no better, but might well have been worse, if the appellant had alighted from the car leaving the ignition switched on. Similarly, I can get no help from the suggested analogies. If one man accidentally treads on another's toe or touches him with a stick, but deliberately maintains pressure with foot or stick after the victim protests, there is clearly an assault; but there is no true parallel between such cases and the present case. It is not, to my mind, a legitimate use of language to speak of the appellant "holding" or "maintaining" the car wheel on the constable's foot. The expression which corresponds to the reality is that used by the justices in the Case Stated. They say, quite rightly, that he "allowed" the wheel to remain.

With a reluctantly dissenting voice, I would allow this appeal and quash the appellant's conviction.

WILSON v. PRINGLE

Court of Appeal [1987] Q.B. 237; [1986] 2 All E.R. 440; [1986] 3 W.L.R. 1; 130 S.J. 468

The plaintiff and defendant, 13-year-old classmates, were walking down the school corridor after a maths class, the plaintiff being in front, when the defendant pulled at the sports bag which the plaintiff was carrying over his right shoulder. The plaintiff fell and suffered a nasty hip injury. The defendant pleaded that the incident was "ordinary horse-play between pupils in the same school and the same class."

The judge held that the defendant was so clearly liable for trespass on these averments that he gave the plaintiff leave to proceed to judgment without a trial, under Order 14. On the defendant's appeal, the Court of Appeal gave him leave to defend.

Croom-Johnson L.J. delivered the judgment of the Court. . . .

It is not possible, even if it were desirable, to ignore the distinction between torts of negligence and torts of trespass strictly so called. This distinction has to be borne in mind in view of a submission made on behalf of the defendant, which would have had the effect of blurring the lines of demarcation between the two causes of action. In a situation (such as the present) in which both causes of action are sought to be raised it is necessary to be as precise as possible in seeing which of the facts giving rise to that situation are appropriate to which cause of action. . . .

The defendant in the present case has sought to add to the list of necessary ingredients. He has submitted that before trespass to the person will lie it is not only the touching that must be deliberate but the infliction of injury. The plaintiff's counsel, on the other hand, contends that it is not the injury to the person which must be intentional, but the act of touching or battery which precedes it: as he put it, what must be intentional is the application of force and not the injury. In support of his contention, counsel for the defendant has relied on passages in the judgments in *Fowler* v. *Lanning* [above p. 285] and *Letang* v. *Cooper* [above p. 288].

[His Lordship discussed those cases.]

In our view, the submission made by counsel for the plaintiff is correct. It is the act and not the injury which must be intentional. An intention to injure is not essential to an action for trespass to the person. It is the mere trespass by itself which is the offence.

That does not answer the question, what does entitle an injured plaintiff to sue for the tort of trespass to the person? Reference must be made to one further case: *Williams* v. *Humphrey* (February 12, 1975, unreported), decided by Talbot J. There the defendant, a boy just under 16, pushed the plaintiff into a swimming pool and caused him physical injury. The judge found the defendant acted negligently and awarded damages. But there was another claim in trespass. Talbot J. rejected the submission that the action would not lie unless there was an intent to injure. He held that it was sufficient, if the act was intentional, that there was no justification for it. In the present Ord. 14 proceedings the judge relied on that decision.

The reasoning in *Williams* v. *Humphrey* is all right as far as it goes, but it does not go far enough. It did not give effect to the reasoning of the older authorities, such as *Tuberville* v. *Savage* ((1669) 86 E.R. 684), *Cole* v. *Turner* ((1704) 90 E.R. 958) and *Williams* v. *Jones* ((1736) 95 E.R. 193) that for there to be either an assault or a battery there must be something in the nature of hostility. It may be evinced by anger, by words or gesture. Sometimes the very act of battery will speak for itself, as where somebody uses a weapon on another.

What, then, turns a friendly touching (which is not actionable) into an unfriendly one (which is)?

We have been referred to two criminal cases. *R.* v. *Sutton* ([1977] 3 All E.R. 476) was decided in the Court of Appeal, Criminal Division. It was a case concerning alleged indecent assaults on boys who consented in fact although in law they were too young to do so. They were asked to pose for photographs. The only touching of the boys by the appellant was to get them to stand in poses. It was touching on the hands, arms, legs or torso but only for the purpose of indicating how he wanted them to pose. It was not hostile or threatening. The court, which was presided over by Lord Widgery C.J., held these were therefore not assaults.

A more recent authority is *Collins* v. *Wilcock* ([1984] 3 All E.R. 374). The facts were that a woman police officer, suspecting that a woman was soliciting contrary to the Street Offences Act 1959, tried to question her. The woman walked away, and was followed by the police officer. The officer took hold of her arm in order to restrain her. The woman scratched the officer's arm. She was arrested, charged with assaulting a police officer in the execution of her duty, and convicted. On appeal by case stated, the appeal was allowed, on the ground that the officer had gone beyond the scope of her duty in detaining the woman in circumstances short of arresting her. The officer had accordingly committed a battery.

The judgment of the Divisional Court was given by Robert Goff L.J. It is necessary to give a long quotation to do full justice to it. He said (at 377–378):

"The law draws a distinction, in terms more easily understood by philologists than by ordinary citizens, between an assault and a battery. An assault is an act which causes another person to apprehend the infliction of immediate, unlawful, force on his person; a battery is the actual infliction of unlawful force on another person. Both assault and battery are forms of trespass to the person. Another form of trespass to the person is false imprisonment, which is the unlawful imposition of constraint on another's freedom of movement from a particular place. The requisite mental element is of no relevance in the present case. We are here concerned primarily with battery. The fundamental principle, plain and incontestable, is that every person's body is inviolate. It has long been established that any touching of another person, however slight, may amount to a battery. So Holt C.J. held in 1704 that 'the least touching of another in anger is a battery.' See *Cole* v. *Turner* ((1704) 90 E.R. 958). The breadth of the principle reflects the fundamental nature of the interest so protected: as Blackstone wrote in his Commentaries, 'the law cannot draw the line between different degrees of violence, and therefore totally prohibits the first and lowest stage of it; every man's person being sacred, and no other having a right to meddle with it, in any the slightest manner' (see 3 Bl.Com. 120). The effect is that everybody is protected not only against physical injury but against any form of physical molestation. But so widely drawn a principle must inevitably be subject to exceptions. For example, children may be subjected to reasonable punishment; people may be subjected to the lawful exercise of the power of arrest; and reasonable force may be used in self-defence or for the prevention of crime. But, apart from these special instances where the control or constraint is lawful, a broader exception has been created to allow for the exigencies of everyday life. Generally speaking, consent is a defence to battery; and most of the physical contacts of ordinary life are not actionable because they are impliedly consented to by all who move in society and so expose themselves to the risk of bodily contact. So nobody can complain of the jostling which is inevitable from his presence in, for example, a supermarket, an underground station or a busy street; nor can a person who attends a party complain if his hand is seized in friendship, or even if his back is (within reason) slapped (see *Tuberville* v. *Savage*). Although such cases are regarded as examples of implied consent, it is more common nowadays to treat them as falling within a general exception embracing all physical contact which is generally acceptable in the ordinary conduct of daily life. We observe that, although in the past it has sometimes been stated that a battery is only committed where the action is 'angry, or revengeful, or rude, or insolent' (see 1 Hawk P.C. c. 62, s.2), we think that nowadays it is more realistic, and indeed more accurate, to state the broad underlying principle, subject to the broad exception. Among such forms of conduct, long held to be acceptable, is touching a person for the purpose of engaging his attention, though of course using no greater degree of physical contact than is reasonably necessary in the circumstances for that purpose. So, for example, it was held by the Court of Common Pleas in 1807 that a touch by a constable's staff on the shoulder of a man who had climbed on a gentleman's railing to gain a better view of a mad ox, the touch being only to engage the man's attention, did not amount to a battery (see *Wiffin* v. *Kincard* (1807) 127 E.R. 713; for another example, see *Coward* v. *Baddeley* (1859) 157 E.R. 927). But a distinction is drawn between a touch to draw a man's attention, which is generally acceptable, and a physical restraint, which is not. So we find Parke B. observing in *Rawlings* v. *Till* (1837) 150 E.R. 1042, with reference to *Wiffin* v. *Kincard*, that 'There the touch was merely to engage a man's attention, not to put a restraint on his person.' Furthermore, persistent touching to gain attention in the face of obvious disregard may transcend the norms of acceptable behaviour, and so be outside the exception. We do not say that more than one touch is never permitted; for example, the lost or distressed may surely be permitted a second touch, or possibly even more, on a reluctant or impervious sleeve or shoulder, as may a person who is acting reasonably in the exercise of a duty. In each case, the test must be whether the physical contact so persisted in has in the circumstances gone beyond generally acceptable standards of conduct; and the answer to that question will depend upon the facts of the particular case."

This rationalisation by Robert Goff L.J. draws the so-called "defences" to an action for trespass to the person (of which consent, self-defence, ejecting a trespasser, exercising parental authority, and statutory authority are some examples) under one umbrella of "a general exception embracing all physical contact which is generally acceptable in the ordinary conduct of daily life." It provides a solution to the old problem of what legal rule allows a casualty surgeon to perform an urgent operation on an unconscious patient who is brought into hospital. The patient cannot consent, and there may be no next of kin available to do it for him. Hitherto it has been customary to say in such cases that consent is to be implied for what would otherwise be a battery on the unconscious body. It is better simply to say that the surgeon's action is acceptable in the ordinary conduct of everyday life, and not a battery. It will doubtless be convenient to continue to tie the labels of the "defences" to the facts of any case where they are appropriate. But the rationalisation explains and utilises the expressions of judicial opinion which appear in the authorities. It also prevents the approach to the facts, which, with respect to the judge in the present case, causes his judgment to read like a ruling on a demurrer in the days of special pleading.

Nevertheless, it still remains to indicate what is to be proved by a plaintiff who brings an action for battery. Robert Goff L.J.'s judgment is illustrative of the considerations which underlie such an action, but it is not practicable to define a battery as "physical contact which is not generally acceptable in the ordinary conduct of daily life."

In our view, the authorities lead one to the conclusion that in a battery there must be an intentional touching or contact in one form or another of the plaintiff by the defendant. That touching must be proved to be a hostile touching. That still leaves unanswered the question, when is a touching to be called hostile? Hostility cannot be equated with ill-will or malevolence. It cannot be governed by the obvious intention shown in acts like punching, stabbing or shooting. It cannot be solely governed by an expressed intention, although that may be strong evidence. But the element of hostility, in the sense in which it is now to be considered, must be a question of fact for the tribunal of fact. It may be imported from the circumstances. Take the example of the police officer in *Collins* v. *Wilcock*. She touched the woman deliberately, but without an intention to do more than restrain her temporarily. Nevertheless, she was acting unlawfully and in that way was acting with hostility. She was acting contrary to the woman's legal right not to be physically restrained. We see no more difficulty in establishing what she intended by means of question and answer, or by inference from the surrounding circumstances, than there is in establishing whether an apparently playful blow was struck in anger. The rules of law governing the legality of arrest may require strict application to the facts of appropriate cases, but in the ordinary give and take of everyday life the tribunal of fact should find no difficulty in answering the question, "was this, or was it not, a battery?" Where the immediate act of touching does not itself demonstrate hostility, the plaintiff should plead the facts which are said to do so.

Although we are all entitled to protection from physical molestation, we live in a crowded world in which people must be considered as taking on themselves some risk of injury (where it occurs) from the acts of others which are not in themselves unlawful. If negligence cannot be proved, it may be that an injured plaintiff who is also unable to prove a battery, will be without redress.

Defences like self-defence, and exercising the right of arrest, are relevant here. Similarly, it may be that allowances must be made, where appropriate, for the idiosyncrasies of individuals or (as was demonstrated in *Walmsley* v. *Humenick* ([1954] 2 D.L.R. 232)) the irresponsibility of childhood and the degree of care and awareness which is to be expected of children.

In our judgment the judge took too narrow a view of what has to be proved in order to make out a case of trespass to the person. It will be apparent that there are a number of questions which must be investigated in evidence.

Accordingly we would allow this appeal, and give unconditional leave to defend.

NASH v. SHEEN

Queen's Bench, *The Times*, March 13, 1953

The plaintiff went to the defendant's hairdressing establishment to obtain a "permanent wave" in her hair. The defendant applied a "tone rinse" which not only dyed the plaintiff's hair an unpleasing colour, but also provoked a painful rash all over her body. The plaintiff did not allege that the rash was a foreseeable consequence of the application of the dye.

Hilbery J.: His Lordship said that the first question to be considered was whether what was applied to the hair, which was called in the trade a "tone-rinse," was applied without the plaintiff's express consent and was a trespass. . . . It was quite clear that she went to the salon for a permanent wave, and he (his Lordship) did not believe that Mrs. Nash consented to the application of the colouring matter . . . in his view that was a trespass. Even on the defendant's account it was plain that the plaintiff never gave consent to the application of any dye or colouring matter to her hair.

The plaintiff recovered £437 damages, including £50 for "her appearance being altered in a way which was distressing to her."

Questions

1. Is this decision still good law after (a) *Fowler* v. *Lanning*, (b) *Wilson* v. *Pringle*, (c) *Collins* v. *Wilcock*?

2. Here there was a contract between the parties. Would it be an implied term of that contract (a) that nothing be applied to the plaintiff's head save what she asked for, or (b) that the defendant should take reasonable care not to apply detrimental substances to her head, or (c) both?

3. Would it have been a trespass if the hairdresser had applied the permanent wave substance in a concentrated form?

4. Did the plaintiff not consent, though mistakenly, to the application of the substance in the hairdresser's hand?

5. Would it have been a trespass if the hairdresser had reasonably thought that the substance being applied was a permanent wave solution?

Section 5.—Trespass to Land

(i) *Title to Sue*

HARPER v. CHARLESWORTH

King's Bench (1825) 4 B. & C. 574; 3 L.J.(o.s.) K.B. 572; 107 E.R. 1174

The defendant claimed to be exercising a public right of footway across land in Staffordshire which belonged to the Crown. The plaintiff paid the Crown 20s. per year in respect of the land, and hunted over it during the appropriate months; he also allowed others to pasture on the land.

At the trial before Garrow B., the jury found a verdict for the plaintiff. The defendant obtained a rule nisi for judgment notwithstanding the verdict, on the ground that the plaintiff was not rightfully in possession of the land in question, inasmuch as since he had no claim against the Crown, he was a mere intruder on Crown land, and could not maintain trespass. The rule was discharged.

Bayley J.: I think that . . . the Crown might at any time, without notice, have removed him from that possession and occupation. Then it becomes a question, whether a person having the actual possession of Crown land can maintain trespass against a mere wrongdoer? Generally speaking, actual possession is sufficient to entitle a party to maintain trespass against a wrongdoer. . . . Apply that doctrine to this case: the plaintiff had no title to enable him to maintain an ejectment, because he had not a legal conveyance from the Crown; but still . . . he would be entitled, by reason of his actual possession, to maintain trespass against a wrongdoer. . . .

Holroyd J.: According to the old rule it was an answer to the action of trespass brought against a wrongdoer for the defendant to show that the right of soil was in a third person. For, although it was necessary for a defendant to allege in his plea that he entered by the command of the owner of the soil, the plaintiff was not at liberty to traverse the command. But that doctrine has been overruled by later cases. The law now is, that an entry on the possession of another cannot be justified, unless it be made by the authority of a person in whom the right of soil is vested.

DELANEY v. T.P. SMITH LTD.

Court of Appeal [1946] K.B. 393; 115 L.J.K.B. 406; 175 L.T. 187; 62 T.L.R. 398; 90 S.J. 296;
[1946] 2 All E.R. 23

The defendant owned a dwelling-house which was bombed. It was agreed orally
that the plaintiff should enter as tenant when the repairs were completed, which
was expected to be in December 1944. In that month, the plaintiff entered clandes-
tinely. One week later the defendant forcibly ejected him and his belongings. In the
county court the defendant pleaded that the oral tenancy could not be relied on by
the plaintiff, by reason of section 40, Law of Property Act 1925, which requires
contracts for an interest in land to be evidenced by a memorandum in writing. The
county court judge held that the defendant's justification for the trespass was
defeated by proof of the agreement, despite its informality. The defendant
appealed, and his appeal was allowed.

Tucker L.J.: . . . It is no doubt true that a plaintiff in an action of trespass to land
need only in the first instance allege possession. This is sufficient to support his
action against a wrongdoer, but it is not sufficient as against the lawful owner, and
in an action against the freeholder the plaintiff must at some stage of the pleadings
set up a title derived from the defendant. . . . I think the plaintiff was at some
stage bound to rely on the oral agreement of tenancy. . . .

WHITE v. BAYLEY

Common Pleas (1861) 10 C.B.(N.S.) 227; 142 E.R. 438

The plaintiff was employed by the trustees of the Swedenborg Society under a contract by which he was to be paid £75 per year for managing and living in premises
rented by the trustees in Bloomsbury Street; the agreement was terminable on six
months' notice. The ground floor of the premises was used as a book-shop, the first
floor as a library and reading-room for the Society, while the upper floors were a
residence for the plaintiff and his family. Over the shop stood the words "Swedenborg Society," and on the door-posts "William White, Bookseller and Publisher."
The trustees gave notice to quit forthwith, and they took possession of the premises
for a time until the plaintiff forcibly re-entered. Then the trustees obtained an
injunction in Chancery, compelling the plaintiff to give up possession. In his action
of trespass the plaintiff was nonsuited, and his motion for a new trial refused.

Byles J.: The first count of the declaration complains of a trespass *quare clausum
fregit*. That clearly does not lie unless the plaintiff has some estate in the land. . . .
I agree with my Brother Willes in thinking that the plaintiff had the use but not the
occupation of the premises: and I do not think he could have maintained trespass
quare clausum fregit even against a stranger. But, assuming the effect of the agreement to have been to give him any estate at all, the utmost it could amount to would
be a tenancy at will. . . .

Willes J.: . . . though generally speaking the relation of master and servant or principal and agent may, where the servant or agent has been guilty of misconduct, be
terminated at a moment, if such an arrangement as this were held to vest in the servant or agent an interest in the employer's premises, the servant might set his
employer at defiance, and, though the latter were perfectly justified in putting an

end to the relation of master and servant between them, the former might insist upon holding on as a tenant until the expiration of a regular notice to quit. . . .

Questions

1. Do you think that Byles J. would have nonsuited the plaintiff if the plaintiff had been suing a burglar?

2. The police want to search the room of X, who is a lodger in Y's house. Do the police, if they have no warrant, require the permission of X as well as Y? If Y gives his permission, can X sue him for (a) trespass, (b) breach of contract?

Note:

Trespass to the person involves no question of title to sue; only the person imprisoned, battered or assaulted may claim. But when the alleged trespass is to a piece of property, the question who can sue in respect of it is very important.

Title to sue in trespass is based on possession. That sounds very simple; it sounds as if one merely had to look at the factual relation of the person and the thing, and ask whether the plaintiff was in control of the thing. One does have to look at that, for if he did not have control, the plaintiff cannot sue. But it does not follow that he can always sue if he did have control of it, for the defendant may be entitled to have the possession from him, either because he owns it or because he is entitled to it under a contract with the plaintiff. Thus it comes about that we have the confusing observations that "possession is title as against a wrongdoer," and that the defendant's plea of "not possessed" means "not possessed as against the defendant." Conversely, a plaintiff who has never actually taken possession of land may be held to have sufficient control to bring suit. In *Portland Managements* v. *Harte* [1977] Q.B. 306, 316, Scarman L.J. took it to be clear law that " . . . when an owner of land is making a case of trespass against a person alleged to be in possession, all that the owner has to prove is his title and an intention to regain possession. If the defendant to the action either admits his ownership or is faced with evidence, which the court accepts, that the plaintiff is in fact the owner, then the burden is on the defendant to confess and avoid; that is to say, to set up a title or right to possession consistent with the fact of ownership vested in the plaintiff." Not long afterwards the same judge said "Trespass is of course a wrong not to ownership, but to possession." *Hesperides Hotel* v. *Aegean Turkish Holidays* [1978] Q.B. 205, 231.

Certain difficulties follow from deciding too much on the question of title to sue. So accustomed were the judges of the nineteenth century to saying that a servant never had possession (lest it be used against the master) that there was some doubt whether the chambermaid could sue a burglar who entered her bedroom. Now perhaps it does not matter, since such an entry is probably a wilful act calculated to cause physical harm such that, if physical harm ensues, the chambermaid can sue the burglar under the principle of *Wilkinson* v. *Downton*.

(ii) *The Act*

SMITH v. STONE

King's Bench (1647) Sty. 65; 82 E.R. 533

Smith brought an action of trespasse against Stone pedibus ambulando, the defendant pleads this speciall plea in justification, viz. that he was carryed upon the land of the plaintiff by force, and violence of others, and was not there voluntarily, which is the same trespasse, for which the plaintiff brings his action. The plaintiff demurs to this plea: in this case Roll Iustice said, that it is the trespasse of the party that carryed the defendant upon the land, and not the trespasse of the defendant: as he that drives my cattel into another mans land is the trespassor against him, and not I who am owner of the cattell.

BASELY v. CLARKSON

Common Pleas (1681) 3 Lev. 37; 83 E.R. 565

Difference *inter* trespass involuntary, and *per* mistake.

Trespass for breaking his closs called the *balk* and the *hade*, and cutting his grass, and carrying it away. The defendant disclaims any title in the lands of the plaintiff, but says that he hath a *balk* and *hade* adjoining to the balk and hade of the plaintiff, and in mowing his own land he involuntarily and by mistake mowed down some grass growing upon the balk and hade of the plaintiff, intending only to mow the grass upon his own *balk* and *hade*, and carried the *grass, &c. quae est eadem, &c. Et quod ante emanationem brevis* he tendered to the plaintiff 2s. in satisfaction, and that 2s. was a sufficient amends. Upon this the plaintiff demurred, and had judgment; for it appears the fact was voluntary, and his intention and knowledge are not traversable; they cannot be known.

Note:
" . . . the fact was voluntary. . . . " Presumably, "fact" is a mistranslation of "fait" and means "act."

A balk is a strip of ground left unploughed between two ploughed areas to serve as a boundary. A hade appears to be the same thing. "Where great Balkes betwixt Lands, Hades, Meares, or Divisions betwixt Land and Land are left," Blithe, *English Improvement,* 13 (1649).

PEACOCK v. YOUNG

Queen's Bench (1869) 21 L.T. 527

During an election at Wisbech in which he was a candidate, the defendant allowed his enthusiastic and rather rowdy supporters to pull him along in his carriage, in which he was standing and waving his hat. He told them not to do any damage, but they smashed the windows of the plaintiff's furniture shop. The plaintiff obtained a verdict in the county court, but the defendant appealed and his appeal was allowed.

Cockburn C.J.: . . . The judge says that if he had stopped the procession and got out of his carriage, there might have been an end put to the whole proceedings of the mob. I may take it, therefore, as found, that Mr. Young was guilty of an act of imprudence, and that is all that is found. But I cannot see, because a gentleman canvassing in the course of his electioneering is accompanied by a crowd of people, that they are therefore his agents, he doing nothing intentionally to encourage them. If he does some act which is no more than an imprudence, he cannot be held responsible for what the mob may do in consequence, in an action of trespass, which this is substantially.

Question
Were the borstal boys in the *Dorset Yacht Co.* case the agents of the Home Office?

Note:
In the 300,000 acres of Exmoor, the League Against Cruel Sports owned 23 "sanctuaries," unfenced areas averaging 52 acres each, or about 500 yards square. Some of the Devon and Somerset Staghounds (the dogs, not the members) used to enter the sanctuaries in pursuit of

deer, without doing any damage to any of the plaintiff's property. The League sued the joint Masters of the Hounds for damages for several such trespasses and sought an injunction against further trespasses. Park J. issued an injunction in respect of one sanctuary, restraining (on pain of imprisonment) the defendants by themselves, their servants or agents, or mounted followers, from causing or permitting hounds to enter or cross the property. Damages totalling £180 for six trespasses were awarded. *League Against Cruel Sports* v. *Scott* [1985] 2 All E.R. 489.

The judge said "Where a master of staghounds takes out a pack of hounds and deliberately sets them in pursuit of a stag or hind knowing that there is a real risk that in the pursuit hounds may enter or cross prohibited land, the master will be liable for trespass if he intended to cause the hounds to enter such land or if by his failure to exercise proper control over them he causes them to enter such land." The Masters were held responsible for the mounted followers and not the followers on foot or in cars, because they have a power of control over the former and not over the latter.

Questions:

1. Was it the hounds or the masters who were the trespassers?

2. If trespass is an intentional tort (see Lord Denning above p. 288), why was the masters' failure to control the followers relevant? And if the tort was negligence, why was the absence of damage not relevant?

3. Should the court have discussed the question of the use to which the plaintiffs were putting their property? Was it really in order to protect their property that the plaintiffs brought suit?

Further Note:

Suppose that a local authority wants to clear gypsies off land which belongs to third parties. It cannot obtain an injunction against them as trespassers, because it is not their land, but it can obtain a court order under certain conditions if the activities of the gypsies constitute a statutory nuisance under s.100 of the Public Health Act 1936 (*Bradford City M.C.* v. *Brown* (1986) 84 L.G.R. 731) and it has standing under s.222 of the Local Government Act 1972 to seek an injunction against the continued commission of a crime: the gypsies' activities might constitute a public nuisance, for example, or the alarming offence contained in s.40 of the Local Government (Misc. Prov.) Act 1982 which can apparently be committed by two glue-sniffers quietly sniffing glue in a deserted playground (*Sykes* v. *Holmes* (1985) 84 L.G.R. 355).

(iii) *The Invasion*

BERNSTEIN OF LEIGH (BARON) v. SKYVIEWS & GENERAL LTD.

Queen's Bench [1978] Q.B. 479; [1977] 3 W.L.R. 136; 121 S.J. 157; 241 E.G. 917; [1977] 2 All E.R. 902

The defendants flew over the plaintiff's house in Kent and took a photograph of it which they tried to sell to him. He sued them for trespass and lost.

Griffiths J.: . . . I turn now to the law. The plaintiff claims that as owner of the land he is also owner of the air space above the land, or at least has the right to exclude any entry into the air space above his land. He relies on the old Latin maxim, *cujus est solum ejus est usque ad coelum et ad inferos,* a colourful phrase often on the lips of lawyers since it was first coined by Accursius in Bologna in the 13th century. There are a number of cases in which the maxim has been used by English judges but an examination of those cases shows that they have all been concerned with structures attached to the adjoining land, such as overhanging buildings, signs or telegraph wires, and for their solution it has not been necessary for the judge to cast his eyes towards the heavens; he has been concerned with the rights of the owner in the air space immediately adjacent to the surface of the land.

That an owner has certain rights in the air space above his land is well established by authority. He has the right to lop the branches of trees that may overhang his boundary, although this right seems to be founded in nuisance rather than trespass: see *Lemmon* v. *Webb* [1894] 3 Ch. 1. In *Wandsworth Board of Works* v. *United Telephone Co.* (1884) 13 Q.B.D. 904 the Court of Appeal did not doubt that the owner of land would have the right to cut a wire placed over his land. Fry L.J. said (at 927): "As at present advised, I entertain no doubt that an ordinary proprietor of land can cut and remove a wire placed at any height above his freehold." Fry L.J. added that the point was not necessary for his decision (it is therefore obiter) and I hasten to add that it would be subject to any statutory rights given to the Post Office and other undertakers to erect telegraph lines or other installations.

In *Gifford* v. *Dent* [1926] 1 W.N. 336 Romer J. held that it was a trespass to erect a sign that projected four feet eight inches over the plaintiff's forecourt and ordered it to be removed. He invoked the old maxim in his judgment. The report reads: " . . . the Plaintiffs were tenants of the forecourt and were accordingly tenants of the space above the forecourt usque ad coelum, it seemed to him that the projection was clearly a trespass upon the property of the plaintiffs." That decision was followed by McNair J. in *Kelsen* v. *Imperial Tobacco Co. Ltd.* [1957] 2 Q.B. 334, in which he granted a mandatory injunction ordering the defendants to remove a sign which projected only eight inches over the plaintiff's property. The plaintiff relies strongly on this case . . .

I do not wish to cast any doubts on the correctness of the decision on its own particular facts. It may be a sound and practical rule to regard any incursion into the air space at a height which may interfere with the ordinary user of the land as a trespass rather than a nuisance. Adjoining owners then know where they stand; they have no right to erect structures overhanging or passing over their neighbours' land and there is no room for argument whether they are thereby causing damage or annoyance to their neighbours about which there may be much room for argument and uncertainty. But wholly different considerations arise when considering the passage of aircraft at a height which in no way affects the user of the land. . . .

I can find no support in authority for the view that a landowner's rights in the air space above his property extend to an unlimited height. In *Wandsworth Board of Works* v. *United Telephone Co.* Bowen L.J. described the maxim, *usque ad coelum,* as a fanciful phrase, to which I would add that if applied literally it is a fanciful notion leading to the absurdity of a trespass at common law being committed by a satellite every time it passes over a suburban garden. The academic writers speak with one voice in rejecting the uncritical and literal application of the maxim: . . . I accept their collective approach as correct. The problem is to balance the rights of an owner to enjoy the use of his land against the rights of the general public to take advantage of all that science now offers in the use of air space. This balance is in my judgment best struck in our present society by restricting the rights of an owner in the air space above his land to such height as is necessary for the ordinary use and enjoyment of his land and the structures on it, and declaring that above that height he has no greater rights in the air space than any other member of the public.

Applying this test to the facts of this case, I find that the defendants' aircraft did not infringe any rights in the plaintiff's air space, and thus no trespass was committed. It was on any view of the evidence flying many hundreds of feet above the ground and it is not suggested that by its mere presence in the air space it caused any interference with any use to which the plaintiff put or might wish to put his land. The plaintiff's complaint is not that the aircraft interfered with the use of his land but that a photograph was taken from it. There is, however, no law against taking a photograph, and the mere taking of a photograph cannot turn an act which is not a trespass into the plaintiff's air space into one that is a trespass.

I was told by counsel that the plaintiff was particularly anxious that his house should not be photographed from the air lest the photograph should fall into criminal hands as it might prove a valuable aid to a terrorist. This anxiety is readily understandable and must attract sympathy, although I should add that it is not suggested that this was a likely consequence as a result of the defendants' activities. Counsel for the plaintiff, however, conceded that he was unable to cite any principle of law or authority that would entitle the plaintiff to prevent someone taking a photograph of his property for an innocent purpose, provided they did not commit some other tort such as trespass or nuisance in doing so. It is therefore interesting to reflect what a sterile remedy the plaintiff would obtain if he was able to establish that mere infringement of the air space over his land was a trespass. He could prevent the defendants flying over his land to take another photograph, but he could not prevent the defendants taking the virtually identical photograph from the adjoining land provided they took care not to cross his boundary, and were taking it for an innocent as opposed to a criminal purpose.

My finding that no trespass at common law has been established is sufficient to determine this case in the defendants' favour. I should, however, deal with a further defence under the Civil Aviation Act 1949, s.40(1) of which provides:

"No action shall lie in respect of trespass or in respect of nuisance, by reason only of the flight of an aircraft over any property at a height above the ground, which, having regard to wind, weather, and all the circumstances of the case is reasonable, or the ordinary incidents of such flight so long as the provisions of Part II and this Part of this Act and any Order in Council or order made under Part II of this Part of this Act are duly complied with."

. . . As I read the section its protection extends to all flights provided they are at a reasonable height and comply with the statutory requirements. And I adopt this construction the more readily because s.40(2) imposes on the owner of the aircraft a strict liability to pay damages for any material loss or damage that may be caused by his aircraft.

It is, however, to be observed that the protection given is limited by the words "by reason only of the flight," so although an owner can found no action in trespass or nuisance if he relies solely on the flight of the aircraft above his property as founding his cause of action, the section will not preclude him from bringing an action if he can point to some activity carried on by or from the aircraft that can properly be considered a trespass or nuisance, or some other tort. For example, the section would give no protection against the deliberate emission of vast quantities of smoke that polluted the atmosphere and seriously interfered with the plaintiff's use and enjoyment of his property; such behaviour remains an actionable nuisance. Nor would I wish this judgment to be understood as deciding that in no circumstances could a successful action be brought against an aerial photographer to restrain his activities. The present action is not founded in nuisance for no court would regard the taking of a single photograph as an actionable nuisance. But if the circumstances were such that a plaintiff was subjected to the harassment of constant surveillance of his house from the air, accompanied by the photographing of his every activity, I am far from saying that the court would not regard such a monstrous invasion of his privacy as an actionable nuisance for which they would give relief. However, that question does not fall for decision in this case and will be decided if and when it arises.

On the facts of this case even if contrary to my view the defendants' aircraft committed a trespass at common law in flying over the plaintiff's land, the plaintiff is prevented from bringing any action in respect of that trespass by the terms of s.40(1) of the Civil Aviation Act 1949.

For these reasons the plaintiff's action fails and there will be judgment for the defendants.

Note:

s.40 of the Civil Aviation Act 1949 has now been replaced by s.76 of the Civil Aviation Act 1982.

PERERA v. VANDIYAR

Court of Appeal [1953] 1 W.L.R. 672; 97 S.J. 332; [1953] 1 All E.R. 1109

The plaintiff was tenant of the defendant's flat, and protected by the Rent Restriction Acts. On October 8, 1952, the defendant cut off the gas and electricity. The plaintiff remained there for two days with his wife and child but without heat or light, and then went to stay with friends. He returned when the utilities were reconnected on October 14.

The plaintiff claimed damages for breach of the tenancy agreement, for which the county court judge awarded £25 general damages and £3 10s. special damages. At the instance of the judge, the plaintiff amended his claim to include an averment that the acts "were done with the intent to evict the plaintiff and did cause the eviction of the plaintiff," whereupon the judge awarded a further £25 punitive damages. The defendant's appeal against the award of this further sum was allowed by the Court of Appeal.

Romer L.J.: . . . The county court judge, after assessing £25 as being the amount which, in his view, would be the right amount to award by way of damages for breach of contract, then held that a further £25 should be added on a certain basis. That basis was, in his own words, that the action of the defendant in cutting off the gas and electricity was a deliberate and malicious tort. That the defendant's action was deliberate is plain, and that it was malicious is, I think, reasonably plain, but I cannot for myself see that it amounted to a tort. It did not constitute an interference with any part of the demised premises and, therefore, could not be regarded as a trespass. It was merely a breach of contract, the object of which was to persuade or induce the tenant to go. That is not a tort. What the defendant did in *Lavender* v. *Betts* ([1942] 2 All E.R. 72) was a tort, because it was a trespass. Although the intention of the defendant here was precisely the same as the intention proved in that case, the defendant in *Lavender* v. *Betts* resorted to trespass for the purpose of getting his own way. It was not because he formed an intention to evict that damages were awarded in *Lavender* v. *Betts*. They were awarded because he trespassed upon his tenant's property.

Eviction might, in certain circumstances, be a tort, and certainly would be if it involved also trespass, but the mere intention to evict cannot, as I see it, be a tort, nor does it become a tort merely because the person who forms the intention hopes to give effect to it by interfering with the tenant's contractual rights. That is what the defendant here did, and in respect of that the first sum of £25 was awarded against him. But he did not bring himself into the area of tort which would justify the awarding of a further sum under the head of punitive damages. Accordingly, though perhaps with some reluctance, I agree that the judgment of the judge went too far in awarding the second sum of £25, and the result which my Lord has already indicated must follow.

Note:
In *Drane* v. *Evangelou* [1978] 2 All E.R. 437 Lord Denning said that this case would be decided differently today, in view of the fact that damages for mental distress may be awarded for breach of contract (see above, p. 77). But the £25 here was awarded as punitive damages, and punitive damages cannot be awarded for breach of contract (*Addis* v. *Gramophone Co.* [1909] A.C. 488). Indeed, the Court of Appeal has now held that damages for annoyance cannot be awarded for breach of contract unless the contract is one to provide peace of mind (*Bliss*, above p. 77); doubtless tenancy will be held to be such a contract. The Court of Appeal had the opportunity in *McCall* v. *Abelesz* [1976] Q.B. 585 to hold that statute (now Protection from Eviction Act 1977, s.1) had made harassment of a tenant into a tort as well as an offence, but decided not to. So there still seems to be a difference between cases like

Drane, where there was a physical trespass, and *Perera,* where there was not. See Gray, *Elements of Land Law,* 957–960 (1987).

Where the landlord is guilty of a physical trespass, exemplary damages can often be awarded against him even after *Rookes* v. *Barnard* because the landlord is evicting the sitting tenant in order to get more money from his successor (as in *Millington* v. *Duffy* (1984) 135 New L.J. 708 (C.A.)).

Chapter 9

DEFENCES

Section 1.—Consent

(i) *Existence*

LATTER v. BRADDELL

Common Pleas Division (1880) 50 L.J.Q.B. 166; Court of Appeal (1881) 50 L.J.Q.B. 448; 44
L.T. 369; 45 J.P. 520; 29 W.R. 366

When Mrs. Braddell returned from holiday the charwoman told her that the plaintiff housemaid was pregnant. The plaintiff denied this, but her mistress sent for the doctor. When the doctor arrived he told the plaintiff to undress and submit to an examination. The plaintiff protested and wept, but took off her clothes and submitted to an examination. She was not pregnant, but was dismissed all the same. She sued Captain and Mrs. Braddell and the doctor. At the trial at Manchester Assizes, Lindley J. withdrew from the jury the case against Captain and Mrs. Braddell, and the jury found in favour of the doctor. The plaintiff obtained a rule nisi for a new trial.

In the Common Pleas Division, Lindley J. upheld his decision, Lopes J. dissenting. On appeal to the Court of Appeal, that court unanimously upheld the decision of Lindley J.

Lopes J.: . . . If the plaintiff voluntarily consented, or if, in other words, the assault was committed with her leave and licence, the action is not maintainable; and to justify the ruling of the learned judge, what was done must have been so unmistakably with the plaintiff's consent that there was no evidence of non-consent upon which a jury could reasonably act. It seems to me there was abundant evidence of non-consent to be left to the jury.

The sending for a doctor by a master or mistress and directing him to examine a female servant, without first apprising her, is, in any circumstances, an arbitrary and high-handed proceeding, and cannot, in my opinion, be justified unless the servant's consent is voluntarily given. A submission to what is done, obtained through a belief that she is bound to obey her master or mistress; or a consent obtained through a fear of evil consequences to arise to herself, induced by her master's or mistress's words or conduct, is not sufficient. In neither case would the consent be voluntarily given: it would be a consent in one sense, but a consent to which the will was not a party. The plaintiff's case is stronger. She swears she did not consent. I know not what more a person in the plaintiff's position could do unless she used physical force. She is discharged without a hearing, forbidden to speak, sent to her room, examined by her mistress's doctor alone, no other female being in the room, made to take off all her clothes and lie naked on the bed. She complains of the treatment, cries continuously, objects to the removal of each garment and swears the examination was without her consent. Could it be said, in these circumstances, that her consent was so unmistakably given that her state of mind was not a question for the jury to consider? I cannot adopt the view that the plaintiff consented because she yielded without her will having been overpowered by force or fear of violence. That, as I have said, is not in my opinion, an accurate definition of consent in a case like this. . . .

Lindley J.: . . . The plaintiff's case cannot be put higher than this, namely, that, without consulting her wishes, her mistress ordered her to submit to be examined by a doctor, in order that he might ascertain whether she (the plaintiff) was in the family way, and that she (the plaintiff) complied with that order reluctantly—that is, sobbing and protesting—and because she was told she must, and she did not know what else to do. There was, however, no evidence of any force or violence, nor of any threat of force or violence, nor of any illegal act done or threatened by the mistress beyond what I have stated; nor did the plaintiff in her evidence say that she was in fear of the mistress or of the doctor, or that she was in any way overcome by fear . . . Under these circumstances I am of opinion that there was no evidence of want of consent as distinguished from reluctant obedience or submission to her mistress's orders, and that in the absence of all evidence of coercion, as distinguished from an order which the plaintiff could comply with or not as she chose, the action cannot be maintained. . . .

In the Court of Appeal

Bramwell L.J.: . . . Very likely the plaintiff thought the defendants had a right to have her examined; but the truth is, she submitted to it, and it is impossible to say the jury were wrong in finding that she submitted. She may have submitted under an eroneous notion of law, but it was not through fear of violence. . . .

Questions
  1. If the plaintiff had been able to prove actual physical damage arising from the outrage, do you think she could have recovered? If so, how would you instruct the jury?
  2. What facts not stated could justify the decision of Lindley J. to withdraw from the jury the case against Captain and Mrs. Braddell, and to leave for their consideration the case against the doctor?
  3. How many housemaids do you think were on the jury?

Note:
  A judge has said that he would not regard as "freely and effectively given" any consent to the removal of property given by the party against whom an Anton Piller order was being enforced unless that party's own solicitor were present. *Columbia Picture Indus.* v. *Robinson* [1986] 3 All E.R. 338, 371.

R. v. DAY

Assizes (1841) 9 C. & P. 722; 173 E.R. 1026

The prosecutrix, a child of 10, was on the way home at seven o'clock one December evening when the prisoner went with her up a dark lane and without any violence made an attempt on her which she did not resist. On being charged with common assault the prisoner argued that the prosecutrix consented to what was done.

Coleridge J. (addressing the jury): . . . There is a difference between consent and submission; every consent involves a submission; but it by no means follows, that a mere submission involves consent. It would be too much to say, that an adult submitting quietly to outrage of this description, was not consenting; on the other hand, the mere submission of a child when in the power of a strong man, and most probably acted upon by fear, can by no means be taken to be such a consent as will justify the prisoner in point of law. You will therefore say whether the submission of the prosecutrix was voluntary on her part, or the result of fear, under the circumstances in which she was placed. If you are of the latter opinion, you will find the prisoner guilty on the second count of the indictment.

The jury found the prisoner guilty.

Note:

Thus a plaintiff is not barred from suing for assault where his apparent consent was really submission induced by fear. What of the case where consent is procured by fraud?

In such a case the plaintiff will have a perfectly good action in deceit, so the question is probably not important although there is now unfortunately authority that exemplary damages cannot be awarded for the tort of deceit (*Mafo* v. *Adams* [1970] 1 Q.B. 548; *Broome* v. *Cassell & Co.* [1972] A.C. 1027). But a plaintiff who has consented to an invasion otherwise trespassory may prefer to bring an action on the theory of trespass where the defendant has suppressed the truth instead of actually telling lies. The form of the action might then conceal the fact that the plaintiff must establish a duty on the defendant to disclose the fact suppressed. That would of course be wrong, but it nearly happened in *Hegarty* v. *Shine* (1878) 4 L.R.Ir. 288; 14 Cox C.C. 145 (C.A.).

The plaintiff had cohabited with the defendant for two years and contracted venereal disease from him. She claimed that he had been assaulting her for those two years, since her consent was vitiated by his failure to disclose his ailment, of which he was perfectly well aware. The judge addressing the jury told them: " . . . an assault implied an act of violence, committed upon a person against his or her will, and that, as a general rule, when the person consented to the act, there was no assault; but that if the consent was obtained by the fraud of the party committing the act, the fraud vitiated the consent, and the act became in view of the law an assault, and that therefore if the defendant, knowing that he had venereal disease, and that the probable and natural effect of his having connection with the plaintiff would be to communicate to her venereal disease, fraudulently concealed from her his condition, in order to induce, and did thereby induce, her to have connection with him; and if but for that fraud she would not have consented to have had such connection; and if he had with her the connection so procured and thereby communicated to her such venereal disease, he had committed an assault. . . . " The jury gave a verdict for the plaintiff; the defendant claimed a misdirection by the judge, and the Queen's Bench Division ordered a new trial. The plaintiff appealed to the Court of Appeal, which upheld the order for a new trial.

AIDS being the modern version of syphilis, the modern tort of negligence will probably be applied rather than the old law of trespass. Doubtless one will be liable for communicating the disease if one knew or should have known that one was infected, subject to a reduction in damages if the plaintiff participated in unsafe sex.

CHATTERTON v. GERSON

Queen's Bench [1981] Q.B. 432; [1980] 3 W.L.R. 1003; [1981] 1 All E.R. 257

Action by patient against doctor for personal injury

The plaintiff, suffering great pain after a hernia operation, was referred to the defendant, a specialist in the treatment of chronic intractable pain. The defendant gave her a spinal injection, which helped the pain for a while but then made her numb in the right leg. Pain returned. The defendant gave a second spinal injection which made the pain no better and the numbness worse. There was dispute regarding the explanation given by the defendant to the plaintiff about the nature and probable effect of the injections.

Bristow J.: . . . It is clear law that in any context in which consent of the injured party is a defence to what would otherwise be a crime or a civil wrong, the consent must be real. Where, for example a woman's consent to sexual intercourse is obtained by fraud, her apparent consent is no defence to a charge of rape. It is not difficult to state the principle or to appreciate its good sense. As so often, the problem lies in its application.

No English authority was cited before me of the application of the principle in the context of consent to the interference with bodily integrity by medical or surgical treatment. . . .

In my judgment what the court has to do in each case is to look at all the circumstances and say, "Was there a real consent?" I think justice requires that in order to vitiate the reality of consent there must be a greater failure of communication between doctor and patient than that involved in a breach of duty if the claim is based on negligence. When the claim is based on negligence the plaintiff must prove not only the breach of duty to inform but that had the duty not been broken she would not have chosen to have the operation. Where the claim is based on trespass to the person, once it is shown that the consent is unreal, then what the plaintiff would have decided if she had been given the information which would have prevented vitiation of the reality of her consent is irrelevant.

In my judgment once the patient is informed in broad terms of the nature of the procedure which is intended, and gives her consent, the consent is real, and the cause of the action on which to base a claim for failure to go into risks and implications is negligence, not trespass. Of course, if information is withheld in bad faith, the consent will be vitiated by fraud. Of course, if by some accident, as in a case in the 1940s in the Salford Hundred Court where a boy was admitted to hospital for tonsilectomy and due to administrative error was circumcised instead, trespass would be the appropriate cause of action against the doctor, though he was as much the victim of the error as the boy. But in my judgment it would be very much against the interests of justice if actions which are really based on a failure by the doctor to perform his duty adequately to inform were pleaded in trespass.

In this case in my judgment even taking Miss Chatterton's evidence at its face value she was under no illusion as to the general nature of what an intrathecal injection of phenol solution nerve block would be, and in the case of each injection her consent was not unreal. I should add that getting the patient to sign a pro forma expressing consent to undergo the operation "the effect and nature of which have been explained to me," as was done here in each case, should be a valuable reminder to everyone of the need for explanation and consent. But it would be no defence to an action based on trespass to the person if no explanation had in fact been given. The consent would have been expressed in form only, not in reality. . . .

Note:

It is sufficient if, in volunteering information about hazards intrinsic to the treatment proposed, the doctor or surgeon conducts himself in accordance with a responsible body of medical opinion which takes due account of the plaintiff's right to make the final decision; if the patient asks for information, the doctor must provide it. *Sidaway* v. *Bethlem Royal Hospital* [1985] A.C. 871 (H.L.). See Brazier, "Patient Autonomy and Consent to Treatment," (1987) 7 L.S. 169.

(ii) *Duration*

HURST v. PICTURE THEATRES LTD.

Court of Appeal [1915] 1 K.B. 1; 83 L.J.K.B. 1837; 111 L.T. 972; 58 S.J. 739

The plaintiff, having paid the entrance fee (as the jury found), entered the defendant's cinema and took a proper seat. The attendant alleged that he had not paid, and asked him to leave. The plaintiff declined. The defendant's manager called a policeman. The policeman refused to act. The defendant's doorkeeper then ejected the plaintiff.

At a trial before Channell J. and a jury, the plaintiff had a verdict, damages £150. The defendant appealed to the Court of Appeal, who dismissed the appeal (Phillimore L.J. dissenting).

Buckley L.J.: . . . The proposition which Mr. Mackinnon sets out to affirm is that if a man has paid for his seat at the opera, or the theatre, and has entered and taken his seat, and is behaving himself quite properly, it is competent to the proprietors of the theatre, merely because they choose so to do, to call upon him to withdraw before he has seen the performance for the enjoyment of which he has paid; that what he has obtained for his money is a mere revocable licence to come upon the land of the proprietor of the theatre, and that the proprietor may, simply because he chooses, say "I revoke your licence; go." If that proposition be true, it involves startling results. Kennedy L.J. has suggested one. Suppose that there be sitting in the stalls a man who is a constant patron of the opera or the theatre, to whom the management pay great deference, whether from his rank or his habit of attendance: he goes to the management and says, "I do not like the person sitting in front of me or next to me; ask him to go." It would be competent to the management to go to that person and say, "Please go; you cannot have your money back, go." Further, if the proposition is right, it follows that, having let the seat to A, the management may come to A at the end of the first act or before and say "I revoke your licence, go," and he has to go. The management may let the seat to B for the rest of the performance, and at the end of the second act or sooner they may come to B and say, "I revoke your licence, go." He will have to go, and they may let the seat a third time to C. Those consequences ensue from this proposition if it be well founded. It was for that reason I said at the outset of my remarks that it seems to me, when the point comes to be considered, it is contrary to good sense. Next it is to my mind contrary also to good law. The proposition is based upon the well-known decision in *Wood* v. *Leadbitter* ((1845) 13 M. & W. 838; 153 E.R. 351). Let me at the outset say what *Wood* v. *Leadbitter* seems to me to have decided. It affirmed that a mere licence, whether or not it be under seal, by which I mean a licence not coupled with an interest or a grant whether it be under seal or not, is revocable. It affirmed also that if there be a licence coupled with an interest or coupled with a grant, it is not, or at any rate in general is not, revocable. For those two propositions, I read these two sentences from the case of *Wood* v. *Leadbitter* (at 844): "A mere licence is revocable; but that which is called a licence is often something more than a licence; it often comprises or is connected with a grant, and then the party who has given it cannot in general revoke it, so as to defeat his grant, to which it was incident. It may further be observed, that a licence under seal (provided it be a mere licence) is as revocable as a licence by parol; and, on the other hand, a licence by parol, coupled with a grant, is as irrevocable as a licence by deed, provided only that the grant is of a nature capable of being made by parol." Those are propositions with which, as it seems to me, no one quarrels or can quarrel. *Wood* v. *Leadbitter* rested, I think, upon one of two grounds—I will indicate them both—but I think it was the second of those which I am going to mention. The first ground is that the man who bought his ticket for the race meeting had not obtained any grant of right to come during the currency of the meeting to see any particular spectacle from its commencement to its termination. If that were the ground, it would, I think, be erroneous. I conceive he had the right to see what was to be seen during the days covered by his ticket. But I do not think that was the ground on which the court decided it. They decided it upon the ground, which will be found at p. 842 and onwards, that no incorporeal inheritance affecting land can be created or transferred otherwise than by deed, a proposition which was discussed with some elaboration in the course of the judgment. What Alderson B. was saying there was:

this man has got no deed; he has got nothing under seal; he has therefore not got a grant; he cannot in this court be heard to say he is a grantee, and because he is not a grantee he is a mere licensee, and being a mere licensee (whether it is under seal or not under seal does not make any difference) the licence is revocable.

Let me for a moment discuss this present case upon the footing that *Wood* v. *Leadbitter* stands as good law at this date. I am going to say presently that to my mind it does not, but suppose it does stand as good law at this date. What is the grant in this case? The plaintiff in the present action paid his money to enjoy the sight of a particular spectacle. He was anxious to go into a picture theatre to see a series of views or pictures during, I suppose, an hour or a couple of hours. That which was granted to him was the right to enjoy looking at a spectacle, to attend a performance from its beginning to its end. That which was called the licence, the right to go upon the premises, was only something granted to him for the purpose of enabling him to have that which had been granted him, namely, the right to see. He could not see the performance unless he went into the building. His right to go into the building was something given to him in order to enable him to have the benefit of that which had been granted to him, namely, the right to hear the opera, or see the theatrical performance, or see the moving pictures as was the case here. So that here there was a licence coupled with a grant. If so, *Wood* v. *Leadbitter* does not stand in the way at all. A licence coupled with a grant is not revocable; *Wood* v. *Leadbitter* affirmed as much.

So far I have been treating it as if *Wood* v. *Leadbitter* were law as now administered in every court. Let us see how that matter stands. *Wood* v. *Leadbitter* was a case decided in a court of law before the Judicature Act; it was a case to be decided, therefore, simply upon the principles which are applicable in a court of law as distinguished from a court of equity. . . .

The position of matters now is that the court is bound under the Judicature Act to give effect to equitable doctrines. The question we have to consider is whether, having regard to equitable considerations, *Wood* v. *Leadbitter* is now law meaning that *Wood* v. *Leadbitter* is a decision which can be applied in its integrity in a court which is bound to give effect to equitable considerations. In my opinion, it is not. . . . The present Lord Parker, then Parker J., in the case of *Jones* v. *Earl of Tankerville*, says this ([1909] 2 Ch. 440, 443): "An injunction restraining the revocation of the licence, when it is revocable at law, may in a sense be called relief by way of specific performance, but it is not specific performance in the sense of compelling the vendor to do anything. It merely prevents him from breaking his contract, and protects a right in equity which but for the absence of a seal would be a right at law, and since the Judicature Act it may well be doubted whether the absence of a seal in such a case can be relied on in any court." What was relied on in *Wood* v. *Leadbitter*, and rightly relied on at that date, was that there was not an instrument under seal, and therefore there was not a grant, and therefore the licensee could not say that he was not a mere licensee, but a licensee with a grant. That is now swept away. It cannot be said as against the plaintiff that he is a licensee with no grant merely because there is not an instrument under seal which gives him a right of law.

There is another way in which the matter may be put. If there be a licence with an agreement not to revoke the licence, that, if given for value, is an enforceable right. If the facts here are, as I think they are, that the licence was a licence to enter the building and see the spectacle from its commencement until its termination, then there was included in that contract a contract not to revoke the licence until the play had run to its termination. It was then a breach of contract to revoke the obligation not to revoke the licence, and for that the decision in *Kerrison* v.*Smith* ([1897] 2 Q.B. 445) is an authority. So far I have dealt with the law. . . .

The defendants had, I think, for value contracted that the plaintiff should see a certain spectacle from its commencement to its termination. They broke that contract and it was a tort on their part to remove him. They committed an assault upon him by law. It was not of a violent kind, because, like a wise man, the plaintiff gave way to superior force and left the theatre. They sought to justify the assault by saying that they were entitled to remove him because he had not paid. He had paid, the jury have so found. Failing on that question of fact, they say that they were entitled to remove him because his licence was revocable. In my opinion, it was not. There was, I think, no justification for the assault here committed. Under the circumstances it was for the jury to give him such a sum as was right for the assault which was committed upon him, and for the serious indignity to a gentleman of being seized and treated in this way in a place of public resort. The jury have found that he was originally in the theatre as a spectator, that the assault was committed upon him, and that it was a wrongful act.

I think that the appeal which has been brought before us, and which is founded simply upon the question of law which I have discussed at the beginning of this judgment, fails and must be dismissed with costs.

Questions

1. May a cinema owner eject a young couple kissing quietly in the back row?

2. Suppose the ticket had said (a) on its face, and (b) in tiny print on the back, "The management reserves the right to eject any person who refuses, when asked, to leave," could the management safely eject a person on the grounds mentioned by Buckley L.J. at the beginning of his judgment?

3. Why was there any difficulty in the case, given that the defendant's act was admittedly a breach of contract and therefore wrongful?

4. £150 in 1915 money is well over £5,000 in 1987 money. Do you think the damages which the jury awarded were aggravated or exemplary?

Note:

"Broadly speaking, a licence does not confer a right; a licence prevents that from being unlawful which, but for the licence, would be unlawful; it is a consent by the owner of a right that another person should commit an act which, but for that licence, would be an infringement of the right of the person who gives the licence; and a bare licence, unless there is some interest in the licensee, is revocable. But it is well settled now—I need only refer to the decision in *Hurst's* case—that once the licensee has an interest, spending money on the faith of the licence—a valuable property or a valuable interest to him—the licence then becomes an irrevocable licence; and when the irrevocable licence is also a sole and exclusive licence, we are getting to the stage when it is difficult to distinguish an exclusive irrevocable licence to do an act from a right to do an act," *per* Scrutton L.J. in *Messager* v. *B.B.C.* (1928) 97 L.J.K.B. 251, 254.

This quotation shows how important it is to limit the apparently excellent decision in the principal case. For example, suppose I contract with a decorator that he should paint my study. He comes and starts working. When he has painted half of it, I tell him I do not like the quality of his work (which is excellent), and that he must take his brushes and go. He declines to go, on the ground that he has invested money on the paint on the wall. I can surely throw him out after the lapse of a reasonable time. For a case where an injunction was issued to prevent a person exercising his contractual right to enter the land of another, see *Thompson* v. *Park* [1944] 1 K.B. 408, which was clearly right on the facts, though the reasons have attracted much flak (*Verrall* v. *Great Yarmouth B.C.* [1980] 1 All E.R. 839).

In *Hounslow* v. *Twickenham Garden Developments* ([1971] Ch. 233) a borough sought an injunction to remove from their site some building contractors whose employment they had tried to terminate. Megarry J. refused the injunction on the ground that it was not clear that the purported termination was contractually valid. He observed that a person who had a contractual right to remain on property could not be physically evicted by the occupier bound by that contract, even if the contract were not specifically enforceable, and held that a court would never issue an injunction to evict such a person. It is to be hoped that neither observation will be treated as authoritative, for they give far too much effect to the mere existence of a contract. The effect of a contract depends on the strength of the right it purports to limit—a point Megarry J. himself recognised in discussing *White & Carter (Councils) Ltd.* v. *McGregor* ([1962] A.C. 413). The learned judge also cast some doubt on the case next following.

VAUGHAN v. HAMPSON

Court of Exchequer (1875) 33 L.T. 15

The defendant, who was a solicitor for a bankrupt, called a general meeting of the creditors, which was attended by the plaintiff, who was acting as proxy for two of them. The defendant ejected him from the meeting, and the plaintiff sued for damages for assault and battery. The defendant pleaded that the plaintiff was a trespasser whom he ejected without unnecessary force. The plaintiff replied that he was a proxy for two of the creditors, and lawfully refused to leave when asked. The defendant demurred to this replication, and his demurrer was overruled.

Cleasby B.: The question is whether or not the plaintiff was a trespasser on the occasion in question. We are of opinion that he was not. He was, on the contrary, one of a number of persons who went to the defendant's office by invitation to attend a meeting of creditors, in order to discuss what steps should be taken in the matter of the liquidation proceedings against the bankrupt, for some of whose creditors the plaintiff was acting as the solicitor and duly appointed proxy on the occasion. The defendant had given the plaintiff leave and licence to be present, and the latter therefore had a right, coupled with an interest, entitling him to be on the defendant's premises. Our judgment must be for the plaintiff.

Pollock B.: I do not think that any question arises here as to whether the defendant had or not any authority as chairman of the meeting to turn the plaintiff out. No such allegation appears in the plea. This case is not governed, in my opinion, by that of *Wood* v. *Leadbitter* ((1845) 13 M. & W. 838; 153 E.R. 351), on which Mr. Herschell seemed to rely as an authority in favour of the defendant here. In that case there was a contract for pleasure. In the present case there was, as my brother Cleasby had said, a right coupled with an interest in the plaintiff to be where he was.

Amphlett B.: I am of the same opinion; and I will only add that if we could come to any other conclusion I think it would be a great scandal to the law.

(iii) *Content*

BURNARD v. HAGGIS

Court of Common Pleas (1863) 14 C.B.(N.S.) 45; 2 New Rep. 126; 32 L.J.C.P. 189; 8 L.T. 320; 9 Jur.(N.S.) 1325; 11 W.R. 644; 143 E.R. 360

The plaintiff let out horses for riding at 7s. 6d. and for jumping at one guinea. The defendant, an infant undergraduate at Trinity College, Cambridge, with rooms in Rose Crescent, went to the plaintiff's stable and asked for a horse for riding to be delivered to Green Street (where his friend Bonner lived). The charge was 7s. 6d., and it was clear that the horse was not to be used for jumping. Bonner, mounted on the plaintiff's mare, and the defendant, otherwise mounted, went out riding over the fields towards Grantchester. Bonner put the plaintiff's mare to a wattle fence and a stake entered her, causing a wound of which she subsequently died.

The plaintiff recovered £30 in the county court, and the defendant's appeal was dismissed.

Willes J.: . . . It appears to me that the act of riding the mare into the place where she received her death-wound was as much a trespass, notwithstanding the hiring for another purpose, as if, without any hiring at all, the defendant had gone into a field and taken the mare out and hunted her and killed her. It was a bare trespass, not within the object and purpose of the hiring. It was not even an excess. It was doing an act towards the mare which was altogether forbidden by the owner. . . .

Byles J.: . . . I am of the same opinion. Here the mare was let for the specific purpose of a ride along the road, and for the purpose of being ridden only by the defendant. The defendant not only allows his friend to mount, but allows him to put the mare to a fence for which he was told she was unfit. Quite independently, therefore, of the question of necessaries, the defendant is clearly responsible for the wrong done.

Question

In *Lord Camoys* v. *Scurr* (1840) 9 C. & P. 383; 173 E.R. 879, the defendant obtained the plaintiff's horse from the plaintiff's agent for sale for the purpose of trial. The defendant tried it and asked a nobleman's groom to try it also. The horse ran away with the groom and was killed. Coleridge J. said: "The defendant had this mare for the purpose of trying her and I think that he was entitled to put a competent person on the mare to try her." Or a person appearing to be competent? Would this apply to the trial of a car?

Note:

This case is not really as simple as it looks. It is difficult to believe that the mere permitting the horse to be jumped could constitute a trespass, but the giving of the horse to Bonner to ride might well be. "There are many bailments in which the bailee is entitled to make a sub-bailment: the repairer of a motor-car for instance, can often quite reasonably send away a part of it to another firm for repairs; a carrier of goods may need to entrust them to another carrier for part of the journey; a hirer may himself often, quite lawfully, sub-hire the goods. It all depends on the circumstances of the particular case," *per* Denning L.J. in *Edwards* v. *Newland & Co.* [1950] 2 K.B. 534, 542.

The liability of a bailee who has deviated from the terms of his holding is absolute in the sense that he becomes an all-risks insurer for the goods. It is not necessary that the damage be a foreseeable consequence of the deviation; if the goods are damaged *during* the deviation, the bailee must pay (*Lilley* v. *Doubleday* (1881) 7 Q.B.D. 510), just as he must if he keeps them too long (*Mitchell* v. *Ealing* [1978] 2 All E.R. 779). In the normal case, the bailee will have promised, as a matter of contract, to adhere to the terms of the holding. Such a promise would not, as a matter of contract, be binding if the contract were illegal, but the bailee might still be liable for deviating from the terms of his holding as a matter of tort.

BYRNE v. KINEMATOGRAPH RENTERS SOCIETY LTD.

Chancery [1958] 1 W.L.R. 762; 102 S.J. 509; [1959] 2 All E.R. 579

The plaintiff cinema-owner was blacklisted and put out of business by the defendant film-distributors whose employees had gone to the plaintiff's cinema not to see the film but simply to check on the number of patrons. The plaintiff claimed damages on the theory that the defendants had deliberately injured him in his trade by means of illegal acts, namely trespasses.

Harman J.: . . . It is alleged by the plaintiff that the investigation conducted by K.R.S. through Belton and his emissaries was illegal because it involved acts of trespass on the plaintiff's property. It was argued that the twenty-three visits of Pinder or Lewis and their assistants to the County Cinema which I have described were all acts of trespass because they went into the cinema not for the purpose for which alone the public was invited to attend but for a different purpose, namely, to obtain evidence against the plaintiff. I cannot think there is anything in this point. The cinema was open to the public who were invited to go in and take tickets, and this is what Pinder and Lewis and their assistants did. Their motives in taking the tickets are, I think, immaterial from this point of view. They did nothing they were not invited to do, and in my judgment it cannot be said that because they may not have wished to see the performance but were merely interested in the numbers on the tickets or in counting the number of patrons they committed acts of trespass. . . .

Questions

1. Suppose that Pinder had injured himself on a nail on one of the seats. Could he recover from the present plaintiff?

2. Suppose that, after their entry to the cinema, the plaintiff had discovered that Pinder and Lewis had come to count the patrons and tickets so as to give evidence inimical to his interests. He asks them to leave. They refuse. He ejects them. Would they succeed in an action of assault? If not, would that be because (a) the contract was induced by fraud, (b) though it was not, equity would not in the circumstances think of ordering specific enforcement, (c) there was an implied term in the contract, or (d) *Hurst's* case was wrongly decided? Would the plaintiff have to give them their money back?

Note:

"A person is guilty of burglary if— . . . (b) having entered any building . . . as a trespasser he steals . . . anything in the building . . . or inflicts . . . on any person therein any grievous bodily harm" (Theft Act 1968, s.9(1)). The term "trespasser" in this enactment is bound to provoke some discussion in the coming years, but great care must be taken before transposing to private law the decisions of criminal courts on such texts. For instance, *mens rea* in relation to the trespass is required for burglary, that is, the accused must have known, or as good as known, that he was trespassing: such knowledge is quite irrelevant in private law.

(iv) *Mistake*

ARMSTRONG v. SHEPPARD & SHORT LTD.

Court of Appeal [1959] 2 Q.B. 384; [1959] 3 W.L.R. 84; 123 J.P. 401; 103 S.J. 508; [1959] 2 All E.R. 651

The defendant building contractors wanted to construct a sewer under a pathway at the back of the plaintiff's house. The plaintiff did not know that he owned this land, and when he was asked by the defendants if he had any objection to their constructing the proposed sewer, he said that he had none. The sewer was built. When the plaintiff discovered that he owned the land, he asked the defendants to remove the sewer. They did not, and continued to discharge effluent through it. The county court judge refused the injunction requested by the plaintiff, but awarded him 20s. damages for trespass. The plaintiff appealed and the defendant cross-appealed.

As to the plaintiff's appeal, the Court of Appeal held that no injunction should be granted because the plaintiff was suffering only trivial damage, and in any case he had tried to deceive the court by denying that he ever gave permission for the construction of the sewer. The cross-appeal also failed.

Evershed M.R.: . . . in an action of common law trespass, it does not, in the circumstances here, matter that the plaintiff was unaware of his proprietary rights when he gave permission: the thing is done: and it has had the lawful justification (in so far as this case is concerned) that it was done with the approval of the man who now tries to complain about it. It follows from that conclusion (as [his counsel] conceded) that [the plaintiff] cannot complain of the presence in the land now of the physical things, the manhole and the pipes. . . .

[His Lordship turned to the trespass by means of the discharge of effluent.] First, if the subject-matter which is alleged to have been granted, is an interest in land, then it cannot be done by parol only. Of course, a licence coupled with a grant, if it is effectively done, will no doubt be irrevocable. But there is nothing in the authorities that [defendant's counsel] cited to support the view that a right to pass water through another's land—which is, as I conceive, a proprietary right—is capable of grant by parol. But, secondly, such a permission to pass effluent down a man's land no doubt might be, as a matter of contract, properly covered as between one individual and another. . . . In my judgment . . . a licence of that kind if it is to be irrevocable during the plaintiff's tenure, must have the necessary qualities of a contract, binding upon the parties: it must be supported by consideration, and must in other respects be the subject of a contract. . . .

. . . by well-established principle the licensee does not become necessarily a trespasser the moment the licensor says "The licence is at an end": the alleged trespasser is allowed a reasonable time . . . to discontinue the act which thereby would become a trespass. . . .

Questions

1. Do you accept the distinction between an act which would constitute a continuing trespass and a series of acts which would constitute repeated trespasses?

2. Was the plaintiff merely estopped from complaining about the presence of the pipes?

Section 2.—Law and Order

(i) *Crime*

POLICE AND CRIMINAL EVIDENCE ACT 1984

PART I

POWERS TO STOP AND SEARCH

1.—(1) A constable may exercise any power conferred by this section—

(*a*) in any place to which at the time when he proposes to exercise the power the public or any section of the public has access, on payment or otherwise, as of right or by virtue of express or implied permission; or

(*b*) in any other place to which people have ready access at the time when he proposes to exercise the power but which is not a dwelling.

(2) Subject to subsection (3) to (5) below, a constable—

(*a*) may search—
    (i) any person or vehicle;
    (ii) anything which is in or on a vehicle,
    for stolen or prohibited articles; and

(*b*) may detain a person or vehicle for the purpose of such a search.

(3) This section does not give a constable power to search a person or vehicle or

anything in or on a vehicle unless he has reasonable grounds for suspecting that he will find stolen or prohibited articles.

(4) If a person is in a garden or yard occupied with and used for the purposes of a dwelling or on other land so occupied and used, a constable may not search him in the exercise of the power conferred by this section unless the constable has reasonable grounds for believing—

(*a*) that he does not reside in the dwelling; and
(*b*) that he is not in the place in question with the express or implied permission of a person who resides in the dwelling.

(5) . . .

(6) If in the course of such a search a constable discovers an article which he has reasonable grounds for suspecting to be a stolen or prohibited article, he may seize it.

. . .

PART II

POWERS OF ENTRY, SEARCH AND SEIZURE

Search warrants

8. . . .

15.—(1) This section and section 16 below have effect in relation to the issue to constables under any enactment, including an enactment contained in an Act passed after this Act, of warrants to enter and search premises; and an entry on or search of premises under a warrant is unlawful unless it complies with this section and section 16 below.

(2) Where a constable applies for any such warrant, it shall be his duty—

(*a*) to state—
    (i) the ground on which he makes the application; and
    (ii) the enactment under which the warrant would be issued;
(*b*) to specify the premises which it is desired to enter and search; and
(*c*) to identify, so far as is practicable, the articles or persons to be sought.

(3) An application for such a warrant shall be made ex parte and supported by an information in writing.

(4) The constable shall answer on oath any question that the justice of the peace or judge hearing the application asks him.

(5) A warrant shall authorise an entry on one occasion only.

(6) A warrant—

(*a*) shall specify—
    (i) the name of the person who applies for it;
    (ii) the date on which it is issued;
    (iii) the enactment under which it is issued; and
    (iv) the premises to be searched; and
(*b*) shall identify, so far as is practicable, the articles or persons to be sought.

(7) Two copies shall be made of a warrant.

(8) The copies shall be clearly certified as copies.

16.—(1) A warrant to enter and search premises may be executed by any constable.

(2) Such a warrant may authorise persons to accompany any constable who is executing it.

(3) Entry and search under a warrant must be within one month from the date of its issue.

(4) Entry and search under a warrant must be at a reasonable hour unless it appears to the constable executing it that the purpose of a search may be frustrated on an entry at a reasonable hour.

(5) Where the occupier of premises which are to be entered and searched is present at the time when a constable seeks to execute a warrant to enter and search them, the constable—

(a) shall identify himself to the occupier and, if not in uniform, shall produce to him documentary evidence that he is a constable;

(b) shall produce the warrant to him; and

(c) shall supply him with a copy of it.

(6) . . .

(7) If there is no person present who appears to the constable to be in charge of the premises, he shall leave a copy of the warrant in a prominent place on the premises.

(8) A search under a warrant may only be a search to the extent required for the purpose for which the warrant was issued. . . .

Entry and search without search warrant

17.—(1) Subject to the following provisions of this section, and without prejudice to any other enactment, a constable may enter and search any premises for the purpose—

(a) of executing—

(i) a warrant of arrest issued in connection with or arising out of criminal proceedings; or

(ii) a warrant of commitment issued under section 76 of the Magistrates' Courts Act 1980;

(b) of arresting a person for an arrestable offence;

(c) of arresting a person for an offence under—

(i) section 1 (prohibition of uniforms in connection with political objects), 4 (prohibition of offensive weapons at public meetings and processions) or 5 (prohibition of offensive conduct conducive to breaches of the peace) of the Public Order Act 1936;

(ii) any enactment contained in sections 6 to 8 or 10 of the Criminal Law Act 1977 (offences relating to entering and remaining on property);

(d) of recapturing a person who is unlawfully at large and whom he is pursuing; or

(e) of saving life or limb or preventing serious damage to property.

(2) Except for the purpose specified in paragraph (e) of subsection (1) above, the powers of entry and search conferred by this section—

(a) are only exercisable if the constable has reasonable grounds for believing that the person whom he is seeking is on the premises; and . . .

(3) The powers of entry and search conferred by this section are only exercisable for the purposes specified in subsection (1)(c)(ii) above by a constable in uniform.

(4) The power of search conferred by this section is only a power to search to the extent that is reasonably required for the purpose for which the power of entry is exercised.

(5) Subject to subsection (6) below, all the rules of common law under which a constable has power to enter premises without a warrant are hereby abolished.

(6) Nothing in subsection (5) above affects any power of entry to deal with or prevent a breach of the peace.

19.—(1) The powers conferred by subsections (2), (3) and (4) below are exercisable by a constable who is lawfully on any premises.

(2) The constable may seize anything which is on the premises if he has reasonable grounds for believing—

(*a*) that it has been obtained in consequence of the commission of an offence; and

(*b*) that it is necessary to seize it in order to prevent it being concealed, lost, damaged, altered or destroyed.

(3) The constable may seize anything which is on the premises if he has reasonable grounds for believing—

(*a*) that it is evidence in relation to an offence which he is investigating or any other offence; and

(*b*) that it is necessary to seize it in order to prevent the evidence being concealed, lost, altered or destroyed.

PART III

ARREST

24.—(1) The powers of summary arrest conferred by the following subsections shall apply—

(*a*) to offences for which the sentence is fixed by law;

(*b*) to offences for which a person of 21 years of age or over (not previously convicted) may be sentenced to imprisonment for a term of five years (or might be so sentenced but for the restrictions imposed by section 33 of the Magistrates' Courts Act 1980); and

(*c*) to the offences to which subsection (2) below applies,

and in this Act "arrestable offence" means any such offence.

(2) [Specifies offences under the Customs and Excise and Official Secrets Acts, offences of corruption, offences against women, taking a motor vehicle without authority and going equipped for stealing, as well as conspiring, attempting and getting others to commit such offences.]

(4) Any person may arrest without a warrant—

(*a*) anyone who is in the act of committing an arrestable offence;

(*b*) anyone whom he has reasonable grounds for suspecting to be committing such an offence.

(5) Where an arrestable offence has been committed, any person may arrest without a warrant—

(*a*) anyone who is guilty of the offence;

(*b*) anyone whom he has reasonable grounds for suspecting to be guilty of it.

(6) Where a constable has reasonable grounds for suspecting that an arrestable offence has been committed, he may arrest without a warrant anyone whom he has reasonable grounds for suspecting to be guilty of the offence.

(7) A constable may arrest without a warrant—

(*a*) anyone who is about to commit an arrestable offence;

(*b*) anyone whom he has reasonable grounds for suspecting to be about to commit an arrestable offence.

25.—(1) Where a constable has reasonable grounds for suspecting that any offence which is not an arrestable offence has been committed or attempted, or is being committed or attempted, he may arrest the relevant person if it appears to him that service of a summons is impracticable or inappropriate because any of the general arrest conditions is satisfied.

(2) In this section "the relevant person" means any person whom the constable has reasonable grounds to suspect of having committed or having attempted to commit the offence or of being in the course of committing or attempting to commit it.

(3) The general arrest conditions are—

(a) that the name of the relevant person is unknown to, and cannot be readily ascertained by, the constable;

(b) that the constable has reasonable grounds for doubting whether a name furnished by the relevant person as his name is his real name;

(c) that—

(i) the relevant person has failed to furnish a satisfactory address for service; or

(ii) the constable has reasonable grounds for doubting whether an address furnished by the relevant person is a satisfactory address for service;

(d) that the constable has reasonable grounds for believing that arrest is necessary to prevent the relevant person—

(i) causing physical injury to himself or any other person;

(ii) suffering physical injury;

(iii) causing loss of or damage to property;

(iv) committing an offence against public decency; or

(v) causing an unlawful obstruction of the highway;

(e) that the constable has reasonable grounds for believing that arrest is necessary to protect a child or other vulnerable person from the relevant person.

. . .

28.—(1) Subject to subsection (5) below, where a person is arrested, otherwise than by being informed that he is under arrest, the arrest is not lawful unless the person arrested is informed that he is under arrest as soon as is practicable after his arrest.

(2) Where a person is arrested by a constable, subsection (1) above applies regardless of whether the fact of the arrest is obvious.

(3) Subject to subsection (5) below, no arrest is lawful unless the person arrested is informed of the ground for the arrest at the time of, or as soon as is practicable after, the arrest.

(4) Where a person is arrested by a constable, subsection (3) above applies regardless of whether the ground for the arrest is obvious.

(5) Nothing in this section is to be taken to require a person to be informed—

(a) that he is under arrest; or

(b) of the ground for the arrest,

if it was not reasonably practicable for him to be so informed by reason of his having escaped from arrest before the information could be given.

29. Where for the purpose of assisting with an investigation a person attends voluntarily at a police station or at any other place where a constable is present or accompanies a constable to a police station or any such other place without having been arrested—

(a) he shall be entitled to leave at will unless he is placed under arrest;

(b) he shall be informed at once that he is under arrest if a decision is taken by a constable to prevent him from leaving at will.

30.—(1) Subject to the following provisions of this section, where a person—

(a) is arrested by a constable for an offence; or

(b) is taken into custody by a constable after being arrested for an offence by a person other than a constable, at any place other than a police station, he shall be taken to a police station by a constable as soon as practicable after the arrest.

(10) Nothing in subsection (1) above shall prevent a constable delaying taking a person who has been arrested to a police station if the presence of that person elsewhere is necessary in order to carry out such investigations as it is reasonable to carry out immediately.

31. Where—

(*a*) a person—
    (i) has been arrested for an offence; and
    (ii) is at a police station in consequence of that arrest; and

(*b*) it appears to a constable that, if he were released from that arrest, he would be liable to arrest for some other offence,

he shall be arrested for that other offence.

117. Where any provision of this Act—

(*a*) confers a power on a constable; and

(*b*) does not provide that the power may only be exercised with the consent of some person, other than a police officer,

the officer may use reasonable force, if necessary, in the exercise of the power.

Note:

Many trespassory acts are legitimated by this important enactment—acts of false imprisonment, battery, trespass to goods and trespass to land.

s.1: Note that these powers may not be exercised in dwellings at all, or in gardens attached to dwellings unless the person is probably trespassing.

s.15(1): Note that breach of the statutory requirements renders the entry unlawful, and that some of the requirements cannot be satisfied until after the entry itself. This is a version of the doctrine of trespass *ab initio*, derided by Lord Denning in *Chic Fashions (West Wales) Ltd.* v. *Jones* [1968] 2 Q.B. 299, but resuscitated by him in *Cinnamond* v. *British Airports Auth'y* [1980] 2 All E.R. 368.

s.17(6): Note that the common law power to enter premises with a view to preventing or quelling a breach of the peace remains unimpaired.

s.24(5): Compare subsections 5 and 6. The restriction on the citizen's right to arrest a suspect (namely that the arrestable offence have actually been committed) stems from *Walters* v. *W.H. Smith & Sons* [1914] 1 K.B. 595.

s.25(6): Anyone may stop a person committing a breach of the peace (*Albert* v. *Lavin* [1982] A.C. 546). Perhaps "arrest" is not quite the right word to describe the act of using reasonable force for this purpose, but it was used by the Court of Appeal in *R.* v. *Howell* [1982] Q.B. 416, 427: " . . . the word 'disturbance' when used in isolation cannot constitute a breach of the peace. We are emboldened to say that there is a breach of the peace whenever harm is actually done or is likely to be done to a person or in his presence to his property or a person is in fear of being so harmed through an assault, an affray, a riot, an unlawful assembly or other disturbance. It is for this breach of the peace, when done in his presence, or the reasonable apprehension of it that a constable, or anyone else, may arrest an offender without warrant." In *R.* v. *Chief Constable of Devon, ex p. Central Elec. Generating Board* [1981] 3 All E.R. 826, Lord Denning felt able to say that it was a breach of the peace "whenever a person who is lawfully carrying out work is unlawfully and physically prevented by another from doing it" (at 832). That is judicial fantasy.

s.26 (not quoted) abolishes all other statutory powers of arrest with warrant except those granted in the 23 enactments listed in Schedule 2.

s.31: What is the mischief against which this section is directed?

CRIMINAL LAW ACT 1967

3.—(1) A person may use such force as is reasonable in the circumstances in the prevention of crime, or in effecting or assisting in the lawful arrest of offenders or suspected offenders or of persons unlawfully at large.

(2) Subsection (1) above shall replace the rules of the common law on the question when force used for a purpose mentioned in the subsection is justified by that purpose.

MAGISTRATES' COURTS ACT 1980

125. . . .
(3) A warrant . . . may be executed by a constable notwithstanding that it is not in his possession at the time; but the warrant shall, on the demand of the person arrested, be shown to him as soon as practicable.

HUSSIEN v. CHONG FOOK KAM

Privy Council [1970] A.C. 942; [1970] 2 W.L.R. 441; [1969] 3 All E.R. 1626

Lord Devlin: . . . This is an appeal in an action for false imprisonment. The three defendants in the action, who are the appellants before the board, are two police officers and the Government of Malaysia. Nothing turns on the separate responsibility of any of the defendants and the action can be described as one brought against the police. The two plaintiffs in the action were arrested on July 11, 1965, for an offence said to have been committed on the previous day against either section 304A of the Penal Code or section 34A of the Road Traffic Ordinance. The former of these sections corresponds to the offence of manslaughter and the latter makes it an offence to cause death by dangerous or reckless driving. The plaintiffs were held in custody overnight and brought before the magistrate on July 12, when he made an order for their retention for seven days under section 117 of the Criminal Procedure Code for further investigation. On the next day the plaintiffs were released, the police having found that there was not sufficient evidence to proceed against either of them. It was agreed that the false imprisonment, if any, was brought to an end by the magistrate's order. The plaintiffs' action was dismissed in the High Court of Malaysia but was successful on appeal in the Federal Court of Malaysia, where judgment was given in their favour for damages of $2,500 each. From this judgment the defendants have appealed to the Board. The plaintiffs have not entered an appearance as respondents to this appeal so that their Lordships have not had the advantage of hearing argument on both sides.

The police inquiry began with a complaint made at the Mentakab police station at 10.15 p.m. on July 10. The complainant stated that at 9.15 p.m., when he was driving home with four friends in his car, he passed a lorry, coming in the opposite direction, with a trailer loaded with timber. As he passed a piece of timber fell off the lorry, hitting his windscreen and two of the men in the car. One of the men died. The lorry did not stop. Police inquiries led them to conclude that the incident had occurred as stated and that the lorry involved in it was numbered PC 8200. It is unnecessary to give details of the inquiry up to this point since it is not disputed that the police had reasonable grounds for reaching this conclusion. Directions were given that the lorry PC 8200 was to be stopped and detained.

At 7.55 a.m. on July 11, PC 22927 of Bukit Tinggi police station found the lorry stationary in front of a coffee shop about a quarter of a mile from the police station. He found and detained the two plaintiffs, one of whom admitted to being the driver of the lorry and the other the attendant. The corporal in charge of the station arrived ten minutes later. According to his evidence (the police evidence generally was accepted by the trial judge) one of the plaintiffs "asked me what wrong he had done. I told him that I had received instructions from Mentakab to detain him on suspicion of a fatal road accident case." This was said in the hearing of the other plaintiff. About 1 p.m. the area inspector from Mentakab and his superior officer, the district superintendent—these are the two individual defendants in the action—arrived at the coffee shop. They interrogated both plaintiffs there. The one who said he was the driver said that they had not met with any accident. The evidence is not very clear, but it is reasonable to infer that he meant by that that they were not at the scene of the accident at the relevant time, for both men were asked to give an account of their movements. The police officers did not regard their explanations as satisfactory and it was decided that they should be taken to Mentakab police station for further investigation. Since an attendant in a lorry is frequently an alternate driver and the police felt doubt about which man was the driver at the relevant time, both men were treated alike. They left about 3 p.m. and arrived at Mentakab at about 5 p.m. Their story was that on the evening in question they had bought food at a shop in Mentakab and that one of them had had his hair cut at a barber's shop. They were taken to the two shops where they pointed out to the police two witnesses, but the witnesses were reluctant to answer any questions. At 6.15 p.m. they were taken back to the police station where, as already recorded, they spent the night and were brought before the magistrate on the following morning.

The law on arrest is contained in the Constitution and the Criminal Procedure Code. For the purposes of this case it is enough to say that under section 23(i)(a) of the Code the police were empowered to arrest the plaintiffs if a reasonable suspicion existed of their having been concerned in an offence of reckless and dangerous driving causing death. In any case of wrongful arrest it is important to identify at the outset the precise time of arrest, not only for the purpose of article 5, clause 3, of the Constitution, which provides that an arrested person shall be informed as soon as may be thereafter of the grounds of his arrest, but also because it is the time when the existence of a reasonable suspicion must be proved. The statement of claim alleges in paragraph 6 that "both plaintiffs were stopped by the police at about 7 a.m. and after prolonged questioning were taken to Bukit Tinggi police station." In paragraph 7 it is alleged that at about 6 p.m. on the same day both the plaintiffs were locked up in separate cells at Mentakab police station and kept falsely imprisoned.

An arrest occurs when a police officer states in terms that he is arresting or when he uses force to restrain the individual concerned. It occurs also when by words or conduct he makes it clear that he will, if necessary, use force to prevent the individual from going where he may want to go. It does not occur when he stops an individual to make inquiries. The moment when it occurred in this case was between 8.05 and 9 a.m. on July 11 when (their Lordships have quoted the relevant passage from the evidence) the corporal told the plaintiffs of the existing suspicion and said that he had instructions to detain them. Mr. Gratiaen, for the appellants, has very fairly conceded that, notwithstanding the pleading—and their Lordships doubt whether it can be construed as alleging an arrest before 6 p.m.—the plaintiffs were arrested by the corporal not later than 9 a.m.

At that point of time the police had good reason to suspect that one or other of the plaintiffs was driving the lorry from whose trailer the piece of timber fell. But there is a wide gap between a suspicion that one of the plaintiffs was the man driving the lorry and a suspicion that he was driving it recklessly or dangerously. The trial judge did not acknowledge the existence of such a gap. He said in his judgment:—"Suspicion focused reasonably enough on the said lorry and it goes without saying on the driver." Granted that the fall of the timber is of itself some evidence of insecure loading, and granted also that it would be reckless driving to drive at any speed or in any manner a lorry with a trailer which the driver knew or ought to have known to be insecurely loaded, the police had in their Lordships' opinion no reasonable grounds for suspecting that either plaintiff had any knowledge, actual or constructive, of the state of the load. Likewise, there was nothing at all to suggest that the lorry was at the time of the accident being driven in a dangerous manner. Mr. Gratiaen has argued that a driver ought to satisfy himself before he sets off that his load is secure. No doubt he ought to notice an obvious danger of collapse, but the fall of a single piece of timber is no evidence of that. Mr. Gratiaen has relied strongly—and it is a strong point—on the fact that the lorry did not stop after the accident. But here again their Lordships must, with respect, differ from the trial judge when he describes it as "clearly a hit and run case." It is quite possible that the fall of a single piece of timber from the trailer might not be noticed at the time, and even if it were and the plaintiffs speculated about it, it might not occur to them that it would lead to the unusual consequences that happened here. Their Lordships conclude that the suspicion that the plaintiffs or either of them was guilty of reckless driving was not reasonable.

Mr. Gratiaen has criticised the test adopted in the Federal Court. Suffian F.J., who delivered the judgment of the court, said that the information available to the police "was insufficient to prove prima facie a case against the plaintiffs under section 304A of the Penal Code or under section 34A of the Road Traffic Ordinance." Mr. Gratiaen submits that this is the test appropriate in actions for malicious prosecution and not in actions for false imprisonment. Whether or not this is so—and their Lordships do not wish to add any further formulae to those already devised for the action of false imprisonment—it would appear to be a much stiffer test than the reasonable suspicion, which is the foundation of the power given in section 23(1)(a) of the Criminal Procedure Code. Suspicion in its ordinary meaning is a state of conjecture or surmise where proof is lacking: "I suspect but I cannot prove." Suspicion arises at or near the starting-point of an investigation of which the obtaining of prima facie proof is the end. When such proof has been obtained, the police case is complete; it is ready for trial and passes on to its next stage. It is indeed desirable as a general rule that an arrest should not be made until the case is complete. But if arrest before that were forbidden, it could seriously hamper the police. To give power to arrest on reasonable suspicion does not mean that it is always or even ordinarily to be exercised. It means that there is an executive discretion. In the exercise of it many factors have to be considered besides the strength of the case. The possibility of escape, the prevention of further crime and the obstruction of police inquiries are examples of those factors with which all judges who have had to grant or refuse bail are familiar. There is no serious danger in a large measure of executive discretion in the first instance because in countries where common law principles prevail the discretion is subject indirectly to judicial control. There is first the power, which their Lordships have just noticed, to grant bail. There is secondly the fact that in such countries there is available only a limited period between the time of arrest and the institution of proceedings; and if a police officer institutes proceedings without prima facie proof, he will run the risk of an action for malicious prosecution. The ordinary effect of this is that a police officer either has something substantially more than reasonable suspicion before he arrests or that, if he has not, he has to act promptly to verify it. In Malaysia the period available is strictly controlled by the Code. Under section 28 the suspect must be taken before a magistrate at the latest within twenty-four hours. If the investigation cannot be completed in twenty-four hours and there are grounds for believing that the accusation or information is well founded, under section 117 the magistrate may order the detention of the accused for a further period not exceeding fifteen days in the whole. By allowing fifteen days after arrest for investigation, the Code shows clearly that it does not contemplate prima facie proof as a prerequisite for arrest.

The test of reasonable suspicion prescribed by the Code is one that has existed in the common law for many years. The law is thus stated in *Bullen and Leake*, 3rd ed. (1868), p. 797, the "golden" edition of (1868): "A *constable* is justified in arresting a person without a warrant, upon a reasonable suspicion of a *felony* having been committed and of the person being guilty of it." Their Lordships have not found any English authority in which reasonable suspicion has been equated with prima facie proof. In *Dumbell* v. *Roberts* ([1944] 1 All E.R. 326), Scott L.J. said (at p. 329): "The protection of the public is safeguarded by the requirement, alike of the common law and, so far as I know, of all statutes, that the constable shall before arresting satisfy himself that there do in fact exist reasonable grounds for suspicion of guilt. That requirement is very limited. The police are not called upon before acting to have anything like a prima facie case for conviction; . . . " There is another distinction between reasonable suspicion and prima facie proof. Prima facie proof consists of admissible evidence. Suspicion can take into account matters that could not be put in evidence at all. There is a discussion about the relevance of previous convictions in the judgment of Lord Wright in *McArdle* v. *Egan* ((1934) 150 L.T. 412). Suspicion can take into account also matters which, though admissible, could not form part of a prima facie case. Thus the fact that the accused has given a false alibi does not obviate the need for prima facie proof of his presence at the scene of the crime; it will become of considerable importance in the trial when such proof as there is is being weighed perhaps against a second alibi; it would undoubtedly be a very suspicious circumstance.

For these reasons the Board considers that Mr. Gratiaen's criticism of the test applied in the Federal Court was well founded. This, of course, does not disturb their Lordships' conclusion that at the time of the arrest in the morning of July 11 there was no reasonable suspicion to justify it. Their Lordships have developed the distinction between reasonable suspicion and prima facie proof because of its materiality at a later stage. The plaintiffs when interrogated denied that they were at the place of the accident. The police, who had admittedly good ground for suspecting that it was the plaintiffs' lorry which was in fact involved, must be credited with equally good grounds for suspecting that the alibi was false. When checked, no corroboration was found for it. These facts, added to the failure to stop, were enough in their Lordships' opinion to raise at this later stage a reasonable suspicion that the plaintiffs were concerned in a piece of reckless driving. But the case falls far short of prima facie proof.

The result of their Lordships' conclusions is that, strictly on the case as pleaded, the claim for false imprisonment fails. Before the plaintiffs were locked up there was a reasonable suspicion. But Mr. Gratiaen has not relied upon the pleading point, quite rightly, their Lordships think, in view of the way the case was argued in the courts below. He has instead, accepting the arrest as being made in the morning of July 11, invited the Board, if it is open to them to do so, to reduce the damages. Undoubtedly their Lordships' conclusion affects the amount of the damages. It is not merely that it cuts in half the period of false imprisonment and excises in particular the night at the police station. Much more important, it alters the character of the arrest. It becomes a premature arrest rather than one that was unjustifiable from first to last. The police made the mistake of arresting before questioning; if they had questioned first and arrested afterwards, there would have been no case against them.

The sum of $2,500 for each plaintiff seems to their Lordships on any view to be extremely high. Judging by the special damage pleaded in the statement of claim, it is equivalent to five months' wages with overtime. On the view that the Board has taken of the facts of this case, this is undoubtedly excessive. On this view the scope for compensatory damages is limited; they must be confined to approximately nine hours' detention in the company of the police. The court is not in this category of case confined to awarding compensation for loss of liberty and for such physical and mental distress as it thinks may have been caused. It is also proper for it to mark any departure from constitutional practice, even if only a slight one, by exemplary damages: but these do not have to be large. The subject has been considered by the House of Lords in *Rookes* v. *Barnard* ([1964] A.C. 1129, 1221). The Board approves also of what was said on this topic by Scott L.J. in *Dumbell* v. *Roberts*. In particular, the Lord Justice said (at p. 329): "The more high-handed and less reasonable the detention is, the larger may be the damages; and, conversely, the more nearly reasonably the defendant may have acted and the nearer he may have got to justification on reasonable grounds for the suspicion on which he arrested, the smaller will be the proper assessment." Their Lordships would not in any event think it right in this case to substitute a figure of their own. What is necessary by way of an award to ensure respect for constitutional principles is a matter that should be settled, at least in the first instance, by the courts of Malaysia. . . .

Question
" . . . if [the police] had questioned first and arrested afterwards, there would have been no case against them." But what power had the police to detain the plaintiffs while the questions were being put to them? Or would a refusal to stay for questioning be in itself a suspicious circumstance which, added to the others, would justify an arrest?

Note:
Lord Devlin emphasises that, given that there are reasonable grounds for suspicion, the policeman has an "executive discretion" whether to arrest or not. Only if this discretion is abused, and not just if it is exercised unreasonably, will the policeman be liable for arresting the suspect. Thus it was not an abuse to arrest a person because she was more likely to confess in the police-station: *Holgate-Mohammed* v. *Duke* [1984] 1 All E.R. 1054 (H.L.), noted 47 M.L.R. 727 (1984) (Dockray), [1984] Camb.L.J. 12 (Smith).

Lord Devlin's observation that there is no harm in allowing an early arrest because the later prosecution, if unfounded, renders the policeman liable must be seen in the light of two facts: (1) there may not be a prosecution; and (2) whereas the defendant sued for false arrest must state the grounds of his suspicion the defendant sued for malicious prosecution need not do so. See *Stapley* v. *Annetts and D.P.P.* ([1969] 3 All E.R. 1541).

Damages
P.C. Walters, an "antiques officer," was keeping an eye on the Portobello Market in London one Saturday afternoon. He saw a man hurrying away carrying a worn suitcase and stopped him. After requiring evidence of Walters's identity, the plaintiff gave his name and address, produced his driver's licence, denied having been fingerprinted, said he had been in the antiques business but was now a fishmonger, and opened the suitcase which contained items of silver, glass and china wrapped in oldish newspapers. Then Walters said "I am not satisfied with your explanation. I am arresting you."

Caulfield J. held that there was no reasonable ground for the arrest, and that even if there had been reasonable ground, the arrest would have been unlawful since the constable's words were insufficient to let the plaintiff know the ground of his arrest. (*Hayward* v. *Comm'r of Police* (1984) 134 New L.J. 24).

On damages the judge said: "Forbes J. in a recent case . . . awarded damages to someone whom he described, I think, as a scoundrel, of £800 for forty-one hours unlawful detention, which works out at about £20 an hour. So that the going rate for unlawful detention could be, it is argued, £20 an hour, which give the plaintiff a little under £100. . . . There have been jury awards . . . as high as £12,000 . . . More recently there have been lesser awards . . . indeed awards of £60 and £40 . . . to two very cultivated young men of perfect character and excellent family who had spent a fair period of time, three or four hours at night, in an unattractive police station. I consider the proper sum to compensate the plaintiff for the pain and frustration and annoyance that he has endured by reason of this unlawful arrest and imprisonment . . . is £1,750."

In *White* v. *Metropolitan Police Comm'r* husband and wife were each awarded £20,000 for false imprisonment and malicious prosecution (see [1985] 2 All E.R. 856). Those who are erroneously convicted fare less well under the Home Office practice.

Judicial Officers
1. For acts within his jurisdiction a judge or magistrate is not under any civil liability even if he acts maliciously and without probable cause. (*McC* v. *Mullan* [1984] 3 All E.R. 908 (H.L.), *per* Lord Bridge at 916, Lord Brandon *dubitante*.)
2. For acts outside his jurisdiction, a magistrate may be liable—for false imprisonment, if imprisonment results—but not every act which may be quashed is outside his jurisdiction for

this purpose. An order which he has no power to give, as where a precondition of his power is unsatisfied, will be outside his jurisdiction, and in such a case the magistrate is liable whether he is to be blamed or not (Lord Templeman *ibid.* at 918.)

3. But if the magistrate, though acting outside his jurisdiction, is acting "in the execution of his office as justice" the amount of his liability is limited by statute to one penny (Justices of the Peace Act 1979, s.52), provided that the plaintiff was actually guilty of the offence or liable to pay the sum in question, and did not receive a larger sentence than that permitted by law. *R.* v. *Waltham Forest Justices, ex p. Solanke* [1986] 2 All E.R. 981 (C.A.), where the plaintiff, who had been locked up for six weeks, sued for £1· million but was awarded only one penny.

Prisoners

Williams was sentenced to 14 years for armed robbery. As he was a "dedicated trouble-maker" he was sent to a segregation or control unit in Wakefield Prison. Of his six months there, he had no company at all for the first month, and none except for exercise for the next two months. It was held that detention in prison is not rendered unlawful by the conditions of the detention, or by breach of the Prison Rules (S.I. 1964 No. 388), as to which the prisoner can complain to the Governor or the Secretary of State, but cannot claim damages. For breach of the Bill of Rights, which did not of itself give any action for damages, the regime must be both cruel and unusual, and this regime, though unusual, was not cruel. *Williams* v. *Home Office* [1981] 1 All E.R. 1211.

Civil Searches

The civil courts have recently taken up issuing search warrants, the part of the policeman being played by the claimant's solicitor, uneasily combining the role of claimant's agent and officer of the court. These warrants, called Anton Piller orders, are open to grave abuse.

It is true that the claimant must give an undertaking in damages and may be held liable thereunder, even for aggravated damages, if its execution is excessive or oppressive (*Columbia Pictures Indus.* v. *Robinson* [1986] 3 All E.R. 338 (Scott J.)), but in *Digital Equipment* v. *Darkcrest* [1984] 3 All E.R. 381 Falconer J. held that entry pursuant to such an order was not trespassory even if the order had been improperly obtained, that no action lay for abuse of process unless it were shown that the claimant had no right to the articles in question, and that, in regard to what he said to the court, the claimant owed no common law duty to the person against whom the order was sought.

R. v. CHIEF CONSTABLE OF DEVON AND CORNWALL, ex p. CENTRAL ELECTRICITY GENERATING BOARD

Court of Appeal [1982] Q.B. 458; [1981] 3 W.L.R. 967; [1981] 3 All E.R. 826

Lord Denning M.R.: The coast of Cornwall is beautiful. Much of the inland is ugly. It is despoiled by china clay workings. Not far from them there is open farmland with small villages dotted around. Pleasant enough but not outstanding. The Central Electricity Generating Board view this as a possible site for a nuclear power station. They wish to survey it so as to compare it with other possible sites. The farmer objected to the survey. So did the villagers. They took up a stand against it. But on being told by the courts that it was unlawful for them to obstruct the survey, they desisted. They moved off the site. They obeyed the law. But then groups of outsiders came in from far and wide. They had no local connection with the place. They came anonymously. They would not disclose their identity. They would not give their names and addresses. They flouted the law. They wilfully obstructed the survey. Can these newcomers be moved off the site so that they obstruct no more?

Can the board move them off? Or, if the board cannot do it, can the police be called in to help? The chief constable feels that he cannot use his force for the purpose. It would put his men in a bad light with the local inhabitants. What then is to be done? . . .

English law upholds to the full the right of people to demonstrate and to make their views known so long as all is done peaceably and in good order (see *Hubbard* v. *Pitt* ([1976] Q.B. 161). But the conduct of these demonstrators is not peaceful or in good order. By wilfully obstructing the operations of the board, they are deliberately breaking the law. Every time they lie down in front of a rig, or put their foot or umbrella down to stop a hole being drilled, or sit on the hole, they are guilty of an offence for which they could be fined up to £50 for every occasion. They must know it is unlawful. They must know of the injunctions granted against the farmers and the local residents. Yet they persist in going on with their unlawful conduct, knowing full well that it is unlawful. Is the law powerless to stop them? Can these people avoid the process of the law by not giving their names and addresses, so that neither a summons nor a writ can reach them? Can they avoid it by bringing in one group after another? I think not. These obstructors should not be in any better position than those against whom injunctions have been obtained. The arm of the law is long enough to reach them despite their attempts to avoid it.

In the first place, I must say that the leaflet issued by the organisers is completely erroneous. The board and their contractors are entitled to manhandle the obstructors so as to move them out of the way. Every person who is prevented from carrying out his lawful pursuits is entitled to use self-help so as to prevent any unlawful obstruction: see *Holmes* v. *Bagge* (1853) 118 E.R. 629 at 631 *per* Lord Campbell C.J. He must, of course, not use more force than is reasonably necessary; but there is no doubt whatever that he can use force to do it.

I go further. I think that the conduct of these people, their criminal obstruction, is itself a breach of the peace. There is a breach of the peace whenever a person who is lawfully carrying out his work is unlawfully and physically prevented by another from doing it. He is entitled by law peacefully to go on with his work on his lawful occasions. If anyone unlawfully and physically obstructs the worker, by lying down or chaining himself to a rig or the like, he is guilty of a breach of the peace. Even if this were not enough, I think that their unlawful conduct gives rise to a reasonable apprehension of a breach of the peace. It is at once likely that the lawful worker will resort to self-help by removing the obstructor by force from the vicinity of the work so that he obstructs no longer. He will lift the recumbent obstructor from the ground. This removal would itself be an assault and battery, unless it was justified as being done by way of self-help. Long years ago Holt C.J. declared that "the least touching of another in anger is a battery" (see *Cole* v. *Turner* (1704) 90 E.R. 958). Salmond on Torts (17th ed., 1977, p. 120) adds that even anger is not essential. An "unwanted kiss may be a battery." So also the lifting up of a recumbent obstructor would be a battery unless justified as being done in the exercise of self-help. But in deciding whether there is a breach of the peace or the apprehension of it, the law does not go into the rights or wrongs of the matter, or whether it is justified by self-help or not. Suffice it that the peace is broken or is likely to be broken by one or another of those present. With the result that any citizen can, and certainly any police officer can, intervene to stop breaches.

If I were wrong on this point, if there was here no breach of the peace or apprehension of it, it would give a licence to every obstructor and every passive resister in the land. He would be able to cock a snook at the law as these groups have done. Public works of the greatest national importance could be held up indefinitely. This cannot be. The rule of law must prevail.

Notwithstanding all that I have said, I would not give any orders to the chief constable or his men. It is of the first importance that the police should decide on their own responsibility what action should be taken in any particular situation. As I said in *R.* v. *Metropolitan Police Comr, ex p. Blackburn* ([1968] 2 Q.B. 118 at 136):

" . . . it is for the Commissioner of Police, or the chief constable, as the case may be, to decide in any particular case where enquiries should be pursued, or whether an arrest should be made, or a prosecution brought. It must be for him to decide on the disposition of his force and the concentration of his resources on any particular crime or area. No court can or should give him direction on such a matter. He can also make policy decisions and give effect to them, as, for instance, was often done when prosecutions were not brought for attempted suicide; but there are some policy decisions with which, I think, the courts in a case can, if necessary, interfere."

The decision of the chief constable not to intervene in this case was a policy decision with which I think the courts should not interfere. All that I have done in this judgment is to give the "definitive legal mandate" which he sought. It should enable him to reconsider their position. I hope he will decide to use his men to clear the obstructors off the site or at any rate help the board to do so.

It is plain that the board can use self-help so as to get rid of this wilful obstruction. To me the obvious solution would be to erect a fence around their place of work, a barbed-wire entanglement if need be, so as to prevent the obstructors getting anywhere near the operations. This is just common sense, so that they should not be a danger to themselves or to others. If they should try and break through the fence, or rush it, the battle would be on. There would be the clearest possible breach of the peace. the police would move in, arrest them, and take them before the magistrates. So I would say to the board, put up a fence and get on with your work. Stand no more of this obstruction.

For the reasons I have given, however, I would make no order against the police. The appeal should be dismissed.

Lawton L.J.: This appeal has two aspects, the general and the particular. The general can be described as follows: can those who disapprove of the exercise by a statutory body of statutory powers frustrate their exercise on private property by adopting unlawful means, not involving violence, such as lying down in front of moving vehicles, chaining themselves to equipment and sitting down where work has to be done. Such means are sometimes referred to as passive resistance. The answer is an emphatic No. If it were otherwise, there would be no rule of law. Parliament decides who shall have statutory powers and under what conditions and for what purpose they shall be used. Those who do not like what Parliament has done can protest, but they must do so in a lawful manner. What cannot be tolerated, and certainly not by the police, are protests which are not made in a lawful manner.

A statutory body can use the minimum of force reasonably necessary to remove those obstructing the exercise of their statutory powers from the area where work has to be carried out. This is the common law remedy of abatement by self-help; but it would involve the statutory body taking the law into its own hands and is, as Lord Wright said in *Sedleigh-Denfield* v. *O'Callaghan* ([1940] A.C. 880 at 911), much to be discouraged. There are many reasons why self-help should be discouraged. Disputes are likely to arise whether the minimum amount of force reasonably necessary was used. In my judgment, based on my understanding of human nature and a long experience of the administration of criminal justice, the most important reason for not using self-help, if any other remedy can be used effectively, is that as soon as one person starts to, or makes to, lay hands on another there is likely to be a breach of the peace. Those obstructing may assert that they will allow themselves to be removed without resisting; but, when the manhandling starts, particularly if a man has to lay hands on a woman, struggling and uproar are likely to begin. I should have expected most police constables to appreciate that this is so; and as they have a duty to deal with breaches of the peace which actually occur or which they have reasonable cause for suspecting are about to occur, those who see what is happening should act either by trying to persuade those obstructing to stop doing so or arresting them if they persist in their unlawful conduct. In many cases those who persist to the point of having to be arrested will commit some other offence in doing so, such as obstructing or assaulting police officers in the execution of their duty: see s.51 of the Police Act 1964. If no other offence is committed, the police constable making the arrest should take the person arrested before the local magistrates to show cause why he should not be bound over, with or without sureties, to keep the peace and be of good behaviour: see s.115 of the Magistrates' Courts Act 1980.

On the evidence it seems likely that the board will have to use self-help if they are to perform their statutory duties at Luxulyan. Civil proceedings have been ineffective. Prosecutions for offences under ss.280 and 281(2) of the Town and Country Planning Act 1971 would serve no useful purpose. When they do decide to use self-help and fix a day for doing so, they should inform the local police who will no doubt be present in sufficient numbers to ensure as best they can that breaches of the peace do not occur and, if they do, that those responsible are removed from the site.

In my judgment this is not a case for making an order of mandamus against the chief constable. It is a case for co-operation between the board and the chief constable and the use of plenty of common sense by all concerned, including those who are on the site obstructing the board's functions.

I would dismiss the appeal.

(ii) *Illness*

MENTAL HEALTH ACT 1983

136.—(1) If a constable finds in a place to which the public have access a person who appears to him to be suffering from mental disorder and to be in immediate need of care or control, the constable may, if he thinks it necessary to do so in the interests of that person or for the protection of other persons, remove that person to a place of safety within the meaning of section 135 above.

(2) A person removed to a place of safety under this section may be detained there for a period not exceeding 72 hours for the purpose of enabling him to be examined by a registered medical practitioner and to be interviewed by an approved social worker and of making any necessary arrangements for his treatment or care.

139.—(1) No person shall be liable, whether on the ground of want of jurisdiction or on any other ground, to any civil or criminal proceedings to which he would have been liable apart from this section in respect of any act purporting to be done in pursuance of this Act or any regulations or rules made under this Act, . . . unless the act was done in bad faith or without reasonable care.

(2) No civil proceedings shall be brought against any person in any court in respect of any such act without the leave of the High Court; . . .

Note:

Until 1983 s.139(2) continued with the words: "and the High Court shall not give leave under this section unless satisfied that there is substantial ground for the contention that the person to be proceeded against has acted in bad faith or without reasonable care." What do you infer from the omission of these words in 1983?

Their effect can be noted in *Carter* v. *Commissioner for Police* [1975] 2 All E.R. 33. Early one morning the plaintiff, who had been born in Jamaica, telephoned the police, as she had done on several previous occasions, to complain of the behaviour of her neighbours in the council block. Four or five policemen arrived and took her to the police station and then to a hospital where doctors confirmed that she was not suffering from any mental disturbance and never had been. The plaintiff maintained that she was calm and collected throughout, while the police asserted that she had been screaming and shouting. Cairns L.J. said: "What seems to me impressive in this case is that one has all these police officers in complete agreement with each other." (!) Lawton L.J. said: " . . . what possible explanation can there be for these police officers behaving as they are said to have behaved? There could not be any rational explanation for them to take a woman who was calm, collected and had done nothing wrong at all, and a stranger to them, into custody." The plaintiff was refused leave to sue (and thus to cross-examine the police).

The vast majority of the people in Britain who are confined against their will are criminals and lunatics, suspected or proved. The average daily population of prisons and like establishments is about 53,000, of whom 9,400 are untried; about 45,000 are detained before trial each year. In the hospitals of England and Wales there are about 89,000 psychiatric patients of whom about 8,000 are there against their will.

In Samuel Butler's *Erewhon* sick people were treated as criminals and criminals as sick. Of course Erewhon is nearly Nowhere backwards, the Utopia to which we progress. So far we have only confused the distinction, not reversed it. But the results are similar. Understandably. Those who hospitalise criminals tend to imprison the sick, since those who discredit free-will disdain the will to be free. A state progressing nowhere might therefore make it an offence to make yourself sick (drugs, smoking).

Section 3.—Self-Defence

ANONYMOUS CASE

Assizes (1836) 2 Lew.C.C. 48; 168 E.R. 1075

Parke B. (to the jury): . . . When a man strikes at another, within a distance capable of the latter being struck, nature prompts the party struck to resist it, and he is justified in using such a degree of force as will prevent a repetition. . . .

ANDERSON v. MARSHALL

Court of Session (1835) 13 S. 1130

The defender was a London businessman who was having difficulties with a firm in Peterhead. At the request of that firm, the pursuer wrote the defender a letter, to which the defender did not reply. The pursuer then wrote another letter, accusing the defender of behaving in a cowardly manner and using other injurious language which he underlined. The defender, on receipt of this letter, went to the pursuer's shop and struck him, not doing any injury.

Lord President Hope (to the jury): This is a case in which there are faults on both sides; and the first fault was committed by the pursuer, in addressing a letter to the defender, containing expressions which, to say the least of them, were extremely ill-judged and foolish. There could be none more intemperate or worse chosen than that which imputed cowardly conduct to the defender. And there were other words of a very insulting character. The defender acted instantaneously, on receipt of the letter; and, if he had merely gone to the pursuer's shop, and abused him, by applying those epithets which he employed, I should have thought there was no ground for a finding in favour of the pursuer at all. But the defender went farther than this, and, in the heat of the moment, he struck the pursuer with his hand. It is my duty to inform you that no verbal provocation whatever can justify a blow. The law on this point is inflexible. I conceive, therefore, that there must be a verdict for the pursuer. But, as verbal provocation is a good ground for mitigating damages, and as the pursuer does not come before you with clean hands, I should conceive that sufficient reparation would be made in this case by a small award of damages. On the proper amount to be awarded you will decide.

The jury found for the pursuer; damages 1s.

TOWNLEY v. RUSHWORTH

Queen's Bench Divisional Court (1963) 62 L.G.R. 95; 107 S.J. 1004

This was an appeal from conviction for assault. The appeal was allowed.

The Mental Health Act 1959, s.31(1), provided that: "An application for the admission of a patient to a hospital under this Part of this Act, duly completed in accordance with the foregoing provisions of this Part of this Act, shall be sufficient authority for the applicant, or any person authorised by the applicant, to take the patient and convey him to the hospital."

Lord Parker of Waddington C.J.: . . . Shortly, what happened in this case was as follows: on April 22, 1963, the defendant's wife signed a form of emergency application; that form bore the words "This application is founded on the medical recommendation forwarded herewith," and it clearly contemplated that, in the case of an emergency certificate, the one medical practitioner would make a medical recommendation for admission on a form, and that that recommendation would be, as it were, annexed to the wife's application.

Having made out the form, the defendant's wife handed it to a Dr. Hardman, who had been the defendant's medical adviser. Although it is not found in the case, I assume that Dr. Hardman deliberately refrained from making the recommendation to be attached to that application until he had in fact seen the defendant. On that same day the doctor went along armed with the wife's application and with a form of recommendation which he would fill up if he felt the condition of the defendant was such that he should do so. He went to the house with a brother-in-law of the defendant, and with two police constables, Kaylor and Major. When they arrived at the house, Dr. Hardman went in first; the defendant heard somebody moving about and then, when told who it was, he told the doctor to get out. Thereupon the doctor went to the door and brought in the other three. The defendant at once said: "You have no right to come in here. You need two doctors. I am going to my bedroom, you can get out." With that he went upstairs to his bedroom. Dr. Hardman and the other three followed him up to the bedroom and, in the bedroom, Dr. Hardman referred to the form of emergency application which he had in his hand, and told the defendant that he, the doctor, was afraid that he, the defendant, would have to go to hospital for a little while whether he wished or not. The defendant then got angry, said: "It's a put up show and a conspiracy to get me out of the way." Then Dr. Hardman went even further; he said to the defendant and to the police constables present that he would have to give the defendant an injection with a sedative, and thereupon left the room to prepare the injection.

While the injection was being prepared the defendant, who was with the other three men in the bedroom, said that he wished to telephone the chief constable, no doubt to remonstrate. Thereupon one of the police constables, Kaylor, stood between the defendant and the door to prevent him from leaving. The defendant tried to push the police constable away and the police constable took the defendant by the arm. At that moment the other police constable, Major, seeing a sort of scuffle going on, came across, as the defendant apparently thought, to strike him, and before he was struck the defendant succeeded in freeing his arm and levelling a fist blow at Major which, most unfortunately, fractured his nose. After that had occurred Dr. Hardman came in, administered the injection and called for an ambulance and then, and then only, did he fill up the recommendation to be attached to the application.

In those circumstances the first question that arises is whether these four men, and in particular police constable Major, were lawfully in the defendant's house and were acting lawfully in keeping him there with a view to taking him against his will to a hospital for observation. In my judgment it is quite clear, and indeed it is conceded, that since the application form was not at the time duly completed by the addition of Dr. Hardman's medical certificate, none of those persons there had any lawful authority to restrain the patient and convey him to hospital. Indeed, they were trespassers in the house. It is as I have said most unfortunate, because I am sure that Dr. Hardman had refrained from filling up the recommendation because he honestly wanted to see whether it was a proper case in which to make the recommendation, and he could not say that until he had seen the defendant during that visit.

The justices state their opinion in this form: "We were of the opinion that although the form of medical recommendation for admission for observation under the Mental Health Act 1959 was not completed at the time Dr. Hardman and the other persons arrived at and entered the defendant's home, the defendant had no proper ground for believing that he was about to be struck and that the force used by the defendant to resist his removal to hospital was unjustified and unreasonable." It is to be noted there that the first matter which influenced them was the fact that the defendant, as they found, had no proper ground for believing that police constable Major was about to strike him. Secondly, it is to be observed that the following words that they used "that the force used by the defendant to resist his removal to hospital was unjustified and unreasonable" are somewhat ambiguous. They do not say so, but I presume that they are intending to convey by that, in effect, that excessive force was used. Be that as it may, I find it very difficult to understand what the justices had in mind.

Here is a case where as the facts turned out, there were four trespassers in the house without any lawful authority, who had been told to get out and had failed to do so—trespassers whom the defendant in the first instance at any rate was not prepared to eject forcibly because he retired; he said he was going to his bedroom, and he went up to his bedroom. He was then pursued; he was told that whether he liked it or not he was going to be taken away, and for that purpose he was going to have an injection and he was further told, while the injection was being prepared, that he was not at liberty even to leave his bedroom; and one officer forcibly restrained him from leaving the bedroom.

Unless it is to be said that a householder is to sit down and submit, not only to his liberty being infringed in his own house, but also to assault by injection, and to his liberty being removed in hospital, I cannot say that to hit out with the fist is an unreasonable use of force.

It is of course, a question of fact for the justices, and this court would hesitate to interfere, but in the present case I am in very grave doubt, from the very wording of the case, what the justices really did have in mind. It may be that they were considering the question whether there were reasonable grounds for belief that police constable Major was going to strike the defendant and were not taking into consideration the full picture that I have tried to outline. It may be also that they were saying to themselves: "well, the fact that the application did not have the recommendation attached at the time was really a mere formality, and the defendant ought to have submitted to his removal." It is, at any rate, those ambiguities in the finding in the case which make me feel justified in saying that although this is a question of fact for the justices, they must have misdirected themselves by not considering the full picture on the basis that these four men were there without any lawful authority. In these circumstances I feel that in this unfortunate case the only course is to quash the conviction.

Questions
    1. Would the defendant have been guilty of assault if the doctor had previously completed his recommendation?
    2. Did the defendant know that the doctor had not completed his recommendation?
    3. Why do you think that this prosecution was brought?

COLLINS v. RENISON

King's Bench (1754) Say. 138; 96 E.R. 830

The plaintiff brought an action of trespass for assault, alleging that the defendant had overturned a ladder upon which the plaintiff was standing and threw the plaintiff from it on to the ground. The defendant pleaded: "that he was in possession of a certain garden; and that the plaintiff, against the will of the defendant, erected a ladder in the garden, and went up the ladder, in order to nail a board to the house of the plaintiff; and that the defendant forbid the plaintiff so to do, and desired him to come down; and that upon the plaintiff's persisting in nailing the board, he gently shook the ladder, which was a low ladder, and gently overturned it, and gently threw the plaintiff from it upon the ground, thereby doing as little damage as possible to the plaintiff."
    The plaintiff demurred to the defendant's plea, and the demurrer was upheld.

Ryder C.J.: Such force, as was used in the present case, is not justifiable in the defence of possession of land. The overturning of the ladder could not answer the purpose of removing the plaintiff out of the garden; since it only left him upon the ground at the bottom of the ladder, instead of being upon it.

Note:
    As Collins had doubtless found, it may be impossible for a person to repair or maintain his house without going a foot or two on to his neighbour's land in order to erect scaffolding or whatever. The neighbour is in principle perfectly entitled to refuse permission and to throw the plaintiff off if he comes on, though the principal case shows that the courts may be a little unsympathetic. Here the Law Commission is making proposals of a very limited nature. (Law Com. No. 151, Cmnd. 9692). See Gray, *Elements of Land Law*, 670.
    It is characteristic of English law to permit property owners (like the League Against Cruel Sports, above p. 317) to behave in a bloody-minded manner if they choose. Thus in one case an outgoing tenant had left on the landlord's premises some chattels which he had hired from the plaintiff. When the plaintiff asked for them the landlord refused either to bring the chattels to the front door or to permit the plaintiff to enter the premises to fetch them (*British Economical Lamp Co.* (1913) 29 T.L.R. 386). Lord Denning believes that this is no longer the law (*Miller* v. *Jackson* [1977] 3 All E.R. 338, 342).

Question
    What may an occupier of land do to motor cars which have been parked there without permission?

WHATFORD v. CARTY

Queen's Bench Divisional Court, *The Times*, October 29, 1960

The appellants, head keeper and game-keepers on the Copped Hall Estate, Epping Forest, laid three informations against the respondent for assault, under Offences against the Person Act 1861, s.42. The justices dismissed the informations on the ground that the respondent had no case to answer. The appeal was dismissed.

Lord Parker C.J.: . . . On Sunday, November 22, 1959, in broad daylight, the respondent was seen by the appellants on a part of the Copped Hall Estate, armed with a bow and arrow. Having seen him, they apparently traced his motor-cycle and went and waited by it until he returned. The moment he got there without any bag, the first appellant took his bow and arrows away from him and handed them to the third appellant, whereupon the respondent said "You are not going to have my bow" and went for the appellants. He pushed the first appellant into a ditch, kicked the second appellant on the leg, took hold of the third appellant and pushed him into a hedge. Unfortunately he kicked their dog and the dog bit him.

His Lordship said that at the end of this momentous case the justices came to the conclusion that the respondent had no case to answer and dismissed the informations. His Lordship entirely agreed. It had been admitted that the first appellant had no right in law to take the bow and arrows. What was said was that once he had taken them peaceably, it was an offence in law for the respondent to attempt to repossess the weapons without making a request for them, and, presumably, without giving a reasonable time for the request to be complied with.

His Lordship thought that it would be wrong to divide up this little episode, which must have taken a matter of seconds, into stages of that sort. It seemed to him that the appellants must have taken the bow and arrows almost before the respondent knew what it was all about. The moment they did, he said "You are not having my bow," and repossession almost immediately took place. The position was perfectly clearly stated in *Russell on Crime*: "If one come forcibly and take away another's goods the owner may oppose him at once, for there is no time to make a request."

Secondly, it has been said that at any rate the assault on the second appellant was not justified because he never handled the bow or the arrows; but the answer to that was that all three appellants were acting in concert.

Finally, it had been said that there was no evidence that the assaults were committed to regain possession of the weapons, but the respondent's immediate reaction was "You are not having my bow."

In his Lordship's view the justices were amply justified in coming to the conclusion they did and would dismiss the appeal.

Section 4.—Protection of Property

CRESSWELL v. SIRL

Court of Appeal [1948] 1 K.B. 241; [1948] L.J.R. 654; 63 T.L.R. 620; 112 J.P. 69; 91 S.J. 653; [1947] 2 All E.R. 730; 46 L.G.R. 109

The defendant was awakened by the noise of barking about midnight one night on his father's farm. He went out and found two excited dogs noisily worrying the sheep. He went back for advice and a gun, and returned with a relative to find that the dogs had by now penned the sheep in a corner of a field and were still worrying them. They flashed a light on to the dogs and the dogs started towards them. When they were about forty yards away, the defendant fired, and the plaintiff's dog was killed.

The county court judge gave judgment for the plaintiff, on the ground that the killing of the dog could be justified only if it was actually attacking the stock at the time and there was no other method of deterring it.

The defendant's appeal to the Court of Appeal was allowed, and the case was remitted to the county court.

Scott L.J.: This is the judgment of the court. This case is of interest since it has involved a consideration by the court—after an interval of more than a hundred years—of the law relating to the justification for the shooting of another's dog. It is also, we think, of no little public importance. To shoot a dog is hateful to anyone fond of animals. On the other hand, those who keep dogs in the country or take dogs to the country are under a real and serious obligation not to allow their dogs to chase sheep or cattle. Even if the sheep or cattle are not physically attacked, serious injury may be done to them if they are frightened and chased, particularly when (as in the present case) the ewes are in lamb or the cattle in calf. . . .

The learned county court judge, whose attention was apparently directed only to certain older cases (presently referred to), treated as a conclusive test of the defendant's liability the question whether at the moment of shooting, the plaintiff's dogs were actually attacking the sheep; and since at that moment, the dogs had admittedly left the sheep and were approaching the defendant and his brother-in-law, he found, on the application of this test, in favour of the plaintiff.

The learned judge derived his test from the case of *Janson* v. *Brown* (1807) 1 Camp. 41; 170 E.R. 869), before Lord Ellenborough C.J. in 1807, to which case he had been referred in argument. According to the very brief report in that case Lord Ellenborough directed the jury that for the defendant to succeed, the plaintiff's dogs must have been "in the very act of killing the fowls" and could not otherwise be prevented from so doing. Upon this direction which, in terms, closely followed the defendant's plea the verdict was for the plaintiff, and it is clear that it was upon the first branch of the direction that the defendant failed. . . . But since that date, and particularly since the date of *Kirk* v. *Gregory* ((1876) 1 Ex.D. 55), the law generally relating to the justification of acts of trespass has been appreciably developed and defined. For the rule that the property in question must be actually under attack has been substituted the more generous rule that it must be in real or imminent danger; and for the absolute criterion that the act of trespass must be shown—in the light of subsequent events—to have been necessary for the preservation of the property has been substituted the more relative standard of reasonable necessity, namely, that any reasonable man would, in the circumstances of the case, have concluded that there was no alternative to the act of trespass if the property endangered was to be preserved. . . .

The whole matter fell to be considered by this court in the case of *Cope* v. *Sharpe (No. 2)* ([1912] 1 K.B. 496). In that case the question was whether the defendant was justified in doing certain acts of trespass on the plaintiff's land for the purpose of preventing the spread of heath fire and consequent loss and damage to the property of the defendant's master. In that case it was shown that the fire never in fact damaged the property of the defendant's master and would not have done so even if the preventive measures adopted by the defendant had not in fact been taken. The risk and danger to the property in question had, however, been "real and imminent" and the steps taken by the defendant, trespassing for the purpose on the plaintiff's land, were held by the jury to have been unnecessary in fact, but nevertheless to have been reasonably necessary. On these findings this court held that the defendant had made out his plea of justification. "The test, I think"—said Buckley L.J.—"is whether . . . there was such real or imminent danger to his" (that is, the defendant's master's) "property as that he was entitled to act and whether his acts were reasonably necessary in the sense [being] acts which a reasonable man would properly do to meet a real danger." And Kennedy L.J. said that danger had been found by the jury to have been "so far imminent that any reasonable person in the circumstances of the defendant would act reasonably in treating it as necessary to adopt the method for the preservation of the property in jeopardy which the defendant adopted."

In our view, the principle underlying the judgment of this court in *Cope* v. *Sharpe* is one of general application to justification of acts of trespass and we do not think that the case of *Janson* v. *Brown* and the other older cases cited to the county court judge should be regarded as laying down any special rules appropriate to the case of shooting dogs. . . .

We come to the conclusion that the law applicable to the facts of the present case is less narrow than the county court judge holds in his judgment. Chasing by dogs which causes any real or present danger of serious harm to the animals chased constitutes an "attack" which entitles the owner to take effective measures of prevention. We think the relevant rules of law may be thus stated: (1) The onus of proof is on the defendant to justify the preventive measure of shooting the attacking dogs. (2) He has, by proof, to establish two propositions, but each proposition may be established in either of two ways: *Proposition No. 1*: That at the time of shooting, the dog was either (a) actually (in the above sense) attacking the animals in question, or (b) if left at large would renew the attack so that the animals would be left presently subject to real and imminent danger unless renewal was prevented. *Proposition No. 2*: That either (a) there was in fact no practicable means, other than shooting, of stopping the present attack or preventing such renewal, or (b) that the defendant, having regard to all the circumstances in which he found himself, acted reasonably in regarding the shooting as necessary for the protection of the animals against attack or renewed attack. . . .

It is clear that, if we have correctly stated the law which is applicable, the learned county court judge did not apply to the facts proved before him the proper tests. As we read his judgment he regarded (on the authority of the case cited to him) as conclusive in the plaintiff's favour his finding that, at the moment of shooting, no actual attack was in progress; and he has not applied himself to the question whether or no, at the time of shooting, the ewes were still in real and imminent peril. Nor are we clear from the terms of his judgment whether he intended to find that, whether or not the shooting was in fact necessary, the defendant acted reasonably in so thinking. . . .

In the circumstances . . . we think that the proper course . . . is to refer the matter back to His Honour with the following directions: If the learned judge finds that the defendant has established both propositions in either of the alternative ways open to him, he should enter judgment for the defendant; but if he finds that the defendant has not so established both propositions, the plaintiff will sustain her judgment.

ANIMALS ACT 1971

. . .

9.—(1) In any civil proceedings against a person (in this section referred to as the defendant) for killing or causing injury to a dog it shall be a defence to prove—

(*a*) that the defendant acted for the protection of any livestock and was a person entitled to act for the protection of that livestock; and

(*b*) that within forty-eight hours of the killing or injury notice thereof was given by the defendant to the officer in charge of a police station.

(2) For the purposes of this section a person is entitled to act for the protection of any livestock if, and only if—

(*a*) the livestock or the land on which it is belongs to him or to any person under whose express or implied authority he is acting; and

(*b*) the circumstances are not such that liability for killing or causing injury to the livestock would be excluded by section 5(4) of this Act.

(3) Subject to subsection (4) of this section, a person killing or causing injury to a

354 DEFENCES

dog shall be deemed for the purposes of this section to act for the protection of any livestock if, and only if, either—

(a) the dog is worrying or is about to worry the livestock and there are no other reasonable means of ending or preventing the worrying; or

(b) the dog has been worrying livestock and is not under the control of any person and there are no practicable means of ascertaining to whom it belongs.

(4) For the purposes of this section, the condition stated in either of the paragraphs of the preceding subsection shall be deemed to have been satisfied if the defendant believed that it was satisfied and had reasonable ground for that belief.

(5) For the purposes of this section—

(a) an animal belongs to any person if he owns it or has it in his possession; and

(b) land belongs to any person if he is the occupier thereof.

Question
How lengthy do you think the Civil Code of England would be if the article relating to liability for killing dogs were as long as this? What rules would apply if I poisoned my neighbour's cat which had made repeated forays into my chicken-run?

Note:
The reader will be glad to learn from the definition in s.11 that "livestock" (a very difficult and abstract concept) includes not only mules but also hinnies. A hinny is a mule whose parents are a male horse and a female donkey instead of the other way round. What a lot one has to know in order to understand an English enactment prompted by a statutory body (the Law Commission) whose duty is to simplify the law!

SOUTHPORT CORPORATION v. ESSO PETROLEUM CO.

Queen's Bench [1953] 3 W.L.R. 773; 118 J.P. 1; 97 S.J. 764; [1952] 2 All E.R. 1204; 52 L.G.R. 22; [1953] 2 Lloyd's Rep. 414

The defendants' tanker ran aground in the Ribble estuary and in order to save life on board the master lightened the ship by discharging a large quantity of oil. This oil was carried on to the plaintiffs' beach, and they spent a great deal of money on clearing it away.

Devlin J. gave judgment for the defendants on the grounds that the plaintiffs must prove negligence and had failed to do so. The plaintiffs' appeal to the Court of Appeal was allowed (Morris L.J. dissenting) on the ground that the defendants must disprove negligence and had failed to do so [1954] 2 Q.B. 182. The House of Lords allowed the defendants' appeal on the ground that the plaintiffs had failed to establish the facts alleged in their pleadings [1956] A.C. 218.

Devlin J.: . . . In my judgment the plaintiffs have a good cause of action in trespass or nuisance subject to the special defences raised by the defendants which I shall next consider.

On the first of these, if one seeks an analogy from traffic on land, it is well established that persons whose property adjoins the highway cannot complain of damage done by persons using the highway unless it is done negligently: *Goodwyn (Goodwin)* v. *Cheveley* ((1859) 28 L.J.Ex. 298), *Tillett* v. *Ward* ((1882) 10 Q.B.D. 17) and *Gayler & Pope Ltd.* v. *Davies (B.) & Son Ltd.* ([1924] 2 K.B. 75). . . .

But there is hardly need to search for exact authority, for the point is covered by two dicta, which may be *obiter* but which bear the great authority of Lord Blackburn and which lay down the same rule on land and water. In *Fletcher* v. *Rylands* ((1866) L.R. 1 Ex. 265, 286) Blackburn J. said: "Traffic on the highways, whether by land or sea, cannot be conducted without exposing those whose persons or property are near it to some inevitable risk; and that being so, those who go on the high-way, or have their property adjacent to it, may well be held to do so subject to their taking upon themselves the risk of injury from that inevitable danger." The judge then went on to say that such persons could not recover "without proof of want of care or skill occasioning the accident." In *River Wear Commissioners* v. *Adamson* ((1877) 2 App.Cas. 743, 767) Lord Blackburn said: "My Lords, the common law is, I think, as follows:— property adjoining to a spot on which the public have a right to carry on traffic is liable to be injured by that traffic. In this respect there is no difference between a shop, the railings or windows of which may be broken by a carriage on the road, and a pier adjoining to a harbour or a navigable river or the sea, which is liable to be injured by a ship. In either case the owner of the injured property must bear his own loss, unless he can establish that some other person is in fault, and liable to make it good. . . . "

Upon this view of the law it is unnecessary for me to consider in detail the alternative defence of necessity, which is in some respects only a variant of the defence which I have already considered. One of the earliest cases of necessity, *Mouse's Case* (1608) 12 Co.Rep. 63; 77 E.R. 1341), was a case of jettison. But the defence of necessity applies irrespective of the situation of the property damaged and so of the principle I have just considered; on the other hand, I am not satisfied that it applies (as it does under the principle I have just considered) if the only object whose salvation is at stake is a ship. I am not prepared to hold without further consideration that a man is entitled to damage the property of another with-out compensating him merely because the infliction of such damage is necessary in order to save his own property. I doubt whether the court in such circumstances can be asked to evaluate the relation of the damage done to the property saved, by inquiring, for example, whether it is permissible to do £5,000 worth of damage to a third party in order to save property worth £10,000. In the ordinary case of jettison the property which is sacrificed is the property of a person who is interested in the venture, and an equitable adjustment is made by the application of general aver-age. The same considerations may not apply to the property of a third party who has no stake in the venture which is being saved.

The defence of necessity would therefore have called for close examination if in fact it had been based solely on the saving of property and if in law I had thought that the plaintiffs' rights of ownership in the foreshore were unqualified by their proximity to the sea. But apart from the law, on which I have already expressed my view, the facts of this case, when examined, show that the peril said to justify the discharge of the cargo is that the ship was in imminent danger of breaking her back. The consequence of that would be not merely that the ship herself would become a total loss, but that in the circumstances of this case the lives of the crew would have been endangered. The safety of human lives belongs to a different scale of values from the safety of property. The two are beyond comparison and the necessity for saving life has at all times been considered a proper ground for inflicting such damage as may be necessary upon another's property. I think, therefore, that if I am wrong in the application of the principle which I have taken from Lord Black-burn, the defence in this case can equally well be put on the ground of necessity.

It is, of course, an answer to either of these defences if the predicament in which the ship found herself was due to her own negligence. Indeed, in the principle I am applying it is necessary, as Lord Blackburn said, for the plaintiffs to prove negli-gence, and so my examination of the law results in the conclusion that this action is to be treated in the same way as any running-down or collision case in which the plaintiff alleges negligence. . . .

Note:
A dangerous psychopath entered the plaintiff's gun-shop in Northampton after closing hours one evening. He armed himself with guns, loaded them and fired them several times. The police decided to flush him out, and fired a canister of CS gas into the shop. A bad fire ensued,

and it took time to put it out because there was no fire engine handy, though a comparable military vehicle had previously been standing by. *Rigby* v. *Chief Constable of Northants.* [1985] 2 All E.R. 985. The trespass was held justifiable by necessity, but the police were held liable as it was unreasonable of them to use the inflammatory canister in the absence of any fire-fighting vehicle.

McPHAIL v. PERSONS UNKNOWN

Court of Appeal [1973] Ch. 447; [1973] 3 W.L.R. 71; 117 S.J. 448; 72 L.G.R. 93; [1973] 3 All E.R. 393

The owner of a house sought an order for possession against persons who had broken into it and were squatting in it. The trial judge granted the order and the defendants appealed, asking for a stay of excecution on the ground that they had nowhere else to live. The Court of Appeal held that it had no power to grant such a stay.

Lord Denning M.R.: . . .

2. *The law as to squatters*
   What is a squatter? He is one who, without any colour of right, enters on an unoccupied house or land, intending to stay there as long as he can. He may seek to justify or excuse his conduct. He may say that he was homeless and that this house or land was standing empty, doing nothing. But this plea is of no avail in law. As we said in *London Borough of Southwark* v. *Williams* [1971] Ch. 734, 744:
   "If homelessness were once admitted as a defence to trespass, no one's house could be safe . . . So the courts must, for the sake of law and order, take a firm stand. They must refuse to admit the plea of necessity to the hungry and the homeless; and trust that their distress will be relieved by the charitable and the good."

(i) *The remedy of self-help*
   Now I would say this at once about squatters. The owner is not obliged to go to the courts to obtain possession. He is entitled, if he so desires, to take the remedy into his own hands. He can go in himself and turn them out without the aid of the courts of law. This is not a course to be recommended because of the disturbance which might follow. But the legality of it is beyond question. The squatters were themselves guilty of the offence of forcible entry contrary to the statute of 1381 [now repealed]. When they broke in, they entered "with strong hand" which the statute forbids. They were not only guilty of a criminal offence. They were guilty of a civil wrong. They were trespassers when they entered, and they continued to be trespassers so long as they remained there. The owner never acquiesced in their presence there. So the trespassers never gained possession. The owner, being entitled to possession, was entitled forcibly to turn them out: see *Browne* v. *Dawson* (1840) 12 Ad. & El. 624, 113 E.R. 950. As Sir Frederick Pollock put it in his book on Torts:
   "A trespasser may in any case be turned off land before he has gained possession, and he does not gain possession until there has been something like acquiescence in the physical fact of his occupation on the part of the rightful owner."
   Even though the owner himself should use force, then, so long as he uses no more force than is reasonably necessary, he is not himself liable either criminally or civilly. He is not liable criminally because it was said in the old times that none of the statutes of forcible entry apply to the expulsion by the owner of the tenant at will: . . . but, even if this is no longer true, in any case the statutes only apply to the expulsion of one who is in possession: see *R.* v. *Child* (1846) 2 Cox C.C. 102. They

do not apply to the expulsion of a trespasser who has no possession. The owner was not civilly liable because the owner is entitled to turn out a trespasser using force, no more than is reasonably necessary: see *Hemmings* v. *Stoke Poges Golf Club* [1920] 1 K.B. 720.

(ii) *The remedy by action*

Although the law thus enables the owner to take the remedy into his own hands, that is not a course to be encouraged. In a civilised society, the courts should themselves provide a remedy which is speedy and effective; and thus make self-help unnecessary. The courts of common law have done this for centuries. The owner is entitled to go to the court and obtain an order that the owner "do recover" the land, and to issue a writ of possession immediately.

3. *The position of tenants*

I must point out, however, that I have referred so far only to squatters who enter without any colour of title at all. It is different with a tenant who holds over after his term has come to an end or after he has been given notice to quit. His possession was lawful in its inception. Even after the tenancy is determined, there is high authority for saying that the owner is not entitled to take the law into his own hands and remove the tenant by force. He should go to the court and get an order for possession. Otherwise he is guilty of a criminal offence. . . .

Note:
The Criminal Law Act 1977 reduces the scope for self-help, as opposed to defence of property. The Act makes it an offence for anyone except a "displaced residential occupier" to use or threaten to use violence in order to secure entry to premises on which he knows there to be any person opposed to his entry, unless he has "lawful authority." "Lawful authority" includes statutory powers and court orders, but not legal rights to possess or occupy the premises. The "displaced residential occupier"—the only person who may still use self-help—is the person who returns home to find it occupied by someone who entered as a trespasser. Instead of resorting to self-help, however, such a person would do better to call the police, for a uniformed policeman can now enter premises and arrest a trespassory intruder who fails to leave when asked to do so by either a displaced residential occupier or a "protected intending occupier." The latter term includes those who have purchased the premises or have been allocated them by a local authority and intend to reside in them. Anyone else who wishes to exercise a right to enter or re-enter premises on which there is a trespasser who wants to stay there must seek a court order: until the court order, the trespasser, who has no right to be there, commits no offence by staying (unless he has an offensive weapon with him), and the party who has a right to enter commits an offence if he tries to do so by force.

PROTECTION FROM EVICTION ACT 1977

3.—(1) Where any premises have been let as a dwelling under a tenancy which is not a statutorily protected tenancy and—

(*a*) the tenancy . . . has come to an end, but
(*b*) the occupier continues to reside in the premises or part of them,

it shall not be lawful for the owner to enforce against the occupier, otherwise than by proceedings in the court, his right to recover possession of the premises.

CONSUMER CREDIT ACT 1974

90.—(1) At any time when—

(*a*) the debtor is in breach of a regulated hire-purchase or a regulated conditional sale agreement relating to goods, and (*b*) the debtor has paid to the creditor one-third or more of the total price of the goods, and

(*c*) the property in the goods remains in the creditor,

the creditor is not entitled to recover possession of the goods from the debtor except on an order of the court.

PART IV

LAW BETWEEN NEIGHBOURS

INTRODUCTION

WHEN Lord Atkin in *Donoghue* wanted to create a relationship between manufacturer and consumer he called them "neighbours," which of course they are not. Neighbours are people who occupy adjacent pieces of land or adjoining flats in the same buildings. They live in constant physical proximity and they did not choose each other. The common law has a special regime for them and it is called "nuisance."

The relationship of neighbours is very "special." First, it has an element of duration; there is a continuous period of mutual exposure; the necessary accommodation of weal and woe must be made with time in mind. (I cannot complain if my neighbour demolishes his house; but I can complain if he does it every year. One late night revel per month is one thing, but one per night is another (*Delvalle* v. *Thompson* (1961) 111 L.J. 276).) Secondly, both parties are at home: at home you should be able to do what you like; but whether you can do what you like (*e.g.* sleep) may depend on what the people next door like doing at home. Thirdly, it is a relationship as fertile in disputes as marriage—if trivial complaints were allowed, the courts would be swamped. These facts are so important, and the real relationship of neighbours so different from the factitious relationship of ships that pass in the night that the law between neighbours is inevitably bound to be very different from the law regulating common users of the highway. It is different in all legal systems and the common law ought not to pretend that it is not.

Of course, the law between neighbours does not comprise nuisance alone. I can sue my neighbour as well as a stranger in trespass; indeed, the law of trespass provides the forum for boundary disputes. But trespass applies only where some "thing" comes across the boundary—you cannot break a close with a smell. And it applies only where the thing comes across directly. Where some thing comes across indirectly or there is no act of the defendant, liability cannot be in trespass. In the latter case there will tend to be no liability at all, and in the former it will be expressed as "nuisance" or the "rule in *Rylands* v. *Fletcher*." When we say that a smell is not a thing, we refer to the quality of tangibility. The more important quality of things for the law, however, is that they do damage, physical damage. But so do fumes, though they are not tangible. So it is not surprising that, though liability in trespass may be restricted to things tangible, liability in nuisance had tended to be strict where physical damage is done, whether by tangible things or not.

We are left with invisible invasions which cause no physical harm. A home may be rendered uninhabitable by the smell of pigs, the pounding of pestles, or even the sight of prostitutes. The law must not stop at guarding the home against tactile invasions or limit its protection to material property. Citizens must be allowed to sleep and relax in their homes (and to watch television?—see below, p. 371). The law of nuisance provides protection against undue discomfort.

The protection given is remarkable in two respects. On the one hand, it does not extend to discomforts which fail to qualify as "intolerable." On the other hand, if the discomfort is sufficiently severe, then protection is given whether or not it was "reasonable" of the defendant to engage in the activity which produced it and whether or not he was making every effort to minimise it. The critical thing is not the behaviour of the defendant, but the suffering of the plaintiff. Thus in cases of occlusion of light "the inquiry is directed not to the amount of light taken but to the amount of light left" (*Carr-Saunders* v. *Dick McNeil Associates* [1986] 2 All E.R. 888, 894). But this does not mean that the defendant's freedom is constrained by unusual susceptibility on the part of the plaintiff: "the right is neither increased nor diminished by the actual use to which the dominant owner has chosen to put his premises . . . " (*ibid.*).

Two special cases call for mention. The first is where, though the discomfort comes from the defendant's land, the defendant did not create it: the trouble was caused either by a trespasser or by an act of nature. Then liability will depend on whether the defendant was under a duty to take positive action to demolish the source of the trouble. The second case is where the defendant was acting under statutory powers. Then again liability will depend on whether the defendant was exercising his powers with a proper regard for his neighbours.

The plaintiff's principal aim in cases of private nuisance is usually to have the court stop the activity complained of, by means of an injunction. Surprisingly little turns on the remedy. There might have been a case for saying that liability in damages depended on fault in the defendant whereas liability to an injunction did not; or that a person exercising statutory powers could not be enjoined but could be made to compensate his victims. Neither case has been made. A court will on occasion grant an injunction to stop behaviour which merely threatens damage, and it will often conditionally suspend an injunction against a public body. But an injunction can always be refused, though damages be given, and damages can be given in lieu of an injunction with the effect of making the continuance of the behaviour no longer actionable.

The cases in this chapter are concerned with the offensive or harmful use or neglect of land. There are other methods of legal control apart from the law of nuisance. In the private law area there are restrictive covenants imposed by the vendor or developer of land which prohibit certain uses of the land in question. Most important, today, as one would expect, are the controls in administrative law. The use of land cannot be changed without permission under planning legislation; those likely to be affected can be consulted. An old use may be a "statutory nuisance" subject to control by the local authority under the Public Health Act 1936, the basic enactment, to which additions have been made, especially as concerns noise (Control of Pollution Act 1974, s.58; see *Hammersmith L.B.* v. *Magnum Automated Forecourts* [1978] 1 All E.R. 401 (C.A.)). Thus the social significance of the private law of nuisance has been reduced, though by no means extinguished.

The case of *Rylands* v. *Fletcher* and its successors are properly in this chapter. Although the original case was a dispute between neighbours, the decision was not based on that fact; it concentrated on the defendant's behaviour and did not deal with the plaintiff's title to sue otherwise than as the victim of the damage, so the case came to be regarded as one of general application. In fact, plaintiffs who are not neighbours usually fail if they cannot prove carelessness, and most of the cases exemplify this.

Public nuisance, on the other hand, has no place in this chapter, and has already been treated (above, p. 174); it is an example of liability for damage caused by a crime. There is no need to perpetuate the difficulties which have been produced by a bad pun.

Chapter 10

NUISANCE

Section 1.—The Elements

BAMFORD v. TURNLEY

Court of Exchequer Chamber (1862) 3 B. & S. 66; 31 L.J.Q.B. 286; 6 L.T. 721; 9 Jur.(N.S.) 377; 10 W.R. 803; 122 E.R. 27

The plaintiff complained of the smoke and smell arising from the burning of bricks by the defendant on his land not far from the plaintiff's house. At the trial, Lord Cockburn C.J. directed the jury, on the authority of *Hole* v. *Barlow* (1858) 4 C.B.(N.S.) 334; 140 E.R. 1113, that if they thought that the spot was convenient and proper, and the burning of bricks was, under the circumstances, a reasonable use by the defendant of his own land, the defendant would be entitled to a verdict, independently of the small matter of whether there was an interference with the plaintiff's comfort thereby. The jury accordingly found a verdict for the defendant. The plaintiff moved for a rule calling upon the defendant to show cause why a verdict should not be entered for the plaintiff for 40s., but the Court of Queen's Bench (Cockburn C.J., Wightman, Hill and Blackburn JJ.) refused the rule. The plaintiff appealed to the Court of Exchequer Chamber, who allowed the appeal and entered judgment for the plaintiff, Pollock C.B. dissenting.

Williams J.: . . . If it be good law, that the fitness of the locality prevents the carrying on of an offensive trade from being an actionable nuisance, it appears necessarily to follow that this must be a reasonable use of the land. But if it is not good law, and if the true doctrine is, that whenever, taking all the circumstances into consideration, including the nature and extent of the plaintiff's enjoyment before the acts complained of, the annoyance is sufficiently great to amount to a nuisance according to the ordinary rule of law, an action will lie, whatever the locality may be, then surely the jury cannot properly be asked whether the causing of the nuisance was a reasonable use of the land.

If such a question is proper for their consideration in an action such as the present, for a nuisance by immitting corrupted air into the plaintiff' house, we can see no reason why a similar question should not be submitted to the jury in actions for other violations of the ordinary rights of property; *e.g.* the transmission by a neighbour of water in a polluted condition. But certainly it would be difficult to maintain, as the law now stands, that the jury, in such an action, ought to be told to find for the defendant if they thought that the manufactory which caused the impurity of the water was built on a proper and convenient spot, and that the working of it was a reasonable use by the defendant of his own land. Again, where an easement has been gained in addition to the ordinary rights of property, *e.g.* where a right has been gained to the lateral passage of light and air, no one has ever suggested that the jury might be told, in an action for obstructing the free passage of the light and air, to find for the defendant if they were of opinion that the building which caused the obstruction was erected in a proper and convenient place, and in the reasonable

365

enjoyment by the defendant of his own land. And yet, on principle, it is difficult to see why such question should not be left to the jury if *Hole* v. *Barlow* was well decided.

We are, however, of opinion that the decision in that case was wrong. . . .

Pollock C.B. (dissenting): The question in this case is, whether the direction of the Lord Chief Justice, professing to be founded on the decision of the Court of Common Pleas in *Hole* v. *Barlow*, was right, and in my judgment substantially it was right, *viz.*, taking it to have been as stated in the case, *viz.*, "that if the jury thought that the spot was convenient and proper, and the burning of the bricks was, under the circumstances, a reasonable use by the defendant of his own land, the defendant would be entitled to a verdict." I do not think that the nuisance for which an action will lie is capable of any legal definition which will be applicable to all cases and useful in deciding them. The question so entirely depends on the surrounding circumstances—the place where, the time when, the alleged nuisance, what, the mode of committing it, how, and the duration of it, whether temporary or permanent, occasional or continual—as to make it impossible to lay down any rule of law applicable to every case, and which will also be useful in assisting a jury to come to a satisfactory conclusion: it must at all times be a question of fact with reference to all the circumstances of the case.

Most certainly in my judgment it cannot be laid down as a legal proposition or doctrine, that anything which, under any circumstances, lessens the comfort or endangers the health or safety of a neighbour, must necessarily be an actionable nuisance. That may be a nuisance in Grosvenor Square which would be none in Smithfield Market, that may be a nuisance at midday which would not be so at midnight, that may be a nuisance which is permanent and continual which would be no nuisance if temporary or occasional only. A clock striking the hour, or a bell ringing for some domestic purpose, may be a nuisance, if unreasonably loud and discordant, of which the jury alone must judge; but although not unreasonably loud, if the owner, from some whim or caprice, made the clock strike the hour every 10 minutes, or the bell ring continually, I think a jury would be justified in considering it to be a very great nuisance. In general, a kitchen chimney, suitable to the establishment to which it belonged, could not be deemed a nuisance, but if built in an inconvenient place or manner, on purpose to annoy the neighbours, it might, I think, very properly be treated as one. The compromises that belong to social life, and upon which the peace and comfort of it mainly depend, furnish an indefinite number of examples where some apparent natural right is invaded, or some enjoyment abridged, to provide for the more general convenience or necessities of the whole community; and I think the more the details of the question are examined the more clearly it will appear that all the law can do is to lay down some general and vague proposition which will be no guide to the jury in each particular case that may come before them.

I am of opinion that the passage in *Comyns' Digest*, "Action upon the Case for a Nuisance (C)," is good law. I think the word "reasonable" cannot be an improper word, and too vague to be used on this occasion, seeing that the question whether a contract has been reasonably performed with reference to time, place and subject matter, is one that is put to a jury almost as often as a jury is assembled. If the act complained of be done in a convenient manner, so as to give no unnecessary annoyance, and be a reasonable exercise of some apparent right, or a reasonable use of the land, house or property of the party under all the circumstances, in which I include the degree of inconvenience it will produce, then I think no action can be sustained, if the jury find that it was reasonable—as the jury must be taken to have found that it was reasonable that the defendant should be allowed to do what he did, and reasonable that the plaintiff should submit to the inconvenience occasioned by what was done. And this gets rid of the difficulty suggested in the judgment just read by my brother Williams; because it cannot be supposed that a jury would find that to be a reasonable act by a person which produces any ruinous effect upon his neighbours. . . .

. . . in my opinion the judgment of the court below ought to be affirmed.

Bramwell B.: I am of opinion that this judgment should be reversed. The defendant has done that which, if done wantonly or maliciously, would be actionable as being a nuisance to the plaintiff's habitation by causing a sensible diminution of the comfortable enjoyment of it. This, therefore, calls on the defendant to justify or excuse what he has done. And his justification is this: He says that the nuisance is not to the health of the inhabitants of the plaintiff's house, that it is of a temporary character, and is necessary for the beneficial use of his, the defendant's, land, and that the public good requires he should be entitled to do what he claims to do.

The question seems to me to be, is this a justification in law—and, in order not to make a verbal mistake, I will say—a justification for what is done, or a matter which makes what is done no nuisance? It is to be borne in mind, however, that, in fact, the act of the defendant is a nuisance such that it would be actionable if done wantonly or maliciously. The plaintiff, then, has a prima facie case. The defendant has infringed the maxim *sic utere tuo ut alienum non laedas*. Then, what principle or rule of law can he rely on to defend himself? It is clear to my mind that there is some exception to the general application of the maxim mentioned. The instances put during the argument, of burning weeds, emptying cesspools, making noises during repairs, and other instances which would be nuisances if done wantonly or maliciously, nevertheless may be lawfully done. It cannot be said that such acts are not nuisances, because, by the hypothesis, they are; and it cannot be doubted that, if a person maliciously and without cause made close to a dwelling-house the same offensive smells as may be made in emptying a cesspool, an action would lie. Nor can these cases be got rid of as extreme cases, because such cases properly test a principle. . . . There must be, then, some principle on which such cases must be excepted. It seems to me that that principle may be deduced from the character of these cases, and is this, *viz.*, that those acts necessary for the common and ordinary use and occupation of land and houses may be done, if conveniently done, without subjecting those who do them to an action. This principle would comprehend all the cases I have mentioned, but would not comprehend the present, where what has been done was not the using of land in a common and ordinary way, but in an exceptional manner—not unnatural nor unusual, but not the common and ordinary use of land. There is an obvious necessity for such a principle as I have mentioned. It is as much for the advantage of one owner as of another; for the very nuisance the one complains of, as the result of the ordinary use of his neighbour's land, he himself will create in the ordinary use of his own, and the reciprocal nuisances are of a comparatively trifling character. The convenience of such a rule may be indicated by calling it a rule of give and take, live and let live.

Then can this principle be extended to, or is there any other principle which will comprehend, the present case? I know of none; it is for the defendant to show it. None of the above reasoning is applicable to such a cause of nuisance as the present. It had occurred to me, that any not unnatural use of the land, if of a temporary character, might be justified; but I cannot see why its being of a temporary nature should warrant it. What is temporary—one, five, or 20 years? If 20, it would be difficult to say that a brick kiln in the direction of the prevalent wind for 20 years would not be as objectionable as a permanent one in the opposite direction. If temporary in order to build a house on the land, why not temporary in order to exhaust the brick earth? I cannot think then that the nuisance being temporary makes a difference.

But it is said that, temporary or permanent, it is lawful because it is for the public benefit. Now, in the first place, that law to my mind is a bad one which, for the public benefit, inflicts loss on an individual without compensation. But further, with great respect, I think this consideration misapplied in this and in many other cases.

The public consists of all the individuals of it, and a thing is only for the public benefit when it is productive of good to those individuals on the balance of loss and gain to all. So that if all the loss and all the gain were borne and received by one individual, he on the whole would be a gainer. But whenever this is the case—whenever a thing is for the public benefit, properly understood—the loss to the individuals of the public who lose will bear compensation out of the gains of those who gain. It is for the public benefit there should be railways, but it would not be unless the gain of having the railway was sufficient to compensate the loss occasioned by the use of the land required for its site; and accordingly no one thinks it would be right to take an individual's land without compensation to make a railway. It is for the public benefit that trains should run, but not unless they pay their expenses. If one of those expenses is the burning down of a wood of such value that the railway owners would not run the train and burn down the wood if it were their own, neither is it for the public benefit they should if the wood is not their own. If, though the wood were their own, they still would find it compensated them to run trains at the cost of burning the wood, then they obviously ought to compensate the owner of such wood, not being themselves, if they burn it down in making their gains. So in like way in this case a money value indeed cannot easily be put on the plaintiff's loss, but it is equal to some number of pounds or pence, £10, £50, or what not: unless the defendant's profits are enough to compensate this, I deny that it is for the public benefit he should do what he has done; if they are, he ought to compensate.

The only objection I can see to this reasoning is, that by injunction or by abatement of the nuisance a man who would not accept a pecuniary compensation might put a stop to works of great value, and much more than enough to compensate him. This objection, however, is comparatively of small practical importance; it may be that the law ought to be amended, and some means be provided to legalise such cases, as I believe is the case in some foreign countries on giving compensation; but I am clearly of opinion that, though the present law may be defective, it would be much worse, and be unjust and inexpedient, if it permitted such power of inflicting loss and damage to individuals, without compensation, as is claimed by the argument for the defendant.

ST. HELEN'S SMELTING CO. v. TIPPING

House of Lords (1865) 11 H.L.Cas. 642, 35 L.J.Q.B. 66; 12 L.T. 776; 29 J.P. 579; 11 Jur.(N.S.) 785; 13 W.R. 1083; 11 E.R. 1483

The plaintiff bought an estate of great value in June 1860. A mile and a half away there was a large smelting works, evidence of whose use prior to that time was uncertain. In September 1860 very extensive smelting operations began on the property of the defendants at St. Helen's, and the vapours exhaled from those works did physical injury to the shrubs and trees on the plaintiff's estate.

At the trial, Mellor J. laid down the law to the jury in the following terms: "That every man is bound to use his own property in such a manner as not to injure the property of his neighbour, unless, by the lapse of a certain period of time, he has acquired a prescriptive right to do so. But that the law does not regard trifling inconveniences; every thing must be looked at from a reasonable point of view; and, therefore, in an action for nuisance to property by noxious vapours arising on the land of another, the injury to be actionable must be such as visibly to diminish the value of the property and the comfort and enjoyment of it. That, in determining that question the time, locality, and all the circumstances should be taken into consideration; that in counties where great works have been erected and carried on, which are the means of developing the national wealth, persons must not stand on extreme rights and bring actions in respect of every matter of annoyance, as, if that were so, business could not be carried on in those places."

The jury found a verdict for the plaintiff, damages £361 18. 4½d. The defendant moved for a rule for a new trial on the ground of misdirection. The Court of Queen's Bench refused the rule (1863) 4 B. & S. 608; 122 E.R. 588; the Court of Exchequer Chamber dismissed the defendant's appeal (1864) 4 B. & S. 616; 122 E.R. 591, and the defendant's appeal to the House of Lords was also dismissed.

Lord Westbury L.C.: . . . My Lords, in matters of this description it appears to me that it is a very desirable thing to mark the difference between an action brought for a nuisance upon the ground that the alleged nuisance produces material injury to the property, and an action brought for a nuisance on the ground that the thing alleged to be a nuisance is productive of sensible personal discomfort. With regard to the latter, namely, the personal inconvenience and interference with one's enjoyment, one's quiet, one's personal freedom, anything that discomposes or injuriously affects the senses or the nerves, whether that may or may not be denominated a nuisance, must undoubtedly depend greatly on the circumstances of the place where the thing complained of actually occurs. If a man lives in a town, it is necessary that he should subject himself to the consequences of those operations of trade which may be carried on in his immediate locality, which are actually necessary for trade and commerce, and also for the enjoyment of property, and for the benefit of the inhabitants of the town and of the public at large. If a man lives in a street where there are numerous shops, and a shop is opened next door to him, which is carried on in a fair and reasonable way, he has no ground for complaint, because to himself individually there may arise much discomfort from the trade carried on in that shop. But when an occupation is carried on by one person in the neighbourhood of another, and the result of that trade, or occupation, or business, is a material injury to property, then there unquestionably arises a very different consideration. I think, my Lords, that in a case of that description, the submission which is required from persons living in society to that amount of discomfort which may be necessary for the legitimate and free exercise of the trade of their neighbours, would not apply to circumstances the immediate result of which is sensible injury to the value of the property.

Now, in the present case, it appears that the plaintiff purchased a very valuable estate, which lies within a mile and a half from certain large smelting works. What the occupation of these copper smelting premises was anterior to the year 1860 does not clearly appear. The plaintiff became the proprietor of an estate of great value in the month of June 1860. In the month of September 1860 very extensive smelting operations began on the property of the present appellants, in their works at St. Helen's. Of the effect of the vapours exhaling from those works upon the plaintiff's property, and the injury done to his trees and shrubs, there is abundance of evidence in the case.

My Lords, the action has been brought upon that, and the jurors have found the existence of the injury; and the only ground upon which your Lordships are asked to set aside that verdict, and to direct a new trial, is this, that the whole neighbourhood where these copper smelting works were carried on, is a neighbourhood more or less devoted to manufacturing purposes of a similar kind, and therefore it is said, that inasmuch as this copper smelting is carried on in what the appellant contends is a fit place, it may be carried on with impunity, although the result may be the utter destruction, or the very considerable diminution, of the value of the plaintiff's property. My Lords, I apprehend that that is not the meaning of the word "suitable," or the meaning of the word "convenient," which has been used as applicable to the subject. The word "suitable" unquestionably cannot carry with it this consequence, that a trade may be carried on in a particular locality, the consequence of which trade may be injury and destruction to the neighbouring property. Of course, my Lords, I accept cases where any prescriptive right has been acquired by a lengthened user of the place.

On these grounds, therefore, shortly, without dilating farther upon them (and they are sufficiently unfolded by the judgment of the learned judges in the court below), I advise your Lordships to affirm the decision of the court below, and to refuse the new trial, and to dismiss the appeal with costs.

Note:
   In his outstanding decision of *Halsey* v. *Esso Petroleum Co.* [1961] 1 W.L.R. 683, Veale J. said this: " . . . liability for nuisance by harmful deposits could be established by proving damage by the deposits to the property in question, provided of course that the injury was not merely trivial. Negligence is not an ingredient of the cause of action, and the character of the neighbourhood is not a matter to be taken into consideration. On the other hand, nuisance by smell and noise is something to which no absolute standard can be applied. It is always a question of degree whether the interference with comfort or convenience is sufficiently serious to constitute a nuisance. The character of the neighbourhood is very relevant and all relevant circumstances have to be taken into account."
   Of course, if prolonged discomfort is caused, the value of the property will diminish; it cannot have been the intention of Lord Westbury to permit a plaintiff to pretend that his discomfort was intolerable on the mere ground that it had economic effects. Accordingly, his distinction must refer to physical damage to property, and not to economic loss only.
   In *Halsey's* case the plaintiffs' life had been made a misery for five years by the constant noise, dirt and commotion from the oil depot near their house in Fulham: all they got by way of damages was £200. In *Bone* v. *Seale* [1975] 1 All E.R. 787 the plaintiffs had been disgusted for 12 years by the nauseating smells from a village pig-farm, and the judge awarded them £500 per year, a total of £6,000 each. The Court of Appeal reduced the award to £1,000. In both cases an injunction was granted as well as damages.

Question
   Can a person recover from a neighbour who has installed a petrol station the amount by which his fire insurance premiums have consequently gone up?

WATT v. JAMIESON

Court of Session, 1954 S.C. 56

The pursuer, an advocate and proprietor of the upper floors of 3, Moray Place, Edinburgh, claimed £3,050 from the defender, a solicitor, and proprietor of the lower floors of 4, Moray Place. The defender had installed a gas water storage heater, the flue of which he connected to the vent in the gable common to the two houses. This flue discharged 2½ gallons of water every six hours, and alarming symptoms of damage appeared on the interior and exterior walls of the pursuer's house. The defender pleaded that the action was irrelevant on the ground that there was no liability for the normal natural and familiar use of property and that this was such a use. A proof before answer was allowed.

Lord President Cooper: . . . From these and other pronouncements I deduce that the proper angle of approach to a case of alleged nuisance is rather from the standpoint of the victim of the loss or inconvenience than from the standpoint of the alleged offender; and that, if any person so uses his property as to occasion serious disturbance or substantial inconvenience to his neighbour or material damage to his neighbour's property, it is in the general case irrelevant as a defence for the defender to plead merely that he was making a normal and familiar use of his own property. The balance in all such cases has to be held between the freedom of a proprietor to use his property as he pleases and the duty on a proprietor not to inflict material loss or inconvenience on adjoining proprietors or adjoining property; and in every case the answer depends on considerations of fact and degree. I cannot accept the extreme view that in order to make a relevant case of nuisance it is always necessary for the pursuer to aver that the type of user complained of was *in itself* non-natural, unreasonable and unusual. Especially when (as in this case) the so-called "locality" principle applies, it must be accepted that a certain amount of inconvenience, annoyance, disturbance and even damage must just be accepted as the price the pursuer pays for staying where he does in a city tenement. The critical question is whether what he was exposed to was *plus quam tolerabile* when due weight has been given to all the surrounding circumstances of the offensive conduct and its effects. If that test is satisfied, I do not consider that our law accepts as a defence that the nature of the user complained of was usual, familiar and normal. *Any* type of use which in the sense indicated above subjects adjoining proprietors to substantial annoyance, or causes material damage to their property, is prima facie not a "reasonable" use. . . .

Note:

But as Lord Fraser said in reference to this case " . . . the fact that the proper approach is from the standpoint of the victim does not mean that the question of fault on the part of the alleged offender can be completely disregarded, so as to make him an insurer . . . " (*R.H.M. Bakeries (Scotland)* v. *Strathclyde R.C.* (1981) S.L.T. 214, 218 (H.L.)).

BRIDLINGTON RELAY LTD. v. YORKSHIRE ELECTRICITY BOARD

Chancery [1965] Ch. 436; [1965] 2 W.L.R. 349; 109 S.J. 12; [1965] 1 All E.R. 264

The plaintiffs had erected a high aerial mast for the reception of sound and television broadcasts which they relayed to the residents of Bridlington, whom the defendants supplied with electricity. The defendants erected a power line which ran within 169 feet of the plaintiffs' mast and the plaintiffs feared that when energised it would interfere with their reception.

The plaintiff's motion for an interlocutory injunction was refused.

Buckley J.: . . . If interference of the kind experienced by the plaintiff during the tests were to recur at all frequently, it is very probable that the plaintiff's business would be damaged. If such damage were established, and it were shown that it would be likely to continue or recur, would the plaintiff have a cause of action in nuisance?

For the plaintiff it is contended that to receive television is now an ordinary use of land and that causing radiation which results in preventing or interfering with the satisfactory reception of television transmissions is something which unwarrantably interferes with the legitimate and reasonable enjoyment of neighbouring property by its owners. It is said that, if that interference is of a sufficiently grave character, it may amount to an actionable nuisance on either or both of two grounds: *viz.*, that it interferes with the beneficial use of the neighbouring property and that it affects the value of that property.

On the other hand, the defendant contends that the plaintiff is using the aerial mast for a purpose requiring exceptional immunity from electrical interference; that not only are the aerials exceptionally sensitive to such interference, but the plaintiff's business is also one of a kind requiring a higher standard of interference-free reception than an ordinary viewer using a domestic aerial would demand.

I was invited and am prepared to take judicial notice of the fact that the reception of television has become a very common feature of domestic life. The evidence has shown that the quality of reception enjoyed in different parts of the country varies widely, mainly for geographical reasons. Where the quality of reception is poor the effect of interference is more serious, for the greater the strength of the wanted signal the less the effect upon the screen of interference of any given strength. Where the strength of the wanted signal is low, interference of even quite moderate intensity will degrade the picture.

In taking judicial notice of the widespread reception of television in domestic circles, I do so upon the footing that in those circles television is enjoyed almost entirely for what I think must be regarded as recreational purposes, notwithstanding that the broadcast programmes include material which may have some educational content, some political content and, it may be, some other content not strictly or exclusively recreational in character. Those programmes, the purposes of which are strictly educational are not, I presume, intended for domestic consumption or very much looked at in private homes.

I mention these matters because, in my judgment, the plaintiff could not succeed in a claim for damages for nuisance if what I may call an ordinary receiver of television by means of an aerial mounted on his own house could not do so. It is, I think, established by authority that an act which does not, or would not, interfere with the ordinary enjoyment of their property by neighbours in the ordinary modes of using such property cannot constitute a legal nuisance. I quote: "A man cannot increase the liabilities of his neighbour by applying his own property to special uses, whether for business or pleasure"—(*Eastern & South African Telegraph Co.* v. *Cape Town Tramways Corporation Ltd.* ([1902] A.C. 381, 393)).

In *Robinson* v. *Kilvert* ((1889) 41 Ch.D. 88, 94) Cotton L.J. stated the principle thus: "If a person does what in itself is noxious, or which interferes with the ordinary use and enjoyment of a neighbour's property, it is a nuisance. But no case has been cited where the doing something not in itself noxious has been held a nuisance, unless it interferes with the ordinary enjoyment of life, or the ordinary use of property for purposes of residence or business."

The dissemination of electrical interference is not, in my judgment, "noxious" in the sense in which I think Cotton L.J. is there using the term. Could such interference as is here in question be held to cause an interference with the ordinary enjoyment of life or the ordinary use of the plaintiff's property for the purposes of residence or business of such a kind as to amount to an actionable nuisance?

There are, of course, many reported cases in which something adversely affecting the beneficial enjoyment of property has been held to constitute a legal nuisance; but I have been referred to no case in which interference with a purely recreational facility has been held to do so. Considerations of health and physical comfort and well-being appear to me to be on a somewhat different level from recreational considerations. I do not wish to be taken as laying down that in no circumstances can something which interferes merely with recreational facilities or activities amount to an actionable nuisance. It may be that in some other case the court may be satisfied that some such inteference should be regarded, according to such plain and sober and simple notions as Knight Bruce V.-C referred to in a well-known passage in his judgment in *Walter* v. *Selfe* ((1851) 4 De G. & Sm. 315, 322; 64 E.R. 849) as detracting from the beneficial use and enjoyment by neighbouring owners of their properties to such an extent as to warrant their protection by the law.

For myself, however, I do not think that it can at present be said that the ability to receive television free from occasional, even if recurrent and severe, electrical interference is so important a part of an ordinary householder's enjoyment of his property that such interference should be regarded as a legal nuisance, particularly, perhaps, if such interference affects only one of the available alternative programmes.

Accordingly, I do not think that even if the conditions which existed during the tests would have produced the same effect on the screen of a householder using an aerial mounted on his own house at the site of the plaintiff's mast, this would have constituted an actionable nuisance. . . .

The plaintiff's complaint is concerned not with interference with domestic amenities; its complaint is that its business will be damaged. But its business is such that to prosper it requires an exceptional degree of immunity from interference. To prosper it must be able to offer its subscribers a better service than they could obtain through aerials of their own. It was not established to my satisfaction that the aerial used by the plaintiff for receiving B.B.C. transmissions from Holme Moss was proportionately more sensitive to interference than domestic aerials are in the same area, but it was established that the business of the plaintiff was exceptionally sensitive in the sense which I have just indicated. The use of its aerial for this particular kind of business was, in my judgment, use of a special kind unusually vulnerable to interference, just as the business carried on by the plaintiff in *Robinson* v. *Kilvert* was exceptionally vulnerable to the effects of heat.

For these reasons as well as the other reasons given earlier in this judgment I am of opinion that the plaintiff cannot succeed in this action.

PUBLIC HEALTH ACT 1936

91.—It shall be the duty of every local authority to cause their district to be inspected from time to time for the detection of matters requiring to be dealt with under the provisions of this Part of this Act as statutory nuisances within the meaning of the next succeeding subsection.

92.—(1) Without prejudice to the exercise by a local authority of any other powers vested in them by or under this Act, the following matters may . . . be dealt with summarily, and are in this Part of this Act referred to as "statutory nuisances," that is to say—

   (a) any premises in such a state as to be prejudicial to health or a nuisance;
   (b) any animal kept in such a place or manner as to be prejudicial to health or a nuisance;
   (c) any accumulation or deposit which is prejudicial to health or a nuisance;
   (d) . . .

Section 2.—Wilfulness

HOLLYWOOD SILVER FOX FARM LTD. v. EMMETT

King's Bench [1936] 2 K.B. 468; 105 L.J.K.B. 829; 155 L.T. 288; 52 T.L.R. 611; 80 S.J. 488; [1936] 1 All E.R. 825

The plaintiff's managing director, Captain Chandler, set up the plaintiff company to breed silver foxes, and erected at the boundary of his land and adjacent to the highway a sign saying "Hollywood Silver Fox Farm." This annoyed his neighbour, the defendant, who was developing the adjoining land as a housing estate, and thought that the sign would deter his customers. Emmett accordingly asked Captain Chandler to remove the sign and when Captain Chandler refused he threatened to shoot along the boundary. This was a serious threat since, as Emmett knew, the effect of loud noises on vixens is to deter mating, impede whelping and provoke infanticide. On four subsequent evenings the threat was carried out by the defendant's son, and damage done. Macnaghten J. gave judgment for the plaintiff in damages, and also issued an injunction.

Macnaghten J.: . . . In these circumstances the decision of the Court of King's Bench in *Keeble* v. *Hickeringill* ((1706) 11 East 574n.; 103 E.R. 1127; 90 E.R. 906), if it be well founded, is a clear authority that the defendant has committed an actionable wrong. In that case the plaintiff, the owner of a duck decoy, brought an action against the defendant for shooting at and disturbing the ducks in his decoy. The jury found a verdict for the plaintiff and the question whether the action was maintainable was argued before the Full Court.

During the argument there was some question whether the defendant had actually trespassed on the plaintiff's land, and according to the report in 11 Mod., p. 74, Lord Holt said: "But suppose the defendant had shot in his own ground, if he had occasion to shoot, it would have been one thing; but to shoot on purpose to damage the plaintiff is another thing and a wrong."

The court decided that the action was maintainable and judgment was entered for the plaintiffs.

Mr. Roche submitted that the defendant was entitled to shoot on his own land, and that even if his conduct was malicious he had not committed any actionable wrong. In support of his argument, Mr. Roche relied mainly on the decision of the House of Lords in the case of *Bradford Corporation* v. *Pickles* ([1894] A.C. 587). In that case the Corporation of Bradford sought to restrain Mr. Pickles from sinking a shaft on land which belonged to him because, according to their view, his object in sinking the shaft was to draw away from their land water which would otherwise come into their reservoirs. Mr. Pickles, they said, was acting maliciously, his sole object being to do harm to the Corporation. The House of Lords decided once and for all that in such a case the motive of the defendant is immaterial.

In the case of *Allen* v. *Flood* ([1898] A.C. 587; below, p. 509) Lord Herschell, commenting on the decision in *Bradford Corporation* v. *Pickles*, said: "It has recently been held in this House, in the case of *Bradford Corporation* v. *Pickles*, that acts done by the defendant upon his own land were not actionable when they were within his legal rights, even though his motive were to prejudice his neighbour. The language of the noble and learned Lords was distinct. The Lord Chancellor said: 'This is not a case where the state of mind of the person doing the act can affect the right. If it was a lawful act, however ill the motive might be, he had a right to do it. If it was an unlawful act, however good the motive might be, he would have no right to do it.' The statement was confined to the class of cases then before the House; but I apprehend that what was said is not applicable only to rights of property, but is equally applicable to the exercise by an individual of his other rights."

Mr. Roche argued that in the present case the defendant had not committed any nuisance at all in the legal sense of the term, and he referred to the case of *Robinson* v. *Kilvert* ((1889) 41 Ch.D. 88). In that case a complaint was made by the tenant of the ground floor of a building that the tenant of the basement was making the basement so warm that the brown paper which he kept on the ground floor suffered damage, and it was held by the Court of Appeal that no actionable wrong had been committed by the defendant, in that the heating was not of such a character as would interfere with the ordinary use of the rest of the house. Mr. Roche submitted that the keeping of a silver fox farm is not an ordinary use of land, and that the shooting would have caused no alarm to the animals which are usually to be found on farms in Kent or done them any harm.

Apart from the case of *Keeble* v. *Hickeringill* there is authority for the view that in an action for nuisance by noise the intention of the person making the noise must be considered. In the case of *Gaunt* v. *Fynney* ((1872) L.R. 8 Ch. 8, 12) Lord Selborne, delivering the judgment of the court, said: "A nuisance by noise (supposing

malice to be out of the question) is emphatically a question of degree." The paren-
thetical statement, "supposing malice to be out of the question," clearly indicated
that his Lordship thought that in the case of an alleged nuisance by noise where the
noise was made maliciously different considerations would apply from those applicable where the defendant had in the words of Lord Holt "occasion" to make the
noise. In *Christie* v. *Davey* ([1893] 1 Ch. 316, 326) the plaintiffs, Mr. and Mrs.
Christie, and the defendant lived side by side in semi-detached houses in Brixton.
Mrs. Christie was a teacher of music, and her family were also musical, and
throughout the day sounds of music pervaded their house and were heard in the
house of their neighbour. The defendant did not like the music that he heard, and
by way of retaliation he took to making noises himself, beating trays and rapping on
the wall. The action came on for trial before North J., who delivered judgment in
favour of the plaintiffs and granted an injunction restraining the defendant from
causing or permitting any sounds or noises in his house so as to vex or annoy the
plaintiffs or the occupiers of their house. In the course of his judgment, he said at
page 326, after dealing with the facts as he found them, "The result is that I think I
am bound to interfere for the protection of the plaintiffs. In my opinion the noises
which were made in the defendant's house were not of a legitimate kind. They were
what, to use the language of Lord Selborne in *Gaunt* v. *Fynney*, 'ought to be
regarded as excessive and unreasonable.' I am satisfied that they were made deliberately and maliciously for the purpose of annoying the plaintiffs." Then come the
significant words: "If what has taken place had occurred between two sets of persons both perfectly innocent, I should have taken an entirely different view of the
case. But I am persuaded that what was done by the defendant was done only for
the purpose of annoyance, and in my opinion it was not a legitimate use of the
defendant's house to use it for the purpose of vexing and annoying his neighbours."

The case of *Ibottson* v. *Peat* ((1865) 3 H. & C. 644; 159 E.R. 684) affords an exact
precedent for the statement of claim in this action. Mr. Ibottson was a landowner in
the parish of Brampton, in Derbyshire, and his land adjoined a grouse moor
belonging to the Duke of Rutland. Mr. Ibottson, for the purpose of inducing the
grouse on the Duke of Rutland's moor to come on to his own land, put down corn
and thereby lured and enticed the grouse to come away from the Duke's land. The
defendant, Peat, was, it appears, a gamekeeper in the employ of the Duke of Rutland, and, in order to prevent Mr. Ibottson from getting any benefit from such
unneighbourly conduct, he let off fireworks, rockets, and bombs as near as he could
get to Mr. Ibottson's land for the purpose of frightening away the grouse which had
been attracted by the corn. In answer to the declaration in that case the defendant
set up as a plea that he was justified in letting off the rockets and bombs because of
the improper conduct of the plaintiff in luring away the Duke's grouse. The question for the consideration of the court was whether that was a good plea, and it was
held to be bad.

The cases to which I have referred were decided before the decision of the House
of Lords in *Bradford Corporation* v. *Pickles*; and the question therefore arises
whether those cases must now be considered as overruled. It is to be observed that
in *Allen* v. *Flood* Lord Watson discussed fully the case of *Keeble* v. *Hickeringill* and
said with reference to that case: "No proprietor has an absolute right to create
noises upon his own land, because any right which the law gives him is qualified by
the condition that it must not be exercised to the nuisance of his neighbours or of
the public. If he violates that condition he commits a legal wrong, and if he does so
intentionally he is guilty of a malicious wrong, in its strict legal sense."

In my opinion the decision of the House of Lords in *Bradford Corporation* v.
Pickles has no bearing on such cases as this. I therefore think that the plaintiff is
entitled to maintain this action. I think also that in the circumstances an injunction
should be granted restraining the defendant from committing a nuisance by the discharge of firearms or the making of other loud noises in the vicinity of the Hollywood Silver Fox Farm during the breeding season—namely, between January 1 and

June 15— so as to alarm or disturb the foxes kept by the plaintiffs at the said farm, or otherwise to injure the plaintiff company.

Question

In view of the terms of the injunction issued, do you think that the defendant could safely shoot any rabbits there might actually be close to the boundary?

Note:

In *Smith* v. *Scott* ([1973] Ch. 314) the plaintiffs had to move out of their house because the problem family next door had made their life intolerable by noise and vandalism. An injunction was naturally issued against the family (but then where do they go?). The local authority which had installed them as tenants was held not liable, although they had known the nature of the tenants they installed. The local authority did not authorise the nuisance because they had inserted a clause forbidding the tenants to create a nuisance, and the nuisance did not result from the purposes for which the premises were let, but only from the persons to whom they were let; there was no duty under *Donoghue* v. *Stevenson* to take care to choose tenants who would not cause harm to their neighbours. The decision would be a surprising one had the second defendant been a private landlord out for profit: as against a local authority which has duties with regard to the housing of poor families, the matter ought to be resolved in terms of the reasonableness of their behaviour in the light of their duties, and even then, one might think, the plaintiffs, effectively evicted by the local authority, should have a claim for compensation.

Donoghue v. *Stevenson* was also put to one side in *Langbrook Properties* v. *Surrey C.C.* [1969] 3 All E.R. 1424. Pursuant to their statutory functions the defendants were doing works which called for excavations near a site which the plaintiffs were developing. The excavations were kept dry by pumping, and the pumping abstracted water from under the plaintiffs' land, which caused buildings there to settle. It was held that the defendants were not liable even if the damage might have been avoided with reasonable care. Plowman J. reviewed the authorities. They clearly established that a landowner has no absolute right to water support as he does to support by land, though in none of them had the defendant by negligent abstraction caused actual damage to property. The judge added that if abstraction of water was not actionable if one intended to cause injury (*Bradford* v. *Pickles* [1895] A.C. 587) it could hardly be actionable if one did not.

The Court of Appeal has endorsed his view that one has an absolute right to drain one's land, though not to dig holes in it, in *Stephens* v. *Anglian Water Auth'y* [1987] 3 All E.R. 379, where on very similar facts the plaintiff sued only "in negligence." The Court's view that the case was covered by *Pickles* is perhaps a little cavalier, since there is surely a relevant difference between a complaint that one has not received water one hoped for and a complaint that one's house is falling about one's ears. Not cited was a decision of the Court of Appeal on March 21, 1984 where the plaintiff's house settled after the defendant had knocked down the house next door; the settlement took place not because the latter house had been propping up the former but because its presence had been preventing the evaporation of water. Dillon L.J. said "I can see no reason in law or sense why the right of support should be curtailed where what has impaired support is the removal by the dominant owner by some act on his own land of water in the clay sub-soil under the plaintiff's building." (*Brace* v. *S.E. Regional Housing Assoc'n.* [1984] C.A.T. 20). See Fleming, 104 L.Q.R. 183 (1988).

Langbrook Properties was not cited in *Home Brewery* v. *Davis & Co.* [1987] 1 All E.R. 637 (Piers Ashworth Q.C.). Here also the defendants had waterlogged land, but instead of draining it they filled it in. The result was that (1) subsequent rainfall was retained on the plaintiff's land up the hill because it could not percolate through the defendant's land as theretofore, and (2) water in an osier bed was squeezed back on to the plaintiff's land. It was held that the defendants were liable for (2), but not for (1) since their conduct was reasonable. The surprising matter is that the defendants would apparently have been liable for (1) if their conduct had been unreasonable.

If one is entitled to drain one's land whatever the external effects, one might have supposed that one would be free to spray one's crops so long as none of the herbicide or pesticide escaped. Not so. Farmer Walter sprayed his rape crop at a time which seemed good to him despite the counterindications noted by the manufacturer, and his neighbours' bees were poisoned when they came to crop his rape and *vice versa*. Farmer Walter was held liable because he had broken a duty of care. If he had given longer warning he might have avoided liability. (*Tutton* v. *A.D. Walter Ltd.* [1985] 3 All E.R. 757, noted [1986] Camb.L.J. 15 (Spencer)).

Section 3.—Inaction

LEAKEY v. NATIONAL TRUST FOR PLACES OF HISTORIC INTEREST OR NATURAL BEAUTY

Court of Appeal [1980] Q.B. 485; [1980] 2 W.L.R. 65; [1980] 1 All E.R. 17; 78 L.G.R. 100

Burrow Mump is a conical hill in Somerset, remarkable enough to be owned by the National Trust. Centuries ago a bit of the West side of the Mump had been sliced off so as to accommodate the plaintiffs' seventeenth-century cottages. For years there had been small falls of earth from the Mump on to the plaintiffs' property directly below, but the summer drought and autumn rains of 1976 caused a really large crack to appear, presaging a major collapse. The National Trust denied liability, but when a serious fall occurred it was required by interlocutory injunction to abate the nuisance. At the trial, to determine who was to bear the cost of these works, the judge held that once the National Trust knew that the condition of its property, wholly natural though it was, constituted a threat to the plaintiffs' property, the Trust was under a duty to take reasonable steps to prevent damage.

The defendant's appeal to the Court of Appeal was dismissed.

Megaw L.J.: This appeal from the judgment of O'Connor J. ([1978] Q.B. 849) raises questions which are of importance in the development of English law. The learned judge held that the defendants are liable to the plaintiffs in damages, on a claim framed in nuisance, based on the fact that soil and other detritus had fallen from property owned and occupied by the defendants onto the plaintiffs' properties. It was accepted by the parties that the instability of the defendants' land which made it liable, and which had caused, and was likely to continue to cause, falls of detritus on the plaintiffs' land, was not caused by, nor was it aggravated by, any human activities on the defendants' land. It was caused by nature: the geological structure, content and contours of the land, and the effect thereon of sun, rain, wind and frost and suchlike natural phenomena. It was held by the learned judge, and is not now in dispute, that, at least since 1968, the defendants knew that the instability of their land was a threat to the plaintiffs' property because of the possibility of falls of soil and other material. Although requested by the plaintiffs to take steps to prevent such falls, the defendants had not taken any action, because they held the view, no doubt on legal advice, that in law they were under no liability in respect of any damage which might be caused to neighbouring property in consequence of the natural condition of their own property and the operation of natural forces thereon.

O'Connor J. has held that that view of the law is wrong. He based his decision on the judgment of the Judicial Committee of the Privy Council in *Goldman* v. *Hargrave* ([1967] 1 A.C. 645). The main issue in this appeal is whether *Goldman* v. *Hargrave* accurately states the law of England. If it does, the appeal fails, and the defendants are liable. . . .

The relevant facts of *Goldman* v. *Hargrave* were simple. A redgum tree, 100 feet high, on the defendant's land was struck by lightning and caught fire. The defendant caused the land around the burning tree to be cleared and the tree was then cut down and sawn into sections. So far there could be no complaint that the defendant had done anything which he ought not to have done or left undone anything which he ought to have done, so as in any way to increase the risk which had been caused by this act of natural forces setting fire to the tree. Thereafter the defendant (this was the state of the facts on which the Judicial Committee based their decision) did not do anything which he ought not to have done. He took no positive action which increased the risk of the fire spreading. But he failed to do something which he could have done without any substantial trouble or expense, which would, if done, have eliminated or rendered unlikely the spreading of the fire, that is, to have doused with water the burning or smouldering sections of the tree as they lay on the ground. Instead the defendant chose to allow or encourage the fire to burn itself out. Foreseeably (again it was the forces of nature and not human action), the weather became even hotter and a strong wind sprang up. The flames from the tree spread rapidly through the defendant's land to the land of neighbours where it did extensive damage to their properties.

The judgment of the Board was delivered by Lord Wilberforce. It was held that the risk of the consequence which in fact happened was foreseeable. This, it is said, "was not really disputed." The legal issue was then defined:

" . . . the case is not one where a person has brought a source of danger on to his land, nor one where an occupier has so used his property as to cause a danger to his neighbour. It is one where an occupier, faced with a hazard accidentally arising on his land, fails to act with reasonable prudence so as to remove the hazard. The issue is therefore whether in such a case the occupier is guilty of legal negligence, which involves the issue whether he is under a duty of care, and, if so, what is the scope of that duty."

It is to my mind clear, from this passage and other passages in the judgment, that the duty which is being considered, and which later in the judgment is held to exist, does not involve any distinction of principle between what, in another sphere of the law, used to be known as misfeasance and non-feasance. A failure to act may involve a breach of the duty, though, since the duty which emerges is a duty of reasonable care, the question of misfeasance or non-feasance may have a bearing on the question whether the duty has been broken. It is to my mind clear, also, that no distinction is suggested in, or can properly be inferred from, the judgment as between a hazard accidentally arising on the defendant's land which, on the one hand, gives rise to a risk of damage to a neighbour's property by the encroachment of fire and, on the other hand, gives rise to such a risk by the encroachment of the soil itself, falling from the bank onto the neighbour's land. There is no valid distinction, to my mind, between an encroachment which consists, on the one hand, of the spread of fire from a tree on fire on the land, and, on the other hand, of a slip of soil or rock resulting from the instability of the land itself, in each case, the danger of encroachment, and the actual encroachment, being brought about by the forces of nature. . . .

I return to the judgment in *Goldman* v. *Hargrave*. The law of England as it used to be is set out in the following passage:

" . . . it is only in comparatively recent times that the law has recognised an occupier's duty as one of a more positive character than merely to abstain from creating, or adding to, a source of danger or annoyance. It was for long satisfied with the conception of separate or autonomous proprietors, each of which was entitled to exploit his territory in a 'natural' manner and none of whom was obliged to restrain or direct the operations of nature in the interest of avoiding harm to his neighbours."

The judgment of the Board then goes on to review the development of the law which, as the Board held, had changed the law so that there now exists "a general duty on occupiers in relation to hazards occurring on their land, whether natural or man-made."

That change in the law, in its essence and in its timing, corresponds with, and may be viewed as being a part of, the change in the law of tort which achieved its decisive victory in *Donoghue* v. *Stevenson*, though it was not until eight years later, in the House of Lords decision in *Sedleigh-Denfield* v. *O'Callaghan* ([1940] A.C. 880), that the change as affecting the area with which we are concerned was expressed or recognised in a decision binding on all English courts, and, even then, the full, logical effect of the decision in altering what had hitherto been thought to be the law was not immediately recognised. But *Goldman* v. *Hargrave* has now demonstrated what that effect was in English law. . . .

In the *Sedleigh-Denfield* case, a local authority had trespassed on the defendant's land, without the defendant's knowledge or consent, and had placed a culvert in a ditch on that land. By the improper placing of a grid at the mouth of the culvert, instead of further back, those who did the work created a danger of flooding which would be likely to spread to the plaintiff's land. The defendant, through his servants, came to know what had been done. He should have realised that it created a real risk of flooding of his neighbour's land. He did nothing. A heavy rainstorm caused the ditch to flood, because of the trespasser's work. The plaintiff's land was damaged. The House of Lords held that the defendant was liable. The defendant himself had not done anything which was an "unnatural user" of his land. He had not himself brought anything "unnatural" onto his land. But when he knew or ought to have known of the risk of flood water from his land encroaching on his neighbour's land he had done nothing towards preventing it. Prevention could have been achieved without any great trouble or expense.

The approval by the House of Lords in the *Sedleigh-Denfield* case of Scrutton L.J.'s judgment in the *Job Edwards* case ([1924] 1 K.B. 341) meant . . . that it was thereafter the law of England that a duty existed under which the occupier of land might be liable to his neighbour for damage to his neighbour's property as a result of a nuisance spreading from his land to his neighbour's land, even though the existence and the operative effect of the nuisance were not caused by any "non-natural" use by the defendant of his own land. But the liability was not a strict liability such as that which was postulated by the House of Lords in *Rylands* v. *Fletcher* [below, p. 391] as arising where damage was caused to another by an "unnatural" user of land. The obligation postulated in the *Sedleigh-Denfield* case, in conformity with the development of the law in *Donoghue* v. *Stevenson*, was an obligation to use reasonable care. A defendant was not to be liable as a result of a risk of which he neither was aware nor ought, as a reasonable careful landowner, to have been aware.

The decision in the *Sedleigh-Denfield* case was in a case where, on the facts, something which might be described as "not natural" had been introduced onto the defendant's land in the building of the culvert, but not by the defendant. It had been done by a trespasser without the defendant's knowledge or consent. It was not a case in which the potential damage to the neighbour's land had been brought about by natural causes. Therefore it may be said that the *Sedleigh-Denfield* case did not decide, so as to bind lower courts in England, that an owner or occupier of land was under a duty to exercise reasonable care where natural causes, as distinct from the act of a trespasser, brought about the dangerous condition of the land, of which he, the owner or occupier, knew or which he should have realised. If I had taken the view that the *Sedleigh-Denfield* case does not bear on the question raised by the present appeal (and therefore also ought not to have influenced the decision in *Goldman* v. *Hargrave*), I should have reached a different conclusion on this appeal. I do not, however, accept the suggested distinction.

My first comment is that the whole tenor of the speeches in the *Sedleigh-Denfield* case suggests that the view of their Lordships, if not their decision, was that the same duty arose. A passage in Lord Wright's speech gives, I believe, a fair reflection of the attitude of their Lordships:

"The liability for a nuisance is not, at least in modern law, a strict or absolute liability. If the defendant, by himself or those for whom he is responsible, has created what constitutes a nuisance, and if it causes damage, the difficulty now being considered does not arise; but he may have taken over the nuisance, ready made as it were, when he acquired the property, or the nuisance may be due to a latent defect or to the act of a trespasser or stranger. Then he is not liable unless he continued or adopted the nuisance, or, more accurately, did not without undue delay remedy it when he became aware of it, or with ordinary and reasonable care should have become aware of it. This rule seems to be in accord with good sense and convenience."

I am confident that Lord Wright's words "latent defect" were intended to include a defect in the land itself. Lord Wright was making the same point, the lack of any valid distinction, in this context, between a trespasser's act and an act of nature, as he had made when he was Wright J., in *Noble* v. *Harrison* ([1926] 2 K.B. 322, 341). There, after referring to *Barker* v. *Herbert* ([1911] 2 K.B. 633), he said:

"The nuisance in that case was caused by the act of a trespasser, but I think the same principle applies to a nuisance (in this case the latent crack in the branch with the resulting risk that some day it would fall) caused by a secret and unobservable operation of nature."

So long as the defect remains "latent" there is no duty on the occupier, whether the defect has been caused by a trespasser or by nature. Equally, once the latent becomes patent, a duty will arise, whether the causative agent of the defect is man or nature. But the mere fact that there is a duty does not necessarily mean that inaction constitutes a breach of the duty.

My second comment on the suggested distinction is that it involves a fallacy. I cite a passage from the judgment in *Goldman* v. *Hargrave* which, I respectfully suggest, makes this clear beyond dispute:

"It was suggested as a logical basis for the distinction that in the case of a hazard originating in an act of man, an occupier who fails to deal with it can be said to be using his land in a manner detrimental to his neighbourhood and so to be within the classical field of responsibility in nuisance, whereas this cannot be said when the hazard originates without human action so long at least as the occupier merely abstains. The fallacy of this argument is that, as already explained, the basis of the occupier's liability lies not in the use of his land: in the absence of "adoption" there is no such use; but in the neglect of action in the face of something which may damage his neighbour. To this, the suggested distinction is irrelevant." . . .

Is there, then, anything in the ratio decidendi of *Rylands* v. *Fletcher*, or in any subsequent authority binding on this court, which requires or entitles us to disregard the decision in the *Sedleigh-Denfield* case or to prevent us from accepting the logical extension of it (so far as it is an extension) which was regarded as proper in *Goldman* v. *Hargrave*.

The application of the decision and of the dicta in *Rylands* v. *Fletcher* has given rise to continual trouble thereafter in the law of England. But, as I see it, the true ratio decidendi of *Rylands* v. *Fletcher* is not relevant to the issue with which we are concerned. In *Rylands* v. *Fletcher* the defendant was held to be liable because he had erected or brought on his land something of an unusual nature, which was essentially dangerous in itself. That, said Wright J. in *Noble* v. *Harrison*, "expresses the true principle of *Rylands* v. *Fletcher*. The decision was that, on such facts, there was strict liability. It would be no answer for the defendant to say "I did not know of the danger and had no reason to know of it." It was no part of the decision, as distinct from dicta, in *Rylands* v. *Fletcher* that one who has not himself brought something of an unusual nature on his land, or used his land in an unnatural way (whatever that may mean or include), is in no circumstances liable if something from his land encroaches on his neighbour's land. That was why Viscount Maugham in the *Sedleigh-Denfield* case said:

"My Lords, I will begin by saying that, in my opinion, the principle laid down in *Rylands* v. *Fletcher* does not apply to the present case. That principle applies only to cases where there has been some special use of property bringing with it increased danger to others, and does not extend to damages caused to adjoining owners as the result of the ordinary use of the land: see *Rickards* v. *Lothian*. ([below p. 395])."

If *Rylands* v. *Fletcher* was thus irrelevant in the *Sedleigh-Denfield* case, it is not relevant in this case. . . .

Is there, then, any subsequent authority binding on this court which prevents it, by the doctrine of precedent, from holding that the law of England, as laid down in the *Sedleigh-Denfield* case, is extended by what the Judicial Committee of the Privy Council regarded as inevitable logic? . . .

In *Davey* v. *Harrow Corpn.* ([1958] 1 Q.B. 60) it was held that the encroachment onto a neighbour's land of roots or branches of trees, causing damage, gives the neighbour an action in nuisance; and that no distinction is to be drawn between trees which may have been self-sown and trees which were deliberately planted on the land. Contrast the decision with *Rouse* v. *Gravelworks Ltd.* ([1940] 1 K.B. 489). There the defendants had dug out gravel from their land, leaving a large hole adjacent to the boundary with the plaintiff's land. It was held by this court, a two judge court consisting of Slesser and Goddard L.JJ., that the plaintiff's claim failed because the damage to his land was caused by "natural agencies." It would seem that the decision would have been different if the water which filled the hole left by the excavation of the gravel had been brought in by pumping or perhaps even by percolation emanating from outside the defendants' land and induced by the excavation to flow into that land. If so, I should have thought that few people would regard this as a satisfactory state of the law. It may, perhaps, be arguable that, following *Rylands* v. *Fletcher*, there is some special doctrine relating to the rights of landowners to dig out coal or gravel from their land as being a "natural user." If there is no such valid distinction, then, in my judgment, the decision in *Rouse* v. *Gravelworks Ltd.* cannot stand with the decision in *Davey* v. *Harrow Corpn*. In that event I have no hesitation in preferring the later decision as stating the law as it now is, subject to the proviso that the duty arising from a nuisance which is not brought about by human agency does not arise unless and until the defendant has, or ought to have had, knowledge of the existence of the defect and the danger thereby created. . . .

Suppose that we are not bound by *Rylands* v. *Fletcher* or any other authority to hold in favour of the defendants where the nuisance arises solely from natural forces; but suppose also that we are not bound by the decision in *Sedleigh-Denfield* or other binding authority to hold that there is a duty on the defendants in a case such as the present. Ought we as a matter of policy to develop the law by holding that there is a duty in a case such as the present?

If, as a result of the working of the forces of nature, there is, poised above my land, or above my house, a boulder or a rotten tree, which is liable to fall at any moment of the day or night, perhaps destroying my house, and perhaps killing or injuring me or members of my family, am I without remedy? (Of course the standard of care required may be much higher where there is risk to life or limb as contrasted with mere risk to property, but can it be said that the duty exists in the one case and not in the other?) Must I, in such a case, if my protests to my neighbour go unheeded, sit and wait and hope that the worst will not befall? . . .

. . . I believe that few people would regard it as anything other than a grievous blot on the law if the law recognises the existence of no duty on the part of the owner or occupier. But take another example, at the other end of the scale, where it might be thought that there is, potentially, an equally serious injustice the other way. If a stream flows through A's land, A being a small farmer, and there is a known danger that in times of heavy rainfall, because of the configuration of A's land and the nature of the stream's course and flow, there may be an overflow, which will pass beyond A's land and damage the property of A's neighbours: perhaps much wealthier neighbours. It may require expensive works, far beyond A's means, to prevent or even diminish the risk of such flooding. Is A to be liable for all the loss that occurs when the flood comes, if he has not done the impossible and carried out these works at his own expense?

In my judgment, there is, in the scope of the duty as explained in *Goldman* v. *Hargrave* a removal, or at least a powerful amelioration, of the injustice which might otherwise be caused in such a case by the recognition of the duty of care. Because of that limitation on the scope of the duty. I would say that, as a matter of policy, the law ought to recognise such a duty of care.

This leads on to the question of the scope of the duty. This is discussed, and the nature and extent of the duty is explained, in the judgment in *Goldman* v. *Hargrave*. The duty is a duty to do that which is reasonable in all the circumstances, and no more than what, if anything, is reasonable, to prevent or minimise the known risk of damage or injury to one's neighbour or to his property. The considerations with which the law is familiar are all to be taken into account in deciding whether there has been a breach of duty, and, if so, what that breach is, and whether it is causative of the damage in respect of which the claim is made. Thus, there will fall to be considered the extent of the risk. What, so far as reasonably can be foreseen, are the chances that anything untoward will happen or that any damage will be caused? What is to be foreseen as to the possible extent of the damage if the risk becomes a reality? It is practicable to prevent, or to minimise, the happening of any damage? If it is practicable, how simple or how difficult are the measures which could be taken, how much and how lengthy work do they involve, and what is the probable cost of such works? Was there sufficient time for preventive action to have been taken, by persons acting reasonably in relation to the known risk, between the time when it became known to, or should have been realised by, the defendant, and the time when the damage occurred? Factors such as these, so far as they apply in a particular case, fall to be weighed in deciding whether the defendant's duty of care requires, or required, him to do anything, and, if so, what.

There is a passage in this part of the judgment in *Goldman* v. *Hargrave* defining the scope of the duty, which, on the one hand, is said to be likely, if accepted, to give rise to insuperable difficulties in its practical working, and, on the other hand, is said to provide a sensible and just limitation on the scope of the duty, avoiding the danger of substantial injustice being caused, even in exceptional cases, by the existence of the duty. The passage in question reads as follows:

" . . . the owner of a small property where a hazard arises which threatens a neighbour with substantial interests should not have to do so much as one with larger interests of his own at stake and greater resources to protect them: if the small owner does what he can and promptly calls on his neighbour to provide additional resources, he may be held to have done his duty: he should not be liable unless it is clearly proved that he could, and reasonably in his individual circumstances should, have done more." . . .

. . . The defendant's duty is to do that which is reasonable for him to do. The criteria of reasonableness include, in respect of a duty of this nature, the factor of what the particular man, not the average man, can be expected to do, having regard, amongst other things, where a serious expenditure of money is required to eliminate or reduce the danger, to his means. Just as, where physical effort is required to avert an immediate danger, the defendant's age and physical condition may be relevant in deciding what is reasonable, so also logic and good sense require that, where the expenditure of money is required, the defendant's capacity to find the money is relevant. But this can only be in the way of a broad, and not a detailed, assessment; and, in arriving at a judgment on reasonableness, a similar broad assessment may be relevant in some cases as to the neighbour's capacity to protect himself from damage, whether by way of some form of barrier on his own land or by way of providing funds for expenditure on agreed works on the land of the defendant.

Take, by way of example, the hypothetical instance which I gave earlier: the landowner through whose land a stream flows. In rainy weather, it is known, the stream may flood and the flood may spread to the land of neighbours. If the risk is one which can readily be overcome or lessened, for example by reasonable steps on the part of the landowner to keep the stream free from blockage by flotsam or silt carried down, he will be in breach of duty if he does nothing or does too little. But if the only remedy is substantial and expensive works, then it might well be that the landowner would have discharged his duty by saying to his neighbours, who also know of the risk and who have asked him to do something about it, "You have my permission to come onto my land and to do agreed works at your expense," or, it may be, "on the basis of a fair sharing of expense." In deciding whether the landowner had discharged his duty of care, if the question were thereafter to come before the courts, I do not think that, except perhaps in a most unusual case, there would be any question of discovery as to the means of the plaintiff or the defendant, or evidence as to their respective resources. The question of reasonableness of what had been done or offered would fall to be decided on a broad basis, in which, on some occasions, there might be included an element of obvious discrepancy of financial resources. It may be that in some cases the introduction of this factor may give rise to difficulties to litigants and to their advisers and to the courts. But I believe that the difficulties are likely to turn out to be more theoretical than practical. I have not heard or seen anything to suggest that the principle laid down in *British Railways Board* v. *Herrington* [1972] A.C. 877 has given rise to difficulties in trespasser cases. If and when problems do arise, they will have to be solved. I do not think that the existence of such potential difficulties justifies a refusal to accept as a part of the law of England the duty as laid down in *Goldman* v. *Hargrave*, including the whole of the exposition as to the scope of the duty. As I have said, no difficulty now arises in this present appeal as regards the application of the *Goldman* v. *Hargrave* scope of the duty, once it is held that the duty exists.

I would dismiss the appeal.

Shaw L.J.: . . . Why should a nuisance which has its origin in some natural phenomenon and which manifests itself without any human intervention cast a liability on a person who has no other connection with that nuisance than the title to the land on which it chances to originate? This view is fortified inasmuch as a title to land cannot be discarded or abandoned. Why should the owner of land in such a case be bound to protect his neighbour's property and person rather than that the neighbour should protect his interests against the potential danger?

The old common law duty of a landowner on whose land there arose a nuisance from natural causes only, without any human intervention, was to afford a neighbour whose property or person was threatened by the nuisance a reasonable opportunity to abate that nuisance. This entailed (1) that the landowner should on becoming aware of the nuisance give reasonable warning of it to his neighbour, (2) that the landowner should give to the neighbour such access to the land as was reasonably requisite to enable him to abate the nuisance.

The principle was relatively clear in its application and served in broad terms to do justice between the parties concerned. The development of "the good neighbour" concept has however blurred the definition of rights and liabilities between persons who stand in such a relationship as may involve them in reciprocal rights and liabilities.

It has culminated in the judgment of the Privy Council in *Goldman* v. *Hargrave*.

. . . with diffident reluctance I would dismiss the appeal.

Cumming-Bruce L.J. agreed with Megaw L.J.

Questions

1. Consider the facts of *Goldman* v. *Hargrave* as given by Megaw L.J. (or, better still, read the decision in [1967] 1 A.C. 645). Would the plaintiff have suffered the same damage if the defendant had been away on holiday, and would the defendant have been liable (a) if no one was left on his premises, (b) there was only a housekeeper, (c) there was no one but a house-guest from town?

2. Does *Leakey* apply in cases of discomfort or only in cases of damage or threatened damage?

3. Does *Leakey* involve that if pheasants spontaneously nest on my land in great numbers, I am to be at the expense of a game-keeper to protect my neighbour's crops?

4. Does the variable duty laid down mean that the plaintiff must take the defendant as he finds him? Is this especially appropriate in cases of neighbours in the true sense? See *Vaughan* v. *Menlove* (1837) 3 Bing.N.C. 468; 132 E.R. 490.

5. Consider the relationship of the ratio of this case and the ratio of *Langbrook Properties* (above p. 376), namely that you may drain your own land even if you know that that will cause actual property damage to your neighbour.

Note:

In *Morgan* v. *Khyatt* [1964] 1 W.L.R. 475, Lord Evershed, speaking for the Privy Council, said " . . . it has . . . long been established as a general proposition that an owner of land may make any natural use of it; but also (and by way of qualification of the general rule) that if an owner of land grows or permits the growth on his land in the natural way of trees whose roots penetrate into adjacent property and thereby cause and continue to cause damage to buildings upon that property, he is liable for the tort of nuisance to the owner of that adjacent property.' In that case, Viscount Simonds approved, *arguendo*, *Davey* v. *Harrow Corp.* [1958] 1 Q.B. 60, where Lord Goddard had said " . . . if trees encroach, whether by branches or roots, and cause damage, an action for nuisance will lie . . . " (at 73).

Now in *Leakey* Megaw L.J. also approved of *Davey* but added a proviso requiring in the defendant knowledge, actual or constructive, of both the encroachment and the damage likely to be caused. The Court of Appeal has now endorsed that qualification and has given judgment for the defendant in a case where the defendant's tree unquestionably caused the plaintiff's house to settle when its roots reached a quite unexpected pocket of clay under the house and dehydrated it in unusual weather conditions (*Solloway* v. *Hants. C.C.* (1981) 79 L.G.R. 449). The questions to be asked are (1) Was there a foreseeable risk that the encroachment of these tree roots would cause damage to the plaintiff's house, and (2) were there any reasonable precautions which the defendants could have taken to prevent or minimise that risk? Dunn L.J. said this: "Although it was not necessary for the decision the proviso suggested by Megaw L.J. puts nuisance by encroachment of tree roots and branches into the same category as any other nuisance not brought about by human agency. It is consistent with *Sedleigh-Denfield* v. *O'Callaghan* [1940] A.C. 880, and confines the strict liability for nuisance to cases where there has been some non-natural user of the land as stated in *Rylands* v. *Fletcher* (1868) L.R. 3 H.L. 330."

This significant change in the basis of liability also means that the judge cannot simply ask "On whose land was this tree?" (not that that is always an easy question, especially where the tree is on the highway), but must inquire into the defendant's geological knowledge, arboreal skills and financial resources. For a case from Hampstead Garden Suburb where the judge had to balance the aesthetic drawbacks of cutting down a century-old oak, with the risk of consequent "heave," the practicalities of encircling the roots, and the efficacy of lopping its limbs, and ignored the fact that the defendants (reasonably) believed that they were not responsible for the tree, see *Russell* v. *Barnet L.B.C.* 271 E.G. 699 and 779 (1984).

It is worth asking why, when dry-rot is so sadly common a natural phenomenon in England, there was no case about its spread until *Bradburn* v. *Lindsay* [1983] 2 All E.R. 408, where the defendant was held liable for not taking steps to prevent its spreading next door when she knew of its existence on her property. She was also held bound to weatherproof the party wall which became exposed to the elements when her house was demolished with her consent by the local authority. As the West German Basic Law pithily observes (and enacts) "Property obliges" (art. 14(2)).

It will be seen that the effect of *Donoghue* v. *Stevenson* has been to reduce the pockets of strict liability and of non-liability which used to be a significant feature of the tort of nuisance. Admittedly one can see the appeal of applying *Donoghue* v. *Stevenson* as between neighbours, but are neighbourly feelings going to be advanced if George, whose kids have broken Harry's window with a cricket ball while playing in their own back garden, can refuse to pay on the ground that it wasn't any fault of his?

Section 4.—Authorised Activities

MANCHESTER CORPORATION v. FARNWORTH

House of Lords [1930] A.C. 171; 99 L.J.K.B. 83; 142 L.T. 145; 94 J.P. 62; 46 T.L.R. 85; 73 S.J. 818; 27 L.G.R. 709; [1929] All E.R. Rep. 90

The plaintiff was a farmer at Barton-on-Irwell whose fields were destroyed by the poisonous fumes emitted from the chimneys of an electric power station erected and operated by the defendant corporation. The defendants pleaded that they were empowered to set up the station by section 32, Manchester Corporation Act 1914.

Talbot J. gave judgment for the defendant. The Court of Appeal (Lawrence L.J. dissenting) granted an injunction and damages [1929] 1 K.B. 533. On appeal by the Corporation, the House of Lords dismissed the appeal, and varied the order by declaring that the plaintiff should have damages until the injunction ceased to be suspended or was dissolved, that the injunction be suspended for one year, with liberty to the defendants to apply for dissolution of the injunction on establishing that all reasonable modes of preventing mischief to the plaintiff had been exhausted and on their submitting to adopt the most effective modes of avoiding such mischief and to replace them by other reasonable but more effective modes of prevention subsequently discovered.

Viscount Dunedin: . . . The serious character of the nuisance naturally makes one reflect on the magnitude of the nuisance which would be caused by stations far bigger than this one, and that such stations are likely in the near future to be established is certain. That brings me to say a word or two on what I conceive to be the well settled law on such matters. The cases are numerous. . . . I believe their whole effect may be expressed in a very few sentences. When Parliament has authorised a certain thing to be made or done in a certain place, there can be no action for nuisance caused by the making or doing of that thing if the nuisance is the inevitable result of the making or doing so authorised. The onus of proving that the result is inevitable is on those who wish to escape liability for nuisance, but the criterion of inevitability is not what is theoretically possible but what is possible according to the state of scientific knowledge at the time, having also in view a certain common sense appreciation, which cannot be rigidly defined, of practical feasibility in view of situation and of expense.

Now it is true that in this case we can hold so far that by their callous indifference in planning the construction of the station to all but its own efficiency, the defendants have not discharged the onus incumbent on them. . . .

Viscount Sumner: . . . My Lords, the conclusion to which a close examination of the evidence has forced me is that the defendants have not shown that a generating station, such as the legislature contemplated in 1914, whatever that may have been, could not have been erected then and cannot be used now without causing a nuisance, but that they have failed to show that they have used all reasonable diligence and taken all reasonable steps and precautions to prevent their operations from being a nuisance to their neighbours, and this for two reasons. (1) At the time of the erection their responsible officers never directed their minds to the prevention of the nuisances, which it was quite obvious might occur, but (2) they were under the impression that, for all practical purposes, so long as their plant was efficiently and successfully conducted, the neighbours must endure their consequent injuries with such stoicism as they could muster. The proof of this is writ large in their answers generally. . . .

Note:
The common law of nuisance is a limitation on activities on one's own land. If one cannot keep 200 horses on one's own land without causing intolerable inconvenience to the neighbours, then the common law says one cannot keep them there at all. But if the legislature has said that something is to be done, the common law cannot say that it is not to be done. What the common law can say is that the thing must be done so as to cause the least damage consistent with its being done. Accordingly, where the defendant in a nuisance case has acted under statutory authority, the common law can demand only that he have acted reasonably so as to minimise the harm; proof of reasonable care will exonerate him, but the proof of that is on him.
Acts of Parliament frequently contain "nuisance clauses," which originated in the Railway Acts of the early nineteenth century. The intention behind these clauses was presumably that the operation should not be enjoined, but that there should be liability for any damage caused by nuisance. That, however, was not their effect. Today, when so many of the bodies providing utilities are either nationalised industries or local authorities, the tendency seems to be to say that there is no liability save for negligence, even when there is a nuisance clause (*Dunne* v. *North-Western Gas Board* [1964] 2 Q.B. 806). The rule that where a nuisance is established, the burden of disproof of negligence is on the defendant may well remain, despite a contrary dictum of Sachs L.J. in *Radstock Co-operative & Industrial Society* v. *Norton-Radstock U.D.C.* [1968] Ch. 605, 634.
Allen v. *Gulf Oil Refining Ltd.* [1981] A.C. 1001 carries the law no further forward.

Section 5.—Established Activities

MILLER v. JACKSON

Court of Appeal [1977] Q.B. 966; [1977] 3 W.L.R. 20; 121 S.J. 287; [1977] 3 All E.R. 338

In 1972 houses were built in an empty field next to a village cricket ground which had been in use for nearly 70 years. That summer the plaintiffs bought one of the houses; its garden wall was only 102 feet from the wicket, so cricket balls kept sailing over it, and they complained bitterly. The cricket club erected the highest possible wire fence atop the wall and instructed the batsmen to try to keep the ball low, but even so five more balls came over in 1975. The plaintiffs refused offers to instal unbreakable glass and to cover the whole garden with a safety net, and sought an injunction to prevent the defendants playing cricket in such a manner that cricket balls came into the plaintiffs' garden. At the trial it appeared that cricket could not be played there at all without the occasional ball going over. The trial judge granted the injunction. The defendants appealed. Although it was held, Lord Denning dissenting, that the defendants were guilty of nuisance notwithstanding that the plaintiffs were aware of the defendants' well-established activity at the time they bought their house, the defendants' appeal was allowed, Geoffrey Lane L.J. dissenting.

Lord Denning M.R.: . . . It has been often said in nuisance cases that the rule is *sic utere tuo ut alienum non laedas.* But that is a most misleading maxim. Lord Wright put it in its proper place in *Sedleigh-Denfield* v. *O'Callaghan* [1940] A.C. 880, 903:

"[It] is not only lacking in definiteness but is also inaccurate. An occupier may make in many ways a use of his land which causes damage to the neighbouring land-owners, and yet be free from liability . . . a useful test is perhaps what is reasonable according to the ordinary usages of mankind living in society, or, more correctly, in a particular society."

I would, therefore, adopt this test: is the use by the cricket club of this ground for playing cricket a reasonable use of it? To my mind it is a most reasonable use. Just consider the circumstances. For over 70 years the game of cricket has been played on this ground to the great benefit of the community as a whole, and to the injury of none. No one could suggest that it was a nuisance to the neighbouring owners simply because an enthusiastic batsman occasionally hit a ball out of the ground for six to the approval of the admiring onlookers. Then I would ask: does it suddenly become a nuisance because one of the neighbours chooses to build a house on the very edge of the ground, in such a position that it may well be struck by the ball on the rare occasion when there is a hit for six? To my mind the answer is plainly No. The building of the house does not convert the playing of cricket into a nuisance when it was not so before. If and in so far as any damage is caused to the house or anyone in it, it is because of the position in which it was built. Suppose that the house had not been built by a developer, but by a private owner. He would be in much the same position as the farmer who previously put his cows in the field. He could not complain if a batsman hit a six out of the ground and, by a million to one chance, it struck a cow or even the farmer himself. He would be in no better position that a spectator at Lord's or the Oval or at a motor rally. At any rate, even if he could claim damages for the loss of the cow or the injury, he could not get an injunction to stop the cricket. If the private owner could not get an injunction, neither should a developer or a purchaser from him.

It was said, however, that the case of the physician's consulting-room was to the contrary (*Sturges* v. *Bridgman* (1879) 11 Ch.D. 852). But that turned on the old law about easements and prescriptions, and so forth. It was in the days when rights of property were in the ascendant and not subject to any limitations except those provided by the law of easements. But nowadays it is a matter of balancing the conflicting interests of the two neighbours. That was made clear by Lord Wright in *Sedleigh-Denfield* v. *O'Callaghan*, when he said:

"A balance has to be maintained between the right of the occupier to do what he likes with his own and the right of his neighbour not to be interfered with."

In this case it is our task to balance the right of the cricket club to continue playing cricket on their cricket ground, as against the right of the householder not to be interfered with. On taking the balance, I would give priority to the right of the cricket club to continue playing cricket on the ground, as they have done for the last 70 years. It takes precedence over the right of the newcomer to sit in his garden undisturbed. After all he bought the house fours years ago in mid-summer when the cricket season was at its height. He might have guessed that there was a risk that a hit for six might possibly land on his property. If he finds that he does not like it, he ought, when cricket is played, to sit in the other side of the house or in the front garden, or go out; or take advantage of the offers the club have made to him of fitting unbreakable glass, and so forth. Or, if he does not like that, he ought to sell his house and move elsewhere. I expect there are many who would gladly buy it in order to be near the cricket field and open space. At any rate he ought not to be allowed to stop cricket being played on this ground.

This case is new. It should be approached on principles applicable to modern conditions. There is a contest here between the interest of the public at large and the interest of a private individual. The *public* interest lies in protecting the environment by preserving our playing fields in the face of mounting development, and by enabling our youth to enjoy all the benefits of outdoor games, such as cricket and football. The *private* interest lies in securing the privacy of his home and garden without intrusion or interference by anyone. In deciding between these two conflicting interests, it must be remembered that it is not a question of damages. If by a million-to-one chance a cricket ball does go out of the ground and cause damage, the cricket club will pay. There is no difficulty on that score. No, it is a question of an injunction. And in our law you will find it repeatedly affirmed that an injunction is a discretionary remedy. In a new situation like this, we have to think afresh as to how discretion should be exercised. On the other hand, Mrs. Miller is a very sensitive lady who has worked herself up into such a state that she exclaimed to the judge:

"I just want to be allowed to live in peace. Have we got to wait until someone is killed before anything can be done?"

If she feels like that about it, it is quite plain that, for peace in the future, one or other has to move. Either the cricket club have to move, but goodness knows where. I do not suppose for a moment there is any field in Lintz to which they could move. Or Mrs. Miller must move elsewhere. As between their conflicting interests, I am of opinion that the public interest should prevail over the private interest. The cricket club should not be driven out. In my opinion the right exercise of discretion is to refuse an injunction; and, of course, to refuse damages in lieu of an injunction. Likewise as to the claim for past damages. The club were entitled to use this ground for cricket in the accustomed way. It was not a nuisance, nor was it negligence of them so to run it. Nor was the batsman negligent when he hit the ball for six. All were doing simply what they were entitled to do. So if the club had put it to the test, I would have dismissed the claim for damages also. But as the club very fairly say that they are willing to pay for any damage, I am content that there should be an award of £400 to cover any past or future damage.

I would allow the appeal, accordingly.

Geoffrey Lane L.J.: . . . Was there here a use by the defendants of their land involving an unreasonable interference with the plaintiffs' enjoyment of *their* land? There is here in effect no dispute that there has been and is likely to be in the future an interference with the plaintiffs' enjoyment of no. 20 Brackenridge. The only question is whether it is unreasonable. It is a truism to say that this is a matter of degree. What that means is this. A balance has to be maintained between on the one hand the rights of the individual to enjoy his house and garden without the threat of damage and on the other hand the rights of the public in general or a neighbour to engage in lawful pastimes. Difficult questions may sometimes arise when the defendants' activities are offensive to the sense, for example by way of noise. Where, as here, the damage or potential damage is physical the answer is more simple. There is, subject to what appears hereafter, no excuse I can see which exonerates the defendants from liability in nuisance for what they have done or from what they threaten to do. It is true no one has yet been physically injured. That is probably due to a great extent to the fact that the householders in Brackenridge desert their gardens whilst cricket is in progress. The danger of injury is obvious and is not slight enough to be disregarded. There is here a real risk of serious injury.

There is, however, one obviously strong point in the defendants' favour. They or their predecessors have been playing cricket on this ground (and no doubt hitting sixes out of it) for 70 years or so. Can someone by building a house on the edge of the field in circumstances where it must have been obvious that balls might be hit over the fence, effectively stop cricket being played? Precedent apart, justice would seem to demand that the plaintiffs should be left to make the most of the site they have elected to occupy with all its obvious advantages and all its equally obvious disadvantages. It is pleasant to have an open space over which to look from your bedroom and sitting room windows, so far as it is possible to see over the concrete wall. Why should you complain of the obvious disadvantages which arise from the particular purpose to which the open space is being put? Put briefly, can the defendants take advantage of the fact that the plaintiffs have put themselves in such a position by coming to occupy a house on the edge of a small cricket field, with the result that what was not a nuisance in the past now becomes a nuisance? If the matter were *res integra*, I confess I should be inclined to find for the defendants. It does not seem just that a long-established activity, in itself innocuous, should be brought to an end because someone chooses to build a house nearby and so turn an innocent pastime into actionable nuisance. Unfortunately, however, the question is not open. In *Sturges* v. *Bridgman* (1879) 11 Ch.D. 852 this very problem arose. The defendant had carried on a confectionery shop with a noisy pestle and mortar for more than 20 years. Although it was noisy, it was far enough away from neighbour-ing premises not to cause trouble to anyone, until the plaintiff, who was a phys-ician, built a consulting-room on his own land but immediately adjoining the confectionery shop. The noise and vibrations seriously interfered with the consult-ing-room and became a nuisance to the physician. The defendant contended that he had acquired the right either at common law or under the Prescription Act 1832 by uninterrupted use for more than 20 years to impose the inconvenience. It was held by the Court of Appeal, affirming the judgment of Jessel M.R. that use such as this which was, prior to the construction of the consulting-room, neither preventible or actionable, could not found a prescriptive right. That decision involved the assump-tion, which so far as one can discover has never been questioned, that it is no answer to a claim in nuisance for the defendant to show that the plaintiff brought the trouble on his own head by building or coming to live in a house so close to the defendant's premises that he would inevitably be affected by the defendant's activi-ties, where no one had been affected previously. See also *Bliss* v. *Hall* (1848) 4 Bing.N.C. 183, 132 E.R. 758. It may be that this rule works injustice, it may be that one would decide the matter differently in the absence of authority. But we are bound by the decision in *Sturges* v. *Bridgman* and it is not for this court as I see it to alter a rule which has stood for so long. . . .

Cumming-Bruce L.J. agreed with Geoffrey Lane L.J. that the defendants were liable in negligence and nuisance, and that *Sturges* v. *Bridgman* was binding. He agreed, however, with Lord Denning M.R. that no injunction should be granted.

Note:
    Here the plaintiff was seeking to enjoin a group activity in the interests of private repose (and safety). So it was also in *Kennaway* v. *Thompson* [1981] Q.B. 88 where the plaintiff had built a nice house by a man-made lake on which the defendant club was just beginning to organise water-skiing and speed-boat racing. By the time of the lawsuit noise organised by the defendants was making life intolerable for the plaintiff. The trial judge refused an injunction, but granted damages of £15,000 in lieu. The Court of Appeal reversed on the basis of a late Victorian decision which held that a mid-Victorian Act permitting the grant of damages in lieu of an injunction had not altered the early Victorian practice of granting an injunction to stop a nuisance in all but very exceptional cases (*Shelfer* v. *City of London Electric Lighting Co.* [1895] 1 Ch. 287). The injunction granted, however, was very qualified in its terms, on the basis that only the excessive noise could be enjoined—a principle which also applies in claims for damages (*Tate & Lyle Indus.* v. *G.L.C.* [1983] 1 All E.R. 1159; *Andreae* v. *Selfridge* [1937] 3 All E.R. 255). However, in *Tetley* v. *Chitty* [1986] 1 All E.R. 663, where residents of Rochester were complaining of the noise from a go-kart track on land across the Medway which the local authority had leased to a go-kart club, go-kart racing was totally enjoined.
    The local authority, having leased the land, was no longer in occupation of it, but was held liable because excessive noise was a very predictable consequence of the use for which the land had been let (contrast *Smith* v. *Scott* above p. 376). A landlord who creates a condition on the premises which renders a nuisance inevitable remains liable, even after he has disposed of his interest; and the person who acquires his interest may become liable for the nuisance although he did not create it. This emerges (rather obscurely) from *Sampson* v. *Hodson-Pressinger* [1981] 3 All E.R. 710. Here X sold the plaintiff a 99-year lease of a flat, and then

constructed a terrace/roof-garden above it for use with the upstairs flat, then vacant, in which he sold a 99-year lease to the first defendant. X then sold the reversion of the whole building to the second defendant. The terrace was badly tiled and the sound of persons walking and talking on it quite normally was intolerable in the plaintiff's sitting room. The first defendant was in principle liable though she was doing absolutely nothing unreasonable, and the second defendant was held liable because he knew of the trouble when he bought the freehold and because by accepting rent he was authorising the nuisance.

Chapter 11

RYLANDS v. FLETCHER

Section 1.—The Rule

RYLANDS v. FLETCHER

House of Lords (1868) L.R. 3 H.L. 330; 37 L.J.Ex. 161; 19 L.T. 220; 33 J.P. 70

Near Ainsworth in Lancashire the defendants had a mill whose water supply they wanted to improve. They obtained permission from Lord Wilton to construct a reservoir on his land and retained reputable engineers to do it. Unknown to the defendants, the plaintiff, who had a mineral lease from Lord Wilton, had carried his workings to a point not far distant, though separated by the land of third parties. In the course of construction the engineers came across some disused mine shafts and did not seal them properly, with the result that when the completed reservoir was filled, water flowed down those shafts and into the plaintiff's coal-mine, causing damage later agreed at £937.

The arbitrator stated a special case for the Court of Exchequer, which found for the defendants (Bramwell B. dissenting) ((1865) 3 H. & C. 774; 159 E.R. 737). The plaintiff took a writ of error to the Court of Exchequer Chamber, which gave him judgment. The defendants' appeal to the House of Lords was dismissed.

In the House of Lords

Lord Cairns L.C.: . . . The reservoir of the defendants was constructed by them through the agency and inspection of an engineer and contractor. Personally, the defendants appear to have taken no part in the works, or to have been aware of any want of security connected with them. As regards the engineer and the contractor, we must take it from the case that they did not exercise, as far as they were concerned, that reasonable care and caution which they might have exercised, taking notice, as they appear to have taken notice, of the vertical shafts filled up in the manner which I have mentioned. However, my Lords, when the reservoir was constructed, and filled, or partly filled, with water, the weight of the water bearing upon the disused and imperfectly filled-up vertical shafts, broke through those shafts. The water passed down them and into the horizontal workings, and from the horizontal workings under the close of the defendants it passed on into the workings under the close of the plaintiff, and flooded his mine causing considerable damage, for which this action was brought.

The Court of Exchequer . . . was of opinion that the plaintiff had established no cause of action. The Court of Exchequer Chamber, before which an appeal from this judgment was argued, was of a contrary opinion, and the judges there unanimously arrived at the conclusion that there was a cause of action, and that the plaintiff was entitled to damages.

My Lords, the principles on which this case must be determined appear to me to be extremely simple. The defendants, treating them as the owners or occupiers of the close on which the reservoir was constructed, might lawfully have used that close for any purpose for which it might in the ordinary course of the enjoyment of land be used; and if, in what I may term the natural user of that land, there had been any accumulation of water, either on the surface or underground, and if, by the operation of the laws of nature, that accumulation of water had passed off into the close occupied by the plaintiff, the plaintiff could not have complained that that result had taken place. If he had desired to guard himself against it, it would have lain upon him to have done so, by leaving, or by interposing, some barrier between his close and the close of the defendants in order to have prevented that operation of the laws of nature.

As an illustration of that principle, I may refer to a case which was cited in the argument before your Lordships, the case of *Smith* v. *Kenrick* in the Court of Common Pleas ((1849) 7 C.B. 515; 137 E.R. 105).

On the other hand if the defendants, not stopping at the natural use of their close, had desired to use it for any purpose which I may term a non-natural use, for the purpose of introducing into the close that which in its natural condition was not in or upon it, for the purpose of introducing water either above or below ground in quantities and in a manner not the result of any work or operation on or under the land—and if in consequence of their doing so, or in consequence of any imperfection in the mode of their doing so, the water came to escape and pass off into the close of the plaintiff, then it appears to me that that which the defendants were doing they were doing at their own peril; and, if in the course of their doing it, the evil arose to which I have referred, the evil, namely, of the escape of the water and its passing away to the close of the plaintiff and injuring the plaintiff, then for the consequence of that, in my opinion, the defendants would be liable. As the case of *Smith* v. *Kenrick* is an illustration of the first principle to which I have referred, so also the second principle to which I have referred is well illustrated by another case in the same court, the case of *Baird* v. *Williamson* ((1863) 15 C.B.(N.S.) 376; 143 E.R. 831), which was also cited in the argument at the Bar.

My Lords, these simple principles, if they are well founded, as it appears to me they are, really dispose of this case.

The same result is arrived at on the principles referred to by Blackburn J. in his judgment in the Court of Exchequer Chamber, where he states the opinion of that court as to the law in these words: "We think that the rule of law is, that the person who, for his own purposes, brings on his land and collects and keeps there anything likely to do mischief if it escapes, must keep it in at his peril; and if he does not do so, is prima facie answerable for all the damage which is the natural consequence of its escape. He can excuse himself by showing that the escape was owing to the plaintiff's default; or, perhaps, that the escape was the consequence of *vis major*, or the act of God; but as nothing of this sort exists here, it is unnecessary to inquire what excuse would be sufficient. The general rule, as above stated, seems on principle just. The person whose grass or corn is eaten down by the escaping cattle of his neighbour, or whose mine is flooded by the water from his neighbour's reservoir, or whose cellar is invaded by the filth of his neighbour's privy, or whose habitation is made unhealthy by the fumes and noisome vapours of his neighbour's alkali works, is damnified without any fault of his own; and it seems but reasonable and just that the neighbour who has brought something on his own property (which was not naturally there), harmless to others so long as it is confined to his own property, but which he knows will be mischievous if it gets on his neighbour's, should be obliged to make good the damage which ensues if he does not succeed in confining it to his own property. But for his act in bringing it there no mischief could have accrued, and it seems but just that he should at his peril keep it there, so that no mischief may accrue, or answer for the natural and anticipated consequence. And upon authority this we think is established to be the law, whether the things so brought be beasts, or water, or filth, or stenches."

My Lords, in that opinion, I must say I entirely concur. Therefore, I have to move your Lordships that the judgment of the Court of Exchequer Chamber be affirmed, and that the present appeal be dismissed with costs.

Lord Cranworth: My Lords, I concur with my noble and learned friend in thinking that the rule of law was correctly stated by Blackburn J. in delivering the opinion of the Exchequer Chamber. If a person brings, or accumulates, on his land anything which if it should escape, may cause damage to his neighbour, he does so at his peril. If it does escape, and cause damage, he is responsible, however careful he may have been, and whatever precautions he may have taken to prevent the damage. . . .

In the Court of Exchequer Chamber (1866) L.R. 1 Ex. 265

Blackburn J.: . . . The plaintiff, though free from all blame on his part, must bear the loss, unless he can establish that it was the consequence of some default for which the defendants are responsible. The question of law therefore arises, what is the obligation which the law casts on a person who, like the defendants, lawfully brings on his land something which, though harmless whilst it remains there, will naturally do mischief if it escape out of his land. It is agreed on all hands that he must take care to keep in that which he has brought on the land and keeps there, in order that it may not escape and damage his neighbours, but the question arises whether the duty which the law casts upon him, under such circumstances, is an absolute duty to keep it in at his peril, or is, as the majority of the Court of Exchequer have thought, merely a duty to take all reasonable and prudent precautions, in order to keep it in, but no more. If the first be the law, the person who has brought on his land and kept there something dangerous, and failed to keep it in, is responsible for all the natural consequences of its escape. If the second be the limit of his duty, he would not be answerable except on proof of negligence, and consequently would not be answerable for escape arising from any latent defect which ordinary prudence and skill could not detect.

Supposing the second to be the correct view of the law, a further question arises subsidiary to the first, *viz.*, whether the defendants are not so far identified with the contractors whom they employed, as to be responsible for the consequences of their want of care and skill in making the reservoir in fact insufficient with reference to the old shafts, of the existence of which they were aware, though they had not ascertained where the shafts went to.

We think that the true rule of law is [here follows the passage cited by Lord Cairns L.C., above, p. 392].

The case that has most commonly occurred, and which is most frequently to be found in the books, is as to the obligation of the owner of cattle which he has brought on his land, to prevent their escaping and doing mischief. The law as to them seems to be perfectly settled from early times; the owner must keep them in at his peril, or he will be answerable for the natural consequences of their escape; that is with regard to tame beasts, for the grass they eat and trample upon, though not for injury to the person of others, for our ancestors have settled that it is not the general nature of horses to kick, or bulls to gore; but if the owner knows that the beast has a vicious propensity to attack man, he will be answerable for that too. . . .

. . . No case has been found in which the question as to the liability for noxious vapours escaping from a man's works by inevitable accident has been discussed, but the following case will illustrate it. Some years ago several actions were brought against the occupiers of some alkali works at Liverpool for the damage alleged to be caused by the chlorine fumes of their works. The defendants proved that they at great expense erected contrivances by which the fumes of chlorine were condensed, and sold as muriatic acid, and they called a great body of scientific evidence to prove that this apparatus was so perfect that no fumes possibly could escape from the defendants' chimneys. On this evidence it was pressed upon the jury that the plaintiff's damage must have been due to some of the numerous other chimneys in the neighbourhood; the jury, however, being satisfied that the mischief was occasioned by chlorine, drew the conclusion that it had escaped from the defendants' works somehow, and in each case found for the plaintiff. No attempt was made to disturb these verdicts on the ground that the defendants had taken every precaution which prudence or skill could suggest to keep those fumes in, and that they could not be responsible unless negligence was shown; yet, if the law be as laid down by the majority of the Court of Exchequer, it would have been a very obvious defence. If it had been raised, the answer would probably have been that the uniform course of pleading in actions on such nuisances is to say that the defendant caused the noisome vapours to arise on his premises, and suffered them to come on the plaintiff's, without stating there was any want of care or skill in the defendant, and that the case of *Tenant* v. *Goldwin* ((1704) 2 Ld.Raym. 1089; 92 E.R. 222)) showed that this was founded on the general rule of law, that he whose stuff it is must keep it that it may not trespass. There is no difference in this respect between chlorine and water; both will, if they escape, do damage, the one by scorching, and the other by drowning, and he who brings them there must at his peril see that they do not escape and do that mischief. . . . But it was further said by Martin B. that when damage is done to personal property, or even to the person, by collision, either upon land or at sea, there must be negligence in the party doing the damage to render him legally responsible; and this is no doubt true, and as was pointed out by Mr. Mellish during his argument before us, this is not confined to cases of collision, for there are many cases in which proof of negligence is essential, as for instance, where an unruly horse gets on the footpath of a public street and kills a passenger: *Hammack* v. *White* ((1862) 11 C.B.(N.S.) 588; 142 E.R. 926); or where a person in a dock is struck by the falling of a bale of cotton which the defendant's servants are lowering, *Scott* v. *London Dock Company* ((1865) 3 H. & C. 596; 159 E.R. 665); and many other similar cases may be found. But we think these cases distinguishable from the present. Traffic on highways, whether by land or sea, cannot be conducted without exposing those whose persons or property are near it to some inevitble risk; and that being so, those who go on the highway, or have their property adjacent to it, may well be held to do so subject to their taking upon themselves the risk of injury from that inevitable danger; and persons who by the licence of the owner pass near to warehouses where goods are being raised or lowered, certainly do so subject to the inevitable risk of accident. In neither case, therefore, can they recover without proof of want of care or skill occasioning the accident; and it is believed that all the cases in which inevitable accident has been held an excuse for what prima facie was a trespass, can be explained on the same principle, *viz.*, that the circumstances were such as to show that the plaintiff had taken that risk upon himself. But there is no ground for saying that the plaintiff here took upon himself any risk arising from the uses to which the defendants should choose to apply their land. He neither knew what these might be, nor could he in any way control the defendants, or hinder their building what reservoirs they liked, and storing up in them what water they pleased, so long as the defendants succeeded in preventing the water which they there brought from interfering with the plaintiff's property.

The view which we take of the first point renders it unnecessary to consider whether the defendants would or would not be responsible for the want of care and skill in the persons employed by them, under the circumstances stated in the case.

We are of opinion that the plaintiff is entitled to recover, . . .

Note:

Everyone has a strong opinion about this decision. Some say it is retrogressive in so far as it declares absence of fault in the defendant to be immaterial (though it is now being treated as an example of liability for independent contractors—*Dunne* v. *North-Western Gas Board* [1964] 2 Q.B. 806, 831). Others say it is a forward-looking example of the imposition of risk of loss on an entrepreneur promoting a dangerous activity; but it has been shown that its results do not always make good sense even in terms of risk—Morris, "Hazardous Enterprises and Risk Bearing Capacity" (1952) 61 Yale L.J. 1172.

What is the extent of the decision? Professor Newark says this: "What was novel in *Rylands* v. *Fletcher*, or at least clearly decided for the first time, was that as between adjacent occupiers on isolated escape is actionable.": "The Boundaries of Nuisance" (1949) 65 L.Q.R. 480, 488. Yet in the United States it has become the starting-point of a liability without fault for the consequences of "ultra-hazardous activities," now called "abnormally dangerous."

The rule as stated by Blackburn J. is in purely factual categories, except for the phrase "for his own purposes" (which may yet have a use in restricting the liability of non-profit-making organisations such as local authorities—see *Dunne*, at 832). But the judgment of Lord Cairns contains the critical term "non-natural use," which allows judges to avoid imposing liability even when the facts of the case satisfy the rule stated in the Exchequer Chamber. It is for this reason that the judgment of Lord Cairns has been said to subvert that of Blackburn J. (Fridman, "The Rise and Fall of *Rylands* v. *Fletcher*" (1956) 34 Can.Bar.Rev. 810, 815).

The reservoir still leaks, according to "Rylands v. Fletcher Revisited," a divertissement by Brian Simpson in *The Lawyer* for September 1983, p. 16. Indeed, the mine, which was abandoned in 1861, was for some time thereafter used as an alternative source of water supply by Rylands's mill. The name of Rylands, at one time the largest private employer in Britain, lives in the minds of scholars as well as less grateful lawyers, for he endowed a marvellous library in Manchester, which the University is now dissipating.

Section 2.—Common User and Third Parties

RICKARDS v. LOTHIAN

Privy Council [1913] A.C. 263; 82 L.J.P.C. 42; 108 L.T. 225; 29 T.L.R. 281; 57 S.J. 281; [1911–13] All E.R.Rep. 71

Action by subjacent tenant against landlord in respect of property damage caused by escaping water

The plaintiff leased second-floor offices in a building occupied by the defendant. One morning he found his stock-in-trade seriously damaged by water. This water came from a fourth-floor lavatory basin, whose outlet had been plugged with nails, soap, pen-holders and string, and whose tap had been turned fully on. The defendant's caretaker testified that all was well at 10.20 the previous evening.

The jury found that the defendant was careless in not providing a lead safe on the floor under the basin, but that the plugging of the outlet and the turning of the tap "was the malicious act of some person." The county court judge at Melbourne entered judgment for the plaintiff. On appeal by the defendant, the Supreme Court of Victoria reversed the judgment, but the High Court of Australia reinstated it. The defendant's appeal to the Judicial Committee of the Privy Council was allowed.

Lord Moulton: . . . Their Lordships are of opinion that all that is . . . laid down as to a case where the escape is due to "*vis major* or the King's enemies" applies equally to a case where it is due to the malicious act of a third person, if indeed that case is not actually included in the above phrase . . . a defendant cannot in their Lordships' opinion be properly said to have caused or allowed the water to escape if the malicious act of a third person was the real cause of its escaping without any fault on the part of the defendant.

It is remarkable that the very point involved in the present case was expressly dealt with by Bramwell B. in delivering the judgment of the Court of Exchequer in *Nichols* v. *Marsland* ((1876) 2 Ex.D. 1). He says: "What has the defendant done wrong? What right of the plaintiff has she infringed? She has done nothing wrong. She has infringed no right. It is not the defendant who let loose the water and sent it to destroy the bridges. She did indeed store it, and store it in such quantities that if it was let loose it would do as it did, mischief. But suppose a stranger let it loose, would the defendant be liable? If so, then if a mischievous boy bored a hole in a cistern in any London house, and the water did mischief to a neighbour, the occupier of the house would be liable. That cannot be. Then why is the defendant liable if some agent over which she has no control lets the water out? . . . I admit that it is not a question of negligence. A man may use all care to keep the water in . . . but would be liable if through any defect, though latent, the water escaped. . . . But here the act is that of an agent he cannot control."

Following the language of this judgment their Lordships are of opinion that no better example could be given of an agent that the defendant cannot control than that of a third party surreptitiously and by a malicious act causing the overflow. . . .

Their Lordships . . . are of opinion that a defendant is not liable on the principle of *Fletcher* v. *Rylands* for damage caused by the wrongful acts of third persons.

But there is another ground upon which their Lordships are of opinion that the present case does not come within the principle laid down in *Fletcher* v. *Rylands*. It is not every use to which land is put that brings into play that principle. It must be some special use bringing with it increased danger to others, and must not merely be the ordinary use of the land or such a use as is proper for the general benefit of the community. To use the language of Lord Robertson in *Eastern and South African Telegraph Co.* v. *Cape Town Tramways Companies* ([1902] A.C. 393), the principle of *Fletcher* v. *Rylands* "subjects to a high liability the owner who uses his property for purposes other than those which are natural." This is more fully expressed by Wright J. in his judgment in *Blake* v. *Woolf* ([1898] 2 Q.B. 426). In that case the plaintiff was the occupier of the lower floors of the defendant's house, the upper floors being occupied by the defendant himself. A leak occurred in the cistern at the top of the house which without any negligence on the part of the defendant caused the plaintiff's premises to be flooded. In giving judgment for the defendant Wright J. says: "The general rule as laid down in *Rylands* v. *Fletcher* is that prima facie a person occupying land has an absolute right not to have his premises invaded by injurious matter, such as large quantities of water which his neighbour keeps upon his land. That general rule is, however, qualified by some exceptions, one of which is that, where a person is using his land in the ordinary way and damage happens to the adjoining property without any default or negligence on his part, no liability attaches to him. The bringing of water on to such premises as these and the maintaining a cistern in the usual way seems to me to be an ordinary and reasonable user of such premises as these were; and, therefore, if the water escapes without any negligence or default on the part of the person bringing the water in and owning the cistern, I do not think that he is liable for any damage that may ensue." . . .

Their Lordships are in entire sympathy with these views. The provision of a proper supply of water to the various parts of a house is not only reasonable, but has become, in accordance with modern sanitary views, an almost necessary feature of town life. It is recognised as being so desirable in the interests of the community that in some form or other it is usually made obligatory in civilised countries. Such a supply cannot be installed without causing some concurrent danger of leakage or overflow. It would be unreasonable for the law to regard those who instal or maintain such a system of supply as doing so at their own peril, with an absolute liability for any damage resulting from its presence even when there has been no negligence. It would be still more unreasonable if, as the respondent contends, such liability were to be held to extend to the consequences of malicious acts on the part of third persons. In such matters as the domestic supply of water or gas it is essential that the mode of supply should be such as to permit ready access for the purpose of use, and hence it is impossible to guard against wilful mischief. Taps may be turned on, ball-cocks fastened open, supply pipes cut, and waste-pipes blocked. Against such acts no precaution can prevail. It would be wholly unreasonable to hold an occupier responsible for the consequences of such acts which he is powerless to prevent, when the provision of the supply is not only a reasonable act on his part but probably a duty. Such a doctrine would, for example, make a householder liable for the consequences of an explosion caused by a burglar breaking into his house during the night and leaving a gas tap open. There is, in their Lordships' opinion, no support either in reason or authority for any such view of the liability of a landlord or occupier. In having on his premises such means of supply he is only using those premises in an ordinary and proper manner, and, although he is bound to exercise all reasonable care, he is not responsible for damage not due to his own default, whether the damage be caused by inevitable accident or the wrongful acts of third persons. . . .

The appeal must therefore be allowed and judgment entered for the defendant. . . .

Note:

This important case holds that the unforeseeable act of a third party can insulate the defendant from the consequences of his negligence, that *Rylands* v. *Fletcher* does not apply to household installations of a normal variety, at least where the plaintiff uses them too, and that even where *Rylands* v. *Fletcher* does apply, the unforeseeable act of a third party provides a defence, on the grounds of causation.

Compare the formulations "likely to do damage if it escapes" and "likely to escape and do damage." The first constitutes a strict liability, the second a liability in negligence. Where liability is easily incurred, its extent is always severely restricted; to put that proposition in another form, we may say that where there are few restrictions at the point of "duty," there are many at the point of "causation." Thus it is no surprise that the act of a third party excludes liability under *Rylands* v. *Fletcher*, just as it does in trespass and in libel. Of course, if the act of the third party is foreseeable, the thing in question then becomes a thing "likely to escape and do damage," and we have a liability effectively based on negligence.

Flooding from upstairs is a common grievance. An occupier is not readily held liable if the flooding is due to vandals, even if they are predictable (*King* v. *Liverpool Corp.* [1986] 3 All E.R. 544); negligence is not presumed, at any rate for a first escape (*Hawkins* v. *Dhawan* (C.A. February 11, 1987); but it is not quite clear for what range of visitors the occupier may be held responsible. In this respect fire is clearer than water.

"*Rylands* v. *Fletcher* has no place in Scottish law, and the suggestion that it has is a heresy which ought to be extirpated.", *per* Lord Fraser of Tullybelton in *R.H.M. Bakeries (Scotland)* v. *Strathclyde R.C.* (1985) S.L.T. 214, 217 (H.L.).

Section 3.—Fire

MASON v. LEVY AUTO PARTS OF ENGLAND LTD.

Assizes [1967] 2 Q.B. 530; [1967] 2 W.L.R. 1384; 111 S.J. 234; [1967] 2 All E.R. 62; [1967] 1 Lloyd's Rep. 372

The defendants kept in their yard large stacks of wooden cases containing greased or wrapped machinery, as well as quantities of petroleum, acetylene and paint. At noon one fine day a fire broke out for an unknown reason, and could not be controlled before it had done damage to the plaintiff's adjoining garden.

MacKenna J.: . . . I come now to the law, beginning with section 86 of the Fires Prevention (Metropolis) Act 1774, whose obscure provisions were foreseeably invoked by the defendants. The section provides that: " . . . no action, suit, or process whatever, shall be had, or prosecuted, against any person in whose house, chamber, stable, barn, or other building, or on whose estate any fire shall . . . accidentally begin, nor shall any recompense be made by such person for any damage suffered thereby; any law, usage, or custom to the contrary notwithstanding. . . . "
. . .

If under the statute the householder may no longer be presumed to have caused the fire, must he be presumed, even rebuttably, to have caused it negligently? I would have said not.

One case only is in the plaintiff's favour, decided by Judge Malcolm Wright, Q.C., in the county court, namely, *Hyman (Sales) Ltd.* v. *Benedyke & Co. Ltd.* ([1957] 2 Lloyd's Rep. 601). But that case is, I think, to be explained as a decision on a bailee's liability to his bailor, which may perhaps be an exception to the general rule prescribed by the Fires Prevention (Metropolis) Act 1774. That the Act expressly excepts the case of landlord and tenant does not, however, make it easy to imply any other exceptions. Nobody argued that any help was to be derived on this point from the repealed provisions about the pleading of the general issue.

In my judgment the plaintiff's first point fails. There is no burden on the defendants of disproving negligence.

Has the plaintiff proved that the defendants were negligent, which is his second point? Or has he brought the case within *Rylands* v. *Fletcher* or any similar principle of liability, which is his third point?

In his particulars the plaintiff charges the defendants with providing no adequate means of detecting or extinguishing fire. I do not think that either of these charges was proved. The defendants were under no duty to maintain a constant lookout for fire, and this fire was in any case detected at an early stage by the defendants' workmen. The appliances recommended by the fire brigade had been provided, and if it proved impossible to control or extinguish the fire by these means that is not the fault of the defendants for failing to provide more or better equipment. Such appliances are, anyhow, intended only as first-aid. That they were ineffective to control or extinguish this fire is not proof of any culpable failure to provide more adequate equipment. Then it is said that the crates were so closely stacked "that there was no reasonable access between them for fire-fighting purposes." That was true of some parts of the yard, but I have no reason to suppose that if it had been otherwise this fire would have been controlled.

As I see it, the plaintiff's real case against the defendants is in the allegation that they "so used their land by cluttering it with combustible material closely packed that the plaintiff's land was endangered." That, like the plaintiff's other allegations, is put against the defendants in alternative ways, including negligence, nuisance, allowing a dangerous thing, namely, fire, to escape from their land, and as a failure so to use their land as not to harm the plaintiff.

I shall consider it under the two last of these heads, beginning, as one must, with *Musgrove* v. *Pandelis* ([1919] 2 K.B. 43) [where petrol in the carburettor of the defendants' garaged car ignited when his servant started it, but no harm would have been done to the plaintiff's flat above if the servant had turned off the petrol flow from the tank as he should]. Bankes L.J. reasoned thus: (a) there were at common law three separate heads of liability for damage done by fire originating on a man's property, "(i) for the mere escape of the fire; (ii) if the fire was caused by the negligence of himself or his servants, or by his own wilful act; (iii) on the principle of *Rylands* v. *Fletcher*." (b) *Filliter* v. *Phippard* decided that the statute did not cover the second case. (c) "Why," Bankes L.J. asked, "if that is the law as to the second head of liability, should it be otherwise as to the third head, the liability on the principle of *Rylands* v. *Fletcher*?" The answer, I would have said with respect, is obvious enough. There were not three heads of liability at common law but only one. A person from whose land a fire escaped was held liable to his neighbour unless he could prove that it had started or spread by the act of a stranger or of God. *Filliter's* case had given a special meaning to the words "accidental fire" used in the statute, holding that they did not include fires due to negligence, but covered only cases of "a fire produced by mere chance, or incapable of being traced to any cause." But it does not follow, because that meaning may be given to "accidental," that the statute does not cover cases of the *Rylands* v. *Fletcher* kind where the occupier is held liable for the escape though no fault is proved against him. In such cases the fire may be "produced by mere chance" or may be "incapable of being traced to any cause." Bankes L.J. was making a distinction unknown to the common law, between "the mere escape of fire" (which was his first head) and its escape under *Rylands* v. *Fletcher* conditions (which was his third), and was imputing an intention to the legislature of exempting from liability in the former case and not in the latter. In holding that an exemption given to accidental fires, "any law, usage, or custom to the contrary notwithstanding," does not include fires for which liability might be imposed upon the principle of *Rylands* v. *Fletcher*, the Court of Appeal went very far. But it is my duty to follow them unless *Musgrove's* case has been overruled, or unless its principle does not apply to the facts proved here.

Musgrove's case has not been overruled; that is certain. . . .

What then, is the principle? As Romer L.J. in *Collingwood's* case pointed out, it cannot be exactly that of *Rylands* v. *Fletcher*. A defendant is not held liable under *Rylands* v. *Fletcher* unless two conditions are satisfied: (i) that he has brought some-thing on to his land likely to do mischief if it escapes, which has in fact escaped, and (ii) that those things happened in the course of some non-natural user of the land. But in *Musgrove's* case the car had not escaped from the land, neither had the petrol in its tank. The principle must be, Romer L.J. said, the wider one on which *Rylands* v. *Fletcher* itself was based, "*sic utere tuo*. . . . "

If, for the rule in *Musgrove's* case to apply, there need be no escape of anything brought on to the defendant's land, what must be proved against him? There is, it seems to me, a choice of alternatives. The first would require the plaintiff to prove (1) that the defendant had brought something on to his land likely to do mischief if it escaped; (2) that he had done so in the course of a non-natural user of the land; and (3) that the thing had ignited and that the fire had spread. The second would be to hold the defendant liable if (1) he brought on to his land things likely to catch fire, and kept them there in such conditions that if they did ignite the fire would be likely to spread to the plaintiff's land; (2) he did so in the course of some non-natural use; and (3) the things ignited and the fire spread. The second test is, I think, the more reasonable one. To make the likelihood of damage if the thing escapes a criterion of liability, when the thing has not in fact escaped but has caught fire, would not be very sensible.

So I propose to apply the second test, asking myself the two questions: (i) did the defendants in this case bring to their land things likely to catch fire, and keep them there in such conditions that if they did ignite the fire would be likely to spread to the plaintiff's land? If so, (ii) did the defendants do these things in the course of some non-natural user of the land?

I have no difficulty in answering "yes" to the first of those questions, but the second is more troublesome. I feel the difficulty which any judge must feel in decid-ing what is a non-natural user of the land, and have prepared myself for answering the question by reading what is said about it in *Salmond on Torts*, 14th ed. (1965), pp. 450–452, and in *Winfield on Torts*, 7th ed. (1963), pp. 449–452. Thus con-ditioned, I would say that the defendants' use of their land in the way described earlier in this judgment was non-natural. In saying that, I have regard (i) to the quantities of combustible material which the defendants brought on their land; (ii) to the way in which they stored them; and (iii) to the character of the neighbour-hood.

It may be that those considerations would also justify a finding of negligence. If that is so, the end would be the same as I have reached by a more laborious, and perhaps more questionable, route.

. . .

Note:

Most people who have an interest in a building keep it insured against fire. Where insurance so fully covers loss, there is less need for the law of tort to intervene; indeed, the curtailment of strict liability for the escape of fire was contemporaneous with the rise of the insurance companies in the eighteenth century. But the law as established will still be used by two classes of person, first, the householder who has underinsured (a large class of persons in times of rapidly increasing building costs) and, secondly, the insurer who has paid the householder and is exercising his rights of subrogation. It is impossible to tell which is which, because insurance companies sue in the name of the person insured.

In a recent case where the landlord's insurer tried to sue the tenant whose carelessness had caused the premises to be burnt, it was held that the tenant was exempted from liability by the clause in the lease whereby the landlord promised to keep the premises insured (with a contribution from the tenant) and to use the proceeds for reinstatement. (*Mark Rowlands* v. *Berni Inns* [1985] 3 All E.R. 473 (C.A.), noted [1986] Camb.L.J. 22 (Clarke)).

Under a fire policy the insurance company pays only the value of the property up to the policy limit; it does not pay for the loss caused to the insured by reason of his inability to use the property until it is repaired or rebuilt. To recover for such loss the owner requires a consequential loss policy or an action in tort.

When a fire escapes because it was negligently started or controlled by someone other than the occupier, the occupier is liable unless that other person is a stranger: a stranger, for this purpose, is a trespasser or a licensee acting in a quite unexpected manner. This was the holding of the Court of Appeal in *H. & N. Emanuel* v. *Greater London Council* ([1971] 2 All E.R. 835). The Council required the Ministry of Housing to remove two prefabricated houses from their land. The Ministry of Works, on the request of the Ministry of Housing, sold the houses to King for removal under a contract forbidding King to light any fires, a thing the Ministry knew King to have done previously despite like prohibitions. King collected the keys from the Council's man and started the work of demolition one Saturday morning. He failed to control the bonfire he lit, and the plaintiff's premises next door were badly burnt. The Court of Appeal unanimously held the Council liable. The holding is perfectly satisfactory, but the asides of their Lordships are worrying. Lord Denning was prepared to hold that both Ministries were also occupiers: that is quite unacceptable. Edmund Davies L.J. held that the Council was personally negligent in not supervising the demolition (on a Saturday morning?). Phillimore L.J. held that the Council was liable for the negligence of the Ministry of Works in failing to supervise the demolition—a double error.

Fire cases are special, and any attempt to incorporate them into the general law will fail: compare, for example, the observations of their Lordships in *Emanuel's* case with the holdings in *Salsbury* v. *Woodland* (above, p. 268) and *Smith* v. *Scott* (above, p. 376).

Section 4.—Limits of the Rule

READ v. J. LYONS & CO.

House of Lords [1947] A.C. 156; [1947] L.J.R. 39; 175 L.T. 413; 62 T.L.R. 646; [1946] 2 All E.R. 471

Action by visitor against occupier in respect of personal injury

By agreement with the Minister of Supply the defendants undertook the management and control of the Elstow Ordnance Factory where they made high-explosive shells for the government. The plaintiff was directed to work as an inspector in the factory, and when she was lawfully in the shell-filling shop on August 31, 1942, there was an explosion which killed one man and injured several others, including the plaintiff.

She did not plead or try to prove that the defendants were negligent, but averred merely that she was lawfully present in the place where the defendants were manufacturing high-explosive shells which they knew to be dangerous things and that she suffered damage when one of them exploded.

The plaintiff succeeded before Cassels J. The defendants' appeal to the Court of Appeal was allowed [1945] 1 K.B. 216. The plaintiff's appeal to the House of Lords was dismissed.

Viscount Simon: My Lords, no negligence was averred or proved against the respondents. The plea of *volenti non fit injuria*, for whatever it might be worth, has been expressly withdrawn before this House by the Attorney-General on behalf of the respondents, and thus the simple question for the decision is whether in these circumstances the respondents are liable, without any proof or inference that they were negligent, to the appellant in damages, which have been assessed at £575 2s. 8d. for her injuries. Cassels J. who tried the case, considered that it was governed by *Rylands* v. *Fletcher*, and held that the respondents were liable, on the ground that they were carrying on an ultra-hazardous activity and so were under what is called a "strict liability" to take successful care to avoid causing harm to persons whether on or off the premises. The Court of Appeal (Scott, MacKinnon, and du Parcq L.JJ.) reversed this decision, Scott L.J. in an elaborately reasoned judgment holding that a person on the premises had, in the absence of any proof of negligence, no cause of action, and that there must be an escape of the damage-causing thing from the premises and damage caused outside before the doctrine customarily associated with the case of *Rylands* v. *Fletcher* can apply. I agree that the action fails. The appellant was a person present in the factory in pursuance of a public duty (like an ordinary factory inspector) and was consequently in the same position as an invitee. The respondents were managers of the factory as agents for the Ministry of Supply and had the same responsibility to an invitee as an ordinary occupier in control of the premises. The duties of an occupier of premises to an invitee have been analysed in many reported cases, but in none of them, I think, is there any hint of the proposition necessary to support the claim of the appellant in this case. The fact that the work that was being carried on was of a kind which requires special care is a reason why the standard of care should be high, but it is no reason for saying that the occupier is liable for resulting damage to an invitee without any proof of negligence at all.

Blackburn J., in delivering the judgment of the Court of Exchequer Chamber in *Fletcher* v. *Rylands*, laid down the proposition that "the person who for his own purposes brings on to his lands and collects and keeps there anything likely to do mischief if it escapes, must keep it in at his peril, and, if he does not do so, is prima facie answerable for all the damage which is the natural consequence of its escape."

It has not always been sufficiently observed that in the House of Lords, when the appeal from *Fletcher* v. *Rylands* was dismissed and Blackburn J.'s pronouncement was expressly approved, Lord Cairns L.C. emphasised another condition which must be satisfied before liability attaches without proof of negligence. This is that the use to which the defendant is putting his land is "a non-natural use." Blackburn J. had made a parenthetic reference to this sort of test when he said: "it seems but reasonable and just that the neighbour, who has brought something on his own property, *which was not naturally there*, harmless to others so long as it is confined to his own property, but which he knows to be mischievous if it gets on his neighbour's, should be obliged to make good the damage which ensues if he does not succeed in confining it to his own property." I confess to finding this test of "non-natural" user (or of bringing on the land what was not "naturally there," which is not the same test) difficult to apply. Blackburn J., in the sentence immediately following that which I have last quoted, treats cattle-trespass as an example of his generalisation. The pasturing of cattle must be one of the most ordinary uses of land, and strict liability for damage done by cattle enclosed on one man's land if they escape thence into the land of another, is one of the most ancient propositions of our law. It is in fact a case of pure trespass to property, and thus constitutes a wrong without any question of negligence. See *per* Lord Coleridge C.J. in *Ellis* v. *Loftus Iron Co.* ((1874) L.R. 10 C.P. 10, 12). The circumstances in *Fletcher* v.

Rylands did not constitute a case of trespass because the damage was consequential, nor direct. It is to be noted that all the counts in the declaration in that case set out allegations of negligence but in the House of Lords Lord Cairns begins his opinion by explaining that ultimately the case was treated as determining the rights of the parties independently of any question of negligence. The classic judgment of Blackburn J., besides deciding the issue before the court and laying down the principle of duty between neighbouring occupiers of land on which the decision was based, sought to group under a single and wider proposition other instances in which liability is independent of negligence, such for example as liability for the bite of a defendant's monkey, *May* v. *Burdett* ((1846) 9 Q.B. 101; 115 E.R. 1213); see also the case of a bear on a chain on the defendant's premises, *Besozzi* v. *Harris* ((1858) 1 F. & F. 92; 175 E.R. 640). There are instances, no doubt, in our law in which liability for damage may be established apart from proof of negligence, but it appears to me logically unnecessary and historically incorrect to refer to all these instances as deduced from one common principle. The conditions under which such a liability arises are not necessarily the same in each class of case. Lindley L.J. issued a valuable warning in *Green* v. *Chelsea Waterworks Co.* ((1894) 70 L.T. 547, 549), when he said of *Rylands* v. *Fletcher* that that decision "is not to be extended beyond the legitimate principle on which the House of Lords decided it. If it were extended as far as strict logic might require, it would be a very oppressive decision." It seems better, therefore, when a plaintiff relies on *Rylands* v. *Fletcher*, to take the conditions declared by this House to be essential for liability in that case and to ascertain whether these conditions exist in the actual case.

Now, the strict liability recognised by this House to exist in *Rylands* v. *Fletcher* is conditioned by two elements which I may call the condition of "escape" from the land of something likely to do mischief if it escapes, and the condition of "non-natural use" of the land. This second condition has in some later cases, which did not reach this House, been otherwise expressed, *e.g.*, as "exceptional" user, when such user is not regarded as "natural" and at the same time is likely to produce mischief if there is an "escape." . . . It is not necessary to analyse this second condition on the present occasion, for in the case now before us the first essential condition of "escape" does not seem to me to be present at all. "Escape," for the purpose of applying the proposition in *Rylands* v. *Fletcher*, means escape from a place where the defendant has occupation of or control over land to a place which is outside his occupation or control. Blackburn J. several times refers to the defendant's duty as being the duty of "keeping a thing in" at the defendant's peril, and by "keeping in" he does not mean preventing an explosive substance from exploding but preventing a thing which may inflict mischief from escaping from the area which the defendant occupies or controls. In two well-known cases the same principle of strict liability for escape was applied to defendants who held a franchise to lay pipes under a highway and to conduct water (or gas) under pressure through them (*Charing Cross Electricity Supply Co.* v. *Hydraulic Power Co.* ([1914] 3 K.B. 772); *Northwestern Utilities Ltd.* v. *London Guarantee and Accident Co.* ([1936] A.C. 108)). In *Howard* v. *Furness Houlder Argentine Lines Ltd.* ((1936) 41 Com.Cas. 290) Lewis J. had before him a case of injury caused by an escape of steam on board a ship where the plaintiff was working. The learned judge was, I think, right in refusing to apply the doctrine of *Rylands* v. *Fletcher*, on the ground that the injuries were caused on the premises of the defendants. Apart altogether from the judge's doubt (which I share) whether the owners of the steamship by generating steam therein are making a non-natural use of their steamship, the other condition upon which the proposition in *Rylands* v. *Fletcher* depends was not present, any more than it is in the case with which we have now to deal. Here there is no escape of the relevant kind at all and the appellant's action fails on that ground. In these circumstances it becomes unnecessary to consider other objections that have been raised, such as the question whether the doctrine of *Rylands* v. *Fletcher* applies where the claim is for damages for personal injury as distinguished from damages to property. It may be noted, in passing, that Blackburn J. himself when referring to the doctrine of *Rylands* v. *Fletcher* in the later case of *Cattle* v. *Stockton Waterworks Co.* ((1875) L.R. 10 Q.B. 453, 457), leaves this undealt with: he treats damages under the *Rylands* v. *Fletcher* principle as covering damages to property, such as workmen's clothes or tools, but says nothing about liability for personal injuries.

. . . I hold that the appellant fails for the reason that there was no "escape" from the respondents' factory. I move that the appeal be dismissed with costs.

Lord Macmillan: My Lords, nothing could be simpler than the facts in this appeal; nothing more far-reaching than the discussion of fundamental legal principles to which it has given rise. . . .

In my opinion the appellant's statement of claim discloses no ground of action against the respondents. The action is one of damages for personal injuries. Whatever may have been the law of England in early times I am of opinion that as the law now stands an allegation of negligence is in general essential to the relevancy of an action of reparation for personal injuries. The gradual development of the law in the matter of civil liability is discussed and traced by the late Sir William Holdsworth with ample learning and lucidity in his *History of English Law* Vol. 8, pp. 446 *et seq.*, and need not here be rehearsed. Suffice it to say that the process of evolution has been from the principle that every man acts at his peril and is liable for all the consequences of his acts to the principle that a man's freedom of action is subject only to the obligation not to infringe any duty of care which he owes to others. The emphasis formerly was on the injury sustained and the question was whether the case fell within one of the accepted classes of common law actions; the emphasis now is on the conduct of the person whose act has occasioned the injury and the question is whether it can be characterised as negligent. I do not overlook the fact that there is at least one instance in the present law in which the primitive rule survives, namely, in the case of animals *ferae naturae* or animals *mansuetae naturae* which have shown dangerous proclivities. The owner or keeper of such an animal has an absolute duty to confine or control it so that it shall not do injury to others and no proof of care on his part will absolve him from responsibility. But this is probably not so much a vestigial relic of otherwise discarded doctrine as a special rule of practical good sense. At any rate, it is too well established to be challenged. But such an exceptional case as this affords no justification for its extension by analogy.

The appellant in her printed case in this House thus poses the question to be determined: "Whether the manufacturer of high-explosive shells is under strict liability to prevent such shells from exploding and causing harm to persons on the premises where such manufacture is carried on as well as to persons outside such premises." Two points arise on this statement of the question. In the first place the expression "strict liability," though borrowed from authority, is ambiguous. If it means the absolute liability of an insurer irrespective of negligence then the answer in my opinion must be in the negative. If it means that an exacting standard of care is incumbent on manufacturers of explosive shells to prevent the occurrence of accidents causing personal injuries I should answer the question in the affirmative, but this will not avail the appellant. In the next place, the question as stated would seem to assume that liability would exist in the present case to persons injured outside the defendants' premises without any proof of negligence on the part of the defendants. Indeed, Cassels J. in his judgment records that ((1944) 170 L.T. 418, 420): "It was not denied that if a person outside the premises had been injured in the explosion the defendants would have been liable without proof of negligence." I do not agree with this view. In my opinion persons injured by the explosion inside or outside the defendants' premises would alike require to aver and prove negligence in order to render the defendants liable.

In an address characterised by much painstaking research Mr. Paull for the appellant sought to convince your Lordships that there is a category of things and operations dangerous in themselves and that those who harbour such things or carry on such operations in their premises are liable apart from negligence for any personal injuries occasioned by these dangerous things or operations. I think that he succeeded in showing that in the case of dangerous things and operations the law has recognised that a special responsibility exists to take care. But I do not think that it has ever been laid down that there is an absolute liability apart from negligence where persons are injured in consequence of the use of such things or the conduct of such operations. In truth it is a matter of degree. Every activity in which man engages is fraught with some possible element of danger to others. Experience shows that even from acts apparently innocuous injury to others may result. The more dangerous the act the greater is the care that must be taken in performing it. This relates itself to the principle in the modern law of torts that liability exists only for consequences which a reasonable man would have foreseen. One who engages in obviously dangerous operations must be taken to know that if he does not take special precautions injury to others may very well result. In my opinion it would be impracticable to frame a legal classification of things as things dangerous and things not dangerous, attaching absolute liability in the case of the former but not in the case of the latter. In a progressive world things which at one time were reckoned highly dangerous come to be regarded as reasonably safe. The first experimental flights of aviators were certainly dangerous but we are now assured that travel by air is little if at all more dangerous than a railway journey. Accordingly I am unable to accept the proposition that in law the manufacture of high-explosive shells is a dangerous operation which imposes on the manufacturer an absolute liability for any personal injuries which may be sustained in consequence of his operations. Strict liability, if you will, is imposed upon him in the sense that he must exercise a high degree of care, but that is all. The sound view, in my opinion, is that the law in all cases exacts a degree of care commensurate with the risk created. It was suggested that some operations are so intrinsically dangerous that no degree of care however scrupulous can prevent the occurrence of accidents and that those who choose for their own ends to carry on such operations ought to be held to do so at their peril. If this were so, many industries would have a serious liability imposed on them. Should it be thought that this is a reasonable liability to impose in the public interest it is for Parliament so to enact. In my opinion it is not the present law of England. . . .

. . . The doctrine of *Rylands* v. *Fletcher*, as I understand it, derives from a conception of mutual duties of adjoining or neighbouring landowners and its congeners are trespass and nuisance. If its foundation is to be found in the injunction *sic utere tuo ut alienum non laedas*, then it is manifest that it has nothing to do with personal injuries. The duty is to refrain from injuring not *alium* but *alienum*. The two prerequisites of the doctrine are that there must be the escape of something from one man's close to another man's close and that that which escapes must have been brought upon the land from which it escapes in consequence of some non-natural use of that land, whatever precisely that may mean. Neither of these features exists in the present case. . . .

Your Lordships' task in this House is to decide particular cases between litigants and your Lordships are not called upon to rationalise the law of England. That attractive if perilous field may well be left to other hands to cultivate. It has been necessary in the present instance to examine certain general principles advanced on behalf of the appellant because it was said that consistency required that these principles should be applied to the case in hand. Arguments based on legal consistency are apt to mislead for the common law is a practical code adapted to deal with the manifold diversities of human life, and as a great American judge has reminded us, "the life of the law has not been logic; it has been experience." For myself, I am content to say that in my opinion no authority has been quoted from case or textbook which would justify your Lordships, logically or otherwise, in giving effect to the appellant's plea. I would accordingly dismiss the appeal.

Lord Simonds: . . . in the appellant's formal case the question was thus stated: "Whether the manufacturer of high-explosive shells is under strict liability to prevent such shells from exploding and causing harm to persons on the premises where such manufacture is carried on as well as to persons outside such premises." The question thus stated assumes that, if the appellant had been outside the premises when she was damaged by the explosion, she would have had a cause of action, and for this assumption it is clear that *Rainham Chemical Works Ltd.* v. *Belvedere Fish Guano Co. Ltd.* is relied on. That case is an authority binding on your Lordships for whatever it decided, but two things at least it did not decide, the first that which is indicated in the question I have cited, *viz.*, whether the respondents have the same liability to those within as to those outside their premises, the second that the liability, to whomsoever it may be owed, extends to purely personal injuries such as the appellant suffered. Holding the view that I do upon the first question I think it inexpedient to express a final view upon the second, but I would not be taken as assenting to the proposition that if, *e.g.* the plaintiff in the *Rainham* case had been a natural person who had suffered personal injury the result would necessarily have been the same.

I turn then to the first question which raises the familiar problem of strict liability, a phrase which I use to express liability without proof of negligence. Here is an age-long conflict of theories which is to be found in every system of law. "A man acts at his peril," says one theory. "A man is not liable unless he is to blame," answers the other. It will not surprise the students of English law or of anything English to find that between these theories a middle way, a compromise, has been found. For it is beyond question that in respect of certain acts a man will be liable for the harmful consequences of those acts, be he never so careful, yet in respect of other acts he will not be liable unless he has in some way fallen short of a prescribed standard of conduct. It avails not at all to argue that because in some respects a man acts at his peril, therefore in all respects he does so. There is not one principle only which is to be applied with rigid logic to all cases. To this result both the infinite complexity of human affairs and the historical development of the forms of action contribute. The House has had the advantage not only of an exhaustive argument in which a large number of cases were cited and discussed and many authoritative textbooks and articles quoted, but also of careful and elaborate judgments in the courts below, and I am left with the impression that it would be possible to find support in decision or dictum or learned opinion for almost any proposition that might be advanced. Yet I would venture to say that the law is that, subject to certain specific exceptions which I will indicate, a man is not in the absence of negligence liable in respect of things, whether they are called dangerous or not, which he has brought or collected or manufactured upon his premises, unless such things escape from his premises and, so escaping, injure another, and, as I have already said, I would leave it open whether, even in the event of such escape, he is liable (still in the absence of negligence) for personal injury as distinguished from injury to some proprietary interest.

My Lords, in this branch of the law it is inevitable that reference should be made to what Blackburn J. said in *Fletcher* v. *Rylands* and what Lord Cairns L.C. said in *Rylands* v. *Fletcher*. In doing so I think it is of great importance to remember that the subject-matter of that action was the rights of adjoining landowners and, though the doctrine of strict liability there enforced was illustrated by reference to the responsibility of the man who keeps beasts, yet the defendant was held liable only because he allowed, or did not prevent, the escape from his land on to the land of the plaintiff of something which he had brought on to his own land, and which he knew or should have known was liable to do mischief if it escaped from it. I agree with the late MacKinnon L.J. ([1945] K.B. 216, 242) that this and nothing else is the basis of the celebrated judgment of Blackburn J., and I think it is no less the basis of Lord Cairns' opinion. For it is significant that he emphasises that, if the accumulation of water (the very thing, which, by its escape in that case, caused the actionable damage) had arisen by the natural user of the defendants' land, the adjoining owner could not have complained. The decision itself does not justify the broad proposition which the appellant seeks to establish, and I would venture to say that the word "escape" which is used so often in the judgment of Blackburn J. meant to him escape from the defendant's premises and nothing else. It has been urged that escape means escape from control and that it is irrelevant where damage takes place if there has been such an escape, but, though it is arguable that that ought to be the law, I see no logical necessity for it, and much less any judicial authority. For, as I have said, somewhere the line must be drawn unless full rein be given to the doctrine that a man acts always at his peril, that "coarse and impolitic idea" as Holmes J. somewhere calls it. I speak with all deference of modern American textbooks and judicial decisions, but I think little guidance can be obtained from the way in which this part of the common law has developed on the other side of the ocean, and I would reject the idea that, if a man carries on a so-called ultra-hazardous activity on his premises, the line must be drawn so as to bring him within the limit of strict liability for its consequences to all men everywhere. On the contrary I would say that his obligation to those lawfully upon his premises is to be ultra-cautious in carrying on his ultra-hazardous activity, but that it will still be the task of the injured person to show that the defendant owed to him a duty of care and did not fulfil it. It may well be that in the discharge of that task he will sometimes be able to call in aid the maxim *res ipsa loquitur*.

My Lords, I have stated a general proposition and indicated that there are exceptions to it. It is clear for instance that if a man brings and keeps a wild beast on his land or a beast known to him to be ferocious of a species generally *mansuetae naturae* he may be liable for any damage occurring within or without his premises without proof of negligence. Such an exception will serve to illustrate the proposition that the law of torts has grown up historically in separate compartments and that beasts have travelled in a compartment of their own. So also it may be that in regard to certain chattels a similar liability may arise though I accept and would quote with respect what my learned and noble friend Lord Macmillan said in *Donoghue* v. *Stevenson*: "I rather regard this type of case as a special instance of negligence where the law exacts a degree of diligence so stringent as to amount practically to a guarantee of safety." There may be other exceptions. Professor Winfield, to whose *Textbook of the Law of Tort*, 3rd ed., I would acknowledge my indebtedness, is inclined to include certain "dangerous structures" within the rule of strict liability. This may be so. It is sufficient for my purpose to say that unless a plaintiff can point to a specific rule of law in relation to a specific subject-matter he cannot, in my opinion, bring himself within the exceptions to the general rule that I have stated. I have already expressed my view that there is no rule which imposes on him who carries on the business of making explosives, though the activity may be "ultra-hazardous" and an explosive "a dangerous thing," a strict liability to those who are lawfully on his premises.

My Lords, it was urged by counsel for the appellant that a decision against her when the plaintiff in the *Rainham* case succeeded would show a strange lack of symmetry in the law. There is some force in the observation. But your Lordships will not fail to observe that such a decision is in harmony with the development of a strictly analogous branch of the law, the law of nuisance, in which also negligence is not a necessary ingredient in the case. For if a man commits a legal nuisance it is no answer to his injured neighbour that he took the utmost care not to commit it. There the liability is strict, and there he alone has a lawful claim who has suffered an invasion of some proprietary or other interest in land. To confine the rule in *Rylands* v. *Fletcher* to cases in which there has been an escape from the defendants' land appears to me consistent and logical. It is worthy of note that so closely connected are the two branches of the law that textbooks on the law of nuisance regard cases coming under the rule in *Rylands* v. *Fletcher* as their proper subject, and, as the judgment of Blackburn J. in that case itself shows, the law of nuisance and the rule in *Rylands* v. *Fletcher* might in most cases be invoked indifferently. . . . In suggesting to your Lordships that except in reference to specific subject-matter the rule in *Rylands* v. *Fletcher* must be confined to the escape of something from the defendants' premises I am pressed by the fact that in the *Charing Cross* case ([1914] 3 K.B. 772) the escape was not strictly from the defendant's premises but from pipes laid in the soil of another. So also in *West* v. *Bristol Tramways Co.* ([1908] 2 K.B. 14) the escape was of creosote from wood-blocks laid in the highway. It is not necessary to pronounce finally upon these cases. It is possible that the rule should be extended to include the case where something has escaped from a pipe or whatever it may be which has been laid and maintained by the defendant by virtue of some right or franchise in the land of another. That is not this case. Nor would I exclude the possibility of a special rule being applicable as between co-users of a highway, for the highway has a law of its own. But that also is not this case. For the present purpose it is sufficient to say negatively that the appellant being on the respondents' premises cannot hold them liable for the damage suffered by her unless she alleges and proves negligence by them in their manufacture of explosives. . . .

Lord Uthwatt: My Lords, the appellant does not allege either negligence or lack of skill on the part of the respondents. Her case is that by reason of the dangerous nature of the business which involved the risk of explosion they owed to her a duty to safeguard her from any harm resulting from its dangerous character. . . .

Is there any good reason consistent with respect for the rights of dominion and user incident to the occupation of land, and with an appreciation of the position of an invitee, for subjecting the occupier carrying on a dangerous but lawful business to an absolute duty to safeguard the invitee from harm? I can see none. In carrying on such a business the occupier may be doing something which is not common, but he is not doing anything which is out of the ordinary course of affairs or which is concealed from the invitee. He is in no way abusing his right to use his land. To subject him to an absolute duty to an invitee would be to my mind to impose an unreasonable limitation on the due exercise of that right. But the relation between the parties is the governing consideration and it is the incidents which the law attaches to that relation that are in question. I can understand an invitee, whatever be the nature of the business carried on, questioning in his own mind whether he is entitled to expect that the occupier will in conducting his business take due care or whether he is to expect only that the occupier will continue to conduct his business in his accustomed manner, whatever that may be. But I do not think that the invitee, any more than the occupier, would assume that, by reason only of the dangerous nature of the business carried on, the occupier guaranteed him freedom from harm. If that be so it is against reason that the law, whose function it is to give effect to reasonable expectations, should impose such a guarantee. A measure of care determined by the degree of danger is in my opinion the utmost that either party would envisage and, in my opinion, the law demands that and no other standard of duty. This denial of absolute liability to an invitee is indeed not inconsistent with the assertion—I do not make it—of an absolute duty towards persons who suffer harm outside the occupier's premises. Matters happening within one's own bounds are one thing and matters happening outside those bounds are an entirely different thing. In the latter case the personal relation is absent and the occupier's dominion over and right to use his land have to be reconciled with the rights of others to use or be present on adjoining lands not subject to his dominion. Unless compelled by authority to come to a contrary conclusion I would, therefore, reject the appellant's contention.

There is no authority which directly supports that contention. The appellant, to some extent, relied on the animal cases, but they are of no real help. Her sheet anchor was *Rylands* v. *Fletcher*. That case on the facts related only to the duty which an occupier of land—nuisance and negligence not being involved and trespass treated as not being involved—owed to an occupier of other land in respect of an intrusion from the land of the one to the land of the other. The accommodation between occupiers of land there laid down was that things liable to escape must be kept by an occupier within his bounds unless their presence within those bounds was due to a natural use of his land. The liability and the excuse both relate to the use of land as affecting other land. I do not regard *Rylands* v. *Fletcher* as laying down any principle other than a principle applicable between occupiers in respect of their land or as reflecting an aspect of some wider principle applicable to dangerous businesses or dangerous things. For the purposes of my opinion, therefore, it is unnecessary to consider whether or not the use of land here in question was a natural use, but I desire to express my agreement with the observations which the noble and learned Lord on the woolsack has made with reference to *Rickards* v. *Lothian* and *Rainham Chemical Works Ltd.* v. *Belvedere Fish Guano Co.* I would only add that "natural" does not mean "primitive." . . .

Note:

As Scott L.J. said at the outset of his excellent judgment in the Court of Appeal, "This case is elemental. It goes to the roots of the common law." Its result he paraphrased by saying " . . . our law of torts is concerned not with activities but with acts." The case decided conclusively that a person injured on the land of another must prove negligence in that other, failing the intervention of the legislature or the attack of a wild beast. But in effect it did more than that. It cast some doubt on the question whether a person could recover damages for personal injuries even in a case where *Rylands* v. *Fletcher* was otherwise a relevant authority, and set a limit to the extension of that doctrine. In other words, if *Donoghue* v. *Stevenson* laid down that negligence is normally sufficient for liability, this case asserts that it is normally necessary. And what could be more important than that?

Question:

A tenant's premises are flooded by water which (a) comes on to the premises because the landlord's gutter is blocked, and (b) stays on the premises because the landlord's drain is blocked. The tenant can recover in (a) but not in (b). (*Duke of Westminster* v. *Guild* [1984] 3 All E.R. 144, 152 (C.A.)). Is this rational?

PART V

ANIMALS

INTRODUCTION

ANIMALS are anomalies. They are things, not people. But, like people, these things are self-propelled; cattle-chattels *stray*—to taste the grass on the far side of the fence or to tangle with a Jaguar on the highway. And, like people, they *attack*—animals bite and scratch, butt and gore. Animals are both tiresome and dangerous. But, even so, pre-industrial society is not going to make the keeper of an animal pay for all the damage it does. Animals are too useful. Alive or dead they give milk and meat, strength and warmth. Or some do. So the law, as is its function, makes distinctions.

It distinguishes first between straying and attacking. As to straying, it mattered both whither and whence. If cattle strayed on to the highway, the keeper used not to be liable even if he was careless; if they strayed on to private land, the keeper was liable even if he was not careless; if they strayed there from the highway, the person who took them on to the highway was liable only if he was careless. Each rule had a separate justification, but the first has been reprobated by those who think the highway is for cars not cows, and their view has prevailed. As to attacking, it mattered what kind of species the animal belonged to; the tiger and the lamb may have the same Creator but they call for different rules. The keeper was not liable to a person attacked by a domesticated animal unless he knew that it was given to attacks of that kind, but a person who kept a wild beast, even a docile one, was liable for all the damage it did.

The subject has fascinated law reformers because it seems unduly complicated, but the legislation resulting from the study and recommendations of the Law Commission (Civil Liability for Animals (Law Com. 13, 1967)) maintains most of the old distinctions and most of the old rules.

Readers of this book who have noted the extent to which the general principles of liability for negligence have subverted existing rules adapted to particular subject-matters such as family, property and governmental administration will not be surprised to learn that the general principles have also entered this area with considerable effect. (See, for example, *Bativala* v. *West* [1970] 1 Q.B. 716 and *Draper* v. *Hodder* [1972] 2 Q.B. 556.) This no doubt reflects the view of the Goddard Committee which said that: "There should be no special rules as to damage done by animals." (Cmnd. 8746 (1953), para. 5.) Considering the distinctive qualities of animals mentioned above, it is hard to see why special rules should be avoided or, indeed, how they could be.

Chapter 12

ANIMALS

ANIMALS ACT 1971

1.—(1) The provisions of sections 2 to 5 of this Act replace—

(*a*) the rules of the common law imposing a strict liability in tort for damage done by an animal on the ground that the animal is regarded as ferae naturae or that its vicious or mischievous propensities are known or presumed to be known;

(*b*) subsections (1) and (2) of section 1 of the Dogs Act 1906 as amended by the Dogs (Amendment) Act 1928 (injury to cattle or poultry); and

(*c*) the rules of the common law imposing a liability for cattle trespass.

(2) Expressions used in those sections shall be interpreted in accordance with the provisions of section 6 (as well as those of section 11) of this Act.

2.—(1) Where any damage is caused by an animal which belongs to a dangerous species, any person who is a keeper of the animal is liable for the damage, except as otherwise provided by this Act.

(2) Where damage is caused by an animal which does not belong to a dangerous species, a keeper of the animal is liable for the damage, except as otherwise provided by this Act, if—

(*a*) the damage is of a kind which the animal, unless restrained, was likely to cause or which, if caused by the animal, was likely to be severe; and

(*b*) the likelihood of the damage or of its being severe was due to characteristics of the animal which are not normally found in animals of the same species or are not normally so found except at particular times or in particular circumstances; and

(*c*) those characteristics were known to that keeper or were at any time known to a person who at that time had charge of the animal as that keeper's servant or, where that keeper is the head of a household, were known to another keeper of the animal who is a member of that household and under the age of 16.

3. Where a dog causes damage by killing or injuring livestock, any person who is a keeper of the dog is liable for the damage, except as otherwise provided by this Act.

4.—(1) Where livestock belonging to any person strays on to land in the ownership or occupation of another and—

(*a*) damage is done by the livestock to the land or to any property on it which is in the ownership or possession of the other person; or

(*b*) any expenses are reasonably incurred by that other person in keeping the livestock while it cannot be restored to the person to whom it belongs or while it is detained in pursuance of section 7 of this Act, or in ascertaining to whom it belongs;

the person to whom the livestock belongs is liable for the damages or expenses, except as otherwise provided by this Act.

(2) For the purposes of this section any livestock belongs to the person in whose possession it is.

5.—(1) A person is not liable under sections 2 to 4 of this Act for any damage which is due wholly to the fault of the person suffering it.

(2) A person is not liable under section 2 of this Act for any damage suffered by a person who has voluntarily accepted the risk thereof.

(3) A person is not liable under section 2 of this Act for any damage caused by an animal kept on any premises or structure to a person trespassing there, if it is proved either—

- (*a*) that the animal was not kept there for the protection of persons or property; or
- (*b*) (if the animal was kept there for the protection of persons or property) that keeping it there for that purpose was not unreasonable.

(4) A person is not liable under section 3 of this Act if the livestock was killed or injured on land on to which it had strayed and either the dog belonged to the occupier or its presence on the land was authorised by the occupier.

(5) A person is not liable under section 4 of this Act where the livestock strayed from a highway and its presence there was a lawful use of the highway.

(6) In determining whether any liability for damage under section 4 of this Act is excluded by subsection (1) of this section the damage shall not be treated as due to the fault of the person suffering it by reason only that he could have prevented it by fencing; but a person is not liable under that section where it is proved that the straying of the livestock on to the land would not have occurred but for a breach by any other person, being a person having an interest in the land, of a duty to fence.

6.—(1) The following provisions apply to the interpretation of sections 2 to 5 of this Act.

(2) A dangerous species is a species—

- (*a*) which is not commonly domesticated in the British Islands; and
- (*b*) whose fully grown animals normally have such characteristics that they are likely, unless restrained, to cause severe damage or that any damage they may cause is likely to be severe.

(3) Subject to subsection (4) of this section, a person is a keeper of an animal if—

- (*a*) he owns the animal or has it in his possession; or
- (*b*) he is the head of a household of which a member under the age of 16 owns the animal or has it in his possession;

and if at any time an animal ceases to be owned by or to be in the possession of a person, any person who immediately before that time was a keeper thereof by virtue of the preceding provisions of this subsection continues to be a keeper of the animal until another person becomes a keeper thereof by virtue of those provisions.

(4) Where an animal is taken into and kept in possession for the purpose of preventing it from causing damage or of restoring it to its owner, a person is not a keeper of it by virtue only of that possession.

(5) Where a person employed as a servant by a keeper of an animal incurs a risk incidental to his employment he shall not be treated as accepting it voluntarily.

Questions

1. Does section 2(1) alter the result of *Weller & Co.* v. *Foot and Mouth Disease Research Institute* [1966] 1 Q.B. 569?

2. Am I liable under section 2(2) when my cat eats my neighbour's goldfish?

3. If a stranger maliciously releases a tiger from a zoo, is the zoo liable for the expenses of the police in warning the local population and catching the tiger?

4. How can damage *caused* by an animal ever be *due* wholly to the fault of the person to whom it is done?

5. What about bees?

6. No fewer than 5,560 postmen were bitten by dogs in 1986. Is it likely that many of them recovered damages?

Note:

We have an instance of the application of the Act in the extempore opinions of the Court of Appeal in *Cummings* v. *Granger* [1977] Q.B. 397, reversing judgment for the plaintiff below. The plaintiff trespassed one night in the defendant's scrapyard and was badly bitten by the untrained Alsatian guard dog which she knew was allowed to roam at large there. Section 2(2)(*a*): The damage was a bite. This Alsatian was not likely to bite, but any bite would likely be severe. Section 2(2)(*b*): This dog was a perfectly normal Alsatian. Like other Alsatians, however, it was excitable (and hence likely to bite) when used as a guard dog ("particular circumstances"). Section 2(2)(*c*): The defendant knew that the dog was excitable when on guard. The requirements of section 2 were accordingly satisfied and the defendant was liable unless he could establish a defence. Section 5(1): The damage was partly, but not wholly, due to the fault of the plaintiff. Section 5(2): The plaintiff did not voluntarily accept the risk of this damage by entering premises without permission when she knew this was apt to excite the dog. Section 5(3): The plaintiff was a trespasser, and although the dog was kept there to protect property (s.5(3)(*a*)), it was not unreasonable to keep it there for that purpose (s.5(3)(*b*)).

Apparently if you fall off a camel, your injuries are damage caused by the animal, which, being of a dangerous species, renders its keeper strictly liable therefor: *Tutin* v. *Mary Chipperfield Promotions Ltd.*, May 23, 1980 (Cantley J.).

The well-bred Lord Justice was nervous and unpredictable, and on one occasion, instead of entering his horse-box in a docile manner, lunged into it and crushed the arm of the plaintiff groom. Lord Justice was not vicious, but his unpredictability was a "characteristic not normally found in horses" and was known to the defendant owner, so the plaintiff's claim succeeded. Similar success would probably not have attended her concurrent claim for negligence. *Wallace* v. *Newton* [1982] 2 All E.R. 106 (Park J.).

Section 2(2) caused puzzlement in the Court of Appeal in *Breeden* v. *Lampard* (March 21, 1985), where Lloyd L.J. said " . . . the concluding words of s.2(2) . . . may be designed to meet an argument by an owner:—'My horse did not have any abnormal characteristics even though it was liable to kick all the time, because all horses are liable to kick some of the time, *e.g.* when crowded from behind.'—in other words, the concluding words are refining what is meant by abnormality, not imposing a head of liability contrary to the main thrust of s.2(2)(b) of the Act." Oliver L.J. said "I cannot believe that Parliament intended to impose liability for what is essentially normal behaviour in all animals of that species."

PART VI

TORTS TO CHATTELS

INTRODUCTION

IF England had a rational system of law there would be no need for a special section on torts to chattels and this chapter could be entirely suppressed. It is quite true that goods get lost or stolen as well as damaged, and that commercial wrongdoing is not exactly like dangerous behaviour, but the tort of negligence can perfectly well embrace cases where a person has been indirectly deprived of a physical asset and the tort of trespass can cope with cases of forthright snatching. In a rational system this would be quite adequate, for a plaintiff who had lost goods would obtain *tort* damages from a defendant only if he was to blame for their loss.

Two conditions would have to be fulfilled before the role of tort could be so sensibly restricted: first, the law of property must provide a means whereby the owner of goods can get them back from whoever is in possession of them; secondly, the law of contract, rather than the law of tort, must regulate the right of contractors to the property they contract about. Neither condition is satisfied in England.

Property

The common law has no special remedy for the owner of a thing who wishes to claim it back from the person in possession of it. This gap has therefore to be filled by a remedy in tort. Unfortunate consequences ensue. The first is to introduce into tort law an area of liability without fault: this is unavoidable, because however innocent a person may be in acquiring possession of a thing he must deliver it up to the true owner unless he has some special right to retain it. The second consequence is to raise problems about who may sue: in a property remedy we would naturally define the plaintiff in terms of his *ownership* or other property right, but when the remedy is in tort one tends to regard the plaintiff's *loss* as a necessary and sufficient criterion of eligibility to sue. This may, thirdly, give rise to multiple plaintiffs when different people have concurrent interests in the thing. Tort has its own problems, as we have seen, when several people suffer loss as a result of injury to person or property, but these problems will be greatly extended if we make tort perform a property role as well. Fourthly, what of the plaintiff's behaviour? In tort cases his contributory negligence has a role to play in reducing the damages he obtains. This can hardly happen in a property remedy: the owner either gets his thing back or he doesn't. Fifthly, what of the defendant? In a property remedy we would insist that the defendant be in actual possession of the thing: after all, an owner who wants his thing back must sue the person who actually has it. In a tort suit we would be more interested in the defendant's past behaviour—what did he do with the thing?—than in his present position or possession. Sixthly, if the owner, not being bound to sue the present possessor, can sue all those through whose hands the goods have passed, there will be grave problems of multiple defendants. We have seen what happens in proper tort cases—the victim may sue any or all of the tortfeasors until he has been paid off, and then those who have paid more than their fair share can claim contribution from those who have paid less (above, p. 66)—but one cannot simply apply this solution to litigation about lost property. Finally, what order is the judge to make? In tort cases he orders the defendant to pay monetary compensation, but in a property remedy he may have to order specific restitution, and if that is impossible he will be tempted to order the defendant to pay the value of the thing even if that differs from the sum which he would award as compensation. These are the problems which arise when tort takes on the role of property law.

Contract

The second condition required for rationality is that tort should not encroach on the role of contract. Where two people are in a voluntary relationship about a thing, the terms of that relationship should control their reciprocal rights in the thing. This is true whether the contract envisages a transfer of the ownership of the thing (as in sale) or only of its possession (as in contracts for hire, repair, carriage etc., all those relationships so usefully called "bailments" in the common law). One would expect a special relationship to make a difference, here as elsewhere: the man you *trust* with a thing (as every equity lawyer knows) is in a different position towards you from the man who just happens to come by your thing. If you pretend to apply the same rules to such different situations, you will have either to bend the rules or to put up with bad results.

Let us test this by contrasting two possessors, one who holds the thing under a contract with the owner and one who does not. If A takes his car to the B garage for repair, a bailment arises between A and B: A has trusted B with his car (more accurately, with the possession of his car). If B now wrongfully sells the car to C and delivers it to him, C will be in possession of A's car, as B was, but C's position *vis-à-vis* A will be different from B's, because A has not trusted C with the car. There is no relationship between A and C, except that C has A's thing, whereas the relationship between A and B is very special, because A permitted B to have his thing.

As we shall see, B is guilty of conversion for selling the car and C is likewise guilty of conversion for buying it, but let us ignore that fact for the moment and concentrate on the differences which arise because of the presence or absence of a contract with the owner. First, B, knowing that the car is not his, must be under a duty to take steps to protect it from harm. C, not knowing that the car is not his, cannot be under any duty to protect it or even to refrain from damaging it: a person who reasonably believes that he owns a car can hardly be liable for wrecking it. Secondly, if the car is destroyed and the possessor receives the insurance money or damages from the tortfeasor responsible, B must—but C will not—hold this money in trust for A in priority to his own creditors. Thirdly, if A demands his car from B, B must, one would have thought, hand it over without the slightest demur regarding A's title to the car: after all, B has promised to return the car to A, and his promise is not conditional on the car's actually belonging to A (though of course B will be bound to give it up to the true owner on demand). C, on the other hand, has never seen A, let alone promised him to return the car, so he can insist that A prove his entitlement. Finally, one can see that unless C is actually in possession when A makes demand on him, C should be under no liabilty to A at all, whereas if B has ceased to be in possession through his wrongful act he will be liable whenever A makes demand on him. These instances sufficiently show that one cannot treat all possessors as equal: much depends on whether the possessor received the thing directly from the claimant or not, that is, on whether there was a special relationship or not. These differences have been rather ignored by English law, which still holds possessors of both types liable in conversion.

Before we turn to the actual English law we must say a word about ownership and possession. The distinction is basically simple: ownership is a legal right, possession a physical fact. The owner is entitled to a thing, whether he has it or not; the possessor has it, whether he is entitled to it or not. Proudhon, the revolutionary, put the point in a neat but nasty way: the husband owns, the lover possesses.

The matter does not stay so simple for long. First, possession is easily proved by witnesses, whereas ownership can only be established by laborious examination of the ownership of predecessors. One is therefore tempted to let a plaintiff rely on his possession rather than require him to establish ownership. Secondly, possession needs to be protected as a matter of public order. Expropriation may be unjust, but dispossession is unruly, so we must give a remedy to people whose possession is invaded, sometimes even if it is invaded by the owner: as Sohm said, the justice of ownership yields to the order of possession.

But now see what we have done. If we let the possessor as such regain or retain possession, possession has itself become a ground of entitlement: the fact of possession gives rise to the right to possess. But ownership itself is important mainly because it gives rise to the right to possess. The concept of "right to possess" thus becomes a sort of half-way house between ownership and possession, blurring both. But it is worse than that, for a right to possess may arise from a contract as well as from ownership and possession, for example, the purchaser of goods to whom delivery has been promised. (And a contract may transfer an owner's right to possess, as when a finance company lets a car on hire-purchase.)

Thus there is a confusion between the categories of property, contract and tort, and also a blurring of the concepts of ownership and possession and of the distinction between the right to possess which arises from each of them and the right to possess which arises from a contract. A case in 1963 (below p. 428) shows how wretchedly the law of England in this area operates. The bona fide purchaser of a stolen car took it to his garage for repair. It was swiped from the garage by a man who thought it belonged to the finance company which employed him. In fact it belonged to an associated company, so he gave the car back to it, the rightful owner. In his suit against the employer, the bona fide purchaser recovered the full value of a car he never owned and which he was in any case about to lose!

This amazing result was reached at a time when there were three torts operating in the area—trespass, detinue and conversion. We need a word about each, since although detinue has been abolished, no existing right of action has thereby been impaired.

As we have seen in an earlier chapter, a person who intentionally interferes with goods in the possession of another is guilty of *trespass* and is liable for any resulting harm unless he can justify his interference. The proper plaintiff in a trespass action is the person in actual possession of the goods at the time; unfortunately people with only a right to possess have sometimes been allowed to sue. It is also unfortunate that people who have misbehaved with a chattel entrusted to them have sometimes been held liable in trespass; such people should be liable on the ground that they cannot excuse their inability to return the thing, but they have not invaded anyone's possession, so they should not be liable as *trespassers*.

A person who treats goods as if they were his when they are not is liable to be sued in *conversion*. This is said to turn on the defendant's *denial of the plaintiff's title*. Some explanation is required.

If I sell a person's goods without his consent, I should certainly be liable to him: it would be quite wrong for me, however innocent I was, to keep the price of someone else's goods. Again, if I buy goods from someone not empowered to sell them, and they do not become mine, I should obviously have to give them up to the true owner: it would be quite wrong for me, however innocent I was, to keep someone else's goods. Thus the seller and the buyer of a third party's goods are rightly held liable to the true owner, though for quite different reasons. The common lawyers, however, with their characteristic penchant for false analysis, decided that there was only one reason, namely that buyer and seller alike were guilty of a denial of the true owner's title. Once this false rationalisation is made, two results follow. First, the buyer becomes liable even if he no longer has the goods, because now the wrong is thought to consist in the purchase, not in the retention after demand. Secondly, the auctioneer becomes liable, although he doesn't keep the price of the goods he sells. This is extremely odd. Just as the auctioneer's very job is to sell other people's goods, so the carrier's is to carry them. Now if A gives B's goods to C for carriage, C is not liable to B for carrying them, so why should C be strictly liable to B for selling goods which A has given him for sale? The answer given, forsooth, is that in selling the goods as A's he is denying B's title to them. Note that the liability of purchaser and seller is strict in the sense that they are liable however carefully they may have checked the title of their vendor or principal. A possessor who refuses to hand over the thing to a person entitled to demand it also commits conversion, and other acts which result in the loss of the goods may be construed as denials of the claimant's title, though in some cases the defendant must have had knowledge that he was doing wrong. However, conversion always required a positive act: losing a thing or letting it get stolen might lead to liability in detinue, but it did not constitute conversion until the 1977 Act, which abolished detinue, came into force (below p. 436).

To be able to bring a claim in conversion it is neither necessary nor sufficient to own the thing: what is required is a "right to immediate possession." Any person who has such a right may sue, even if his right arises only by contract; a person who has no such right cannot sue, even if he is the owner. An owner may give up his right to immediate possession by contracting it away; whether he has actually given it up depends on the bailment—the gratuitous lender is always entitled to repossess, as is the bailor whose bailee has misconducted himself, so in such cases bailors can sue notwithstanding the bailment.

Detinue, which has now been abolished, could be brought by a bailor against his bailee or by a person entitled to possess a thing against the person in actual possession of it. This form of action was especially useful to a claimant who wanted the goods themselves rather than money damages, since only in detinue could the judge order specific delivery. If the defendant no longer had the thing, he obviously could not hand it over, but the bailee would be liable in damages if his inability to return the thing was due to his positive act, such as giving it to someone else, or his failure to look after it properly. Detinue thus had two advantages: it gave rise, as against a possessor, to a right to have the thing back, and it made a bailee liable for carelessly ceasing to possess. The 1977 Act allows a judge to order the redelivery of the thing in any appropriate case, and it turns the wrongful failure to look after a thing into an act of conversion. So detinue has gone only in name.

In 1967 the Lord Chancellor asked the Law Reform Committee to consider the law of detinue and conversion; trespass was added to the brief at the Committee's request, and in 1971 the Committee produced its Eighteenth Report (Cmnd. 4774), with the following principal recommendations:

(1) that the three existing torts should be replaced by a new tort;

(2) that in general there should continue to be liability wherever there was liability under any of the old torts, and that in particular the strict liability imposed in conversion should remain;

(3) that any person with a possessory or proprietary interest in the chattel (other than a purely equitable interest) should be entitled to sue;

(4) that the measure of recovery in each case should be the amount of the plaintiff's loss;

(5) that so far as possible all interested parties should be brought into the suit, and that the defendant should therefore be permitted to show that others had a better interest than the plaintiff;

(6) that contributory negligence should not be a defence;

(7) that the court should have discretion to order the return of the chattel as an alternative to payment of damages;

(8) that remedies in this tort should continue to concur with remedies for breach of contract.

By no means all of these recommendations are implemented in the Torts (Interference with Goods) Act 1977. Only detinue is abolished: tort liability in conversion and trespass remains exactly as before. Certainly the Act introduces "wrongful interference with goods" but this is not a new tort, it is just a new term, a simple way of referring to all torts which involve lost or damaged goods, not only conversion and trespass but also negligence and any other tort. Such a term was useful because the Act applies to all such torts a number of new rules, mainly procedural in character. One such rule empowers a judge to order specific delivery in any suitable case. Another rule, which provides that a claimant's title is extinguished on full payment or settlement, will be useful where there are several possible defendants. Where there are several possible claimants, it is best if they all join in a single suit, so that each can receive the right amount. Provision is therefore made for the amalgamation of suits begun in different courts. Further, the defendant is allowed to mention, and the plaintiff may be required to disclose, the existence of other possible claimants: these may forfeit their rights if they fail, after notification, to join in the suit. If a second claimant appears after a first claimant has already been paid, the first must account for any excess to the second, and if this results in over-payment to the second, he must hand over the excess to the wrongdoer.

Two proposals in particular were not implemented by the Act: (1) that anyone could sue if he had a possessory or proprietary interest in the goods, and (2) that the measure of recovery in all cases should be the amount of the plaintiff's loss. It is therefore necessary, in order to ascertain the existing law on these important topics, to familiarise oneself with the law as it was before the Act.

Chapter 13

TORTS TO CHATTELS

Section 1.—Title to Sue

(i) *Conversion*

LORD v. PRICE

Court of Exchequer (1873) L.R. 9 Exch. 54; 43 L.J.Ex. 49; 30 L.T. 271; 22 W.R. 318

The plaintiff bought two lots of cotton at an auction. He thereby became owner of them. The terms of the sale were that payment should be made immediately after the auction, but the plaintiff paid only the deposit. He collected one lot, but when he returned for the other, he discovered that the defendant had taken it in mistake for a lot which he had purchased at the same sale.

The plaintiff was nonsuited at the Passage Court, Liverpool. He moved for a new trial, but the rule was discharged.

Bramwell B.: I am of opinion that this rule must be discharged, on the ground that the action cannot be maintained without a right of present possession in the plaintiff. Here there is no evidence that the plaintiff had any right of possession; that right was in the vendor, who was entitled to retain possession of the goods until the balance of the purchase-money was paid, and, on non-payment, to resell the goods and recoup himself for any loss sustained on re-sale. Therefore, if the goods were tortiously removed (and there is no evidence that the vendor assented to their removal) it is manifest that the vendor could have maintained an action. But it cannot be that two men can be entitled at the same time to maintain an action of trover for the same goods. It is, therefore, abundantly manifest that the vendor could, and that the plaintiff cannot, maintain this action.

Whether, by paying the balance of the price now, or tendering it, the buyer can, either in an action of trover or by a special action on the case, have any remedy at Common Law in his own name, or whether he is limited to an action in the name of the vendor, it is not necessary now to pronounce. It is sufficient to say that, on the facts shewn here, the plaintiff cannot recover.

Note:

It seems very hard that the owner of goods should not be able to get them from a person who possesses them and has no title to them. But if the plaintiff had been allowed to recover in this action, he would have been in the very happy position of having a bale of cotton (or its value) for which he had not paid and for which he could not be made to pay. Conversion actions cannot be regarded as involving just the plaintiff and the defendants. Here the plaintiff could not sue because he did not have possession of the goods at the time of the defendant's act, and he did not at that time have the right to their immediate, that is, unconditional, possession. He could only get possession by paying the vendor the balance of the price. But Bramwell B. was wrong in saying that it is never possible for two persons to have the right to maintain conversion in respect of the same goods at the same time. Whenever there is a bailment such that the bailor may resume possession on demand, either party to the bailment may sue a stranger in conversion. (*Nicolls* v. *Bastard* (1835) 2 Cr.M. & R. 659; 150 E.R. 279, Parke B., *arguendo*.)

If the vendor had *delivered* the cotton to the defendant, then the plaintiff could have main-tained his action; for the act of the vendor would have destroyed his lien for the price (*Chinery v. Viall* (1860) 5 H. & N. 288; 157 E.R. 1192).

On the facts as they were, there seems little reason to doubt that if the plaintiff had paid the price to the auctioneer, he could then demand the goods of the defendant, and, if he did not deliver them up, sue him for the conversion constituted by the refusal to deliver. But if the defendant had sold them already, he would have to find the person with the goods, or a per-son who had had dealings with them after the payment of the price, as the plaintiff must have had title to sue at the moment of the conversion founded upon.

MOORGATE MERCANTILE CO. v. FINCH (and READ)

Court of Appeal [1962] 1 Q.B. 701; [1962] 3 W.L.R. 110; 106 S.J. 284; [1962] 2 All E.R. 467

Finch (who later disappeared without trace) took a car on hire-purchase terms from the plaintiff company on October 5, 1960, but did not pay the instalment due on November 5. On November 9 he left it at a garage for repairs, and when he came to fetch it the garage owner asked him to lend it to a person unnamed. Finch agreed, since he owed the garage owner some money. The man in question was Read, the second defendant and the only one served. He used it to carry 675 Swiss watches which had been smuggled into the country. He was caught, charged, convicted and imprisoned, and the car was forfeited and sold under the Customs and Excise Act 1952.

The plaintiff company claimed damages for conversion, the value of the car; they said they were entitled to the immediate possession of the car under clause 11 of the agreement, since Finch had defaulted on his payments, had lent the car to an unknown person and had permitted it to be used for an illegal purpose; and they said that Read's act constituted a conversion because he used it in such a way that it became liable to forefeiture.

Judgment was given for the plaintiff, and the second defendant appealed. In unreserved judgments the Court of Appeal dismissed the appeal.

Danckwerts L.J.: . . . The first question to decide is whether what the second defendant did constituted a conversion. What he did, of course, was to go to the place where the car happened to be, to borrow it and then fill it up with uncustomed goods, which conduct was likely to result in the consequence, which indeed in fact happened, that the car was seized by the Customs authorities and sold. I think it is clear, and it seems to me to be an irresistible inference, that when he went to bor-row the car, he had already in his mind the intention of using it for the illegal pur-poses for which he did in fact use it, and I think that if he had not deceived the persons who were concerned with the car about his intentions, that is to say, the hirer and the garage owner, they would not have allowed him to take it. In any case it seems to me that the consequences of what he did resulted in a conversion of the car in question.

The county court judge cited a passage from *Salmond on Torts*, 13th ed., (1961), p. 262: "Conversion Defined: A conversion is an act of wilful interference, without lawful justification, with any chattel in a manner inconsistent with the right of another, whereby that other is deprived of the use and possession of it. Two elements are combined in such interference: (1) a dealing with the chattel in a man-ner inconsistent with the right of the person entitled to it, and (2) an intention in so doing to deny that person's right or to assert a right which is in fact inconsistent with such right."

What the second defendant did in fact was to take the car and use it in a way which necessarily resulted, or might, at any rate, in all probability, result in the owners being deprived of the car for ever, because he had placed the watches in the car, and that, if it was found out, would inevitably give the Customs authorities a right to confiscate the car with, of course, a final loss of it to the plaintiffs if that event occurred. It seems to me that whether the second defendant intended that consequence to follow or not—presumably he did not intend it, but hoped he would not be found out—nonetheless, he must be taken to intend the consequences which were likely to happen from the conduct of which he was guilty, and which did in fact result in the loss of the car to the plaintiffs. To my mind, there is no doubt whatever that there was a conversion by the second defendant.

The next point which arises is, had the plaintiffs an immediate right to possession at the time of the conversion, so that they were entitled to sue the second defendant. That depends on clause 11 of the agreement. It is really sufficient to take the first part of the clause. "In case of any and every breach of any term or condition hereof the owners shall forthwith without notice or demand become entitled immediately to recover possession of the vehicle," and then certain options are given to them.

If that applies—that is to say, if there had been a breach by the hirer—they were entitled immediately to recover possession of the vehicle. There were three breaches which had been committed by the hirer, or might have been committed by the hirer. The question remains whether they were or were not in fact breaches. There was an instalment of the hire-purchase payments in arrear. That was a plain breach. Secondly, there was a question whether there was a breach by the loan of the car to the second defendant in the circumstances of this case. Thirdly, there might be a breach by using the car for an illegal purpose.

The county court judge rejected the last as a breach, I think rightly, because the second defendant never made known the illegal purpose for which he intended to use the car to either the hirer or the garage owner. The judge was inclined to doubt whether lending the car in the circumstances would amount to a breach of the contract of hire-purchase. I feel some doubt whether he did reach the right conclusion on that matter, but it is not necessary to pursue it further, because there was plainly a breach by the failure to pay the hire-purchase instalment when it became due.

Then on the face of clause 11 of the agreement the plaintiffs became immediately entitled to possession of the vehicle in question, . . .

It says: "In case of any and every breach of any term or condition hereof the owners shall forthwith without notice or demand become entitled to recover possession of the vehicle." It seems to me, therefore, that they were entitled to recover possession of the vehicle on the terms of that clause, and could clearly sue the second defendant in conversion.

That disposes of the point whether there was any conversion and whether the plaintiffs had any immediate right under the terms of this clause which enabled them to sue the second defendant.

Questions

1. Suppose that Read did not know that the watches were uncustomed. Would the risk of forfeiture be any the less? Would the result of the case have been the same?

2. Would Finch have had any claim against Read?

3. The plaintiff was held to have title to sue because he could immediately repossess the vehicle from the first defendant. Would the plaintiff have been able to sue if the contract had fallen within the Consumer Credit Act 1974, and no notice of default had been served in accordance with section 87? Suppose that Finch had paid more than one-third of the hire-purchase price, so as to exclude the right of the plaintiffs to repossess without a court order, under section 90. Could the plaintiffs have recovered against Read? Do your answers make any kind of practical sense? How do you explain the holding of the Court of Appeal in *Union Transport Finance* v. *British Car Auctions* [1978] 2 All E.R. 385 that a hire-purchase contract

which provided that it could be terminated after notice of default could be terminated for
default even without notice?

Note:

By agreement between the plaintiff factors and a company the company was to hand over to
the plaintiff any cheque paid to it by a debtor. At a time when the company, now in liquidation, was in difficulties, the defendant director received four cheques from debtors to the
company and paid them into the company account, knowing that this was in breach of the
company's agreement with the plaintiff. The plaintiff sued him in conversion, and to the
defendant's objection that the plaintiff had no title to sue, the answer was that if not a contractual right, then an equitable right as *cestui que trust* was sufficient. *International Factors Ltd.*
v. *Rodriguez* [1979] Q.B. 351 (C.A.). (This is contrary to the proposals of the Law Reform
Committee (18th Report, para. 34)).

Why did the plaintiff not sue for inducing breach of contract (below p. 499)?

(ii) *Trespass*

WILSON v. LOMBANK LTD.

Assizes [1963] 1 W.L.R. 1294; [1963] 1 All E.R. 740

The plaintiff unsuspectingly bought a Renault Dauphine car from a person who had
no right to sell it. He took it to his garage for repairs. The defendant's servant saw it
there, and thought it belonged to the finance company which employed him. He
accordingly took it, without the assent of the garage owner. In fact it belonged to
another finance company, to whom the defendant then returned it.

The plaintiff was held entitled to recover the value of the car as repaired.

Hinchcliffe J.: . . . It is in these circumstances that the plaintiff submits that he was
in possession of the motor-car; that the defendants had no right to take the car
away; and that since the plaintiff was in possession and the defendants had no legal
title, it is not open to the defendants to assert that the title rests in another person.
In other words, the plaintiff says that possession here is title.

The defendants, through their counsel, Mr. Fox-Andrews, present an interesting
argument. They concede that an action for trespass in respect of a personal chattel
would lie if, at the time of the taking of the chattel, the plaintiff was in possession of
it. It is submitted that a person is in possession in law if he has actual possession,
constructive possession, or an immediate right to possession. In the circumstances
of this case Mr. Fox-Andrews contends that the plaintiff did not have actual possession and he did not have constructive possession, since the motor-car was in the
hands of a garage for repairs. And he further submits that the plaintiff did not have
an immediate right to possession since this is something which only arises in the
case of a gratuitous bailment, which this was not. Furthermore, it is submitted that
because the motor-car was in for repairs, the garage had a lien on it, and therefore
the plaintiff could not have had an immediate right of possession. In support of this
argument my attention was drawn to *United States of America and Republic of
France* v. *Dollfus Mieg et Cie S.A. and Bank of England* ([1952] A.C. 582). Also I
was referred to Vol. 2 and Vol. 38 of *Halsbury's Laws of England*, 3rd ed., pp. 133
and 787 respectively.

Mr. Fox-Andrews further submits that even if the plaintiff did have an immediate
right of possession, his claim is defeated by virtue of the fact that on April 16, 1960,
the defendants returned the motor-car to the true owners. . . .

Mr. Best, on behalf of the plaintiff, agrees that "possession" includes constructive possession; the right to immediate possession; and, of course, actual possession. Mr. Best relies on *United States of America and Republic of France* v. *Dolfus Mieg et Cie S.A. and Bank of England*, to which I have already referred, and he draws my attention to certain observations in the speech of Lord Porter ([1952] A.C. 582, 611). Lord Porter referred to a portion of the judgment of Mellish L.J. in *Ancona* v. *Rogers* ((1876) 1 Ex.D. 285), and after he had quoted those words Lord Porter went on as follows: "It is urged, however, that these 'dicta' are 'obiter,' and wrong; that, in any case, the judgment was not concerned with 'possession' as opposed to property and that the true view is that the rule applies only in a case where the bailor has the property and the bailee has the possession. In such a case it is maintained that the bailor can sue in right of his property but that an action in right of possession belongs to the bailee only. This contention may be true where the bailor has no right to demand an immediate return of the article at his will, but the better opinion is, I think, that where the bailor can at any moment demand the return of the object bailed, he still has possession."

Mr. Best also submits that as to the question of lien, here there was a monthly account between the plaintiff and the Haven Garage Co. Ltd. The repairs had been completed. The motor-car was on the forecourt awaiting collection and there therefore was an implied term between the plaintiff and the Haven Garage that there was to be no lien.

I have summarised the submissions as briefly as I can, and I hope accurately. Giving those submissions the best consideration I can, in my judgment the plaintiff was in possession of the car; not only did he have the right to immediation possession, but I do not think that in the circumstances of this case he ever lost possession of the car. In my view the plaintiff at all times could have demanded the return of the car, and I would, with respect, like to adopt the words of Lord Porter in his speech which I have just quoted. I do not think there was a lien on the motor-car, having regard to the course of dealing between the plaintiff and the Haven Garage over a period of eight years, during which time there existed this monthly credit. On the view I have formed, that the plaintiff never lost possession of the motor-car, it seems to me that the defendants wrongfully took the car and that the plaintiff is entitled to recover damages.

As to the damages, the plaintiff submits that he is entitled to recover the sum of £470, that is to say, the amount that he paid for the motor-car, plus the cost of the repairs—£27 14s., plus the loss of profit that he would have made. The defendants submit that only the cost of the repairs is recoverable. In my judgment this is certainly not a case for exemplary damages. I am of the opinion that the plaintiff is entitled to recover the full value of the article wrongfully taken by the defendants. Here the full value was £470. To that sum there should be added the sum of £27 14s., the cost of the repairs. I am not prepared to speculate what the loss of profit would have been. In my judgment the plaintiff is entitled to recover the total of those two sums.

Questions

1. Could the plaintiff have sued in conversion?

2. What is the measure of damages in (a) conversion, (b) trespass?

3. What is the value of a car? How much damage does a person suffer if he loses the use of a car which he has no right to retain, or property which he is in fact soon going to lose? (See *Burmah Oil* v. *Lord Advocate* [1964] 2 All E.R. 348, 362).

4. If the owner of the car could sue both the plaintiff and the defendant in conversion, would they be tortfeasors "liable in respect of the same damage?" (See above, p. 67.) If so, how much damage has an owner suffered who has got his thing back? How would that damage be divided as between the plaintiff and the defendant?

5. See now Torts (Interference with Goods) Act 1977 (below p. 444) s.8(1). Does it affect the result of the principal case?

Section 2.—The Act of Conversion

HIORT v. BOTT

Court of Exchequer (1874) L.R. 9 Exch. 86; 43 L.J.Ex. 81; 30 L.T. 25; 22 W.R. 414

The defendant, a licensed victualler in Birmingham, had never had any dealings with the plaintiffs, who were corn-merchants in Hull, or with a broker they sometimes used, named Grimmett. He was therefore surprised one day to receive from them an invoice and a delivery order empowering him to collect from the railway station 83 quarters of barley, said to have been ordered by him through Grimmett. Grimmett had indeed put in the order, but as a fraud. A day or two later Grimmett called on the defendant, said that it was all a mistake, and asked the defendant to endorse over the delivery order so that it could be put right. The defendant did endorse over the delivery order and gave it to Grimmett. Grimmett collected the barley, sold it and made off with the proceeds.

The jury found that the defendant had no intention of appropriating the barley to his own use, but was anxious to correct a supposed error, with a view to returning the barley to the plaintiffs. Archibald J. directed a verdict for the defendant with leave to the plaintiffs to move to enter a verdict for £180, the value of the barley. The plaintiffs obtained a rule accordingly, and the rule was made absolute by the Court of Exchequer. That is, the plaintiffs won.

Bramwell B.: . . . I think the plaintiffs are entitled to recover; though, so far as concerns the defendant, whose act was well meant, I regret the result. Mr. Bosanquet gave a good description of what constitutes a conversion when he said that it is where a man does an unauthorised act which deprives another of his property permanently or for an indefinite time. The expression used in the declaration is "converted to his own use"; but that does not mean that the defendant consumed the goods himself; for, if a man gave a quantity of another person's wine to a friend to drink, and the friend drank it, that would no doubt be as much a conversion of the wine as if he drank it himself. Now here the defendant did an act that was unauthorised. There was no occasion for him to do it; for the delivery order made the barley deliverable to the order of the consignor or consignee, and if the defendant had done nothing at all it would have been delivered to the plaintiffs. And there is no doubt that by what he did he deprived the plaintiffs of their property; because, by means of this order so indorsed, Grimmett got the barley and made away with it, leaving the plaintiffs without any remedy against the railway company, who had acted according to the instructions of the plaintiffs in delivering the barley to the order of the consignee. The case, therefore, stands thus: that by an unauthorised act on the part of the defendant, the plaintiffs have lost their barley, without any remedy except against Grimmett, and that is worthless. It seems to me, therefore, that this was assuming a control over the disposition of these goods, and a causing them to be delivered to a person who deprived the plaintiffs of them. The conversion is therefore made out.

Various ingenious cases were put as to what would happen if, for instance, a parcel were left at your house by mistake, and you gave it to your servant to take back to the person who left it there, and the servant misappropriated it. Probably the safest way of dealing with that case is to wait until it arises; but I may observe that there is the difference between such a case and the present one, that where a man delivers a parcel to you by mistake, it is contemplated that if there is a mistake, you will do something with it. What are you to do with it? Warehouse it? No. Are you to turn it into the street? That would be an unreasonable thing to do. Does he not impliedly authorise you to take reasonable steps with regard to it—that is, to send it back by a trustworthy person? And when you say, "Go and deliver it to the person who sent it," are you in any manner converting it to your own use? That may be a question. But here the defendant did not send the order back; but at Grimmett's request indorsed it to him, though, no doubt, as the jury have found, with a view to the barley being returned to the plaintiffs. There is therefore a distinction between the case put and the present one. And there is also a distinction between the case of *Heugh* v. *London and North Western Ry.* ((1870) L.R. 5 Ex. 51), which was cited for the defendant, and the present case; because there it was taken that the plaintiff authorised the defendants to deliver the goods to a person applying for them, if they had reasonable grounds for believing him to be the right person.

On these considerations I think the plaintiffs are entitled to recover. But I must add one word. This is an action for conversion, and I lament that such a word should appear in our proceedings, which does not represent the real facts, and which always gives rise to a discussion as to what is, and what is not, a conversion. But supposing the case were stated according to a non-artificial system of pleading, thus: "We, the plaintiffs, had at the London and North Western Railway station certain barley. We had sent the delivery order to you, the defendant. You might have got it, if you were minded to be the buyer of it; you were not so minded, and therefore should have done nothing with it. Nevertheless, you ordered the London and North Western Railway Co. to deliver it, without any authority, to Grimmett, who took it away." Would not that have been a logical and precise statement of a tortious act on the part of the defendant, causing loss to the plaintiffs? It seems to me that it would. I think, but not without some regret, that this rule should be made absolute, to enter the verdict for the plaintiffs.

Cleasby B.: . . . It should be particularly noticed in this case that the plaintiffs had not, by what they had done, placed the defendant in any position of difficulty, as is often the case with an involuntary bailee (an expression often used in the argument) who has received property into his possession for a purpose which cannot, as it afterwards appears, be exactly carried into effect, and who does his best and acts in a reasonable manner for carrying into effect the purpose of the bailment. In such cases the bailee has a duty to perform in relation to the goods, and he is placed in a difficulty in the discharge of that duty by the default of the plaintiff, who ought not to be allowed to complain if, under that difficulty, the bailee has acted in a manner which is considered reasonable and proper.

But no difficulty of that sort arises here, . . .

It is also to be observed that the present case is different from a class of cases referred to in the argument, in which some act is done to goods, such as shoeing a horse, packing goods, or forwarding them on. In these cases no act is done having reference to the property in the goods or the right to the possession of them. The act is consistent with the title of any person. But in the present case the act of the defendant transfers the title to the possession of the goods, so as to cause them to be lost to the real owner.

. . .

It was not left to the jury in this case to say whether the conduct of the defendant was reasonable and proper, but I do not think that this was necessary. No objection was made in the argument that this had not been done; but it was unnecessary, because to transfer voluntarily the title to the possession of goods, in which you have no interest whatever, to a third person is, in my opinion, under the circumstances of the present case, obviously improper and unreasonable; and that is the ground of my judgment.

Questions
1. Did the defendants in this case behave reasonably? Would it be reasonable for them to behave in the same way today?
2. Would you describe the defendant's conduct as a cause of the plaintiff's loss?

3. Suppose that the defendants had wired the plaintiffs to discover if delivery to Grimmett were in order. Could they recover the cost of the telegram? See *The Winson* [1982] A.C. 939.

4. In *Elvin & Powell* v. *Plummer Roddis* (1934) 50 T.L.R. 158 the same fraud was tried with equal success, with a bundle of coats worth £350 instead of a delivery order. Hawke J. said: "If persons were involuntary bailees and had done everything reasonable they were not liable to pay damages if something which they did resulted in the loss of the property," and gave judgment for the defendant. Which case would you follow if a similar fraud involved a diamond ring?

ENGLAND v. COWLEY

Court of Exchequer (1873) L.R. 8 Exch. 126; 42 L.J.Ex. 80; 28 L.T. 67; 21 W.R. 337

Miss Morley owed money to both the defendant and the plaintiff. The defendant was her landlord, and she owed him six months' rent; the plaintiff had lent her money which she had not repaid. The dispute between them was over Miss Morley's furniture, which the plaintiff was empowered to take by a Bill of Sale signed by Miss Morley, and which the defendant could distrain on at common law, but only while the goods were on the premises and only during the hours of daylight. The plaintiff had put a man in the house in early August, and after sunset on the eleventh he sent round two men with vans to pick up the furniture. The defendant forbade them to take it away, and stationed a policeman at the gate to make sure they did not.

A verdict was entered for the defendant on instructions by Bramwell B. The plaintiff obtained a rule to enter a verdict for himself. The rule was discharged by the Court of Exchequer.

Bramwell B.: . . . I think no action is maintainable, because the defendant did no act, but only threatened that, in a certain event, he would do something. The plaintiff should either have proceeded with the removal of the goods, or at least have commenced to remove them, leaving the defendant to stop him at his peril, when there might have been a cause of action of some sort. But further, even if the defendant had prevented the removal of the goods by physical force, I do not think trover would have been maintainable. The substance of that action is the same as before the Common Law Procedure Act, 1852, and although in the form of declaration there given in sch. B the words used are, "converted to his own use, or wrongfully deprived the plaintiff of the use and possession of the plaintiff's goods," the gist of the action is the conversion, as for example, by consuming the goods or by refusing the true owner possession, the wrong-doer having himself at the time a physical control over the goods. Now here the defendant did not "convert" the goods to his own use, either by sale or in any other way. Nor did he deprive the plaintiff of them. All he did was to prevent, or threaten to prevent, the plaintiff from using them in a particular way. "You shall not remove them," he said, but the plaintiff still might do as he pleased with them in the house. Assume that there was actual prevention, still I think this action cannot be maintained. Take some analogous cases, by way of illustration. A man is going to fight a duel, and goes to a drawer to get one of his pistols. I say to him, "You shall not take that pistol of yours out of the drawer," and hinder his doing so. Is that a conversion of the pistol by me to my own use? Certainly not. Or, again, I meet a man on horseback going in a particular direction, and say to him, "You shall not go that way, you must turn back"; and make him comply. Who could say that I had been guilty of a conversion of the horse? Or I might prevent a man from pawning his watch, but no one would call that a conversion of the watch by me. And really this case is the same with these. Illustrations of my meaning might be easily multiplied. The truth is that, in order to maintain trover, a plaintiff who is left in possession of the goods must prove that his dominion over his property has been interfered with, not in some particular way, but altogether; that he has been entirely deprived of the use of it. It is not enough that a man should say that *something* shall not be done by the plaintiff; he must say that *nothing* shall. Now here there was no interference with the plaintiff's rights except the statement by the defendant that he would prevent the goods from being removed. This is not sufficient to furnish a basis for the present action. For it must be remembered that if the defendant is liable at all, it is for the value of the goods. But how unjust that would be! The plaintiff's man was left in possession. Miss Morley could not legally take away the goods. If she did, the plaintiff could maintain an action against her for their wrongful removal. Yet he is also to be able to recover their full value against the defendant. Moreover, I cannot but think that the jury really negatived all idea of conversion. "If you are of opinion," they were told, "that the defendant did not deprive the plaintiff of his goods, did not take possession of, nor assume dominion over them, but merely prevented the plaintiff from removing them from one place to another, allowing the plaintiff to remain in possession of them if he liked," then there is no cause of action. The jury answered this question in favour of the defendant. There had, therefore, been no general assertion of right to the exclusion of the plaintiff.

Questions

1. Would the answer have been the same if the defendant had had no claim in respect of the property whose removal he prohibited? Would it be the same if he had not owned the premises on which the goods were situated?

2. How far was the consideration that the measure of damages in conversion was then the whole value of the goods a factor which led to this result?

3. What would have happened if, the following morning, the plaintiff's man had stopped the defendant from taking possession of the goods?

4. Did the plaintiff act unreasonably?

Note:

In *Bird* v. *Jones* (above, p. 296) a similar attempt to use a form of strict liability failed, since the proper remedy for a person obstructed on the highway is public nuisance and not false imprisonment. Given that the plaintiff here had suffered financial loss by the improper act of the defendant but could not sue him in conversion, what form of action could he use?

Compare also *Herring* v. *Boyle* (above, p. 299) for the argument that the defendant was not liable since he only threatened to do a prohibited act, and did not actually do it. In which case was the argument more convincing?

R. H. WILLIS & SON v. BRITISH CAR AUCTIONS

Court of Appeal [1978] 1 W.L.R. 438; [1978] 2 All E.R. 392

Croucher, a publican, paid the plaintiff motor dealers £350 towards a car priced at £625, and they let him have it on hire-purchase terms, making it clear that he must not sell it before the balance was paid. Croucher nevertheless took the car to the defendant auctioneers and asked them to sell it for at least £450. The highest bid at the auction was only £410. After the auction Croucher was asked in the defendants' office if he would accept the £410, and after the defendants had reduced their commission he did so. Croucher went bankrupt, the purchaser and the car disappeared, and the plaintiffs sued the defendants for conversion.

The plaintiffs obtained judgment for £275 in the county court, and the Court of Appeal dismissed the defendants' appeal.

Lord Denning M.R.: . . . The question that arises is the usual one: which of the two innocent persons is to suffer? Is the loss to fall on the motor car dealers? They have been deprived of the £275 due to them on the car. Or on the auctioneer? They sold it believing that Mr. Croucher was the true owner. In answering that question in cases such as this, the common law has always acted on the maxim: *nemo dat quod non habet*. It has protected the property rights of the true owner. It has enforced them strictly as against anyone who deals with the goods inconsistently with the dominion of the true owner. Even though the true owner may have been very negligent and the defendant may have acted in complete innocence, nevertheless the common law held him liable in conversion. Both the "innocent acquirer" and the "innocent handler" have been hit hard. That state of the law has often been criticised. It has been proposed that the law should protect a person who buys goods or handles them in good faith without notice of any adverse title, at any rate where the claimant by his own negligence or otherwise has largely contributed to the outcome. Such proposals have however been effectively blocked by the decisions of the House of Lords in the last century of *Hollins* v. *Fowler* (1875) L.R. 7 H.L. 757 and in this century of *Moorgate Mercantile Co. Ltd.* v. *Twitchings* [1977] A.C. 890, to which I may add the decision of this court in *Central Newbury Car Auctions Ltd.* v. *Unity Finance Ltd.* [1957] 1 Q.B. 371.

In some instances the strictness of the law has been mitigated by statute, as for instance, by the protection given to private purchasers by the Hire Purchase Acts. But in other cases the only way in which the innocent acquirers or handlers have been able to protect themselves is by insurance. They insure themselves against their potential liability. This is the usual method nowadays. When men of business or professional men find themselves hit by the law with new and increasing liabilities, they take steps to insure themselves, so that the loss may not fall on one alone, but be spread among many. It is a factor of which we must take account: see *Post Office* v. *Norwich Union Fire Insurance Society Ltd.* [1967] 2 Q.B. 363, 375 and *Morris* v. *Ford Motor Co. Ltd.* [1973] Q.B. 792, 801.

The position of auctioneers is typical. It is now, I think, well established that if an auctioneer sells goods by knocking down his hammer at an auction and thereafter delivers them to the purchaser—then although he is only an agent—then if the vendor has no title to the goods, both the auctioneer and the purchaser are liable in conversion to the true owner, no matter how innocent the auctioneer may have been in handling the goods or the purchaser in acquiring them: see *Barker* v. *Furlong* [1891] 2 Ch. 172, 181, *per* Romer J. and *Consolidated Co.* v. *Curtis & Son* [1892] 1 Q.B. 495. This state of the law has been considered by the Law Reform Committee in 1966 as to innocent acquirers (Twelfth Report, Transfer of Title to Chattels, Cmnd. 2958); and in 1971 as to innocent handlers (Eighteenth Report, Conversion and Detinue, Cmnd. 4774). But Parliament has made no change in it; no doubt it would have done so in the Torts (Interference with Goods) Act 1977 if it had thought fit to do so.

Such is the position with sales "under the hammer." What about sales which follow a "provisional bid?" I see no difference in principle. In each case the auctioneer is an intermediary who brings the two parties together and gets them to agree on the price. They are bound by the conditions of sale which he has prepared. He retains the goods in his custody. He delivers them to the purchaser on being paid the price. He pays it over to the vendor and deducts his commission. So in principle, I think that on a "provisional bid" an auctioneer is liable in conversion, just as when he sells under the hammer. There are two decisions, however, which suggest a difference. Each followed a dictum of Bramwell L.J. in *Cochrane* v. *Rymill* (1879) 40 L.T. 744, 746. One is the decision of the Court of Appeal in *National Mercantile Bank Ltd.* v. *Rymill* (1881) 44 L.T. 767. The other is the decision of the Divisional Court in *Turner* v. *Hockey* (1887) 56 L.J.Q.B. 301. In those two cases it was held that the auctioneer was not liable in conversion, because he had not actually effected the sale. It had been made by the parties themselves. I doubt whether those decisions are correct. Although the auctioneer had not actually effected the sale, his intervention in each case was an efficient cause of the sale and he got his commission for what he did. To my mind those two decisions are a departure from the principles stated by Blackburn J. in *Hollins* v. *Fowler*. That is the principle which should guide us, especially as it was inferentially accepted by the House of Lords. I cannot help thinking that in those two cases the courts were anxious to protect the auctioneer, as an innocent handler, from the strictness of the law. In doing so they introduced fine distinctions which are difficult to apply. I do not think we should follow those two cases today, especially when regard is had to the insurance aspect to which I now turn. It is clear that the auctioneers insure against both kinds of sale equally. On every one of the sales, under the hammer or on provisional bids, the auctioneers charge an "indemnity fee" to the purchaser. He has to pay a premium of £2 on each vehicle purchased. In return for it the auctioneers, British Car Auctions Ltd., through an associate company, the Omega Insurance Co. Ltd., insures the purchaser against any loss he may suffer through any defect in title of the seller. So if the true owner comes along and retakes the goods from the purchaser or makes him pay damages for conversion, the auctioneers (through their associate company) indemnify the purchaser against the loss. The premium thus charged by the auctioneers (through their associate company) is calculated to cover the risk of the seller having no title or a defective title. That risk is the same no matter whether the true owner sues the auctioneer or the purchaser. The auctioneer collects £2 from every purchaser to cover that risk. We are told it comes to £200,000 a year. Seeing that they receive these sums, they ought to meet the claims of the true owners out of it. This system is the commercial way of doing justice between the parties. It means that all concerned are protected. The true owner is protected by the strict law of conversion. He can recover against the innocent acquirer and the innocent handler. But those innocents are covered by insurance so that the loss is not borne by any single individual but is spread through the community at large. The insurance factor had a considerable influence on the Law Reform Committee. In view of it they did not recommend any change in the law. So also it may properly have an influence on the courts in deciding issues which come before them.

My conclusion is that, where goods are sold by the intervention of an auctioneer, under the hammer or as a result of a provisional bid, then if the seller has no title, the auctioneer is liable in conversion to the true owner. I would dismiss the appeal accordingly.

Roskill and Browne L.JJ. agreed.

Note:

This case shows that when goods are sold without the owner's consent, the seller commits a tort. The buyer usually commits a tort as well. It is common to describe the buyer's position in terms of the law of property—"the buyer acquires no better title to the goods than the seller had" (Sale of Goods Act 1979, s.21); this is precisely equivalent to saying that the buyer is just as liable as the seller. In certain situations, however, an exception is made and the buyer does get a better title than the seller; in other words, the buyer is sometimes not liable although the seller had no authority to sell. For example, although one is normally liable to the finance company if one buys goods, however innocently, from a person who has taken them on hire-purchase terms, an exception is made if the chattel in question is a motor vehicle and the buyer is not a dealer (Hire Purchase Act 1964, s.27). The rules are too complicated to go into here, but they may be found in the Twelfth Report of the Law Reform Committee (Cmnd. 2958 (1966)). The Committee's principal recommendation, still unimplemented, was that people in good faith should not be liable for buying goods in a shop or at a public auction.

In *Hiort* v. *Bott* (above, p. 420) all the defendant did was to handle a document, but he was held liable for the conversion of the barley to which it related. Unidentified money cannot be converted, but one may be liable for converting a document which relates to money (for a superb off-the-cuff exposé see Diplock L.J. in *Marfani & Co.* v. *Midland Bank* [1968] 1 W.L.R. 956, 970–973). The Law Reform Committee considered the question and said: "It is true that a claim against a banker for conversion of a cheque has a somewhat artificial air, because what the true owner is in substance complaining about is that the bank has diverted his money, and if it were theoretically possible the obvious claim would be for the conversion of the money. But . . . We are satisfied that the present application of the law of conversion to such instruments is sound in principle and is not merely a legal fiction." (Eighteenth Report (Cmnd. 4774), para. 98).

Sound in principle it may be, but it would be impossible in practice if bankers, who spend all their time paying out on cheques (*i.e.* buying them) and collecting on them (*i.e.* selling them), were vulnerable to a conversion claim every time they accepted a cheque from a person not entitled to it. Bankers therefore have protection of two kinds. First, cheques are negotiable instruments, and unless their negotiability has been impaired in some way, the acquiring bank can often obtain a better title than the person presenting it. Secondly, bankers now have statutory protection in most cases if they can prove that they acted normally and without negligence (Bills of Exchange Act 1882, ss.60, 80; Cheques Act 1957, s.4).

In modern times the value of property may be greatly enhanced if its owner obtains permission to use it in certain ways (licences, planning permissions etc.). It is sometimes possible for a person to appropriate such a benefit to himself without handling the property to which it relates or even any document vested in the other party. In such a case there should be liability if the conduct is improper, but conversion is not the right tort since guilty knowledge is not a prerequisite. *Douglas Valley Finance Co.* v. *Hughes* [1969] 1 Q.B. 738 is an interesting case in this connection.

TORTS (INTERFERENCE WITH GOODS) ACT 1977

2.—(1) Detinue is abolished.

(2) An action lies in conversion for loss or destruction of goods which a bailee has allowed to happen in breach of his duty to his bailor (that is to say it lies in a case which is not otherwise conversion, but would have been detinue before detinue was abolished).

CAPITAL FINANCE COMPANY LTD. v. BRAY

Court of Appeal [1964] 1 W.L.R. 323; 108 S.J. 95; [1964] 1 All E.R. 603

The plaintiff let a car on hire-purchase terms to the defendant, and when the defendant defaulted on his payments, repossessed the car in the middle of the night. The defendant immediately informed them, correctly, that they had no right to repossess the car without a court order, since he had paid more than one-third of the purchase price, and threatened to bring an action to recover all that he had paid. The plaintiffs returned the car, and the defendant used it without paying. Nine months later, on March 1, 1963, the plaintiffs demanded the return of the car to one of three addresses within 10 days, and payment of the outstanding instalments of £89. The defendant did nothing. On April 11 the company claimed the return of the car on the basis of the original contract. The defendant answered that the contract was terminated by the illegal repossession of the car, and counterclaimed for the £113 he had paid. The plaintiff added a claim in detinue and damages for detention up to the time of the hearing.

The county court judge gave judgment for the plaintiff on the ground of the defendant's failure to return the car as demanded, and gave damages from the date of that failure up to the date on which the plaintiff initiated proceedings. The defendant appealed, and the Court of Appeal allowed his appeal; the defendant had judgment on the counterclaim.

Lord Denning M.R.: . . . Now comes the point in the case. What was the position after March 1, 1963? Was there a wrongful detention of the car by Bray so as to give rise to a claim in detinue? The judge held that there was. The key sentence in his judgment in this: "When, however, in response to the plaintiffs' solicitor's letter of March 1, 1963, he failed to deliver the car on March 11, as demanded, then it seems to me a claim arose in detinue." While I agree with much of the judgment, I cannot agree with this. This claim in detinue was only raised at the last moment and I do not think the judge had the benefit of the authorities as we have had. In my judgment the letter of March 1, was not a sufficient demand to found a claim in detinue. It was a demand to deliver up in accordance with the hire-purchase agreement. It demanded delivery up by Bray at his own expense to one of three named places, Edinburgh, Waterloo Place in London, or Stone Buildings, Lincoln's Inn. But once the hire-purchase agreement was determined and not reinstated, Bray was under no obligation to take the goods to the finance company. He could leave the goods at his house until the owner came to collect them. He would not be guilty of any unlawful detention unless, when the owner came to collect them, he prevented him taking possession of them. It is rather like the case which was put in argument. Suppose a trader leaves some article on my premises—it may be a photograph or even a grand piano—hoping I will buy it. If I am unwilling to buy it, he cannot demand that I post the picture back to him or that I load the grand piano on a haulage contractor's van and take it back to him. I can leave it where it is. Or I can put it out of my way, if I like, without being guilty of any wrongdoing at all. If he comes to collect it, I must let him have it: but that is all. There is no obligation on a person who has another person's goods to return them to him, except by contract. The rule is accurately stated in *Salmond on Torts*, 13th ed., at p. 264: "No one is bound, save by contract, to take a chattel to the owner of it. His only obligation is not to prevent the owner from getting it when he comes for it." That has been the law ever since the case to which we were referred of *Clements* v. *Flight* ((1846) 16 M. & W. 42, 49; 153 E.R. 1090). The judgment of the court makes it quite clear that, in order that there should be a wrongful detention of goods, the defendant must withhold the goods and prevent the plaintiff from having possession of them. He is not bound to be active and send the goods back unless there is an obligation by contract to do so. It seems to me, therefore, that this demand of March 1, 1963, was not a good demand such as to found a claim in detinue. It did not merely demand delivery up. It demanded that the hirer should take the car back to one of these three addresses. He was under no obligation to do so.

The only way in which a claim in detinue might be made here was the way Mr. Shaw put it. He said that if a man uses a car in defiance of the owner's rights, that may give a claim in detinue. I agree. It may. No doubt after receiving the letter of March 1, 1963, Bray had no right to use the car. The owners had withdrawn their consent to it. And if he did use it after March 1, 1963, there might be a claim to detinue. But what evidence of that is there here? There is no evidence of any user by Bray after March 1, 1963. It was argued that the judge inferred user from that time: but I am not all sure that he did. In any event if he did, there was no evidence of it: and I do not think it should be inferred. So there is no claim on that score.

This means that in my judgment the cross appeal should be allowed and the claim of the finance company should be dismissed. Bray is entitled to the £113 on his counterclaim.

Questions

1. Debts are payable at the domicile of the creditor. Why is there a different rule where the object of a debt is a chattel?

2. Suppose that, after March 1, the car had been stolen from Bray's garage, the door of which he had failed to lock. Would he be liable? Suppose that it is not clear whether Bray was careless or not. Would he have to prove that he was not, or must the plaintiffs prove that he was?

3. Lord Denning said elsewhere in his judgment that Bray was not liable to pay for the use

of the car between the time it was returned to him and the time it was demanded back from him. Can this be right?

4. Lord Denning said that Bray might have been liable in detinue if he had used the car after March 1. Would he be liable now? If so, under what head of liability?

HOUGHLAND v. R. R. LOW (LUXURY COACHES) LTD.

Court of Appeal [1962] 1 Q.B. 694; [1962] 2 W.L.R. 1015; 106 S.J. 243; [1962] 2 All E.R. 159

The plaintiff and her husband were old age pensioners who went on a trip to Jersey organised by the Good Companions Club. Back in Southampton, the party boarded one of the defendant's coaches to return to Hoylake, Cheshire, and the plaintiff's suitcase was put in the boot along with the others. After a tea-stop at Ternhill, Shropshire, the coach would not start again. Three hours later the relief coach arrived and the luggage was transferred, the passengers unloading it without supervision and the defendant's driver packing it expertly in the boot. At Hoylake the plaintiff's suitcase could not be found.

The plaintiff claimed "delivery up of the said suitcase and the contents thereof or £82 10s. their value." Alternatively she claimed damages in a similar amount on the grounds of negligence. The county court judge found that it was probably at Ternhill that the suitcase was either taken or lost, and gave judgment for the plaintiff. The defendant appealed, and the Court of Appeal dismissed the appeal in unreserved judgments.

Ormerod L.J.: The judge, according to the note that we have of his judgment . . . found in the first place that the driver of the coach was a bailee of the suitcase, and that the bailment was a gratuitous bailment. I am not sure that there is any evidence for the latter finding; and indeed, I might well, I think, have come to a different conclusion. . . . The judge then found that it was probably at Ternhill that the suitcase was either taken or lost, and in the circumstances he decided that the defendants were liable to pay the plaintiff £82 10s. 11d.

The objection made to the judgment, as I understand it, is that, as this was a gratuitous bailment, the high degree of negligence required, otherwise called gross negligence in some of the cases, has not been established; that the judge made no finding of negligence, and that, in the circumstances, the judgment should not stand. I am bound to say that I am not sure what is meant by the term "gross negligence" which has been in use for a long time in cases of this kind. There is no doubt, of course, that it is a phrase which has been commonly used in cases of this sort since the time of *Coggs* v. *Bernard*, when the distinction was made in a judgment of Lord Holt C.J. ((1703) 2 Ld.Raym. 909, 913; 92 E.R. 107), which has been frequently referred to and cited; but as we know from the judgment of Lord Chelmsford in *Giblin* v. *McMullen* ((1869) L.R. 2 P.C. 317, 336), that it was said, after referring to the use of the term "gross negligence" over a long period: "At last, Lord Cranworth (then Baron Rolfe) in the case of *Wilson* v. *Brett* ((1843) 11 M. & W. 113, 115; 152 E.R. 757) objected to it, saying that he 'could see no difference between negligence and gross negligence; that it was the same thing, with the addition of a vituperative epithet.' And this critical observation has been since approved of by other eminent judges."

For my part, I have always found some difficulty in understanding just what was "gross negligence," because it appears to me that the standard of care required in a case of bailment, or any other type of case, is the standard demanded by the circumstances of that particular case. It seems to me that to try and put a bailment, for instance, into a watertight compartment—such as gratuitous bailment on the one hand, and bailment for reward on the other—is to overlook the fact that there might well be an infinite variety of cases, which might come into one or the other category. The question that we have to consider in a case of this kind, if it is necessary to consider negligence, is whether in the circumstances of this particular case a sufficient standard of care has been observed by the defendants or their servants.

First, I think I should deal with the question of detinue. It has been admitted by Mr. Somerset Jones on behalf of the defendants that this is a case where a prima facie case has been established by the plaintiff. If that be so, I find it difficult to appreciate that there can be any grounds for appeal. Mr. Somerset Jones has endeavoured to establish, and he has done it by reference to authority, that to found a prima facie case is not sufficient—that there must, in addition, be affirmative evidence before the plaintiff can succeed. I am bound to say that is a doctrine which rather surprises me. If a prima facie case is once established, it is something which may be rebutted easily, but it can only be rebutted by evidence, and that is not present in this case; and therefore the prima facie case having been established, still remains.

Supposing that the claim is one in detinue, then it would appear that once the bailment has been established, and once the failure of the bailee to hand over the articles in question has been proved, there is a prima facie case, and the plaintiff is entitled to recover, unless the defendant can establish to the satisfaction of the court a defence; and that, I think, is very clear from the words used by Bankes L.J. in *Coldman* v. *Hill* ([1919] 1 K.B. 443, 449) in a passage that appears to me to be important in this case: "I think the law still is that if a bailee is sued in detinue only, it is a good answer for him to say that the goods were stolen without any default on his part, as the general bailment laid in the declaration pledges the plaintiff to the proof of nothing except that the goods were in the defendant's hands and were wrongfully detained." So far, so good, but it is, of course, in those circumstances for the defendants to establish affirmatively, not only that the goods were stolen, but that they were stolen without default on their part; in other words, that there was no negligence on their part in the care which they took of the goods.

Applying that principle here, Mr. Somerset Jones has been at pains to point out that the judge has made no finding that these goods were in fact stolen. The only view that the judge has expressed on the point is: "It is impossible to say what happened to this suitcase when it was lost on its journey," and with that I am bound to agree. It was put on the coach at Southampton, and it was not in the boot of the relief coach when it arrived at Hoylake. The judge has come to the conclusion that, on the probabilities, and again I agree with him, something happened to that suitcase when the transfer took place at Ternhill, or when the coach was delayed for some considerable period of time there. There seems to be no doubt that for something like three hours in the darkness that coach remained there unattended.

In these circumstances, I find it difficult to appreciate what substance there is in the complaint made by Mr. Somerset Jones that in this case the judge, in treating this as a case of detinue, was in error. But let us suppose for a moment that the issue here is an issue in negligence: then he admits, and I think properly admits, that there is a prima facie case against the defendants derived from the fact that the suitcase was found by the judge to have been put on the coach at Southampton, and was not on the second coach when it arrived at its destination at Hoylake. In those circumstances, it is for the defendants to adduce evidence which will rebut a presumption of negligence. . . .

Willmer L.J.: . . . The burden was on the defendants to adduce evidence in rebuttal. They could discharge that burden by proving what in fact did happen to the suitcase, and by showing that what did happen happened without any default on their part. They certainly did not succeed in doing that, for the judge was left in the position that he simply did not know what did happen to the suitcase.

Alternatively, the defendants could discharge the burden upon them by showing that, although they could not put their finger on what actually did happen to the suitcase, nevertheless, whatever did occur occurred notwithstanding all reasonable care having been exercised by them throughout the whole of the journey. Clearly

the judge was not satisfied that they had proved the exercise of any such degree of
care throughout the whole of the journey. . . .

Note:
   There is no harm in saying that a bailee of whatever nature must take reasonable care in all
the circumstances, provided that it is remembered that the relevant circumstances include not
only the circumstances surrounding the *loss* but also those surrounding the *bailment*. The
inception of a voluntary relationship controls its consequences. If that is forgotten, dire things
will happen, because there is a real difference between the person who does a favour—like
looking after your cat while you are away—and the person performing a service by way of
trade. The Civil Codes insist that a gratuitous depositee is liable only for gross negligence
(French Civil Code, art. 1927: German Civil Code, § 690). But the distinction between gratuitous and remunerated bailments is not really the right one, since a business man may not
make a separate charge for a particular service. In *Coughlin* v. *Gillison* [1899] 1 Q.B. 145,
149, Collins L.J. suggested that liability might be higher in bailments of mutual benefit, but in
Andrews v. *Home Flats* [1946] 2 All E.R. 698, Scott L.J. preferred to ask whether the transaction was a "business arrangement." That seems a very good test, and brings it into line with
Hedley Byrne, above, p. 44.
   The duty of the bailee to look after the goods does not depend on the existence of a contract
with the owner (*Gilchrist Watt & Sanderson Pty.* v. *York Products Pty.* [1970] 1 W.L.R. 1262
(P.C.); *Morris* v. *Martin* (above, p. 248), but a contract very commonly does exist, and it may
contain an exemption or limitation clause which purports to protect the bailee. Such a clause,
if reasonable, is not invalidated by the Unfair Contract Terms Act 1977 (above, p. 222).
   In *A.V.X.* v. *E.G.M. Solders* (*The Times*, July 7, 1982) the defendants were expecting to
receive from the plaintiffs a single package of tiny solder spheres which were being returned
to them as sub-standard goods and which the defendants were naturally going to scrap on
arrival. However, at the same time as the plaintiffs handed that package to carriers for
delivery to the defendants, they also handed them 21 other packages addressed to their
own depot, containing brand-new capacitors for sale to customers. By error the carriers
delivered all 22 packages to the defendants with a delivery note indicating that the defendants
were the consignees of the whole consignment. The defendants' store-man asked his boss
what to do with the goods from the plaintiffs and was told to scrap them. Scrapped they were,
to the tune of $100,000 and more, or at any rate inextricably intermingled and commercially
destroyed.
   Staughton J. held that this was a case of "unconscious bailment," and, somehow invoking
Houghland v. *Low*, held that one must not destroy anything until one has taken reasonable
steps to ascertain that it is one's own property. "Simply to entrust boxes of goods to the factory staff for destruction, without ascertaining what was in them, cannot be other than a
breach of the duty owed by E.G.M."
   Your view of the merits of this decision ought to be affected by the considerations (i) that
the plaintiffs at interest were not the owners of the goods but their insurers, and (ii) that the
carriers, whose entire fault it was, had a limitation clause in their contract with the plaintiffs.
   Another case which gives one pause is *Awad* v. *Pillai* ([1982] R.T.R. 266 (C.A.)). In that
case the plaintiff had bailed his car to X in order to have it resprayed. X lent it to the defendant, saying that it belonged to him and was fully insured. The defendant damaged the car by
careless driving. The Court of Appeal held that the defendant owed to the owner of the car,
unknown though he was, a duty to take care of it, and was liable to him for its breach. Is this
case just the same as *Moorgate Mercantile Co.* v. *Finch* (above, p. 416), or does the switch
from conversion to negligence betoken a widening of liability?
   Normally the bailee has the burden of proving that he was not negligent. What the effect of
an exemption clause on the burden of proof may be is not clear now that the substantive doctrine of fundamental breach has gone (*Photo Production* v. *Securicor* [1980] A.C. 827).

SORRELL v. PAGET

Court of Appeal [1950] 1 K.B. 252; 65 T.L.R. 595; 93 S.J. 631; [1949] 2 All E.R. 609

The plaintiff and defendant had adjoining farms alongside the main London to
Dover railway line. The plaintiff's heifer kept straying. One morning the defendant

found it on the railway line, drove it off, and delivered it, with a protest, to the plaintiff's servants. That very evening at dusk the defendant saw it on the railway line again, telephoned the station and had the *Golden Arrow* stopped. He drove the heifer into his own stubble field, where it went to sleep. During the night or early morning the beast left that field, went along the highway, and entered a field where the defendant kept his T.T. herd. The defendant removed it, put it in a barn and fed it on hay and water. He did not inform the plaintiff. Four days later the plaintiff discovered its whereabouts and sent two men to fetch it. The defendant demanded £2 salvage and one shilling per day for keep. No money was offered to him, so he kept the heifer. Three days later the heifer died, having been driven mad, according to the plaintiff, by the defendant's negligence.

The county court judge held that the taking possession of the heifer was not wrongful, that the refusal to deliver up was not wrongful, and that the plaintiff had failed to prove negligence; he accordingly gave judgment for the defendant. The plaintiff appealed to the Court of Appeal, and his appeal was dismissed in unreserved judgments.

Bucknill L.J.: The first question that arises is: Did the defendant commit any wrong to the plaintiff when he took possession of the plaintiff's heifer? In my opinion he did not. It was getting dark at the time and the defendant, rightly, in my opinion, in the interests of the plaintiff and his heifer and of the common safety of the public using the railway, drove the heifer again for the second time that day off the railway and, on this occasion, into one of his own fields, which the county court judge has described as a place of "comparative safety." Unfortunately, that night the heifer escaped from that field on to a highway and thence strayed into another field of the defendant where was his T.T. herd. The defendant saw the heifer there in the morning to his dismay, because he was anxious to keep his herd free from all possible infection. The defendant then impounded the heifer in his barn. I think that the second question in the case is: Was he entitled to do so? In my opinion he was. He fed the heifer with baled hay and gave it water. Since, apparently, the plaintiff and the defendant were not on good terms, the defendant did not communicate with the plaintiff and tell him that the heifer was in his barn.

The third question is whether, when the plaintiff ascertained that his heifer was in the defendant's barn and sent his men to fetch her, the defendant was wrong in refusing to hand over the heifer. The county court judge has dealt with that point in his judgment where he said: "No actual money was offered to the defendant for the keep or damage. He told the men to go and get the whole of the money, keep and compensation. It was open to the men to do one of two things: hand the defendant three shillings"—I think he must mean 1s. a day—"for keep, or go away and return, and tender the keep money. It had been argued that they should be excused because they were told to go and get the money. There was never in this case any kind of offer to pay any sum at all, and therefore no legal tender." I think that the learned judge's view there was right.

During the course of the case a discussion took place as to the use of the word "salvage." There is no doubt that, strictly speaking, salvage on land is not a recognised head of claim in the common law as it is by maritime law, at sea. I need only refer to the judgment of Bowen L.J. in *Falcke* v. *Scottish Imperial Insurance Co.* ((1886) 34 Ch.D. 234, 248) to show what is the position. He said: "The general principle is, beyond all question, that work and labour done or money expended by one man to preserve or benefit the property of another do not according to English law create any lien upon the property saved or benefited, nor, even if standing alone, create any obligation to repay the expenditure. Liabilities are not to be forced upon people behind their backs any more than you can confer a benefit upon a man against his will." Then he goes on to deal with maritime salvage. Unfortunately, in this case, although it is admitted that the defendant did ask for salvage, there is nothing in the judge's notes to show that he was asked what he meant by salvage. There is no evidence to show that he made any claim for damage apart from salvage, and I think he clearly would be entitled to damage if he could prove it; damage, for instance, done by the heifer in getting into this field and grazing, and possible damage to the herd. But, assuming that the defendant was putting forward a claim, which included a claim for salvage proper, and that such a claim was not recognisable by law, I think that the cases do establish that it was the duty of the plaintiff to make a tender in respect of any damage done by the animal. He never did make a tender, and until the tender was made the defendant was justified in keeping the heifer in the barn.

The only other point is whether the defendant was negligent in keeping the heifer in that barn for a week before it died. If she was lawfully there, it was for the plaintiff to prove that the defendant was negligent, and that the death of the animal was the result of that negligence. That is a question of fact. It was a question which, I suspect, was argued with great vigour before the judge, and he has come to the conclusion, as he says in his judgment, that "the plaintiff has not got anywhere near proving that the animal died as a result of the defendant's fault. I am satisfied that the barn was a large, well-ventilated one and a suitable place to impound the animal." He was satisfied that she had been properly attended to all the time she was alive. So the plaintiff failed on this issue. For these reasons, in my judgment, this appeal should be dismissed.

Questions

1. What is the principal difference between this case and the last case?
2. Why was it not a trespass for the defendant to remove the plaintiff's heifer from the railway line? Would it have been a trespass if the defendant had left the heifer on the highway instead of putting it in his field?
3. Why did the defendant not have the burden of disproving negligence?
4. Suppose that a car is left parked on my property where I have erected a notice saying "No Parking." May I put the car on the highway? If so, is that the result of the principal case? Suppose, in putting it there, I damage the car. Must I disprove negligence?

Note:

The commonest ground of lien (that is, the right to detain a chattel until a money claim is paid) arises from the repair of chattels. Here the defendant had no such lien, because he did not improve the cow; he only fed it (*Re Southern Livestock Producers* [1964] 1 W.L.R. 24). For the circumstances in which the repairer's lien can be asserted against the owner of the chattel when the chattel was received from someone else, see *Tappenden* v. *Artus* [1964] 2 Q.B. 185. Only an innkeeper has a lien over stolen goods (*Marsh* v. *Commissioner of Police* [1944] W.N. 204, where the inn was The Ritz Hotel). There is no lien on people (*Herring* v. *Boyle*, above, p. 299).

Changes in the law relating to the seizure and detention of stray livestock are contained in the Animals Act 1971, s.7. It appears to apply only if the stray animal is taken on the land occupied by the person seizing it, and therefore it would not apply on the facts of the principal case. Under the Act, the person detaining the livestock is bound to inform the police and the owner, if known, within 48 hours, to treat the beast properly (there is no mention of burden of proof) and to return it on payment of a sum sufficient to satisfy any claim under section 4 of the Act for damage done by the beast. A power of sale after 14 days is given.

Section 3.—The Remedies

TORTS (INTERFERENCE WITH GOODS) ACT 1977

1. In this Act "wrongful interference," or "wrongful interference with goods," means—

    (*a*) conversion of goods (also called trover),
    (*b*) trespass to goods,

(*c*) negligence so far as it results in damage to goods or to an interest in goods,

(*d*) subject to section 2, any other tort so far as it results in damage to goods or to an interest in goods.

. . .

3.—(1) In proceedings for wrongful interference against a person who is in possession or in control of the goods relief may be given in accordance with this section, so far as appropriate.

(2) The relief is—

(*a*) an order for delivery of the goods, and for payment of any consequential damages, or

(*b*) an order for delivery of the goods, but giving the defendant the alternative of paying damages by reference to the value of the goods, together in either alternative with payment of any consequential damages, or

(*c*) damages.

(3) Subject to rules of court—

(*a*) relief shall be given under only one of paragraphs (*a*), (*b*) and (*c*) of subsection (2),

(*b*) relief under paragraph (*a*) of subsection (2) is at the discretion of the court, and the claimant may choose between the others.

(4) If it is shown to the satisfaction of the court that an order under subsection (2)(*a*) has not been complied with, the court may—

(*a*) revoke the order, or the relevant part of it, and

(*b*) make an order for payment of damages by reference to the value of the goods.

(5) Where an order is made under subsection (2)(*b*) the defendant may satisfy the order by returning the goods at any time before execution of judgment, but without prejudice to liability to pay any consequential damages.

(6) An order for delivery of the goods under subsection (2)(*a*) or (*b*) may impose such conditions as may be determined by the court, or pursuant to rules of court, and in particular, where damages by reference to the value of the goods would not be the whole of the value of the goods, may require an allowance to be made by the claimant to reflect the difference.

For example, a bailor's action against the bailee may be one in which the measure of damages is not the full value of the goods, and then the court may order delivery of the goods, but require the bailor to pay the bailee a sum reflecting the difference.

. . .

7.—(1) In this section "double liability" means the double liability of the wrongdoer which can arise—

(*a*) where one of two or more rights of action for wrongful interference is founded on a possessory title, or

(*b*) where the measure of damages in an action for wrongful interference founded on a proprietary title is or includes the entire value of the goods, although the interest is one of two or more interests in the goods.

(2) In proceedings to which any two or more claimants are parties, the relief shall be such as to avoid double liability of the wrongdoer as between those claimants.

(3) On satisfaction, in whole or in part, of any claim for an amount exceeding that recoverable if subsection (2) applied, the claimant is liable to account over to the other person having a right to claim to such extent as will avoid double liability.

(4) Where, as the result of enforcement of a double liability, any claimant is unjustly enriched to any extent, he shall be liable to reimburse the wrongdoer to that extent.

For example, if a converter of goods pays damages first to a finder of the goods, and then to the true owner, the finder is unjustly enriched unless he accounts over to the true owner under subsection (3); and then the true owner is unjustly enriched and becomes liable to reimburse the converter of the goods.

8.—(1) The defendant in an action for wrongful interference shall be entitled to show, in accordance with rules of court, that a third party has a better right than the plaintiff as respects all or any part of the interest claimed by the plaintiff, or in right of which he sues, and any rule of law (sometimes called jus tertii) to the contrary is abolished.

(2) Rules of court relating to proceedings for wrongful interference may—

   (*a*) require the plaintiff to give particulars of his title,
   (*b*) require the plaintiff to identify any person who, to his knowledge, has or claims any interest in the goods,
   (*c*) authorise the defendant to apply for directions as to whether any person should be joined with a view to establishing whether he has a better right than the plaintiff, or has a claim as a result of which the defendant might be doubly liable,
   (*d*) where a party fails to appear on an application within paragraph (*c*), or to comply with any direction given by the court on such an application, authorise the court to deprive him of any right of action against the defendant for the wrong either unconditionally, or subject to such terms or conditions as may be specified.

(3) Subsection (2) is without prejudice to any other power of making rules of court.

. . .

11.—(1) Contributory negligence is no defence in proceedings founded on conversion, or on intentional trespass to goods.

. . .

Note:

Section 11(1) is a very silly piece of legislation. It has already had to be disapplied in suits against a banker where he is by statute liable only on proof of negligence (Banking Act 1979, s.47; and see above p. 425).

But worse, it bars judicial reversal of the very bad common law rule that a person who carelessly facilitates the theft of his goods can nevertheless sue a third party bona fide purchaser. An owner of goods may sometimes be estopped from denying that the person from whom the defendant purchased the goods was authorised to sell them, but carelessness does not ground such an estoppel unless the plaintiff owed the defendant a duty to be careful, which is hardly ever the case, except in cases of representation, as the defendant is usually a stranger and the harm in issue financial only.

Thus in *Moorgate Mercantile Co.* v. *Twitchings* [1977] A.C. 890 the defendants bought a car which was offered to them for sale; before buying it they had checked with H.P. Information but had drawn a blank because the plaintiffs had carelessly failed to register the fact that the car was theirs and that it was the subject of a hire-purchase transaction. All their Lordships agreed that if the plaintiffs had owed the defendants a duty to take care to register their interest (which a bare majority denied), then the action in conversion must fail. But if a third member of the House had held that the plaintiffs owed the defendants a duty to take care, and the plaintiffs had accordingly lost their suit, would this not be an instance of "contributory negligence" now barred by the Act?

THE WINKFIELD

Court of Appeal [1902] P. 42; 71 L.J.P. 21; 85 L.T. 668; 50 W.R. 246; 18 T.L.R. 176; 46 S.J. 163; 9 Asp.M.L.C. 259; [1900–3] All E.R. Rep. 346

Collins M.R.: This is an appeal from the order of Sir Francis Jeune dismisssing a motion made on behalf of the Postmaster-General in the case of *The Winkfield*.

The question arises out of a collision which occurred on April 5, 1900, between the steamship *Mexican* and the steamship *Winkfield*, and which resulted in the loss of the former with a portion of the mails which she was carrying at the time.

The owners of the *Winkfield* under a decree limiting liability to £32,514 17s. 10d. paid that amount into court, and the claim in question was one by the Postmaster-General on behalf of himself and the Postmasters-General of Cape Colony and Natal to recover out of that sum the value of letters, parcels, etc., in his custody as bailee and lost on board the *Mexican*.

The case was dealt with by all parties in the court below as a claim by a bailee who was under no liability to his bailor for the loss in question, as to which it was admitted that the authority of *Claridge* v. *South Staffordshire Tramway Co.* ([1892] 1 Q.B. 422) was conclusive, and the President accordingly, without argument and in deference to that authority, dismissed the claim. The Postmaster-General now appeals.

The question for decision, therefore, is whether *Claridge's* case was well decided. . . . For the reasons which I am about to state I am of opinion that *Claridge's* case was wrongly decided, and that the law is that in an action against a stranger for loss of goods caused by his negligence, the bailee in possession can recover the value of the goods, although he would have had a good answer to an action by the bailor for damages for the loss of the thing bailed.

It seems to me that the position, that possession is good against a wrongdoer and that the latter cannot set up the *jus tertii* unless he claims under it, is well established in our law, and really concludes this case against the respondents. As I shall show presently, a long series of authorities establishes this in actions of trover and trespass at the suit of a possessor. And the principle being the same, it follows that he can equally recover the whole value of the goods in an action on the case for their loss through the tortious conduct of the defendant. I think it involves this also, that the wrongdoer who is not defending under the title of the bailor is quite unconcerned with what the rights are between the bailor and bailee, and must treat the possessor as the owner of the goods for all purposes quite irrespective of the rights and obligations as between him and the bailor.

I think this position is well established in our law, though it may be that reasons for its existence have been given in some of the cases which are not quite satisfactory. I think also that the obligation of the bailee to the bailor to account for what he has received in respect of the destruction or conversion of the thing bailed has been admitted so often in decided cases that it cannot now be questioned; and, further, I think it can be shown that the right of the bailee to recover cannot be rested on the ground suggested in some of the cases, namely, that he was liable over to the bailor for the loss of the goods converted or destroyed. It cannot be denied that since the case of *Armory* v. *Delamirie* ((1722) 1 Stra. 504; 93 E.R. 664), not to mention earlier cases from the Year Books onward, a mere finder may recover against a wrongdoer the full value of the thing converted. That decision involves the principle that as between possessor and wrongdoer the presumption of law is, in the words of Lord Campbell in *Jeffries* v. *Great Western Ry.* ((1856) 5 E. & B. 802, 806; 119 E.R. 680), "that the person who has possession has the property." In the same case he says: "I am of opinion that the law is that a person possessed of goods as his property has a good title as against every stranger, and that one who takes them from him, having no title in himself, is a wrongdoer, and cannot defend himself by showing that there was title in some third person, for *against a wrongdoer possession is title.* The law is so stated by the very learned annotator in his note to *Wilbraham* v. *Snow*" ((1670) 2 Wms.Saund. 47f.; 85 E.R. 624). Therefore it is not open to the defendant, being a wrongdoer, to inquire into the nature or limitation of the possessor's right, and unless it is competent for him to do so the question of his relation to, or liability towards, the true owner cannot come into the discussion at all; and, therefore, as between those two parties full damages have to be paid without any further inquiry. The extent of the liability of the finder to the true owner not being relevant to the discussion between him and the wrongdoer, the facts which would ascertain it would not have been admissible in evidence, and therefore the right of the finder to recover full damages cannot be made to depend upon the extent of his liability over to the true owner. To hold otherwise would, it seems to me, be in effect to permit a wrongdoer to set up a *jus tertii* under which he cannot claim. But, if this be the fact in the case of a finder, why should it not be equally the fact in the case of a bailee? Why, as against a wrongdoer, should the nature of the plaintiff's interest in the thing converted be any more relevant to the inquiry, and therefore admissible in evidence, than in the case of a finder? It seems to me that neither in one case nor the other ought it to be competent for the defendant to go into evidence on that matter. . . .

Note:
   This rule was recently confirmed by Lord Brandon in *The Jag Shakti* [1986] 1 All E.R. 480, 485–486. Is it still good law in England after s.8 of the 1977 Act?

WICKHAM HOLDINGS LTD. v. BROOKE HOUSE MOTORS LTD.

Court of Appeal [1967] 1 W.L.R. 295; [1967] 1 All E.R. 117

A finance company sued for conversion of a car in respect of which only £274.50 was still due under the hire-purchase contract. The trial judge gave judgment for £440, including the full value of the car at the time of the conversion plus £75 as damages for detention. The amount of the judgment was reduced on appeal.

Lord Denning M.R.: . . .
   Even so, there remains the important question: what is the proper measure of damage? It is a familiar situation. The hirer of a motor car, who has got it on hire-purchase wrongfully sells it to someone else. The hiring is thereupon automatically determined. The finance company claims the return of the car and damages for detention or, alternatively, damages for conversion. In such a case the finance company in my opinion is not entitled to the full value of the car. The finance company is only entitled to what it has lost by the wrongful act of the defendant. I am well aware, of course, that prima facie in conversion the measure of damages is the value of the goods at the date of the conversion. That does not apply, however, where the plaintiff, immediately prior to the conversion, has only a limited interest in the goods: see *Edmondson* v. *Nuttall* (1864) 17 C.B.N.S. 280, 294; 114 E.R. 113, 118–119, *per* Willes J. Take this case. The hirer had a most valuable interest in the car. He had paid already £615 10s. towards the purchase price and had the right to buy it outright on paying another £274 10s. The interest of the finance company was limited correspondingly. Its interest was limited to securing the payment of the outstanding £274 10s. It is entitled to be compensated for the loss of that interest, and no more. This was so held by Channell J., in the well known case of *Belsize Motor Supply Co.* v. *Cox* [1914] 1 K.B. 244. As Winn L.J., pointed out in the course of the argument, immediately prior to the wrongful sale, the high probability was that the finance company would only get out of this transaction another £274 10s.; either because Mr. Pattinson would complete the purchase, or because a purchaser would pay the "settlement figure." That is all that the finance company has lost and all that it should recover. It would be most unjust that the finance company should recover twice as much as it has lost.
   As against this view, we were referred to *United Dominions Trust (Commercial) Ltd.* v. *Parkway Motors Ltd.* [1955] 2 All E.R. 557. In that case the hire-purchase

price of a van was £626 3s. The hirer paid £529 19s. and resold it when the outstanding balance was only £96 4s. The finance company refused to accept this £96 and claimed the full value of the van, £350. McNair J., awarded them the £350. That was four times as much as the finance company had lost. He was referred to the *Belsize* case, but distinguished it on this ground. In the *Belsize* case the hire-purchase agreement contained a simple prohibition that "the hirer shall not re-let sell or part with the possession" of the goods. In the *United Dominions Trust* case, it contained a prohibition that the hirer "shall not sell, offer for sale, assign or charge the goods or the benefit of the agreement." The only distinction is that in the *United Dominions Trust* case the printed form contained the extra words "or the benefit of the agreement." This distinction, said McNair J., made all the difference: and entitled him to award the finance company the full value of the van. I must confess that this distinction drawn by McNair J., is too fine for me. I cannot subscribe to it. . . . I think that the *United Dominions Trust* case was wrongly decided.

I base my decision on this. In a hire-purchase transaction there are two proprietary interests, the finance company's interest and the hirer's interest. If the hirer wrongfully sells the goods or the benefit of the agreement in breach of the agreement, then the finance company are entitled to recover what they have lost by reason of this wrongful act. That is normally the balance outstanding on the hire-purchase price; but they are not entitled to more than they have lost.

I would, therefore, allow the appeal. The judgment below should be varied by substituting for the figure of £440, the sum of £274 10s. We were told, however, that the finance company has claimed another instalment of £54 10s. from Mr. Pattinson, and has received it. So this must come off too.

Questions

1. If the Post Office in *The Winkfield* could recover more than it had lost, why not the finance company in this case?

2. The trial judge awarded £75 as damages for detention. Why could the plaintiff not retain this sum?

3. Would it now be right to say that a hire-purchaser has a transferable "proprietary interest" even if the contract forbids both the transfer of possession and the assignment of any contract rights? What kind of interest does the hire-purchaser have—a chose in possession or a chose in action?

4. The X Co. lets a car on hire-purchase to A. B steals it and wrecks it. Can the X Co. sue B (a) in trespass, (b) in conversion, (c) at all? How much can be recovered from B by (a) the X Co., (b) A? Suppose that the X Co. and A had each insured the car under separate policies. How much would each receive from his insurer? If the X Co. received the full value of the car from its insurer, would A still owe anything under the hire-purchase contract?

5. If the fact that the auctioneer is insured is a good reason for making him pay though he is not to blame (*Willis*, above, p. 423), why is it not a good reason for making him pay too much?

Note:

In distraining on X's property for non-payment of VAT the defendant bailiffs auctioned off for £178 a cash-register which X said was his. In fact X had taken it on hire-purchase terms from the plaintiff: the plaintiff owned it and X owed £1,200 on it. The plaintiff was able to recover only the market value of the thing, taken to be £178, and not, as the trial judge had held, the sum of £950 which C's default rendered the plaintiff liable to pay to the factors to whom they had assigned the right to receive the instalments. (*Chubb Cash* v. *John Crilley & Son* [1983] 2 All E.R. 294 (C.A.)).

In *Hillesden Securities* v. *Ryjak* [1983] 2 All E.R. 184 the plaintiffs obtained much more than the value of the chattel. They got £13,282.50 as well as the Rolls Royce which the defendants had bought from their lessee in September 1980, when its value was £7,500, and continued to use despite demand in February 1981 until returning it in December 1982. As the car was a profit-making asset in the plaintiff's hands the defendants were treated as if they were hiring the vehicle at £115 per week.

PART VII

DEFAMATION

INTRODUCTION

ALL law gets difficult when important interests come into conflict. In the tort of false arrest the suspect's interest in liberty conflicts with the policeman's interest in repressing crime. In conversion the owner's interest in keeping his property conflicts with the purchaser's interest in acquiring it. In defamation the conflict is between my interest in what people think of me and yours in telling people what you think. Defamation is arguably the most difficult of all torts. It is certainly the oddest. For instance, defamation is the only tort in which (a) liability is extinguished by the death of either party, (b) trial by jury is available at the instance of either party, and (c) legal aid is not available to either party. These are marginal matters, perhaps, but defamation is odd throughout. It allows a plaintiff to claim damages for a statement without having to prove (a) that the statement was false, (b) that the defendant was in any way at fault, or (c) that the statement did him any harm. Loss may have to be proved in a few cases of spoken defamation (slander), but usually the plaintiff is only required to show that the defendant made an observation to a third party (and not just to his wife) which was apt to make people think worse of the plaintiff, to lower him in their opinion.

The primary question is "Were the words defamatory?" That involves discovering the meaning of the words. Even in dictionaries words have more than one meaning; in the varied contexts of life, words can mean almost anything. (This is one reason, and perhaps the best one, for the distinction between slander and libel—see *Broome* v. *Agar* (1928) 138 L.T. 698, 701. Written words have at least a fixed partial context.) When can words be said to be very likely to cause other people, reasonable people, to think so much worse of the plaintiff that their behaviour towards him would be affected? The answer is, when they are critical of his conduct, his competence or his character, for the addressee is apt, such is the frailty of human nature, to visit the victim with hatred, ridicule or contempt. In law, uttered words are held to mean what the addressee would reasonably have supposed the utterer to have intended to convey; in fact people relate what they read and hear to what they already know and believe, and they may know more than the speaker or writer; it is thus quite possible for words to be defamatory of a person although the publisher had no idea that such a person even existed, let alone that the words defamed him.

Publication itself does not present many real difficulties. Just as carriers and warehousemen tend to be free from liability in conversion, so booksellers and lending libraries are free from liability in defamation if they have no reason to suspect that the works they propagate contain defamatory matter. A great many publications take place. The text of a book is published by the author of a manuscript to his typist, by the author to the publisher, by the publisher to the printer, and by the publisher to the purchaser. And a person is liable for every publication he intended, though it is made by another.

451

Thus liability in defamation is extremely easy to incur. But there are defences.

The first defence is "justification" or truth. The law has an extraordinary regard for truth, and just as it makes a person liable for a white lie, it makes a person immune in respect of a black truth. Truth is a total defence, in the sense that it rebuts the presumption that what the defendant said was false. It is thus irrelevant why the defendant published the unpalatable fact; the plaintiff has no right to a reputation based on concealment; put otherwise, the public has a right to know all. Truth may out. To this there is now one exception: if a person's conviction for an offence is "spent" by the lapse of the appropriate period, a malicious reference to it is actionable despite its truth (Rehabilitation of Offenders Act 1974, s.8). Apart from this a defendant who makes a single imputation goes free if he proves it to be substantially true, that is, if he justifies its "sting"; where the words of which the plaintiff makes complaint contain several imputations, failure to justify them all is not fatal to the defendant "if the words not proved to be true do not materially injure the plaintiff's reputation having regard to the truth of the remaining charges" (Defamation Act 1952, s.5); and if the plaintiff complains of one of several charges in the same publication the defendant can justify others which have a "common sting."

This being so, can the defendant say "Well, I find I can't prove that what I said was true, but there were true things I might have said which would have done no more harm than what I did say?" The answer is that he cannot. He can only lead evidence about such of the plaintiff's behaviour as is publicly known, so as to show that he had not much reputation to lose (*Plato Films* v. *Speidel* [1961] A.C. 1090). This is not justification but mitigation. However, if one tries to justify and fails, any facts proved may be relied on by way of mitigation; counsel are therefore on their honour not to seek to justify unless they think they can succeed.

Secondly, there is the defence of privilege. In some situations communication is so important that its flow must not be impeded by fear of lawsuits. Thus in Parliament and the courts speech is absolutely privileged, and an action in respect of words spoken there is foredoomed: the people who make our law have protected themselves, with good reason, from its effects. In other cases communications are protected only if they were made bona fide: the privilege is qualified in the sense that it is open to the plaintiff to show, if he can, that the occasion was abused. Of course the defendant will be liable if he knew that what he was saying was false, but "malice" will be established also if he was using the occasion just to hurt the plaintiff. To test whether or not an individual has a privilege in a particular situation, imagine that X comes to you and says "Look, I know this bad thing about Z. Should I tell Y?"; if as a reasonably sensitive and responsible member of society you would think it right that X should tell Y, and Y is the right person to tell, X's communication to him is privileged.

This common law privilege is of little use to newspapers and television companies, since hardly any of what they publish is of interest to the whole world. They have, however, a statutory privilege to publish fair and accurate reports of the proceedings and decisions of various public bodies and meetings, and to communicate notices from certain public officers; sometimes this privilege is conditional on their publishing a reasonable statement from the plaintiff by way of explanation or contradiction (Defamation Act 1952, s.7).

If matters are of public interest, however, anyone is free to express his opinion on them, however daft his opinion may be and however prejudicial to others. Public discussion of matters of public interest should be encouraged. But not public error. So the defence of "fair comment" applies only to comments, not to facts. If one gets one's facts wrong, one is strictly liable for stating them; but if the facts are right, then any honest comment is protected. Truth is the criterion of fact, honesty of opinion. The distinction between statement and comment—important because reasonableness of statement is insufficient and reasonableness of comment is not required—appears to be whether the addressee would suppose he was being given a piece of information or a personal value-judgment. A hint for the future may be contained in the following observation of Stephenson L.J.: "No privilege attaches yet to a statement on a matter of public interest believed by the publisher to be true in relation to which he has exercised reasonable care" (*Blackshaw* v. *Lord* [1983] 2 All E.R. 311, 327).

Many people are dissatisfied by the present law of defamation in England. It seems to give too much protection to reputation and to impose too great a restriction on the freedom of speech. Reputation, the cousin of respectability, is now regarded as less important than it was, since one is not supposed to care what other people think. Freedom of speech, on the other hand, is now regarded as more important than it was: to the utilitarian view that its effects are good ("the truth shall make you free") is added the more modern hedonistic view that self-expression is fun. The law of England is certainly stricter than that of any other free country, though it must be said that England does not feel much less free on that account. In France the criminal law is much used against those who abuse and vilify others: this is not as bad a solution as might at first sight appear. In the United States the Supreme Court has held that it is unconstitutional to impose liability in damages on the media, or perhaps on anyone, for speaking out on a matter of public concern unless it is proved that what he said was false and that he was at fault in saying it; even so, damages are limited to proved loss unless actual malice is shown, as it must be by a public figure who wants any damages at all.

It is not for want of attention that the English law of defamation is as it is. The Porter Committee looked at it after the war (Cmd. 7536 (1948)) and many of its recommendations were implemented in the Defamation Act 1952. This Act helped plaintiffs by increasing the number of slander cases where they need not prove any damage, and helped defendants by tempering the defences of "justification" and "fair comment," introducing the procedure of "offer of amends" for innocent publishers and extending the range of matters of which newspapers and broadcasters could safely give a fair and accurate report.

Less than 20 years later the Faulks Committee was set up to reconsider the whole topic. Its Report, which was produced in 1975 (Cmnd. 5909), contains many recommendations, but few of them are radical as to substance. The proposed abolition of the distinction between libel and slander would mean that no human plaintiff would ever have to prove any damage: institutional plaintiffs, however, would always have to prove that the words actually caused them loss or were likely to do so. Death would cease to have its extinctive effect on liability: if the critic died, his estate would be liable; if the plaintiff died, his action could continue; if the victim died before suing, his representatives could claim compensation for the loss caused to his estate; if the victim died before the libel (but less than five years before it) his relatives could sue for a declaration. Litigants would doubtless be delighted to receive legal aid and be able to sue in the county court for the first time, but they would lose their right to demand a jury. Even if the judge decided to empanel a jury, its only role as to damages would be to say whether they should be substantial, moderate, nominal or contemptuous. The latter categories might be used more often since the defendant would be allowed greater latitude with regard to evidence in mitigation of damages. No punitive damages would be allowed, and the judge's figure would be subject to alteration in the Court of Appeal. The procedure of "offer of amends" would be tidied up, but remain available only in the case of a wholly innocent publication. The range of matters on which a fair and accurate report could safely be made would be increased again, and the privilege extended to all publishers, not just to newspapers and broadcasters. Printers would share with booksellers, newsagents and lending libraries the defence of "innocent dissemination."

Now in so far as these proposals are helpful to plaintiffs, they are to be deprecated: the incidence of liability in this rampant tort should be curtailed and not enlarged in any respect. Take the distinction between libel and slander, for example. Admit that it is irrational, though there are some other areas of the law where a distinction is made between speech and writing. Even so, until the happy day comes when all plaintiffs in search of damages have to show that they suffered some provable or probable harm (as the Committee rightly recommends for institutional plaintiffs), we should retain those few cases where such proof is required at present precisely because slander and not libel is involved. To enfranchise the scatheless but irritated objects of backyard gossip and to give them public money to sue with is a really dotty proposal; so is the proposal to protect the reputation of the dead. Trivialities of this kind are of no use. Here, much more than elsewhere, radical change is required.

The defects of the present law arise because it uses a single remedy, the action for damages, in order to perform three distinct purposes: (a) to permit people to clear their reputation from unfounded allegations; (b) to allow people to claim compensation for the harm they suffer because others have abused their freedom of speech, and (c) to repress gratuitous vituperation, scurrilous disparagement and malignant calumny.

Only for (b) is damages the appropriate remedy. For (a) we need a procedure for retraction or correction, and for (c) we need the public stocks. Diplock L.J. once said that the law of defamation "has passed beyond redemption by the courts" ([1968] 2 Q.B. 157, 179). Redemption by Committee seems equally impossible.

Chapter 14

DEFAMATION

Section 1.—The Meaning of Words

LEWIS v. DAILY TELEGRAPH LTD.

House of Lords [1964] A.C. 234; [1963] 2 W.L.R. 1063; 107 S.J. 356; [1963] 2 All E.R. 151

Just before Christmas 1958, the *Daily Mail* published a paragraph headed "Fraud Squad Probe Firm" and the *Daily Telegraph* one headed "Inquiry on Firm by City Police," both on the front page. The paragraphs identified the corporate plaintiff as the company in question and the individual plaintiff as its chairman.

The plaintiffs alleged that the words were defamatory in the ordinary and natural meaning, and this the defendants did not dispute. But the plaintiffs said that the words in their ordinary meaning indicated that the plaintiffs were guilty of, or were suspected by the police of being guilty of, fraud or dishonesty, whereas the defendants said the words meant only that there was an inquiry on foot, and this meaning they sought to justify as being true.

Salmon J. rejected the defendants' submission that the meaning put on the words by the plaintiffs was impossible, and instructed the jury that they might find that the words meant what the plaintiffs said they meant. He did not point out the absence of cogent evidence of financial loss, and asked them only two questions: (1) whether they found for the plaintiffs or for the defendants, and (2) if for the plaintiffs, what damages. In the first action, against the *Daily Telegraph*, the jury awarded £25,000 to the chairman and £75,000 to the company; in the second action, against the *Daily Mail*, a different jury awarded £17,000 to the chairman and £100,000 to the company. It was accepted that the size of the awards indicated that the juries took the words to impute guilt and not merely suspicion.

The Court of Appeal allowed the defendants' appeals, and ordered new trials [1963] 1 Q.B. 340. The plaintiffs' appeal to the House of Lords was dismissed.

Lord Morris of Borth-y-Gest: . . . My Lords, I turn to consider the question whether the words were capable of bearing the meaning that the affairs of the company and/or its subsidiaries were conducted fraudulently or dishonestly. I do not understand any of your Lordships to be of the view that the words were not capable of bearing the meaning that the police suspected that the affairs of the company or its subsidiaries were conducted fraudulently or dishonestly: nor did I understand any submission to be made that the words were not so capable.

It is a grave thing to say that someone is fraudulent. It is a different thing to say that someone is suspected of being fraudulent. How much less wounding and damaging this would be must be a matter of opinion depending upon the circumstances. Similarly in the case of the personal plaintiff the submission is made that the words, while capable of bearing some of the alleged meanings, were not capable of bearing the meanings that Mr. Lewis had been guilty of fraud or dishonesty in connection with the affairs of the company or its subsidiaries or had caused or permitted the affairs to be conducted fraudulently or dishonestly.

My Lords, the only question that now arises is not whether the words did bear but whether they were capable of bearing the meanings to which I have referred.

455

What could ordinary reasonable readers think? Some, I consider, might reasonably take the view that there was just an inquiry to find out whether or not there had been any fraud or dishonesty. Some, I consider, might reasonably take the view that the words meant that there was an inquiry because the police suspected that there had been fraud or dishonesty. Some, I consider, might reasonably take the view that the words meant that there was an inquiry because there had been fraud or dishonesty which occasioned or required the inquiry by the police. Some, I consider, might reasonably take the view that the words meant that the inquiry was either (a) because there had been fraud or dishonesty or (b) because of a suspicion that there had been.

My Lords, it is not for me to say what I think was the meaning which the words conveyed to the ordinary reasonable reader of a newspaper, nor is it for me to express any opinion as to what conclusion a jury should reach as to this matter, but I do not consider that that meaning which involved that there had been fraud or dishonesty was a meaning which the jury should have been prohibited from considering on the basis that it was a meaning of which the words were not capable. I do not think that it can be said that 12 jurors could not reasonably have come to the conclusion that the words bore the meaning now being considered. In using this language I am following the approach suggested by Lord Porter in his speech in *Turner* v. *Metro-Goldwyn-Mayer Pictures Ltd.* ((1950) 66 T.L.R. (Pt. 1) 342; [1950] 1 All E.R. 449).

My Lords, a reasonable reader will probably be a fair-minded reader. The fair-minded reader would assume that a responsible newspaper would also be fair. If there was some private police inquiry in progress, the purpose of which was to ascertain whether or not there had been fraud or dishonesty, what possible justification could there be for proclaiming this far and wide to all the readers of a newspaper? If confidential information was received to the effect that there was a police inquiry, on what basis could the publishing of such information be warranted? There is no suggestion that the police had asked that any notice should be published. Under certain circumstances a newspaper may enjoy qualified privilege if it publishes a notice issued for the information of the public by or on behalf of a chief officer of police. (See section 7 of the Defamation Act 1952). If there was a police inquiry by a "Fraud Squad" which might result in the conclusion that any suspicion of fraud or dishonesty was wholly unwarranted, how manifestly unfair it would be to make public mention of the inquiry. What purpose could there be in doing so? With these thoughts and questions in his mind, a reasonable reader might well consider that no responsible newspaper would dare to publish, or would be so cruel as to publish, the words in question unless the confidential information, which in some manner they had obtained, was not information merely to the effect that there was some kind of inquiry in progress but was information to the effect that there was fraud or dishonesty. Some reasonable readers might therefore think that the words conveyed the meaning that there must have been fraud or dishonesty.

Furthermore, a reasonable reader might reflect that while the police may be concerned with inquiries as to whether some crime has or has not been committed, they are probably more often only concerned after a crime has been committed. They have to inquire whether they possess the necessary evidence for the launching of a prosecution. Reasonable readers might also think that inquiries into the affairs of a company if such inquiries were not concerned with fraud or dishonesty would not be conducted by the police at all. They would be conducted by persons or departments having no connection with the City of London Police Fraud Squad. Some of such readers might therefore be led to believe that if there was an inquiry by the City of London Fraud Squad, which a newspaper felt justified in mentioning, it must have been an inquiry to collect and marshal evidence in order to launch a prosecution for some offence involving fraud or dishonesty which had been committed.

My Lords, it was for the jury to determine what they consider was the meaning that the words would convey to ordinary men and women: we have only to decide as to the limits of the range of meanings of which the words were capable. For the reasons that I have given I have the misfortune to differ from your Lordships as to this very important part of the case. I consider that the learned judge was fully entitled to leave the matter to the jury in the way in which he did, and I consider that his directions concerning liability were clear and correct and fair. . . .

Lord Hodson: . . . The defendants having admitted that the words are defamatory in their ordinary meaning have always maintained that their ordinary meaning does not go so far as to include actual guilt of fraud. They have sought to justify by proving that an inquiry was in fact held, not by proving actual suspicion of fraud.

This is the gist of the whole case. Salmon J., who tried both pairs of actions, took the view that the words were capable of imputing guilt of fraud. Davies L.J. was inclined to the same opinion, and my noble and learned friend, Lord Morris of Borth-y-Gest, has expressed the same opinion as Salmon J. Holroyd Pearce L.J. and Havers J. took the contrary view. In view of this difference of judicial opinion, one naturally hesitates before expressing a concluded opinion of one's own, but after listening to many days of argument I am myself satisfied that the words cannot reasonably be understood to impute guilt. Suspicion, no doubt, can be inferred from the fact of the inquiry being held if such was the case, but to take the further step and infer guilt is, in my view, wholly unreasonable. This is to draw an inference from an inference and to take two substantial steps at the same time.

The distinction between suspicion and guilt is illustrated by the case of *Simmons* v. *Mitchell* ((1880) 6 App.Cas. 156) which decided that spoken words which convey a mere suspicion that the plaintiff has committed a crime punishable by imprisonment will not support an action without proof of special damage.

It has been argued before your Lordships that suspicion cannot be justified without proof of actual guilt on the analogy of the rumour cases such as *Watkin* v. *Hall* ((1868) L.R. 3 Q.B. 396). Rumour and suspicion do, however, essentially differ from one another. To say something is rumoured to be the fact is, if the words are defamatory, a republication of the libel. One cannot defend an action for libel by saying that one has been told the libel by someone else, for this might be only to make the libel worse. The principle as stated by Blackburn J. in *Watkin* v. *Hall* is that a party is not the less entitled to recover damages from a court of law for injurious matter published concerning him because another person previously published it. It is wholly different with suspicion. It may be defamatory to say that someone is suspected of an offence, but it does not carry with it that that person has committed the offence, for this must surely offend against the ideas of justice which reasonable persons are supposed to entertain. If one repeats a rumour one adds one's own authority to it and implies that it is well founded, that is to say, that it is true. It is otherwise when one says or implies that a person is under suspicion of guilt. This does not imply that he is in fact guilty but only that there are reasonable grounds for suspicion, which is a different matter.

Having reached the conclusion that the innuendo should not have been left to the jury as a separate issue and that the natural and ordinary meaning of the words does not convey actual guilt of fraud, I agree with the Court of Appeal that there must be a new trial for the learned judge left the question to the jury "Did they find for plaintiffs or defendants?" without a direction that the words were incapable of the extreme meaning which I have rejected. . . .

The responsibility of the judge to exclude a particular meaning which the plaintiff seeks to ascribe to words in their natural or ordinary meaning is, I think, clearly established by the decision of this House in *Capital and Counties Bank Ltd.* v. *Henty & Sons* ((1882) 7 App.Cas. 741). Henty & Sons had sent out a circular to a number of their customers giving notice that they would not receive in payment cheques drawn on any of the vouchers of the bank. There was no evidence to support the innuendo that the words imputed insolvency to the bank, and it was held that in their natural and ordinary meaning the words were not libellous. Lord Blackburn said (at 776): "Since Fox's Act at least, however the law may have been before, the prosecutor or plaintiff must also satisfy a jury that the words are such, and so published, as to convey the libellous imputation. If the defendant can get either the court or the jury to be in his favour, he succeeds. The prosecutor, or plaintiff, cannot succeed unless he gets both the court and the jury to decide for him." . . .

Lord Devlin: . . . If it is said of a man that he is a fornicator the statement cannot be enlarged by innuendo. If it is said of him that he was seen going into a brothel, the same meaning would probably be conveyed to nine men out of ten. But the lawyer might say that in the latter case a derogatory meaning was not a necessary one because a man might go to a brothel for an innocent purpose. An innuendo pleading that the words were understood to mean that he went there for an immoral purpose would not, therefore, be ridiculous. To be on the safe side, a pleader used an innuendo whenever the defamation was not absolutely explicit. That was very frequent, since scandalmongers are induced by the penalties for defamation to veil their meaning to some extent. . . . I have said that a derogatory implication might be easy or difficult to detect; and, of course, it might not be detected at all, except by a person who was already in possession of some specific information. Thus, to say of a man that he was seen to enter a named house would contain a derogatory implication for anyone who knew that the house was a brothel but not for anyone who did not. . . .

The real point, I think, that Mr. Milmo makes is that whether the libel is looked at as a statement or as a rumour, there is no difference between saying that a man is suspected of fraud and saying that he is guilty of it. It is undoubtedly defamatory, he submits, to say of a man that he is suspected of fraud, but it is defamatory only because it suggests that he is guilty of fraud: so there is no distinction between the two. This is to me an attractive way of putting the point. On analysis I think that the reason for its attraction is that as a maxim for practical application, though not as a proposition of law, it is about three-quarters true. When an imputation is made in a general way, the ordinary man is not likely to distinguish between hints and allegations, suspicion and guilt. It is the broad effect that counts and it is no use submitting to a judge that he ought to dissect the statement before he submits it to the jury. But if on the other hand the distinction clearly emerges from the words used it cannot be ignored. If it is said of a man: "I do not believe that he is guilty of fraud but I cannot deny that he has given grounds for suspicion," it seems to me to be wrong to say that in no circumstances can they be justified except by the speaker proving the truth of that which he has expressly said he did not believe. It must depend on whether the impression conveyed by the speaker is one of frankness or one of insinuation. Equally, in my opinion, it is wrong to say that, if in truth the person spoken of never gave any cause for suspicion at all, he has no remedy because he was expressly exonerated of fraud. A man's reputation can suffer if it can truly be said of him that although innocent he behaved in a suspicious way; but it will suffer much more if it is said that he is not innocent.

It is not, therefore, correct to say as a matter of law that a statement of suspicion imputes guilt. It can be said as a matter of practice that it very often does so, because although suspicion of guilt is something different from proof of guilt, it is the broad impression conveyed by the libel that has to be considered and not the meaning of each word under analysis. A man who wants to talk at large about smoke may have to pick his words very carefully if he wants to exclude the suggestion that there is also a fire; but it can be done. One always gets back to the fundamental question: what is the meaning that the words convey to the ordinary man: you cannot make a rule about that. They can convey a meaning of suspicion short of guilt; but loose talk about suspicion can very easily convey the impression that it is a suspicion that is well founded.

In the libel that the House has to consider there is, however, no mention of suspicion at all. What is said is simply that the plaintiff's affairs are being inquired into. That is defamatory, as is admitted, because a man's reputation may in fact be injured by such a statement even though it is quite consistent with innocence. I dare say that it would not be injured if everybody bore in mind, as they ought to, that no man is guilty until he is proved so, but unfortunately they do not. It can be defamatory without it being necessary to suggest that the words contained a hidden allegation that there were good grounds for inquiry. A statement that a woman has been raped can affect her reputation, although logically it means that she is innocent of any impurity: *Yousoupoff* v. *Metro-Goldwyn-Mayer Pictures Ltd.* ((1934) 50 T.L.R. 581). So a statement that a man has been acquitted of a crime with which in fact he was never charged might lower his reputation. Logic is not the test. But a statement that an inquiry is on foot may go further and may positively convey the impression that there are grounds for the inquiry, that is, that there is something to suspect. Just as a bare statement of suspicion may convey the impression that there are grounds for belief in guilt, so a bare statement of the fact of an inquiry may convey the impression that there are grounds for suspicion. I do not say that in this case it does; but I think that the words in their context and in the circumstances of publication are capable of conveying that impression. But can they convey an impression of guilt? Let it be supposed, first, that a statement that there is an inquiry conveys an impression of suspicion; and, secondly, that a statement of suspicion conveys an impression of guilt. It does not follow from these two suppositions that a statement that there is an inquiry conveys an impression of guilt. For that, two fences have to be taken instead of one. While, as I have said, I am prepared to accept that the jury could take the first, I do not think that in a case like the present, where there is only the bare statement that a police inquiry is being made, it could take the second in the same stride. If the ordinary sensible man was capable of thinking that wherever there was a police inquiry there was guilt, it would be almost impossible to give accurate information about anything: but in my opinion he is not. I agree with the view of the Court of Appeal. . . .

In the result I think that all your Lordships are now clearly of the opinion that the judge must rule whether the words are capable of bearing each of the defamatory meanings, if there be more than one, put forward by the plaintiff. . . .

Questions

1. Lord Reid said this: "To my mind, there is a great difference between saying that a man has behaved in a suspicious manner and saying that he is guilty of an offence, and I am not convinced that you can only justify the former statement by proving guilt. I can well understand that if you say there is a rumour that X is guilty you can only justify it by proving that he is guilty, because repeating someone else's libellous statement is just as bad as making the statement directly. . . . " Is the difference not simply between saying "A thinks B is guilty" and saying "A says B is guilty?" If this is true, is the difference as material as is suggested? And which is wrong—the rumour or the suspicion rule?

2. Why did the juries award such enormous damages, very much higher in real terms than the £500,000 awarded in 1987 to Jeffrey Archer who was alleged to have used the services of a prostitute, or the £450,000 collected by a British journalist defamed in a Greek newspaper of which about 50 copies were sold in this country (see *Packard* v. *Andricopoulos* (1987) 137 New L.J. 609)?

3. Can a person be libelled by an obvious misprint? (*e.g.* the General who was referred to as battle-scared (or bottle-scarred)).

Notes:

1. It is now safe to say, until the conviction is "spent," that a person was guilty of an offence if he has been convicted of it by a court in the United Kingdom (Civil Evidence Act 1968, s.13(1)); in other words, a person erroneously convicted cannot establish his innocence in a defamation action. Had other recommendations of the Law Reform Committee been imple-

mented, an acquittal would be conclusive of innocence, which would have been equally bad, though for different reasons (Fifteenth Report, Cmnd. 3391, 1967, draft clause 3(1)).

2. The plaintiff ought in all cases to state the defamatory meaning which he alleges the defendant's publication to bear (*Allsop* v. *Church of England Newspaper* [1972] 2 Q.B. 161 (C.A.)), and while, oddly, he need not say which parts he claims to be false (*Viscount de l'Isle* v. *Times Newspapers* [1987] 3 All E.R. 499, 509), he must, in the case of a long unitary publication, identify which parts he claims to be defamatory (*D.D.S.A. Pharmaceuticals* v. *Times Newspapers* [1973] Q.B. 21 (C.A.)). He may not, however, by omitting to claim a particular portion as defamatory, prevent the defendant's attempting to justify it (*Polly Peck (Holdings)* v. *Trelford* [1986] 2 All E.R. 84 (C.A.)), though the defendant must make it clear precisely what it is that he is seeking to justify (*Lucas-Box* v. *News Group Newspapers* [1986] 1 All E.R. 177 (C.A.)). Furthermore, if only a person already acquainted with certain facts would attribute any defamatory meaning to words, the plaintiff must show that the words were brought to the attention of such a person (*Fullam* v. *Newcastle Chronicle* [1977] 3 All E.R. 32 (C.A.)).

Section 2.—Reference to the Plaintiff

E. HULTON & CO. v. JONES

House of Lords [1910] A.C. 20; 79 L.J.K.B. 198; 101 L.T. 831; 26 T.L.R. 128; 54 S.J. 116; [1908–10] All E.R. Rep. 29

The defendants published in the *Sunday Chronicle* an article by their Paris correspondent describing a motor festival at Dieppe. It contained the following passages: "Upon the terrace marches the world, attracted by the motor races—a world immensely pleased with itself, and minded to draw a wealth of inspiration—and, incidentally, of golden cocktails—from any scheme to speed the passing hour . . . 'Whist! there is Artemus Jones with a woman who is not his wife, who must be, you know—the other thing!' whispers a fair neighbour of mine excitedly into her bosom friend's ear. Really, is it not surprising how certain of our fellow-countrymen behave when they come abroad? Who would suppose, by his goings on, that he was a churchwarden at Peckham? No one, indeed, would assume that Jones in the atmosphere of London would take on so austere a job as the duties of a churchwarden. Here, in the atmosphere of Dieppe on the French side of the Channel, he is the life and soul of a gay little band that haunts the Casino and turns night into day, besides betraying a most unholy delight in the society of female butterflies."

The plaintiff was a barrister on the North Wales Circuit who was baptised as Thomas Jones but on confirmation took, on the ground of its distinctiveness, the additional name of Artemus. Until being called to the Bar in 1901 he had contributed signed articles to the defendant's paper, but he accepted that the writer of the article and the editor of the paper knew nothing of him and that they did not intend the article to refer to him. Witnesses called by the plaintiff testified that they took the article to refer to him.

The jury awarded £1,750 damages, and Channell J. entered judgment for the plaintiff in that amount. The defendant's appeal to the Court of Appeal was dismissed (Fletcher Moulton L.J. dissenting) [1909] 2 K.B. 444. The defendant further appealed to the House of Lords, and that appeal was also dismissed in unreserved judgments.

Lord Loreburn L.C.: My Lords, I think this appeal must be dismissed. A question in regard to the law of libel has been raised which does not seem to me to be entitled to the support of your Lordships. Libel is a tortious act. What does the tort consist in? It consists in using language which others knowing the circumstances would reasonably think to be defamatory of the person complaining of and injured by it. A person charged with libel cannot defend himself by showing that he intended in his own breast not to defame, or that he intended not to defame the plaintiff, if in fact he did both. He has none the less imputed something disgraceful and has none the less injured the plaintiff. A man in good faith may publish a libel believing it to be true, and it may be found by the jury that he acted in good faith believing it to be true, and reasonably believing it to be true, but that in fact the statement was false. Under those circumstances he has no defence to the action, however excellent his intention. If the intention of the writer be immaterial in considering whether the matter written is defamatory, I do not see why it need be relevant in considering whether it is defamatory of the plaintiff. The writing, according to the old form, must be malicious, and it must be of and concerning the plaintiff. Just as the defendant could not excuse himself from malice by proving that he wrote it in the most benevolent spirit, so he cannot show that the libel was not of and concerning the plaintiff by proving that he never heard of the plaintiff. His intention in both respects equally is inferred from what he did. His remedy is to abstain from defamatory words.

It is suggested that there was a misdirection by the learned judge in this case. I see none. He lays down in his summing-up the law as follows: "The real point upon which your verdict must turn is, ought or ought not sensible and reasonable people reading this article to think that it was a mere imaginary person such as I have said—Tom Jones, Mr. Pecksniff as a humbug, Mr. Stiggins, or any of that sort of names that one reads of in literature used as types? If you think any reasonable person would think that, it is not actionable at all. If, on the other hand, you do not think that, but think that people would suppose it to mean some real person—those who did not know the plaintiff of course would not know who the real person was, but those who did know of the existence of the plaintiff would think that it was the plaintiff—then the action is maintainable, subject to such damages as you think under all the circumstances are fair and right to give to the plaintiff."

I see no objection in law to that passage. The damages are certainly heavy, but I think your Lordships ought to remember two things. The first is that the jury were entitled to think, in the absence of proof satisfactory to them (and they were the judges of it), that some ingredient of recklessness, or more than recklessness, entered into the writing and the publication of this article, especially as Mr. Jones, the plaintiff, had been employed on this very newspaper, and his name was well known in the paper and also well known in the district in which the paper circulated. In the second place the jury were entitled to say this kind of article is to be condemned. There is no tribunal more fitted to decide in regard to publications, especially publications in the newspaper Press, whether they bear a stamp and character which ought to enlist sympathy and to secure protection. If they think that the licence is not fairly used and that the tone and style of the libel is reprehensible and ought to be checked, it is for the jury to say so; and for my part, although I think the damages are certainly high I am not prepared to advise your Lordships to interfere, especially as the Court of Appeal have not thought it right to interfere, with the verdict.

Questions

1. Is the true question (a) whether the defendant intended to be understood as referring to the plaintiff; (b) whether the words used by the defendant fitted the plaintiff; or (c) whether reasonable people might believe that the defendant was intending to refer to the plaintiff? Is your answer affected by the fact that mere vulgar abuse is not actionable, and by the result of *Blennerhassett* v. *Novelty Sales Services Ltd.* (1933) 175 L.T.J. 393?

2. The jury awarded £1,750 in 1909. In the values of 1987 this represents over £63,000. Libel damages are not taxed. Do you think that anyone who knew Artemus Jones believed the

libel, or that anyone who did not know him cared in the least? Did Artemus Jones embellish his reputation by this lawsuit?

Notes:

1. The decision in the House of Lords was given in unreserved judgments. Accordingly, the careful judgments in the Court of Appeal should be read, especially the furious dissenting judgment of Fletcher Moulton L.J., who said: "It is . . . to my mind, settled law that a defendant is not guilty of libel unless he wrote and published the defamatory words 'of and concerning the plaintiff'—in other words, unless he intended them to refer to the plaintiff. . . . To say that when the common law required it to be alleged and proved that the defendant wrote and published the words of and concerning the plaintiff it meant only that it must be shewn that some people might think so is, to my mind, to give up all pretence of interpreting language and arbitrarily to create new torts which the law never did and should not now recognize as such. . . . If this be the law, then a person who makes a statement about Mr. A.B. which is perfectly true, but which if not true would be libellous, can be made liable to every person of the name of A.B. except the person of and concerning whom the words were written. . . . It cannot be pretended that any actual damage has been suffered by the plaintiff."

Farwell L.J. approached the question from the point of view of recklessness and carelessness in the publication: " . . . [the defendant] has, therefore, for his own purposes chosen to assert a fact of a person bearing the very unusual name of Artemus Jones, recklessly, and caring not whether there was such a person or not, or what the consequences might be to him. . . . Negligence is immaterial on the question of libel or no libel, but may be material on the question of damages. The recklessness to which I have referred, founding myself on *Derry* v. *Peek* (below, p. 489), is quite different from mere negligence." He also said: "If the libel was true of another person and honestly aimed at and intended for him, and not for the plaintiff, the latter has no cause of action, although all his friends and acquaintances may fit the cap on him."

(In *Newstead* v. *London Express* [1940] 1 K.B. 377, the case of the Camberwell bigamist, the Court of Appeal disapproved this last remark, and gave damages to a person in respect of a statement true of someone else; thus the consequence followed which Fletcher Moulton L.J. foretold and Farwell L.J. denied and both regarded as absurd.)

Lord Alverstone C.J. said: "The question, if it be disputed whether the article is a libel upon the plaintiff, is a question of fact for the jury; and in my judgment this question of fact involves not only whether the language used of a person in its fair and ordinary meaning is libellous or defamatory, but whether the person referred to in the libel would be understood by persons who knew him to refer to the plaintiff." This was adopted by Lord Shaw of Dunfermline in the House of Lords.

2. This problem of "innocent defamation" was considered by both the Porter Committee and the Faulks Committee, and the proposals of the former were enacted in Defamation Act 1952, s.2. This section provides that a publisher who makes a prompt "offer of amends," including an offer to publish a suitable correction and apology, may avoid liability if he can prove that neither he nor any of his agents could reasonably have known that the words might be taken to be defamatory of the plaintiff. The provision has been a dead letter, probably because of the requirement for the newspaper defendant to disclose its sources.

3. After the success of *The Second Mrs. Tanqueray* Sir Arthur Pinero decided to write a play about *The Notorious Mrs.*—, but he wanted to be sure that there was no first Mrs. —. He looked through *Crockford's Clerical Dictionary*, and was struck by the name of Canon Flood-Jones; he therefore called his play *The Notorious Mrs. Ebbsmith*. His caution did him no good, for there was a lady of that improbable name who considered herself defamed.

4. Artemus Jones was mentioned by name, or, more accurately, the name Artemus Jones was mentioned. The name of the plaintiff in *Morgan* v. *Odhams Press* ([1971] 1 W.L.R. 1239) was not. All the newspaper had said was that Miss X had been kidnapped by a dog-doping gang and kept in a flat in Kilburn during a specified week. The plaintiff had in fact had Miss X staying with him in his flat in Cricklewood the previous week, and claimed that people who knew this fact would suppose that the newspaper was saying that he was connected with the gang. The jury awarded him £4,750. The Court of Appeal reversed on the ground that the plaintiff must find in the words used some key or pointer to him. The House of Lords disagreed with this, and ordered a new trial on damages only: the jury might reasonably find that readers of *The Sun* would ignore the discrepancies of time and place, and think of the plaintiff while reading the story. A further point arose. One of the plaintiff's witnesses said that though

he thought the story referred to the plaintiff he did not believe it. Lord Reid said of this, with the emphatic approval of Lord Morris: "It was argued that . . . no tort is committed by making a defamatory statement about X to a person who utterly disbelieves it. That is plainly wrong." So we now have powerful authority for the ludicrous proposition that a person may be sued for making a true statement about X which anyone can, despite its terms, suppose to be a false statement about Y.

5. Another extraordinary case of reference is *Boston* v. *Bagshaw* ([1966] 1 W.L.R. 1126). The defendants broadcast the true statement that at a recent auction a man had bid for pigs, given his name as Boston of Rugeley, and made off with the pigs without paying. The true Boston of Rugeley claimed damages and nearly got them. Is it defamatory of X to say that a person masquerading as X has done something disgraceful? Is it defamatory of X to masquerade as X and do something disgraceful? (Note that a person to whom statements are falsely ascribed has a remedy in damages under the Copyright Act 1956, s.43(2)).

6. It is actionable to be rude about an unspecified person and then identify him later, as is shown by the very thrilling case of *Hayward* v. *Thompson* [1981] 3 All E.R. 450.

7. In France a newspaper which refers to a person, even in a non-defamatory way, is bound, on pain of a fine, to allow that person the right of reply (Law of the Press, July 29, 1881, Art. 13). The Faulks Committee dismissed this idea as one "which entitles a person, who may be without merits, to compel a newspaper to publish a statement extolling his non-existent virtue" (para. 623). It is worth noting that under our own dear system no plaintiff *ever* leaves court with his reputation cleared: even the award of massive damages is no indication that what the defendant said was false, only that the defendant did not prove it to be true: in other words, the successful plaintiff may be every bit as bad as the defendant said.

KNUPFFER v. LONDON EXPRESS NEWSPAPER LTD.

House of Lords [1944] A.C. 116; 113 L.J.K.B. 251; 170 L.T. 362; 60 T.L.R. 310; 88 S.J. 143; [1944] 1 All E.R. 495

The *Daily Express* of July 1, 1941, carried an article entitled "Hitler's Littlest Kaiser" and containing the following words: "The quislings on whom Hitler flatters himself he can build a pro-German movement within the Soviet Union are an emigré group called 'Mlado Russ' or 'Young Russia.' They are a minute body professing a pure Fascist ideology who have long sought a suitable fuehrer—I know with what success. . . . The vast majority of Russian emigrés repudiate these people, but Hitler is accustomed to find instruments among the despised dregs of every community. . . . "

The plaintiff, a Russian resident in London, proved that he was the head of the British branch of the Young Russia party, which counted 24 members in Britain and about 2,000 in the world. Four of his witnesses were asked "To whom did your mind go when you read that article?" and they all replied "To the plaintiff."

Stable J., who tried the action without a jury, held that the words referred to the plaintiff, and gave judgment for the plaintiff with £3,500 damages. The Court of Appeal held that the words could not be regarded as referring to the plaintiff, and allowed the defendant's appeal [1943] K.B. 80. The plaintiff appealed to the House of Lords, who dismissed his appeal.

Viscount Simon L.C.: . . . There are two questions involved in the attempt to identify the appellant as the person defamed. The first question is a question of law—can the article, having regard to its language, be regarded as capable of referring to the appellant? The second question is a question of fact—does the article, in fact, lead reasonable people, who know the appellant, to the conclusion that it does refer to him? Unless the first question can be answered in favour of the appellant, the second question does not arise, and where the trial judge went wrong was in treating evidence to support the identification in fact as governing the matter, when the first question is necessarily, as a matter of law, to be answered in the negative. I move that this appeal be dismissed.

Lord Atkin: . . . I venture to think that it is a mistake to lay down a rule as to libel on a class, and then qualify it with exceptions. The only relevant rule is that in order to be actionable the defamatory words must be understood to be published of and concerning the plaintiff. It is irrelevant that the words are published of two or more persons if they are proved to be published of him, and it is irrelevant that the two or more persons are called by some generic or class name. There can be no law that a defamatory statement made of a firm, or trustees, or the tenants of a particular building is not actionable, if the words would reasonably be understood as published of each member of the firm or each trustee or each tenant. The reason why a libel published of a large or indeterminate number of persons described by some general name generally fails to be actionable is the difficulty of establishing that the plaintiff was, in fact, included in the defamatory statement, for the habit of making unfounded generalisations is ingrained in ill-educated or vulgar minds, or the words are occasionally intended to be a facetious exaggeration. Even in such cases words may be used which enable the plaintiff to prove that the words complained of were intended to be published of each member of the group, or, at any rate, of himself. Too much attention has been paid, I venture to think, in the textbooks and elsewhere to the ruling of Willes J. in 1858 in *Eastwood* v. *Holmes* ((1858) 1 F. & F. 347; 175 E.R. 758), a case at nisi prius in which the judge non-suited the plaintiff both because he thought there was no evidence that the words were published of the plaintiff and for other reasons, and, so far as the first ground is concerned, it appears to me on the facts to be of doubtful correctness. His words "it only reflects on a class of persons" are irrelevant unless they mean "it does not reflect on the plaintiff," and his instance "All lawyers were thieves" is an excellent instance of the vulgar generalisations to which I have referred. It will be as well for the future for lawyers to concentrate on the question whether the words were published of the plaintiff rather than on the question whether they were spoken of a class. I agree that in the present case the words complained of are, apparently, an unfounded generalisation conveying imputations of disgraceful conduct, but not such as could reasonably be understood to be spoken of the appellant. It becomes unnecessary to deal with the question of excessive damages. I content myself by saying that, if the libel had been published of the appellant, while the damages awarded are possibly too high, I do not find myself in any degree in accord with the estimate of the damages suggested by the Court of Appeal.

Questions
1. Why, *precisely*, does a person who says "All lawyers are thieves" not defame every lawyer who is not?
2. Is there a class of people called Artemus Jones?
3. Did the defendant intend to refer to the plaintiff?
4. Is it defamatory to say that the plaintiffs in defamation suits during the past 20 years have, with very few exceptions, been thoroughly undeserving claimants? Is it true?

Notes:
1. The Court of Appeal has held it arguable that if an unidentified member of a group is defamed, each member of the group may sue (*Farrington* v. *Leigh*, *The Independent*, December 14, 1987).
2. In *Riches* v. *News Group Newspapers* [1985] 2 All E.R. 845 the defendant repeated a madman's grotesque allegations against "the Banbury CID." The Banbury CID had 11 male members, and 10 of them sued. The jury awarded each plaintiff £300 compensatory and £25,000 exemplary damages—a total of £253,000. The verdicts for exemplary damages were reversed by the Court of Appeal: only one sum could be awarded if compensatory damages were insufficient to punish the defendant, and it must be divided equally.

Section 3.—Qualified Privilege

WATT v. LONGSDON

Court of Appeal [1930] 1 K.B. 130; 98 L.J.K.B. 711; 142 L.T. 4; 45 T.L.R. 619; 73 S.J. 544;
[1929] All E.R. Rep. 284

Longsdon was liquidator of the Scottish Petroleum Company. He received from Browne, manager of their office in Casa Blanca, a letter relating that Watt, the managing director, had been living in sin for two months with the housemaid, who was described as old, deaf and nearly blind and was said to dye her hair; the letter also stated that Watt had planned to seduce Mrs. Browne. Longsdon sent this letter to Singer, the chairman of the board of directors. Longsdon also replied to Browne, saying that he had long suspected Watt of immorality and that, in his view, Mrs. Watt (whom he knew well, as she had nursed him through an illness) ought to be told; he himself would tell her, if only Browne would obtain a sworn statement, by bribery, if need be. Before that statement was obtained, Watt himself returned to England, and Longsdon sent Browne's original letter to Mrs. Watt. The result was a separation and proceedings for divorce.

Watt sued Longsdon in respect of the publications to Singer, Browne and Mrs. Watt. The learned judge held that the occasion of all three publications was privileged, and held further that there was no evidence of malice fit to be left to the jury. The plaintiff appealed; the Court of Appeal allowed his appeal and ordered a new trial.

Scrutton L.J.: This case raises, amongst other matters, the extremely difficult question, equally important in its legal and social aspect, as to the circumstances, if any, in which a person will be justified in giving to one partner a marriage information which that person honestly believes to be correct, but which is in fact untrue, about the matrimonial delinquencies of the other party to the marriage. The question becomes more difficult if the answer in law turns on the existence or non-existence of a social or moral duty, a question which the judge is to determine, without any evidence, by the light of his own knowledge of the world, and his own views on social morality, a subject-matter on which views vary in different ages, in different countries, and even as between man and man. . . .

The learned judge appears to have taken the view that the authorities justify him in holding that if "there is an obvious interest in the person to whom a communication is made which causes him to be a proper recipient of a statement," even if the party making the communication had no moral or social duty to the party to whom the communication is made, the occasion is privileged. . . . He has therefore found in the present case that the occasion of each of the three communications, to Singer, to the wife, and to Browne, was privileged, and that there is no evidence of excess of communication or of malice to be left to the jury. "No nice scales should be used," as Lord Dunedin said in *Adam* v. *Ward* ([1917] A.C. 309, 330).

By the law of England there are occasions on which a person may make defamatory statements about another which are untrue without incurring any legal liability for his statements. These occasions are called privileged occasions. A reason frequently given for this privilege is that the allegation that the speaker has "unlawfully and maliciously published," is displaced by proof that the speaker had either a duty or an interest to publish, and that this duty or interest confers the privilege. But communications made on these occasions may lose their privilege: (1) they may exceed the privilege of the occasion by going beyond the limits of the duty or interest, or (2) they may be published with express malice, so that the occasion is not being legitimately used, but abused. . . . The question whether the occasion was privileged is for the judge, and so far as "duty" is concerned, the question is: Was there a duty, legal, moral, or social, to communicate? As to legal duty, the judge should have no difficulty; the judge should know the law; but as to moral or social duties of imperfect obligation, the task is far more troublesome. The judge has no evidence as to the view the community takes of moral or social duties. All the help the Court of Appeal can give him is contained in the judgment of Lindley L.J. in *Stuart* v. *Bell* ([1891] 2 Q.B. 341, 350): "The question of moral or social duty being for the judge, each judge must decide it as best he can for himself. I take moral or social duty to mean a duty recognised by English people of ordinary intelligence and moral principle, but at the same time not a duty enforceable by legal proceedings, whether civil or criminal. My own conviction is that all or, at all events, the great mass of right-minded men in the position of the defendant would have considered it their duty, under the circumstances, to inform Stanley of the suspicion which had fallen on the plaintiff." Is the judge merely to give his own view of moral and social duty, though he thinks a considerable portion of the community hold a different opinion? Or is he to endeavour to ascertain what view "the great mass of right-minded men" would take? It is not surprising that with such a standard both judges and text-writers treat the matter as one of great difficulty in which no definite line can be drawn. . . .

. . . In 1855, in *Harrison* v. *Bush* ((1855) 5 E. & B. 344, 348; 119 E.R. 509), Lord Campbell C.J. giving the judgment of the Court of Queen's Bench accepted a principle stated thus: "A communication made bona fide upon any subject-matter in which the party communicating has an interest, or in reference to which he has a duty, is privileged, if made to a person having a corresponding interest or duty, although it contain criminatory matter which, without this privilege, would be slanderous and actionable." This is the first of a series of statements that both parties, the writer and the recipient, must have a corresponding interest or duty. . . . Lord Atkinson in *Adam* v. *Ward* ([1917] A.C. 309, 334) expresses it thus: "It was not disputed, in this case on either side, that a privileged occasion is, in reference to qualified privilege, an occasion where the person who makes a communication has an interest or a duty, legal, social, or moral, to make it to the person to whom it is made, and the person to whom it is so made has a corresponding interest or duty to receive it. This reciprocity is essential." With slight modifications in particular circumstances, this appears to me to be well-established law, but, except in the case of communications based on common interest, the principle is that either there must be interest in the recipient and a duty to communicate in the speaker, or an interest to be protected in the speaker and a duty to protect it in the recipient. Except in the case of common interest justifying intercommunication, the correspondence must be between duty and interest. There may, in the common interest cases, be also a common or reciprocal duty. It is not every interest which will create a duty in a stranger or volunteer. . . .

In *Stuart* v. *Bell* ([1891] 2 Q.B. 341) there was again a difference of opinion . . . Stanley, the explorer, and his valet, Stuart, were staying with the mayor of Newcastle, Bell. The Edinburgh police made a very carefully worded communication to the Newcastle police that there had been a robbery in Edinburgh at an hotel where Stuart was staying, and it might be well to make very careful and cautious inquiry into the matter. The Newcastle police showed the letter to the mayor, who after consideration showed it to Stanley, who dismissed Stuart. Stuart sued the mayor. Lindley and Kay L.JJ. held that the mayor had a moral duty to communicate, and Stanley a material interest to receive the communication; Lopes L.J. held that in the circumstances there was no moral duty to communicate, though in some circumstances there might be such a duty in a host towards a guest. I myself should have agreed with the majority, but the difference of opinion between such experienced judges shows the difficulty of the question.

In my opinion Horridge J. went too far in holding that there could be a privileged occasion on the ground of interest in the recipient without any duty to communicate on the part of the person making the communication. But that does not settle the question, for it is necessary to consider, in the present case, whether there was, as to each communication, a duty to communicate, and an interest in the recipient.

First as to the communication between Longsdon and Singer, I think the case must proceed on the admission that at all material times Watt, Longsdon and Browne were in the employment of the same company, and the evidence afforded by the answer to the interrogatory put in by the plaintiff that Longsdon believed the statements in Browne's letter. In my view on these facts there was a duty, both from a moral and a material point of view, on Longsdon to communicate the letter to Singer, the chairman of his company, who, apart from questions of present employment, might be asked by Watt for a testimonial to a future employer. Equally, I think Longsdon receiving the letter from Browne, might discuss the matter with him, and ask for further information, on the ground of a common interest in the affairs of the company, and to obtain further information for the chairman. I should therefore agree with the view of Horridge J. that these two occasions were privileged, though for different reasons. Horridge J. further held that there was no evidence of malice fit to be left to the jury, and, while I think some of Longsdon's action and language in this respect was unfortunate, as the plaintiff has put in the answer that Longsdon believed the truth of the statements in Browne's and his own letter, like Lord Dunedin in *Adam* v. *Ward*, I should not try excess with too nice scales, and I do not dissent from his view as to malice. As to the communications to Singer and Browne, in my opinion the appeal should fail, but as both my brethren take the view that there was evidence of malice which should be left to the jury, there must, of course, be a new trial as to the claim based on these two publications.

The communication to Mrs. Watt stands on a different footing. I have no intention of writing an exhaustive treatise on the circumstances when a stranger or a friend should communicate to husband or wife information he receives as to the conduct of the other party to the marriage. I am clear that it is impossible to say he is always under a moral or social duty to do so; it is equally impossible to say he is never under such a duty. It must depend on the circumstances of each case, the nature of the information, and the relation of speaker and recipient. It cannot, on the one hand, be the duty even of a friend to communicate all the gossip the friend hears at men's clubs or women's bridge parties to one of the spouses affected. On the other hand, most men would hold that it was the moral duty of a doctor who attended his sister in law, and believed her to be suffering from a miscarriage, for which an absent husband could not be responsible, to communicate that fact to his wife and the husband. . . . If this is so, the decision must turn on the circumstances of each case, the judge being much influenced by the consideration that as a general rule it is not desirable for any one, even a mother in law, to interfere in the affairs of man and wife. Using the best judgment I can in this difficult matter, I have come to the conclusion that there was not a moral or social duty in Longsdon to make this communication to Mrs. Watt such as to make the occasion privileged, and that there must be a new trial so far as it relates to the claim for publication of a libel to Mrs. Watt. The communications to Singer and Browne being made on a privileged occasion, there must be a new trial of the issue as to malice defeating the privilege. There must also be a new trial of the complaint as to publication to Mrs. Watt, the occasion being held not to be privileged.

Greer L.J.: . . . In my judgment no right minded man in the position of the defendant, a friend of the plaintiff and of his wife, would have thought it right to communicate the horrible accusations contained in Mr. Browne's letter to the plaintiff's wife. . . . A man may believe in the truth of a defamatory statement, and yet when he publishes it be reckless whether his belief be well-founded or not. His motive for publishing a libel on a privileged occasion may be an improper one, even though he believes the statement to be true. He may be moved by hatred or dislike, or a desire to injure the subject of the libel, and may be using the occasion for that purpose, and if he is doing so the publication will be maliciously made, even though he may believe the defamatory statements to be true. . . .

Questions

1. If a statement is false, how can there ever be a duty to communicate it?

2. Would the outcome of the case have been the same if Longdson had sent the defamatory letter in response to an inquiry from Mrs. Watt whether he had any news of her husband? Or asking if what she had heard about him were true? Or asking if he could help her obtain evidence for a forthcoming divorce suit? If there were a privilege in any of these cases, what would be its source?

3. If A defames B to C, and B retaliates by defaming A to C, can B, when sued by A, claim (a) that he had any kind of duty to make the statement in question, and (b) that C had any interest in hearing it? See *Turner* v. *M.G.M. Pictures Ltd.* [1950] 1 All E.R. 449 (H.L.).

4. Would it be safe for a disgruntled customer to write to the manager of a store that in his view its employees were incompetent and insolent?

5. Is it not odd that speech is free only where there is a duty to speak or to listen? Can you think of a better technique than qualified privilege to distinguish socially desirable communications from gratuitous gossip and mere muck-raking?

Notes:

1. As Blackburn J. said in *Davies* v. *Snead* (L.R. 5 Q.B. 608, 611 (1870)): "where a person is so situated that it becomes right in the interests of society that he should tell to a third person certain facts, then if he bona fide and without malice does tell them it is a privileged communication." The test of the existence of privilege is objective: it must be right in the interests of society, and it is not enough that the defendant honestly supposed that it was right; furthermore, the person to whom he makes the communication must be the right person to receive it, and it is not enough that the defendant should honestly think that he is. If these objective criteria are satisfied, then the defendant is protected if he honestly believed what he said, even if he got his facts wrong. Indeed, if he got his facts wrong, privilege is the only possible defence, even if the matter is one of public interest.

2. A businessman who dictates a letter "publishes" its contents to his secretary. If the letter was destined for a third party, privilege attaches to the dictation if actual publication to that third party would be privileged. If the letter is addressed to the plaintiff, there is the difficulty that since publication to the party defamed is not a tort at all, it cannot strictly be called privileged; even so, the dictation of such a letter appears to be privileged unless the letter was quite unwarranted. If the secretary has any particular interest in the subject-matter, the dictation may be privileged in its own right, but otherwise no privilege attaches to the dictation situation as such. *Bryanston Finance* v. *de Vries* [1975] Q.B. 703 contains a fascinating conflict of opinion on the matter between Lord Denning and Lord Diplock.

(It might be better to say that there is no publication at all between businessman and secretary, just as there is none between husband and wife (Spencer [1975] Camb.L.J. 195)).

3. A man who was divorcing his third wife sued his doctor for writing, in reply to his solicitor's request for a medical report, that the plaintiff was paranoid, especially in relation to his first two wives. The latter part of this statement was not proved. The letter was held to attract not only qualified privilege, in view of the reciprocity of interest between the plaintiff's two professional advisers, but also absolute privilege, since the defendant's possible evidence in the forthcoming divorce proceedings was in issue. *Guske* v. *Cooke*, November 19, 1980 (Skinner J.).

4. The privilege, absolute or qualified, which attaches to the occasion of a communication must be distinguished from the immunity or privilege which may attach to a document so as to render it inadmissible as evidence of what was communicated. Thus one may not found a libel suit on a document compulsorily disclosed in prior litigation (*Riddick* v. *Thames Board Mills* [1977] 3 All E.R. 677). This was extended in *Hasselblad (G.B.)* v. *Orbinson* [1985] 1 All E.R. 173. The defendant bought a camera manufactured by the plaintiff and then complained to the shop that the plaintiff refused to repair it because it had come from an unauthorised dealer. The shop sent the letter to its supplier, the supplier sent it to the European Commission which it had previously notified of the plaintiff's possible breach of Article 86 of the Treaty of Rome, and the Commission, as it was bound to do, sent a copy of it to the plaintiff. The plaintiff sued for defamation. The Court of Appeal held that the absolute privilege which

attaches to evidence given to a judicial or quasi-judicial body did not apply since the Commission's procedure rendered it administrative rather than in any way judicial, but that Hasselblad should be prevented from using the letter as the foundation of a libel suit as it had been mandatorily disclosed to it for a limited purpose. The suit therefore collapsed. Those who ask, with May L.J., why qualified privilege was not sufficient protection for the defendant may ponder the words of Sir John Donaldson M.R.: "It is only the very rich, the very foolish, the very malicious or the very dedicated who will knowingly put themselves in a position in which they have to defend a libel action, even with the benefit of qualified privilege as a defence. The anxieties would be enormous and, even if ultimately successful, the difference between actual and recoverable costs would be very substantial indeed." May L.J. was struck by the fact that no similar case had come up in any of the other member states of the E.E.C. That is because none of them has a law of defamation as dotty as ours, or as susceptible of wicked abuse.

Abuse is likely when plaintiffs are provided with funds by unions or others. Such funds are available to policemen who want to sue citizens who complain about their conduct. While statements made in the course of an investigation are absolutely privileged and non-disclosable, the complaint which initiates the investigation may be disclosed and sued on (*Conerney* v. *Jacklin* [1985] Crim.L.R. 234, criticised *ibid.*) The House of Lords should reverse this, perhaps on the basis that the Police Complaints Board has been replaced by the Police Complaints Authority under the Police and Criminal Evidence Act 1984 (Part IX). The complaint does, of course, attract qualified privilege, but one must remember the words of the Master of the Rolls quoted above.

5. Where X has been employed by Y and now seeks employment with Z, a reference supplied by Y to Z is supplied on a privileged occasion. X therefore cannot sue Y simply for saying disagreeable things about him: he must prove malice. But if X can prove that Y took no care over the reference, that, for example, he did not check his files or confused X with another employee, X can, if he proves loss, claim damages in negligence: after all, one owes some duty to those who have served one (*Lawton* v. *BOC Transhield* [1987] 2 All E.R. 608) (*contra* Tettenborn [1987] Camb.L.J. 390).

HORROCKS v. LOWE

House of Lords [1975] A.C. 135; [1974] 2 W.L.R. 282; 118 S.J. 149; [1974] 1 All E.R. 662; 72 L.G.R. 251

At a meeting of the Bolton town council the defendant, a Labour alderman, proposed that the plaintiff, a Conservative councillor, be removed from a committee because of his interests as a property developer. In particular, the defendant referred to an incident in which the corporation had had to pay the Conservative Club over £17,000 in compensation because the land it had leased from the corporation could not be used for building owing to a refusal by the plaintiff's company to release a restrictive covenant.

The trial judge held that the occasion was privileged but that the defendant, being in the grip of gross and unreasonable prejudice, was guilty of malice, although he really believed what he was saying and was not actuated by any personal spite or ill-will against the plaintiff. He gave judgment for the plaintiff, damages £400. The defendant's appeal to the Court of Appeal was allowed unanimously, on the ground that a defendant who believed in the truth of what he said on a privileged occasion could not be held liable ([1972] 3 All E.R. 1098). The plaintiff's appeal to the House of Lords was dismissed unanimously.

Lord Diplock: . . . Mr. Lowe and other members of the Labour caucus took the view that because of his personal interest in the development of land in Bolton Mr. Horrocks ought not to be a member of the Management and Finance Committee. He had expressed this view at the meeting of that committee on 27th October 1969 but was powerless to obtain acceptance of it by the committee because of the Conservative majority on the committee and in the council itself. He gave notice that he intended to raise the matter again at the council meeting on 5th November on the occasion of the statement by Alderman Telford about the Bishops Road site. This he did and what he said at that meeting of the council is the slander in respect of which this action has been brought. It consisted in large part of a recital of what he understood to be the facts about the Bishops Road affair. It was hard hitting criticism of Mr. Horrocks's conduct. The sting of it was in the words quoted by Stirling J.:

"I don't know how to describe his attitude whether it was brinkmanship, megalomania or childish petulance . . . I suggest that he has misled the town, the Leader of the party and his political and club colleagues some of whom are his business associates. I therefore request that he be removed from the Committee to some other where his undoubted talents can be used to the advantage of the Corporation."

My Lords, as a general rule, English law gives effect to the ninth commandment that a man shall not speak evil falsely of his neighbour. It supplies a temporal sanction: if he cannot prove that defamatory matter which he published was true, he is liable in damages to whomsoever he has defamed, except where the publication is oral only, causes no damage and falls outside the categories of slander actionable *per se*. The public interest that the law should provide an effective means whereby a man can vindicate his reputation against calumny has nevertheless to be accommodated to the competing public interest in permitting men to communicate frankly and freely with one another about matters with respect to which the law recognises that they have a duty to perform or an interest to protect in doing so. What is published in good faith on matters of these kinds is published on a privileged occasion. It is not actionable even though it be defamatory and turns out to be untrue. With some exceptions which are irrelevant to the instant appeal, the privilege is not absolute but qualified. It is lost if the occasion which gives rise to it is misused. For in all cases of qualified privilege there is some special reason of public policy why the law accords immunity from suit—the existence of some public or private duty, whether legal or moral, on the part of the maker of the defamatory statement which justifies his communicating it or of some interest of his own which he is entitled to protect by doing so. If he uses the occasion for some other reason he loses the protection of the privilege.

So, the motive with which the defendant on a privileged occasion made a statement defamatory of the plaintiff becomes crucial. The protection might, however, be illusory if the onus lay on him to prove that he was actuated solely by a sense of the relevant duty or a desire to protect the relevant interest. So he is entitled to be protected by the privilege unless some other dominant and improper motive on his part is proved. "Express malice" is the term of art descriptive of such a motive. Broadly speaking, it means malice in the popular sense of a desire to injure the person who is defamed and this is generally the motive which the plaintiff sets out to prove. But to destroy the privilege the desire to injure must be the dominant motive for the defamatory publication; knowledge that it will have that effect is not enough if the defendant is nevertheless acting in accordance with a sense of duty or in bona fide protection of his own legitimate interests.

The motive with which a person published defamatory matter can only be inferred from what he did or said he knew. If it be proved that he did not believe that what he published was true this is generally conclusive evidence of express malice, for no sense of duty or desire to protect his own legitimate interests can justify a man in telling deliberate and injurious falsehoods about another, save in the exceptional case where a person may be under a duty to pass on, without endorsing, defamatory reports made by some other person.

Apart from those exceptional cases, what is required on the part of the defamer to entitle him to the protection of the privilege is positive belief in the truth of what he published or, as it is generally though tautologously termed, "honest belief." If he publishes untrue defamatory matter recklessly, without considering or caring whether it be true or not, he is in this, as in other branches of the law, treated as if he knew it to be false. But indifference to the truth of what he publishes is not to be equated with carelessness, impulsiveness or irrationality in arriving at a positive belief that it is true. The freedom of speech protected by the law of qualified privilege may be availed of by all sorts and conditions of men. In affording to them immunity from suit if they have acted in good faith in compliance with a legal or moral duty or in protection of a legitimate interest the law must take them as it finds them. In ordinary life it is rare indeed for people to form their beliefs by a process of logical deduction from facts ascertained by a rigorous search for all available evidence and a judicious assessment of its probative value. In greater or less degree according to their temperaments, their training, their intelligence, they are swayed by prejudice, rely on intuition instead of reasoning, leap to conclusions on inadequate evidence and fail to recognise the cogency of material which might cast doubt on the validity of the conclusions they reach. But despite the imperfection of the mental process by which the belief is arrived at it may still be "honest," *i.e.* a positive belief that the conclusions they have reached are true. The law demands no more.

Even a positive belief in the truth of what is published on a privileged occasion—which is presumed unless the contrary is proved—may not be sufficient to negative express malice if it can be proved that the defendant misused the occasion for some purpose other than that for which the privilege is accorded by the law. The commonest case is where the dominant motive which actuates the defendant is not a desire to perform the relevant duty or to protect the relevant interest, but to give vent to his personal spite or ill-will towards the person he defames. If this be proved, then even positive belief in the truth of what is published will not enable the defamer to avail himself of the protection of the privilege to which he would otherwise have been entitled. There may be instances of improper motives which destroy the privilege apart from personal spite. A defendant's dominant motive may have been to obtain some private advantage unconnected with the duty or the interest which constitutes the reason for the privilege. If so, he loses the benefit of the privilege despite his positive belief that what he said or wrote was true.

Judges and juries should, however, be very slow to draw the inference that a defendant was so far actuated by improper motives as to deprive him of the protection of the privilege unless they are satisfied that he did not believe that what he said or wrote was true or that he was indifferent to its truth or falsity. The motives with which human beings act are mixed. They find it difficult to hate the sin but love the sinner. Qualified privilege would be illusory, and the public interest that it is meant to serve defeated, if the protection which it affords were lost merely because a person, although acting in compliance with a duty or in protection of a legitimate interest, disliked the person whom he defamed or was indignant at what he believed to be that person's conduct and welcomed the opportunity of exposing it. It is only where his desire to comply with the relevant duty or to protect the relevant interest plays no significant part in his motives for publishing what he believes to be true that "express malice" can properly be found.

There may be evidence of the defendant's conduct on occasions other than that protected by the privilege which justifies the inference that on the privileged occasion too his dominant motive in publishing what he did was personal spite or some other improper motive, even although he believed it to be true. But where, as in the instant case, conduct extraneous to the privileged occasion itself is not relied on, and the only evidence of improper motive is the content of the defamatory matter itself or the steps taken by the defendant to verify its accuracy, there is only one exception to the rule that in order to succeed the plaintiff must show affirmatively that the defendant did not believe it to be true or was indifferent to its truth or falsity. Juries should be instructed and judges should remind themselves that this burden of affirmative proof is not one that is lightly satisfied.

The exception is where what is published incorporates defamatory matter that is not really necessary to the fulfilment of the particular duty or the protection of the particular interest on which the privilege is founded. Logically it might be said that such irrelevant matter falls outside the privilege altogether. But if this were so it would involve the application by the court of an objective test of relevance to every part of the defamatory matter published on the privileged occasion; whereas, as everyone knows, ordinary human beings vary in their ability to distinguish that which is logically relevant from that which is not and few, apart from lawyers, have had any training which qualifies them to do so. So the protection afforded by the privilege would be illusory if it were lost in respect of any defamatory matter which on logical analysis could be shown to be irrelevant to the fulfilment of the duty or the protection of the right on which the privilege was founded. As Lord Dunedin pointed out in *Adam* v. *Ward* the proper rule as respects irrelevant defamatory matter incorporated in a statement made on a privileged occasion is to treat it as one of the factors to be taken into consideration in deciding whether, in all the circumstances, an inference that the defendant was actuated by express malice can properly be drawn. As regards irrelevant matter the test is not whether it is logically relevant but whether, in all the circumstances, it can be inferred that the defendant either did not believe it to be true or, though believing it to be true, realised that it had nothing to do with the particular duty or interest on which the privilege was based, but nevertheless seized the opportunity to drag in irrelevant defamatory matter to vent his personal spite, or for some other improper motive. Here, too, judges and juries should be slow to draw this inference.

My Lords, what is said by members of a local council at meetings of the council or of any of its committees is spoken on a privileged occasion. The reason for the privilege is that those who represent the local government electors should be able to speak freely and frankly, boldly and bluntly, on any matter which they believe affects the interests or welfare of the inhabitants. They may be swayed by strong political prejudice, they may be obstinate and pig-headed, stupid and obtuse; but they were chosen by the electors to speak their minds on matters of local concern and so long as they do so honestly they run no risk of liability for defamation of those who are the subjects of their criticism.

In the instant case Mr. Lowe's speech at the meeting of the Bolton borough council was on matters which were undoubtedly of local concern. With one minor exception the only facts relied on as evidence from which express malice was to be inferred had reference to the contents of the speech itself, the circumstances in which the meeting of the council was held and the material relating to the subject-matter of Mr. Lowe's speech which was within his actual knowledge or available to him on enquiry. The one exception was his failure to apologise to Mr. Horrocks when asked to do so two days later. A refusal to apologise is at best but tenuous evidence of malice, for it is consistent with a continuing belief in the truth of what he said. Stirling J. found it to be so in the case of Mr. Lowe.

So the judge was left with no other material on which to found an inference of malice except the contents of the speech itself, the circumstances in which it was made and, of course, Mr. Lowe's own evidence in the witness box. Where such is the case the test of malice is very simple. It was laid down by Lord Esher himself, as Brett L.J. in *Clark* v. *Molyneux* (1873) 3 Q.B.D. 237. It is: has it been proved that the defendant did not honestly believe that what he said was true, *i.e.* was he either aware that it was not true or indifferent to its truth or falsity? In *Royal Aquarium & Summer & Winter Garden Society* v. *Parkinson* [1892] 1 Q.B. 431 Lord Esher M.R. applied the self-same test. In the passage cited by Stirling J. he was doing no more than disposing of a suggestion made in the course of the argument that reckless disregard of whether what was stated was true or false did not constitute malice unless it were due to personal spite directed against the individual defamed. All Lord Esher M.R. was saying was that such indifference to the truth or falsity of what was stated constituted malice even though it resulted from prejudice with regard to the subject-matter of the statement rather than with regard to the particular person

defamed. But however gross, however unreasoning the prejudice it does not destroy the privilege unless it has this result. If what it does is to cause the defendant
honestly to believe what a more rational or impartial person would reject or doubt
he does not thereby lose the protection of the privilege.

I know of no authority which throws doubt on this proposition apart from a Del-
phic dictum in the judgment of Greer L.J. in *Watt* v. *Longsdon* where he gives as an
example of state of mind which constitutes malice: "A man may believe in the truth
of a defamatory statement, and yet when he publishes it be reckless whether his
belief be well founded or not." If "reckless" here means that the maker of the
statement has jumped to conclusions which are irrational, reached without
adequate enquiry or based on insufficient evidence, this is not enough to constitute
malice if he nevertheless does believe in the truth of the statement itself. The only
kind of recklessness which destroys privilege is indifference to its truth or falsity.

My Lords, in his judgment Stirling J. rejected the inference that Mr. Lowe was
actuated by personal spite against Mr. Horrocks. He found, however, that Mr.
Lowe was—

"so anxious to have the plaintiff removed from the Management and Finance
Committee that . . . he did not consider fairly and objectively whether the evidence that he had of the plaintiff's conduct over Bishops Road came anything like
far enough to justify his conclusions or comments."

He then gave some examples of Mr. Lowe's jumping to conclusions and failing to
make further enquiries and to his omission to refer to the dilemma in which Mr.
Horrocks found himself *vis-à-vis* those who had purchased from his company building plots with the benefit of the restrictive covenant against building on the land
leased by the corporation to the Conservative Club.

It was no misuse of the occasion to use the Bishops Road fiasco in an attempt to
obtain the removal of Mr. Horrocks from the Management and Finance Committee
even though the prospects of success may have been slender until the balance of
political power on the council changed. The other matters referred to by the
learned judge as showing Mr. Lowe to be grossly and unreasoningly prejudiced
might have warranted the inference that he was indifferent to the truth or falsity of
what he said, if his own evidence as to his belief had been unconvincing. But it was
an inference the judge, who heard and saw Mr. Lowe in the witness box, did not
feel able to draw. "I am prepared," he said "to accept what the defendant reiter-
ated in his evidence that he believed and still believes that everything he said was
true and justifiable."

However prejudiced the judge thought Mr. Lowe to be, however irrational in
leaping to conclusions unfavourable to Mr. Horrocks, this crucial finding of Mr.
Lowe's belief in the truth of what he said on that privileged occasion entitled him to
succeed in his defence of privilege. The Court of Appeal so held. I would myself do
likewise and dismiss this appeal.

Lord Wilberforce, Lord Hodson and Lord Kilbrandon agreed with Lord Diplock.
Viscount Dilhorne delivered a concurring opinion.

Question

If it is proposed that the holder of an office be removed from it on the ground that he is unfit
to continue in it, is it possible without defaming him (a) to make the proposal, (b) to speak in
its favour, (c) to vote for it? Does it matter whether the alleged unfitness is moral, intellectual,
political or physical?

Note:

Since Lord Denning could not persuade the other members of the Court of Appeal in *Riddick* v. *Thames Board Mills* [1977] Q.B. 881 that an employer should not have to pay when
one of his employees defames another to a third, the usual rules of vicarious liability apply in

defamation: a principal or employer, although entirely free from fault, is liable if his agent or servant utters actionable defamations in the scope of his authority or the course of his employment. This remains true where the occasion of publication is privileged and the defamation is actionable only because the subordinate is malicious. In such a case principal and agent or master and servant are joint tortfeasors.

This does not, however, apply in all cases of joint publication. If A and B jointly draft and send a letter, that is doubtless a joint publication such that if there were no privilege both would be liable; but if privilege does prima facie attach to the communication, B, if innocent, will not be rendered liable just because A is malicious. This is true whether B is an equal or a subordinate. *Egger* v. *Viscount Chelmsford* [1965] 1 Q.B. 248 (C.A.).

Section 4.—Fair Comment

CAMPBELL v. SPOTTISWOODE

Nisi Prius (1862) 3 F. & F. 421; 176 E.R. 188
Queen's Bench (1863) 3 B. & S. 769; 32 L.J.Q.B. 185; 8 L.T. 201; 27 J.P. 501;
9 Jur. 1069; 122 E.R. 288

The plaintiff, Dr. Campbell, ran a religious newspaper, *The Ensign*. Its columns carried letters, many purporting to come from a Mr. Thompson, which urged readers to subscribe for copies of the paper to be sent to China to convert the heathen. The suggested scheme, and Dr. Campbell himself, were roundly attacked in *The Saturday Review* for June 14, 1862, published by the defendant. The article contained the following passages: "The doctor refers frequently to Mr. Thompson as his authority—so frequently that we must own to having had a transitory suspicion that Mr. T. was nothing more than another Mrs. Harris, and to believe, with Mrs. Gamp's acquaintance, that 'there never was no such person.' . . . To spread the knowledge of the Gospel in China would be a good and an excellent thing, and worthy of all praise and encouragement; but to make such a work a mere pretext for puffing an obscure newspaper into circulation, is a most scandalous and flagitious act, and it is this act, we fear, we must charge against Dr. Campbell. . . . There have been many dodges tried to make a losing paper 'go,' but it remained for a leader in the Non-conformist body to represent the weekly subscription as an act of religious duty. Moreover, the well-known device is resorted to of publishing lists of subscribers, the authenticity of which the public have, to say the least, no means of checking. . . . No doubt it is deplorable to find an ignorant credulity manifested among a class of the community entitled, on many grounds, to respect; but now and then this very credulity may be turned to good account. Dr. Campbell is just now making use of it for a very practical purpose, and tomorrow some other religious speculator will cry his wares in the name of Heaven, and the mob will hasten to deck him out in purple and fine linen. . . . In the meanwhile, there can be no doubt that he is making a very good thing indeed of the spiritual wants of the Chinese."

Cockburn C.J. (to the jury): The article, no doubt, is pungent, bitter and caustic; at the same time public men, and, above all, public writers, must not complain if they are sometimes rather roughly treated. Public writers, who expose themselves to criticism, must not complain that such criticism is sometimes hostile. The writers of the "Review" might have thought Dr. Campbell's view a legitimate object of hostile observation. Nor is it matter of complaint that the article was written in a spirit and tone of hostility, ridicule and satire. But particular passages are complained of as libellous; and it is said that they impute to the plaintiff that he acted on sordid and base motives, and that therefore he is entitled to damages. It will be for you to judge of the effect of those passages. They may be divided under two heads: first, as to suggestions that Dr. Campbell had made certain untrue statements as to sources

whence he had derived subscriptions, and used them as decoys to get further subscriptions; that he was in the habit of referring to fictitious persons; and that this
was suggested to be a fraud on those whom he induced, by the supposed example of
persons represented as contributors, to put their names down as subscribers. And
then, under the second head, it is complained that it is said that the plaintiff put forward to the public the great religious enterprise of converting the Chinese to Christianity, and asked for contributions for that purpose, when it was not intended to
get them for that purpose, but to increase the circulation of his newspaper, and that
thus he was using a great and powerful motive—appealing to the highest considerations and the most solemn duties, as a means, not of promoting the spread of
Christianity, but his own sordid interests. Such is the second head of complaint. It is
said, on the other hand, that this was only legitimate criticism, and discussion, of
the fair merits of this scheme of the plaintiff's, with a view to show that it was idle
and absurd and must end in disappointment and delusion, and that the "Review"
had a right so to comment upon it.

Now, it is not to be disputed that the plaintiff's proposal is open, to the fullest
extent, to discussion and criticism of a severe and hostile character. Dr. Campbell
made an appeal to the public on a subject not only of public interest but of sacred
and universal interest—the spread of Christianity throughout the heathen world,—
and he did so through the columns of his newspaper. It is impossible to conceive
any subject on which comment and criticism might more fairly be made, and any
writer who thought that this proposal of the plaintiff could only end in disappointment to the public who might be induced to subscribe to his paper, and that they
would be throwing away their money, would have a perfect right to comment upon
it, with some latitude of criticism and comment. But the question is, whether the
one or the other of the two views suggested of the effect of the article is correct. Is
the effect of these passages merely to comment on the reasonableness of the plaintiff's proposal, or do they impute, not only that it was delusive, but then it was
induced by the base and sordid motive of promoting his own pecuniary interest?
First, with reference to Mr. Thompson, is it represented that he is a fictitious person, so that it is an imputation upon the character of the plaintiff for veracity and
integrity in his referring to an imaginary and non-existing person? Is that the effect
of the passage in the libel? Or is it no more than to detract, in a tone of banter, from
the authority of a person so often referred to? If the former is the meaning, certainly it was a misstatement. But might not the passage receive a milder construction? This is of less importance than the other part of the libel complained of; but it
is for you to consider, and if you think that it was intended to charge against Dr.
Campbell the intentionally putting forward of fictitious persons to deceive and
delude the public, it is for you to say what importance you attach to it.

But there is another matter under the same head which is of more serious import;
for to say of a man that he is appealing to the public for subscriptions, and that, to
obtain them, he puts down the names of non-existing subscribers, is surely to
charge him with fraud. Let every man judge for himself whether he would not deem
it a reflection on his character and honour; and it is for the jury to say whether this
is the meaning of the article. "Moreover, a well-known device is adopted," etc.
"There have been dodges tried to make a losing paper pay," etc. It is for you to
judge of these expressions, how far they made this serious imputation upon the
plaintiff's character. Then, coming to the next head of libel—that which related to
the proposal to subscribe to the plaintiff's newspaper—it is not to be taken as if all
that the doctor proposed was that persons should send their subscriptions to his
paper; and the fair mode of putting it is, that they should support a journal which
would stimulate subscriptions for the missions. It would be absurd for the plaintiff
to ask persons to co-operate in the work of missions merely by buying copies of his
paper. It must be taken as his meaning, and the meaning of the subscribers, that
these letters were intended to arouse the religious world to a sense of their duty to
make every effort to support missions. The parties interested in missions might very

fairly believe that an appeal to the public on the subject might produce great effects. But it was perfectly lawful for a public writer to say that it was an idle scheme, and that it was a delusion to suppose that by forcing these papers into circulation by free distribution the great cause of missions would be promoted, and, in short, to denounce the whole scheme as pernicious and delusive. And if you think that this is all which has really been done in this case, then it is within the fair and legitimate scope of criticism, and then you ought to find your verdict for the defendant. But the question is, whether the writer has not gone beyond these limits, and whether he has not gone the length of imputing to Dr. Campbell, not merely that he has proposed a delusive and mischievous scheme, but that he has done so with the sordid motive of abusing the confidence of the public on subjects the most holy and sacred, and for the pitiful purpose of increasing the subscriptions to his newspaper. If you think that, then the case assumes a different character. It is said that the circumstances were such as not only to entitle the writers of the "Review" to criticise in a hostile spirit the scheme of the plaintiff, but also to impute to him sordid and base motives in putting it forward, for that it is obvious that it could do good to nobody but the proprietors of the paper. I own, however, that my view of the law does not accord with this. A public writer is fully entitled to comment upon the conduct of a public man, and this was a public matter and a fair subject of comment. But it cannot be said that because a man is a public man a public writer is entitled not only to pass a judgment upon his conduct, but to ascribe to him corrupt and dishonest motives. That, in my view, is not the law, and the privilege of comment does not go to that extent. Take the case of a statesman. His public conduct is open to criticism in speeches or in writings. But has anyone a right to say that he has sold himself, or that he has been inspired by base and sordid motives, unless prepared to justify those allegations as true? Take the case of a general in command of a fortress, who has surrendered it earlier than the necessity of the case, in the opinion of others, required. His conduct in so doing would be open to the most severe criticism, but would there be a right to say that he had betrayed the fortress into the hands of the enemy for a corrupt consideration? Surely not. Take the case of a treaty concluded by a statesman with a foreign power; suppose its terms to be disastrous to the country. Its terms would be open to the most severe criticism and the most righteous condemnation; but would there be a right to say that the statesman had sold his country? I think not. At the same time I feel the great importance of the question. No doubt the liberty of the press is of very vast importance, and the privilege of commenting on the public conduct of public men cannot be too highly appreciated; and if you see your way to the conclusion that the writer here had a sincere belief that the plaintiff, in his invitations to the public to subscribe, was actuated by desire, not to promote the cause of Christianity, but his own sordid interests, although I should still say that it is not a ground on which you could find a verdict for the defendant, yet you may find that matter specially in his favour; for it is a question of such great importance that, although my own opinion upon it is clear, still, as it is now for the first time raised in a Court of Justice, I will give the defendant leave to raise it in the Full Court, by moving to enter the verdict for him upon the matter so found in his favour; should your finding be such as thus to raise the question. Even, however, although your verdict should be for the plaintiff, yet, when you come to consider the question of damages, you must take into account all the circumstances of the case. And it is to be regretted that the means proposed by the plaintiff to carry out his ends should have been of a somewhat doubtful character. It certainly does at first sight seem to be so when a man says, "Here is a great work—a work in which all Christians should unite." And how is it to be accomplished? "Subscribe to my newspaper." It does sound odd, and provokes the suggestion that it is not so much the interests of religion which the man has in his mind as the promotion of the circulation of his own paper. And when a person not imbued with his religious views comments upon the case it might easily suggest itself to his mind in that point of view. You may think that there was no ground for it, but still, if it might naturally suggest itself to the mind, you must make some allowance for the position of the writer, who may have been influenced by a sense of public duty; for I cannot help saying that I think the counsel for the plaintiff went too far when he stated that the object of the article was to injure and crush the plaintiff. There, then, was a strong spirit of antagonism naturally aroused by these very conflicting views on a matter connected with religious opinions, and the writer in the "Review," no doubt, sat down to attack the plaintiff, not as the individual, but as the journalist, and as an upholder of particular views. And if he has, in doing what he might conceive to be his duty, unjustly aspersed the plaintiff, we must still look at the matter as one arising out of a public controversy, and not as one in which there was any intention to wound and injure the plaintiff.

If you think that the only effect of the article was fairly to discuss the proposal of the plaintiff, then find for the defendant. If you think that the effect is to impute base and sordid motives, then your verdict ought to be for the plaintiff. If, at the same time, you are of opinion that the writer did so under an honest and genuine belief that the plaintiff was fairly open to these charges, I invite you, while you find your verdict for the plaintiff with such damages as you think proper, to find that matter of fact specially, and I shall, in that event, reserve leave to the defendant to move to enter the verdict for him, if the Court should be of the opinion that the matter of fact so found in his favour entitles him to the verdict.

Verdict for the plaintiff for £50, the jury finding, specially, "that the writer in the 'Saturday Review' believed his imputations to be well founded."

The defendant moved to enter verdict for himself, or for a new trial on the ground of misdirection. The Court of Queen's Bench refused the motion.

Queen's Bench

Lord Cockburn C.J.: . . . In the present case, the charges made against the plaintiff were unquestionably without foundation. It may be that, in addition to the motive of religious zeal, the plaintiff was not wholly insensible to the collateral object of promoting the circulation of his newspaper, but there was no evidence that he had resorted to false devices to induce persons to contribute to his scheme. That being so, Mr. Bovill is obliged to say that, because the writer of this article had a bona fide belief that the statements he made were true, he was privileged. I cannot assent to that doctrine. It was competent to the writer to have attacked the plaintiff's scheme; and perhaps he might have suggested, that the effect of the subscriptions which the plaintiff was asking the public to contribute would be only to put money into his pocket. But to say that he was actuated only by the desire of putting money into his pocket, and that he resorted to fraudulent expedients for that purpose, is charging him with dishonesty: and that is going farther than the law allows.

It is said that it is for the interests of society that the public conduct of men should be criticised without any other limit than that the writer should have an honest belief that what he writes is true. But it seems to me that the public have an equal interest in the maintenance of the public character of public men; and public affairs could not be conducted by men of honour with a view to the welfare of the country, if we were to sanction attacks upon them, destructive of their honour and character, and made without any foundation. I think the fair position in which the law may be settled is this: that where the public conduct of a public man is open to animadversion, and the writer who is commenting upon it makes imputations on his motives which arise fairly and legitimately out of his conduct so that a jury shall say that the criticism was not only honest, but also well founded, an action is not maintainable. But it is not because a public writer fancies that the conduct of a public man is open to the suspicion of dishonesty, he is therefore justified in assailing his character as dishonest. . . .

Crompton J.: . . . It must be taken that the jury have found that the imputations made were not within the range of fair argument or criticism on the plaintiff's publication of his scheme. Nothing is more important than that fair and full latitude of discussion should be allowed to writers upon any public matter, whether it be the conduct of public men, or the proceedings in courts of justice or in Parliament, or the publication of a scheme or of a literary work. But it is always to be left to a jury to say whether the publication has gone beyond the limits of a fair comment on the subject-matter discussed. A writer is not entitled to overstep those limits and impute base and sordid motives which are not warranted by the facts, and I cannot for a moment think that, because he has a bona fide belief that he is publishing what is true, that is any answer to an action for libel. With respect to the publication of the plaintiff's scheme, the defendant might ridicule it and point out the improbability of its success; but that was all he had a right to do. . . .

Questions
1. Was the objectionable matter actionable because it was not "fair comment" or because it was not "comment" at all?
2. See the charge to the jury in the comparable modern case of *Silkin* v. *Beaverbrook Newspapers Ltd.* [1958] 1 W.L.R. 743. Is that summing-up of Diplock J. more or less favourable to the defendant than that of Lord Cockburn C.J.?
3. Does the following dictum of Lord Denning (in *Slim* v. *Daily Telegraph* [1968] 2 Q.B. 157, 169) conflict with the ratio of *Campbell's* case? "Even if the words did convey the imputation, by way of comment, that the plaintiff's conduct was dishonest, insincere or hypocritical, the defence of fair comment was still available."

Note:
The Faulks Committee proposed that "Any special limitation of the defence of comment in cases where base or sordid motives are imputed should be abolished." The Faulks Committee also proposed that the defence be renamed simply "Comment," since the comment need not be fair at all, though it must be honest.

KEMSLEY v. FOOT

House of Lords [1952] A.C. 345; [1952] 1 T.L.R. 532; 96 S.J. 165; [1952] 1 All E.R. 501

An article published in the *Tribune* of March 10, 1950, was entitled "Lower than Kemsley by Michael Foot" and continued: "The prize for the foulest piece of journalism perpetrated in this country for many a long year, and that is certainly saying something, must go to Mr. Herbert Gunn, editor of the *Evening Standard*, and all those who assisted him in the publication of an attack on John Strachey last week." The article proceeded with a savage attack on the *Evening Standard*, a paper with which Viscount Kemsley had no connection at all, though he was a well-known proprietor of other newspapers. The plaintiff alleged that the words meant that he "used his position as a director of newspaper companies to procure the publication of statements he knew to be false and that his name was a byword in this respect." The defendants in paragraph 5 of their pleadings claimed that the words were "fair comment made in good faith and without malice upon a matter of public interest namely the control by the plaintiff of . . . newspapers."
The plaintiff applied to strike out this defence. The Master refused. On appeal by the plaintiff, Parker J. ordered the paragraph struck out. The Court of Appeal allowed the defendant's appeal and restored the Master's order [1951] 2 K.B. 34. The plaintiff's appeal to the House of Lords was dismissed.

Lord Porter: . . . It is not, as I understand, contended that the words contained in that article are fact and not comment: rather it is alleged that they are comment with no facts to support it. The question for your Lordships' decision is, therefore, whether a plea of fair comment is only permissible where the comment is accompanied by a statement of facts upon which the comment is made and to determine the particularity with which the facts must be stated.

Before one comes to consider the general question it is, I think, desirable to determine what the language of the alleged libel can be held to assert. It may, in my opinion, be construed as containing an inference that the Kemsley Press is of a low and undesirable quality and that Lord Kemsley is responsible for its tone. Indeed, as I understand the defence and such particulars as have been delivered, an imputation no less severe has been accepted by the defendants as being a true interpretation of the words used.

Although the article complained of uses the phrase "Lower than Kemsley," that language is accompanied by an attack on Lord Beaverbrook's papers, and it is at least arguable that the attack is on the Kemsley Press and not on Lord Kemsley's personal character save in so far as it is exhibited in the press for which he is responsible. Nevertheless, libel must reflect upon a person and Lord Kemsley is held up as worthy of attack on the ground that he is a newspaper proprietor who prostitutes his position by conducting his newspapers or permitting them to be conducted in an undesirable way. In this sense the criticism does not differ from that which takes place when what is called literary criticism comes in question. In such case the attack is not on the personal character of the person libelled, it is upon him as responsible for certain productions, e.g. an article in the press, a book, a musical composition, or an artistic work.

Later, I shall have to come back to the truth and accuracy of this analogy but I have thought it right to set out the basis of literary criticism at this point, because a distinction is sought to be drawn and, indeed, in some of the decided cases, has been drawn between literary criticism and a personal attack upon the character of an individual.

If an author writes a play or a book or a composer composes a musical work, he is submitting that work to the public and thereby inviting comment. Not all the public will see or read or hear it but the work is public in the same sense as a case in the Law Courts is said to be heard in public. In many cases it is not possible for everyone who is interested to attend a trial, but in so far as there is room for them in the court all are entitled to do so, and the subject-matter upon which comment can be made is indicated to the world at large.

The same observation is true of a newspaper. Whether the criticism is confined to a particular issue or deals with the way in which it is in general conducted, the subject-matter upon which criticism is made has been submitted to the public, though by no means all those to whom the alleged libel has been published will have seen or are likely to see the various issues. Accordingly, its contents and conduct are open to comment on the ground that the public have at least the opportunity of ascertaining for themselves the subject-matter upon which the comment is founded. I am assuming that the reference is to a known journal: for the present purpose it is not necessary to consider how far criticism without facts upon which to base it is subject to the same observation in the case of an obscure publication.

A further ground for the distinction sought to be drawn between an attack on an individual and criticism of a literary work appears to suggest that comment upon the literary production must be confined to criticism of it as literature. This is not so; a literary work can be criticised for its treatment of life and morals as freely as it can for bad writing, e.g. it can be criticised as having an immoral tendency. The fairness of the criticism does not depend upon the fact that it is confined to form or literary content.

The question, therefore, in all cases is whether there is a sufficient substratum of fact stated or indicated in the words which are the subject-matter of the action, and I find my view well expressed in the remarks contained in *Odgers on Libel and Slander* (6th ed., 1929), at p. 166. "Sometimes, however," he says, "it is difficult to distinguish an allegation of fact from an expression of opinion. It often depends on what is stated in the rest of the article. If the defendant accurately states what some public man has really done, and then asserts that 'such conduct is disgraceful,' this is merely the expression of his opinion, his comment on the plaintiff's conduct. So, if without setting it out, he identifies the conduct on which he comments by a clear reference. In either case, the defendant enables his readers to judge for themselves how far his opinion is well founded; and, therefore, what would otherwise have been an allegation of fact becomes merely a comment. But if he asserts that the plaintiff has been guilty of disgraceful conduct, and does not state what that conduct was, this is an allegation of fact for which there is no defence but privilege or truth. The same considerations apply where a defendant has drawn from certain facts an inference derogatory to the plaintiff. If he states the bare inference without the facts on which it is based, such inference will be treated as an allegation of fact. But if he sets out the facts correctly, and then gives his inference, stating it as his inference from those facts, such inference will, as a rule, be deemed a comment. But even in this case the writer must be careful to state the inference as an inference, and not to assert it as a new and independent fact; otherwise, his inference will become something more than a comment, and he may be driven to justify it as an allegation of fact."

But the question whether an inference is a bare inference in this sense must depend upon all the circumstances. Indeed, it was ultimately admitted on behalf of the appellant that the facts necessary to justify comment might be implied from the terms of the impugned article and therefore the inquiry ceases to be—Can the defendant point to definite assertions of fact in the alleged libel upon which the comment is made? and becomes—Is there subject-matter indicated with sufficient clarity to justify comment being made? and was the comment actually made such as an honest, though prejudiced, man might make?

Is there, then, in this case sufficient subject-matter upon which to make comment? In an article which is concerned with what has been described as "the Beaverbrook Press" and which is violently critical of Lord Beaverbrook's newspapers, it is, I think, a reasonable construction of the words "Lower than Kemsley" that the allegation which is made is that the conduct of the Kemsley Press was similar to but not quite so bad as that of the press controlled by Lord Beaverbrook, *i.e.* it is possibly dishonest, but in any case low. The exact meaning, however, is not, in my opinion, for your Lordships but for the jury. All I desire to say is that there is subject-matter and it is at least arguable that the words directly complained of imply as fact that Lord Kemsley is in control of a number of known newspapers and that the conduct of those newspapers is in question. Had the contention that all the facts justifying the comment must appear in the article been maintainable, the appeal would succeed, but the appellant's representatives did not feel able to and, I think, could not support so wide a contention. The facts they admitted, might be implied, and the respondents' answer to their contention is: "We have pointed to your press. It is widely read. Your readers will and the public generally can know at what our criticism is directed. It is not bare comment; it is comment on a well-known matter, much better known, indeed, than a newly printed book or a once-performed play." . . .

Question
  What can Lord Kemsley have sought to achieve, or to indulge, by bringing this lawsuit at the expense of so much time and money?

Note:

About suing in defamation the barons of the press, possibly the nastiest tycoons of all, seem to have no compunction: but perhaps one has to be shameless to get to be so rich. One press baron sued *Private Eye* for implying that he was seeking a real barony with more than thimbles and hope, and had the gall to celebrate his £55,000 victory by getting his hacks to write a book about it (see *Maxwell* v. *Pressdram* [1987] 1 All E.R. 656). One is reminded of Lord Bernstein, the TV mogul, suing the people who photographed his house, of Hedley Byrne, the advertising agents, complaining of misrepresentation, of Caliban seeing his face in the glass. A pity that it was not Maxwell's tabloid that had to pay £500,000 to Jeffrey Archer, politician and writer, for saying that he had used the services of a prostitute when he had only paid her to leave the country. Another sensitive familiar of the law courts is the tycoon Sir James Goldsmith, ludicrously characterised by a judge as an "ordinary citizen" (*Goldsmith* v. *Sperrings* [1077] 2 All E.R. 557, 566; *Goldsmith* v. *Pressdram* [1987] 3 All E.R. 485).

The publicity and drama of the court are naturally alluring to actors and actresses. Liberace had the nerve to sue the *Daily Mirror* for calling him "fruit-flavoured' (a word whose meaning the judge had to have explained to him) and collected £7,000 for this allusion to his evident proclivities; Telly Savalas exacted a load of money from those who suggested a habit of arriving on set late and unsober; and an actress who sued one of Maxwell's papers for featuring her as "Wally of the Week" and describing her as having a "big bum" got £10,000, though not for long, as this verdict was reversed by the Court of Appeal which sent the case back for a further waste of everyone's time (*Cornwell* v. *Myskow* [1987] 2 All E.R. 504).

Politicians are another class of person whom ambition or success has rendered insensitive to all but criticism and whose taste for publicity does not seem to have inured them to any obloquy. One prime minister was not ashamed to resort to a defamation suit in order to silence the only member of the opposition, and he was supported therein by the Privy Council, a success not publicised in the law reports (*Jeyaretnam* v. *Lee*, February 24, 1982).

Disgusting though all these proceedings are, one might ask why the law should not provide a forum in which really awful people can gird at each other with a chance of scooping the pool? After all, counsel at the libel bar, scandalously overpaid though they are for an activity entirely without social merit, are paid by the parties themselves (or is it by newspaper readers?). But the judges are paid by decent people, and they have better things to do. Worse still, ordinary people get caught up in these despicable goings-on, dragged away from their activities and pleasures to attend as jurymen to boring harangues, lying testimony and idiotic instructions. In the *Orme* case about the "Moonies," the trial with jury lasted no less than 100 days, and the appeal was expected to last 50. This prompted two eminent judges to move in a debate in the House of Lords that a judge should have discretion to decide whether there should be a jury or not. It remains the rule, however, that unless there are masses of documents (rather than the 118 witnesses in the *Orme* trial) either party to a defamation suit has the right to demand trial by jury (Supreme Court Act 1981, s.69(1); *Viscount de l'Isle* v. *Times Newspapers* [1987] 3 All E.R. 499).

DEFAMATION ACT 1952

6. In an action for libel or slander in respect of words consisting partly of allegations of fact and partly of expression of opinion, a defence of fair comment shall not fail by reason only that the truth of every allegation of fact is not proved if the expression of opinion is fair comment having regard to such of the facts alleged or referred to in the words complained of as are proved.

Questions

1. In *Broadway Approvals* v. *Odhams Press* [1965] 1 W.L.R. 805 the trial judge said to the jury: "And, needless to say, if the facts are untrue, then the criticism based upon those facts cannot in its very nature be fair, can it?" Do you accept that a comment is rendered unfair simply by reason of an innocent misapprehension of the facts?

2. How valuable is the right to comment on matters of public interest if one is liable for unavoidable errors of fact?

3. Is it so that one may flatter or may criticise the persons implicated in matters of public interest that one is given the right to state one's views?

PART VIII

WRONGFULLY CAUSING LOSS

INTRODUCTION

How far does the law protect a man's interest in earning his living—the trader's interest in trading and the workman's interest in working? Some protection—indeed, a good deal—is incidentally afforded by the torts already studied, although their main purpose may be something else. Thus the tort of negligence protects a man's body, which is, in this connection, his human capital. It also protects the material tools of his trade from damage; conversion protects them from theft. Nuisance ensures comfort to do business as well as take relaxation. In guarding the highways, public nuisance protects the means of access to offices, factories and shops. Defamation protects the character of businessmen as well as *rentiers*—rather better, indeed, in slander. The liability imposed for misrepresentation helps the man who invests money or lays out goods on credit. But is any general protection given to a man's interest in earning?

But what exactly *is* this interest in earning? How should it be analysed? We can hardly say that there is a legal *right* to one's living in the way that there is a right in property, because although neither interest is unqualified, the former is qualified almost to the point of extinction by the existence of a similar right in one's competitors. For example, even the littlest of the Three Bears can properly speak of "*my* bowl of porridge," for they have separate bowls. If they ate from a communal bowl, as all traders and earners do, he could not speak of "*my* bowl of porridge," for it is not. Nor could he speak of "*my* next spoonful," since, if the biggest bear eats quickly, there won't be one. Even the "right to dip in the bowl" is not a useful notion, because the biggest bear must have an identical right and may leave nothing. All that "right to dip in the bowl" suggests is that there may be circumstances where it is a wrong in the biggest bear to prevent baby bear from dipping; we must discover what those circumstances are.

Of course, if anything can be discovered which can be called "property" or a "right," even if it is not a thing in fact or a right in the general law, it tends to be more strongly protected. Thus an author's copyright, an inventor's patent and a manufacturer's registered trade-mark are very strongly protected. A trade secret and an unregistered mark or name are protected less strongly, but still quite well. So also with a "right." An employer has a right to the services of his employee during the period of the contract, but not after that period, however likely it may be that the employee would remain. He can therefore sue a competitor who lures his employee away during that period, not one who offers the employee a larger salary at the end of it. But in the absence of anything which can, however transferentially, be called "property" or a "right," the interest in earning one's living appears to be merely an expectation of benefit from a third party—the hope that the public will come and buy, or that the colliery will be kept going by the National Coal Board.

It is essential to remember that people depend on other people for their livelihood: the employee depends on his employer for his wages, just as the employer himself depends on his customers for his income, as well as on his suppliers for the materials and on his workforce for the labour which help

485

him earn it. Thus if you want to hurt the barmaid, you get at the publican, and if you want to close the pub, you disaffect the patrons, alienate the barmaid or interrupt the supply of beer. The element of indirection in these torts is at the level of action only: at the level of intention the line is direct, for as we have seen, there is no liability for causing business loss by byblow. The element of indirection involves that the facts in the following cases have a triangular structure, which makes them slightly difficult, as the law tends to think along straight lines, as between plaintiff and defendant.

We have already seen a triangular situation in defamation; but there the third party disappears when he has been published to, and is replaced by a hypothetical one. In conversion there are appalling difficulties in the triangular situation where the apex is the disappearing rogue. In public nuisance the third party presented difficulties, where the plaintiff complained, not that he himself had been obstructed in his use of the highway, but that his customers had been. So it is not surprising that the third party causes trouble in the trade torts; he adds to the conceptual difficulties in an area where the policy is not at all clear.

The difficulty of policy is to find a minimum principle of liability, the analogue of the principle of *Wilkinson* v. *Downton* for acts causing personal damage. One might suppose that intentionally to damage another in his trade would be wrong, but a moment's consideration shows that this cannot be. When a vast supermarket opens in town next to a small family grocer, the latter cannot complain just because the former has been successful in its avowed aim of ruining him. Price wars are not like gang-wars; bystanders benefit from them (at least for a time).

What, then, is the law to say? It could have said that the supermarket prima facie committed a wrong in intentionally ruining the man at the corner, but that it could justify itself on the ground of trade competition. It refused to say that. It could have said that the supermarket must act fairly in its competition (*e.g.*, must not sell goods at a loss); but it specifically declined to say that. It might have said (indeed, it nearly did) that the plaintiff could recover if, in addition to proving intentional damage, he proved malice, in the sense of indirect motive or absence of justification; but it didn't (since a jury of shop-keepers might have had an extensive notion of "malice").

In fact, the minimum general principle has not yet emerged. It may, however, be useful to consider the cases which follow on the view that it is actionable *intentionally* to cause *harm* to another by *wrongful* means. That may seem tautologous, but it is not. The reason it is not tautologous is that these situations are triangular, and wrongfulness is a quality attaching to straight lines. Thus we must examine the line between the plaintiff and the defendant to discover if the latter intended to hurt the plaintiff; and, in order to discover whether he used wrongful means, we must examine *both* the other sides of the triangle, both that linking the defendant and the third party, whom we call "X," and that linking the third party with the plaintiff.

Let us first examine the line between X and the defendant, bearing in mind that all that is done is designed by the defendant. If the defendant gets X to commit a wrong against the plaintiff, the defendant will be liable just as where A tells B to strike C. If what X does at the defendant's instigation is a tort, the defendant is liable as a joint tortfeasor; if the defendant gets X to break his contract with the plaintiff (*e.g.*, persuades X to dismiss him without notice), the defendant is equally liable, for the tort of inducing breach of contract. The only difference is that, whereas the defendant is taken to know the general law of tort, he must be proved to have knowledge or suspicion of the contract between X and the plaintiff. Note particularly that in such cases X will always have broken his contract *deliberately* if not freely; and if there is one kind of breach of contract which is wrongful, it must be the deliberate breach.

Now let us suppose that X is in a position to hurt the plaintiff without committing any wrong (*e.g.*, to give him notice or to stop frequenting his shop). If the defendant persuades him by lawful means, and X hurts the plaintiff by lawful means, there will be no liability, save in the very rare case where both the defendant and X are actuated solely by "disinterested malevolence." But the means of persuasion used by the defendant on X must be studied. For example, he may have *misled* X into hurting the plaintiff. Those lies will constitute wrongful means; what in a two-party situation is called deceit is called malicious falsehood in a three-party situation. Or, absent fraud, the defendant may have used duress, may have *threatened* X with some evil if he did not hurt the plaintiff. If the evil threatened would be a wrong against X if it were committed, then those threats are wrongful means, whether the evil threatened would be a tort or a breach of contract. But if the evil threatened is one which the defendant is at liberty to produce, then there is no use of wrongful means so far as the line between X and the defendant is concerned. In either case, of course, the plaintiff will suffer harm only if X hurts him, in consequence of being taken in by the lie or coerced by the threat.

Now suppose that the defendant, in his aim of hurting the plaintiff, strikes *at* X instead of *through* him. Rather than threaten to assault the plaintiff's customers if they remain loyal, the defendant actually batters them. Rather than threaten to break his contract, he deliberately breaks it in order to hurt the plaintiff. There again we have wrongful means successfully employed to harm the plaintiff, and the defendant is liable (to the plaintiff as well as to X).

This basic common law is overlaid and obscured by statutes which outlaw commercial excess or legitimate industrial action. Even so, it is a pity that in most tort courses cases such as those in this chapter are rather overshadowed by regular negligence cases, for while the rules of negligence just give people "out," as it were, like an umpire in a cricket match, these decisions lay down the rules of the game, rules as a basis for action, determining what is permitted and what is not. They are therefore concerned with the limits of freedom, rather like those cases which turn on defences to trespass claims: but here the freedom of action is, and should be, very much greater, because the plaintiff is complaining of only financial harm, not of an invasion of one of his primary rights.

The common law principles, developed at rather a high level of abstraction, apply to all cases where one person has deliberately caused financial loss to another. If one wants to make a distinction between losing wages and losing profits, that is, between jobs and businesses, or between the various means of interference, such as withdrawal of labour, cutting off of supplies or dissuasion of customers, then legislation is required.

Chapter 15

SHARP PRACTICES AND POWER PLAYS

EDGINGTON v. FITZMAURICE

Court of Appeal (1885) 29 Ch.D. 459; 55 L.J.Ch. 650; 1 T.L.R. 326; 53 L.T. 369; 33 W.R. 911

The Rev. Charles Edgington was a shareholder of the Army & Navy Provision Market (Ltd.). He received a prospectus issued by the defendant officers of that company, inviting him to subscribe for debenture bonds, and he did so, to the amount of £1,500. The prospectus stated that the sums were wanted "To enable the society to complete the present alterations and additions to the buildings and to purchase their own horses and vans . . . and to further develop the arrangements at present existing for the direct supply of cheap fish from the coast." It also stated that the society had purchased a London property subject to a mortgage on which £21,500 was outstanding, repayable in instalments.

The plaintiff now seeks the return of his £1,500 on the ground of fraud.

Bowen L.J.: This is an action for deceit, in which the plaintiff complains that he was induced to take certain debentures by the misrepresentations of the defendants, and that he sustained damage thereby. The loss which the plaintiff sustained is not disputed. In order to sustain his action he must first prove that there was a statement as to facts which was false; and secondly, that it was false to the knowledge of the defendants, or that they made it not caring whether it was true or false. For it is immaterial whether they made the statement knowing it to be untrue, or recklessly, without caring whether it was true or not, because to make a statement recklessly for the purpose of influencing another person is dishonest. It is also clear that it is wholly immaterial with what object the lie is told. That is laid down in Lord Blackburn's judgment in *Smith* v. *Chadwick* ((1884) 9 App.Cas. 201), but it is material that the defendant should intend that it should be relied on by the person to whom he makes it. But, lastly, when you have proved that the statement was false, you must further show that the plaintiff has acted upon it and has sustained damage by so doing; you must show that the statement was either the sole cause of the plaintiff's act, or materially contributed to his acting. . . .

The alleged misrepresentations were three. First, it was said that the prospectus contained an implied allegation that the mortgage for £21,500 could not be called in at once, but was payable by instalments. I think that upon a fair construction of the prospectus it does so allege; and therefore that the prospectus must be taken to have contained an untrue statement on that point; but it does not appear to me clear that the statement was fraudulently made by the defendants. It is therefore immaterial to consider whether the plaintiff was induced to act as he did by that statement.

Secondly, it is said that the prospectus contains an implied allegation that there was no other mortgage affecting the property except the mortgage stated therein. I think there was such an implied allegation, but I think it is not brought home to the defendants that it was made dishonestly; accordingly, although the plaintiff may have been damnified by the weight which he gave to the allegation, he cannot rely on it in this action: for in an action of deceit the plaintiff must prove dishonesty. Therefore if the case had rested on these two allegations alone, I think it would be too uncertain to entitle the plaintiff to succeed.

But when we come to the third alleged misstatement I feel that the plaintiff's case is made out. I mean the statement of the object for which the money was to be raised. These were stated to be to complete the alterations and additions to the buildings, to purchase horses and vans, and to develop the supply of fish. A mere suggestion of possible purposes to which a portion of the money might be applied would not have formed a basis for an action of deceit. There must be a misstatement of an existing fact: but the state of a man's mind is as much a fact as the state of his digestion. It is true that it is very difficult to prove what the state of a man's mind at a particular time is, but if it can be ascertained it is as much a fact as anything else. A misrepresentation as to the state of a man's mind is, therefore, a misstatement of fact. Having applied as careful consideration to the evidence as I could, I have reluctantly come to the conclusion that the true objects of the defendants in raising the money were not those stated in the circular. I will not go through the evidence, but looking only to the cross-examination of the defendants, I am satisfied that the objects for which the loan was wanted were misstated by the defendants, I will not say knowingly, but so recklessly as to be fraudulent in the eye of the law.

Then the question remains: Did this misstatement contribute to induce the plaintiff to advance his money. Mr. Davey's argument has not convinced me that they did not. He contended that the plaintiff admits that he would not have taken the debentures unless he had thought they would give him a charge on the property, and therefore he was induced to take them by his own mistake, and the misstatement in the circular was not material. But such misstatement was material if it was actively present to his mind when he decided to advance his money. The real question is, what was the state of the plaintiff's mind, and if his mind was disturbed by the misstatement of the defendants, and such disturbance was in part the cause of what he did, the mere fact of his also making a mistake himself could make no difference. It resolves itself into a mere question of fact. I have felt some difficulty about the pleadings, because in the statement of claim this point is not clearly put forward, and I had some doubt whether this contention as to the third misstatement was not an afterthought. But the balance of my judgment is weighed down by the probability of the case. What is the first question which a man asks when he advances money? It is, what is it wanted for? Therefore I think that the statement is material, and that the plaintiff would be unlike the rest of his race if he was not influenced by the statement of the objects for which the loan was required. The learned judge in the court below came to the conclusion that the misstatement did influence him, and I think he came to a right conclusion.

Questions

1. In what ways is it possible *carelessly* to misrepresent one's present intentions?

2. " . . . if his mind was disturbed by the misstatement of the defendants, and such disturbance was in part the cause of what he did, the mere fact of his also making a mistake himself could make no difference." Would this be true where the defendants' misstatement was not deceitful but careless?

Note:

Four years later the House of Lords confirmed that "To found an action for damages there must be a contract and breach, or fraud" (*Derry* v. *Peek* (1889) 14 App.Cas. 337, 347 *per* Lord Bramwell). Seventy-five years thereafter *Hedley Byrne* v. *Heller & Partners* (above p. 44) showed that there was a middle ground of liability where there was neither contract nor fraud, but a special relationship and negligence. Does the tort of deceit still have a role? Yes, just as contract does. For just as there are special relationships where there is no contract (as in *Hedley Byrne* itself) and therefore no possible guarantee liability, so there may be fraud where there is no special relationship, and therefore no possible liability for mere negligence.

We have seen that the duty to take care is more easily found where an answer is given to a particular questioner than when a statement is made to the world at large (above p. 50).

Again, a duty is not apt to be found unless the statement is made on a business occasion. There are accordingly many situations where statements are made but no duty to take care arises; a person who suffers loss from reliance on such a statement may have to prove fraud in order to recover damages, but if he proves fraud, he will certainly recover. Is there any advantage, if one is in a duty situation, in trying to prove that the defendant was not just negligent but fraudulent, that not only should he not have believed what he said but that he actually did not? There may be an advantage with regard to damages, aggravated or exemplary, or where the plaintiff has himself been uncircumspect (since a liar can hardly complain that his dupe was gullible) or even infringed some law (for the defendant has wickedly disregarded the basic rule of honesty) (*Saunders* v. *Edwards* [1987] 2 All E.R. 651, 659–660 (C.A.)).

If the statement in question induced a contract between the parties, the effects of fraud occur unless the maker of the statement can prove that he believed and had good reason to believe that the statement was true at the time of the contract (Misrepresentation Act 1967 s.2(1)). That is perhaps the middle ground between special relationship and contract.

Quotations:

> "Oh what a tangled web we weave,
> When first we practise to deceive":
> (Sir Walter Scott, *Marmion* xvii)

"Fraud unravels all" (Lord Denning, *passim*).

RATCLIFFE v. EVANS

Court of Appeal [1892] 2 Q.B. 524; 61 L.J.Q.B. 535; 66 L.T. 794; 56 J.P. 837; 40 W.R. 578; 8 T.L.R. 597; 36 S.J. 539

The defendant's newspaper, a local weekly, announced that the firm of Ratcliffe & Sons had gone out of business, whereas in fact Ratcliffe & Sons, the plaintiff's engineering and boilermaking firm, was still trading. The plaintiff was able to prove that he suffered a diminution in trade in consequence of the publication, but not that he lost any particular customer or order.

The jury found that, though the words were not libellous in the sense of reflecting on the plaintiff's character, they were not published bona fide and had caused damage to the plaintiff's business to the extent of £120. Mr. Commissioner Bompas Q.C. entered judgment for the plaintiff for £120. The defendant appealed to the Court of Appeal, but his appeal was dismissed.

Bowen L.J.: . . . The only proof at the trial of such damage consisted, however, of evidence of general loss of business without specific proof of the loss of any particular customers or orders, and the question we have to determine is, whether in such an action such general evidence of damage was admissible and sufficient. That an action will lie for written or oral falsehoods, not actionable *per se* nor even defamatory, where they are maliciously published, where they are calculated in the ordinary course of things to produce, and where they do produce, actual damage, is established law. Such an action is not one of libel or of slander, but an action on the case for damage wilfully and intentionally done without just occasion or excuse, analogous to an action for slander of title. To support it, actual damage must be shewn, for it is an action which only lies in respect of such damage as has actually occurred. It was contended before us that in such an action it is not enough to allege and prove general loss of business arising from the publication, since such general loss is general and not special damage, and special damage, as often has been said, is the gist of such an action on the case. Lest we should be led astray in such a matter by mere words, it is desirable to recollect that the term "special damage," which is found for centuries in the books, is not always used with reference to similar subject-matter, nor in the same context. At times (both in the law of tort and contract) it is employed to denote that damage arising out of the special circumstances of the case which, if properly pleaded, may be superadded to the general damage which the law implies in every breach of contract and every infringement of an absolute right: see *Ashby* v. *White* ((1703) 2 Ld.Raym. 938; 92 E.R. 126). In all such cases the law presumes that *some* damage will flow in the ordinary course of things from the mere invasion of the plaintiff's rights, and calls it general damage. Special damage in such a context means the particular damage (beyond the general damage), which results from the particular circumstances of the case, and of the plaintiff's claim to be compensated, for which he ought to give warning in his pleadings in order that there may be no surprise at the trial. But where no actual and positive right (apart from the damage done) has been disturbed, it is the damage done that is the wrong; and the expression "special damage," when used of this damage, denotes the actual and temporal loss which has, in fact, occurred. Such damage is called variously in old authorities, "express loss," "particular damage," "damage in fact," "special or particular cause of loss."

The term "special damage" has also been used in actions on the case brought for a public nuisance, such as the obstruction of a river or a highway, to denote that actual and particular loss which the plaintiff must allege and prove that he has sustained beyond what is sustained by the general public, if his action is to be supported, such particular loss being, as is obvious, the cause of action. In this judgment we shall endeavour to avoid a term which, intelligible enough in particular contexts, tends, when successively employed in more than one context and with regard to different subject-matter, to encourage confusion in thought. The question to be decided does not depend on words, but is one of substance. In an action like the present, brought for a malicious falsehood intentionally published in a newspaper about the plaintiff's business—a falsehood which is not actionable as a personal libel, and which is not defamatory in itself—is evidence to show that a general loss of business has been the direct and natural result admissible in evidence, and, if uncontradicted, sufficient to maintain the action? In the case of a personal libel, such general loss of custom may unquestionably be alleged and proved. Every libel is of itself a wrong in regard of which the law, as we have seen, implies general damage. By the very fact that he has committed such a wrong, the defendant is prepared for the proof that some general damage may have been done . . . Akin to, though distinguishable in a respect which will be mentioned from, actions of libel are those actions which are brought for oral slander, where such slander consists of words actionable in themselves and the mere use of which constitutes the infringement of the plaintiff's right. The very speaking of such words, apart from all damage, constitutes a wrong and gives rise to a cause of action. The law in such a case, as in the case of libel, presumes, and in theory allows, proof of general damage. But slander, even if actionable in itself, is regarded as differing from libel in a point which renders proof of general damage in slander cases difficult to be made good. A person who publishes defamatory matter on paper or in print puts in circulation that which is more permanent and more easily transmissible than oral slander. Verbal defamatory statements may, indeed, be intended to be repeated, or may be uttered under such circumstances that their repetition follows in the ordinary course of things from their original utterance. Except in such cases, the law does not allow the plaintiff to recover damages which flow, not from the original slander, but from its unauthorised repetition: *Ward* v. *Weeks* ((1830) 7 Bing. 211; 131 E.R. 81). General loss of custom cannot properly be proved in respect of a slander of this kind when it has been uttered under such circumstances that its repetition does not flow directly and naturally from the circumstances under which the slander itself was uttered. The doctrine that in slanders actionable *per se* general damage may be alleged and proved with generality must be taken, therefore, with the qualification that the words complained of must have been spoken under circumstances which might in the ordinary course of things have directly produced the general damage that has in fact occurred . . .

From libels and slanders actionable *per se*, we pass to the case of slanders not actionable *per se*, where actual damage done is the very gist of the action. Many old authorities may be cited for the proposition that in such a case the actual loss must be proved specially and with certainty: *Law* v. *Harwood* ((1627) Cro.Car. 140; 79 E.R. 724) . . .

In all actions accordingly on the case where the damage actually done is the gist of the action, the character of the acts themselves which produce the damage, and the circumstances under which these acts are done, must regulate the degree of certainty and particularity with which the damage done ought to be stated and proved. As much certainty and particularity must be insisted on, both in pleading and proof of damage, as is reasonable, having regard to the circumstances and to the nature of the acts themselves by which the damage is done. To insist upon less would be to relax old and intelligible principles. To insist upon more would be the vainest pedantry. The rule to be laid down with regard to malicious falsehoods affecting property or trade is only an instance of the doctrines of good sense applicable to all that branch of actions on the case to which the class under discussion belongs. The nature and circumstances of the publication of the falsehood may accordingly require the admission of evidence of general loss of business as the natural and direct result produced, and perhaps intended to be produced. An instructive illustration, and one by which the present appeal is really covered, is furnished by the case of *Hargrave* v. *Le Breton* ((1769) 4 Burr. 2422; 98 E.R. 269), decided a century and a half ago. It was an example of slander of title at an auction. The allegation in the declaration was that divers persons who would have purchased at the auction left the place; but no particular persons were named. The objection that they were not specially mentioned was, as the report tells us, "easily" answered. The answer given was that in the nature of the transaction it was impossible to specify names; that the injury complained of was in effect that the bidding at the auction had been prevented and stopped, and that everybody had gone away. It had, therefore, become impossible to tell with certainty who would have been bidders or purchasers if the auction had not been rendered abortive. This case shows, what sound judgment itself dictates, that in an action for falsehood producing damage to a man's trade, which in its very nature is intended or reasonably likely to produce, and which in the ordinary course of things does produce, a general loss of business, as distinct from the loss of this or that known customer, evidence of such general decline of business is admissible. In *Hargrave* v. *Le Breton* it was a falsehood openly promulgated at an auction. In the case before us today, it is a falsehood openly disseminated through the press—probably read, and possibly acted on, by persons of whom the plaintiff never heard. To refuse with reference to such a subject-matter to admit such general evidence would be to misunderstand and warp the meaning of old expressions; to depart from, and not to follow, old rules; and, in addition to all this, would involve an absolute denial of justice and of redress for the very mischief which was intended to be committed . . . In our opinion, therefore, there has been no misdirection and no improper admission of evidence, and this appeal should be dismissed with costs.

DEFAMATION ACT 1952

3.—(1) In an action for slander of title, slander of goods or other malicious falsehood, it shall not be necessary to allege or prove special damage—

    (*a*) if the words upon which the action is founded are calculated to cause pecuniary damage to the plaintiff and are published in writing or other permanent form; or (*b*) if the said words are calculated to cause pecuniary damage to the plaintiff in respect of any office, profession, calling, trade or business held or carried on by him at the time of the publication.

Questions

1. The Court of Appeal has decided that where a plaintiff takes advantage of this statutory rule, he may not at the trial produce evidence of specific pecuniary damage at all. *Calvet* v. *Tomkies* [1963] 1 W.L.R. 1397. Can you think of any justification for that ruling?

2. The defendant has a notice outside his petrol station saying 'Last Petrol before the Motorway." As the defendant knows, the plaintiff has a petrol station closer to the motorway. Can the plaintiff sue? Does it make any difference if (i) the defendant erected the notice before the plaintiff built his petrol station, or (ii) the notice says "Last Good Petrol before the Motorway"? If the plaintiff has just established his petrol station, how can he prove the loss he has suffered? Does it matter if the statement is a false trade description under the Trade Descriptions Act 1968, s.2? Or constitutes any other offence under that Act?

Note:

This is no new tort. Centuries ago the defendant said that if he gave his mare malt, it would piss better beer than the plaintiff brewed. The plaintiff's action failed because he could not prove that he had suffered any loss (*Dickes* v. *Fienne* (1639) March 59; 82 E.R. 411). The tort often takes the form of slander of title or slander of goods or disparagement of their quality, but these are just examples of the application of the general principle stated in the principle case.

The tort is structurally different from deceit, where the false statement is made by the defendant to the plaintiff, who then hurts himself in reliance on it by spending money either on a third party or on the defendant. Here the false statement is made to a third party who relies on it and consequently fails to confer an expected benefit on the plaintiff. The nature of the damage makes it difficult to prove.

The tort is qualitatively different from defamation, where also the statement is made to a third party. Defamation is limited to the case where the words are a reflection on the character or competence of the plaintiff. It is not always easy to tell disparagement of property from defamation of person. Lord Halsbury once said: "Could it be gravely argued that to say of a fishmonger that he was in the habit of selling decomposed fish would not be a libel upon him in the way of his trade? And, if so, would it not be a mere juggle with language to alter the form of that allegation to say that all the fish in A's shop is decomposed?" (*Linotype Co.* v. *British Empire Typesetting Machine Co.* (1899) 15 T.L.R. 524, 526). Yet if the goods in question had been canned fish, it is not clear that there would have been a defamation. It would perhaps have been better if corporations had not been allowed to sue in defamation, but had been limited to this tort which guards not honour but wealth, which is all they have.

In this tort the plaintiff must prove the falsity of the words, and show "malice" in the defendant. What is "malice"? Of course it is satisfied by the case where the defendant had no belief in the truth of what he said, but it probably also includes the case where, though he believed what he said to be true, he had no interest in saying it. There is a case in Coke (4 Co.Rep. 17a; 76 E.R. 899) where it is observed that to say "You are a bastard" is actionable, whereas to say "You are a bastard, and I am the true heir" is not, even if it is false. In the second case the words demonstrate the interest claimed by the speaker. A consumers' association presumably has an interest in communicating to its members the characteristics of the goods tested. We come here quite close to qualified privilege in defamation, but here, of course, the privilege should be wider.

As between competitors, the scope of the tort was rather cut down by the House of Lords in *White* v. *Mellin* [1895] A.C. 154. There the defendant, Timothy White the chemist, had bought from the plaintiff who manufactured it some bottles of an invalid food. To these bottles the defendant physically attached leaflets singing the praises of another proprietary food in which he had an interest. When the plaintiff, who sought an injunction, failed to establish a contract to sell his goods in the form in which they were delivered, he was non-suited. The Court of Appeal allowed his appeal ([1894] 3 Ch. 276), but the House of Lords upheld the trial judge. Lord Shand said: "when all that is done is making a comparison between the plaintiff's goods and the goods of the person issuing the advertisement, and the statement made is that the plaintiff's goods are inferior in quality or inferior, it may be, in some special qualities, I think this cannot be regarded as a disparagement of which the law will take cognisance." In *De Beers Abrasive Products* v. *International General Electric Co.* [1975] 2 All E.R. 599, Walton J. presents a useful review of the authorities and offers the test "Did the defendant make observations about the plaintiffs' product in relation to his own which a reasonable person would take as being seriously intended?" If so, and if malice is shown, an action will lie.

Question

In *Grappelli* v. *Derek Block (Holdings) Ltd.* [1981] 2 All E.R. 272 the defendant agents had booked concerts for the plaintiff jazz violinist, allegedly without his authority, and in cancelling those arrangements had told the concert hall managers that the plaintiff was very ill and would probably never tour again. This statement, which was passed on to members of the public, was a complete fabrication. What damages could the plaintiff obtain for injurious falsehood? Would the defendant be liable in defamation, either before or after the publication of the plaintiff's authorised concert schedule, which included some concerts on the very same dates? If there is liability in injurious falsehood, why does it matter if there is concurrent liability in defamation?

ERVEN WARNINK B.V. v. TOWNEND (J.) & SONS (HULL)

House of Lords [1979] A.C. 731; [1979] 3 W.L.R. 68; (1979) 123 S.J. 472; [1979] 2 All E.R. 927; [1980] R.P.C. 31

Advocaat differs from egg-flip in being made with spirits rather than with fortified wine, which is cheaper. In 1974, in order to profit from the popularity of advocaat, the defendants decided to call their egg-flip "Keeling's Old English Advocaat." They thereby made a hole in the market for true advocaat, of which the plaintiffs had a very large share, almost all the competitors being from the Netherlands also.

The trial judge found that while no one buying Keeling's drink would suppose that he was buying Warnink's advocaat or indeed any Dutch advocaat, many people did suppose, as Keelings intended, that the drink they were buying was advocaat rather than egg-flip.

The trial judge granted an injunction. The Court of Appeal allowed the defendant's appeal, but the House of Lords restored the injunction.

Lord Diplock: My Lords, this is an action for "passing off", not in its classic form of a trader representing his own goods as the goods of somebody else, but in an extended form first recognised and applied by Danckwerts J. in the Champagne case (*Bollinger* v. *Costa Brava Wine Co. Ltd.* ([1960] Ch. 262)). The radio decidendi of that case was subsequently adopted as correct by Cross J. in the Sherry case (*Vine Products Ltd.* v. *Mackenzie & Co. Ltd.* ([1969] R.P.C. 1)) and by Foster J. in the Scotch Whisky case (*John Walker & Sons Ltd.* v. *Henry Ost & Co. Ltd.* ([1970] 2 All E.R. 106)).

The facts of the instant case as found by Goulding J. after a protracted trial make it, in my view, impossible to draw a rational distinction between the instant case and the Champagne case which could reconcile acceptance of the reasoning in the Champagne case with dismissal of the plaintiff's action in the instant case . . . and if this be so, the question of law for your Lordships is whether this House should give the seal of its approval to the extended concept of the cause of action for passing off that was applied in the Champagne, Sherry and Scotch Whisky cases. This question is essentially one of legal policy . . .

My Lords, the findings of fact accepted by the Court of Appeal and not challenged in your Lordship's House . . . seem to me to disclose a case of unfair, not to say dishonest, trading of a kind for which a rational system of law ought to provide a remedy to other traders whose business or goodwill is injured by it.

Unfair trading as a wrong actionable at the suit of other traders who thereby suffer loss of business or goodwill may take a variety of forms, to some of which separate labels have become attached in English law. Conspiracy to injure a person in his trade or business is one, slander of goods another, but most protean is that which is generally and nowadays, perhaps misleadingly, described as "passing off." The forms that unfair trading takes will alter with the ways in which trade is carried on and business reputation and goodwill acquired. Emerson's maker of the better mousetrap if secluded in his house built in the woods would today be unlikely to find a path beaten to his door in the absence of a costly advertising campaign to acquaint the public with the excellence of his wares.

The action for what has become known as "passing off" arose in the 19th century out of the use in connection with his own goods by one trader of the trade name or trade mark of a rival trader so as to induce in potential purchasers the belief that his goods were those of the rival trader. Although the cases up to the end of the century had been confined to the deceptive use of trade names, marks, letters or other indicia, the principle had been stated by Lord Langdale M.R. as early as 1842 as being: "A man is not to sell his own goods under the pretence that they are the goods of another man . . . " (*Perry v. Truefitt* ((1842) 6 Beav. 66, 73, 49 Enq.Rep. 749, 752)). At the close of the century in *Reddaway v. Banham*, ([1896] A.C. 199), it was said by Lord Herschell that what was protected by an action for passing off was not the proprietary right of the trader in the mark, name or get-up improperly used. Thus the door was opened to passing-off actions in which the misrepresentation took some other form than the deceptive use of trade names, marks, letters or other indicia; but as none of their Lordships committed themselves to identifying the legal nature of the right that was protected by a passing-off action it remained an action sui generis which lay for damage sustained or threatened in consequence of a misrepresentation of a particular kind.

Reddaway v. Banham, like all previous passing-off cases, was one in which Banham had passed off his goods as those of Reddaway, and the damage resulting from the misrepresentation took the form of the diversion of potential customers from Reddaway to Banham. Although it was a landmark case in deciding that the use by a trader of a term which accurately described the composition of his own goods might nevertheless amount to the tort of passing off if that term were understood in the market in which the goods were sold to denote the goods of a rival trader, *Reddaway v. Banham* did not extend the nature of the particular kind of misrepresentation which gives rise to a right of action in passing off beyond what I have called the classic form of misrepresenting one's own goods as the goods of someone else nor did it provide any rational basis for an extension.

This was left to be provided by Lord Parker of Waddington in *A.G. Spalding & Bros. v. A.W. Gamage Ltd.* ((1915) 32 R.P.C. 273, 284). In a speech which received the approval of the other members of this House, he identified the right the invasion of which is the subject of passing-off actions as being the "property in the business or goodwill likely to be injured by the misrepresentation." The concept of goodwill is in law a broad one which is perhaps best expressed in the words used by Lord Macnaghten in *Inland Revenue Comrs. v. Muller & Co.'s Margarine Ltd.* ([1901] A.C. 217, 223)): "It is the benefit and advantage of the good name, reputation and connection of a business. It is the attractive force which brings in custom."

The goodwill of a manufacturer's business may well be injured by someone else who sells goods which are correctly described as being made by that manufacturer but being of an inferior class or quality are misrepresented as goods of his manufacture of a superior class or quality. This type of misrepresentation was held in *A.G. Spalding & Bros. v. A.W. Gamage Ltd.* to be actionable and the extension to the nature of the misrepresentation which gives rise to a right of action in passing off which this involved was regarded by Lord Parker as a natural corollary of recognising that what the law protects by a passing-off action is a trader's property in his business or goodwill . . .

My Lords, *A.G. Spalding & Bros.* v. *A.W. Gamage Ltd.* and the later cases make it possible to identify five characteristics which must be present in order to create a valid cause of action for passing off: (1) a misrepresentation (2) made by a trader in the course of trade, (3) to prospective customers of his or ultimate consumers of goods or services supplied by him, (4) which is calculated to injure the business or goodwill of another trader (in the sense that this is a reasonably foreseeable consequence) and (5) which causes actual damage to a business or goodwill of the trader by whom the action is brought or (in a quia timet action) will probably do so.

In seeking to formulate general propositions of English law, however, one must be particularly careful to beware of the logical fallacy of the undistributed middle. It does not follow that because all passing-off actions can be shown to present these characteristics, all factual situations which present these characteristics give rise to a cause of action for passing off. True it is that their presence indicates what a moral code would censure as dishonest trading, based as it is on deception of customers and consumers of a trader's wares, but in an economic system which has relied on competition to keep down prices and to improve products there may be practical reasons why it should have been the policy of the common law not to run the risk of hampering competition by providing civil remedies to everyone competing in the market who has suffered damage to his business or goodwill in consequence of inaccurate statements of whatever kind that may be made by rival traders about their own wares. The market in which the action for passing off originated was no place for the mealy mouthed: advertisements are not on affidavit; exaggerated claims by a trader about the quality of his wares, assertions that they are better than those of his rivals, even though he knows this to be untrue, have been permitted by the common law as venial "puffing" which gives no cause of action to a competitor even though he can show that he has suffered actual damage in his business as a result.

Parliament, however, beginning in the 19th century has progressively intervened in the interests of consumers to impose on traders a higher standard of commercial candour that the legal maxim caveat emptor calls for, by prohibiting under penal sanctions misleading descriptions of the character or quality of goods; but since the class of persons for whose protection the Merchandise Marks Acts 1887 to 1953 and even more rigorous later statutes are designed are not competing traders but those consumers who are likely to be deceived, the Acts do not themselves give rise to any civil action for breach of statutory duty on the part of a competing trader even though he sustains actual damage as a result: *Cutler* v. *Wandsworth Stadium Ltd.* ([1949] A.C. 398); and see *London Armoury Co. Ltd.* v. *Ever Ready Co. (Great Britain) Ltd.* ([1941] 1 K.B. 742). Nevertheless the increasing recognition by Parliament of the need for more rigorous standards of commercial honesty is a factor which should not be overlooked by a judge confronted by the choice whether or not to extend by analogy to circumstances in which it has not previously been applied a principle which has been applied in previous cases where the circumstances although different had some features in common with those of the case which he has to decide. Where over a period of years there can be discerned a steady trend in legislation which reflects the view of successive Parliaments as to what the public interest demands in a particular field of law, development of the common law in that part of the same field which has been left to it ought to proceed on a parallel rather than a diverging course . . .

My Lords, in the Champagne case the class of traders between whom the goodwill attaching to the ability to use the word "champagne" as descriptive of their wines was a large one, 150 at least and probably considerably more, whereas in the previous English cases of shared goodwill the number of traders between whom the goodwill protected by a passing-off action was shared had been two . . .

It seems to me, however, as it seemed to Danckwerts J., that the principle must be the same whether the class of which each member is severally entitled to the goodwill which attaches to a particular term as descriptive of his goods is large or small. The larger it is the broader must be the range and quality of products to which the descriptive term used by the members of the class has been applied, and the more difficult it must be to show that the term had acquired a public reputation and goodwill as denoting a product endowed with recognisable qualities which distinguish it from others of inferior reputation that compete with it in the same market. The larger the class the more difficult it must also be for an individual member of it to show that the goodwill of his own business has sustained more than minimal damage as a result of deceptive use by another trader of the widely-shared descriptive term. As respects subsequent additions to the class, mere entry into the market would not give any right of action for passing off; the new entrant must have himself used the descriptive term long enough on the market in connection with his own goods and have traded successfully enough to have built up a goodwill for his business.

For these reasons the familiar argument that to extend the ambit of an actionable wrong beyond that to which effect has demonstrably been given in the previous cases would open the floodgates or, more ominously, a Pandora's box of litigation leaves me unmoved when it is sought to be applied to the actionable wrong of passing off.

I would hold the Champagne case to have been rightly decided and in doing so would adopt the words of Danckwerts J. where he said ([1960] Ch. 262, 284):

> "There seems to be no reason why such licence [sc. to do a deliberate act which causes damage to the property of another person] should be given to a person, competing in trade, who seeks to attach to his product a name or description with which it has no natural association so as to make use of the reputation and goodwill which has been gained by a product genuinely indicated by the name or description. In my view, it ought not to matter that the persons truly entitled to describe their goods by the name and description are a class producing goods in a certain locality, and not merely one individual. The description is part of their goodwill and a right of property. I do not believe that the law of passing off, which arose to prevent unfair trading, is so limited in scope." . . .

Of course it is necessary to be able to identify with reasonable precision the members of the class of traders of whose products a particular word or name has become so distinctive as to make their right to use it truthfully as descriptive of their product a valuable part of the goodwill of each of them; but it is the reputation that that type of product itself has gained in the market by reason of its recognisable and distinctive qualities that has generated the relevant goodwill. So if one can define with reasonable precision the type of product that has acquired the reputation, one can identify the members of the class entitled to share in the goodwill as being all those traders whose have supplied and still supply to the English market a product which possesses those recognisable and distinctive qualities.

It cannot make any difference in principle whether the recognisable and distinctive qualities by which the reputation of the type of product has been gained are the result of its having been made in, or from ingredients produced in, a particular locality or are the result of its having been made from particular ingredients regardless of the provenance, though a geographical limitation may make it easier (a) to define the type of product, (b) to establish that it has the qualities which are recognisable and distinguish it from every other type of product that competes with it in the market and which have gained for it in that market a reputation and goodwill and (c) to establish that the plaintiff's own business will suffer more than minimal damage to its goodwill by the defendant's misrepresenting his product as being of that type.

In the instant case it is true that all but a very small portion of the alcoholic egg drink which gained for the name "advocaat" a reputation and goodwill on the English market was imported from the Netherlands where, in order to bear that name, the ingredients from which it was made had to conform to the requirements of official regulations applicable to it in that country; but that is merely coincidental, for it is not suggested that an egg and spirit drink made in broad conformity with the Dutch official recipe for "advocaat," wherever it is made or its ingredients produced, is not endowed with the same recognisable and distinctive qualities as have gained for "advocaat" its reputation and goodwill in the English market.

So, on the findings for fact by Goulding J. to which I referred at the beginning of this speech, the type of product that has gained for the name "advocaat" on the English market the reputation and goodwill of which Keelings are seeking to take advantage by misrepresenting that their own product is of that type is defined by reference to the nature of its ingredients irrespective of their origin. The class of traders of whose respective businesses the right to describe their products as advocaat forms a valuable part of their goodwill are those who have supplied and are supplying on the English market an egg and spirit drink in broad conformity with an identifiable recipe. The members of that class are easily identified and very much fewer in number than in the Champagne, Sherry or Scotch Whisky cases. Warnink with 75 per cent. of the trade have a very substantial stake in the goodwill of the name "advocaat" and their business has been showed to have suffered serious injury as a result of Keelings putting on the English market in competition with Warnink and at a cheaper price an egg and wine based drink which they miscall advocaat instead of egg-flip which is its proper name.

My Lords, all the five characteristics that I have earlier suggested must be present to create a valid cause of action in passing off today were present in the instant case. Prima facie, as the law stands today, I think the presence of those characteristics is enough, unless there is also present in the case some exceptional feature which justifies, on grounds of public policy, withholding from a person who has suffered injury in consequence of the deception practised on prospective customers or consumers of his product a remedy in law against the deceiver. On the facts found by the judge, and I stress their importance, I can find no such exceptional feature in the instant case.

I would allow this appeal and restore the injunction granted by Goulding J.

Lord Fraser of Tullybelton delivered a concurring speech; Viscount Dilhorne, Lord Salmon and Lord Scarman agreed with both speeches.

Note:
A skirmish in the Great Hamburger War reached the courts. Burgerking put advertisements in London Tube trains headed "It's Not Just Big, Mac" and asserting that Burgerking burgers were 100 per cent. beef. More than half the thousand travellers polled said they took the advertisements to be for McDonald's "Big Mac" hamburgers, one in ten thinking they could be had at Burgerking outlets. The trial judge found that passing-off was established but that, for want of malice, trade libel was not (*McDonald's Hamburgers* v. *Burgerking (U.K.)* [1986] F.S.R. 45). The Court of Appeal ordered an enquiry as to damages (likely to be costly to the plaintiff) for the passing-off ([1987] F.S.R. 112).

If a person's competitors are restrained, his market position is strengthened, even if their competition is unfair. But the competition so restrained does not benefit the public if customers do not get what they are led to expect. Thus deception of the public is an important component of this tort. If there is no deception, there is no liability for taking advantage of a market created by another. Thus by means of a very expensive advertising campaign which stressed the muscularity of yesteryear, Cadbury Schweppes created public demand in Australia for their drink "Solo." The defendant decided to horn in on this market with his own drink "Pub Squash," also associated with macho nostalgia. He was held not liable since no one thought that Pub Squash was Solo. *Cadbury Schweppes* v. *Pub Squash Co.* [1981] 1 All E.R. 213 (P.C.)

LUMLEY v. GYE

Queen's Bench (1853) 2 E. & B. 216; 22 L.J.Q.B. 463; 17 Jur. 827; 1 W.R. 432; 118 E.R. 749

The plaintiff was manager of Her Majesty's Theatre and the defendant ran The Royal Italian Opera, Covent Garden; the dispute was over a prima donna, Richard Wagner's niece Johanna.

The law was decided on demurrer, *i.e.*, on the defendant's objection that the plaintiff's declaration disclosed no cause of action. The first count stated that the plaintiff contracted and agreed with Johanna Wagner to perform in his theatre for a certain time, with a condition, amongst others, that she should not sing or use her talents elsewhere during the term without the plaintiff's consent in writing: yet the defendant, well knowing the premises, and maliciously intending to injure the plaintiff, whilst the agreement with Wagner was still in force, and before the expiration of the term, enticed and procured Wagner to refuse to perform: by means of which enticement and procurement of the defendant, Wagner wrongfully refused to perform, and did not perform during the term.

The plaintiff had judgment on the demurrer, but since the defendant had obtained leave to plead as well as demur, the case went to trial on the facts and the plaintiff lost. The contract between the plaintiff and Wagner is contained in *Lumley* v. *Wagner* (1852) 1 De G.M. & G. 604; 42 E.R. 687.

Erle J.: . . . The question raised upon this demurrer is, whether an action will lie by the proprietor of a theatre against a person who maliciously procures an entire abandonment of a contract to perform exclusively at that theatre for a certain time; whereby damage was sustained? And it seems to me that it will. The authorities are numerous and uniform, that an action will lie by a master against a person who procures that a servant should unlawfully leave his service. The principle involved in those cases comprises the present; for, there, the right of action in the master arises from the wrongful act of the defendant in procuring that the person hired should break his contract, by putting an end to the relation of employer and employed; and the present case is the same. If it is objected that this class of actions for procuring a breach of contract of hiring rests upon no principle, and ought not to be extended beyond the cases heretofore decided, and that, as those have related to contracts respecting trade, manufactures or household service, and not to performance at a theatre, therefore they are no authority for an action in respect of a contract for such performance; the answer appears to me to be, that the class of cases referred to rests upon the principle that the procurement of the violation of the right is a cause of action, and that, when this principle is applied to a violation of a right arising upon a contract of hiring, the nature of the service contracted for is immaterial. It is clear that the procurement of the violation of a right is a cause of action in all instances where the violation is an actionable wrong, as in violations of a right to property, whether real or personal, or to personal security: he who procures the wrong is a joint wrong-doer, and may be sued, either alone or jointly with the agent, in the appropriate action for the wrong complained of. Where a right to the performance of a contract has been violated by a breach thereof, the remedy is upon the contract against the contracting party; and, if he is made to indemnify for such breach, no further recourse is allowed; and, as in case of the procurement of a breach of contract the action is for a wrong and cannot be joined with the action on the contract, and as the act itself is not likely to be of frequent occurrence nor easy of proof, therefore the action for this wrong, in respect of other contracts than those of hiring are not numerous; but still they seem to me sufficient to show that the principle has been recognised. In *Winsmore* v. *Greenbank* (Willes, 577) it was decided that the procuring of a breach of the contract of a wife is a cause of action. The only distinction in principle between this case and other cases of contracts is that the wife is not liable to be sued: but the judgment rests on no such grounds; the procuring a violation of the plaintiff's right under the marriage contract is held to be an actionable wrong. In *Green* v. *Button* (2 C.M. & R. 707) it was decided that the procuring a breach of a contract of sale of goods by a false claim of lien is an actionable wrong. *Sheperd* v. *Wakeham* (1 Sid. 79) is to the same effect, where the defendant procured a breach of a contract of marriage by asserting that the woman was already married. In *Ashley* v. *Harrison* (1 Peake's N.P.C. 194; 1 Esp.N.P.C. 48) and in *Taylor* v. *Neri* (1 Esp. N.P.C. 386) it was properly decided that the action did not lie, because the [libel], in the first case, and the [battery], in the second case, upon the contracting parties were not shown to be with intent to cause those persons to break their contracts, and so the defendants by the wrongful acts did not procure the breaches of contract which were complained of. If they had so acted for the purpose of procuring those breaches, it seems to me they would have been liable to the plaintiffs. To these decisions, founded on the principle now relied upon, the cases for procuring breaches of contracts of hiring should be added; at least Lord Mansfield's judgment in *Bird* v. *Randall* (3 Burr. 1345) is to that effect. This principle is supported by good reason. He who maliciously procures a damage to another by violation of his right ought to be made to indemnify; and that, whether he procures an actionable wrong or a breach of contract. He who procures the non-delivery of goods according to contract may inflict an injury, the same as he who procures the abstraction of goods after delivery; and both ought on the same ground to be made responsible. The remedy on the contract may be inadequate, as where the measures of damages is restricted; or in the case of non-payment of a debt where the damage may be bankruptcy to the creditor who is disappointed, but the measure of damage against the debtor is interest only; or, in the case of the non-delivery of the goods, the disappointment may lead to a heavy forfeiture under a contract to complete a work within a time, but the measure of damages against the vendor of the goods for non-delivery may be only the difference between the contract price and the market value of the goods in question at the time of the breach. In such cases, he who procures the damage maliciously might justly be made responsible beyond the liability of the contractor.

With respect to the objection that the contracting party had not begun the performance of the contract, I do not think it a tenable ground of defence. The procurement of the breach of the contract may be equally injurious, whether the service has begun or not, and in my judgment ought to be equally actionable, as the relation of employer and employed is constituted by the contract alone, and no act of service is necessary thereto.

The result is that there ought to be, in my opinion, judgment for the plaintiff.

Wightman J.: . . . It was undoubtedly prima facie an unlawful act on the part of Miss Wagner to break her contract, and therefore a tortious act of the defendant maliciously to procure her to do so; and, if damage to the plaintiff followed in consequence of that tortious act of the defendant, it would seem, upon the authority of the two cases referred to . . . as well as upon general principle, that an action on the case is maintainable . . .

Crompton J. used the illuminating phrase "wrongfully and maliciously, or, which is the same thing, with notice."

Coleridge J. (dissenting strongly): . . . there would be such a manifest absurdity in attempting to trace up the act of a free agent breaking a contract to all the advisers who may have influenced his mind, more or less honestly, more or less powerfully, and to make them responsible civilly for the consequences of what after all is his own act, and for the whole of the hurtful consequences of which the law makes him directly and fully responsible, that I believe it will never be contended for seriously . . . To draw a line between advice, persuasion, enticement and procurement is practically impossible in a court of justice.

Grace Note:

Johanna Wagner was not the only donna traviata at the time, and Lumley was not always the innocent party. Jenny Lind, the Swedish Nightingale, had an exclusive contract with Drury Lane but sang at Her Majesty's Theatre in a performance of Meyerbeer's *Robert le Diable*, attended by Queen Victoria and Mendelssohn. The Queen wrote about it in her diary, and Jenny Lind paid £2,500 for breach of contract.

Questions

1. Was it a material factor that the defendant here was trying to appropriate a benefit the plaintiff had secured for himself by contract? Would the answer be the same if the defendant had been the prima donna's manager who, on second thoughts, believed that it would not be in her professional interests to sing at the plaintiff's theatre?

2. What is the difference between saying "Break your contract, and I shall pay you more" and saying "You will earn more if you break your contract"? Should there be a difference in the two cases? If so, is the difference that between advising a person not to fulfil his contract and procuring that he does not?

3. If the defendant had kidnapped Miss Wagner in order to prevent her appearance at the plaintiff's theatre, could the plaintiff sue Miss Wagner for breach of contract? Could he sue the defendant?

Note:

This well-established tort has been deployed against extractors of trade secrets and other confidences (*British Industrial Plastics* v. *Ferguson*, [1938] 4 All E.R. 504); against persons persuading agents to exceed the terms of their agency (*Jasperson* v. *Dominion Tobacco Co.* [1923] A.C. 709); against a tenant who persuaded other tenants not to pay their rent because the building was in bad repair (*Camden Nominees* v. *Forcey* [1940] Ch. 353); and against a person who offered to buy the Aintree racecourse for development from a person who had promised not to sell it for that purpose (*Sefton (Earl)* v. *Topham's Ltd.* [1964] 1 W.L.R. 1408, reversed on other grounds [1967] 1 A.C. 50).

A modern example is *Rickless* v. *United Artists* [1987] 1 All E.R. 699 (C.A.). Pursuant to contracts between his loan-out company and various production companies, Peter Sellers starred in the *Pink Panther* films on the terms that his performance was not to be used for any other film without his consent; after his death the defendants knowingly obtained clips and take-outs from the production companies and were held liable for making another film with them.

This tort also has the honour of giving rise to the largest award of damages in history. A Texas jury awarded Pennzoil (a Texas company) the sum of $10,530,000,000 ($10·53 bn.) against Texaco (a New York company) for interfering, by offering a higher price, with Pennzoil's contract to buy stock in Getty Oil (729 S.W.2d 768 (Tex.App. 1987)). Texaco, unable to raise even the interest on this sum, filed for bankruptcy and finally agreed to pay Pennzoil $3,000,000,000. Very arguably, Texaco should not have been held liable at all, since when its offer was accepted by Getty Texaco had no idea that Getty was already bound to Pennzoil.

Employees are usually members of a union. Loyalty to the union may well conflict with obedience to the employer. Union officials would be powerless if they were liable simply for getting their members to break their contracts of employment, by striking or otherwise. Accordingly ever since 1906 certain conduct which would otherwise have been actionable under *Lumley* v. *Gye* has been legitimised if done "in contemplation or furtherance of a trade dispute."

The immunity originally attached only to inducing breach of a contract of employment, since only employees were union members. But then the courts very tiresomely held that one was guilty of inducing breach of A's contract to supply B if one persuaded A's employees not to co-operate (*Thomson* v. *Deakin* [1952] Ch. 646) and the statutory immunity was extended to inducing breach of commercial contracts. The position now is that if there is a trade dispute, the inducing of breaches of contracts of employment is not wrongful in itself or as a means of causing harm unless the aim and effect is to interfere with commercial contracts to which the other party to the dispute is not a party.

The tort can be approached in two ways, by concentrating either on the plaintiff's right or on the defendant's wrong. Lord Macnaghten did the former in *Quinn* v. *Leathem* [1901] A.C. 495, 510: "A violation of a legal right committed knowingly is a cause of action, and . . . it is a violation of a legal right to interfere with contractual relations recognised by law if there be no sufficient justification for the interference." Lord Haldane in *Jasperson's* case concentrated on the defendant's wrong: "What was laid down long ago in *Lumley* v. *Gye* reaches all wrongful acts done intentionally to damage a particular individual, and actually damaging him." ([1923] A.C. 709, 712). Lord Haldane's analysis is preferable, especially after *Rookes* v. *Barnard* (below p. 517) where it was held that even though no "right" of the plaintiff had been infringed, he could sue a defendant who by threatening to break his contract with another had procured that other to hurt him. Lord Macnaghten's formula has led to a deplorable expansion of this tort (see below p. 520).

In the classical version of this tort the defendant uses no wrongful means against the promise-breaker: Gye did not lie to Johanna nor threaten to beat her, he just offered her a raise, and there is nothing wrong with that. But what it was offered for made it not a simple raise but a bribe, for he persuaded her to do what they both knew was wrong: it was a kind of commercial adultery. But suppose that wrongful means *are* used. Suppose Gye had threatened Miss W. with g.b.h. if she sang for Lumley as promised. Of course there would be liability, but it would not be liability for inducing breach of contract, since Gye would be just as liable if there had been no breach at all, if Miss Wagner had been entirely free not to sing for Lumley, but would in fact have done so, but for the unlawful threat. Gye's liability would be for causing intentional harm by wrongful means, not for inducing breach of contract.

In such a case it is not simply inelegant to emphasise the contract and breach, but positively harmful. Despite anything to the contrary in cases given below, to *cause* an involuntary breach of contract is not wrongful in itself: for causing an involuntary breach of contract there should be no liability unless unlawful means are used, and if unlawful means are used there is liability whether a contract is broken or not. The tort under *Lumley* v. *Gye* is of *persuading* a contractor to defect. Of course that is a wrong, and because it is a wrong it may constitute wrongful means for the other tort, as where, in order to hurt A, the defendant persuades B to break his contract with C (as in *Merkur Island*, below p. 526).

As a defendant guilty of using unlawful means is liable for intended harm even if no contract of the plaintiff's is affected, one may wonder why the courts bother to ask whether any such contract has been aborted, frustrated or broken. The answer is that Parliament has couched the defendant's immunities in terms of the plaintiff's contracts, and the courts have deliberately turned one tort into the other in order to deprive defendants of those immunities. Now that the immunities have been so seriously reduced, the courts should back up.

MOGUL STEAMSHIP CO. v. McGREGOR, GOW & CO.

House of Lords [1892] A.C. 25; 61 L.J.Q.B. 295; 66 L.T. 1; 56 J.P. 101; 40 W.R. 337; 8 T.L.R. 182; 7 Asp.M.L.C. 120. Court of Appeal (1889) 23 Q.B.D. 598; 58 L.J.Q.B. 465; 61 L.T. 820; 53 J.P. 709; 37 W.R. 756; 5 T.L.R. 658; 6 Asp.M.L.C. 455. Queen's Bench (1888) 21 Q.B.D. 544

On the facts given in the judgment of Bowen L.J., the plaintiffs failed at first instance, and on appeal to the Court of Appeal (Lord Esher M.R. dissenting), and on further appeal to the House of Lords.

In the Court of Appeal

Bowen L.J.: We are presented in this case with an apparent conflict or antinomy between two rights that are equally regarded by the law—the right of the plaintiffs to be protected in the legitimate exercise of their trade, and the right of the defendants to carry on their business as seems best to them, provided they commit no wrong to others. The plaintiffs complain that the defendants have crossed the line which the common law permits; and inasmuch as, for the purposes of the present case, we are to assume some possible damage to the plaintiffs, the real question to be decided is whether, on such an assumption, the defendants in the conduct of their commercial affairs have done anything that is unjustifiable in law. The defendants are a number of shipowners who formed themselves into a league or conference for the purpose of ultimately keeping in their own hands the control of the tea carriage from certain Chinese ports, and for the purpose of driving the plaintiffs and other competitors from the field. In order to succeed in this object, and to discourage the plaintiffs' vessels from resorting to those ports, the defendants during the "tea harvest" of 1885 combined to offer to the local shippers very low freights, with a view of generally reducing or "smashing" rates, and thus rendering it unprofitable for the plaintiffs to send their ships thither. They offered, moreover, a rebate of 5 per cent. to all local shippers and agents who would deal exclusively with vessels belonging to the Conference, and any agent who broke the condition was to forfeit the entire rebate on all shipments made on behalf of any and every one of his principals during the whole year—a forfeiture of rebate or allowance which was denominated as "penal" by the plaintiffs' counsel. It must, however, be taken as established that the rebate was one which the defendants need never have allowed at all to their customers. It must also be taken that the defendants had no personal ill-will to the plaintiffs, nor any desire to harm them except such as is involved in the wish and intention to discourage by such measures the plaintiffs from sending rival vessels to such ports. The acts of which the plaintiffs particularly complained were as follows: First, a circular of May 10, 1885, by which the defendants offered to the local shippers and their agents a benefit by way of rebate if they would not deal with the plaintiffs, which was to be lost if this condition was not fulfilled. Secondly, the sending of special ships to Hankow in order by competition to deprive the plaintiffs' vessels of profitable freight. Thirdly, the offer at Hankow of freights at a level which would not repay a shipowner for his adventure, in order to "smash" freights and frighten the plaintiffs from the field. Fourthly, pressure put on the defendants' own agents to induce them to ship only by the defendants' vessels, and not by those of the plaintiffs. It is to be observed with regard to all these acts of which complaint is made that they were acts that in themselves could not be said to be illegal unless made so by the object with which, or the combination in the course of which, they were done; and that in reality what is complained of is the pursuing of trade competition to a length which the plaintiffs consider oppressive and prejudicial to themselves. We were invited by the plaintiffs' counsel to accept the position from which their argument started—that an action will lie if a man maliciously and wrongfully conducts himself so as to injure another in that other's trade. Obscurity resides in the language used to state this proposition. The terms "maliciously," "wrongfully," and "injure" are words all of which have accurate meanings, well known to the law, but which also have a popular and less precise signification, into which it is necessary to see that the argument does not imperceptibly slide. An intent to "injure" in strictness means more than an intent to harm. It connotes an intent to do wrongful harm. "Maliciously," in like manner, means and implies an intention to do an act which is wrongful, to the detriment of another. The term "wrongful" imports in its turn the infringement of some right. The ambiguous proposition to which we were invited by the plaintiffs' counsel still, therefore, leaves unsolved the question of what, as between the plaintiffs and defendants, are the rights of trade. For the purpose of clearness, I desire, as far as possible, to avoid terms in their popular use so slippery, and to translate them into less fallacious language wherever possible.

The English law, which in its earlier stages began with but an imperfect line of demarcation between torts and breaches of contract, presents us with no scientific analysis of the degree to which the intent to harm, or, in the language of the civil law, the *animus vicino nocendi*, may enter into or affect the conception of a personal wrong: see *Chasemore* v. *Richards* ((1859) 7 H.L.C. 349, 388; 11 E.R. 140). All personal wrong means the infringement of some personal right. "It is essential to an action in tort," say the Privy Council in *Rogers* v. *Rajendro Dutt* ((1860) 13 Moore P.C. 209; 15 E.R. 78), "that the act complained of should under the circum-

stances be legally wrongful as regards the party complaining; that is, it must preju-
dicially affect him in some legal right; merely that it will, however indirectly, do a
man harm in his interests, is not enough." What, then, were the rights of the plaintiffs as traders as against the defendants? The plaintiffs had a right to be protected
against certain kind of conduct; and we have to consider what conduct would pass
this legal line or boundary. Now, intentionally to do that which is calculated in the
ordinary course of events to damage, and which does, in fact, damage another in
that other person's property or trade, is actionable if done without just cause or
excuse. Such intentional action when done without just cause or excuse is what the
law calls a malicious wrong (see *Bromage* v. *Prosser* ((1825) 4 B. & C. 247; 107
E.R. 1051); *Capital and Counties Bank* v. *Henty, per* Lord Blackburn ((1882) 7
App.Cas. 741, 772)). The acts of the defendants which are complained of here were
intentional, and were also calculated, no doubt, to do the plaintiffs damage in their
trade. But in order to see whether they were wrongful we have still to discuss the
question whether they were done without any just cause or excuse. Such just cause
or excuse the defendants on their side assert to be found in their own positive right
(subject to certain limitations) to carry on their own trade freely in the mode and
manner that best suits them, and which they think best calculated to secure their
own advantage.

What, then, are the limitations which the law imposes on a trader in the conduct
of his business as between himself and other traders? There seem to be no burdens
or restrictions in law upon a trader which arise merely from the fact that he is a
trader, and which are not equally laid on all other subjects of the Crown. His right
to trade freely is a right which the law recognises and encourages, but it is one
which places him at no special disadvantage as compared with others. No man,
whether trader or not, can, however, justify damaging another in his commercial
business by fraud or misrepresentation. Intimidation, obstruction, and molestation
are forbidden; so is the intentional procurement of a violation of individual rights,
contractual or other, assuming always that there is no just cause for it. The intentional driving away of customers by show of violence: *Tarleton* v. *M'Gawley* ((1793)
Peek, N.P.C. 270; 170 E.R. 153); the obstruction of actors on the stage by preconcerted hissing: *Clifford* v. *Brandon* ((1810) 2 Camp. 358; 170 E.R. 1183); *Gregory*
v. *Brunswick* (1843) 6 Man. & G. 205; 134 E.R. 866); the disturbance of wild fowl
in decoys by the firing of guns: *Carrington* v. *Taylor* ((1809) 11 East 571; 103 E.R.
1126) and *Keeble* v. *Hickeringill* ((1706) 11 East 574n.; 103 E.R. 1127); the impeding or threatening servants or workmen: *Garret* v. *Taylor* ((1620) Cro.Jac. 567; 79
E.R. 485); the inducing persons under personal contracts to break their contracts:
Bowen v. *Hall* ((1881) 6 Q.B.D. 333); *Lumley* v. *Gye* ((1853) 2 E. & B. 216; 118
E.R. 749; above, p. 499); all are instances of such forbidden acts. But the defendants have been guilty of none of these acts. They have done nothing more against
the plaintiffs than pursue to the bitter end a war of competition waged in the interest of their own trade. To the argument that a competition so pursued ceases to
have a just cause or excuse when there is ill-will or a personal intention to harm, it
is sufficient to reply (as I have already pointed out) that there was here no personal
intention to do any other or greater harm to the plaintiffs than such as was necessarily involved in the desire to attract to the defendants' ships the entire tea freight
of the ports, a portion of which would otherwise have fallen to the plaintiffs' share.
I can find no authority for the doctrine that such a commercial motive deprives of
"just cause or excuse" acts done in the course of trade which would but for such a
motive be justifiable. So to hold would be to convert into an illegal motive the
instinct of self-advancement and self-protection, which is the very incentive to all
trade. To say that a man is to trade freely, but that he is to stop short at any act
which is calculated to harm other tradesmen, and which is designed to attract business to his own shop, would be a strange and impossible counsel of perfection. But
we were told that competition ceases to be the lawful exercise of trade, and so to be
a lawful excuse for what will harm another, if carried to a length which is not fair or

reasonable. The offering of reduced rates by the defendants in the present case is said to have been "unfair." This seems to assume that, apart from fraud, intimidation, molestation, or obstruction, of some other personal right *in rem* or *in personam*, there is some natural standard of "fairness' or "reasonableness" (to be determined by the internal consciousness of judges and juries) beyond which competition ought not in law to go. There seems to be no authority, and I think, with submission, that there is no sufficient reason for such a proposition. It would impose a novel fetter upon trade. The defendants, we are told by the plaintiffs' counsel, might lawfully lower rates provided they did not lower them beyond a "fair freight," whatever that may mean. But where is it established that there is any such restriction upon commerce? And what is to be the definition of a "fair freight"? It is said that it ought to be a normal rate of freight, such as is reasonably remunerative to the shipowner. But over what period of time is the average of this reasonable remunerativeness to be calculated? All commercial men with capital are acquainted with the ordinary expedient of sowing one year a crop of apparently unfruitful prices, in order by driving competition away to reap a fuller harvest of profit in the future; and until the present argument at the bar it may be doubted whether shipowners or merchants were ever deemed to be bound by law to conform to some imaginary "normal" standard of freights or prices or that Law Courts had a right to say to them in respect of their competitive tariffs, "Thus far shalt thou go and no further." To attempt to limit English competition in this way would probably be as hopeless an endeavour as the experiment of King Canute. But on ordinary principles of law no such fetter on freedom of trade can in my opinion be warranted. A man is bound not to use his property so as to infringe upon another's right. *Sic utere tuo ut alienum non laedas.* If engaged in actions which may involve danger to others, he ought, speaking generally, to take reasonable care to avoid endangering them. But there is surely no doctrine of law which compels him to use his property in a way that judges and juries may consider reasonable: see *Chasemore* v. *Richards* (1859) 7 H.L.C. 349). If there is no such fetter upon the use of property known to the English law, why should there be any such a fetter upon trade?

It is urged, however, on the part of the plaintiffs, that even if the acts complained of would not be wrongful had they been committed by a single individual, they become actionable when they are the result of concerted action among several. In other words, the plaintiffs, it is contended, have been injured by an illegal conspiracy. Of the general proposition, that certain kinds of conduct not criminal in any one individual may become criminal if done by combination among several, there can be no doubt. The distinction is based on sound reason, for a combination may make oppressive or dangerous that which if it proceeded only from a single person would be otherwise, and the very fact of the combination may show that the object is simply to do harm and not to exercise one's own just rights. In the application of this undoubted principle it is necessary to be very careful not to press the doctrine of illegal conspiracy beyond that which is necessary for the protection of individuals or of the public; and it may be observed in passing that as a rule it is the damage wrongfully done, and not the conspiracy, that is the gist of actions on the case for conspiracy: see *Skinner* v. *Gunton* ((1668) 1 Wms.Saund. 229; 85 E.R. 249). But what is the definition of an illegal combination? It is an agreement by one or more to do an unlawful act, or to do a lawful act by unlawful means: *O'Connell* v. *The Queen* ((1844) 11 Cl. & F. 155; 8 E.R. 1061); *R.* v. *Parnell* ((1881) 14 Cox Crim. Cas. 508); and the question to be solved is whether there has been any such agreement here. Have the defendants combined to do an unlawful act? Have they combined to do a lawful act by unlawful means? A moment's consideration will be sufficient to show that this new inquiry only drives us back to the circle of definitions and legal propositions which I have already traversed in the previous part of this judgment. The unlawful act agreed to, if any, between the defendants must have been the intentional doing of some act to the detriment of the plaintiffs' business without just cause or excuse. Whether there was any such justification or excuse for the defendants is the old question over again, which, so far as regards an individual trader, has been already solved. The only differentia that can exist must arise, if at all, out of the fact that the acts done are the joint acts of several capitalists, and not of one capitalist only. The next point is whether the means adopted were unlawful. The means adopted were competition carried to a bitter end. Whether such means are unlawful is in like manner nothing but the old discussion which I have gone through, and which is now revived under a second head of inquiry, except so far as a combination of capitalists differentiates the case of acts jointly done by them from similar acts done by a single man of capital. But I find it impossible myself to acquiesce in the view that the English law places any such restriction on the combination of capital as would be involved in the recognition of such a distinction. If so, one rich capitalist may innocently carry competition to a length which would become unlawful in the case of a syndicate with a joint capital no larger than his own, and one individual merchant may lawfully do that which a firm or a partnership may not. What limits, on such a theory, would be imposed by law on the competitive action of a joint-stock company limited, is a problem which might well puzzle a casuist. The truth is, that the combination of capital for purposes of trade and competition is a very different thing from such a combination of several persons against one, with a view to harm him, as falls under the head of an indictable conspiracy. There is no just cause or excuse in the latter class of cases. There is such a just cause or excuse in the former. There are cases in which the very fact of a combination is evidence of a design to do that which is hurtful without just cause—is evidence—to use a technical expression—of malice. But it is perfectly legitimate, as it seems to me, to combine capital for all the mere purposes of trade for which capital may, apart from combination, be legitimately used in trade. To limit combinations of capital, when used for purposes of competition, in the manner proposed by the argument of the plaintiffs, would, in the present day, be impossible—would be only another method of attempting to set boundaries to the tides. Legal puzzles which might well distract a theorist may easily be conceived of imaginary conflicts between the selfishness of a group of individuals and the obvious well-being of other members of the community. Would it be an indictable conspiracy to agree to drink up all the water from a common spring in a time of drought; to buy up by preconcerted action all the provisions in a market or district in times of scarcity: see *R.* v. *Waddington* ((1800) 1 East 143; 102 E.R. 56); to combine to purchase all the shares of a company against a coming settling-day; or to agree to give away articles of trade gratis in order to withdraw custom from a trader? May two itinerant match-vendors combine to sell matches below their value in order by competition to drive a third match-vendor from the street? In cases like these, where the elements of intimidation, molestation, or the other kinds of illegality to which I have alluded are not present, the question must be decided by the application of the test I have indicated. Assume that what is done is intentional, and that it is calculated to do harm to others. Then comes the question, Was it done with or without "just cause or excuse"? If it was bona fide done in the use of a man's own property, in the exercise of a man's own trade, such legal justification would, I think, exist not the less because what was done might seem to others to be selfish or unreasonable: see the summing-up of Erle J. and the judgment of the Queen's Bench in *R.* v. *Rowlands* ((1851) 17 Q.B. 671; 117 E.R. 1439). But such legal justification would not exist when the act was merely done with the intention of causing temporal harm, without reference to one's own lawful gain, or the lawful enjoyment of one's own rights. The good sense of the tribunal which had to decide would have to analyse the circumstances and to discover on which side of the line each case fell. But if the real object were to enjoy what was one's own, or to acquire for one's self some advantage in one's property or trade, and what was done was done honestly, peaceably, and without any of the illegal acts above referred to, it could not, in my opinion, properly be said that it was done without just cause or excuse. One may with advantage borrow for the benefit of traders what was said by Erle J. in *R.* v. *Rowlands*, of workmen and of masters: "The intention of the law is at present to allow either of them to follow the dictates of their own will, with respect to their own actions, and their own property; and either, I believe, has a right to study to promote his own advantage, or to combine with others to promote their mutual advantage."

Lastly, we are asked to hold the defendants' Conference or association illegal, as being in restraint of trade. The term "illegal" here is a misleading one. Contracts, as they are called, in restraint of trade, are not, in my opinion, illegal in any sense, except that the law will not enforce them. It does not prohibit the making of such contracts; it merely declines, after they have been made, to recognise their validity. The law considers the disadvantage so imposed upon the contract a sufficient shelter to the public . . . No action at common law will lie or ever has lain against any individual or individuals for entering into a contract merely because it is in restraint of trade . . . If indeed it could be plainly proved that the mere formation of "conferences," "trusts," or "associations" such as these were always necessarily injurious to the public—a view which involves, perhaps, the disputable assumption that, in a country of free trade, and one which is not under the iron régime of statutory monopolies, such confederations can ever be really successful—and if the evil of them were not sufficiently dealt with by the common law rule, which held such agreements to be void as distinct from holding them to be criminal, there might be some reason for thinking that the common law ought to discover within its arsenal of sound common-sense principles some further remedy commensurate with the mischief. Neither of these assumptions are, to my mind, at all evident, nor is it the province of judges to mould and stretch the law of conspiracy in order to keep pace with the calculations of political economy. If peaceable and honest combinations of capital for purposes of trade competition are to be struck at, it must, I think, be by legislation, for I do not see that they are under the ban of the common law.

In the result, I agree with Lord Coleridge C.J., and differ, with regret from the Master of the Rolls. The substance of my view is this, that competition, however severe and egotistical, if unattended by circumstances of dishonesty, intimidation, molestation, or such illegalities as I have above referred to, gives rise to no cause of action at common law. I myself should deem it to be a misfortune if we were to attempt to prescribe to the business world how honest and peaceable trade was to be carried on in a case where no such illegal elements as I have mentioned exist, or were to adopt some standard of judicial "reasonableness," or of "normal" prices, or "fair freights," to which commercial adventures, otherwise innocent, were bound to conform.

In my opinion, accordingly, this appeal ought to be dismissed with costs.

Fry L.J.: . . . It was forcibly urged upon us that combinations like the present are in their nature calculated to interfere with the course of trade, and that they are, therefore, so directly opposed to the interest which the state has in freedom of trade, and in that competition which is said to be the life of trade, that they must be indictable. It is plain that the intention and object of the combination before us is to check competition; but the means it uses is competition, and it is difficult, if not impossible, to weigh against one another the probabilities of the employment of competition on the one hand and its suppression on the other; nor is it easy to say how far the success of the combination would arouse in others the desire to share in its benefits, and by competition to force a way into the magic circle . . . To draw a line between fair and unfair competition, between what is reasonable and unreasonable, passes the power of the courts . . .

Lord Esher M.R. (dissenting): . . . the act of the defendants in lowering their freights far beyond a lowering for any purpose of trade—that is to say, so low that if they continued it they themselves could not carry on trade—was not an act done in the exercise of their own free right of trade, but was an act done evidently for the purpose of interfering with, *i.e.*, with intent to interfere with, the plaintiffs' right to a free course of trade, and was therefore a wrongful act as against the plaintiffs' right; and as injury ensued to the plaintiffs, they had also in respect of such act a right of action against the defendants. The plaintiffs, in respect of that act, would have had a right of action if it had been done by one defendant only . . .

In the House of Lords

Lord Halsbury L.C.: . . . upon a review of the facts, it is impossible to suggest any malicious intention to injure rival traders, except in the sense that in proportion as one withdraws trade that other people might get, you, to that extent, injure a person's trade when you appropriate the trade to yourself. If such an injury, and the motive of its infliction, is examined and tested, upon principle, and can be truly asserted to be a malicious motive within the meaning of the law that prohibits malicious injury to other people, all competition must be malicious and consequently unlawful, a sufficient *reductio ad absurdum* to dispose of that head of suggested unlawfulness . . .

Lord Bramwell: . . . what is the definition of "fair competition"? What is unfair that is neither forcible nor fraudulent? . . .

At first instance

Lord Coleridge C.J.: . . . It must be remembered that all trade is and must be in a sense selfish; trade not being infinite, nay, the trade of a particular place or district being possibly very limited, what one man gains another loses. In the hand to hand war of commerce, as in the conflicts of public life, whether at the Bar, in Parliament, in medicine, in engineering, (I give examples only,) men fight on without much thought of others except a desire to excel or to defeat them. Very lofty minds, like Sir Philip Sidney with his cup of water, will not stoop to take an advantage, if they think another wants it more. Our age, in spite of high authority to the contrary, is not without its Sir Philip Sidneys; but these are counsels of perfection which it would be silly indeed to make the measure of the rough business of the world as pursued by ordinary men of business. The line is in words difficult to draw, but I cannot see that these defendants have in fact passed the line which separates the reasonable and legitimate selfishness of traders from wrong and malice . . .

Note:
    Lord Bramwell's brutal question marks the heart of this important decision; where no specific right has been infringed, everything in trade is fair save force and fraud. Unfair competition is not unlawful; only unlawful competition is. It is a strong case, for the tactics used by the Conference were implacably used and cripplingly effective—predatory price-cutting, "fighting-ships" and pressure on agents. It is curious that Lord Esher M.R. in his dissent focused on the first of these—the short-term uneconomic lowering of freights—when the law of contract was based on the view that a man might charge what he liked for his goods or services (see Lord Bramwell in *Manchester, Sheffield & Lincolnshire Ry.* v. *Brown* (1883) 8 App.Cas. at 716). In their other methods, the Conference sailed closer to the wind. By shadowing rival ships, they risked a liability of public nuisance which had been incurred by London bus companies for similar practices (*Green* v. *London General Omnibus Co.* (1859) 7 C.B.(N.S.) 290; 141 E.R. 828). In their approaches to the agents, they risked liability under *Lumley* v. *Gye*.
    The French courts did not believe, with Fry L.J., that it passed their power to say what was reasonable in matters of competition and what was not. They developed, as a matter of pure case law, an extensive system of control of *concurrence déloyale*. When the judges in Germany declined to do likewise, the legislature passed a special Act in very general terms in 1909 (*unlauterer Wettbewerb*), which the German judges now apply in addition to the rules of tort:

"A person who in the course of business for purposes of competition acts in a manner which offends against good morals is liable to be enjoined or cast in damages." (Note that if Lord Bramwell's "force" could be extended to cover any "abuse of power" and his "fraud" to include all "dirty tricks," most offences against good morals would be reached).

At the very time of the *Mogul* case, the United States Congress was passing the *Sherman Act*: "Every contract, combination in the form of trust or otherwise, or conspiracy in restraint of trade or commerce . . . is declared to be illegal," and any person suffering business loss in consequence may now recover threefold damages in a civil action. This Act was to keep competition alive; to keep it fair, Congress enacted the Federal Trade Commission Act in 1914, whereunder "Unfair methods of competition in commerce, and unfair or deceptive acts or practices in commerce, are declared unlawful." The regulatory device is an administrative tribunal empowered to enjoin and fine, and not the civil action for damages. Some of the several states, unlike England, evolved a prima facie tort theory from the following dictum of Bowen L.J.: "Now intentionally to do that which is calculated in the ordinary course of events to damage, and which does, in fact, damage another, is actionable if done without just cause or excuse." But even this principle is incapable of producing a tort of unfair competition which has had, therefore, to develop from the rule that it is wrongful to take away someone's trade by selling your goods as his (passing-off): see above, p. 494.

In comparison with these jurisdictions, the English law was slow to develop. The Restrictive Trade Practices Act 1976 makes it generally unlawful and sometimes actionable for suppliers of goods and designated services to restrain trade in particular ways, and the Resale Prices Act 1976 gives an action to a retailer whose supplies are cut off because he undersold. But the aim of these statutes is to maintain competition, not to curb its nastier excesses.

When Britain joined France and Germany in the Common Market, the picture changed, at any rate in relation to trade between member states. Article 85 of the Treaty of Rome prohibits and avoids as incompatible with the common market "all agreements between undertakings, decisions by associations of undertakings and concerted practices . . . which have as their object or effect the prevention, restriction or distortion of competition . . . " Article 86 prohibits "Any abuse by one or more undertakings of a dominant position within the common market or in a substantial part of it . . . " The Luxembourg Court has asserted that these articles generate individual rights which national courts must safeguard.

A claim for damages almost certainly lies in England (*Garden Cottage Foods* v. *Milk Marketing Board* [1983] 2 All E.R. 770 (H.L.)). It is patterned on the action for breach of statutory duty (see above p. 173) but it is quite uncertain yet who may sue, what conduct constitutes an abuse, how dominant the position must be and in how substantial a part of the market. An English brewery must have been surprised to run into difficulties for instructing the pubs it had just bought to terminate their contracts with the plaintiff for the hire of slot-machines (*Cutsforth* v. *Mansfield Inns* [1986] 1 All E.R. 575).

ALLEN v. FLOOD

House of Lords [1898] A.C. 1; 67 L.J.Q.B. 119; 77 L.T. 717; 62 J.P. 595; 46 W.R. 258; 14 T.L.R. 125; 42 S.J. 149

The *Sam Weller* was under repair by the Glengall Iron Co. in the Regent Dock at Millwall; the woodwork was being done by shipwrights, including the plaintiffs Flood and Taylor, members of the tiny Shipwrights' Provident Union, and the ironwork was being done by about 40 boilermakers, belonging to the huge Independent Society of Boiler Makers and Iron and Steel Ship Builders, whose London delegate was the defendant Allen. The boilermakers discovered that Flood and Taylor had been employed on ironwork by another company and wired for Allen, who came and talked to the boilermakers. He then told the company's manager that the boilermakers would go on strike unless Flood and Taylor were dismissed. Flood and Taylor were dismissed that very day. It was assumed that all the contracts were determinable at will.

Kennedy J. ruled that there was no evidence of conspiracy, or of intimidation or coercion or of breach of contract. The jury found that Allen maliciously induced the Glengall Co. to discharge Flood and Taylor from their employment, and also not to engage them again, and that each plaintiff had suffered damage amounting to £20.

After consideration, Kennedy J. gave judgment for the plaintiffs for £40 [1895] 2 Q.B. 21. The Court of Appeal (Lord Esher M.R., Lopes and Rigby L.JJ.) affirmed that decision [1895] 2 Q.B. 21, in judgments whose effect is stated by the headnote, which reads: "An action will lie against a person who maliciously induces a master to discharge a servant from his employment if injury ensues thereby to the servant, though the discharge by the master does not constitute a breach of the contract of employment. An action will also lie for maliciously inducing a person to abstain from entering into a contract to employ another, if injury ensures thereby to that other."

Allen appealed to the House of Lords. The case was argued before Lord Halsbury L.C., and Lords Watson, Herschell, Macnaghten, Morris and Shand. Eight judges answered a summons to attend (Hawkins, Mathew, Cave, North, Wills, Grantham, Lawrance and Wright JJ.) and the case was reargued before all of them, with the addition of Lord Ashbourne and Lord James of Hereford. The appeal was allowed (Lords Watson, Herschell, Macnaghten, Shand, Davey and James of Hereford; Lord Halsbury L.C., Lord Ashbourne and Lord Morris dissenting). Of the judges who wrote opinions at the request of the House, only Wright and Mathew JJ. were in favour of the defendant. Accordingly, of the 21 judges who wrote opinions on this case, only eight were in favour of the defendant who ultimately won.

Lord Watson: . . . There are, in my opinion, two grounds only upon which a person who procures the act of another can be made legally responsible for its consequences. In the first place, he will incur liability if he knowingly and for his own ends induces that other person to commit an actionable wrong. In the second place, where the act induced is within the right of the immediate actor, and is therefore not wrongful in so far as he is concerned, it may yet be to the detriment of a third party; and in that case . . . the inducer may be held liable if he can be shown to have procured his object by the use of illegal means directed against that third party . . . [The iron-men] were not under any continuing engagement to their employers, and, if they had left their work and gone out on strike, they would have been acting within their right, whatever might be thought of the propriety of the proceeding. Not only so; they were, in my opinion, entitled to inform the Glengall Iron Company of the step which they contemplated, as well as of the reasons by which they were influenced, and that either by their own mouth, or as they preferred, by the appellant as their representative . . .

Lord Herschell: . . . I can imagine no greater danger to the community than that a jury should be at liberty to impose the penalty of paying damages for acts which are otherwise lawful, because they choose, without any legal definition of the term, to say that they are malicious . . . [His Lordship referred to the "fair-minded man" test propounded by Wills J., below, p. 516.] . . . this suggested test makes men's responsibility for their actions depend on the fluctuating opinions of the tribunal before whom the case may chance to come as to what a right-minded man ought or ought not to do in pursuing his own interests. . . . It was said that there seemed to be no good reason why, if an action lay for maliciously inducing a breach of contract, it should not equally lie for maliciously inducing a person not to enter into a contract. So far from thinking it a small step from the one decision to the other, I think there is a chasm between them . . . Even . . . if it can be said without abuse of language that the employers were "intimidated and coerced" by the appellant, even if this be in a certain sense true, it by no means follows that he committed a wrong or is under any legal liability for his act. Everything depends on the nature of the representation or statement by which the pressure was exercised. The law cannot regard the act differently because you choose to call it a threat or coercion instead of an intimation or warning.

I understood it to be admitted at the Bar . . . that it would have been perfectly lawful for all the ironworkers to leave their employment and not to accept a subsequent engagement to work in the company of the plaintiffs. [His Lordship discussed the cases.] In all of them the act complained of was in its nature wrongful; violence, menaces of violence, false statements . . . everything depends on the nature of the act, and whether it is wrongful or not . . . I am aware of no ground for saying that competition is regarded with special favour by the law . . . Even if a misrepresentation by the appellant to the Glengall Company would be sufficient in any circumstances to afford a right of action to the plaintiffs, I think it could scarcely be contended that it could do so, unless the misrepresentation were wilful and intentional . . .

Lord Macnaghten: . . . Even if I am wrong in my view of the evidence and the verdict, if the verdict amounts to a finding that Allen's conduct was malicious in every sense of the word, and that he procured the dismissal of Flood and Taylor, that is, that it was his act and conduct alone which caused their dismissal, and if such a verdict were warranted by the evidence, I should still be of opinion that judgment was wrongly entered for the respondents. I do not think that there is any foundation in good sense or in authority for the proposition that a person who suffers loss by reason of another doing or not doing some act which that other is entitled to do or to abstain from doing at his own will and pleasure, whatever his real motive may be, has a remedy against a third person who, by persuasion or some other means not in itself unlawful, has brought about the act or omission from which the loss comes, even though it could be proved that such person was actuated by malice towards the plaintiff, and that his conduct if it could be inquired into was without justification or excuse.

The case may be different where the act itself to which the loss is traceable involves some breach of contract or some breach of duty, and amounts to an interference with legal rights. There the immediate agent is liable, and it may well be that the person in the background who pulls the strings is liable too, though it is not necessary in the present case to express any opinion on that point.

But if the immediate agent cannot be made liable, though he knows what he is about and what the consequences of his action will be, it is difficult to see on what principle a person less directly connected with the affair can be made responsible unless malice has the effect of converting an act not in itself illegal or improper into an actionable wrong. But if that is the effect of malice, why is the immediate agent to escape? Above all, why is he to escape when there is no one else to blame and no one else is answerable? And yet many cases may be put of harm done out of malice without any remedy being available at law. Suppose a man takes a transfer of a debt with which he has no concern for the purpose of ruining the debtor, and then makes him bankrupt out of spite, and so intentionally causes him to lose some benefit under a will or settlement—suppose a man declines to give a servant a character because he is offended with the servant for leaving—suppose a person of position takes away his custom from a country tradesman in a small village merely to injure him on account of some fancied grievance not connected with their dealings in the way of buying and selling—no one, I think, would suggest that there could be any remedy at law in any of those cases. But suppose a customer, not content with taking away his own custom, says something not slanderous or otherwise actionable or even improper in itself to induce a friend of his not to employ the tradesman any more. Neither the one nor the other is liable for taking away his own custom. Is it possible that the one can be made liable for inducing the other not to employ the person against whom he has a grudge? If so, a fashionable dressmaker might now and then, I fancy, be plaintiff in a very interesting suit. The truth is that questions of this sort belong to the province of morals rather than to the province of law.

Against spite and malice the best safeguards are to be found in self-interest and public opinion. Much more harm than good would be done by encouraging or permitting inquiries into motives when the immediate act alleged to have caused the loss for which redress is sought is in itself innocent or neutral in character, and one which anybody may do or leave undone without fear of legal consequences. Such an inquisition would, I think, be intolerable, to say nothing of the probability of injustice being done by juries in a class of cases in which there would be ample room for speculation and wide scope for prejudice.

In order to prevent any possible misconstruction of the language I have used I should like to add that in my opinion the decision of this case can have no bearing on any case which involves the element of oppressive combination. The vice of that form of terrorism commonly known by the name of "boycotting," and other forms of oppressive combination, seems to me to depend on considerations which are, I think, in the present case conspicuously absent.

As regards authority, there is, I think, very little to be said. It is hardly necessary to go further back than *Lumley* v. *Gye* ((1853) 2 E. & B. 216; 118 E.R. 749) in 1853. There is not much help to be found in the earlier cases that were cited at the Bar, not even, I think, in the great case about frightening ducks in a decoy, whatever the true explanation of that decision may be. In *Lumley* v. *Gye* it was held that an action would lie for procuring a person to break a contract for personal service. The subsequent cases of *Bowen* v. *Hall* (1881) 6 Q.B.D. 333) and *Temperton* v. *Russell* ([1893] 1 Q.B. 715) are authorities for the proposition that the principle is not confined to contracts for personal service. There is no doubt much to be said for that proposition. But the judgment under appeal does not depend on *Lumley* v. *Gye* or on any decision before or after that case . . .

Lord Shand: . . . If anything is clear on the evidence, it seems to me to be this— that the defendant was bent, and bent exclusively, on the object of furthering the interests of those he represented in all he did—that this was his motive of action, and not a desire, to use the words of the learned judge, "to do mischief to the plaintiffs in their lawful calling. . . . "

The case was one of competition in labour, which, in my opinion, is in all essentials analogous to competition in trade, and to which the same principles must apply . . . Threats may, like false or fraudulent representations, be of such a nature, if used, as to amount to improper and unlawful means used to induce action which may be injurious to others, causing them loss and damage, and I should not for a moment say that damages might not in cases of such threats be recoverable. But this can only apply to threats of violence, intimidation, obstruction, or the like—threats which may be described as menace which improperly affects freedom of action in the person who is induced to act or to refrain from acting. The boiler-makers were quite entitled to resolve that they would not then or at any future time work at the same vessel, or even in the same yard, with the plaintiffs. No one can dispute their right so to resolve. They were quite entitled, having formed that resolution, to inform their employers that they had done so; indeed, I should say that the defendant Allen was only doing what was right and proper in intimating this resolution to the employers, in place of allowing the men to leave without notice to the employers of what would certainly cause them great inconvenience and loss. There was no threat of the nature of menace so as to amount to the use of illegal means to induce the employers to act—no threat to do anything beyond the exercise of their legal right. A master who warns his servant that a repetition of certain faults will result in dismissal may be said to use a threat; but he is not only acting lawfully, but in most cases is to be commended for so doing in place of giving an instant dismissal.

One of the learned judges—the late Cave J.—has expressed the opinion that if a butler who, for some reason or another, has made up his mind that he will no longer continue in service with the cook, with whom he has been in the same employment, should intimate his resolution to the employer, and the services of the cook should thereupon be dispensed with, the cook will have in law a claim of damages against the butler. If this view were sound, then the plaintiffs in this case might be entitled to succeed. Indeed, I have always thought throughout the course of the argument that the case put by the learned judge is perhaps the simplest form in which the very question now under discussion could be raised. But, with great deference to the opinion of the learned judge, no such claim could arise in such circumstances, because it cannot be truly said that on the part of the butler there was either an unlawful act, or unlawful means used in the doing of a lawful act. A servant is surely entitled, for any reason sufficient in his judgment, or even from caprice, I should say, to resolve that he will no longer continue, after the expiry of a current engagement, in service with another servant in the same employment. This being unquestionable, the only limitation on his right to act is that he must not use unlawful means to induce his employer to dispense with the services of his fellow-servant. Should his master ask him the reason for his giving up the service, he is surely entitled to give the true reason, leaving the master to act as he thinks best in determining with which of the two servants he will part; and the notion of a claim of damages by his fellow-servant would be extravagant. It can make no difference that he thinks it right at his own hand to inform his master of the resolution he has taken, and I must add, with reference to what I have immediately to say, that this action being lawful, and no unlawful means being used in carrying it out, the motive, even if it be personal ill-will to another, would not, in my opinion, create liability to a claim of damages.

Coming now directly to the merits of the question in controversy in the case, the argument of the plaintiffs and the reasons for the opinions of the majority of the consulted judges seem to me to fail, because, although it is no doubt true that the plaintiffs were entitled to pursue their trade as workmen "without hindrance," their right to do so was qualified by an equal right, and indeed the same right, on the part of other workmen. The hindrance must not be of an unlawful character. It must not be by unlawful action. Amongst the rights of all workmen is the right of competition. In the like manner and to the same extent as a workman has a right to pursue his work or labour without hindrance, a trader has a right to trade without hindrance. That right is subject to the right of others to trade also, and to subject him to competition—competition which is in itself lawful, and which cannot be complained of where no unlawful means (in the sense I have already explained) have been employed. The matter has been settled in so far as competition in trade is concerned by the judgment of this House in the *Mogul Steamship Co.* case ([1892] A.C. 25; (above, p. 502). I can see no reason for saying that a different principle should apply to competition in labour. In the course of such competition, and with a view to secure an advantage to himself, I can find no reason for saying that a workman is not within his legal rights in resolving that he will decline to work in the same employment with certain other persons, and in intimating that resolution to his employers.

It is further to be observed, distinguishing the case from one in which a contract might have subsisted between the plaintiffs and their employers for a definite period, or for the work, it might be, on a particular ship until the whole was completed (in which case the refusal to continue to give the work would be a breach of contract on the employers' part), that there was here no such breach of contract. The employers' act in dispensing with the services of the plaintiffs at the end of the day was a lawful act on their part. The defendant induced them only to do what they were entitled to do, and, in the absence of any fraud or other unlawful means used to bring this about, the action fails.

As already fully explained, there was no case of malice in the ordinary sense of the term, as meaning personal ill-will, presented to the jury; but I agree with those of your Lordships who hold that, even if such a motive had existed in the mind of the defendant, this would not have created liability in damages. On the grounds already stated, I think the defendant only exercised a legal right in intimating that the boiler-makers would leave work if the plaintiffs were continued; he used no fraud or illegal means in the assertion of that right; and the exercise by a person of a legal right does not become illegal because the motive of action is improper or malicious: *Bradford Corporation* v. *Pickles* ([1895] A.C. 587) and the *Mogul Steamship Co.* case . . .

Lord Davey: . . . Nor can I agree that there is no legal difference between persuasion to break a contract and persuasion not to enter a contract . . . In the one case there is a violation of right; in the other case there is not . . . It was, however, argued that the act of the appellant in the present case was a violation of the right which every man has to pursue a lawful trade and calling, and that the violation of this right is actionable. I remark in passing that, if this be so, the right of action must be independent of the question of malice, except in the legal sense. The right which a man has to pursue his trade or calling is qualified by the equal right of others to do the same and compete with him, though to his damage. And it is obvious that a general abstract right of this character stands on a different footing from such a private particular right as the right to performance of a contract into which one has entered. A man has no right to be employed by any particular employer, and has no right to any particular employment if it depends on the will of another.

But is there any such general cause of action irrespective of the means employed or mode of interference? I think it unnecessary to comment on all the cases which have been cited by counsel, and are referred to by the learned judges. I have read them carefully, and I am satisfied that in no one of them was anything decided which is an authority for the abstract proposition maintained. In every one of them you find there was either violence or the threat of violence, obstruction of the highway, or the access to the plaintiff's premises, nuisance, or other unlawful acts done to the damage of the plaintiff. Nor does it appear to me that the gist of the action in those cases was that the plaintiff was a trader or exercised a profitable calling. That circumstance, no doubt, afforded evidence of the damage. But I suppose that if a person obstructed the access to my house or to my vessel by molesting and firing guns at persons resorting thither on their lawful occasions, I may have my action against him, though I do not keep a school, or I am not a trader, but sailing in my yacht for my own pleasure. Or, if a person obstructs my free use of the highway, and I suffer damage thereby, I have a right of action, though my carriage does not ply for hire, but is used only for my own purposes. It is strange that if there be any such right of action for interference with trade, there is not to be found some clear authority in the law books in its favour. And, as remarked by one of the learned judges, if those who argued and those who decided *Lumley* v. *Gye* had been aware of any such general doctrine, it would have disposed of that case without the elaborate consideration to be found in the judgments. I do not think that the well-known action for slander of a trader's goods supports the larger proposition attempted to be founded on it. Blackstone treats that action as a particular example of slanderous words. And it appears to me an obvious fallacy to argue backwards from the existence of some recognised and well-known cause of action to a larger and wider legal proposition of which the cause of action in question might be treated as a particular case if the larger proposition had been generally recognised.

The authority most relied on in support of the proposition maintained by the respondents is the well known case of *Keeble* v. *Hickeringill* (1706) 11 East 574n.; 103 E.R. 1127; or, more properly, the dicta of Lord Holt as reported in the note to 11 East. That case was an action by the owner of a decoy pond against the defendant for driving away his wild fowl by firing guns with intent to damnify the plaintiff. It appears to have been twice argued, and there are four separate reports of it, which do not altogether agree as to the grounds of the judgment. But I think it was decided on the ground that the act of the defendant was a wilful disturbance of the enjoyment by the plaintiff of his own land for a lawful and profitable purpose, and what is called in law a nuisance. The reported cases in which the case has been followed, *Carrington* v. *Taylor* ((1809) 11 East 571; 103 E.R. 1126) and *Ibbotson* v. *Peat* ((1865) 3 H. & C. 644; 159 E.R. 684), support this view. If this be a correct view of the decision, it is no authority for the larger proposition founded on it by the respondents; and the dicta of Lord Holt, however much entitled to respect, are inadequate to support the weight which it is sought to place upon them . . .

Lord Morris (dissenting): . . . The plaintiffs were only day-labourers, but with a certainty of their employment being continued *de die in diem* for a considerable time. In my opinion it is actionable to disturb a man in his business by procuring the determination of a contract at will, or even by preventing the formation of a contract, when the motive is malicious and damage ensues . . .

Lord Halsbury (dissenting): . . . My difference is founded on the belief that in denying these plaintiffs a remedy we are departing from the principles which have hitherto guided our courts in the preservation of individual liberty for all. I am encouraged, however, by the consideration that the adverse views appear to me to overrule the views of most distinguished judges, going back now for certainly 200 years, and that up to the period when this case reached your Lordships' House there was an unanimous consensus of opinion; and that of eight judges who have given us the benefit of their opinions, six have concurred in the judgment which your Lordships are now asked to overrule . . .

The following are extracts from the opinions of judges who were asked to state them.

Hawkins J. (for the plaintiff): . . . I can imagine a state of things in which the defendant might have rightfully, in the bona fide exercise of a privilege or a duty, done and said what he did, but having acted and spoken under the prompting of malice or bad motive, those actions and words were wrongful, and without any privilege to excuse or justify them . . .

Mathew J. (for the defendant): . . . in the judgments under review, no distinction is drawn between inducing a breach of contract and preventing a contract from being entered into. It seems to me the distinction is all-important. . . . I am not aware of any authority for the proposition that the law recognises a man's interest in his trade, profession or business as analogous to property in land or to a right created by contract . . .

Cave J. (for the plaintiff): . . . It was asked by one of your Lordships, "If a cook says to her master, 'Discharge the butler or I leave you,' is that actionable?" With submission I say that it is, if the master does discharge the butler in consequence; and I hardly understand why it should not be . . . Another question put in the course of the argument was this: "Will an action lie if A., out of ill-will to B., induces C. not to leave him a legacy?" I answer, Certainly not, because there is no such recognised trade or profession as that of a legacy-hunter . . . [Allen's] motive was not to secure the work they were then doing . . . but to punish the respondents for what they had previously done . . .

North J. (for the plaintiff) held that there was no distinction to be drawn between a contract for a determinate time and a contract determinable at will, provided that as a matter of fact it was probable that the contractual relationship would not be determined: . . . one can readily divine what the answer of a layman would be who was told that the law made a distinction between the two cases, and the officious intermeddling of Allen would be justifiable in the one but not in the other . . .

Wills J. (for the plaintiff): . . . If no interference with ancient lights . . . be involved, a man may erect upon his own land a building which may ruin his neighbour's industry exercised upon the adjoining land. No action could be maintained, though it were demonstrated that his only purpose in making the erection was to spite and damage his neighbour . . . Equally any right given by contract may be exercised against the giver by the person to whom it is granted, no matter how wicked, cruel or mean the motive may be which determines the enforcement of the right . . . I think the question whether the act complained of was malicious would depend upon whether the defendant had in pursuing his own interests done so by such means and with such a disregard of his neighbour as no honest and fair-minded man ought to resort to . . . The distinction between inducing people to break contracts and inducing them not to enter into contracts cannot, in my opinion, be ignored; but it appears to me that it is one of circumstance rather than one of essence . . .

Note:

This is arguably the most important case in the book, and it is certainly the one which was most argued, and on which most judicial opinions were written, the speeches extending to nearly 200 pages. The background of the participants is splendidly laid out in Heuston, "Judicial Prosopography," (1986) 102 L.Q.R. 90. If the decision had gone the other way, then in every case of industrial strife a jury would have been permitted to find that the acts of the defendants, workmen or masters, had been malicious in the sense that they had some motive of which the jury disapproved: it was better that injustice be done in shipyards and factories than in Her Majesty's courts.

On one view the decision is simply an application of the ratio of the *Mogul* case: both cases involved the deliberate infliction of purely economic loss without the use of any unlawful means. But in other respects the cases are very different. Mogul was a company, Flood a human being. In *Mogul* the plaintiff was complaining of lost freight, in *Allen* v. *Flood* of lost wages. While Mogul lost cargoes, Flood lost his job.

Should an individual's job not be better protected than a company's trading profits? Under special legislation nowadays it is, but the labour legislation, originating in 1906, tended to equate "trade and business" with "employment" and a person's right to dispose of his capital with his right to dispose of his labour, though in collateral respects it distinguishes the contract of employment from contracts of other kinds. The common law, which is curiously reluctant to distinguish between companies and individuals, is certainly capable, as we saw in the chapter on vicarious liability, of distinguishing the contract of employment from the contracts under which independent persons and non-persons obtain their income. Perhaps it should have done so in the present case.

Another distinction between *Mogul* and *Allen* v. *Flood* is that there were several defendants in the former case and only one in the latter. In *Mogul* the defendants were palpably acting in their own group interests at the expense of Mogul's. In *Allen* v. *Flood* the single defendant's motivation was held immaterial. *Quinn* v. *Leathem* [1901] A.C. 495, the next case, involved several defendants acting in concert not to advance their own interests (so the jury found) but to hurt the plaintiff out of malevolence. The defendants wanted the plaintiff, a meat wholesaler, to fire his existing employees and replace them with union members. This the plaintiff refused to do, though he was perfectly willing for them to join the union and indeed was prepared to pay their fines and dues. The defendants were not satisfied with this and struck at him by getting their men at his best retail customer to refuse to handle any more meat from the plaintiff and by paying three of his men to quit their jobs. No breach of contract was induced or threatened, but the defendants were held liable. This is the tort of civil conspiracy, on which see *Lonrho* v. *Shell* below p. 529.

ROOKES v. BARNARD

House of Lords [1964] A.C. 1129; [1964] 2 W.L.R. 269; 108 S.J. 93; [1964] 1 All E.R. 367;
[1964] 1 Lloyd's Rep. 28

The plaintiff was employed by B.O.A.C. as a skilled draughtsman at London Airport. He left his union, the Association of Engineering and Shipbuilding Draughtsmen, after a dispute. There was a meeting of the airport branch of the union, at which a resolution was passed that B.O.A.C. should be informed that all labour would be withdrawn unless the plaintiff were removed from the design office. The defendants spoke in favour of this resolution; two of them were employed by B.O.A.C. and the third, Silverthorne, was a union official. In consequence of this resolution, B.O.A.C. first suspended and then dismissed the plaintiff, with the lawful period of notice. Agreements between B.O.A.C. and the union provided for 100 per cent. union membership, and also that there should be neither strike nor lock-out. By reason of the conceded fact that this last term was incorporated in the individual contracts of employment, the threat by the employees to withhold their labour constituted a threat to break their contracts.

The trial took place before Sachs J. and a jury, who returned a verdict for the plaintiff for £7,500 after an instruction permitting them to award exemplary damages [1961] 3 W.L.R. 438. The Court of Appeal reversed this decision on the ground that the tort of intimidation was limited to threats of violence, and was not satisfied with threats to break contracts [1963] 1 Q.B. 623. The House of Lords allowed the plaintiff's appeal on the merits, but remanded the case for re-trial on the point of damages. (The case was later settled for £4,000 plus costs ([1966] 1 Q.B. 176).

Lord Reid: . . . This case raises the question whether it is a tort to conspire to threaten an employer that his men will break their contracts with him unless he dismisses the plaintiff, with the result that he is thereby induced to dismiss the plaintiff and cause him loss. The magnitude of the sum awarded by the jury shows that the appellant had every prospect of retaining his employment with B.O.A.C. if the respondents and the other conspirators had not interfered: leaving the Trade Disputes Act 1906, out of account, if B.O.A.C. had been induced to dismiss the appellant in breach of their contract with him then there is no doubt that the respondents would have committed a tort and would have been liable in damages (*Lumley* v. *Gye*). Equally, there is no doubt that men are entitled to threaten to strike if that involves no breach of their contracts with their employer, and they are not trying to induce their employer to break any contract with the plaintiff. The question in this case is whether it was unlawful for them to use a threat to break their contracts with their employer as a weapon to make him do something which he was legally entitled to do but which they knew would cause loss to the plaintiff.

The first contention of the respondents is very far reaching. They say there is no such tort as intimidation. That would mean that, short of committing a crime, an individual could with impunity virtually compel a third person to do something damaging to the plaintiff which he does not want to do but can lawfully do: the wrongdoer could use every kind of threat to commit violence, libel or any other tort, and the plaintiff would have no remedy. And a combination of individuals could do the same, at least if they acted solely to promote their own interests. It is true that there is no decision of this House which negatives that argument. But there are many speeches in this House and judgments of eminent judges where it is assumed that that is not the law and I have found none where there is any real support for this argument. Most of the relevant authorities have been collected by Pearson L.J. and I see no need to add to them. It has often been stated that if people combine to do acts which they know will cause loss to the plaintiff, he can sue if either the object of the conspiracy is unlawful or they use unlawful means to achieve it. In my judgment, to cause such loss by threat to commit a tort against a third person if he does not comply with their demands is to use unlawful means to achieve their object.

That brings me to the second argument for the respondents, which raises a more difficult question. They say that there is a distinction between threats to commit a tort and threats to break a contract. They point out that a person is quite entitled to threaten to do something which he has a legal right to do and they say that breach of contract is a private matter between the contracting parties. If the plaintiff cannot sue for loss to him which results from an actual breach of a contract to which he is not a party, why, they ask, should he be entitled to sue for loss which results from a threat to break a contract to which he is not a party?

A somewhat similar argument failed in *Lumley* v. *Gye*. The defendant had induced a singer to break her contract with the plaintiff and he knew that this would cause loss to the plaintiff. The plaintiff had his action against the singer for breach of contract and he was held also to have a cause of action against the defendant for the tort of unjustifiably interfering so as to cause him loss. The fact that the direct cause of the loss was a breach of a contract to which the defendant was not a party did not matter. So, too, the plaintiff's action in the present case does not sound in contract: in fact there was no breach of contract because B.O.A.C. gave in.

The appellant in this case could not take a benefit from contracts to which he was not a party or from any breach of them. But his ground of action is quite different. The respondents here used a weapon in a way which they knew would cause him loss, and the question is whether they were entitled to use that weapon—a threat that they would cause loss to B.O.A.C. if B.O.A.C. did not do as they wished. That threat was to cause loss to B.O.A.C. by doing something which they had no right to do, breaking their contracts with B.O.A.C. I can see no difference in principle between a threat to break a contract and a threat to commit a tort. If a third party could not sue for damage caused to him by the former I can see no reason why he should be entitled to sue for damage caused to him by the latter. A person is no more entitled to sue in respect of loss which he suffers by reason of a tort committed against someone else that he is entitled to sue in respect of loss which he suffers by reason of breach of a contract to which he is not a party. What he sues for in each case is loss caused to him by the use of an unlawful weapon against him—intimidation of another person by unlawful means. So long as the defendant only threatens to do what he has a legal right to do he is on safe ground. At least if there is no conspiracy he would not be liable to anyone for doing the act, whatever his motive might be, and it would be absurd to make him liable for threatening to do it but not for doing it. But I agree with Lord Herschell (*Allen* v. *Flood*) that there is a chasm between doing what you have a legal right to do and doing what you have no legal right to do, and there seems to me to be the same chasm between threatening to do what you have a legal right to do and threatening to do what you have no legal right to do. It must follow from *Allen* v. *Flood* that to intimidate by threatening to do what you have a legal right to do is to intimidate by lawful means. But I see no good reason for extending that doctrine. Threatening a breach of contract may be a much more coercive weapon than threatening a tort, particularly when the threat is directed against a company or corporation, and, if there is no technical reason requiring a distinction between different kinds of threats, I can see no other ground for making any such distinction.

I have not set out any of the passages cited in argument because the precise point which we have to decide did not arise in any of the cases in which they occur, and it does not appear that any of the authors of these passages had this point in mind. Sometimes the language seems to point one way and sometimes another and it would, I think, be wrong in such circumstances to use a judge's language as authority for a proposition which he did not have in mind. The Court of Appeal ([1963] 1 Q.B. 623) in this case were unwilling to go beyond existing authorities. Sellers L.J. said: "Unless authority requires it, I would resist enlarging the tort of intimidation in the manner sought before and accepted by the judge," and Pearson L.J. said: "Should this obscure, unfamiliar and peculiar cause of action, which has its roots in cases of physical violence and threats of violence, be extended to cover a case in which there is only a threat to break a contract?" I am afraid I take a different view. Intimidation of any kind appears to me to be highly objectionable. The law was not slow to prevent it when violence and threats of violence were the most effective means. Now that subtler means are at least equally effective I see no reason why the law should have to turn a blind eye to them. We have to tolerate intimidation by means which have been held to be lawful but there I would stop. Accordingly, I would hold that on the facts found by the jury the respondents' actions in this case were tortious . . .

Questions

1. A contracts to sell to B some goods of which he has a monopoly; he then discovers that B *plans* to deliver them to C, whom A hates. A deliberately, and with the intention of hurting C, refuses to deliver the promised goods to B. Can C sue A? Does it make any difference if B has *contracted* to deliver the goods in question to C, and A knows this?

2. What is the difference between this case and *Allen* v. *Flood*, above, p. 509? If the difference is that here the defendants had a contractual right to continued employment, do you think it fair that their freedom of action should be correspondingly curtailed?

Note:

This decision caused a fearful furore. Perhaps it was not perfectly understood. Or perhaps the objectors were lucid but malignant. The general proposition that A is liable for using unlawful pressure on B so as to hurt C is surely acceptable. Doubtless there might be circumstances in which such action by A might be justified, but a justification is called for. Parliament immediately provided such a justification by enacting that to act like Barnard and his friends was not unlawful in contemplation or furtherance of a trade dispute. See below, p. 528.

In this case Rookes was hurt when B.O.A.C. yielded to the defendants' pressure, but B.O.A.C. itself was unscathed. Commonly, however, the person leant on does suffer harm by complying with the demands of the person doing the leaning, often by conferring a benefit on him: thus the traveller enriches the highwayman and the policeman collects the protection money from the porno-dealer. Can the victim of blackmail or duress reclaim what he has paid?

In *Universe Tankships* v. *International Transport Workers' Federation* [1982] 2 All E.R. 67, a trade union blacked a ship and exacted a sum as the price of its release. Unless legitimised by the Trade Unions and Labour Relations Act 1974, s.13 (below p. 527), the blacking would have been tortious (inducing the tug-men to break their contracts of employment with the harbour authorities); if so legitimised, the House of Lords held, the restitutionary claim was also barred. Often duress is brought to bear on a party by his contractor; on this see *The Atlantic Baron* [1979] Q.B. 705 and *Pao On* v. *Lau Yiu* [1980] A.C. 614.

It may be useful to recapitulate the effect of the last four cases excerpted: there is no liability simply for frustrating a person's economic prospects, even by bringing pressure on third parties (*Mogul, Allen* v. *Flood*), but in doing so not only must you eschew the use of force and fraud, you must also respect people's binding engagements, your own (*Rookes*) as well as other people's (*Lumley* v. *Gye*). If one recognises that one's liberty to beggar one's neighbour is conditioned upon one's using no unlawful means, it is far from clear that any further common law liability is required. In fact no further liability has ever been imposed, but methods have been used which are objectionable and pregnant with danger, exemplified in the next case.

TORQUAY HOTEL CO. v. COUSINS

Court of Appeal [1969] 2 Ch. 106; [1969] 2 W.L.R. 289; (1969) 113 S.J. 52; [1969] 1 All E.R. 522

Angry at what they took to be an intervention by the manager of the plaintiff's Imperial Hotel in a dispute they were having with another hotel in the area, the defendant union officials telephoned Esso, with whom the Imperial Hotel had a bulk contract for the delivery of oil, and said that no further deliveries should be made. Esso told the manager that there was little point in ordering further oil since none could be delivered as the tanker drivers, being members of the defendant union, would not cross the picket lines. Instead, the manager ordered oil from Alternative Fuels, who made a delivery in the temporary absence of the pickets; the defendants then telephoned the firm and threatened unspecific repercussions if further deliveries were attempted. After a solicitor's letter to the defendants, the manager ordered 3,000 gallons of oil from Esso; that oil was delivered but the defendants refused to give any undertaking that further deliveries would not be stopped.

Stamp J. granted an interlocutory injunction restraining the named defendants from "doing any act which, whether directly or indirectly, causes or procures a breach or breaches by any supplier of fuel oil of contracts made now or hereafter by such supplier, with the plaintiff company for the delivery of oil to the plaintiff company, and picketing at or near the entrance or entrances near the Imperial Hotel for the purpose of persuading drivers of oil tankers not to deliver fuel oil there." ([1969] 2 Ch. 106, 112).

The defendants' appeal to the Court of Appeal was dismissed, subject to the injunction being vacated as to the defendant union.

Lord Denning M.R.: . . . The reason why the Imperial Hotel apply for an injunction is essentially *quia timet*. No oil has in fact been stopped from reaching the Imperial Hotel: but the Imperial Hotel fear that the union and their officials will try to stop it unless the court intervenes. To obtain an injunction, the plaintiffs must show that the defendants are proposing to do something unlawful.

Many grounds of unlawfulness have been canvassed before us, including breach of contract, conspiracy and intimidation. The judge put the case on the broad ground that the defendants were proposing, without justification, to interfere with the contractual relations of the Imperial Hotel. He granted an injunction to restrain the defendants from procuring a breach by any supplier of oil of contracts made or hereafter to be made for delivery of fuel-oil to the hotel. On the appeal the argument covered many points which I will take in order.

1. WAS THERE A "TRADE DISPUTE"?
[His Lordship held that no statutory immunity attached because the defendants' acts were not done in furtherance of a trade dispute with the plaintiff] . . . The position must be judged at common law.

2. CAN THE DEFENDANTS TAKE ADVANTAGE OF THE FORCE MAJEURE CLAUSE?
The Imperial Hotel had a contract with Esso under which the Imperial Hotel agreed to buy their total requirements of fuel-oil from Esso for one year, the quantity being estimated at 120,000 gallons, to be delivered by road tank wagon at a minimum of 3,000 gallons a time. Under the contract there was a *course of dealing* by which the Imperial Hotel used to order 3,000 gallons every week or 10 days, and Esso used to deliver it the next day. But there was a *force majeure* or *exception clause* which said that: "neither party shall be liable for any failure to fulfil any term of this agreement if fulfilment is delayed, hindered or prevented by any circum-

stance whatever which is not within their immediate control, including . . . labour disputes."

It is plain that, if delivery was hindered or prevented by labour disputes, as, for instance, because their drivers would not cross the picket line, Esso could rely on that exception clause as a defence to any claim by Imperial. They would not be liable in damages. And I am prepared to assume that Esso would not be guilty of a breach of contract. But I do not think that would exempt the trade union officials from liability if they unlawfully hindered or prevented Esso from making deliveries. The principle of *Lumley* v. *Gye* [above, p. 499] extends not only to inducing breach of contract, but also to preventing the performance of it. That can be shown by a simple illustration taken from the books. In *Lumley* v. *Gye*, Miss Wagner, an actress, was engaged by Mr. Lumley to sing at Her Majesty's Theatre. Mr. Gye, who ran Covent Garden, procured her to break her contract with Mr. Lumley by promising to pay her more: see *Lumley* v. *Wagner* ((1852) 1 De G.M. & G. 604). He was held liable to Mr. Lumley for inducing a breach of contract. In *Poussard* v. *Spiers & Pond* ((1876) 1 Q.B.D. 410) Madam Poussard was under contract with Spiers to sing in an opera at the Criterion Theatre. She fell sick and was unable to attend rehearsals. Her non-performance, being occasioned by sickness, was not a breach of contract on her part: but it was held to excuse the theatre company from continuing to employ her. Suppose now that an ill-disposed person, knowing of her contract, had given her a potion to make her sick. She would not be guilty of a breach herself. But undoubtedly the person who administered the potion would have done wrong and be liable for the damage suffered by them. So here I think the trade union officials cannot take advantage of the *force majeure* or exception clause in the Esso contract. If they unlawfully prevented or hindered Esso from making deliveries, as ordered by Imperial, they would be liable in damages to Imperial, notwithstanding the exception clause. There is another reason too. They could not rely on an excuse of which they themselves had been "the mean" to use Lord Coke's language: see *New Zealand Shipping Co. Ltd.* v. *Société des Ateliers et Chantiers de France* ([1919] A.C. 1, 7, 8).

The principles of law

The principle of *Lumley* v. *Gye* is that each of the parties to a contract has a "right to the performance" of it: and it is wrong for another to procure one of the parties to break it or not to perform it. That principle was extended a step further by Lord Macnaghten in *Quinn* v. *Leathem* ([1901] A.C. 495), so that each of the parties has a right to have his "contractual relations" with the other duly observed. "It is," he said at p. 510, "a violation of legal right to interfere with contractual relations recognised by law if there be no sufficient justification for the interference." That statement was adopted and applied by a strong board of the Privy Council in *Jasperson* v. *Dominion Tobacco Co.* ([1923] A.C. 709). It included Viscount Haldane and Lord Sumner. The time has come when the principle should be further extended to cover "deliberate and direct interference with the execution of a contract without that causing any breach." That was a point left open by Lord Reid in *Stratford (J.T.) & Son Ltd.* v. *Lindley* ([1965] A.C. 269, 324). But the common law would be seriously deficient if it did not condemn such interference. It is this very case. The principle can be subdivided into three elements:

First, there must be *interference* in the execution of a contract. The interference is not confined to the procurement of a *breach* of contract. It extends to a case where a third person *prevents* or *hinders* one party from performing his contract, even though it be not a breach.

Second, the interference must be deliberate. The person must know of the contract or, at any rate, turn a blind eye to it and intend to interfere with it: see *Emerald Construction Co.* v. *Lowthian* [1966] 1 W.L.R. 691.

Third, the interference must be *direct*. Indirect interference will not do. Thus, a man who "corners the market" in a commodity may well know that it may prevent others from performing their contracts, but he is not liable to an action for so doing. A trade union official, who calls a strike on proper notice, may well know that it will prevent the employers from performing their contracts to deliver goods, but he is not liable in damages for calling it. *Indirect* interference is only unlawful if unlawful means are used. I went too far when I said in *Daily Mirror Newspapers Ltd.* v. *Gardner* ([1968] 2 Q.B. 762, 782) that there was no difference between direct and indirect interference. On reading once again *Thomson (D.C.) & Co. Ltd.* v. *Deakin* ([1952] Ch. 646), with more time, I find there is a difference. Morris L.J., at p. 702, there draws the very distinction between "*direct* persuasion to breach of contract" which is unlawful in itself: and "the intentional bringing about of a breach by *indirect* methods involving wrongdoing." This distinction must be maintained, else we should take away the right to strike altogether. Nearly every trade union official who calls a strike— even on due notice, as in *Morgan* v. *Fry* ([1968] 2 Q.B. 710)—knows that it may prevent the employers from performing their contracts. He may be taken even to intend it. Yet no one has supposed hitherto that it was unlawful: and we should not render it unlawful today. A trade union official is only in the wrong when he procures a contracting party *directly* to break his contract, or when he does it indirectly *by unlawful means*. On reconsideration of the *Daily Mirror* case ([1968] 2 Q.B. 762), I think that the defendants there interfered directly by getting the retailers as their agents to approach the wholesalers.

I must say a word about unlawful means, because that brings in another principle. I have always understood that if one person deliberately interferes with the trade or business of another and does so by unlawful means, that is, by an act which he is not at liberty to commit, then he is acting unlawfully, even though he does not procure or induce any actual breach of contract. If the means are unlawful, that is enough. Thus in *Rookes* v. *Barnard* ([1964] A.C. 1129) (as explained by Lord Reid in *Stratford* v. *Lindley* [1965] A.C. 269, 325, and Lord Upjohn, at p. 337) the defendants interfered with the employment of Rookes—and they did it by unlawful means, namely, by intimidation of his employers—and they were held to be acting unlawfully, even though the employers committed no breach of contract as they gave Rookes proper notice. And in *Stratford* v. *Lindley* ([1965] A.C. 269), the defendants interfered with the business of Stratford—and they did it by *unlawful means*, namely, by inducing the men to *break their contracts* of employment by refusing to handle the barges—and they were held to be acting unlawfully, even in regard to *new business* of Stratford which was not the subject of contract. Lord Reid said, at p. 324: "The respondents' action made it practically impossible for the appellants to do any new business with the barge hirers. It was not disputed that such interference is tortious if any unlawful means are employed."

So also on the second point in *Daily Mirror* v. *Gardner* ([1968] 2 Q.B. 762), the defendants interfered with the business of the *Daily Mirror*—and they did it by a collective boycott which was held to be *unlawful* under the Restrictive Trade Practices Act 1956—and they were held to be acting unlawfully.

This point about unlawful means is of particular importance when a place is declared "black." At common law it often involves the use of unlawful means. Take the Imperial Hotel. When it was declared "black," it meant that the drivers of the tankers would not take oil to the hotel. The drivers would thus be induced to break their contracts of employment. That would be unlawful at common law. The only case in which "blacking" of such a kind is lawful is when it is done "in contemplation or furtherance of a trade dispute."It is then protected by section 3 of the Trade Disputes Act 1906: see *Thomson (D.C.) & Co. Ltd.* v. *Deakin* [1952] Ch. 646, 662, 663, by Upjohn J.; for, in that event, the act of inducing a breach of a contract of employment is a lawful act which is not actionable at the suit of anyone; see *Stratford* v. *Lindley* [1965] A.C. 269, 303, by Salmon L.J., and *Morgan* v. *Fry* [1968] 2 Q.B. 710, 728, by myself. Seeing that the act is lawful, it must, I think, be lawful for the trade union officials to tell the employers and their customers about it. And this is so, even though it does mean that those people are compelled to break their commercial contracts. The interference with the commercial contracts is only indirect, and not direct: see what Lord Upjohn said in *Stratford* v. *Lindley* [1965] A.C. 269, 337. So, if there had been a "trade dispute" in this case, I think it would have protected the trade union officials when they informed Esso that the dispute with Imperial was an "official dispute" and said that the hotel was "blacked." . . .

APPLYING THE PRINCIPLE IN THIS CASE

Seeing that there was no "trade dispute" this case falls to be determined by the common law. It seems to me that the trade union officials deliberately and directly interfered with the execution of the contract between the Imperial Hotel and Esso. They must have known that there was a contract between the Imperial Hotel and Esso. Why otherwise did they on that very first Saturday afternoon telephone the bulk plant at Plymouth? They may not have known with exactitude all the terms of the contract. But no more did the defendants in *Stratford* v. *Lindley*, at p. 332. They must also have intended to prevent the performance of the contract. That is plain from the telephone message: "Any supplies of fuel-oil will be stopped being made." And the interference was direct. It was as direct as could be—a telephone message from the trade union official to the bulk plant.

Take next the supplies from Alternative Fuels. The first wagon got through. As it happened, there was no need for the Imperial Hotel to order any further supplies from Alternative Fuels. But suppose they had given a further order, it is quite plain that the trade union officials would have done their best to prevent it being delivered. Their telephone messages show that they intended to prevent supplies being made by all means in their power. By threatening "repercussions" they interfered unlawfully with the performance of any future order which Imperial Hotel might give to Alternative Fuels. And the interference was direct again. It was direct to Alternative Fuels. Such interference was sufficient to warrant the grant of an injunction *quia timet* . . .

Conclusion

Other wrongs were canvassed, such as conspiracy and intimidation, but I do not think it necessary to go into these. I put my decision on the simple ground that there is evidence that the defendants intended to interfere directly and deliberately with the execution of the existing contracts by Esso and future contracts by Alternative Fuels so as to prevent those companies supplying oil to the Imperial Hotel. This intention was sufficiently manifest to warrant the granting of an injunction. The form of the injunction was criticised by Mr. Pain, but it follows the form suggested by Lord Upjohn in *Stratford* v. *Lindley* [1965] A.C. 269, 339, and I think it is in order.

I find myself in substantial agreement with the judge and would dismiss this appeal.

Russell L.J.: . . . I turn now to the main aspects of the case. Is it a case in which an interlocutory injunction should be ordered pending trial on the ground that the defendants or some of them have so conducted themselves as to indicate that they are likely unless restrained to take steps against the plaintiff company damaging to it and which in law those defendants are not entitled to take? . . .

The bulk supply contract between Esso and the Imperial Hotel was such as might be expected for an establishment the size of the latter. It was argued that the exception clause had the effect that Esso could not be in breach of its supply contract if failure to deliver was due to labour disputes. In my view, the exception clause means what it says and no more: it *assumes* a failure to fulfil a term of the contract—*i.e.*, a breach of contract—and excludes liability—*i.e.*, in damages— for that breach in stated circumstances. It is an exception from liability for non-performance rather than an exception from obligation to perform. If over a considerable period Esso failed to deliver for one of the stated reasons it seems to me that the hotel would be entitled to repudiate the contract on the ground of failure by Esso to carry out its terms: otherwise the hotel would be unable to enter into another bulk supply contract until the Esso contract was time expired. I will not repeat the facts as to Esso and Alternative Fuels, but it seems to me that, as they appear at present, they demonstrate an attitude on the part of the union officials of willingness directly to induce breaches of contract for the supply of fuel oil to the Imperial Hotel in order to carry out a policy of punishing Mr. Chapman for his temerity in being critical of the union. This justifies a continuance of the injunction pending trial. At trial the evidence may appear in a different light, and other considerations such as conspiracy and intimidation will have to be dealt with in the light of the full evidence. In the meantime, the plaintiff company should be protected against what could be virtual destruction of its undertaking . . .

Winn L.J.: . . . The evidence does not establish that in consequence any quantity of fuel which had been ordered was not delivered: no breach of contract by Esso was induced. However, the argument of Mr. Pain that clause 10 of the written contract between Esso and the hotel company for a year's supply would have operated to prevent a failure or failures to deliver ordered instalments of fuel thereunder from being a breach does not seem to me to be sound. As I construe the clause it affords only an immunity against any claim for damages; it could not bar a right to treat the contract as repudiated by continuing breach: despite the clause Esso could well have been held to have committed a breach by non-delivery and Mr. Pedley came close to committing a tort of the *Lumley* v. *Gye*, 2 E. & B. 216, type.

It is not necessary in the instant case to consider to what extent the principle of that case may cover conduct which Lord Reid described in *Stratford* v. *Lindley* ([1965] A.C. 269, 324) as "deliberate and direct interference with the execution of a contract without that causing any breach." For my part I think that it can at least be said, with confidence, that where a contract between two persons exists which gives one of them an optional extension of time or an optional mode for his performance of it, or of part of it, but, from the normal course of dealing between them, the other person does not anticipate such postponement, or has come to expect a particular mode of performance a procuring of the exercise of such an option should, in principle, be held actionable if it produces material damage to the other contracting party.

It was one of Mr. Pain's main submissions that mere advice, warning or information cannot amount to tortious procurement of breach of contract. Whilst granting *arguendi causa* that a communication which went no further would, in general, not, in the absence of circumstances giving a particular significance, amount to a threat or intimidation, I am unable to understand why it may not be an inducement. In the ordinary meaning of language it would surely be said that a father who told his daughter that her fiancé had been convicted of indecent exposure, had thereby induced her, with or without justification, by truth or by slander, to break her engagement. A man who writes to his mother-in-law telling her that the central heating in his house has broken down may thereby induce her to cancel an intended visit.

The court is not concerned in this case with any indirect procuring of breach, or non-performance of a contract, or with the adoption of indirect means to produce such a result: it is therefore not appropriate to consider whether such a mode of procuring such a result is only actionable, as Mr. Pain submitted, where unlawful means, involving, for example, breaches of contract, or actionable breaches of contract, are involved.

It is equally irrelevant, in my view, as a matter of logic, whether or not there was a trade dispute in furtherance of which the defendants were intending to act: the relevant contracts or contractual relationships—Esso and Imperial, Imperial and

Alternative Fuels—did not arise from contracts of employment and are therefore outside the scope of section 3 of the Act of 1906 . . .

Note:

Take the confident dictum of Winn L.J. He says that if (i) B has an option under a contract with A, and (ii) B plans to exercise the option and A expects him to, and (iii) C persuades B not to and A suffers loss, then A can sue C. This, if true, would mean that one may not by a surprise offer of a large wage persuade a long-standing and valuable employee to give notice to the employer who expected to retain and exploit him. This cannot be. The dictum is fundamentally false. It is also irreconcilable with *Allen* v. *Flood*, a decision of rather greater authority, which counsel should force the courts to face one of these days before liberty has gone beyond recall.

Winn L.J. is wrong on "inducing" and he is wrong on "breach." As to the latter it is simply perverse (and as English as the Mad Hatter) to say that a man who has promised to deliver if possible has promised to deliver whether delivery is possible or not, with an immunity in the latter eventuality. As to the former, the defendants certainly *prevented* Esso from performing (and, as they used unlawful means, they should be liable), but they did not *induce* Esso not to perform. My mother-in-law is certainly induced to defer her visit by the indication of a chilly welcome, but that is because she could come if she nevertheless chose. Esso could not have delivered oil if they had chosen; their being told made no difference. After all, if I tie a man up and tell him not to move, it is the rope and not my instruction which induces immobility. Only Tweedledum would say the man was not moving because he had been told not to.

The defendants were rightly held liable, given that there was no trade dispute, but the proper ground of liability is for causing intended harm to the plaintiff by unlawful means, namely persuading Esso's men to break their contracts of employment. Had there been a trade dispute, then under the existing law the defendants should have been immune, for to induce breach of a contract *of employment* was then not unlawful. Indeed Lord Denning, though on erroneous grounds, correctly held that if there had been a trade dispute they would have been immune, whereas Winn L.J. managed to be wrong on that point also. That the defendants *should* be so immune is clear since even under our present law, where the immunities are so much restricted, there would be no liability, as this would be permitted secondary action.

Lord Denning held that the defendants were liable for directly interfering with the plaintiff's contractual expectations. The distinction between directness and indirectness is inappropriate, dangerous and incomprehensible. This can be seen from Lord Denning's judgment itself. For he holds that on the facts the interference was direct, and says that had there been a trade dispute the interference would have been indirect. But the existence of a trade dispute cannot conceivably make indirect what in its absence would be direct interference. So what is direct and what is indirect? If it is indirect, as Lord Denning says, to suborn the personnel and pre-empt the goods (and presumably to block the road) required for the execution of a contract for the delivery of goods, it seems that the only direct interference is an approach, perhaps through agents, to the contractor himself.

The proper and useful distinction is not between directness and indirectness, but between persuasion and prevention, between getting a man not to perform his contract and causing him not to. If you persuade a man not to do something he would otherwise have done, you are liable only if he was bound to do it; if he is not bound to do it, he must be free not to do it and you must be free to persuade him not to do it by all lawful means. (Of course, in our case Esso were not free to deliver oil when they could, and if the defendants had persuaded Esso not to deliver oil when they could, Esso would have been in breach and the defendants consequently liable under *Lumley* v. *Gye*.) If you prevent a man doing something, you are liable only if you use wrongful means, and if you use wrongful means you are liable whether or not he was bound to do it. Accordingly, even if Esso had guaranteed delivery of oil to Imperial, come what might, the defendants here would not be liable under *Lumley* v. *Gye*; they would be liable on another principle, if they used wrongful means, as they did, by threatening to induce or inducing Esso's drivers to disobey orders.

The court here has treated a case of using unlawful means to cause harm to expectations as a case of interfering directly with contractual relations, a thing said to be wrongful in itself; by ignoring the unlawfulness of the means used, they have extended liability in a way contrary to authority and inimical to freedom. The dicta in this case suggest that you are liable for persuading a contractor not to do what is expected of him; but the very point decided in *Allen* v. *Flood* was that it was not tortious to discourage a person from maintaining an existing contract which would otherwise have been maintained. It appears that *Allen* v. *Flood* was not cited to the Court of Appeal, and it was certainly not cited by them. It would be gratifying if the present decision could be regarded as having been rendered *per incuriam*. Unfortunately the same is true of the next case . . .

MERKUR ISLAND SHIPPING v. LAUGHTON

House of Lords [1983] A.C. 570; [1983] I.C.R. 490; [1983] 2 W.L.R. 778; [1983] 2 All E.R. 189 (noted by Wedderburn, 46 M.L.R. 632 (1983))

The plaintiff's ship was let on a time-charter to X and on sub-charter to Y who contracted with Z to have it towed out of port. The ship was unable to leave port however, because the defendants, in furtherance of their dispute with the plaintiff, persuaded Z's men not to do the towing. The charter provided that the ship was to proceed with the utmost despatch, so performance was disrupted though no breach was caused. The trial judge granted an interlocutory injunction which was upheld by the Court of Appeal [1982] 1 All E.R. 334; the defendants' appeal to the House of Lords was dismissed.

Lord Diplock: . . . My Lords, your Lordships have had the dubious benefit during the course of the argument in this appeal of having been referred once more to many of those cases, spanning more than a century, that were the subject of analysis in the judgment of Jenkins L.J. in *D.C. Thomson & Co.* v. *Deakin* ([1952] Ch. 646) and led to his statement of the law as to what are the essential elements in the tort of actionable interference with contractual rights by blacking. That statement has, for 30 years now, been regarded as authoritative, and for my part, I do not think that any benefit is gained by raking over once again the previous decisions. The elements of the tort as stated by Jenkins L.J. were (at 697):

" . . . first, that the person charged with actionable interference knew of the existence of the contract and intended to procure its breach; secondly, that the person so charged did definitely and unequivocally persuade, induce or procure the employees concerned to break their contracts of employment with the intent I have mentioned; thirdly, that the employees so persuaded, induced or procured did in fact break their contracts of employment; and, fourthly, that breach of the contract forming the alleged subject of interference ensued as a necessary consequence of the breaches by the employees concerned of their contracts of employment."

D.C. Thomson & Co. v. *Deakin* was a case in which the only interference with contractual rights relied on was procuring a *breach* by a third party of a contract between that third party and the plaintiff. That is why in the passage that I have picked out for citation Jenkins L.J. restricts himself to that form of actionable interference with contractual rights which consists of procuring an actual breach of the contract that formed the subject matter of interference; but it is evident from the passages in his judgment which precede the passage I have cited . . . that Jenkins L.J., though using the expression "breach," was not intending to confine the tort of actionable interference with contractual rights to the procuring of such non-performance of primary obligations under a contract as would necessarily give rise to secondary obligations to make monetary compensation by way of damages. All prevention of due performance of a primary obligation under a contract was intended to be included even though no secondary obligation to make monetary compensation thereupon came into existence, because the secondary obligation was excluded by some *force majeure* clause.

If there were any doubt about this matter, it was resolved in 1969 by the judgments of the Court of Appeal in *Torquay Hotel Co.* v. *Cousins* [above p. 520]. That was a case in which the contract the performance of which was interfered with was one for the delivery of fuel. It contained a *force majeure* clause excusing the seller from liability for non-delivery if delayed, hindered or prevented by, *inter alia,* labour disputes. Lord Denning M.R. stated the principle thus:

" . . . there must be *interference* in the execution of a contract. The interference is not confined to the procurement of a *breach* of contract. It extends to a case where a third person *prevents* or *hinders* one party from performing his contract, even though it be not a breach." (Lord Denning's emphasis.)

Parliamentary recognition that the tort of actionable interference with contractual rights is as broad as Lord Denning M.R. stated in the passage I have just quoted is, in my view, to be found in s.13(1) of the 1974 Act itself, which refers to inducement not only "to break a contract," but also "to interfere with its performance," and treats them as being *pari materia.*

So I turn to the four elements of the tort of actionable interference with contractual rights as Jenkins L.J. stated them, but substituting "interference with performance" for "breach," except in relation to the breaking by employees of their own contracts of employment where such breach has as its necessary consequence the interference with the performance of the contract concerned.

[His Lordship considered the facts] . . . I accordingly agree with the Court of Appeal that the shipowners, on the evidence that was before Parker J., have made out a strong prima facie case that the ITF committed the common law tort of actionable interference with contractual rights.

I should mention that the evidence also establishes a prima facie case of the common law tort, referred to in s.13(2) and (3) of the 1974 Act, of interfering with the trade or business of another person by doing unlawful acts. To fall within this genus of torts the unlawful act need not involve procuring another person to break a subsisting contract or to interfere with the performance of a subsisting contract. . . .

Note:
Each one of the first three paragraphs cited contains an error. As to the first, there is nothing in the speech of Jenkins L.J. to justify the supposition that he would have envisaged imposing liability for causing disruption of a contract without causing a breach of it, much less granting an action to a frustrated *debtor.* As to the second, doubt does remain despite the decision in *Torquay Hotel,* because of the three judges in that case only Lord Denning made his decision on the basis that there was no breach. As to the third, it is absurd to state that when Parliament accords immunity for certain conduct it is thereby endorsing the liability from which the immunity is accorded. From a judge who proceeds to berate the Parliamentary draftsman and say, truly enough, "Absence of clarity is destructive of the rule of law," this is sorry work indeed.

The defendants' conduct, it was held, was wrongful at common law under two heads—indirect interference with the charterparty by unlawful means, *viz.* inducing the tugmen to break their contracts of employment, and interference with the plaintiff's business by the same unlawful means. While there was statutory immunity for the latter tort there was none for the former (!). Both sets of lawmakers are to blame for this foolishness.

Question:
If in *Lumley* v. *Gye* it was the plaintiff's right to Miss Wagner's services which was interfered with, what right of the plaintiff's was interfered with in this case?

TRADE UNION AND LABOUR RELATIONS ACT 1974

13.—(1) An act done by a person in contemplation or furtherance of a trade dispute shall not be actionable in tort on the ground only—

(*a*) that it induces another person to break a contract or interferes or induces any other person to interfere with its performance; or

(*b*) that it consists in his threatening that a contract (whether one to which he is a party or not) will be broken or its performance interfered with, or that he will induce another person to break a contract or to interfere with its performance.

[(2) For the avoidance of doubt it is hereby declared that an act done by a person in contemplation or furtherance of a trade dispute is not actionable in tort on the ground only that it is an interference with the trade, business or employment of another person, or with the right of another person to dispose of his capital or his labour as he wills.

(3) For the avoidance of doubt it is hereby declared that—

(*a*) an act which by reason of subsection (1) or (2) above is itself not actionable;

(*b*) a breach of contract in contemplation or furtherance of a trade dispute;

shall not be regarded as the doing of an unlawful act or as the use of unlawful means for the purpose of establishing liability in tort.]

(4) An agreement or combination by two or more persons to do or procure the doing of any act in contemplation or furtherance of a trade dispute shall not be actionable in tort if the act is one which, if done without any such agreement or combination, would not be actionable in tort.

Note:

s.13(1)(*a*) grants immunity from liability under *Lumley* v. *Gye* (inducing) and *Torquay Hotel Co.* v. *Cousins* (interfering). S.13(1)(*b*) grants immunity from liability under *Rookes* v. *Barnard*. S.13(4) grants immunity from liability under *Quinn* v. *Leathem* (above, p. 516).

Contemplation or furtherance

If in fact there is a trade dispute (as now defined by s.18 of the Employment Act 1982), conduct qualifies for immunity if the actor genuinely believed it would help his side (*Express Newspapers* v. *McShane* [1980] A.C. 672). As Lord Diplock said in *NWL Ltd.* v. *Woods*, "Immunity under s.13 is not forfeited by being stubborn or pig-headed" ([1979] 3 All E.R. 614, 624).

S.13(2) and 13(3), now repealed, purported to be purely declaratory, and actually were so. As to s.13(2), it is clear common law that no conduct is actionable *simply* because it interferes with a person's economic freedom, whether or not there is a trade dispute on foot: as we have seen, something more is required, such as the use or threat of force, fraud, breach of contract or a gratuitously noxious combination. The repeal of this subsection by s.19 of the Employment Act 1982 would therefore have been legally irrelevant had it not been for the astonishing (and quite unsupportable) observation by Lord Diplock in *Hadmor Productions* v. *Hamilton* [1982] 1 All E.R. 1042, 1053 that the subsection granted immunity for causing business loss even where the means used were unlawful.

The repeal of s.13(3) by s.17(8) of the Employment Act 1980 is also irrelevant, because it seems quite clear now that conduct legitimised by s.13(1) cannot be treated as unlawful by anyone (*Hadmor Productions*, where Lord Diplock reviews the entire legislative history).

The immunity granted by section 13 of the 1974 Act has been removed in several situations by subsequent legislation. First, section 16 of the Employment Act 1980 introduced a new s.15 into the main Act which renders the common law applicable to conduct in the course of picketing elsewhere than at one's actual or former place of work (*News Group Newspapers* v. *SOGAT 82* [1987] I.C.R. 181). Secondly, section 18 of the 1980 Act restricts the statutory immunity for conduct which is aimed at raising union membership in other businesses. Thirdly, action by a trade union attracts no immunity unless it is pursuant to action endorsed by a prior ballot (Trade Union Act 1984, ss.10–11). Finally section 17 of the 1980 Act restores common law liability for conduct involving breaches of commercial contracts through "secondary action" (*i.e.* getting at the employees of someone other than the other party to the dispute): if your dispute is with A, you must not suborn B's men unless B is A's immediate supplier or customer.

This last rule operates irrationally in a context where there are interlocking companies. For example, in *Merkur* the defendants got the tugmen to refuse to tow a ship belonging to the plaintiff, with whom they were in dispute. That seems fair enough, but it was rendered unlawful just because the contract for towage was not with the plaintiff but with the sub-charterer. Again, in *Dimbleby & Sons* v. *N.U.J.* [1984] 1 All E.R. 751 (H.L.) the defendants thought that TBF1, with whom they were in dispute, was going to print newspapers for the plaintiff, so they told members who were employed by the plaintiff not to co-operate. They were held liable when it transpired that it was not TBF1 that was to do the printing, but its subsidiary TBF2.

The legislative practice of regulating, or deregulating, industrial conflict by means of granting limited immunity from common law liabilities and then derogating from that grant is not a convenient one. This is especially true now that actions in tort may be brought against trade unions (Employment Act 1982, ss.15, 16). See Elias and Ewing, Economic Torts and Labour Law: Old Principles and New Liabilities, 1982 Camb. L.J. 321 (an excellent review).

LONRHO LTD. v. SHELL PETROLEUM LTD.

House of Lords [1982] A.C. 173; [1981] 3 W.L.R. 33; [1981] 2 All E.R. 456

The claimants owned a pipeline, leading from the Mozambique coast to Southern Rhodesia, which the respondent oil companies paid to use. After the government of that country had declared itself independent, Orders in Council in the United Kingdom rendered it an offence to supply crude oil to Southern Rhodesia, and oil ceased to flow along the claimants' pipeline to their loss. In arbitration proceedings the claimants claimed over £100m. on the basis that the illegal regime would have collapsed and the profitable use of their pipeline recommenced much sooner had the respondents not supplied the regime with oil in breach of the Orders. It was held by the House of Lords that none of the claimants' allegations stated a cause of action, and the extract printed below gives the opinion of Lord Diplock in answer to Question 5(b), namely " . . . if there were breaches by the respondents of the 1965 and 1968 Orders [sc. the sanctions orders] (b) Whether the Claimants have a cause of action for damage alleged to have been caused by such breaches by virtue only of the allegation that there was an agreement to effect them."

[Lord Diplock's answer to question 5(a) is given above p. 153.]

Lord Diplock: . . . Question 5(b), to which I now turn, concerns conspiracy as a civil tort. Your Lordships are invited to answer it on the assumption that the purpose of Shell and BP in entering into the agreement to do the various things that it must be assumed they did in contravention of the sanctions order was to forward their own commercial interests, *not* to injure those of Lonrho. So the question of law to be determined is whether an intent by the defendants to injure the plaintiff is an essential element in the civil wrong of conspiracy, even where the acts agreed to be done by the conspirators amount to criminal offences under a penal statute. It is conceded that there is no direct authority either way on this question to be found in the decided cases; so if this House were to answer it in the affirmative, your Lordships would be making new law.

My Lords, conspiracy as a criminal offence has a long history. It consists of "the agreement of two or more persons to effect any unlawful purpose, whether as their ultimate aim, or only as a means to it, and the crime is complete if there is such agreement, even though nothing is done in pursuance of it." I cite from Viscount Simon L.C.'s now classic speech in *Crofter Hand Woven Harris Tweed Co. Ltd.* v. *Veitch* ([1942] A.C. 435, 439). Regarded as a civil tort, however, conspiracy is a highly anomalous cause of action. The gist of the cause of action is damage to the plaintiff; so long as it remains unexecuted, the agreement, which alone constitutes the crime of conspiracy, causes no damage; it is only acts done in execution of the agreement that are capable of doing that. So the tort, unlike the crime, consists not of agreement but of concerted action taken pursuant to agreement.

As I recall from my early years in the law, first as a student and then as a young barrister, during its chequered history between Lord Coleridge C.J.'s judgment at first instance in *Mogul Steamship Co.* v. *McGregor, Gow & Co.* [above p. 502] and the *Crofter* case, the civil tort of conspiracy attracted more academic controversy than success in practical application. Why should an act which causes economic loss to A but is not actionable at his suit if done by B alone become actionable because B did it pursuant to an agreement between B and C? An explanation given at the close of the nineteenth century by Bowen L.J. in the *Mogul* case [above p. 505] when it was before the Court of Appeal was: "The distinction is based on sound reason, for a combination may make oppressive or dangerous that which if it pro- ceeded only from a single person would be otherwise . . . " But to suggest today that acts done by one street-corner grocer in concert with a second are more oppressive and dangerous to a competitor than the same acts done by a string of supermarkets under a single ownership or that a multinational conglomerate such as Lonrho or oil company such as Shell or BP does not exercise greater economic power than any combination of small businesses is to shut one's eyes to what has been happening in the business and industrial world since the turn of the century and, in particular, since the end of the 1939–45 war. The civil tort of conspiracy to injure the plaintiff's commercial interests where that is the predominant purpose of the agreement between the defendants and of the acts done in execution of it which caused damage to the plaintiff must I think be accepted by this House as too well- established to be discarded, however anomalous it may seem today. It was applied by this House eighty years ago in *Quinn* v. *Leathem* ([1901] A.C. 495), and accepted as good law in the *Crofter* case in 1942, where it was made clear that injury to the plaintiff and not the self-interest of the defendants must be the predominant purpose of the agreement in execution of which the damage-causing acts were done.

My Lords, in none of the judgments in decided cases in civil actions for damages for conspiracy does it appear that the mind of the author of the judgment was directed to a case where the damage-causing acts, although neither done for the purpose of injuring the plaintiff nor actionable at his suit if they had been done by one person alone, were nevertheless a contravention of some penal law. I will not recite the statements in those judgments to which your Lordships have been referred by Lonrho as amounting to dicta in favour of the view that a civil action for conspiracy does lie in such a case. Even if the authors' minds had been directed to the point, which they were not, I should still find them indecisive. This House, in my view, has an unfettered choice whether to confine the civil action of conspiracy to the narrow field to which alone it has an established claim or whether to extend this already anomalous tort beyond those narrow limits that are all that common sense and the application of the legal logic of the decided cases require.

My Lords, my choice is unhesitatingly the same as that of Parker J. and all three members of the Court of Appeal. I am against extending the scope of the civil tort of conspiracy beyond acts done in execution of an agreement entered into by two or more persons for the purpose not of protecting their own interests but of injuring the interests of the plaintiff. So I would answer question 5(b) No.

Questions

1. Suppose that the sanctions order had said: "No oil shall be supplied to Rhodesia, on pain of penalty, save through the Lonrho pipeline" and the defendants had supplied oil by air. Would Lonrho have been able to sue? Would this be because the order would have been held to give Lonrho a right to sue or for some other reason? Is it right that one should be able to advance one's own interests at another's expense by deliberate breach of the law? If a claim were granted to those adversely affected thereby, should the claim be limited to those foresee- able to the reasonable man or to those foreseen by the legislator?

2. What do you think of Lord Diplock's attempt to disprove what was said by Bowen L.J.? Did Bowen L.J. suggest that two pygmies were bigger than one giant or than one pygmy? Would McGregor Gow by itself have been able to ruin the Mogul Steamship Co.? Would the threat to withdraw the labour of one draughtsman have swayed B.O.A.C.? Why is a boycott effective? Has it ceased to be so? What is a lynch mob? Does the principle that "two against one is unfair" depend on the size of the one?

Notes:

1. It is rather taken for granted in the West today that there is a right to combine with others in order to advance common interests. It was not always so even in England (the Combination Acts were in force from 1802 till 1824), and it is not so elsewhere now. But if the right to combine in order to advance common interests is accepted, surely it must be an abuse of that right if one combines with others not to advance common interests but to cause wanton harm. Is not this the explanation of the rule that while it is permissible for an individual to aim to hurt someone and hurt him, for a group to do so is not?

2. None of the defendants in *Rookes, Torquay Hotel* and *Merkur Island* was guilty of a statutory offence, though they were all aiming at the plaintiff, out to worst him if they could, not from what Holmes J. once called "disinterested malevolence," but in order to advance their own interests. Suppose that in their efforts to disgruntle the plaintiff they had committed some crime instead of merely running afoul of contract or tort? Would they be liable on that ground? Although *Lonrho* deals with deliberate unlawful conduct and consequent economic loss this is a question it does not answer. As Lord Wedderburn observes " . . . there is . . . an element of uncertainty . . . about the real effect of the judgment." (*The Worker and the Law*, (3rd ed. 1986) 639).

Let us see. The plaintiff's claim, namely, "We were hurt by your action which was (a) illegal, and (b) concerted," was dismissed because (a) the victim of a statutory offence cannot sue on that ground alone unless such was the intention of the legislature (above p. 153), and (b) concert does not by itself render even illegal conduct actionable.

The decision therefore clearly demonstrates that, absent contrary legislative intention, no claim vests in the fall-out victim of deliberate or concerted crime: the bystander cannot sue, however predictable, even inevitable, his (financial) injury. *Lonrho* does not deal with the case of the plaintiff who was the very object of the deliberate illegal conduct. So it may still be true that a person can sue a defendant who deliberately infringes the law with the aim of hurting him. But does that have to be the defendant's predominant aim, as it admittedly does where there is a conspiracy using no unlawful means? Here one must distinguish between (a) going out of your way to knock someone down; (b) knocking someone down because he is in your way; and (c) proceeding on your way regardless of who may be in the way. "Predominant aim" exists only in (a), intention to hurt in (b) as well, but not in (c), which was the *Lonrho* situation. It would be a strong thing to say that in one's efforts to disgratify one's enemy one must respect the rules of contract and tort but may blithely flout the criminal law. *Lonrho* does not force us to say this: it is only in cases where persons acting in concert are not employing any unlawful means that *Lonrho* requires that the desire to hurt the plaintiff be the predominant aim. In other words, the House of Lords has not said that self-advancement by illegal means, whether by many or by one, is not actionable at the instance of the intended victim.

3. *Lonrho* may be useful if it concentrates our attention on "aiming." No such emphasis was necessary until *Torquay Hotel* because (a) under *Lumley* v. *Gye* only the disappointed creditor in the contract "interfered with" could sue and he was always squarely in the defendant's sights, (b) liability under *Rookes* v. *Barnard* existed only if the defendant had said to the middleman "Sack the plaintiff, or else!," thereby showing his aim, and (c) in conspiracy an unalloyed desire to screw the plaintiff was required. *Torquay Hotel*, however, has rendered it necessary to stress the "aiming" requirement, since both parties to a contract "interfered with" are interfered with, though only one is aimed at. In *Merkur Island* and *Torquay Hotel* the shipowner and the hotelkeeper were aimed at and should therefore have title to sue: the charterer and Shell were merely incidental victims and should not.

The decision in *Barretts & Baird* (below p. 535) is satisfactory in this regard. There the meat-traders were possibly beneficiaries of the MFC's statutory duty to run the service properly and therefore poised to complain if the defendants had deliberately prevented MFC's performance of their statutory duty (!), but since it was MFC the defendants were aiming at and not the plaintiffs, the plaintiff meat-traders could not sue.

4. The tort of conspiracy was sadly misused in *Gulf Oil (G.B.)* v. *Page* [1987] 3 All E.R. 14

(C.A.). The Page brothers ran a company which owned a few filling stations. In a dispute with their supplier, Gulf, the Pages, or their company, had lost one lawsuit and won another. The brothers, or the company, hired a plane to fly over a race-course towing a sign saying "Gulf exposed in fundamental breach," and Gulf, who admitted the truth of the statement, sought to enjoin them.

The trial judge correctly refused the injunction: the courts are rightly slow to stop a person saying something he asserts is true. This practice naturally developed in defamation suits, which have two characteristics, (a) that the plaintiff asserts the falsehood of what was said, and (b) that the defendant is frequently out to hurt the plaintiff. The Court of Appeal granted the injunction. Parker L.J. held that the practice did not apply where the plaintiff admits the truth of the assertion (!!) and where the assertion was being made by two or more people whose predominant aim was to hurt the plaintiff, because that was CONSPIRACY, A TORT. So much for freedom of speech: *vox clamantis* is permitted, *voces clamantium* are enjoined; truth is for solo voices, not a chorus. The learned Lord Justice refused point-blank to discuss whether directors could be said to conspire with their company. After all, "The matter was of great urgency because the Cheltenham Gold Cup was due to be run at 3 p.m. . . . . "(!)

Questions:

1. Did the directors of Gulf conspire to sue the Page brothers? What do you think of their conduct in doing so?

2. How does the scenario in this case (*Giant* v. *Two Pygmies*) square with Lord Diplock's observations about the tort of conspiracy?

Chapter 16

ABUSE OF PUBLIC AND CIVIL POWERS

BOURGOIN S.A. v. MINISTRY OF AGRICULTURE

Court of Appeal [1986] Q.B. 716; [1985] 3 All E.R. 585; [1985] 3 W.L.R. 1027; [1986] 1
C.M.L.R. 267

In August 1981 the Minister of Agriculture revoked the general licence under which the plaintiffs' frozen turkeys had been imported from France, on the ostensible ground that the control of Newcastle disease by vaccination as was done in France (and had been done in Britain between 1964 and 1981) was insufficiently effective. The Court of Justice of the European Communities held that this was in breach of the United Kingdom's obligations under art. 30 Treaty of Rome, saying *inter alia*, that "Certain established facts suggest that the real aim of the 1981 measures was to block, for commercial and economic reasons, imports of poultry from other Member States, in particular from France."

The plaintiffs, French turkey exporters, alleged that the defendant "misconducted itself in the discharge of its public duties and in its public office, in that it exercised its powers to withdraw the said licences for a purpose that (as the Defendant knew) was contrary to Article 30 and/or was calculated to and did unlawfully damage the Plaintiffs in their business and/or was not the purpose for which the said powers had been conferred upon the Defendant." The defendant argued that this disclosed no cause of action, but Mann J. held that it did, and the Court of Appeal unanimously agreed with him on this point.

Oliver L.J.: . . . The third way in which the case is formulated on the pleadings is as a claim for damages against the minister for misfeasance in public office, a tort which was described by Lord Diplock in *Dunlop* v. *Woollahra Municipal Council* ([1981] 1 All E.R. 1202, 1210), as "well-established." That is not in dispute. The difference between the parties rests only in their respective appreciations of the essential ingredients of the tort. For the purposes only of the preliminary issue, it was accepted that the minister's purpose in revoking the general licence was to protect English turkey producers, and that he knew at the time (i) that this involved a failure to perform the United Kingdom's obligations under art. 30, (ii) that the revocation would cause damage to the plaintiffs in their business and (iii) that the protection of English producers from foreign competition was not one for the achievement of which powers were conferred on him by the enabling legislation or the 1980 order. The Solicitor General's submission, however, was that it was an essential allegation, and one not made on the pleadings, that the minister acted with the purpose of inflicting harm on the plaintiffs. This has been referred to conveniently as an allegation of "targeted malice."

The court has been referred to a large number of cases both in this country and in Canada and Australia from which, it is said, the inference can be drawn that in order to constitute the tort it is necessary to show an improper motive specifically aimed at the plaintiff. The authorities were extensively reviewed by the judge and it would, I think, be a work of supererogation to repeat the exercise here. There are in certain of the older cases phrases in the judgments or pleadings which might be taken to suggest that "targeted malice" was regarded as essential. I say "might," because in my judgment they are entirely inconclusive. There are also strong indications in the other direction, particularly in the older election cases. For instance in *Cullen* v. *Morris* (1819) 171 E.R. 741, 744 Abbott C.J. observed:

"On the part of the defendant it has been contended, that an action is not maintainable for merely refusing the vote of a person who appears afterwards to have really had a right to vote, unless it also appears that the refusal resulted from a malicious and improper motive, and that if the party act honestly and uprightly according to the best of his judgment, he is not amenable in an action for damages. I am of opinion, that the law, as it has been stated by the counsel for the defendant, is correct."

Again later, he said (at 745):

"If a vote be refused with a view to prejudice either the party entitled to vote, or the candidate for whom he tenders his vote, the motive is an improper one, and an action is maintainable."

Coming to more modern times, there is the Privy Council case of *Dunlop* v. *Woollahra Municipal Council*, where the allegation was one of damage caused to the plaintiff by passing planning resolutions, which were in fact invalid, restricting the height of his proposed building. Paragraph 15A of the statement of claim in that case was (so far as material) in these terms (at 1208):

" . . . [the council] was a public corporate body which occupied a public office and was incorporated by a public statute . . . and [the council] abused its said office and public duty under the said Statute by purporting to pass each of the said resolutions with the consequence that damage was occasioned to [Dr. Dunlop]."

In delivering the judgment of the Board Lord Diplock said (at 1210):

"In pleading in para. 15A of the statement of claim that the council abused their public office and public duty Dr. Dunlop was relying on the well-established tort of misfeasance by a public officer in the discharge of his public duties . . . their Lordships . . . agree with [the trial judge's] conclusion that, in the absence of malice, passing without knowledge of its invalidity a resolution which is devoid of any legal effect is not conduct that of itself is capable of amounting to such 'misfeasance' as is a necessary element in this tort."

Of this case Sir William Wade Q.C. in his book *Administrative Law* (5th ed., 1982) pp. 672–673 comments that the Privy Council held that the tort "required as a necessary element either malice or knowledge . . . of the invalidity," a view which is in line with that expressed by Smith J. in *Farrington* v. *Thomson and Bridgland* ([1959] V.R. 286), which was carefully considered by Mann J. in the course of his judgment in the instant case. Having concluded his review of the authorities, Mann J. concluded thus:

"I do not read any of the decisions to which I have been referred as precluding the commission of the tort of misfeasance in public office where the officer actually knew that he had no power to do that which he did, and that his act would injure the plaintiff as subsequently it does. I read the judgment in *Dunlop* v. *Woollahra Municipal Council* in the sense that malice and knowledge are alternatives. There is no sensible reason why the common law should not afford a remedy to the injured party in circumstances such as are before me. There is no sensible distinction between the case where an officer performs an act which he has no power to perform with the object of injuring A (which the defendant accepts is actionable at the instance of A) and the case where an officer performs an act which he knows he has no power to perform with the object of conferring a benefit on B but which has the foreseeable and actual consequence of injury to A (which the defendant denies is actionable at the instance of A). In my judgment each case is actionable at the instance of A and, accordingly, I determine that paras. 23 and 26 of the amended statement of claim do disclose a cause of action."

For my part, I too can see no sensible distinction between the two cases which Mann J. mentions.

If it be shown that the minister's motive was to further the interests of English turkey producers by keeping out the produce of French turkey producers, an act which must necessarily injure them, it seems to me entirely immaterial that the one purpose was dominant and the second merely a subsidiary purpose for giving effect to the dominant purpose. If an act is done deliberately and with knowledge of its consequences, I do not think that the actor can sensibly say that he did not "intend" the consequences or that the act was not "aimed" at the person who, it is known, will suffer them. In my judgment, the judge was right in his conclusion also on this point.

Questions:

1. The Minister did what he did in deference to pressure from English turkey producers. Would they be liable to the plaintiff? Could they be described as interfering with the plaintiffs' statutory rights? If so, would the Minister have a claim against them?

2. Suppose that The Talking Turkey Delicatessen could have sold more turkeys if delicious French ones had been available instead of fishy English ones. Could it claim damages from the Minister for the profits lost through the unlawful embargo?

Notes:

1. The plaintiffs failed in their argument that the Minister would be liable to them even if he had been in good faith, for infringing their rights under Art. 30 Treaty of Rome. See above p. 173. But they were doubtless content with the £3,500,000 which our government paid out in order to avoid further embarrassing litigation on the misfeasance/abuse/bad faith point here reported.

2. In *Barretts & Baird* v. *IPCS* [1987] I.C.L.R. 3, the MLC, a quango, had a statutory duty to run a system for certifying meat so as to enable producers and traders to claim subsidies of about £300m. annually. Their 630 employees, civil servants, went on strike for more pay after the statutory ballot, and this disrupted the business of the plaintiff abattoir owners and other meat traders. The plaintiffs sought an injunction to prevent the strike on the ground, *inter alia*, that the civil servants were damaging them by wrongful means, namely inducing breach of statutory duty on the part of their employer, the MLC. The judge held that the plaintiffs could probably sue for breach of statutory duty but that no breach had been induced; furthermore, even if a breach had been provoked, an injunction should not issue as the defendants were not aiming at the plaintiffs. (See Townshend-Smith, "Breach of Statutory Duty and the Economic Torts," [1987] New L.J. 371, and notes at [1987] Camb.L.J. 222 (Napier), 104 L.Q.R. 176 (Fredman), 50 M.L.R. 506 (Simpson)). It seems clear that the ricochet (unintended if foreseeable) victims of unlawful strikes should not be able to sue, but a County Court judge has allowed a passenger to recover £153 from the railwaymen's union whose unlawful strike caused him to be benighted away from home (*Falconer* v. *ASLEF* [1986] I.R.L.R. 331).

SUTTON v. JOHNSTONE

Exchequer Chamber (1785) 1 Term Rep. 544; 99 E.R. 1243

The defendant was a commodore of the British fleet, engaged in warfare with the French in the West Indies. After one engagement, he ordered the captains of his ships to ship their cables and pursue a squadron of the French. The plaintiff, one of those captains, failed to do so, because his top-mast was damaged. The defendant had the plaintiff imprisoned for two years, and court-martialled for delaying the public service and for disobeying orders.

At trials at Guildhall, the plaintiff had a verdict for £5,000 on the first occasion and £6,000 on the second. The defendant moved in arrest of judgment, but the Court of Exchequer discharged the rule (1785) 1 Term Rep. 501; 99 E.R. 1220. The defendant brought error to the Exchequer Chamber and succeeded. The plaintiff brought error to the House of Lords, and the decision of the Court of Exchequer Chamber was affirmed (1787) 1 Term Rep. 784; 99 E.R. 1377.

Lord Mansfield C.J. and Lord Loughborough C.J.: . . . There is no similitude or analogy between an action of trespass, or false imprisonment, and this kind of action. An action of trespass is for the defendant's having done that, which, upon the stating of it, is manifestly illegal. This kind of action is for a prosecution, which, upon the stating of it, is manifestly legal. The essential ground of this action is, that a legal prosecution was carried on without a probable cause. We say this is emphatically the essential ground; because every other allegation may be implied from this; but this must be substantively and expressly proved, and cannot be implied. From the want of probable cause, malice may be, and most commonly is, implied. The knowledge of the defendant is also implied. From the most express malice, the want of probable cause cannot be implied.

A man, from a malicious motive, may take up a prosecution for real guilt, or he may, from circumstances which he really believes, proceed upon apparent guilt; and in neither case is he liable to this kind of action.

The question of probable cause is a mixed proposition of law and fact. Whether the circumstances alleged to show it probable, or not probable, are true and existed, is a matter of fact; but whether, supposing them true, they amount to a probable cause, is a question of law . . .

We have no difficulty to give our opinion, that, in law, the commodore had a probable cause to bring the plaintiff to a fair and impartial trial . . . The person unjustly accused is not without his remedy . . . Reparation is done to him by an acquittal.

Note:
Malicious prosecution is not so much a ground of liability as an exception to the general immunity for putting the criminal law into force. A person is not liable for prosecuting another, and putting him to the expense and shame of defending himself against a criminal charge, unless the prosecutor is shown to be both a knave and a fool. If one person thinks another guilty, and prosecutes him out of a passion for justice (for the destructive qualities of which see Kleist's *Michael Kohlhaas*), then no matter how foolish and stupid the prosecutor was, he will not be liable; his bona fides will save him. Equally, where there exists against a person evidence which justifies the putting in force of the criminal procedure, a prosecutor who knows and accepts that evidence is not deprived of his immunity because to him the duty is also a pleasure. It is only where there is a devious motive and also either no belief or an unreasonable belief in the merits of the case that the prosecutor will be liable.

The question of reasonable and probable cause is for the judge. As Lord Bramwell said in *Abrath* v. *North Eastern Ry.* (1886) 11 App.Cas. 247, 252: "A man brings an action for a malicious prosecution; he gives evidence which shews or goes to shew that he is innocent. You may tell the jury over and over again that that is not the question, but they never or very rarely can be got to understand it. They think that it is not right that a man should be prosecuted when he is innocent, and in the end they pay him for it."

British naval history is full of such excitements. Augustus, Viscount Keppel, was court-martialled for his conduct of operations off Brest in 1779. The prosecution was pronounced "malicious and ill-founded," and he was subsequently made First Lord of the Admiralty.

GLINSKI v. McIVER

House of Lords [1962] A.C. 726; [1962] 2 W.L.R. 832; 106 S.J. 261; [1962] 1 All E.R. 696

The plaintiff (who recovered £100 damages for false imprisonment, as to which no question arose) also alleged that the defendant, a police detective, maliciously and without reasonable and probable cause charged him with conspiracy to defraud and obtaining with false pretences. The plaintiff was acquitted of those charges by the direction of the court.

There was evidence on which the jury could find that the defendant charged the plaintiff in order to punish him for having given unwelcome evidence in a previous case, and the jury did find that the defendant was actuated by a motive other than to bring the plaintiff to justice. The trial judge also asked the jury "Did the defendant honestly believe . . . that the plaintiff was guilty of the offence of conspiracy to defraud?" They answered that he did not.

Cassels J. accordingly found that there was no reasonable and probable cause for the prosecution, and gave judgment for the plaintiff for £2,500, the sum found by the jury. The defendant appealed to the Court of Appeal who reversed the judgment. The plaintiff's appeal to the House of Lords was dismissed.

Lord Radcliffe: My Lords, one must suppose that the answers returned by the jury to the first two questions left to them at the trial meant that they considered that the prosecution of the appellant was a put-up job on the part of the police. To the first question they answered that the respondent in starting the prosecution had been actuated by a motive other than a desire to bring the appellant to justice. In my view, there was evidence capable of supporting this finding and I do not think that it can be upset or ignored. The whole point of the present appeal, as I see it, is whether there was any evidence capable of supporting their second finding that on September 29, 1955 (which is agreed to be the relevant date), the respondent did not honestly believe that the appellant was guilty of the offence of conspiracy to defraud. For, if there was no such evidence, then no question ought to have been put to them on this issue and the learned trial judge, instead of concluding, as I think that he must have, that their answer required him to hold that there was an absence of reasonable and probable cause moving the respondent, should have considered independently whether there was such reasonable and probable cause for the action that the respondent took. Had he done so, I agree with the view taken by the Court of Appeal that the correct answer should have been that there was such cause.

The action for malicious prosecution is by now a well-trodden path. I take it to be settled law that if the defendant can be shown to have initiated the prosecution without himself holding an honest belief in the truth of the charge (I must, of course, refine on this phrase later) he cannot be said to have acted upon reasonable and probable cause. The connection between the two ideas is not very close at first sight, for one would suppose that there might well exist reasonable and probable cause in the objective sense, what one might call a good case, irrespective of the state of the prosecutor's own mind or his personal attitude towards the validity of the case. The answer is, I think, that the ultimate question is not so much whether there is reasonable or probable cause in fact as whether the prosecutor, in launching his charge, was motivated by what presented itself to him as a reasonable and probable cause. Hence, if he did not believe that there was one, he must have been in the wrong.

On the other hand, I take it to be equally well settled that mere belief in the truth of his charge does not protect an unsuccessful prosecutor, given, of course, malice, if the circumstances before him would not have led "an ordinarily prudent and cautious man" to conclude that the person charged was probably guilty of the offence. This is involved, I think, in the formula from *Hicks* v. *Faulkner* (1878) 8 Q.B.D. 167) adopted by this House in *Herniman* v. *Smith* ([1938] A.C. 305); and, while the state of the prosecutor's mind or belief or opinion, if a disputed issue, is a question of fact properly to be left to the jury, the question whether the circumstances reasonably justified a belief in the truth of the charge is a question for the judge himself to decide, whether you call the question one of fact or one of law.

I cannot say that I see any special difficulty in keeping separate the respective

functions of judge and jury, nor do I wish to approach this matter with any precon-
ception that the judge has a duty to lean towards protecting a prosecutor, *ex
hypothesi* unsuccessful and malicious, from the possible injudiciousness of a jury. If
there really is some evidence founded on speech, letters or conduct that supports
the case that the prosecutor did not believe in his own charge, the plaintiff is, in my
view, entitled as of right to have the jury's finding upon it. On the other hand, if
there is not any such evidence, I do not think that an issue can be raised for the jury
out of the mere argument that the facts known to the prosecutor were so slender or
unconvincing that he could not have believed in the plaintiff's guilt. To argue in
that way is no more than to say: "No reasonable or prudent man could have supposed that on these facts the plaintiff was probably guilty: the defendant is a
reasonable and prudent man: therefore you must conclude on the evidence that the
defendant did not believe in the plaintiff's guilt." To put a question to the jury as to
the defendant's state of mind when it is only to be deduced by inference from the
alleged feebleness of the case, is, I think, to put to them indirectly exactly the same
issues as the judge himself has to decide directly when he rules that there is or is not
an absence of reasonable and probable cause. To do that is to confuse the respective functions of judge and jury, and would allow the jury on occasions to usurp the
function that ought to be reserved for the judge. It has always been recognised that
the issue as to the defendant's belief (more properly, his lack of belief) does not
necessarily arise in every action for malicious prosecution (see *Blachford* v. *Dod*
((1831) 2 B & Ad. 179, 181; 109 E.R. 1110)), so that in any particular trial there
may be no question that can rightly go to the jury upon it. In my opinion, it does
not arise unless there is some contested evidence bearing directly upon the defendant's belief at the relevant date, apart from anything that could merely be inferred
as to his belief from the strength or weakness of the case before him.

Was there, then, any such evidence at the trial before Cassels J.? Before I say
what my view is upon this, however, I must notice what was the respondent's main
argument on this appeal, an argument to the effect that in considering whether
there was an issue for the jury one should realise that the true question is whether
there was a dispute "as to the main facts which formed the foundation of the prosecution complained of," and not whether there was a dispute as to what was the
prosecutor's actual belief when he made his charge. In this case, it was said, there
was no dispute as to these main facts and therefore no issue to go to the jury: on the
other hand, to dispute about the prosecutor's belief in the plaintiff's guilt was to dispute about his opinion on a question of law which, given the facts, he was entitled
to bring before the court, without himself forming an opinion or holding a belief
about it one way or the other.

My Lords, I dare say that I have not done proper justice to the force of the
respondent's argument in the way that I have now stated it. The cause of my failure, if there is one, lies in the fact that, despite the full and meticulous review of
numerous past decisions in malicious prosecution cases which was offered to us by
the respondent's counsel, I was never able to see that there was anything amiss with
the various formulae such as "belief in guilt," "belief in the case laid," "belief in
the truth or propriety of the charge" or "belief that the facts amounted to the
offence charged," which judges have habitually used when putting a question to a
jury on this issue, or that there is any useful or maintainable distinction between
belief in the facts upon which the guilt is thought to be founded and belief in the
guilt dependent on those facts. To try to maintain such a distinction in practice
would involve impossible permutations in the separation and combination of facts
or groups of facts and in the inferences to be drawn from them, separated or combined. But, after all, the facts that are to be attended to cannot be just any set of
facts; they must be such facts as, taken together, point to a case of the offence
charged. They must be fraud facts, or theft facts or conspiracy facts. No doubt to
take a view as to what these amount to is in a sense to form an opinion on a question of law, for it implies an idea as to what are the requisite conditions of the legal

offence. But I do not see any complication in this, for an ordinary sensible man does have a general idea as to what these offences consist in; and if in a particular case an intending prosecutor has no such idea or the offence in question is complicated or special, I take it that he would be expected to suspend action until he had resorted to legal advice upon it.

To put it shortly, I do not think that the elucidation of the law upon the tort of malicious prosecution is likely to be assisted by hypothesising the instance of a prosecutor who believes in the existence of certain undisputed facts but has no personal opinion or belief as to whether they constitute a legal offence or not. I should like to come across an actual case of that nature before taking a view about it. For if the man has prosecuted, though unsuccessfully and has been acting merely from a sense of public duty, then he is not guilty of malice, so there has been no malicious prosecution; whereas, if he has prosecuted for some reason other than a desire to vindicate justice and so has been malicious, I see no compelling reason why the law should give any protection to him on the ground of the alleged neutrality of his attitude. If we fine the matter down to police prosecutions, I think that the rights and wrongs may well depend on the nature of the explanation, if any, offered by the prosecutor in his evidence. I dare say that he may say that, having satisfied himself as to the existence of certain facts, he took action either on the strength of legal advice given to him or in accordance with the orders of some official superior. If his belief is said to rest on legal advice, I think that the court is entitled to know positively, not merely by inference, what that advice was and upon what instructions it was obtained. If, on the other hand, his action is attributed to departmental instructions, I can only say that my present view is that it would be undesirable in the public interest to allow such a reason to serve as a substitute for the belief in guilt that has habitually been required. Scotland Yard itself is not a possible defendant in these actions, nor is any police force as such. If any particular officer comes forward to make a charge it is not unreasonable, I think, if the issue arises, to hold him to the belief that the person he is prosecuting is guilty of the charge preferred.

In any event, the case now before us is not in the least that of a neutral officer moved by no personal view as to the plaintiff's guilt. The respondent was insistent in his evidence that he preferred his charge against the appellant because he considered that the facts and circumstances then before him pointed to the appellant as guilty of conspiracy to defraud, and we come back, therefore, to the straightforward question whether there was any countervailing evidence produced at the trial which made it a disputed issue, to be submitted to the jury, whether he honestly entertained that belief or not.

I have not found it easy to decide on this but, on the whole, I think that there was no such evidence . . .

If the jury's finding in answer to question 2 does not stand, I do not feel any doubt that the Court of Appeal were correct in holding that there was no lack of reasonable and probable cause to move the respondent when he preferred his charge on September 29, 1955.

I agree that the appeal must be dismissed.

SPEED SEAL PRODUCTS v. PADDINGTON

Court of Appeal [1986] 1 All E.R. 91; [1986] F.S.R. 309; 135 New L.J. 935

After working for the plaintiff on the design of oil-pipe couplings, the defendant left that employment and set up in business on his own. When he applied for a patent for an oil-pipe coupling and started advertising it, the plaintiff sought an injunction to prevent further advertisement or use of information allegedly confidential. In addition to defending, the defendant applied to bring a counterclaim for the tort of abuse of court process.

The trial judge struck out the plaintiff's claim as unlikely to succeed, and allowed the defendant to counterclaim for damages. The plaintiff's appeal was allowed on the first point but not on the second.

Fox L.J.: . . . The proposed counterclaim asserts that the action was brought in bad faith for the ulterior motive of damaging the defendants' business, and not for the protection of any legitimate interest of the plaintiffs. This is particularised by the assertions (i) that the plaintiffs falsely pleaded that the first defendant had the idea which is the subject-matter of the action in the course of his employment by them at the meeting on February 25, 1981, whereas they knew that he had brought the idea with him at a time when he was not an employee of the plaintiffs and (ii) that the plaintiffs made use of the action for the purpose of deterring potential customers from dealing with the defendants. Reliance is placed on the undated telex sent by the plaintiffs to Woodfield Systems Ltd. which stated that the action had been commenced, that it related to the defendants' coupling devices and that it claimed an injunction restraining the defendants from misusing the alleged confidential information. It is asserted that all this, though true, implied that the design and sale of the defendants' coupling did infringe the plaintiffs' confidential information and that an injunction would, in due course, be granted to restrain the supply of such products. That implication, it is said, was false and was made maliciously.

Further it is alleged that since this action was started on July 21, 1983 the second defendants have not succeeded in securing a single contract, though they have tendered for 24 at a value of over £950,000 and their product is cheaper than its competitors.

The plaintiffs' contentions on this part of the case are, broadly, as follows. (i) The nature of the motive with which an act is done does not make the act unlawful (see *Bradford Corp.* v. *Pickles* [1895] A.C. 587). (ii) To bring legal proceedings is *per se* a lawful act. It is wrongful only if the proceedings are brought without reasonable and probable cause. (iii) There is no absence of reasonable and probable cause, at least where the alleged abuse is an action, unless such action has determined in favour of the person who is alleging the tortious act.

Now in the present case, say the plaintiffs, the proceedings have not determined in favour of the defendants. And further, there is no pleaded allegation that the plaintiffs commenced or continued the action without reasonable and probable cause. Accordingly, it is contended the counterclaim is not sustainable.

The defendants' response to that is as follows. They say, first, that if the allegations in the draft counterclaim are proved at the trial, they will establish the following: (i) that the plaintiffs started the action without any bona fide belief in its chance of success; (ii) that the plaintiffs intended to use and did use the existence of the action as a weapon to persuade the defendants' potential customers not to deal with them; (iii) that the defendants have suffered and, they emphasise, are still suffering serious damage as a result.

It would, say the defendants, be a serious defect in the law if it were powerless to protect the defendants in the original action itself on proof of those facts. They are suffering continuing damage and there should be no delay.

The defendants accept that, so far as the tort of malicious prosecution is concerned, it is necessary for the person asserting the tort to prove (a) the commencement of a suit, (b) malice, (c) damage to that person, (d) absence of reasonable and proper cause for the suit and (e) termination of the suit in that person's favour.

The defendants contend that, on the true construction of the pleading, absence of reasonable and probable cause is in fact pleaded, and that, in any event, the defect can be cured by amendment. And, so far as the requirement of determination of the proceedings is concerned, there is no reason why the point should not await the trial of the counterclaim. If at that stage the defendants cannot establish prior termination, they will fail.

But, quite apart from these contentions, the defendants advance a further argument. They say that there is a tort of abuse of process of the court established by *Grainger* v. *Hill* (1838) 132 E.R. 769. In that case the plaintiff had borrowed £80 from the defendants on the mortgage of a ship which he owned. The debt was repayable on September 28, 1837. The defendants, being apparently apprehensive as to their security, decided in November 1836 (*i.e.* before the debt was repayable) to possess themselves of the ship's register, without which the plaintiff could not go to sea. They therefore called on the plaintiff to pay the debt (which was not due) and threatened to arrest him if he failed to pay. The defendants then made an affidavit of debt and sued out a writ of capias indorsed for bail in the sum of some £95, and sent in two sheriff's officers with the writ to the plaintiff, who was ill in bed and attended by a surgeon. One of the officers then told the plaintiff that they had not come to take him but to get the ship's register, but that if he failed to deliver the register either they must take him or leave one of the officers with him. The plaintiff, being unable to procure bail and being alarmed, gave up the register. The plaintiff claimed damages for the loss of voyages which he could not undertake because of the loss of the register, and also the recovery of the register.

The plaintiff succeeded at the trial, and there was an appeal to the Exchequer Chamber, which dismissed it. Tindal C.J. said (at 773):

"The second ground urged for a nonsuit is, that there was no proof of the suit commenced by the Defendants having been terminated. But the answer to this, and to the objection urged in arrest of judgment, namely, the omission to allege want of reasonable and probable cause for the Defendants' proceeding, is the same: that this is an action for abusing the process of the law, by applying it to extort property from the Plaintiff, and not an action for malicious arrest or malicious prosecution, in order to support which action the termination of the previous proceeding must be proved . . . "

Tindal C.J. went on to say that, the complaint being that the process of the law had been abused, it was "immaterial whether the suit which that process commenced has been determined or not, or whether or not it was founded on reasonable and probable cause."

Park J. said that the argument as to the omission to prove the determination of the defendant's suit and to allege want of reasonable and probable cause for it proceeded on an erroneous analogy between the case and an action for malicious arrest (see 132 E.R. 773). Bosanquet J. said that "the process was enforced for an ulterior purpose" (at 774).

It is clear that the court distinguished the case from one of malicious prosecution, and accordingly rejected the arguments based on non-determination of the original proceedings. It regarded the wrong as abuse of the process. And the abuse, as I understand it, was that the purpose of the original proceeding was not the recovery of the debt (which was not due) but the extortion of the register.

Grainger v. *Hill* has not been much referred to in the subsequent authorities, but it has not been disapproved.

In *Goldsmith* v. *Sperrings Ltd.* [1977] 2 All E.R. 566, 574, Lord Denning M.R. (in a dissenting judgment) said:

"What may make it [the legal process] wrongful is the purpose for which it is used. If it is done in order to exert pressure so as to achieve an end which is improper in itself, then it is a wrong known to the law. This appears distinctly from the case which founded this tort. It is *Grainger* v. *Hill* . . . "

And Scarman L.J. said (at 582):

"In the instant proceedings the defendants have to show that the plaintiff has an ulterior motive, seeks a collateral advantage for himself beyond what the law offers, is reaching out 'to effect an object not within the scope of the process': *Grainger* v. *Hill* . . . "

The American Second Restatement of the Law of Tort (1977) § 682 states the following principle, under the heading "Abuse of Process":

"One who uses a legal process, whether criminal or civil, against another primarily to accomplish a purpose for which it is not designed, is subject to liability to the other for harm caused by the abuse of process."

Grainger v. *Hill* is cited in the Restatement for the proposition that termination of the proceeding in favour of the plaintiff need not be shown.

It seems to me that, if allegations of fact pleaded in the draft counterclaim are established at the trial, the decision in *Grainger* v. *Hill* provides a basis for an arguable case that there has been an actionable abuse of the process of the court. I express no view as to the strength of the defendants' case. It is enough to say that I think that a sufficiently arguable case has been demonstrated to justify giving leave to amend the defence by adding a counterclaim, as asked. It will be open to the defendants to support it by such arguments as may be available, whether based on *Grainger* v. *Hill* or not.

Lloyd L.J. and **Sir George Waller** agreed.

Question
Is this decision reconcilable with the rule that no claim for damages lies in respect of false evidence given with a view to litigation?

Note:
The case is noted in [1986] Camb.L.J. 200 (Tettenborn) and 102 L.Q.R. 9 (1986) (Wells).

It was in cases such as this that the German courts invented a new head of liability in tort, for unreasonably harming an "established and operative business" (Markesinis, The German Law of Torts 35–36). In England the need was less great by reason of the rule that a person seeking an interlocutory injunction must undertake to pay damages if he ultimately proves unentitled to it. If the plaintiff here had simply said that the defendant was not entitled to his invention, he would have been liable only on proof of malice (trade libel, above p. 490) and no injunction would be granted if the plaintiff sought to justify his statement (*Sterling-Winthrop Group* v. *Scott* (C.A. *The Independent*, February 23, 1987, applying *Bestobell Paints* [1975] F.S.R. 421).

An attempt to deploy negligence law in the area of litigation was foiled in *Business Computers International* v. *Registrar of Companies* [1987] 3 All E.R. 465, where the plaintiff company was unaware that it was being wound up because the petitioner had carelessly sent the papers to the wrong address: "The safeguards against impropriety are to be found in the rules and procedure that control litigation and not in tort." (Scott J.). The abuse of litigation is well shown in *Fitzroy* v. *Cave* [1905] 2 K.B. 364. The plaintiff obtained from five of the defendant's creditors an assignment of their debts, on the terms that after collection he would pay them the net proceeds. On cross-examination the plaintiff admitted that his sole purpose in suing was to bankrupt the defendant in order to have him removed from the board of directors of the Cork Mineral Development Company. The trial judge dismissed the claim as savouring of maintenance and as being otherwise contrary to public policy, but the Court of Appeal reversed: "I fail to see that we have anything to do with the motives which actuated the plaintiff." This was only 30 years after the assignment of debts, previously banned as suspect, was legitimated. Even now an assignment can be avoided if the purpose is deplorable (*Trendtex Trading Corp.* v. *Crédit Suisse* [1981] 3 All E.R. 520 (H.L.)).

PART IX

DAMAGES

Chapter 17

DAMAGES

Section 1.—Personal Injuries

TAYLOR v. BRISTOL OMNIBUS CO.

Court of Appeal [1975] 1 W.L.R. 1054; 119 S.J. 476; [1975] 2 All E.R. 1107

Lord Denning M.R.: This case is to be considered as at the date of the trial in February 1974. I will state the facts as then proved.

The plaintiff, Paul Taylor, is nine years of age. He is a hopeless cripple. It is all due to an accident six years ago, when he was only 3½ years. He was a bright little boy. His parents had taken him for a drive in the car. He was sitting in the back seat. It was along the road from Huntingdon to Cambridge. His father had stopped the car before turning right. But it was then run into from behind by a coach. Paul was thrown from the back seat and hit his head. There was not much injury to the rest of his body, but to his head. His skull was fractured extensively and his brain was damaged severely. The consequences have been terrible. He cannot control his legs or his arms, or his speech. He cannot walk. He can only get around on his knees or by pushing himself around in a sitting position. His left arm is useless. He cannot feed himself. He makes attempts to dress himself, but without much success. He can understand what people say to him, but he is not much good at making himself understood. He cannot formulate his words properly. He knows the letters of the alphabet and figures, but he cannot add or subtract above four. He has had three major epileptic attacks. He is taken each day to a school for disabled children. At home he sits and watches television. He needs constant supervision and nursing care day and night. His mother and father look after him with the utmost devotion. He will never be able to be employed by anyone. But his expectation of life is not reduced to any great extent. His intellectual capacity is sufficient for him to be aware of his helplessness and of his utter dependence on others. His sister, who is three years older, has been much affected. His grandparents too, because they help look after him.

The question is, what is the proper figure of damages? The judge assessed them as:

	£	£
Special damages (agreed)		500
Adaptation of accommodation (agreed)		1,000
Electrically-propelled chair (agreed)		500
Home help at £15 a week for the next eight years	6,000	
Less one-third for present payment	2,000	
	4,000	4,000

Thereafter in a Cheshire Home, or similar home at £30 a week (£1,500 a year) from eight years hence to the end of his life. Take a multiple of 16.	24,000	
Less five-twelfths for present payment	10,000	
	14,000	14,000
Loss of future earnings from age 19 for rest of his working life. Average £2,000 a year. Take a multiple of 16.	32,000	
Less one-half for present payment.	16,000	
	16,000	16,000
Pain and suffering and loss of amenities of life	27,500	27,500
	TOTAL:	63,500
Interest in accordance with *Jefford* v. *Gee*		8,300
		£71,800

Counsel for the defendants said that the total figure of £63,500 was too high. He suggested that it was about £10,000 too much.

Now, there is one matter that I would mention at the outset. These damages were assessed by Shaw J. in February 1974. We are deciding this appeal in May 1975. In the intervening 15 months there has been a big drop in the value of money; and the rate of inflation has increased greatly. Nevertheless, it is our duty to throw our minds back, if we can, to February 1974, and assess the damages as at that date. No one should be encouraged to appeal by the idea that the Court of Appeal will take into account changes in values since the trial. We are not asked to take it into account. I think this was right. The question has been much discussed, notably by the High Court of Australia in *O'Brien* v. *McKean* (1968) 42 A.J.L.R. 223, by the House of Lords in *Taylor* v. *O'Connor* [1971] A.C. 115 and by this court in *Mitchell* v. *Mulholland (No. 2)* [1972] 1 Q.B. 65. It must be remembered that, when assessing compensation for loss of future earnings, the court is not seeking to replace week by week the sums which the plaintiff would have earned. It is only giving compensation for loss of future earning capacity. And when it is assessing compensation for expense of nursing and attendance, it is not calculating ahead what that expense will be. It is only giving compensation for the fact that in the future extra expense will be incurred. This compensation could become altogether excessive if it were based on the expectation of future inflation. To keep it within bounds, it must be based on the value of money at the date of the trial.

Another matter which I would mention is the splitting up of the award into items. At one time this was thought to be undesirable: see *Watson* v. *Powles* [1968] 1 Q.B. 596; but it is now recognised as necessary, if only so as to enable the interest to be calculated: see *Jefford* v. *Gee* [1970] 2 Q.B. 130. Yet at the end the judges should look at the total figure in the round, so as to be able to cure any overlapping or other source of error.

Finally, at the outset I would mention the parents. They were in the car which was struck in the back by the coach. There was a breach of duty to them as well as to their baby. If they had themselves been injured or had suffered nervous shock, they could have recovered damages for themselves. They did not so suffer, but the tragedy is for them even greater. Before this accident they could have looked forward to a future of happiness, bringing up their baby son with the joy it brings, seeing him through his schooldays, marrying and having children of his own, and then his caring for them in their old age. Now, in consequence of this accident, they are deprived of it all. They have nursed him day and night. They have watched over him. They have carried him everywhere. They have taught him to do little things for himself. They have devoted their lives to him and will continue to do so. Yet they are not entitled to recover any damages for all their grief and suffering. Not a penny. Nor would they ask it.

With these matters in mind, I turn to the items in his case.

1. *Pain and suffering etc.*

The judge awarded £27,500. Counsel for the defendants says that that figure is very high but he recognises that it is not so high that this court should interfere with it. It is difficult to find any comparable cases. In *S*. v. *Distillers Co. (Biochemicals) Ltd.* [1970] 1 W.L.R. 114 Hinchcliffe J., in 1969, for badly deformed infants, awarded £18,000 and £28,000. In *Daish* v. *Wauton* [1972] 2 Q.B. 262 for a boy of five, with severe brain damage, this court, in 1971, awarded £20,000. Seeing that the value of money has fallen much since those awards were made, I do not think we should interfere with the award here of £27,500. This little boy is ruined for life. He can do nothing. He can enjoy nothing. He can take part in none of the activities of others. And he is aware of it—to his great distress.

2. *Cost of future nursing and attendance*

In *Cunningham* v. *Harrison* [1973] Q.B. 942 we said that, if and in so far as a disabled person is likely to be provided for by the state free of charge, he cannot claim it as part of his damages. But in this case we have been referred to section 29(5) of the National Assistance Act 1948. It says that a local authority may recover such charges as they may determine. And we are told that in this present case they may make a charge for any services rendered by them. So it would not be right to regard their services as free.

The judge divided the figure into two parts: (i) for the next eight years Paul would be at home, but his parents would reasonably spend £15 a week for help in the house; (ii) for the rest of his life he would be in a Cheshire or similar home at £30 a week.

Counsel for the defendants directed some criticism at those figures. He said that it was a mistake to divide up Paul's life into two parts—the next eight years at home—and the rest thereafter in an institution. I think that criticism is justified. The doctor said that it would be better for Paul to be with the family as long as possible. Most of us have known of similar sad cases. I should have thought that these devoted parents would have kept Paul at home with them as long as they could. They would do so until they themselves were too old to do it. They would give their own lives to him. And then someone else in the family would do it.

If such is the future, the question arises: is his compensation to be less because he is looked after at home instead of in an institution? I do not think so. I am glad to say that as a result of recent cases, compensation can be given in money for services rendered by the parents. It has been so held when a wife gave up work to look after her husband: see *Wattson* v. *Port of London Authority* [1969] 1 Lloyd's Rep. 95; when she did not give up work but, nevertheless, devoted her life to looking after him: see *Cunningham* v. *Harrison*; and when a mother gave up work to look after her child: see *Donnelly* v. *Joyce* [1974] Q.B. 454. In *Hay* v. *Hughes* [1975] 1 All E.R. 257, Lord Edmund-Davies said that "the injured plaintiff can recover the value of nursing and other services gratuitously rendered to him by a stranger to the proceedings."

Approaching the case on those broad principles, the boy was only 3½, his father 30 at the time of the accident, and his mother a little younger. Taking values at the date of trial, the cost of a home help and compensation for the parents' services can be put together at £20 a week. That is £1,000 a year. All this is over his whole life. I would take a multiplier of 18. Thus arriving at the figure of £18,000 in all. That is the very figure arrived at by the judge, although by a different route. I would add that, although this sum is only recoverable by Paul, it is really for the costs incurred and services rendered by the parents. If a trust is created, as it should be, this fact should be borne in mind in administering the trust.

3. *Loss of future earnings*

The judge assumed that Paul would start earning at the age of 19. He took the yardstick of his father's position. He took an average figure of £2,000 a year and used a multiplier of 16. Thus making £32,000. Less one-half for present payment: making £16,000.

Counsel for the defendants urged us to adopt a new attitude in regard to babies who are injured. He suggested that the loss of future earnings was so speculative that, instead of trying to calculate it, we should award a conventional sum of say £7,500. He suggested that we might follow the advice given by Lord Devlin in *H. West & Son Ltd.* v. *Shephard* [1964] A.C. 326, 357, that is: (i) give him such a sum as will ensure that for the rest of his life, this boy will not, within reason, want for anything that money can buy; (ii) give him, too, compensation for pain and suffering and loss of amenities; (iii) but do not, in addition, give him a large sum for loss of future earnings. At his very young age these are speculative in the extreme. Who can say what a baby boy will do with his life? He may be in charge of a business and make much money. He may get into a mediocre groove and just pay his way. Or he may be an utter failure. It is even more speculative with a baby girl. She may marry and bring up a large family, but earn nothing herself. Or, she may be a career woman, earning high wages. The loss of future earnings for a baby is so speculative that I am much tempted to accept the suggestion of counsel for the defendants.

This suggestion is, however, contrary to present practice. In the children's cases hitherto the courts have made an estimate of loss of future earnings. In *S.* v. *Distillers Co. (Biochemicals) Ltd.* Hinchcliffe J. took a loss of wages at £1,500 a year and assessed an annuity value on that basis of £13,700. In *Daish* v. *Wauton* this court took an annual loss of £1,000 a year for 20 years and arrived at £6,000. Those cases were decided four or five years ago; and wages and salaries have gone up much since then. I cannot say that the judge was wrong in taking an average of £2,000 a year. Counsel for the defendants said that the judge did not allow for Paul's reduced expectancy of life. The doctor said it was reduced by 5 to 10 per cent. But that would have little impact on his working life. I think the judge was entitled to take a loss of £2,000 a year from age 19 to 60 or 65. This might well give a figure of £16,000.

I feel that we must follow the accepted practice in the cases. I would not dispute the judge's figure of £16,000 for loss of future earnings.

4. *Overlapping*

It was suggested that there might be some overlap in that, if he was earning wages he would have had to spend some of them in keeping himself; and also his family, if he married. This was considered by this court in *Daish* v. *Wauton*. The court then pointed out that in most cases an injured man will have living expenses after he is injured which are roughly equivalent to those he would have had to pay if he had not been injured. The expenses, therefore, cancel out. And so far as the cost of wife and children are concerned, if he had married, this should not be deducted: any more than if he had remained a bachelor: see *Fletcher* v. *Autocar & Transporters Ltd.* [1968] 2 Q.B. 322 by Diplock L.J. The only deduction which might be made is, if he was in an institution and getting his board and lodging included in his expenses. That, however, is not this case, because it is probable that Paul will stay at home and not go into an institution.

5. *Conclusion*

I must confess that at first I thought that the £63,500 was too high. Looked at in the round, I thought that counsel for the defendants was right and that it should have been about £55,000. But, on analysis, and considering it with my brethren, I have come to the conclusion that the figure was not out of the way. At any rate, not so much that this court should interfere with it. I would, therefore, dismiss this appeal. But I would like to say that these huge lump sums give food for thought. Our present system of assessing and awarding compensation for injuries such as these calls for radical re-appraisement; and I hope that the Royal Commission presided over by Lord Pearson will do this.

Stamp and Orr L.JJ. delivered concurring opinions.

Note:
This is not in any way a leading case, but it provides a good instance of the various items for which one may claim damages in a personal injury suit. Translated into 1987 prices, the economic loss (lost income and increased expenditure) totalled £101,801 and the human loss (pain and suffering, loss of amenities) £111,055. In personal injury cases as a whole, economic loss and human harm come out about 50–50.

Important cases include *Lim Poh Choo* v. *Camden H.A.* [1979] 2 All E.R. 910 (H.L.), where Lord Scarman refused to follow Lord Denning's "radical reappraisal," which would have reduced the award by 45 per cent., but deplored the actual position and implored the legislature to improve it; also *Housecroft* v. *Burnett* [1986] 1 All E.R. 332 (C.A.), where awards for human loss were upgraded to take account of inflation.

These cases involved largish sums (about £520,000 and £350,000 in 1987 prices), and doubtless awards will increase substantially as well as nominally as doctors get even cleverer at keeping human wrecks expensively afloat so that their non-enjoyment of life may be maximally prolonged. Medical negligence claims tend to be the most expensive, and local health authorities are more than occasionally facing claims of £1 million or more; as they do not insure, the effect of the incidence of such liabilities is not spread through the country or across the years, and the impact in a particular area on, say, new hospital buildings or equipment may be severe.

But the great majority of claims are much smaller, for a variety of reasons (free medical treatment, net income loss, deductions for collateral benefits, ungenerous judges): nearly half the successful plaintiffs in the High Court get less than £5,000, the maximum that can be awarded in the County Court, where most awards are naturally smaller. The expense is much greater than the award, since most lawyers are paid by the parties even if most doctors are paid by the state, and costs, which exceed awards in the County Court, nearly equal them in the smaller High Court cases. The relationship between awards to victims and rewards to their lawyers may be seen in the offer by the manufacturers of the noxious drug Opren: £2,275,000 for the victims and £4,000,000 for their lawyers.

Economic Loss

A. *Lost Income*
(1) *For how long?* Although in this case the plaintiff's normal earning life was not shortened, a victim may die early as a result of his injuries. Can such a victim claim only what he would have earned during the years now left to him, or can he also claim what he would have earned, and not spent on himself, during the years of which he has been deprived? The House of Lords opted for the latter solution in *Pickett* v. *British Rail Engineering* [1980] A.C. 136, which leads to tiresome discussions about how much the claimant would have spent on himself/actual dependants/possible dependants, etc. This claim no longer transmits to the victim's estate, as it did at the time of *Hill* v. *Chief Constable of West Yorkshire* [1987] 1 All E.R. 1173 (above p. 32).

(2) *How much?*
(i) Income is taxed and damages are not. So the defendant makes good only the plaintiff's "take-home" pay. As to tax this was decided in *Gourley's* case [1956] A.C. 185 (not followed in Australia, (*Atlas Tiles* v. *Briers*, (1978) 21 A.L.R. 129 (H.Ct.Aus.)) and as to contractual pension contributions by *Dews* v. *N.C.B.* [1987] 2 All E.R. 545 (H.L.).

(ii) People's income often rises as they grow older because of (a) inflation and (b) promotion and seniority. The courts generally ignore (a) (*Auty* v. *N.C.B.* [1985] 1 All E.R. 930 (C.A.)), and take account of (b). Overpaid but insecure Yuppies may present problems.

(iii) Future gains are birds in the bush, while present damages are birds in the hand. Folk-wisdom operates. Courts award a plaintiff less than he would probably have earned, because he might not have earned it.

(iv) The plaintiff is receiving money now in place of income and expenditure in the future. A discount is therefore applied. On the other hand, he is receiving money now that he was entitled to receive when he was injured, or, in deference to Englishry, at the moment he formally demanded it. He must therefore obtain interest, a matter which has given rise to not very interesting discussion.

(3) *Earnings, ability to earn, or ability to work?* If the victim continues to receive wages during his incapacity to work (and he has a statutory right to it now for 28 weeks—Social Security Act 1985 s.18(1)), he suffers no "loss of earnings" with which to charge the tortfeasor. It can, however, be said that he has nevertheless suffered a "loss of earning capacity," as may also be said of a person who has not lost his job but would have difficulty in finding another as good. Just as the courts are prepared to give damages for "need for medical treatment" though there have been no "medical expenses," so they give damages for "loss of earning capacity" though it is not proved that any earnings will be lost. These are called "*Smith* v. *Manchester*" damages, after the case at (1974) 17 K.I.R. 1, confirmed in *Moeliker* v. *Reyrolle* [1977] 1 All E.R. 9 (C.A.). Such damages may be substantial (£35,000 in *Foster* v. *Tyne & Wear C.C.* [1986] 1 All E.R. 567); and £5,000 (worth £10,000 at age 18) was awarded to an infant injured at one month, whose future was entirely speculative (*Mitchell* v. *Liverpool H.A.* (C.A., *The Times*, June 17, 1985)).

Some people, of course, work without being paid. The housewife is the classic example. Until recently the housewife had no claim for her inability to do the housework. The husband, on the other hand, was able to claim something for the loss of her assistance in the home. The husband's action is abolished by the Administration of Justice Act 1982, s.2. S.9 of the same enactment makes the tortfeasor liable for the victim's inability to perform gratuitous family services, but applies to Scotland only. In England such a claim had been endorsed by *Daly* v. *General Steam Navigation Co.* [1980] 3 All E.R. 696 (C.A.).

B. *Increased outgoings*

(1) *Medical expenses.* Although treatment under the National Health Service is free, patients who go to a private specialist can send the bill to the defendant (Law Reform (Personal Injuries) Act of 1948, s.2(4)). The rule in the Criminal Injuries Compensation Scheme is much more stringent (above p. 159).

(2) *Nursing.* The plaintiff may need attention after leaving hospital. Having a nurse to live in costs a lot. Having a member of the family do the nursing costs the patient nothing (though it may cost the family something if someone has to give up a job to do the nursing). The Court of Appeal adheres to its view, shared by the Pearson Commission, that the victim's *need for treatment* is one of the items of his loss and that the defendant must pay its value, even if that need is met without cost to the plaintiff himself. The damages, which belong to the plaintiff and are unaffected by any private agreement between the victim and the family nurse, need not equal the commercial value of the services and must not exceed it (*Housecroft* v. *Burnett* [1986] 1 All E.R. 343).

H. WEST & SON v. SHEPHARD

House of Lords [1964] A.C. 326; [1963] 2 W.L.R. 1359; 107 S.J. 454; [1963] 2 All E.R. 625

The plaintiff, a woman of 41 years of age, was dreadfully injured in a street accident brought about by the negligence of the defendant's servant. She suffered from cerebral atrophy and paralysis of all four limbs. She could not speak, but was able to move her right hand, and changes in her facial expression testified to a capacity to distinguish different foods and recognise people. She needed constant hospital nursing, and there was no prospect of improvement during the five years she was expected to live.

Paull J. gave £500 for loss of expectation of life, and £17,500 general damages. This sum he reached by referring to *Wise* v. *Kaye* [1962] 1 Q.B. 638, where the

Court of Appeal had upheld an award of £15,000 to a plaintiff rendered permanently unconscious.

The defendant's appeal to the Court of Appeal was dismissed, and his further appeal to the House of Lords was also dismissed (Lord Reid and Lord Devlin dissenting).

Lord Reid (dissenting): . . . I can go straight to the question of general importance—What is the basis on which damages for serious injuries are awarded? The determination of that question in the ordinary case where the injured person is fully conscious of his disability will go far to decide how to deal with a case like *Wise* v. *Kaye* ([1962] 1 Q.B. 638) where the injured person was wholly unconscious with no prospect of ever regaining consciousness or like the present case where the respondent is only conscious to a slight extent.

In the ordinary case of a man losing a leg or sustaining a permanent internal injury, he is entitled to recover in respect of his pain and suffering: if he is fortunate in suffering little pain he must get a smaller award. So it is not disputed that where an injured person does not suffer at all because of unconsciousness he gets no award under this head. Nothing was awarded in *Wise's* case and nothing has been awarded in this case. On the other hand no one doubts that damages must be awarded irrespective of the man's mental condition or the extent of his suffering where there is financial loss. That will cover the cost of treatment or alleviation of his condition just as much as it covers the cost of repairing or renewing his property. And it will cover loss of earning power: there may be a question whether some deduction should be made where his outgoings will be less than they would have been if there had been no accident, so as to reach his net financial loss, but that does not arise in the present case.

The difficulty is in connection with what is often called loss of amenity and with curtailment of his expectation of life. If there had been no curtailment of his expectation of life the man whose injuries are permanent has to look forward to a life of frustration and handicap and he must be compensated, so far as money can do it, for that and for the mental strain and anxiety which results. But I would agree with Sellers L.J. in *Wise's* case that a brave man who makes light of his disabilities and finds other outlets to replace activities no longer open to him must not receive less compensation on that account.

There are two views about the true basis for this kind of compensation. One is that the man is simply being compensated for the loss of his leg or the impairment of his digestion. The other is that his real loss is not so much his physical injury as the loss of those opportunities to lead a full and normal life which are now denied to him by his physical condition—for the multitude of deprivations and even petty annoyances which he must tolerate. Unless I am prevented by authority I would think that the ordinary man is, at least after the first few months, far less concerned about his physical injury than about the dislocation of his normal life. So I would think that compensation should be based much less on the nature of the injuries than on the extent of the injured man's consequential difficulties in his daily life. It is true that in practice one tends to look at the matter objectively and to regard the physical loss of an eye or a limb as the subject for compensation. But I think that is because the consequences of such a loss are very much the same for all normal people. If one takes the case of injury to an internal organ, I think the true view becomes apparent. It is more difficult to say there that the plaintiff is being paid for the physical damage done to his liver or stomach or even his brain, and much more reasonable to say that he is being paid for the extent to which that injury will prevent him from living a full and normal life and for what he will suffer from being unable to do so.

If that is so, then I think it must follow that if a man's injuries make him wholly unconscious so that he suffers none of these daily frustrations or inconveniences, he ought to get less than the man who is every day acutely conscious of what he suffers and what he has lost. I do not say that he should get nothing. This is not a question that can be decided logically. I think that there are two elements, what he has lost and what he must feel about it, and of the two I think the latter is generally the more important to the injured man. To my mind there is something unreal in saying that a man who knows and feels nothing should get the same as a man who has to live with and put up with his disabilities, merely because they have sustained comparable physical injuries. It is no more possible to compensate an unconscious man than it is to compensate a dead man. The fact that the damages can give no benefit or satisfaction to the injured man and can only go to those who inherit the dead man's estate would not be a good reason for withholding damages which are legally due. But it is, in my view, a powerful argument against the view that there is no analogy between a dead man and a man who is unconscious and that a man who is unconscious ought to be treated as if he were fully conscious.

It is often said that it is scandalous that it should be cheaper to kill a man than to maim him, and that it would be monstrous if the defendant had to pay less because in addition to inflicting physical injuries he had made the plaintiff unconscious. I think that such criticism is misconceived. Damages are awarded not to punish the wrongdoer but to compensate the person injured, and a dead man cannot be compensated. Loss to his estate can be made good, and we can give some compensation to those whom he leaves behind. Perhaps we should do more for them—but not by inflating the claim of the dead man's executor, for then the money may go to undeserving distant relatives or residuary legatees or even to the Treasury if he dies intestate and without heirs. And it is already the case that it may benefit the defendant to injure the plaintiff more severely. If he is injured so severely that he can only live a year or two at most the damages will be much less than if he is less severely injured so that he may survive for many years. . . .

Coming to the facts of this case I would accept the sum of £1,600 which has been awarded to cover special damage, loss of earnings and loss of expectation of life but I would reduce the general damages of £17,500. I would consider separately the objective and the subjective element arising from the respondent's injuries. Accepting that in view of her shortened expectation of life £17,500 would be a fair sum if the respondent were fully conscious of her position. I would think that not more than £5,000 of that ought to be attributed to the actual physical injuries, and then the question is to what extent the respondent is conscious and suffering. Unfortunately we have nothing to go by except three medical reports and on this matter they do not take us very far. It would seem that the respondent has some but not very much appreciation of her surroundings and she seems to suffer no pain. I think that perhaps £4,000 would be appropriate here. And then perhaps insufficient attention has been given to expense which her husband may incur in tending her and providing amenities if her condition should improve slightly. So I would substitute a figure in the region of £10,000 for the sum of £17,500 which has been awarded.

Lord Devlin also dissented.

Lord Morris: . . . The fact of unconsciousness is therefore relevant in respect of and will eliminate those heads or elements of damage which can only exist by being felt or thought or experienced. The fact of unconsciousness does not, however, eliminate the actuality of the deprivations of the ordinary experiences and amenities of life which may be the inevitable result of some physical injury. . . .

Lord Tucker agreed with Lord Morris.

Lord Pearce: . . . The loss of happiness of the individual plaintiffs is not, in my opinion, a practicable or correct guide to reasonable compensation in cases of personal injury. A man of fortitude is not made less happy because he loses a limb. . . .

Note:

The Pearson Commission recommended that "non-pecuniary [*sic*] damages should no longer be recoverable for permanent unconsciousness." It also recommended that damages should no longer be awarded for the mere fact, as opposed to the knowledge, that one's life has been shortened. Both these recommendations are sound. Unfelt losses need no compensation. Only the second recommendation has been implemented: Administration of Justice Act 1982, s.1.

The Commission's main proposal about non-economic loss is, however, entirely unacceptable: no damages whatever for the first three months of pain, suffering and loss of amenity. But the first three months are the worst; that is when people pain and suffer most; indeed, there is often no pain at all thereafter—19 out of 20 injured workmen are back at work before the three months are up. Quite so. The saving in pay-outs would be immense. What would be done with the money thus saved? Most of it would go to those whose awards are already very large, but not quite large enough to make up fully for the fancy job they no longer do. Did the Commission not realise that money is the great divider, suffering the great equaliser? Why ignore so much human harm while meeting every money loss? Is getting and spending more important than feeling? Is it because personal injury *costs* or because it *hurts* that it rated a Royal Commission? If the former, why was property damage not included in their brief? Or did the Commission just feel that damages *in* money must be damages *for* money? At any rate the recommendation is nauseating in its implications and miserable in its effect—to free the rapist and the minor thug from all civil responsibility. Principle ousted by slide-rule.

Mrs. Shephard could not use what the House of Lords held her entitled to. Recently it has been said that a plaintiff, at any rate if permanently incapacitated, should receive what he will need, not what he has lost. The political implications of the slogan "To each according to his needs" may not have been appreciated. The other suggestion that damages should be paid in instalments rather than in a lump sum also smacks of paternalism.

It is worth observing that although awards of damages have got bigger (as the pound got smaller), the cost of liability insurance is still quite low for persons apt to cause personal injuries. This is largely due to the fact that the tortfeasor does not have to reimburse the state for the cost of curing the victim through the National Health Service nor for maintaining him through social security payments. In other countries of Western Europe the social insurer pays the victim and then claims from the tortfeasor. Our system is better.

One way to cut down the total of damages is to find that the component items "duplicate" each other, or "overlap." Spot the fallacy in the following passage: " 'Future care' is awarded on the footing that [the plaintiff] is completely incapacitated and has to be kept at great expense all his future life. 'Future earnings' are awarded on the footing that he was not incapacitated at all and would be earning all his future life. I cannot think it right in principle that he should have both." *Croke* v. *Wiseman* [1981] 3 All E.R. 852, 856, *per* Lord Denning M.R.

PARRY v. CLEAVER

House of Lords [1970] A.C. 1; [1969] 2 W.L.R. 821; [1969] 1 All E.R. 555; [1969] 1 Lloyd's Rep. 183

The plaintiff policeman was on point duty when the defendant motorist carelessly ran into him. He consequently had to leave the police force at age 36, with an invalid pension for life. He took a civilian job, but not only were the civilian wages less than his police wages but the civilian retirement pension was smaller than his police pension would have been, and payable from age 65, not age 48.

The question was whether the invalid pension he was receiving was to be set off against his loss as regards wages as well as against his loss as regards retirement pension. The trial judge held not, but the Court of Appeal reversed ([1968] 1 Q.B. 195). The House of Lords, by a majority, held that the invalid pension should be set off against the pension loss but not against the loss of wages.

Lord Pearce: My Lords, the appellant was discharged from the police force as a result of his injuries. He took civilian employment at a lower wage. There is no dispute that the respondent must recompense him for the difference between the wages he would have earned and the wages which he did in fact earn for the period until he would in any event have retired from the police force. But from that time onwards he will no longer be losing any wages as a result of the accident since he would, in any event, have ceased to earn them. But owing to his having had to leave the force early his pension will be lower than it would have been if he had continued in the force until his proper retiring age of 48. There is no dispute that he is entitled to recompense from the age of 48 for the difference between the pension which he would have got but for the accident and the pension which he will in fact receive. That is a simple comparison of pensions. Since he is claiming for that period in respect of diminution of pension it is obvious that he must give credit for the smaller pension which he will get against the larger pension which he would have got.

The problem here is whether, during the period when he is under the age of 48 and is still claiming a loss of wages, he must give credit for the premature pension which he receives from his employers during what should have been, but for the accident, his working time on full pay in the force. The fact that he must give credit after the age of 48 for his actual pension during the period when he is claiming, as a pensioner in any event, in respect only of a diminution of pension, does not shed light on the problem.

The cases on this subject show a conflict of view, each side of which has been attractively presented to us. One may summarise the two points of view in this way. On behalf of the appellant it is said that an insurance, or a pension, are the product of a man's service or a man's thrift. Their character, like that of charitable gifts, is such that it was never intended, nor is it just, that a tortfeasor should take over the benefit of them by getting a credit for them in the account of damages that he must pay. And it is they rather than the accident which are the true source of the benefit. For the respondent it is said that damages are not to be punitive; that *Gourley's* case ([1956] A.C. 185) had laid down that only a plaintiff's actual loss to his pocket can be recovered; that since the accident caused the pension as well as the losses, both must be taken into account; and that for good or ill, the smooth with the rough, a defendant takes a plaintiff as he finds him; so that if he knocks down a pensionable plaintiff he gets the benefit of the pension.

The word "punitive" gives no help. It is simply a word used when a court thinks it unfair that a defendant should be saddled with liability for a particular item. There is nothing punitive in calling on a defendant to pay that which the law says is a just recompense for the injury the plaintiff has caused. Nor does causation, I think, really provide an answer. The pension could not have arisen had not the man by the terms of his employment earned it or by his own thrift provided for it outside his employment. That is the real source of the pension. On the other hand, the potential pension thus provided would not have come into play had not the accident occurred. Each is certainly a *causa sine qua non* and probably each is entitled to be called a *causa causans*. Strict causation seems to provide no satisfactory line of demarcation. It would only lead one to a compromise like that contained in the [Law Reform (Personal Injuries)] Act 1948, whereby both a plaintiff and a defendant were given some advantage from national insurance benefits. This was quite a sensible compromise, but it is difficult to find any legal principle to justify it.

Again, *Gourley's* case does not, nor was it intended to, throw light on this problem. By a convention (rather than any clear principle) which the weight and idiosyncrasies of modern taxation had made obsolete, tax was disregarded in assessment of damages. *Gourley's* case corrected this and laid down that in a plaintiff's claim for damages it was his actual net loss of wages, not his theoretical gross loss which must be regarded. The real loss must be measured. But that case was not directed to considering how far adventitious payments received by a plaintiff must be introduced into the credit side of his account. In dealing with the point before them in *Gourley's* case their Lordships relied on the dominant rule that there should be *restitutio in integrum*. A man should be put financially in the position in which he would have been but for the accident. But if they were intending to say that that general rule applied strictly to all benefits from every source received by a plaintiff, then the plaintiff must clearly bring into account all benefits from public subscription or kindness of relatives or private insurance. Clearly they had no such intention. . . .

The maxim that a defendant must take a plaintiff as he finds him does not solve this problem. True, if he knocks down a high wage earner he must take the consequences; and if he knocks down a low wage earner or a man of character who will go on earning wages in spite of disabilities, a defendant gains thereby. But, if pressed to its logical conclusion, that maxim would entitle the defendant to say that he takes the plaintiff as he finds him in respect of generous relatives who will subsidise him in misfortune and thrifty private insurances which have cancelled out the losses caused by the defendant. One may cut down the maxim by saying that a defendant takes a plaintiff as he finds him in respect of all potential benefits from the [plaintiff's] employment. There is no inherent logic in this. It may provide a convenient line to draw if, but only if, the line is one which there is reason to draw at that particular point. And on which side of that line does one put gifts of a generous employer?

One must, I think, start with the firm basis that *Bradburn* v. *Great Western Railway Co.* ((1874) L.R. 10 Ex. 1) was rightly decided and that the benefits from a private insurance by the plaintiff are not to be taken into account. . . .

No help can be derived from various cases where courts have drawn a distinction between pensions where there was a discretion to withhold the pension and pensions where there was no such discretion. If pensions in general are to be taken into account, then such a discretion does not take them out of the account. It merely calls for some large or small or negligible discount in the value to be attached to the pension, according to whether the withholding of it is a real practical danger or (as in most cases) a mere theoretical danger.

Nor do I think that a dividing line can be drawn between contributory and non-contributory pensions. It would be unreal. The present case is an example of the unreality. There was no pension fund and the employers did not pay their contribution. The whole arrangement was merely a part of the wage structure, and no doubt for bargaining about wages it was useful to allocate notional contributions to employers and employed. What the employer pays actually or notionally to a pensions fund is part of the total cost which he is prepared to pay in respect of the employee's service. . . .

Throughout the whole subject . . . run equitable considerations. It seems to me possible that on those grounds there might be some difference of approach where it is the employer himself who is the defendant tortfeasor, and the pension rights in question come from an insurance arrangement which he himself has made with the plaintiff as his employee.

If one starts on the basis that *Bradburn's* case ((1874) L.R. 10 Ex. 1), decided on fairness and justice and public policy, is correct in principle, one must see whether there is some reason to except from it pensions which are derived from a man's contract with his employer. These, whether contributory or non-contributory, flow from the work which a man has done. They are part of what the employer is prepared to pay for his services. The fact that they flow from past work equates them to rights which flow from an insurance privately effected by him. He has simply paid for them by weekly work instead of weekly premiums.

Is there anything else in the nature of these pension rights derived from work which puts them into a different class from pension rights derived from private insurance? Their "character" is the same, that is to say, they are intended by payer and payee to benefit the workman and not to be a subvention for wrongdoers who will cause him damage.

In *National Insurance Co. of New Zealand Ltd.* v. *Espagne* ((1961) 105 C.L.R. 569, 573), Dixon C.J. said of pension rights that they had the additional and "dis-

tinguishing characteristic, namely they are conferred on him not only independently of the existence in him of a right of redress against others but so that they
may be enjoyed by him although he may enforce that right: they are the product of
a disposition in his favour intended for his enjoyment and not provided in relief of
any liability in others fully to compensate him."

This view was accepted by the High Court of Australia in *Jones* v. *Gleeson*
((1965) A.L.J.R. 258) . . . ; a police disability pension was there disregarded as
irrelevant to damages.

Moreover, one of the aspects of a service pension, and even more so of a policeman's pension, is that they are not intended necessarily as any substitute for the
capacity to earn. The familiar pattern is that a man may earn in a civilian employment when his service ends (whether prematurely or not) and thus enjoy both his
pension and his civilian wage. His pension is thus a personal benefit additional to
anything that he may be able to earn by way of wages. In this case the plaintiff
would from the age of 48 be receiving his full pension as well as earning civilian
wages.

In my opinion, the character of the pension rights in this case brings them within
the general principle of *Bradburn's* case ((1874) L.R. 10 Ex. 1), and there is no
adequate equitable reason to exclude them from it.

Parliament in 1959 has by implication expressed a similar view on the fairness
and justice of the matter and the question of public policy inherent in it. The cases
under Lord Campbell's Act had taken a different turn and, unlike the cases under
the common law, had brought pensions into account in assessing damages. The
Fatal Accidents Act 1959 directed that pensions should *not* be taken into account.
It may have done this, regardless of what should be the fair and just principle,
simply in order to bring cases under that Act into line with common law cases. If so,
it would be unfortunate that the common law cases should now change direction
and get out of line once more. It is, however, far more likely that Parliament
excluded the taking into account of pensions because it thought that the principle of
exclusion laid down in common law cases was fairer and more in accordance with
public policy and that, therefore, cases under Lord Campbell's Act should be
brought into line with it. If this be so, it is some confirmation of the view which I
have expressed.

I would, therefore, allow the appeal. . . .

Lord Wilberforce: . . . On the two related grounds, each of which would separately
justify the conclusion, namely (a) that the police pension is payable in any event
and is not dependent on loss of earning capacity and (b) that the pension is to be
regarded as the reward or earning of pre-injury service and therefore not entering
into the computation of lost post-injury wages, I would reach the conclusion that it
should not be deducted against damages recoverable from a third person for a
proved loss of earning capacity.

Lord Reid: . . . So by having to leave the police force the appellant lost two things:
first, the wage which he would actually have received until his retirement from the
police force if he had not been injured, *i.e.* his gross wage of £21 18s. 3d. minus
the sum which would have been retained as a contribution £1 3s. 1d.; and secondly,
the opportunity, by continuing to serve and to make this contribution, to obtain his
full retirement pension. On the other hand, he gained two things, the wage which
he received as a clerk, which must admittedly be set-off against the wage which he
lost, and the ill-health pension. The main question in the case is whether this pension must be brought into account, and for the reasons which I have given I am of
opinion that it must not. That is the position up to the retiring age from the police
force. Thereafter the position is different.

For a time after retirement from the police force he would still have been able to
work at other employment, so allowance must be made for that. As regards police

pension his loss after reaching police retiring age would be the difference between the full pension which he would have received if he had served his full time and his ill-health pension. It has been asked why his ill-health pension is to be brought into account at this point if not brought into account for the earlier period. The answer is that in the earlier period we are not comparing like with like. He lost wages but he gained something different in kind, a pension. But with regard to the period after retirement we are comparing like with like. Both the ill-health pension and the full retirement pension are the products of the same insurance scheme; his loss in the later period is caused by his having been deprived of the opportunity to continue in insurance so as to swell the ultimate product of that insurance from an ill-health to a retirement pension. There is no question as regards that period of a loss of one kind and a gain of a different kind.

Lord Morris (dissenting): . . . When the plaintiff, after leaving the police force, very properly obtained the best employment that he could get, his successful efforts were in one sense in relief of the wrongdoer. Yet it is beyond question that the new earned salary is a relevant fact to be taken into account in calculating the plaintiff's economic loss. Nor is anything achieved by saying that the plaintiff's police pension is something that he had earned. So he had. Most good positions and good entitlements have been earned. The arrangements concerning the pension were essentially a part and an integral part of his condition of employment. By his work and his labour he earned both his pay and his prospects of having a pension or of having other benefits. But it is with earnings and receipts that we are concerned. In his new employment the plaintiff earned his money. Yet regard must be had to that money in deciding as to economic loss. In his new employment he has a pension scheme, and in future he will have a pension: that he will have earned by his work and by entering into a contract which provides for a pension. But all these matters are the facts in the economic situation. Though in advancing the claim of the plaintiff reference is made to the terms of his service in the police force in order to base a claim for loss, it is nevertheless said that certain sums which he received pursuant to those terms of service and which offset his loss are to be ignored. In my view, that is quite unwarranted. As Lord Denning M.R. said ([1968] 1 Q.B. 195, 207), the contract for a contributory pension was "part and parcel of his employment." I agree also with Winn L.J. when he said, at p. 212: "In my judgment, where a plaintiff asserts that a tort has deprived him of the whole or part of what he formerly earned from an employment, we must reduce his claim to the extent not only of all he is earning or able to earn in another employment but also of all that his former employment still produces in the form of pension as a set-off against lost earnings, no less than against loss of potential pension."

The view which I have accepted does not in any way conflict with or diminish acceptance of *Bradburn's* case and does not involve that gifts from benevolent persons need be brought into consideration. If someone makes a purely voluntary and personal decision to insure himself against accidents he is choosing to use some of his money or some of his savings in a particular way just as he would be doing if he saved some of his money and invested it. If he insures against accidents he will hope that no accident will befall him and he will be well content to have no return from the expenditure which is involved in the payment of premiums. He may be one in whose case there is already some provision against sustaining economic loss. He may feel that in the event of accident befalling him he would welcome the receipt of a sum of money to compensate him in ways that would not be possible as a result of a successful claim at law. He may contemplate situations in which no claim against anyone would be possible or would succeed. I think that it would seem to most people, as it seemed to Bramwell B. and Pigott B., that there would be neither reason nor justice in any suggestion that money received under such a contract of insurance should be taken into consideration. So, also, would it seem to most people to be contrary to reason and justice if the impulses of sympathy and of concern which prompt gifts or benevolent arrangements lead to the result that a claim against a defendant has to be diminished. All these matters are purely the personal and private affairs of a plaintiff. It is not for a defendant to inquire what use a plaintiff has in the past made of his own money. If a defendant who is sued asks the plaintiff whether or not he had had a gift from a friend or whether or not he had saved money and invested it and whether his investments had prospered and, if so, to what extent, or whether or not he had taken out any insurance policies the reply, firm though courteous, could well be that the defendant should only concern himself with his own affairs. The position will be entirely different if the plaintiff, in asserting his loss, himself stated that he has a contract with an employer and claims that he has lost the remuneration for which that contract provided. If a plaintiff sets up a contract of employment as the basis of his claim and asserts that he has lost his salary under the contract, he must for the sake of completeness acknowledge, if it be the fact, that under the very same contract he is receiving some sum less than his salary. If under the contract he continues, in the events that have happened, to receive half his pay he cannot assert that he has lost all his pay. If he receives part of his pay, even if it is given the name of sick pay, he cannot assert that he has lost all his pay. Nor can he say that, because he had the wisdom to obtain a contract under which it was provided that he would get his half pay or sick pay, he may ignore their receipt and claim the amount of his full pay. Nor can he say that it was because of his service in the past or because he had earned them that his half pay or his sick pay came to him with the result that he could claim his whole pay as lost pay. He would not have lost his whole pay. If, under the terms of a contract of employment the time comes when instead of having full pay or half pay or sick pay a person retires with a pension, the loss which he suffers is the difference between the amount of his pay and the amount of his pension. If it is said that a pension is neither pay nor insurance benefit, then I would say that where there is no discretionary element, and where the arrangements leading to a pension are an essential part of the contract of employment, then the pension payments are very much more akin to pay than to anything else. Indeed, it is often asserted that a pension is a form of deferred pay and is taken into account in fixing remuneration. A man would measure his loss by comparing what he used to get under his contract with what he now gets under his contract. That is the financial loss that he has suffered. That is the loss which the defendant should make good. . . .

Lord Pearson (dissenting): . . . As to causation, was the pension in the present case too remote in the sense that it was caused by something remote from and wholly collateral to the accident and its direct and natural train of consequences? The accident disabled the plaintiff, and it caused his compulsory retirement, and as the employment was pensionable—had pension rights attached to it—his retirement was not a retirement with nothing to live on but a retirement on pension. By reason of the accident his salary ceased and his pension began. The pension was intended to take the place *pro tanto* of his salary. I do not see how you can reasonably separate the cessation of the employment from the commencement of the pension. Both salary and pension were payable under the same contract, both were derived from the same employment, the one being current remuneration for present services and the other being deferred remuneration for past services, but each being part of the reward for his services under that contract in that employment. The plaintiff claims that the cessation of salary was caused by the accident, and it must follow, in my opinion, that the commencement of the pension was equally caused by the accident, because the two events coincided in time and were linked together. In the circumstances it is grievously artificial to contend that the loss of salary is admissible and to be taken into account but the receipt of the pension is to be excluded and disregarded. Moreover, it is conceded that the salary earned in the new clerical employment under a different employer is to be taken into account and deducted from the lost salary in ascertaining the net loss. That clerical employment is a new employment coming into existence under a new contract made some time after the old salary had ceased. If that new salary is not too remote, how can the pension under the old contract be too remote? . . .

Note:

This marginal decision, which made P.C. Parry better off by £3.92 per week, is very regrettable (and arguably regretted—see *Hussain* v. *New Taplow Paper Mills* [1988] 1 All E.R. 541 (H.L.)). It gives a special bonus to people whose terms of employment provide for an invalidity or disablement pension, *i.e.* those, such as policemen and firemen, whose job exposes them to particular risk. Sometimes that risk results from carelessness on someone's part. When such carelessness occurs, it is idiotic to give the victim more than enough (and the Criminal Injuries Compensation Scheme does not: see above p. 160). He may not have accepted the risk, but he has been paid for it already. This consideration entirely justifies the "firemen's rule," whereby a fireman injured in a fire cannot claim damages from the person who negligently started it. The rule, adopted by the two most liberal jurisdictions in the United States, was rejected by our House of Lords in *Ogwo* v. *Taylor* [1987] 3 All E.R. 961. The combination of *Parry* and *Ogwo* is quite unacceptable.

The state provides a bewildering variety of social security benefits. Sometimes the recipient has a tort claim. Should the tort damages be reduced because the claimant has received a social security benefit? The Pearson Commission adopted the very sound view-point that all such benefits should be taken into account. The present statutory scheme, which may shortly be changed, is that in personal injury cases only one-half of certain social security benefits are deducted, and for the first five years only; in death cases benefits are ignored altogether. Where there is no statutory provision, the courts tend to deduct the value of ascertainable social security benefits (*Lincoln* v. *Hayman* [1982] 2 All E.R. 819 (C.A.)).

The state may also provide benefits in kind. It has now been laid down by the Administration of Justice Act 1982, s.5 that if a victim of personal injuries is maintained in a hospital at public expense, any saving attributable thereto must be deducted from his claim for lost income.

Section 2.—Fatal Accidents

MALLETT v. McMONAGLE

House of Lords [1970] A.C. 166; [1969] 2 W.L.R. 767; 113 S.J. 207; [1969] 2 All E.R. 178; [1969] 1 Lloyd's Rep. 127; 6 K.I.R. 322

Lord Diplock: My Lords, the purpose of an award of damages under the Fatal Accidents Acts is to provide the widow and other dependants of the deceased with a capital sum which with prudent management will be sufficient to supply them with material benefits of the same standard and duration as would have been provided for them out of the earnings of the deceased had he not been killed by the tortious act of the respondents . . .

. . . it has become usual both in England and in Northern Ireland to arrive at the total award by multiplying a figure assessed as the amount of the annual "dependency" by a number of "year's purchase." If the figure for the annual "dependency" remained constant and could be assessed with certainty and if the number of years for which it would have continued were also ascertainable with certainty it would be possible in times of stable currency, interest rates and taxation to calculate with certainty the number of years' purchase of the dependency which would provide a capital sum sufficient to produce an annuity equal in amount to the dependency for the number of years for which it would have continued. If the estimated "dependency" did not remain constant but altered at intervals during the period of its enjoyment an accurate assessment of the appropriate award would involve calculating the present value of a series of annuities for fixed periods progressively deferred. For reasons to which I shall advert this is seldom if ever done.

Anticipated future variations in "dependency" are normally dealt with by an adjustment in the multiplicand to be multiplied by the single multiplier—the number of years' purchase. . . .

The starting point in any estimate of the number of years that a dependency would have endured is the number of years between the date of the deceased's death and that at which he would have reached normal retiring age. That falls to be reduced to take account of the chance not only that he might not have lived until retiring age but also the chance that by illness or injury he might have been disabled from gainful occupation. The former risk can be calculated from available actuarial tables. The latter cannot. There is also the chance that the widow may die before the deceased would have reached the normal retiring age (which can be calculated from actuarial tables). . . . But in so far as the chances that death or incapacitating illness or injury would bring the dependency to an end increase in later years when, from the nature of the arithmetical calculation their effect on the present capital value of the annual dependency diminishes, a small allowance for them may be sufficient where the deceased and his widow were young and in good health at the date of his death. . . . In cases such as the present where the deceased was aged 25 and the appellant, his widow, about the same age, courts have not infrequently awarded 16 years' purchase of the dependency. It is seldom that this number of years' purchase is exceeded. It represents the capital value of an annuity certain for a period of 26 years at interest rates of 4 per cent., 29 years at interest rates of $4\frac{1}{2}$ per cent. or 33 years at interest rates of 5 per cent. Having regard to the uncertainties to be taken into account 16 years would appear to represent a reasonable maximum number of years' purchase where the deceased died in his twenties. Even if the period were extended to 40 years, $i.e.$ when the deceased would have attained the age of 65, the additional number of years' purchase at interest rates of 4 per cent. would be less than four years, at $4\frac{1}{2}$ per cent. would be less than $2\frac{1}{2}$ years, and at 5 per cent. would be little more than one year.

The starting point in any estimate of the amount of the "dependency" is the annual value of the material benefits provided for the dependants out of the earnings of the deceased at the date of his death. But quite apart from inflation with which I have already dealt there are many factors which might have led to variations up or down in the future. His earnings might have increased and with them the amount provided by him for his dependants. They might have diminished with a recession in trade or he might have had spells of unemployment. As his children grew up and became independent the proportion of his earnings spent on his dependants would have been likely to fall. But in considering the effect to be given in the award of damages to possible variations in the dependency there are two factors to be borne in mind. The first is that the more remote in the future is the anticipated change the less confidence there can be in the chances of its occurring and the smaller the allowance to be made for it in the assessment. The second is that as a matter of the arithmetic of the calculation of present value, the later the change takes place the less will be its effect on the total award of damages. Thus at interest rates of $4\frac{1}{2}$ per cent. the present value of an annuity for 20 years of which the first 10 years are at £100 per annum and the second 10 years at £200 per annum is about 12 years' purchase of the arithmetical average annuity of £150 per annum, whereas if the first 10 years are at £200 per annum and the second 10 years at £100 per annum the present value is about 14 years' purchase of the arithmetical mean of £150 per annum. If therefore the chances of variations in the "dependency" are to be reflected in the multiplicand of which the years' purchase is the multiplier variations in the dependency which are not expected to take place until after 10 years should have only a relatively small effect in increasing or diminishing the "dependency" used for the purpose of assessing the damages.

At the date of his death on 21st November 1964, the deceased, Mr. William John Mallett, then aged 25, was employed in his home town of Londonderry as a machine operative by Monarch Electric, Ltd., at an average weekly wage of £12

16s. 7d. From these wages his average weekly contribution to the maintenance of the appellant, his wife, then aged 24, and his three infant children was £9 10s. a week. But for six weeks before his death he was receiving an additional £6 to £10 per week for spare-time work as a vocalist in a dance band and from these (untaxed) receipts he gave the appellant for household expenses another £3 10s. on the average. Thus up to six weeks before his death the total "dependency" of the appellant and the children had been £338 per annum but for the last six weeks had risen to £520 per annum.

Between the date of his death and the date of the trial of the appellant's action for damages under the Fatal Accidents Acts (Northern Ireland) 1846–1959 on 18th September 1967, two things happened. Up to January 1967, the average weekly wages of operatives of the grade of the deceased had risen by 17s., but the company by which he was employed had closed down in that month. Londonderry is an area of high unemployment but there was evidence of a witness who said that if the deceased had lived and been out of a job he would have employed him as an asphalter at an average weekly wage of £22 10s. though he would have had to work very long hours at times in order to earn this average wage. These hours would seem to be incompatible with spare-time work with the band, but his average weekly earnings would have been about £2 per week more than during the last six weeks of his life when the "dependency" was £520 per annum.

The jury awarded a total of £22,000 damages. By a majority (Lord MacDermott C.J., and McVeigh L.J.; Curran L.J., dissenting) the Court of Appeal of Northern Ireland set aside this verdict and ordered a new trial. Both Curran L.J. (in his dissenting judgment), and McVeigh L.J., considered that the loss of dependency during the two years and ten months up to the date of the trial might be reasonably assessed at £1,500. This leaves £20,500 for future loss. Accepting, as would be appropriate for a deceased who have been 27 years old at the date of the assessment, 16 years' purchase as the multiplier this means that the multiplicand was a "dependency" of £1,281 per annum or almost two and a half times the actual dependency at the date of the death.

I can see no possible justification for an award of this magnitude. I would dismiss the appeal.

Lord Reid, Lord Morris, Lord Pearce and Lord Wilberforce agreed in dismissing the appeal.

Note:
The award in this case was in respect of economic harm only. That is because between 1846 and 1982 English law did not accept the humane view of Mr. Grewgious in *Edwin Drood* that "Death is *not* a matter of pounds, shillings and pence." The Administration of Justice Act 1982 added the new s.1A to the Fatal Accidents Act 1976 (above p. 79). It is still true that there is no claim for bereavement or grief except under that section, *i.e.* by a spouse for the death of a spouse or a parent for the death of an unmarried minor child. The amount to be awarded is £3,500, subject to variation only for the decedent's contributory negligence. Thus although a resident lover of two years standing can claim for economic loss, subject to reduction if the relationship might not have lasted, there can be no claim for bereavement.

Where the husband is killed, as in *Mallett's* case, the widow can claim the money he would have given her. In *Howitt* v. *Heads* [1973] Q.B. 64 this came to £15,000 (£70,000 in 1987 money) though the husband was killed before the honeymoon was over: the longer you have your husband the less you get for him. Where the wife is killed, the husband can claim the value of her services: if he reasonably gives up his job to mind the kids, then the lost wages (*Mehmet* v. *Perry* [1977] 2 All E.R. 529); if he hires a housekeeper, then the cost of that plus a little extra. Where both parents are killed, the orphans get damages for both the father's money and the mother's services: in *Hay* v. *Hughes* [1975] Q.B. 790 this worked out at £7,900 for the father and £8,500 for the mother (over £29,000 and £31,000 in 1987 money).

Maternal care for the orphans in that case was being supplied by their grandmother, much as marital support may be provided for a widow by a second husband. Parliament has enacted that no account may be taken of the widow's remarriage, and the court ignored the grand-mother's contributions. Not very much is left of the old rule that in wrongful death cases compensation is given only for the net loss attributable to the death after giving credit for any gains thereby accruing to the claimant.

Section 3.—Property Damage

OWNERS OF THE STEAMSHIP MEDIANA v. OWNERS OF LIGHTSHIP COMET (THE "MEDIANA")

House of Lords [1900] A.C. 113; 69 L.J.P. 35; 82 L.T. 95; 16 T.L.R. 194; 48 W.R. 398; 9 Asp.M.L.C. 41

The Mersey Docks and Harbour Board were under a statutory duty to light four stations on the approaches to the River Mersey. For this purpose they had six light-ships, one of which was kept to replace any lightship withdrawn for overhaul and one of which, the *Orion*, was kept for emergencies, at a cost of £1,000 per year, including interest on the capital invested in her.

The *Mediana* collided with the *Comet* and sank her. The Board towed the *Orion* out to take her place, which she occupied for 74 days, a period during which there was no other call for the *Orion's* services. The Board claimed, *inter alia*, "Loss of use of the lightship *Comet*, or hire of the services of the lightship *Orion*—74 days at £4 4s.—£310 6s."

The registrar allowed this item. Phillimore J. disallowed it. The Court of Appeal allowed it [1899] P. 127, and the owners of the *Mediana* appealed without success to the House of Lords.

Earl of Halsbury L.C.: . . . Now, in the particular case before us, apart from a circumstance which I will refer to immediately, the broad proposition seems to me to be that by a wrongful act of the defendants the plaintiffs were deprived of their vessel. When I say deprived of their vessel, I will not use the phrase "the use of the vessel." What right has a wrongdoer to consider what use you are going to make of your vessel? More than one case has been put to illustrate this: for example, the owner of a horse, or of a chair. Supposing a person took away a chair out of my room and kept it for 12 months, could anybody say you had a right to diminish the damages by showing that I did not usually sit in that chair, or that there were plenty of other chairs in the room? The proposition so nakedly stated appears to me to be absurd; but a jury have very often a very difficult task to perform in ascertaining what should be the amount of damages of that sort. I know very well that as a matter of common sense what an arbitrator or a jury very often do is to take a perfectly artificial hypothesis and say, "Well, if you wanted to hire a chair, what would you have to give for it for the period"; and in that way they come to a rough sort of conclusion as to what damages ought to be paid for the unjust and unlawful withdrawal of it from the owner. Here, as I say, the broad principle seems to me to be quite independent of the particular use the plaintiffs were going to make of the thing that was taken, except—and this I think has been the fallacy running through the arguments at the Bar—when you are endeavouring to establish the specific loss of profit, or of something that you otherwise would have got which the law recognises as special damage. In that case you must show it, and by precise evidence, so much so that in the old system of pleading you could not recover damages unless you had made a specific allegation in your pleading so as to give the persons responsible for making good the loss an opportunity of inquiring into it before they came into court. But when we are speaking of general damages no such principle applies at all, and the jury might give whatever they thought would be the proper equivalent for the unlawful withdrawal of the subject-matter then in question. It seems to me that that broad principle comprehends within it many other things. There is no doubt in many cases a jury would say there really has been no damage at all: "We will give the plaintiffs a trifling amount"—not nominal damages, be it observed, but a trifling amount; in other cases it would be more serious.

It appears to me, therefore, that what the noble and learned Lords [in *The Greta Holme* [1897] A.C. 596] . . . intended to point out, and what Lord Herschell gives expression to in plain terms, was that the unlawful keeping back of what belongs to another person is of itself a ground for real damages, not nominal damages at all. Of course, I observe that it has been suggested that this was not an action for trover or detinue; but although those are different forms of action, the principle upon which damages are to be assessed does not depend upon the form of action at all. I put aside cases of trespass where a high-handed procedure or insolent behaviour has been held in law to be a subject of aggravated damages, and the jury might give what are called punitive damages. Leaving that aside, whatever be the form of action, the principle of assessing damages must be the same in all courts and for all forms of what I may call the unlawful detention of another man's property.

My Lords, that seems to me to be so plain that I confess I have been somewhat puzzled to learn that it has been decided in the Admiralty Courts that the loss of the use of a vessel under the circumstances of this case had been treated (if it has really been so treated I have serious doubt about it) as something for which no moneys counted could possibly be allowed. I can only say that I am very glad such a principle has not been affirmed by your Lordships' House, because it seems to me to be inconsistent with principle and very unreasonable in itself. . . .

Note:

In view of the very clear terms of this decision of the House of Lords, it is with some surprise that one finds a recent decision of the Court of Appeal thus represented in the headnote: " . . . since the plaintiffs had not proved that they would have used the copper during the period of detention . . . they were entitled only to nominal damages . . . " *Brandeis Goldschmidt* v. *Western Transport* [1981] Q.B. 864. Intriguing though it is that the plaintiffs recovered only £5 from defendants who wrongly detained 42 tons of their copper for over seven months, during which period its market value fell by £3,588, the decision seems to have turned on the view that if you try to prove you have lost a specific sum and fail to prove it, you can recover nothing; it is a warning for barristers rather than a lesson for students.

Insurance companies do not readily admit that a person whose car has been damaged by the carelessness of their insured is entitled to claim anything for the loss of use of his car, unless he hires a substitute for it and it is reasonable for him to do so (*Moore* v. *D.E.R. Ltd.* [1971] 1 W.L.R. 1476). The decision of *Darbishire* v. *Warran*, below, p. 565, suggests that the courts today might agree with them.

If a person is deprived of the use of a thing owing to another's breach of contract, the contractor is liable only for the value of the use which might foreseeably have been made of the thing: *Cory* v. *Thames Ironworks* (1868) L.R. 3 Q.B. 181.

OWNERS OF DREDGER LIESBOSCH v. OWNERS OF STEAMSHIP EDISON

House of Lords [1933] A.C. 449; 102 L.J.P. 73; 149 L.T. 49; 49 T.L.R. 289; 77 S.J. 176; 38 Com.Cas. 267; 18 Asp.M.L.C. 380; 45 Ll.L.R. 123

The defendants admitted liability for sinking the plaintiff's dredger. The question was how much they had to pay. The history of the case is given in the words of Scrutton L.J. in *The Edison (No. 2)* (1934) 151 L.T. 279, 281: "The plaintiffs, who had bought the dredger for £4,000 and had taken her out to Patras for another

£2,000, making £6,000 in all, and insured her for £5,500, discovered that by her loss that had lost some £23,500, which they proceeded to claim. The claim was made up on the basis: We are very poor, consequently we cannot do what a rich man would have done, and so we have had to make a series of elaborate and expensive arrangements of finance, in order to carry out our harbour contract. Langton J. gave judgment, confirming a reference on those lines for a sum of £19,000 odd, and I can quite understand the defendants' anger, as it was rather provocative to claim for an old dredger more than twice its value on the plaintiffs' own computation. The matter then came to the Court of Appeal, which took the line that it is well established that the damages one can recover for the total loss of a ship are: her value to the owner at the time of the loss, taking into account her engagements, plus interest from the time of the loss; and we assessed the value at £9,000, being of opinion that that more than amply paid the plaintiffs for what they had lost. On appeal, the House of Lords laid down the same principle on which we thought we were acting, dismissed the appeal, and made the plaintiffs pay three-quarters of the costs, but sent the matter to the registrar to assess the damages on the principles they had laid down. The registrar gave £11,000 odd; so that the plaintiffs got £2,000 more on the judgment of the House of Lords."

Lord Wright: . . . The respondents' tortious act involved the physical loss of the dredger; that loss must somehow be reduced to terms of money. But the appellants' actual loss in so far as it was due to their impecuniosity arose from that impecuniosity as a separate and concurrent cause, extraneous to and distinct in character from the tort; the impecuniosity was not traceable to the respondents' acts, and in my opinion was outside the legal purview of the consequences of these acts. The law cannot take account of everything that follows a wrongful act; it regards some subsequent matters as outside the scope of its selection, because "it were infinite for the law to judge the cause of causes," or consequences of consequences. Thus the loss of a ship by collision due to the other vessel's sole fault, may force the shipowner into bankruptcy and that again may involve his family in suffering, loss of education or opportunities in life, but no such loss could be recovered from the wrongdoer. In the varied web of affairs, the law must abstract some consequences as relevant, not perhaps on grounds of pure logic but simply for practical reasons. In the present case if the appellants' financial embarrassment is to be regarded as a consequence of the respondents' tort, I think it is too remote, but I prefer to regard it as an independent cause, though its operative effect was conditioned by the loss of the dredger. The question of remoteness of damage has been considered in many authorities and from many aspects, but no case has been cited to your Lordships which would justify the appellants' claim. A dictum was quoted by Mr. Raeburn from the speech of Lord Collins in *Clippens Oil Co.* v. *Edinburgh and District Water Trustees* ([1907] A.C. 291, 303): "It was contended that this implied that the defenders were entitled to measure the damages on the footing that it was the duty of the company to do all that was reasonably possible to mitigate the loss, and that if, through lack of funds, they were unable to incur the necessary expense of such remedial measures the defenders ought not to suffer for it. If this were the true construction to put upon the passage cited, I think there would be force in the observation, for in my opinion the wrongdoer must take his victim *talem qualem*, and if the position of the latter is aggravated because he is without the means of mitigating it, so much the worse for the wrongdoer, who has got to be answerable for the consequences flowing from his tortious act." But, as I think it is clear that Lord Collins is here dealing not with measure of damage, but with the victim's duty to minimise damage, which is quite a different matter, the dictum is not in point. . . . Nor is the appellants' financial disability to be compared with that physical delicacy or weakness which may aggravate the damage in the case of personal injuries, or with the possibility that the injured man in such a case may be either a poor labourer or a highly paid professional man. The former class of circumstances goes to the extent of actual physical damage and the latter consideration goes to interference with profit-earning capacity; whereas the appellants' want of means was, as already stated, extrinsic.

. . . it follows that the value of the *Liesbosch* to the appellants, capitalised as at the date of the loss, must be assessed by taking into account: (1) the market price of a comparable dredger in substitution; (2) costs of adaptation, transport, insurance, etc., to Patras; (3) compensation for disturbance and loss in carrying out their contract over the period of delay between the loss of the *Liesbosch* and the time at which the substituted dredger could reasonably have been available for use in Patras, including in that loss such items as overhead charges, expenses of staff, equipment, and so forth thrown away, but neglecting any special loss due to the appellants' financial position. On the capitalised sum so ascertained, interest will run from the date of the loss. . . .

Note:

" . . . the authority of what Lord Wright said in *The Edison* is consistently being attenuated in more recent decisions of this court," *per* Kerr L.J. in *Perry* v. *Sidney Phillips & Son* [1982] 3 All E.R. 705, 712 (C.A.). Indeed, it had been ignored in *Martindale* v. *Duncan* [1973] 2 All E.R. 355, where the plaintiff delayed having his car repaired until it became clear that the defendants would pay the cost, and charged them for the hire of a substitute during that period.

Distaste for *The Edison* is probably attributable to two considerations. First, that it was decided in terms of causation rather than remoteness, *i.e.* it smacks of *Re Polemis* rather than *The Wagon Mound*. Secondly, it draws a distinction which, though perfectly valid, has been unfashionable, namely the distinction between the physical and the financial.

The Edison does, however, illustrate the problem which arises when there is a great discrepancy between the value of property and the loss caused by its destruction: the dredger was "worth" £6,000 or so, yet the plaintiffs claimed that its destruction had cost them £23,500. It seems right as a basic principle that the person whose capital good has been destroyed should receive the cost of a replacement plus an indemnity for incidental outgoings and temporary lost profits, *i.e.* its value as a going concern. Consider also the facts of *Wimpey* (above p. 43) where the damaged crane-barge was the lynch-pin of a huge construction programme in which others than its hirer were very heavily implicated. The subsequent reassertion of the rule that only the owner or possessor of a thing may sue for loss due to its destruction may perhaps confirm *The Edison*'s emphasis on the value of the thing rather than the plaintiff's loss. So, too, in cases where there is concurrent liability in tort and contract, the relatively limited quantum of recovery in contract cases may have a moderating effect on the concurrent tort claim.

Recent cases have been concerned with the date of valuation of the loss (*Dodd Properties* v. *Canterbury C.C.* [1980] 1 All E.R. 928) and the currency in which the loss is to be expressed (*The Despina R* [1979] A.C. 685).

Valuation of property is a complex matter with a specialist profession to resolve it. Lawyers should not expect to be able to apply rules of thumb. Some things are especially difficult to value, like component parts (*e.g.* a propeller screw or a crankshaft) or unique things (*e.g.* houses or family photographs) or things whose conventional value is much higher than their manufacturing cost (*e.g.* holiday stamps). Those who insure property against damage normally have to pay less than those who tortiously damage it. (But see *Taylor (C.R.) (Wholesale) Ltd.* v. *Hepworths Ltd.* [1977] 2 All E.R. 784). Why should this be?

DARBISHIRE v. WARRAN

Court of Appeal [1963] 1 W.L.R. 1067; 107 S.J. 631; [1963] 3 All E.R. 310; [1963] 2 Lloyd's Rep. 187

Pearson L.J.: In August 1958 the plaintiff bought a used motor-car for about £330. It was a 1951 Lea Francis shooting brake. Being a mechanical engineer the plaintiff maintained it well and it was reliable. There was no special adaptation of it. On July 26, 1962, it was seriously damaged in a collision caused by the defendant's negligence. The plaintiff sued the defendant in the Haywards Heath County Court for damages for negligence, and the defendant admitted liability but denied the alleged loss and damage.

The issue in the appeal arises in this way. The judge included in his assessment of the damages a sum of £180, being the cost of repairing the damage to the vehicle, but he also made a finding that the market value was £80. It is contended by Mr. O'Connor for the defendant that the assessment should have been based on the market value and not on the cost of repair. The other figures can be mentioned briefly. The plaintiff is admittedly entitled to a sum of £25 for the cost of temporary hiring of a substitute vehicle. The plaintiff gives credit for £80 received from his own insurance company. As between the plaintiff and his insurance company the market value was taken at £85, but the plaintiff under his policy bore the first £5 of the loss. This point is unimportant, but I think the judge's figure of £80 for the market value should be adjusted to £85, and Mr. O'Connor does not contest that.

There is no complete definition of the expression "market value" in the evidence or the judgment, but I understand it as meaning standard replacement market value, that is to say, the retail price which a customer would have to pay in July 1962 on a purchase of an average vehicle of the same make, type and age or a comparable vehicle. It is not the price for a sale to a dealer or between dealers. It appears from a passage in the judgment that the "market value" does not include any allowance for the good maintenance and reliability of the plaintiff's vehicle.

What are the principles applicable? The first and main principle is that the plaintiff is entitled to receive as damages such a sum of money as will place him in as good a position as he would have been in if the accident had not occurred. In *Liesbosch Dredger* v. *Edison S.S. (Owners)* ([1933] A.C. 449, 459) Lord Wright said: "It is not questioned that when a vessel is lost by collision due to the sole negligence of the wrongdoing vessel the owners of the former vessel are entitled to what is called *restitutio in integrum*, which means that they should recover such a sum as will replace them, so far as can be done by compensation in money, in the same position as if the loss had not been inflicted on them, subject to the rules of law as to remoteness of damage."

Now, but for the accident, the plaintiff would have continued to have the use of his existing motor-car, the 1951 Lea Francis shooting brake, undamaged. The accident deprived him of it. To be restored to substantially the same position, he needed such sum of money as would enable him to provide himself with an equivalent vehicle either by having the existing damaged vehicle repaired or by finding and acquiring another vehicle equally good.

There is, however, a second principle which was stated by Viscount Haldane in *British Westinghouse Electric and Manufacturing Co. Ltd.* v. *Underground Electric Railways Company of London Ltd.* ([1912] A.C. 673, 689): "The fundamental basis is thus compensation for pecuniary loss flowing from the breach; but this first principle is qualified by a second, which imposes on a plaintiff the duty of taking all reasonable steps to mitigate the loss consequent on the breach, and debars him from claiming any part of the damage which is due to his neglect to take such steps. In the words of James L.J. in *Dunkirk Colliery Co.* v. *Lever* ((1878) 9 Ch.D. 20, 25), 'The person who has broken the contract not being exposed to additional cost by reason of the plaintiffs not doing what they ought to have done as reasonable men, and the plaintiffs not being under any obligation to do anything otherwise than in the ordinary course of business.' "

For the purposes of the present case it is important to appreciate the true nature of the so-called "duty to mitigate the loss" or "duty to minimise the damage." The plaintiff is not under any actual obligation to adopt the cheaper method: if he wishes to adopt the more expensive method, he is at liberty to do so and by doing so he commits no wrong against the defendant or anyone else. The true meaning is that the plaintiff is not entitled to charge the defendant by way of damages with any greater sum than that which he reasonably needs to expend for the purpose of making good the loss. In short, he is fully entitled to be as extravagant as he pleases but not at the expense of the defendant.

Now did the plaintiff in this case take all reasonable steps to mitigate the loss consequent on the breach? He knew from his dealings with the insurance company that they assessed the replacement market value at £85, and he accepted payment from them on that basis. The insurance company advised against repairs. He was told, at one time at any rate, by the repairers that it was uneconomic to have the vehicle repaired. He had estimates of the cost and there is no evidence of the estimates being inaccurate. After spending about £180, he would have a vehicle worth only about £85. And yet he made no attempt to find another car. It is true he said in his evidence in chief that he could not replace the car with one of similar type and quality for £85, nor for less than £192, but that evidence cannot carry conviction, as he admitted in cross-examination that he did not attempt to find another car. The witness Langley, the works manager of the repairers, said in evidence that he would not have expected to get anything reliable for £100 in September 1962. He also said that the plaintiff discussed the repairs with their manager Redhouse and that Redhouse said it was not an economic proposition. Barnes, the defendant's expert witness, gave the figures of prices from Glass's Guide, and said that in July to September 1962 it would be difficult to find a Lea Francis but you could find other estate cars. Then in the notes of his evidence there is the word "uneconomic."

In my view it is impossible to find from the evidence that the plaintiff took all reasonable steps to mitigate the loss, or did all that he reasonably could do to keep down the cost. He was fully entitled to have his damaged vehicle repaired at whatever cost because he preferred it. But he was not justified in charging against the defendant the cost of repairing the damaged vehicle when that cost was more than twice the replacement market value and he had made no attempt to find a replacement vehicle.

The judge in his judgment stated his view very cogently and at first I thought it was right; but after consideration of the arguments in this appeal I am unable to accept it, because he was not giving due effect to the principles of mitigation of loss or minimising of damage. He was not paying sufficient regard to the economic aspect of the matter. He said: "Evidence has been given on behalf of the defence that it was uneconomical to repair, but I do not think that kind of phrase really helps. What was reasonable for the plaintiff to do?" Later he said: "What would a reasonable man do? I do not think I ought to look at it merely from the point of view of a lawyer or a hard-headed businessman or of the precise mathematician. What would the ordinary man in the street do in a case like this?" In my opinion there is an error of principle involved in these passages. It is vital, for the purpose of assessing damages fairly between the plaintiff and the defendant, to consider whether the plaintiff's course of action was economic or uneconomic, and if it was uneconomic it cannot (at any rate in the absence of special circumstances, of which there is no evidence in this case) form a proper basis for assessment of damages. The question has to be considered from the point of view of a businessman. It seems to me the practical business view is that if the cost of repairing your damaged vehicle is greatly in excess of the market price, you must look around for a replacement and you would expect to find one at a cost not far removed from the market price, although unless you were lucky you might have to pay something more than the standard market price to obtain a true equivalent of a well-maintained and reliable vehicle.

In my view the defendant succeeds on the issue of principle. The assessment should be based on the market price and not on the much higher cost of repairing the damaged vehicle, and therefore the judge's assessment was made on a wrong basis and should be reduced.

In considering what reduction should be made, it may not be appropriate to take the exact figure of the market price, which I understand to be the standard market price of an average vehicle of the make, type and age of the plaintiff's vehicle. There should be an element of flexibility in the assessment of damages to achieve a result which is fair and just as between the parties in the particular case. In the *Liesbosch* case Lord Wright quoted Lord Sumner in *Admiralty Commissioners* v. *S.S. Chekiang (Owners)* ([1926] A.C. 637, 643): " 'The measure of damages ought never to be governed by mere rules of practice, nor can such rules override the principles of the law on this subject.' " Lord Wright went on to say: "Lord Sumner also distinguishes 'a rule of thumb' from what is binding law. In these cases the dominant rule of law is the principle of *restitutio in integrum*, and subsidiary rules can only be justified if they give effect to that rule." Although I am not able to agree with the judge that £180, the cost of repair, can be regarded as a reasonable figure as between the parties, I do agree with him that the bare market value seems too low, as he accepted the plaintiff's evidence as to good maintenance and reliability, and there was the evidence of Langley that he would not have expected to get anything reliable for £100 in September 1962. I am impressed by this passage in the judgment: "Did the plaintiff act reasonably? What would a jury say? Would a jury sy that the plaintiff had acted so unreasonably that he is not entitled to a pennypiece more than the market value of the car? I do not think they would. Certainly if they had had any experience of buying an old second-hand car they would not."

As it would be no kindness to either party to order a new trial on this merely residual question as to what the exact figure should be, it would be appropriate for this court to fix it by a rough and ready estimate. I would fix it at £105 less £80 received by the plaintiff from his own insurance company plus £25 for hiring charges, and the resulting figure is £50. I would allow the appeal, reducing the damages to £50. However, as both my brethren take a different view as to the extent of the reduction which should be made on the evidence given in this case, their view as to the final figure of damages prevails.

I should add this. In *O'Grady* v. *Westminster Scaffolding Ltd.* ([1962] 2 Lloyd's Rep. 238) the decision was justified by the very unusual facts, which made the vehicle unique, so that the standard market value was irrelevant. . . .

Questions

1. "The question has to be considered from the point of view of a business man" says Pearson L.J. But what is this "business" business? The plaintiff here was not a businessman and his car was not a company car. If the law can distinguish between contracts for pleasure and other contracts in order to award damages for annoyance (see *Bliss*, above p. 77), can it not distinguish between chattels for pleasure and chattels for business? Why should actual people of flesh and blood and *feeling* be subjected to a test possibly appropriate to insensate nonentities incorporated simply to make profits and limit the liability of the profiteers? Are judges actually *incapable* of seeing whether the plaintiff is human or not, or is it just that they don't care?

2. The defendant here was apparently given credit for the £80 received by the plaintiff from his own insurer. But we have seen, most recently in *Parry* v. *Cleaver*, above p. 553, that a defendant is not entitled to benefit from the plaintiff's insurance. The law is that a person who tortiously damages property cannot object that the plaintiff could be or has been paid by his insurer, though the insurer who has actually paid the insured victim is entitled *pro tanto* to the tort claim or its proceeds. But insurers like to contract out of the law (or to contract despite the law—see *Phoenix General* [1987] 2 All E.R. 152)—and they have knock-for-knock agreements (see Lewis, "The Private Settlement of Disputes Between Insurers," [1984] New L.J. 947). In our case, therefore, not only the defendant's insurer but also the plaintiff's insurer, which was certainly not bound to pay more than the market value of the wreck, had an interest in the result which the Court of Appeal obligingly gave them. The only person to get screwed was the human plaintiff.

3. A poor widow has a cat worth about sixpence on the open market. A driver whose negligence can be established has run it over, and it is very badly injured. The veterinary surgeon reports that the bill for the treatment necessary to effect a cure would amount to £50. Would you, as legal adviser to the widow, recommend the expenditure of that sum? Would you seek to invoke *Jarvis* v. *Swans Tours* [1973] Q.B. 233 and the other cases cited above p. 77?

INDEX

569